AF661379

# Frontiers of Electronic Commerce

*Ravi Kalakota*
The University of Rochester, New York

*Andrew B. Whinston*
The University of Texas at Austin

PEARSON

Many of the designations used by manufacturers and sellers to distinguish their products are claimed as trademarks. Where those designations appear in this book, and Pearson Education was aware of a trademark claim, the designations have been printed in initial caps or all caps.

**Copyright © 1996 by Pearson Education, Inc.**
**This edition is published by arrangement with Pearson Education, Inc. and Dorling Kindersley Publishing Inc.**

This book is sold subject to the condition that it shall not, by way of trade or otherwise, be lent, resold, hired out, or otherwise circulated without the publisher's prior written consent in any form of binding or cover other than that in which it is published and without a similar condition including this condition being imposed on the subsequent purchaser and without limiting the rights under copyright reserved above, no part of this publication may be reproduced, stored in or introduced into a retrieval system, or transmitted in any form or by any means (electronic, mechanical, photocopying, recording or otherwise), without the prior written permission of both the copyright owner and the above-mentioned publisher of this book.

ISBN 978-81-7758-392-2

First Impression, 2006
Thirteenth Impression, 2013
**Fourteenth Impression**

***This edition is manufactured in India and is authorized for sale only in India, Bangladesh, Bhutan, Pakistan, Nepal, Sri Lanka and the Maldives. Circulation of this edition outside of these territories is UNAUTHORIZED.***

Published by Dorling Kindersley (India) Pvt. Ltd., licensees of Pearson Education in South Asia.

Head Office: 7th Floor, knowledge Boulevard, A-8(A) Sector-62, Noida – 201309 (U.P), India.
Registered Office: 11 Community Centre, Panchsheel Park, New Delhi 110 017, India.

Printed in India by Sai Print O Pack.

# Preface

Every individual or company that wants to make money and become the next Microsoft needs to understand the market potential, business implications, and technological foundations of electronic commerce. Recently, the CEO of a very large retail organization in Hong Kong asked us, "What is this electronic commerce everybody is talking about? How does it affect my organization's way of doing business? What sort of technical and business skills are needed to be successful?" These questions are not unique to one firm or one industry.

Clearly, companies and consumers are discovering that global networking and other technological innovations are powerful assets if used as competitive weapons in their day-to-day activities. These activities range from being entertained and educated by material on the USENET and World Wide Web to building a business serving customers on the Internet. These activities also permeate organizations where increased demands for the efficient collection, dissemination, and processing of information are evident because of various economic factors—global competition and other market forces—and consumer demands for high service and improved quality. These demands are forcing companies to integrate previously isolated "islands of automation" into coherent weapons.

This book is an introduction to the many facets of electronic commerce and is aimed at any person who wants to understand the changes taking place. It explains what electronic commerce is and what the various business strategies and management issues are, and it describes pertinent technology standards and protocols. The first part of the book is devoted to the network infrastructure and the second to business-related issues. In the third part of the book, we explain the key technological ideas that form the bedrock for the applications.

It can be argued that consumers or business professionals are not interested in technology per se but in solutions to their problems. In emerging topics like electronic commerce, however, business and technological issues are becoming increasingly inseparable. To truly understand available solutions and to choose the correct strategy for a given environment and application, there must also be some understanding of the underlying technology. It is also important to understand the implications of technological trends, as they will affect the management qualifications or skills that are needed, the character of jobs that will be created, and the type of high-tech training or credentials needed in the coming years.

It is often difficult to write a book about a fast-moving subject. Describing the past is relatively easy. Predicting the future with reasonable accuracy is possible if the discussion is based on a good understanding of the fundamentals. The real problem with the analysis of the present is that it tends be be out of date, and significant new developments are taking place almost every day in electronic commerce. We have tried to make the description of the present as robust as possible without tieing it too closely to any particular product or development. Our goal is simple: to provide a single source for persons interested in electronic commerce. Articles in magazines and newspapers can give a more up-to-date picture of events, but sometimes there is need for a book to pull everything together, to act as a single source of reference, and to separate the forest, trees, and wood.

## Audience

This book is written for business professionals—students, investors, executives, developers, managers, and other professionals—seeking an understanding of the fit between electronic commerce technology and business applications. It can also serve as a text or professional reference for educators and business school students.

The style has been tailored to bring out the key points and reach those who feel intimidated by the jargon found in the current literature. The typical reader is assumed to have a background in technology that corresponds to the audience that reads the technology sections in popular newspapers such as the *New York Times, Wall Street Journal,* or *Investor's Business Daily* or weekly magazines such as *Business Week, Time,* or *Newsweek.* A number of chapters are of more general interest, and some portions of the book necessarily get technical. Readers with a casual interest can safely skip the technical chapters and still enjoy the rest of the book.

We also hope to reach engineers and other technology-oriented individuals, as many of the issues and problems raised are directly related to the design of software for business applications. A clearer understanding of the business issues will result in better system design and implementation.

## What You Will Learn

We go beyond merely describing the latest technology; we examine in detail the underlying concepts and show how the pieces fit together in business applications. These applications will give you a practical understanding of how to exploit the synergy (and avoid the pitfalls) of the new technology.

This book covers a lot of ground and caters to diverse individual interests:

- For senior executives it lays out the key players—their capabilities and limitations—in the strategic convergence of technology (e.g., telecommunications, computing, and databases) and business (e.g., manufacturing, entertainment, and banking).
- For marketing executives it describes the radical changes taking place in advertising, real-time promotion, and new product introduction.
- For manufacturing and production executives it describes the implications of changes taking place in EDI and its role in supply chain management and integrated logistics.
- For the finance and accounting executive it lays out the developments in the area of electronic currency, secure electronic payments, and remittance, which form the basis for buying or selling products and services in the electronic world.
- For IS executives it introduces new technologies (e.g., structured and compound documents, software agents and mobile computing, networked multimedia databases, and security and encryption) that must be mastered to support their companies' entry into the world of electronic commerce.
- For entrepreneurs it describes various lucrative niches that are emerging such as interactive catalogs, CD-ROM publications, and targeted on-line newsletters and magazines.

Our examples and discussion unabashedly relate to the current business environment, management practices, systems, and programs. Our aim is to show that, when properly employed, these technologies offer astute managers new options for lowering costs, restructuring work flows, streamlining operations, and redefining their strategic focus. Those who ignore the opportunities, in contrast, will surely sacrifice competitive advantages to their more farsighted rivals.

## Organization

This book is divided into three parts. Chapters 1 through 5 discuss the network infrastructure. We begin by introducing the concept of electronic commerce and the various types of consumer and organizational applications (Chapter 1). The Information Superhighway (I-way), which serves as the network infrastructure for electronic commerce, is introduced in Chapter 2. We compare and contrast the various network infrastructure alternatives: the various types of on-ramps being built for the Information Superhighway. We also discuss the immediate future and provide guidelines for experimenting with various access methods. The Internet, from its genesis in the 1960s to its rapidly changing configuration today, is then surveyed (Chapter 3), before we walk the potential implementor or user through the existing options for commercial Internet access (Chapter 4). Rounding off the discussion about network infrastructure are network and transaction security issues that concern both the individual consumer or the organization protecting its perimeter (Chapter 5).

Chapters 6 through 15 are a wide-ranging discussion of the business applications of the Information Superhighway and the technologies, rules, and regulations involved in designing electronic commerce applications. We begin with the architectural framework for electronic commerce and focus on the World Wide Web as a technology infrastructure (Chapter 6). We then look at three broad applications of electronic commerce:

- Comsumer-oriented electronic commerce (Chapter 7) whose implementation requires on-line electronic payment systems (Chapter 8).
- Inter-organizational electronic commerce (Chapter 9) whose implementation is based on the technology, protocols, and standards related to electronic data interchange (EDI) (Chapter 10).
- Intra-organizational electronic commerce (Chapter 11), which is implemented on the concepts of corporate digital libraries and data warehouses (Chapter 12).

We then examine the emerging changes in marketing and advertising that have been facilitated by technology (Chapter 13). Chapter 14 discusses the development and implementation of electronic commerce interfaces, namely, interactive catalogs, directories, and information search and retrieval methods. We wrap up this section with an in-depth look at education on demand and issues related to intellectual copyrights (Chapter 15).

The last part of the book deals with the technological building blocks used in the construction of electronic commerce applications: software agents (Chapter 16); the Internet protocol suite with focus on Mobile IP, IP Multicast, and IPng (Chapter 17); and followed by desktop and broadband multimedia (Chapter 18). We take an in-depth look at emerging broadband telecommunications technology (Chapter 19) and mobile and cellular networks

(Chapter 20). We conclude with a description of document technology: structured documents (Chapter 21) and active documents (Chapter 22).

## Acknowledgments

Many people deserve our thanks for helping with this book. We are indebted to Susan Kutor who reviewed the manuscript and made innumerable corrections in structure, grammar, and style. We thank our reviewers: Wayne Hathaway, Jack Kessler, Edward Krall, Fred Patterson, Keith Porterfield, and Ting Vogel. We also thank our editors: Tom Stone, Debbie Lafferty, and Juliet Silveri. Acting on all of the comments we received was painful but has made this a better book. Of course, we bear the blame for any errors, not these intrepid readers.

Ravi Kalakota
kalakota@uhura.cc.rochester.edu

Andrew Whinston
abw@uts.cc.utexas.edu

# Contents

Preface 3

## 1 Welcome to Electronic Commerce 15

1.1 Electronic Commerce Framework 17
1.2 Electronic Commerce and Media Convergence 21
1.3 The Anatomy of E-Commerce Applications 23
1.4 Electronic Commerce Consumer Applications 36
1.5 Electronic Commerce Organization Applications 44
1.6 Summary 54

## 2 The Network Infrastructure for Electronic Commerce 57

2.1 Market Forces Influencing the I-Way 60
2.2 Components of the I-Way 64
2.3 Network Access Equipment 65
2.4 The Last Mile: Local Roads and Access Ramps 70
2.5 Global Information Distribution Networks 90
2.6 Public Policy Issues Shaping the I-Way 92
2.7 Summary 97

## 3 The Internet as a Network Infrastructure 99

3.1 The Internet Terminology 100
3.2 Chronological History of the Internet 103
3.3 NSFNET: Architecture and Components 112
3.4 National Research and Education Network 120
3.5 Globalization of the Academic Internet 129
3.6 Internet Governance: The Internet Society 134
3.7 An Overview of Internet Applications 137
3.8 Summary 144

## 4 The Business of Internet Commercialization 147

4.1 Telco/Cable/On-Line Companies 151
4.2 National Independent ISPs 156
4.3 Regional-Level ISPs 162

4.4 Local-Level ISPs 164

4.5 Service Providers Abroad 168

4.6 Service Provider Connectivity: Network Interconnection Points 171

4.7 Internet Connectivity Options 174

4.8 Logistics of Being an Internet Service Provider 177

4.9 Summary 188

**5 Network Security and Firewalls** 191

5.1 Client–Server Network Security 191

5.2 Emerging Client–Server Security Threats 196

5.3 Firewalls and Network Security 199

5.4 Data and Message Security 206

5.5 Challenge-Response Systems 217

5.6 Encrypted Documents and Electronic Mail 221

5.7 U.S. Government Regulations and Encryption 224

5.8 Summary 226

**6 Electronic Commerce and World Wide Web** 229

6.1 Architectural Framework for Electronic Commerce 231

6.2 World Wide Web (WWW) as the Architecture 231

6.3 Web Background: Hypertext Publishing 244

6.4 Technology behind the Web 248

6.5 Security and the Web 257

6.6 Summary 264

**7 Consumer-Oriented Electronic Commerce** 267

7.1 Consumer-Oriented Applications 268

7.2 Mercantile Process Models 287

7.3 Mercantile Models from the Consumer's Perspective 288

7.4 Mercantile Models from the Merchant's Perspective 302

7.5 Summary 306

**8 Electronic Payment Systems** 309

8.1 Types of Electronic Payment Systems 310

8.2 Digital Token-Based Electronic Payment Systems 313

8.3 Smart Cards and Electronic Payment Systems 326
8.4 Credit Card-Based Electronic Payment Systems 331
8.5 Risk and Electronic Payment Systems 340
8.6 Designing Electronic Payment Systems 343
8.7 Summary 344

**9 Interorganizational Commerce and EDI 347**

9.1 Electronic Data Interchange 348
9.2 EDI Applications in Business 356
9.3 EDI: Legal, Security, and Privacy Issues 374
9.4 EDI and Electronic Commerce 377
9.5 Summary 381

**10 EDI Implementation, MIME, and Value-Added Networks 383**

10.1 Standardization and EDI 384
10.2 EDI Software Implementation 389
10.3 EDI Envelope for Message Transport 393
10.4 Value-Added Networks (VANs) 401
10.5 Internet-Based EDI 409
10.6 Summary 414

**11 Intraorganizational Electronic Commerce 417**

11.1 Internal Information Systems 420
11.2 Macroforces and Internal Commerce 424
11.3 Work-Flow Automation and Coordination 433
11.4 Customization and Internal Commerce 437
11.5 Supply Chain Management (SCM) 441
11.6 Summary 452

**12 The Corporate Digital Library 455**

12.1 Dimensions of Internal Electronic Commerce Systems 457
12.2 Making a Business Case for a Document Library 466
12.3 Types of Digital Documents 469
12.4 Issues behind Document Infrastructure 475
12.5 Corporate Data Warehouses 479
12.6 Summary 486

**13 Advertising and Marketing on the Internet** 489
13.1 The New Age of Information-Based Marketing 492
13.2 Advertising on the Internet 499
13.3 Charting the On-Line Marketing Process 510
13.4 Market Research 522
13.5 Summary 524

**14 Consumer Search and Resource Discovery** 527
14.1 Search and Resource Discovery Paradigms 531
14.2 Information Search and Retrieval 533
14.3 Electronic Commerce Catalogs or Directories 543
14.4 Information Filtering 557
14.5 Consumer-Data Interface: Emerging Tools 559
14.6 Summary 565

**15 On-Demand Education and Digital Copyrights** 567
15.1 Computer-Based Education and Training 568
15.2 Technological Components of Education On-Demand 580
15.3 Digital Copyrights and Electronic Commerce 599
15.4 Summary 607

**16 Software Agents** 609
16.1 History of Software Agents 612
16.2 Characteristics and Properties of Agents 614
16.3 The Technology behind Software Agents 617
16.4 Telescript Agent Language 626
16.5 Safe-Tcl 616
16.6 Applets, Browsers, and Software Agents 632
16.7 Software Agents in Action 635
16.8 Summary 640

**17 The Internet Protocol Suite** 643
17.1 Layers and Networking 644
17.2 Internet Protocol Suite 647
17.3 Desktop TCP/IP: SLIP and PPP 654

17.4 Other Forms of IP-Based Networking 659
17.5 Mobile TCP/IP-Based Networking 660
17.6 Multicast IP 665
17.7 Next Generation IP (IPng) 668
17.8 Summary 671

**18 Multimedia and Digital Video** 673

18.1 Key Multimedia Concepts 674
18.2 Digital Video and Electronic Commerce 684
18.3 Desktop Video Processing 695
18.4 Desktop Video Conferencing 699
18.5 Summary 708

**19 Broadband Telecommunications** 709

19.1 Broadband Background Concepts 710
19.2 Frame Relay 718
19.3 Cell Relay 720
19.4 Switched Multimegabit Data Service (SMDS) 722
19.5 Asynchronous Transfer Mode (ATM) 724
19.6 Summary 740

**20 Mobile and Wireless Computing Fundamentals** 743

20.1 Mobile Computing Framework 745
20.2 Wireless Delivery Technology and Switching Methods 746
20.3 Mobile Information Access Devices 755
20.4 Mobile Data Internetworking Standards 760
20.5 Cellular Data Communications Protocols 764
20.6 Mobile Computing Applications 767
20.7 Personal Communication Service (PCS) 772
20.8 Summary 776

**21 Structured Documents** 779

21.1 Structured Document Fundamentals 780
21.2 Standard Generalized Markup Language (SGML) 788
21.3 Summary 802

**22 Active/Compound Document Architecture** 805

22.1 Defining Active Documents 806
22.2 Approaches to Active Documents 812
22.3 Object Linking and Embedding 818
22.4 OpenDoc 819
22.5 CORBA: Distributed Objects 821
22.6 Summary 823

References 825
Index 831

## Chapter 1

# Welcome to Electronic Commerce

The cutting edge for business today is electronic commerce (e-commerce). Broadly defined, *electronic commerce* is a modern business methodology that addresses the needs of organizations, merchants, and consumers to cut costs while improving the quality of goods and services and increasing the speed of service delivery. The term also applies to the use of computer networks to search and retrieve information in support of human and corporate decision making.

More commonly, e-commerce is associated with the buying and selling of information, products, and services via computer networks today and in the future via any one of the myriad of networks that make up the *Information Superhighway* (*I-way*). Projections anticipate that the I-way will transform information transport technology for electronic commerce applications and provide an economic windfall similar to what the interstate highway system did for productivity in the nation's manufacturing, travel, and distribution systems [NII93]. The I-way is not a U.S. phenomenon but a global one, as reflected by its various labels worldwide. For instance, it is also called the National Information Infrastructure (NII) in the United States, *data-dori* in Japan, and *jaring*, which is Malay for "net," in Malaysia [AW94].

Factors fueling the avid interest in e-commerce run the gamut of the business process. From the broad perspective, e-commerce is well suited to facilitate the current reengineering of business processes occurring at many firms. The broad goals of reengineering and e-commerce are remarkably similar: reduced costs, lower product cycle times, faster customer response, and improved service quality. One major goal of the reengineering effort is to use electronic messaging technologies—a key building block of e-commerce—to streamline business processes by reducing paperwork and increasing automation. For example, electronic data interchange (EDI)—a fast and dependable way to deliver electronic transactions by computer-to-computer communication—combined with just-in-time (JIT) manufacturing methods, enables suppliers to deliver components directly to the factory floor, resulting in savings in inventory, warehousing, and handling costs. And while EDI is primarily interorganizational, electronic mail (e-mail) does much the same thing, enabling firms to accelerate the document-based business processes both inside and across the organizational boundaries from simple order processing to complete supply chain mangement.

Technologies such as EDI and e-mail, widely used for years in work-flow and reengineering applications, are now diffusing into other aspects of commerce. The efforts of the late 1980s and early 1990s focused primarily on moving existing nonelectronic methods to an electronic platform to improve internal business process efficiency. Today, the emphasis has shifted from this narrow focus to the invention of entirely new business applications for reaching and getting close to the customer. The Information Superhighway and yet-to-be developed technologies will be key elements in this business transformation. And while earlier efforts resulted in small gains in productivity and efficiency, integrating them into the Information Superhighway will fundamentally change the way business is done. These new ideas demand radical changes in the design of the entire business process.

The effects of e-commerce are already appearing in all areas of business, from customer service to new product design. It facilitates new types of information-based business processes for reaching and interacting with customers—on-line advertising and marketing, on-line order taking, and on-line customer service, to name a few. It can also reduce costs in managing orders and interacting with a wide range of suppliers and trading partners, areas that typically add significant overhead to the cost of products and services. Finally, e-commerce enables the formation of new types of information-based products such as interactive games, electronic books, and information on-demand that can be very profitable for content providers and useful for consumers. In sum, companies believe that e-commerce can result in improved efficiency in finding and interacting with customers, in communicating with trading partners, and in developing new products and markets.

Clearly, a key element of e-commerce is information processing. All steps of commerce, except for production, distribution, and delivery of physical goods, are forms of information gathering, processing, manipulation, and distribution, which computers and networks are perfectly suited to handle. This information processing activity is usually in the form of business transactions, for which several broad categories can be observed:

- Transactions between a company and the consumer over public networks for the purpose of home shopping or home banking using encryption for security and electronic cash, credit, or debit tokens for payment (Chapter 7)

- Transactions with trading partners using EDI (Chapter 9)
- Transactions for information gathering such as market research using bar-code scanners, information processing for managerial decision making or organizational problem solving, and information manipulation for operations and supply chain management (Chapter 11)
- Transactions for information distribution with prospective customers, including interactive advertising, sales, and marketing (Chapter 13)

From a management perspective, all of these transactions require tight coordination and control among many participating organizations in order to minimize the exposure to risk. If we look at managing these transactions in light of global sourcing, an integral part of the increasingly global market, the complexity is compounded by long transportation distances, currencies, customs regulations, and language barriers. Codifying these transactions and coordinating them through software via the I-way can reduce the complexity of the task.

Many predict that electronic commerce will propel global computer networks from the fringe into the core of business. Despite the many unknowns in this rapidly changing area, e-commerce stands poised to make a momentous contribution to the way government, business, and individuals conduct business. To understand the various components of electronic commerce, we will first present a framework within which we can examine the various interlocking elements. Then we will examine electronic commerce applications, first in light of the supporting technology infrastructure, then in view of the various consumer and organizational needs.

## 1.1 ELECTRONIC COMMERCE FRAMEWORK

From the business activity already taking place, it is clear that e-commerce applications will be built on the existing technology infrastructure—a myriad of computers, communications networks, and communication software forming the nascent Information Superhighway. Figure 1.1 shows a variety of possible e-commerce applications, including both interorganizational and consumer-oriented examples. None of these uses would be possible without each of the building blocks in the infrastructure:

- Common business services, for facilitating the buying and selling process
- Messaging and information distribution, as a means of sending and retrieving information

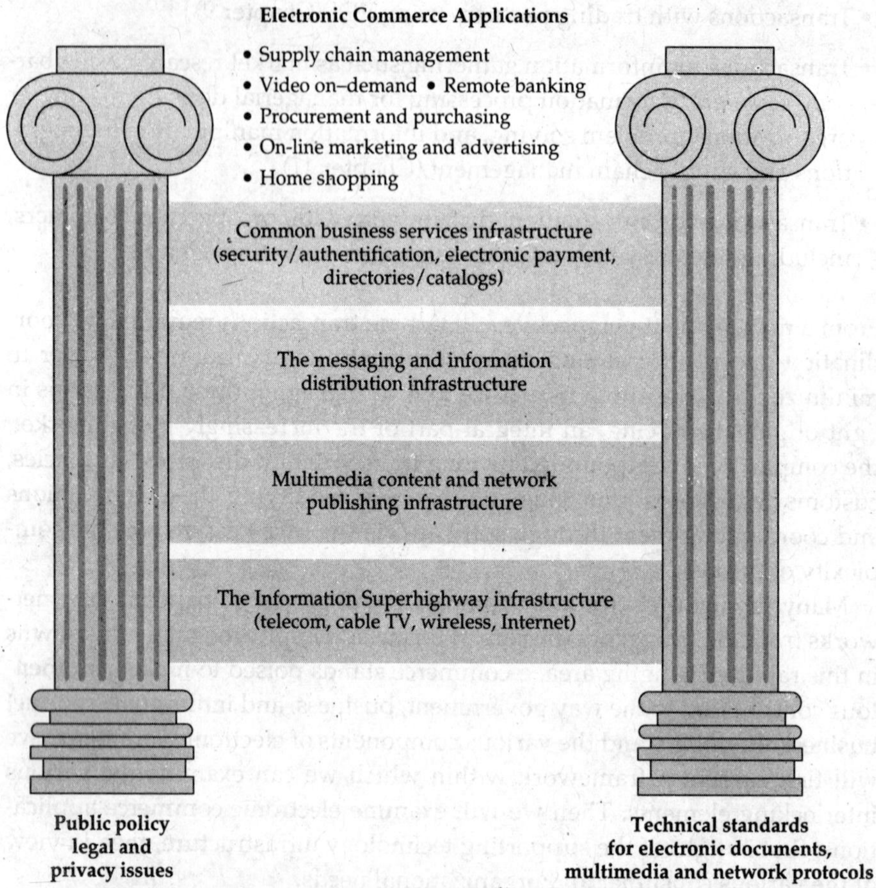


**Figure 1.1** Generic framework for electronic commerce

- Multimedia content and network publishing, for creating a product and a means to communicate about it
- The Information Superhighway—the very foundation—for providing the highway system along which all e-commerce must travel

The two pillars supporting all e-commerce—applications and infrastructure—are just as indispensable:

- Public policy, to govern such issues as universal access, privacy, and information pricing

- Technical standards, to dictate the nature of information publishing, user interfaces, and transport in the interest of compatibility across the entire network

To better understand the integration of the various infrastructure components in our framework, let us use the analogy of a traditional transportation business. Any successful e-commerce application will require the I-way infrastructure in the same way that regular commerce needs the interstate highway network to carry goods from point to point. You must travel across this highway, whether you are an organization purchasing supplies or a consumer ordering a movie on demand. Understand, however, that the I-way is not one monolithic data highway designed according to long-standing, well-defined rules and regulations based on well-known needs. Rather, still under construction, the I-way will be a mesh of interconnected data highways of many forms: telephone wires, cable TV wires, radio-based wireless—cellular and satellite.

Far from complete, the I-way is quickly acquiring new on-ramps and even small highway systems. The numerous constructors are either in competition with or in alliance with one another, all in an effort to convince traffic to use their on-ramps or sections of the highway because, like tollways, revenues in e-commerce are based on vehicular traffic, in our case, vehicles transporting information or multimedia content. The myriad transactions among businesses means that the ultimate winner must select the technology for the I-way that best matches future business needs by using today's tools. Building an access road to a ghost town or a highway too narrow to handle the traffic will yield equally little return on investment for those who have been less successful at matching needs with the infrastructure.

Building the various highways is not enough. Transport vehicles are needed, routing issues must be addressed, and of course the transportation costs must be paid. On the I-way, the nature of vehicular traffic is extremely important. The *information and multimedia content* determines what type of vehicle is needed. A breakdown of potential everyday e-commerce vehicles into their technological components shows that they vary widely in complexity and may even need to travel different routes on the I-way, much the way an eighteen-wheeler may be restricted from traveling roads that cannot accommodate it:

Movies = video + audio
Digital games = music + video + software
Electronic books = text + data + graphics + music + photographs
+ video.

Once these vehicles (multimedia content) are created, where are they housed? What sort of distribution warehouses are needed to store and deliver their multimedia cargo? In the electronic "highway system" multimedia content is stored in the form of electronic documents. These documents are often digitized, compressed, and stored in computerized libraries or multimedia storage warehouses called *servers* that are linked by transport networks to each other and to the software/hardware clients that allow customers to access them.

Exactly how do the vehicles move from one distribution warehouse to another? In a traditional transportation business, diesel engines or gasoline-powered motors move the trucks along the roadways. On the I-way, *messaging software* fulfills this role, in any number of forms: e-mail, EDI, or point-to-point file transfers.

In addition to the development of new vehicles and systems, other key components of commercial transactions need to be examined. How can businesses assure customers of safe delivery? How can customers pay for using the I-way? The Common Business Services block of Fig. 1.1 addresses these supporting issues. Encryption and authentication methods have been developed to ensure security of the contents while traveling the I-way and at their destination (Chapter 5), and numerous electronic payment schemes are being developed to handle highly complex transactions with high reliability.

These logistical issues are difficult to address in long-established transportation systems. That complexity is compounded in the nascent world of electronic commerce by the unique interplay among government, academia, and private commercial endeavors as well as by the challenge of integrating otherwise incompatible transportation systems while maintaining an uninterrupted flow of traffic. And whereas traditional businesses are governed by the Commercial Code and detailed case histories, very basic policy and legal questions are materializing in relation to e-commerce. In the case of vehicular traffic over the interstate highway system, public policy issues concern pollution, consumer protection from fraud, environmental impact, and taxation. Similarly, in information traffic, public policy issues deal with the cost of accessing information, regulation to protect consumers from fraud and to protect their right to privacy, and the policing of global information traffic to detect information pirating or pornography. Again the issues themselves, let alone the solutions, are just now evolving and will become increasingly important as more and more people with variable intent enter the electronic marketplace.

The final pillar on which the e-commerce framework rests is *technical standards,* without which the impact of this revolution would be minimized. For instance, returning to our analogy with traditional transportation systems, railroads would not have flourished had each state established a separate track standard (meter gauge versus broad gauge, for example) and goods would have to be constantly moved from one train to another every time the standard changed, as they do today at the border between Russia and Western Europe. Similar differences in standards exist today in electricity distribution (110 versus 200 volts) and video distribution (Sony Beta versus VHS), limiting worldwide use of many products.

Standards are crucial in the world of global e-commerce, to ensure not only seamless and harmonious integration across the transportation network but access of information on any type of device the consumer chooses—laser disc, PCs, portable hand-held devices or television + set-top boxes (cable converter boxes)—and on all types of operating systems. For example, without the adoption of video standards, video conferencing will never become widespread, as each manufacturer will attempt to develop equipment that maximizes their short-term profits rather than working toward customer goals such as interoperability.

While we have strived to limit our initial discussion of the elements of a framework for electronic commerce to an understanding of what part they play within this complex network, it is no accident that we have ended with a convergence of technical, policy, and business concerns. The concept of "convergence" is essential to the operation of the Information Superhighway and to the way the business world is gearing up to deal with it. It is only fitting that we preface our discussion of the one element of our framework we have not yet discussed in detail—e-commerce applications themselves—with a clarification of the concept of convergence.

## 1.2 ELECTRONIC COMMERCE AND MEDIA CONVERGENCE

The effects of convergence are already being felt. Many companies are pooling their resources and talents through alliances and mergers with other companies to make the electronic marketplace a reality. Part of their motivation may include reducing their risk in light of the uncertainty about what form this eventual global marketplace and e-commerce applications will take.

The term *e-commerce* has become irrevocably linked with the idea of convergence of industries centered on information that until today has been isolated—content, storage, networks, business applications, and consumer devices. *Convergence*, broadly defined, is the melding of consumer electronics, television, publishing, telecommunications, and computers for the purpose of facilitating new forms of information-based commerce. The public can be forgiven for finding the concept perplexing, since the popular press uses the terms *multimedia* and *cross-media* interchangeably. *Multimedia convergence* applies to the conversion of text, voice, data, image, graphics, and full-motion video into digital content. *Cross-media convergence* refers to the integration of various industries—entertainment, publication, and communication media—based on multimedia content.

These two types of convergence are often closely related. For instance, in a new era of interactive TV, the lines between advertisements, entertainment, education, and services often become blurred. While watching an Olympic soccer match between Nigeria and Ireland, you may develop an urge to know more about Nigeria. Instead of running to the local bookstore and purchasing a book, you can link to an on-line database and search while not missing any part of the match. The information in these on-line databases is not limited to text but also provide photographs and digital videos (multimedia). In short, convergence requires removing the barriers between the telecommunications, broadcasting, computing, movie, electronic games, and publishing industries to facilitate interoperability.

Driving the phenomenon of convergence are some simple technological advances:

- *Convergence of content* translates all types of information content—books, business documents, videos, movies, music—into digital information. Once converted into digital form, that information can easily be processed, searched, sorted, enhanced, converted, compressed, encrypted, replicated, transmitted, and so on, in ways that are conveniently matched to today's information processing systems.

- *Convergence of transmission* compresses and stores digitized information so it can travel through existing phone and cable wiring. New switching techniques and other technological breakthroughs enable all types of information to travel to the home. Here we see a convergence of communication equipment that provides the "pipelines" to transmit voice, data, image, and video—all without rewiring the neighborhood.
- *Convergence of information access devices* have the sophistication to function as both computers and televisions. Other examples are the ubiquitous telephone, with internal fax machine, modem, and video monitor, capable of receiving fax, e-mail, and video.

Convergence is also being driven by of certain market conditions including the following:

- The widespread availability of increasingly low-cost, high-performance enabling component technologies, including semiconductors, storage and display devices, communications systems, and operating systems, among others

- Entrepreneurs who are feeding on anticipated end-user demand for new applications—both products and services—that rely on the aforementioned enabling technologies
- Aggressive regulatory actions that are introducing competition in monopoly markets—local and long-distance communications, telecommunication and cable equipment, and right-of-way to customer's curb—and that serve to facilitate the rapid deployment of these new applications.

## 1.3 THE ANATOMY OF E-COMMERCE APPLICATIONS

Although no one knows what applications of electronic commerce will be successful in the long run, the potential payback for those who hold the winning numbers is a powerful driving force behind the development of the infrastructure and the convergence of numerous industries that we have examined in the previous sections. In Fig. 1.1 we showed e-commerce applications situated at the very top, and this is indeed indicative of how most applications rest on the entire infrastructure and reach out to consumers. It is important to understand, however, that applications can be found at all levels of the infrastructure itself. Not only is multimedia content a part of the infrastructure that will enable consumers to enjoy video on demand, but creation of that content is in itself an e-commerce application. Similarly, e-mail can be considered both a messaging infrastructure and a purchasable end product.

In the following subsections we will revisit many parts of the infrastructure we have already presented, this time in light of the business applications. Once again we have provided a point of reference, in Fig. 1.2. We will examine electronic commerce applications, multimedia content and multimedia storage servers as well as the information delivery system, the network service providers that serve as access points, and the devices that function as interfaces for various e-commerce applications.

### Multimedia Content for E-Commerce Applications

Multimedia content can be considered both fuel and traffic for electronic commerce applications. The technical definition of multimedia is the use of

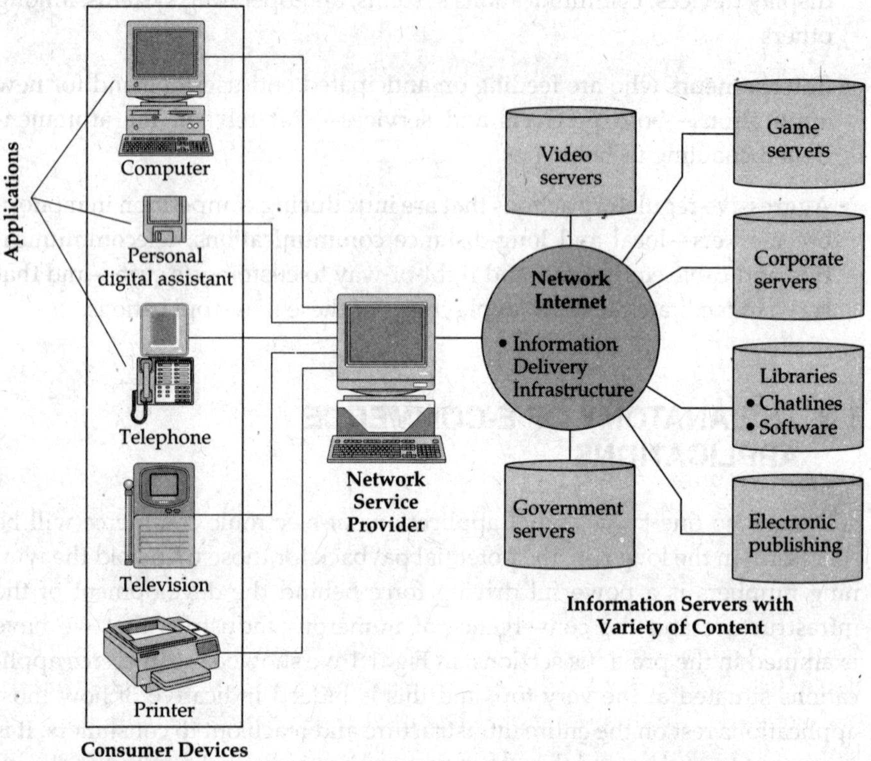


**Figure 1.2** Elements of electronic commerce applications

digital data in more than one format, such as the combination of text, audio, video, and graphics in a computer file/document (see Fig. 1.3).

Multimedia mimics the natural way people communicate. Its purpose is to combine the interactivity of a user-friendly interface with multiple forms of content. In the popular press, multimedia is associated with the hardware convergence taking place in the telecommunications, computer, and cable industry as the next generation of digital, interactive home entertainment nears technical completion. From this perspective, multimedia has come to mean the combination of computers, television, and telephone capabilities in a single device.

Multimedia systems do much more than conventional database systems, which are oriented toward numeric processing (or number crunching). Business professionals are well aware that more than 90 percent of the information that firms use for business operations and decision making lives outside the "traditional" database systems. This external information—in the form of technical manuals, memos, e-mail, problem reports, sales brochures, and product design—is crucial for smooth organizational functioning.

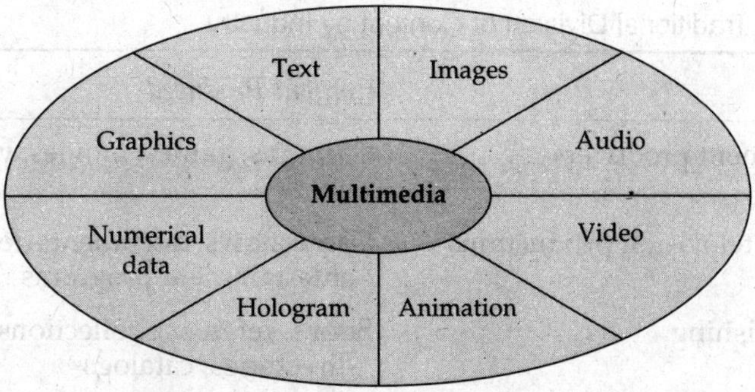


**Figure 1.3** Possible components of multimedia

Because most business systems support only a fraction of the information and communications found in the workplace, the goal of multimedia is to increase the utility of all information through the processing and distribution of new forms such as images, audio, and video.

Thus many managers charting strategic directions now ask, Which applications of multimedia will have the greatest impact on their particular business operations? That question is being asked more frequently because computing and networking have advanced to the point where the distribution of multimedia is not only possible but also inexpensive. Although everyone agrees that multimedia represents the next generation of computing, few have a clear idea of what multimedia is all about, what it can do, and where it is heading. This is understandable since, the term *multimedia* covers so many things that it is often difficult to conceptualize. And, adding to the turmoil, telecommunications, cable/broadcasters, computer software and hardware providers each have a different view of what multimedia means. Everyone does agree, however, that whatever multimedia proves to be, business must be involved in it one way or another.

The traditional, separate business divisions, presented in Table 1.1, no longer hold true in the world of multimedia. For instance, an electronic book, no longer text only, often includes photographs, voice, video clips, animation, and a host of other things. In other words, every form of content is interrelated to other forms.

Access to multimedia content depends on the hardware capabilities of the customer. For a long time, the capability of the computer hardware was well ahead of the needs of software applications available to run on it. This gap is narrowing rapidly, however, with resource-hogging "application software" rich in multimedia content: electronic books, real-time information, movies, videos, and interactive services such as CD-ROM titles.

Telecommunications and cable companies, now aware of the importance of content for the future of e-commerce applications, have begun to acquire

**Table 1.1** Traditional Division of Content by Industry

| *Industry* | *Content Produced* |
|---|---|
| Entertainment producers | Cartoons, games, movies, video, music |
| Broadcast television productions | Gameshows, documentaries, entertainment programs |
| Print publishing | Books, reference collections, directories, catalogs |
| Computer software | Software programs: animation, games, productivity-enhancing tools |

rights to the content they believe will have great value. This direction is evident in the protracted bidding war running into several billions of dollars between Viacom and QVC for Paramount Studios. The target: Paramount's library of movies, television series, and copyrights. The press and Wall Street have picked up on the programming-content theme with a vengeance, painting all content providers as winners and differentiating very little between possession and application.

This simplistic view fails to consider the key issue in e-commerce application development: What does the consumer want? For instance, the real catalysts to the business computing boom in the 1980s proved to be productivity-enhancing software like spreadsheets, word processing, desktop publishing programs, icon-based user interface, and graphics. Consumer acceptance will be positive if the technology is an e-commerce "killer" application that meets some suppressed need, as did the Lotus 1-2-3 spreadsheet for the IBM PCs and Nintendo's Super Mario Brothers for video games. These applications rapidly filled a need that the consumer never knew existed. No one has yet developed the "killer" application for e-commerce, and it is unlikely that an uncontested winner will emerge until the technical infrastructure is in place, clearly defined, or at least articulated.

The success of e-commerce applications also depends on the variety and innovativeness of multimedia content and packaging. The advantage goes to the current providers (or packagers) of multimedia content—to entertainment, broadcast television productions, traditional print publications, and software and information services. Supporting these content providers are the hidden brigade of small businesses or individuals producing content—writing articles, creating videos, developing software programs, and other important entrepreneurial activities. Plenty of opportunity, remains, however, for new players who can provide innovative content that meets consumer demands not fulfilled by existing providers.

## Multimedia Storage Servers and Electronic Commerce Applications

Electronic commerce requires robust servers to store and distribute large amounts of digital content to consumers. These multimedia storage servers are large information warehouses capable of handling various content, ranging from books, newspapers, advertisement catalogs, movies, games, and x-ray images. These servers, deriving their name because they serve information upon request, must handle large-scale distribution, guarantee security, and complete reliability.

Digitized content eliminates the bulkiness and mechanical unreliability found in past equipment. Steady advances in digital memory technology are making mass-storage devices technologically feasible and increasingly cost-effective. For example, with the 256-megabyte and 1-gigabyte memory chips now under development, an entire feature-length movie could be stored on four to ten memory chips. Frequently requested or accessed content will be stored on such relatively expensive chips; content requested less often will be housed on less expensive media, such as optical disks and magnetic tape.

### *Client–Server Architecture in Electronic Commerce*

All e-commerce applications follow the client–server model (see Fig. 1.4). Clients are devices plus software that request information from servers. The client–server model replaces traditional mainframe-based models that worked well for a long time. Mainframe computing, which traditionally meant "dumb" terminals attached to a computer housed in a glass house, is too costly and slow to cope with new data types like audio and video. In contrast, the dominant model of client–server architecture links PCs to a storage (or database) server, where most of the computing is done on the client. Even existing client–server models based on PC servers, while providing back-end technology for scalable and flexible database management, have to be reengineered to accommodate new data types.

The client–server model, allows the client to interact with the server through a request-reply sequence governed by a paradigm known as *message passing*. The server manages application tasks, handles storage and security, and provides scalability—ability to add more clients as needed for serving more customers—and client devices (from personal digital assistants to PCs) handle the user interface (see Fig. 1.4). In effect, the multime-

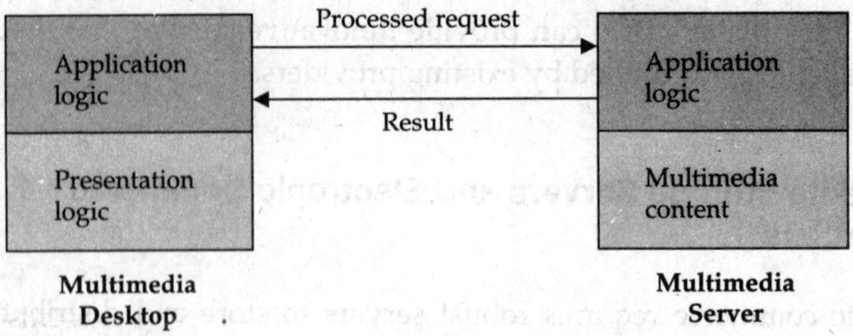


**Figure 1.4** Distribution of processing in multimedia client–server world

dia server handles the critical elements (distribution, connectivity, security, accounting), and so is expected to simplify and make scaling more cost-effective.

Be aware, however, that the full impact of the fundamental shift in the computing paradigm from a host-terminal architecture to a networked client–server architecture will take several more years to be realized. There is a long way to go before the installed base of mainframes and minicomputers is networked or replaced by workstations and PCs. Commercial users have only recently begun downsizing their applications to run on client–server networks, a trend that electronic commerce is expected to accelerate.

### *Internal Processes of Multimedia Servers*

The internal processes involved in the storage, retrieval, and management of multimedia data objects are integral to e-commerce applications. In general terms, a *multimedia server* is a hardware and software combination that converts raw data into usable information and then "dishes out" this information where and when users need it. It captures, processes, manages, and delivers text, images, audio, and video. Most multimedia servers provide a core set of functions to display, create, and manipulate multimedia documents; to transmit and receive multimedia documents over computer networks, and to store and retrieve multimedia documents.

To make interactive multimedia a reality, a server must do the following: handle thousands of simultaneous users; manage the transactions of these users (e.g., purchases, specific information requests, customer billing); and deliver information streams to consumers at affordable costs. The technical challenge is obvious when one realizes that traditional models of information management do not lend themselves to the new paradigm. First, the data differ radically; we are no longer dealing with only table-formatted, alphanumeric data. Second, the computing platforms pose bottlenecks when trying to deliver large pieces of complex data.

Let us illustrate the issues by looking at video on-demand. Here, a single 90-minute video consuming over 100 gigabytes of storage space must be distributed to a large number of consumers. For these new requirements, platform choices include high-end symmetric multiprocessors, clustered architecture, and massive parallel systems. Massive parallel systems harness the power of cheap processors and intricately chain them to create a web that behaves as one single unit, although each processor has its own communications pathway to the outside world. This process avoids the congested pathways of traditional models while affording thousands of users information from the server. And finally one of the most compelling technical challenges is the management of enormous storage capacity required for these new forms of data, in particular digital video. Economical storage and manipulation of digital video is impossible without several magnitudes of compression accomplished by using video compression standards such as Motion Picture Expert Group (MPEG) (see Chapter 18). To address these technical challenges, new types of video servers are being developed.

### Video Servers and Electronic Commerce

The electronic commerce applications related to digital video will include telecommuting and video conferencing, geographical information systems that require storage and navigation over maps, corporate multimedia servers, postproduction studios, and shopping kiosks. Consumer applications will include video on-demand and a range of interactive services such as shopping, video navigation (e.g., interactive TV guides), and directories (e.g., interactive telephone yellow pages).

The need for large-scale video storage has led to a unique business partnership between technology/transport and media companies in interactive TV trials and has resulted in the development of new video servers. *Video servers* (see Fig. 1.5 for a block diagram of a video server architecture) are an important link between the content providers (entertainment/media) and transport providers (telcos/wireless/cable operators). One important difference between video servers and the current client–server computer systems used extensively for data processing is that video servers are designed to deliver information to hundreds of consumers simultaneously via public telecommunications and cable networks. Video servers tackle the "simultaneous overlapping" supply problem that arises when providing on-demand services to large numbers of homes. Numerous households will want to

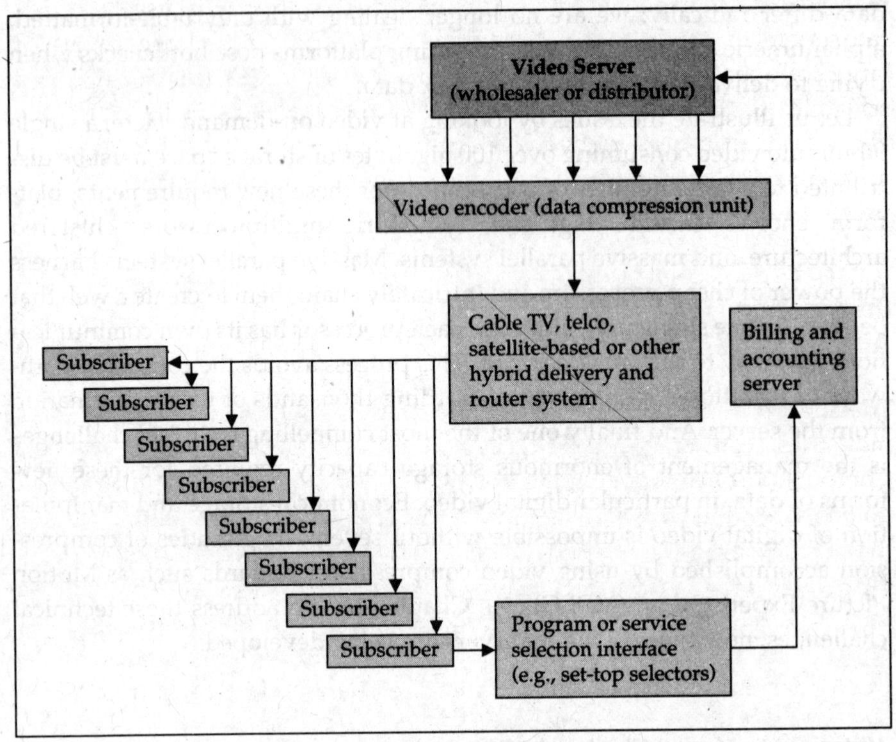


**Figure 1.5** Block diagram of a generic video on-demand system

watch the film either simultaneously or at overlapping times. This problem can be approached from either the hardware or software end.

In the case of hardware solutions, servers can harness the power of massive parallel architecture—that is, using thousands of inexpensive microprocessors that are interlinked to create the illusion of one large computer. Each processor acts as a "video pump" and distributes a portion of the film so that a single film can be viewed by numerous households on-demand. One example of such a video server is nCube, which contains 512 processors, each equivalent to an Intel Pentium chip. The total random-access memory in such an architecture is 16,000 megabytes (16 gigabytes)—dwarfing the typical 8 megabytes found in a desktop computer.

All video servers need not be hardware-based. Rather than looking at the delivery of continuous media on-demand (e.g., audio and video) as a hardware problem solved with massive parallel machines, Microsoft has approached the problem as a customizable software issue. This software architecture, being developed under the code-name Tiger, is based on the Windows NT operating system. Tiger is expected to be implemented in many ways—on personal PCs for individual or work-group use, as corporate servers for small- or mid-sized private networks, and as large servers for large-scale consumer use. The goal is to provide the power, functionality, and scalability to give users split-second access to thousands of media files and to allow laser disc–type functions such as pause, reverse, fast-forward, and jump-ahead to user-specified locations. Only time, economics, and customer preferences will decide which approach will dominate.

## Information Delivery/Transport and E-Commerce Applications

Transport providers are principally telecommunications, cable, and wireless industries; computer networks including commercial networks such as CompuServe or America Online; and public networks such as the Internet. As noted earlier, the transport system does not function as a monolithic system, in the sense that there is no single Interstate 80 that connects the digital equivalent of New York's George Washington Bridge to San Francisco's Bay Bridge. Instead, the architecture is a mix of many forms of high-speed network transport whether it be land-based telephone, air-based wireless, modem-based PCs, or satellite transmissions (see Table 1.2). Literally, the transport routes for e-commerce applications are boundless.

The distribution of information has become a competitive market with a combination of offense and defense. Playing on the defense are telephone companies and cable television companies, providers that have enjoyed monopoly positions for decades. Now, however, their enormous investments in wiring and equipment have become vulnerable to new competition.

**Table 1.2** Transport Routes

| *Information Transport Providers* | *Information Delivery Methods* |
|---|---|
| Telecommunication companies | Long-distance telephone lines; local telephone lines |
| Cable television companies | Cable TV coaxial, fiber optic, and satellite lines |
| Computer-based on-line servers | Internet; commercial on-line service providers |
| Wireless communications | Cellular and radio networks; paging systems |

Playing offense are computer companies that offer new hardware capabilities and software programs with the potential to define new markets. The computer companies are banking on public networks such as the Internet, which is expanding at an astounding pace (see Chapter 3). Another emerging threat will be wireless communications known as *personal communications services*, a form of walkaround telephony that bypasses the traditional telecommunications companies and uses wireless communications.

Each highway route provider faces a different but no less daunting set of challenges:

- *Telecom-based.* These providers, the most visible (and vocal) of all competitors, include long-distance and local telephone service providers. For the phone companies, the breakthrough for e-commerce applications delivery came in 1991 when scientists found a way to do what everybody had assumed was impossible: squeeze a video signal through a telephone wire. The technology, known as *asymmetric digital subscriber line (ADSL)*, has some unresolved drawbacks: It cannot handle live transmissions, and the picture it produces is not as clear as that provided by a well-tuned cable hookup. Researchers have recently improved the quality of the picture and with further compression expect to accommodate several channels of live video over a single telephone wire.

- *Cable-based.* These providers depend on coaxial cable as transport roads and will help determine which broadband applications and services the viewing public prefers. All leading cable providers are conducting trials with a variety of hardware and software, and most are expected to use fiber optic cable and coaxial wire as the delivery medium. The strategy among cable companies is to develop a "network neutral" content that uses digital compression and is adaptable to alternative delivery systems, such as wireless and satellites (see Chapter 2).

- *Computer network-based.* These providers are often dial-up linkages of lower bandwidth when compared to telecom and cable highways. Bandwidth is analogous to the number of lanes on a highway. Examples of on-line transport architectures are CompuServe, Prodigy, and America Online (see Chapter 2), which often tend to serve as both a transport road and content providers.

- *Wireless.* These operators are typically radio-based—cellular, satellite and light-based—infra-red. In fact, some of the most exciting transport architectures are invisible. New wireless-based systems require new ways of thinking about information delivery. The 1990s have been characterized by record-breaking growth in most wireless segments, including cellular, paging, and specialized mobile radio. This thriving market, considered to have enormous growth potential through the year 2000 and beyond, was further boosted in 1993–1994 by a series of legislative and regulatory developments encouraging emerging wireless technologies.

Currently, about 65 percent of e-commerce applications are delivered online via computers equipped with modems, but the percentage of information delivered on CD-ROM continues to grow. Information delivery by telephone, called *audiotext*, is a promising medium, generating about $590 million in revenue in 1993 despite government regulations that have curtailed its growth [USIO94]. Audiotext is especially popular for delivery, in real time, of certain types of information such as stock quotes, mortgage rates, sports and lottery results, weather, and news. One major newspaper publisher estimated that more than one million calls will be made monthly to its audiotext service. However, the next generation of delivery media is expected to be interactive multimedia, a technology that combines computer, telephone, and television services. This technology could attract more home users to information services.

## Consumer Access Devices

Which consumer devices provide the on-ramps to the transport architectures? Will the digital on-ramps be through existing televisions, personal computers, multimedia PCs, or televisions with so-called set-top boxes? or through all four? What computer operating systems will be the engines in these access devices?

Over the next decade hundreds of billions of private and tax dollars will fund the integration of the different (and often incompatible) communications systems and the creation of new software and hardware navigation tools for improved information access. How the majority of users will access e-commerce applications, as yet unknown, is heavily linked to the access device they opt to use. A myriad of devices can provide access to information: videophones, PCs capable of handling multimedia, personal digital assistants like Apple's Newton, televisions capable of two-way transmission, cellular phones, mobile and portable computers. (See Table 1.3.)

Of all these devices, interactive TV has been touted as the information access device of the future. The argument is simple: Almost everyone has a TV, and everyone is far more comfortable using a TV than a PC. Does this sound like the argument advanced by radio manufacturers after TV was introduced fifty years ago? Just as improvements in TV made it far more appealing and affordable, advances in computers are making it much easier to operate, much more useful, and much less expensive. The newest genera-

**Table 1.3** Information Access Devices

| *Information Consumers* | *Access Devices* |
|---|---|
| Computers with audio and video capabilities | Personal/desktop computing (workstations, multimedia PC)<br>Mobile computing (laptop and notebook)<br>CD-ROM-equipped computers |
| Telephonic devices | Videophone |
| Consumer electronics | Television + set-top box<br>Game systems |
| Personal digital assistants (PDAs) | Pen-based computing<br>Voice-driven computing<br>Software agents |

tion of PCs, for example, operates microprocessors powerful enough to run video with the resolution of a television picture. All access devices need not be hardware based, moreover. A new breed of software-based devices called software agents is being created that will act as the consumer's personal digital assistants (see Chapter 16).

Some issues remain unresolved. For instance, which operating system will be the dominant player on these access devices? Who will define the user interface (and earn the staggering royalties likely to accrue from it)? The operating system of choice will depend to some extent on which transport highway consumers ride and the user interface they prefer. If on-line services are used, then there is high probability that PC-based access may predominate. Here, Microsoft is well positioned with its Windows 95 operating system.

Adding to the realm of uncertainty about the future configuration of various access devices is the nature of the interface between the consumer and the content. Having access to a veritable cornucopia of interactive information and entertainment is useless to the average consumer who is petrified by technology. A common joke in movies and late night talk shows concerns "flashing twelves," a reference to consumers' inability to program VCRs.

To illustrate difficulties in interface design in e-commerce applications, let's look at some specifics, beginning with on-line newspapers and magazines. Stories abound about *Time, The New York Times,* and many other publications going on-line. Clearly, these offerings have a long way to go. At this point they are best used for looking up specific information they are known to contain rather than browsing or skimming as done with normal reading.

One major drawback is readers' inability to decide which stories to read. Readers of printed magazines can browse the headline, the subheads, the photos, the captions, or perhaps read three paragraphs and then hop to another story, all within a few seconds.

On-line browsing is not easy. Often, users are confronted with a menu of brief headlines, each describing a story. One selects the story by typing a number at the keyboard, or if confronted with a graphical user interface, by clicking on a mouse pointer. Often, the menu doesn't yield enough information to make an informed decision, so time is wasted opening up stories and then finding that they are not relevant. Even if the material is relevant, it is not that much fun reading copy on a screen because the colors and layout are often not attractive.

On the positive side, these early systems represent the first generation of on-line publications, and in another few years things probably won't be the same. Eventually, we will figure out how to design effective interface with pictures, text, probably sound, movies (and smell!). In other words, at this point the whole area is nascent with tremendous potential.

Home shopping, video on-demand, or other services present similar challenges. Bell Atlantic estimates that, to make these applications attractive, the consumer must be in a position to make a purchase decision within four "clicks" of the remote control. A number of firms are tackling the challenge of making life easy for the confused consumer in a world of many choices, using software agents that act on the consumer's behalf through voice commands. Some of the most recent thinking in this area suggests that the set-top box will actually have to become a broker, a machine that delivers the consumer's typical preferences to a number of other computer systems in the networks. This raises two issues: The need for additional computer systems to track consumer preferences will boost application and network costs; and the increasingly feature-rich software content will present a vast variety of choices and increase the chance of major software bugs, which will damage the attractiveness of the products in consumers' eyes.

A *Wall Street Journal* survey of the complexity of user interface design illustrates the gap between what seems obvious to application developers but makes no sense to the user. The newspaper presented a random selection of all but meaningless icons from popular desktop software in "what do these mean?" quiz form. The respondents understood only 30 percent of the icons, on the average. Detailed analysis of the results reveals that icons have to be extremely obvious to be of any use to the consumer.

To delve into interface design further, consider video on-demand. It is clear that simply presenting the consumer with 500 films (about the size of the selection found at a combined corner convenience/video store) without any clips would be a highly ineffective marketing method. On the other hand, playing a continuous cycle of 15-second clips for 500 movies would require almost two hours and would be just as ineffective as a list of 500 titles sorted by category. Currently, companies are bypassing the entire issue of effective user interface design and focusing on getting the basics to work, as evidenced in the early on-demand trial services being conducted. Time Warner's Quantum system, for instance, asks the user to choose a film and responds to the user's selection by giving the time of the next screening; to watch a film, the user pushes a button on the remote control and is charged a fee between two and four dollars. Special events such as major sporting events or concerts cost up to thirty dollars to watch. This is by no means a complete video on-demand service, but it does provide some experience in this emerging market and allows companies to assess the potential demand.

In the meantime, Blockbuster Video, Disney, and others are actively researching customer-technology interfaces. Both companies have done studies that demonstrate some interesting aspects of consumer behavior: 65 percent of customers cannot accurately remember the name of the video they rented a week or two before, and consumers like to hold the video boxes in their hands and read the labels when choosing viewing material. Both observations indicate the need for facilitating better recall. In other words, the interfaces will have to be very effective at re-creating the experience of browsing an electronic shelf to provide some sort of memory by association. In the end, many of these issues may be overcome, but it does seem premature to assume that they will not be sorted out without a number of costly experiments in terms of both time and money. This does not condemn interactive multimedia to death, but it does suggest a slower-than-expected scenario for widespread adoption.

## 1.4 ELECTRONIC COMMERCE CONSUMER APPLICATIONS

Businesses looking to get involved in the electronic marketplace want fast answers to some very basic questions. What type of services do consumers really want or are willing to pay for? Do they want applications that bring about social change, that entertain, that are educational, or that educate as well as entertain? What amount is the consumer willing to pay for these services? How should the product be priced so that firms are competitive as well as profitable? We address these questions in the following sections.

Consumer desires are very hard to predict, pinpoint, or decipher in electronic markets whose shape, structure, and population are still in the early stages. Needs envisioned include entertainment on-demand, including 500-channel TV, video on-demand, games on-demand, and news on-demand;

electronic retailing via catalogs and kiosks and home shopping networks; interactive distance education; collaboration through desktop videoconferencing; medical consultations, and many more. Predicting which applications will be the winners and which will be "duds" resulting in huge losses will not be easy until experiments are done, but those experiments require an infrastructure. To plan the infrastructure, however, hard choices about a winning application have to be made—a classic chicken/egg problem.

Currently, the application of choice among the cable and telecom providers who are developing the infrastructure is video on-demand. Why are most companies betting heavily on this? Let's look at some statistics from the United States:

- Ninety-three million homes have television. That's 98 percent of households. About two-thirds of the homes have more than one television, and about the same number are connected to cable.
- Americans spend nearly half their free time watching television. According to Nielsen, the market research firm, the average television is on about seven hours a day, and the average American watches television between three to four and a half hours a day. The only other activities that take up more time than watching television are work and sleep.
- At almost any moment every evening, more than one-third of the population is in front of a television—not all watching the same channel, of course. This huge TV audience is made up of a multitude of moving targets, namely, consumers wielding remotes.
- Sight, sound, and motion combine to make television a powerful means of marketing. As proven by the success of home shopping networks, television can move mountains of merchandise.

Video on-demand is seen as part of an overall long-term trend from the passive delivery vehicles of movies, radio, and TV to "consumer-interactive" platforms. How will it work? To see a video, consumers would pick one from a wide selection and would be billed later. As currently envisioned, video on-demand is merely a cheaper or more convenient replacement for the corner video store.

In the future, viewers will decide what they want to see and when they want to participate. Consumers will be given greater control over scheduling these activities. The changing trends in consumer choice can be seen in other areas of entertainment besides movies, namely, in the consumption of sports, TV shows, and educational programs. This movement is evident in the popularity of CNN, whose 24-hour newscast frees the consumer from having to watch the six or eleven o'clock news. However, video on-demand is not a sure bet by any means (or a killer application for e-commerce), as we will see in later sections.

## Consumer Applications and Social Interaction

In the long run, the e-commerce application winners will be those that can change the way consumers think and the way they do business. One example might be applications oriented toward social interaction. Lessons from history indicate that the most successful technologies are those that make their mark socially.

Television, the most successful technological miracle since the automobile, quickly became so vital that people, even those who couldn't even afford shoes, bought sets in the millions. In 1945 almost no one in the U.S. had a TV; by 1960 about 86 percent of households did. Now contrast this with the telephone. Bell invented the telephone in 1876 and by 1940, 40 percent of U.S. households and by 1980 about 95–98 percent of households were connected.

Penetration was slower for the telephone than for TV because of the effort needed to set up the wiring infrastructure. Nevertheless, both technologies are equally significant in their impact. The impact of the telephone on business and social communications is without doubt one of the most significant events of the twentieth century. The same is true of the influence of television on consumer behavior and entertainment habits.

Other social revolutions have bearing on the e-commerce applications. For instance, the current trends in radio and television talk shows can be seen replicated in the on-line news groups. All-talk radio began in 1960 at KABC in Los Angeles, and by 1989, almost three decades later, just 319 radio stations followed the news and mostly chat format. In 1994, their numbers exceeded 1000, and virtually every one of the nearly 12,000 radio stations in the United States had a talk show. Incidentally, talk shows began on TV by serendipity, when Phil Donahue leapt into the audience of his new talk show to let a woman ask his guest a question. Since then, talk shows have become a national pastime. But it was the presidential campaign of 1992 that enlarged the conversation by pulling even the presidency down to street level. While his opponents flew from primary to primary, independent billionaire Ross Perot popped up on "Donahue," "Larry King Live," and C-SPAN. Soon, Bill Clinton was answering questions on MTV and taking calls. The newly elected Bill Clinton was then responding to questions from the e-mail address president@whitehouse.gov.

Social interactions were also promoted by the introduction of the 800 toll-free service around 1968. By 1993, AT&T's 800-number business represented

40 percent of total calls made—some 12 billion 800 calls. Providing contrast to the toll-free services is the caller-paid 900 service known as audiotext, which allows callers to access a live, prerecorded, or interactive program. The four major 900 services are fax-back, interactive, recorded—sports scores, financial services and weather, opinion polling, and conferencing or simultaneous conversation using Group Access Bridging (GAB). In the corporate world, marketers are exploring 900 services as a way to offset costs in areas like customer service by getting callers to pay. The nature of these audiotext services may change as computers are used to access the information with modems doing the dialing.

In sum, the most successful marketplaces are expected to be those that cater to consumers' loneliness, boredom, education, and career. For instance, look at the success of on-line chat services and home shopping channels. In a highly competitive society, where neighbors seldom talk to one another, these outlets give consumers someone to talk to after going home. One can add video on-demand, adult entertainment (sports, sex, and gambling), electronic malls, grocery shopping, and local news to that list. Newspaper publishers with on-line services have already found a successful niche: the personal ads. But turf battles emerge as debates rage over whether interactive TV or on-line computer services will become the pivotal medium for solving consumer loneliness.

## What Do Consumers Really Want?

Two key questions still need to be addressed: Do consumers want new services and will they pay for them? Having set out the proposition that the e-commerce applications cannot be built overnight and probably will emerge more slowly than many now assume, we now analyze how the consumer will react to the promised multimedia cornucopia.

Some cable TV and telecommunication network operators seem to be taking a "build it and they will come" attitude. Plans for video on-demand and other applications are predicated on imaginary customers who are expected to buy multimedia services. If history has taught us anything about imaginary customers, it is that they have a way of doing unexpected things.

To accurately gauge consumer intentions with respect to services they do not yet understand is very difficult. Interestingly, focus groups and limited-market tests suggest consumers show no pressing demand for additional services or for a 500-channel interactive TV. Nonetheless, several very successful businessmen are convinced that the public will gobble up interactive services if they are made available.

It would be to the peril of e-commerce application creators to forget that people always gravitate toward doing things in the easiest possible way. The February 1994 issue of *Direct Marketing* [JS94] featured a speech on the challenges facing marketers in electronic markets made by Joseph Segel, founder of both QVC Network and the Franklin Mint. Some of the key comments from the transcript of his speech are summarized here:

- Consumers are generally satisfied with the range of choices (approximately 50 channels) now available on cable television. The main complaint is not lack of choices, but quality and cost of service.
- Many of the concepts being promoted are solutions in search of a problem. Most successful present-day systems are about as simple as they can be. People, for instance, are comfortable with the way televisions and telephones work. If a new system requires more steps to do essentially the same things, consumers may resist it.
- Television viewers are passive by nature. Some system developers and their software programmers assume that consumers are itching to be converted from passive to interactive television watchers. Certainly, some people fit that mold, but most of the public prefers to lay back and just watch television and let someone else do the work of figuring out the sequence of television programming.

The convenience factor is also critical. In 1993 Americans bought $60 billion worth of goods through catalogs, TV shopping networks, and other direct marketing alternatives. Although only 2.8 percent of the $2.1-trillion-a-year retail marketplace (which includes supermarkets, drugstores, mall outlets, car dealerships, department stores, warehouse clubs, boutiques), direct marketing represents the fastest growing segment of retailing [JS94].

The bottom line seems to be that new interactive services must be easy to use, inexpensive, and appealing in terms of satisfying a need before consumers will use them and buy them.

## What Are Consumers Willing to Spend?

As in all commerce, economics is a key issue. How much are consumers willing to spend and how should products be priced? Right now, the $3.50 charge for a rental video is a cash, out-of-pocket item. Video on-demand, in contrast, would necessitate monthly billing, raising the question of "sticker shock." Consider the following projected cable subscriber bill projected for the year 2000 [ABS94], for example:

*Recurring fees:*

| | |
|---|---|
| Standard service channels | $9.75 |
| Expanded basic video | 7.00 |
| Premium channels | 8.00 |
| Audio music broadcasts | 0.25 |
| Converter boxes | 8.75 |
| | Subtotal: $33.75 |

*Usage fees:*

| | |
|---|---|
| Pay-per-view | $0.75 |
| Movies-on-demand | 13.00 |
| Time-shifted television | 2.75 |
| Music videos-on-demand | 2.50 |
| Interactive games | 5.50 |
| Educational programs | 2.75 |
| | Total monthly charges: $61.00 |

Contrast this charge with a current cable bill for basic service of about $30. Discretionary spending on cable in the United States has been flat for ten years, at an adjusted $124 per annum per subscriber line. This raises some interesting questions about the affordability of video on-demand, particularly if the cable bill is doubled from $30 to $65 a month. Now look at the economics for the service provider: (1) the cost to the network operator to run fiber to the home is around $1000; (2) the cost of a intelligent set-top box is around $1000; and (3) the cost of network enhancements per subscriber is around $1000. A GTE Corporation study showed that, above $4 a film, video on-demand's popularity decreases very rapidly. Even if we assume that the economic cost projected for the year 2000 can be halved, and the technological cost per subscriber is $1000, will the consumer be willing to spend (assuming rapid depreciation at 30 percent to allow for technological obsolescence) the $400-plus per annum needed to recover these costs? At $120 access charges, that is at least 70 films a year!

If consumers are unwilling to spend the amounts needed to fully recover the costs of bringing entertainment to their homes, then network operators might look to advertisers to fill the gap. A study by *The Economist* noted that consumers already absorb $30 a month in built-in advertising costs to pay for supposedly "free" television. Television is truly a broadcast medium; however, interactive multimedia is anything but that. In theory, network operators could target consumers with advertising, but this would raise technical and privacy issues not easily resolved. The issues of how customer data will be collected, stored, and who will have access to it are enough to keep the courts busy for the foreseeable future. Our conclusion: Don't bet too heavily on video on-demand being the dominant application.

## Delivering Products to Customers

In addition to developing e-commerce applications, packaging and distribution must be considered. Blockbuster Video, for instance, believing that its traditional distribution through stores could become obsolete, is actively exploring electronic media as a distribution channel. Clearly, Blockbuster knows what consumers want in entertainment: It has the rental and purchase history on its 40 million members and is adding 300,000 new members each week. While positioning itself to be the provider of new media, the company is collecting extensive information about this emerging market. Blockbuster's research shows that the typical consumer: (1) spends $12 a month on home video expenditures; (2) wants to go to the video store to select a video; (3) is on a limited budget; (4) has time to kill; and (5) only periodically expends a large sum of money on entertainment. If we compare this profile with that presented earlier, of a $200-a-month home entertainment delivery wherein users needn't leave their couch, the two approaches seem quite contradictory.

Clearly, then, extenuating factors such as the attraction of video stores and the ability to browse are sometimes overlooked. Until user interfaces become sophisticated, the process of scrolling through dozens of menus to select a video may prove to be as time consuming as, and substantially more frustrating than, going to the video store. Most current thinking ignores the actual "excursion" element of choosing a video, for children and adults alike. Cocooning may be a very valid concept, but it does not mean that people will never want to leave their homes.

## Consumer Research and Electronic Commerce

Evaluating customer preference is the main uncertainty facing application designers. What mix of voice, data, video, entertainment, education, information, geographic coverage, mobility, and interactivity will consumers demand? How much time and money will they be willing to spend to use these networks? How much will regional or cultural differences influence application architectures? The answers to these questions lie in consumer research.

Many businesses are navigating the electronic marketplace without proper consumer and market research. This can be disastrous, given that even preliminary research shows some surprising results. Let's look at one specific example: interactive television. Surveys by Chilton Research Services and *CBS News/New York Times* suggest some degree of consumer interest and perhaps a willingness to pay less than $20 a month for a selection of interactive television services. Movies on-demand attract the most interest, followed by news, which fares relatively well. A Chilton poll of 1000 adults found 63 percent at least somewhat interested in interactive television services. Of that group, 68 percent said they would probably or definitely use "a news channel that allows you to pick the topic" [QUILL94].

A CNN/Gallup poll of consumer opinion about interactive TV yielded the following results [SBS94]:

- 46 percent would be "willing to pay for personalized news summaries" on an interactive television service.
- 39 percent want video phone calls.
- 63 percent would pay for movies on-demand.
- 57 percent would pay for television shows on-demand.
- 78 percent said their greatest worry about interactive TV is that they will have to pay for something that they previously received free of charge.
- 64 percent are concerned that interactive television will make it harder for viewers to protect their privacy.
- 41 percent are concerned that it will be too confusing to use.

On a similar note, *Macworld* magazine (October 1994) reported a telephone survey of consumer interests that showed people are more interested in facts than in the growing number of entertainment services envisioned for the electronic marketplace. The eight-month investigation showed that in the sample of 600 adults (375 randomly selected and 225 *Macworld* subscribers) consumers rate high-tech entertainment and shopping networks lower than information access, community involvement, self-improvement, and communication computer services. Only 28 percent rated a video on-demand service as highly desirable. The most desirable on-line capability was voting in elections, with half the sample in favor. The public also favors taking part in on-line public opinion polls and interactive electronic townhall political meetings. The poll dramatically demonstrates that gaining access to reference and government information and educational courses is preferable to entertainment services. Movies and television-on-demand services were ranked only tenth among 26 possible on-line capabilities [MW94].

These results contradict the directions of most companies. These companies argue that surveys are misleading in that they indicate consumers don't yet know what interactive television is and so can't be sure they will pay for it or use it. These polls do reveal a split between commercial applications being promoted by business and the public's needs and interests. If the corporate world is wrong, some spectacular failures could result. The history of home interactive services has already been marked by several multimillion-dollar failures. Most notable among these:

- The QUBE Cable Network, offered by Warner Communications and American Express from 1977 to 1984, was a $20-million investment offering polling services, games, viewer conferencing, and limited access to data banks. Although drawing plenty of publicity, the system attracted few users.
- In the early 1980s, the Times-Mirror Company introduced teletext services, called Gateway, with much fanfare. Teletext offered news and other information using television sets as display terminals. The Times-Mirror Company lost an estimated $30 million on this service.
- In 1983, the Knight-Ridder newspaper chain introduced Viewtron, which was the first attempt at delivering news, banking, shopping, and other interactive services via computer. It offered data over a telephone line, complete with graphics and color. The videotext technology, crude by today's standards, was based on a $600 terminal that plugged into television sets. The menus were unwieldy, the scrolling too slow, and the dedicated terminals too expensive. Three years and $50 million later, the service was discontinued.

Why did these services fail? The people did not seem to need videotext services. As the novelty wore off, usage of most services except on-line games and electronic mail dropped off. In sum, the consumer discredited expert predictions that "videotext" would transform society.

## 1.5 ELECTRONIC COMMERCE ORGANIZATION APPLICATIONS

Just as consumer appeal is not certain, it is not clear which e-commerce applications corporations will use internally. Corporations do not buy information and communications technology simply because it is new or because it is interesting to writers in the press. Companies adopt technology to save money and improve the bottom line. Managers are asking: How can electronic markets be utilized to further such organizational goals as better internal coordination, faster problem solving, and improved decision making?

How can it help us better serve our customers? How can we use it to better interact with our suppliers and distributors? How will these new applications impact business processes currently established internally? Developers of organizational electronic commerce applications must address these questions if they are to be successful.

## Changing Business Environment

The traditional business environment is changing rapidly as customers and businesses seek the flexibility to change trading partners, platforms, carriers, and networks at will. Many companies are looking outside their organization as well as within when shaping their business strategies. These activities include establishing private electronic connections to customers, suppliers, distributors, industry groups, and even competitors, to increase the efficiency of business communications, to help expand market share, and to maintain long-term viability in today's business environment. The Information Superhighway will expand this trend to another level all together: It will allow business to exchange information among constantly changing sets of customers, suppliers, and research collaborators in government and academia on a global basis. It will indeed become a powerful business tool that no organization can do without.

This trend has been reinforced in George Salk's interesting *Harvard Business Review* (HBR) article "Time—The Next Source of Competitive Advantage" (July/August 1988) and, more recently, in the March/April 1992 HBR (Salk, Evans, and Shulman) article, "Competing on Capabilities: The New Rules of Corporate Strategy." According to Salk, "competitive strategies based on flexible manufacturing, rapid response, expanding variety, and increasing innovation are time-based. Inter-networking, whether internally or externally with customers and business partners, can be a useful tool to facilitate time-based competitive strategies." Internetworking via a public network infrastructure provides a firm with the pathways to conduct e-commerce between trading partners, support collaboration with partners who can supply needed capabilities, and stay close to the customer.

Interestingly, traditional firms and financial institutions such as banks and credit institutions view electronic commerce with a mix of eagerness, fear, and confusion. Many large and successful organizations fear that their vision of business no longer seems to apply. The story is a familiar one: A company doing well suddenly finds itself stagnating and frustrated as fleet-footed competitors take away market share. The root cause of these crises is not that things are being done poorly. It is not even that the wrong things are being done very well. Indeed, in most cases, the right things are being done—but fruitlessly. What accounts for this paradox is that the assumptions on which the organization was founded and according to which it is being run no longer fit reality. Take, for instance, the classic cases of IBM and Digital Equipment Corporation (DEC) in the computer industry. IBM based its philosophy on the success of mainframe computers, and DEC clung to its VAX line of minicomputers for close to a decade. Much painful surgery befell before these companies' managements finally changed their theory of business and shifted to new foundations based on the PC revolution, which began around 1981 and which these companies had missed exploiting for almost a decade. Now, e-commerce is bringing about another revolution that no company can afford to miss.

In general, firms utilize consumer and market research to form the assumptions that shape its strategy, dictate its decisions about what to do and what not to do, and define what it considers meaningful results. These assumptions are what Peter Drucker [PD94] calls a company's theory of the business. This raises interesting issues: Which assumptions of e-commerce may force you to develop a new theory of business? If you are a computer company, what should you change to adapt? Likewise, if you are a bank, what should you do? These are tricky but fundamental questions that every company must address with candor and thoroughness. Finding the right answers will mean survival in the twenty-first century, and not answering them adequately will lead to chapter 11 filings for bankruptcy protection.

On the issue of developing a theory of business in the electronic marketplace, the *Washington Post* carried a series of articles dealing with economic growth and the structure of what they term the *New Economy*. It stated that new growth is coming from thousands of small, fleet-footed companies. At the same time, the old giants are reshaping to be in the vanguard of a productivity revolution that is refashioning the economy. The article went on to state that "with the aid of new technology and new forms of corporate organization, firms are finding ways to do things faster, better and cheaper, revitalizing entire industries and redefining the terms of economic competition at the same time" [WP94].

The reaction to numerous business pressures are depicted in Fig. 1.6. Companies are restructuring. Lean and mean is the battle cry of companies seeking increased market share to offset decreasing profit margins and to gain competitive global positioning through reduced operational costs. Organizations see major work force reductions or "downsizings" as the way to gain operational efficiency and agility. The need for faster reaction times to environmental events (customer requests, competitive new products) typically results in a decrease in middle management and line employees, whom top management visualizes as hampering organizational flexibility and not contributing directly to the bottom line.

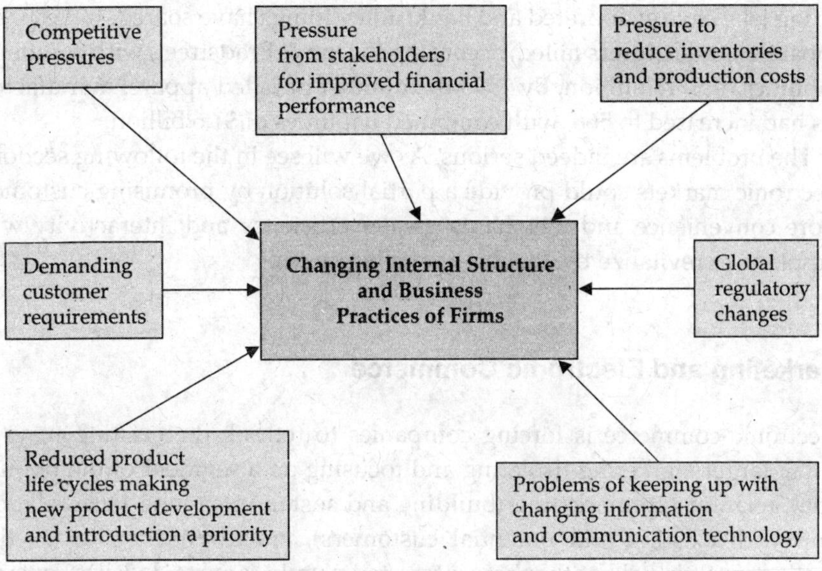


**Figure 1.6** Pressures influencing business

## Electronic Commerce and the Retail Industry

Let's take a look at the changing conditions in the "new economy" with respect to the retail industry. Consumers are pushing retailers to the wall, demanding lower prices, better quality, a large selection of in-season goods. Retailers are scrambling to fill the order. They are slashing back-office costs, reducing profit margins, reducing cycle times, buying more wisely, and making huge investments in technology. They are revamping distribution channels to make sure that warehouse costs are down by reducing their average inventory levels and coordinating the consumer demand and supply patterns. In the push to reduce prices, more and more retailers are turning to overseas suppliers, in part because of cheaper labor costs. For example, apparel retailers in the U.S. buy roughly half their merchandise overseas each year. In 1993, they increased the amount of merchandise purchased abroad by about 7 percent while holding the line on total purchasing.

Retailers are in the immediate line of fire and were first to bear the brunt of cost cutting. They are putting that pressure on the manufacturing and supplier end of the pipeline. At the same time, the quest for efficiencies has led to turmoil and consolidation within the retail industry. The pressure experienced by retailers and suppliers can be seen in the disappearance of jobs, in mergers, and in the increase in business failures in the manufacturing sector. During the past ten years in the United States, 2.5 million apparel manufacturing jobs have evaporated and bankruptcy filings have soared. In 1989, 204 apparel manufacturers failed, according to Dun & Bradstreet, with combined liabilities of $148 million. By 1993 the number of failed apparel manufacturers had increased to 566, with combined liabilities of $1.6 billion.

The problems are indeed serious. As we will see in the following sections, electronic markets could provide a partial solution by promising customers more convenience and merchants greater efficiency and interactivity with suppliers to revitalize the troubled retailing sector.

## Marketing and Electronic Commerce

Electronic commerce is forcing companies to rethink the existing ways of doing target marketing (isolating and focusing on a segment of the population), relationship marketing (building and sustaining a long-term relationship with existing and potential customers), and even event marketing (setting up a virtual booth where interested people come and visit). Consider the case of conventional direct marketers, who devote some 25 percent of their revenues to such costs as printing and postage for catalogs. Interactive marketing could help cut such expenses and may even deliver better results.

Interactive marketing is accomplished in electronic markets via interactive multimedia catalogs that give the same look and feel as a shopping channel. Users find moving images more appealing than still images and listening more appealing than reading text on a screen. Those are two powerful reasons why every text-based and still-picture-based interactive experiment like videotext has failed in the past. It is also why no computer terminal–based service has ever generated anywhere near the volume of retail merchandise orders that televised shopping channels have achieved. Maximum public acceptance will require that interactive catalog services have a more entertaining visual appearance than traditional text-intensive catalogs have had. Ideally, an interactive shopping program should produce full-motion demonstrations of the selected products, but such a practical and economical technology has yet to be developed.

Consumer information services are a new type of catalog business. An example is CUC International, of Stamford, Connecticut, whose Comp-U-Card shopping service produces annual revenues of some $850 million. The company's primary mission is not to sell products but to provide the information people need to comparison shop. CUC maintains databases with detailed information on some 250,000 products, such as cars, TV sets, and air conditioners. In return for a $49 annual fee, each of the service's 30 million subscribers gets unlimited access to the information—usually by dialing an 800 number and speaking to a live person who consults the computer database. Those who wish to order products through CUC can do so by phone or computer; the company relays the order to the manufacturer. According to CEO Walter Forbes (*Fortune*, April 18, 1994): "This is virtual-reality inventory. We stock nothing, but we sell everything."

## Inventory Management and Organizational Applications

With borders opening up and companies facing stiff global competition for the first time in decades, managers know they need to catch on quickly to better ways of doing international business. Adaptation would include moving toward computerized, "paperless" operations, to reduce trading costs and facilitate the adoption of new business processes.

One often-targeted business process is inventory management. Solutions for these processes go by different names. In the manufacturing industry, they're known as just-in-time inventory systems, in the retail industry as quick response programs, and in the transportation industry as consignment tracking systems. Inventory reduction is often a target as it averages 2 percent of sales; and when the cost of inbound warehousing of raw materials or the cost of warehousing work-in-process inventory is included, the total often reaches 6 percent to 30 percent of sales. Electronic commerce projects seek to reduce this cost by as much as 90 percent [TD95].

### *Just-in-Time Manufacturing*

Just-in-time (JIT) is viewed as an integrated management system consisting of a number of different management practices dependent on the characteristics of specific plants. The JIT management system, an evolution of the Japanese approach to manufacturing and initially introduced for the Toyota production system, is based on two principles: elimination of waste and empowering workers. The first principle refers to the elimination of all waste (time, materials, labor, and equipment) in the production cycle. The following management practices are typically associated with JIT systems: focused factory, reduced set-up times, group technology, total productive maintenance, multifunction employees, uniform workloads, JIT purchasing, *kanban*, total quality control, and quality circles.

JIT purchasing, considered an integral part of JIT, has received considerable attention in electronic commerce. It allows a manufacturer to incorporate its suppliers' efforts toward eliminating waste in the upstream portion of the manufacturing cycle. JIT purchasing focuses on the reduction of inventories throughout the logistical systems of the manufacturing firms involved and provides a careful audit of the production process. Basically, it optimizes supplier and customer relations. In a production plant the needed materials are to be supplied just in time, no earlier or later than is demanded for processing. Production costs will decrease as the required level of stock is reduced. Materials from the supplier will be ordered only if the production plant can sell its product. Market risks are therefore passed on through the supplier chain. Furthermore, quality control of production is considerably enhanced. All stages of production are closely monitored, enabling an adequate assessment of imperfections. Such close collaboration between suppliers and customers has introduced the concept of co-makership. The companies involved in overall production are integrated and combine their efforts through long-term trade relations as evident in the Japanese system of *kieretsu*.

To achieve JIT savings, many large corporations have installed private communications networks. The I-way makes this practice more affordable and easily available to a number of small firms..

### Quick Response Retailing

Quick response (QR) is a version of JIT purchasing tailored for retailing. Most often, keeping a store filled with merchandise is a task most shoppers never consider—until the product they want is out of stock. The frustration that shoppers experience sometimes gives way to thoughts of "How do retailers buy and stock products anyway?" The process is quite complex, given that a single retailer may purchase merchandise from thousands of vendors in a global market. The failure to stock merchandise that matches customer demand can be extremely costly. For example, in the soft goods industry alone, excess inventories, inadequate information, and related inefficiencies resulted in lost sales of more than $25 billion in 1991 [IBD95].

To reduce the risk of being out of stock, retailers are implementing QR systems. QR provides for a flexible response to product ordering and lowers costly inventory levels. QR retailing focuses on market responsiveness while maintaining low levels of stocks. It creates a closed loop encompassing the retailer, vendor, and consumer chain, and as consumers make purchases the vendor automatically orders new deliveries from the retailer through its computer network. The bar-coded articles are logged by the cash registers at the point of sale, the inventory system of the store then determines the needed supply, and the system transmits an order message to the retailer. The availability of accurate information with respect to the current sales enables sophisticated marketing capable of responding to consumers' preferences. Figure 1.7 illustrates the various steps of the quick response chain.

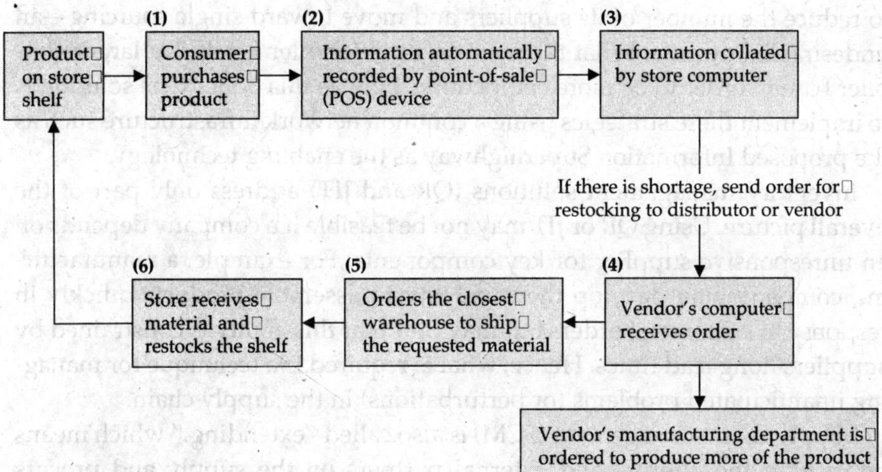


**Figure 1.7** The quick response chain

One of the famous examples of QR systems was implemented in the 1980s by Wal-Mart. Wal-Mart invested half a billion dollars in computer and satellite communications networks, bar-code systems, scanners, and other QR equipment linking each point-of-sale terminal to distribution centers and headquarters in Bentonville, Arkansas. Many believe that it was this system that enabled Wal-Mart to manage the explosive retail sales growth that catapulted the company to number one position in the U.S. retail business. The system enabled the company to maintain high service levels and increase sales while reducing the inventory costs to one-fourth of previous levels. Also by empowering its individual stores to order directly from suppliers, even overseas, individual Wal-Mart stores reduced inventory restocking time from an industry average of six weeks to thirty-six hours. Moreover, by tracking every sale through the point-of-sales devices to see what product was selling in large quantities, Wal-Mart stores were better able to keep their stores well stocked while maintaining tight inventories and low prices [MN94].

## Supply Chain Management

Until recently, these inventory management strategies were implemented through very expensive computer systems and private networks. The cost was an insurmountable barrier for many small businesses, and these new business strategies created many side effects. For instance, because of the vast investments needed to implement JIT/QR, the manufacturer/retailer tended to reduce the number of its suppliers and move toward single sourcing—an undesirable outcome. What the manufacturer/retailer needs is a larger supplier base in order to be more competitive. How is this done? One solution is to implement these strategies using a common network infrastructure such as the proposed Information Superhighway as the enabling technology.

Inventory management solutions (QR and JIT) address only part of the overall picture. Using QR or JIT may not be feasible if a company depends on an unresponsive supplier for key components. For example, a manufacturing company may develop the capability to assemble products quickly in response to customers' orders but may find that this ability is constrained by suppliers' long lead times. Hence, what is required is a technique for managing unanticipated problems (or perturbations) in the supply chain.

Supply chain management (SCM) is also called "extending," which means integrating the internal and external partners on the supply and process chains to get raw materials to the manufacturer and finished products to the consumer. Most companies fail to integrate their supply chain strategies for a number of reasons, among them a lack of system integration due to fragmented supply chain responsibilities. But in neglecting integration and the broader concept of supply chain management, firms might be missing an opportunity to cut costs and boost customer service. SCM rests on the premise that product excellence alone fails to guarantee corporate success. In fact, customers expect many services, including the prompt delivery of products to precise locations with near-perfect administrative and physical quality (see Chapter 11).

Supply chain management includes the following functions:

- *Supplier management*. The goal is to reduce the number of suppliers and get them to become partners in business in a win/win relationship. The benefits are seen in reduced purchase order (PO) processing costs, increased numbers of POs processed by fewer employees, and reduced order processing cycle times.

- *Inventory management*. The goal is to shorten the order-ship-bill cycle. When a majority of partners are electronically linked, information faxed or mailed in the past can now be sent instantly. Documents can be tracked to ensure they were received, thus improving auditing capabilities. The inventory management solution should enable the reduction of inventory levels, improve inventory turns, and eliminate out-of-stock occurrences.

- *Distribution management*. The goal is to move documents related to shipping (bills of lading, purchase orders, advanced ship notices, and manifest claims). Paperwork that typically took days to cycle in the past can now be sent in moments and contain more accurate data, thus allowing improved resources planning.

- *Channel management.* The goal is to quickly disseminate information about changing operational conditions to trading partners. In other words, technical, product, and pricing information that once required repeated telephone calls and countless labor hours to provide can now be posted to electronic bulletin boards, thus allowing instant access. Thus electronically linking production with their international distributor and reseller networks eliminates thousands of labor hours per week in the process.

- *Payment management.* The goal is to link the company and the suppliers and distributors so that payments can be sent and received electronically. This process increases the speed at which companies can compute invoices, reducing clerical errors and lowering transaction fees and costs while increasing the number of invoices processed (productivity).

- *Financial management.* The goal is to enable global companies to manage their money in various foreign exchange accounts. Companies must work with financial institutions to boost their ability to deal on a global basis. They need to assess their risk and exposure in global financial markets and deal with global information as opposed to local market information.

- *Sales force productivity.* The goal is to improve the communication and flow of information among the sales, customer, and production functions. Linking the sales force with regional and corporate offices establishes greater access to market intelligence and competitor information that can be funneled into better customer service and service quality. Companies need to collect market intelligence quickly and analyze it more thoroughly. They also need to help their customers (relationship management) introduce their products to market faster, giving them a competitive edge.

In sum, the supply chain management process increasingly depends on electronic markets because of global sourcing of products and services to reduce costs, short product life cycles, and increasingly flexible manufacturing systems resulting in an variety of customizable products.

## Work Group Collaboration Applications

For work group applications, e-commerce represents the holy grail of connectivity: a ubiquitous internetwork that enables easy and inexpensive connection of various organizational segments to improve communications and information sharing among employees and to gather and analyze competitive data in real-time. E-commerce also facilitates sales force automation by enabling salespeople to carry product and reference information in one portable device. Other applications, such as videoconferencing, document sharing, and multimedia e-mail, are expected to reduce travel and encourage telecommuting. Businesses might also save big on reduced processing costs by improving the distribution channel for documents and records to suppliers, collaborators, and distributors.

Video conferencing is now the best-established application, and is expected to grow in the coming years. Video conferencing allows distant business colleagues to communicate without the expense, time, and inconvenience of traveling. Already in hospitals and health clinics, video conferencing allows surgeons to examine computerized video x-rays and CAT scans of distant patients whose doctors need a second opinion. Because video conferencing still requires significant investments in equipment and often entails the use of dedicated facilities with special communications lines, its applicability and appeal to small businesses have been limited.

Video conferencing is beginning to penetrate the desktop PC market, although technical limitations will limit that growth. What is needed are faster chips for processing video—namely, compressing and decompressing. In the past, high video conferencing start-up costs—at least $25,000—have kept it a product for large corporations. This could change dramatically with the introduction of cheaper video conferencing for less than $500. A small camera mounted on the top of the computer monitor and two add-on boards can transform a PC into a video-phone. Also, as the price of point-to-point or point-to-multipoint video conferencing drops, video conferencing is expected to continue its penetration into the corporate marketplace (see Chapter 18).

In sum, organizational applications of electronic commerce have to meet the challenges of the new business environment where the emphasis is on service quality, flexibility, and customization of production to meet customer needs.

## 1.6 SUMMARY

Broadly speaking, electronic commerce is a new way of conducting, managing, and executing business transactions using computer and telecommunications networks. Electronic commerce is expected to improve the productivity and competitiveness of participating businesses by providing unprecedented access to an on-line global marketplace with millions of customers and thousands of products and services. Another goal is to provide participating companies with new, more cost- and time-efficient means for working with customers, suppliers, and development partners. For instance, if everything works as planned, network-based e-commerce will enable companies to (1) shorten procurement cycles through on-line catalogs, ordering, and payment; (2) cut costs on both stock and manufactured parts through efficient JIT and QR systems that reduce inventory and facilitate automatic replenishment; and (3) shrink product development cycles and accelerate time-to-market through collaborative engineering and product customization.

The emerging electronic marketplace is expected to support all business services that normally depend on paper-based transactions. Buyers can browse multimedia catalogs, solicit bids, and place orders. Sellers will respond to bids, schedule production, and coordinate deliveries. A wide array of value-added information services will spring up and bring buyers and sellers together. These services will include specialized directories, broker and referral services, vendor certification and credit reporting, network notaries and repositories, and financial and transportation services. Although many of these transactions and services already occur electronically, they require dedicated lines or prior arrangements. The use of a network-based infrastructure reduces the cost and levels the playing field for both small and large businesses.

Chapter 2

# The Network Infrastructure for Electronic Commerce

To become a reality, electronic commerce needs a network infrastructure to transport the content. Also known as the electronic, interactive, or multimedia superhighway, the I-way has become the leading buzzword that has no precise definition. Basically, the term describes a high-capacity (broadband), interactive (two-way) electronic pipeline to the home or office that is capable of simultaneously supporting a large number of electronic commerce applications and providing interactive phonelike connectivitv between users and services and between users and other users.

The principal shortcoming of the existing communications infrastructure lies in its inability to provide integrated voice, data, and video services. Historically, the voice and data networks have evolved separately, with voice networks relying on circuit switching and data networks using packet switching techniques. Thus a business user requiring voice, data, and video conferencing services often had to use three separate networks—a voice network, a data network, and a videoconferencing network. The emergence of integrated electronic commerce applications in health care, manufacturing, education, and other industries is paving the way for a network infrastructure capable of supporting multiple types of information.

Few concepts have caught the attention of financial markets, news media, government bureaucrats, and the public at large with as much sound and fury as the I-way. Fueling media and business interest is the fascination with the future of e-commerce and the profit potential for "first-mover" companies that are expected to capture a market share. We already see billion-dollar companies and global conglomerates (e.g., AT&T, Sony, Time Warner, Microsoft, Viacom) frantically maneuvering, through mergers, acquisitions, and joint ventures, to prepare for a future they dimly perceive but are anxious to understand and influence. These firms have begun making investments in technology to construct the new infrastructure. As we will see shortly, however, interest in the I-way is slowly diffusing to other industries as the investment in new information technologies and tools accelerates. Still, projections indicate that anywhere from $100 to $200 billion will be spent on constructing the I-way infrastructure over the next 10 to 15 years [NII93].

The pace of activity is frantic in all spheres. Companies are upgrading their network infrastructure or creating new products, and reorganizing through mergers and acquisitions to better prepare for life on the I-way. For instance, long-distance and local telephone operators are laying new high-speed fiber optic links to the home. Cable television providers are either upgrading their coaxial cable or installing fiber optic links. To access the information, computer companies are building sophisticated PCs with much more functionality, and TV manufacturers are building televisions and set-top boxes (cable boxes with embedded microprocessors with the digital processing power of fast computers). Traditional publishers and movie producers are rushing to create content for delivery. And software companies are racing to build the tools and programs to make it all work together. On the nontechnology front, courts are stepping in, declaring certain regulatory statutes unconstitutional and so paving the way for more competitive markets. Worldwide, governments are proposing new laws to eliminate restrictions on competition [GAO94].

The initial euphoria about the I-way is being tempered as everyone involved realizes the technological complexity and the multiyear R&D effort needed to make it a reality. The collapse of the Bell Atlantic/TCI $30 billion merger in early 1994, which would have combined telephone and cable networks in the Northeast to create a large segment of the I-way, was the first event to bring this to the fore. Initial articles often described the I-way as either already existing or right around the corner, but it is now acknowledged that the I-way has attracted attention beyond its abilities to deliver.

Even the business moguls who rushed to make deals earlier are now stepping back and admitting that constructing the I-way is not as easy as initial ly expected. By the same token, perceptions of the I-way have progressed from hazy unfamiliarity to jaundiced skepticism, often in the space of about six weeks. Initially, the thesis was "the development of the I-way is the next industrial revolution"—and then the dismissive antithesis, "The I-way is off track, it is delayed and it is not meeting anyone's expectations." This quote is attributed to Barry Diller, CEO of QVC, who fought bitterly with Viacom in a takeover battle for Paramount Studios [IWK94].

Some cynicism should have been expected after the initial euphoria, especially among those who discount the technological complexity of crafting an integrated infrastructure consisting of millions of complicated parts. Many people familiar with technology know that constructing the I-way is a painstakingly slow and arduous process. In fact, the abandonment of the Bell Atlantic/TCI merger and other early setbacks probably served to blow a welcome cooling breeze of reality over what had become an overheated market. Although much of the present skepticism is justified given the hype, it is nonetheless important not to underestimate the scale and import of the changes that are occurring daily.

For a preponderance of the general public the I-way remains shrouded in mystery despite the constant supply of TV, newspaper, and magazine stories about cyberspace. Most people just don't understand what the I-way is or how it works and how it will change their lives. According to a poll reported in *Folio Magazine*, 66 percent of Americans say they have not seen, read, or heard anything about the I-way. The survey of 1255 adults also revealed that even among the 34 percent of people aware of the topic, most claim to have very little understanding of what it all means and believe the technology has little or nothing to do with their everyday lives [FM94]. Meanwhile, a Gallup poll found that 78 percent of Germans and 57 percent of Britons didn't know what the I-way was, while 73 percent of the French demonstrated a basic understanding (*Wall Street Journal*, April 10, 1995, p. B6). An MCI survey of 800 adults found that 50 percent didn't even recognize the term *interactive media*, which is extensively associated with the I-way [SIMBA94].

Likewise, most businesses do not understand how the I-way will change the way they advertise, market, or sell their products and services, how it will change their relationship with customers, what sort of new arrangements will be possible with suppliers and collaborators, how it will affect information sharing between various parts of the organization, and how it will impact individual productivity and efficiency. These are the very issues that have been neglected in the media coverage.

The lack of comprehension can be attributed in part to the paucity of electronic commerce applications that the consumer has personally experienced. Technologists, moreover, are creating applications with little emphasis on marketing or consumer education. We believe that the technology lacks a suitable framework for capturing new events, events moving so rapidly and in so many directions that it is practically impossible to keep up with changes. To understand the changes taking place, a big picture needs to be developed that can put all the pieces into proper perspective.

In this chapter, we will present such a framework, one that integrates the various components of the I-way. Our goal is to understand broadly the various changes occurring in the industries that comprise the I-way. Our focus is on the convergence of business acumen, strategy, technology directions, and capital requirements. We will end the chapter with a discussion of the important public policy issues that need to be addressed in the I-way construction.

## 2.1 MARKET FORCES INFLUENCING THE I-WAY

### Demands and Requirements of Market Participants

The success or failure of any innovation, product, or service is a factor of market forces. In this section, we will chart the forces that are influencing the construction of the I-way. This understanding is important because e-commerce applications are dependent on the underlying I-way. For instance, if we choose cable TV as our access ramp, we may be limiting ourselves to certain applications such as video on-demand and may not be able to develop two-way interactive applications such as small business information publishing using tools like the World Wide Web (WWW).

Such limitations raise the question of which user roles the I-way will eventually support. The possibilities include:

- Users who become information publishers by setting up on-line servers
- Consumers, end users, or businesses consuming and paying for information products/services
- Information service providers, who are commercial, government, or private providers or publishers of information goods and services
- Value-added information providers, including third-party brokers and other intermediaries, as well as originators of services who add value by packaging or building on services provided by others

From this list, we see that users and firms play multiple roles as consumers and producers of information. These roles are not fixed but can be combined or bundled in various ways such that firms can, for example, concurrently be information consumers and providers. Examination of the various user roles provides an indication of the market structure and could explain why many companies are merging or realigning themselves.

Until recently, the marketplace was fragmented into communication, entertainment, and information sectors. Companies once narrowly focused on one type of user role now seek to broaden their markets and serve as many users as possible. Two points are worth considering here:

1. The boundaries among communication, entertainment, and information are not absolute. For instance, video is part of information, entertainment, and communication (via video conferencing).
2. The boundaries among equipment are not absolute. Today, technology exists to allow television sets and PCs to interact or exchange any sort of

data. This emerging compatibility results in the flexibility needed to take advantage of new services. In the next generation of consumer equipment, this will become more evident as new devices for telephony, entertainment, and data all interact.

Predicting the most successful form and function of the infrastructure requires examining the overlap between user roles and conflicting technical perspectives brought forth by the companies competing to create, support, and exploit specific components of the information infrastructure. Among these competitors are telephone companies, cable distributors, computer makers, and content providers, each based on different technologies and points of view.

The telcos want to see an I-way that can support a variety of applications: on-demand publishing, real-time video conferencing, including distance learning and tele-everything—telemedicine, telemarketing, and telecommuting—where individuals work from home through the extensive use of telephone hookups. The telcos are driven by the fear that they could be out of business if they are complacent in providing new products and services. Although the seven Regional Bell Operators (RBOCs or Baby Bells) reach an estimated 90 percent of the U.S. population, they cannot sit still as improvements in cellular and other technology and upstarts such as the cable companies cut into their market share. To head off competition, the telcos have invested heavily in fiber optics and sophisticated switching technology. Between 1985 and 1992, long-distance companies are estimated to have installed 95,000 miles of fiber optic cable nationwide [GAO94].

The cable industry wants to expand services from TV programming or pay-per-view services such that the consumer can pay bills, shop, reference encyclopedias, or check stock prices—all without leaving the couch. The cable companies see a market for new consumer offerings in enhanced entertainment services such as interactive TV (e.g., video on-demand, information on-demand, and education on-demand) and in business services such as voice and data communications and access to on-line services. Most of all, they see the I-way as a chance to exploit their primary asset: coaxial cables stretching into an estimated 61 percent of U.S. households and around 20 percent of Japanese and European homes. Most cable companies, however, tend to see the I-way as a 500-channel one-way distribution vehicle (from local cable head-end to customer premises) for audio and video. If they were solely responsible for linking users to the network backbone, their concept of I-way might favor entertainment delivery over two-way interactive communication that the telephone companies want. In short, driving the cable companies is a desire to truck entertainment into homes. They want a highway optimized for digital entertainment, and it is not clear whether this fits the needs of businesses or consumers.

The on-line services (Prodigy, CompuServe, America Online) and computer companies want to see an I-way that involves a lot of two-way interaction such as electronic mail, information search and retrieval, and more forums, chat lines, and bulletin boards. The computer industry is determined to shape a market, substantially broader than that for computers—the success story of the 1980s. The I-way is expected to spark a "gold rush" for powerful desktop computers with networking and multimedia capabilities. This in turn would boost sales of system and application software that would provide the services need to work with these computers.

The demands and requirements various participants place on the network infrastructure are bound to be very different. To support as many roles as possible, an increasing number of alliances are developing between telecommunication, cable television, and entertainment companies. These partnerships provide the synergy to spur consumer demand for advanced information, entertainment services, and the equipment and devices necessary to provide them.

## Strategic Alliances and the I-Way Infrastructure

To ensure construction of a broadly useful I-way, strategic planning should take into account the needs of the communication, entertainment, and information sectors. However, the resource requirements of building these three segments of the I-way are driving companies to make maximum use of existing facilities through alliances to control costs and create test markets.

Alliances, particularly among large firms, are dominant for several reasons: They reduce risks, spread costs, and allow firms to acquire costly expertise in different areas instantly. Two aspects of these alliances are worth noting. First, they cut across industry lines, a diversity suggesting that member companies will perform different roles within the alliances. For example, studios provide the content, telephone or cable companies deliver the information, and computer hardware and software firms provide the access hardware and applications to use the data. Second, many alliances are international, signaling that the I-way will be global from the start.

During 1993 and 1994, cable operators, telcos, computer hardware manufacturers, software developers, and instrument manufacturers announced alliances almost on a weekly basis. Envisioning a future of programming and data services sent to homes, the competitive cable and telcos have been warily sniffing at each other for years. Besides the AT&T–McCaw, Rogers–Maclean Hunter, and Viacom–Paramount alliances, there has been substantial activity on a more modest scale, including the following:

- Southwestern Bell became the first telephone company to own cable systems with its acquisition of Hauser Communications Systems in Washington D.C, Maryland, and Virginia, for $650 million.
- Liberty Media purchased 75 percent of Home Shopping Network. QVC network announced a 2.4 billion stock swap merger for Home Shopping Network. BellSouth invested $2.5 billion in QVC to buy out Liberty Media interest. (This is as complicated as it gets.)
- US West invested $2.5 billion for a 25.5 percent stake in Time Warner. The strategic alliance, the first ever between a telco and a cable operator, will allow them to build full-service, fiber optic data networks.
- The Paramount–Viacom merger, worth $16 billion, gives Viacom access to content and assures Paramount access to consumers for its content. NYNEX invested $2.2 billion in Viacom in support of this merger. Paramount acquired publisher Macmillan for $533 million.
- Other mergers and acquisitions: British Telecom bought into MCI ($4.0 billion); BellSouth bought 22.5 percent of Prime Cable ($0.3 billion); Bell Atlantic bought into Lusacell ($0.4 billion); SW Bell bought Associated Communications domestic cellular business ($0.5 billion).

As you can see, a majority of the alliances are between telcos and cable companies. Why? Today, cable companies have the bandwidth to the home that the telcos lack, but they don't have the telcos sophisticated switching equipment and operational support systems to provide interactive, point-to-point communications. The phone companies bring their vast investment in switching equipment to the table but lack cable operators' know-how in packaging, pricing, and distributing entertainment and information services. Both parties, then, need each other.

These mergers are expected to result in significant long-term opportunities to achieve economies of scale by providing cable and telephony access to more customers. More important, it would give the new alliance increased leverage, from both a cost and timeliness perspective, in the purchase of content or programming. Phone companies need cable/programming assets for two reasons. First, new regulations will allow telcos to be cable operators (to carry and even own programming content) in their assigned region. Thus access and ownership of programming is valuable. Cable companies such as Time Warner, which includes Warner Brothers Studios and Home Box Office (HBO), and Viacom, which includes MTV, VH-1, Showtime, and Paramount Studios, are examples of cable operators that own content and copyright. Second, given the inevitable loss of market share for RBOCs in telephony due to the easing of government regulations and out-of-region competition, alliances are key to putting pressure on other cable/telco competitors, as well as generating incremental revenue. Confusion could remain the watchword for the telecommunications industry through the mid-1990s, as these companies try to figure out market conditions and understand how to deliver a variety of content, rather than simply audio conversations, over phone lines.

In short, major players will continue acquiring smaller players on the presumption that the following will be necessary for success: an active presence in a variety of markets (cellular, cable, and telephony); large pools of geographically contiguous consumers; and content for the network.

## 2.2 COMPONENTS OF THE I-WAY

Three major components make up the I-way infrastructure, as shown in Fig. 2.1: consumer access equipment, local on-ramps, and global information distribution networks.

*Consumer access equipment* is often ignored in discussions of the I-way but represents a critical category, the absence or slow progress of which is holding up other segments of the I-way. For instance, interactive TV is uncommon, not because of a lack of wiring, but because of a lack of affordable equipment on the customer's side for access and on the provider's side for

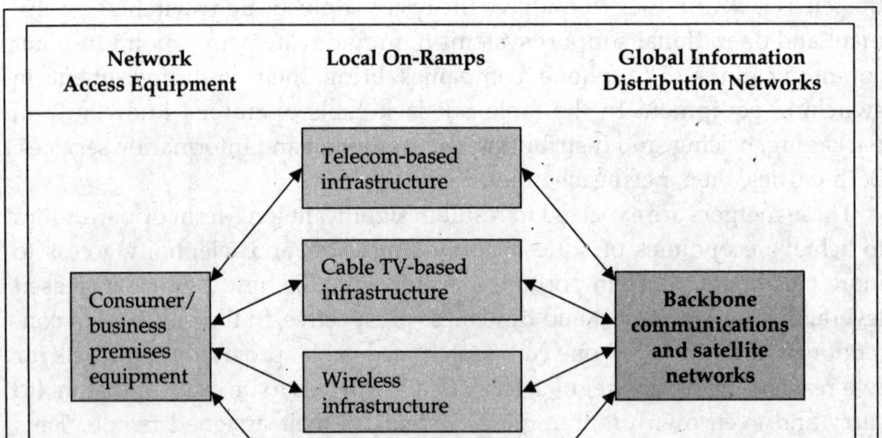


**Figure 2.1** Components of the Information Superhighway infrastructure

distribution. This segment of the I-way includes hardware and software vendors, who provide physical devices such as routers and switches, access devices such as computers and set-top boxes, and software platforms such as browsers and operating systems.

*Local or access roads, or on-ramps,* simplify linkages between businesses, schools, and homes to the communications backbone. This component is often called the "last mile" in the telecommunications industry. The providers of access ramps can be differentiated into four categories: telecom-based, cable TV–based, wireless-based, and computer-based on-line information services that include value-added networks (VANs). Benefits and limitations accompany each method. These backbone access providers link users and e-commerce application providers. Before consumers select a provider, they should decide which services they want to access in the electronic marketplace and then research which options best suit their needs. Business must give careful consideration to the applications deployed or accessed, objectives and costs, and security and privacy. All these factors will influence the choice of tools and the access ramp consumers/business choose.

*Global information distribution networks* represent the infrastructure crisscrossing countries and continents. Most of the infrastructure for the I-way already exists in the vast network of fiber optic strands, coaxial cables, radio waves, satellites, and copper wires spanning the globe. This backbone, put in place over the last three decades by the telephone and cable companies, includes such networks as long-distance telephone lines, satellite networks, and the Internet. Although the Internet uses the same hardware (leased telephone lines), the history, protocols, and regulations surrounding it warrant its placement in another category.

Linking all the components of the I-way will require large capital investments in "open" systems (interoperable equipment that uses common standards) and installing gateways between various networks. A final requirement is switching hardware and software to move huge amounts of data effortlessly over such a complex network.

## 2.3 NETWORK ACCESS EQUIPMENT

One important, often ignored component of the I-way is the customer premises equipment (CPE) industry. *CPE, or terminal equipment,* is a generic term for privately owned communications equipment that is attached to the network. For clarity of discussion, we divide this broad category into three parts: cable TV set-top boxes; computer-based telephony; and hubs, wiring closets, and routers or digital switches.

## Set-Top Boxes

A key hardware platform for I-way access will be cable converter boxes, also known as set-top boxes, converter boxes, and converters/descramblers. They will be the gateway for information services, commercial transactions, and 500-digitally compressed channels. These boxes will have greater intelligence and more features than the existing converter boxes, such as enabling users to make phone calls, surf the Internet, and even plan their viewing schedule for the week. Because virtually all cable boxes are owned not by cable subscribers but by the cable systems that deliver programming, the type of boxes consumers get in the next few years will ultimately be decided by the local cable company. Major suppliers of set-tops are building them with varying degrees of capabilities to serve the more than 10,000 cable systems across the United States, each with a different expectation of what the future will bring.

The simplest set-top boxes will feature on-screen text menus enabling features like parental lockout, favorite-channel grazing, and time-delay programming for unattended VCR recording. At the high end might be a box with a menu system based on icons for navigating through various activities—to shop, access a bank account, play videogames, watch a pay-per-view movie, or examine an on-screen TV schedule. Cable operators will be able to download software through the cable system into the set-tops. Set-tops will have slots for add-on cards that can be used to change or add applications, provide security, or expand the unit's memory. They will also have a serial data port that can be hooked up to a printer. The main goal is to be flexible for the applications of tomorrow.

For more sophisticated transactions, much of the intelligence will be in the set-top device, as opposed to residing in a central computer. For instance, General Instrument has devised a standardized module that could be included in set-top boxes for delivery of interactive services ranging from home banking and electronic yellow pages to baseball statistics and stock quotes. Developed in cooperation with Intel and Microsoft, the module, dubbed the LinX, is based on the 486 chip and will have a real-time operating system developed by Microsoft.

The following is a comparison of accessing the I-way via a set-top versus a PC:

- *The display.* The standard television display, a low-resolution video image, has not changed in 30 years. TV is well adapted to showing full-motion video to viewers sitting several feet away, but its text display is extremely limited. High-definition television, still getting off the ground, is sharper but still too poor for text. Computer displays, which are essentially improved television tubes, on the other hand, have evolved to the point where the latest high-resolution models easily display video, text, and graphics crisply to a viewer seated a foot and a half away. Displays suitable for a roomful of people are less advanced. In sum, computers won't have to adapt much to match television's strengths, but television is a long way from matching a computer monitor's strengths.

- *The controls.* The set-top will use a hand-held remote control—possibly a joystick, trackball, or other hand-held cursor control borrowed from video games—that permits selections from menus. The computer has a full-function keyboard; most also have a mouse for pointing, clicking, and highlighting; other devices such as joysticks, trackballs, light pens, and voice recognition systems are widely available. In sum, there are far more flexible and powerful ways to interact with a computer than with a television.

- *The pipeline.* Existing cable television systems can deliver a huge amount of information rapidly one way—to the home—but must be modified to allow a significant return flow. Computers traditionally talk to each other over phone lines, which have sharply limited capacity compared with cable. But new modems and networks let them communicate over high-capacity cable lines. The ultimately dominant system will need high-capacity lines to deliver the vast volume of data needed for digitized video like movies on-demand.

- *The brains.* The set-top box is really a special-purpose computer with powerful graphics and communications features but limited versatility: Users can do nothing else with it. The box is largely a slave to the central computers of the interactive system. PCs are very versatile; interactive applications are only a small part of what they can do. They are powerful in their own right and not dependent on the system's central computers with which they communicate. In the history of new technologies, single-use hardware has usually lost out to more versatile hardware, and centralized control has usually given way to autonomy for users.

- *The accessibility.* Nearly every household has a television and is familiar and comfortable with using it. Video games, the closest analog to the set-top box's interface with the user, are commonplace, and more than half of all households receive cable service. PCs are rapidly gaining acceptance in the home and are selling briskly, especially those that are easiest and most comfortable to use. The people most likely to use interactive systems may be the same ones most attracted to computers. The leap to interactive use is greater from passive television watching than from active computer use, so the universality of television is less advantageous than it appears. But a significant part of the public remains uncomfortable with computers.

## Computer-Based Telephony

The largest CPE product sectors are private branch exchanges (PBXs), telephones, facsimile products, modems, voice processing equipment, and video communication equipment. Most CPE product sectors such as modems are mature and evolving markets characterized by intense competition and declining unit prices. While shipment declines are being noticed in such product groups as telephones and telephone answering machines, shipments of modems, voice processing and video communication equipment are booming [USI94]. Personal communicators are beginning to emerge as a commercially viable CPE product group. These devices combine voice, data, and facsimile functions and enable users to send, store, and receive information over either wireline or wireless networks.

These software-intensive CPE products have been well received because they improve business productivity by reducing communications and travel expenses. CPE equipment will continue to become more compatible with computing equipment. For instance, AT&T reached agreement with Novell to develop a PBX-LAN interface. A similar agreement was reached between Intel and Microsoft. The open software interfaces developed through these agreements promise to enable businesses and personal computer users to transfer data, video, image, and voice messages through the telephone switches more efficiently.

## Digital Switches, Routers, and Hubs

The digital switches industry has a major impact on the I-way. To understand switching better, examine the six distinct generations (see Table 2.1) of technological developments in the switching industry from the 1880s to the 1990s. In the 90s, the switching technology is finally in place to offer sophisticated services.

How does switching work? All digital bits are essentially alike, whether they represent a movie, an opera, an electronic newspaper, or a phone call. A video program, once digitized, looks like any other digital data. In a computer network, data move from one point to their intended destination(s) because they are tagged on the front with a small bundle of identifying digits known as a *header*. Video programming is no different. Like any other data (CD-quality music, video games, or video conferencing), the digital data pass through switches that route them to their intended destination—either one or multiple recipients. Since the bundles of data are known as *packets* and the packets move through a network at very high speeds, this routing technique is known as *fast packet switching*. Cable companies are evaluating and testing

**Table 2.1** Six Generations of Switching Technology

| | |
|---|---|
| 1880s to 1920s | Manual operator controlled |
| 1920s to 1940s | Step-by-step electromechanical switches (called Strowger design); developed at the turn of the century; placed in common use beginning in the 1920s |
| 1940s to 1960s | Crossbar electromechanical; developed in the 1930s; in heavy use in the 1950s and into the 1960s to replace step-by-step |
| 1960s to 1970s | Semielectronic switching stored-program-control computers, analog and digital |
| 1970s to 1990s | Totally electronic solid state digital, increasingly software driven |
| 1990s | Fiber optic-based integrated switching and transmission systems enabling distributed architecture, multimedia systems |

different switching techniques, including asynchronous transfer mode (ATM), a method quickly gaining acceptance as an international standard.

Capacity expansions (fiber optic upgrades and digital compression) have served only to enlarge the pipeline so that more content can be sent to everyone in a "broadcast" or "point-to-multipoint" style of communication. But a longer-term benefit of the digitization of program content will be the growing ability to switch or route content from a sender to a single receiver (known in telecommunications as "point-to-point" communication). If 400 to 1000 channels can be sent to a neighborhood of 300 homes, channel capacity will become so great that individual channels can be sent to individual homes, or even individual viewers within that home—a true video-on-demand capability.

For building internetworks, routers play a major role. *Routers* are internetworking devices that intelligently connect the local area networks (LANs) and backbone wide area networks (WANs) of various providers. The major benefits of internetworks include communication between separate networks and access to computing resources distributed throughout an organization. Currently businesses with many disparate protocols running in their computing environment require multiprotocol routers to process their LAN and WAN traffic. Routers allow companies to departmentalize and segment their networks so that a problem on one segment does not bring down another department.

In contrast to routers, *hubs* act as the wiring centers for large LANs—they can diagnose line failures, measure and manage traffic flow, and greatly simplify reconfiguring large LANs. Adding switching technology to hubs solves both the efficiency and predictability problems with the Ethernet LAN topology. Essentially, a switched hub gives each user on the network his/her own private line, a feature that can eliminate collisions (two stations trying to talk at once) and allow traffic to flow more evenly. Switched hubs can improve network efficiency by more than an order of magnitude. As technology develops, the fine line between the two technologies will blur, and the hub and the router will likely become one box.

## 2.4 THE "LAST MILE": LOCAL ROADS AND ACCESS RAMPS

One of the key forces shaping the dynamics of the I-way infrastructure is the "last mile" wiring linking homes with the backbone. Four types of "last mile" connections are currently in existence: plain old telephone system (POTS) wires, cable TV coaxial cable, electricity wires, and wireless (a radio-based cellular or satellite connection). The "last mile" connections represent a tremendous "sunken" investment that cannot be easily replaced or overlooked in any network strategy [BY94].

The huge investment needed for wiring and upgrades will come only after sufficient consumer demand for the e-commerce services. The investment is enormous, given that an estimated 98 percent of U.S. households have a telephone line that connects them to the local telephone company's network, and outside 90 percent of these homes is a cable laid by the local cable TV operator. In addition, almost 99 percent of the households have electricity lines that connect them to the local power company. And, the cellular industry is estimated to have 30–35 million users and is growing rapidly.

Eventually, consumers may get two or three upgraded links into the home: one from the telcos, one from the cable TV industry, and one from the electric power utility industry. However, companies laying the last mile need a "right of way" to wire neighborhoods or homes. In the United States, except for telephone, telegraph, cable, and electric companies, few others have the legal rights called "right of way." Some points to consider:

- The telephone and cable providers are expected to spend $5 billion per year over the next twenty years in their distribution loops alone to upgrade their "last mile" networks.
- The size of the market, the multitude of potential products and solutions, and operator insistence on multiple sources will ensure that several vendors will be winners in this environment.

- There is a trend toward the integration of voice and video within a single network. While hybrid fiber/coax networks are becoming the preferred architecture, this is not a universal choice. Wireless is a strong competitor. In short, multiple ways exist to implement/migrate to the hybrid architecture.
- Migration from an existing cable system is relatively straightforward. By upgrading the trunk portion of the cable network, channel capacities can be upgraded substantially and switched voice can be added at a relatively low cost.
- Most important, subscriber equipment needs to be upgraded only in those homes that are willing to pay for the incremental services. Migration for the telcos is more complicated. Because of the limited bandwidth available over existing telephone lines, the telcos must increase their last mile capacity.

In sum, companies can expect to upgrade the last mile only once in the next decade due to the tremendous cost. Hence, the last-mile economics is the most important of the issues that impel a unified vision of the I-way.

## Telecom-Based Last Mile

The telephone companies are eyeing the last mile and trying to determine the best way to spin the final web to provide a high-speed "pipe" capable of carrying high volumes of interactive voice, data, and video to homes and businesses. Telcos are the vanguard of I-way construction; their lines into homes and businesses represent the most common access ramps to the backbone. They also control the world's largest switched distributed network providing point-to-point voice, fax, data, and video-conferencing services to hundreds of millions of subscribers. This network appears to be the primary foundation for the I-way for two reasons: It is capable of handling millions of simultaneous calls, and it provides accurate usage tracking and billing. However, the telephone network suffers from two problems: lack of digital transmission capability and uneven distribution [GAO94].

Although the industry is rapidly introducing advanced digital communication technologies, the telephone network continues to be dependent on analog transmission. Much of today's telephone service is based on two analog-oriented transmission technologies: the analog voice frequency (VF) systems and the digital T-carrier system. The VF system supports voice transmission over a pair of copper wires—also known as the local loop—connecting millions of residential and business subscribers with the local telephone company's central offices. The T-carrier system plays a major role in the first step in the transition from analog to digital capabilities. The basic building block of the T-carrier technology is a single VF voice channel digitized into a 64-Kbps data stream; a T-1 line carries 24 digitized voice channels, an aggregate of 1.544 Mbps. (See Chapter 19.)

The current telco network suffers from uneven capacity distribution. For years, telcos have been weaving high-capacity fiber throughout their networks. Long-distance carriers were first, laying it for intercity trunks. Then, local carriers used fiber to connect to the long-distance carrier's points of presence. Today, much of the backbone (trunk) infrastructure is comprised of fiber. These trunk lines, making up long-distance or the local area interoffice networks, are capable of carrying interactive video and other bandwidth-intensive applications. But the local loops from the local switching center into businesses and homes are still two- or four-wire unshielded copper wire with limited capacity. In short, the bandwidth available to residential subscribers is constrained by the limited capacity of the wire linking the local telco's central office with the subscriber's equipment.

Huge investments are needed to replace the last-mile copper wires with high-capacity fiber to handle the expected flood of information from e-commerce applications. The strongest candidate for the "local wire" job seems to be fiber. A typical fiber optic cable contains 40 strands, each the size of a human hair, and is capable of carrying nearly 1.3 million phone conversations or 1920 TV channels. Fiber has successfully replaced the old microwave technology (radio waves transmitted between towers) that carried 15,000 phone conversations or 22 TV channels as the premier information delivery vehicle. To take advantage of the vast bandwidth offered by fiber networks, local telcos need to upgrade existing digital switches used to route calls to even faster technology.

Clearly, telephone companies are in a bind. On one hand, they want to extend the life of their investment in switching plant and equipment that connects residential and business telephones. On the other hand, they need more traffic for their huge networks of high-speed fiber optic trunk lines that are now operating at only a fraction of full capacity. This trade-off between more investment and better utilization of existing investment is creating very interesting dynamics in the marketplace. As a BellSouth executive put it, "We're dealing with entirely new paradigms of what constitutes a telecommunications company" [TELE94].

What will likely be offered to consumers is probably far different from what is being proposed today. We feel that two commonsense principles will likely apply:

1. There is too much existing investment, and too little money, to see very many networks start from a clean piece of paper. Networks will be built with a considerable amount of adhocracy, and will likely be a hybrid mix.

**Table 2.2** Total U.S. Access Lines, 1984–1993

| *Year* | *Lines* | *Percent Change* |
|---|---|---|
| 1984 | 114,348,800 | – |
| 1985 | 118,275,000 | 3.4 |
| 1986 | 122,202,600 | 3.3 |
| 1987 | 126,725,000 | 3.7 |
| 1988 | 130,000,000 | 2.6 |
| 1989 | 135,010,686 | 3.9 |
| 1990 | 138,059,000 | 2.2 |
| 1991 | 141,209,000 | 2.3 |
| 1992 | 145,117,000 | 2.8 |
| 1993 | 147,584,000 | 1.7 |

*Source:* United States Telephone Association [USITC94].

**Table 2.3** Network Digitalization (access lines connected to digital switches)

| *Company* | *Percent* |
|---|---|
| Hong Kong Telecom | 100.0 |
| Telokom Malaysia | 82.0 |
| Telefonos de Chile | 76.0 |
| Bell Canada | 65.0 |
| British Telecom | 64.0 |
| TELMEX (Mexico) | 57.0 |
| RBOC average (USA) | 56.1 |
| NTT (Japan) | 50.0 |
| STET (Italy) | 48.4 |
| Telefonica de Argentina | 34.0 |

*Source:* Merrill Lynch [USITC94].

2. Given the hybrid nature of networks, and given the current regulatory laws in the United States, networks might vary in design even between neighboring service areas. This will generate confusion and will to some degree hinder consumer adoption.

In many countries, the technological upgrades required seem daunting. Across Asia, for instance, only Hong Kong and Singapore enjoy telecommunications facilities comparable to that found in the United States and in Japan. Thailand and the Philippines are just beginning to develop high-speed data backbones. Take developing countries such as India. At the moment, on-line services that require telephone access are limited because there are too few lines and too many people. Nonetheless, many countries, including India, are taking telecom development more seriously than ever before. For instance, the Malaysian private sector is planning to invest more than $20 billion in the next ten years to establish the "Malaysian information highway"[AW94]. Tables 2.2 and 2.3 indicate the amount of sunken investment in terms of number of telephone lines in the United States and level of digitalization in telephone switching in several countries.

### Structure of the U.S. Telecommunications Industry

To understand the infrastructure challenges and changes taking place, it's essential that you comprehend the structure of the telecom industry. In the United States, voice, data, and video-conferencing services are provided by the local exchange carriers (local telephone companies) serving the local access and transport areas, and by the interexchange carriers (long-distance carriers) providing long-distance and international dialing services through their long-distance networks. At the top the Federal Communications Commission (FCC) regulates interstate common carrier communications, and individual state public utility commissions (PUCs) regulate local communications. The FCC also regulates the use of radio frequencies through a system of spectrum allocation and licensing.

The common carrier network has been divided into 161 local access transport areas (LATAs). Communications among LATAs are handled by long-distance carriers, while intra-LATA telecommunications (both local and toll calling) are the responsibility of the local exchange carriers (LECs). Private telecommunications networks, which serve specific customers rather than offering services to the public at large, are not regulated as common carriers. In 1984 the telecommunications infrastructure was changed when the monopolistic reign of Ma Bell (AT&T) was broken up. The divestiture of AT&T not only has revolutionized the U.S. telecom market, but its effects have been felt worldwide, as it took a stodgy, bureaucratic monopoly and turned it into a lean, mean fighting machine. For instance, in 1984 it would have taken up to eighteen months to install a leased line at a customer site and six to eight weeks to provide a private circuit connecting various parts of the organization. Today, it takes less than four weeks [MM94].

Local services in the United States are provided by about 1325 local telephone companies, including 7 Regional Bell Operating Companies; other telcos owned by GTE, Sprint (United Telecom and Centel franchises); and independent local telephone companies. Many of these small, local companies operate as rural telephone cooperatives. For over a decade, the RBOCs have enjoyed one of the last true monopolies in the United States. Each still has exclusive rights to provide a basic, local telephone service. However, that too is changing. At the time of the creation of the Modified Final Judgment (MFJ) in 1984, RBOCs were prevented from providing any type of information or long-distance services. However, in 1988, after much lobbying, the FCC reversed itself and allowed the RBOCs to provide information transmissions—the ability to carry data over their networks. Then, in 1990, the FCC further relaxed regulations to enable RBOCs to provide information services as well.

For the first time in 1993, the RBOCs confronted increasing competitive pressures in certain local services they had monopolized for decades. Hence, they are examining new ways to construct local loops and provide services in a marketplace that is no longer a "natural monopoly." Conditions in the local market today resemble those in the long-distance arena twenty years ago, when AT&T first began to face limited competition from carriers like MCI. In response to possible competition from cable TV companies and others for local exchange telephone service itself, the RBOCs have stepped up their campaign to obtain authority to enter the long-distance and telecommunications equipment manufacturing businesses and to offer video programming services.

How successful RBOCs will be in the I-way creation still it is not clear. Some historical examples show their less-than-enviable record in the information business:

- US West entered the computer retailing business in 1989, with several dozen stores. In 1992 it wrote off the entire $245-million adventure to nothing. NYNEX and Bell Atlantic also entered this market before absorbing large losses and selling out, respectively, to ComputerLand and MicroAge.
- Ameritech hailed its move into software services with a $215-million acquisition that later sold for only $170 million.
- NYNEX was savaged in the information market after an acquisition designed to combine software and telecom services and consulting backfired. The firm acquired AGS Computer for $300 million and later sold it for $100 million (necessitating a $275-million charge in November 1993).

These examples indicate that RBOCs might trumpet truly massive expansion plans, leap into a costly initial phase of growth in new markets, take a financial bloodbath, and withdraw. So in the I-way, careful planning and strategy must be coupled with flawless execution.

### RBOCs' I-Way Strategy

Cutting through the noise and defining the current network plans of various RBOCs is extremely difficult. Absent a definitively superior or ideal network architecture, there is no simple answer. The earlier strategy was not clear due to regulatory constraints that forbid RBOCs from offering video services in their region. These regulations are being dismantled, however, making the whole situation very fluid.

Basically, telcos are following two strategies in their expansion: in-territory and out-of-territory. Some RBOCs are actually implementing only one strategy, some are implementing both. However, very interesting dynamics regarding the competition and market structure are coming to light.

To compete with the existing cable operator and offer "video dialtone," Ameritech, PacTel, and several other RBOCs are focusing on in-territory growth and plan to expend significant investment into deploying basically traditional cable (a hybrid fiber/coax wire). Video dial tone (VDT) systems are expected to be open carrier networks (like computer networks) available to any programmer who wishes to use the network to deliver video programming to consumers. The VDT platform has two types of customers: multiple programmers who sell their services directly to consumers, and consumers who subscribe to one or more services from different programmers. Each service may consist of one or more channels, video on-demand, or two-way interactive service.

The main advantage touted for the VDT service is the lack of regulation or censorship (like unmoderated news groups). Any programmer, civic organization, or governmental authority can obtain access to the VDT platform for any type of content, and unsatisfied consumers can switch to other programmers' offerings over the VDT platform. In contrast to VDT, traditional cable systems are closed networks that control the distribution system and make the editorial decisions concerning what programming consumers see. A cable system has two types of customers—advertisers and consumers who subscribe to a package of programming offered by the cable operator. Cable operators can refuse to carry certain programming but are required by law to provide public, educational, and governmental channels. Due to the traditional monopoly over provision of cable service, consumers have no recourse if disappointed by the price, quality, or content. In short, VDT avoids making programming choices for consumers.

To provide VDT, RBOCs are expanding out-of-territory by acquiring cable operators. While still unable to own or operate cable TV services or companies in their own regions, the moves have laid the groundwork for the RBOCs to be big players in other regions of the country (out of state). At the same time the seven U.S. RBOCs are investing worldwide in cable television, entertainment, and wireless (Pacific Telesis in Belgium and BellSouth in Germany, Bell Atlantic and Ameritech in New Zealand, and Southwestern Bell in Mexico).

Out-of-territory also implies that they are encroaching on other RBOCs' territory. In effect, we are no longer seeing what would be called traditional cable versus telco competition. Instead, we are seeing an in-territory RBOC competing against an out-of-territory RBOC. For example, Bell Atlantic teamed with TCI to compete against Comcast within the Philadelphia area, while out-of-territory, Southwestern Bell, with its investment in Hauser, is competing against Bell Atlantic.

If the strategy works, the implications are very significant for the cable industry. It implies another significant level of growth and activity on the equipment side as two things happen. To compete with the million miles of existing cable company wire, which in effect is overbuilt, the in-territory telco players are laying additional wiring. The cable operators, who are working without out-of-territory telco assistance, will react by upgrading and rebuilding their wiring to compete against the in-territory players. Thus competitive pressure is increasing on upgrading installed wiring/equipment to ward off potential competition by making market entry less attractive to any competitor. The telcos' competitive or redundant activities will be a major factor in the shaping of the I-way.

### Broadband to the Loop "Video–Dial Tone" Strategy

In the near term, the primary challenge is to provide broadband digital services over the existing plant—the hundreds of thousands of miles of copper wire—although ultimately it may be preferable to provide fiber optics to each residence. The replacement cost for this "last mile" of the I-way linking the broadband backbone with homes, businesses, and institutions continues to be high, not only because there is so much copper wire to be replaced, but also because of the need for special equipment to process the signal on the customer's premises.

The telephone companies are adopting a mix of technologies and strategies to cope with the bottleneck in the local loop—the portion of the telephone communication circuit connecting individual subscribers with the telephone company's central office. For the telephone companies, the most promising approaches are the asymmetrical digital subscriber line (ADSL) (copper) and the fiber-to-the-curb architectures: a switched digital fiber-to-the-curb (fiber) and switched digital hybrid fiber-coax (HFC) (fiber and coaxial).

ADSL allows telephone companies to use a single copper wire to simultaneously transmit video and telephone signals by increasing the downstream transmission speed from 64 Kbps to 1.5 Mbps while providing an upstream channel between 16 and 384 Kbps. Digital compression and coding techniques permit a video signal to be transmitted over a bandwidth of 1.5 Mbps. With ADSL such a signal can be sent over several miles of ordinary twisted pair telephone wire. The ADSL central office unit works with an ADSL remote terminal located at the customer's premises. The remote terminal separates the POTS or ISDN (integrated services digital network) signal from the compressed video signal. The POTS signal is transported over standard customer premises wiring to a telephone; the broadband signal is delivered via standard twisted pair copper facilities to a set-top terminal. Advances in both ADSL technology and video decoding techniques are expected to provide real-time broadcast capability at channel rates of 3 Mbps up to 6 Mbps over a single twisted copper pair. ADSL's disadvantage is that it limits the customer to one video channel.

The fiber-to-the-curb architecture provides high-capacity switched digital network services to optical network units serving multiple residences A switched digital fiber-to-the-curb system provides video programming and information in a digitally compressed format (MPEG) and transports digitally by fiber optic equipment to the central office. The digital video signals from all providers are combined on a video distribution element known as a *host digital terminal (HDT)*. Fibers are extended from the HDT to the local pedestal (similar to cable head-end). The pedestal is an optical network unit that houses the necessary equipment to convert the optical signals to electrical impulses and distribute them to individual homes over a copper wire or coaxial cable. Only programs that are requested by the subscriber are transmitted.

Most of the newer or rebuilt cable systems use a hybrid fiber optics/coaxial cable architecture, commonly known as fiber optic feeder. Switched digital HFC combines properties of fiber and coaxial architectures and can provide 100 or more analog channels using a bus architecture. This tree and branch structure allows many customers access to the same information, thereby reducing requirements for both the transport medium and the associated electronics as compared to a switched star type architecture. For instance, in a Bell Atlantic's testbed system, 20 channels of analog video and over 650 digital signals are combined in the HFC system at the central office. A linear analog laser transmitter converts the radio frequency (RF) electrical signal to an optical one. The optical signal splits and travels downstream over multiple fibers in the feeder network to an optical node, where an optical receiver converts the signal back to an RF electrical signal. The electrical signal is amplified and broadcast over a large diameter coaxial backbone cable to individual subscribers. This system allows for maximum flexibility, including interactive multimedia connections that allow each consumer to choose his or her own programs.

The ADSL approach is expected to be the least expensive and the fiber-to-the-curb the most expensive. However, it is not yet clear which architecture will be the winner.

## Cable TV-Based Last Mile

The second major contender in the last-mile provider battle, cable is vigorously pushing the concept that high-speed data to the home is best served by running over cable networks, not on telephone analog and more recent ISDN connections. Supporters reason that cable runs through 90 percent of U.S. homes today and offers capacity that has not been fully utilized. Unlike the telephone companies, cable companies already have the high-capacity wiring in the form of coaxial cable for broadcasting analog video. But the cable companies want to provide important business services, too, such as voice telephony, data communications, and access to on-line services. A major hindrance is that cable systems tend to be proprietary and not well interconnected.

### *Wired Cable TV*

The cable television network links thousands of cable systems with millions of subscribers via broadband coaxial cable. This web of coaxial cables is, in many respects, a counterpart of the local loop linking telephone subscribers with the local telephone companies. However, there are considerable differences between the transmission technologies and network architectures deployed in the telephone and the cable systems. The telephone system is based on a switched, distributed network architecture and uses standard switching and transmission protocols capable of supporting global, narrowband, two-way, point-to-point communications. The cable systems, on the other hand, are based on a tree-and-branch network architecture and proprietary transmission protocols designed to support one-way broadband analog transmission with little or no provision for "upstream" communications.

Cable in the United States is the major video service provider, serving 62 percent of U.S. TV households, almost 55 million homes, who pay $20 billion annually for the service. Of all 93 million U.S. households, 91 million have coaxial cable running at or near their property line ("homes passed," in cable terminology). Almost 95 percent of cable subscribers have access to 30–54 channels, while 35 percent of subscribers receive 54 or more channels. See Table 2.4.

**Table 2.4** Cable Growth

| | *1975* | *1980* | *1985* | *1990* | *1992* |
|---|---|---|---|---|---|
| TV households (millions) | 69 | 77 | 85 | 92 | 93 |
| Cable subscribers (millions) | 8.5 | 15 | 38 | 54 | 56 |
| Homes passed (millions) | 23 | 35 | 65 | 83 | 89 |
| Average channel capacity | 12 | 20 | 25 | 35 | 38 |
| Network miles (thousands) | 321 | 375 | 740 | 864 | 1089 |

*Source:* A.C. Nielsen and *Television Digest.*

Time Warner, TCI, and other larger cable operators, called MSOs (multiple system operators), are taking two approaches to the development and roll-out of new services on the I-way. The first approach is holistic, anticipating a major paradigm shift in communications and entertainment where the goal is to develop and use a single system for a full array of services such as shopping, banking, entertainment, and education. Time Warner is pursuing the first strategy in Orlando, Florida, as is Viacom in its testbed efforts in Castro Valley, California. The second approach is more incremental, relying on joint ventures and partnerships to develop and test new services by investing in new networks and equipment. However, everyone is increasing channel capacity, and both approaches are likely to reach the same conclusion.

Table 2.5 provides an overview of the cable strategy. The key to the strategy lies in digital compression of signals discovered during 1991 and 1992 by cable competitors in the high-definition television (HDTV) and by designers of early direct broadcast satellite (DBS) systems. Digital compression would replace the traditional method of TV transmission (analog waves) with digital transmission, a system in which a computer takes frequent numeric samples of the analog waves and transmits this information as a string of digital ones and zeroes. To transmit the massive information content of a TV picture, these digits are compressed, meaning much of their bulk is harmlessly discarded by mathematical processes to save space on the pipeline. Cable engineers have devised a scheme for superimposing compressed, digitized channels onto the same fiber optic wire or coaxial cable that is also carrying conventional "analog" TV signals. Space savings in the pipeline can be dramatic: Anywhere

**Table 2.5** Three Phases of Cable Strategy

| | |
|---|---|
| Phase 1: 1994–1996 | Digital compression and fiber deployment expand channel capacity from current 60 channels; computing power used on system periphery; software user interface for program navigation is introduced; interactivity is limited. |
| Phase 2: 1996–1998 | Interactivity advances between subscriber and head-end; computing power deployed throughout interior of network; video servers offering true video on-demand come on line. |
| Phase 3: 1998–2000 | Cable becomes a fully implemented interactive national digital network; subscriber-to-subscriber communications available; cable networks open to wide array of new interactive services including video telephony and switched high-speed data transmission. |

from 4 to 16 video channels can go into space that had carried one analog channel, depending on the subject matter and the required picture quality. The bandwidth allocated to a single analog channel—typically 6 MHz—will carry multiple channels to the set-top box for decompression.

Cable systems traditionally use coaxial cable and a series of amplifiers throughout the distribution network. Today, most large-scale upgrades replace traditional components with fiber optic technology in the trunk sections of the network. A fiber optic system can send its signals greater distances and with less signal degradation than can the traditional coaxial system. Because fiber optic cable has a greater bandwidth capacity than coaxial cable, it can send more channels to subscribers' homes. This system also eliminates the need for expensive electronic amplifiers. In addition, fiber optic transmission offers greater security from illegal signal tapping. Cable companies are cooperating to establish fiber networks involving different operators so that they can compete with the telephone companies. Their goal is to offer alternative access for business data transport services and eventually to provide local switched residential services when regulatory hurdles are lowered.

It seems inevitable that some time in the future cable TV companies will compete with the local telephone companies. New digital and fiber optic technologies will allow them to provide telephone services over their networks, something cable companies already are doing in Britain. In the United States, state or local governments issue franchises to cable operators, and in most areas cable TV services are offered under a legal or de facto monopoly. Cable companies are not legally prohibited from offering telecommunications services, although they would probably need approval from the state public utility commissions to provide any intrastate telecommunications services.

As new entrants in the telephony business, cable companies are beginning to turn to wireless as the most cost-effective means of hooking up customers. Previous designs, by contrast, focused on integrating telephone onto the existing hybrid fiber/coaxial network all the way to the home [MCN94]. The new design would make sense if cable companies were to offer an all-wireless approach to telephone connectivity in the home, using digital technology to carve out a new service niche that would distinguish cable phone service from that of the telcos. In such a case, the voice signals would be integrated on the fiber/coax but would be propagated to several homes in a neighborhood from strand-mounted transceivers, much like cellular telephones.

### Wireless Cable TV

Direct broadcast satellite (DBS) is just starting to move into the collective consciousness of the big players as a potential threat. DBS uses super high frequency (SHF) channels to transmit satellite cable programming over the air instead of through overhead or underground wires. Technically, DBS is a name given to a service that is called multichannel multipoint distribution service (MMDS). MMDS is a fairly new service that evolved from MDS (multipoint distribution service), which could only send one or two channels. Created in the early 1970s and originally used to send business data, MDS has recently become increasingly popular in distributing entertainment programming.

DBS offers two benefits to the customer: availability and affordability. It can be made available in rural areas and other areas of scattered population where it is too expensive to build a traditional cable infrastructure, and those savings can be passed on to the subscribers.

DBS works by sending scrambled satellite cable programming to a central location where it is processed and fed into special SHF transmitters for distribution throughout the coverage area. The signals are received by special antennas installed on subscribers' roofs, combined with the existing VHF and UHF (very- and ultra- high frequency) channels from the subscriber's existing antenna, and distributed within the home or building through coaxial cable into a channel program selector located near the television set. However, some technical problems exist. For instance, rain fade, a phenomenon of rain droplets absorbing the signals being sent to the satellite dish receiver, results in picture quality degradation and/or interruption. The more dish area available for the signal to reach, the better quality picture will be, even during inclement weather or heavy rain.

Currently two types of DBS wireless cable are available: PrimeStar and Direct Satellite System—Hughes DirecTV:

- *PrimeStar Direct Broadcast Satellite Service.* Founded in 1990, PrimeStar is a partnership of six U.S. cable companies (Comcast Cable, Continental Cablevision, Cox Cable Communications, Newhouse Broadcasting, Tele-Communications Inc., and Time Warner Cable) and G.E. American Communications. G.E. American Communications owns the satellite used by PrimeStar. PrimeStar works by beaming its digital programming up to its satellite from several transmission locations in Colorado and New Jersey. The signal reaches the satellite, is boosted in power, and then travels to subscribers' 32–39 inch receiver dishes on earth, where it is channeled to decoding boxes inside subscribers' houses, and then to their televisions. Unlike Hughes DirecTV, PrimeStar customers needn't buy any equipment, but receive a mini satellite dish and a decoder box attached to the TV set as part of the service. When complete, the service is expected to offer subscribers over 100 channels of programming, for an average fee of $28 per month, excluding the dish rental.

- *Direct Satellite System (DSS)—Hughes DirecTV.* DirecTV and USSB, the respective subsidiaries of GM Hughes Electronics and Hubbard Broadcasting, provide this service with subscriber dish equipment provided by Thompson Electronics. The dish itself bears the RCA brand name and is sold together with a set-top converter. These programming services are available to anyone in the United States who has the equipment to receive their signal, but marketing of receiver equipment and service is initially limited to these markets. Programming includes most major cable services, sports, pay per view (PPV) movies, and specialized niche programming aimed at smaller audiences. The service providers claim near-laser-disc-quality pictures and near-CD-quality sound.

  Here's how it works. Hughes has launched two Ku-band satellites each containing sixteen 120-watt transponders. DBS uses digital compression to allow from four to eight channels per transponder for a total of about 140 to 180 channels, depending on what is being shown. The satellites are more powerful than the current generation of satellites and are spaced 9 degrees from others broadcasting in the same frequency range. This positioning allows interference-free reception from anywhere within the viewing area. On the customer end, signal decoders are needed and the hardware is called Digital Satellite System or DSS.

Let us examine some economics of DBS. The upfront cost to DBS subscribers is likely to be prohibitive for most current and potential wireless cable subscribers. Anybody subscribing to DirecTV pays at least $700 per TV set for the dish and set-top box, or $900 for a dish that allows a two-set hook-up, then incurs an installation fee of approximately $150, bringing the total to $850. Once the service is set up, subscribers pay a monthly programming fee, with basic packages ranging from $5.95 to $22.95 for DirecTV or $7.95 to $34.95 for USSB. Additional services, like pay per view, can add to this cost. In contrast, PrimeStar operators do not charge subscribers for the customer premises equipment nor do they commonly charge more than $25 for installation. The average cost for the service varies greatly but generally runs at a 25 percent to 40 percent discount to the wired operators in the market. In a nutshell, wireless operators are expected to be the low-cost providers in the video to the home market.

## Radio-Based Wireless Last Mile

Radio-based wireless networks, made up of cellular, microwave, and specialized mobile radio data networks, represent an important piece of the last-mile puzzle. The cellular and satellite networks have advantages over terrestrial (wired) networks because they are potentially accessible from any point on the globe without the cost of installing wire or a cable. These systems provide users with an unprecedented degree of mobility and flexibility.

The rapid growth of cellular, paging, and other wireless services tends to give the (false) impression that radio technology itself is some sort of recent development. Radio technology, of course, has been around for a long time, having first been developed on an experimental basis late in the last century. However, the technology was crude by modern standards, relatively expensive, and suffered from the "chicken and egg" syndrome, in that it took decades for a base of users to develop.

Two applications of radio technology led to its widespread usage. The first was radio broadcasting. Originally intended to bring culture and education to the masses, early radio broadcasting developers viewed the new technology as a means of developing a market for broadcast radio receivers. Eventually someone thought up the idea of charging for advertising, and the broadcasting business rapidly developed into its current structure as a profit-making industry.

The second application of radio technology was to warfare. The military establishment quickly recognized the superiority of wireless communications over earlier technologies (written messages, homing pigeons, hard-wired systems) and, by World War I, had developed a rudimentary two-way radio communications capability. World War II saw this capacity advance tremendously, as the importance of radio detection and ranging (RaDaR) and other applications of wireless technology spurred research and development at ever-higher frequencies. But through all this, applications of radio technology to public communications service lagged, and it was not until the post–World War II era that any significant services came to be available to the general public.

### Factors Influencing Wireless Growth

Over the last decade, three factors have come together to produce very rapid growth in the deployment of wireless telecommunications technology and service throughout a market traditionally served by the hard-wired public switched telephone network (PSTN). Technology is the first of these factors. Cellular technology is not a new concept; some authorities have traced its origins to 1947. Barring its growth (prior to the development of modern microelectronic devices) was impossibly bulky and expensive hardware implementation. Much of the functionality of cellular systems lies in the microprocessors that operate both the subscriber units and the infrastructure.

Regulation was the second necessary condition for the development of wireless service. Prior to the adoption of cellular technology, the FCC was reluctant to allocate significant amounts of radio spectrum to radiotelecommunications service because it was viewed as a relatively wasteful use of scarce spectrum. As a result, prior to the cellular authorization, only some fifty-four channels were allocated for mobile telephone service nationwide. In the extreme case, the entire New York City metropolitan area had only twelve channels available for mobile telephone service, and New York Telephone company had only 800 units in service and more than 1200 on the waiting list.

Propelled by the increased spectral efficiency of cellular architecture, the FCC in the late 1970s reallocated a chunk of spectrum from the upper UHF channels (70 to 83) and assigned 40 MHz of spectrum to cellular. This increased the number of available channels by several orders of magnitude and made modern, high-capacity service possible. (The allocation has since been increased to 50 MHz, which gives each of the two licensees in a given service area up to 295 two-way voice channels, plus 21 system signaling channels.)

Demand for mobile radio service has been the third factor needed to support the growth experienced by cellular in recent years. It seems hard to believe today, but when cellular was first introduced, there was considerable opinion, even among experts, that only the larger markets could support systems. Actual subscriber behavior has proven otherwise, of course, and the subscriber base has grown rapidly.

Price is also a factor in stimulating demand, as seen in the decline of monthly subscriber bills, from $120 to $150 in 1983 to today's monthly averages of $60 to $75. The price of the cellular telephones themselves has likewise declined, from the $4000 1983 quote on the original Motorola "Dyna-TAC" hand-held unit to $700 or less for the top-of-the-line MicroTAC, which has vastly improved features, greatly reduced weight and size, and improved battery life. Adjusted for inflation, it can be argued that the prices of both equipment and service have declined, in real terms, between 70 percent and 80 percent since the early days of the industry, thus stimulating demand.

In short, wireless can give consumers a mix of mobility and convenience unparalleled in the wired world. From an infrastructure angle, wireless entails less infrastructure and environmentally disruptive construction activities than the more labor-intensive fiber optic and coaxial systems that require underground cabling. So it's no surprise that despite wireless being more costly, an ever-growing number of people are expected to tread the wireless path because of its convenience.

### Cellular Network Infrastructure

The growth in cellular telecommunications has been astounding and as prices decline, Americans are subscribing to cellular telephone service in droves, boosting the total number of U.S. customers to a record 19 million. It took the industry nine years to attract its first 10 million subscribers. So while wireless data services may be fairly new, they appear to be logical extensions to existing and trusted services. Another important trend in the cellular telephone market is the availability of new features made possible by technological advances and the increasing intelligence built into the cellular network. These features include voice dialing and alphanumeric display for short messaging, among others.

Anyone who's been observing the emergence of wireless services can attest that vendors are storming the market with as much zeal as the gold prospectors who descended on California during the 1849 gold rush. For instance, long-distance companies, barred from directly offering local services, see a way of offering local phone service in conjunction with a wireless industry—to enter the "last-mile" game in competition with the RBOCs. The biggest news in this context is AT&T's estimated $12.6 billion acquisition of McCaw Cellular Communications; wireless technology provides a means to bypass the RBOCs and connect customers directly to long-distance points of presence, or PoPs.

One of the shortcomings of cellular infrastructure has been the lack of a seamless national network. This concept of being able to make and receive calls any time, any place—known to wireless providers as seamless roaming—is not new. It has been a much-discussed, much-pursued objective. But now, with customers expecting more, creating a seamless roaming environment and providing enhanced services will be the key. This translates into increased air time usage, greater customer loyalty, and competitive differentiation in a marketplace that will soon have several more wireless providers. One obstacle to the creation of a national architecture is the proliferation of competing standards in the cellular market.

Two trends—digital networks and competition—are now changing the cellular landscape. Cellular operators are upgrading their analog networks to digital to provide greater capacity at lower cost as well as increase the quality and functionality of the cellular network. However, it appears that, given the plethora of standards, the digital cellular environment will not have a single technology platform as was present with analog. This raises two immediate issues: roaming and costs. With roaming, since the initial phones are dual mode (they will operate in both analog and digital), if a user travels into a network operating on a different digital platform (or none at all) then his or her phone will revert to analog mode. This presents a different level of quality of service and perhaps even a loss of functionality. While not an issue, it is certainly going to be an annoyance for heavy roaming customers (who, in general, happen to be the higher-revenue-generating customers). Also, this will present the need for dual-mode phones, rather than a single-digital-mode-only phone, which raises extra cost issues.

One of the cellular industry's major competitors is the specialized mobile radio.

### Specialized Mobile Radio

The specialized mobile radio (SMR) is a conventional two-way radio system that can be configured in a manner that provides so-called "interconnect" service, which is functionally very similar to cellular. The SMR providers (NEXTEL, Dial Page, CenCall) are known today as the providers of analog, dispatch private radio services. These are the services that are common in fleets of vehicles (anything from police/emergency services to taxis and limousines).

The major SMR industry players are rapidly consolidating the industry as well as building state-of-the-art digital wireless systems. These companies are making significant investments in digital technology to convert existing SMR systems in major markets to a digital cellularlike architecture. The converted systems, known in the industry as enhanced specialized mobile radio or ESMR, use a digital technology developed by Motorola. That technology, known as Motorola integrated radio service or MIRS, is believed to expand the call-carrying capacity of a set of SMR channels by as much as a factor of six.

Coupled with the establishment of a cellularlike system architecture employing frequency reuse and handoff, ESMR technology is expected to increase the call-carrying capacity of a set of SMR channels by a factor of 15 or more. With the roll-out of ESMR networks, cellular operators will find themselves competing for the first time. ESMR is offering a whole plethora of wireless features and functions. Thus we believe that a successful roll-out of ESMR systems will result in cellular operators rapidly developing and deploying their own digital wireless networks. The FCC has begun to license radio spectrum. These auctions, referred to as the PCS auctions, have recently been completed (See Chapter 20).

### Mobile Data Networks

Mobile data networks have been built on SMR infrastructure. Advances in portable computers are an important factor that is likely to lead to increased use of mobile data communication. Most companies have developed information systems that help make employees more productive in the office. Millions of dollars have been invested to create computer networks and to help employees gain access to the corporate database while at their desks. Centralized databases make information more uniform and up to date, thereby helping to improve customer service. However, few existing applications facilitate the exchange of messages or data directly with mobile workers. As a result, workers on the road typically receive instructions and collect information in written form or by voice. Voice instructions may be heard incorrectly and/or misinterpreted, however, and information collected must be entered into the database later at the home office, increasing the possibility of inaccuracies and delaying database updates. Wireless data networks have the ability to connect mobile workers to the central database directly.

To the extent that wireless communications become a key on-ramp to the data highway, the long-distance carriers—as well as wireless providers such as RAM Mobile Data and the IBM/Motorola Ardis joint venture—want a piece of the action. The result for customers could be fierce price competition and an explosion of service options.

## Commercial On-Line Services-Based Last Mile

### *Applications and Growth*

On-line services are a major part of the I-way infrastructure. They provide customers with both the e-commerce applications as well as the ramps to access the I-way. The big on-line services, set up before the popularity of global networks, were designed to provide all the goods and information services any paying customer might want—all under one computing platform. Their goal is to become the one-stop shopping mall of cyberspace. With a single telephone call, customers can read or download the news, look up a stock quote, give some advice, make a friend, book a flight, check the weather, buy a raincoat, or order a bunch of flowers. The benefit of the computer-based on-line approach is that services are packaged better and appear less complex than other infrastructure options.

On-line services tend to be general-purpose, for-profit networks that are available nationwide, regionally, or in some cases locally. They are analogous to twenty-four-hour "supermarkets" or "corner drugstores" of computer-based, on-line industry, supplying a wide array of information services—e-mail, real-time communication, file transfer, database access, reference tools, and gateways to other services. They attract an audience with varied interests and offer on-line access to the greatest number of users throughout the United States.

The demand for on-line services is driven in part by growing numbers of PCs in homes and businesses, primarily spurred by lower hardware prices and increased functionality in the form of enhanced graphics, animation, sound, and speech capabilities. In addition to processing power, consumers are actively seeking a direct link to the I-way by which content (entertainment, education, or shopping services) reaches the home or business through electronic distribution channels. These channels act as on-ramps to the Internet or other on-line information services.

The on-line industry newsletter *Information & Interactive Services Report* (September 1994) reported that subscribers to on-line computer services in the United States total 5.52 million. According to a *Times-Mirror* poll (October 1995), the number of on-line subscribers has passed 12 million. Similar growth in Asian markets is reported by the New Media Development Association. The number of subscribers in Japan totaled 2.6 million at the end of June 1994, up 32 percent from a year earlier. Women accounted for 10.3 percent of subscribers, according to the study. The reason for growth can be attributed to the fact that when users go on-line, they are experiencing the first glimmer of what it's going to be like when the I-way becomes a reality.

### The Microsoft Network

To provide a more in-depth look at commercial on-line service providers, we examine the Microsoft Network, which provides an access ramp to the I-way for the millions of expected Windows 95 users. This system is unique, as it is the first desktop PC to have I-way access built into the operating systems, through a built-in feature of Windows 95.

Microsoft states in its white paper that customers will find it easy to sign up and access the network as a feature of the operating system. Ease of use is expected to come by extending the familiar feature set and graphical interface of Windows 95, to facilitate easier exploration and interaction in the on-line world. For example, the on-line services can be browsed using the Explorer feature in Windows 95. Actions such as downloading files are simple copy operations accomplished by drag and drop. Short-cuts enable personalized and efficient navigation. The Microsoft Network's e-mail and rich-text content documents are managed through the Information Exchange and WordPad services built into Windows 95, with the same familiar user interface carried through all core communications functionality.

According to Microsoft, the on-line service will be accessible in more than thirty-five countries, and its client application will be localized in twenty languages. Subscribers will be able to access the I-way with a local phone call and connect at speeds of up to 28.8 Kbps. The data center for the Microsoft Network is located in the Seattle area and based on PCs running the Microsoft Windows NT Server operating system.

Microsoft is estimated to be targeting the 50 million or so potential users of the Windows operating system. It is basing its marketing on the fact that while on-line services are well publicized throughout the media, their user populations are fairly small. For example, while 40 percent of Microsoft Windows users have modems, fewer than 10 percent of Windows users and 4 percent of U.S. households subscribe to any on-line service. While many details remain sketchy, the success of this on-line service could be an important landmark in the I-way access.

## 2.5 GLOBAL INFORMATION DISTRIBUTION NETWORKS

The two major technologies underpinning high-speed global information distribution networks are fiber optic long-distance networks and satellites.

### Long-Distance Networks

Long-distance connectivity is available via cable (coaxial or fiber) owned by long-distance or interexchange carriers (IXCs). Experience suggests that the importance of fiber optic cable for international transmission is likely to grow. Submarine cables provide an attractive economic advantage for selected routes where the growth in demand for communications capacity is high. One reason is cable's provision of better-quality service for interactive applications. The current large-scale capacity of fiber optic connections between the United States and Europe (TAT-8) is being enhanced to operate at gigabit rates. In the Pacific Rim, there are several large-capacity fiber optic cables (TransPac 3 and 4) similar to the TAT-8 series of cables. TransPac 5, scheduled to be in operation by 1996, will offer gigabit rates.

The IXCs also play a significant role in the local access market by teaming with firms in the wireless and cable TV business. IXCs are exploring alternative arrangements that would lower their cost of using the local network, an expense that exceeded $30 billion in 1993, or even allow them to provide such access themselves through business partnerships or acquisitions. The IXCs have advanced switched networks nationwide that can serve as a backbone for alternative local access networks, and they have the financial and human resources that can help the small, competitive access firms grow.

U.S. long-distance services are provided by AT&T, MCI, Sprint, WilTel, Metromedia Communications, Litel Telecommunications, Allnet, and more than 475 smaller carriers. At the time of the divestiture in 1984, AT&T owned nearly 90 percent of the long-distance business, but in the months and years that followed, its chief competitors, MCI and Sprint, invested in new technology to chip away at that market share. MCI first started deploying fiber optic cable in 1984, when it had revenues close to $ 2 billion and nearly 5 percent of the long-distance market. In 1993, MCI was an $11-billion company and owned nearly 17 percent of the long-distance business. Sprint was also growing so fast in 1984 that it stopped accepting orders in the 35 markets in which it operated because its network had reached capacity. Today, Sprint owns nearly 10 percent of the total U.S. market and has tripled in size since 1984.

Similar events have occurred elsewhere. In the early 1980s British Telecom became a private corporation and competitor Mercury was established. Since then, countries such as France, Germany, and Spain have opened their markets to competition. Internationally, service providers continue to build alliances in efforts to build a global network and offer worldwide the advanced telecommunications services available in the U.S. markets. Until October 1, 1994, telecom lines in Europe had been state monopolies and prices varied considerably from country to country. With liberalization came fierce competition for user accounts and the perception that competition is the key to homogenize services, lower costs, improve levels of technology, and increase efficiency levels across Europe. The fear of pending competition has forced network operators to spend heavily on upgrades. For a single business market to develop in Europe, however, uniform speed, efficiency, levels of technology, and cost of telecom services are necessary for both voice and data services. At present, wide disparities remain among different network operators in terms of both efficiency and pricing.

As we mentioned earlier, the major long-distance carriers have focused their attention on wireless technologies and made plans to work with or acquire companies in the wireless market. This would enable them to provide long-distance services to cellular users and possibly to develop a more economical local access network to reach their own subscribers. For instance, AT&T is on the verge of once again re-creating itself into a national communications company through both cellular and circuit-switched networks. AT&T got a foothold in the emerging cellular marketplace by buying McCaw Cellular, the largest U.S. cellular carrier. This buyout gives AT&T a presence in the wireless market as well as local access to customers.

### Satellite Networks

The role of satellites in the communications industry has changed substantially during the past fifteen years. Initially, satellites were used to transport long-distance telecommunications and one-way video broadcasts. The advent of fiber optics in the early 1980s, however, changed the role of satellites in the global communications industry. Fiber optics has emerged as the technology of choice, not only because it is capable of providing higher bandwidth than satellites, but also because it is immune to electromagnetic interference. Consequently, fiber has been extensively deployed in the U.S. long-distance infrastructure and is now being deployed underseas to carry international traffic.

Satellite networks do have some advantages over terrestrial networks, however. They are accessible from any spot on the globe; can provide broadband digital services, including voice, data, and video, to many points without the cost of acquiring right-of-way and wire installation; and can add receiving and transmitting sites without significant additional costs. Commercially available since 1965, communications satellites are a crucial part of the global communications infrastructure. Today, about 150 communications satellites in geosynchronous orbit (GEO) are providing a wide range of services, including broadcast video and overseas telephone links. GEO satellites are placed in a high circular orbit 22,300 miles above the equator. Because GEO satellites rotate with the earth, they appear to be stationary.

In general, geosynchronous satellites are designed to broadcast a wide beam to ensure the wide area coverage. Although such a large broadcast "footprint" allows only three GEO satellites to provide nearly global coverage, the network's receiving stations require large antennas to capture the relatively weak signal. In addition, satellites can provide services to areas that cannot be reached by fiber. Earth blanketing satellite services, such as Motorola's Iridium low-earth orbit satellite telephony project and the Teledesic championed by Microsoft and McCaw Cellular, are expected to provide the basic infrastructure to beam data and voice practically anywhere in the world.

In the 1980s, industry introduced a new class of satellites using a narrow beam to focus the transmitted energy on a small geographic area. Known as very small aperture terminal (VSAT) satellites, the new breed uses small ground antennas to provide low data rate point-to-point network services. VSAT networks are being increasingly used by large corporations to link hundreds of retail sites. (See Chapter 20.)

## 2.6 PUBLIC POLICY ISSUES SHAPING THE I-WAY

It is expected that governments will play a crucial role in defining the I-way. There are seven major issues: cost, subsidies, allocation of scarce resources, regulation, universal access, privacy, and social issues.

*Cost.* The primary concern is cost: Who will pay for constructing the I-way? With estimates as high as $200 billion, this is a very important question. Some favor the interstate highway model, with government construction, ownership, and maintenance. Others support the current regulated telephone system model. But giant telecommunications firms that have already pledged tens of billions for highway construction favor a less regulated market.

*Subsidies.* Developers might hope for subsidies, tax breaks, government business, or other forms of encouragement. This raises an open question: What will these tax subsidies actually subsidize? For example, if many of the new services can be received only through souped-up "smart" TVs or computer boxes, would subsidies be used to underwrite the cost of hardware so that low-income families could buy it? If "telecommuting" takes off over the new network, should rate payers subsidize "work-at-home" employees, much as public transportation systems are subsidized now? Who will pay to extend the networks to nonprofit institutions such as schools, hospitals, and police and fire departments?

*Allocation of scarce resources.* Some economists wonder whether huge investments in all aspects of the I-way will be wasted because there is no strong evidence that markets exist for the services it would offer. They point to costly commercial failures like the Bell Laboratories Picture Phone fiasco of the late 1960s as well as the failure of the SBS broadband corporate satellite network of the late 1970s. On the other hand, some economists and industry executives argue that this kind of spending would help create markets that are not now being pursued by private industry because of the prohibitive costs of developing new technologies.

*Regulation.* Some free enterprises argue that if the highway is built with private funds, there should be no government regulation. The Clinton administration seems to be steering toward the middle of the road: open competition among highway operators, but regulation to provide public access, privacy, and reasonable tolls. Some issues remain undecided: What are the rules? Who writes them? Who enforces them?

*Universal access.* In the debate about the I-way architecture, one issue dominates all others: universal access. This has become almost as sacred as the first amendment right of free speech. No politician can talk about telecom policy without first endorsing "equal access." What does that mean? Probably that cable and phone companies deploying upgraded networks will be required to serve some consumers at prices below cost and to extend wires to places where other technologies (like satellite, perhaps) would make more sense.

Economists argue that the market should decide who gets access to the I-way. Others insist that highway operators must provide universal access at reasonable cost. The U.S government seems to favor regulation requiring universal access, both to ensure that poorer citizens can afford to buy information and so that information vendors cannot be denied network access by competing networks—to avoid creating a society of information 'haves" and "have-nots." The inclusionary emphasis isn't all bad. Networks are inherently collectivist: A broader reach benefits everyone (a concept known as *network externality* in economics).

Perhaps the organizations most concerned about losing out are the nonprofits—libraries, schools, hospitals, and other public institutions. If the I-way is built and run by private interests without significant government investment, these institutions might not be able to afford hooking up to the network. Indeed, in the final analysis the success of the I-way won't be measured by capacity or capability but by who has access and on what terms. Those are the important policy questions. Still undecided: How are firms "encouraged" to provide universal access? Are they compensated for losses in unprofitable areas? How universal is universal: just nationwide or international access?

*Information privacy issues.* If people knew where you drove and why, they could form a picture of your activities. Maybe too well. The same applies to the I-way: Every keystroke—interests, purchases, and inquiries—can be tracked by companies. In late 1994, America Online was assailed for marketing customer information, after lists containing detailed information on the firm's 1 million subscribers were advertised for sale in a trade magazine. AOL's subscriber list offered information on its subscribers' computer equipment, gender, children, income, and other personal details. AOL and other on-line services invite members to create on-line profiles of such information as marital status, hobbies, occupation, geographical location, computer equipment and software used, as well as personal comments. These profiles are accessible to all other members. It is obvious that the potential for abuse is great, and so are the open questions: Can vendors keep track of customer preferences? Can they sell this information to others? Can network managers read electronic mail or ads to root out fraud or pornography? On what grounds can they deny access? When will police surveillance be allowed? Expect much contention and new legislation in these areas.

*Social and religious barriers.* Cyberspace is considered by many to be a representation of free speech and democracy. It is very hard to police because bypassing even the strongest barrier is quite easy. As for censorship, some governments will be more protective of their cyberspace than others. For many countries where free speech is alien, the Internet presents interesting problems and policy issues. For other strongly religious countries where women have been denied voice and access to media for many years, the Internet, which does not distinguish between sexes, causes many headaches. Other social and religious conflicts include topics such as sex. For instance, some countries have very strict pornographic laws. With the Internet, it is very hard to control the influx of pornographic material as it's hard to distinguish one byte from another.

## Public Policy and Global Connectivity

Achieving global connectivity has policy implications: (1) access to distribution (local infrastructure and access points) within countries, including bilateral or multilateral agreements on technical issues (addressing, routing); and (2) usage policy issues (rules about acceptable use, management, financing); and (3) technology standards that are adopted by various countries. Let us examine each component in detail.

### *Access to Local Infrastructure*

Local infrastructure within a country is a matter of local policy and investment and it is the area of greatest unevenness across countries. The disparity between developed and developing data communications environments (including networks and associated hardware and software) is a source of operational frustration to businesses when they seek to effect or use international connections.

In other countries the problems are mostly political. In such countries, state-owned telcos control both domestic and international communications. It can be nearly impossible to acquire a direct link into a specific site, and often use of an expensive telco-operated network is mandated. When available, obtaining leased line service may involve substantial delays and/or costs that are very high compared to U.S. costs.

One possibility for overcoming shortcomings in local distribution is wireless communication technology, including microwave cellular telephony. In addition, cable telephone technology might also enhance local infrastructure in some countries. It is important to keep in mind that local infrastructure is a national issue for each of the countries involved. It is not appropriate for international private or government groups to try to dictate national network approaches to other countries despite the fact that many companies are competing in foreign countries for business. Moreover, although policies such as those cited have limited communications, they have also had the effect of stifling the development of national industries to compete globally.

### *Global Subsidies*

Since many countries simply cannot afford the massive investments required to finance telecom development, the richer countries may have to subsidize the infrastructure through the World Bank. In fact, the word "massive" is an understatement, as the investments required are really beyond the means of many developing countries. For instance, the planned investments in the Philippines amount to P102 billion or about $4 billion annually, the amount equivalent to 35 percent of the total budget of the Philippine government for 1995. The breakdown of investments required for upgrading: telephone system, P1.165 trillion; public data networks, P610 billion; CMTS (cellular mobile telephone systems), P530 billion (approximately $20 billion).

Conditions are far worse in most of Africa and parts of Asia and Latin America. Several governments have initiated changes to improve their telecommunications infrastructures, such as the move from analog to digital circuits and the passage of legislation to encourage investments by companies marketing products and services in telecommunications. Despite these gains, significant investments are required to bring these nations to "telco equality" with developed nations. These investments depend to a large degree on the ability of these countries to promote market economies and to demonstrate a business environment that will provide investors a reasonable risk and return on their investments.

### Cost and Pricing of "Universal Access" Transmission Capacity

Any effort to create a high-speed network to Asia, Europe, and to the Pacific Rim nations must first consider who will pay and how payment will be made. Network users in Asia and Europe spend, on the average, ten times more for circuits than similar users in the United States; and in some regions of Asia and Europe leased lines service is unobtainable at any price. The disparity between the costs of international circuits initiated in the United States and those of other countries seriously constrains the cost-sharing efforts of government agencies using these circuits. Today some government agencies pick up the costs of the long-haul transmission channels and their international partners pay for the local distribution circuits within their own countries. For example, when DOE or NASA arrange international connections, they have typically provided the international circuit in exchange for provision of distribution by the foreign partner.

An important policy question is involved here: To what extent should U.S. agencies, and therefore U.S. taxpayers, support non-U.S. networking facilities even though this support might help U.S.business? It is likely that there will be different answers for different countries. A related issue is the degree to which the U.S.-supported facilities carry traffic other than that dedicated to the particular application that justified the link.

### Adoption of Technology Standards

Adoption of standards is a major barrier to the I-way construction. This environment was a form of "religious/political wars" wherein government bureaucrats decided which protocols are "politically correct." For reasons of competitiveness or, in some cases, to avoid adopting what has been perceived as a U.S. standard (the Internet protocols), some groups in Europe and Japan decreed that local networks must use the ISO/CCITT OSI-compliant protocol suite. However, OSI software has not been readily available and some of the standards have been slow in coming, leading to implementation delays.

The infrastructure issue is made even more complex because of the different standards in place and being planned. Achieving consensus on standards in the current international environment has been difficult at best. Standards developed by slow-moving international committees over many years are seen as not serving the needs of the user community; yet, these governments, commissions, and research funding organizations representing one or more countries often mandate the acceptance of these standards.

## 2.7 SUMMARY

The I-way is defined as universal, affordable access to high-performance networks capable of carrying billions of bits per second in the context of e-commerce. The development of new telecommunications technologies and the continued deployment of fiber optic facilities have resulted in higher transmission speeds at significantly lower costs. The end result is a seamless web called the I-way of communications networks, computers, digital libraries, and consumer electronics that will put vast amounts of information at users' fingertips.

Let us summarize some of the business issues concerned with network infrastructure investments. There is general agreement that an open, competitive architecture is the desirable long-term objective, but there is a trade-off between open networks and incentive for large investments. An open environment is good for consumers because it promotes the introduction of new services and applications, and it promotes lower prices. An open environment is good for the industry because it promotes innovation and cost reduction, which in turn promote competitiveness. It also promotes reuse of deployed assets in new ways, which leads to increased revenue opportunities for those who have deployed I-way assets.

There is also a trade-off during the initial deployment due to the rapid economic depreciation of investments because the technologies associated with the I-way (computer and communication technologies) are continually and rapidly being improved and cost reduced. At the same time, because an advanced I-way is in the process of being conceived and deployed, the market for applications and services is still developing. Those who make the initial investments face a combination of uncertainty as to which applications and services will experience good market acceptance, as well as a learning perioa during which the market for products and services will develop and mature.

In the context of an open architecture, some competitors can wait on the sidelines while the pioneering competitors make substantial investments to enter and develop the market. Then these sideline competitors can pick and choose where to enter the market, taking full advantage of the open architecture and of the improved, cost-reduced technologies that are then at their disposal. This creates a disincentive for pioneering investment, and those who choose to be pioneering investors will be reluctant to make their I-way investments so open as to make it easy for competitors to enter later and destroy the value of their pioneering investments. This trade-off underscores a serious tension between open architecture and investment incentive during the initial deployment and development of the I-way. This issue needs to be closely examined to determine the correct balance between initial openness of the I-way architecture and investment incentives.

The achievement of an open architecture and the achievement of interoperability among applications, services, and technologies within an open architecture involve substantial technological challenges. For example, the core networks and services that support applications must be extremely reliable. Downtime is not consistent with many of the applications envisioned for the I-way. Yet the technology to create an open architecture that is resistant to accidental or intentionally induced outages does not exist at this time. Similarly, the technology to achieve interoperability or to substantially mitigate the problems associated with achieving interoperability among applications, services, and technologies also does not exist at this time. Thus much research and development effort remains to create the technological capabilities needed to realize the objectives of open architecture and interoperability.

Since the benefits of this technology flow primarily to consumers of I-way applications and services, and typically do not produce a proprietary advantage for any I-way application or service provider (by definition, open architecture principles and interoperability technologies are useful only it they are widely adopted by all competitors), there is a natural role for government, as the representative of the public, in providing a portion of the funding of the necessary R&D and in taking a leadership role in public policy issues.

Finally, as a note of caution, it is easy to overestimate the speed with which technological innovation will assume the substance of reality in the context of the I-way. The market has traditionally misjudged the pace of penetration of new technology and the potential impact of applications.

## Chapter 3

# The Internet as a Network Infrastructure

The Internet is the most well-known component of the Information Superhighway network infrastructure. Today, the Internet (*Inter*connected *net*works) is an information distribution system spanning several continents. Its very general infrastructure targets not only one electronic commerce application, such as video on-demand or home shopping, but a wide range of computer-based services, such as e-mail, EDI, information publishing, information retrieval, and video conferencing. Simply put, the Internet environment is a unique combination of postal service, telephone system, research library, supermarket, and talk show center that enables people to share and purchase information. This interchange takes place rapidly, usually in a matter of seconds, using fairly inexpensive and commonly available technology. In short, the Internet is viewed as a prototype for the emerging I-way of which it will become one component.

The Internet began around 1965 when the U.S. Department of Defense financed the design of a computer network to link a handful of universities and military research laboratories. Since then, this network, linked by leased telephone lines, has mushroomed into a matrix of several thousand connections in over one hundred countries. Until 1991, most of these networks were used primarily for research by academics, government agencies, and research laboratories to communicate and share information.

During 1992–1993 the spotlight on the I-way propelled the Internet from a virtual unknown to a chic media cliché. Many who heard about this "technology of the future" attempted to get onto the Internet and see what all the fuss was about. So in a short span of time, the Internet quickly became a front-page story in every major newspaper; a cover story for magazines such as the *BusinessWeek*, *Time*, and the *New Republic*; a standing reference on CNN; and, inevitably, the inspiration for a *New Yorker* cartoon—two dogs at a keyboard, with one canine saying to the other, "On the Internet, nobody knows you're a dog."

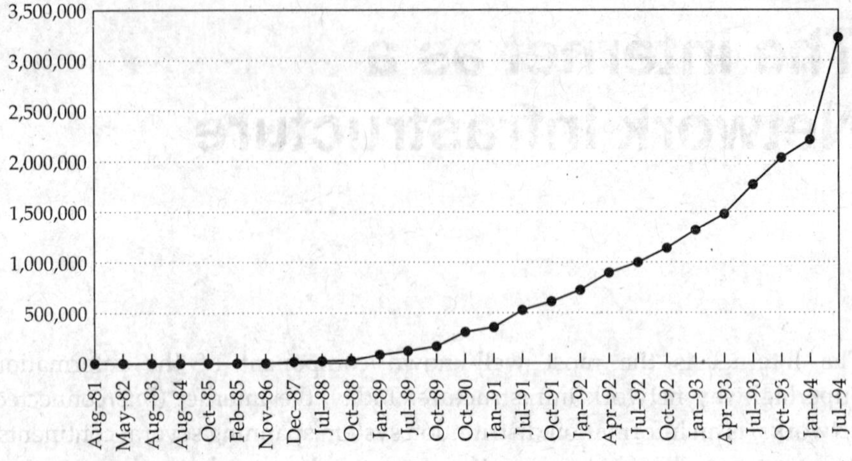


**Figure 3.1** Internet host growth

Estimates by the Internet Society (http://www.isoc.org/) indicate a doubling of subscribers annually. Educated guesses indicate 20–30 million users in 1995, although an exact count is impossible given that the network is decentralized and has no central agency to monitor users. Figure 3.1 charts the growth of host computers linked to the Internet from 1981 to 1994. In July 1995, the number of connected hosts has passed 6.642 million.

Before delving into details of the Internet, we need to define the terminology used in the rest of this chapter.

## 3.1 THE INTERNET TERMINOLOGY

Today, the Internet is a mesh that envelops thousands of interconnected networks linking approximately 4 million computers worldwide. It is estimated that every thirty minutes a major network links into the Internet. These networks belong to several domains—universities, government institutions, large private companies, and small entrepreneurial start-ups. The interconnected computers include stand-alone computers, LANs (local area networks—networks whose span is limited to one building), MANs (metropolitan area networks—networks that span an area up to 100 square miles), and WANs (wide area networks that cover large geographic distances).

A LAN is characterized by its small geographic location, which allows resource sharing and work-group interaction within a single building, has total management control residing with the local manager (who bought and installed the technology), and consists of a limited number of users (anywhere from 50 to 1000) sharing resources (print server, post office servers). Sometimes the term MAN is used to describe campus networks or "Big-LANs," which connect 1000–10,000 computers that could be a combination of PCs, servers, and mainframes. MANs are usually segregated hierarchically into smaller LANs that are interconnected using devices called bridges. A WAN links several dispersed MANs and extends the principles of information resource sharing to several locations. It is characterized by multiorganizational control; in other words, a company may own the LAN host, but various carriers (telcos) own communications subnetworks on which the WAN operates.

Broadly speaking, the Internet can be differentiated based on the language spoken (protocol) by inhabitants (host computers) into two classifications: Academic and Business. In the *Academic Internet* (also known in the literature as *core Internet*), all the host computers speak the language Transport Control Protocol/Internet Protocol (TCP/IP). In the *Business Internet* the host computers can speak a variety of languages other than TCP/IP, including ISO/OSI X.25-based packet switching networks (popular in Europe and with telcos), SNA-based BITNET (now defunct, was once popular with universities and other value-added network providers who use IBM mainframes), and other languages for networks run by such commercial providers as CompuServe, Prodigy, and America Online; FidoNet, AppleLink, Minitel, and UUCP networks.

Figure 3.2 captures the distinction between Academic and Business Internet. Academic Internet consists of various government networks, regional networks, campus networks, and some international networks. These

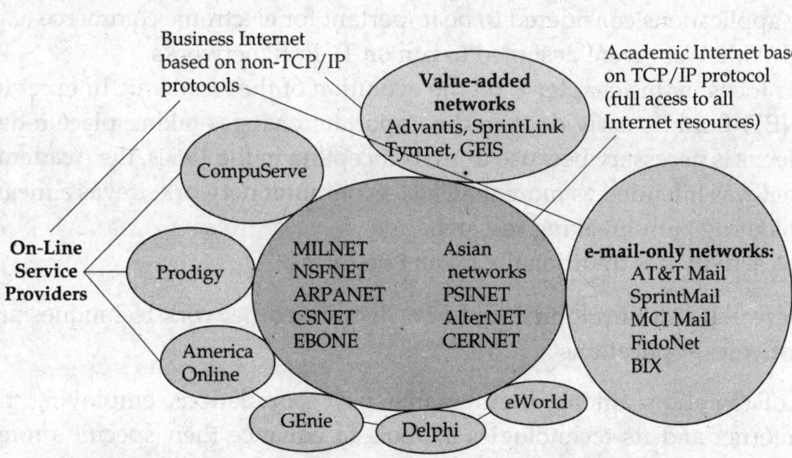


**Figure 3.2** Networks making up the Internet

include NSFNET the premier group of research IP networks in the United States; EBONE, the European group of IP networks; and, more recently, private IP networks run by for-profit organizations (e.g., PSINet, UUNET).

The Business Internet consists of on-line services, value-added networks, and other e-mail-only services. The Academic and Business networks can talk to each other through language (protocol) translators, called *gateways*, stationed at the network border. In the past, because only mail gateways were widely implemented and deployed, the most interoperable application or the least common denominator for the entire Internet was electronic mail. In this capacity, "The Internet" is a universal electronic messaging infrastructure spanning more than 154 countries.

The various Business Internet providers soon realized that implementing gateways for every useful application that runs on the Academic Internet would be too costly. The Academic Internet's massive size, high performance, open connectivity, valuable information and rich set of applications have proven to be a magnet to the customers of nearly every other kind of computer network. Bowing to their customers' demand, many Business Internet networks have attached themselves to the core Internet's periphery. More recently, Business Internet providers have begun to adopt the TCP/IP as the standard protocol on their own networks, thus allowing smooth linkage with the Academic Internet.

How is the I-way related to the Internet? Think of the I-way as a superset that includes both the Academic and Business Internet categories and extends the boundaries further to encapsulate non-IP-based networks such as telecom carrier networks, cable TV, mobile and cellular networks. Which languages (protocols) will be spoken on all these networks is not yet clear. It is clear though that they will have to speak some dialect of TCP/IP as many of the applications considered to be important for electronic commerce (e.g., World Wide Web) were designed to run on TCP/IP networks.

Our focus in this chapter is on the evolution of the Academic Internet (or NSFNET) from its early days to the important changes taking place today. This focus is necessary because from its inception in the 1960s, the Academic Internet was intended as more than just a computer network. It was a means of facilitating path-breaking research.

This activity has traditionally taken two forms:

1. Research and development of new distributed network techniques and software applications
2. Collaboration among innumerable user populations employing the Internet and its technologies as tools to enhance their specific professional activity or other interests significantly.

Hence, we take the position that the changes taking place today in the Academic Internet, such as gigabit networking, will be influential in the future direction of electronic commerce and therefore must be understood.

## 3.2 CHRONOLOGICAL HISTORY OF THE INTERNET

The beginnings of the Internet hark back to the late 1960s, when the Advanced Research Projects Agency (ARPA) of the Department of Defense (DOD) formed ARPANET. The agency was established in the late 1950s to develop information technologies to help the United States to counter the Soviet launch of *Sputnik*. Consequently, the early ARPANET consisted primarily of research universities and military contractors with computers linked by telephone lines leased from AT&T. The chronological development of the ARPANET and the milestones leading to the Internet reflect a history of top-down government-sponsored initiatives (see Table 3.1).

**Table 3.1** Internet Milestones

| | |
|---|---|
| Early 1960s | Genesis of networking at The RAND Corporation in a series of reports by Paul Baran. Also, Leonard Kleinrock's thesis "Communication Nets: Stochastic Message Flow and Delay" at MIT created the model for performance evaluation and network design. The concept of a "mesh network" of minicomputers that would use packet switching (in contrast to circuit switching used in phone connections) to communicate over phone lines was a revolutionary notion at the time. Until then, computer communications had centered on mainframes and point-to-point links. |
| 1965 | One of the first networking experiments took place when the TX-2 computer at M.I.T.'s Lincoln Laboratory was connected to a Scientific Data Systems Q-23 computer in Santa Monica, California [HAF96]. |
| 1968 | A request for proposal was floated to create the ARPANET; Bolt, Beranek, and Newman (BBN) was awarded the prime contract. ARPA awarded other contracts to AT&T for communications circuits, Network Analysis Corporation for designing the network topology, the University of California at Los Angeles (UCLA) for a "network measurement center," and Stanford Research Institute (SRI) for a "network information center." Other sites on the nationwide net included the University of Utah in Salt Lake City and the University of California at Santa Barbara (UCSB). |

**Table 3.1** Internet Milestones (Continued)

| | |
|---|---|
| 1969 | The first ARPANET node was installed at UCLA in September 1969, thus launching the first packet switching network connecting SRI, UCSB, and University of Utah. The actual ARPANET network that resulted used special-purpose computers known as IMPs (interface message processors) to dismantle information into small chunks called packets, transmit the packetized information to a destination computer known by an address, check for transmission errors, retransmit damaged packets, and reassemble packets at the destination sites. To interface between the IMPs and proprietary software on the multivendor host computers, the ARPANET researchers created Network Communication Protocol (NCP). |
| 1971 | In just two short years approximately twenty nodes were installed, and ARPA was funding thirty different university sites as part of the ARPANET program. |
| 1972 | E-mail was invented by accident, when two programmers at BBN decided to send each other messages, not merely transfer files. Ray Tomlinson of BBN is credited with using the ARPANET to place the world's first e-mail message in 1973. |
| 1973–1974 | In the mid-1970s, the Transport Control Protocol/Internet Protocol (TCP/IP) protocol was developed by Vint Cerf to link different packet networks. The purpose of TCP/IP was to connect different networks (copper wire, radio, microwave) and still enable the host computers to talk to each other coherently. TCP/IP is capable of connecting multiple independent networks through routers (or gateways). |
| 1975 | In July 1975 ARPA transferred management of ARPANET and Network Measurement Center from BBN and UCLA to the Defense Communications Agency (DCA; now called Defense Information Systems Agency). It was expected that direct experience with packet switching by DCA would ultimately be of wider benefit to the Department of Defense. |
| 1978 | The U.S. government decreed that TCP/IP be the preferred way to send information from one computer to another. This caused computer vendors to wake up and realize that TCP/IP is here to stay. |
| 1980 | DARPA funded the development of Berkeley UNIX. TCP/IP was made part of the operating system. The government had considered buying AT&T UNIX but felt that it didn't have enough features, primarily TCP/IP. |

**Table 3.1** Internet Milestones (Continued)

| | |
|---|---|
| 1983 | Transition from the original ARPANET protocol, the Network Communication Protocol (NCP), to TCP. At this time only a few hundred host computers were on the nascent Internet. |
| 1980–1986 | From 1980 to 1986, NSF supported the development of CSNET, a computer science research network. CSNET was a network of networks, one component of which used the TCP protocols over an X.25 public data network showing the power of a layered architecture. CSNET also included the ARPANET and PHONENET, a telephone-based electronic mail relaying system. By 1985, CSNET had links to over 170 university, industrial, and government research organizations and numerous gateways to networks in other countries. |
| 1982–1986 | In 1982 a report, "Large Scale Computing in Science and Engineering," recommended the establishment of NSF-funded supercomputing centers as well as a high-speed network to connect them. These centers would offer an opportunity to make progress in science and engineering research. By early 1985, NSF announced five awards, and by 1986 the Cornell Theory Center, the Illinois National Center for Supercomputing Applications (NCSA), the Pittsburgh Supercomputing Center, the San Diego Supercomputer Center, and the Princeton John von Neumann Center were up and running. |
| 1986 | NSF initiated a new program of networking and computer support for supercomputing centers to be used by researchers. This program began with a memorandum of understanding with ARPA to allow NSF-funded supercomputer centers and selected researchers to use the ARPANET. Believing that ARPANET was not suitable, NSF instituted the NSF Connections program in 1986 to broaden the base of network users with their own computer facilities and eventually to help universities achieve access to supercomputers (by supplying hardware and telecommunications lines for direct, point-to-point connections). In 1986, it launched the NSFNET network backbone program. |
| 1987 | CSNET merged with BITNET, a worldwide network connecting IBM mainframes that was initiated in 1980–1981. CSNET operations were continued under the Corporation for Research and Education Networking (CREN), whose operating costs were completely covered by member organizations' dues. |

**Table 3.1** Internet Milestones (*Continued*)

| | |
|---|---|
| 1987 | After significant congestion was experienced in 1987, the backbone was upgraded from 56 kbps to T1 service (1.5 Mbps) and became operational in 1988. |
| 1988 | The Internet virus is unleashed by a graduate student at Cornell University, focusing attention on network vulnerability to security threats. Immediate steps were taken to make the network more secure. |
| 1990 | Twenty years after its birth at UCLA, ARPANET was officially decommissioned; its descendant, the NSFNET, inherited its role as the research and education communities' backbone network. The first relay between a commercial electronic mail carrier (MCI Mail) and the Internet took place through the Clearinghouse for Networked Information. |
| 1991 | Its mission accomplished, CSNET service was discontinued. For the first time, commercial networks were connected to the NSFNET backbone through the Commercial Internet eXchange (CIX) Association. CIX was formed by General Atomics (CERFnet), Performance Systems International, Inc. (PSINet), and UUNET Technologies, Inc. (AlterNet). (See Chapter 4.)<br>A new breed of distributed information services called Wide Area Information Servers (WAIS) released by the now-bankrupt Thinking Machines Corporation; Gopher was released by the University of Minnesota, and the World Wide Web was announced on alt.hypertext by Tim Berners-Lee of CERN.<br>The U.S. government made a decision to turn NSFNET into a faster research network called National Research and Education Network (NREN) as defined in the High-Performance Computing Act of 1991. |
| 1993 | National Information Infrastructure announcement sparks interest in the Information Superhighway. Businesses and media suddenly realized there was something called the Internet and began to take an interest in its exploitation. |
| 1993–1994 | Two million copies of a freeware Mosaic—a multimedia browser for the WWW, written by Marc Andreesen, at that time an undergraduate student at the University of Illinois at Urbana Champaign—were distributed over the Internet and attained incredible popularity. This milestone event represents a new chapter in electronic commerce. |
| 1995 | The old NSFNET backbone is decommissioned and a new architecture based on Network Access Points (NAPs) is installed. |

## Six Stages of Internet Growth

The incredible growth of the Internet can be divided into several stages (see Table 3.2). The first stage, *experimental networking*, covers the early years (from 1965) under the aegis of the DOD ARPA and the province of a relatively small technical community. That group developed not only the technology but the cooperative mechanisms that made it possible to scale and allow further innovation to occur. The second stage, *discipline-specific research* (1980–1985), grew out of the more general ARPANET and began to build international on-line communities. CSNET, for instance, linked computer science researchers from all over the world.

The third stage, *general research networking* (1985–1991) and called the NSFNET program, unfolded following the explosive growth in the mid-1980s. The NSFNET program was established chiefly to allow exchange of information and access to remote resources within the research and education community. Since the backbone network was launched, its traffic has doubled each year and its transmission capacity has increased more than thirtyfold to 45 million bits per second.

The NSFNET program has dramatically impacted the way science is conducted. Prior to 1985 collaboration and information sharing between colleagues in different institutions was difficult, time-consuming, and costly. That changed as NSFNET backbone network services and the associated regional networks extended connectivity throughout institutions in the United States, and scientists, students, and other researchers very quickly discovered the ease with which they could communicate with their colleagues, exchange data and results, and seek new information.

As early as 1990, Internet connectivity had become an essential tool for the conduct of scientific research. This stage represented a period of major devel-

**Table 3.2** Evolution of Purpose over the Years

| *Type and Scope of Network* | *Examples* |
|---|---|
| Experimental networking | ARPANET |
| Discipline-specific research | CSNET, MILNET, HEPnet, MFEnet |
| General research networking | Early NSFNET, BITNET |
| Privatization and commercialization | Present NSFNET |
| Restricted public data networks for research and education | National Research and Education Network (NREN) and HPCC |
| National information infrastructure | Information Superhighway (I-way) |

opment by (1) vendors for a growing data communications market, (2) the scaling of the network to support global academic and research activities, and (3) early innovators in the business sector who began providing public access services.

In 1991 the NSFNET program was deemed to have outgrown its initial vision as stipulated in 1985: to provide access to NSF's supercomputing centers for researchers with data- or algorithm-intensive projects. The successor program was established by the High Performance Computing Act of 1991 (P.L. 102–194), resulting in three parallel activities (see Fig. 3.3): commercialization of network services, creation of a national information infrastructure; and research in high-performance computing and networking technologies whose goals include development of teraops computing systems capable of performing trillions of operations per second and the demonstration of gigabit networks, high-speed networks capable of moving billions of bits per second.

The fourth stage, *privatization and commercialization* (1991–present), involves removing government subsidies to regional networks and dismantling the barriers imposed by restrictive acceptable usage policies. The network extends far beyond the research community and today supports not only the expanding backbone services, but also commercial transactions and extensive connections for commercial organizations. (see Chapter 4).

The fourth stage recognizes the changing nature of the networking marketplace. During 1987–1991, high-bandwidth Internet services were not available commercially. There were neither suppliers nor markets. By 1991 a number of comparable commercial services had arisen, catalyzed in part by the market generated by the NSFNET backbone and growing interest from commercial users. This stage calls for the development of a new backbone architecture that will allow the research and education communities to take

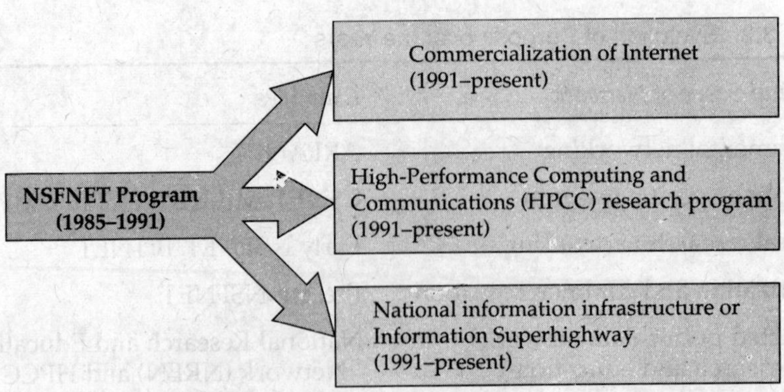


**Figure 3.3** Evolution of the NSFNET program

advantage of the services available from commercial suppliers while NSF concentrates on introducing an experimental very high speed backbone network service (or vBNS). The vBNS backbone's speed is around 155 Mbps compared to the earlier backbone speed of 45 Mbps.

Running in parallel to the fourth stage are *high performance computing and communications (HPCC)* programs linked to fundamental research on computer science and engineering, the prerequisite to the development of future computing, communications, and information systems.

HPCC is an R&D program wherein each new set of technologies forms the foundation for the next. As high-performance computing hardware is built, the systems software to make it usable is developed, then the applications software. As advanced networking technologies are developed and deployed, software developers at remote locations access this hardware by using systems software to develop applications. This work doesn't proceed sequentially—systems software development may sometimes begin before hardware is available, for example. Applications programs cannot be executed on multiple systems until the systems and networks are in place. Hence, progress on all fronts is required because all these areas are so closely linked.

HPCC has five basic interrelated objectives. The first two focus on advancing the computing infrastructure for scïence and engineering researchers by supporting access to high-speed networks and to supercomputers. The others focus on technology transfer issues such as discovery and transfer of pertinent knowledge and the education and training of people who can apply the new capabilities to a broad array of problems and issues—academic, industrial, and economic. Specifically, these five objectives are as follows:

1. To develop, provide, and support advanced research and education networking services and capabilities for connecting researchers, educators, and students in universities, high schools, research laboratories, libraries, and businesses. An example of this phase is the National Research and Education Network (NREN) described in Section 3.4.

2. To provide access to state-of-the-art high-performance computing environments and to incorporate new generations of scalable, parallel high-performance computers and software technologies into important application areas. These systems are expected to have the potential to perform one trillion computer calculations per second to help in the solution of major scientific and engineering problems. This involves developing critical expertise in scalable computing areas such as components, interconnects, computing architectures, and systems software. This will enable distributed computing over heterogeneous platforms, from workstations and clusters to large-scale, high-performance systems. This effort aims to help vendors see the strengths and weaknesses

of their products and users see the types of problems those products can effectively address. An example of this phase is gigabit networking, described in Section 3.4.

3. To generate fundamental knowledge that can lay the foundation for future advances in high-performance computing and communications. Capabilities resulting from new knowledge uncovered by basic research have made dramatic impacts on the offerings of the computer industry, on the power and extent of use of computers, and on the range of applications of the technologies.
4. To enhance innovation, technology transfer, productivity, and industrial competitiveness through academic–industrial partnerships. This also involves education and training of a cadre of scientists, engineers, technical personnel, and students who are prepared to take advantage of these new capabilities.
5. To make advanced computing and communications information infrastructure available to—and usable by—a larger segment of the society. By demonstrating solutions to problems with broad societal impact, these efforts may have the most impact on commercial markets because of the large number of people affected. This leads into stage six: The Information Superhighway.

The sixth stage, *national information infrastructure*, or the I-way, is the ultimate goal. The objective is to extend networking everywhere (ubiquitous) and enable new consumer applications. The I-way is rather broad in scope and represents the convergence of computing, entertainment, telecommunications, the Internet, cable TV, publishing, and information-provider industries. New niche markets and synergies emerge as these intersections occur.

## The Internet and Network Structure

The impact of NSFNET on the computer and communications industry has been extraordinary. Prior to 1986 only a small handful of networks existed within the research and education community. The introduction of NSFNET stimulated the rapid deployment of regional networks throughout the world and a growing demand for high-speed connectivity. In turn, this stimulated development of switches and routers to accommodate the increasing demands of the networks. What has arisen from this activity is a clear market for data communications networks.

Paralleling the evolution of the Internet has been an increasing generalization of its physical structure (see Table 3.3). If the first stage took us to 2000 hosts over the first ten years and the second and third stages scaled the connectivity from 2000 to 1 million over eight years, the fourth stage of Internet growth is now marked by host counts that will likely increase from 1 million to 100 million over the next five years. In the first stage, we primarily dealt with homogeneous networks, then moved to internetworks that are heterogeneous in nature. The next generation signified by the I-way is expected to involve even more diversified, multifunctional networks.

The last decade has seen the following exponential progression in the NSFNET bandwidth, paving the way for many new applications.

| | |
|---|---|
| 1969 | 9.6 Kbps |
| 1985 | 56 Kbps |
| 1987 | 1.544 Mbps |
| 1989 | 45 Mbps |
| 1995–1999 (expected) | 155–1000 Mbps |

Today, the NSFNET has become the core for more recent developments, NREN and commercialization. To understand the changes taking place, we need to take a closer look at the overall architecture of NSFNET and delve into its backbone structure and component networks.

**Table 3.3** Generalization of the Internet Structure

| *Type and Scope of Network* | *Examples* |
|---|---|
| Stand-alone computers | Time-sharing hosts |
| Early networks | ARPANET |
| Internetwork | ESNET, NSFNET (tiered), EBONE |
| Multiple internetworks | The Internet |
| Multiple-function internetworks (cable TV, telecom, computer networks) | Information Superhighway |

## 3.3 NSFNET: ARCHITECTURE AND COMPONENTS

In the mid-1980s the National Science Foundation (NSF) created five supercomputer centers on the presumption that the availability of supercomputer power greatly expands computational possibilities and stimulates a wider range of scientific explorations. Until then, availability of supercomputers was limited to military researchers and others who could afford to buy time on them. NSF wanted to make supercomputing resources widely available for academic research and so mandated that the five centers' expensive computing resources be shared—the logic being that complex research projects require the sharing of knowledge, databases, software, and results. This mandate created a communications problem: NSF needed a way to interconnect these centers and to allow the clients of these centers to access them.

NSF initially tried to use the ARPANET, but this strategy failed because of the military bureaucracy and other staffing problems. In response to these problems, NSF decided to build its own network, based on the ARPANET's IP (internet protocol) technology. The NSFNET backbone initially connected the five supercomputing centers with 56 kbps telephone leased lines. While slow by modern standards, it was considered fast in 1985.

As it became evident that every university could not be connected directly to a supercomputing center, NSF realized it had to provide an access structure. Each campus joined the regional network that was connected to the closest supercomputing center and acted as an access ramp onto the network. With this architecture, any computer could communicate with any other by routing the traffic through its regional networks, closest access ramp, and then on the backbone to the destination network where the process was reversed to reach the destination. This is depicted in the three-level hierarchical model shown in Fig. 3.4.

The abstraction in Fig. 3.4 is not completely accurate, as it ignores commercial network providers, international networks, and interconnections that bypass the strict hierarchy. For the sake of discussion, commercial Internet providers and international networks best fit into the mid-level network abstraction, since they use the NSFNET and other agency backbones.

Water distribution systems may be a useful analogy in understanding the technology and economics of the NSFNET program. We can think of the data circuits as pipes that carry data rather than water. The cost to an institution was generally a function of the size of the data pipe entering the campus. The campuses installed plumbing and appliances—computers, workstations, and routers—and funded these services as they did other parts of campus infrastructure such as classrooms, libraries, and water fountains. There was no extra charge for data use [CONG94].

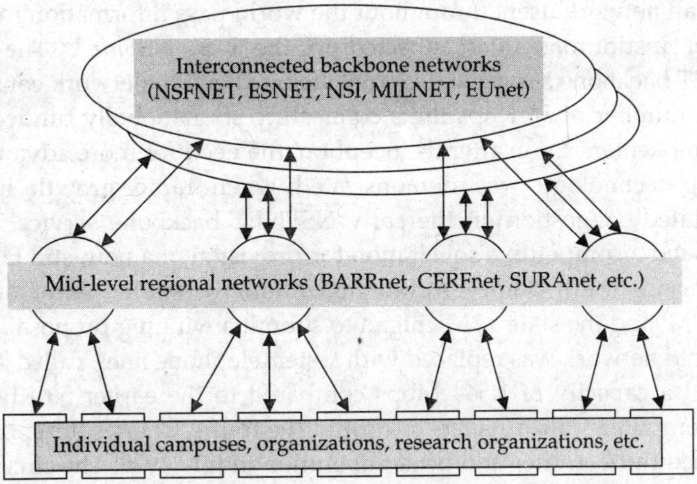


**Figure 3.4** Structure of the Internet hierarchy from national backbone to campus networks

The mid-level networks acted like cooperatives that distributed data from the national backbone to the campuses. The mid-levels leased data pipes from the telephone companies, and added services and management, so each member of the co-op could access the pipe and either consume or send data. If the supply of data slowed due to excess use, the cooperative could purchase larger pipes for all to share. Data in essence were a free and renewable resource contributed by members of the cooperative and cooperatives like them around the world. The federal government provided some of the funding for these pipes, largely through the NSF's investment in nationwide infrastructure (backbone services) and some seed money for these mid-level networks.

This model was a huge success—and, like any successful solution, a time came when it became a victim of its own success and was no longer effective. The original target of sharing supercomputers was subsumed by the growing use of the network to do several tasks never envisioned initially. Everyone discovered e-mail for communication and news groups for sharing information, files, and expertise. The network's traffic increased until, eventually, the computers controlling the network and the telephone lines connecting them became saturated. The network was upgraded several times over the last decade to accommodate the increasing demand.

## The NSFNET Backbone

The NSFNET backbone service was the largest single government investment in the NSF-funded program. The backbone is important because almost all network users throughout the world pass information to or from member institutions interconnected to the U.S. NSFNET. The current NSFNET backbone service dates from 1986, when the network consisted of a small number of 56-Kbps links connecting six nationally funded supercomputer centers. Soon after its inception, the need for more advanced networking technology was demonstrated when rapid growth in traffic precipitated congestion on the early NSFNET backbone service. In 1987, NSF issued a competitive solicitation for provision of a new, still faster network service. Merit, a non-profit organization, worked in partnership with MCI, IBM, and the state of Michigan to submit a winning proposal.

The old network was replaced with faster telephone lines, called T-1 lines, that had a capacity of 1.544 Mbps compared to the earlier 56 Kbps, with faster computers called *routers* to control the traffic. The resulting backbone connected thirteen sites and began operation in July 1988. The circuits were provided by MCI, and the routers were based on IBM RT technology. The congestion–network upgrade cycle continues to this day. Unlike changes to a typical highway system where we see "at work" signs restricting traffic, most changes on the Internet are transparent to users. Perhaps even more important: The congestion–network upgrade cycle has resulted in a technological framework that has proven to be resilient.

By 1989, the NSFNET was reengineered by increasing the number of T1 circuits and improving router performance. This expanded bandwidth and speed was not just a matter of buying more capacity, for new routing methods had to be developed, tested, and proven. The speed and capability encouraged new and innovative uses of the network for research and education, resulting in more than a 15 percent increase in network traffic per month. To meet the expanding demands, Advanced Network & Services (ANS) was created by Merit, IBM, and MCI. During ANS's stewardship, the backbone capacity expanded from T-1 to T-3 45 Mbps, or by a factor of more than 30.

By the end of 1991, all NSFNET backbone sites were connected to the new ANS-provided T-3 backbone. In just a few years' time, the increase in the number of NSFNET users has reaffirmed the need for this high-speed data network. That increase is reflected in the number of local, state, and regional networks connected to the network. From an initial 170 networks in July 1988 to over 38,000. In the same period, traffic went from an initial 195 million packets during the first full month of operation to over 15 terabytes.

Another statistic that is even more interesting and germane to the discussion of electronic commerce is the economic factor. The cost to the NSF for transport of information across this network has decreased by two orders of magnitude, falling from approximately $10 per megabyte in 1987 to less then $1.00 in 1989. At the end of 1993, the cost was 13 cents. These cost reductions occurred gradually over a six-year period. While there were some reductions in the cost of data circuits, the majority of savings resulted from industry equipment vendors incorporating what was learned and developing new faster and more efficient hardware and software technologies. In the case of NSFNET, the annual federal investment covers only a minor part of the backbone and the regional networks.

In some respects, the Internet is already privatized, as the physical circuits are owned by the private sector and the routing (logical networks) is usually managed and operated by the private sector. The nonprofit regional networks of the NSFNET increasingly contract out routine operations, including network information centers, while retaining control of policy and planning functions. This helps develop expertise, resources, and competition in the private sector and so facilitates the development of commercial services.

Figure 3.5 shows the NSFNET backbone architecture. The NSFNET backbone connects core nodal traffic switching substations (CNSS) located at thirteen sites around the country. Each CNSS then serves the regional networks through exterior nodal switching stations (ENSS).

## Mid-Level Regional Networks

Mid-level networks, often referred to as regional networks, are one element of the three-tier NSFNET architecture (see Fig. 3.4). They provide a bridge

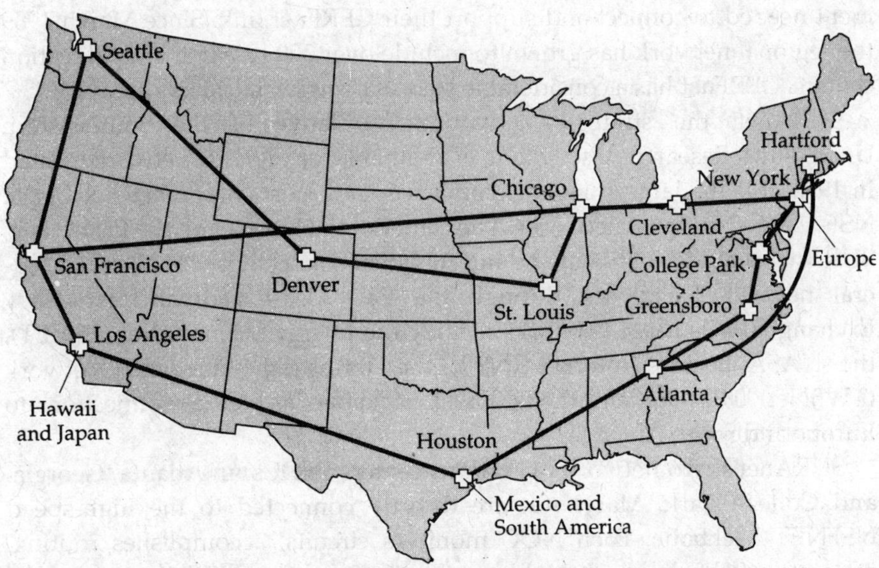


**Figure 3.5** Structure of the old NSFNET backbone (1989–1995)

between local organizations, such as campuses and libraries, and the federally funded NSFNET backbone service. The service area of mid-level networks tends to vary from substate, statewide, and multistate coverage. They deserve special consideration in our discussion, since they have taken the lead in providing network access to a much broader population of scholars. Mid-level networks have been the primary vehicle for connecting K–12 schools, libraries, and hospitals to the Internet. This is not to say that all U.S libraries and school systems have Internet access—the majority are yet to be connected.

Regional networks evolved from networks that originally connected geographically proximate universities. In the past, most regional networks were funded by NSF. NSF provided close to 40 percent of the operating costs of the mid-level networks, with the remainder covered by membership and connection fees, funding from state governments, and in-kind contributions. Anecdotal evidence compiled informally by FARNET and NSF suggests that about 80 percent of network traffic is usually intraregional and the remainder interregional.

To illustrate, let's look at creation of one regional network, California Education and Research Federation Network (CERFnet). In June 1988 the San Diego Supercomputer Center and General Atomics submitted a proposal to the NSF to establish the CERFnet. Thirty-four of the leading research and education centers in California participated in the proposal effort. In March 1989 NSF awarded $3.8 million to initiate CERFnet. The institutions contributed additional funds in membership fees, support personnel (such as training, consultation, and documentation), and maintenance of equipment needed to connect and support their CERFnet link. Since March 1989 the regional network has grown to include over 300 research and education centers. CERFnet has a considerable base of commercial clients as well.

SURAnet, the strategic networking initiative of the Southeastern Universities Research Association, is another large regional network created in 1986. It is the largest, most experienced, and most comprehensive of the NSF-assisted regional networks. The center of the Internet on the East Coast, SURAnet provides national and international connectivity for all major federal network backbones through the East Coast Federal Interagency Exchange (FIX). These networks include the Energy Sciences Net (ESNET), the NASA Science Internet (NSI), the Terrestrial Wideband Network (TWBNet), MILNET, and the NSFNET backbone, as well as connections to Europe and South America.

SURAnet's two network operations centers (NOCs) in Atlanta, Georgia, and College Park, Maryland, are directly connected to the high-speed NSFNET backbone. Each NOC monitors circuits, accomplishes routing, interacts with federal networking agencies such as ANS (which runs the NSFNET backbone), and provides technical coordination among the sites within the region. The NOCs also test new technologies and plan for their deployment. In general, the NOCs are responsible for the performance and the reliability of the network within the region and for technical assistance to the sites under its jurisdiction.

Internet access within a mid-level network is accomplished within the individual states, sometimes through the state networking entities and sometimes through individual sites. Internet access can be accomplished in two ways: (1) via a dedicated connection that brings the network to the site, or (2) via dial-in. A dedicated connection requires that the site have a router connected to an NOC router through a dedicated connection (usually a digital circuit). Dedicated connections may be at various speeds, ranging from very slow speed access through modems running at 14,400 baud over an ordinary phone circuit, or at higher speeds through a digital circuit. Dedicated connections are appropriate when a number of people wish simultaneous access to the Internet. Table 3.4 summarizes the connection capabilities and technology.

Generally, direct connections are made to the state backbone nodes. For instance, Westnet's region encompasses Arizona, Colorado, New Mexico, Utah, and Wyoming and the southern half of Idaho; the state backbones are interconnected at T-1 speeds, ensuring good network access. These state backbones are connected directly to the NSFNET backbone via the NSFNET site at the University of Utah. Dial-in connections of a variety of types are possible, including simple terminal access (this is the "old" manner of dialing in via an asynchronous modem and is usually used to access a computer on the network), SLIP (serial line internet protocol), PPP (point-to-point protocol), or UUCP. (See Chapter 17.)

Each regional network serves about 100 to 200 state and campus sites (research and educational institutions). The financial health and viability of regional networks varies. With the shift toward commercial traffic plus diminishing federal support, most regional providers have to evolve to fill

**Table 3.4** Direct Connection Types and Technologies

| *Speed* | *Type of Circuit* | *Line* | *Approximate No. of Users* |
|---|---|---|---|
| Very slow speed | 14,400 baud | Ordinary phone line | 12 |
| Slow speed | 56,000 bps | 56 kbps digital | 40 |
| High speed | 1.544 Mbps | T-1 digital | 1000 |
| Very high speed | 45 Mbps | T-3 digital | 100,000 |

new roles. A list of regional networks that maintained network operations centers (NOCs) for connecting local networks to the Internet is given in Table 3.5. It remains to be seen whether regional providers, as they are currently known, are a temporary phenomenon or will become competitive providers of network service. Toward that end, eight regional networks have recently organized themselves as the Corporation for Regional and Enterprise Networking (CoREN), to provide voice, data, and video services, including TCP/IP networking, between regions and nationwide.

## State and Campus Networks

State and campus networks link into regional networks. The mandate for state networks is to provide local connectivity and access to wider area services for state governments, K–12 schools, higher education, and research institutions.

Campus networks include university and college campuses, research laboratories, private companies, and educational sites such as K–12 school districts. These are the most important components of the network hierarchy, as the investment in these infrastructures far exceeds that of the government's investments in the national and regional networks. NSF funds institutional or campus connections to the NSFNET, which includes payments by the institution to the regional network (see Fig. 3.6).

The campus-level networks at academic institutions probably represent a 7–10 times larger annual investment than the mid-level networks and the

**Table 3.5** Regional Networks that Maintained NOCs

| | |
|---|---|
| CERFnet, Southern California | NevadaNet |
| THEnet, Texas | Concertnet, North Carolina |
| BARRnet, Northern California | PSCnet (Pittsburgh Supercomputing Center) |
| Westnet, Colorado | OARnet (Ohio Supercomputer Center) |
| Northwestnet, Washington State | SDSCnet (San Diego Supercomputer Center) |
| SURAnet, SouthEastern network | Sesquinet (Rice University SuperComputer Center) |
| NYSERnet, New York | JVNCnet (Cornell SuperComputer Center) |

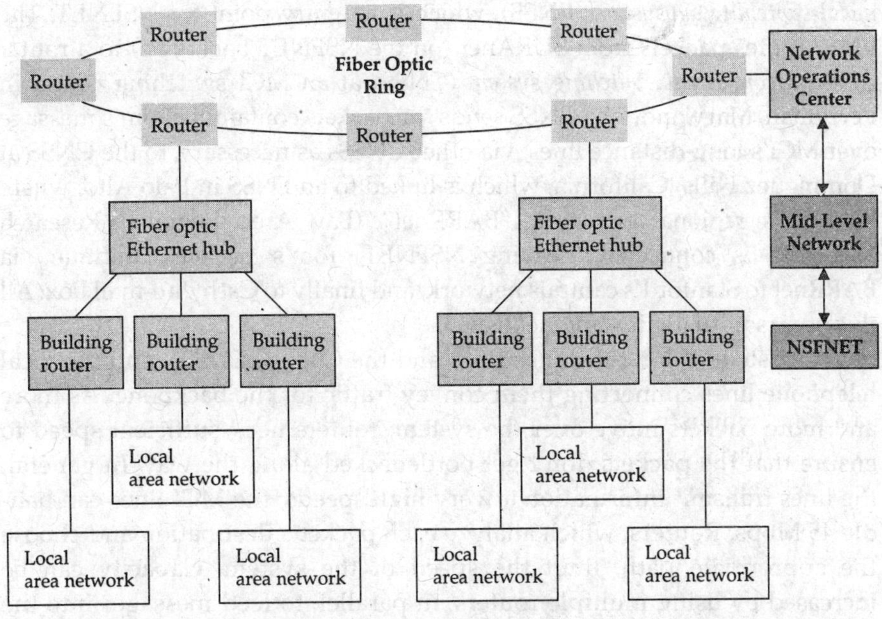


**Figure 3.6** Network hierarchy in a campus network interconnecting multiple local area networks to the Internet

backbone together, yet there is little federal funding program at this level. Furthermore, since these local networks must be built by the institution rather than leased, the institutions incur an additional capitalization cost that, annualized and aggregated, is perhaps another 20–50 times the annual costs of the mid-level and backbone networks. (These numbers are the roughest of estimates, intended only for illustration.)

## Movement of Information on the NSFNET

NSFNET is used for a variety of applications. For example, electronic mail provides a way of sending person-to-person messages almost instantaneously, enabling researchers separated by thousands of miles to collaborate. But how exactly does this happen?

As an example, imagine Tom, sitting at a PC in Washington, D.C., sending a message to Cathy, at a terminal at Stanford University in Palo Alto, California. Tom is connected to a local network, which serves about 1000 users. Recall that the local network breaks the e-mail message into pieces called "packets" and sends the packets through a type of switch, called a router, which is part of a regional network called SURAnet. SURAnet has a router in College Park, Maryland, that is linked to a router called an *external nodal switching subsystem* (ENSS), which is an entry point for NSFNET. The ENSS routes packets from SURAnet (on the NSFNET backbone) to a router called a *core nodal switching system* (CNSS) at an MCI switching center in Perryman, Maryland. The CNSS sends the packets containing Tom's message over MCI's long-distance lines, via other CNSSs as necessary, to the CNSS at Dominguez Hills, California, which is linked to an ENSS in Palo Alto, where Stanford's regional network, "BARRnet" (Bay Area Regional Research Network) is connected. Leaving NSFNET, Tom's packets continue via BARRnet to Stanford's campus network, and finally to Cathy's e-mail box. All this occurs virtually instantaneously.

The system of long-distance lines and the CNSSs, ENSSs, and the local telephone lines connecting them convey traffic for the backbone. As more and more packets move over the system, routers need sufficient speed to ensure that the packets don't get bottlenecked along the way. In general, the lines transmit information at very high speeds; the MCI lines can handle 45 Mbps. Routers, which analyze each packet's destination and choose the appropriate path, limit the speed of the system. Capacity can be increased by using multiple routers, in parallel, to feed messages into the lines.

## 3.4 NATIONAL RESEARCH AND EDUCATION NETWORK

The NSFNET has evolved into the National Research and Education Network (NREN). The NREN is a five-year project approved by Congress as part of the High Performance Computing and Communications Act in fall 1991. NREN represents the first phase of the HPCC project. The intent is to create a next-generation Internet to interconnect the nation's education and research communities at more than one gigabit (one billion bits per second) data rates, thereby facilitating enhanced access to information resources and computational capabilities.

Development and deployment of NREN is planned to occur in three phases. The first phase, begun in 1988, involved upgrading all telecommunications links within the NSFNET backbone to 1.544 Mbps (T-1). This upgrade has been completed for most agencies. In phase two, which began in 1991, the NSFNET backbone was upgraded to 45 Mbps (T-3). The second phase also provides upgraded services for 200 to 300 research facilities directly linked to this backbone. The third phase, which will result in a phased implementation of a gigabit-speed network operating at roughly 20–50 times T-3 speeds, is expected to begin during the mid-1990s if the necessary technology and funding are available.

NREN activities can be broadly split into two classifications:

1. Establishment and deployment of a new network architecture for *very high bandwidth networks* (vBNS).
2. Research to yield insights into the design and development of *gigabit network* technology.

The following sections give more details on these activities, beginning with the new network architecture for NSFNET.

## New Architecture for NSFNET Backbone

The level of commercialization of the Internet has prompted NSF to define a new architecture for NSFNET to serve the needs of many communities, including government, research, education, and commercial users.

In its effort to further evolve the Internet, NSF issued a solicitation [NSF92] on June 15, 1992, for a high-speed network architecture that would substantially change the nature of Internet routing and operations. This solicitation set forth a new architecture for providing NSFNET backbone services, including regional networks and network service providers. The solicitation was for a "Network Access Point (NAP) Manager and Routing Arbiter (RA) organization; and a provider of very high speed Backbone Network Services (vBNS)." We will explain each of these in the following subsections. To understand how all these three fit together, see Fig. 3.7. The new architecture became operational on April 30, 1995.

The previous NSFNET backbone architecture illustrated in Fig. 3.5 contained thirteen core nodal stations. They have been replaced by three "priority" network access points connected by very high bandwidth networks running at minimum speeds of 155 Mbps, replacing the earlier technology running at 45 Mbps.

To each NAP, a variety of commercial networks, international networks, and federal networks can be connected. They are required by NSF to operate at a minimum of 1.544 Mbps. The mid-level networks, which were dominant players in the previous NSFNET architecture, have lost lustre and can now connect to the NSFNET backbone only through commercial network providers such as SprintNet. In fact, NSF funding for mid-level networks has been terminated. The new architecture calls for regional networks to secure vBNS backbone access services from network access points (NAPs) run by commercial network providers. To ensure transition, there has been a four-year phasing out of NSF's funding for the regionals that ended on April 30, 1995.

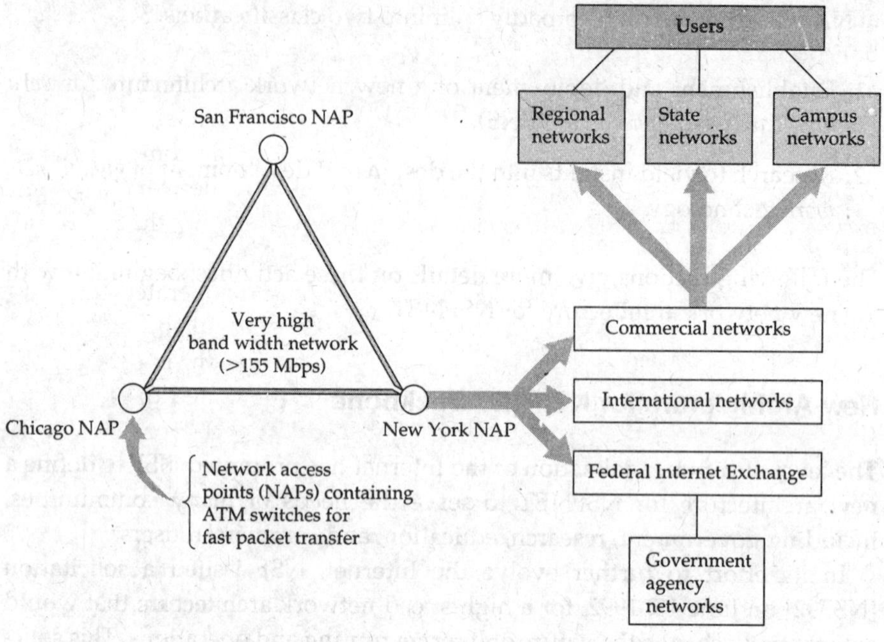


**Figure 3.7** Network access points (NAPs) and very high bandwidth architecture (vBNS)

### *Network Access Points (NAPs)*

A network access point is a high-speed network or switch to which a number of routers can be connected for the purpose of traffic exchange and interoperation. NAPs are locations where other networks can connect to the vBNS. It is anticipated that many types of networks will eventually connect to the NAPs. Examples of such networks include other federally sponsored networks, other service providers for research and education, service providers for traffic not limited to the support of research and education, and international networks. NAPs must be able to operate at speeds of at least 100 Mbps, and networks that attach to NAPs must operate at speeds of at least 1.544 Mbps (T-1).

According to NSF, NAPs will not be subject to the Acceptable Usage Policy (AUP) and will permit, for example, two attached networks to exchange traffic without violating the AUP of any other attached network. The Internet's Acceptable Use Policy states that only data whose content type falls under the category of research and education is allowed on the Internet backbone; commercial business data content is not. This policy, however, created a need for commercial network providers to bypass the NSFNET backbone as much as possible.

The NAP is a conceptual evolution of other successful models, namely, Federal Information Exchanges (FIX) and the Commercial Information Exchange (CIX). An interconnection point where multiple commercial networks meet and exchange traffic, CIX was created to let network providers exchange traffic directly without concern about violating the AUP (see Chapter 4).

Today, the primary NAPs are located in San Francisco, operated by Pacific Bell; in Chicago, operated by Ameritech; and in Pennsauken, New Jersey, operated by Sprint. A fourth access point, in Washington, is operated by Metropolitan Fiber Systems. The NAPs are fiber distributed data interface (FDDI)–based rings to which other carriers connect at T-1 or T-3 speeds. Traffic meeting AUP guidelines would be allowed on the vBNS 155-Mbps backbone, but commercial traffic would have to use alternative delivery services that may also be connected to the NAPs. In other words, a single NAP could be connected to multiple backbones, each serving different customers.

The internal details of each NAP are beyond the scope of this book. They can be obtained from the following addresses:

- San Francisco—Pacific Bell (http://www.pacbell.com/)
- Chicago—Ameritech (http://www.ameritech.com/)
- New York—Sprint (http://www.sprint.com/)
- Washington, D.C.—Metropolitan Area Fiber (http://www.mfsdatanet.com/)

### Routing Arbiter (RA)

Routing arbiter (RA) is an entirely new element introduced into the NAP architecture. RA organization implements the concept of policy-based network routing that enables routing of traffic between different network operators. This is now recognized as a key for network efficiency. In the past, although several tools were available to apply routing algorithms, they were not used in a well-coordinated way. In a large network such as the Internet, applying individual routing policies without proper coordination and simulation of the consequences leads to an unmanageable situation. The solution for controlling the chaos is the routing arbiter (RA).

RA will maintain databases of routing services that have networks attached to the NAPs backbone access points. They can be used to obtain information on network topology, policy, and interconnection information in order to construct routing tables. This job will fall to an organization chosen to handle a number of routing tasks that formerly were part and parcel of the role of backbone provider. In fact, the solicitation warns that the routing arbiter and the 155-Mbps backbone provider cannot be the same organization. According to the NSF solicitation, "this component of the architecture will provide for an unbiased routing scheme which will be available [but not mandatory] for all attached networks" [NSF92].

Under the new NSF architecture, Merit and Information Sciences Institute (ISI) have been selected to jointly implement the role of routing arbiter (http://www.ra.net). Merit will have the central role in technical coordination for Internet service providers who need to interchange traffic. This function is needed to assure smooth operations and stability for the Internet during the transition to the new technologies resulting from this award program and beyond. Merit will also work with ISI to implement new technologies for routing traffic among Internet networks, using high-powered workstations as "route servers." Merit will be responsible for deploying the new routing technologies that are expected to be a key to accommodating continued Internet growth and complexity resulting from the many new users of the Internet in the next few years. For instance, a key task for the routing arbiter will be to enhance the use of new switched services offered by the telco carriers, such as ATM, in place of the dedicated point-to-point technology that is widely deployed in wide-area internetworks.

The major goals for the routing arbiter include advancement of Internet routing algorithms with respect to scaling and stability issues, routing information registration and dissemination for the network service providers serving the Internet, deployment of route servers to aid in the dissemination and real-time maintenance of the global routing system, and coordination and sharing of technical information in support of the Internet operations community. A key element for enabling information sharing is the routing arbiter database (RADB). Data from the RA database may be used by anyone worldwide to help with debugging, configuring, and engineering Internet routing and addressing.

### *Very High Speed Backbone Network Services (vBNS)*

MCI was selected to provide the NSFNET very high speed backbone network service (vBNS). This service will be operated from MCI's production telecommunications infrastructure based on SONET transport technology and asynchronous transfer mode (ATM) switching technology. The technical details of SONET and ATM are presented in Chapter 19.

The vBNS provider is responsible for establishing and maintaining a vBNS to accept traffic from the five supercomputing centers (SCCs) and the

NSF-designated network access points (NAPs). The vBNS provider is also required to provide for high-speed connectivity between regions, facilitate distributed computing applications, facilitate multimedia applications, and promote development and utilization of advanced routing technologies.

Access to the MCI vBNS will commence at data rates of 155 Mbps and will increase to gigabit-per-second rates over the five-year award period. Access of 655 Mbps is estimated to be available by 1996. By 1998 a 960-Gbps SONET backbone with 2.4-Gbps access to SCCs is anticipated. MCI will make a Testnet available in support of experimentation with new telecommunications technologies. Although vBNS traffic must comply with the AUP, the vBNS can have connections and customers beyond those specified by NSF as long as the quality and quantity of required services for NSF-specified customers are not affected.

## Gigabit Network Research

Currently, the NREN community has access to a variety of networks operating at speeds ranging from those obtained with dial-up modems (14.4 Kbps) to high-speed LANs (100 Mbps). In the realm of wide area networks, regional networks typically offer 1.5-Mbps access lines and national level backbone networks such as the NSFNET, and other networks operated by the government offer 45 Mbps. It is recognized that gigabit networks (>1000 Mbps) have the potential of becoming a major part of the internetworking infrastructure during the next decade.

In light of this, gigabit network research has two goals: (1) to advance the technology and understanding of requirements for high-speed networking by developing architectural alternatives in determining the possible structure of a next generation wide area gigabit network, and (2) to explore the potential applications for such a network that are of importance to business and society in general. Applications for gigabit networks will probably evolve from various experimental applications being developed in universities and in government and industrial research testbeds.

### *High-Speed Gigabit Wide Area Network Architecture*

Creating a wide area gigabit network is expected to require major departures from existing network technology along several dimensions:

- The network speed will overwhelm the processing capabilities of most existing supercomputers and workstations. Existing operating systems and protocols will be unable to respond quickly without radical design changes.

- Since the total delay across a gigabit network is expected to be small, applications requiring large bandwidth and whose quality deteriorates with delays are enabled easily. Applications such as video conferencing requiring the exchange of large amounts of data at regular intervals can be deployed.
- The volume of data in the network can be huge. The task of managing the reliable flow of such large amounts of data in a network environment with thousands of users requires research in algorithms for storage, routing, and retransmission required to recover from anomalies such as errors, failures, and congestion.
- Switching protocols must be designed and developed that can operate at gigabit speeds while dealing with the propagation delays and processing constraints specific to gigabit networks. New switches will be required that have the ability to handle traffic loads of several gigabits per second (or more) and to switch millions of application data representing the combined traffic load.

In short, although gigabit networks can provide many benefits and enable new applications that are required in a information-dominated society, they also pose many technical challenges. The physical layer of the gigabit network (cabling and wiring) may well be the simplest of these hurdles to overcome. In addition to physical data transport, networks running at these speeds will require changes in almost every network element at all levels to eliminate bottlenecks that reduce the speed of information flow. This will require major architectural changes in workstation hosts, packet switches, gateways, and routers, both in hardware design and software.

### *Gigabit Applications: Challenges Ahead*

The key issue to be considered is this: Will the world of the researcher, the educator, and the industry employee be fundamentally altered by the existence of gigabit networks and if so, how? More specifically, what network-based applications can be envisioned that need the gigabit speeds to be effective? Two of the criteria for determining potential applications in this context are (1) real-time processing and synchronization of information and (2) distributed applications.

Applications in the realm of real-time processing and synchronization of information require that the time needed to complete a task using the network must be influenced by gigabit speeds. In other words, waiting for results to arrive in the mail or over slow-speed networks may be too slow to be useful. Examples of this application include group collaboration and video conferencing. Generally, it is conjectured that the use of gigabit networks will enable a major paradigm shift to image-based communication from the older text-based modes of communication.

Although not exclusively a gigabit networking problem, real-time processing of multiple high-speed data streams that are interrelated first requires the synchronization of multiple streams to align and integrate them. The resulting streams are intended to be viewed by a user at a workstation. Synchronization is a key problem, since the communication paths can introduce widely differing delays both among different remote points and among different user media being communicated.

Applications in the realm of distributed computing use multiple computational resources (supercomputers and workstations) in parallel, all interacting at gigabit speeds to significantly improve our ability to solve particular problems related to electronic commerce. Examples include virtual reality and large-scale simulations.

Distributed computing applications often require programs running simultaneously on multiple machines on the network. These programs pass data back and forth to each other at speeds determined by the nature of the computation, the speed of the network, and the delay between the computers. A major research challenge in this area is dealing with the relatively long latency, or propagation delay, present over long distances between processors. This latency factor can be a major problem relative to the data exchange required for computational efficiency.

## Gigabit Research Testbeds

Today, gigabit testbed facilities are being developed, and work on the gigabit network applications has begun. However, the classical "chicken and egg" problem applies to gigabit networks in the sense that they won't be economically viable until a market for them exists and a market won't develop until users have a chance to experiment with such higher-speed networks.

The NSF established several testbeds to provide a focal point for needed technical interaction that is driven by user needs. These testbeds have pioneered some of the technical discussion and publications concerned with the evolving architectures. The initial goal was to concentrate on end-to-end upper-layer issues (user impact, applications, transport and higher-layer protocols, operating systems, and host–network interface architecture best suited for imaging, visualization, multimedia, remote backup, and other emerging applications) so that usage of networks is understood.

The current gigabit research revolves around a set of six testbeds (Aurora, Blanca, CASA, MAGIC, Nectar, and VISTAnet) funded by the NSF and the Defense Advanced Research Projects Agency, each with its own research objective and staff. Here are some details of the six NREN testbeds:

*Aurora.* The network links four sites located in the Northeast using 622-Mbps SONET (data transmission standard) channels: the University of Pennsylvania in Philadelphia; Bellcore in Morristown, New Jersey; IBM's T.J. Watson Research Center in Hawthorne, New York, and the Massachusetts Institute of Technology in Cambridge, Massachusetts. This testbed will explore alternative network technologies, investigate distributed system/network service paradigms, and experiment with gigabit network applications. A key objective is to provide a platform on which other researchers can explore both business and scientific applications of such networks as well as develop the network architecture to meet the needs of these new applications.

*Blanca.* The network connects sites at AT&T Bell Labs in New Jersey; the University of Wisconsin and the University of Illinois in the Midwest; and the University of California–Berkeley and Lawrence Livermore Laboratories in California. AT&T is providing long-distance T-3 circuits and experimental switches and hardware, and local exchange carriers are providing higher-speed regional links. The emphasis will be on widely distributed supercomputing and high-bandwidth visualization. Specifically, the applications to be studied include multiple remote visualization and control of simulations; radio astronomy imaging; multimedia digital library; and medical imaging.

*CASA.* The network connects four sites in California and New Mexico: the major ones being the San Diego Supercomputer Center and the Los Alamos National Laboratory. Network links are provided by MCI, Pacific Bell, and US West. Applications here focus on using gigabit networks to combine the processing power of multiple supercomputers for climate and chemical reaction modeling.

*MAGIC.* The network ties together a wide variety of government and university sites. Sprint and Southwestern Bell are among the carriers providing links. The network will be used by the U.S. Army and others to test interactive simulations of real-life landscapes.

*Nectar.* The network will provide a high-speed link connecting two local area networks at Carnegie-Mellon University and the Pittsburgh Supercomputer Center. Fiber links will be provided by Bell Atlantic, and Bellcore and CMU are collaborating on hardware design. The network will link high-performance parallel interface LANs over ATM- and SONET-based networks.

*VISTAnet.* The network uses SONET/ATM links from BellSouth and GTE to link supercomputer center MCNC, North Carolina State University, and University of North Carolina–Chapel Hill. The network focuses on a single application: networking powerful computers to help doctors plan radiation therapy for cancer treatment.

These testbeds are exploring two different technological approaches to developing gigabit switching systems: asynchronous transfer mode (ATM) and packet transfer mode (PTM). A prototype ATM switch was provided by Bellcore, and IBM has provided a packet transfer mode switch. High-speed network links are provided by MCI, NYNEX, and Bell Atlantic. The first approach, ATM switching, uses small, fixed-size data elements (called cells) and is expected to form the basis for the next generation of network switching technology. The second approach, PTM, is based on variable-sized packets and is a method being pursued within a smaller segment of the data communications industry. Each approach has its advantages, and these and other options may coexist in the network of tomorrow. In addition, various issues associated with interoperability between these two switching technologies, as well as the development of higher-layer protocols and application service models, need further research.

## 3.5 GLOBALIZATION OF THE ACADEMIC INTERNET

By the late 1980s, the Internet had spread globally, including Canada, Australia, Europe, South Africa, South America, Asia, and Japan. Although we have discussed the development, implementation, and network infrastructure in the United States, the Internet has always been an international network. Today the global network environment reaches over 140 countries, each with its own slant. Asian countries see the Internet as way of expanding business and trade. Eastern European countries, longing for western scientific ties, have long wanted to participate but were excluded by government regulation. Since this ban was relaxed, development is progressing rapidly. Third World countries that formerly did not have the means to participate now view the Internet as a way to raise their education and technology levels.

At present, the Internet's international expansion is hampered by the lack of a good supporting infrastructure, namely, a decent telephone system. In Eastern Europe and in several developing nations, a reliable phone system capable of handling continuous data transmission is virtually nonexistent. Even in major capital cities, fast connections are often limited to the speeds available to the average home anywhere in the United States, 9600 bps. Typically, even if one of these countries is "on the Internet," only a few sites representing the top institutions have access—usually, the major technical university for that country. However, telecom infrastructure is a major priority in most developing countries and is expected to improve rapidly [NAS93].

## International Computer Networks

International computer networks have flourished since the mid 1970s when sites in the United Kingdom and Norway were connected to the ARPANET. An early national network project outside the United States was JANET (Joint Academic Network) in the United Kingdom. Later, several national network projects were initiated in numbers of countries on every continent. Examples include JUNET in Japan, DFN (Deutsche Forschungsnetz) in Germany, UNINET in Norway, and SDN in Korea. International collaborations included NORDUNET in the Nordic countries (regional networks such as Swedish SUNET are part of NORDUNET), EARN and EUNET in Europe, and PACOM in the Pacific Rim.

In the early 1980s, the CSNET (Computer Science Network), BITNET (Because It's Time Network), and UUCP (UNIX to UNIX Copy) all developed international links. For example, by 1984 CSNET was operating e-mail gateways between the United States and Canada, Korea, Israel, Japan, France, Germany, Australia, and Scandinavia. In the same time period, BITNET spread to Europe, via the European Academic Research Network (EARN) and the other regions such as GULFNET in the Persian Gulf region. Similarly, the UUCP network developed a gateway to the EUNET (European UNIX networks) via Amsterdam [NAS93].

By the mid-1980s, when the NSFNET backbone was being discussed, e-mail gateways already connected the various U.S. networks to a robust and growing global networking infrastructure. Today, the NSFNET and European networks are connected by two high-speed circuits linking the NSFNET at New York to INRIA, a French research network in Sophia-Antipoles, and NORDUNET, a Scandinavian research network in the Royal Institute of Technology in Stockholm.

In Europe, the development of the Internet was hampered by national policies mandating OSI protocols. These policies prevented development of large-scale Internet infrastructures everywhere except for the Scandinavian countries (Sweden, Finland, and Norway) that embraced the TCP/IP protocols and became well connected. In fact, Scandinavian countries are the heaviest users of the Internet after the United States. In 1989, RIPE (Reseaux IP Europeans) began coordinating the Internet operation in Europe, and today about 25 percent of all hosts hooked to the Internet are estimated to be in Europe.

Other international links to NSFNET were established in 1991. For example, the Federal University of Rio de Janeiro (UFRJ) came on-line in December 1991. The connection between California's regional network CERFnet and UFRJ is intended to provide Internet access to a regional network located within the state of Rio de Janeiro. Mexico was also linked to the

NSFNET in November 1991 with a 64-Kbps satellite link to the CERFnet via the Mexican satellite, *Morelles II*. And, the System Engineering Research Institute (SERI), Seoul, Korea, was brought on-line in March 1991. The link between SERI and CERFnet provides Internet access to the Korean National Research Network (KREONet).

Networking in developing countries such as China presents a cross-sectional view of the importance these countries place on computer networks. For instance, the major wide area network in China was CNPAC (China National Public Data Network). CNPAC was designed to carry data at speeds varying between 1.2 and 9.6 Kbps. The network hub was in Beijing, where the network management center is located. Since 1993, China has been installing a new network, CHINAPAC. CHINAPAC covers all provincial capital cities of the mainland and is intended to be the major public data network backbone. CHINAPAC and its international link runs at a 64-Kbps backbone rate. User links vary from 1200 bps through 64 Kbps. Users can connect to CHINAPAC through leased lines (9.6 through 64 Kbps) or through dial-up (9.6 Kbps; 1200/2400 bps). It is expected that high-speed fiber will soon blanket China. China is expected to invest approximately $60 billion in telecom infrastructure through the end of the decade. It is anticipated that $18.39 billion will be invested during the Eighth Five Year Plan (1990–1995) and $41.37 billion during the Ninth (1996–2000).

## EBONE: European Backbone

EBONE is a European international network backbone connecting research network service providers. A not-for-profit cooperative effort, EBONE is set up as a consortium whose members share the costs of management and operation based on respective access speeds. EBONE began in September 1991 when representatives of several European academic and research networks met to resolve long-standing connectivity problems. Their approach was to evaluate existing available links and to look for opportunities to bring these links together quickly under a unified approach. The effort was formally started in January 1992 and has proved successful. The need for bandwidth and high-speed connectivity to the U.S. backbone had long been recognized in the European community. Until late 1991 such connectivity was available only to individual national and international research networks. Among EBONE's advantages are simplified network interconnection, increased bandwidth, improved connections to the United States, and greater economy of scale in terms of operations and transmission cost.

EBONE provides two types of service: backbone services and interconnect services. According to the EBONE Consortium, the focus in the coming years will be on the interconnect (Global Neutral Interconnect) service as other backbones come into existence, providing networking services for research.

EBONE operates a core backbone among London, Stockholm, Amsterdam, Geneva, and Paris, as shown in Fig. 3.8. Intercontinental links to the United States are provided from London, Paris, Stockholm, and Geneva. The European links initially operated at speeds between 256 Kbps and 512 Kbps, but the demand for EBONE services has grown such that the Stockholm–Amsterdam–Geneva links are now being upgraded to 1.5 Mbps, Paris–Geneva will become 2 Mbps, and the Paris–U.S. link will be 1.5 Mbps. A new core site in Bonn is being set up and one in Vienna is being investigated to support extension of the network to the central and eastern European countries. Please note that the network speeds in Fig. 3.8 are probably outdated and are used to illustrate the structure at one point in time.

EBONE is managed by the EBONE Management Committee, which is elected by the participating organizations. Operational support is provided by core sites and other sites in cooperation with EBONE Network Operations Center at the Royal Institute of Technology (KTH) in Stockholm. Development is planned by the EBONE Action Team, which consists of technical representatives from the participating organizations. Some of the member organizations of the EBONE Consortium are listed in Table 3.6.

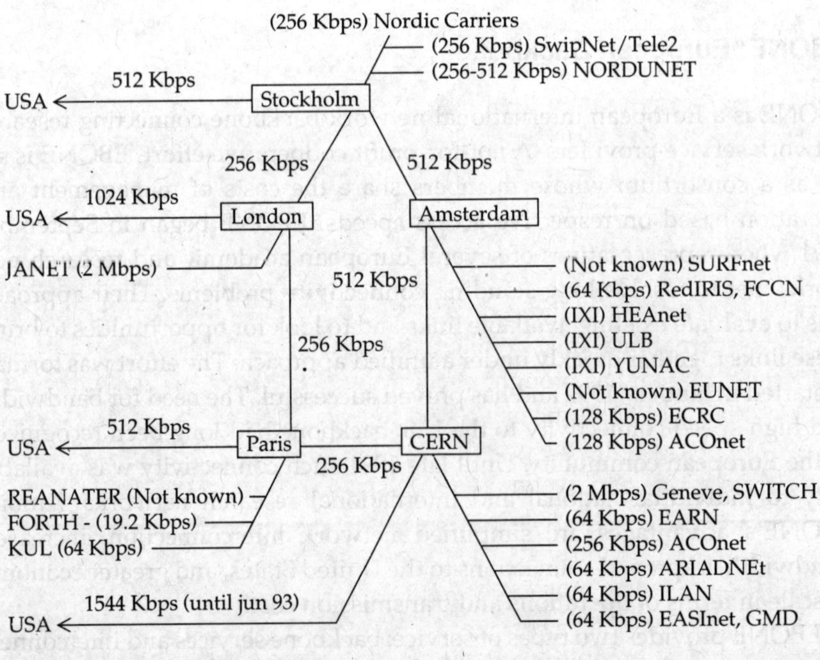


**Figure 3.8** EBONE (European backbone) structure

**Table 3.6** EBONE Consortium Members

| | |
|---|---|
| ACOnet, Austria | KTH, Sweden |
| ARIADnet, Greece | NFSR, Belgium |
| EARN | NORDUNET |
| ECRC | PIPEX, U.K. |
| EUNET/EurOpen | RedIRIS, Spain |
| FCCN, Portugal | Renater, France |
| FORTH, Greece (Crete) | SURFnet, Netherlands |
| GMD, Germany | SwipNet, Sweden |
| HEANET, Ireland | SWITCH, Switzerland |
| ILAN, Israel | TIPnet/Telecom Finland |
| JANET/JNT, UK | |

### Barriers to International Internetworking

Historically, three barriers have slowed the development of international networks. The principal barrier has been the high cost of international communications. Another important factor has been the high cost of installing and maintaining the physical infrastructure, coupled with the limited capacity of such facilities. With the advent of optical transmission and the introduction of new technical innovations, however, capacity is increasing and hence costs can be amortized over an enlarged user base. The third reason has been the lack of competition. Until recently, most governments have exercised either direct or indirect control over national telecommunications as well as international links. While this is still the case in some parts of the world, deregulation has brought about a significant increase in competition and the opening of domestic markets to foreign companies [NAS93].

Nevertheless, despite the growing availability of capacity, the cost differential between U.S. and overseas service is not something that is likely to be resolved soon, although change seems inevitable. In almost every country telcos operate in a "contrived" economic system, that is, a system of cross-subsidization in which monies are collected to support a wide range of government goals. One of the goals in the United States is "universal service," or the provision of affordable telephone service for the greatest number of people. The Swiss, and many other governments throughout western Europe, use monies collected from telecommunications services to subsidize postal and transportation services. Introducing competition into these countries does not appear in the best interests of many of these governments and, in fact, the telcos are discouraging anyone from building his own network employing leased lines. In short, two factors—possible loss of control and income—have made the telcos reluctant to enter into a market economy in which competition is encouraged.

## 3.6 INTERNET GOVERNANCE: THE INTERNET SOCIETY

### Governance Hierarchy

Because the Internet is not a single, unified network, it is not surprising that no one body controls it. Although there are standards, no Internet police exists to enforce them. In effect, the system itself polices such things: If any organization strays from the collective standards, it loses the benefits of global connectivity—which was the whole point of becoming part of the Internet in the first place. Groups do exist that carry out central management functions for the Internet, such as the InterNIC (www. internic.net), which, among other things, registers companies that are connected to the Internet, and the Internet Society (www.isoc.org). The Internet Society has various engineering committees that help make technical recommendations for the future development of the Internet. But none has the power to force a particular direction or action on the Internet community.

The ultimate authority for the technical direction of the Internet rests with the Internet Society (ISOC). This professional society is concerned with the growth and evolution of the worldwide Internet, with the way in which the Internet is and can be used, and with the social, political, and technical issues. It is a voluntary organization whose goal is to promote global information exchange. The four groups in the structure are the ISOC and its Board of Trustees, the Internet Architecture Board (IAB), the IESG, and the IETF itself (see Fig. 3.9). The ISOC Trustees are responsible for approving appointments to the IAB from among the nominees submitted by the IETF nominating committee.

ISOC appoints a council—IAB—that has responsibility for the technical management and direction of the Internet. The IAB is responsible for overall architectural considerations in the Internet. It also serves to adjudicate disputes in the standards process and is responsible for setting the technical

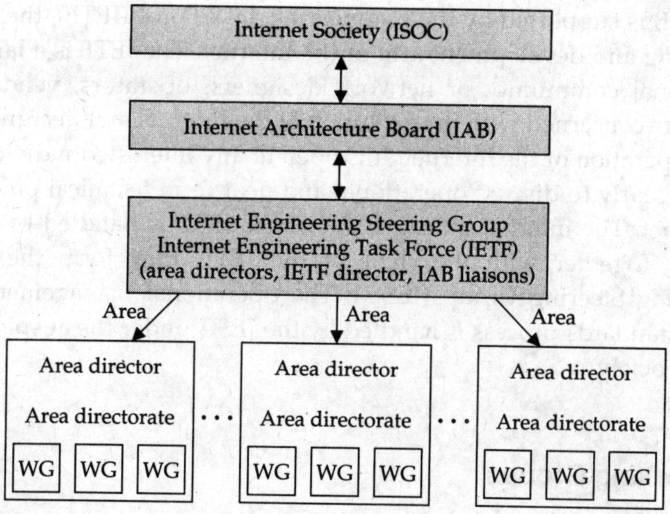


**Figure 3.9** Internet governance hierarchy

direction, establishing standards, and resolving problems in the Internet. The IAB meets regularly to discuss Internet standards. Since the Internet is not an IBM-only, Intel-only, or PowerPC-only network, it can work only if standard ways exist for computers and software applications to talk to each other. This allows computers from different vendors to communicate or interoperate without problems. The IAB is responsible for these standards; it decides when a standard is necessary, considers the problem, adopts a standard, and announces it via the network.

The IAB also keeps track of various network addresses. Each host computer has a unique 32-bit address called an IP address; no two computers in the world can have the same address. The IP address is similar to a telephone number, no two customers can have the same number. The IAB worries about problems like how to develop rules for assigning IP numbers. In other words, it doesn't actually assign the addresses, but it makes the rules about how to assign them. An interesting side effect of the rapid growth of the Internet is that the 32-bit IP address space is becoming insufficient. While it is true that the Internet is running out of 32-bit IP addresses, this problem is being addressed with the IP next generation (IPng) extensions (see Chapter 17). In short, IPng seeks to add digits to the IP address. This is somewhat like the U.S. phone system, which has run out of numbers several times. Ten years ago local calls were dialed with seven digits; today, in some metropolitan areas, local calls now require dialing ten digits.

The IAB is supported by the Engineering Task Force (IETF), the protocol engineering and development arm of the Internet. The IETF is a large open international community of network designers, operators, vendors, and researchers concerned with the evolution of the Internet architecture and the smooth operation of the Internet. It is open to any interested individual and meets regularly to discuss operational and near-term technical problems of the Internet. The internal management of the IETF is handled by the area directors. Together with the chair of the IETF, they form the Internet Engineering Steering Group (IESG). The operational management of the Internet standards process is handled by the IESG under the auspices of the Internet Society.

## IETF Working Groups

The IETF is currently divided into eight functional areas: applications, internet, network management, operational requirements, routing, security, transport, and user services. Each area has one or two area directors. When it considers a problem important enough to merit concern, the IETF sets up a working group (a group of people who work under a charter to achieve a certain goal) for further investigation.

The actual technical work of the IETF is done in its working groups, which are organized by topic into several areas (routing, network management, security). Their goal may be the creation of an informational document, the creation of a protocol specification, or the resolution of problems in the Internet. Most working groups have a finite lifetime and are disbanded after the initial goal is achieved. As in the IETF, there is no official membership for a working group.

Each area has several working groups and may also have birds of a feather (BOF) sessions. BOF generally have the same goals as working groups, except that they have no charter and usually meet only once or twice. BOFs are often held to determine whether there is enough interest to form a working group. The purpose of BOFs is to provide an informal forum for discussing the latest trends in the marketplace that may necessitate a working group for more detailed inquiry. This process is outlined in Fig. 3.10.

Output of the IETF working groups is usually a request for comments (RFC) that is floated in the Internet community for comments and criticism. The early RFCs were meeting minutes and messages between the ARPANET architects about how to resolve certain problems. Two special subseries of the RFCs exist: FYIs and STDs. The For Your Information (FYI) RFC subseries was created to present overviews and introductory topics. Often, FYIs are

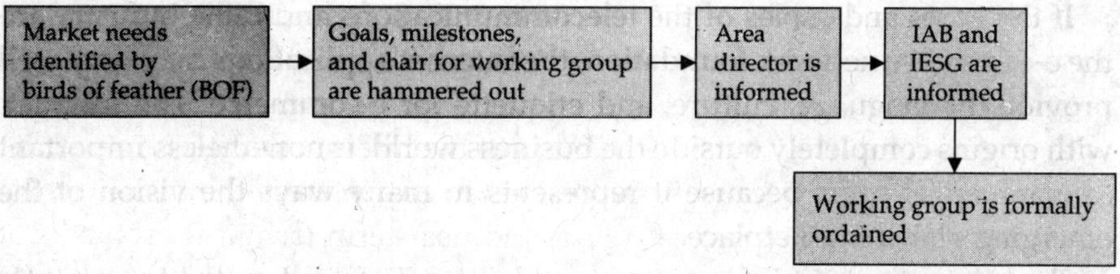


**Figure 3.10** Process of working group creation that culminates in an Internet standard document

created by groups within the IETF User Services Area. The standard (STD) RFC subseries was created to identify Internet standards.

There is another category called Internet-Drafts. These are working documents of the IETF. Any group or individual may submit a document for distribution as an Internet-Draft. These documents are valid for six months and may be updated, replaced, or made obsolete at any time. Guidelines require that an expiration date appear on every page of an Internet-Draft. It is not appropriate to use Internet-Drafts as reference material or to cite them, other than as "working drafts" or "works in progress." Figure 3.11 details the process of draft creation and standardization.

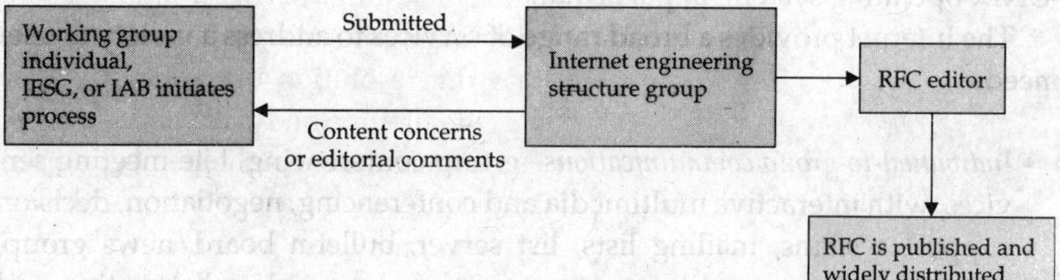


**Figure 3.11** Process of request for comments (RFC) publication

## 3.7 AN OVERVIEW OF INTERNET APPLICATIONS

To understand why the Internet is being commercialized, we need to understand what Internet applications people are interested in and are actively seeking. This section will provide an overview of the popular applications found on the Internet. These applications serve as the inspiration and harbinger to the vision of electronic commerce on the I-way.

If the wires and cables of the telecommunications and cable industry are the e-commerce network foundation, the Internet applications may very well provide the language, culture, and etiquette for e-commerce. The Internet, with origins completely outside the business world, is nonetheless important to commercial users because it represents in many ways the vision of the emerging global marketplace.

Two major types of information are likely to be found on the Internet: (1) public (or free) information (stock quotes, company annual reports, product and customer service information, government documents, works with expired copyrights, works in the public domain, and works that authors make available to the Internet community on an experimental basis); and (2) fee-based information, access to which is billed (financial information, and electronic newspapers such as the *San-Jose Mercury Times*). For understandable reasons, some types of information not likely to be found on the Internet, most notably, commercial works that are protected by copyright law. However this too may change as better security and information protection methods become available (See Chapter 15).

To navigate through the wealth of information resources, Internet users traditionally had to know cryptic operating system commands for UNIX, which is the dominant operating system on the Internet. Today, sophisticated user interfaces are being developed that shield the end user from much of the complexity that was associated with the Internet in general and with the UNIX operating system, in particular.

The Internet provides a broad range of services to address a variety of user needs:

- *Individual-to-group communications.* group conferencing, tele-meeting services, with interactive multimedia and conferencing, negotiation, decision support systems; mailing lists, list server, bulletin board/news group, directories/resource discovery services—for research collaboration and distance education (interactive tutorials) across institutional, state, and national boundaries

- *Information transfer and delivery services.* text-based e-mail, multimedia e-mail, e-mail/fax interface e-mail/EDI interface; news groups/bulletin boards/directories; digital (packet) audio and video communications

- *Information databases.* access to citation, full-text databases and "virtual" libraries containing both text and multimedia information. These databases are accessible using Internet tools like Gopher, World Wide Web (WWW), file transfer, remote log-in, resource discovery services, and news-gathering agents

- *Information processing services.* remote access to a variety of software programs including operations research (OR) tools, statistics, simulation, and visualization tools
- *Resource-sharing services.* access to printers, fax machines, and other processing services that enable the utilization of spare capacity on underutilized machines.

Within these categories the most commonly used services and tools are e-mail, bulletin boards, search and retrieval tools (Archie), and information publishing tools (Gopher and World Wide Web). These tools are described next.

*Electronic mail.* The bulk of the traffic that crosses the Internet and by far its most widely used service is interpersonal communication in the form of electronic mail. The ability to send messages in a few seconds to a computer anywhere in the world is a big reason for getting on and staying on the Internet. e-mail is handled by a variety of programs with names like *elm, pine,* and *Eudora* that allow users to send and receive messages (see Fig. 3.12). As it becomes easy and inexpensive to access the Internet, rather than setting up private systems, e-mail is being increasingly used for both internal and external corporate communication between enterprises and their customers, suppliers, and collaborators.

*E-mail to fax.* Other services (e-mail to fax and fax to e-mail) offer a variation of the e-mail theme, allowing users to send and receive a fax via e-mail. Some services are free. In general, it works in the following manner: The user sends an e-mail to a special address including the phone number of the recipient's fax machine. A computer looks at the phone number and decides

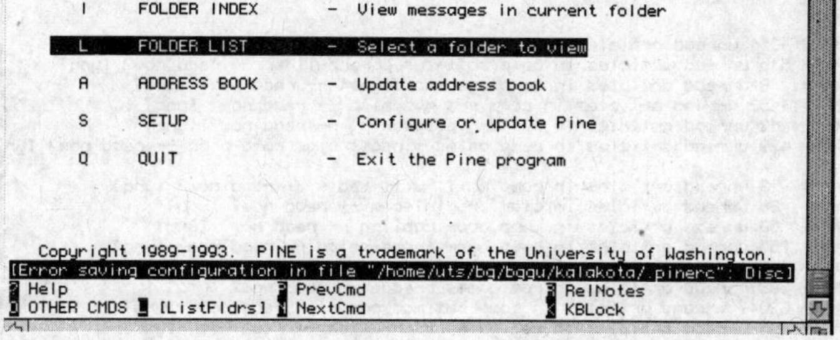


**Figure 3.12** Screen shot of an e-mail program, PINE, developed at the University of Washington

whether any of the participating fax machines cover the destination. If so, the message is routed to the appropriate location. Also, faxes can be sent to multiple fax machines—a fax mail-out—or faxes and traditional e-mail can be combined. After the deed is done, the sender receives an e-mail containing the outcome, namely, success or failure to deliver. Certain limitations still apply. You cannot send a fax just anywhere with this service, only to those companies, institutions, and individuals that have linked a computer and fax modem to the network. This innovative use of the Internet is an example of the digital convergence trend—in this case the two technologies being facsimile and electronic mail.

*Collaboration via bulletin boards.* Another major source of the Internet's allure is that anyone can post and retrieve information in *news groups,* which are essentially global bulletin boards. One important source of information is the USENET service, a massive collection of topic-specific forums in which participants can send and receive news, debate issues, ask questions, and provide answers. Thousands of news groups are filled with experts discussing various aspects of their fields. Several discussion groups focus on software, hardware, medicine, politics, manufacturing, education, pets, movies, sex, cooking, humor, and a host of other topics (see Fig. 3.13). In the figure, the comp. groups are computer groups, rec. groups are recreation-oriented groups, and alt. is usually reserved for groups that do not fit the traditional hierarchy.

*Information publishing and databases.* Most on-line database information on the Internet is free for the taking and the quantity is mind boggling. Highly

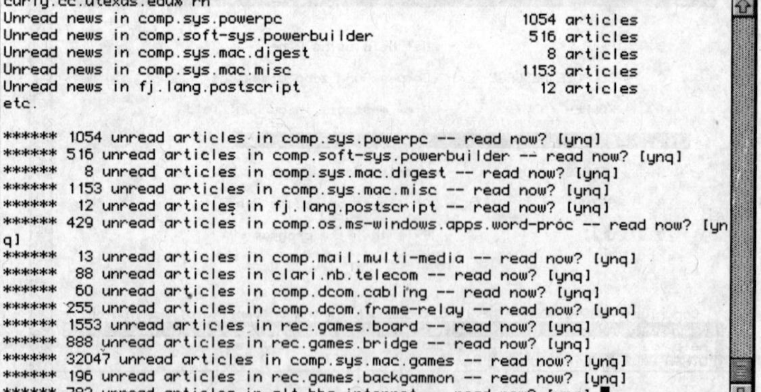

```
uts.cc.utexas.edu
curly.cc.utexas.edu% rn
Unread news in comp.sys.powerpc                      1054 articles
Unread news in comp.soft-sys.powerbuilder             516 articles
Unread news in comp.sys.mac.digest                      8 articles
Unread news in comp.sys.mac.misc                     1153 articles
Unread news in fj.lang.postscript                      12 articles
etc.

****** 1054 unread articles in comp.sys.powerpc -- read now? [ynq]
****** 516 unread articles in comp.soft-sys.powerbuilder -- read now? [ynq]
******   8 unread articles in comp.sys.mac.digest -- read now? [ynq]
****** 1153 unread articles in comp.sys.mac.misc -- read now? [ynq]
******  12 unread articles in fj.lang.postscript -- read now? [ynq]
****** 429 unread articles in comp.os.ms-windows.apps.word-proc -- read now? [yn
q]
******  13 unread articles in comp.mail.multi-media -- read now? [ynq]
******  88 unread articles in clari.nb.telecom -- read now? [ynq]
******  60 unread articles in comp.dcom.cabling -- read now? [ynq]
****** 255 unread articles in comp.dcom.frame-relay -- read now? [ynq]
****** 1553 unread articles in rec.games.board -- read now? [ynq]
****** 888 unread articles in rec.games.bridge -- read now? [ynq]
****** 32047 unread articles in comp.sys.mac.games -- read now? [ynq]
****** 196 unread articles in rec.games.backgammon -- read now? [ynq]
****** 782 unread articles in alt.bbs.internet -- read now? [ynq]
```

**Figure 3.13** Screenshot of a small subset of news groups accessible via command "rn"

prized information that is freely accessible includes Securities and Exchange Commission (SEC) databases containing valuable information on the health of companies, the NASDAQ stock exchange, the Federal Reserve and many other government agencies, esoteric information such as National Weather Service satellite photos, on-line searches of the largest library in the world—the Library of Congress catalog—and a host of other sources too numerous to list comprehensively. In addition to information, users can download software called freeware and shareware (for which a small amount is requested by the author). Although shareware applications are not very polished, they match the functionality of applications bought shrink-wrapped from the store at prices in the hundreds of dollars.

Several tools—Gopher/Veronica, FTP/Archie, WWW—exist for accessing information. The Gopher, developed at the University of Minnesota, is an information organization method for facilitating easy search and access of files through menulike interfaces (see Fig. 3.14). The Gopher program lists different host computers and the subject areas of information they contain. The user can select any one of these menu choices and will be transported to the submenus in that category. Gopher servers are available on many host machines around the world. Each version provides information about files on the machine it is on, as well as on other interconnected computers.

Another very popular tool for accessing information databases is anonymous FTP (file transfer protocol), which allows the user to connect and download files from one computer to another. Figure 3.15 shows a typical log-in session for doing anonymous FTP. The user name is always "anony-

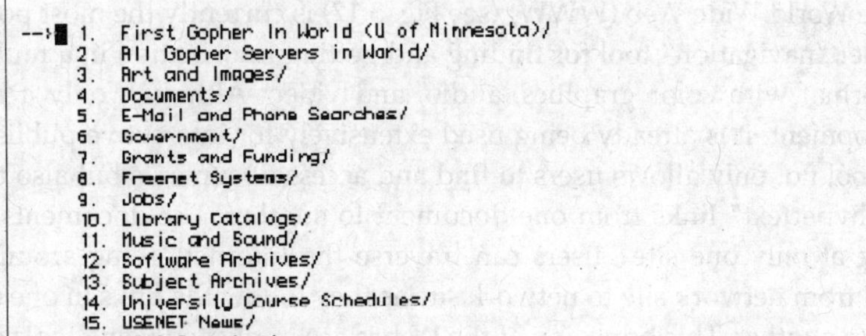


**Figure 3.14** A screen shot of a Gopher session

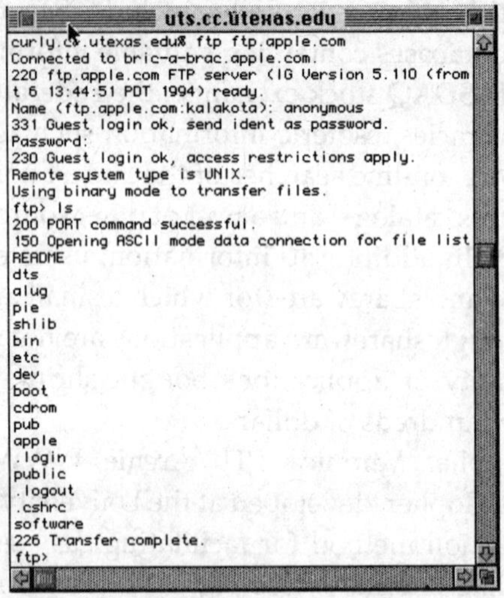


**Figure 3.15** Anonymous FTP session

mous" and the password is either "guest" or your personal log-in name and @. For example, "kalakota@." Any of the files listed with a "ls" command can be retrieved by using the command "get filename."

But to make effective use of anonymous FTP, we must first find the files we are looking for. The Internet tool used for this purpose is Archie, a service that finds the location of specific files at remote Internet sites. For example, the Archie command "archie Mosaic" can be used to see a listing of files throughout the Internet that contain the word "Mosaic." The screen shot in Fig. 3.16 indicates the result of a search for the string "Mosaic." It shows the sites that have that particular file. To avoid receiving a huge list, the user should use good word descriptors to narrow the scope of the search.

The World Wide Web (WWW) (see Fig. 3.17) is currently the most popular Internet "navigation" tool for finding and getting information in a multimedia format with color graphics, audio, and video. Although only a recent development, it is already being used extensively for interactive publishing. This tool not only allows users to find and access documents but also to follow "hypertext" links from one document to another. The documents need not be at only one site—users can traverse the Internet, going around the world from network site to network site as they follow the links in one document to another. This browsing of the Web is accomplished using tools called universal browsers, e.g., NetScape (ftp://ftp.mcom.com/), NCSA Mosaic (ftp://ftp.ncsa.uiuc.edu/) and others. These tools provide access to World Wide Web, Gopher, and FTP information servers via one common interface.

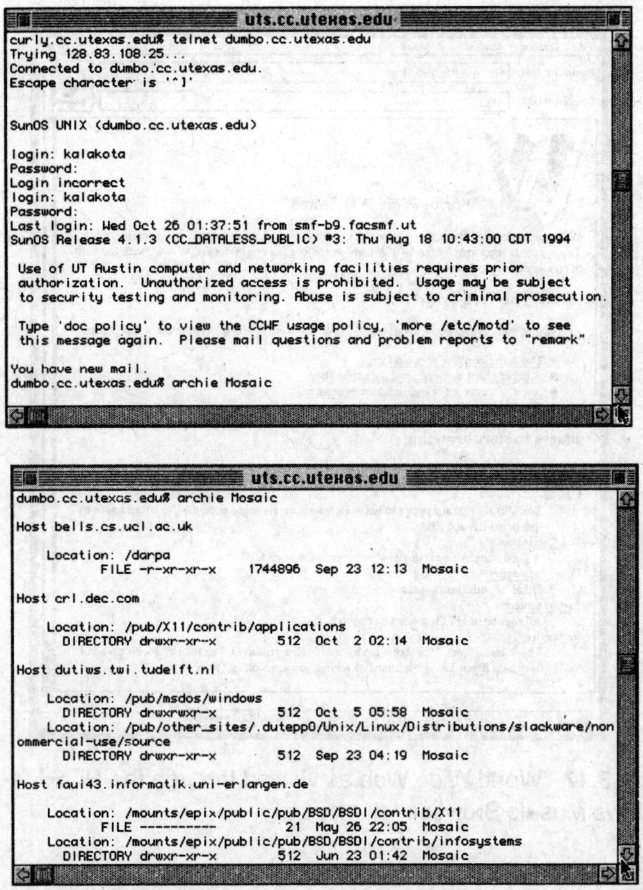


**Figure 3.16** Archie, anonymous FTP search tool

In addition to the information publishing services, the Internet is also used for a variety of business purposes such as buying and selling products and services on-line (see Fig. 3.18).

## 3.8 SUMMARY

During the course of this chapter, we discussed the architecture of the Internet. However, the Internet is more about the sharing and exchange of ideas in a free manner than about data transfer between machines. The Internet has transformed the way network infrastructures are conceptualized and created. In the past, network infrastructures were built around

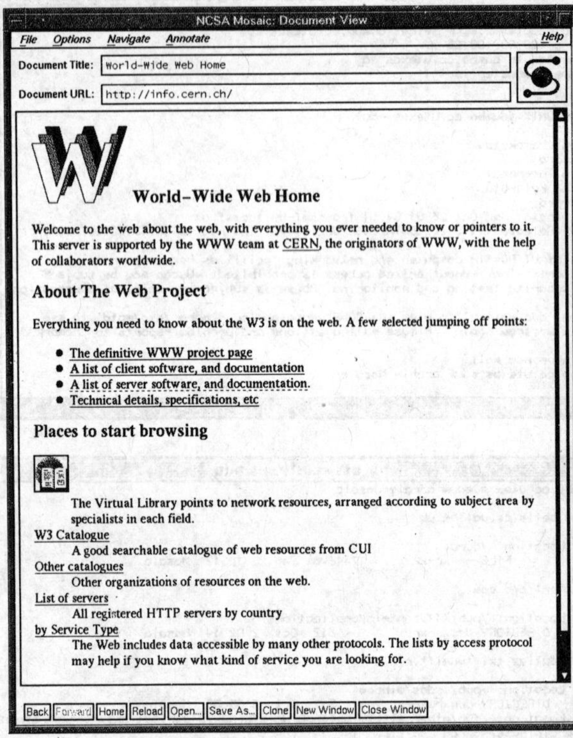


**Figure 3.17** World Wide Web as viewed through the NCSA X-Windows Mosaic Browser

highly structured architectures that were planned, created, and operated by government, telcos, and big corporations. The basic infrastructure flowed "top-down" from formal meetings and standards that purported to chart the future requirements for decades to come. They provided abstractions such as open systems interconnection (OSI) that were vague, under the aegis of concepts that were never quite defined or implemented. Enormous capital flowed into these projects in the hope that the network infrastructure would eventually settle into place.

Under pressure from rapid technological change, competition, and decreasing prices of hardware, the world of network infrastructure began a speedy transformation. New technological advancements such as VLSI, PCs, workstations, local area networks, robust protocols, routers, and user-friendly software found an enormous marketplace that motivated individual initiative to experiment with networking, the likes of which had never been seen before. At the same time, long-haul network technology offered increasingly cheap bandwidth that was absorbed by an expanding consumer market fueled by price competition among various vendors.

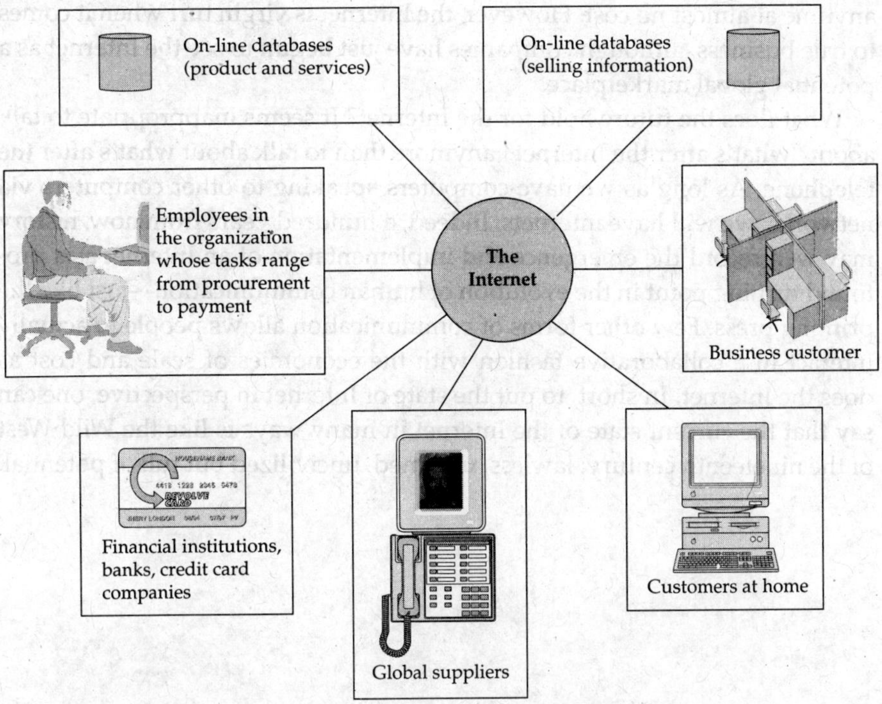


**Figure 3.18** The commercial uses of the Internet

Massive bottom-up infrastructure sprouted all over the world in bits and pieces, proliferated, and a new paradigm was created. As a result, enterprise networks, distributed network management, and unusual software applications were implemented in parallel worldwide. This is not to say that there was no top-down activity or that all bottom-up activity will produce meaningful infrastructure. Similarly, there is a lot more to network infrastructure than just the Internet. However, the Internet provides some invaluable models and lessons about key components of national and global information infrastructure. The most prominent of these lessons is that bottom-up infrastructure succeeds and sometimes even spectacularly.

Interestingly, the Internet incorporates several paradoxes. It is a network for the elite, yet it is very egalitarian. It has valuable information, yet there is no extra charge. There's no real government, yet there is no real anarchy. It is a creature of government bureaucrats, yet it is the soul of new enterprise and entrepreneurship. It has pornography and also the word of God (the Koran and the Bible). People have best friends there, but they've never met in person. In other words, the Internet has been flourishing because it represents an ideal where information is free to be disseminated to anyone, anywhere, and anytime at almost no cost. However, the Internet is virgin turf when it comes to true business, although companies have just begun to see the Internet as a potential global marketplace.

What does the future hold for the Internet? It seems inappropriate to talk about "what's after the Internet" anymore than to talk about what's after the telephone. As long as we have computers speaking to other computers via networks, we will have internets. Indeed, a hundred years from now, history may well record the emergence and implementation of an Internet as a profound turning point in the evolution of human communication—just like the printing press. Few other forms of communication allows people to actually interact in a collaborative fashion with the economies of scale and cost as does the Internet. In short, to put the state of Internet in perspective, one can say that the current state of the Internet in many ways is like the Wild West of the nineteenth century: lawless, untamed, uncivilized but full of potential.

Chapter 4

# The Business of Internet Commercialization

The U.S. government's 1991 decision to end subsidizing the NSFNET backbone beginning in 1995 sparked a massive restructuring aimed at shaping the Internet into a faster and more productive tool for the business. This ongoing evolution of the Internet has ramifications for the types of commercial activities it can offer. In the past, because of government sponsorship, the Internet followed a voluntary policy called Acceptable Usage Policy (AUP) that allowed only nonprofit, educational, and government use: no commercial activities (see Table 4.1). For example, AUP rules prohibited users from sending unsolicited e-mail messages urging people to buy their products.

These policies were relaxed in 1991 by the National Science Foundation, which footed the bill for the U.S. backbone and roughly 10 percent of the leased lines that connect sites to the backbone. The new policies allowed many commercial uses, including "announcements of new products or services for use in research or instruction, but not advertising of any kind." This easing of restrictions opened the floodgates for commercial Internet access. Today, many Internet sites allow commercial messages across their own regional networks, which are considered non-NSF lines. As a result, the Internet is seeing enormous growth in the number of people and businesses using its services. To serve these new customers, an entirely new industry called Internet service providers (ISP) has emerged.

Commercialization of the Internet was first discussed at a workshop held in March 1990 at the John F. Kennedy School of Government at Harvard University. This workshop discussed the various economic and technical issues pertaining to the commercialization of the Internet. It was at this workshop that Stephen Wolff, then director of the NSF Division of Networking and Communications Research and Infrastructure, distinguished between "commercialization" and "privatization." He defined commercialization as permitting commercial users and providers access to and use of Internet facilities and services, and privatization as the elimination of

**Table 4.1** NSF's Acceptable Usage Policy for the Internet [AUP92]

*Specifically Acceptable Uses:*

- Communication with foreign researchers and educators in connection with research or instruction, as long as any network that the foreign user employs for such communication provides reciprocal access to U.S. researchers and educators
- Communication and exchange for professional development, to maintain currency, or to debate issues in a field or subfield of knowledge
- Use for disciplinary-society, university-association, government-advisory, or standards activities related to the user's research and instructional activities
- Use in applying for or administering grants or contracts for research or instruction, but not for other fund-raising or public relations activities
- Any other administrative communications or activities in direct support of research and instruction
- Announcements of new products or services for use in research or instruction, but not advertising of any kind
- Any traffic originating from a network of another member agency of the Federal Networking Council if the traffic meets the acceptable use policy of that agency
- Communication incidental to otherwise acceptable use, except for illegal or specifically unacceptable use

*Unacceptable Uses:* Use for for-profit activities, unless covered by the General Principle or as a specifically acceptable use and/or extensive use for private or personal business.

This statement applies to use of the NSFNET backbone only. NSF expects that connecting networks will formulate their own use policies.

---

the federal role in providing or subsidizing network services. In principle, privatization was to be achieved by shifting the federal subsidy from network providers to users, thus spurring private sector investment in network infrastructure. The participants of this workshop felt that the creation of a market for private vendors would in turn defuse concerns among the R&D community about acceptable use and commercialization of the NSFNET backbone [RFC1192].

Few workshop participants anticipated the fantastic growth of commercial users and providers. In 1993 alone, with the increasing media publicity, commercial membership on the Internet skyrocketed more than 300 percent, from 485 to 1590 member companies and organizations. Also, in a span of one year, the Internet service provider world has changed dramatically. The Internet Network Information Center's (InterNIC) compilation of public access dial-up providers listed 80 vendors in December 1993. One year later, the list cited more than 1500 providers. Today, most major cities in the world have accessible service. In short, the commercialization of the Internet promises to produce profound transformation of business and economic forces in the global marketplace. Broadly speaking, commercialization of the Internet has taken place in two spheres: commercialization of users and commercialization of Internet service providers (ISPs). These spheres are explained in the following sections.

### Commercialization of Internet Users

Commercial usage of the Internet for companies is nothing new—how they are using it is new. Although corporations have been on the Internet for several years, their participation has been limited to their R&D or engineering departments engaged in research and educational uses. This was in line with the NSF-instituted Acceptable Use Policy (see Table 4.1) that states that "for-profit" and "extensive use for private or personal business" are unacceptable uses of the Internet. However, the AUP permits the use of the Internet by for-profit organizations where this use is "covered by the General Principles or as a specifically acceptable use." This opens the door wide enough to allow the engineering departments of many companies to use the Internet, especially those in computer and communications companies.

For-profit business communications corporations used other networks (usually a private network operated by a value-added network provider). These corporations used interconnected mainframes (e.g., IBM 3081), which handled their commercial data processing and did networking using a protocol suite called system network architecture (SNA). For a long time, corporate executives felt that the Internet was only an academic toy for bored graduate students. They are rapidly changing their minds as they discover the obvious: Running multiple networks is expensive. Some are also beginning to look to the Internet for "one-stop" shopping to satisfy connectivity needs, e-mail, news, and other information services.

At first, companies that accessed the Internet through the existing non-profit mid-level networks were offered a lower level of membership than the academic members. As restrictions are dismantled, commercial use of the Internet is becoming more common. This is especially good for small businesses. For instance, IBM or Exxon can afford to run international and nationwide private networks connecting their sites, but a start-up company

(CornerStore Mom & Pop) couldn't. If CornerStore has a New York office and a Miami office, all it needs is an Internet connection on each end. For all practical purposes, it has a nationwide corporate network, just like the big firms.

Besides enjoying the intra- and interorganizational connectivity advantages offered by the Internet, companies want to do business on the Internet in ways the likes of which have never been seen before. But this revolutionary change will not be painless. The culture of the Internet is still academically oriented, with sometimes "an antibusiness flavor" that frowns upon blatant promotion. Most of the early Internet users, not recognizing that this was an artificial environment created by military and government subsidies, believed in free goods to everybody. Some of the Internet oldtimers lament the inevitable change that commercialization will wreak on the unique subculture. The general feeling among this community is that if Internet access is no longer free, the Internet will lose its communal spirit. Only time will rule on this issue.

### Commercialization of Internet Service Providers

Commercial Internet service providers (ISPs) exist to provide for-pay access to the various Internet applications and resources for both companies and individuals. There are four general categories of ISP: telco/cable/on-line companies, national independents, regionals, and local ISPs:

- *Telco/cable/on-line companies.* These are long-distance telephone companies (AT&T, MCI, and Sprint), RBOCs (Ameritech, Pacific Bell), Cable TV (Time Warner, TCI), and on-line service operators (CompuServe, America Online, Prodigy). Their common factor is company size, with balance sheets of billions of dollars. They are rapidly entering the Internet service provider marketplace. Sprint was first to enter in 1991, with ATT in 1993, MCI and Ameritech in 1994, CompuServe and Prodigy in early 1995, and others announcing monthly.
- *National independents.* These are commercial, for-profit entities offering connectivity services nationwide or internationally in some cases, which are positioned to compete in the evolving commercial marketplace. PSI and UUNET are among the firms presently competing in this market.
- *Regionals.* In the past, these were nonprofit university-affiliated enterprises that offered services within one state or within regional interstate areas. With the elimination of NSF subsidies, however, these enterprises are aggressively entering the commercial marketplace. SURAnet, NEARnet, NYSERnet, and BARRnet are examples.

- *Local Service Providers.* Commonly called "mom and pop shops," these are small businesses that support 10–1000 customers. They usually operate in one physical location and offer services to business and individual consumers within a single metropolitan area.

## 4.1 TELCO/CABLE/ON-LINE COMPANIES

Established telcommunications, cable companies, and commercial on-line services are attempting to take advantage of their existing networks and brand name to become the Internet service providers offering residential and business customers dial-up access to the Internet.

These companies have not been aggressive entrants in the past, for the following reasons:

- The Internet service provider market is relatively small, totaling only $150 million in 1994 and estimated at $450 million in 1995.
- The technology changes very often, perhaps as often as once a year. Since large firms chose to open hundreds (or thousands) of sites, they cannot move as quickly in the upgrade cycle as can the more firms.
- The efficiencies of the Internet technology, such as video and audio, might put price and performance pressure on existing telephone company services that could produce a net decrease in revenues.

The big companies view the growth of the Internet as more of an opportunity than a threat, however. Telecom firms, on-line services, and other big companies already offer an easy-to-use on-ramp with their existing infrastructure, but to be competitive, they have to improve their service options.

### Telephone Companies

More and more telco/cable companies are emerging from behind the curtain and showing their face to a growing base of Internet users. Although they are at dramatically different stages of deployment, they are expected to be very competitive.

All the large U.S. telcos are participants in the Internet infrastructure. Sprint, Pacific Bell, Ameritech, and Bellcore are building some of the key new components, network access points (NAPs), for the new NSFNET architecture in the United States. Metropolitan Fiber Systems, a competitive access provider in major metropolitan areas, is building another of these

NAPs in the Washington D.C. area under a cooperative agreement with the NSF. AT&T also became a participant when it successfully competed for a cooperative agreement to provide database directory services to the NSFNET community. MCI has contributed by providing reduced rates for the NSFNET backbone circuits and investing in developing the new switching technology that is used today. In addition, MCI will build the vBNS (the very high speed 155-Mbps network for high bandwidth applications) under a cooperative agreement with the NSF. MCI has also entered the commercial Internet business through its InternetMCI services. Sprint, an early entrant into the commercial Internet, has a rapidly growing Internet services business.

We will examine the services provided by one of the major players: MCI. The company is involved at three levels: Internet Backbone Services, Internet Backbone Access Provider, Internet Service Provider for individuals and companies. MCI has been involved with the Internet since 1987, when it was awarded the contract to upgrade the backbone's data transfer speed from 9.6 Kbps. to 56 Kbps. Today, MCI is a major player because it is currently completing the implementation activities for the vBNS under a cooperative agreement with the NSF.

MCI offers a service called Internet Backbone Access Provider that provides connectivity to the network access points. MCI has also been selected by seven of the eight regional Internet providers (SURAnet, CICnet, NEARnet, BARRnet, NorthwestNet, MIDnet, and Sesquinet) carrying more than 40 percent of all the Internet traffic. Several international Internet networks have also established connections to MCI's network, including the Canadian CA*net and the Japanese WIDE network.

MCI provides an InternetMCI service that lets it deal directly with individuals and businesses. A company need not operate its own computer to establish a presence on the Internet and can instead lease space on an MCI server. With an expensive ad campaign, MCI is educating the general public about the various aspects of the Internet. These ads show businesses using a variety of the Internet applications such as consulting bulletin boards or launching on-line merchandising projects with the potential to reach literally millions of people worldwide.

## Large Commercial On-Line Services

Many of the larger commercial on-line services have also begun offering Internet-based dial-up services. In early 1995, CompuServe, Prodigy, and America Online began providing direct Internet Protocol (IP) dial-up accounts. These large companies have obvious advantages in the service provider business because of their well-known brand names. Other consumer choices include Microsoft Network, AT&T Interchange, Delphi, and Apple Computer's eWorld.

### CompuServe

CompuServe, a subsidiary of H&R Block since 1980, offers Internet access along with a host of other services. From its origins in 1969 as a computer time-sharing firm, CompuServe has become a leading provider of computer-based information and communications services. As of 1994, CompuServe's telecommunications network extended to 369 metropolitan local-access points in the United States and, through the use of supplementary networks, provides total coverage in approximately 97 foreign countries.

CompuServe operates through four divisions: Information Services, Network Services, Support Services, and Software Products. CompuServe Information Services (CIS) is the leading provider of on-line services for PC owners. It offers comprehensive information services (shopping services, stock market brokerage services, airline reservation services) that enable users to play computer games, conduct research, send and receive messages, and exchange helpful tips about computer use through special interest bulletin boards called "forums." It has also developed a wide range of business services that enable companies to link their employees with information needed to conduct commerce. Service offerings include e-mail, internal corporate information systems for diverse applications, and a variety of business-related databases.

CompuServe's Network Services Division provides corporations with a packet data network that offers customers a fast data communications system. A primary focus of CompuServe was the continued development of its frame relay service FRAME-Net, a high-speed network used for information transfer between LANs. One of the many applications and an area of continued success for this division is providing the network component for point-of-sale (POS) transaction authorization of credit card purchases. Using the network, a merchant can pass a customer's credit card through a computer terminal and determine instantly whether the card is valid.

CompuServe's Support Services Division provides knowledge through forums, which are similar to moderated news groups on the Internet. For instance, a user seeking advice on how to fix a software product will probably talk to the tech support people on the CIS forum. If they can't answer the question, someone else probably can. Many CIS forum hosts make a living that way: CIS gives them up to 10 percent of the connect charges accumulated by people who spend time in their forums. This approach differs from other services and reflects CompuServe's desire to steer clear of responsibility for the on-line activity.

CIS has slowly been moving away from its hobbyist/game playing roots toward a professional audience. Low-key and conservative, CIS got where it is by emphasizing execution over flash and by investing in technological advances that have made its system more efficient and profitable. For example, CIS developed GIF (the graphics interchange format) and CompuServe B, a file-transfer protocol, two widely supported applications by communications software vendors and other service providers. Both are more efficient ways for subscribers to download and upload more and larger files, thus increasing network usage. In 1982, a few subscribers who were fed up with having to read and post messages while they were spending money on-line wrote off-line readers such as TAPCIS (for DOS) and Navigator (for Macs). This was the beginning of the browser market.

### Prodigy

Prodigy, a joint venture between Sears and IBM (CBS dropped out before the service, then called Trintex, was actually launched), has suffered plenty of losses since it was launched in 1990. It started out with all the wrong assumptions about users and their habits and has paid the price in subscriber unrest. Estimates are that 10 million people actually tried the service but few have been loyal. Having lost $70 million in 1992, Prodigy is at a pivotal moment in its history as its parent companies are in a downsizing crunch and lack the cash to spend unwisely.

Prodigy is the only service that reserves a part of almost every screen for advertising. Vendors find it works: Being on the opening screen can bring in 50 percent more business than advertising deeper in the service. Until recently, all Prodigy services except e-mail were untimed. Hypothetically, you could keep Prodigy running all day at no extra cost; of course, the service would log you out. However, Prodigy has instituted hourly charges (after two cumulative free hours) for bulletin boards, Eaasy Sabre, Dow Jones News Retrieval, and stock quotes.

Prodigy's interface offers flashy features, such as attractive marquees framing screens with diverse but low-resolution graphics and a market snapshot that appears automatically when a user logs in, including selected stocks from her portfolio. Prodigy has attracted popular family services, such as Sesame Street, Nova, National Geographic, and the Weekly Reader (yes, the same one kids read in school). Prodigy has special pricing plans for support groups, such as those that link doctors with families and social workers, or those based on dependencies. Prodigy has just begun using members as forum co-hosts; they get preferred rates but no pay, unlike CompuServe.

To be competitive, Prodigy is working to achieve feature parity with other on-line services in the near term. Prodigy has no chat feature, partly because its network is centralized and partly because of its policy of censoring content: Every message goes through a software filter; borderline postings are reviewed by staff, who return offensive ones to their originators. Prodigy is gradually removing the human censors and will rely on a software filter that bounces messages back until they are appropriately sanitized, with no check on the writer's intent. It allows a preview feature that lets users see the first lines of a series of postings, off-line reading functions, an Exclude Member feature to silence the bothersome, plus (most notably) useful new formats for its forums. Most forums or conferences consist of lists of topics, nothing more. Prodigy will actually show links between related features on the screen, making it far easier to jump from, say, car classifieds to the automotive enthusiasts' group to the "showroom" or car-loan department.

### America Online

America Online, headquartered in Vienna, Virginia, is a leading independent and the fastest growing provider of on-line services to U.S. consumers. Originally called Quantum Communication Services, America Online started its official life in 1988 on Apple II computers as the Personal Edition of AppleLink (Apple's on-line system for developers and staff, since expanded to include customers). In 1989, AOL relaunched the service independently as America Online (AOL) and introduced front-end software for Macs. By 1991, PC users could log in with GeoWorks front end; in 1993 it delivered a Windows front end. All of them are simple to install; all are given away to promote trial.

Of the major on-line services, AOL is the only pure player; the other large players are part of larger companies in other industries. It is also one of the few left that has not created a two-tier price structure, separating services such as e-mail or airline reservations from others. This would go against AOL's populist ethic, anyway: It wants to focus on individuals, providing them an easy, appealing service with a variety of interesting activities and resources, all without hidden charges. It offers subscribers a wide variety of services, including e-mail, conferencing, news, sports, weather, stock quotes, software, computing support, and on-line classes. It focuses on the interactive nature of its offerings by providing services that encourage users to share information and ideas of common interest. A strategic alliance with Sprint allows AOL to keep its communications costs low for its subscribers and to remove premium pricing for daytime use. Although AOL still offers alternative access via Tymnet owned by British Telecom/MCI, the SprintNet access will cost less. Today, SprintNet carries the vast majority of AOL traffic.

Recently, AOL has announced a number of Internet-related acquisitions—BookLink Technologies (developer of InternetWorks a Windows-based browser) and NaviSoft (developer of software tools for content/publishing)—that are expected to accelerate efforts to leverage its brand name and experience into growth opportunities related to the Internet. These two companies will form the core of AOL's Internet Services Company, which will be responsible for Internet strategy. AOL also acquired Advance Network & Services (ANS) for $35 million and expanded its agreement with Sprint. ANS's backbone network (ANSnet) is one of the fastest public data networks in the United States and includes 12,000 miles of leased T-3 (45-Mbps) fiber optic circuits. The network has 15 PoPs (points-of-presence) at MCI facilities nationally. Importantly, AOL plans to add more high-speed access at 14.4 Kbps. This move should help eliminate some of the log-on difficulties experienced by AOL users due to the capacity constraints.

It remains to be seen how AOL and others will fare once the Microsoft Network becomes fully operational. Microsoft bundled a basic on-line service (code-named Marvel) with Windows 95. It is believed that, initially, Marvel would be used primarily as an on-line help system for Microsoft's customers and as a gateway for e-mail and for downloading of software (such as demos, upgrades, and patches). This plan was later shelved and Microsoft came out with a full-blown on-line service. The variables that Microsoft can capitalize on include its current base of 70 million Windows users; its bundling/distribution capability; a multitude of software development tools and products; nearly $4 billion in corporate cash; and past, pending, and future mergers. All of these assets ensure that other on-line services must run fast and hard. We, as others, believe that Microsoft will be a big factor in shaping the on-line market.

## 4.2 NATIONAL INDEPENDENT ISPs

The telco/cable/on-line combo faces a strong challenge from well-entrenched existing Internet service providers called national independents who pioneered the commercial Internet marketplace. These are the dominant players in the Internet access hierarchy and provide other smaller service providers with backbone connectivity. To provide an analogy, think of the national independents as the Interexchange Carriers (IXCs) of the telephone business that connect the local providers. In this sense, the national independents are commercial entities that specialize in dealing with wide-area networks. However, this category competes with the telco/cable providers for the same pool of customers. The importance of this category was brought to the fore when Microsoft bought a 20-percent stake in UUNET technologies as a service provider for its Microsoft Network.

The major U.S. service providers include Performance Systems International (PSI), Advanced Networks and Services (ANS) (which has been bought by America Online), and UUNET Technologies. Non-U.S. providers include EUNET (Europe), SWIPnet (Sweden), Datalink (Finland), and PIPEX (U.K.). Much like the value-added networks of the past such as TELENET (now called SprintNet) and Tymnet (now MCI Tymnet), these early pioneers recognized a business need not addressed by existing suppliers of networking services, namely, the telephone companies. Utilizing facilities and routers located outside of the telecom carriers, they built large public data networks (PDNs) based on TCP/IP much like TELENET and Tymnet did with X.25 switches. In a short five-year period, this technical model has became a huge success.

None of these networks have restrictions on their use. One goal of the ISP vendors is to provide all customers of their collective markets the ability to communicate with each other without restrictions imposed by the Acceptable Usage Policy. Consequently, a common point of interconnection has been deployed: the Commercial Internet Exchange (CIX). Like a border checkpoint, CIX serves as an entry point for traffic into the Internet. As alluded to earlier, there are hundreds of other networks whose use is "restricted" to a particular purpose (research, education, a specific mission). In general, national ISP customers may access resources on these restricted networks as long as the specific instance of usage conforms to the network's acceptable use policy.

Figure 4.1 shows the structure of the national independents. National ISPs offer very high speed connections to the Internet, up to 45 Mbps. Firms planning to capitalize on the Internet will find national ISPs providing connections (also called points of presence) in major centers that provide a direct linkage to backbone networks. These PoPs are usually equipped with routers for dedicated connections and modems for dial-up connections. In other words, national ISPs extend high-speed connections to users just about anywhere, bypassing the existing telco infrastructure. Users simply connect to a national provider's nearest switching facility. The national ISP then transports the Internet traffic across its own network to a router with a connection into the rest of the Internet.

At the regional and local levels are tens of thousands of organizations of every conceivable kind that have built their own private internetworks that are connected to the national backbones via an ISP. Most of these small networks are operated by organizations that provide Internet access to their internal staff or specialize in providing widespread public access to end users. But along with high-bandwidth connections comes the need for cus-

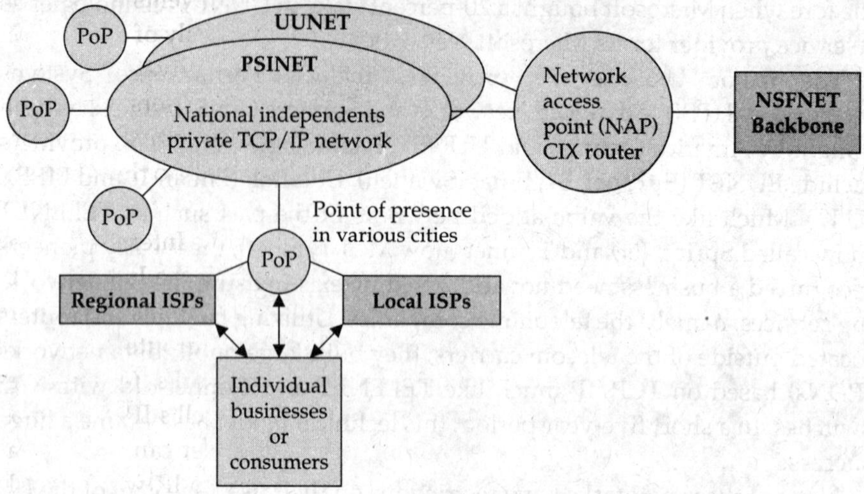


**Figure 4.1** Architecture of national level Internet service providers

tomer premises equipment (CPE) that is complicated to configure and manage. This is where systems integration and consultancy services could become a key criterion in the service provider selection process. National ISPs often provide advice needed to make the Internet connections easy, but that advice comes with a fee attached.

National ISPs offer several advantages that may lead a firm to connect all of its corporate sites to a national ISP instead of maintaining the connection internally. The ISP is usually a wide area network configured in a star topology. This structure requires only one leased line from each corporate location to the nearest ISP hub, rather than leased dedicated phone connections from each site to every other site. Also, by getting an ISP to manage a geographically dispersed wide area network, significant cost savings can accrue from staff reductions and the elimination of the need to purchase expensive network management hardware and software. By off-loading the network management responsibility to the ISP's skilled personnel, companies can reduce overhead and increase the reliability of the network.

The ISPs also offer value-added services beyond Internet connectivity. PSI, for instance, offers Clarinet, a service that provides professional news and information, including news wire services. UUNET offers USENET archive services (ftp://ftp.uu.net/) with publicly available UNIX software and information. Many are offering video conferencing services.

To deal with corporate concerns for security, ISPs have come up with a variety of solutions. PSI, for instance, uses its frame relay service to define fixed private connections across its own network and prevents access from the public Internet. ANS offers the InterLock service, a family of application-level security services that establishes a barrier between a private IP network and the public Internet. It works both ways: Unauthorized users cannot gain access from the Internet to proprietary data residing on the private network, and unauthorized communication from the private network to the Internet is filtered out.

ISPs also offer gateways that load non-IP traffic into the Internet Protocol (IP) packets for transmission across the Internet, allowing the Internet to be used as a transparent connection between non-TCP/IP systems. This opens many possibilities for users. For instance, companies can route traffic destined for the Internet across internal backbone networks (e.g., Novell NetWare) using an existing backbone protocol (e.g., Novell's IPX) to a host computer that has a direct connection into an ISP. The user can then use an internal or ISP-provided gateway to convert that traffic to IP, which would then be routed across the Internet. Some ISPs enable users to send and receive Open Systems Interconnection (OSI) traffic over the Internet. For instance, ANS offers gateways that encapsulate Novell's IPX and IBM's Systems Network Architecture (SNA) traffic into TCP/IP packets for routing over the Internet.

Some acceptable usage policy issues must be considered if extensive commercial activity is involved. For example, a firm connected to a PSINet might desire to work with one of the many Korean companies and universities connected to the Korean academic network (KRnet) or with a German company/university connected to DFNnet. Given that KRnet and DFNnet have acceptable use policies restricting their usage to research and education, it would be inappropriate for the firm to exchange invoices or purchase orders with the foreign firm via KRnet or DFNnet, but it is allowable to exchange messages and files that address research or education. Acceptable use policies of non-ISPs are published and are usually easily available in the network information service centers of the target network. No such precautions are necessary when the path consists solely of ISPs. For example, if a firm connected to PSINet or SprintLink desires to exchange invoices with a firm connected to UUNET or DataLink in Finland, because these ISPs connect to the CIX, there are no restrictions on what they can exchange.

And finally, moving traffic from a corporate private network to an Internet access point and vice versa can be quite complex. Users must have the technical knowledge to manage the bandwidth requirements of the Internet traffic to avoid adversely affecting corporate backbone traffic. Users also need to be prepared to upgrade their backbones as more and more people access the Internet facilities. In short, to reduce the headaches of dealing with constantly changing technology, more and more corporations are looking toward ISPs to offload their network management. Table 4.2 provides a summary of the services offered by national level ISPs.

To better understand the national ISPs, let us examine two major players—UUNET/AlterNet and PSI—in more depth. Both are for-profit organizations that offer TCP/IP network services and access to the Internet.

## UUNET/AlterNet

UUNET, founded in May 1987, was the first company to provide business professionals access to the Internet. In addition, UUNET sells computer-related books and makes available to the world an extensive collection of freely distributable UNIX source archives and software (ftp://ftp.uu.net/).

With respect to the Internet, the company's initial goal was to revitalize the overburdened UUCP electronic mail and USENET news networks. UUNET introduced a full-time communications service for its customers to connect to the Internet to send and receive electronic mail and news. Shortly afterward, in January 1990, UUNET launched AlterNet, one of the first commercial networks to use TCP/IP protocol.

AlterNet customers use dial-up or high-speed leased lines for direct access to the full range of services available over the Internet. AlterNet operates its own network and maintains direct connections to most other component net-

**Table 4.2** Large ISP Service Summary

| | |
|---|---|
| Hourly fees | Cap is generally 20 hours; only a few charge for every hour used. |
| Bandwidth to rest of the Internet | Often run their own national or international backbone with a direct feed into network access points, such as Metropolitan Area Ethernet-East in Washington and CIX-West in San Jose, Calif., with a T-3 (45 Mbps) connection. |
| Local dial-up numbers | Offer numbers for many cities. |
| Preconfigured software | Most offer some kind of package or special interface for click-and-log-in first-time entry. |
| High-speed access | 9600 bps is top rate in many cities, especially those using public X.25 networks; 14.4 Kbps is being deployed by all of them; 28.8 Kbps is the next step. |

works of the Internet. In contrast to publicly funded networks such as the NSFNET, AlterNet places no restrictions on its customers' traffic. This permits AlterNet customers to communicate with virtually any other individual or organization that is connected to the global Internet, for whatever purpose they wish. AlterNet offers a multitude of Internet connectivity options: UUCP and dial-up SLIP/PPP, dedicated SLIP/PPP, and dedicated 56K, T-1, and 10-Mbps service. AlterNet service also sells a full range of equipment used for the Internet connections: modems, routers, and terminal servers.

UUNET operates a national 45-Mbps ATM network and maintains PoPs in more than fifty U.S. cities. In addition, users can reach AlterNet through Sprint or Wiltel PoPs located in over 450 cities. For dial-up connections, UUNET offers toll-free 800 number service and access through CompuServe. All PoPs connect to the network at a minimum speed of T-1 (1.544 Mbps). All major PoPs have redundant T-1 and/or 10-Mbps access to the network.

UUNET is the founding member of the CIX, an interconnection point for most major regional, national, and foreign Internet service providers. It is also the founding member of MAE-East—an interconnection point for service providers in the Washington, D.C. area and in Europe.

More recently, UUNET has become prominent due to the Microsoft Network. To provide network access to its new on-line network called Microsoft Network (MSN), Microsoft has purchased an interest in UUNET and struck an accord with UUNET to expand the company's existing network PoPs so that dial-up access is easier for Microsoft's customers. This network will augment the UUNET's core 45-Mbps backbone.

### Performance Systems International (PSI)

PSI was formed in 1989 as a spin-off from the NYSERnet, a non-profit academic network based in Syracuse, New York. NYSERnet continues to use PSI as its network service supplier. Beginning with just 40 customers on this new network, PSINet had grown to nearly 5000 customers by the end of 1993, more than any other the Internet service provider in the world. PSI's network has grown to the point that it now has PoPs in over 100 U.S. metropolitan areas and Japan.

PSI's commercialization of the Internet began in 1990 with leased-line service for corporations on a coast-to-coast basis, defying the model imposed by regional Internet service providers. PSI introduced Internet access for individuals with a preliminary PSILinkSM service in the fall of 1990, offering simple electronic mail service to PC users.

PSI's services range from a series of low-cost dial-up network access options using normal telephone lines and modems, to ISDN access at 64

Kbps, to a set of high-performance customer access services using dedicated (leased) high-speed circuits from 56 Kbps to 4 Mbps. All are connected to a national router-based network deployed in 1990, which was upgraded to ATM (asynchronous transfer mode) switches with T-3 (45-Mbps) circuits in its backbone internetwork.

PSI has been aggressively expanding and looking for new avenues of growth. For instance, the company is attempting to bring Internet access to a mass consumer audience through an agreement with Continental Cablevision. Under the agreement, Continental provides several channels of cable TV bandwidth dedicated to PSI's customers in several regions of the United States. For each metropolitan area's cable head-end (distribution site), ten separate 4-Mbps cable segments (channels) are distributed to different customer locations.

Each channel is shared by ten to twenty organizations, providing up to 4-Mbps peak performance between subscribers. Each subscriber (organization or home) then uses the amount of performance needed, anywhere from 128 Kbps to 1.5 Mbps, to connect to the Internet. Through such partnerships, the term "telecommuter" may soon be superseded by a new concept: the "cableTV commuter." The bandwidth provided by cable will allow customer connections to the Internet at speeds greater than those provided by telephone company facilities. This greater bandwidth will encourage the use of capacity-hogging services such as continuous audio and video.

## 4.3 REGIONAL-LEVEL ISPs

In contrast to national ISPs, regional ISP coverage is usually limited to a handful of contiguous states, but many of them can match national ISP service levels. For the most part, however, regional ISPs do not have the existing infrastructure of the national providers and therefore can't offer connections everywhere in the country. Instead, regional ISPs have the Internet access points that are concentrated in their coverage area. Examples of regional ISP include CERFnet, Netcom, and Global Enterprise Services.

The service providers that operated CERFnet, JvNCNet, and other regional backbone networks lost their status as regional monopolies operating under a grant from the U.S. government, to enter a more competitive open market where several service providers were allowed to operate concurrently. Today, all regional providers carry commercial traffic. In fact, some of the first commercial ISPs were spin-offs from organizations funded by the NSF. PSI, for example, emerged from the New York Educational and Research Network (NYSERnet). ANS resulted from the Merit Network, IBM, and MCI partnership that now manages the NSFNET operations. JvNCNet spun off from

Princeton University Network. Regional providers supply inter-networking without the restriction of the NSF acceptable use.

JvNCNet, is a representative example of a regional Internet service provider in the Northeast. It became a commercial entity called Global Enterprise Services (GES) with the intention of providing commercial unrestricted access to the Internet. GES offers a dedicated line leasing option to meet any level of the Internet usage, and thus provides easy service expansion as members use dictates.

GES even provides the hardware and telephone line necessary to connect to the nearest JvNCNet Access Point with unlimited usage. Members may connect to JvNCNet at any of the following bandwidths: 3 T-1 (4.5 Mbps), 2 T-1 (3 Mbps), T-1 (1.544 Mbps), 512 Kbps, 256 Kbps, 128 Kbps, 56 Kbps, and 19.2 Kbps. GES also offers Dialin'Gateway, a "dial-on-demand" gateway service. Unlike the individual dial-up connections, Dialin'Gateway allows multiple hosts at a site to access the network through the same connection. A flat monthly fee and unlimited usage and a lower monthly fee with usage charges are both available, facilitating cost-effective network access.

GES also offers host connection services. The host services are an ideal way for any organization or individual to take advantage of the many resources available on the Internet at a low cost. Members may choose to dial into local numbers or use an 800 number, making these ideal services for the traveler. Members must provide their own modem. The Host Connection Services offer two pricing options—a fixed monthly fee and unlimited usage—or usage based pricing. Members choose the option that best fits their Internet usage needs. Table 4.3 summarizes the service features of regional ISPs.

**Table 4.3** Regional ISP Service Summary

| | |
|---|---|
| Hourly fees | If metered, fees usually begin after first 30 hours. |
| Bandwidth to rest of the Internet | Usually a T-1 (1.544 Mbps); sometimes as little as 56 Kbps, other times as great as multiple T-1 lines. |
| Local dial-up numbers | Regional providers offer some way to access without a long-distance call when you are out of the area; those that do not currently offer out-of-area dialing plans. |
| Preconfigured software | Only a few offer a tailored package; others may offer or point users to commercial packages that include easy access to their services. |
| High-speed access | All offer 14.4 Kbps; many offer banks of 28.8 Kbps; several now offer single-channel ISDN. |

## 4.4 LOCAL-LEVEL ISPs

In contrast to national and regional ISPs, local ISP providers offer low-speed service to users in confined areas, usually within a city or metropolitan area, by subleasing circuits from regional or national ISPs and adding their own application services and support. In the early phase, local ISPs represent the corner stores in the ISP business and are often run by technical experts in their homes or basements.

The big difference between regional and local providers is found in customer service and support: Few local ISPs offer 24-hour technical support; many of the regional and national providers have around-the-clock, seven-days-per-week network operations centers. Almost all regional providers have people on call twenty-four-hours a day, seven-days-per-week for network outages and related emergencies.

In the past, local ISPs, saddled with an unsavory reputation for being fly-by-night operations, were not considered viable alternatives for users with enterprisewide networks. They are taking steps to shed that image by improving support and other services. Many local providers now have thousands of subscribers, and some are growing at more than 1000 new accounts per month. They are able to offer customers the same level of access as regional providers to Internet news groups and e-mail, often at lower costs. And, because local providers serve only a specific area, they may offer better, faster connections for customers. In short, the increased user base has fostered more professionalism and accountability, making the choice between a national and a regional/local ISP solely dependent on competitive prices, services, and availability in a given area.

One main reason for the growth of local ISPs is the freedom of expression. Some of the larger service providers tend to restrict the activities of users on the Internet from their networks. Another reason is that local ISPs tend to be more innovative and adapt more quickly to the rapidly changing Internet application world than the slower-moving regional and national ISPs. The World Wide Web, for instance, became popular and widely available in 1993 on most local ISPs. The national ISPs and bigger on-line service providers made this service available to their customers only in 1995.

While the size of local ISPs varies, the founders often have much in common. Many start out running bulletin board systems, or BBSs, to allow local users to exchange messages, information, and programs. Most BBSs are run out of living rooms and basements—anyone with a computer and a modem can start one. Early Internet providers tended to be an unconventional bunch. One of the first was Stewart Brand, the first publisher of *The Whole Earth Catalog*, founded in the 1960s as a kind of counterculture mail-order guide. In 1985 he founded The WELL, a San Francisco–based provider and bulletin board that now serves more than 10,000 customers nationwide. Another is Digital Express Group (DIGEX), which provides Internet access in Washington and Baltimore from its Greenbelt headquarters. With $4000, two engineers started DIGEX in the unfinished basement of a home.

The growth of some local access providers has been astounding. Take, for instance, MCSNet in Chicago. MCSNet began in February 1993 on an investment of approximately $5000 as a provider of Internet services to both individuals and businesses. The company purchased its first dedicated connection (a 14.4 Kbps SLIP line) to the Internet and began selling accounts to the general public. Others soon followed, but MCSNet was able to sustain its growth and achieve approximately 400 subscribers by the end of the 1993 year. At this point, MCSNet had 24 modems and two computers. MCSNet ended 1993 with a significant net profit. In January 1994, MCSNet obtained its first T-1 connection to the Internet and began offering full-service connectivity to individuals and businesses. In the first ten months of 1994, growth was estimated at 650 percent annually. By the end of 1994, MCSNet had over 2200 individual customers and nearly 50 corporate and public-sector clients. To cover the ever-expanding demand, MCSNet is deploying more routers, fault-tolerance storage using disk mirrors for backing up information, powerful computers, CPU, disk resources, and more people.

To better understand the types of services provided, consider those offered by Digital Express (Washington D.C). This ISP has one option that provides e-mail and full news-group access for $15 per month. For many people, this is enough. If not, an account with complete Internet access (TELNET, IRC, WWW) costs $25 per month. The customer is given 5 megabytes of diskspace on their system for free in order to save e-mail or some articles from news groups that customers want to keep around for future reference. Additional disk space is a dollar or two per megabyte per month, depending on total amount. All accounts include six hours per day of connect time. Additional connect time after this is one dollar per hour. There are no extra charges for messages or file transfers. A special offer of a year's access (12 months) for the price of 10 months is also available. Thus, for the E-mail and Netnews-only account, a year is $150 (payment in advance) and for the Internet Services account (which also includes e-mail and Netnews) it is $250 for a year (also, in advance). There is a one-time set-up fee of $20 per account.

A major segment of local ISPs is the thousands of bulletin board systems catering to different interest groups.

## Bulletin Boards or Niche Services

These ISPs are the on-line version of a grass-roots, rapidly growing, low-cost segment. BBSs often earned a bad reputation because of their association with pornography. Once a struggling industry where most of the system software was shareware, BBSs have emerged as a vital industry in their own right. Over the past couple of years, several of the leading BBS system vendors have adopted "doors," which are standard sockets into which third parties can plug their wares. Soon service providers will be able to run a 1000-modem BBS from several PCs, which will open the market to many new entrants.

BBSs are not meant for a mass audience but for a specialized group of people who share common interests. For instance, there are niche on-line BBSs that appeal to women (Women's Wire and Echo), the digitally hip (Transom, Pipeline, and @Wired), older hipsters (Senior Net), homosexuals (Digital Queers and Eye Contact), sports buffs (USA Today Information Center), game players (The Imagination Network and Novalink), and computer buffs (Interchange and Applelink). Some charge for access while others are free. The most controversial and heavily used bulletin boards usually involve groups dealing with pornography. The cost to the users is the telephone charges, which can be substantial if the bulletin board is not local. Most of the major on-line services have local access telephone numbers, however, and their communication costs are about $1.25 per hour.

In cyberspace, women represent 10 percent to 15 percent of on-line users and often feel unwelcome as men tend to dominate on-line conversations. To reduce the imbalance, several services that cater exclusively to women have emerged. For example, WIRE, the Women's Information & Resource Exchange, is one such on-line service devoted to women. WIRE started operation from offices in San Francisco, offering a mix of news, entertainment, bulletin board conversations, and electronic messaging. The goal is to present information and connections that are beneficial to women, along with a "no stupid questions" policy for helping all users learn how to use the network. Competing with WIRE are services like Echo (East Coast Hang Out), which was started in 1990 with an investment of $20,000. Echo has a New York flavor (to send an Echoid, an instant message, for example, type "yo <username>"), an artsy bent (the most active conferences are "culture" and "panscan"), and an unusually large proportion of women on-line. Women also moderate half of Echo's conferences. This is in large part by design, to make the system more hospitable to women. Echo's market differentiation is not achieved by better system software but by careful conference host selection and to connections made on-line in conferences such as WIT (women in telecommunications) which have then spread by word of mouth to new subscribers.

## Free-Nets, Libraries, and Government as ISPs

Free-nets are mostly open-access, free, community, or municipal computer systems that typically carry information on city services, including job postings, park reservations, and civic calendars. They represent the "electronic city streets" that link homes, schools, libraries, hospitals, and small businesses to the ever-growing Internet. More importantly, they provide access to community members who otherwise would not be on the Net at all. One such system is the Cleveland Freenet, sponsored by CWRU (Case Western Reserve University). Anyone and everyone is allowed to join, and there's no charge for the registration process or to use the system. Users are required only to fill out a form and send it in through the Postal Service—log-in ID and password will be created a few days later. At that point users are free to use the system as they wish.

Libraries are rapidly becoming more than book warehouses. Viewing the Internet as a vast digital library, more and more libraries are taking on the mantle of a local Internet service provider. For instance, three dozen public libraries in New Jersey began offering free access to the Internet in mid-1994 as part of a two-year experiment that some hope will serve as a model.

Now that the I-way is coming, many states and towns want to be ready to take advantage of it. History teaches that the lack of a railroad stop condemned many towns to a lingering death a hundred years ago. Thirty years ago, interstate interchanges helped many communities to prosper, while those on backroads stagnated. In an effort to keep in step with the electronic transportation of today, many states are exploring the possibility of providing access to the Internet.

The first state to offer residents free access to the Internet was Maryland. All it costs is a local phone call, but there is a catch: The system is capable of handling only 192 dial-in users at a time. For residents who don't get a busy signal, the Internet will offer a world of information, from job listings, to stock market reports, to travel advisories. The service was set up through the state's public libraries using $2 million in federal funds and another $800,000 a year from the state to keep it going. Popular features, such as e-mail and the ability to transfer files, will cost extra. The state will charge about $35 a year for e-mail, while a package including other options will cost about $100 a year.

The possibility of state-provided Internet services bothers many local service providers, who feel that the tax dollars they pay are being used to try to put them out of business. The state justifies the service by saying that, just as electricity, streets, and sewers are core infrastructures that serve residents, businesses, and government alike, so too is access to the information infrastructure a communitywide need. Internet access could soon become a hotly contested issue in local elections or referendums.

## Challenges in the Local ISP Business

Although small Internet providers are flourishing now, their future is far from secure. Like the thousands of small video shops that opened during the

VCR boom of the 1980s, the mom and pops of the Internet business are finding that the on-line equivalents of Blockbuster are poised to move in. All major on-line services have offered access to the Internet news groups and now have direct links to remote systems. The on-line services aren't alone. Regional telephone companies, long-distance carriers, and cable television operators are among the giants considering Internet forays.

In the face of these challenges, Dial-N-Cerf, Netcom, and other local and regional access providers are aiming to go national. To attract nontechnical users, they're adding graphical interfaces that don't require the user to learn how to use UNIX, the operating system whose arcane command language scares users. Some small providers dismiss predictions of doom, arguing that customers require extensive personal contact and support that large companies can't deliver. But critics say that small providers are often overcome by their own success. Many experts predict a consolidation of the industry, but see a "differentiation" favoring small providers who are able to carve out a specialized niche.

## 4.5 SERVICE PROVIDERS ABROAD

Around the world, access to the Internet is fast becoming a necessity for individuals and organizations. As seen from the following examples taken from the nascent Far East marketplace, numerous opportunities exist.

### The Far East

Japanese researchers began studying the feasibility of bringing the emerging Internet technology to Japan around 1984. Japan's participation increased in 1987, with the establishment of the WIDE network, which was created for R&D of internetworking technologies. The connection of WIDE to the rapidly expanding Internet brought Japan fully into the international networking community. In the years that followed, many other Japanese networks were created under the auspices of various groups, expanding the use of internetworking technology. However, each of these networks was restricted to use for academic or research purposes, and no commercial AUP-free internetworking services provider existed.

The Japanese commercial Internet began in June 1992, when AT&T Jens became the first general provider of corporate commercial AUP-free connectivity with its Spin services, which offered UUCP connectivity with the rest of the Internet world. The Spin network was expanded with the introduction of IP connectivity in 1993, under the name InterSpin. It provides the following types of services: (1) leased-line connections that provide a high-speed, continuous connection to the Internet, allowing access to resources as well as the capability to offer full-time access to servers or services at the customer's site (Gopher, FTP, WWW, etc.); (2) dial-up ISDN connections that provide the user with a fully digital connection on demand (the on-demand capability provides the high-speed communication of a digital leased-line connection without the high monthly charges); and (3) dial-up connection provides access over the public telephone network (called PSTN service) without the added cost of special ISDN network equipment. Ideal for the customer with limited access and bandwidth needs, the dial-up connection service is the least costly direct Internet connection service, as shown in the Table 4.4. Keep in mind that the prices may have changed.

Hong Kong has also connected to the Internet using three ISP providers: HK Supernet, HK Internet, and Gateway Services and Internet-On-line HK (IOHK). All three provide a basic dial-in UNIX shell to a machine with all the basic services such as e-mail, TELNET, USENET news, and IRC. They are connected to the global Internet through leased lines. For instance, HK Supernet operates a dedicated 64-Kbps, private leased circuit connecting its Hong Kong facilities to PSI in Santa Clara, California. PSI provides HK Supernet with high reliability connectivity to all the major interexchanges (CIX West and MAE East). Table 4.5 compares some of the prices and costs of competing ISPs.

**Table 4.4** Pricing of Internet Services in Japan.

| *InterSpin (IP service) Subscription Cost: 50,000 yen (including manuals and domain name registration)* | | | *Dial-Up Connections—ISDN and PSTN* | | |
|---|---|---|---|---|---|
| *Speed* | *Type A** | *Type B* | *Speed* | *Type A* | *Type B*** |
| 64 Kbps | 425,000 yen | 385,000 yen | 19.2 Kbps (PSTN) | 180,000 yen | 150,000 yen |
| 128 Kbps | 620,000 yen | 580,000 yen | | | |
| 192 Kbps | 830,000 yen | 770,000 yen | 64 Kbps (ISDN) | 283,000 yen | 248,000 yen |
| 256 Kbps | 985,000 yen | 925,000 yen | | | |

*Type A includes provision and maintenance of networking equipment (router, CSU) at the customer site.

**For Type B service, the customer is responsible for networking equipment. Also, the customer is responsible for leased-line charges to the InterSpin access point, which are not included above.

**Table 4.5** Hong Kong Service Providers Monthly Minimum Fees

| | *Basic Shell $/mo** | *Hourly Connect Time $/hr** |
|---|---|---|
| HKIGS | 100 (no connect time) | 20 (above and beyond their $100/month basic shell charge) |
| IOHK | 33 (no connect time); 80 (w/15 hr per month connect time); 120 (w/30 hr per month connect time) | 6 |
| HK Supernet | 145 (if you prepay 12 months includes w/7 hr peak or 17.5 hrs off-peak) | 25 (between 9 AM and 9 PM); 10 (all other times) |

*All amounts in Hongkong dollars.

## Europe

In Europe, one of the major ISPs is EUNET, a private network run by a group originally known as the European UNIX Users Group, an organization that repackaged itself as EurOpen in a marketing move to reflect the diverse interests of the group more accurately. EurOpen is composed of national UNIX user groups in member countries ranging from Ireland to Algeria. Each country runs a national network that links to a host computer in a research institution that acts as a national hub. The national hubs, in turn, set up links to the EUNET operations center in Amsterdam. High and widely varying international tariffs in Europe were the reason why this star topology makes sense. EUNET flouts the conventional wisdom in Europe that the only way to make an operational network is with government subsidies. Despite high tariffs and political traps set by bureaucratic opponents, EUNET continues to thrive. EUNET has been one of the major forces behind EBONE, the European backbone consortium that is finally providing a more comprehensive regional solution to European connectivity.

Many of EUNET's national networks have grown to be quite extensive, running TCP/IP protocols over leased-line backbones instead of dial-up lines. In all cases, the networks make extensive use of volunteers and the users pay their own way. The national networks all pitch in to keep the EUNET operation in Amsterdam going. EUNET not only links all the national networks together, but also plays a major role in global connectivity. EUNET shares line costs with organizations like UUNET in the United States and NORDUNET in the Nordic countries, letting one fat pipe be put in where otherwise there might be lots of skinny ones.

In many countries in Eastern Europe and Northern Africa, EUNET is the first network to be put in place, providing valuable connectivity until corporations can put in their own internal nets or scientists are able to establish a national research network. As networking matures in a country, other networks have typically joined EUNET, but have never replaced it. Even if educational users go to national research networks, there is always a need for ways to connect small and medium-sized businesses, not to mention providing a way for research groups in corporations to link up.

## 4.6 SERVICE PROVIDER CONNECTIVITY: NETWORK INTERCONNECTION POINTS

Because the Internet is a collaborative collection of networks that exchange information, connectivity between all the various service providers—telco/cable/on-line service, national independents, regional/local ISPs, and the Internet backbone—is crucial so that information can flow easily from one point to another. A good analogy is the world's telephone system. The different public systems have evolved a set of standards that allows calls to be connected between any two points on the global phone network. The Internet is the same: it consists of hundreds of service providers—some complementary and many competitive—which adhere to certain basic standards when exchanging information among themselves. This allows users to communicate in various ways with others on participating network systems.

For the sake of efficiency, connectivity of service providers must be designed such that information must traverse only a few intermediate networks. To create this efficient architecture, the NSF mandated that commercial networks pool all their traffic together at one or two points and then connect these points directly to the Internet backbone. This effectively creates a limited number of entry points into the backbone and simplifies network management. Examples of such network interconnection points that give commercial operators a way to forward traffic to one another include the Commercial Internet Exchange (CIX, pronounced "kicks") in the United States and the London Internet Exchange (LINX).

### Commercial Internet Exchange (CIX)

CIX (http://www.cix.org/) was formed in March 1991 by General Atomics (operator of CERFnet), Performance Systems International (PSI), and UUNET Technologies. The initial agreement allowed all customers of CERFnet and PSINET and AlterNet to exchange Internet traffic directly, regardless from which network the customer obtains service, and at no additional cost. These three competing firms provided nearly 100 percent of the commercial TCP/IP services in the United States in 1990 and were not subject to government-mandated "acceptable use" restrictions on their traffic. The CIX concept was found useful and the membership expanded from three members to over 155 members as of May 1995. The concept has also been adopted in the design of NSFNET's Network Access Points (NAPs). Although many aspects of CIX are now encapsulated in the NAP architecture, it is important to understand the business model surrounding it.

The initial goal of CIX was to provide a path for customers of member networks to communicate with each other and not be restricted by the NSF Acceptable Usage Policy. Prior to the formation of CIX, the three networks were interconnected by the NSFNET backbone. This meant, for example, that a PSI customer communicating with a UUNET customer had to conform to the NSF AUP. These three networks were isolated islands of commercialization that somehow needed to be bridged. Hence the establishment of CIX. CIX maintains a hub or connectivity point in San Francisco called CIX West.

How does it work? Commercial Internet traffic might start on a local LAN, go through a regional provider, and be routed to the CIX hub, where it gets shipped through another commercial carrier to its final destination without ever using NSFNET. CIX also provides connection from its hubs to the NSFNET and networks in Europe, Australia, Canada, and elsewhere.

## Membership of CIX

For its members, CIX imposed two important business models:

1. An agreement that an ISP could sign with the CIX and gain access to other ISP networks. This allows traffic to flow smoothly between networks.
2. A financial agreement that states that there are no settlement fees. This model is unlike the telephone networks, where payment settlement is a critical part.

Members pay CIX an annual membership fee of $10,000 and a one-time start-up fee of $5,000. Each member arranges for its own connection to the CIX-West hub. Fundamentally the large U.S. ISPs subsidize the smaller U.S. ISPs through the CIX, by providing them access to their customers.

All sellers of IP transit are expected to join CIX. An individual or organization is considered to be selling IP transit if they accept IP traffic from another individual or organization and route it to a different individual or organization in exchange for a fee. According to CIX, an individual or organization is *not* selling IP transit if they are selling time-sharing services on a system that offers connectivity as part of the time-sharing service (e.g., BBS systems or shell account systems). For example:

- An individual or organization that operates a computer on which people log in directly and are able to receive Internet access is not required to join unless they are also selling IP transit.
- An individual or organization that sells one or more dial-up PPP/SLIP accounts is required to join to receive membership services.
- An individual or organization that sells dial-up PPP/SLIP access only to its own systems and that does not transmit those IP packets outside its internal networks is not required to join.

Commercial Internet providers offer the advantage of handling all types of traffic, without requiring their users to route commercial traffic differently from noncommercial traffic (research and education). While one division of a company may have access to the Internet, other divisions of the company may not and must route their traffic to another network. When using CIX member networks, all company traffic goes over the same network. Network managers need maintain only one external network, which connects to a CIX member.

The ISP market has been boosted by the availability of inexpensive PCs, modems, and decreasing connection costs. The lower costs are enabling individuals and small businesses to use the Internet facilities in search of improved efficiency, reduced costs, and the need to create a global corporate identity and broaden their markets.

## Future of Network Interconnection Points

The CIX initially represented a small commerical interconnection point in an environment dominated by a research and education mindset. With that phase becoming history, CIX represents one of the few stable and open interconnection points. It is providing a guaranteed access to its members, and a simple multilateral agreement to do commercial internetworking.

Today, there are several other interconnection points in the United States: CIX West, MAE East, FIX (Federal Internet Exchange), and the proposed NAP (Network Access Points). The NAP is an architecture of the U.S. government. The government is using economic incentives to make all of the R&E networks appear at the NAPs, although it is not clear whether there will be much participation of the commercial ISPs at the NAPs. The argument against the NAP model is that it costs about $20 to $25,000 per month to connect to all three NAPs, as there is no multilateral agreement in place to provide access to anyone once you get there.

PSI has proposed an AsianCIX and EuroCIX interconnection point operated and owned by the CIX corporation so that the overall technical direction and the financial stability of the CIX is available outside of North America (see Fig. 4.2). The assumption is that the various Internet models will continue to be in place through the end of the decade and that the CIX is integral in supporting or providing those models. Of the several models proposed, the one that appears to be of interest is the model where CIXs are interconnected with members fitting into two categories: transnational, and single-nation ISPs.

## 4.7 INTERNET CONNECTIVITY OPTIONS

The ISP marketplace offers a wide range of connectivity options designed to give customers (individuals, small businesses, or large organizations) the needed performance. The choices available can be broadly classified into three categories: (1) individual and light usage options; (2) small business or midrange options; and (3) high-volume options.

The cost of all types of connections is often based on the amount of bandwidth. Bandwidth on a network is analogous to number of lanes on a high-

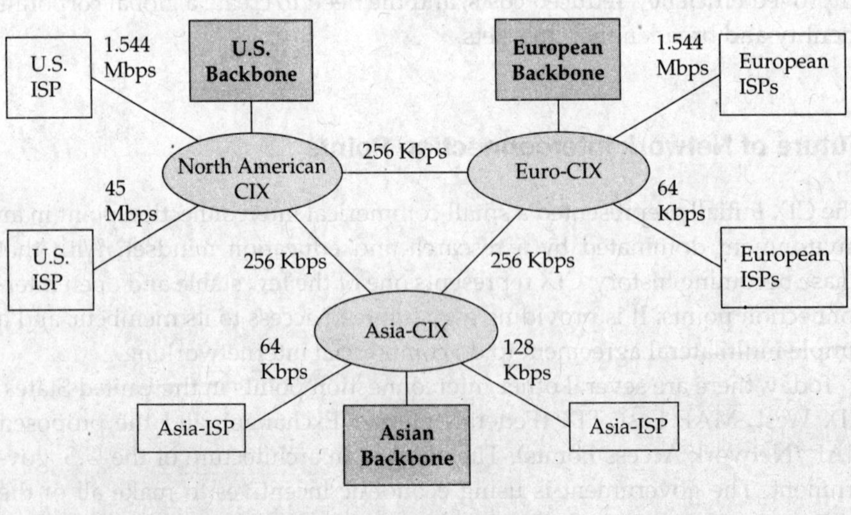


**Figure 4.2** Structure of the proposed international Internet interconnection points

way. At the other end of the spectrum is the metered dial-up rates where individuals or light users are charged based on the number of hours of usage. At the other end, heavy users can purchase dedicated unmetered flat rates for unlimited usage for about $10,000 per connection.

## Individuals and Light Usage Options

Dial-up connections are the most cost-effective method of accessing the Internet for lower volume, intermittent use, from anywhere. This service option requires the customer to have a single telephone line and hardware/software, such as a modem and a TCP/IP package. See Fig. 4.3.

Selecting an Internet service provider is not simple, and you still have to consider types of protocols, phone and access charges, and connection speeds. If you thought choosing a long-distance phone carrier was tough, wait until you select a service provider. Given that all the different categories of ISPs offer services for the individual, choosing one over the other often becomes a tricky proposition. The good news for customers is that as more people connect to the Internet, the service providers are becoming more accountable and professional.

Two types of connections are possible: plain vanilla connections provided by standard terminal emulation packages (Kermit, Z-modem) and sophisticated connection methods called direct IP (e.g., SLIP and PPP) service.

The direct IP service requires that a version of the TCP/IP protocol stack called SLIP or PPP be running on the computer. SLIP and PPP are two similar methods of encapsulating TCP packets to go over a modem line, ISDN, or another telecommunications connection. SLIP, the older of the two, can be confusing to set up for even an advanced user. PPP by comparison is simpler to set up, taking just a fraction of the time. It can also handle more types of traffic. PPP's more robust nature and ease of configuration have made it the method of choice for most national providers; many local providers are turning to it as well.

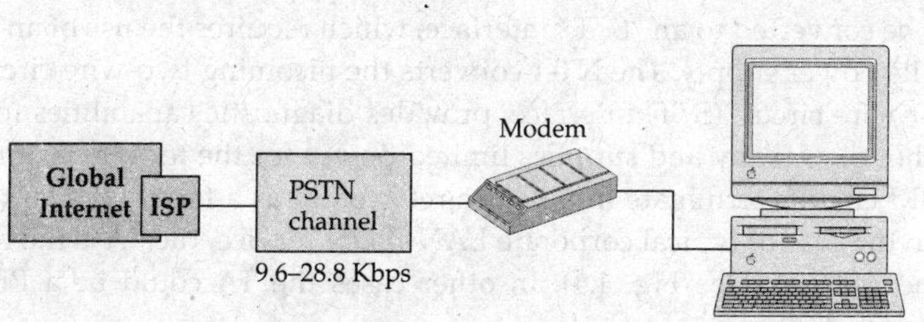


**Figure 4.3** Dial-up connection

SLIP and PPP provide a way of packaging information for easy movement between many different kinds of computers, large and small. They also enable the PC to become part of the Internet and get an IP address that allows users to publish information by running their own WWW or Gopher servers on the PCs. This means that people from other sites can access information from the PC.

In other words, the TCP/IP stack provides the capability to make the telephone line connection two-way. Direct IP links enable users to send and receive TCP/IP traffic over the Internet. With IP connections, any computer that a user links into the Internet can become an Internet host, which makes it possible for individual personal computers and workstations to become Internet hosts alongside the most powerful supercomputers.

## Mid-Range Options

ISDN is ideal for intermittent access to the Internet for high-volume data applications like video. There are two types of ISDN connections: basic rate interface ISDN (BRI) and primary rate interface ISDN (PRI). The BRI maximizes the transmission capability of existing copper wires, allowing for the simultaneous transmission of voice and data over a single twisted pair connection. It allows a maximum speed range of 64–128 Kbps (compared to the 14.4 Kbps of the analog modem). The ISDN PRI is an international standard for sending voice, video, or data over T-1 (1.544 Mbps) phone lines, in digital format, with 24 separate 64-Kbps channels. Since the PRI has a lot more capacity than the BRI, it can act as a network hub that can concentrate multiple incoming ISDN BRI data calls to a PRI line at the host, which can be a LAN or a computer.

The technical details of ISDN are as follows. A BRI circuit from the local telephone company will use a "U" interface when the circuit comes into the building and connects to the terminal equipment called NT-1 (Network Terminator–1). This incoming "U" interface is composed of two wires and carries data but no power for the terminal equipment. The "U" interface must be converted to an "S/T" interface, which requires the use of an NT-1 with its power supply. The NT-1 converts the incoming two-wire circuit to a four-wire circuit (S/T) interface, provides diagnostic capabilities for the telephone company and supplies limited power for the terminals, if needed. BRI circuits terminate in a device referred to as a terminal adapter, or TA. In the case of typical corporate LAN-ISDN service, the TA is the router on the network (see Fig. 4.4). In other cases the TA could be a PBX or modem.

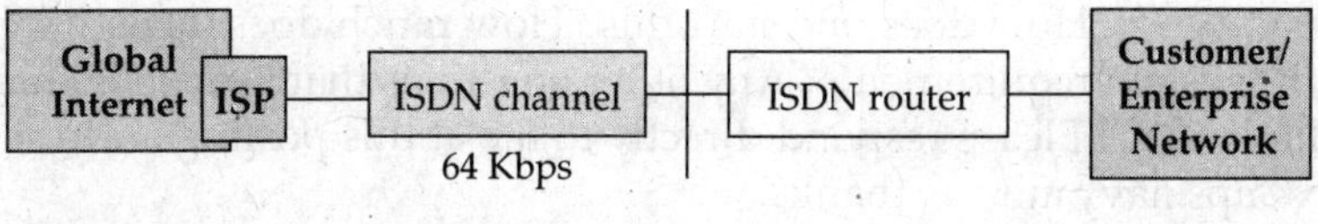


**Figure 4.4** ISDN connection

### Heavy-Volume Users

Private circuits are ideal for those who want to make extensive use of the Internet and require a dedicated line to operate at high bandwidth. These circuits are aimed primarily at business planning to make extensive use of the Internet. This service is often intended for companies that have extensive computer facilities or experience and are seeking to augment existing enterprisewide communication capability with the Internet connections.

Figure 4.5 shows that a dedicated connection requires a leased line from the service provider—a dedicated, point-to-point telecommunications circuit—and an IP router (a dedicated networking device), linking the subscriber to the Internet. Line speeds range from 9.6 Kb to 45 Mb, with the most common connection speeds being 56 Kb and 1.544 Mb. In this case, providers usually charge a flat-rate connection fee and no usage charge.

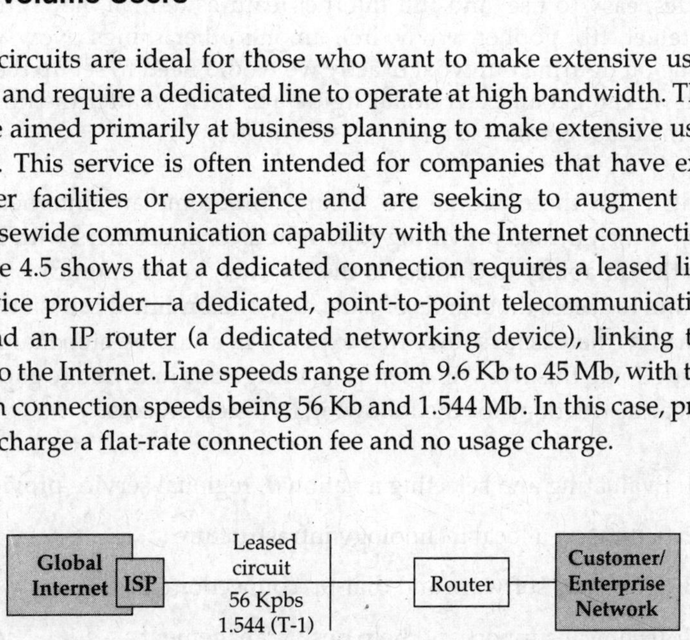


**Figure 4.5** Leased connection

## 4.8 LOGISTICS OF BEING AN INTERNET SERVICE PROVIDER

The phenomenal increase in consumers seeking access to the Internet has spurred entrepreneurs to examine ways of getting involved in this fast-growing business. Look, for example, at two postings on the alt.bbs.offered and alt.internet.services news groups:

> I am working with an international nonprofit organization that would like to start a BBS (bulletin board service) connected to the Net to publish information, track members, put out information, provide database

> access, etc. . . . How does one start this? How much does it cost? What are the system requirements? Any other questions that I'm too ignorant to think of. . . . Please respond directly to me at this posting address or xxxx@nps.navy.mil. . . . thanks.
>
> Myself and a couple associates have decided that it is time to bring a true Net system to our area, and we've been looking into that for some time now. We've got all the easy stuff down, such as what we want in it: 30 nodes, easy to use, and full Internet features (e-mail, newsgroups, open telnet, ftp, gopher, www, irc), among other things. Now we're working on figuring out what exactly we would need to set up the system so we can get an exact dollar figure and then go after the funding to get the beast going.

It is evident that these people are seeking to become an "Internet service provider," which means providing to hundreds of consumers with PCs and modems the capability to connect to the Internet, to communicate with one another, and to access thousands of databases and on-line discussion groups. Unfortunately, there is no source that explains in a step-by-step manner how to go about doing this. We will attempt to bridge this knowledge gap by providing clear instructions for the following five-step process:

Step 1: Evaluating and selecting a national/regional service provider

Step 2: Setting up a local technology infrastructure

Step 3: Setting up software and dial-up connection lines

Step 4: Technical support and help desk management

Step 5: Targeting and keeping customers

## Step 1: Evaluating and Selecting a National/Regional ISP

The first thing that any local ISP wants is access to the Internet backbone. For this, determine which national or regional ISP has a point of presence in that area. The choice of the service provider, the middleman, to be responsible for ensuring the vital connection to the Internet backbone is an important decision. This depends on the speed of connection needed and the reputation of the vendor that provides the service. The following are some selection criteria to be used in evaluating and choosing ISPs.

Network topology is one of the most important criteria to consider when choosing a provider. Looking at the network topology aids in understanding how vulnerable the network is to outages, how much capacity is available when the network is loaded more heavily than usual, and most importantly, how well the provider understands wide area networking. Most providers will provide details of their network topology and explain what service can be expected in various times of the day. Look closely at the speeds of the links from the PoP to the other nodes and to the Internet backbone. Note that any network connection offered to customers is dependent on the slowest link in the path. It doesn't matter if you are connected to a 45-Mbps node if there is a 56-Kbps link between you and the backbone. This is like linking a half-inch hose to a fire hydrant. The limit is the size of the hose, not how much the hydrant can deliver.

Then look at the external links of the ISP's backbone. Does the provider have a single connection to the Internet backbone? This is a potential point of failure. Look for multiple, direct connections to other network providers. The more, the better. This shows that the provider is concerned about external connectivity and does not want to be dependent on one third party for interconnection. If the provider has a single connection to the outside world, ask how often it fails and the length of downtime.

The next criterion is the cost to connect to the backbone. All service providers require you to buy the local loop segment from your facility to their closest PoP. You will have to buy this directly or indirectly from one of the telephone companies serving your local area. Think of the water hose analogy again. If you're limited by the local loop speed, then a high-speed backbone is not very useful.

Many providers claim impressive number of PoPs. Evaluate what constitutes a PoP in their book. Some providers claim a PoP anywhere they deliver service. Find out if many of their PoPs are single customers at the end of low-speed lines or if those PoPs house high-end routers linked by physically redundant high-speed connections. Network PoPs should be designed to scale with additional customers who, themselves, have growing requirements. The structure of a PoP is shown in Fig. 4.6.

Most PoPs offer Internet connectivity ranging from 14.4 Kbps to 45 Mbps. To determine which option is right for you, use the following guidelines: Estimate the number of customers who will be using the link, the types of applications they will be using, and the frequency with which they will be sending and receiving data.

Bandwidth requirements depend on the types of usage. For example, a typical e-mail message contains about 10 to 20 kilobits of data. This amount of data will be transmitted over a connection operating at 14.4 kilobits per second in just over two seconds, so a large number of users can share such a link for e-mail only and receive acceptable service. However, a single quality picture might contain 500–1000 kilobits of data. It would take almost five

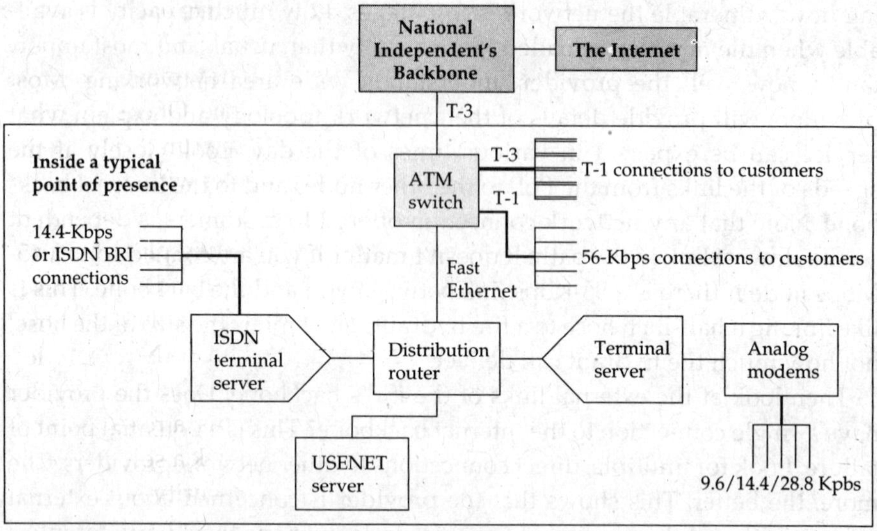


**Figure 4.6** Structure of a point of presence

minutes to transmit such an image over a 14.4-Kbps link, about 20 seconds over a 56-Kbps link, and 1 second over a T-1 (1.5-Mbps) link. Take the preceding estimates, multiply by the number of users who might simultaneously transmit data, and divide by the connection speed to come up with transmission time. Settle on a connection type that will meet your transmission time requirements.

Customer service is an important concern. Make sure that the provider offers documentation, consultation, and ongoing support. Also, make sure that the provider works with customers to integrate their computer systems. Also, as TCP/IP and Internet capabilities and technology become broadly used, the need for one-stop shopping for all products is becoming apparent. Products required include modems, routers, and networking software that streamlines the LAN and Internet integration process. The customer service group must be able to help in the purchase of needed equipment.

Finally, do some comparison shopping and a price/benefit analysis. Some providers may appear to be priced less than others. Make sure you do an "oranges to oranges" comparison. Don't compare one provider's bare-bones service with another's full-service offering. What one provider thinks is basic may be minimal or useless to you. Ask for customer references. See what complaints current customers have. Find out where their new customers come from. The most interesting statistic is how many of their customers have switched from other providers.

## Step 2: Setting Up a Local Technology Infrastructure

The technology used to operate the network is crucial. Today, plenty of commercial-quality routers, switches, and modems are available. Of course, part of the hardware decision depends on what software is being run on it. Figure 4.7 shows the architecture of a local Internet service provider with its various components.

The most important part of the architecture is the operating platforms (or servers). A typical local ISP needs servers that can easily handle a 30-customer system and all the activity that would come with it. Possible hardware includes UNIX machines or several Pentium-90s in a small LAN to handle the load.

In addition to computers, you also need three major items: a router, a terminal server, and a modem farm. Some standard advice: Pick a secure operating system and computer platform. Check the CERT security advisories

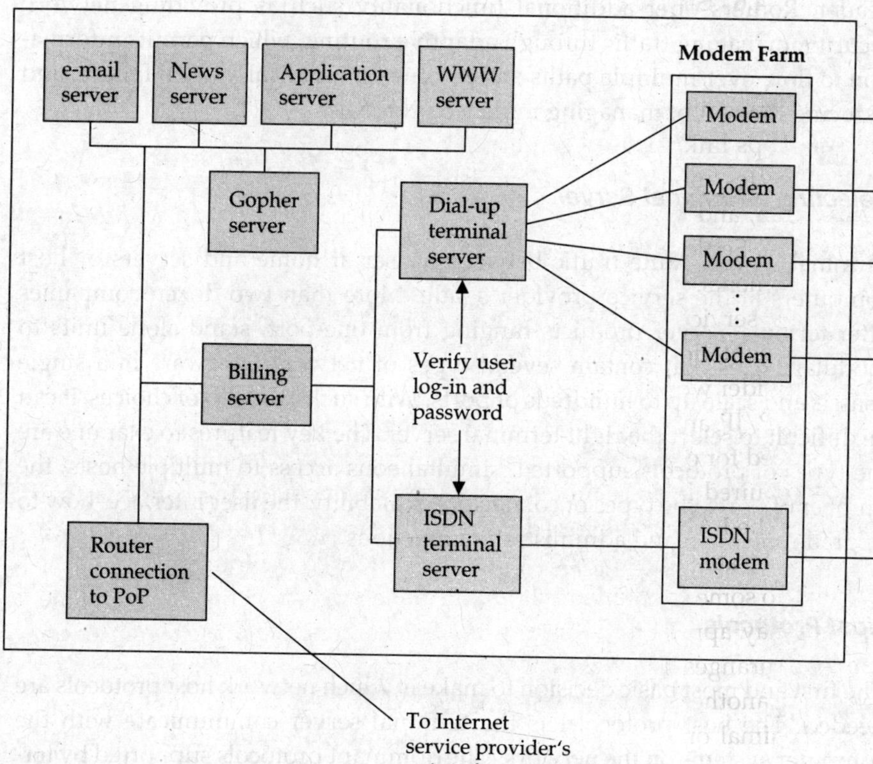


**Figure 4.7** Architecture of public access providers

(ftp://ftp.cert.org/) for the operating system with the fewest risk entries and successful hacker attacks, and don't be surprised if it's not a dialect of UNIX. Invest in uninterrupted power supply (UPS) for every server. Have dual paths to the local telco's central office so that a part-time gardener with a backhoe is not able to bring the entire network down.

### Selecting a Router

As the size of the local ISP increases, there is a need for an on-site router that connects to the PoP. The router is often a box with a modem, network interface card (NIC), and a small PC running the router software. More sophisticated routers support multiple modems and connections between networks running a variety of protocols. Information arriving from the network comes in packets, rather like envelopes, each with its own header bearing the address of its destination. As these packets come along the wiring, the router snags them and shoots them off to their destination based on the packet header. Routers offer additional functionality such as providing network security; managing traffic through adaptive routing, which permits information to flow over multiple paths and reroute automatically upon failure; and reducing the cost of managing multiple protocols.

### Selecting a Terminal Server

Terminal servers route traffic between a user at home and servers or host computers at the service provider's side. More than two dozen companies offer terminal-server products ranging from one-port, stand-alone units to modular boxes that contain several types of network hardware in a single chassis and scale up to hundreds of ports. With such a wealth of choices, it can be difficult to select the right terminal server. The key features to examine are the types of protocols supported, simultaneous access to multiple hosts, the number of ports, the types of connectors, scalability, the user interface, how to upgrade software, and administrative functions.

### Host Protocols

The first and most basic decision to make is which network host protocols are needed. The host protocol lets the terminal server communicate with the computer systems on the network. The dominant protocols supported by terminal servers are *Telnet*, which is part of the TCP/IP suite, SLIP/PPP, and more recently ISDN for dial-up access. Most terminal servers also support the Serial Line Internet Protocol (SLIP), another part of the TCP/IP suite. SLIP allows network services that use TCP/IP—mail, netnews, X Windows—to run over a serial line. An alternative to SLIP is the point-to-point protocol (PPP), which offers much the same services but has the reputation of being more robust and comprehensive (see Chapter 17).

The *Telnet* protocol used between a terminal server and a host system is no different from the protocol used between two computer systems. A terminal server that supports *Telnet* generally appears on the network as just another TCP/IP host from which connections are being made to other TCP/IP systems. UNIX environments demand that a terminal server support *Telnet* since almost every UNIX system uses this protocol for basic networking. Most terminal servers include *Telnet* as a basic feature, and those that do not usually will offer it at an extra cost.

A few terminal servers also support the TN3270 protocol, which allows ASCII terminals or PCs to access IBM mainframes using TCP/IP and IBM's 3270 terminal protocol. This ability is particularly useful in a heterogeneous environment that includes IBM host systems. Installations that run a variety of operating systems and networking protocols need terminal servers that can simultaneously run multiple protocols. With multiple protocols, for example, one user can connect to a UNIX host via *Telnet*, while someone else can use the same terminal server to connect to a IBM host with TN3270.

## Terminal Ports

Once host protocols are decided, the number of ports must be determined. Each port represents one dial-up user. For each port, a decision must be made whether modem control on the serial ports is required. If you are connecting local terminal users or LAN PCs through a terminal server, modem control is not required. If, however, you plan to attach modems to your terminal servers to allow dial-in access by remote users or dial-out access by your host systems, make sure that a sufficient number of ports support modem control.

## Terminal Sessions

Next evaluate the maximum number of sessions for the entire terminal server. A manufacturer may not explicitly specify or implement a limit for the server as a whole. But a limit does exist, generally determined by the amount of memory in the device. One powerful feature of terminal servers is that they let a user at a single terminal simultaneously log on to many host systems. Some users never open more than one session at a time, but a power user could tie up the whole server. An important feature in a terminal server is the ability to allow the network administrator to set a maximum number of simultaneous sessions per port.

### Terminal Connections

Other issues involve speed and reverse connections. Most terminal servers support serial connections at speeds of at least 19.2 kilobits per second (Kbps) and some have extremely high-speed models that achieve 115.2 Kbps. Most terminal servers also support a reverse connection, in which the connection originates from the host system, not the terminal side. Reverse connections are necessary if printers are attached on serial lines. The types of reverse-connection protocols mirror those of host protocols.

### Selecting a Modem Farm

Customer computers cannot link to the terminal server without a modem on the service provider's side. Modems come with all types of capabilities and speeds and in two basic forms: asynchronous and synchronous. *Synchronous modems* establish an end-to-end connection (like a telephone call) and begin sending information. *Asynchronous modems*, however, send information in small "blocks," then check to make sure that there were no errors before sending the next "block" of information. Until recently, synchronous modems were far more reliable than asynchronous, but with advancement in telephone line quality and other standards, asynchronous modems are catching up. The following types of modems are in use:

- *V.32bis (14.4 Kbps).* The current standard for corporate dial-up modems. Most bulletin boards and public-access UNIX systems offer this speed. The typical 50-percent speed boost over V.32 modems comes at only an incremental price premium.
- *V.32 (9600 bps).* Largely made obsolete by V.32bis technology, V.32 modems can still offer inexpensive access to on-line services. Most on-line services do not yet offer V.32bis speeds, so for this application exclusively, paying more for the extra speed of V.32bis may not make sense.
- *V.34 (28.8 Kbps).* V.34 modems are available today. These modems will probably command a high price premium over V.32bis modems, so expect both to coexist for a long time.
- *V.32 terbo (19.2 Kbps).* A new "standard" offered by a coalition of modem vendors including AT&T, Penril, and Data Race. V.32 terbo modems exist

today and often cost only a little more than V.32bis modems. V.32 terbo looks like a good bet to supplant V.32bis, but many modem vendors are resisting it.

The type of modem selected is closely related to telephone charges, which can dominate the cost of access to the Internet. Check first for telco providers with metro or regional dial-ins that necessitate a local call (no per-minute phone charges). If there aren't any, move on to comparing prices for 800 and direct-dial long-distance charges. Make sure to compare all the available options. For instance, in the United States calling long distance out-of-state or across the country is often cheaper than just calling 30 miles away.

## Step 3: Setting Up Software and Dial-Up Connection Lines

Several types of services can be provided to the customer. The most basic service gives the customer access to all of the Internet services such as e-mail, USENET news, FTP, *Telnet*, and all of the UNIX tools such as emacs, Tex, C, C++. In addition to application access, customers receive a 5-Mb working directory, with more available for a fee.

The SLIP/PPP service provides the customer with an IP connection to the Internet. This service is available only to individual persons wishing to connect PCs to the Internet to execute programs such as Mosaic. Providers can offer this service with both dial-up pools and private lines.

Other services include:

- *Gopher Server Service.* Allows the customer to display information files on the provider's Gopher server. It is used to display information about the customer business, the customer product, or the customer services.
- *WWW Server Service.* Allows the customer to display hypertext documents on the web server. These documents can display pictures, animation, and sound. It is used to display information about the customer business, the customer product, or the customer services.
- *FTP Archive Service.* Gives the customer an archive directory on the anonymous FTP server. It distributes the customer software or other information easily.
- *Mailing List Service.* Allows the customer to set up a mailing list. Most providers provide archive and digest service for the customer mailing list.

Additional services include UUCP Service, which provides the customer or the customer's organization with domain name and a mail and news feed to the customer site. The service provider will register the domain name for the customer and act as the customer mail forwarder. This service is great for BBSs or small businesses that need mail and news service.

### Step 4: Technical Support and Help Desk Management

An area where variation is great among service providers is in the level and quality of the customer service they offer. This is often a very important consideration with customers in choosing providers. There is nothing more frustrating in using a computer than encountering a problem, being focused on finding the solution, and then running into a brick wall because there is no one available to help. Some access providers offer little in the way of customer support other than a recorded message on an answering machine and an eventual call-back. On the other end of the spectrum are the full-service providers who have a customer assistance hotline and who offer proactive support in the form of users meetings, workshops, and newsletters. In looking at a support structure, there are at least five basic areas that a prospective customer should evaluate:

1. *Documentation.* Does the ISP have a user manual? Is it written in standard English or computerese? Does it adequately explain how to use all the functionalities (e-mail, *Telnet*, FTP) that are provided?

2. *Telephone support.* Is there someone to call if the customer runs into problems or has questions? What hours is telephone support available? Is there any additional charge for it?

3. *Training and workshops.* Few front-end interfaces are so simple that a new user cannot benefit from some initial training, and learning about resources available through the Internet is facilitated through educational opportunities. Are they willing to provide start-up training? advanced training? general and specialized workshops focusing on resources available on the Internet?

4. *Ongoing communication.* Most providers publish an ongoing newsletter or memos that discuss the state of the system and include information about new resources on the Internet. Are they budgeting for that?

5. *Technical enhancements.* Does the ISP have a track record of enhancing the system to make it easier to use? When changes are made, how are users kept informed? Have they acted on users' suggestions for improvements?

As with any complex electronic information system or service, a strong support structure can make an enormous difference in customer satisfaction. Probably the most costly and important aspect to consider when becoming a provider is the quality of technical staff and help desk personnel. Most service providers do not budget for this part of the business and often are shocked to see how much it costs. However, it is probably the most important investment, as these people will be interacting with the customer to provide service and solve technical problems. Most of the customers will be attempting to surf the Internet for the very first time and will need a lot of hand holding and guidance to get things right. The technical staff are the ones who will get customer connections running to begin with and then keep them and the network running in the future. Make sure that your "technical" staff consists of people who are experienced with TCP/IP.

The help desk is also the network operations center (NOC). It should be staffed by at least one person around the clock, as computing is a 24-hour activity. While it is normal to have only junior people on duty at odd hours of the night, it is crucial that senior personnel be on site from at least 8 A.M. to 8 P.M. Monday through Friday. If a customer's connection fails during normal business hours, senior people must be available to work on it. An amazing number of providers claiming twenty-four-hour, seven-day operations really mean that someone will answer the phone, not that they will have someone capable of dealing with the customer's problem. An answering service or beeper number is no substitute for a trained network engineer.

The problems users have with the Internet lie in two areas: tools and organization. Although the current generation of GUI-based clients is a large step beyond the dark ages of UNIX command lines and teletype display access, they fall short in several areas. For example, the applications for file transfer protocol (FTP), e-mail, news groups, and other common functions suffer from an immediately apparent lack of features and usability. The average user may not even get to the applications, given the difficulty of configuring a serial communications protocol such as a SLIP or PPP link. Even if supplied with a preconfigured software disk, a user is still likely to face inadequate documentation trying to determine whether the simple mail transport protocol gateway is the same as the POP (post office protocol) gateway, which is the same as the host address. It is the service provider's job to supply clear and legible instructions.

The user who overcomes the tools barrier will run headlong into another: the Internet's lack of organization. It has no central directory service for locating information or people. Customers can spend hours browsing up and down Gopher menus or Web links without ever finding a specific piece of information. Wide Area Information Server (WAIS, software that allows users to find and retrieve information from databases using keywords) shows some promise, except that it expects people to first decide which of several hundred esoteric databases should be searched. Archie software that lets users find information on FTP servers may find what the customer wants if it is the name of a file and one can guess what it might have been called. It is no coincidence that there is a booming industry in on-line Internet guides. Unfortunately, it is still true that the easiest way to find something on the Internet is to post the question to a news group or mailing list.

### *Step 5: Targeting and Keeping Customers*

The astonishing growth of the Internet as a public access computer network has all kinds of new users, large and small, exploring the virtues of "getting on the Internet." More and more companies are using the Internet to conduct their business, communicate with and support their customers, exchange electronic mail with hundreds of thousands of users, and seek and find valuable information leading to sustainable competitive advantage.

These are the customers who will find the Internet indispensable once connected. The challenge for the new service providers will be to develop services that differentiate themselves in terms of quality of service, coverage, support, ease of use, and value-added services. As they grow and start to compete with the established value-added network providers such as CompuServe and Prodigy, the commercial Internet providers will have an even more difficult challenge to face.

To answer these challenges, any budding access provider will need to develop strong marketing strategies and programs to support future growth. They need to differentiate themselves from their current and future competitors. Even more importantly, they must define a strong market position for themselves and for the Internet to continue their growth in the long term. There are still too many people who really do not know what the Internet is or how they can connect to it, even among sophisticated users. Educating end users will not be easy. The current revenue levels probably do not generate enough profits to finance the growth, the product development, and the marketing programs required for long-term success. The challenge for the providers will be to finance and manage their growth so that they end up among the winners of this new game.

## 4.9 SUMMARY

To support electronic commerce and on-line businesses, an entire new industry called the internet service providers (ISPs) has emerged. These service providers do not offer their own content (files to download, on-line stock reports, and shopping malls); rather, they provide a door through which users travel to reach the content. These providers are mostly entrepreneurs who view themselves as analogous to the railroad men who helped develop and commercialize the Wild West frontiers or as on-line "real-estate property developers."

The steady commercialization and privatization of the Internet through commerce service providers fortells the growth of electronic commerce to a much greater extent than seen today. The ability to do business over the Internet will benefit the Internet community in several ways: Many new and valuable services will be available to the users of the Internet; it will drive the Internet growth to a large extent; it will foster market efficiency by facilitating small vendors' entry into large markets and by providing consumers with broader ranges of choice. An infrastructure for conducting business will enable automated transactions between consumers and service providers ranging from department stores, mail order stores (e.g., the Home Shopping Club and L.L. Bean), news and broadcast networks (e.g., CNN and AP News), and even business-to-business commerce.

Chapter 5

# Network Security and Firewalls

Complex issues of security, privacy, authentication, and anonymity have been thrust into the forefront as confidential information increasingly traverses modern networks. Confidence, reliability, and protection of this information against security threats is a crucial prerequisite for the functioning of electronic commerce. A security threat is defined as a circumstance, condition, or event with the potential to cause economic hardship to data or network resources in the form of destruction, disclosure, modification of data, denial of service, and/or fraud, waste, and abuse.

The discussion of security concerns in electronic commerce can be divided into two broad types:

1. *Client–server security* uses various authorization methods to make sure that only valid users and programs have access to information resources such as databases. Access control mechanisms must be set up to ensure that properly authenticated users are allowed access only to those resources that they are entitled to use. Such mechanisms include password protection, encrypted smart cards, biometrics, and firewalls.
2. *Data and transaction security* ensures the privacy and confidentiality in electronic messages and data packets, including the authentication of remote users in network transactions for activities such as on-line payments. The goal is to defeat any attempt to assume another identity while involved with electronic mail or other forms of data communication. Preventive measures include data encryption using various cryptographic methods.

## 5.1 CLIENT–SERVER NETWORK SECURITY

Client–server network security is one of the biggest headaches system administrators face as they balance the opposing goals of user maneuverability and easy access and site security and confidentiality of local information. According to the National Center for Computer Crime Data, computer security violations cost U.S. businesses half a billion dollars each year. The concerns are real, and doing nothing is analogous to leaving a door unlocked in a high-crime neighborhood.

Network security on the Internet is a major concern for commercial organizations, especially top management. Recently, the Internet has raised many new security concerns. By connecting to the Internet, a local network organization may be exposing itself to the entire population on the Internet. As Fig. 5.1 illustrates, an Internet connection effectively breaches the physical security perimeter of the corporate network and opens itself to access from other networks comprising the public Internet.

That being the case, the manager of even the most relaxed organization must pay some attention to security. For many commercial operations, security will simply be a matter of making sure that existing system features, such as passwords and privileges, are configured properly. They need to audit all access to the network. A system that records all log-on attempts—particularly the unsuccessful ones—can alert managers to the need for stronger measures. However, where secrets are at stake or where important corporate assets must be made available to remote users, additional measures must be taken. Hackers can use password guessing, password trapping, security

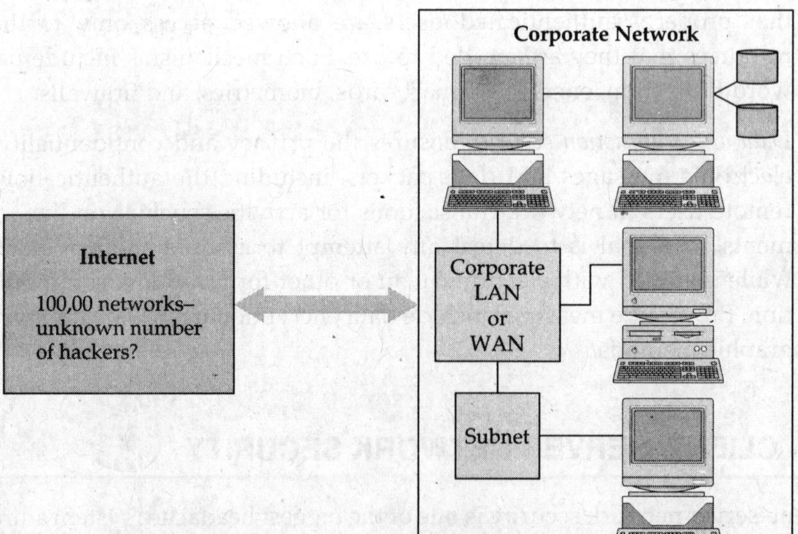


**Figure 5.1** Unprotected Internet connection

holes in programs, or common network access procedures to impersonate users and thus pose a threat to the server.

Client–server network security problems manifest themselves in three ways:

1. *Physical security holes* result when individuals gain unauthorized physical access to a computer. A good example would be a public workstation room, where it would be easy for a wandering hacker to reboot a machine into single-user mode and tamper with the files, if precautions are not taken. On the network, this is also a common problem, as hackers gain access to network systems by guessing passwords of various users.

2. *Software security holes* result when badly written programs or "privileged" software are "compromised" into doing things they shouldn't. The most famous example of this category is the "sendmail" hole, which brought the Internet to its knees in 1988. A more recent problem was the "rlogin" hole in the IBM RS-6000 workstations, which enabled a cracker (a malicious hacker) to create a "root" shell or superuser access mode. This is the highest level of access possible and could be used to delete the entire file system, or create a new account or password file resulting in incalculable damage.

3. *Inconsistent usage holes* result when a system administrator assembles a combination of hardware and software such that the system is seriously flawed from a security point of view. The incompatibility of attempting two unconnected but useful things creates the security hole. Problems like this are difficult to isolate once a system is set up and running, so it is better to carefully build the system with them in mind. This type of problem is becoming common as software becomes more complex.

To reduce these security threats, various protection methods are used. At the file level, operating systems typically offer mechanisms such as access control lists that specify the resources various users and groups are entitled to access. Protection—also called *authorization* or *access control*—grants privileges to the system or resource by checking user-specific information such as passwords. The problem in the case of e-commerce is very simple: If consumers connect a computer to the Internet, they can easily log into it from anywhere that the network reaches. That's the good news. The bad news is that without proper access control, anyone else can too.

Over the years, several protection methods have been developed, including trust-based security, security through obscurity, password schemes, and biometric systems.

### Trust-Based Security

Quite simply, *trust-based security* means to trust everyone and do nothing extra for protection. It is possible not to provide access restrictions of any kind and to assume that all users are trustworthy and competent in their use of the shared network. This approach assumes that no one ever makes an expensive breach such as getting root access and deleting all files (a common hacker trick). This approach worked in the past, when the system administrator had to worry about a limited threat. Today, this is no longer the case.

### Security Through Obscurity

Most organizations in the mainframe era practiced a philosophy known as *security through obscurity* (STO)—the notion that any network can be secure as long as nobody outside its management group is allowed to find out anything about its operational details and users are provided information on a need-to-know basis. Hiding account passwords in binary files or scripts with the presumption that "nobody will ever find them" is a prime case of STO (somewhat like hiding the housekey under the doormat and telling only family and friends). In short, STO provides a false sense of security in computing systems by hiding information. Although admittedly sound in theory, this philosophy can mean lifelong trust of a small group of people. In reality; however better pay from competitors means that the knowledge goes with employees, reducing the effectiveness of the method.

This method was quite successful with stand-alone systems that ran operating systems such as IBM MVS or CMS and DEC VAX. But its usefulness is minimal in the UNIX world, where users are free to move around the file system, have a great understanding of programming techniques, and have immense computing power at their fingertips. Widespread networking necessitates greater need for details of how the system works, rendering STO less effective. Many users today have advanced knowledge of how their operating system works and through experience can guess at the bits of knowledge considered confidential. This bypasses the whole basis of STO and makes this method of security useless.

### Password Schemes

One straightforward security solution, a *password scheme*, erects a first-level barrier to accidental intrusion. In actuality, however, password schemes do little about deliberate attack, especially when common words or proper names are selected as passwords. For instance, network administrators at a Texas air force base discovered that they could crack about 70 percent of the passwords on their UNIX network with tools resembling those used by hackers. The simplest method used by most hackers is *dictionary comparison*—comparing a list of encrypted user passwords against a dictionary of encrypted common words [GCN94]. This scheme often works because users tend to choose relatively simple or familiar words as passwords. To beat the dictionary comparison method, experts often recommend using a minimum of eight-character length mixed-case passwords containing at least one non-alphanumeric character and changing passwords every 60 to 90 days.

Even so, because passwords in a remote log-in session usually pass over the network in unencrypted form, any eavesdropper on the network (which means anyone with any control at all of his or her hardware) can simply record the password any time it is used. Having distinct passwords for distinct devices is sometimes a problem, because people will write them down (making them easy for others to find), share them (with people on the same project), or include them in automatic scripts (eliminating the inconvenience of typing them and also eliminating the protection from accidental access).

To counter these threats, various approaches have been suggested for creating one-time passwords, including smart cards, randomized tokens, and challenge-response schemes. For example, a hand-held smart card can generate a token that a computer system can recognize—the token is derived from a cryptographic function of the clock time and some initialization information, and a personal identification number (PIN) is required to complete the authentication process. Some devices generate a visually displayed token that can be entered as a one-time password, and others provide direct electronic input. These devices typically use one-key symmetric cryptographic algorithms or two-key algorithms with public and private keys (see Section 5.4). A less high-tech approach merely provides an item from a preprinted codebook of passwords [PNMAY94].

### Biometric Systems

Biometric systems, the most secure level of authorization, involve some unique aspect of a person's body. Past biometric authentication was based on comparisons of fingerprints, palm prints, retinal patterns, or on signature verification or voice recognition. Biometric systems are very expensive to implement: At a cost of several thousand dollars per reader station, they may be better suited for controlling physical access—where one biometric unit can serve for many workers—than for network or workstation access. Many biometric devices also carry a high price in terms of inconvenience; for example, some systems take 10 to 30 seconds to verify an access request. Moreover, users see such systems as unduly intrusive; people are reluctant to stick a finger or a hand into a slot, or sign their name, or sit still while an optical system scans their eyeball. Biometric device variations are appearing, such as systems that recognize keyboard-typing patterns or read infrared facial patterns from passersby using only a simple video camera for image capture [RKBY94].

## 5.2 EMERGING CLIENT–SERVER SECURITY THREATS

Another security threat that is emerging in the electronic commerce world is mobile code (software agent), which in many ways resembles a more traditional virus threat. Mobile code is an executable program that has the ability to move from machine to machine and also to invoke itself without external influence. To circumvent this threat, organizations are installing firewalls that filter incoming data packets. These threats can be divided into two major categories: (1) threats to local computing environment from mobile software and (2) access control and threats to servers that include impersonation, eavesdropping, denial of service, packet replay, and packet modification.

### Software Agents and Malicious Code Threat

The major threat to security from running client software results because of the nature of the Internet: Client programs interpret data downloaded from arbitrary servers on the Internet. In the absence of checks on imported data, the potential exists for this data to subvert programs running on the systems. The security threat arises when the downloaded data passes through local interpreters (such as PostScript) on the client system without the user's knowledge. A similar problem existed in the UNIX mail system, whereby a remote user, through various escape sequences, could invoke the shell program (csh or sh) on the recipient's machine. This potential security breach has been plugged in most of the new mail systems.

In short, client threats mostly arise from malicious data or code. Malicious code refers to viruses, worms, Trojan horses, logic bombs, and other deviant software programs (see Table 5.1). Malicious code is sometimes mistakenly associated only with stand-alone PCs but can also attack computer networks easily. In the latter case, actual costs attributed to the presence of malicious code have resulted primarily from system outages and staff time to repair the systems. Nonetheless, these costs can be significant.

**Table 5.1** Examples of Malicious Code

*Virus.* A code segment that replicates by attaching copies of itself to existing executables (.EXE files). The new copy of the virus is executed when a user executes the host program. The virus may include additional "payload" that triggers when specific conditions are met. For example, some viruses display a text string or delete all files on the hard disk on a particular date. Many types of viruses fall into categories known as variants, overwriting, resident, stealth, and polymorphic.

*Trojan Horse.* A program that performs a desired task but also includes unexpected (and undesirable) functions. Consider as an example an editing program for a multiuser system. This program could be modified to randomly delete one of the users' files each time they perform a useful function (editing); these deletions are unexpected and definitely undesired.

*Worm.* A self-replicating program that is self-contained and does not require a host program. The program creates a copy of itself and causes it to execute; no user intervention is required. Worms commonly utilize network services to propagate to other host systems.

---

Clients must scan for malicious data and executable program fragments (such as MIME mail messages and PostScript files) that are transferred from the server to the client. It is conceivable that the client may need to filter out data and programs known to be dangerous, although it is not possible to do so conclusively: Automatic determination of program behavior is not computable and is generally referred to in computer science as the "halting problem." It is possible, however, to perform some heuristics on known dangers.

## Threats to Servers

Threats to servers consist of unauthorized modification of server data, unauthorized eavesdropping or modification of incoming data packets, and compromise of a server system by exploiting bugs in the server software. Compared to stand-alone systems, network servers are much more susceptible to attacks where legitimate users are impersonated. For example:

- Hackers have potential access to a large number of systems. As a result, computers that are not properly configured and/or are running programs with security holes are particularly vulnerable.
- Hackers can use popular UNIX programs like Finger, rsh, or ruser to discover account names and then try to guess simple passwords using a dictionary or more sophisticated password guessing methods (e.g., a hacker

could use a password guessing program in which multiple computer systems are used simultaneously for comparison purposes).

- Hackers can use electronic eavesdropping to trap user names and unencrypted passwords sent over the network. They can monitor the activity on a system continuously and impersonate a user when the impersonation attack is less likely to be detected.
- Hackers can *spoof*, or configure, a system to masquerade as another system, thus gaining unauthorized access to resources or information on systems that "trust" the system being mimicked.

Hackers can eavesdrop using software that monitors packets sent over the network. Many network programs, such as *Telnet* and ftp, are vulnerable to eavesdroppers who obtain passwords, which are often sent across the network unencrypted. Eavesdropping often allows a hacker to make a complete transcript of network activity and thus obtain sensitive information, such as passwords, data, and procedures for performing functions. A cracker can also eavesdrop using wiretapping, radio, or auxiliary ports on computers, which are used by network programs. In most cases, it is difficult to detect that someone is eavesdropping. Network programs that involve remote file transfer are especially susceptible to eavesdroppers gaining access to the contents of files. Encryption can prevent eavesdroppers from obtaining data traveling over unsecured networks. (See section 5.6.)

Servers can also be attacked with threats such as denial of service, where a user can render the system unusable for legitimate users by "hogging" a resource or by damaging or destroying resources so that they cannot be used. The two most common forms of denial-of-service attacks are service overloading and message flooding.

Servers are especially vulnerable to *service overloading*. For instance, one can easily overload a WWW server by writing a small loop that sends requests continually for a particular file, for example, a home page. The server tries to respond to the request in good faith as it assumes that all requests are legitimate. Hence, denial-of-service attacks may be caused intentionally or unintentionally by "runaway" software programs such as those caught in an infinite loop.

*Message overloading* occurs when someone sends a very large file to a message box every few minutes. The message box rapidly grows in size and begins to occupy all the space on the disk and increases the number of receiving processes on the recipient's machine, tying it up even more and often causing a disk crash. The best way to avoid message overloading is to provide separate areas for different programs and to make provisions for graceful failure.

Although hard to prevent, service attacks can be reduced by restricting access to critical accounts, resources, and files and protecting them from unauthorized users. It is important for administrators to protect against denial-of-service threats without denying access to legitimate users.

Other sophisticated threats like packet replay and modification are harder to guard against. *Packet replay* refers to the recording and retransmission of message packets in the network. This is a significant threat for programs that require authentication sequences, because a hacker could replay legitimate authentication sequence messages to gain access to a secure system. Packet replay is frequently undetectable, but can be prevented by using methods like packet time-stamping and sequence counting. Packet modification is an integrity threat involving one computer intercepting and modifying a message packet destined for another system. In many cases, packet information may not only be modified, but its contents may be destroyed before the legitimate users can see them.

To counter some of these server threats, a new concept is emerging in the area of network security on the Internet called firewalls.

## 5.3 FIREWALLS AND NETWORK SECURITY

The most commonly accepted network protection is a barrier—a firewall—between the corporate network and the outside world (untrusted network). The term *firewall* can mean many things to many people, but basically it is a method of placing a device—a computer or a router—between the network and the Internet to control and monitor all traffic between the outside world and the local network. Typically, the device allows insiders to have full access to services on the outside while granting access from the outside only selectively, based on log-on name, password, IP address or other identifiers (see Fig. 5.2).

Generally speaking, a firewall is a protection device to shield vulnerable areas from some form of danger. In the context of the Internet, a firewall is a system—a router, a personal computer, a host, or a collection of hosts—set up specifically to shield a site or subnet from protocols and services that can be abused from hosts on the outside of the subnet. A firewall system is usually located at a gateway point, such as a site's connection to the Internet, but can be located at internal gateways to provide protection for smaller collection of hosts or subnets.

Firewalls come in several types and offer various levels of security. Generally, firewalls operate by screening packets and/or the applications that pass through them, provide controllable filtering of network traffic, allow restricted access to certain applications, and block access to everything

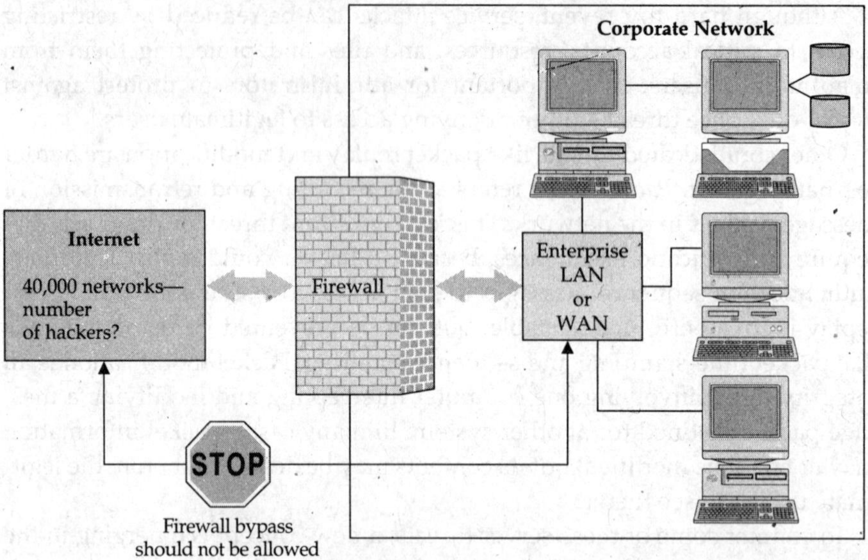


**Figure 5.2** Firewall-secured Internet connection

else. The actual mechanism that accomplishes filtering varies widely, but in principle, the firewall can be thought of as a pair of mechanisms: one to block incoming traffic and the other to permit outgoing traffic. Some firewalls place a greater emphasis on blocking traffic, and others emphasize permitting traffic.

In short, the general reasoning behind firewall usage is that, without a firewall, network security is a function of each host on the network and all hosts must cooperate to achieve a uniformly high level of security. The larger the subnet, the less manageable it is to maintain all hosts at the same level of security. As mistakes and lapses in security become more common, break-ins can occur not as the result of complex attacks, but because of simple errors in configuration and inadequate passwords.

## Firewalls in Practice

Firewalls range from simple traffic logging systems that record all network traffic flowing through the firewall in a file or database for auditing purposes to more complex methods such as IP packet screening routers, hardened firewall hosts, and proxy application gateways. The simplest firewall is a packet-filtering gateway or screening router. Configured with filters to restrict packet traffic to designated addresses, screening routers also limit the types of services that can pass through them.

More complex and secure are application gateways. They are essentially PCs or UNIX boxes that sit between the Internet and a company's internal network to provide proxy services to users on either side. For example, a user who wants to FTP in or out through the gateway would connect to FTP software running on the firewall, which then connects to machines on the other side of the gateway. Screening routers and application gateway firewalls are frequently used in combination when security concerns are very high. In cases of heavy traffic, subnetworks or hardened firewall machines are set up between the Internet and a company's private network.

## IP Packet Screening Routers

This is a static traffic routing service placed between the network service provider's router and the internal network. The traffic routing service may be implemented at an IP level via screening rules in a router or at an application level via proxy gateways and services. Figure 5.3 shows a secure firewall with an IP packet screening router.

The firewall router filters incoming packets to permit or deny IP packets based on several screening rules. These screening rules, implemented into the router are automatically performed. Rules include target interface to which the packet is routed, known source IP address, and incoming packet protocol (TCP, UDP, ICMP). ICMP stands for Internet Control Message Protocol, a network management tool of the TCP/IP protocol suite (see Chapter 17).

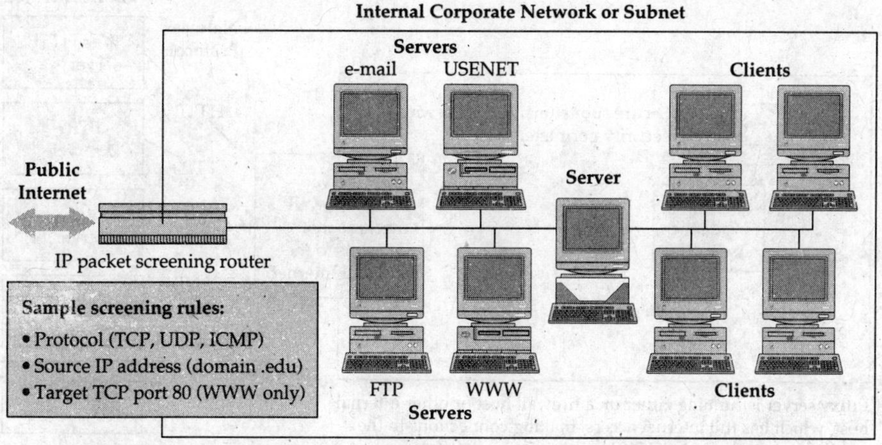


**Figure 5.3** Secure firewall with IP packet screening router

Although properly configured routers can plug many security holes, they do have several disadvantages. First, screening rules are difficult to specify, given the vastly diverse needs of users. Second, screening routers are fairly inflexible and do not easily extend to deal with functionality different from that preprogrammed by the vendor. Lastly, if the screening router is circumvented by a hacker, the rest of the network is open to attack.

### Proxy Application Gateways

A *proxy application gateway* is a special server that typically runs on a firewall machine. Their primary use is access to applications such as the World Wide Web from within a secure perimeter (see Fig. 5.4). Instead of talking directly to external WWW servers, each request from the client would be routed to a proxy on the firewall that is defined by the user. The proxy knows how to get through the firewall. An application-level proxy makes a firewall safely permeable for users in an organization, without creating a potential security hole through which hackers can get into corporate networks. The proxy waits for a request from inside the firewall, forwards the request to the remote server outside the firewall, reads the response, and then returns it to the client. In the usual case, all clients within a given subnet use the same proxy. This makes it possible for the proxy to execute efficient caching of documents that are requested by a number of clients.

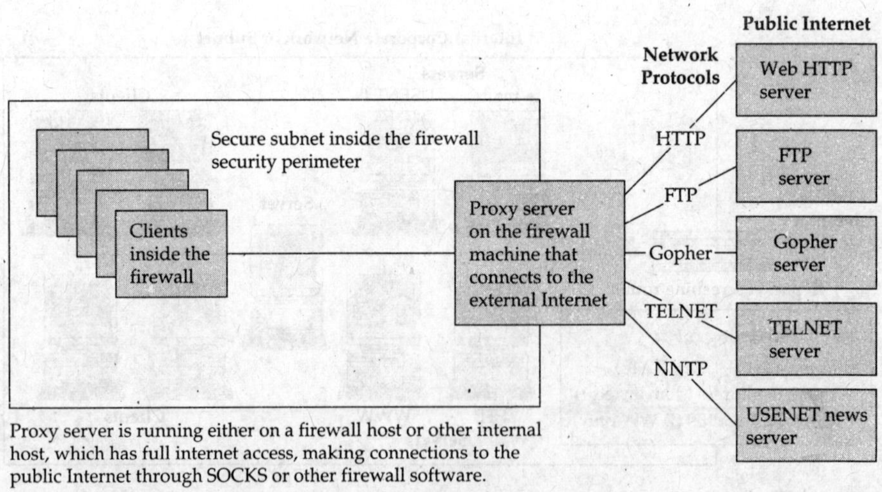


**Figure 5.4** Proxy servers on the World Wide Web

Proxy gateways have several advantages. They allow browser programmers to ignore the complex networking code necessary to support every firewall protocol and concentrate on important client issues. For instance, by using HTTP between the client and proxy, no protocol functionality is lost, since FTP, Gopher, and other Web protocols map well into HTTP methods (see Chapter 6). This feature is invaluable, for users needn't have separate, specially modified FTP, Gopher, and WAIS clients to get through a firewall—a single Web client with a proxy server handles all of these cases.

Proxies can manage network functions. Proxying allows for creating audit trails of client transactions, including client IP address, date and time, byte count, and success code. Any regular fields and meta-information fields in a transaction are candidates for logging. The proxy also can control access to services for individual methods, host and domain, and the like.

Given this firewall design in which the proxy acts as an intermediary, it is natural to design security-relevant mediation within the proxy. Proxy mediation helps mitigate security concerns by (1) limiting dangerous subsets of the HTTP protocol (a site's security policy may prohibit the use of some of HTTP's methods); (2) enforcing client and/or server access to designated hosts (an organization should have the capability to specify acceptable web sites); (3) implementing access control for network services that is lost when the proxy is installed (to restore the security policy enforced by the firewall); and (4) checking various protocols for well-formed commands. A bug existed in a previous version of the Mosaic browser that permitted servers to download a "Trojan horse" URL to the client that would cause the client to run an arbitrary program. The proxy must be in a position to filter dangerous URLs and malformed commands.

### Hardened Firewall Hosts

A *hardened firewall host* is a stripped-down machine that has been configured for increased security. This type of firewall requires inside or outside users to connect to the trusted applications on the firewall machine before connecting further. Generally, these firewalls are configured to protect against unauthenticated interactive log-ins from the external world. This, more than anything, helps prevent unauthorized users from logging into machines on the network.

Creating a hardened host requires several steps, among them:

- Removing all user accounts except those necessary for operation of the firewall, the logic being that, if users cannot log in to the firewall host, they cannot subvert the security measures

- Removing all noncrucial files and executables, especially network server programs and client programs like FTP and *Telnet*
- Extending traffic logging and monitoring to check remote access
- Disabling IP forwarding to prevent the firewall from forwarding unauthorized packets between the Internet and the enterprise network

The hardened firewall host method can provide a greater level of audit and security, in return for increased configuration cost and decreased level of service (because a proxy needs to be developed for each desired service). The old trade-off between ease of use and security must therefore be addressed.

Hardened firewall hosts also offer specific advantages, for example:

- *Concentration of security.* All modified software and logging is located on the firewall system as opposed to being distributed on many hosts.
- *Information hiding.* A firewall can "hide" names of internal systems or e-mail addresses, thereby revealing less information to outside hosts.
- *Centralized and simplified network services management.* Services such as FTP, e-mail, Gopher, and other similar services are located on the firewall system(s) as opposed to being maintained on many systems.

Given these advantages, there are some design problems, the most obvious being that certain types of network access may be blocked for some hosts, including *Telnet*, FTP, and X Windows. These disadvantages, are not unique to firewalls, however; network access could be restricted at the host level as well, depending on a site's security policy. A second problem with a firewall system is that it concentrates security in one spot as opposed to distributing it among systems; thus a compromise of the firewall could be disastrous to other less-protected systems on the subnet. This weakness can be countered, however, with the argument that lapses and weaknesses in security are more likely to be found as the number of systems in a subnet increases, thereby multiplying the ways in which subnets can be exploited. Another potential problem is that relatively few vendors have offered firewall systems until very recently. Most firewalls have been handcrafted by site administrators; the time and effort that could go into constructing a firewall is quite significant.

## Security Policies and Firewall Management

The firewall method of protection spans a continuum between ease of use and paranoid security. Before putting a firewall in place, the administrator who has the responsibility of designing, specifying, and implementing or overseeing the installation of a firewall must address a number of management issues [IW94].

The first issue reflects the security policy of the organization: Is the firewall in place explicitly to deny all services except those integral to the mission of connecting to the Internet, or is the firewall in place to provide a metered and audited method of regulating access in a nonthreatening manner? There are various degrees of paranoia between these positions; the final stance may be more the result of political and/or financial reasoning than technical or engineering. In short, many corporations and data centers have computing security policies and practices that dictate how data must be protected. A firewall is an embodiment of this security policy.

The second issue is: What is the level of monitoring, redundancy, and control? Having established the acceptable risk level by resolving the first issue, a checklist is made of what should be monitored, permitted, and denied. For instance, the firewall computer can control access based on time of day, organizations might allow employees to run e-mail or FTP at any time, but to read USENET news groups only between 7 P.M. and 8 A.M. In other words, the administrator begins by figuring out the overall objectives, combines a needs analysis with a risk assessment, then sorts out the conflicting requirements into a list to guide the implementation.

Frequently, technical design is dictated by financial concerns: How much will it cost either to buy or to implement? For example, a complete firewall product may cost anywhere between $0 to $200,000. At the low end, configuring the router will probably cost staff time. Implementing a high-end firewall from scratch might cost several man-months of effort. The systems management overhead is also a consideration. It's important, in other words, to evaluate firewalls not only in terms of what they cost now, but in terms of continuing maintenance costs such as support and upgrades.

Finally, firewall policies must be realistic reflections of the level of security in the entire network. For example, a site with top secret or classified data should not be hooking up to the Internet in the first place; or the systems with the really secret data should be isolated from the rest of the corporate network. Firewalls are poor protection against threats such as viruses. The ways of encoding binary files for transfer over networks are too numerous, and the formats and viruses too varied, to monitor them all. In other words, a firewall cannot replace user security-consciousness. In general, a firewall cannot protect against data-driven attacks—attacks in which something is mailed or copied to an internal host and then executed. This form of attack has occurred in the past against various versions of Sendmail.

Often, the hardest part of hooking to the Internet is not justifying the expense or effort, but convincing management that it is beneficial to do so. A firewall provides more than real security—it often plays an important role as a security blanket for management. A firewall also acts as the corporate "ambassador" to the other users of Internet. Many corporations use their firewall systems as a place to store public information about corporate products and services, files to download, bug-fixes, and so forth. Several of these systems have become important parts of the Internet service structure (e.g., instead of ftp.uu.net, gatekeeper.dec.com) and have reflected well on their corporate sponsors.

## 5.4 DATA AND MESSAGE SECURITY

The lack of data and message security on the Internet has become a high-profile problem due to the increasing number of merchants trying to spur commerce on the global network. For instance, credit card numbers in their plain text form create a risk when transmitted across the Internet where the possibility of the number falling into the wrong hands is relatively high. Would you be willing to type in your credit card number knowing the risk? Even worse, would you expose your customers to that risk? Just the thought of "sniffer" programs that collect credit card numbers en masse is enough to keep merchants away from on-line shopping given the possible lawsuits and other liability issues. In short, the lack of business transaction security is widely acknowledged as a major impediment to widespread e-commerce.

Historically, computer security was provided by the use of account passwords and limited physical access to a facility to bona fide users. As users began to dial in from their PCs and terminals at home, these measures were deemed sufficient. With the advent of remote users on internetworks, commercial transactions, mobile computers, and wireless technologies, simple password schemes are not sufficient to prevent attacks from sophisticated hackers.

Interestingly, the security problems plaguing network administrators resemble the problems facing transaction-based electronic commerce. Credit card numbers are similar to passwords in many ways. A growing threat on today's public (and sometimes even private) networks is the theft of passwords and other information that passes over them. Today's hacker has an array of tools to reach and manipulate information from remote sites as well as to engage in unauthorized eavesdropping. Unsuspecting and amateur users logging into remote hosts are the most vulnerable.

Transaction security issues can be divided into two types: data and message security. These are discussed below.

## Data Security

Electronic data security is of paramount importance at a time when people are considering banking and other financial transactions by PCs. Also, computer industry trends toward distributed computing, and nomadic or mobile computer users, only exacerbate security challenges. One major threat to data security is unauthorized network monitoring, also called *packet sniffing*.

Sniffer attacks begin when a computer is compromised and the cracker installs a packet sniffing program that monitors the network to which the machine is attached. The sniffer program watches for certain kinds of network traffic, typically for the first part of any *Telnet*, FTP, or rlogin sessions—sessions that legitimate users initiate to gain access to another system. The first part of the session contains the log-in ID, password, and user name of the person logging into another machine, all the necessary information a sniffer needs to log into other machines. In the course of several days, the sniffer could gather information on local users logging into remote machines. So, one insecure system on a network can expose to intrusion not only other local machines but also any remote systems to which the users connect.

The fact that someone can extract meaningful information from network traffic is nothing new. The problem has been magnified because this knowledge is no longer limited to a small set of responsible people but to a much larger set of potentially malicious folks. If the compromised system is on a backbone network, intruders can monitor any transit traffic traversing between nodes on that network. Network monitoring can rapidly expand the number of systems intruders are able to access, all with only minimal impact on the systems on which the sniffers are installed and with no visible impact on the systems being monitored. Users whose accounts and passwords are collected will not be aware that their sessions are being monitored, and subsequent intrusions will happen via legitimate accounts on the machines involved.

## Message Security

Threats to message security fall into three categories: confidentiality, integrity, and authentication.

### Message Confidentiality

Confidentiality is important for uses involving sensitive data such as credit card numbers. This requirement will be amplified when other kinds of data, such as employee records, government files, and social security numbers, begin traversing the network. Confidentiality precludes access to, or release of, such information to unauthorized users.

The environment must protect *all* message traffic. After successful delivery to their destination gateways, messages must be removed (expunged) from the public environment. All that remains is the accounting record of entry and delivery, including message length, authentication data, and perhaps the audit trail of message transfer agents that processed the message, but no more. All message archiving must be performed in well-protected systems. Provision must be made for the irrevocable emergency destruction of stored, undelivered messages, where necessary and when needed.

The vulnerability of data communications and message data to interception is exacerbated with the use of distributed networks and wireless links. The need for securing the communications link between computers via encryption is expected to rise.

### *Message and System Integrity*

Business transactions require that their contents remain unmodified during transport. In other words, information received must have the same content and organization as information sent. It must be clear that no one has added, deleted, or modified any part of the message. Unauthorized combining of messages either by intermixing or concatenating during submission, validation, processing, or delivery should not be allowed. One exception would be the capability of reformatting messages if requested by the message originator or the receiving party.

While confidentiality protects against the passive monitoring of data, mechanisms for integrity must prevent active attacks involving the modification of data. Error detection codes or checksums, sequence numbers, and encryption techniques are methods to enhance information integrity. Error detection codes operate on the entire message or selected fields within a message. Sequence numbers prevent reordering, loss, or replaying of messages by an attacker. Encryption techniques such as digital signatures can detect modifications of a message.

### *Message Sender Authentication/Identification*

For e-commerce, it is important that clients authenticate themselves to servers, that servers authenticate to clients, that both authenticate to each other. Authentication is a mechanism whereby the receiver of a transaction or message can be confident of the identity of the sender and/or the integrity of the message. In other words, authentication verifies the identity of an entity (a user or a service) using certain encrypted information transferred from the sender to the receiver.

The form of authentication, such as cryptographically signed certificates, must not be easily spoofed (falsified). The client and server must compare the origination address of transactions and messages with information associated with each service gateway to ascertain that the origination address is valid with respect to the gateway across which the message enters.

Whenever a message enters the public Internet for transfer, it must bear some unambiguous identification of the system from which it came. On the network this identification often takes the form of the IP address. If the identification is lacking, the delivery program will insert it. Sender authentication will be performed at the time a sender submits a message and/or by a gateway system when a message has been delivered to it. Consumer devices attached to the Internet will be expected to generate an unambiguous origin identification. The assignment of identifiers and their management will become an important responsibility.

Authentication in e-commerce basically requires the user to prove his or her identity for each requested service. The race among various vendors in the e-commerce today is to provide an authentication method that is easy to use, secure, reliable, and scalable. Third-party authentication services must exist within a distributed network environment where a sender cannot be trusted to identify itself correctly to a receiver. In short, authentication plays an important role in the implementation of business transaction security.

## Encryption as the Basis for Data and Message Security

Sensitive information that must travel over public channels (such as the Internet) can be defended by encrypting it. Encryption is the mutation of information in any form (text, video, graphics) into a representation unreadable by anyone without a decryption key. First, some elementary terminology. Suppose Anne wants to send you a message but doesn't want anyone but you to read it. Anne can *encrypt*, or *encipher*, the message, which means that Anne can scramble it in a hopelessly complicated way, rendering it unreadable to anyone except you, the intended recipient. Anne then supplies a cryptographic "key" to encrypt the message, and you have to use the same key to decipher or decrypt it [PGP94]. These are the basics of single-key cryptography.

The general scenario in the case of business transactions is as follows: A wishes to send a purchase order (PO) to B in such a way that only B can read it. A encrypts the PO, called the plaintext, with an encryption key and sends the encrypted PO, called the ciphertext, to B. B decrypts the ciphertext with the decryption key and reads the PO. A hacker, C, may obtain the ciphertext as it passes on the network, but without the decryption key it is impossible to recover the message even if C has access to supercomputers.

Broadly speaking, there are two types of encryption methods: secret-key cryptography and public-key cryptography [SCHN96].

### *Secret-Key Cryptography*

Secret-key cryptography involves the use of a shared key for both encryption by the transmitter and decryption by the receiver. Shared-key techniques suffer from the problem of key distribution, since shared keys must be securely distributed to each pair of communicating parties. Secure-key distribution becomes cumbersome in large networks.

To illustrate secret-key cryptography, A encrypts a message with a secret key and e-mails the encrypted message to B. On receiving the message, B checks the header to identify the sender, then unlocks his electronic key storage area and takes out the duplicate of the secret key. B then uses the secret key to decrypt the message.

The Achilles heel of secret-key cryptography is getting the sender and receiver to agree on the secret key without a third party finding out. This is difficult because if A and B are in separate sites, they must trust not being overheard during face-to-face meetings or over a public messaging system (a phone system, a postal service) when the secret key is being exchanged. Anyone who overhears or intercepts the key in transit can later read all encrypted messages using that key.

The generation, transmission, and storage of keys is called key management; all cryptosystems must deal with key management issues. Although the secret-key method is quite feasible and practical for one-on-one document interchange, it does not scale. In a business environment where a company deals with thousands of on-line customers, it is impractical to assume that key management will be flawless. Hence, we can safely assume that secret-key cryptography will not be a dominant player in e-commerce given its difficulty providing secure key management.

### *Data Encryption Standard (DES)*

A widely-adopted implementation of secret-key cryptography is Data Encryption Standard (DES). The actual software to perform DES is readily available at no cost to anyone who has access to the Internet. DES was introduced in 1975 by IBM, the National Security Agency (NSA), and the National Bureau of Standards (NBS) (which is now called NIST). DES has been extensively researched and studied over the last twenty years and is definitely the most well-known and widely used cryptosystem in the world.

DES is a secret-key, symmetric cryptosystem: When used for communication, both sender and receiver must know the same secret key, which is used both to encrypt and decrypt the message. DES can also be used for single-user encryption, for example, to store files on a hard disk in encrypted form. In a multiuser environment, however, secure-key distribution becomes difficult; public-key cryptography, discussed in the next subsection, was developed to solve this problem.

DES operates on 64-bit blocks with a 56-bit secret key. Designed for hardware implementation, its operation is relatively fast and works well for large bulk documents or encryption. Instead of defining just one encryption algorithm, DES defines a whole family of them. With a few exceptions, a different algorithm is generated for each secret key. This means that everybody can be told about the algorithm and your message will still be secure. You just need to tell others your secret key, a number less than $2^{56}$. The number $2^{56}$ is also large enough to make it difficult to break the code using a brute force attack (trying to break the cypher by using all possible keys).

DES has withstood the test of time. Despite the fact that its algorithm is well known, it is impossible to break the cypher without using tremendous amounts of computing power. A new technique for improving the security of DES is triple encryption (Triple DES), that is, encrypting each message block using three different keys in succession. Triple DES, thought to be equivalent to doubling the key size of DES, to 112 bits, should prevent decryption by a third party capable of single-key exhaustive search [MH81]. Of course, using triple-encryption takes three times as long as single-encryption DES. If you use DES three times on the same message with different secret keys, it is virtually impossible to break it using existing algorithms. Over the past few years several new, faster symmetric algorithms have been developed, but DES remains the most frequently used.

### Public-Key Cryptography

A more powerful form of cryptography involves the use of public keys. Public-key techniques involve a pair of keys; a private key and a public key associated with each user. Information encrypted by the private key can be decrypted only using the corresponding public key. The private key, used to encrypt transmitted information by the user, is kept secret. The public key is used to decrypt information at the receiver and is not kept secret. Since only the bona fide author of an encrypted message has knowledge of the private key, a successful decryption using the corresponding public key verifies the identity of the author and ensures message integrity.

Public keys can be maintained in some central repository and retrieved to decode or encode information. Public-key techniques alleviate the problem of distribution of keys [DH76]. Let's examine how this process works.

Each party to a public-key pairing receives a pair of keys, the public key and the private key. When A wishes to send a message to B, A looks up B's public key in a directory, A then uses the public key to encrypt the message and mail it to B. B uses the secret private key to decrypt the message and read it. Anyone can send an encrypted message to B but only B can read it. Unless, a third party, say C, has access to B's private key, it is impossible to decrypt the message sent by A. This ensures confidentiality.

Clearly, one advantage of public-key cryptography is that no one can figure out the private key from the corresponding public key. Hence, the key management problem is mostly confined to the management of private keys. The need for sender and receiver to share secret information over public channels is completely eliminated: All transactions involve only public keys, and no private key is ever transmitted or shared. The secret key never leaves the user's PC. Thus a sender can send a confidential message merely by using public information and that message can be decrypted only with a private key in the sole possession of the intended recipient.

Furthermore, public-key cryptography can be used for sender authentication, known as *digital signatures*. Here's how authentication is achieved using public-key cryptography: A, to digitally sign a document, puts his private key and the document together and performs a computation on the composite (key+document) to generate a unique number called the digital signature. For instance, when an electronic document, such as an order form with a credit card number, is run through the method, the output is a unique "fingerprint" of the document.

This "fingerprint" is attached to the original message and further encrypted with the signer A's private key. The result of the second encryption is then sent to B, who then first decrypts the document using A's public key. B checks whether the message has been tampered with or is coming from a third party C, posing as A. To verify the signature, B does some further computation involving the original document, the purported signature, and A's public key. If the results of the computation generate a matching "fingerprint" of the document, the digital signature is verified as genuine; otherwise, the signature may be fraudulent or the message altered, and they are discarded. This method is the basis for secure e-commerce, variations of which are being explored by several companies.

Several implementations of these popular encryption techniques are currently employed. In public-key encryption, the RSA implementation dominates and is considered very secure, but using it for overseas traffic conflicts with the U.S. government's position on export of munitions technology of military importance. Clearly, the government has not reckoned with the Internet and transborder data flow.

### RSA and Public-Key Cryptography

RSA is a public-key cryptosystem for both encryption and authentication developed in 1977 by Ron Rivest, Adi Shamir, and Leonard Adleman. RSA's system uses a matched pair of encryption and decryption keys, each performing a one-way transformation of the data. RSA is also developing digital signatures, which are mathematical algorithms that encrypt an entire document.

The security of RSA is predicated on the fact that it is extremely difficult—even for the fastest computers—to factor large numbers that are the products of two prime numbers (keys), each greater than $2^{512}$. RSA is important because it enables digital signatures, which can be used to authenticate electronic documents the same way handwritten signatures are used to authenticate paper documents. Here's how a digital signature works for an electronic document to be sent from the sender X to the receiver Y: X runs a program that uses a hash algorithm to generate a digital fingerprint—a pattern of bits that uniquely identifies a much larger pattern of bits—for the document and encrypts the fingerprint with his private key.

This is X's digital signature, which is transmitted along with the data. Y decrypts the signature with X's public key and runs the same hash program on the document. If the digital fingerprint output by the hash program does not match the fingerprint sent by X (after that has been decrypted), then the signature is invalid. If the fingerprints do match, however, then Y can be quite sure that the digital signature is authentic. If the document were altered en route, the fingerprints will not match (the output from the hash programs will be different) and the receiver will know that data tampering occured. If the sender's signature has been forged (encrypted with the wrong private key), the fingerprints won't match either. Therefore the digital signature verifies both the identity of the sender and the authenticity of the data in the document.

The use of RSA is undergoing a period of rapid expansion and may become ubiquitous. It is currently used in a wide variety of products, platforms, and industries around the world. It is being incorporated into the World Wide Web browsers such as NetScape, giving it a wider audience. In hardware, RSA can be found in secure telephones, on Ethernet network cards, and on smart cards. Adoption of RSA seems to be proceeding more quickly for authentication (digital signatures) than for privacy (encryption), perhaps in part because products for authentication are easier to export than those for privacy.

### Mixing RSA and DES

RSA allows two important functions not provided by DES: secure key exchange without prior exchange of keys, and digital signatures. For encrypting messages, RSA and DES are usually combined as follows: first the message is encrypted with a random DES key, then, before being sent over an insecure communications channel, the DES key is encrypted with RSA. Together, the DES-encrypted message and the RSA-encrypted DES key are sent. This protocol is known as an *RSA digital envelope*.

Why not just use RSA to encrypt the whole message and not use DES at all? Although RSA may be fine for small messages, DES (or another cipher) is preferable for larger messages due to its greater speed. In some situations, RSA is not necessary and DES alone is sufficient, for example, in multiuser environments where secure DES-key agreement can take place (the two parties meeting in private). Also, RSA is usually not necessary in a single-user environment; for example, if you want to keep your personal files encrypted, just do so with DES using, say, a password as the DES key.

RSA, and public-key cryptography in general, is best suited for a multiuser environment. Also, any system in which digital signatures are desired needs RSA or some other public-key system.

### Digital Public-Key Certificates

The most difficult aspect of creating an effective multiparty transaction system is the distribution of public keys. Because the keys are intended to be public and widely distributed, secrecy is not a concern; anyone should be able to get a copy of a public key. Rather, the primary concern is authenticity. An impostor could easily create a private/public key pair and distribute the public key, claiming it belonged to someone else. For instance, if A in England is doing business with B in Canada and wants to encrypt information so that only B can read it, A must first get the public key of B from a key directory. That's where the problem lies. There is nothing that says that this public key information is valid and not a forgery put there by C impersonating B.

One solution to this problem is a public-key certificate. A *public-key certificate* is a data structure, digitally signed by a certification authority (also known as the certificate issuer), that binds a public-key value to the identity of the entity holding the corresponding private key. The latter entity is known as the *subject of the certificate*. In essence, a certificate is a copy of a public key and an identifier (number), digitally signed by a trusted party.

The problem is then transformed into finding a trusted third party to create these certificates. A public-key user needs to obtain and validate a certificate containing the required public key. This is where it gets complicated. If the public-key user does not already have a copy of the public key of the trusted party that signed the certificate, then the user may need an additional certificate to get that public key. In such cases, a chain of multiple certificates may be needed, comprising a certificate of the public-key owner signed by one certification authority, and additional certificates of certification authorities signed by other certification authorities.

### Clipper Chip

Clipper is an encryption chip developed as part of the Capstone project. Announced by the White House in April 1993, Clipper was designed to balance the competing concerns of federal law enforcement agencies with those of private citizens and industry. Law enforcement agencies wish to have access—for example, by wire-tapping—to the communications of suspected criminals, and these needs are threatened by secure cryptography.

Clipper technology attempts to balance these needs by using escrowed keys. The idea is that communications would be encrypted with a secure algorithm, but the keys would be kept by one or more third parties (the "escrow agencies") and made available to law enforcement agencies when authorized by a court-issued warrant. Thus, for example, personal communications would be impervious to recreational eavesdroppers and commercial communications would be impervious to industrial espionage, and yet the FBI could listen in on suspected terrorists or gangsters.

Skipjack, designed by the NSA, is the encryption algorithm contained in the Clipper chip. It uses one 80-bit key to encrypt and decrypt 64-bit blocks of data. Skipjack can be used in the same way as DES and may be more secure than DES, since it uses 80-bit keys and scrambles the data for 32 steps, or "rounds"; by contrast, DES uses 56-bit keys and scrambles the data for only 16 rounds.

The details of Skipjack are classified. The decision not to make the details of the algorithm publicly available has been widely criticized, and many are suspicious that Skipjack is not secure, either due to design oversight or to deliberate introduction of a secret trapdoor. By contrast, the many failed attempts to find weaknesses in DES over the years have made people confident in the security of DES. Since Skipjack is not public, the same scrutiny cannot be applied, and thus a corresponding level of confidence may not arise.

Aware of such criticism, the government invited a small group of independent cryptographers to examine the Skipjack algorithm. Their report stated that, although their study was too limited to reach a definitive conclusion, they nevertheless believe that Skipjack is secure [CACM94]. Another consequence of Skipjack's classified status is that it cannot be implemented in software, but only in hardware by government-authorized chip manufacturers.

### Digital Signatures

In the case of business transactions, authentication refers to the use of digital signatures, which play a function for digital documents similar to that played by handwritten signatures for printed documents: The signature is an unforgeable piece of data asserting that a named person wrote or otherwise agreed to the document to which the signature is attached.

Unlike encryption, digital signatures are a recent development, the need for which has arisen with the proliferation of electronic commerce. The recipient, as well as a third party, can verify that the document did indeed originate from the person whose signature is attached and that the document has not been altered since it was signed.

A secure digital signature system thus consists of two parts: a method of signing a document such that forgery is infeasible, and a method of verifying that a signature was actually generated by whomever it represents. Furthermore, secure digital signatures cannot be repudiated; that is, the signer of a document cannot later disown it by claiming it was forged.

**Digital Signature Standard (DSS).** The Digital Signature Standard specifies a Digital Signature Algorithm (DSA) as part of the U.S. government's Capstone project. It was selected to be the digital authentication standard of the U.S. government; whether the government should in fact adopt it as the official standard is still under debate. The Internal Revenue Service pushed for DSS because all its efforts to conduct electronic commerce under Tax Systems Modernization depend on the ability to send signatures over networks electronically. For a detailed description of DSS, see [NIST92].

DSS has been controversial in the computer industry, which had hoped the government would choose the RSA algorithm as the official standard since RSA has become the most widely used authentication algorithm. The DSS is also controversial, because vendors seeking to use DSS face lawsuits from Public Key Partners Inc., which alleges the government infringed on its patented public-key encryption methods.

Criticism of DSS has focused on a few main issues: It lacks key exchange capability; the underlying cryptosystem is too recent and has been subject to too little scrutiny for users to be confident of its strength; verification of signatures with DSS is too slow; the existence of a second authentication standard will cause hardship to computer hardware and software vendors, who have already standardized on RSA; and the process by which DSS was chosen in too secretive and arbitrary. In the DSS system, signature generation is faster than signature verification, whereas in the RSA system, signature verification is faster than signature generation. NIST claims that it is an advantage of DSS that signing is faster, but many people in cryptography think that it is preferable for verification to be the faster operation.

The most serious criticisms of DSS involve security. DSS was originally proposed with a fixed 512-bit key size, but after much criticism that this is not secure enough, NIST revised DSS to allow key sizes up to 1024 bits (yes $2^{1024}$). More critical, however, is the fact that DSS has not been around long enough to withstand repeated attempts to break it; although the algorithm is old, the particular form of the algorithm used in DSS was first proposed for cryptographic use in 1989 by Schnorr [CACM94] and has not received much public study.

In general, any new cryptosystem could harbor serious flaws that are discovered only after years of scrutiny by cryptographers. DES and RSA have withstood over fifteen years of vigorous examination. In the absence of mathematical proofs of security, nothing builds confidence in a cryptosystem like sustained attempts to crack it. Although DSS may well turn out to be a strong cryptosystem, its relatively short history will leave doubts for years to come. Some researchers warned about the existence of "trapdoor" primes in DSS, which could enable a key to be broken. These trapdoor primes are rare and are avoidable if proper key generation procedures are followed.

## 5.5 CHALLENGE-RESPONSE SYSTEMS

Today, with the notion of boundaries between networks fast disappearing, user authentication is becoming increasingly important in client–server access. Also, business transactions on the network are taking the form of a client–server interaction. So, what we effectively have is a hybrid where the same method is being used to guard network resources as well as business transactions.

For instance, if a client (user) accesses a for-pay information publishing server, the server (merchant) must make sure that the client is a bona fide user. The merchant will therefore use some form of authentication to ensure that the client is indeed who it claims to be. The merchant can choose from several challenge-response authentication methods: smart cards or third-party authentication.

## Token or Smart-Card Authentication

Whereas memorized passwords had been sufficient in the past to authenticate users (a sharp-eyed observer might learn the password when users log on), smart cards will be used to enhance security. A *smart card* computes a password or encryption key and furnishes it directly to the computer for the log-on procedure.. When a user wants to access the computer, he or she logs on with a stagnant password, which then quickly issues an eight-character password. The user then types the eight-character password into the card, which resembles a hand-held calculator running the same mathematical equations as the computer. Finally, the card kicks out a one-time password that's acceptable. To defend against loss or theft, the cards usually require the user to enter a personal identification number as well.

These hand-held password generators (HPGs) are about the size of a pocket calculator and generate a random password for each access attempt. The algorithm in the HPG is initialized with "seed" data unique to the user and is synchronized with the algorithm running on the host. HPGs typically work on a challenge-response basis where, on an access attempt, the host presents the remote user with some numeric code. The user then enters that code into the HPG, which responds with the password to be used during this access attempt. Access is granted by the host if the password returned by the user is what would have been calculated by the HPG's algorithm.

## Third-Party Authentication

In third-party authentication systems, the password or encryption key itself never travels over the network. Rather, an "authentication server" maintains a file of obscure facts about each registered user. At log-on time, the server demands the entry of a randomly chosen fact—mother's maiden name is a traditional example—but this information is not sent to the server. Instead, the server uses it (along with other data, such as the time of day) to compute a token. The server then transmits an encrypted message containing the token, which can be decoded with the user's key. If the key was properly computed, the user can decrypt the message. The message contains an authentication token that allows users to log on to network services.

There are many variations on this theme. For example, users can tell the authentication server with which remote computer they want to converse. It sends two encrypted tokens: one for the user and another to send to the remote computer. This second token is doubly encrypted, and users pass it along after peeling off one layer of encryption. The remote machine, which has also authenticated itself with the server, supplies the second layer of decoding.

**Kerberos.** *Kerberos* is a popular third-party authentication protocol. Kerberos is an encryption-based system that uses secret key encryption designed to authenticate users and network connections. It was developed at MIT's Project Athena in the 1980s and is named after the three-headed dog of Greek mythology that guards the entrance to Hades. Like its namesake, Kerberos is charged with preventing unauthorized access and does it so well that it is now a de facto standard for effecting secure, authenticated communications across a network.

The assumption of Kerberos is that the distributed environment is made up of unsecured workstations, moderately secure servers, and highly secure key-management machines. Kerberos provides a means of verifying the identities of requestor (a workstation user or a network server) on an unprotected network. The goal is to accomplish security without relying on authentication by the host computer, without basing trust on the IP addresses, without requiring physical security of all the hosts on the network, and under the assumption that IP packets on the network can be read, modified, and inserted at will. Kerberos performs authentication under these conditions as a trusted third-party authentication service by using conventional cryptography (secret key).

The authentication process proceeds as follows: Client A sends a request to the Kerberos authentication server (KAS) requesting "credentials" for a given server, B. The KAS responds with the following information, which is encrypted in A's key:

- A "ticket" for the server. This ticket contains B's key.
- A temporary encryption key (often called a "session key").

A then transmits—the client's identity and a copy of the session key, both encrypted in B's key—to B.

The session key (now shared by the client and server) is used to authenticate the client and used to authenticate the server in future transaction. The session key is then used to encrypt further communication between the two parties or to exchange a separate subsession key to be used to encrypt further communication.

How about attacks from other parties? To verify the identities of the principals in a transaction, the client transmits the ticket to the server. Since the ticket is sent "in the clear" (parts of it are encrypted, but this encryption does not thwart replay) and might be intercepted and reused by an attacker, additional information is sent to prove that the message was originated by the principal to whom the ticket was issued. This authenticator information is encrypted in the session key and includes a timestamp. The timestamp proves that the message was recently generated and is not a replay from some stored value. Encrypting the authenticator in the session key proves that it was generated by a party possessing the session key. Because no one except the requesting client and the server know the session key (it is never sent over the network in the clear), the identity of the client is guaranteed.

This approach provides detection of both replay attacks and message stream modification attacks. It is accomplished by generating and transmitting a collision-proof checksum (called a hash or digest function) of the client's message, encrypted with the session key. Privacy and integrity of the messages exchanged between principals can be secured by encrypting the data to be passed using the session key passed in the ticket and contained in the credentials [RFC1510].

Kerberos, like other secret-key systems, requires trust in a third party (in this case the Kerberos server) to perform centralized key management and administrative functions. The server maintains a database containing the secret keys of all users, generates session keys whenever two users wish to communicate securely, and authenticates the identity of a user who requests certain network services. If the server were compromised, the integrity of the whole system would fail.

Kerberos may be adequate for those who do not need the more robust functions and properties of public-key systems. Unlike a public-key authentication system, Kerberos does not produce digital signatures: Kerberos was designed to authenticate requests for network resources rather than to authenticate authorship of documents. Kerberos provides real-time authentication in a distributed environment, but does not provide for future third-party verification of documents.

In the electronic commerce world, Kerberos can be used for third-party payment servers that grant tickets to clients for usage of some server resource. Implementations that depend entirely on Kerberos are NetCash [MN93] and NetCheque [http://nii-server.isi.edu/info/NetCheque/]. NetCash is a framework that supports real-time electronic payments with provision of anonymity over an unsecure public network. Users registered with NetCheque (Kerberos) accounting servers are able to write checks to other users. When deposited, the check authorizes the transfer of account balances from the account against which the check was drawn to the account to which the check was deposited (see Chapter 8).

## 5.6 ENCRYPTED DOCUMENTS AND ELECTRONIC MAIL

E-mail users who desire confidentiality and sender authentication are using encryption. Encryption is simply intended to keep personal thoughts personal. Some users are already using Pretty Good Privacy (PGP); others are starting to use Privacy Enhanced Mail (PEM). Both will be described.

E-mail is typically encrypted for the reason that all network correspondence is open for eavesdropping. Internet e-mail is obviously far less secure than the postal system, where envelopes protect correspondence from casual snooping. A glance at the header area of any e-mail message, by contrast, will show that it has passed through a number of nodes on its way to you. Every one of these nodes presents the opportunity for snooping.

Everyday communication over phone and fax lines entails security risks. Despite leaps in technology and wide usage, fax transmissions are not yet widely encrypted. The main reason is the inconvenience of equipping both the sending and receiving machines with compatible encryption before facsimile transmission; the fax protocol has no convenient place for inserting nonfax functions such as encryption, and until recently there has been little awareness of security threats among fax users. However, increasing use of fax transmissions by businesses who wish to keep their corporate information and finances confidential and an increasing awareness of the security problems will increase the availability of products that encrypt fax communications [CACM94].

E-mail software is increasingly incorporating specific options that simplify encryption and decryption. Examination of encrypted information is nontrivial; each file must be decrypted even before it can be examined. If the file itself proves to contain embedded, compressed, encrypted files, those too must be expanded and decrypted. This process may need repeating several times before the innermost files' contents are discernible. Let's look at two e-mail encryption schemes that are being deployed on the Internet.

### Privacy Enhanced Mail Standard

PEM is the Internet Privacy Enhanced Mail standard, designed, proposed, but not yet officially adopted, by the Internet Activities Board to provide secure electronic mail over the Internet. Designed to work with current Internet e-mail formats, PEM includes encryption, authentication, and key management, and allows use of both public-key and secret-key cryptosystems. The system supports multiple cryptographic tools: for each mail message, the specific encryption algorithm, digital signature algorithm, hash function, and so on are specified in the header. PEM explicitly supports only a few cryptographic algorithms; others may be added later. It uses the DES algorithm for encryption and the RSA algorithm for sender authentication and key management. PEM also provides support for nonrepudiation, which allows the third-party recipient of a forwarded message to verify the identity of the message originator (not just the message forwarder) and to verify whether any of the original text has been altered.

Although PEM is not yet widespread, a number of vendors are offering versions of it in conjunction with or integrated into their commercial e-mail applications. Trusted Information Systems, Inc. has developed a free non-commercial implementation of PEM, and other implementations should soon be available as well. RIPEM, a program developed by Mark Riordan, enables secure Internet e-mail; it provides both encryption and digital signatures, using RSA and DES routines from RSAREF (a set of routines provided by RSA). RIPEM is not fully PEM-compatible; for example, it does not currently support certificates. However, future versions will include certificates and will be fully compliant with the PEM standard. RIPEM is available free for noncommercial use in the United States and Canada. To get RIPEM, FTP into ripem.msu.edu. The details of PEM can be found in Internet RFCs (requests for comments) 1421 through 1424.

## Pretty Good Privacy (PGP)

Pretty Good Privacy (PGP) is an implementation of public-key cryptography based on RSA. It is a free software package developed by Phillip Zimmerman [PGP94] that encrypts e-mail. Since being published in the United States as freeware in June 1991, PGP has spread rapidly and has since become the de facto worldwide standard for encryption of e-mail. It is freely available for DOS, Macintosh, UNIX, Amiga, VMS, Atari, and OS/2 systems. The latest version is available from MIT via FTP://net-dist.mit.edu, in the pub/PGP directory.

PGP provides secure encryption of documents and data files that even advanced supercomputers are hard pressed to "crack." The process is simple enough that anyone with a PC can do it with almost no effort. For authentication, PGP employs the RSA public-key encryption scheme and the MD5 (Message Digest version 5) developed by Rivest, a one-way hash function to form a digital signature that assures the receiver that an incoming message is authentic (that it comes from the alleged sender and that it has not been altered).

The transaction sequence begins when the sender types an e-mail and MD5 is used to generate a digital signature of the e-mail. The digital signature is then encrypted with RSA using the sender's private key, and the result is prepended to the e-mail. The receiver uses RSA with the sender's public key to decrypt and recover the digital signature. The receiver then generates a new digital signature for the recovered e-mail and compares it with the decrypted digital signature. If the two match, the message is accepted as authentic. Don't worry, all this is done automatically by the program.

The combination of MD5 and RSA provides an effective digital-signature scheme. RSA's strength assures the receiver that only the possessor of the private key can generate the signature, and MD5's strength assures the receiver that no one else can generate a message that matches the content of the original message.

PGP provides confidentiality by encrypting messages to be transmitted or to be stored locally as files. In both cases, the conventional encryption algorithm known as IDEA (international data encryption algorithm) is used. Relatively new, IDEA is considered to be much stronger than the widely used DES and is not subject to government-imposed cryptographic controls.

Any secret-key encryption system must address the problem of key distribution; in PGP, each key is used only once. That is, a new key is generated as a random number for each message. This key is bound to the message and transmitted with it. Let's examine the process.

When the sender generates a message, the system generates a random 128-bit number as a session key for that message only. The message is encrypted, using IDEA with the session key. The session key is encrypted with RSA, using the receiver's public key, and is prepended to the message. The receiver uses RSA with his or her private key to decrypt and recover the session key. The session key then decrypts the message.

IDEA is much faster than RSA and reduces message encryption time as only the key is encrypted using RSA. The IDEA/RSA combination is used in preference to simply using RSA to directly encrypt the message. Also, the use of RSA solves the session-key distribution problem, because only the receiver is able to recover the session key that is prepended to the message. Thus, to the extent that RSA is secure, the entire scheme is secure. To this end, PGP provides the user with several RSA key-size options: casual (384 bits)—known to be breakable, but with much computing effort; Commercial (512 bits)—possibly breakable by supercomputer running for several days; military (1024 bits)—generally believed to be unbreakable.

Both confidentiality and authentication services can be used for the same message. First, a signature is generated for the plain text message and is prepended to the message. Then, the plaintext message, along with the signature, is encrypted using IDEA, and the session key is encrypted using RSA. In summary, when both services are used, the sender first signs the message with his or her own private key, then encrypts the message with a session key, and then encrypts the session key with the receiver's public key.

Message encryption is often applied after compression to strengthen cryptographic security. The compression technique used for PGP is PKZIP, a popular compression algorithm originally developed for DOS. As a default, PGP compresses a message after applying the signature but before encryption. Compression reduces the size of an e-mail transmission. Because the compressed message has less information than the original plaintext, cryptanalysis is more difficult.

One of the bottlenecks for PGP is key management. In the PGP documentation, Phil Zimmerman captures the importance of this problem: "This whole business of protecting public keys from tampering is the single most difficult problem in practical public-key applications. It is the Achilles' heel of public-key cryptography, and a lot of software complexity is tied up in solving this one problem."

A number of approaches are possible within PGP for minimizing the risk of a user's public-key file containing false public keys, such as physically passing the key via surface mail or floppy disk, verifying a key by telephone, or transferring and confirming the key through a trusted third party. But another, more likely method is already being used: The use of a trusted key server and verification by monitoring the sender's PGP fingerprints in postings to USENET news groups and other public forums.

In summary, PGP is already being widely used, and its growth is being fueled by the rapid growth in Internet use and the increasing reliance on e-mail for everything from legal documents to love letters. Many people now routinely include their PGP fingerprint in e-mail messages.

## 5.7 U.S. GOVERNMENT REGULATIONS AND ENCRYPTION

Several cryptographic protocols cannot be exported from the United States because they come under the category of weapons. This restriction creates a barrier for global electronic commerce. The challenge is to work around the existing law to enable various electronic commerce applications.

The U.S. government has been reluctant to grant export licenses for encryption products stronger than some basic level (not publicly stated).

Under current regulations, a vendor seeking to export a product using cryptography first submits a request to the State Department's Defense Trade Control office.

All cryptographic products need export licenses from the State Department, acting under authority of the International Traffic in Arms Regulation (ITAR), which defines cryptographic devices, including software, as munitions.

Export jurisdiction may then be passed to the Department of Commerce, whose export procedures are generally simple and efficient. If jurisdiction remains with the State Department, further review will be required before export is either approved or denied; the National Security Agency (NSA) may become involved at this point. The NSA has de facto control over export of cryptographic products. The State Department will not grant a license without NSA approval and routinely grants licenses whenever NSA does approve. Therefore the policy decisions over exporting cryptography ultimately rest with the NSA.

Export policy is currently a matter of great controversy, as many vendors consider current export regulations overly restrictive and burdensome. The Software Publishers Association (SPA) has been negotiating with the government to ease export license restrictions; one agreement was reached that allows simplified procedures for export of two bulk encryption ciphers, RC2 and RC4, when the key size is limited. Also, the export policy was made less restrictive for foreign subsidiaries and overseas offices of U.S. companies.

U.S. export policy is expected to undergo significant change in the next few years [CACM94]. A public debate is the only way to reach a consensus policy to best satisfy competing interests: national security and law enforcement agencies want restrictions on cryptography, especially for export, whereas other government agencies and private industry want greater freedom to use and export cryptography. In the past, export policy has been decided solely by agencies concerned with national security, without much input from those who wish to encourage commerce.

## Business and Legal Issues

Currently, commercial use of encryption is concentrated within financial institutions, where encryption both protects the contents of messages and ensures their authenticity. If a bank receives an encrypted money transfer and can successfully decrypt it using the sending bank's key, it can be sure the transfer is authentic.

Three problems deter widespread acceptance of encryption. First, successful encryption requires that all participating parties use the same encryption scheme. Within an organization, or a group expected to cooperate (such as banks), standards have to be established that make encryption feasible.

The distribution of keys has been a second barrier to wider use of encryption, as there is no easy way to distribute the secret key to a person not known. The only safe way to communicate the key is in person, and then the distributor must provide a different secret key for each person. Even public key schemes require a method for key distribution.

The final deterrent to widespread acceptance of encryption is its difficulty to use. The user interface to encryption must be simplified. For encryption to flourish an average consumer (Joe or Jane Consumer) must find the software easy to use for commercial applications. Currently, it is well known that consumer will not wait more than a few seconds for information access or retrieval. So, in the future we can expect encryption to be done by fast hardware rather than software.

As encryption becomes user friendly and commonplace in the commercial world, a new legal problem is expected to surface: Employers will be confronted with the problem of producing documents that only certain employees can decrypt. With modern labor force mobility, the problem will become an order of magnitude more severe: A company will be confronted with the task of producing documents encrypted by an ex-employee who may not wish to cooperate.

Will courts tolerate the production of pivotal evidence in encrypted form? Will a party's counsel produce it without first having it dycrypted, leaving the opposing counsel with the task of "cracking" the encryption? On what basis could counsel claim such a data file was irrelevant or privileged? Or will the producer have the onus of contacting the ex-employee in the hope that the employee will remember the password necessary for decryption? Will the courts compel individuals to provide their passwords? Imagine the problems if all employees routinely used encryption and changed their passwords regularly—both are considered good practice in security-minded organizations.

It may not be unusual, in the years ahead, to find that 100 percent of all electronic mail messages, and perhaps 30 to 50 percent of computer-based documents, are stored in encrypted form [AJL94].

## 5.8 SUMMARY

Today's computer systems, linked by global networks, face a variety of security threats that can result in significant financial and information losses.

Threats vary considerably, from threats to system availability from malicious hackers attempting to crash a system, to data or transaction integrity threats. An understanding of the types of threats in today's computing environment can assist a security manager in selecting appropriate cost-effective controls to protect valuable information resources. An overview of many of today's common threats will be useful to organizations studying their own threat environments with a view toward developing solutions specific to their organization.

Chapter 6

# Electronic Commerce and the World Wide Web

We have broadly defined electronic commerce as a modern business methodology that addresses the desire of firms, consumers, and management to cut costs while improving the quality of goods and increasing the speed of services. The need for electronic commerce stems from the demand within business and government to make better use of computing, that is, to better apply computer technology to improve business processes and information exchange both within an enterprise and across organizations. In short, electronic commerce appears to be an integrating force that represents the digital convergence of twenty-first century business applications and computing technologies.

Electronic commerce applications emphasize the generation and exploitation of new business opportunity and, to use the popular buzzword, "generate business value." For instance, when buyer–seller transactions occur in the electronic marketplace, information is accessed, absorbed, arranged, and sold in different ways. In fact, the information about a product or service is separated from the physical product or service and has become important on its own. In some cases, this information can become as crucial as the actual product or service in terms of its effect on a company's profits. A good example of this is 900-based customer service, where a customer is charged (from $1.00 to $3.99 per minute) for access to derived information or even secondary information about a product or service. In short, information-based business transactions are creating new ways of doing business and even new types of business.

Electronic commerce applications are quite varied. In its most common form, e-commerce is also used to denote the paperless exchange of business information using EDI, electronic mail (e-mail), electronic bulletin boards, electronic funds transfer (EFT), and other similar technologies. These technologies are normally applied in high-payoff areas, recognizing that paper-handling activities usually increase expenses without adding value. On the other hand, the term *electronic commerce* is used to describe a new on-line approach to performing traditional functions such as payment and funds transfer, order entry and processing, invoicing, inventory management, cargo tracking, electronic catalogs, and point-of-sale data gathering. More recently, companies have realized that the advertising, marketing, and customer support functions are also part of the electronic commerce application domain. These business functions act as initiators to the entire order management cycle that incorporates the more established notions of electronic commerce. In short, what we are witnessing is the use of the term *electronic commerce* as an umbrella concept to integrate a wide range of new and old applications (see Fig. 6.1).

Despite the changes taking place, businesses have three goals: stay competitive, improve productivity, and deliver quality service. These goals are the guiding buoys for firms plotting their course in the turbulent waters of electronic commerce. There are other factors that companies need to keep in mind. First, most companies have already made enormous information technology investments to automate their key internal processes such as pur-

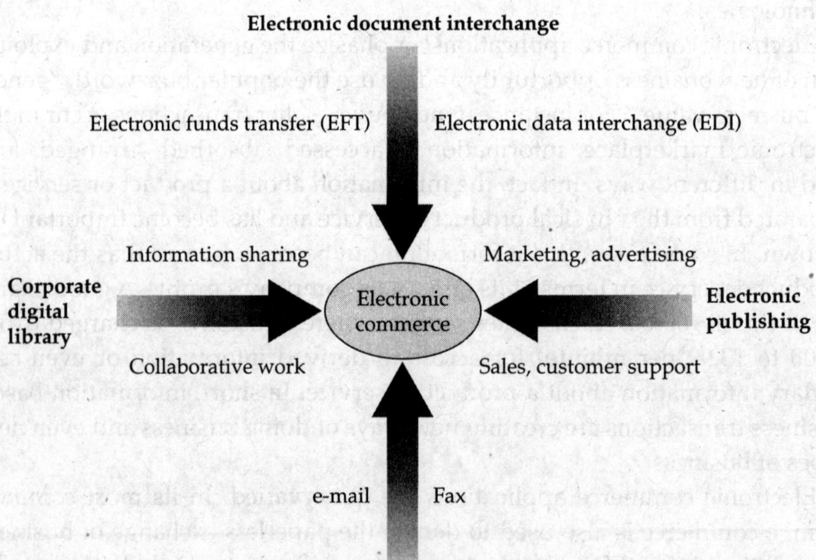


**Figure 6.1** Convergence of previously disparate functions around electronic commerce

chasing, invoicing, and other similar functions. So, some aspects of the technical infrastructure for electronic commerce are already in place. The challenge now becomes: How to effectively leverage this investment. Second, prices for computer hardware and network equipment continue to fall, making information technology an appealing investment for many businesses, especially when it's used for high-impact applications such as linking their distributed operations. However, investment without a clear idea of the electronic commerce architecture being built would be akin to driving with blinders on. As a result, companies that have decided that electronic commerce applications represent one of the best strategic investments they can make must first exert some effort to understand the technology underlying electronic commerce applications.

At first glance, it appears that messaging-based technologies such as EDI and mail-enabled applications, combined with database and information management services, form the technical foundation for effective electronic commerce solutions. No single one of these technologies can deliver the full potential of electronic commerce, however. What we require is an integrated architecture the likes of which has never been seen before. This integrated architecture is emerging in the form of the World Wide Web (WWW). As electronic commerce becomes more mature, we are beginning to see sophisticated applications being developed on the WWW. Technically and commercially, the WWW client–server model seems poised to become a dominant technology. In this chapter, we will first provide an overview of the different parts of a software application architecture. We will then build on it by expounding on the World Wide Web technology.

## 6.1 ARCHITECTURAL FRAMEWORK FOR ELECTRONIC COMMERCE

The software framework necessary for building electronic commerce applications is little understood in existing literature. In general a framework is intended to define and create tools that integrate the information found in today's closed systems and allow the development of e-commerce applications. It is important to understand that the aim of the architectural framework itself is not to build new database management systems, data repository, computer languages, software agent-based transaction monitors, or communication protocols. Rather, the architecture should focus on synthesizing the diverse resources already in place in corporations to facilitate the integration of data and software for better applications.

We propound that the electronic commerce application architecture consists of six layers of functionality, or services: (1) applications; (2) brokerage services, data or transaction management; (3) interface and support layers; (4) secure messaging, security, and electronic document interchange; (5) middleware and structured document interchange; and (6) network infrastructure and basic communications services (see Fig. 6.2).

These layers cooperate to provide a seamless transition between today's computing resources and those of tomorrow by transparently integrating information access and exchange within the context of the chosen application. As seen in Fig. 6.2, electronic commerce applications are based on several elegant technologies. But only when they are integrated do they provide uniquely powerful solutions.

In the ensuing discussion of each of these layers, we will not elaborate on the various aspects of the network infrastructure that transports information. These were discussed extensively earlier and will not be addressed here. We begin our discussion with the application level services.

## Electronic Commerce Application Services

The application services layer of e-commerce will be comprised of existing and future applications built on the innate architecture. Three distinct classes

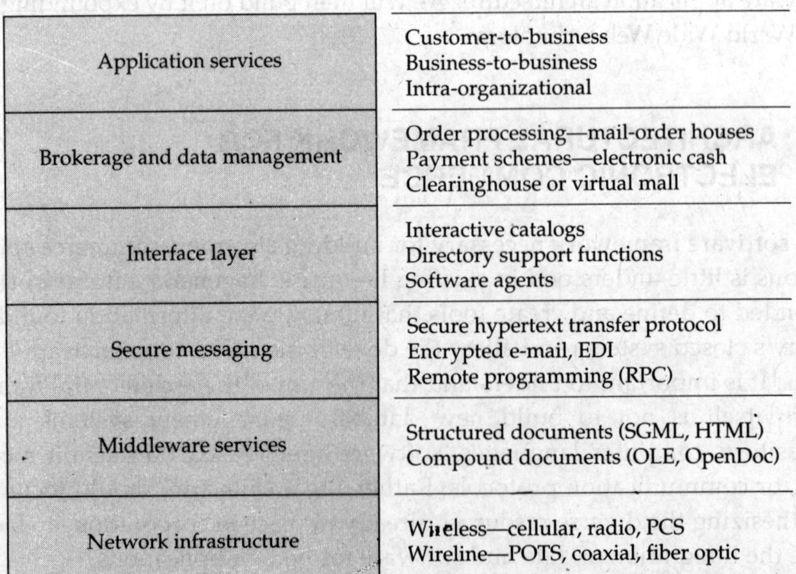


**Figure 6.2** Electronic commerce: a conceptual framework

of electronic commerce applications can be distinguished: customer-to-business, business-to-business, and intraorganization (see Fig. 6.3.).

### Consumer-to-Business Transactions

We call this category marketplace transaction. In a marketplace transaction, customers learn about products differently through electronic publishing, buy them differently using electronic cash and secure payment systems, and have them delivered differently. Also, how customers allocate their loyalty may also be different.

In light of this, the organization itself has to adapt to a world where the traditional concepts of brand differentiation no longer hold—where "quality" has a new meaning, where "content" may not be equated to "product," where "distribution" may not automatically mean "physical transport." In this new environment, brand equity can rapidly evaporate forcing firms to develop new ways of doing business (see Chapters 7 and 8).

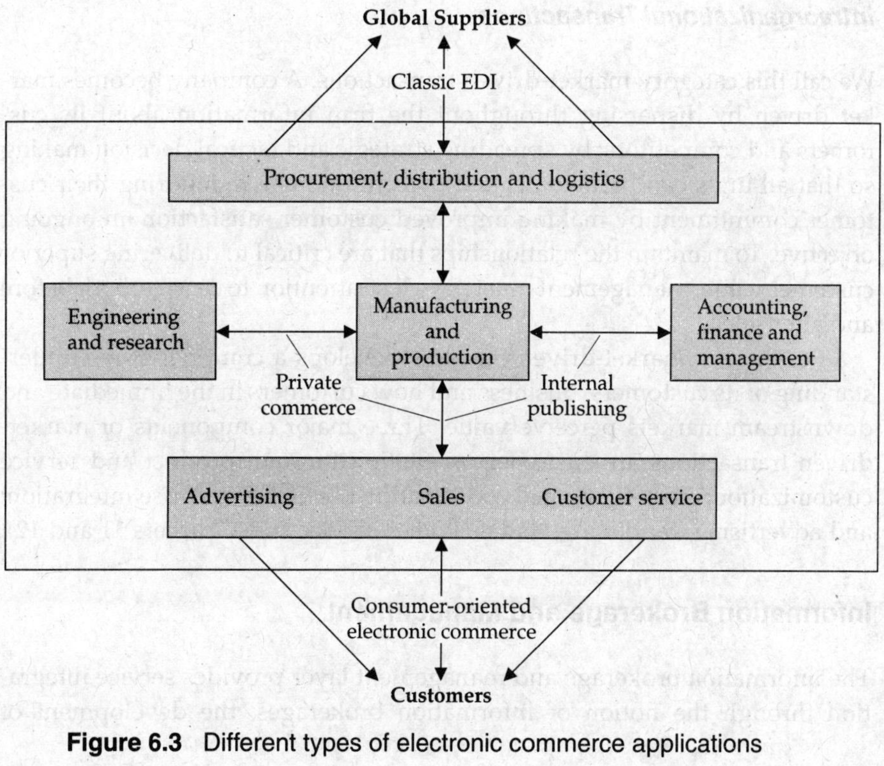


**Figure 6.3** Different types of electronic commerce applications

### Business-to-Business Transactions

We call this category market-link transaction. Here, businesses, governments, and other organizations depend on computer-to-computer communication as a fast, an economical, and a dependable way to conduct business transactions. Small companies are also beginning to see the benefits of adopting the same methods. Business-to-business transactions include the use of EDI and electronic mail for purchasing goods and services, buying information and consulting services, submitting requests for proposals, and receiving proposals.

Examine this scenario. The current accounts payable process occurs through the exchange of paper documents. Each year the trading partners exchange millions of invoices, checks, purchase orders, financial reports, and other transactions. Most of the documents are in electronic form at their point of origin but are printed and key-entered at the point of receipt. The current manual process of printing, mailing, and rekeying is costly, time-consuming, and error-prone. Given this situation and faced with the need to reduce costs, small businesses are looking toward electronic commerce as a possible savior (see Chapters 9 and 10).

### Intraorganizational Transactions

We call this category market-driven transactions. A company becomes market driven by dispersing throughout the firm information about its customers and competitors; by spreading strategic and tactical decision making so that all units can participate; and by continuously monitoring their customer commitment by making improved customer satisfaction an ongoing objective. To maintain the relationships that are critical to delivering superior customer value, management must pay close attention to service, both before and after sales.

In essence, a market-driven business develops a comprehensive understanding of its customers' business and how customers in the immediate and downstream markets perceive value. Three major components of market-driven transactions are customer orientation through product and service customization; cross-functional coordination through enterprise integration; and advertising, marketing, and customer service (see Chapters 11 and 12).

## Information Brokerage and Management

The information brokerage and management layer provides service integration through the notion of information brokerages, the development of which is necessitated by the increasing information resource fragmentation. We use the notion of information brokerage to represent an intermediary who provides service integration between customers and information providers, given some constraint such as a low price, fast service, or profit maximization for a client.

Information brokers, for example, are rapidly becoming necessary in dealing with the voluminous amounts of information on the networks. As on-line databases migrate to consumer information utilities, consumers and information professionals will have to keep up with the knowledge, and ownership, of all these systems. Who's got what? How do you use it? What do they charge? Most professionals have enough trouble keeping track of files of interest on one or two database services. With all the complexity associated with large numbers of on-line databases and service bureaus, it's impossible to expect humans to do the searching. It will have to be software programs—information brokers or software agents, to use the more popular term—that act on the searcher's behalf.

Information brokerage does more than just searching. It addresses the issue of adding value to the information that is retrieved. For instance, in foreign exchange trading, information is retrieved about the latest currency exchange rates in order to hedge currency holdings to minimize risk and maximize profit. In other words, the act of retrieving the information is the input to other transactions. With multiple transactions being the norm in the real world, service integration becomes critical. Taking the same foreign exchange example further, service integration allows one to link the hedging program (offered on a time-sharing basis by a third party) with the search program (could be another vendor) that finds the currency rates from the cheapest on-line service to automatically send trades to the bank or financial services company. In effect, a personalized automated trading system can be created without having to go to any financial institution. This is just one example of how information brokerages can add value.

Another aspect of the brokerage function is the support for data management and traditional transaction services. Brokerages may provide tools to accomplish more sophisticated, time-delayed updates or future-compensating transactions. These tools include software agents, distributed query generator, the distributed transaction generator, and the declarative resource constraint base—which describes a business's rules and environment information. At the heart of this layer lies the work-flow scripting environment built on a software agent model that coordinates work and data flow among support services.

As pointed out earlier, software agents are used to implement information brokerages. Software agents are mobile programs that have been called "healthy viruses," "digital butlers," and "intelligent agents." Agents are encapsulations of users' instructions that perform all kinds of tasks in electronic marketplaces spread across networks. Information brokerages dispatch agents capable of information resource gathering, negotiating deals, and performing transactions. The agents are intelligent because they have contingency plans of action. They examine themselves and their environment and if necessary change from their original course of action to an alternative plan. For example, suppose you send an agent to an on-line store with a request to order a bouquet of roses for $25 or less. If the shop offers roses starting at $30, your agent can either choose a different bouquet or find a different store by consulting an on-line "Yellow Pages" directory, depending on prior instructions.

Although the notion of software agents sounds very seductive, it will take a while to solve the problems of interagent communication, interoperable agents, and other headaches that come with distributed computing and networking. To some critics, the prospect of a single-agent language like Telescript as a world standard is disturbing. They worry that agents sound a bit too much like computer viruses, which instead of running errands may run amok. Vendors such as General Magic go to great lengths to explain the precautions it has taken to make this impossible: the limits placed on the power of agents, the "self-destruct" mechanism built into their codes. Yet until electronic commerce services are up and running on a large scale, it is impossible to know how well software agents will work. We will discuss these and other agent-related issues in Chapter 16.

## Interface and Support Services

The third layer, interface and support services, will provide interfaces for electronic commerce applications such as interactive catalogs and will support directory services—functions necessary for information search and access. These two concepts are very different. Interactive catalogs are the customized interface to consumer applications such as home shopping. An interactive catalog is an extension of the paper-based catalog and incorporates additional features such as sophisticated graphics and video to make the advertising more attractive.

Directories, on the other hand, operate behind the scenes and attempt to organize the enormous amount of information and transactions generated to facilitate electronic commerce. Directory services databases make data from any server appear as a local file. A classic example of a directory is the telephone White Pages, which allows us to locate people and telephone numbers. In the case of electronic commerce, directories would play an important role in information management functions. For instance, take the case of buying an airline ticket with several stopovers with the caveat that the time between layovers be minimized. This search would require several queries to various on-line directiories to find empty seats on various airlines and then the availability of seats would be coordinated with the amount of time spent in the airport terminals.

The primary difference between the two is that unlike interactive catalogs, which deal with people, directory support services interact directly with software applications. For this reason, they need not have the multimedia glitter and jazz generally associated with interactive catalogs.

From a computing perspective, we can expect that there will be no one common user interface that will glaze the surface of all electronic commerce applications, but graphics and object manipulation will definitely predominate. Tool developers and designers might incorporate common tools for interface building, but the shape of catalogs or directories will depend on the users' desires and functional requirements.

## Secure Messaging and Structured Document Interchange Services

The importance of the fourth layer, secured messaging, is clear. Everyone in business knows that electronic messaging is a critical business issue. Consider a familiar business scenario: You hand over an urgent fax Monday and find out Tuesday that it's still sitting on your fax operator's desk. What happened? The line was busy and he thought he'd try again later. Or, the number was wrong, but he forgot to let you know. Or you're in London and you need to send a spreadsheet that details a marketing plan for a product introduction strategy to a co-worker in New York. This must be done today, not tomorrow when the courier service would deliver. There is a solution to these common and frustrating problems. It's called integrated messaging: a group of computer services that through the use of a network send, receive, and combine messages, faxes, and large data files. Some better-known examples are electronic mail, enhanced fax, and electronic data interchange.

Broadly defined, messaging is the software that sits between the network infrastructure and the clients or electronic commerce applications, masking the peculiarities of the environment. Others define messaging as a framework for the total implementation of portable applications, divorcing you from the architectural primitives of your system. In general, messaging products are not applications that solve problems; they are more enablers of the applications that solve problems.

Messaging services offer solutions for communicating nonformatted (unstructured) data—letters, memos, reports—as well as formatted (structured) data such as purchase orders, shipping notices, and invoices. Unstructured messaging consists of fax, e-mail, and form-based systems like Lotus Notes. Structured documents messaging consists of the automated interchange of standardized and approved messages between computer applications, via telecommunications lines. Examples of structured document messaging include EDI.

Messaging is gaining momentum in electronic commerce and seems to have many advantages. It supports both synchronous (immediate) and asynchronous (delayed) message delivery and processing. With asynchronous messaging, when a message is sent, work continues (software doesn't wait for a response). This allows the transfer of messages through store-and-forward methods.

Another advantage of messaging is that it is not associated with any particular communication protocol. No preprocessing is necessary, although there is an increasing need for programs to interpret the message. Messaging is well suited for both client–server and peer-to-peer computing models. In distributed systems, the messages are treated as "objects" that pass between systems.

Messaging is central to work-group computing that is changing the way businesses operate. The ability to access the right information at the right time across diverse work groups is a challenge. Today, with the messaging tools, people can communicate and work together more effectively—no matter where they are located. When an employee sends an electronic mail form, the information travels along with the form. So one person can start the form, mail it to the next person, fill it in/sign it, mail it to the next, and so on. This is known as *message-enabled work-flow solutions*.

The main disadvantages of messaging are the new types of applications it enables—which appear to be more complex, especially to traditional programmers —and the jungle of standards it involves. Because of the lack of standards, there is often no interoperability between different messaging vendors leading to islands of messaging. Also, security, privacy, and confidentiality through data encryption and authentication techniques are important issues that need to be resolved for ensuring the legality of the message-based transactions themselves.

## Middleware Services

Middleware is a relatively new concept that emerged only recently. Like so many other innovations, it came into being out of necessity. Users in the

1970s, when vendors delivered homogeneous systems that worked, didn't have a need for middleware. When conditions changed—along with the hardware and the software the organizations couldn't cope: The tools were inadequate, the backlog was enormous, and the pressure was overwhelming. And, the users were dissatisfied. Something was needed to solve all the interface, translation, transformation, and interpretation problems that were driving application developers crazy.

With the growth of networks, client–server technology, and all other forms of communicating between/among unlike platforms, the problems of getting all the pieces to work together grew from formidable to horrendous. As the cry for distributed computing spread, users demanded interaction between dissimilar systems, networks that permitted shared resources, and applications that could be accessed by multiple software programs. In simple terms, middleware is the ultimate mediator between diverse software programs that enables them talk to one another.

Another reason for middleware is the computing shift from application centric to data centric. That is, remote data controls all of the applications in the network instead of applications controlling data. To achieve data-centric computing, middleware services focus on three elements: transparency, transaction security and management, and distributed object management and services (see Chapter 22).

### Transparency

Transparency implies that users should be unaware that they are accessing multiple systems. Transparency is essential for dealing with higher-level issues than physical media and interconnection that the underlying network infrastructure is in charge of. The ideal picture is one of a "virtual" network: a collection of work-group, departmental, enterprise, and interenterprise LANs that appears to the end user or client application to be a seamless and easily accessed whole.

Transparency is accomplished using middleware that facilitates a distributed computing environment. This gives users and applications transparent access to data, computation, and other resources across collections of multivendor, heterogeneous systems. The strategic architectures of every major system vendor are now based on some form of middleware. The key to realizing the theoretical benefit of such an architecture is transparency. Users need not spend their time trying to understand where something is. Nor should application developers have to code into their applications the exact locations of resources over the network. The goal is for the applications to send a request to the middleware layer, which then satisfies the request any way it can, using remote information.

### *Transaction Security and Management*

Support for transaction processing (TP) is fundamental to success in the electronic commerce market. Security and management are essential to all layers in the electronic commerce model. At the transaction security level, two broad general categories of security services exist: authentication and authorization. Transaction integrity must be a given for businesses that cannot afford any loss or inconsistency in data. Some commercial sites have had gigantic centralized TP systems running for years. For electronic commerce, middleware provides the qualities expected in a standard TP system: the so-called ACID properties (atomicity, consistency, isolation, and durability).

### *Distributed Object Management and Services*

Object orientation is proving fundamental to the proliferation of network-based applications for the following reasons: It is too hard to write a network-based application without either extensive developer retraining or a technology that camouflages the intricacies of the network. Objects are defined as the combination of data and instructions acting on the data. Objects are an evolution of the more traditional programming concept of functions and procedures.

A natural instance of an object in electronic commerce is a document. A document carries data and often carries instructions about the actions to be performed on the data. Today, the term *object* is being used interchangeably with *document* resulting in a new form of computing called *document-oriented computing*. Here, the trend is to move away from single data-type documents such as text, pictures, or video toward integrated documents known as *compound document architectures*.

The best example of this approach is an active document. If you create a new document that is an integration of the spreadsheet, word processor, and presentation package, what you'll see in the next generation of operating systems is that as you scroll through your document, the tool bar will automatically change from a spreadsheet tool bar, to a word processing tool bar, to a presentation package tool bar. These applications will also be able to access and retrieve data from any file in the computing network. The implications are clear: We're going to see a gradual movement toward active documents that will be designed out of linked applications.

Evidence of the emergence of document-oriented computing is everywhere. The next generation of operating systems (Apple System 8, Microsoft 95 and IBM Taligent) enable users to create applications that take little "applets" and put them together to make "hyperapps," or bundles of complex functionality. The document orientation provides the ability to build applications from applets. It will provide the necessary ease of development through capabilities of reuse and customization. In addition, document orientation is expected to provide scalability as the addition (or modification) of underlying infrastructure should have no impact on application logic or response time in electronic commerce applications.

In sum, middleware acts as an integrator for the various standard protocols already in use, or soon to be available. These protocols include TCP/IP, Open Software Foundation's distributed computing environment, and the emerging distributed object computing frameworks for creating compound documents such as Common Object Request Broker Architecture (CORBA), Object Linking and Embedding (OLE), and OpenDoc (see Chapter 22).

## 6.2 WORLD WIDE WEB (WWW) AS THE ARCHITECTURE

The electronic commerce framework outlined in the last section is being built on the World Wide Web (WWW) architecture. To provide a human analogy, think of the network infrastructure as the skeleton and the Web as the flesh, veins, and skin that shape the human body. Carrying the analogy further, the functions carried out by the human body would be the electronic commerce applications. In short, the Web provides the functionality necessary for electronic commerce.

Electronic commerce depends on the unspoken assumption that computers cooperate efficiently for seamless information sharing. Unfortunately, this assumption of interoperability has not been supported by the realities of practical computing. Computing is still a world made up of many technical directions, product implementations, and competing vendors. This diversity, while good for innovation, causes problems as the e-commerce applications try to impose a certain discipline on the proliferating computers and networks. It is ironic that the real effect of computing is all too often the prevention of data sharing due to incompatibilities—architectures, data formats, and communications protocols.

The Web community of developers and users is tackling these complex problems. The Web began in March 1989, when Tim Berners-Lee of the European Laboratory for Particle Physics (known as CERN, an R&D group of European high-energy physics researchers) proposed the Web project for research collaboration. Information sharing has been a goal of CERN, whose members are located in a number of European countries, for many years.

The initial proposal outlined a simple system of using networked hypertext to quickly disseminate documents among colleagues. There was no intention of supporting sound, video, or images in this proposal. By the end of 1990, an implementation of the Web was placed on a NeXT machine at CERN. The software had the capability to serve documents to other people on the Internet and came with the capability to edit documents on the screen using a very primitive line-mode browser (tool for examining Web documents).

The project quickly expanded beyond all imagination as others understood the potential for global information sharing. Hundreds of people throughout the world have contributed by writing and modifying Web software and documents. In a way never envisioned by the original project group, the project reached global proportions by the middle of 1993 with the introduction of the NCSA Mosaic—a multimedia front-end to all the information served by the Web.

Figure 6.4 shows a block diagram depicting the numerous pieces that constitute a Web architecture. The architecture is made up of three primary entities: client browser, Web server, and third-party services. The client browser usually interacts with the WWW server, which acts as an intermediary in the interaction with third-party services.

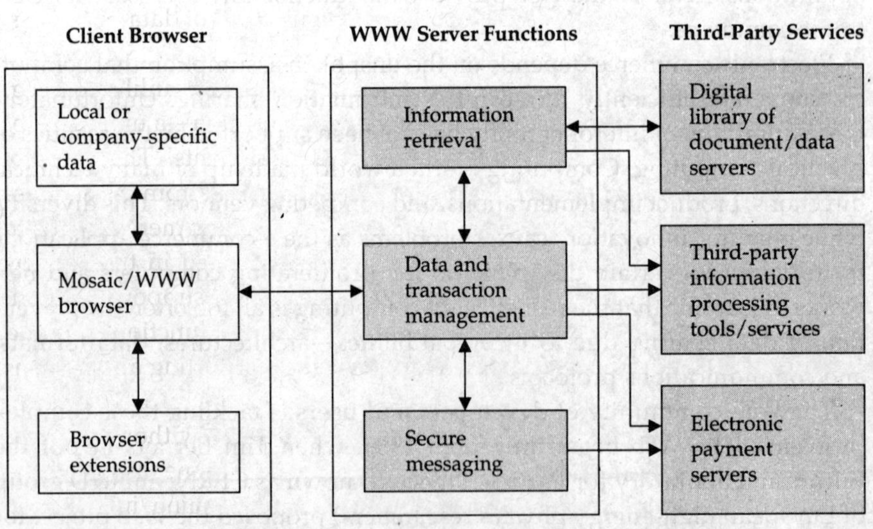


**Figure 6.4** Block diagram depicting an electronic commerce architecture

The client browser resides on the user's PC or workstation and provides an interface to the various types of content. For instance, if the user retrieves a graphics file from a Web server, the browser automatically starts up the browser extension to display the graphics file. Remember that many types of graphics files are available—JPEG, GIF, TIFF, BMP, among others. The browser has to be smart enough to understand what file it is downloading and what browser extension it needs to activate to display the file. Browsers are also capable of manipulating local files.

Web server functions can be categorized into information retrieval, data and transaction management, and security. The third-party services could be other Web servers that make up the digital library, information processing tools, and electronic payment systems.

## What Does the Web Encompass?

The Web has become an umbrella for a wide range of concepts and technologies that differ markedly in purpose and scope. These include the global hypertext publishing concept, the universal reader concept, and the client–server concept.

The *global hypertext publishing concept* promotes the idea of a seamless information world in which *all* on-line information can be accessed and retrieved in a consistent and simple way. To access information in this seamless world, we will need the ability to address many types of data—text files, images, sound files, animation sequences.

The *universal readership concept* promotes the idea that, unlike the segmented applications of the past, we can use one application—a universal (or common) user interface—to read a variety of documents. This concept implies that once information is published it is accessible from any type of computer, in any country, and that any (authorized) person merely needs to use one simple program to access it. This is accomplished in the Web by using a core browser or application that is augmented by supporting applications. The core browser implements only minimal functionality and attempts to offload more specialized work onto the supporting applications (see Fig. 6.5).

The *client–server concept* allows the Web to grow easily without any centralized control. Anyone can publish information, and anyone (as long as he or she is authorized) can read and download it. Publishing information requires a server program, and reading data requires a client browser. All the clients and all the servers are connected to one another by the Internet. The

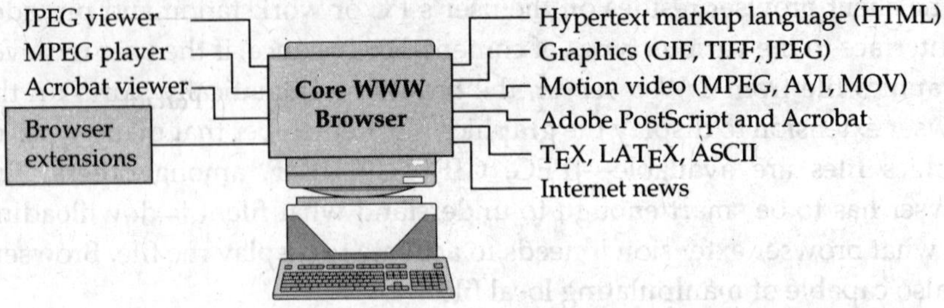


**Figure 6.5** Universal readership supported by core WWW browser

various standard protocols allow all clients to communicate with all servers. The client–server architecture of the Web is illustrated in Fig. 6.6.

In practice the Web hangs on a number of essential concepts, including the following:

- The addressing scheme known as uniform resource locator (URL) makes the hypermedia world possible despite many different protocols.
- A network protocol known as hypertext transfer protocol (HTTP) used by the client browsers and servers offers performance and features not otherwise available.
- A mark-up language (HTML), which every Web client is required to understand, is used for the representation of hypertext documents containing text, list boxes, and graphics information across the net.

## 6.3 WEB BACKGROUND: HYPERTEXT PUBLISHING

During the last few years, interest in hypermedia on the Internet (called distributed or global hypermedia) has accelerated sharply following the success of the Web and browsers such as the NCSA Mosaic. This success has been aided by more powerful workstations, high-resolution graphics displays, faster network communications, and decreased costs for large on-line storage. This section provides a brief introduction aimed at providing readers unfamiliar with hypertext with sufficient background information so that they can see the potential of hypertext in digital publishing and also follow the discussion in later sections.

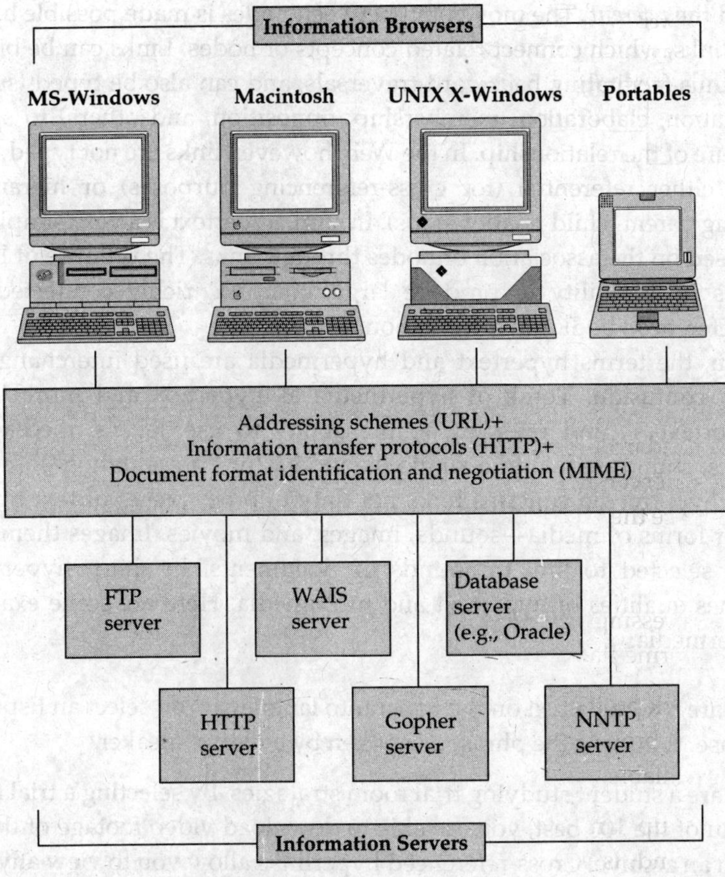


**Figure 6.6** Client–server structure of the Web

## Hypertext Versus Hypermedia

Hypertext is an approach to information management in which data are stored in a network of documents connected by links. These links represent relationships between nodes. A hypermedia system is made of nodes (documents) and links (pointers). A node usually represents a single concept or idea. Nodes can contain text, graphics, animation, audio, video, images, or programs. The nodes, and in some systems the network itself, are meant to be viewed through an interactive browser and manipulated through a structure editor.

Nodes are connected to other nodes by links. The node from which a link originates is called the *reference* or *anchor*, and the node at which a link ends is called the *referent*. The movement between nodes is made possible by activating links, which connect related concepts or nodes. Links can be bidirectional, thus facilitating backward traversals, and can also be typed (such as specification, elaboration, membership, opposition, and others) to specify the nature of the relationship. In the Web, however, links are not typed. Links can be either referential (for cross-referencing purposes) or hierarchical (showing parent–child relationships). In sum, hypertext is a very simple concept based on the association of nodes through links. The promise of hypertext lies in its ability to produce large, complex, richly connected, and cross-referenced bodies of information.

Often, the terms hypertext and hypermedia are used interchangeably, causing confusion. Think of hypermedia as hypertext and more (a sort of hypertext++) and referring to the ability to use several media (text, graphics, sound, video) in a single document (or "presentation"). In other words, hypermedia contains links not only to other pieces of text but also to other forms of media—sounds, images, and movies. Images themselves can be selected to link to sounds or documents. In short, hypermedia combines qualities of hypertext and multimedia. Here are some examples of hypermedia:

- You are reading a text on the Esperanto language. You select an Esperanto phrase, then hear the phrase as spoken by a native speaker.
- You are a student studying trial room strategies. By selecting a trial from a menu of the 100 best, you are able to download video footage of the trial from an archive. Cross-referenced hyperlinks allow you to view any reference with audio annotations.
- You are a customer who has a complaint about a product. By selecting the appropriate customer service representative, you are able to video conference with the representative in some other part of the country and discuss the problem.

Although still in its infancy, hypermedia has already enabled many of these examples. For instance the Web facilitates the easy exchange of hypermedia through networked environments from anything as small as two PCs connected together to something as large as the global Internet.

## Benefits of Hypermedia Documents

Hypermedia documents are much more flexible than conventional documents. For example, one can read a hypermedia article just as one reads

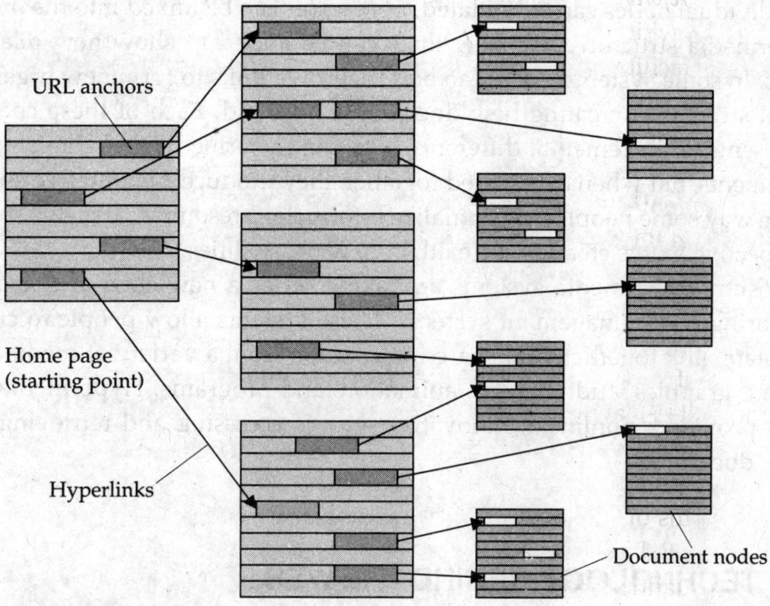


**Figure 6.7** Hypertext information network

a conventional newspaper article, by first reading the overview node, then the first section node(s), the second section, and so forth. However, one can also read the sections in different order depending on what captures the reader's interest.

Hypermedia documents are also convenient. Hypermedia documents offer sound, video sequences, animation, even computer programs that execute when the links are selected. Following the cross references in a modern encyclopedia often means moving among many volumes. Readers do it, but it is a slow, frequently laborious, task. While following a cross-reference in a 30-volume encyclopedia can take several minutes, many hypermedia systems can deliver the next node in less than a second and from a much larger body of information that might encompass thousands of volumes in print. While hypermedia provides greater flexibility and convenience than conventional documents, its power and appeal increase dramatically when it is implemented in computing environments that include networked microcomputers and workstations, high-resolution displays, and large on-line storage.

Another advantage is dynamic organization. While the organizational and cross-reference structures of conventional documents are fixed at the time of printing, hypermedia links and nodes can change dynamically. Information in individual nodes can be updated, new nodes can be linked into the overall hypermedia structure, and new links can be added to show new relationships. In some systems, users can add their own links to form new organizational structures, creating new documents from old. Each of these changes represents an incremental difference between hypermedia and conventional documents, but when considered together, they produce a qualitative change in the way some people conceptualize information resources. It is this shift in perspective that is creating a wealth of new possibilities.

In sum, hypermedia systems are taking off as a new class of document authoring and management systems. These systems allow people to create, annotate, link together, and share information from a variety of media such as text, graphics, audio, video, animation, and programs. Hypermedia systems provide a nonlinear, innovative way of accessing and retrieving network documents.

## 6.4 TECHNOLOGY BEHIND THE WEB

Information providers (or publishers) run programs (called servers) from which the browsers (clients) can obtain information. These programs can either be Web servers that understand the hypertext transfer protocol (HTTP), "gateway" programs that convert an existing information format to hypertext, or a non-HTTP server that Web browsers can access—anonymous FTP or Gopher servers.

Web servers are composed of two major parts: the hypertext transfer protocol for transmitting documents between servers and clients and the hypertext markup language (HTML) format for documents. The link between HTML files and the HTTP servers is provided by the uniform resource locators (URLs). A detailed, technical discussion of the specifics of URL, HTTP, and HTML is beyond the scope of this book, but some of the key properties of these features will be described next.

### Uniform Resource Locators

The documents that the browsers display are hypertext that contains pointers to other documents. The browsers let you deal with the pointers in a transparent way—select the pointer and you are presented with the text to which it points. This pointer is implemented using a concept that is central to Web browsers: uniform resource locators (URLs). One way to think about URLs is to use the libraries and location on a shelf as a metaphor. A URL for a digital library would be a unique call number that provides the exact location of every book in the world, including the country, city, street, and library shelf location.

In practice, URLs are the strings used as addresses of objects (documents, images) on the Web. Think of them as analogous to your e-mail address. Just as your address is unique and may be used by any other Internet user to send you mail without knowing exactly where you are, a URL marks the unique location on the Internet where a file or service can be found.

URLs follow a fairly consistent pattern. The first part describes the type of resource; the second part gives the name of the server housing the resource; and the third part gives the full file name of the resource. URLs are universal in that they provide access to a wide range of network services which required separate applications in the past. For a new network protocol one can easily form an address as the set of parameters necessary to retrieve the object. If these parameters are encoded into a concise string, with a prefix to identify the protocol and encoding, one has a new URL scheme. Take a look at the URL formats below:

| | |
|---|---|
| FTP: | ftp://server.address/complete.file.name |
| Gopher: | gopher://server.address:port/directory/filename |
| TELNET: | telnet://server.address:port |
| HTTP: | http://server.address:port/homepage.html |
| News: | news: misc. stocks. invest |

There are URLs for Internet news articles and newsgroups (the NNTP protocol), and for HTTP archives, for TELNET destinations, email addresses, and so on. The same can be done for names of objects in a given name space. For example, the URL of the main page for the Web project happens to be: http://web.w3.org/hypertext/Web/TheProject.html. The prefix "http" in the preceding example indicates the address space and defines the interpretation of the rest of the string. The HTTP protocol is to be used, so the string contains the address of the server to be contacted, and a substring to be passed to the server.

As noted earlier, different protocols use different syntaxes, but they do have a small amount in common. For example, the common URL syntax reserves the solidus (/) as a way of representing a hierarchical space, the pound label (#) as a way of pointing inside the document, and the question mark (?) as a separator between the address of an object and a query operation applied to it. Hierarchical spaces are useful for hypertext, where one "work" may be split up into many interlinked documents. The # allows relative names to exploit the hierarchical structure and allows links to be made within the work independent of the higher parts of the URL, such as the server name.

URLs are central to the Web architecture. The fact that it is easy to address an object anywhere on the Internet is essential for the system to scale and for the information space to be independent of the network and server topology.

## Hypertext Transfer Protocol (HTTP)

Hypertext transfer protocol (HTTP) is a simple request/response protocol that is currently run over TCP and is the basis of the World Wide Web. In short, HTTP is a protocol for transferring information efficiently between the requesting client and server. The data transferred may be plain text, hypertext, images, or anything else. When a user browses the Web, objects are retrieved in rapid succession from often widely dispersed servers. For small documents, the limitations to the response time stem mainly from the number of round trip delays across the network necessary before the rendition of the object can be started.

HTTP does more than transfer HTML documents. Although HTML comprehension is required of WWW clients, HTTP is used for retrieving documents in an unbounded and extensible set of formats. To achieve this, the client sends a list of the formats it can handle, and the server replies with data in any of those formats that it can produce. This function allows proprietary formats to be used between consenting programs in private, without the need for standardization of those formats. This is important both for high-end users who share data in sophisticated forms and as a method for formats that have yet to be invented.

HTTP is an Internet protocol. It is similar in its readable, text-based style to the file transfer (FTP) and network news (NNTP) protocols that have been used to transfer files and news on the Internet for many years. Unlike these protocols, however, HTTP, is stateless (it runs over a TCP connection held only for the duration of one operation). The stateless model is efficient when a link from one object may lead equally well to an object stored on the same server or to another distant server. The purpose of a reference such as a URL is that it should always refer to the "same" (in some sense) object. This also makes a stateless protocol appropriate, as it returns results based on the URL but irrelevant of any previous operations performed by the client.

The HTTP request from the client starts with an object request method and the URL of the object. The most often used methods are GET and POST. A

GET method is defined for front-end update, and a POST method for the attachment of a new document to the Web, or submission of a filled-in form or other object to some processor.

When objects are transferred over the network, information about them ("meta-information") is transferred in HTTP headers. The set of headers is an extension of the multipurpose Internet mail extensions (MIME) set. This design decision was taken to open the door to integration of hypermedia mail, news, and information access. In HTTP, unlike in e-mail, transfer in binary, and transfer in nonstandard but mutually agreed document formats, is possible. This allows, for example, servers to indicate links from, and titles of, documents (such as bit-map images) whose data format does not otherwise include such information.

The convention that unrecognized HTTP headers and parameters are ignored has made it easy to try new ideas on working production servers. This has allowed the protocol definition to evolve in a controlled way by the incorporation of tested ideas.

### HTTPD Servers

Because information publishing is an important element of electronic commerce, organizations must learn how to publish information via World Wide Web servers (called httpd servers). Installing and maintaining a Web server is not a trivial matter, however, given the security and administrative issues involved. There are now a number of Web servers to choose from, and several are very easy to install and administer. In fact, the difficulty lies not so much in installing and maintaining a Web server but in choosing a server that best fits the organization's needs. Issues to be considered include the following:

- What platform and operating system is the right choice?
- What kind of traffic loads are anticipated on the Web server—heavy or light?
- What kind of security features are envisioned?
- How flexible and robust does the server need to be?

Flexibility, ease of administration, security features, and familiarity often rank much higher in the decision process than other criteria, such as raw performance. It is also important to evaluate the tasks for which the Web server will be used. A server used for Internet-based marketing and technical-support tasks will need more robust resources than a Web server used internally within a firewall for distributing memos and bulletins. New security features such as encryption are also making it possible to consider the Web as a commercial transaction channel, and the Web server will have to support those features.

Another important consideration when choosing a Web server is the amount of traffic that it will be expected to handle. The number of users on the Web is exploding, and even a moderately popular site can generate several million connections a month. With a high-speed connection to the Internet, such as a T-1 leased line, a Web server can bog down very quickly and begin to refuse connections. If you are doing business on the Internet, it is probably not a good idea to turn away potential customers.

Httpd servers are ideal for companies that want to provide a multitude of services ranging from product information to technical support. The way to provide other services via the Web is with HTML pages (see a later section) and CGI scripts. These simple scripts, which can be written or acquired over the Internet, allow the Web server to act as a gateway to other Internet services such as databases (Oracle or Sybase), Gopher, and news.

### Format/Content Negotiation and HTTP

Format/content negotiation is the ability to serve clients of varying sophistication automatically with HTML and other document types that offer the best representation of information that the client is capable of accepting. Format negotiation allows the Web to be generic and distance itself from the technical and political battles that surround the various data formats.

Format negotiation is an interesting feature of HTTP standard. Here the client (Mosaic, Netscape, or other browsers) sends a list of the representations it understands or data formats it is prepared to accept along with its request. The intention is that when information is available in multiple variants (in different data formats), a server can use this information to ensure that it replies in a suitable way. This feature necessarily copes with the existing mass of document formats. For example, in the graphics world we have to deal with GIF, TIFF, JPEG, BMP, and so on.

A spin-off of this feature involves high-level formats (also called MIME application formats) for handling specific data. In certain fields, special data formats have been designed for handling such applications as chemistry codes, the spectra of stars, classical Greek, or the design of bridges. Those working in the field use software enabling them not only to view this data but to manipulate it, analyze it, and modify it. When the server and the client both understand such a high-level format, then they can take advantage of it, and the data are transferred in that way. At the same time, other people without the special software can still view the data, if the server can convert it into an inferior but still useful form. In other words, we can adhere to the Web goal of "universal readership" without compromising total functionality at the high level.

## Hypertext Markup Language (HTML)

At the heart of the Web is a simple page description language called hypertext markup language (HTML). HTML is a common basic language of interchange for hypertext that forms the fabric of the Web. HTML is based on an international electronic document standard called Standard Generalized Markup Language (SGML) (see Chapter 21).

HTML enables document creation for the Web by embedding control codes in ASCII text to designate titles, headings, graphics, and hypertext links, making use of SGML's powerful linking capabilities. HTML was designed to be sufficiently simple so as to be produced easily by people and automatically generated by programs.

Familiarity with UNIX text-formatting languages such as troff, Tex, or LaTex simplifies HTML coding pickup. Even otherwise, HTML coding is very easy and can be mastered in a few hours. HTML tags, embedded within the body of the text, are used to define a document and guide its display.

There are three ways to produce HTML documents: Writing them yourself, which is not a very difficult skill to acquire; using an HTML editor, which assists in doing the above; and converting documents in other formats to HTML. Another way to produce HTML files is to choose a template and modify it. The fastest way to produce HTML is to learn by example. That is, you can use the built-in "view source" option (usually under the file menu of most browsers) to view the HTML commands that make up some of your favorite pages on the Web. We are not advocating that you outright steal documents or violate copyright, but study the document structure and formatting commands that are used and try to use the same techniques in your own documents.

HTML is evolving rapidly in various directions. The specification is currently at document type definition (DTD) level 2, which includes support for forms within standard hypertext documents. (The DTD describes the logical structure of possible document instances.) This includes features for more sophisticated on-line documentation, form templates for the entry of data by users, tables, and mathematical formulae. Work is also underway for DTD level 3, which is focusing on a "scalable HTML."

In short, HTML was meant to be a language of communication, which actually flows over the network. HTML use is not restricted to HTTP, but can be used in hypertext e-mail (it is proposed as a format for MIME), news, and anywhere basic hypertext is needed. It includes simple structure elements, such as several levels of headings, lists, menus, and compact lists, all of which are useful when presenting choices, and in on-line documents. Also, there is no rule that all httpd files are stored in HTML. Servers may store files in other formats, or in variations on HTML that include extra information of local interest only, and then generate HTML on the fly with each request. To generate HTML on the fly, servers make use of an essential service for dealing with HTML forms known as CGI (Common Gateway Interface).

### HTML Forms

Form support is an important element for doing on-line business. In fact, most of an organization's time will be spent writing HTML forms and CGI scripts to process these forms. Forms are necessary for gathering user information, conducting surveys, or even providing interactive services. Forms make Web browsing an interactive process for the user and the provider. Before the advent of HTML forms, information flow was unidirectional. Forms provide the means to collect and act on data entered by the end user. They also open up a number of possibilities for on-line transactions, such as requesting specific news articles, specifying search requests, soliciting customer feedback, or ordering products.

Forms must be supported by both the client and the server for successful implementation. A number of features are available for building forms, including text boxes, radio buttons, and check boxes. A user can enter text, select items from a list, check boxes, and then submit the information to the server. A program on the server then interprets the data and acts on it appropriately, either by returning information in hypertext form, downloading a file, or electronically notifying the company of your order.

The process of going from HTML forms to constructing a query to send to the server consists of four steps:

*Step 1.* The form structure is read as an HTML file.

*Step 2.* The form is displayed on the screen and the user fills it out.

*Step 3.* The user-entered information is aggregated and assembled into a query.

*Step 4.* The query is directed by the httpd server to the specified CGI script.

To understand this process better, let's consider an example of a simple purchase order.

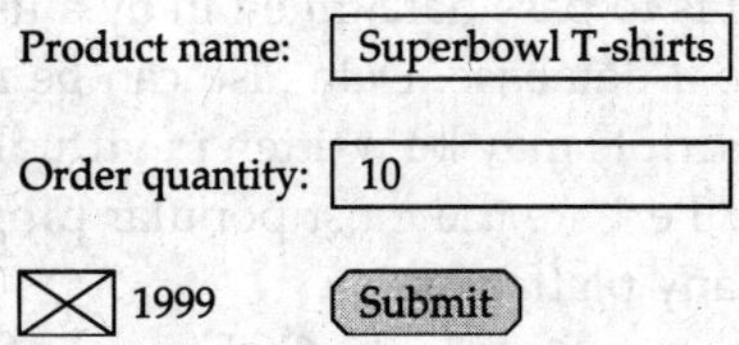


This HTML form corresponds to the following HTML code:

```
<form method="post" action="/cgi-bin/purchase.cgi">
Product Name: <input name="product_name" value="Super-bowl T-
  Shirts"><p>
Order Quantity: <input name="order_quantity" value="10"><p>
<input type="checkbox" name="year" checked>1999
<input type="submit" value="submit"><p>
```

The query URL that is assembled looks like this:

```
http://server/cgi-bin/purchase.cgi?product_name=Super-bowl+
  T-Shirts&order_quantity=10&year=on
```

In this example, the http://server/cgi-bin/purchase.cgi part of the query URL comes from the action attribute of the form. The product_name= part of the query URL comes from the name attribute of the input tag. The order_quantity= and year= attributes are similar. Nonprinting characters in the input ("Super-bowl T-Shirts") are processed; whitespace is replaced by +.

Generating forms in HTML is only half the battle. The harder part is to decode the input data submitted from the form. All the programs that use data submitted from an HTML form must conform to the specification called Common Gateway Interface (CGI).

### CGI Gateway Services

Today, an important aspect of Web server development is application gateways, more specifically, CGI, which is a specification for communicating data between an information server, in this case a Web server, and another application. CGI is used wherever the Web server needs to send or receive data from another application, such as a database. A CGI script is a program that negotiates the movement of data between the Web server and an outside application. Information on the CGI specification can be found on-line at http://hoohoo.ncsa.uiuc.edu/cgi/interface.html.

A typical use of CGI is to pass data, filled in by a user in an HTML form, from the Web server to a database. Data also can be returned to the user's browser via CGI. CGI scripts may be written in virtually any high-level language, although C and Perl are the most popular programming languages, since they run on so many platforms.

Let's examine the various steps in the CGI process (see Fig. 6.8).

*Step 1.* When any HTML form is filled out, the client browser assembles the query and forwards it onto the designated server using the HTTP protocol. To enable this action, forms begin with the construct: <FORM METHOD=POST ACTION="cgi-bin/program">...</FORM>. The ACTION should be a URL pointing to the script (or program) that will be processing the data collected by the form.

*Step 2.* The server passes the data to an executable program. The server activates the script and passes to the script the various values filled out by the user in the HTML form. On a UNIX httpd server, the CGI program will receive the form data from the stdin—provided that the METHOD=POST

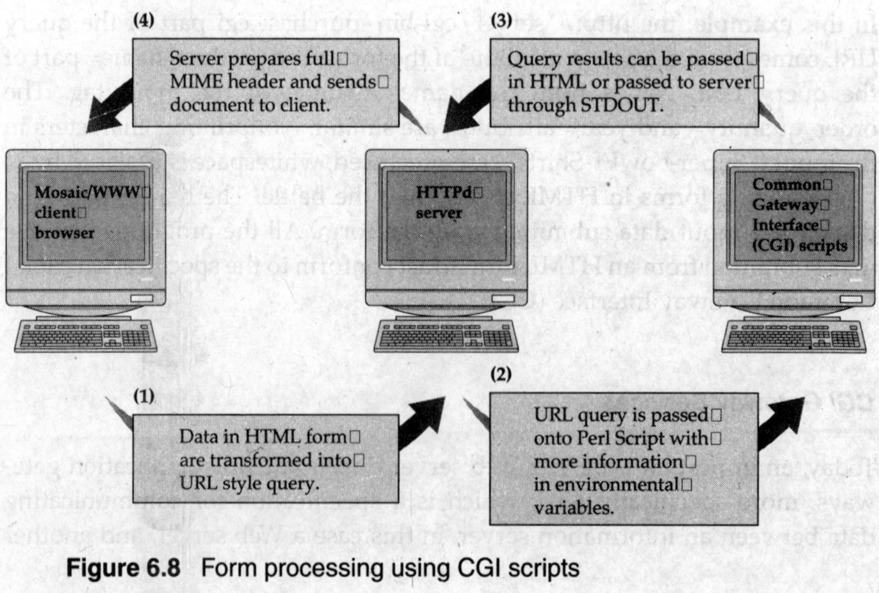


**Figure 6.8** Form processing using CGI scripts

receive the form data from the stdin—provided that the METHOD=POST attribute was used. If the METHOD=GET attribute was used, all the form data are encoded in the environment variable QUERY_STRING. This is not recommended because it is unreliable for large strings of data.

*Step 3.* The script then processes the incoming query. Its task is to return an answer in the form of a document that the server can pass back to the client browser. Typically the document will be in HTML or text, but other types are allowed. To differentiate between various document types, the script must specify the type of the document by printing a MIME content-type header as the first line.

*Step 4.* The server takes the document from the script, then sends this package back to the client browser via the HTTP protocol. The output generated by the CGI program sent to httpd, which will be sent back to the browser.

## 6.5 SECURITY AND THE WEB

The ability to conduct business on a public network has strong attraction—and the potential for big savings. Security and confidentiality are essential, however, before businesses can conduct financial transactions over the Internet, and a lack of widespread security measures remains at this time. At present, credit card numbers, financial records, and other important information are not encrypted and can be intercepted by any savvy Internet hacker (a severe problem for anyone planning to perform commerce over the Net).

The lack of data security on the Internet has become a high-profile problem due to the increasing number of applications oriented toward commerce. Many commercial applications require that the client and server be able to authenticate each other and exchange data confidentially. This exchange has three basic properties [MCOM94a]:

1. Clients are confident about servers they are communicating with (server authentication).
2. Client conversation with the server is private (privacy using encryption).
3. Clients' conversations cannot be tampered or interfered with (data integrity).

Several software companies and electronic marketplace providers are tackling the issue of secure HTTP implementations by developing additional data security measures that involve encryption—the digital coding of sensitive data, such as credit card numbers between the client (user) and server (merchant). Encrypted information can be "unlocked" only by the intended recipient through a digital key. (See Chapter 5 for detailed discussion of security issues and encryption methods.)

## Categories of Internet Data and Transactions

Several categories of data must be encrypted, making Internet data security an interesting challenge [PHB94b]:

- *Public data* have no security restrictions and can be read by anyone. Such data should be protected from unauthorized tampering or modification, however, because a reader may perform damaging actions on its content.
- *Copyright data* have content that is copyrighted but not secret. The owner of the data is willing to provide it but wishes to ensure that the user has paid for it. The objective is to maximize revenue and security.
- *Confidential data* contain material that is secret but whose existence is not a secret. Such data include bank account statements, personal files, and the like. Such material may be referenced by public or copyright data.
- *Secret data*'s existence is a secret. Such data might include algorithms. It is necessary to monitor and log all access to secret data.

Despite the variety of data, security and verification are necessary for all types because of the sensitivity of information being transferred and to protect the consumer from various forms of fraud and misconduct.

### WWW-Based Security Schemes

Several methods can provide security in the Web framework. These include the following:

- *Secure HTTP (S-HTTP)* is a revision of HTTP that will enable the incorporation of various cryptographic message formats, such as DSA and RSA standards, into both the Web client and the server; most of the security implementation will take place at the protocol.
- *Security socket layer (SSL)* uses RSA security to wrap security information around TCP/IP-based protocols. This implementation, while different from S-HTTP, accomplishes the same task. The benefit of SSL over S-HTTP

is that SSL is not restricted to HTTP, but can also be used for security for FTP and TELNET, among other Internet services.

- *SHEN* is a security scheme for the Web sponsored by the W3 consortium. It is a noncommercial or more research oriented security and is similar to S-HTTP.

Because these three security camps are currently working on different proposals and approaches, it is likely that in the near future they will collaborate to develop a single standard.

In fact, the transport of information needs to be decoupled from higher-layer mercantile protocols such as electronic payment services. Approaches that decouple commercial transactions from implementation and transport service accounting not only simplify the latter but also may provide cost recovery for transport services. For example, the dynamic of the user's interaction with a bank, using the postal service as transport, is completely decoupled from the interaction between the transacting parties. In mail-order transactions, costs for the postal service are recovered in a variety of ways that can be matched to the accounting overhead and market strategies of the parties.

## Existing Basic Authentication Features

NCSA has already implemented extensions by which the client and NCSA httpd server call external programs that encrypt and decrypt their communications and thus provide secure communications between the server and the client. These programs also provide authentication to ensure that users are who they say they are.

This system has hooks for PEM (Privacy Enhanced Mail) as well as PGP (Pretty Good Privacy) encryption (see Chapter 5). PGP and PEM (both of which use RSA encryption) are programs that allow a sender and a receiver to communicate in a way that does not allow third parties to read them and that certify that senders are really who they claim to be. Currently, this protocol with PEM and PGP uses local key files on the server side. The client side with PEM uses the "finger" program to retrieve the server's public key, but parties who wish to use Mosaic and httpd with PEM or PGP encryption will need to communicate beforehand and find a secure way to exchange their public keys.

We illustrate a sample exchange between client and server [NCSA93a]. The first illustration shows a request without an authorized password that is rejected by the server. Once a server receives a request without an authorization field to access a document that is protected, it sends an Unauthorized 401 status code and a set of Web-authenticate fields containing valid authentication schemes and their scheme-specific parameters. After receiving unauthorized status code, the browser prompts for user name and password (if they are not already given by the user) and constructs a string containing those two separated by a colon: username:password. This string is then encoded into printable characters and sent along with the next request in the authorization field as follows: Authorization: Basic encoded_string.

```
Client:                                  Server:

GET /docs/protected.html HTTP/1.0        HTTP/1.0 401 Unauthorized
UserAgent: Mosaic/X 2.5                  Web-Authenticate:PEM
                                          entity="webmaster@cism.bus.utexas.edu"
                                         Server: NCSA/1.1
```

The following exchange is a valid one with a request with a PEM key being delivered in encrypted form. The server performs an access request validation procedure [CERN93a] and then decrypts the message using the public key and responds with the body of the reply also encrypted.

```
Client:                                  Server:

GET / HTTP/1.0                           HTTP/1.0 200 OK
Authorization: PEM entity=               Content-type: application/x-Web-pem-reply
 "ram@cism.bus.utexas.edu"
Content-type: application/
x-Web-pem-request

—BEGIN PRIVACY-                          —BEGIN PRIVACY-
 ENHANCED MESSAGE—                        ENHANCED MESSAGE—
this is the real request, encrypted      this is the real reply, encrypted
END PRIVACY-ENHANCED                     —END PRIVACY-ENHANCED
 MESSAGE—                                    MESSAGE—
```

However, this simple protocol has been used for (1) user name/password-level access authorization; (2) rejection or acceptance of connections based on the Internet address of the client; or (3) a combination of these two methods. This protocol is deemed insufficient for dealing with the needs of commerce, where strong authentication and message integrity are necessary.

## Secure Sockets Layer (SSL)

Netscape Communications has proposed a protocol for providing data security layered between high-level application protocols and TCP/IP. This security protocol, called secure sockets layer (SSL), provides data encryption, server authentication, message integrity, and optional client authentication for a TCP/IP connection.

SSL is layered beneath application protocols such as HTTP, SMTP, TELNET, FTP, Gopher, and NNTP (see Fig. 6.9) and above the Internet connection protocol TCP/IP. SSL provides a security "handshake" to initiate the TCP/IP connection. This handshake results in the client and server agreeing on the level of security they will use and fulfills any authentication requirements for the connection. Thereafter, SSL's only role is to encrypt and decrypt the message stream.

This protocol fully encrypts all the information in both the HTTP request and the HTTP response, including the URL the client is requesting, any submitted form contents (including things like credit card numbers), any HTTP access authorization information (user names and passwords), and all the data returned from the server to the client. In other words, SSL provides encryption that creates a secure channel to prevent third parties on the network from being able to tamper with and read messages being exchanged between the client and server and authentication that uses a digital signature to verify the legitimacy of the server.

The server implements server-side support for HTTP over SSL, including support for acquiring a server certificate and communicating securely with

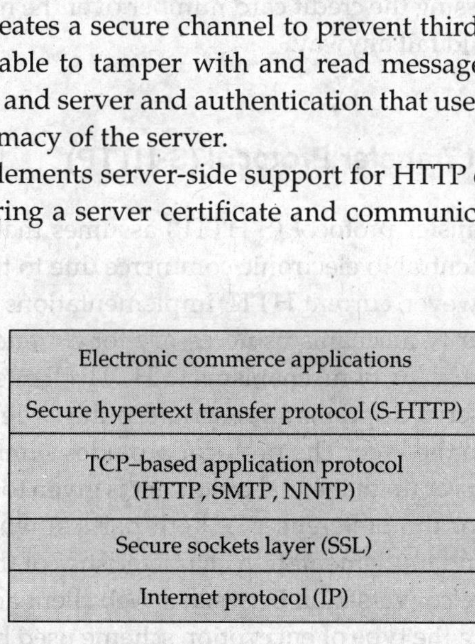


**Figure 6.9** Web security layers

SSL-enabled browsers. To provide security, the Netscape Navigator supports a new URL access method, https, for connecting to HTTP servers using SSL (https is a protocol that is simply SSL underneath HTTP). You need to use "https://" for HTTP URLs with SSL, whereas you continue to use http:// for HTTP URLs without SSL.

Because HTTP+SSL (or https) and HTTP are different protocols and typically reside on different ports (443 and 80, respectively), the same server system can run both secure and insecure HTTP servers simultaneously. This means that HTTP can provide some information to all users using no security, and https can provide information only securely. For instance, the "storefront" and merchandise catalog could be insecure and the ordering payment forms could be secure.

Browsers who do not implement support for HTTP over SSL will not be able to access https URLs. One of the benefits of using a different URL access method (https instead of just http) is so that non-SSL browsers can refuse to allow insecure submission of forms that expect to be submitted securely. That is, if a document served by a normal HTTP server contains a fill-out form that allows a user to enter his/her credit card number and that form's submission action is an https URL (because the document's author expects the form to be submitted securely), a non-SSL browser will not even try to submit the form (typically giving a "cannot submit" error message instead). Were a separate URL access method not being used, the browser would try to submit the form, passing the credit card number over the net in the clear, and the submission would fail anyway.

## Secure Hypertext Transfer Protocol (S-HTTP)

Secure hypertext transfer protocol (S-HTTP) assumes that the Web and the HTTP protocol are central to electronic commerce due to their installed base and ease of use. However, current HTTP implementations have only modest support for the security mechanisms necessary for commerce. Secure HTTP supports a variety of security mechanisms to HTTP clients and servers, providing the security service options appropriate to the wide range of potential end uses possible on the Web. The protocol provides symmetric capabilities to both client and server (in that equal treatment is given to both requests and replies, as well as for the preferences of both parties) while preserving the transaction model and implementation characteristics of the current HTTP.

To ensure a secure conversation between a Web client and server, S-HTTP works by negotiating the type of encryption scheme used between client and server. Several cryptographic message format standards can be incorporated into S-HTTP clients and servers. Option negotiation is used to allow clients and servers to agree on transaction modes (Should the request be signed? encrypted? both? What about the reply?); cryptographic algorithms; and certificate selection (please sign with your "VISAcard certificate").

S-HTTP-secured clients can talk to S-HTTP-oblivious servers and vice-versa, although such transactions obviously would not use S-HTTP security features. S-HTTP does not require client-side public key certificates (or public keys). This is significant because it means that spontaneous private transactions can occur without requiring individual users to have an established public key. While S-HTTP will be able to take advantage of ubiquitous certification infrastructures, its deployment does not require it.

One advantage of S-HTTP is that it supports end-to-end secure transactions. This means that multiple encryption/decryption need not be done at every intermediate point. Clients may initiate a secure transaction, typically using information supplied in HTML fill-out forms. With S-HTTP, no sensitive data need ever be sent over the network in the clear.

### *SSL versus S-HTTP*

What about the relationship between SSL and S-HTTP? Secure HTTP and SSL address different pieces of the security puzzle, but they are not technologically incompatible. That is, SSL and S-HTTP are not mutually exclusive; one could in fact layer S-HTTP on top of SSL. S-HTTP provides capabilities SSL does not, as SSL provides capabilities S-HTTP does not. Figure 6.9 shows the relationship between the different security standards.

SSL and S-HTTP have different motivations: SSL layers security beneath application protocols such as HTTP, FTP, and TELNET, whereas S-HTTP adds message or transaction-based security to HTTP by drawing on the approaches and philosophies of the message encryption standards such as PEM and PGP. SSL simply encrypts the data in a given file, such as a customer information form with a credit card number, and decrypts it at the other end of the transaction. Secure HTTP is a more comprehensive security package that includes authentication of the client's identity by the server through digital signature verification and other features. But secure HTTP only works with transactions that use the HTTP transfer protocol.

## SHEN Security Scheme for the Web

Because of U.S. government export restrictions, browser software with encryption algorithms cannot be sent overseas. To get around this problem, the W3 consortium is developing SHEN, which in many ways mirrors S-HTTP. SHEN provides for three separate security-related mechanisms [PHB94a].

1. *Weak authentication with low maintenance overhead and without patent or export restrictions.* A user identity must be established as genuine. Unauthorized access must be improbable but need not be secure from all possible forms of attack.
2. *Strong authentication via public key exchange.* A user identity must be established as genuine. Unauthorized access must be impossible except by random chance or by access to unknown technology.
3. *Strong encryption of message content.* The data must not be transmitted in a form comprehensible to a third party; an identified party acts as guarantor in this respect.

Though SSL and S-HTTP are the Web security schemes that have the most clout, other proposals and implementations are currently research projects aimed at providing more comprehensive security than SSL or S-HTTP currently offer.

## 6.6 SUMMARY

We see electronic commerce as the integration of network infrastructure, data management, and security services, to allow business applications within different organizations to interchange information within the context of business processes automatically. Communications services transfer the information from the originator to the recipient. Data management services define the interchange format of the information. Security services authenticate the source of information, verify the integrity of the information received by the recipient, prevent disclosure of the information to unauthorized users, and verify that the intended recipient received the information.

Electronic commerce applications are being built on a foundation of global hypertext. Developers long believed that hypertext is just another user-interface approach. However, distributed hypertext systems such as the World Wide Web are interesting computing hybrids that span traditional boundaries. The Web has the following characteristics: It is a networking technology plus an information management method that provides a novel way of directly accessing and manipulating information. It is also provides an information representation scheme. It is an interface that integrates security and payment schemes that can be arbitrarily embedded with the contents and can be used for on-line buying and selling.

In short, the Web provides a totally different and unique method of accessing information. Whereas traditional databases have some structure to them, a hypertext database has no regular structure. The user is free to explore and assimilate information in different ways, an immense flexibility that is making electronic commerce a reality.

# Chapter 7

# Consumer-Oriented Electronic Commerce

The convergence of money, commerce, computing, and networks is laying the foundation for a global consumer marketplace. Consumer-oriented e-commerce is still in its early stages, but the question is no longer whether it will occur but rather how fast and how widely it will spread.

In this nascent electronic marketplace only an infinitesimal fraction of business transactions are currently handled on the I-way. However, the profit potential of an untapped consumer market is tantalizing scores of corporations. For instance, Microsoft, which had revenues of $4.6 billion in fiscal 1994, is attempting to position itself with various alliances to become a provider of both consumer-oriented products and services. The spending power of the consumer market is evident when one examines consumer products giants such as Procter & Gamble (over $30 billion in sales), or even a niche player such as video game maker Nintendo, whose estimated worldwide revenue totals over $9 billion.

Consumer applications such as on-line stores and electronic shopping malls are burgeoning but access is still cumbersome and basic issues need to be resolved. Customers can browse (net-surf) at their PCs, traveling through electronic shops viewing products, reading descriptions, and sometimes trying samples. For instance, if customers are interested in buying CD-ROMs with racy pictures, they can download sample pictures before purchasing. However, these early systems are not consumer friendly or well integrated. For instance, although it is certainly feasible to browse "The ABC" store's catalog via the Web, there are no directories or catalogs that guide the customer to that particular store. This lack of integration puts the burden on the consumer, who has to spend time and money searching for stores and on-line information.

These early systems sometimes provide information only and lack the means to accept orders via the keyboard. Ideally, consumers should be able to execute a transaction by clicking on the BUY button to authorize payment, and the on-line store's bank account would then automatically receive it from the customer's preferred payment mode (credit, debit, or check). Security of on-line payments remains a major barrier to this feature. Customers could pay by credit card, by transmitting the necessary data via modem, but intercepting messages on the Internet is easy for a smart hacker, so sending a credit card number in an unscrambled message is inviting trouble. It would be relatively safe to send an encrypted credit card number, but that would require either adoption of encoding (or encryption) standards or ad hoc arrangements between buyers and sellers.

Since these capabilities have not yet been worked out even in cases where product selection and delivery are quite sophisticated, certain aspects of the business transaction—negotiation, order processing, payment, and customer service—are still conducted via traditional means, losing much of the advantage of the electronic component. For instance, bills and payment for on-line information products/services are still delivered in most cases via the telephone or postal service. The overall transaction is no longer fully automated, and most of the problems of the nonautomated paradigm remain.

Some fundamental business issues must be addressed before consumer-oriented e-commerce can become widespread, including:

- Establishment of standard business processes for buying and selling products and services in electronic markets
- Development of widespread and easy-to-use implementations of mercantile protocols for order-taking, on-line payment, and service delivery similar to those found in retail/credit card based transactions
- Development of transport and privacy methods that will allow parties that have no reason to trust one another to carry on secure commercial exchanges

In other words, to make consumer-oriented e-commerce more effective, we need a better understanding of the components of the business process from the initial search and discovery of the product/services via on-line catalogs to the management of the order-to-delivery cycle, including the all-important payment/settlement component.

Before delving into the details of the on-line mercantile processes, we need to understand the genre of applications that these business processes are attempting to serve.

## 7.1 CONSUMER-ORIENTED APPLICATIONS

The wide range of applications envisioned for the consumer marketplace can be broadly classified into entertainment, financial services, information, essential services, and education and training (see Table 7.1). The operational rule of evolution for consumer-oriented electronic commerce is simple: Whenever the physical transfer of information is replaced with digital transmission, a winner might emerge as long as the cost is comparable or less, use is more convenient or faster, or the provider has the muscle or strategic partner(s) to underwrite technology investments, along with a vision to understand the demands of these new media.

Let's examine four types of applications that illustrate the operational rule of evolution in very different areas: (1) personal finance management (or remote banking), (2) home shopping, (3) home entertainment, (4) microtransactions of information.

## Personal Finance and Home Banking Management

It is estimated that Americans write 55 billion checks every year. Although experts have been predicting the demise of paper checks for a number of years, paper checks still outnumber electronic checks nearly 30 to 1. The newest technologies—direct deposit of payroll, on-line bill payment and telephone transfers—do not yet have wide acceptance, even though they promise to cut the amount of time spent balancing checkbooks. Only 4 percent of bills are paid by phone, and it is estimated that only 1 percent of consumers use computers for home banking, even though more than 25 percent of American households have PCs. These figures have prompted *American Demographics* to dub "home banking" as one of the ten top marketing blunders of the 1980s [RJ94].

The technology for paying bills, whether by computer or telephone, is infinitely more sophisticated than anything on the market a few years ago. The

**Table 7.1** Consumer-Oriented Services

| *Consumer Life-Style Needs* | *Complementary Multimedia Services* |
|---|---|
| Entertainment | Movies on demand, video cataloging, interactive ads, multiuser games, on-line discussions |
| Financial services and information | Home banking, financial services, financial news |
| Essential services | Home shopping, electronic catalogs, telemedicine, remote diagnostics |
| Education and training | Interactive education, multiuser games, video conferencing, on-line databases |

1980s were the days of "stone age" technology compared to what exists today. In the 1980s, technology choices for accessing services were limited to touch-tone phones and in some very advanced cases PCs. The range of options has expanded to include PCs, interactive television, and even personal digital assistants (PDAs). It would be myopic indeed to predict that choices will stop with these. Consumer interest in home banking has resumed, fueled by growing comfort—or at least familiarity—with electronics, by greater demands on consumers' time, and by the expanding need for information to manage the increasing complexity of household finances [HBB94].

Home banking services are often categorized as basic, intermediate, and advanced. Basic services are related to personal finance: checking and savings account statement reporting, round-the-clock banking with automated teller machines (ATM), funds transfer, bill payment, account reconciliation (balancing checkbooks), and status of payments or "stop payment requests." Intermediate services include a growing array of home financial management services, which include household budgeting, updating stock portfolio values, and tax return preparation. More advanced services include stock and mutual fund brokerage or trading services, currency trading, and credit or debit card management.

### Basic Services

Let's take a look at the evolution in banking from live tellers to ATM machines and now to home banking. Banks introduced ATMs in the 1970s to automate two functions: deposits and cash extraction. Citicorp first installed ATMs to serve customers with low bank balances. Initially the thinking in banking circles was that the high-balance customers would do business with bank tellers and ATMs would be used by the less wealthy. Customers soon discovered, however, that ATMs were more convenient than live tellers because they were open late and often didn't have a long queue. In addition, with transaction volume growing steadily, banks discovered that ATMs resulted in real cost savings. According to an ATM survey conducted by the *American Banker*, customer use of ATMs has been rising significantly with a concomitant decrease in bank operating costs.

As ATMs proliferated, banks saw the business need for a network that could be accessed by a broader range of people transacting from nontraditional places like airports and supermarkets and for a wider array of activities, such as bank balance inquiries or loan applications. As the ATM network expanded, an unintended consequence emerged: Customer loyalty became a thing of the past as customers began to look at technology and service as the differentiator, not the individual bank's name. Banks found themselves caught in a vicious circle: Customers demanded greater ATM services, but in furnishing those services, banks became the faceless providers of commodities. Their hard-won brand equity was swept away by the power of the marketplace transactions. Indeed, as banks linked and branded their networks for added customer convenience (e.g., CIRRUS or OTTO), the net effect was further homogenization of ATMs and declining consumer brand loyalty to individual retail banks.

The ATM network (Fig. 7.1) can be thought of as analogous to the Internet, with banks and their associations being the routers and the ATM machines being the heterogeneous computers on the network. This interoperable network of ATMs has created an interface between customer and bank that changed the competitive dynamics of the industry. Today, the ATM interface is an integral part of a bank's communications and market strategy. Bankers, applying traditional, time-honored management models, originally saw only automation in the ATM network, however. They did not see that such automation would change the entire process of retail banking itself.

Increased ATM usage and the consequent decrease in teller transactions does not necessarily mean the demise of branches. There will always be customers who will prefer a live teller to a machine, but it will be bank officers with their sophisticated software who will, with increased efficiency, meet new customers, handle their questions, and sell them new products.

While few would argue that consumers on average are currently more comfortable with ATMs and phones than with PCs, many believe that the future of home banking lies with PCs, which are fast becoming household items.

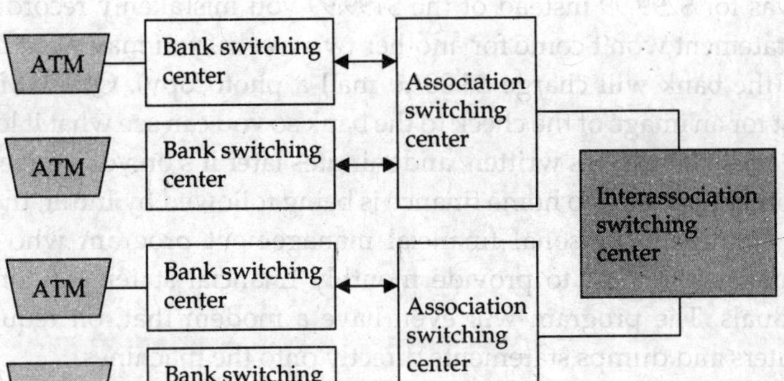


**Figure 7.1** Structure of ATM network

### Intermediate Services

The problems associated with home banking in the 1980s were long believed to prevail in the 1990s, namely, that it is a relatively expensive service that requires a PC, a modem, and special software. These problems are being solved rather quickly. For the sophisticated customer, home banking offers the facility of paying bills, transferring funds, and opening new accounts from home. As the equipment becomes less and less expensive and as banks offer a broader array of services, home banking could develop into a comprehensive package that could even include such nonbank activities as insurance, entertainment, travel, and business news.

Experts predict that as home banking matures it will include a mixture of delivery mechanisms from phones, computers, to even televisions. The PC-based products allow the customer to maintain account data in a local database on their hard drive and to perform import/export between the banking application and others on the PC such as accounting and check register. Some of the more robust products offer specialized services for businesses, such as direct payroll deposit and cash concentration. At the high end of this category are the more sophisticated cash management packages offered to the bank's large corporate customers.

Whether large or small, the underlying principles remain the same. Say you use the Quick & Dirty Personal Money Management (QDPMM) program for keeping track of your finances. It allows you to pay the bills (electronically and by check), reconcile your checking accounts, reconcile your credit card accounts, move money between investment accounts, and so forth. The program can pass data to/from any bank that can provide data in "standard" formats. QDPMM pulls down a list of paid checks from your bank and reconciles the checking account. It shows you that check number 1234 was for $299.99 instead of the $199.99 you mistakenly recorded. Since your statement won't come for another two weeks, you may want to see the check (the bank will charge $5.00 to mail a photocopy). QDPMM sends a request for an image of the check to the bank so you can see what it looks like, where and when it was written, and minutes later it's on your screen.

Another approach to home finance is being followed by Intuit, the makers of the "Quicken" personal financial management program who have an agreement with VISA to provide monthly financial statements on disk to individuals. The program will even have a modem that, on request, calls computers and dumps statements directly onto the machines.

Consider the following computerized on-line bill-paying system offered by CheckFree, an Ohio-based service with an estimated 140,000 clients. Once the software is loaded and the user sends his or her bank account number—writing checks takes only seconds. Say you owe your local telephone company $75. You click on the check-writing software and a picture of a check pops up. You fill in the name, the amount, and the date you want the bill paid. Once you've written checks to everyone you need to pay, you instruct the computer to transmit them. The modem dials the CheckFree computer with payment instructions. Each evening, CheckFree processes those payments, verifies that money exists to cover them, then either electronically notifies the Federal Reserve Board to transfer that amount from customer account in bank A to the merchants' accounts in bank B or, if a payee isn't set up to receive electronic payments, will mail a check. (See Fig. 7.2.)

More sophisticated options are also possible. One can actually program a computer to pay certain monthly bills automatically on a specified day. The computer keeps track of these commands and never forgets to record a payment. The cost for all this convenience: $ 9.95 a month for the first 20 payments, $3.50 for each additional batch of 10 payments (plus the software for around $29.95).

### Advanced Services

The goal of many financial services firms is to offer their on-line customers a complete portfolio of life, home, and auto insurance along with mutual funds, pension plans, home financing, and other financial products. Barriers to this goal lie not only on the customer's side but in the fact that the systems in place at many financial services firms are not interoperable. Even within

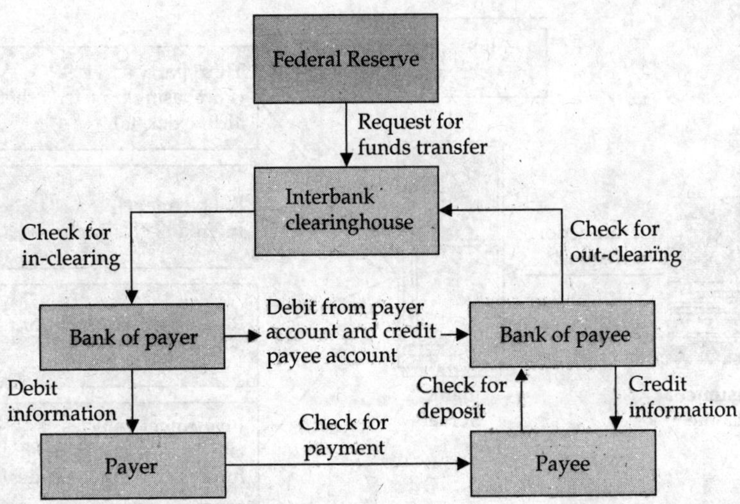


**Figure 7.2** Check-clearing process

most companies offering a range of financial products, each line of business typically has separate accounting and customer record systems.

There is a growing push in the banking and brokerage community to develop systems that support advanced services. Figure 7.3 illustrates the range of services that may well be offered by banks in the future. These services range from on-line shopping to real-time financial information from anywhere in the world. Some of these services are already being offered and others are planned for the future. Although some of these services may appear simple enough, they require extraordinary integration of computer systems at the branch, central office, and partners levels.

In short, home banking allows consumers to avoid long lines and gives them the flexibility of doing their banking at any time. For bankers, it's an opportunity to avoid building more bank branches and cut office expenses. It is estimated that processing an electronic transaction costs six times less than the cost of processing a check.

On the customer side, factors are working both for and against home banking. Growing familiarity with technology to access bank accounts and to handle financial affairs is boosting interest. And the oft-cited time squeeze on consumers (long commutes, heavy workload, family obligations, household management) is also pushing consumers toward services that can ease the burden. But perhaps the key issue driving consumer acceptance is pricing. Home banking services can be expensive to implement and operate, yet consumers are rarely willing to pay much more than $10 or $15 per month. The companies offering these services have to provide incen-

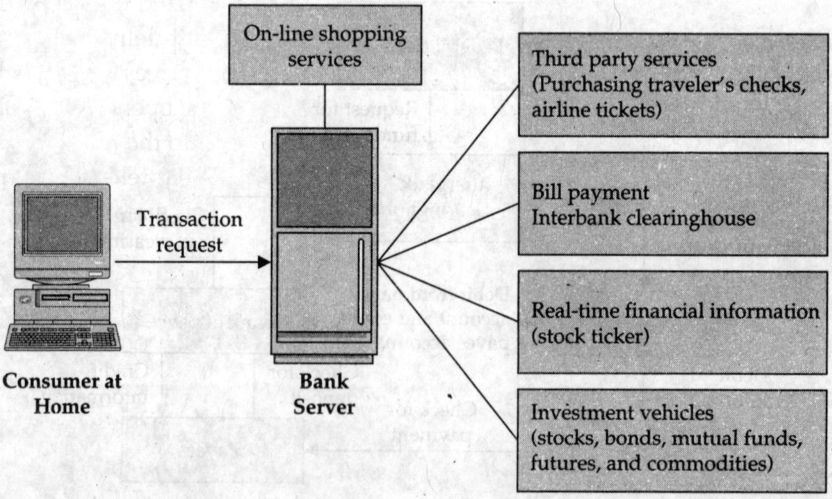


**Figure 7.3** Advanced services and home banking

tives such as low fees to customers to use the service. Banks must also look beyond consumers for home banking. Many regard small businesses as the next target for these services. While the issues surrounding home banking appear to be growing in complexity, so are the opportunities and challenges for bankers.

Indeed, it can be said that the evolution in personal finance over the last twenty-five years is as much the byproduct of new network technologies as the result of deregulating old financial institutions. For example, technology enabled the transformation of the regional BankAmericard into the global VISA, as banks collaborated to create a technical standard for credit transactions and settlements. The 1980s saw an explosion of ATMs—in no small part due to the recognition that networks of ATMs made more sense than each bank having its own proprietary technology.

One thing is certain: All of these technologies have combined and converged to create the infrastructures for today's overwhelming array of personal financial services. Intriguingly, these network technologies frequently demand new organizational structures to manage them [MSLA94], and we are bound to witness some very interesting dynamics in the financial services industry in the next few years.

## Home Shopping

Another oft-cited example of electronic commerce, home shopping, is already in wide use and has generated substantial revenues for many companies racing to develop on-line malls. These malls will enable a "customer" to enter on-line stores, look at products, try on computerized clothes, see a reflection in a digital mirror, and purchase with overnight delivery against credit card billing. The exact operating method of these services has yet to be determined, but the retailers are well aware of the potential opened up by the ability to transmit huge amounts of digital information into the home and to provide interactive control to the shopper. And the current television- and catalog-based shopping processes are expected to undergo major changes to take advantage of the technology.

### *Television-Based Shopping*

The home shopping concept gained ground with the amazing popularity of television-based shopping. Launched in 1977 by the Home Shopping Network (HSN), television-based shopping enjoyed revenues of $1.2 billion in 1993. To put this into perspective, consider that in 1992 U.S. consumers bought $42 billion of merchandise from home through mail-order houses and television channels. It is estimated that this market crossed the $100-billion mark in 1994 [HSN94].

Who is the target audience sitting before the TV? A survey of 450 home shoppers by WSL Marketing that appeared in *Broadcasting and Cable Magazine* showed that 75 percent of home shoppers were women. Almost half (48 percent) of the respondents said that price was the main factor in their buying decisions, and only 7 percent cited convenience as a factor. More than 25 percent of respondents said they had no specific reason for their purchases. Interestingly, more than 10 percent of the respondents replied, "TV shopping is for lazy, stupid people" [HSN94].

TV shopping has evolved over the years to provide a wide variety of goods ranging from collectibles, clothing, small electronics, housewares, jewelry, and computers. When HSN started in Florida in 1977, it mainly sold factory overruns and discontinued items. Today, it and QVC, the other major home shopping network, operate more like traditional retailers and offer many of the same services. Both networks have liberal return policies—up to 30 days after the buyer receives the item—and money-back guarantees. Both offer installment plans for more expensive purchases, accept most major credit cards, and offer their own credit card. Like other merchants, the TV shopping networks try to hook consumers by offering exclusive lines of merchandise. If you yearn for some celebrity's shoes or covet her sweaters, you'll have to buy them from HSN. Aside from their appeal to some viewers, exclusive lines and private labels are popular with television retailers because viewers can't comparison-shop.

How does this type of shopping work? A customer uses her remote control to shop different channels with the touch of a button. To target customers, channels are often specialized. For example, one would be a fashion channel to show the latest styles and a variety of merchandise. The sports fashion channel would feature men's apparel, both casual and dresswear, and women's casual or career sportswear. The style channel would feature a talk show with fashion tips. There would be home furnishings, electronics, and audio and video and fitness channels. A spotlight channel would give in-depth information on new and interesting products, and a specialty catalog channel would feature women's sizes, big and tall, bridal gowns, and accessories. And the customer service channel would provide the viewer with information on payment, delivery, how to order the proper size, customer inquiry, return policies, and other consumer protection details.

At this time, cable shopping channels are not truly interactive because they use phone lines to take orders. But soon they will be interactive, offering intriguing new possibilities. For instance, you may be able to scan your picture into the TV and see how the latest outfit looks on your body before making a decision.

Well aware of the enormous potential of electronic retailing, many firms have announced their intention to enter some hybrid of the developing interactive business. The biggest barrier to entry into the video shopping arena has been the lack of available channels offering variety to customers. As a result, many of the electronic shopping ventures will initially generate only very modest results because most will not reach any more than 10 million homes. This constraint will fade over the next few years as more cable operators upgrade their systems and add more services.

### Catalog-Based Shopping

Let's visualize the following scenario in the on-line consumer marketplace of the future. A consumer is planning to buy a car. Using a computer connected to the Internet, she launches an inquiry using a knowledge-gathering software assistant (in technical terms a mobile software agent) that roams the global networks and identifies cars in various vendor catalogs that fit certain specified parameters such as safety, price, and quality.

Some of the necessary information needed for objective decision making, such as third-party ratings, could be located on a *Consumer Reports* commercial archival service, which our consumer has never accessed before. She would like to retrieve copies of these reports to read on her computer. The archive service informs her that there will be a $5 charge for the consumer report. Our fictional consumer cannot buy on credit because she doesn't have an account with this service and the service doesn't accept credit cards for charges under $10. So she places her smart card containing electronic cash provided as part of a bank service into the smart-card reader. She transfers $5 worth of these electronic tokens to the archival service. The service validates the tokens as authentic and sends the reports to the consumer. Upon receipt of the requested reports, the consumer in turn completes the transaction by transferring ownership of $5 in tokens to the service.

After reading the reports and deciding that her dream car is too expensive, our consumer decides to buy jewelry. While browsing, she sees an advertisement for diamond rings and sends a request to the advertising distributor to buy the "XYZ" diamond ring. The distributor notifies her that the charge will be $1399.99. She places her smart card into her card reader and transfers $1399.99 in electronic tokens. The shopping service attempts to validate these tokens and discovers that her bank has put a bar on the tokens, meaning that she cannot use them to shop for expensive products. The service returns the tokens to the customer with an explanation. To enable this scenario, traditional paper-based shopping catalogs have to be replaced, at least in part, by on-line catalogs. Also, new payment instruments are required.

The on-line catalog business consists of brochures, CD-ROM catalogs, and on-line interactive catalogs. Currently, most on-line catalogs are some form of electronic brochures. Also known as *softads* or *interads*, electronic brochures are a multimedia replacement for direct mail paper and diskette brochures used in the business-to-business marketing arena. Basically, they consist of a highly interactive program using still images, graphics, animation, sound, text, and data. Motion picture video is seldom used due to storage and performance limitations. According to the Direct Marketing Association, electronic brochures frequently evoke considerably better responses (up to 12 percent) than traditional mail methods, where a 1 percent response rate is considered to be successful. One of the drawbacks of this catalog is prohibitive cost, ranging from $10,000 to $1,000,000, depending on the creativity shown in advertising, quality of graphics, and so forth. Even a simple interactive catalog can cost anywhere from $20,000 to $30,000.

An extension of the electronic brochure concept is a multiproduct comprehensive on-line catalog system typically put in kiosks. These interactive kiosks let shoppers browse through video presentations of products and go one step further—into the future of interactive advertising. These catalogs are very similar to electronic brochures and have no added benefit except for more storage capacity (they often use CD-ROM for storage). Some kiosk catalogs also incorporate order-taking through an instore Electronic Data Interchange (EDI). Examples include DisplayNet used by Sears Roebuck, Nordstrom, and Mervyn's department stores. CD-ROM-based catalogs can also range in cost from $10,000 to $1,000,000, depending on the quality and originality shown.

One of the most active areas of on-line shopping is distributed component catalogs. Electronic access to component information is essential during the design and manufacturing processes for almost all products. Component information often includes schematic symbols, logical circuit diagrams, timing circuit diagrams, and thermal simulation models for manufacturing, electrical/mechanical parameters, part footprint, costing, reliability models, and ordering and delivery information. Distributed component catalogs seek to address three aspects of electronic component commerce: the component information itself, transfer of the information from vendor to user, and information integration into the customer's CAD/CAM (computer-aided design and manufacturing). The goal is to eliminate the current paper path for component information and avoid investing resources into correcting the deficiencies of paper-based information transfer. Achieving this goal is expected to help organizations focus their resources directly on producing higher-quality products in less time and at lower cost.

## Home Entertainment

Another application area of e-commerce is that of home entertainment. Consider the following scenario. A customer wishes to watch a movie. She browses through an on-line movie archive guide containing thousands of movies, music videos, award-winning documentaries, soap opera episodes, concerts, and sporting events. After selecting an artistic French movie from a distributor who operates a server in France, she sends a request to the movie distributor with the cost of the movie (e.g., $2.99) in the form of electronic tokens. The distributor informs her that he accepts only credit cards, not tokens as they are hard to change into European currency. The customer then sends her credit card number with expiration date using an encrypted message (e.g., privacy-enhanced mail message). The distributor validates the credit card and transfers the movie to her TV set-top with the necessary safeguards that prevent any copying or reproduction of the movie.

Movie on-demand represented in this scenario is very similar in technology and characteristics to interactive games. The on-line gaming services industry in turn parallels the television industry, where the consumer is primarily interested in good quality programming and is not loyal to any one network. New developments related to on-line gaming include on-demand gaming services such as the Sega channel, a video game channel launched in the middle of 1994 with the aid of Time Warner and TCI [WSJ94]. Subscribers to the Sega channel can download Sega games from their cable TV, including test versions of games new to the market and complete versions of older games. Multiplayer games are also available, allowing viewers to compete against distant friends or relatives on the network. Gaming is expected to be a winning application as more and more sophisticated games are developed and the popularity of the medium increases among adults and children.

In the entire home entertainment area, the key element is the notion of customer control over programming. Entertainment on-demand is expected to give each viewer total control over what, when, and where to watch. Table 7.2 illustrates what will be required in terms of television-based technology for this telemart to become a reality.

In addition to game technology, we are witnessing the emergence of entertainment support functions such as on-screen catalogs, such as *TV Guide*, that inform users "what's on TV." TV Guide On Screen lets cable system subscribers download program schedules and other information from cable system satellite feeds. These catalogs are a convenient way for viewers to scan program options, find specific shows, change channels, order pay-per-view and premium services, lock out programming they do not want, and set reminders for programs they do want to see. Due to the enormous variety of

**Table 7.2** The Telemart: Present and Future Functions

| | |
|---|---|
| Compressing and decoding a digital signal (Images are compressed in order to reduce the quantity of information traveling on the network) | The transition to digital satellite and cable network head broadcasting involves linking the television set to a decoder to reconvert the digital signal into an analog signal (the only type of signal adapted to current television receivers). |
| Decoding a scrambled signal | The broadcasting of a pay channel requires the encryption or scrambling of the signal on emission and the unscrambling on reception. An increase in the number of pay channels could result either in the bundling of the decoders (1 per pay channel received) or the creation of a unique scrambling standard. |
| Rapid loading of a program on a memory medium | An increase in the number of individual interactive services is possible only if network overloading is kept to a strict minimum. It will thus be necessary to download a high-speed broadcast in order to free the network and then let it run at "normal speed" on the screen. The decoder would be fitted with a memory medium (RAM, hard disk, CD-ROM). |
| Electronic money or card payment terminal | Once separated from the telephone, telemart will need a keyboard linked up to the television set in order to ensure interactivity. The keyboard will have a payment connection to simplify the billing process. |

choices (local, national, and even international), customers need to inform the system what they like and don't like. In return, the system will customize a personalized electronic menu of entertainment options.

### Size of the Home Entertainment Market

Entertainment services are expected to play a major role in e-commerce. This prediction is underscored by the changing trends in consumer behavior. Notice the critical importance of home video to Hollywood revenues in Table 7.3. In 1990 home video accounted for an estimated 10.4 percent of movie industry revenues. By 1993 that number had risen to almost 35 percent.

**Table 7.3** Industry Estimates of Consumer Expenditures

| | *1980 ($4.7 bln)* | | *1990 ($31.0 bln)* | | *1993 ($37.8 bln)* | |
|---|---|---|---|---|---|---|
| Theaters | 49.0% | $2.3 | 14.5% | $ 4.5 | 13.2% | $ 5.0 |
| Basic cable | 35.0% | $1.6 | 34.5% | $10.7 | 36.9% | $13.9 |
| Premium cable | 16.0% | $0.8 | 16.5% | $ 5.1 | 14.0% | $ 5.3 |
| Home video | — | — | 33.8% | $10.5 | 34.8% | $13.2 |
| Pay per view | — | — | 0.7% | $ 0.2 | 1.1% | $ 0.4 |

Global video revenues are estimated to account for five times the wholesale revenues realized by the studios from their share of studio receipts. On the other hand, pay per view, video on-demand's technologically less advanced cousin, has been around for fifteen years and generates less than $100 million of film revenue (most pay-per-view revenues come in the "event area" such as sports) [PW94].

Although an accurate assessment of the potential size of the e-commerce entertainment market is very difficult, preliminary research by telco, cable TV, and computer firms indicates that the entertainment market is potentially a multibillion-dollar one. These studies indicate that the key to success may well depend on the ability to tap the large pool of discretionary income within medium–high-income households. Several interesting issues present some food for thought, however. For instance, data on TV, cable and VCR ownership, and usage patterns indicate that high-income households have a higher penetration of all three media, yet are relatively light users. In fact, the statistics suggest that TV and cable usage declines but that video rental increases with increasing income, which could mean that the market for video on-demand may be greater in higher-income households. In addition, service providers offering games, home shopping, home banking, and other services would prefer to target their services, particularly in the early stages of marketing, at those end users with high discretionary income [NS94]. However, there is very little research in how computer shopping patterns vary across different income groups on which to base strategic decisions. In short, more research in consumer buying and behavior in emerging electronic markets is clearly needed.

The good economic news for the entertainment business is that the net effect of the proliferation of electronic distribution channels created by the I-way will further smooth the risk inherent in any undertaking. For instance, because revenues generated by releasing movies into theaters, overseas markets, home video, and other distribution windows often more than offset the effects of underperformers in the studio's portfolio, major studios have been increasingly willing to produce bigger-budget films. This leads to increased spending on advertising. By increasing the number of prints, expanding the release schedule, and concentrating high-cost advertising campaigns at the earliest stage of distribution, the studios garner consumer awareness and assure a continued source of revenue from the increasingly important ancillary markets—no matter how well the film does in initial release.

### Impact of Home Entertainment on Traditional Industries

The impact of the new forms of entertainment on the traditional movie industry presents a case study that is likely to be repeated in many other industries. The movie exhibition industry clearly needs to understand the implications of the convergence of several technologies into a functioning "home theater." Eventually, it is expected that the average subscriber will sit on the couch, order a first-run film through a computerized set-top box, and watch it on a high-definition television that matches the sound and visual quality of any theatrically released feature. This scenario could have devastating effects on the theater business, but it appears that the technology may not become available as rapidly as some proponents would have us believe. Currently, only a third of the nation's cable subscribers receive more than fifty-three channels; even the most ambitious cable companies, including Time Warner and Tele-Communications, are not promising nationwide, interactive, 500-channel cable systems until the first decade of the twenty-first century [PW94].

Although industry executives fear that home-delivered premiere films will cannibalize the movie market, movie revenues are not dependent on their theatrical releases. In fact, box office grosses account for only about 35 percent of a movie's total revenues, while pay per view, cable, video, and television generate the remaining 65 percent of total worldwide receipts. Consequently, rather than cannibalize the market, pay-per-view premieres may simply change the order in which movies reach the public, with theaters taking a backseat to pay per view. Either way, it remains to be seen whether cable subscribers will be willing to pay the exorbitant pay-per-view price tag of approximately $25 per film that industry executives have suggested they will charge for new pictures.

To get around this problem, cable companies are actually buying movie production houses. For instance, Tele-Communications (TCI) and Carolco Pictures entered into an agreement whereby TCI would gain the rights to broadcast premiere films (first-runs) over its expansive cable system. TCI agreed to invest $90 million in Carolco Pictures in exchange for four pay-per-view films over the 1995–1999 period. The movie company will receive another $10 million in licensing fees when each film is delivered. Finally, Carolco will be paid a third of TCI's revenues from the televised premiere movies up to $60 million, plus $0.50 on every dollar beyond that [PW94].

Similarly, other business strategy questions now debated in the boardrooms will define who will be successful in the future. Consider the following examples of strategic questions. Sony generates billions of dollars a year in sales of VCRs and VCR tapes. Should it work enthusiastically toward changing the distribution channels? Should Blockbuster Video, by far the largest video chain in North America, rush to dismantle its existing business? These and other business strategy issues are among those being hotly debated.

Ultimately, economic issues might allow theaters to maintain an important role in the movie industry given the higher cost of 500-channel, interactive cable systems and HDTVs versus today's 50-odd channel systems and the traditional color TV and pricey pay-per-view events. Today, the average cable bill is approximately $30 a month. If the TCI/Carolco venture succeeds, it is estimated that the cable company would charge about $25 for each initial release offered. In addition, if a cable subscriber were to buy other pay-per-view events or use interactive services, including home shopping and two-way video games, monthly cable bills could soar into the $100 range. Of course, viewers desiring the full "home theater" effect would also have to buy a high-definition television for around $2000. It is unlikely that today's average cable subscriber would be willing to spend that much money just to avoid going to the movies. For the moment, movie theaters are faring reasonably well, and there is little reason to believe that the industry will be decimated either in the near future or further down the line with the arrival of home entertainment.

## Microtransactions of Information

To serve the information needs of the consumer, service providers whose product is information delivered over the I-way are creating an entirely new industry. Most sell any form of digital information that can be sent down a network of one sort or another: data, pictures, computer programs and services. A few sell products—sex, music, books, lingerie—through on-line catalogs.

One significant change in traditional business forced by the on-line information business is the creation of a new transaction category called small-fee transactions for microservices. For example, if company X charged 5 cents to download a customer service file "cs123.txt" from its FTP server and 20,000 people chose to do it every day, then X would have $1000 added to its bank account just for that one file. Now assume that there are 1000 files with similar activity. This volume of activity entails $1,000,000 changing hands in one day.

Such a high daily volume of transactions is currently not feasible because of the overhead involved. Processing even a 5-cent transaction could cost a bank as much as $1.00. Why is the overhead so high? Electronic funds transfer (EFT) means that the accounting systems of several banks have to be able to respond to a message of the format "transfer 5 cents from account #1231 of Bank X [the purchaser] to account #5432 of Bank Y [the service provider]." Although the transaction itself is not complex, the surrounding issues of settlement between the payor and payee banks and verification of funds to cover the transaction add to the overall cost. (See Chapter 8 for more detail.)

First, let's examine the process of verifying the authenticity of the transaction. Once the bank verifies that the purchaser has a balance or credit limit sufficient to make the transfer, the bank determines whether the purchaser authorized the transfer. To protect against fraud, merchants and banks rely on redundant information and reverification. In traditional banking, redundant information can be a signature, a PIN (personal identification number), a driver's license number, or a mother's maiden name. On the network, redundant information could include IP address of the computer, the phone number of the modem, a password, or an encryption key. When the basic message to transfer funds between accounts is supplemented with this redundant information, it can be checked against the bank's database to reduce the likelihood of fraud.

One solution for this problem is to entice the customer by giving some information away for free and provide information bundles (collection of related chunks) that cover the transaction overhead. For example, users can download a demo from a software archive, try it out, and if they like it send their credit card number by e-mail. In return the company will send a software key to activate the program. Several potential problems keep this from being an effective solution.. First and foremost is the potential for massive fraud. As credit card numbers float around the network, some fly-by-night operator will emerge, set up a plausible front, collect credit card numbers, and begin defrauding people. By collecting only 1000 valid credit card numbers in a week, this operator could ring up a lot of charges before having to close up shop. So, in the long run, a small company starting to sell services over the network will find that not many people are going to trust it with their credit card numbers.

Another problem is the inability of the credit card model to deal with those network services that don't cost a lot of money. Say a public WWW server wants to recoup some money from the tens of thousands of people who access it every day. The server wants to charge $.01 for every file downloaded. With the advent of the World Wide Web customers tend to retrieve information in small chunks so the challenge from a business perspective is: How to price such small chunks? How to collect and process the transactions based on small-chunk retrieval so that a profit can be shown?

Answers to these questions represent the future of electronic commerce. The growth of small-money transfers could foster a boom in other complementary information services. For instance, Joe Consumer downloads file "XX" and finds a reference to file "YY" on another server. He clicks on the hyperlink to the location of "YY" and browses through that file and finds another reference. Each time Joe Consumer retrieves a file from a commercial server, the payment meter is ticking. This type of continuous payment is necessary—as opposed to a fixed fee—for several reasons. First, better quality of information will be served. Second, reduction in excessive network traffic could lead to better resource management of public networks, because if A knows that he might be charged, he might not retrieve the file. However, the negative aspect of this is that without people browsing freely, the magic of public networks will disappear.

The complexity of selling microservices increases further when additional activities like account reverification are factored in. Reverification means checking on the validity of the transaction after it has been approved. For example, individuals can verify the validity of transactions using their monthly checking account and credit card statements. In the electronic world, these statements could be received daily, or within five minutes of the occurrence of a transaction, or at some other interval. In cases like information purchase for immediate consumption, "round trip" (in which the bank sends a verification statement/query to the purchaser and receives an okay in response) is not feasible without invoking the ire of the customer. For the transfer of goods, however, the vendor may require that a "round trip" be completed before providing the goods or services to the customer. Not all transactions use the same redundant information and the same reverification process. Transactions involving large dollar amounts and/or high risk of fraud require more sophisticated fraud-prevention procedures. The amount of redundant information and real-time reverification for transactions will depend on their risk classes, and the system must be intelligent enough to recognize and investigate anomalies. The systems have to be fine-tuned to prevent fraud and at the same time impose transaction costs of only 2 or 3 percent (or less) on people dealing with small amounts.

As if the environment is not complex enough, additional possible components for the cost of just doing e-commerce include transport costs; processing costs at endpoints and by agents; if applicable, cost of maintaining and/or setting up/tearing down (TCP) connections to effect transactions; transaction record keeping for auditing and billing; and the costs of running accounting and billing software (to produce statements). Given all this overhead, multiple small transactions, instead of one large one, are likely to be more costly to handle.

Functional small-money transactions require an inexpensive safety and settlement process or a major portion of the transaction value will be consumed in the verification process. Also, most of the arguments in favor of using encryption are aimed at ensuring the integrity of transactions and authentication of transactions, not at economic issues that form a significant factor of business thinking. This is one of the reasons banks are reticent about electronic commerce, fearing it will not be profitable. Banks would rather deal with the evil they understand, like credit card fraud, than the lesser evil they don't comprehend, like a tamper-proof electronic cash system based on encryption.

In sum, the potential usefulness of small-money transfers in generating a steady cash flow, combined with the inability of traditional banks to meet this need, has created a vacuum. Some entrepreneurs appear to be moving in to fill the vacuum and to supply a form of electronic cash that can be used on the Internet. To make small-money transfers work, we need to develop the concept of small-fee banking transaction in the electronic banking world. Unfortunately, the gap is not only technical, given that many bankers do not understand the complex information environment and the rapidly changing business paradigm that is sprouting. Similarly, software experts are suggesting and developing approaches that may be technologically elegant but financially infeasible from a business perspective. What is required is a satisfactory balance between technology for enabling secure transactions and the economic processing of these transactions.

## Desirable Characteristics of an Electronic Marketplace

To summarize the discussion of the electronic marketplace for consumers, let's identify some of the desirable features. Some of these features are unique, while others are the same as in any market. The following criteria are essential for consumer-oriented electronic commerce:

- *Critical mass of buyers and sellers.* The trick is getting a critical mass of corporations and consumers to use electronic mechanisms. In other words, the electronic marketplace should be the first place customers go to find the products and services they need.
- *Opportunity for independent evaluations and for customer dialogue and discussion.* In the marketplace, not only do users buy and sell products or services, they also compare notes on who has the best products and whose prices are outrageous. And, of course, there are usually one or two shrewd

impartial sources whose opinions and endorsements are sought by many. The ability to openly evaluate the wares offered is a fundamental principle of a viable marketplace.

- *Negotiation and bargaining.* No marketplace is complete if it does not support negotiation. Buyers and sellers need to be able to haggle over conditions of mutual satisfaction, including money, terms and conditions, delivery dates, and evaluation criteria.
- *New products and services.* In a viable marketplace, consumers can make requests for products and services not currently offered and have a reasonable expectation that someone will turn up with a proposed offering to meet that request. In short, an electronic marketplace is an interactive information service that supports the entire innovation process.
- *Seamless interface.* The biggest barrier to electronic trade is having all the pieces work together so that information can flow seamlessly from one source to another. This requires standardization. For example, for consumers to find benefit in making all transactions electronically, they need their bank statements delivered to them electronically. These statements need to be compatible with the home finance software so that bills can be paid and checkbooks balanced. On the corporate side, companies need compatible EDI software and network services in order to send electronic purchase orders, invoices, and payments back and forth.
- *Recourse for disgruntled buyers.* A viable marketplace must have a recognized mechanism for resolving disputes among buyers and sellers. Markets typically include a provision for resolving disagreements by returning the product or through arbitrage in other cases.

Many early attempts at electronic markets have failed because these basic conditions were not met. To be successful, companies must know their customers and be able to demonstrate that they can meet their needs. As the number of computer/audio video techno-literate consumers increases every day, business opportunities will emerge and those who identify a need and satisfy it will prosper.

## 7.2 MERCANTILE PROCESS MODELS

Mercantile processes define interaction models between consumers and merchants for on-line commerce. This is necessary because to buy and sell goods, a buyer, seller, and other parties must interact in ways that represent some standard business processes. We, like many others, believe that a common way of doing business over the I-way will be essential to the future growth of e-commerce. A well-established standard process for processing credit card purchases has contributed to the widespread dissemination of credit cards. The war against escalating on-line transaction-processing costs requires new weapons. And designing and implementing new mercantile processes is the most powerful weapon available to wage that war effectively.

The establishment of a common mercantile process (or set of processes) is expected to increase convenience for consumers who won't have to figure out a new business process for every single vendor. The absence of a common process for managing and completing transactions will result in electronic commerce being entangled in a mesh of bilateral ad hoc mechanisms that are specific to every company doing business on-line.

Before rushing off and developing new mercantile process models, it is prudent to review existing business process models used in the manufacturing and retailing industries. The review would provide the understanding required to determine the features needed in an architectural model designed specifically for electronic commerce. Then, of course, within the scope of such an architecture, we must demonstrate the ability to solve all the problems that the current consumer-oriented business processes require and any new ones we may have identified for the future. The idea behind a general architecture is that it would lead to a set of methods and tools from which specific protocols can be easily implemented.

## 7.3 MERCANTILE MODELS FROM THE CONSUMER'S PERSPECTIVE

The on-line consumer expects quality, convenience, value, low price, and control. To meet these expectations and understand the behavior of the online shopper, there is a need for a business process model that provides a standard product/services purchasing process from an interactive services and merchandising point of view. The business process model from a consumer's perspective consists of seven activities that can be grouped into three phases: prepurchase phase, purchase consummation, and postpurchase interaction (see Fig. 7.4):

1. The *prepurchase preparation phase* includes search and discovery for a set of products in the larger information space capable of meeting customer requirements and product selection from the smaller set of products based on attribute comparison.

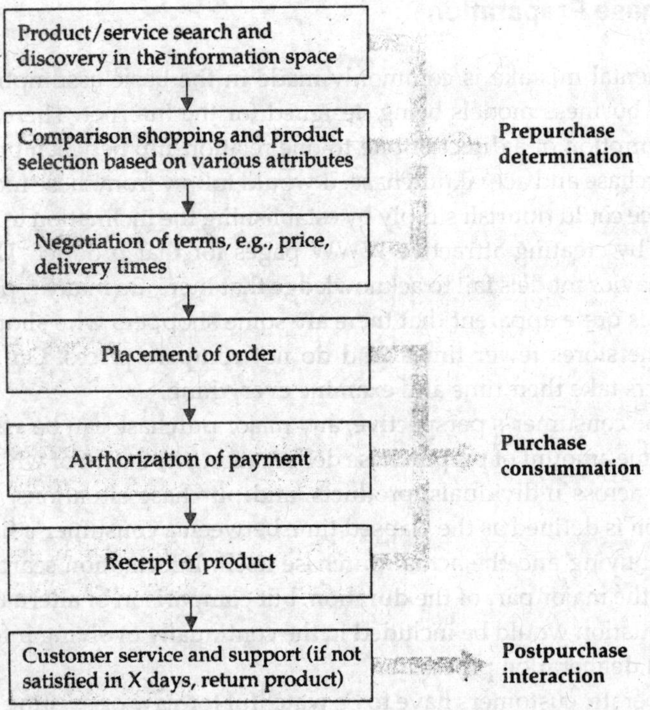


**Figure 7.4** Steps taken by customers in product/service purchasing

2. The *purchase consummation phase* includes mercantile protocols that specify the flow of information and documents associated with purchasing and negotiation with merchants for suitable terms, such as price, availability, and delivery dates; and electronic payment mechanisms that integrate payment into the purchasing process.
3. The *postpurchase interaction phase* includes customer service and support to address customer complaints, product returns, and product defects.

The specialization of this model to particular cases would help merchants and others understand: why consumers shop on-line, where they shop, and what they buy. Just answering these basic questions can be eye-opening: What products and sizes do consumers purchase, and why? How often do they shop? How do they respond to promotions? Who shops the competition, and why? Although each consumer has a distinct way of doing business and different criteria define various products and services, some generalizations can be made about the way consumers make on-line purchasing decisions. These generalizations are essential for understanding the broad consumer dynamics. Let's consider each of the consumer purchasing phases in detail.

## Prepurchase Preparation

A fundamental mistake is commonly made in the basic assumptions of e-commerce business models being designed for the Internet. There seems to be an assumption of a direct or one-to-one relationship between predisposition to purchase and actual purchase. It would follow from these models that e-commerce could flourish simply by establishing the inclination to purchase a product by creating attractive WWW pages for that product. These consumer behavior models fail to acknowledge that there are many types of consumers. It is quite apparent that there are some shoppers who shop quickly, visit on-line stores fewer times, and do not compare prices. On the other hand, others take their time and examine everything.

From the consumer's perspective, any major purchase can be assumed to involve some amount of prepurchase deliberation, the extent of which is likely to vary across individuals, products, and purchase situations. Purchase deliberation is defined as the elapsed time between a consumer's first thinking about buying and the actual purchase itself. Information search should constitute the major part of the duration, but comparison of alternatives and price negotiation would be included in the continually evolving information search and deliberation process.

To deliberate, customers have to be watchful for new or existing information regarding variables that are important for the purchase decision process. Consider a consumer who is currently active in the information search and deliberation process for a new automobile. Unlike the purchase of groceries, which is considered an impulse purchase, typically the purchase of a new car involves an appreciable time lag between the initiation of the information search process and the decision. Through time, information gathered during the search process as well as changing exogenous conditions (an unexpected increase in income, the existence of a promotional sale) can either speed up the purchase decision or encourage the consumer to postpone the purchase decision in some fashion (because prices encountered were too high).

The answers to several important questions about the purchase deliberation process can shape the way on-line shopping environments are designed and created: How much time are buyers allocating and spending on their purchasing decisions with respect to various products? What factors account for the differences in consumer decision time? What technology can be used or designed to reduce decision time? What is the right shopping environment that keeps customers happy and wanting to return? Moreover, information on customer characteristics associated with reduced purchase deliberation times can be quite valuable when attempting to target selective communications to desired audiences properly. In short, not much attention has been paid to this important research area, which may dictate the success or failure of on-line shopping.

In general, consumers can be categorized into three types:

1. *Impulsive buyers,* who purchase products quickly
2. *Patient buyers,* who purchase products after making some comparisons
3. *Analytical buyers,* who do substantial research before making the decision to purchase products or services

Impulse buying (or unplanned purchasing) fits particularly uneasily into current predisposition models of on-line consumer behavior. There is no doubt that unplanned purchasing is a major factor in retailing and is said to account for around a third of total purchasing in nonelectronic markets. In fact, in grocery sectors, impulse buying is in the region of one half or more of total purchases. While the figures for different industries are not entirely compatible, there is little doubt that in most retailing sectors, impulse/unplanned purchasing is a major factor.

In fact, marketing researchers have isolated several types of purchasing:

- *Specifically planned purchases.* The need was recognized on entering the store and the shopper bought the exact item planned.
- *Generally planned purchases.* The need was recognized, but the shopper decided in-store on the actual manufacturer of the item to satisfy the need.
- *Reminder purchases.* The shopper was reminded of the need by some store influence. This shopper is influenced by in-store advertisements and can substitute products readily.
- *Entirely unplanned purchases.* The need was not recognized entering the store.

The key role of the in-store influences on purchasing is indisputable. Thus, to assume that the creation of a predisposition to buy is a sufficient explanation of buyer behavior seems untenable. Creating a predisposition is merely one side of the equation.

In many cases search and discovery technology as well as organized catalogs or directories are necessary inducements to purchasing decisions. Often, search and discovery mechanisms are oriented toward dynamic environments where change makes organization difficult. Directories or catalogs are oriented toward fairly static environments (see Chapter 14).

While the technology for supporting search is important, we still need to understand the actual process that consumers and organizations employ in gathering information. In fact, the promise of electronic commerce could remain unsatisfied unless more effective methods of information search and retrieval based on consumer preferences and behavior are implemented.

### The Consumer Information Search Process

Information search is defined as the degree of care, perception, and effort directed toward obtaining data or information related to the decision problem. Earlier research on information search, primarily in the area of economics, focused on understanding search outcomes or results rather than the specific nature of the underlying search processes. The emphasis was on what rather than how. In e-commerce markets, the outcomes may be identical to those obtained in traditional markets, but the process of reaching them is significantly different. In short, the nature of consumer search behavior is undocumented in the existing literature and represents an area that must be better understood before e-commerce applications can be effectively designed.

Purchase behavior in electronic markets differs from traditional retail settings in two ways. First, a retailer is concerned with simply inducing purchase through the use of marketing mix variables (retail and/or manufacturer rebates, list price discounts, trade-in allowances). Second, a retailer is interested in inducing purchase now, rather than later. Thus coupon books and other tools likely to induce a consumer to make decisions quickly can have important implications on the purchasing process.

In electronic markets, in contrast, we have limited understanding of the marketing mix variables effective in inducing purchases. Also, the issue of information dissemination is a major problem. If we create coupon books, how do we get them to the on-line customer without flooding the network with junk mail. To solve both problems, a better understanding of consumer behavior in on-line markets technology is essential.

In the context of e-commerce, information search can be classified into two categories: organizational and consumer search.

### The Organizational Search Process

Organizational search can be viewed as a process through which an organization adapts to such changes in its external environment as new suppliers, new products, and new services. More narrowly, purchasing departments inside organizations search for information about specific courses of action, such as the purchase of equipment.

In general, organizational search is an activity designed to balance the cost of acquiring information with the benefits of improved final decisions. The search can be characterized in terms of the overall effort made by the buyer to obtain information from the external environment and in terms of the overall duration, or the length of time between the first initiation of information gathering activities and the time when all of the information considered necessary to make a decision has been collected.

The organizational search process is determined in part by market characteristics (such as pace of change and technological complexity) and by certain aspects of a firm's present buying situation (switching costs and prior experience). Together, these dimensions impose a series of demands on the search process used.

Certain forces may represent disincentives to search. For example, organizational buyers commonly have strong vertical vendor relationships based on prior purchases of previous versions of a particular product. Such vendor relationships may involve nontrivial levels of switching costs that represent a disincentive for buyers to search outside the established vendor portfolio and may result in constrained search processes. Furthermore, current vendor relationships may constrain buyers' search processes indirectly by insulating them from market information. As a consequence, buyers with strong vendor relationships may generally perceive less change to be taking place and hence have a low incentive to engage in search.

The rate of information change in the marketplace imposes additional demands on a firm's search process. Though change can be argued in a general sense to constitute uncertainty, its particular time-dependent nature may create needs above and beyond the traditional information needs. Specifically, under rapidly changing market conditions, acquired information is time-critical and tends to have a shorter lifetime. That is, information about a product received today may be relatively less valuable tomorrow to the extent that the product's features or underlying technology is improving quickly. For a buyer, the implication of fast-paced change may be a disincentive to prolong a search process. In cost-benefit terms, fast-paced change implies that distinct benefits are associated with search effort, yet costs are associated with prolonging the process. Therefore firms may respond to high-paced information change by constraining search process time.

Another influence on market change and organizational search processes is the pace of technological change, defined as the rate at which the product and its features are changing. For instance, in the product category of computers, rapidly improving Intel ×86 and PowerPC/RISC microprocessors are forcing organizational buyers to consider a series of fast and ongoing changes in computer architecture, memory capacity, and graphics capabilities. In a general sense, a perception of a rapid pace of technological change creates uncertainty and gives rise to an information processing problem for potential buyers. A rapid pace of change can be "competence destroying" for an organization, necessitating the initiation of search efforts to acquire new information continuously. In other words, organizations may respond to uncertainty or information processing problems by deliberately increasing their search effort.

### *Consumer Search Experiences*

An understanding of the nature of search and discovery in the context of on-line shopping necessitates knowing what motivates various types of search (e.g., impulse purchasing, compulsive shopping, window shopping, or browsing). Consumer motivation can be viewed in terms of two questions: "Why is the consumer shopping" and "What was in it for the consumer?" These questions imply that an on-line shopping experience can be valuable, or valueless, "fun" or a "chore." Broadly speaking, on-line shopping experiences can be categorized into two distinct dimensions: utilitarian and hedonic value. These dimensions reflect the distinction between carrying out a shopping activity "to achieve a goal" (utilitarian) as opposed to doing it because "you love it" (hedonic). Marketing experts acknowledge that shopping experiences can produce both utilitarian and hedonic value.

In general, shopping's utilitarian aspects have garnered the majority of attention in the design of today's systems. Utilitarian behavior has often been portrayed as task-related and rational, implying that a product is purchased in a deliberate and efficient manner. It is also conceivable that a purchase is not a necessary motivator of shopping. For example, value may result from a consumer collecting information to get some ideas and prices on various possibilities. The utilitarian dimension is often equated with a work mentality and may be useful in explaining the "chore aspect of shopping" alluded to earlier. For example, utilitarian value may help explain why few consumers browse through on-line stores, which most feel is an arduous and time-consuming process. Organizational search is often considered utilitarian.

Compared to utilitarian aspects, the fun or hedonic aspect of shopping has not been explored much in the context of electronic commerce. Hedonic value is more subjective and personal than its utilitarian counterpart and results from fun and playfulness rather than from task completion. Thus hedonic shopping value reflects shopping's potential entertainment, increased arousal, heightened involvement, perceived freedom, fantasy fulfillment, and escapism. Here the purchase of products may be incidental to the entire experience of shopping. In other words, people buy so they can shop, not shop so they can buy. Furthermore, vicarious consumption through virtual reality can provide hedonic value by allowing a consumer to enjoy a product's benefits without purchasing it. Consumers may also receive hedonic value through bargain perceptions. Some people like to hunt for bargains and when they find a really cheap "bargain," that fact alone can provide increased sensory involvement and excitement.

In sum, to understand consumer search, we also need to examine how particular aspects of the buyers' present buying situation and the shopping experience that is being sought affect the search process. It is evident that an understanding of hedonic and utilitarian shopping can provide insight into many electronic commerce consumption behaviors that are normally not taken into account in the design and layout of electronic marketplaces.

### *Information Brokers and Brokerages*

To facilitate better consumer and organizational search, intermediaries called information brokers or brokerages are coming into existence. Information brokerages are needed for three reasons: comparison shopping, reduced search costs, and integration. Information formerly found at more or less the same high prices on all the on-line database search services can sometimes be found at other service bureaus at minute fractions of those charges. Why pay more when you can get information for less if you comparison shop? This is a good thing for consumers who want to save money and for business professionals whose bosses like to see more value for budget expenditures.

Searching for information on some on-line services is not cheap. America Online, for example, charges $48/connect-hour for archive searching during the daytime, but only $6 evenings and weekends, and then adds $2.50/connect-hour to both figures after the five free hours are used up each month. We are going to see more and more nonexpert consumers offload their searching tasks to professional searchers, who can get the job done faster and cheaper.

The plethora of on-line services are creating a segregation of consumers by the computer platforms (the hardware and software) they run. Some services use fancy facades so only the subscribers (those with special software) can get on board. You want America Online? You must use AOL software. Ditto for CompuServe. But the era when the customer could get all the on-line data available from one source using one basic telecommunications program and a modem is ending. Most traditional on-line services have operated in a "lowest common denominator" mode that would even support access with dumb terminals. Now, searchers need not only a microcomputer and a modem but also a mouse, a GUI (graphic user interface) operating system, and multimedia peripherals, not to mention the memory and storage to run it all. This complexity means that consumers will have to go to a third-party brokerage that can provide the tools and services needed to integrate the various services.

Today, many on-line information providers are moving to a consumer services model, where they provide not only inexpensive access but lots of free information. If information brokers are so great, why are we not seeing more of them? The primary reason is that most on-line services allow subscribers or account holders to utilize the information for their own betterment as long as they don't resell the information or claim it as their own. Nothing prohibits corporate or university librarians from checking stock quotes, researching newspapers, or reading PR Newswire, but information brokers are usually not welcome. This mindset has to change if electronic commerce is to proliferate and become more efficient.

## Purchase Consummation

After identifying the products to be purchased, the buyer and seller must interact in some way to actually carry out the mercantile transaction. A *mercantile transaction* is defined as the exchange of information between the buyer and seller followed by the necessary payment. Depending on the payment model mutually agreed on, they may interact by exchanging currency that is backed by a third party (a central bank) or by transferring authorizations for a credit billing organization (VISA, MasterCard). Clearly, the actual details of the interaction would be different for these payment models.

A single mercantile model will not be sufficient to meet the needs of everyone. Just as there are multiple mercantile models in the nonelectronic world, it is quite possible that multiple mercantile models will eventually be used. In very general terms, a simple mercantile protocol would require the following transactions. Although there may be many variants of this protocol, the basic flow remains the same.

1. Buyer contacts vendor to purchase product or service. This dialogue might be interactive on-line—through World Wide Web (WWW), e-mail, off-line through an electronic catalog and telephone.
2. Vendor states price.
3. Buyer and vendor may or may not engage in negotiation.
4. If satisfied, buyer authorizes payment to the vendor with an encrypted transaction containing a digital signature for the agreed price.
5. Vendor contacts his or her billing service to verify the encrypted authorization for authentication.

6. Billing service decrypts authorization and checks buyer's account balance or credit and puts a hold on the amount of transfer. (Billing service may need to interact with buyer's bank.)
7. Billing service gives the vendor the "green light" to deliver product and sends a standardized message giving details of transaction (e.g., authorization number) for merchant's records.
8. On notification of adequate funds to cover financial transaction, vendor delivers the goods to buyer or in the case of information purchase provides a cryptokey to unlock the file.
9. On receiving the goods, the buyer signs and delivers receipt. Vendor then tells billing service to complete the transaction.
10. At the end of the billing cycle, buyer receives a list of transactions. Buyer can then either deny certain transactions or complain about overbilling. Suitable audit or customer service actions are then initiated depending on the payment scheme.

Figure 7.5 shows a simplified diagram of this mercantile process.

Customers, typically have two choices: to pay before receiving goods or services (by cash, debit card) or to receive goods or services and consume them before paying (by credit card). Note that in the first case there is no way of knowing the quality of goods or services until consumption, which occurs *following* payment. For instance, a customer who views a movie in a theater after paying in cash risks that the movie's technical quality is insufficient and then will have to spend time trying to convince the movie provider to refund the cash. Alternatively in a pay-per-view situation, the customer can view the movie and then pay, with the option of refusing to pay if the quality is not satisfactory. The provider has to provide better customer service in the second case than in the first because the customer can inform the bank or credit card company to stop payment.

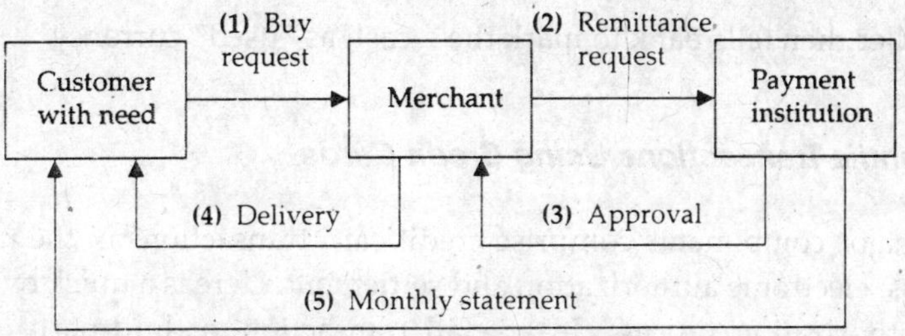


**Figure 7.5** Simplified on-line mercantile model

Hence, depending on the payment form chosen, the specifics of the mercantile protocol vary. To understand the purchase process better, let us examine two types of the mercantile protocols where the payment is the form of electronic cash and credit cards.

### Mercantile Process Using Digital Cash

In this scenario, a bank (or a consortium of banks) mints electronic currency (e-cash). Such currency is simply a series of bits that the issuing bank can verify to be valid. This currency is kept secure (unforgeable) by the use of cryptographic techniques. (For details of e-cash, see Chapter 8.) After being issued some e-cash, a buyer can transfer it to a seller in exchange for goods. Upon receiving the e-cash, the seller can verify its authenticity by sending it to the issuing bank for verification. E-cash issuing banks make money by charging either buyers or sellers a transaction fee for the use of their e-cash.

Electronic cash is similar to paper currency and has the benefits of being anonymous and easily transmitted electronically. It still entails the risk of theft or loss, however, and so requires significant security by the buyer when storing e-cash. The following is a generic mercantile protocol based on the use of e-cash:

1. Buyer obtains anonymous e-cash from issuing bank.
2. Buyer contacts seller to purchase product.
3. Seller states price.
4. Buyer sends e-cash to seller.
5. Seller contacts his bank or billing service to verify the validity of the e-cash.
6. Bank gives okay signal to seller after ensuring that the e-cash hasn't been duplicated or spent on other products.
7. Seller delivers the product to buyer.
8. Seller then tells bank to mark the e-cash as "used" currency.

### Mercantile Transactions Using Credit Cards

Two major components comprise credit card transactions in the mercantile process: electronic authorization and settlement. Here is a quick overview of the authorization process. In a retail transaction, a third-party processor (TPP) captures information at the point of sale; transmits the information to the credit card issuer for authorization, communicates a response to the merchant, and electronically stores the information for settlement and reporting. Once the information leaves the merchant's premises, the entire process takes two to five seconds. The benefits of electronic processing include the reduction in credit losses, lower merchant transaction costs, and faster consumer checkout and merchant-to-bank settlement.

Credit authorization is processed at point-of-sale terminals using dial-up telephone access into the TPP networks such as GEIS or Advantis network. The credit card number is checked against the database and the transaction is either approved or denied, typically within seven seconds. A similar procedure is also used for debit cards and check verification. The transaction data are recorded at the time of authorization at both the point-of-sale location and the processor's data center in order to protect against potential loss of data. In addition to data capture redundancy, TPP provides multiple routing capabilities for a high level of access to electronic authorization. Once the electronic authorization function is completed, the information is processed within the system for client reporting. The data are then transmitted for settlement to the appropriate institution or processor. A step-by-step account of a retail transaction follows:

*Step 1.* A customer presents a credit card for payment at a retail location. The card reader—either a freestanding "credit card terminal," the store's electronic cash register, or a PC-based point-of-sale device—scans the information on the card's magnetic stripe.

*Step 2.* The point-of-sale software directs the transaction information to the local network access point. If the primary local point cannot make a connection to accept the transaction, it is automatically rerouted to a secondary access point.

*Step 3.* Once in the network, the system verifies the source of the transaction and routes it to the appropriate authorization source, where the cardholders' account record is reviewed. An authorization code is then sent back through the network for display on the point-of-sale device. System redundancy provides alternative routing paths and data center processing capability if primary routing is unavailable. Transaction information is captured both in the network system and in the point-of-sale device.

*Step 4.* Periodically, the retail location initiates a "close-out" transaction that bundles completed transaction information into a "batch." Transaction count and financial totals are confirmed between the terminal and the network, and a series of reports can be printed out at the retail location. This transaction clears the terminal software for a new batch of transactions.

*Step 5.* The system gathers all completed batches and processes the data in preparation for settlement. The process identifies for each merchant the appropriate settlement location by card type and prepares detailed reports and files that are routed to the designated settlement bank for VISA and MasterCard transactions. For the Discover Card, American Express, and other card types, settlement information is provided directly to the card issuer. For private label transactions, settlement occurs within the system.

After the transaction is complete, a set of activities related to account settlement are initiated. In a credit or debit transaction, the merchant's account is credited and either the card issuer is notified to enter the transaction on the cardholder's monthly statement or the cardholder's checking account is debited automatically. VISA and MasterCard transaction data are transmitted to the settlement institution selected by the client (Citibank, for example). The settlement institution then enters the transaction data into the settlement process. In addition to data capture and settlement functions, the electronic transaction processing business also provides other services including a twenty-four-hour network "help" desk, which responds to inquiries from merchant locations regarding terminal, communication, and training issues. Other services include terminal sales and maintenance of point-of-sale equipment, customized reporting, debit card processing, check verification, and check guarantee.

What does all this cost? The pricing of electronic transaction services provided by TPP to merchant clients takes one of two forms:

1. In the first form, merchants are charged a flat fee per transaction for authorization and data capture services. A merchant discount rate for the settlement function is contracted separately. The merchant discount rate is the difference between the amount charged by the cardholder and the amount the settlement institution pays to the merchant, usually expressed as a percentage of the credit card sale.

2. The other form of billing allows merchants to pay a "bundled" price for authorization, data capture, and settlement. The merchant pays one fee in the form of a merchant discount rate to the settlement institution. An agreed-upon fee is then paid by the settlement institution to TPP.

As technology improves, credit card usage is on the rise, even though card-based transactions carry higher direct costs than cash transactions. These costs accrue from sophisticated cash registers with modem attachments, phone charges for calls to the transaction center, bank charges, and staff time for paperwork completion. According to a recent study, the average direct cost of cash transactions is 7 cents, compared with 30 cents for on-line debit transactions and 81 cents for credit card transactions.

### Costs of Electronic Purchasing

On the surface, cash seems to be preferable to electronic payments. A more careful examination reveals why retailers are embracing electronic payment methods, such as on-line debit, credit, and electronic check authorization. When indirect elements such as float gains, allocation of equipment costs, and accounting costs are factored in, many firms are finding that accepting debit is less expensive than pocketing cash for transactions. Another reason that firms may be attracted to electronic payment options is that consumers appear to spend more when using cards than when spending cash. A study on supermarket purchasing revealed that the value of the average sale on a debit card is $31.61, compared with $13.83 for cash purchases. Consumers using credit cards tended to purchase even more—$35.56 on average—than debit users. Despite these benefits, electronic payment options have found acceptance slow. This is expected to change as the cost of the necessary equipment decreases, expertise becomes widely available, and consumers become familiar with technology [ECA94].

## Postpurchase Interaction

As long as there is payment for services, there will be refunds, disputes, and other customer service issues that need to be considered. Returns and claims are an important part of the purchasing process that impact administrative costs, scrap and transportation expenses, and customer relations. In the ongoing relationship with the customer, this step can produce some of the most heated disagreements; every interaction becomes a zero-sum game that either the company or the customer wins. To compound the problem, most companies design their mercantile processes for one-way merchandise flow: outbound to the customer. That means returns and claims must flow upstream, against the current, creating logistical messes and transactional snarls—and extremely dissatisfied customers.

Other complex customer service challenges arise in customized retailing that we have not fully understood or resolved:

- *Inventory issues.* To serve the customer properly, a company should inform a customer right away when an item ordered is sold out—not with a rain check or back-order notice several days later. On the other hand, if the item is in stock, a company must be able to assign that piece to the customer immediately and remove it from available inventory. Otherwise, the company will have a disappointed customer who knows he or she doesn't have to put up with such problems and tries to find alternative products.

- *Database access and compatibility issues.* Unless the customer can instantly access all the computers of all the direct-response vendors likely to advertise on the Information Superhighway—on a real-time basis, with compatible software—he or she is not likely to get the kind of service that customers normally get by calling an 800 number. Generally, when consumers call an 800 number, they are connected directly to an operator who has instant access to the merchant's inventory and database.
- *Customer service issues.* Customers often have questions about the product (color, size, shipment), want expedited delivery, or have one of a myriad of other things in mind that can be resolved only by talking to an order entry operator.

In sum, ordering merchandise simply by pushing a button on a remote control device is inherently complex and is not likely for all types of products or services—despite the promises and hype.

## 7.4 MERCANTILE MODELS FROM THE MERCHANT'S PERSPECTIVE

The order-to-delivery cycle from the merchant's perspective has been managed with an eye toward standardization and cost. This view, developed over the last five decades, is based on the assumption that an organization must create a set of operating standards for service and productivity, then perform to those standards while minimizing the cost of doing so. Often, when orders are delivered, the company measures how the actual delivery stacks up against the guidelines for that activity and what the action costs. If the service standards are met with minimal expense, the company judges the delivery successful. The strengths of this philosophy lie in (1) a company's ability to take the position of low-cost provider, (2) its stress on benchmarking service, and (3) its emphasis on responsiveness as well as continuous improvement.

Unfortunately, this model is incomplete for e-commerce. As an operations-focused, inward-looking vision, it's out of sync with the e-commerce accent on flexibility, customization, and customer service. Those companies concentrating on performance standards and cost metrics may be headed for big trouble in the e-commerce environment, because the nature of products and services is dramatically different. Instead of asking whether the customer's needs were met effectively, the traditional view is concerned with the percentage of cases of products that were shipped on time and at what cost. To fully realize and maintain a competitive advantage in the on-line environment, a company must build a robust vision of what its order-to-delivery cycle, and all the business processes that support it, should be.

To achieve a better understanding, it is necessary to examine the order management cycle (OMC) that encapsulates the more traditional order-to-delivery cycle. The typical OMC includes eight distinct activities, although overlapping may occur. The actual details of OMC vary from industry to industry and may differ for individual products and services. However, OMC has the following generic steps (see Fig. 7.6).

### Order Planning and Order Generation

The business process begins long before an actual order is placed by the customer. What happens in the first step, order planning, already shows how and why lack of cohesive operations can cripple a company: Those farthest from the customer make crucial decisions and open up debate between interdependent functions right from the start. For example, people close to the customer, either in the sales force or in a marketing group at company headquarters, develop a sales forecast. At the same time, a group in the operations or manufacturing function drafts a capacity plan that specifies how much money will be spent, how many people will be hired, and how much inventory will be created. The production planners often develop the final forecast used to hire workers and build inventory. The lack of internal communication can cause the final result to differ significantly from what is actually needed.

Order planning leads into order generation. Orders are generated in a number of ways in the e-commerce environment. The sales force broadcasts ads (direct marketing), sends personalized e-mail to customers (cold calls), or creates a WWW page. Regardless of the specific marketing approach, the result is almost always the same: The sales and marketing functions worry about order generation, and the other functions stay out of the way. Little coordination takes place across functional boundaries.

### Cost Estimation and Pricing

Pricing is the bridge between customer needs and company capabilities. But most companies do not understand how to execute order-based pricing in on-line markets. Pricing at the individual order level depends on understanding the value to the customer that is generated by each order, evaluating the cost

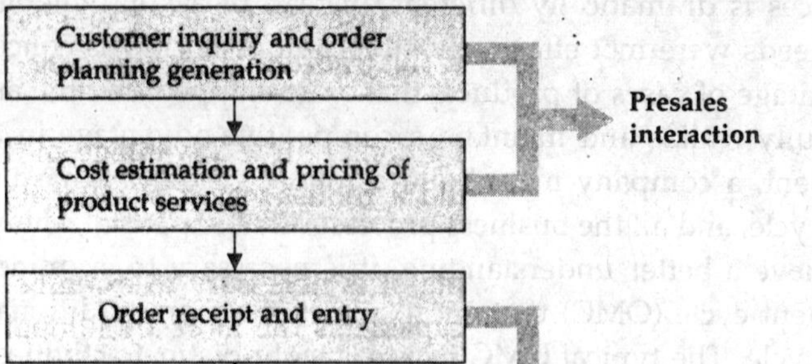


**Figure 7.6** Order management cycle in e-commerce

of filling each order; and instituting a system that enables the company to price each order based on its value and cost. Although order-based pricing is difficult work that requires meticulous thinking and deliberate execution, the potential for greater profits is simply worth the effort. Often, battles erupt between engineers who do the estimation, accountants who tabulate costs, management that oversees pricing, and the sales force that actually quotes a price. Each group questions the judgment, competence, and goals of the others. Meanwhile, of course, the customer waits for the bid or quote, unattended.

### Order Receipt and Entry

After an acceptable price quote, the customer enters the order receipt and entry phase of OMC. Traditionally, this was under the purview of departments variously titled customer service, order entry, the inside sales desk, or customer liaison. These departments are staffed by customer service representatives, usually either very experienced, long-term employees or totally inexperienced trainees. In either case, these representatives are in constant contact with customers.

### Order Selection and Prioritization

Customer service representatives are also often responsible for choosing which orders to accept and which to decline. In fact, not all customer orders are created equal; some are simply better for the business than others. In particular, the desirable orders are those that fit the company's capabilities and offer healthy profits. These orders fall into the "sweet spot" region, which represents a convergence of great customer demand and high customer satisfaction, which in turn translates into customer retention.

Another completely ignored issue concerns the importance of order selection and prioritization. Companies that put effort into order selection and link it to their business strategy stand to make more money, regardless of production capacity. In addition, companies can make gains by the way they handle order prioritization—that is, how they decide which orders to execute faster. These decisions are usually made not by top executives who articulate corporate strategy but by staff who have no idea what that strategy is. While customer service reps decide which order gets filled when, they often determine which order gets lost in limbo. In sum, there is little recognition of the importance that should be placed on order selection and prioritization in e-commerce.

### Order Scheduling

During the ordering scheduling phase the prioritized orders get slotted into an actual production or operational sequence. This task is difficult because the different functional departments—sales, marketing, customer service, operations, or production—may have conflicting goals, compensation systems, and organizational imperatives: Production people seek to minimize equipment changeovers, while marketing and customer service reps argue for special service for special customers. And if the operations staff schedule orders unilaterally, both customers and their reps are completely excluded from the process. Communication between the functions is often nonexistent, with customer service reporting to sales and physically separated from production scheduling, which reports to manufacturing or operations. The result is lack of interdepartmental coordination.

### Order Fulfillment and Delivery

During the order fulfillment and delivery phase the actual provision of the product or service is made. While the details vary from industry to industry, in almost every company this step has become increasingly complex. Often, order fulfillment involves multiple functions and locations: Different parts of an order may be created in different manufacturing facilities and merged at yet another site, or orders may be manufactured in one location, warehoused in a second, and installed in a third. In some businesses, fulfillment includes third-party vendors. In service operations, it can mean sending individuals with different talents to the customer's site. The more complicated the task, the more coordination required across the organization. And the more coordination required, the greater the chance that the order is delayed.

### Order Billing and Account/Payment Management

After the order has been fulfilled and delivered, billing is typically handled by the finance staff, who view their job as getting the bill out efficiently and collecting quickly. In other words, the billing function is designed to serve the needs and interests of the company, not the customer. Often customers don't understand the bill they receive, or they believe it contains inaccuracies. The bill may not be inaccurate, but it is usually constructed in a way more convenient for the billing department than for the customer.

### Postsales Service

This phase plays an increasingly important role in all elements of a company's profit equation: customer value, price, and cost. Depending on the specifics of the business, it can include such elements as physical installation of a product, repair and maintenance, customer training, equipment upgrading, and disposal. Because of the information conveyed and intimacy involved, postsales service can affect customer satisfaction and company profitability for years. But in most companies, the postsales service people are not linked to any marketing operation, internal product-development effort, or quality assurance team.

## 7.5 SUMMARY

There are four principal reasons why consumer-oriented e-commerce's time has come. First, the cost of processing many types of financial and retail transactions has been rising so rapidly that it is imperative to develop new ways to handle those transactions. Second, competition in banking and retailing has become so intense that only those organizations that can provide superior customer services, which in turn require sophisticated transaction management, will continue to grow and prosper. Third, consumers themselves are feeding the fires of competition by demanding more services and greater convenience in their banking and shopping activities. Finally, the technology is at last in place to process electronic transactions at faster speeds more easily and at less cost than we can process paper transactions.

Traditional companies have a product looking for a market, whereas consumer-oriented e-commerce is that rare thing, a vast market visibly hungry for a fairly well-defined mercantile process. As such, it is proving to be a tremendous forcing-ground for ideas and experiments that, if successful, will have implications extending far beyond the Internet itself. For instance, dozens of groups are proposing solutions to the problem of electronic payment. Some have concepts alone, others are undertaking experimental trials, and one or two are declaring themselves open for business. The proposal that meets the needs of the consumer will be an instant killer application that will surely revolutionize commerce as we know it.

In this chapter we explained the basics of the business mechanisms that will be at the heart of electronic commerce on the I-way. The larger goal, however, is to get people thinking about the impact of consumer-oriented e-commerce and its ability to change our lives in the next decade. The design and development of mercantile business processes that are fast, flexible and global is going to become one of the hottest topics in management and computing.

# Chapter 8

# Electronic Payment Systems

Electronic payment systems are becoming central to on-line business process innovation as companies look for ways to serve customers faster and at lower cost. Emerging innovations in the payment for goods and services in electronic commerce promise to offer a wide range of new business opportunities.

Electronic payment systems and e-commerce are intricately linked given that on-line consumers must pay for products and services. Clearly, payment is an integral part of the mercantile process (Chapter 7) and prompt payment (or account settlement) is crucial. If the claims and debits of the various participants—individuals, companies, banks, and nonbanks—are not balanced because of payment delay or, even worse default, then the entire business chain is disrupted. Hence an important aspect of e-commerce is prompt and secure payment, clearing, and settlement of credit or debit claims. But on-line sellers face a problem: How will buyers pay for goods and services? What currency will serve as the medium of exchange in this new marketplace?

The current state of on-line electronic payments is in many ways reminiscent of the medieval ages. The merchants of Asia and Europe faced a similar problem while trying to unlock the commercial potential of the expanding marketplace. Those ancient traders faced a number of obstacles (e.g., conflicting local laws and customs regarding commercial practices and incompatible and nonconvertible currencies) that restricted trade. To circumvent some of these problems, traders invented various forms of payment instruments (promissory notes, bills of exchange, gold coins, and barter). The merchants also developed commercial law surrounding the use of these instruments that proved to be one of the turning points in the history of trade and commerce. We are on the verge of a similar sort of development today, but one that is unlikely to take anywhere near the centuries it took for the traditional payment system to evolve.

Everyone agrees that the payment and settlement process is a potential bottleneck in the fast-moving electronic commerce environment if we rely on conventional payment methods such as cash, checks, bank drafts, or bills of exchange. Electronic replicas of these conventional instruments are not well suited for the speed required in e-commerce purchase processing. For instance, payments of small denominations (micropayments) must be made and accepted by vendors in real time for snippets of information. Conventional instruments are too slow for micropayments and the high transaction costs involved in processing them add greatly to the overhead. Therefore new methods of payment are needed to meet the emerging demands of e-commerce. These neo-payment instruments must be secure, have a low processing cost, and be accepted widely as global currency tender.

We will examine these demands by looking at the following issues:

- What form and characteristics of payment instruments—for example, electronic cash, electronic checks, credit/debit cards—will consumers use?
- In on-line markets, how can we manage the financial risk associated with various payment instruments—privacy, fraud, mistakes, as well as other risks like bank failures? What security features (authentication, privacy, anonymity) need to be designed to reduce these risks?
- What are the step-by-step procedures and institutional arrangements that form the fabric of the electronic payment business processes that link consumers and organizations?

To answer these questions, we will draw on examples of various electronic payment systems that have been proposed, prototyped, or actually deployed.

## 8.1 TYPES OF ELECTRONIC PAYMENT SYSTEMS

Electronic payment systems are proliferating in banking, retail, health care, on-line markets, and even government—in fact, anywhere money needs to change hands. Organizations are motivated by the need to deliver products and services more cost effectively and to provide a higher quality of service to customers. This section will briefly describe the pertinent developments in various industries to provide an overall picture of electronic payment systems of the past and present. A timeline showing the evolution of payment systems is presented in Table 8.1.

Research into electronic payment systems for consumers can be traced back to the 1940s, and the first applications—credit cards—appeared soon after. In the early 1970s, the emerging electronic payment technology was labeled electronic funds transfer (EFT). EFT is defined as "any transfer of

**Table 8.1** Timeline of Innovations in Payment Systems

| *Period* | *Innovation* |
|---|---|
| 700 BC | Earliest coins produced in western Turkey to pay mercenaries or taxes. |
| 1400 | First banks open, in Italy and Catalonia, honoring checks against cash reserves. |
| 1694 | The Bank of England opens, creating deposits on the principle that not all deposit receipts will be presented for redemption simultaneously. The bank monopolizes the issuing of bank notes. |
| 1865 | A sample of payments into British banks shows that 97 percent are made by check. |
| 1887 | The phrase *credit card* is coined in *Looking Backward*, a novel by Edward Bellamy. |
| 1880–1914 | Heyday of the gold standard as major currencies are pegged to gold at fixed rates. |
| 1945 | Bretton Woods agreement links currencies to gold via their fixed parities with the U.S. dollar. |
| 1947 | Flatbush National Bank issues first general-purpose credit card, for use in select New York shops. |
| 1950 | Diners Club Charge Card introduced |
| mid 1950s | The development of magnetic ink character recognition (MICR), facilitating more timely processing of checks, sealed the check's standing as the preferred noncash payment option. |
| 1958 | BankAmerica, in Fresno, California, executes the first mass mailing of credit cards. |
| 1967 | Westminster Bank installs first automated teller machine at Victoria, London, branch. |
| 1970 | The New York Clearing House launches CHIPS—the Clearing House Interbank Payments System—which provides U.S.-dollar funds-transfer and transaction settlements on-line and in real time. |
| late 1970s | Chemical Bank launches its Pronto system providing 3000 computer terminals to customers' homes linked to its central computers by telephone. It offers a range of facilities: balance inquiries, money transfers between Chemical Bank accounts, and bill payments to selected local stores. The stumbling block for first-generation home-banking systems in general was who is to pay for the terminals at home. |

*(continues)*

**Table 8.1** (Continued)

| *Period* | *Innovation* |
|---|---|
| 1985 | Electronic data interchange (EDI) extensively used in bank-to-bank payment systems. |
| 1994 | Digital cash trials by DigiCash of Holland conducted on-line. |
| 1995 | Mondex electronic currency trials begin in Swindon, England. |

funds initiated through an electronic terminal, telephonic instrument, or computer or magnetic tape so as to order, instruct, or authorize a financial institution to debit or credit an account." EFT utilizes computer and telecommunication components both to supply and to transfer money or financial assets. Transfer is information-based and intangible. Thus EFT stands in marked contrast to conventional money and payment modes that rely on physical delivery of cash or checks (or other paper orders to pay) by truck, train, or airplane.

Work on EFT can be segmented into three broad categories:

1. Banking and financial payments
   - Large-scale or wholesale payments (e.g., bank-to-bank transfer)
   - Small-scale or retail payments (e.g., automated teller machines and cash dispensers)
   - Home banking (e.g., bill payment)
2. Retailing payments
   - Credit cards (e.g., VISA or MasterCard)
   - Private label credit/debit cards (e.g., J.C. Penney Card)
   - Charge cards (e.g., American Express)
3. On-line electronic commerce payments
   - Token-based payment systems

     Electronic cash (e.g., DigiCash)

     Electronic checks (e.g., NetCheque)

     Smart cards or debit cards (e.g., Mondex Electronic Currency Card)
   - Credit card–based payment systems

     Encrypted credit cards (e.g., World Wide Web form–based encryption)

     Third-party authorization numbers (e.g., First Virtual)

Retail payments were covered in Chapter 7 and will not be elaborated here. Large-scale payments between banks and business, widely recognized as the pioneering efforts in electronic commerce that involve the extensive use of EDI for transferring payment information, will be discussed in Chapter 9. Our focus in the following sections will be on the remaining category: on-line electronic commerce payment.

## 8.2 DIGITAL TOKEN-BASED ELECTRONIC PAYMENT SYSTEMS

None of the banking or retailing payment methods are completely adequate in their present form for the consumer-oriented e-commerce environment. Their deficiency is their assumption that the parties will at some time or other be in each other's physical presence or that there will be a sufficient delay in the payment process for frauds, overdrafts, and other undesirables to be identified and corrected. These assumptions may not hold for e-commerce and so many of these payment mechanisms are being modified and adapted for the conduct of business over networks.

Entirely new forms of financial instruments are also being developed. One such new financial instrument is "electronic tokens" in the form of electronic cash/money or checks. Electronic tokens are designed as electronic analogs of various forms of payment backed by a bank or financial institution. Simply stated, electronic tokens are equivalent to cash that is backed by a bank.

Electronic tokens are of three types:

1. *Cash or real-time.* Transactions are settled with the exchange of electronic currency. An example of on-line currency exchange is *electronic cash (e-cash).*

2. *Debit or prepaid.* Users pay in advance for the privilege of getting information. Examples of prepaid payment mechanisms are stored in smart cards and electronic purses that store electronic money.

3. *Credit or postpaid.* The server authenticates the customers and verifies with the bank that funds are adequate before purchase. Examples of postpaid mechanisms are *credit/debit cards* and *electronic checks.*

The following sections examine these methods of on-line payment. But we must first understand the different viewpoints that these payment instruments bring to electronic commerce. Here are four dimensions that are useful for analyzing the different initiatives.

1. *The nature of the transaction for which the instrument is designed.* Some tokens are specifically designed to handle micropayments, that is, payments for small snippets of information. Others are designed for more traditional products. Some systems target specific niche transactions; others seek more general transactions. The key is to identify the parties involved, the average amounts, and the purchase interaction.

2. *The means of settlement used.* Tokens must be backed by cash, credit, electronic bill payments (prearranged and spontaneous), cashier's checks, IOUs, letters and lines of credit, and wire transfers, to name a few. Each option incurs trade-offs among transaction speed, risk, and cost. Most transaction settlement methods use credit cards, while others use other proxies for value, effectively creating currencies of dubious liquidity and with interesting tax, risk, and float implications.

3. *Approach to security, anonymity, and authentication.* Electronic tokens vary in the protection of privacy and confidentiality of the transactions. Some may be more open to potentially prying eyes—or even to the participants themselves. Encryption can help with authentication, nonrepudiability, and asset management.

4. *The question of risk.* Who assumes what kind of risk at what time? The tokens might suddenly become worthless and the customers might have the currency that nobody will accept. If the system stores value in a smart card, consumers may be exposed to risk as they hold static assets. Also electronic tokens might be subject to discounting or arbitrage. Risk also arises if the transaction has long lag times between product delivery and payments to merchants. This exposes merchants to the risk that buyers don't pay—or vice-versa that the vendor doesn't deliver.

## Electronic Cash (e-cash)

Electronic cash (e-cash) is a new concept in on-line payment systems because it combines computerized convenience with security and privacy that improve on paper cash. Its versatility opens up a host of new markets and applications. E-cash presents some interesting characteristics that should make it an attractive alternative for payment over the Internet.

E-cash focuses on replacing cash as the principal payment vehicle in consumer-oriented electronic payments. Although it may be surprising to some, cash is still the most prevalent consumer payment instrument even after thirty years of continuous developments in electronic payment systems. Cash remains the dominant form of payment for three reasons: (1) lack of trust in the banking system, (2) inefficient clearing and settlement of noncash transactions, and (3) negative real interest rates paid on bank deposits.

These reasons seem like issues seen primarily in developing countries. Not true. Even in the most industrialized countries, the ratio of notes and coins in circulation per capita is quite large and is estimated to range from $446 to $2748. Consider the situation in two of the most industrialized nations in world: the United States and the United Kingdom. In the United States, there supposedly was about $300 billion of notes and coins in circulation in 1992. Interestingly, this number is not shrinking but growing at approximately 8 percent per year. Deposits by check are growing by only 6 percent per year. It has been reported that in the United Kingdom about a quarter of all "spontaneous" payments over 100 pounds sterling are still made with cash. For payments under five pounds sterling, the percentage is 98 percent [AB94].

The predominance of cash indicates an opportunity for innovative business practice that revamps the purchasing process where consumers are heavy users of cash. To really displace cash, the electronic payment systems need to have some qualities of cash that current credit and debit cards lack. For example, cash is negotiable, meaning it can be given or traded to someone else. Cash is legal tender, meaning the payee is obligated to take it. Cash is a bearer instrument, meaning that possession is prima facie proof of ownership. Also, cash can be held and used by anyone even those who don't have a bank account, and cash places no risk on the part of the acceptor that the medium of exchange may not be good.

Now compare cash to credit and debit cards. First, they can't be given away because, technically, they are identification cards owned by the issuer and restricted to one user. Credit and debit cards are not legal tender, given that merchants have the right to refuse to accept them. Nor are credit and debit cards bearer instruments; their usage requires an account relationship and authorization system. Similarly, checks require either personal knowledge of the payer or a check guarantee system. Hence, to really create a novel electronic payment method, we need to do more than recreate the convenience that is offered by credit and debit cards. We need to develop e-cash that has some of the properties of cash.

### *Properties of Electronic Cash*

Of the many ways that exist for implementing an e-cash system, all must incorporate a few common features. Specifically, e-cash must have the following four properties: monetary value, interoperability, retrievability, and security [OO91].

E-cash must have a monetary value; it must be backed by either cash (currency), bank-authorized credit, or a bank-certified cashier's check. When e-cash created by one bank is accepted by others, reconciliation must occur without any problems. Stated another way, e-cash without proper bank certification carries the risk that when deposited, it might be returned for insufficient funds.

E-cash must be interoperable—that is, exchangeable as payment for other e-cash, paper cash, goods or services, lines of credit, deposits in banking accounts, bank notes or obligations, electronic benefits transfers, and the like. Most e-cash proposals use a single bank [MN93]. In practice, multiple banks are required with an international clearinghouse that handles the exchangeability issues because all customers are not going to be using the same bank or even be in the same country.

E-cash must be storable and retrievable. Remote storage and retrieval (e.g., from a telephone or personal communications device) would allow users to exchange e-cash (e.g., withdraw from and deposit into banking accounts) from home or office or while traveling. The cash could be stored on a remote computer's memory, in smart cards, or in other easily transported standard or special-purpose devices. Because it might be easy to create counterfeit cash that is stored in a computer, it might be preferable to store cash on a dedicated device that cannot be altered. This device should have a suitable interface to facilitate personal authentication using passwords or other means and a display so that the user can view the card's contents. One example of a device that can store e-cash is the Mondex card—a pocket-sized electronic wallet.

E-cash should not be easy to copy or tamper with while being exchanged; this includes preventing or detecting duplication and double-spending. Counterfeiting poses a particular problem, since a counterfeiter may, in the Internet environment, be anywhere in the world and consequently be difficult to catch without appropriate international agreements. Detection is essential in order to audit whether prevention is working. Then there is the tricky issue of double spending [DFN88]. For instance, you could use your e-cash simultaneously to buy something in Japan, India, and England. Preventing double-spending from occurring is extremely difficult if multiple banks are involved in the transaction. For this reason, most systems rely on post-fact detection and punishment.

### *Electronic Cash in Action*

Electronic cash is based on cryptographic systems called "digital signatures" (see Chapter 5). This method involves a pair of numeric keys (very large integers or numbers) that work in tandem: one for locking (or encoding) and the other for unlocking (or decoding). Messages encoded with one numeric key can only be decoded with the other numeric key and none other. The encoding key is kept private and the decoding key is made public.

By supplying all customers (buyers and sellers) with its public key, a bank enables customers to decode any message (or currency) encoded with the bank's private key. If decoding by a customer yields a recognizable message, the customer can be fairly confident that only the bank could have encoded it. These digital signatures are as secure as the mathematics involved and have proved over the past two decades to be more resistant to forgery than handwritten signatures. Before e-cash can be used to buy products or services, it must be procured from a currency server.

**Purchasing E-cash from Currency Servers.** The purchase of e-cash from an on-line currency server (or bank) involves two steps: (1) establishment of an account and (2) maintaining enough money in the account to back the purchase. Some customers might prefer to purchase e-cash with paper currency, either to maintain anonymity or because they don't have a bank account.

Currently, in most e-cash trials all customers must have an account with a central on-line bank. This is overly restrictive for international use and multicurrency transactions, for customers should be able to access and pay for foreign services as well as local services. To support this access, e-cash must be available in multiple currencies backed by several banks. A service provider in one country could then accept tokens of various currencies from users in many different countries, redeem them with their issuers, and have the funds transferred back to banks in the local country. A possible solution is to use an association of digital banks similar to organizations like VISA to serve as a clearinghouse for many credit card issuing banks.

And finally, consumers use the e-cash software on the computer to generate a random number, which serves as the "note." In exchange for money debited from the customer's account, the bank uses its private key to digitally sign the note for the amount requested and transmits the note back to the customer. The network currency server, in effect, is issuing a "bank note," with a serial number and a dollar amount. By digitally signing it, the bank is committing itself to back that note with its face value in real dollars.

This method of note generation is very secure, as neither the customer (payer) nor the merchant (payee) can counterfeit the bank's digital signature (analogous to the watermark in paper currency). Payer and payee can verify that the payment is valid, since each knows the bank's public key. The bank is protected against forgery, the payee against the bank's refusal to honor a legitimate note, and the user against false accusations and invasion of privacy.

How does this process work in practice? In the case of DigiCash, every person using e-cash has an e-cash account at a digital bank (First Digital Bank) on the Internet. Using that account, people can withdraw and deposit e-cash. When an e-cash withdrawal is made, the PC of the e-cash user calculates how many digital coins of what denominations are needed to withdraw the requested amount. Next, random serial numbers for those coins will be generated and the blinding (random number) factor will be included. The result of these calculations will be sent to the digital bank. The bank will encode the blinded numbers with its secret key (digital signature) and at the same time debit the account of the client for the same amount. The authenticated coins are sent back to the user and finally the user will take out the blinding factor that he or she introduced earlier. The serial numbers plus their signatures are now digital coins; their value is guaranteed by the bank.

Electronic cash can be completely anonymous. Anonymity allows freedom of usage—to buy illegal products such as drugs or pornographic material or to buy legal product and services. This is accomplished in the following manner. When the e-cash software generates a note, it masks the original number or "blinds" the note using a random number and transmits it to a bank. The "blinding" carried out by the customer's software makes it impossible for anyone to link payment to payer. Even the bank can't connect the signing with the payment, since the customer's original note number was blinded when it was signed. In other words, it is a way of creating anonymous, untraceable currency. What makes it even more interesting is that users can prove unequivocally that they did or did not make a particular payment. This allows the bank to sign the "note" without ever actually knowing how the issued currency will be used.

For those readers who are mathematically inclined, the protocol behind blind signatures is presented [XIWT94].

1. The customer's software chooses a blinding factor, $R$, independently and uniformly at random and presents the bank with $(XR)^E$ (mod PQ),where $X$ is the note number to be signed and $E$ is the bank's public key.
2. The bank signs it: $(XR^E)^D = RX^D$ (mod PQ). $D$ is the bank's private key.
3. On receiving the currency, the customer divides out the blinding factor: $(RX^D)/R = X^D$ (mod PQ).
4. The customer stores $X^D$, the signed note that is used to pay for the purchase of products or services. Since $R$ is random, the bank cannot determine $X$ and thus cannot connect the signing with the subsequent payment.

While blinding works in theory, it remains to be seen how it will be used in the real business world.

**Using the Digital Currency.** Once the tokens are purchased, the e-cash software on the customer's PC stores digital money undersigned by a bank.

The user can spend the digital money at any shop accepting e-cash, without having to open an account there first or having to transmit credit card numbers. As soon as the customer wants to make a payment, the software collects the necessary amount from the stored tokens.

Two types of transactions are possible: bilateral and trilateral. Typically, transactions involving cash are bilateral or two-party (buyer and seller) transactions, whereby the merchant checks the veracity of the note's digital signature by using the bank's public key. If satisfied with the payment, the merchant stores the digital currency on his machine and deposits it later in the bank to redeem the face value of the note. Transactions involving financial instruments other than cash are usually trilateral or three-party (buyer, seller, and bank) transactions, whereby the "notes" are sent to the merchant, who immediately sends them directly to the digital bank. The bank verifies the validity of these "notes" and that they have not been spent before. The account of the merchant is credited. In this case, every "note" can be used only once.

In many business situations, the bilateral transaction is not feasible because of the potential for double spending, which is equivalent to bouncing a check. Double spending becomes possible because it is very easy to make copies of the e-cash, forcing banks and merchants to take extra precautions.

To uncover double spending, banks must compare the note passed to it by the merchant against a database of spent notes. Just as paper currency is identified with a unique serial number, digital cash can also be protected. The ability to detect double spending has to involve some form of registration so that all "notes" issued globally can be uniquely identified. However, this method of matching notes with a central registry has problems in the online world. For most systems, which handle high volumes of micropayments, this method would simply be too expensive. In addition, the problem of double spending means that banks have to carry added overhead because of the constant checking and auditing logs. (See Fig. 8.1.)

Double spending would not be a major problem if the need for anonymity were relaxed. In such situations, when the consumer is issued a bank note, it is issued to that person's unique license. When he or she gives it to somebody else, it is transferred specifically to that other person's license. Each time the money changes hands, the old owner adds a tiny bit of information to the bank note based on the bank note's serial number and his or her license. If somebody attempts to spend money twice, the bank will now be able to use the two bank notes to determine who the cheater is. Even if the bank notes pass through many different people's hands, whoever cheated will get caught, and none of the other people will ever have to know. The downside is that the bank can tell precisely what your buying habits are since it can check the numbers on the e-cash and the various merchant accounts that are being credited. Many people would feel uncomfortable letting others know this personal information.

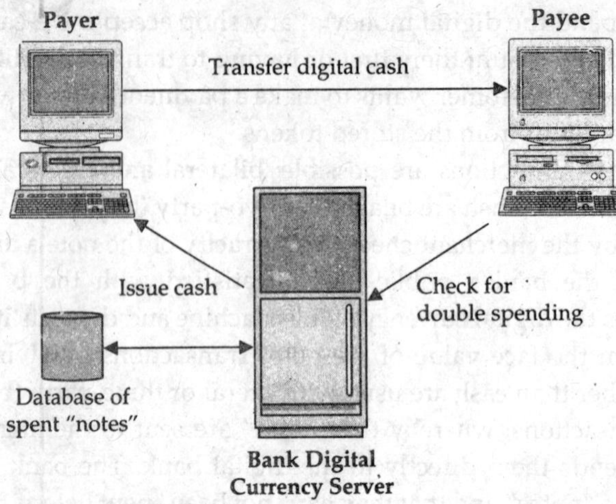


**Figure 8.1** Detection of double spending

One drawback of e-cash is its inability to be easily divided into smaller amounts. It is often necessary to get small denomination change in business transactions. A number of variations have been developed for dealing with the "change" problem. For the bank to issue users with enough separate electronic "coins" of various denominations would be cumbersome in communication and storage. So would a method that required payees to return extra change. To sidestep such costs, customers are issued a single number called an "open check" that contains multiple denomination values sufficient for transactions up to a prescribed limit. At payment time, the e-cash software on the client's computer would create a note of the transaction value from the "open check."

### Business Issues and Electronic Cash

Electronic cash fulfills two main functions: as a medium of exchange and as a store of value. Digital money is a perfect medium of exchange. By moving monetary claims quickly and by effecting instant settlement of transactions, e-cash may help simplify the complex interlocking credit and liabilities that characterize today's commerce. For instance, small businesses that spend months waiting for big customers to pay their bills would benefit hugely from a digital system in which instant settlement is the norm. Instant settlement of micropayments is also a tantalizing proposition [ECON94].

The controversial aspects of e-cash are those that relate to the other role, as a store of value. Human needs tend to require that money take a tangible form and be widely accepted, or "legal tender." In most countries, a creditor by law cannot refuse cash as settlement for a debt. With the acceptability of cash guaranteed by law, most people are willing to bank their money and settle many of their bills by checks and debits, confident that, barring a catastrophe, they can obtain legal tender (cash) on demand. If e-cash had to be convertible into legal tender on demand, then for every unit there would have to be a unit of cash reserved in the real economy: or, to look at it the other way round, there would be cash in the real world for which digital proxies were created and made available. This creates problems, because in an efficient system, if each e-cash unit represents a unit of real cash, then positive balances of e-cash will earn no interest; for the interest they might earn would be offset by the interest foregone on the real cash that is backing them.

The enormous currency fluctuations in international finance pose another problem. On the Internet, the buyer could be in Mexico and the seller in the United States. How do you check that the party in Mexico is giving a valid electronic currency that has suitable backing? Even if it were valid today, what would happen if a sudden devaluation occurs such as the one in December 1994 where the peso was devalued 30 percent overnight. Who holds the liability, the buyer or the seller? These are not technological issues but business issues that must be addressed for large-scale bilateral transactions to occur. Unless, we have one central bank offering one type of electronic currency, it is very difficult to see e-cash being very prominent except in narrow application domains.

From a banker's point of view, e-cash would be a mixed blessing. Because they could not create new money via lending in the digital world, banks would see electronic money as unproductive. They might charge for converting it, or take a transaction fee for issuing it, but on-line competition would surely make this a low-profit affair. In the short term, banks would probably make less from this new business than they would lose from the drift of customers away from traditional services.

It seems unlikely that e-cash would be allowed to realize its potential for bypassing the transaction costs of the foreign-exchange market. If you pay yen for e-cash in Osaka and buy something from a merchant based in New York who cashes them for francs, a currency conversion has taken place. That, however, is an activity toward which most governments feel highly defensive; and if e-cash started to bypass regulated foreign exchange markets by developing its own gray market for settlement, then governments might be provoked into trying to clamp down on it. Because of these obstacles, e-cash in its early forms may be denominated in single currencies and exchanged at conventional market rates.

## Operational Risk and Electronic Cash

Operational risk associated with e-cash can be mitigated by imposing constraints, such as limits on (1) the time over which a given electronic money is valid, (2) how much can be stored on and transferred by electronic money, (3) the number of exchanges that can take place before a money needs to be redeposited with a bank or financial institution, and (4) the number of such transactions that can be made during a given period of time.

These constraints introduce a whole new set of implementation issues. For example, time limits could be set beyond which the electronic money would expire and become worthless. The customer would have to redeem or exchange the money prior to the expiration deadline. For this feature to work, electronic money would have to be time-stamped, and time would have to be synchronized across the network to some degree of precision.

The objective of imposing constraints is to limit the issuer's liability. A maximum upper limit could be imposed on the value that could be assigned to any single transaction or that could be transferred to the same vendor within a given period of time. Since the user's computer could be programmed to execute small transactions continuously at a high rate over the network, a strategy of reporting transactions over a certain amount would be ineffective for law enforcement.

However, a well-designed system could enforce a policy involving both transaction size and value with time. For example, an "anonymous coin-purse" feature might be capable of receiving or spending no more than $500 in any twenty-four-hour period. Alternatively, the "rate ceiling" for the next twenty-four hours could be made dependent on the rate of use or on the number of exchanges that could be permitted before any electronic money would have to be redeposited in a bank or financial institution and reissued.

Finally, exchanges could also be restricted to a class of services or goods (e.g., electronic benefits could be used only for food, clothing, shelter, or educational purposes). The exchange process should allow payment to be withheld from the seller upon the buyer's instructions until the goods, or services are delivered within a specified time in the future. Conversely, it should allow delivery to be withheld upon the seller's instructions until payment is received.

## Legal Issues and Electronic Cash

Electronic cash will force bankers and regulators to make tough choices that will shape the form of lawful commercial activity related to electronic commerce. As a result of the very features that make it so attractive to many, cash has occupied an unstable and uncomfortable place within the existing taxation and law enforcement systems.

Anonymous and virtually untraceable, cash transactions today occupy a place in a kind of underground economy. This underground economy is generally confined to relatively small-scale transactions because paper money in large quantities is cumbersome to use and manipulate—organized crime being the obvious exception. As long as the transactions are small in monetary value, they are tolerated by the government as an unfortunate but largely insignificant by-product of the modern commercial state. As transactions get larger the government becomes more suspicious and enlists the aid of the banks, through the various currency reporting laws, in reporting large disbursements of cash so that additional oversight can be ordered.

Consider the impact of e-cash on taxation. Transaction-based taxes (e.g., sales taxes) account for a significant portion of state and local government revenue. But if e-cash really is made to function the way that paper money does, payments we would never think of making in cash—to buy a new car, say, or as the down payment on a house—could be made in this new form of currency because there would be no problem of bulk and no risk of robbery. The threat to the government's revenue flow is a very real one, and officials in government are starting to take cognizance of this development and to prepare their responses [AL95].

To prevent an underground economy, the government through law may prevent a truly anonymous and untraceable e-cash system from developing. But that raises its own problems because the vision of "Big Brother" rears its ugly head. Just as powerful encryption schemes permit the design of untraceable e-cash systems, so, too, do powerful electronic record-keeping tools permit the design of traceable systems—systems in which all financial transactions are duly recorded in some database, allowing those with access to know more about an individual than anyone could know today.

Anything that makes cash substantially easier to use in a broader range of transactions holds the potential to expand this underground economy to proportions posing ever more serious threats to the existing legal order. Under the most ambitious visions of e-cash, we would see a new form of currency that could be freely passed off from one computer to another with no record, yet incapable of being forged. A consumer could draw such e-cash electronically from his or her bank. The bank would have a record of that transaction, just as a withdrawal or check is recorded now. But after that, the encrypted e-cash file could be handed off without the knowledge of anyone but the parties to the transaction.

However, as the politics and business play out, the technology is forcing legal as issues to be reconsidered. The question e-cash poses is not, "Should the law take notice of this development?" but rather, "How can it not?" By impacting revenue-raising capabilities, e-cash cannot escape government scrutiny and regulation; but it is going to take some serious thinking to design a regulatory scheme that balances personal privacy, speed of execution, and ease of use. Without a functioning system, what the government will do remains a mystery. Moreover, it is not even clear yet that the market as a whole will adopt an anonymous e-cash standard. For now, we are mainly watching and trying to educate ourselves about the likely path of the transition to electronic cash.

## Electronic Checks

Electronic checks are another form of electronic tokens. They are designed to accommodate the many individuals and entities that might prefer to pay on credit or through some mechanism other than cash. In the model shown in Fig. 8.2, buyers must register with a third-party account server before they are able to write electronic checks. The account server also acts as a billing service. The registration procedure can vary depending on the particular account server and may require a credit card or a bank account to back the checks.

Once registered, a buyer can then contact sellers of goods and services. To complete a transaction, the buyer sends a check to the seller for a certain amount of money. These checks may be sent using e-mail or other transport methods. When deposited, the check authorizes the transfer of account bal-

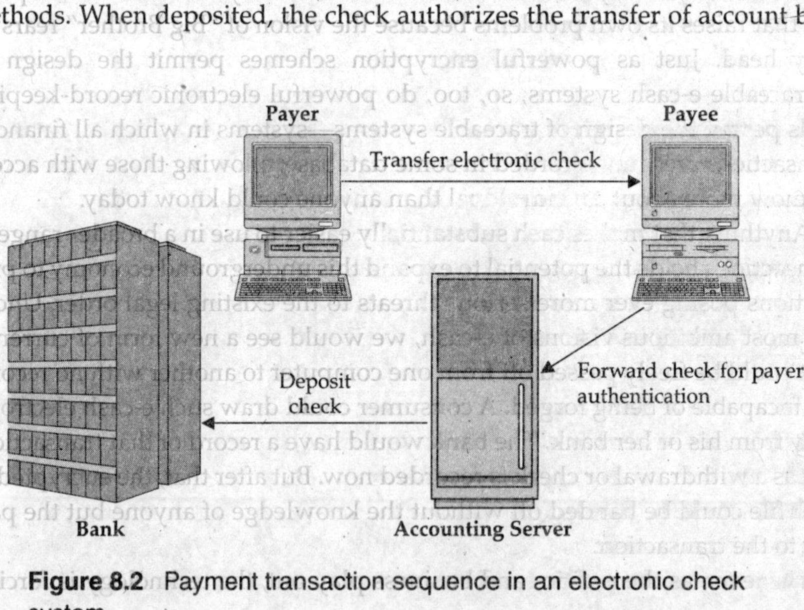


**Figure 8.2** Payment transaction sequence in an electronic check system

ances from the account against which the check was drawn to the account to which the check was deposited.

The e-check method was deliberately created to work in much the same way as a conventional paper check. An account holder will issue an electronic document that contains the name of the payer, the name of the financial institution, the payer's account number, the name of the payee and the amount of the check. Most of the information is in uncoded form. Like a paper check, an e-check will bear the digital equivalent of a signature: a computed number that authenticates the check as coming from the owner of the account. And, again like a paper check, an e-check will need to be endorsed by the payee, using another electronic signature, before the check can be paid. Properly signed and endorsed checks can be electronically exchanged between financial institutions through electronic clearinghouses, with the institutions using these endorsed checks as tender to settle accounts.

The specifics of the technology work in the following manner: On receiving the check, the seller presents it to the accounting server for verification and payment. The accounting server verifies the digital signature on the check using the Kerberos authentication scheme (see Chapter 5). In the language of Kerberos, an electronic check is a specialized kind of "ticket" created by the Kerberos system. A user's digital "signature" is used to create one ticket—a check—which the seller's digital "endorsement" transforms into another—an order to a bank computer for fund transfer. Subsequent endorsers add successive layers of information onto the tickets, precisely as a large number of banks may wind up stamping the back of a check along its journey through the system.

Electronic checks have the following advantages:

- They work in the same way as traditional checks, thus simplifying customer education.
- Electronic checks are well suited for clearing micropayments; their use of conventional cryptography makes it much faster than systems based on public-key cryptography (e-cash).
- Electronic checks create float and the availability of float is an important requirement for commerce. The third-party accounting server can make money by charging the buyer or seller a transaction fee or a flat rate fee [illegible] it can act as a bank and provide deposit accounts and make money on the deposit account po[illegible]
- Financial risk is assumed by the accounting server and may result in easier acceptance. Reliability and scalability are provided by using multiple accounting servers. There can be an interaccount server protocol to allow buyer and seller to "belong" to different domains, regions, or countries.

A prototype electronic check system called " NetCheque" was developed at Information Sciences Institute by Clifford Neumann [MN93]. NetCheque will include software for writing and depositing checks independent of other applications and an application programming interface that will allow common functions to be called automatically when integrated with other programs. ISI is expected to make available "accounting server" software that will allow organizations to set up their own in-house, on-line "banks," which would accept paper checks or credit card payments in exchange for crediting a customer's NetCheque account. Such accounting servers will enable large organizations to pay bills and settle accounts with NetCheques written with their own banks, in effect integrating their own internal accounting system with the external financial hierarchy.

The interesting implication of NetCheque is that it can be used as a resource management tool inside organizations, a form of an internal cash. For instance, each user in the organization could be given an account and allowed to use various resources and be billed for it. Thus organizations will be able to manage resources more effectively using accounting mechanisms. This will become important in the future as corporate networks become more congested and such qualities of e-cash as anonymity are not major requirements.

## 8.3 SMART CARDS AND ELECTRONIC PAYMENT SYSTEMS

The enormous potential of electronic tokens is currently stunted by the lack of a widely accepted and secure means of transferring money on-line. In spite of the many prototypes developed, we are a long way from a universal payment system because merchants and banks have to be signed up and a means has to be developed to transfer money. Such a system moreover must be robust and capable of handling a large number of transactions and will require extensive testing and usage to iron out all the [illegible]

In the meantime, thousands of would-be sellers of electronic commerce services have to pay one another and are actively looking for payment substitutes. One such substitute is the smart card. Smart cards have been in existence since the early 1980s and hold promise for secure transactions using existing infrastructure. *Smart cards* are credit and debit cards and other card products enhanced with microprocessors capable of holding more information than the traditional magnetic stripe. The chip, at its current state of development, can store significantly greater amounts of data, estimated to be 80 times more than a magnetic stripe. Industry observers have predicted that, by the year 2000, one-half of all payment cards issued in the world will have embedded microprocessors rather than the simple magnetic stripe.

The smart card technology is widely used in countries such as France, Germany, Japan, and Singapore to pay for public phone calls, transportation, and shopper loyalty programs. The idea has taken longer to catch on in the United States, since a highly reliable and fairly inexpensive telecommunications system has favored the use of credit and debit cards.

Smart cards are basically of two types: relationship-based smart credit cards and electronic purses. Electronic purses, which replace money, are also known as debit cards and electronic money.

## Relationship-Based Smart Cards

Financial institutions worldwide are developing new methods to maintain and expand their services to meet the needs of increasingly sophisticated and technically smart customers, as well as to meet the emerging payment needs of electronic commerce. Traditional credit cards are fast evolving into smart cards as consumers demand payment and financial services products that are user-friendly, convenient, and reliable.

A relationship-based smart card is an enhancement of existing card services and/or the addition of new services that a financial institution delivers to its customers via a chip-based card or other device. These new services may include access to multiple financial accounts, value-added marketing programs, or other information cardholders may want to store on their card. The chip-based card is but one tool that will help alter mass marketing techniques to address each individual's specific financial and personal requirements. Enhanced credit cards store cardholder information including name, birth date, personal shopping preferences, and actual purchase records. This information will enable merchants to accurately track consumer behavior and develop promotional programs designed to increase shopper loyalty.

Relationship-based products are expected to offer consumers far greater options, including the following:

- Access to multiple accounts, such as debit, credit, investments or stored value for e-cash, on one card or an electronic device
- A variety of functions, such as cash access, bill payment, balance inquiry, or funds transfer for selected accounts
- Multiple access options at multiple locations using multiple device types, such as an automated teller machine, a screenphone, a personal computer, a personal digital assistant (PDA), or interactive TVs

Companies are trying to incorporate these services into a personalized banking relationship for each customer. They can package financial and nonfinancial services with value-added programs to enhance convenience, build loyalty and retention, and attract new customers. Banks are also attempting to customize services on smart cards, offering a menu of services similar to those that come up on ATM screens. As with credit cards, banks may link up with health care providers, telephone companies, retailers, and airlines to offer frequent shopping and flyer programs and other services.

## Electronic Purses and Debit Cards

Despite their increasing flexibility, relationship-based cards are credit based and settlement occurs at the end of the billing cycle. There remains a need for a financial instrument to replace cash. To meet this need, banks, credit card companies, and even government institutions are racing to introduce "electronic purses," wallet-sized smart cards embedded with programmable microchips that store sums of money for people to use instead of cash for everything from buying food, to making photocopies, to paying subway fares.

The electronic purse works in the following manner. After the purse is loaded with money, at an ATM or through the use of an inexpensive special telephone, it can be used to pay for, say, candy in a vending machine equipped with a card reader. The vending machine need only verify that a card is authentic and there is enough money available for a chocolate bar. In one second, the value of the purchase is deducted from the balance on the card and added to an e-cash box in the vending machine. The remaining balance on the card is displayed by the vending machine or can be checked at an ATM or with a balance-reading device. Electronic purses would virtually eliminate fumbling for change or small bills in a busy store or rush-hour toll booth, and waiting for a credit card purchase to be approved. This allows customers to pay for rides and calls with a prepaid card that "remembers" each transaction.

And when the balance on an electronic purse is depleted, the purse can be recharged with more money. As for the vendor, the receipts can be collected periodically in person—or, more likely, by telephone and transferred to a bank account. While the technology has been available for a decade, the cards have been relatively expensive, from $5 to $10. Today the cards cost $1, and special telephones that consumers could install at home to recharge the cards are projected to cost as little as $50. A simple card reader would cost a merchant less than $200.

## Smart-Card Readers and Smart Phones

The benefits of smart cards will rely on the ubiquity of devices called smart-card readers that can communicate with the chip on a smart card. In addition to reading from and writing to smart cards, these devices can also support a variety of key management methods. Some smart-card readers combine elements of a personal computer, a point-of-sale terminal, and a phone to allow consumers to quickly conduct financial transactions without leaving their homes.

In the simplest form, the card reader features a two-line by 16-character display that can show both a prompt and the response entered by the user. Efficiency is further enhanced by color-coded function keys, which can be programmed to perform the most frequently used operations in a single keystroke. It can communicate via an RS-232 serial interface with the full range of transaction automation systems, including PCs and electronic cash registers (ECRs).

Card readers in the form of screen phones are becoming more prominent. Proponents of screen phone applications have long stated that consumer familiarity with phones gives screen phones an entrée th[illegible] computers cannot match. Some screen-based phones feature a four-[illegible] screen, a magnetic stripe card reader, and a phone keypad that folds [illegible] to reveal a keyboard for use in complex transactions. The phone pr[illegible]pts users through transactions using menus patterned after th[illegible]ound on automated teller machines.

Many bankers maintain that scre[illegible]sed phones are more convenient to use than PC-based home banki[illegible]plications, which require users to boot up their systems and establi[illegible]dem connection before conducting transactions. Other features of [illegible] phones include advanced telephone functions such as a two-w[illegible]ker phone capability, a dialing directory, and a phone log for trac[illegible]s. Several financial institutions have teamed up with local phone[illegible]nies in an effort to use these functions as a marketing tool for scree[illegible]s.

Smart c[illegible]aders can be customized for specific environments. The operatin[illegible]vironment allows programmers to use the C programming languag[illegible]reate and modify applications without compromising the device's se[illegible]y functions. The development system for most card readers even [illegible]mes with precoded modules for accelerated application development [PRNW94]. To promote smart card usage, the Smart Card Forum—a group of about 130 bu[illegible]esses and government agencies—is drawing up common specifications to promote the use of multiple application smart cards useable for everyth[illegible] from toll gates to hospitals [REB94].

## Business Issues and Smart Cards

For merchants, smart cards are a very convenient alternative to handling cash, which is becoming a nightmare. Cash is expensive to handle, count, and deposit and incurs *slippage,* a commercial term for theft, fraud, or misplacement. Long-range planners in the banking industry see the weaning of small businesses and consumers from cash as the last step to closing many expensive branches and conducting virtually all business by telephone, through cash machines and perhaps home computers. In fact, it is estimated that 4 percent of the value of cash that is deposited gets eaten up in handling costs. Banks and card issuers also expect to cut down on fraud, given that an embedded microchip is harder to tamper with than magnetic stripe technology.

What is the estimated market size for debit cards? MasterCard, which began putting chips into its cards in 1994, estimates that Americans make more than 237 billion cash purchases totaling $600 billion each year. Of this, 84 percent is for purchases costing less than $20. Given these figures, there appears to be enormous potential for a debit card with a prepaid feature that replaces coins and small bills. Debit cardholders may transfer up to $50, for example, into the "electronic purse" segment of their smart card either at ATMs or at a store or restaurant. Although anyone who picks up a lost prepaid card may use it, consumers can also preserve their anonymity—a welcome feature if one is worried that ATM cards and identification numbers could give strangers access to personal history.

Electronic purses are already being used to pay for photocopies, laundry machines, and parking meters. A [illegible] advanced usage of smart cards, known as Mondex—electronic purses that can be loaded with five currencies at one time—is under trial by 40,000 card[illegible] and 1,000 merchants in Swindon, England; its debut is imminent. Unlike [illegible] other electronic purse systems, Mondex, like cash, is anonymous. The [illegible] that issue Mondex cards will not be able to keep track of who makes o[illegible] payments (two cardholders can transfer money to each other as long a[illegible] [illegible]ve card readers, which is analogous to cash exchange between two people). While bankers are concerned that the system may open the doors [illegible] fraud and abuse, others say anonymity and flexibility are vital to acceptance.

The most extensive deployment of the electronic purses so far has [illegible] in Denmark, where a consortium of banks and telephone companies, known [illegible] Danmont, has issued more than 150,000 stored-value cards, [illegible]ed at very small transactions like those at parking meters and soda machines. [illegible] most popular application has been in laundromats, where the cards reduce [illegible] and [illegible]ism and increase sales. Danmont makes money by earning inte[illegible] [illegible]

ey it holds on the cards, called the *float*, and by charging vending mac
ers who use the system about 3 cents a transaction. Some bankers e
the security of smart cards and their ability to authenticate thems
make them useful for payments related to electronic commerce servic

## 8.4 CREDIT CARD-BASED ELECTRONIC PAYMENT SYSTEMS

To avoid the complexity associated with digital cash and electronic checks, consumers and vendors are also looking at credit card payments on the Internet as one possible time-tested alternative. There is nothing new in the basic process. If consumers want to purchase a product or service, they simply send their credit card details to the service provider involved and the credit card organization will handle this payment like any other.

We can break credit card payment on on-line networks into three basic categories:

1. *Payments using plain credit card details.* The easiest method of payment is the exchange of unencrypted credit cards over a public network such as telephone lines or the Internet. The low level of security inherent in the design of the Internet makes this method problematic (any snooper can read a credit card number, and programs can be created to scan the Internet traffic for credit card numbers and send the numbers to its master). Authentication is also a significant problem, and the vendor is usually responsible to ensure that the person using the credit card is its owner. Without encryption there is no way to do this.

2. *Payments using encrypted credit card details.* It would make sense to encrypt your credit card details before sending them out, but even then there are certain factors to consider. One would be the cost of a credit card transaction itself. Such cost would prohibit low-value payments (micropayments) by adding costs to the transactions.

3. *Payments using third-party verification.* One solution to security and verification problems is the introduction of a third party: a company that collects and approves payments from one client to another. After a certain period of time, one credit card transaction for the total accumulated amount is completed.

Table 8.2 lists some of the companies or consortiums that are attempting to provide the infrastructure for on-line credit card processing.

Players in On-Line Credit Card Transaction Processing

| | |
|---|---|
| ual Holdings | San Diego-based start-up offers an Internet payment system to process credit card transactions on the Internet. It's allied with EDS for data processing and First USA Merchant Services in Dallas for card processing services. |
| Interactive Transactions Partners | Joint venture of EDS, France Telecom, USWest, and H&R Block for home banking and electronic payment services. |
| MasterBanking | A home banking service started by MasterCard and Checkfree Corp., an on-line payments processor. |
| VISA Interactive | VISA International acquired US Order, a screen phone manufacturer. VISA Interactive has signed up more than 30 banks, including NationsBank. |
| Block Financial | This H&R Block unit owns Managing Your Money personal-finance software and CompuServe. Provides electronic-banking services for VISA member banks. |
| Prodigy | Teaming up with Meridian Bank and others to offer PC-based home banking via its on-line service. |

## Encryption and Credit Cards

Encryption is instantiated when credit card information is entered into a browser or other electronic commerce device and sent securely over the network from buyer to seller as an encrypted message. This practice, however, does not meet important requirements for an adequate financial system, such as nonrefutability, speed, safety, privacy, and security. To make a credit card transaction truly secure and nonrefutable, the following sequence of steps must occur before actual goods, services, or funds flow:

1. A customer presents his or her credit card information (along with an authenticity signature or other information such as mother's maiden name) securely to the merchant.
2. The merchant validates the customer's identity as the owner of the credit card account.
3. The merchant relays the credit card charge information and signature to its bank or on-line credit card processors.

4. The bank or processing party relays the information to the customer's bank for authorization approval.
5. The customer's bank returns the credit card data, charge authentication, and authorization to the merchant.

In this scheme, each consumer and each vendor generates a public key and a secret key. The public key is sent to the credit card company and put on its public key server. The secret key is reencrypted with a password, and the unencrypted version is erased. To steal a credit card, a thief would have to get access to both a consumer's encrypted secret key and password. The credit card company sends the consumer a credit card number and a credit limit. To buy something from vendor X, the consumer sends vendor X the message, "It is now time *T*. I am paying *Y* dollars to *X* for item *Z*," then the consumer uses his or her password to sign the message with the public key. The vendor will then sign the message with its own secret key and send it to the credit card company, which will bill the consumer for *Y* dollars and give the same amount (less a fee) to X. (See Fig. 8.3)

Nobody can cheat this system. The consumer can't claim that he didn't agree to the transaction, because he signed it (as in everyday life). The vendor can't invent fake charges, because he doesn't have access to the consumer's key. He can't submit the same charge twice, because the consumer included

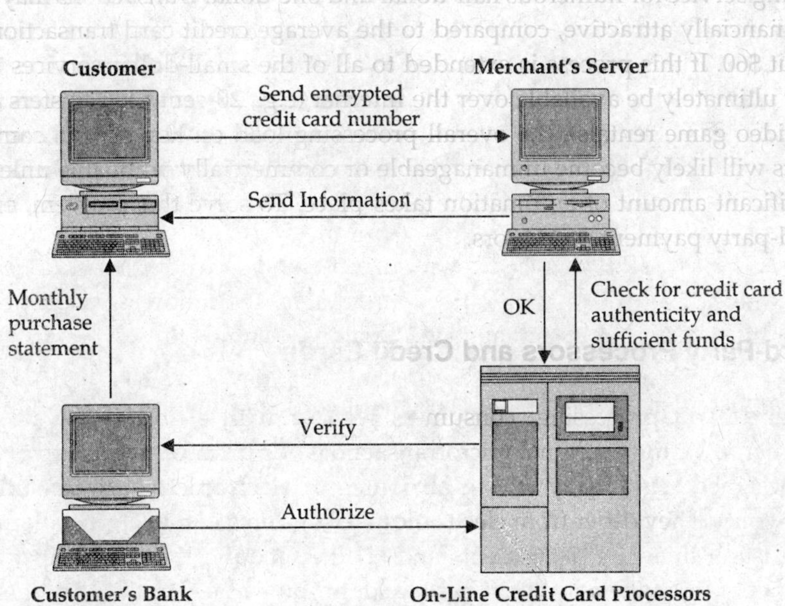


**Figure 8.3** Processing payments using encrypted credit cards

the precise time in the message. To become useful, credit card systems will have to develop distributed key servers and card checkers. Otherwise, a concentrated attack on these sites could bring the system to a halt.

Support for Privacy Enhanced Mail (PEM) and Pretty Good Privacy (PGP) encryption has been built into several browsers. Both of these schemes can be substantially bolstered with the addition of encryption to defeat snooping attacks. Now any vendor can create a secure system that accepts credit card numbers in about an hour.

Unfortunately, whether existing credit card companies will accept digital signatures as replacements for real signatures is not clear, so vendors will still have a difficult time when customers dispute charges made using encrypted credit card numbers over the Internet. When credit card companies do decide to accept digital signatures, they will need to maintain a public server with all of the public keys. This method assumes that the credit card company will keep the vendor honest, as is the case in traditional credit card transactions. Electronic payment processing is not an inexpensive proposition, however. But neither is fraud. If electronic commerce takes off and small transactions increase without a fully encrypted system in place, fraud will become even more expensive.

Although they are a positive step, encrypted credit card transactions may not be micro enough for purchasing information. Providing credit card processing service for numerous half-dollar and one-dollar transactions may not be financially attractive, compared to the average credit card transaction of about $60. If this process is extended to all of the small-dollar services that may ultimately be available over the Internet (e.g., 20-cent file transfers and $1 video game rentals), the overall processing load on key system components will likely become unmanageable or commercially nonviable unless a significant amount of automation takes place. To solve this problem, enter third-party payment processors.

## Third-Party Processors and Credit Cards

In third-party processing, consumers register with a third party on the Internet to verify electronic microtransactions. Verification mechanisms can be designed with many of the attributes of electronic tokens, including anonymity. They differ from electronic token systems in that (1) they depend on existing financial instruments and (2) they require the on-line involvement of at least one additional party and, in some cases, multiple parties to ensure extra security. However, requiring an on-line third-party connection for each transaction to different banks could lead to processing bottlenecks that could undermine the goal of reliable use.

Examples of companies that are already providing third-party payment services on the Internet are First Virtual (http://www.fv.com/) and Open Market (http://www.openmarket.com/). Both companies claim that their payment system is the first to link credit cards, banks, processing agents, and the Internet. Payments can be made by credit card or by debiting a demand deposit account via the automated clearinghouse. For the sake of brevity, we refer to them as on-line third-party processors (OTPPs) since both methods are fairly similar in nature.

OTPPs have created a six-step process that they believe will be a fast and efficient way to buy information on-line:

1. The consumer acquires an OTPP account number by filling out a registration form. This will give the OTPP a customer information profile that is backed by a traditional financial instrument such as a credit card.

2. To purchase an article, software, or other information on-line, the consumer requests the item from the merchant by quoting her OTPP account number. The purchase can take place in one of two ways: The consumer can automatically authorize the "merchant" via browser settings to access her OTPP account and bill her, or she can type in the account information.

3. The merchant contacts the OTPP payment server with the customer's account number.

4. The OTPP payment server verifies the customer's account number foı the vendor and checks for sufficient funds.

5. The OTPP payment server sends an electronic message to the buyer. This message could be an automatic WWW form that is sent by the OTPP server or could be a simple e-mail. The buyer responds to the form or e-mail in one of three ways: Yes, I agree to pay; No, I will not pay; or Fraud, I never asked for this.

6. If the OTPP payment server gets a Yes from the customer, the merchant is informed and the customer is allowed to download the material immediately.

7. The OTPP will not debit the buyer's account until it receives confirmation of purchase completion. Abuse by buyers who receive information a product and decline to pay can result in account suspension.

To use this system, both customers and merchants must be registered with the OTPP. In the case of First Virtual, this registration costs $2 for buyers and $10 for sellers. Sellers also pay a fee of 29 cents for each transaction plus 2 percent. Sellers also pay a $1 processing fee when aggregated payments (several transactions) are made to their account.

An on-line environment suitable for microtransactions will require that many of the preceding steps be automated. World Wide Web browsers capable of encryption can serve this purpose. Here the two key servers are merchant server and payment server (see Fig. 8.4). Users first establish an account with the payment server. Then, using a client browser, a user makes a purchase from a merchant server by clicking on a payment URL (hyper-

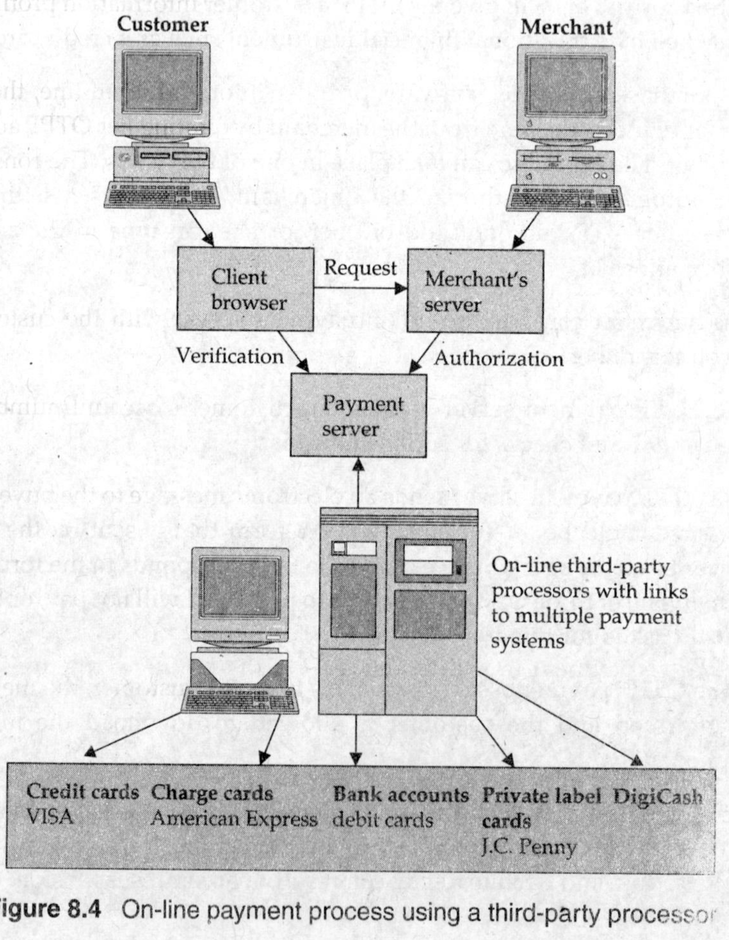


**Figure 8.4** On-line payment process using a third-party processor

links), which is attached to the product on a WWW page. Unknown to the customer, the payment URL encodes the following details of purchase: price of item, target URL (for hard goods, this URL is usually an order status page; for information goods, this URL points to the information customers are purchasing), and duration (for information goods, it specifies how long customers can get access to the target URL).

Payment URLs send the encoded information to the payment server. In other words, the payment URL directs the customer's browser to the payment server, which authenticates the user by asking her for the account number and other identification information. If the information entered by the customer is valid and funds are available, the payment server processes the payment transaction. The payment server then redirects the user's browser (using an HTTP redirect operation) to the purchased item with an access URL, which encodes the details of the payment transaction (the amount, what was purchased, and duration).

The access URL is effectively a digital invoice that has been stamped "paid" by the payment server. It provides evidence to the merchant that the user has paid for the information and provides a receipt that grants the user access. The access URL is the original target URL sent by the merchant's server, with additional fields that contain details of the access: expiration time (optional), user's address (to prevent sharing).

The merchant runs an HTTP server that is modified to process access URLs (HTTP redirects). The server checks the validity of the URL and grants access if the expiration time has not passed. If access has expired, the server returns a page that may give the user an opportunity to repurchase the item. The payment system can also generate access URLs in a format that can be parsed by CGI scripts running on an unmodified HTTP server.

Once a customer is authenticated, the payment is automatically processed. The payment server implements a modular payment architecture where accounts can be backed by different types of financial instruments, credit card accounts, prepaid accounts, billed accounts, debit cards, and other payment mechanisms. For credit card accounts, the payment system has a real-time connection to the credit card clearing network. The system can authorize payment in real time based on the profile of the transaction and the user. The system supports small transactions by accumulating them and settling them in aggregate. All transactions are recorded in a user's online statement. The statement is a summary of recent purchases, and each summary line is a hypertext link. For information goods, this is a link back to the purchased item. If access has expired, the merchant's server will give the user the opportunity to repurchase the item. For noninformation goods, the link may point to an order status or summary page.

## Business Pros and Cons of Credit Card-Based Payment

Third-party processing for credit cards entails a number of pros as well as cons. These companies are chartered to give credit accounts to individuals and act as bill collection agencies for businesses. Consumers use credit cards by presenting them for payment and then paying an aggregate bill once a month. Consumers pay either by flat fee or individual transaction charges for this service. Merchants get paid for the credit card drafts that they submit to the credit card company. Businesses get charged a transaction charge ranging from 1 percent to 3 percent for each draft submitted.

Credit cards have advantages over checks in that the credit card company assumes a larger share of financial risk for both buyer and seller in a transaction. Buyers can sometimes dispute a charge retroactively and have the credit card company act on their behalf. Sellers are ensured that they will be paid for all their sales—they needn't worry about fraud. This translates into a convenience for the buyer, in that credit card transactions are usually quicker and easier than check (and sometimes even cash) transactions. One disadvantage to credit cards is that their transactions are not anonymous, and credit card companies do in fact compile valuable data about spending habits.

Record keeping with credit cards is one of the features consumers value most because of disputes and mistakes in billing. Disputes may arise because different services may have different policies. For example, an information provider might charge for partial delivery of a file (the user may have abandoned the session after reading part of the file), and a movie distributor might charge depending on how much of the video had been downloaded. The cause of interrupted delivery needs to be considered in resolving disputes (e.g., intentional customer action versus a problem in the network or provider's equipment). In general, implementing payment policies will be simpler when payment is made by credit rather than with cash.

The complexity of credit card processing takes place in the verification phase, a potential bottleneck. If there is a lapse in time between the charging and the delivery of goods or services (for example, when an airline ticket is purchased well in advance of the date of travel), the customer verification process is simple because it does not have to be done in real time. In fact, all the relaying and authorizations can occur after the customer–merchant transaction is completed, unless the authorization request is denied. If the customer wants a report (or even a digital airline ticket), which would be downloaded into a PC or other information appliance immediately at the time of purchase, however, many message relays and authorizations take place in real time while the customer waits. Such exchanges may require many sequence-specific operations such as staged encryption and decrypting and exchanges of cryptographic keys.

Encryption and transaction speed must be balanced, however, as research has shown that on-line users get very impatient and typically wait for 20 seconds before pursuing other actions. Hence, on-line credit card users must find the process to be accessible, simple, and fast. Speed will have design and cost implications, as it is a function of network capabilities, computing power, available at every server, and the specific form of the transaction. The infrastructure supporting the exchange must be reliable. The user must feel confident that the supporting payment infrastructure will be available on demand and that the system will operate reasonably well regardless of component failures or system load conditions. The builders and providers of this infrastructure are aware of customer requirements and are in fierce competition to fulfill those needs.

## Infrastructure for On-Line Credit Card Processing

Transaction processing is an extremely lucrative business and on-line retail transaction processing on the I-way is expected to be even more so. To get an idea of the market size, consider the fact that global transaction services generated $1.6 billion in 1993 revenues to Citicorp alone. Principal players in the electronic credit card transaction processing business include Card Establishment Services, Envoy, First Data Corporation, First Financial Management, National Processing Company, J.C. Penney Business Services and SPS Transaction Services.

There is also no question that banks and other financial institutions must resolve many key issues before offering on-line processing services in e-commerce markets. Should they go it alone or form a partnership—and with whom? What technology to use? What services to offer? Which consumers are interested and who should be targeted? A wide variety of organizations are jumping into the fray. Regional electronic funds transfer (EFT) networks, credit card associations, equipment vendors, data processors, software developers, bill payment companies, and telecommunications providers are all wooing banks with the goal of building the transaction processing infrastructure on the Internet (see Table 8.2).

Competition among these players is based on service quality, price, processing system speed, customer support, and reliability. Most third-party processors market their services directly to large regional or national merchants rather than through financial institutions or independent sales organizations. Barriers to entry include (1) large initial capital requirements, (2) ongoing expenses related to establishing and maintaining an electronic transaction processing network, (3) the ability to obtain competitively priced access to an existing network, and (4) the reluctance of merchants to change processors.

What exactly is at stake here? A lot. In the emerging world of e-commerce, the companies that own the transaction infrastructure will be able to charge a fee, much as banks do today with ATMs. This could be extremely profitable. Microsoft, VISA, and other companies understand that they have to do something. If they wait for a clear path to emerge, it will be "too little too late." They know all too well that e-commerce transaction architectures (similar to MS-DOS or Windows) on which other e-commerce applications are developed will be very profitable.

Many companies are developing advanced electronic services for home-based financial transactions, and software companies are increasingly allying with banks to sell home banking. Eventually, the goal would be to offer everything from mutual funds to brokerage services over the network. Many banks are concerned about this prospect and view it as an encroachment on their turf. After years of dabbling, mostly unsuccessfully, with remote banking [BW94], banking is receiving a jarring message: Get wired or lose customers.

The traditional roles are most definitely being reshuffled, and electronic payment on the Internet can have a substantial effect on transaction processing in the "real" (nonelectronic) world. According to some estimates, transaction processing services account for as much as 25 percent of noninterest income for banks, so banks clearly stand to lose business. Why banks are on the defensive is obvious if we look at banking in the last ten years. A decade ago, banks processed 90 percent of all bank card transactions, such as VISA and MasterCard [BW94]. Today, 70 percent of those transactions are processed by nonbanks such as First Data Resources. If software companies and other interlopers become electronic toll-takers, banks could become mere homes for deposits, not the providers of lucrative value-added services. Even more worrisome, banks could lose the all-important direct link to be the customer's primary provider of financial services that lets them hawk profitable services. The effect of electronic commerce on the banking industry has been one of total confusion. To be fair, things are happening so fast in this area that it's hard to keep up with it all.

## 8.5 RISK AND ELECTRONIC PAYMENT SYSTEMS

One essential challenge of e-commerce is risk management. Operation of the payment systems incurs three major risks: fraud or mistake, privacy issues, and credit risk. Preventing mistakes might require improvements in the legal framework. Dealing with privacy and fraud issues requires improvements in the security framework. Curtailing credit risk requires devising procedures to constrict or moderate credit and reduce float in the market.

## Risks from Mistake and Disputes: Consumer Protection

Virtually all electronic payment systems need some ability to keep automatic records, for obvious reasons. From a technical standpoint, this is no problem for electronic systems. Credit and debit cards have them and even the paper-based check creates an automatic record. Once information has been captured electronically, it is easy and inexpensive to keep (it might even cost more to throw it away than to keep it). For example, in many transaction processing systems, old or blocked accounts are never purged and old transaction histories can be kept forever on magnetic tape.

Given the intangible nature of electronic transactions and dispute resolution relying solely on records, a general law of payment dynamics and banking technology might be: No data need ever be discarded. The record feature is an after-the-fact transcription of what happened, created without any explicit effort by the transaction parties. Features of these automatic records include (1) permanent storage; (2) accessibility and traceability; (3) a payment system database; and (4) data transfer to payment maker, bank, or monetary authorities.

The need for record keeping for purposes of risk management conflicts with the transaction anonymity of cash. One can say that anonymity exists today only because cash is a very old concept, invented long before the computer and networks gave us the ability to track everything. Although a segment of the payment-making public will always desire transaction anonymity, many believe that anonymity runs counter to the public welfare because too many tax, smuggling, and/or money laundering possibilities exist. The anonymity issue raises the question: Can electronic payments happen without an automatic record feature?

Many recent payment systems seem to be ambivalent on this point. For instance, the Mondex electronic purse touts equivalence with cash, but its electronic wallets are designed to hold automatic records of the card's last twenty transactions with a statement built in. Obviously, the card-reading terminals, machines, or telephones could all maintain records of all transactions and they probably ultimately will. With these records, the balance on any smart card could be reconstructed after the fact, thus allowing for additional protection against loss or theft. This would certainly add some value versus cash.

In sum, anonymity is an issue that will have to be addressed through regulation covering consumer protection in electronic transactions. There is considerable debate on this point. An anonymous payment system without automatic record keeping will be difficult for bankers and governments to accept. Were the regulation to apply, each transaction would have to be reported, meaning it would appear on an account statement making mistakes and disputes easier to resolve. However, customers might feel that all this record keeping is an invasion of privacy resulting in slower than expected adoption of electronic payment systems.

## Managing Information Privacy

The electronic payment system must ensure and maintain privacy. Every time one purchases goods using a credit card, subscribes to a magazine or accesses a server, that information goes into a database somewhere. Furthermore, all these records can be linked so that they constitute in effect a single dossier. This dossier would reflect what items were bought and where and when. This violates one the unspoken laws of doing business: that the privacy of customers should be protected as much as possible.

All details of a consumer's payments can be easily be aggregated: Where, when, and sometimes what the consumer buys is stored. This collection of data tells much about the person and as such can conflict with the individual's right to privacy. Users must be assured that knowledge of transactions will be confidential, limited only to the parties involved and their designated agents (if any).

Privacy must be maintained against eavesdroppers on the network and against unauthorized insiders. The users must be assured that they cannot be easily duped, swindled, or falsely implicated in a fraudulent transaction. This protection must apply throughout the whole transaction protocol by which a good or service is purchased and delivered. This implies that, for many types of transactions, trusted third-party agents will be needed to vouch for the authenticity and good faith of the involved parties.

## Managing Credit Risk

Credit or systemic risk is a major concern in net settlement systems because a bank's failure to settle its net position could lead to a chain reaction of bank failures. The digital central bank must develop policies to deal with this possibility. Various alternatives exist, each with advantages and disadvantages.

A digital central bank guarantee on settlement removes the insolvency test from the system because banks will more readily assume credit risks from other banks.

Without such guarantees the development of clearing and settlement systems and money markets may be impeded. A middle road is also possible, for example, setting controls on bank exposures (bilateral or multilateral) and requiring collateral. If the central bank does not guarantee settlement, it must define, at least internally, the conditions and terms for extending liquidity to banks in connection with settlement.

## 8.6 DESIGNING ELECTRONIC PAYMENT SYSTEMS

Despite cost and efficiency gains, many hurdles remain to the spread of electronic payment systems. These include several factors, many nontechnical in nature, that must be addressed before any new payment method can be successful:

- *Privacy.* A user expects to trust in a secure system; just as the telephone is a safe and private medium free of wiretaps and hackers, electronic communication must merit equal trust.
- *Security.* A secure system verifies the identity of two-party transactions through "user authentication" and reserves flexibility to restrict information/services through access control. Tomorrow's bank robbers will need no getaway cars—just a computer terminal, the price of a telephone call, and a little ingenuity. Millions of dollars have been embezzled by computer fraud. No systems are yet fool-proof, although designers are concentrating closely on security.
- *Intuitive interfaces.* The payment interface must be as easy to use as a telephone. Generally speaking, users value convenience more than anything.
- *Database integration.* With home banking, for example, a customer wants to play with all his accounts. To date, separate accounts have been stored on separate databases. The challenge before banks is to tie these databases together and to allow customers access to any of them while keeping the data up-to-date and error free.
- *Brokers.* A "network banker"—someone to broker goods and services, settle conflicts, and facilitate financial transactions electronically—must be in place.

- *Pricing.* One fundamental issue is how to price payment system services. For example, should subsidies be used to encourage users to shift from one form of payment to another, from cash to bank payments, from paper-based to e-cash. The problem with subsidies is the potential waste of resources, as money may be invested in systems that will not be used. Thus investment in systems not only might not be recovered but substantial ongoing operational subsidies will also be necessary. On the other hand, it must be recognized that without subsidies, it is difficult to price all services affordably.
- *Standards.* Without standards, the welding of different payment users into different networks and different systems is impossible. Standards enable interoperability, giving users the ability to buy and receive information, regardless of which bank is managing their money.

None of these hurdles are insurmountable. Most will be jumped within the next few years. These technical problems, experts hope, will be solved as technology is improved and experience is gained. The biggest question concerns how customers will take to a paperless and (if not cashless) less-cash world.

## 8.7 SUMMARY

From one angle, electronic commerce sounds like a great opportunity—low overhead, no physical location needed, and few employees. But several important questions need to addressed that revolve around the issue of payment: How will businesses be paid? Or will consumers pay for what they buy?

Electronic payment systems are widely used in commerce and include wholesale payments, wire transfers, recurring bill payments, the automated clearinghouse, electronic draft capture, and electronic check presentment. Can currency remain immune to this trend forever? Maybe. Maybe not. To answer these questions, this chapter examined the emerging area of cashless payment and the various payment options that are currently being examined. These payment options include e-cash, electronic checks, smart cards, and electronic purses.

A world with electronic payment systems will be very different from today's world. New opportunities will arise for consumers, banks, and others. If record keeping were part of the payment instrument, several innovative uses could be visualized. For instance, consumers could tally up everything they spent with little effort. They could do realistic expense analysis and even negotiate with merchants based on volume. Even small merchants could know who actually utilizes their stores and how much they spend. Possible benefits to banks and other firms would be a better understanding of the financial behavior of their customers. Governments might monitor prices, inflation, and the velocity of money more accurately and more quickly than today. Income taxes might even become integrated with the payment system.

In sum, just as ATM machines revolutionized consumer banking services, safe electronic payment systems are expected to catalyze sales of on-line goods and services. The challenge for the future is to come to the right vision of how electronic payment systems will augment or replace paper-based payment methods. The next step is to figure out how to make a profit on that vision.

Chapter 9

# Interorganizational Commerce and EDI

As a cost-conscious, highly competitive electronic commerce environment comes of age, businesses are looking at electronic data interchange (EDI) in a new light. EDI is defined as the interprocess communication (computer application to computer application) of business information in a standardized electronic form. In short, EDI communicates information pertinent for business transactions between the computer systems of companies, government organizations, small businesses, and banks.

Over the last decade, EDI has changed not only how firms do business, but with whom they do business in a global marketplace. Prior to EDI, purchase orders, acknowledgments, and invoices depended on postal systems and communication with trading partners was restricted to the few hours of the workday that overlap from time zone to time zone. Today, computers simplify and enhance communication between North American, Asian, and European trading partners and enable new business practices like global procurement and sourcing.

Using EDI, trading partners establish computer-to-computer links that enable them to exchange information electronically. This allows businesses to better cope with a growing avalanche of paperwork: purchase orders, invoices, confirmation notices, shipping receipts, and other documents. With the aid of EDI, all these documents are in electronic form, which allows more work automation to occur and even alters the way business is done.

Many industries see EDI as essential for reducing cycle and order fulfillment times. Manufacturers work with customers and suppliers to convert to an electronic exchange the huge volume of orders and records that now crawl back and forth on paper. In retailing, EDI can provide vendors with a snapshot of what stores are selling, enabling them to recognize and meet their customer's needs much faster than in the past. In addition, it enables retailers and vendors to place orders and pay bills electronically, reducing time and the expense of paperwork.

The primary benefit of EDI to business is a considerable reduction in transaction costs, by improving the speed and efficiency of filling orders. Studies show that it takes up to five times as long to process a purchase order manually as it does electronically. In addition, the common interaction channel between trading partners can foster closer relationships. All this can result in important competitive and strategic advantages.

Ironically, despite these advantages, EDI is not (yet) widely used. It is estimated that out of millions of businesses in the United States, only 44,000 companies exchange business data electronically. Only about 10 percent of these companies use EDI for financial transactions. Moreover, no more than fifty banks have the capability of providing complete financial EDI services to their corporate customers [KWY94]. The joke in industry is that most companies are so unfamiliar with EDI they don't even know how to spell it. The reality is they d better learn quickly. With an annual growth rate of more than 45 percent, and with more than 90 percent of Fortune 1000 companies currently using EDI and more expected in the near future as networking becomes pervasive, EDI is rapidly becoming key to the way business is done in interorganizational electronic commerce [TBW94].

This chapter will focus on defining EDI, its advantages, the interorganizational business scenarios involving EDI, new forms of EDI dealing with e-commerce requirements, and EDI standardization. Chapter 10 will deal with EDI implementation issues.

## 9.1 ELECTRONIC DATA INTERCHANGE

EDI developed in the 1960s as a means of accelerating the movement of documents pertaining to shipments and transportation. Not until the mid-1980s, however, was the technique used in a wide range of industries—automotive, retail, transportation, and international trade. Its use is growing and it is set to become the standard by which organizations will communicate formally with each other in the world of electronic commerce.

Electronic commerce is often equated with EDI, so it is important to clarify that electronic commerce embraces EDI and much more. In electronic commerce, EDI techniques are aimed at improving the interchange of information between trading partners, suppliers, and customers by bringing down the boundaries that restrict how they interact and do business with each other. In short, EDI is aimed at forging *boundaryless relationships*.

Technically speaking, EDI is one well-known example of structured document interchange which enables data in the form of document content to be exchanged between software applications that are working together to process a business transaction. Emphasis must be placed on the fact that EDI only specifies a format for business information, that the actual transmission of the information is tackled by other underlying transport mechanisms such as e-mail or point-to-point connections.

### Defining EDI

Because of the different approaches in the development and implementation of EDI, there is no consensus on a definition of EDI. A review of some of the prevailing definitions follows:

> Electronic data interchange is the transmission, in a standard syntax, of unambiguous information of business or strategic significance between computers of independent organizations. [*The Accredited Standards Committee for EDI of the American National Standards Institute*]
>
> Electronic data interchange is the interchange of standard formatted data between computer application systems of trading partners with minimal manual intervention. [*UN/EDIFACT Training Guide*]
>
> Electronic data interchange is the electronic transfer, from computer to computer, of commercial and administrative data using an agreed standard to structure an EDI message. [*Article 2.1. of the European Model EDI agreement*]
>
> Electronic data interchange is the electronic transfer from one computer to another of computer processable data using an agreed standard to structure the data. [*International Data Exchange Association, The EDI Handbook: Trading in the 1990s*]

Another aspect of EDI that often causes confusion is its usage in one context as a technological solution that focuses on the mechanical transport and assembly of business forms and in another context as a business methodology that focuses on the content and structure of forms. This confusion can be cleared by examining the layered architecture of EDI.

## EDI Layered Architecture

EDI architecture specifies four layers: the semantic (or application) layer, the standards translation layer, the packing (or transport) layer, and the physical network infrastructure layer.

The *EDI semantic layer* describes the business application that is driving EDI. For a procurement application, this translates into requests for quotes, price quotes, purchase orders, acknowledgments, and invoices. This layer is specific to a company and the software it uses. In other words, the user interface and content visible on the screen are tailored or customized to local environments.

The information seen at the EDI semantic layer must be translated from a company-specific form to a more generic or universal form so that it can be sent to various trading partners, who could be using a variety of software applications at their end. To achieve this, companies must adopt universal EDI standards that lay out the acceptable fields of business forms. What complicates matters is the presence of two competing standards that define the content and structure of EDI forms: the X12 standard, developed by the American National Standards Institute (ANSI), and EDIFACT, developed by United Nations Economic Commission for Europe (UN/ECE), Working Party for the Facilitation of International Trade Procedures.

To facilitate the transfer of computer files between two "trading partners" requires that the computer applications of both sender and receiver use a compatible format for EDI document exchange. The sender must use a software application that creates an EDI file format similar to what the recipient's computer application can read. It is not mandatory that both have identical file processing systems. When the trading partner sends a document, the EDI translation software converts the proprietary format into a standard mutually agreed on by the processing systems. When a company receives the document, their EDI translation software automatically changes the standard format into the proprietary format of their document processing software so that the company can manipulate the information in whatever way it chooses to.

*EDI standards* specify business form structure and to some extent influence content seen at the application layer. For instance, a purchase order name field in an X12 standard might be specified to hold a maximum of 50 charac-

| | | |
|---|---|---|
| EDI semantic layer | Application level services | |
| EDI standard layer | EDIFACT business form standards | |
| | ANSI X12 business form standards | |
| EDI transport layer | Electronic mail | X.435, MIME |
| | Point to point | FTP, TELNET |
| | World Wide Web | HTTP |
| Physical layer | Dial-up lines, Internet, I-way | |

**Figure 9.1** Layered architecture of EDI

ters. An application using 75-character field lengths will produce name truncation during the translation from the application layer to the standard layer. In short, the EDI standards and application level, although separate, are closely intertwined. (See Fig. 9.1.)

The *EDI transport layer* corresponds closely with the nonelectronic activity of sending a business form from one company A to company B. The business form could be sent via regular postal service, registered mail, certified mail, or private carrier such as United Parcel Service (UPS) or simply faxed between the companies. In other words, the content and structure of the form are separated from the transport carrier. More and more, the EDI transport carrier of choice is becoming e-mail. Here, EDI documents are exchanged rapidly over electronic networks using the existing e-mail programs and infrastructure.

*EDI document transport* is far more complex than simply sending e-mail messages or sharing files through a network, a modem, or a bulletin board. These EDI documents are more structured than e-mail and typically are manipulated or processed more than e-mail messages by the sending and receiving software.

The relationship between EDI and e-mail can be ambiguous as e-mail systems become very sophisticated and incorporate more and more form-based features (see Table 9.1). A good example is Lotus Notes, which started as a simple form-based mail system but has evolved into a very sophisticated environment. Lotus Notes lack flexibility, however, and require trading partners to use the same software application at both ends. This goes against the EDI goal of openness.

**Table 9.1** EDI Versus e-mail

| *Electronic Data Interchange (EDI)* | *Electronic Mail* |
|---|---|
| There is typically no human involvement in the processing of the information, as the interface has software-to-software orientation. The data are structured in a software-understandable way. | The data are not necessarily structured to be software-understandable. A human-to-software interface is involved at a minimum of one end of the interchange. |
| The interchange is composed by one software for interpretation by another software. If a reply is involved, it is composed by a software to be interpreted by another software. | The message is composed by a human and/or interpreted by a human and/or a reply is composed by a human and/or interpreted by a human. |

What really differentiates EDI from messaging is its emphasis on the automation of business transactions conducted between organizations. In addition, EDI messages have certain legal status. For instance, if a buyer sends a supplier EDI purchase orders that specify the requirements, time of delivery, and quantity and the supplier does not uphold its end of the contract, it can be taken to court with the EDI trading agreements serving as evidence. Table 9.1 indicates some EDI properties which distinguish it from e-mail.

## EDI in Action

The idea behind EDI is very simple. EDI seeks to take what has been a manually prepared form or a form from a business application, translates that data into a standard electronic format, and transmit it. At the receiving end, the standard format is "untranslated" into a format that can be read by the recipient's application. Hence output from one application becomes input to another through the computer-to-computer exchange of information. The result is an elimination of the delays and the errors inherent in paper-based transactions.

Benefits of EDI can be seen by comparing the flow of information between organizations before and after its implementation. For this purpose the purchasing application provides an ideal scenario. In general, EDI has been used extensively in the procurement function to streamline the interaction between the buyer and seller. Other uses for EDI are also prevalent. Universities use EDI to exchange transcripts quickly. Auto manufacturers use EDI to transmit large, complex engineering designs created on specialized computers. Large multinational firms use EDI to send on-line price catalogs to customers listing products, prices, discounts, and terms. EDI-capable businesses can compare prices and terms and make direct orders by EDI

Figure 9.2 shows the information flow when paper documents are shuffled between organizations via the mailroom. When the buyer sends a purchase order to a seller, the relevant data must be extracted from the internal database and recorded on hard copy. This hard copy is then forwarded to the seller after passing through several intermediate steps. Sellers receive information in the form of letters and in some cases a vast number of facsimiles. This information is manually entered into the internal information systems of the recipient by data entry operators. This process generates a considerable amount of overhead in labor costs and time delays. The reproduction of information also increases the risk of errors caused by incorrect data entries.

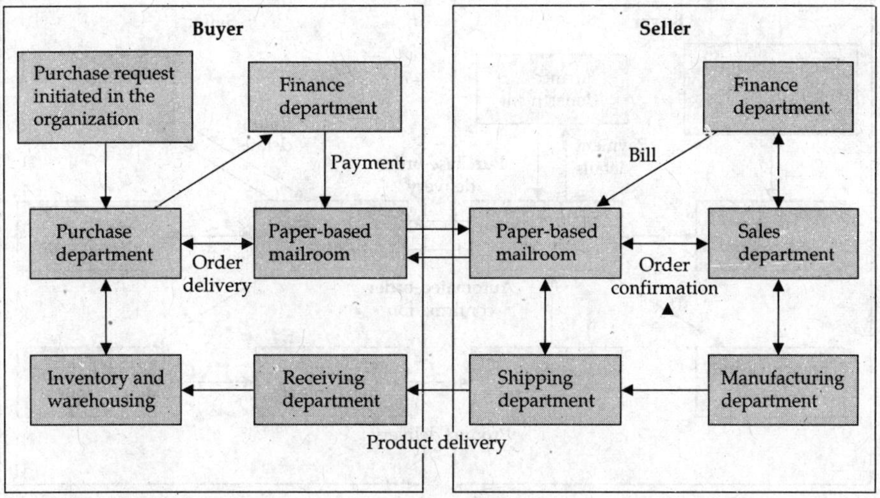


**Figure 9.2** Information flow without EDI

This pervasive practice of converting digital data into hard copy data that is reconverted into electronic information again on the receiving end generates unnecessary costs. It is quite possible to exchange the information in its electronic format by means of other carriers. Such carriers include magnetic tapes and diskettes and, more recently, the EDI third-party services. The use of EDI carriers saves substantial administration costs by eliminating the bulk of circulating paperwork. Furthermore, the accessibility of the information is improved manifold, which enables a more efficient audit of the operations.

EDI can substantially automate the information flow and facilitate management of the business process, as illustrated in Fig. 9.3. The EDI transactions for a purchase, shipment, and corresponding payment are as follows:

*Step 1.* Buyer's computer sends *Purchase Order* to seller's computer.

*Step 2.* Seller's computer sends *Purchase Order Confirmation* to buyer's computer.

*Step 3.* Seller's computer sends *Booking Request* to transport company's computer.

*Step 4.* Transport company's computer sends *Booking Confirmation* to seller's computer.

*Step 5.* Seller's computer sends *Advance Ship Notice* to buyer's computer.

*Step 6.* Transport company's computer sends *Status* to seller's computer.

*Step 7.* Buyer's computer sends *Receipt Advice* to seller's computer.

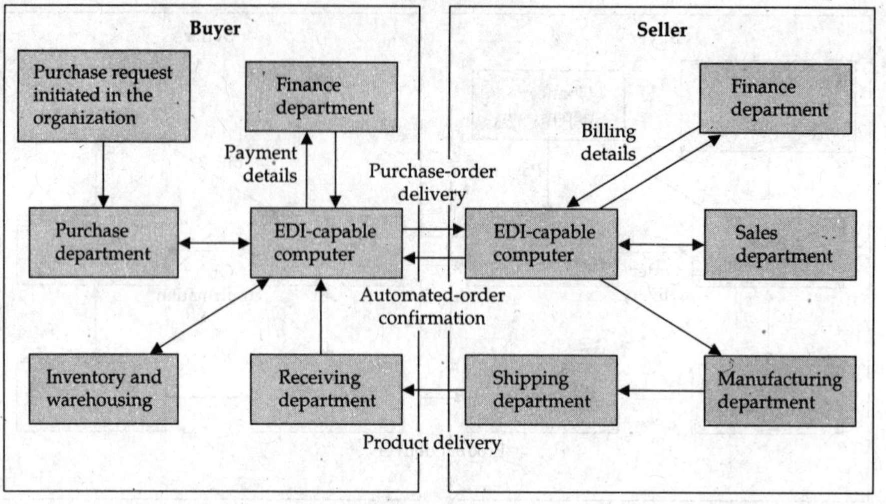


**Figure 9.3** Information flow with EDI

*Step 8.* Seller's computer sends *Invoice* to buyer's computer.

*Step 9.* Buyer's computer sends *Payment* to seller's computer

The Purchase Order Confirmation is the seller's acceptance of the price and terms of sale. Note that the various internal departments are aggregated and called buyer and seller to simplify the description. All the interactions occur through EDI forms and in most cases are generated automatically by the computer.

In sum, firms are adopting EDI as a fast, inexpensive, and safe method of sending invoices, purchase orders, customs documents, shipping notices, and other frequently used business documents. We can think of EDI as a strategic tool that enhances the competitiveness of the companies involved. The improved ability to exchange huge amounts of data in a fast and effective manner tends to speed up business processes. Furthermore, these processes can be closely monitored, providing the companies with the ability to trace, manage, and audit the operations. Such flexibility allows firms to adopt business techniques aimed at removing the bottlenecks and making the business processes more efficient.

## Tangible Benefits of EDI

EDI can be a cost- and time-saving system, for many reasons. The automatic transfer of information from computer to computer reduces the need to rekey information and as such reduces costly errors to near zero. EDI transactions produce acknowledgments of receipt of data. Many firms are now finding that this acknowledgment can make the invoice obsolete and save many efforts now devoted to acquiring, receiving, and paying for goods.

For companies dealing with thousands of suppliers and tens of thousands of purchase orders a year, the savings from EDI are significant. For example, RJR Nabisco figures that purchase orders that previously cost between $75 and $125 to process now cost 93 cents. Companies can also pay each other through "automated receipts settlement" or financial EDI, whereby electronic purchase order acknowledgments and shipping notices provide the data necessary for payment, further reducing paper.

Savings also accrue from the following improvements:

- *Reduced paper-based systems.* EDI can impact the effort and expense a company devotes to maintaining records, paper-related supplies, filing cabinets, or other storage systems and to the personnel required to maintain all of these systems. Electronic transactions take over most of the functions of paper forms and through automation drastically reduce the time spent to process them. EDI can also reduce postage bills because of the amounts of paper that no longer need be sent.

- *Improved problem resolution and customer service.* EDI can minimize the time companies spend to identify and resolve interbusiness problems. Many such problems come from data-entry errors somewhere along the way, and EDI can eliminate many of them. EDI can improve customer service by enabling the quick transfer of business documents and a marked decrease in errors (and so can fill orders faster) and by providing an automatic audit trail that frees accounting staff for more productive activities.

  An example of problem resolution and customer service facilitated by EDI is the Vendor Stock Replenishment (VSR) initiated by retailers such as Wal Mart. This program requires that vendors maintain appropriate inventory levels in all stores. With VSR, stores do not run out of a product while suppliers or distributors wait for a purchase order from the headquarters. Suppliers and distributors send stock as soon as the store EDI system reports it is necessary and automatically bill the client. It cuts days, even weeks, from the order fulfillment cycle and ensures that the product is always on the shelf. The time savings come from not having to copy and fax/mail copies of invoices or purchase orders.

- *Expanded customer/supplier base.* Many large manufacturers and retailers with the necessary clout are ordering their suppliers to institute an EDI program. However, these are isolated islands of productivity because they are unable to build bridges to other companies. With the advent of electronic commerce, the bridge is now available. Today, when evaluating a new product to carry or a new supplier to use, the ability to implement EDI is a big plus in their eyes. These same companies tend to stop doing business with suppliers who do not comply.

## 9.2 EDI APPLICATIONS IN BUSINESS

Although EDI was developed to improve transportation and trade, it has spread everywhere. Some idea of the breadth of EDI's coverage may be obtained from a sample of EDI applications currently in development or under consideration. This sample includes railway rolling stock monitoring; ship "bay plans" (cargo plans for container ships); ship berthing/scheduling notices; notification of the presence of dangerous/hazardous goods on ships/trains/planes; the exchange of CAD/CAM documents; tender tracking; lodgment of law court documents; notification of the lodgment of archive documents; the exchange and lodgment of trade documents such as ship manifests/airway bills/customs clearances; airline ticket settlements—in addition to the more commonly considered exchange of documents concerned with the purchase and supply of goods (such as purchase orders or invoices). In short, EDI has grown from its original (and somewhat limited) use as expediter of the transfer of trade goods to facilitator of standard format data between any two computer systems.

An examination of EDI usage in various industries provides insight into the business problems that EDI is attempting to solve. We will present four very different scenarios in industries that use EDI extensively: international or cross-border trade, electronic funds transfer (EFT), health care EDI for insurance claims processing, and manufacturing and retail procurement. As these examples illustrate, companies have applied a number of EDI-based solutions to improve business processes—for both strategic and competitive advantages. In some cases, EDI has transformed operational aspects of a company's business. Increased quality and cost reductions can significantly change industry standards of competition as innovators exert greater pressure on competitors to meet new standards of customer satisfaction and productivity. In others, EDI has shaped a company's marketing and distribution efforts by helping to create new distribution channels, develop new merchandising and market research methods, and introduce better customer service. In sum, major improvements in product manufacturing and customer service response time allow companies to be more competitive.

## International Trade and EDI

EDI has always been very closely linked with international trade. In fact, the origins of EDI have been traced to the 1948 Berlin Airlift, where the monumental task of coordinating air freighted consignments of food arriving with differing packaging, languages, and forms was addressed by devising a standard form to be filled in by all aircraft personnel before unloading.

Over the last few years, significant progress has been made toward the establishment of more open and dynamic trade relations. Recent years have brought the General Agreement on Tariffs and Trade (GATT); the Free Trade Agreement (NAFTA) among the United States, Canada, and Mexico; and the creation of the European Union. These developments have meant the lifting of long-standing trade restrictions. Many countries, and in particular developing countries, have made significant efforts to liberalize and adjust their trade policies. In this context, trade efficiency, which allows faster, simpler, broader and less costly transactions, is a necessity. It is a widely held view that trade efficiency can be accomplished only by using EDI as a primary global transactions medium.

### *Role of EDI in International Trade*

EDI attempts to facilitate the smooth flow of information. Often, those of us not closely involved in international trade tend to think only of its physical aspects—the movement of goods, containers, vehicles, ships, and aircraft. Underlying, controlling, and regulating the physical movement, however, is an invisible deluge of information handling and exchange manifested by a variety of documents or their electronic equivalents. The purpose of the information flow is not merely to provide data but to facilitate timely delivery. The best quality information, which arrives days after the cargo, is not very helpful. Such delays can be caused by poorly designed documents, mistakes in document handling, or bad management upstream where a bureaucrat sits on the document.

EDI replaces paper, which has been the mainstay for carrying trade-related information. Undoubtedly, paper-based communication is inefficient and costly because of the labor involved, error rates, and associated delays. The problem of paper is significant in national trade but becomes far more acute in international trade. It is estimated that a minimum of twelve participants are involved in the simplest international trade transaction. All want information about what is being moved or paid for, and the core of that information is the same. Vast amounts of time and resources are often spent transferring and checking the information from one paper document to another. Errors occur frequently; for example 319 may unwittingly become 399. This may sound like a small problem, but if a ship or aircraft is being loaded based on an inaccurate waybill, time and money would be spent looking for the missing 80 crates and may even result in claims letters and repudiations sent back and forth before the mistake is realized. The United Nations has estimated that error rates in excess of 50 percent have been consistently recorded in letters of credit and error rates of 30 percent are not uncommon in manual processing of customs entries [UN94a].

According to the U.N. Conference on Trade and Development (UNCTAD), the costs of voluminous paperwork, complex formalities, and associated delays and errors amount to about 10 percent of the final value of goods. A typical international trade transaction may involve 30 different parties, 60 original documents, and 360 document copies, all of which have to be checked, transmitted, re-entered into various information systems, processed, and filed. For small companies, this can be daunting, even without the additional handicaps faced by many Third World exporters such as poor infrastructure and cumbersome, sometimes corrupt, bureaucracies [FRAN94]. UNCTAD argues that transaction costs—totaling perhaps $400 billion a year by the end of the decade—could be sliced by 25 percent by streamlining procedures and expanding paperless trading.

EDI is expected to reduce the entry barrier for small traders. Small and medium-sized traders are confined to the margins of international trade because of lack of efficient procedures, lack of access to information and information networks, or inadequate support services or trade logistics. Although the needs vary from one country to the next, most firms can greatly benefit from efficient business practices and trade facilitation measures. Since all such improvements need not be technology-intensive, they can generate substantial benefits at all levels.

EDI benefits for international trade include (1) reduced transaction expenditures; (2) quicker movement of imported and exported goods; (3) improved customer service through "track and trace" programs that quickly identify to the many participants in a trade deal—companies, customs, banks, insurers, transport agents, and so on—where things are located or being handled; and (4) faster customs clearance and reduced opportunities for corruption, a huge problem in trade.

### The Components of International Trade

International trade is structured around thousands of freight forwarders who are sometimes called travel agents for freight. Freight forwarders act as middlemen for shippers and consumers. Freight forwarding is a highly specialized industry in which the provider handles large freight shipments and customs clearance for customers. Freight forwarders provide a wide range of services, including cargo booking, air cargo documenting, and consolidating cargo from numerous shippers. The provider finds capacity for the freight on trucks, aircraft, or ocean-going vessels. Freight forwarders usually do not own aircraft, but book space on commercial and cargo airlines on behalf of companies around the world that manufacture or supply virtually every type of product. The provider arranges for customs brokers to prepare import customs documentation once it arrives at its final destination (see Fig. 9.4).

These international trade agencies—shippers, airlines, forwarders, and customs in various countries—are supported by EDI and computer networks that tie them together. EDI facilitates the transmittal of commercial documents and the associated freight information sent via modem from the foreign exporter to both the importer and his customs broker. The importer's computer and software would automatically receive the data and produce an exception report showing only those items that are late when compared to the importer's internal manufacturing due dates. This alerts the importer to any items requiring special attention. Simultaneously, the broker's computer

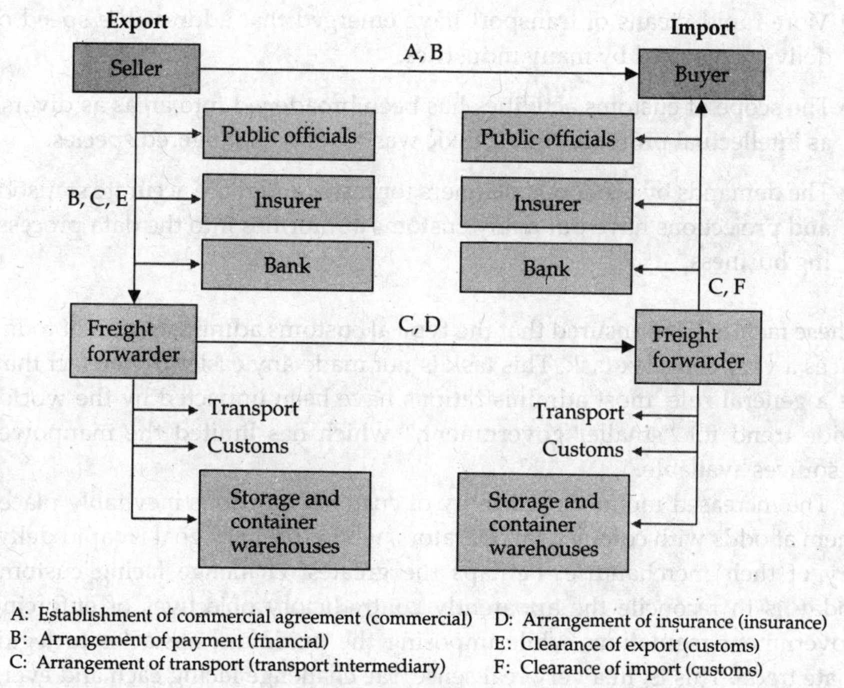


**Figure 9.4** Internals of international trade

and software receives the data, strips out all required data, and prepares ABI (automated broker interface) entry data, which is transmitted to customs for clearance. No faxing, copying, rekeying, or manual data input is required.

In addition to freight forwarders, other important functions of international trade include banking and insurance, customs, and logistics and transport. We will defer the discussion of the banking and insurance functions until later in this chapter. Numerous EDI forms are involved in all these functions. Fully elaborating on them in the limited space available is impossible. Instead we focus on the challenges and business issues involved.

### *Customs and International Trade*

Customs plays a key role in international trade. Every international trade transaction involves at least two customs clearances, export and import. The environment in which customs operates is changing rapidly and many new challenges have emerged, including the following:

- A tremendous volume of goods is being traded in an increasingly global economy.
- More rapid means of transport have emerged that address the speed of delivery required by many industries.
- The scope of customs activities has been broadened into areas as diverse as intellectual property rights, toxic wastes, and endangered species.
- The demands by economic planners for faster and more accurate statistics and projections have put many customs authorities into the data processing business.

These factors have ensured that the typical customs administration of today faces a very complex task. This task is not made any easier by the fact that, as a general rule, most administrations have been impacted by the worldwide trend for "smaller government," which has limited the manpower resources available.

The increased monitoring activity of customs functions inevitably places them at odds with commercial operators, whose primary goal is rapid delivery of their merchandise. Perhaps the greatest challenge facing customs today is to reconcile the apparently contradictory objectives of enforcing government regulations while imposing the minimum obstacles to legitimate trade. This is, in a very real sense, the challenge facing each and every customs authority worldwide.

The response of customs has been greater use of EDI as authorities grasp its importance. A growing number of countries now offer traders the option of submitting their customs documentation in electronic format rather than on paper.

### The Logistics of Transport

Let's look at one example of transport—air cargo. As in many other industries, the rules are changing in the air cargo field too. Just-in-time manufacturing, global sourcing, new markets, and downsizing have all had their effect on how companies view the movement of goods. JIT demands tight delivery windows. Global sourcing means coordinating vendors worldwide. New markets require new distribution programs. And downsizing leaves fewer people to do the work.

The players in the industry are changing. In the past decade, several air carriers have been squeezed out of the market due to competition. New carriers have emerged and integrators—forwarders who own their own aircraft, such as United Parcel Service and Federal Express—have emerged, especially in the small-package overnight market. Small local branches have been replaced by international transportation providers that offer a full range of services, including inventory and distribution management, materials requirement planning, protective cargo packing, insured warehousing, foreign trade zone operations, marine insurance, air and ocean freight forwarding, and customs brokerage.

Today, the stakes are higher. Time-critical deliveries often save enormous amounts of money. For example, the Harper Group, a freight agent, expedited a machine part from Philadelphia to Scotland in less than one day to avoid a plant closure that could have cost the customer $4 million [TN93]. With the growing trend toward purchasing just-in-time, delays in delivery increasingly imply lost business. If local suppliers can produce and deliver inputs within a deadline, remote suppliers must do likewise or they will lose market share. With all these changes and competition, it is no wonder that EDI is critical.

### Trade Point Global Network: The Future of Trade

In industrialized countries EDI is used by fewer than 7.5 percent of companies, and in developing countries this number is far lower. For exporters in developing countries, poor telecommunications may make EDI impractical. To help reduce this gap, UNCTAD came up with the idea of a worldwide network of trade points [UN94b].

Trade points attempt to bring together under one roof all the services needed by exporters, such as government departments, customs authorities, chambers of commerce, banks, insurers, and freight forwarders. Trade points will enable companies to use EDI as well as gain access to computerized information on markets, potential clients and investment partners, tariffs, and trade rules worldwide. A trade point typically consists of the following services:

- A trade facilitation center, where participants in foreign trade transactions (customs, foreign trade institutes, freight forwarders, transport companies, banks, and insurance companies) are grouped together under a single physical or virtual roof.
- A source of trade-related information that provides actual and potential traders with data about business and market opportunities, potential clients and suppliers, trade regulations, and requirements.
- A gateway to global networking, whereby all trade points will be interconnected and equipped with computing and telecommunication tools to link up with other global networks.

The main objective of the trade points is to entice more small and medium-sized enterprises to embark on international commerce. At the trade point, market opportunities are targeted, government formalities are cleared, and business transactions are carried out. This "one stop shopping" lowers the transaction costs of importing and exporting. It also reduces the procedural barriers to trade, thus encouraging new entrants into the trade arena. Pilot centers are being built in more than one hundred countries.

## Financial EDI

Financial EDI comprises the electronic transmission of payments and remittance information between a payer, payee, and their respective banks. This section examines the ways business-to-business payments are made today and describes the various methods for making financial EDI payments.

Financial EDI allows businesses to replace the labor-intensive activities associated with issuing, mailing, and collecting checks through the banking system with automated initiation, transmission, and processing of payment instructions. Thus it eliminates the delays inherent in processing checks. Financial EDI also improves the certainty of the payment flows between corporate bank accounts because the payee's bank can credit its account on the scheduled payment date and the payer's bank can debit its account on the same day.

Despite the significant benefits of financial EDI and electronic funds transfer (EFT) to business and the banking efficiency, traditional methods continue to be used for business-to-business payments. Most firms continue to bill their customers with paper invoices and to mail their suppliers paper checks with remittance information. Creating and processing these documents consumes costly resources—labor and transportation. For instance, the buyer must manually enter data from invoices into its automated accounts payable system, track the receipt of supplies, print remittance documents, and issue and mail checks. After receiving payment, the supplier must manually enter payment data into its automated accounts receivable system and deposit the check with its bank for collection.

To collect payment for its customer, the supplier's bank (the collecting bank) must transport the financial instrument such as checks to the bank on which the purchaser drew it (the payer bank). Collecting banks frequently route checks through intermediaries, which ultimately deliver the checks to the payer banks. Thus the transportation of checks through the collection chain and the repetitive handling of them at each bank in the chain contribute significantly to the cost of processing checks. Just imagine the extra steps and paperwork involved when the payer and payee banks are in different countries with different regulatory environments.

### Types of Financial EDI

Traditionally, wholesale or business-to-business payment is accomplished using checks, EFT, and automated clearinghouses (ACH) for domestic and international funds transfer. ACH provides two basic services to industrial and financial corporate customers (including other banks): (1) fast transmission of information about their financial balances throughout the world, and (2) the movement of money internationally at rapid speed for settlement of debit/credit balances. Banks have developed sophisticated cash management systems on the back of these services that essentially reduce the amount of money companies leave idly floating in low-earning accounts.

Let's provide a quick overview of the three principal types of noncash payment instruments currently used for business-to-business payments: checks, electronic funds transfers, and automated clearinghouse (ACH) transfers.

### Bank Checks

Checks are instruments for debit transfers where payees collect funds from payers. Funds made available by banks to depositors of checks are provisional and may be reversed if the payer does not have sufficient funds in its account to pay the check when it is received by the payer's bank.

Businesses use checks to make payments for two main reasons. First, they are a familiar and readily accepted form of payment despite some uncertainty about receiving final payment. Second, businesses benefit from the float created by the delays in the check-collection process. Businesses find float valuable because they can continue to use or invest funds for several days after they have issued a check.

Float is created when a delay occurs between the initiation of a payment and the availability of the funds to the recipient. Delays occur because checks are delivered through the mail, require human handling, and must be transported among banks in the collection chain. Some companies increase the float benefit of checks by drawing checks on banks located in remote locations or by otherwise imposing barriers to the timely collection of checks. These practices add to the expenses incurred in collecting checks and delay recipients' access to the funds. In 1993 more than 96 percent of all noncash payments in the United States were made by paper checks. Consumers issued about 55 percent of these checks, businesses about 40 percent, and the government about 5 percent.

### *Interbank Electronic Funds Transfer (EFT)*

Electronic funds transfer (EFT) are credit transfers between banks where funds flow directly from the payer's bank to the payee's bank. They are same-day, almost instantaneous payments. EFT is one of the earliest examples of payment systems that use on-line transactions, although these transactions are carried out on private networks.

The two biggest funds transfer services in the United States are the Federal Reserve's system, Fedwire, and the Clearing House Interbank Payments System (CHIPS) of the New York clearinghouse. Because the Federal Reserve guarantees Fedwire funds transfers, transfers cannot be revoked after the receiving bank is advised that a reserve bank has credited its account. The members of CHIPS, on the other hand, pledge collateral to ensure settlement of CHIPS transfers, and payments become final only at the close of business when all members settle their net positions using Fedwire transfers.

Funds transfers account for an extremely small portion of the total number of noncash payments. In 1993, for example, they accounted for about 0.2 percent of all noncash payments in the United States. At the same time, however, they accounted for nearly 86 percent of the value of all noncash payments [FRB87]. Businesses use EFT when timeliness and certainty of payment are paramount, rarely to pay suppliers for goods and services. For this, they use ACH transfers.

### *Automated Clearinghouse (ACH) Transfers*

In contrast to the EFT process, ACH transfers are used to process high volumes of relatively small-dollar payments for settlement in one or two business days. An ACH provides the following services: preauthorized credits, such as the direct deposit of payrolls; preauthorized debits, such as repetitive bill payments; and consumer-initiated payments (called GIRO in banking circles). This is primarily a high-volume/low-dollar, consumer-oriented product.

To provide these and other services, banks not only have set up their own systems but also have shared ACH systems with other banks. For example:

- BankWire, the pioneer network, owned and operated by banks in over 200 American cities. In addition to money transfers, it offers information on such things as loans and account balances.
- FedWire, the Federal Reserve Board's system, is the biggest funds transfer system in the United States. It handles a majority of American domestic transactions by value. Banks use it to transfer funds to each other.
- CHIPS (Clearing House Interbank Payments System), operating out of New York, processes 90 percent of all international dollar transfers made.
- SWIFT (Society for Worldwide Interbank Financial Telecommunications) was initiated in Brussels in 1973 and began operation in 1977. SWIFT has been a leader in providing standard EDI formats for funds-transfer instructions and administrative messages.

Two types of ACH transfers are used: credit transfers and debit transfers. Credit transfers are similar to large-dollar funds transfers in that funds flow directly from the payer's bank to the payee's. The funds received by the payee's bank are generally provisional until the morning of the business day following the settlement. The reserve bank may revoke payment if the sending bank does not have sufficient funds in its account to fund them on the settlement day. When ACH debit transfers are used, the payee's bank initiates the transfer and receives funds immediately from the payer's. As with checks, funds made available by banks to collecting businesses are provisional and may be revoked if sufficient funds in the payer's account are not available to cover the transfer on the scheduled settlement day.

In sum, use of the ACH for business-to-business payments is growing rapidly. Businesses typically use ACH credit transfers to pay for goods or services and to make tax payments to state and local governments. They use ACH debit transfers to concentrate funds from the bank accounts of widely dispersed affiliates and subsidiaries to the company's primary bank account. Some businesses also use ACH debit transfers to collect funds from businesses that distribute their products. Firms are concerned about permitting other companies to initiate debits on their accounts as this eliminates float. Thus ACH debit transfers are used less often than credit transfers for business-to-business payments.

### How Financial EDI Payments Are Made

Corporations use various approaches when implementing financial EDI. The most fundamental decision a business must make is whether payment instructions and remittance data should flow together through the banking system or whether payment instructions should flow through the banking system while remittance data are transmitted over a direct data communications link with a trading partner or over a value-added network (VAN). VANs facilitate the exchange of electronic data by accepting data in a variety of formats and by converting the incoming data to a format usable by the receiver of the information. VANs also manage transmission schedules and hold data until receivers are ready to accept them.

The choices businesses make are based on differences in electronic transmission costs, the extent to which the two trading partners are able to exchange business documents electronically, and the types of electronic payment services offered by their banks.

**Payment and Remittance Information Flowing Together.** In Fig. 9.5, the purchasing company (company X), which is the payer, transmits remittance data to instruct its bank (bank X) to pay its supplier. Bank X creates an ACH credit transfer instruction, indicating the specified payment date, and attaches the appropriate electronic remittance data. Bank X transmits the payment instruction with the remittance data to an ACH operator. After receiving the payment instructions and remittance information, the ACH operator edits the payment instructions, extracts accounting data from them, and transmits the payment instructions and remittance data to the seller's bank (bank Y). Bank Y then transmits a payment advice and the remittance data to the selling company (company Y), which is the payee.

When ACH credit transfers are processed by the Federal Reserve, on the scheduled payment date the reserve banks maintaining the accounts of banks X and Y debit and credit the reserve or clearing accounts of banks X and Y, respectively, for the total value of transfers sent or received. If a private sector ACH operator processed the ACH transfers, the value of all ACH transfers processed for the banks using that operator would be netted, and each participant would settle its net position through its account maintained on the books of a Federal Reserve bank. (Banks that do not have a reserve or

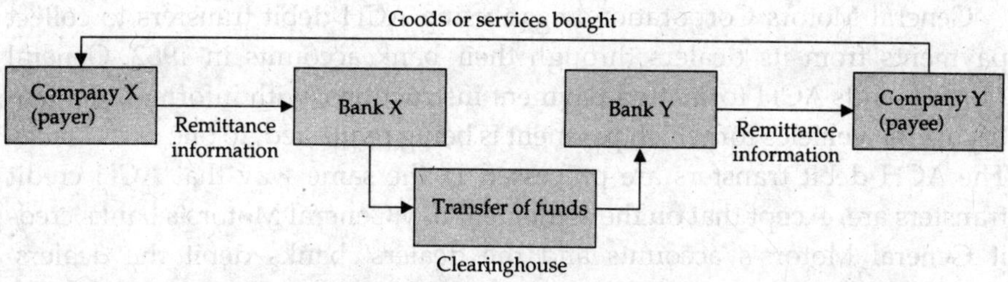


**Figure 9.5** Payment and remittance information flowing together

clearing account settle ACH transfers through correspondent banks' reserve or clearing accounts.) Banks X and Y then debit and credit their respective customers' accounts.

**Payment and Remittance Information Flowing Separately.** As shown in Fig. 9.6, the payer transmits payment instructions to its bank (bank X) and remittance information to the payee through a VAN. The payment instructions are processed through the banking system and settled as described for funds flowing together, with the exception that remittance data are not attached.

The following examples illustrate how financial EDI payments are made using ACH credit and debit transfers. Sears Roebuck and Company's Merchandise Group began using ACH credit transfers to pay its suppliers in 1983. Sears uses EDI format standards to transmit payment instructions and remittance information to its banks. The banks convert the data to ACH payment formats, which are then processed. If Sears's supplier requests that remittance data be sent separately, rather than with the payment, Sears transmits the remittance data to the trading partner through the same network used for exchanging other business data with that trading partner. The ACH transfer is then processed by Sears's bank as shown in Fig. 9.6.

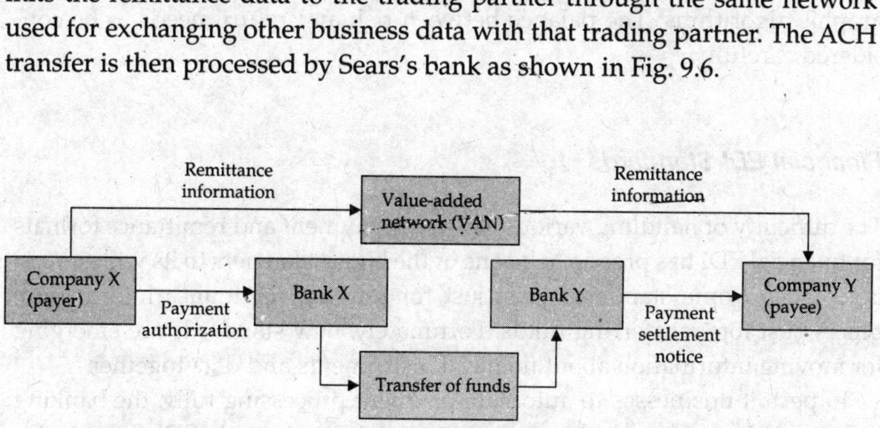


**Figure 9.6** Payment and remittance information flowing separately

General Motors Corporation began using ACH debit transfers to collect payments from its dealers through their bank accounts in 1982. General Motors sends ACH formatted payment instructions, with information identifying the vehicles for which payment is being requested, to one of its banks. The ACH debit transfers are processed in the same way that ACH credit transfers are, except that on the settlement day General Motors's banks credit General Motors's accounts and the dealers' banks debit the dealers' accounts. In 1993, using this method, General Motors collected 600,000 payments from its dealers, with a value of $12 billion. General Motors also uses ACH credit transfers to make payments to suppliers. Besides transmitting remittance information to suppliers through the banking system or a VAN, General Motors will mail it directly to a supplier if the supplier's bank cannot receive EDI data. In 1993, General Motors made 700,000 ACH credit payments valued at $38 billion to suppliers [KWY94].

To facilitate the use of financial EDI, some banks provide VAN-like services with payment services to their corporate customers. Some of these banks have developed their own networks for communicating data to their corporate customers, and some also contract with VANs to transmit remittance information to their corporate customers' trading partners.

Interestingly, the growing volume of EFT between banks has necessitated the increasing use of security and message authentication systems to determine whether a message has originated from its proper source and whether there have been any modifications. One institution alone, the Clearing House Interbank Payment System, currently moves an average of one trillion dollars each day via wire and satellite. Strong cryptography is necessary to provide authentication for these fund transfers. It is not clear whether we will ever see EFT on public networks even with strong cryptographic algorithms. The balance between risk and return needs to be considered carefully.

### Financial EDI Standards

The difficulty of handling various electronic payment and remittance formats for financial EDI has proven to be one of the biggest barriers to its widespread acceptance. Some standards exist just for sending remittance information; others, just for transferring funds. Fortunately, new standards are emerging for moving information about financial instruments and data together.

To permit businesses to automate payment processing fully, the banking industry has combined electronic payment formats with EDI formats for remittance data. The following are among the most commonly used formats in the industry today:

- *BAI.* Developed by the Bank Administration Institute (BAI), these proprietary standards have been used by U.S. banks for sending and receiving invoice and remittance information (no funds transfers) for several decades.
- *820 and 823.* In the 1980s, the American National Standards Institute (ANSI), whose standards apply to most regular EDI transactions in the United States, created the ANSI X12 820 and 823 formats for payment orders and remittance advice.
- *CCD.* NACHA's first U.S. standards effort, the cash concentration and disbursement format offers electronic funds transfer capabilities, but can be used only for corporate payments requiring minimal remittance information.
- *CTP.* The corporate trade payments format overcame the 94-character restriction of standard ACH transfers by accommodating remittance information in additional predefined 94-character blocks.
- *CCD+.* In 1987, NACHA introduced CCD+, which allows companies to transmit funds and single ANSI X12 820 remittance advice in the same transaction.
- *CTX.* NACHA's Corporate Trade Exchange is essentially ANSI X12 820 information tucked into an ACH funds-transfer envelope. CTX is the only format that enables U.S. companies to move dollars and data together. The biggest problem with CTX is that few banks have the systems required to process these transactions.
- *EDIFACT.* EDIFACT is being used for the international financial EDI pilot project currently being conducted by SWIFT.

Despite technological progress, it must be made clear that the development and adoption of universal EDI formats takes many years. For example, the ATM networks in the banking industry required almost twenty years to progress from experimental ATM networks in the 1960s to the use of standard formats allowing for interconnection of networks in the 1980s.

## Health Care and Insurance EDI

Providing good and affordable health care is a universal problem. In 1994, the American public spent $1 trillion on health care, nearly 15 percent of the gross domestic product (GDP). National health care expenditures have risen by 10.5 percent each year for the past eight years—more than double the rate of increase in the consumer price index [HCFA93]. It is estimated that $3.2 billion in administrative savings are expected to be achieved by switching from being paper-based to an EDI implementation. Employers could save $70 million to $110 million by using EDI for enrollment and to certify that a prescribed procedure is covered under the subscriber's health insurance contract [WEDI93].

EDI is rapidly becoming a permanent fixture in both insurance and health care industries as medical providers, patients, and payers increasingly process claims via electronic networks. Electronic claim processing is quick and reduces the administrative costs of health care. In most cases, claims can be sent to payers within 24 hours. Fewer errors translates to decreased turnaround time. In addition to processing claims for billing purposes, EDI enables doctors to communicate with other physicians, laboratories, hospitals, and other health care settings. In short, it leads to better managed care.

Other transactions targeted for electronic transmission include claims submission or billing, payment and payment posting, eligibility verification, and primary care member enrollment. EDI could reduce labor intensive activities of providers and payers involved with submitting, adjudicating, processing, and paying claims. In short, the most innovative efforts involving EDI go considerably beyond claims administration.

To understand the role of EDI, let's consider the claims process. The normal process executed without EDI begins with a claim filled out manually by the health care provider. It is then photocopied, filed, placed in an envelope, and mailed via regular postal service to the insurance company. Along with thousands of other claims, the envelope is then opened manually and the claim is microfilmed and keyed into the insurer's database system. In the mean time if the provider wants to find out the status of the claim, she would have to phone the company and wait till the customer service representative locates the claim (assuming that it was entered into the database) and checks on its status. If a discrepancy or error shows up, the process would start all over again. The entire process could take weeks. The complexity in form handling is further increased when we take into account the fact that each provider has many subsets of claims—hospital claims (in-patient care, emergency care, outpatient care) and medical claims (surgery and other types such as optical and dental).

Now let us look at the process using EDI. Using the EDI software, service providers prepare the necessary forms and submit claims via telecommunication lines to the value-added network service provider. The company then edits, sorts, and distributes properly formatted forms to the appropriate payer organization. If necessary, the insurance company computer can electronically route transactions to a third-party organization for price evaluation, additional review of the case, and so forth, prior to sending it to the payer. Claims submission also receives acceptance/rejection reports that may contain payer-initiated messages regarding claim status and requests for additional information, unprocessed claims, zero balances, and settlements.

The advantages of the EDI-based process are clear. On the payer side, claims are received in a standard data format, which increases quality and eliminates the extra data entry of the claims office and mailroom mess that is part of the manual process. Turnaround for processed EDI-based claims is estimated at two to four working days. Actual payment takes longer because payment settlements are done either weekly or fortnightly, so providers probably receive payment only 14 to 20 days after the claim was submitted electronically. Now contrast this to a paper environment where the initial processing alone would take 10 to 15 days.

In sum, to achieve significant administrative cost reductions, the health care community must adopt EDI. Although the business and operational efficiencies achieved using EDI can produce significant savings, the health care community has been reluctant to migrate to EDI because guidelines defining specific data requirements have not been developed. In addition, there has not been full acceptance by all health care providers to implement standardized EDI. However, this situation is changing with the creation of EDI standards for the health care industry. Today, several of the ASC X12 Health Care Workgroups [WEDI93] are developing new transaction standards for patient information, certification and utilization management, expanded claims formats, coordination of benefits, and claims status.

## Manufacturing/Retail Procurement Using EDI

Both manufacturing and retail procurement are already heavy users of EDI. In manufacturing, EDI is used to support just-in-time. In retailing, EDI is used to support quick response.

### *Just-in-Time and EDI*

Companies using JIT and EDI no longer stock thousands of large parts in advance of their use. Instead, they calculate how many parts are needed each day based on the production schedule and electronically transmit orders and schedules to suppliers every day or in some cases every 30 minutes. Parts are delivered to the plant "just in time" for production activity.

EDI has changed the whole manufacturing environment. For example, stock-holding used to be planned months ahead. Today this is no longer feasible. Delivery has to be responsive, or it will cost too much in money and time. Small quantities, as opposed to massive shipments, must be delivered more frequently. That means getting data to suppliers quickly. Not all parts require the immediacy of EDI, however, and plants still stock a few components in inventory. In other words, different parts dictate different delivery schedules. For example, in the automobile industry, small fixings like nuts don't need to be delivered just-in-time or even close.

A major benefit of JIT and EDI is a streamlined cash flow. When a company receives an invoice, it pays for parts that are actually in use, in a product ready to be sold, instead of paying for large, costly items stored in inventory.

### Quick Response and EDI

Taking their cue from the efficiencies manufacturers have gained from just-in-time manufacturing techniques, retailers are redefining practices through the entire supply chain using quick response (QR) systems. For the customer, QR means better service and availability of a wider range of products. For the retailer and suppliers, QR may mean survival in a competitive marketplace.

Much of the focus of QR is in reduction of lead times using event-driven EDI. Occurrences such as inventories falling below a specified level immediately trigger a chain of events including automatic ordering from one company's application directly into the other's application. Batch EDI, whereby an organization may group a set of transactions from various departments and mail them at one time in order to save money, may no longer suffice under these time pressures. In QR, EDI documents include purchase orders, shipping notices, invoices, inventory position, catalogs, and order status. Some of the innovations originally targeted for improving distribution are also improving effectiveness in other areas. The data generated can be used, for example, in customer information systems to provide better marketing.

Often, point-of-sale (POS) scanning is the starting point in the EDI chain that allows retailers to track merchandise at the item level and provides detailed information for demand forecasting. This way of managing inventory can eliminate the need to remark merchandise for discounts and promotion to reduce inventory levels.

POS systems feed data to automatic replenishment systems that constantly monitor inventory levels and trigger EDI transactions. These systems support smaller, more frequent deliveries, which improve in-stock position and reduce on-hand inventory. Scanning is a valuable part of warehouse operations, as this expedites the rapid flow of goods through the distribution center by reducing manual receiving and checking procedures. When scanning is used with predistribution techniques such as packing directly for an individual store, merchandise can be "cross-docked" within the distribution center or be sent directly to the store.

Perhaps the most dramatic effect of EDI can be seen in the relationship between retailer and supplier. The retailer is responsible for providing a detailed sales history for vendor planning and for developing model stock plans based on a forecast of total unit sales that the suppliers use for their planning. The supplier is responsible for implementing EDI and helps to shorten the order-to-delivery pipeline further and commits to quality by improving shipping accuracy and on-time delivery. The results of the partnership make it well worth the risk involved in sharing information more completely between companies. The retailer reduces inventory carrying costs, increases in-stock position, and enjoys greater dependability and accuracy from the supplier. The supplier gains the retailer's commitment and has access to information for better planning.

## Business Information, Product Design, and Procurement

The development of global sourcing has been closely intertwined with the rapid evolution of business information. Business information is defined in the broad sense as all information required by enterprises for the efficient planing, execution, and monitoring of product manufacturing and marketing. This includes not only raw data (statistics and contact data), but also product data for design and engineering. Figure 9.7 shows the movement of information from external component information producers to what we call customized product design brokerages.

Business information and information technology are to a large extent responsible for the emergence of global markets. Business practices and strategies such as lead time reductions (e.g., "just-in-time") or global sourcing would simply not be feasible in the absence of comprehensive business information and software to analyze it.

In this sense, business information has become indispensable for the transition from a passive to an active or strategic approach toward global markets. The utility of business information is immediately obvious: obtaining detailed insight into specific market requirements before full-scale production, identifying the most suitable foreign vendors rather than relying on casual contacts; knowing about import regulations or packaging requirements before goods are shipped; finding the most competitive source for imported inputs—all have a major impact on the efficiency of manufacturing and trade.

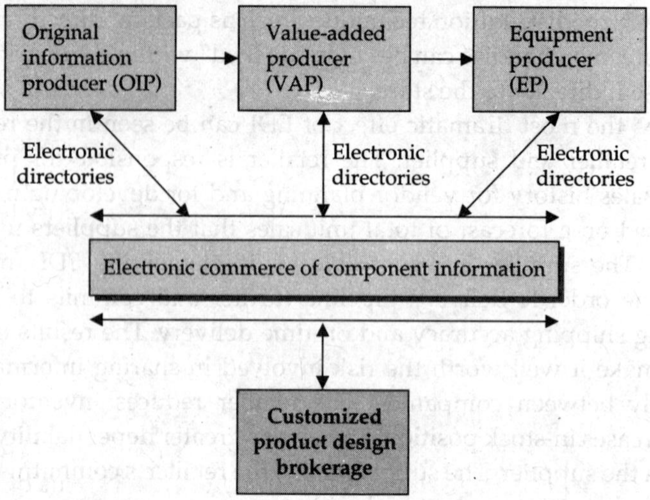


**Figure 9.7** Business information in product design

A whole new discipline in business, referred to as *competitive intelligence*, focuses on the importance of business information for the competitiveness of enterprises. This does not imply that business information can replace the engineering or entrepreneurial dimension. It cannot. Its contribution consists of providing the required data for informed decisions.

The market for business information is slowly emerging as a big chunk of electronic commerce. It is characterized by rapid technological change; highly differentiated arrays of products and services; and information in a large variety of forms, from informal documents to traditional publications and on-line databases.

Suppliers of business information range from a company's in-house marketing unit to independent information brokers and government institutions such as trade promotion organizations or departments of statistics. The standardization of business information—which would improve availability and facilitate the exchange and comparison of business information across countries—is still only at the starting stage.

## 9.3 EDI: LEGAL, SECURITY, AND PRIVACY ISSUES

Since in the case of EDI, we are dealing with trade between countries and corporations, issues of legal admissibility and computer security are paramount. Companies that deal with EDI often retain the services of a lawyer during the design of an EDI application so that the appropriate evidentiary/admissibility safeguards are implemented. Indeed, these concerns are real and must be addressed.

Analyzing the security requirements of particular applications can be aided by considering the security characteristics the application should possess as well as the sensitivity level for each. As enhanced security techniques become more cost effective and increasingly ubiquitous, the task will become easier. However, careful assessment of the trade-offs must be part of this process and should satisfy legal requirements.

## Legal Status of EDI Messages

There has been considerable debate concerning the legal status of EDI messages and electronic messages in general. Although a lot of work is being done on legal framework, nothing concrete has come out these efforts. No rules exist that indicate how electronic messages may be considered binding in business or other related transactions.

The establishment of such a framework is essential if EDI is to become widespread. To understand the terrain better, let's take a quick look at contract law. It distinguishes three modes of communication types: instantaneous communication, delayed communication via the U.S. Postal Service (USPS), and delayed communication via non-USPS couriers:

1. *Instantaneous.* If the parties are face to face or use an instantaneous communication medium such as the telephone, an offer or acceptance is deemed communicated and operable when spoken.
2. *Delayed (USPS).* The "mailbox rule" provides that an acceptance communicated via USPS mail is effectively communicated when dispatched, or physically deposited in a USPS mailbox.
3. *Delayed (non-USPS).* Offers or acceptances transmitted (other than through USPS mail) via telegram, mailgram, and probably electronic messaging systems, are deemed communicated and operable upon receipt. Couriers fall within this category. The legal disparity between USPS and non-USPS services requires reexamination, as the difference is no longer there.

Messaging systems combine features of both instantaneous and delayed communications. A message's delay is a function of the specific application, message routing, network(s) traversed, system configuration, and other technical factors typically unknown to the user. So, who assumes liability? If the U.S. mail or an overnight express service does not deliver a contract to the right addressee, it can be held responsible for any business losses caused by the error. Of course, liability also depends on the situation. In the case of EDI, however, the courts haven't decided who is liable if an EDI network fails to transmit a document or transmits a document to the wrong party. There is no legal precedence in this area (yet!).

## Digital Signatures and EDI

The cryptographic community is exploring various technical uses of digital signatures by which messages might be time-stamped or digitally notarized to establish dates and times at which a recipient might claim to have had access or even read a particular message. If digital signatures are to replace handwritten signatures, they must have the same legal status as handwritten signatures (documents signed with digital signatures must be legally binding). For example, an on-line "notarized time-stamping" service has been suggested that would accept a message and return one showing the date, time, and a digital signature binding the notarized message content and received date and time to the digital public notary. The digital signature provides a means for a third party to verify that the notarized object is authentic.

Interestingly, the U.S. federal government purchase orders will be signed by the digital signature standard (DSS); this implies that the government will support the legal authority of digital signatures in the courts. Although there is no legal precedence, some preliminary research has also resulted in the opinion that digital signatures would meet the requirements of legally binding signatures for most purposes, including commercial use as defined in the Uniform Commercial Code (UCC). A GAO (Government Accounting Office) decision states that digital signatures will meet the legal standards of handwritten signatures [GAO91]. However, since the validity of documents with digital signatures has never been challenged in court, their legal status is not yet well defined. Through such challenges, the courts will issue rulings that collectively define which digital signature methods, key sizes, and security precautions are acceptable for a digital signature to be legally binding.

Digital signatures should have greater legal authority than handwritten signatures. For instance, if a ten-page contract is signed by hand on the tenth page, one cannot be sure that the first nine pages have not been altered. If the contract was signed by digital signatures, however, a third party can verify that not one byte of the contract has been altered. Currently, if two people wish to digitally sign a series of contracts, they may wish to first sign a paper contract in which they agree to be bound in the future by any contracts digitally signed by them with a given signature method and minimum key size.

It is not an exaggeration to say that legal consideration of digital notarizing and the binding strength of electronic interchange is a topic well deserving of prompt, qualified, and intense attention. Without such a framework, it is hard to see how EDI can fulfill the role envisioned for it in the future.

## 9.4 EDI AND ELECTRONIC COMMERCE

The economic advantages of EDI are widely recognized. But until recently, companies have been able to improve only discrete processes such as automating the accounts payable function or the funds transfer process. While important in their own right, such improvements are limited in their ability to help businesses transform themselves. Companies are realizing that to truly improve their productivity they need to automate their external processes as well as their internal processes. This is the thrust of new directions in EDI.

New EDI services for electronic commerce are seen as the future bridge that automates external and internal business processes, enabling companies to improve their productivity on a scale never before possible. They present information management solutions that allow companies to link their trading community electronically—order entry, purchasing, accounts payable, funds transfer, and other systems interact with each other throughout the community to link the company with its suppliers, distributors, customers, banks, and transportation and logistics operations.

Another goal of new EDI services is to reduce the cost of setting up an EDI relationship. These costs are still very high because of the need for a detailed bilateral agreement between the involved business partners and for the necessary technical agreements. EDI links in short-term partnerships are rarely realized because the costs of the establishment of such an agreement are too high. EDI links with many partners are also rarely realized, because the negotiation and agreement between partners is not easily manageable. Therefore most successful EDI implementations are either in long-term partnerships or among a limited number of partners.

With the advent of interorganizational commerce, several new types of EDI are emerging that can be broadly categorized as traditional EDI and open EDI.

### Traditional EDI

Traditional EDI replaces the paper forms with almost strict one-to-one mappings between parts of a paper form to fields of electronic forms called transaction sets. Traditional EDI covers two basic business areas:

1. *Trade data interchange (TDI)* encompasses transactions such as purchase orders, invoices, and acknowledgments.
2. *Electronic funds transfer (EFT)* is the automatic transfer of funds among banks and other organizations.

Today, traditional EDI is divided into two camps: old EDI and new EDI. Old EDI is a term created by those working on the next generation of EDI standards in order to differentiate between the present and the future.

### Old EDI

Old EDI refers to the current practice of automating the exchange of information pertinent to the business activity. Information that is generated by the business process of one computer is transferred electronically and effects a corresponding business process in another computer. For instance, a retail application, under low stock conditions, automatically generates a purchase order and transfers it electronically to the sales order processing system of the supplier. The sales order is then automatically processed through customer credit checking, allocation of stock, and transport planning and results in the transfer of an order acknowledgement/dispatch advice electronically back to the retailer.

Old EDI is also used to refer to the current EDI-standardization process (e.g., X12, EDIFACT) where tens of thousands of people in groups (or working committees) all around the world are attempting to define generic document interchanges (e.g., purchase orders) that allow every company to choose its own, unique, proprietary version (that is a subset of the original transaction set). The nature of these proprietary structures is such that it is extremely difficult for general application programs to handle/understand them, forcing the design and implementation of specialized application programs. This makes EDI implementation needlessly expensive and very narrowly specialized. See Section 10.1 for a discussion of old-EDI standards.

### New EDI

New EDI is really a refocus of the standardization process. With old EDI, the standardization is focused on the interchange structure, on the transaction set in X12 or the message in EDIFACT. With new EDI the structure of the interchanges is determined by the programmer who writes the business application program, not by the lengthy standards process. New EDI makes

EDI work for electronic commerce by removing the long standardization process that is impeding it.

The goal of new EDI is to produce standardization at the document processing level in the context of a business work flow rather than at the document interchange level. To produce business applications that can talk to each other and perform a business transaction, the business practices at both ends need to understand one another or operate in the same way. Hence they need to devise a set of standards for business practices.

For those familiar with work in structured documents, new EDI is proposing constructs similar in many ways to the document type definition (DTD) used in SGML and HTML. The idea is that DTDs, which are written by document authors, are exchanged with tagged or marked-up documents so that browsers can understand the document structure easily. This will require several steps, broadly defined as follows:

1. Shift the focus of the EDI standardization process away from the low-level interchange structure and onto more high-level business work flows involving many low-level interchange activities.

2. Allow customization (or massaging) of information by enabling application programs to use the interchange structures that best suit their local environment.

To make new EDI work, we have to address a standard bridge between the language of business and the programming languages used in expressing the interchange standards. This is where a database that captures business semantics comes in. It standardizes the way programmers handle the business specifications in the programs they write to make the computers do what the business managers want them to do. It also enables programmers to leave a note inside the computer in the form of an EDIFACT message called ICSDEF to describe the interchange structure that the program uses or accepts.

Another aspect of new EDI is the interactive query response (also called interactive EDI), which is a form of EDI used by travel agents to book airline flights. Interactive EDI is aimed at starting and completing the business process using an open channel of communication (point-to-point) between the customer and supplier for the period of the business transaction(s). This type of interaction eliminates the current intermediary, namely, the value-added network. For instance, a customer's purchasing system opens with an inquiry to the supplier, the supplier's sales order processing system provides availability, the customer's system purchases, and the supplier's system closes with confirmation details. This type of interaction is being implemented using the World Wide Web.

## Open EDI

Open EDI provides a framework where two potential trading partners can whip out an EDI structure for their potential partnership in the short time frame that it takes them to draw up and negotiate the legal contracts. The increased interest in open EDI is a result of dissatisfaction with traditional EDI. The big difference between the traditional EDI model and the needs of today is that business today has a much larger component of rapid project-based partnerships that are created and dissolved in time scales too small to permit a full-blown standards process to play out its consensus building. Many businesses do not want to wait or cannot wait literally years for a standard to be developed, voted on, and go through the entire standardization process.

Open EDI is a business procedure that enables electronic commerce to occur between organizations where the interaction is of short duration. In essence, open EDI is the process of doing EDI without the upfront trading partner agreement that is currently signed by the trading partners before they commence trying to do business by EDI. The goal is to sustain ad hoc business or short-term trading relationships using simpler legal codes.

In other words, open EDI is a business process for automating the operation of the law of contract within the context of electronic commerce where transactions are not repeated or sustained over a long period of time. An example is an automatic transmission of graphics, which allows for engineering drawings, prepared with computer-aided design systems, to be exchanged among all parties involved in their creation. This facilitates revisions and aids in more speedy agreement on a final version.

To implement open EDI, the ISO has developed an open EDI reference model, which consists of two distinct views. The first of them, the business operational view (BOV), supports the semantics of (1) business data in business transactions and the associated data interchanges and (2) business conventions and business rules in business transactions. This includes operational conventions, agreements, and mutual obligations that apply to the business needs of open EDI.

The second, the functional service view (FSV), addresses the framework for services meeting the mechanistic needs of open EDI. It is focused on the IT aspects as service capabilities, service interfaces, and protocols required for the inner working of organizations, whatever the business content and conventions. Such services and protocols include but are not limited to EDI syntax and control reconciliation services, name/address resolution, audit tracking, and security mechanism handling.

In short, the first class of standards addresses the business problems of open EDI and the second class of standards addresses the information technology problems. Therefore each class of standards corresponds to different standardization activity. However, these are still in the early stages and much work needs to be done.

## 9.5 SUMMARY

A look at some of the lessons that EDI history has taught us will show that the key to EDI implementation is often dictated by business issues rather than technology considerations. It is often stated that EDI is 20 percent technology and 80 percent business. However, EDI is often viewed as a technology without realizing or understanding the important business implications. In the past, companies often threw the technology bucket at the problem without determining where EDI fits into organizational processes.

Even on the Internet, similar trends can be seen, with technology often leading the charge. While this is good, it is also important to realize that EDI has been around for well over twenty years without catching on because of certain inherent limitations other than technology and standardization. Not until we can find a cheap and widely used EDI-based "killer application" will it become accepted.

There are several other reasons why EDI is still only used by a handful of companies. EDI is expensive and quite difficult to implement, and its pitfalls are considerable. Success often depends on getting a majority of the suppliers to hook up, or the investment won't justify the returns.

Another problem is the lack of a single good standard for EDI transactions. Like any other communications problem, EDI is plagued by an excess number of industry and de facto standard "solutions" that make connectivity a real chore. There's the US ANSI X12 standard, with all of its industry-specific variants. There's the international EDIFACT standard, which is only partially defined and accepted. There are European standards and a whole slew of proprietary specifications.

EDI implementation policy in the past has been one of coercion. That is, unless you're big enough to browbeat your vendors, plow through standards problems, or cough up equipment and software for your vendors to use, you won't soon get to implement your own EDI program. For this reason, most of the EDI links in place today are hub-and-spoke arrangements with a big customer at the middle and large numbers of suppliers hanging on the spokes. But the question remains: Is it good for vendors to be locked into one company? Add to this natural reluctance of business to enter into uncharted waters and the prognosis for EDI remains cloudy. It makes sense, and it can save us money, so it will happen sooner or later. The big question is when.

EDI holds promise for the conduct of on-line business. A considerable amount of technical progress has been made in support of that promise, but there are important organizational, legal, and international barriers that impede progress. The effort to provide a satisfactory infrastructure for e-commerce within which EDI can flourish is timely and essential and will require the dedicated efforts of a diversity of technical, legal, political efforts to achieve fruition.

Chapter 10

# EDI Implementation, MIME, and Value-Added Networks

EDI implementation starts with an agreement between a company and its trading partner. The two parties decide which standard (ANSI X.12 or UN/EDIFACT) will be used, the nature of the information to be exchanged (invoice, purchase order, payment order/remittance), the network carrier (or value-added network), and the mode of information transmission (e-mail: X.400, X.435; Internet e-mail standards: RFC 822, MIME; Internet point-to-point connections: TELNET, FTP, World Wide Web).

An efficient EDI system requires that the data be input only once, and the system manages the rest. In other words, the data moves without much intervention to the trading partner's application, with no additional steps to slow the process. To achieve this, both parties exchange messages based on a structured format—that is, for each type of message a standard format has been agreed on by the exchanging parties. These messages are exchanged by means of electronic transfer between autonomous computer application systems of the involved trading partners.

EDI relies on the use of standards for the structure and interpretation of electronic business transactions. All trading partners must use a common standard, to reduce errors and ensure accurate translation of data, regardless of the computer systems involved. The basic kit necessary for EDI implementation includes the following:

- *Common EDI standards* dictate syntax and standardize on the business language. EDI standards basically specify transaction sets—complete sets of business documents (invoice, a purchase order, or a remittance advice, for example).
- *Translation software* sends messages between trading partners, integrates data into and from existing computer applications, and translates among EDI message standards.

- *Trading partners* are a firm's customers and suppliers with whom business is conducted.
- *Banks* facilitate payment and remittance.
- *EDI value-added network services (VANs).* A VAN is a third-party service provider that manages data communications networks for businesses that exchange electronic data with other businesses.
- *Proprietary hardware and networking* if it is a hub company. *Hubs,* also called *sponsors,* are large companies, very active in EDI, that facilitate their business partners' use of EDI. Often-cited examples of hubs are in the auto industry: Ford, GM, and Toyota.

An important feature of EDI is that software evaluates and processes structured messages. For instance, when a message is received, the system checks its integrity automatically and then sends an acknowledgment to the originator of the message. The information system then proceeds to act upon the message. The requested goods are shipped to the buyer, or information is forwarded to other in-house computer applications.

The generation of messages might also be done automatically. In EDI, it is quite common to find a chain of automated actions and reactions because they are easy to implement. Human intervention can be minimized and is often limited to the overall management of the operations. A computer might be programmed, for example, to request the consent of a human operator only for transactions that exceed a certain monetary value. Or an inventory control application that manages inventory levels in a production plant may request additional supplies if the stock has reached a preset minimal level. Hence, the software system continuously evaluates a set of parameters in its program to verify whether the plant has reached low inventory levels.

In short, the key implementation issues in the EDI process are EDI interchange standards, EDI software, third-party value-added network services, and data transport standards. These topics will be the focus of our attention in this chapter.

## 10.1 STANDARDIZATION AND EDI

Connecting trading partners is not enough for EDI. All software, hardware, and networks must work together so that information flows from one source to another. In fact, the standard joke says: "The most appealing attribute of standards is that there are so many to choose from." Indeed, the computer industry has spawned a multitude of de facto, often overlapping standards, because many independent groups develop them. The result has been slow deployment and restricted implementation of EDI between companies.

The advantages of standardization are numerous. One field that has benefited immensely from standardization is the electronics industry. In the 1960s and 1970s electronic components were designed without concern for compatibility. This created a lot of confusion and spurred the Institute of Electrical and Electronics Engineers (IEEE) to issue guideline standards for capacitors, resistors, power supplies, and all other components. As components became substitutable, production boomed, competition increased, and prices deflated. Likewise, standardization is expected to promote "interoperability" between EDI implementations.

Today, two major EDI standards exist: the American National Standards Institute (ANSI) X.12 Committee and the United Nations EDI for Administration, Commerce, and Trade (EDIFACT) standards for international usage.

### *ANSI X.12*

The ANSI chartered the Accredited Standards Committee in 1979 to research and develop standards for business documents. The X.12 committee develops standards to facilitate EDI relating to such business transactions as order placement and processing; shipping and receiving; invoicing, payment, and cash application processing for products and services. The X.12 transaction sets generally map a traditional paper document to an electronic format that can move easily over telecommunication networks. Each transaction format includes many data segments needed for the business function as well as instructive information to ensure that the telecommunication system routes the data correctly. Examples of ANSI ASC X.12 transactions include (form number 838) Vendor Registration; (840) Request for Quotation; (843) Response to Request for Quotation; (850) Purchase Order or Delivery Order; (855) Purchase Order Acknowledgment; and (997) Functional Acknowledgment. These X.12 transactions are transmitted to the trading partner (TP) through either the X400 e-mail protocol, or the multipurpose Internet mail extensions (MIME) protocols (see Section 10.3).

### *EDIFACT*

Developed by the United Nations, EDIFACT is a family of standards similar to ANSI X.12. EDIFACT was based on TRADECOMS, developed by the U.K. Department of Customs and Excise with the assistance of SITPRO (the British Simplification of Trade Procedures Board). It was further developed by the United Nations Economic Commission for Europe—Working Party (Four) on Facilitation of International Trade Procedures (UN/ECE/WP4). EDIFACT is becoming widely accepted as the foremost international EDI standard. Today, EDIFACT and ANSI are working towards compatibility.

## EDI Standards Selection

Those seeking to implement electronic systems for electronic commerce are sometimes unsure about which standards to use. International standards such as EDIFACT? National Standards such as ANSI X.12? Specific industry standards such as TDCC (Transportation Data Coordination Committee) including a series of releases for Air, Freight, Motor, Ocean, Rail, Tariff, General, and AIAG (Automotive Industry Action Group) standards? All of these?

The diversity among electronic standards calls to mind the confusion and pandemonium of the Tower of Babel. How has this quagmire been created? To understand the situation better, let's briefly trace the history of EDI.

During the 1960s rail and road transport industries began to think about standardizing documents and replacing paper-based methods of communication. In these very early days of EDI, North American transportation providers investigated ways of moving information from shippers, carriers, receivers, banks, and others. The TDCC set out to develop a unified set of EDI standards for transportation documents (bills of lading, shipment status reports, freight invoices). Contrary to the belief of several industry experts that the developers would abandon their efforts, in 1975 the TDCC published the first set of draft standards for air, motor, ocean, and rail documents. Due in part to the success of TDCC, through the 1970s and into the 1980s other industries began to develop, publish, and implement EDI standards.

As EDI became widely used in industries other than transportation, ANSI created a working group, ASC X.12, to oversee EDI standard creation. Out of this effort, several sets of industry-specific EDI message standards based on ANSI X.12 were created for intercompany transactions. Examples include VICS for pharmaceuticals, UCS for food and groceries, and WINS for warehousing. Specific industry groups, such as EIDX for the electronics industry, use the ANSI standards but decide which optional segments and elements to use for each transaction set and which table values to use. For example, ANSI has several hundred unit-of-measure values such as *each*, *piece*, *box*, *set*, and *unit*. EIDX has adopted *each* as the only unit of measure the electronics industry needs. In short, an industry-specific transaction set simplifies exchanges within the industry.

Over the years, the United States has adopted X.12. Many Pacific Rim nations also support it. Most industry-specific standards have committed to aligning themselves with X.12, which consists of a number of underlying standards and addresses a wide range of business requirements. Because most EDI information exchanges are domestic and X.12 is more widely used than EDIFACT in the United States, U.S. companies doing business overseas must subscribe to EDIFACT. Although EDIFACT is similar to ASC X.12 in both purpose and approach, sufficient technical differences exist that may inhibit interoperability. As global trade expands, most U.S. companies will require implementation of both standards.

Complicating matters further are the business issues. ANSI X.12 has been around for over thirty years and the tremendous investment made in its implementation makes transition from it difficult. Companies would have to rewrite software and even change business practices. In this age of lean and mean, companies simply do not have the resources to undertake such costly efforts.

Ultimately, this situation will become untenable and will require a migration strategy from the national standard (X.12) to the international standard (EDIFACT). Fortunately, an awareness of commerce's international nature and the desirability of a single EDI standard have resulted in a decision by the ASC X.12 committee to align its standard with EDIFACT by 1997. Although the implementation plan is not final, it appears that sometime after 1997 all new standards will follow EDIFACT syntax. However, a straightforward, cost-effective, and low-risk migration strategy is yet to be found.

## Structure of EDI Transactions

EDI standards are very broad and general because they have to meet the needs of all businesses. EDI messages, however, share a common structure:

1. *Transaction set* is equivalent to a business document, such as a purchase order. Each transaction set is made up of data segments.

2. *Data segments* are logical groups of data elements that together convey information, such as invoice terms, shipping information, or purchase order line.

3. *Data elements* are individual fields, such as purchase order number, quantity on order, unit price.

The concept and theory of EDI has evolved from the transmission of data in "fixed-length" proprietary formats to the transmission of data in "variable length" standard formats. Without these standard formats, industry utilization of computer-to-computer communication technology would be encumbered by the use of different formats and data contents.

EDI in the early years was limited to single applications such as purchasing, one or two transaction sets such as invoices or purchase orders, and a predictably narrow trading partner population. The most recent development of cross-industry standards allows multiple applications and hundreds of transaction sets for varying groups of business transactions.

## Comparison of EDIFACT and X.12 Standards

Both EDIFACT and X.12 are comprised of strings of data elements called segments. A transaction set (or message, in EDIFACT terminology) is a set of segments ordered as specified by the standard.

ANSI standards require each element to have a very specific name, such as *order date* or *invoice date*. EDIFACT segments, in contrast, allow for generic, or multiuse elements, such as *date*. A qualifier, such as order or invoice, accompanies the generic element identifying what the date relates to. In essence, EDIFACT has fewer data elements and segments and only one beginning segment (header), but it has more composites (a group of two or more data elements that give meaning to another data element, such as price).

EDIFACT's use of fewer components facilitates updating and expanding a system—which proves to be a shortcoming as well as a benefit. Fast update makes EDIFACT an ever-evolving platform, so trading partners often use different versions of the standard. The standard version is usually dictated by a major trading partner, but unfortunately that can mean one vendor is using numerous versions to communicate with various major trading partners. This imposes its own set of problems. A vendor needs several different versions to communicate within its own industry.

The following messages illustrate a sample payment message in EDIFACT and ANSI X.12. These messages show that company A is paying company B's bank account 98765432 U.S. $59,400 for three invoices in the amounts of $10,000, $20,000, and $30,000. Each invoice receives a 1 percent discount.

### ANSI and EDIFACT Transaction Sets Payment Messages

```
EDIFACT PAYORD, version 91.2 UNH+1+PAYEXT:2:912:UN'
   BGM+451+0101+137:920515:101+9' NAD+OY+COMPANY A'
      FII+BF+98765432+COMPANY
   B+BANKXX:25:5' DTM+203+920515:101' MOA+7+9:59400:USD' UNS+S'
      DOC+380+101'
   MOA+7+9:10000+52:100+12:9900 DOC+380+102' MOA+7+9:20000+52:200+12:19800
   DOC+380+103' MOA+7+9:30000+52:300+12:29700 MOA+3+128:59400:USD'
      UNT+15+0101'

ANSI X12 820, version 003.020 ST*820*0101
   BPR*C*59400*C*SWT*******02*BANKXX*DA*98765432 TRN*1*0101
      DTM*007*920515
   ENT**0101 N1*PR*COMPANY A N1*PE*COMPANY B
      RMR*IV*101*PO*9900*10000*100
   RMR*IV*102*PO*19800*20000*200 RMR*IV*103*PO*29700*30000*300 SE*11*0101
```

## 10.2 EDI SOFTWARE IMPLEMENTATION

EDI software has four layers, as shown in Fig. 10.1: business application, internal format conversion, EDI translator, and EDI envelope for document messaging. These four layers package the information and send it over the value-added network to the target business, which then reverses the process to obtain the original information. Assume that the message flows from company A to trading partner company B. Before company B can receive and process the message content, the message has to go through several intermediary steps, as detailed in the following sections

### EDI Business Application Layer

The first step in the EDI process (see Fig. 10.2) creates a document—in this case, an invoice—in a software application. This software application then sends the document to an EDI translator, which automatically reformats the invoice into the agreed-on EDI standard. If these two pieces of software are from different vendors, it is very important that the document preparation application seamlessly integrate with the EDI translation software.

If both the EDI translator and business application are on the same type of computer, the data will move faster and more easily from one to another. The

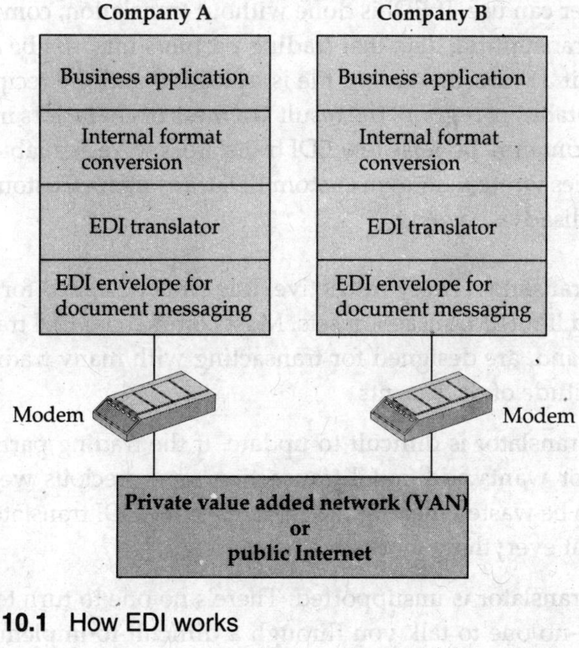


**Figure 10.1** How EDI works

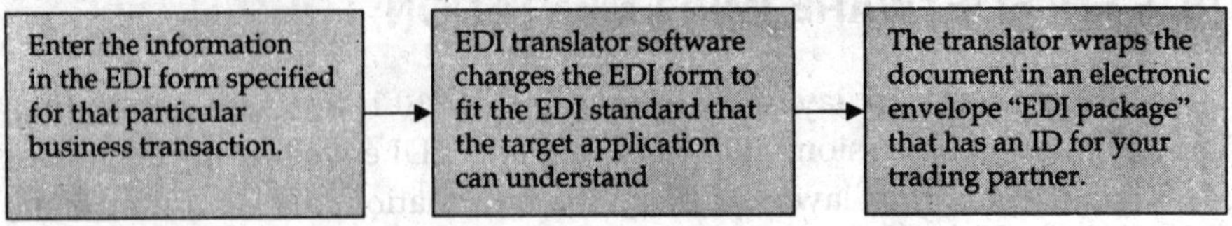


**Figure 10.2** The preparation process followed by the application software

translator creates and wraps the document in an electronic envelope "EDI package" that has a mailbox ID for the company's trading partner. The EDI wrapper software can be a module to the translator, a programming tool to write to different communications protocols, or a separate application.

## EDI Translator Layer

Translation is an integral part of the overall EDI solution. Translators describe the relationship between the data elements in the business application and the EDI standards. For instance, a purchase order specific to a company must be mapped onto the data fields defined by the generic representation of purchase order as specified by the EDI standard.

The translator ensures that the data are converted into a format that the trading partner can use. If EDI is done without translation, companies run a great risk of transmitting data that trading partners may not be able to read. For example, if a word processing file is uploaded and the recipient tries to open it in a database program, the result is a mess of characters instead of the expected information. Because few EDI translators were available in the past, large companies wrote their own custom EDI translators. Custom translators have several disadvantages.

- A custom translator is very restrictive. It is often designed for one trading partner and limited transaction sets. Most commercial EDI translators, on the other hand, are designed for transacting with many trading partners and a multitude of documents.
- A custom translator is difficult to update. If the trading partner changes standards or wants additional transaction sets, precious weeks or even months can be wasted making the changes to the EDI translator and making sure that everything works correctly.
- A custom translator is unsupported. There's no one to turn to when help is needed—no one to talk you through a difficult-to-implement require-

ment from your trading partner. Providers of commercial EDI translators offer telephone support with industry experts. Some software companies put customers in touch with someone who can solve their problem and walk the client through the tricky areas.

However, all these advantages of commercial translators come with a hefty price tag.

## EDI Communications Layer

The communications portion—which could be part of the translation software or a separate application—dials the phone number for the value-added network service provider or other type of access method being used. Three main types of EDI access methods are available: (1) direct dial or modem to modem connection; (2) limited third-party value-added network services, and (3) full-service third-party VANs. These networks could be private networks or public networks such as the Internet.

Direct-dial systems are by far the simplest and most common. The user has direct access to the partner's modem and communicates by using the modem to dial the modem of the other party. A direct computer-to-computer transfer of documents (uploading and downloading) through a modem requires that both computer applications read the same format, such as ASCII text, or use translators.

Limited VANs are regional and international communications services similar to those used with e-mail (MCIMail, AT&T Mail). These VANs often provide only the very basic technical services such as protocol conversion and data error detection and correction, directing and delivering EDI traffic to thousands of buyers and sellers. They receive the envelope containing the document (e.g., purchase order), read the ID on the envelope, and place it in the correct trading partner's mailbox.

Full third-party services provide more than just communication between two or more parties. Electronic mailboxes and associated extra features are the heart of these third-party services. Extra features include access control for security and document tracking, which allows users to track their own documents as they pass through the system. This feature supports audit needs.

A third-party network can also provide a "gateway" to interconnect with other third-party networks. This facilitates communication between businesses having accounts with different third-party networks running a variety of protocols and systems. Some third-party networks can also connect internationally, an increasingly valuable feature.

Companies use EDI VAN service providers because they provide a central post office function, directing message traffic to the appropriate recipient and often providing additional functions such as data translation between different computers or message standards. EDI VANs also automatically set up an "audit trail" to enable an organization to check and validate traffic.

On the receiving end, the process is reversed. The trading partner's modem calls the VAN network and retrieves everything in the mailbox. The EDI translator opens the envelope and translates the data from the standard form to the format read by their application. The business layer (e.g., accounts payable) software creates a check from the electronic invoice form and completes the EDI transaction.

## How Much Will an EDI Implementation Cost?

Prices for EDI products vary from no cost (for very simple one-function products) to several thousands of dollars for full-function applications. The final cost depends on several factors:

- *The expected volume of electronic documents.* Generally speaking, PC products cost less but handle only a few documents and trading partners. Mid-range EDI packages can be a little more expensive but can handle a larger volume of multiple document types or multiple trading partners.
- *Economics of the EDI translation software.* Some products initially look like a bargain, but as needs grow, hidden costs suddenly appear. These costs can range from new transaction sets for doing different forms to expensive upgrades.
- *Implementation time.* Some applications are easier to learn and use than others. The more time spent in training, the more time it takes to get into production mode. If the implementation time frame is tight, it is wise to look for a translator that doesn't require training before implementation.

Maintenance fees and VAN charges can vary considerably and as such can affect the cost of EDI systems:

- *Maintenance fees.* Most companies charge an annual maintenance fee, usually a percentage of the translator's list price. This fee should include software updates, standards updates, technical support, and customer service.
- *VAN charges.* VANs bill for data transmission, similar to long-distance phone calls. Some base their billing per document (such as 25 cents per

document transmitted); others charge based on the number of kilo-characters in each document. Some also bill for connect time. In this case, a fast modem, which reduces connect time by transferring information faster, can lower transmission costs. Most VANs charge a monthly fee for maintaining a mailbox on their network (fee structures for VANs are discussed later in the chapter).

## 10.3 EDI ENVELOPE FOR MESSAGE TRANSPORT

Nearly all of the applications for which EDI transactions have been defined can be modeled as the exchange of electronic mail between computer programs. To differentiate EDI from regular mail, some special conventions have been devised in the form of message headers or envelopes. Two types of EDI envelopes are used: X.435 (derived from ISO X.400 mail standard and primarily used in VANs) and Internet EDI based on MIME (based on widely used Internet e-mail standard known as RFC 822).

### The X.400 and X.435 Envelopes

The X.400 standard was meant to be the universal answer to e-mail interconnectivity. Born from a desire to solve such recurring problems as binary file transfers and to produce a single, consistent addressing scheme, X.400 promises much and, to date, delivers little. Work on X.400 began in 1980 when corporations discovered that message transmission between heterogeneous computers required a translator or gateway between each computer's electronic mail system. For example, a company with Lotus cc:Mail, IBM's Professional Office System, DEC's All-In-One, and Hewlett-Packard's HP Mail had to install four separate gateways to connect its systems. The goal of X. 400 is to allow companies to connect all electronic mail systems with a single gateway.

Even though most of the work on the X.400 standard was completed and ratified at a 1984 ISO meeting, X.400 acceptance has only trudged along, primarily due to lack of market demand. Still, X.400 is the one open standard for mail interchange that has the blessing of such official standards organizations as ISO and CCITT.

The standard exists in three versions: 1984, 1988, and 1992. The 1984 version is a basic transfer system for the storing and forwarding of messages. The 1988 version added a variety of enhanced services to the basic message transfer system (security and remote message storage). The 1992 version expanded the types of messages that can be transferred, including store and forward services, so important for communication between heterogeneous computers.

In short, X.400 tries to be a universal mail standard for fax, paper mail, and software binaries. In theory, X.400 provides a way to send anything. In practice, it is another matter. For instance, binary file or fax transmission between networks is unreliable due to the existence of several differing versions of X.400. Other interconnection problems exist because there is enough latitude in the standard for incompatibilities to creep in.

A subset of the overall X.400 recommendations, designated X.435, contains services specifically for electronic commerce. Specifically aimed at support for EDI within the X.400 framework, X.435 specifies how EDI content is distinguished within an X.400 message.

Two methods based on header information have been developed to carry EDI traffic on the X.400 network. A header is always placed at the top of the message when information is sent from one computer to another. The header acts as an address on the outside of an envelope. The network acts as a post office and moves the data between computers until it reaches a destination.

The first method wraps the X.400 header around an EDI header and EDI data. This technique, which some call *double bagging*, represents the simplest method of carrying EDI messages over an X.400 network and will meet the needs of many. The shortcoming of this approach is the duplicate information contained in EDI and X.400 headers. In many networks duplication is not a major issue, but in networks with large volumes of EDI traffic, network performance would be slow.

The second method, called X.435, inserts a special field in an X.400 envelope to identify an EDI message. This approach is preferred because it eliminates duplication and therefore allows EDI transactions to take advantage of all X.400 capabilities. In contrast, the first technique enables messages to use only EDI services, which are not as robust as X.400. An important function of X.435 is its ability to handle multiple body parts. For example, a purchase order can move with a CAD/CAM drawing attached to it in the same envelope, with the purchase order sent to the EDI system and the CAD/CAM drawing to the design application.

X.435 offers many features. It lets companies leverage their existing X.400 infrastructure and service provider contracts to handle EDI. Other features include data encryption; integrity (proof documents have not been altered); notification of message delivery and nondelivery; and nonrepudiation of delivery (ability to prove the delivery of documents). In short, the X.435 was designed to be a secure, reliable way to send EDI and accompanying files within the same message. Purchase orders, invoices, drawings, e-mail—all could be sent with end-to-end acknowledgment of message receipt.

X.435 does not seem be making much headway given the ice-cold response with which the marketplace—end users and vendors—have greeted the standard. What is more, the spotlight is on MIME—a standard that is turning the Internet into a viable channel, for EDI and related multimedia documents. Sensing more customer interest in the emerging MIME Internet standard than in X.435, service providers are pouring more resources into their Internet EDI product lines. Whether this is the right strategy, only time will tell.

To provide an overview of the terminology commonly used in X.400 systems, a brief list of definitions is provided in Table 10.1.

**Table 10.1** X.400 and X.435 Terminology

| *Term* | *Definition* |
|---|---|
| X.400 1984 | An ISO standard defining a store-and-forward messaging application |
| X.400 1988 | A revised version of X.400 including new additions: message store and new message contents |
| X.400 downgrading | Interworking between X.400 1988 and 1984 systems as defined in the 1988 standard |
| X.400 1992 | Minor enhancements to X.400, including voice body parts and a new file attachment |
| X.435 | Standard for transmission of electronic data interchange messages over X.400 |
| MTA | Message Transfer Agent: a store-and-forward node in an X.400 network |
| MTS | Message Transfer System: a set of interconnected MTAs |
| UA | User Agent: the software that interacts with the X.400 network on behalf of a user |
| MS | Message Store: a component in the X.400 network that stores messages until they are retrieved by a UA |
| MHS | Message Handling System: the complete X.400 network including MTAs, UAs, and MSs |
| P2 | The content of an interpersonal (electronic mail) message as defined in X.400 1984 |
| P22 | An extended X.400 message content as defined in X.400 1988 |
| BP | Body Part: the specific type of content contained within a P2/P22 message |

## MIME-Based EDI

Even as VANs upgrade their networks to let customers exchange EDI transactions wrapped in X.435 mail envelopes, the Internet community is hard at work on new ways to tie EDI into mail messages using Multipurpose Internet Mail Extensions (MIME). MIME dictates how multimedia message attachments such as spreadsheets, word processing documents, or EDI transaction sets can be sent as enveloped messages using the Internet Simple Mail Transport Protocol (SMTP).

SMTP provides a common specification for the exchange of e-mail messages between systems and networks. Whether they know it or not, most Internet e-mail users use SMTP. SMTP defines not only how messages are addressed but their format as well. No authentication, confidentiality, or data integrity properties are provided in SMTP or MIME. Persons desiring any or all of those security properties should look into the use of Privacy Enhanced Mail (PEM), an Internet standard that uses a combination of security techniques to assure privacy, integrity, and nonrepudiation of messages. With PEM, all or part of a message can be digitally signed or encrypted with the Data Encryption Standard (DES) and Public Key cryptography (see Chapter 5).

### *Multipurpose Internet Mail Extensions (MIME)*

Why multimedia mail extensions? Multimedia is rapidly becoming part and parcel of network applications—in electronic mail, EDI, World Wide Web. In the case of e-mail, users are no longer satisfied with sending simple, plain-text messages. Today, users want to send spreadsheets, word processing files, graphics, and other complex data files—digital audio and video—as part of e-mail messages. And they want to avoid the hassle of encoding/decoding or transforming information to the plain ASCII text as required by mail systems of the past.

Data transmission would be less complex if all users dealt with a single computing platform, but few applications rely on only one computing technology and one set of network protocols. Today's technology requires interconnecting different workstations with different networking capabilities running on different operating systems. Such complexity requires a standards-based information exchange system—a common language that bridges a variety of applications and disparate platforms.

Enter MIME, a specification that offers a way to interchange text in languages with different character sets and multimedia e-mail among many different computer systems. MIME allows users to create and read e-mail messages containing the following:

- Character sets other than ASCII such as Arabic, Kanji, Mandarin
- Enriched text with special symbols such as mathematics
- Graphics images
- Audio files or sounds
- Binary files—PostScript and compressed files such as tar or zip files
- Other not-yet-invented data or information types

MIME not only supports several predefined types of nontextual message contents, such as GIF image files and PostScript programs, but also permits users to define their own types of message parts easily. This flexibility is essential for communicating EDI-related information where the information content may not fit exactly what the standard specifies.

The MIME specification defines four different header fields:

1. *A MIME-version header* labels a message as MIME-conformant. This header allows different MIME-aware mail user agents to process the message appropriately.
2. *A content-type header field* specifies the data types within the message. Within the content-type header various fields are used to describe different message types and subtypes. So far, there is a text type, a multipart type (for multiple parts in a single message), an application type (for data shared between applications, such as a spreadsheet), a message type (for encapsulated messages), an image type, an audio type, and a video type.
3. *A content-transfer-encoding header field* specifies the encoding used to get the message through a given message transport system, such as the Internet.
4. Two optional header fields, a *content-ID* and a *content-description header* serve to label and identify the data in the message.

### MIME User Agent (UA)

The real key of any MIME -based mail system is the MIME-capable mail user agent, MIME UA. In fact, the MIME standard describes how mail user agents identify different message types, so that the user's mail interface can properly display the data for the user. A MIME UA can handle complex multipart messages regardless of the mail transport agent, computer operating system, or network operating system. The trick, however, is finding a MIME-compatible user agent that is not only MIME-aware (able to interpret incoming

MIME messages) but also MIME-capable (able to create as well as read MIME e-mail messages).

A MIME UA differs from a conventional mail user agent. Where most mail agents have a simple viewer to display text e-mail messages, the MIME UA has a MIME parser and a dispatcher. To display a multipart/multimedia message, the MIME UA first passes the message through a parser, which identifies the different components of the message from the header information. The UA's dispatcher then accesses a specific viewer for each message type, specifying output as a graphic, text, PostScript, and so forth. MIME capabilities can be added to an existing e-mail user agent, or a new user agent with built-in MIME support can be installed.

The MIME UA offers real advantages because it means that MIME-compatible applications can be extended easily. For example, to support new image formats, the user can purchase new viewer software and then tell the MIME UA how and under what conditions to invoke it; a new user agent is unnecessary, as would be the case with a conventional e-mail system. Furthermore, add-on viewers can be provided by virtually any vendor. So as needs change and expand, the multimedia e-mail support can change and expand as well.

### Computing Components of Mail-Handling Systems

Any mail system has four major components: user agents, message store, message transfer agent (MTA), and directory services. See Fig. 10.3.

The user agent creates, responds to, and receives mail, all in an interface through which a user performs the equivalent task of placing mail in a mailbox on a street corner. In host-based systems, such as UNIX ELM or PINE, the user agent resides wholly on the mini or mainframe. In LAN-based e-mail, such as cc:Mail and Microsoft Mail, the user agent resides on the PC and is called the mail client.

The second component, the message store, queues up undelivered messages and receives mail even when mail clients are off-line. Private user mailboxes are part of the massage store. A collection of user mailboxes on the same server and the queue of messages waiting to be delivered on that server are called a post office. EDI applications may either use their own mailboxes or share the mailboxes of other applications or users. With shared mailboxes, the mail messages intended for a particular application usually carry an identifier in either the header or the body of the mail, which enables the application to recognize and retrieve its mail when it periodically checks the mailbox.

The third component, the message transfer agent (MTA), sorts and routes messages among mailboxes and post offices. The MTA uses a mail protocol

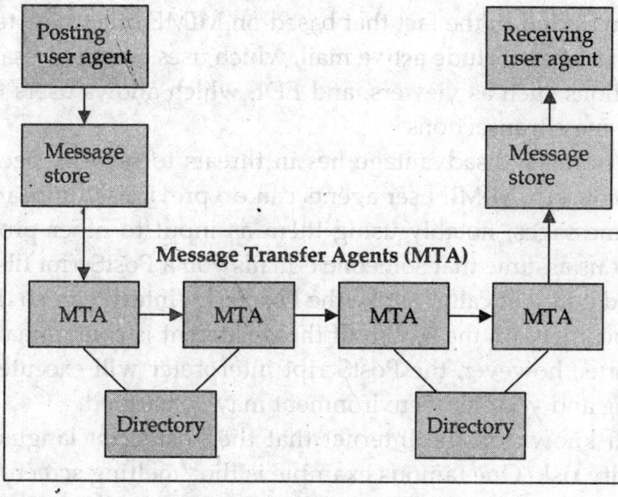


**Figure 10.3** The message-handling model

that defines the format of the message's envelope, address, contents, and attachments. Simple Mail Transfer Protocol (SMTP) is the de facto standard for UNIX systems, and X.400 is another standard for commercial e-mail systems. In the case of EDI, MIME will serve as the Internet standard.

The fourth component is directory services. With users entering the Internet in increasing numbers, EDI service directories will become essential for looking up mail addresses.

### *MIME Advantages and Disadvantages*

The advantages offered by MIME are numerous. Users have already discovered that MIME is the perfect vehicle to ship binary files around the Internet. For example, IETF document announcements (RFCs, Internet Drafts, etc.) are structured as multipart MIME messages. The first part contains the document abstract. The second part is itself a multipart message, containing external references to the actual document itself (one reference via a mail server, one reference via anonymous FTP). Thus, with a suitable UA (usually the end user's mail program, e.g., MH, PINE, ELM), users can read the abstract and then retrieve the complete document (by the most appropriate method) at the press of a button.

The strength of MIME comes from its careful design to survive the different variations of mail transport protocols (SMTP, UUCP, BITNET, X.400) that like to slice, dice, and stretch the headers and bodies of e-mail messages. This strength is reflected in the fact that based on MIME other new technologies are emerging. They include active mail, which uses e-mail messages to initiate applications such as viewers, and EDI, which allows users to utilize e-mail for business transactions.

MIME's primary disadvantage lies in threats to security because of the user agent concept. MIME user agents can do previously unheard of things with mail messages, notably using them as input to other programs. For instance, let us assume that someone e-mails you a PostScript file. Your user agent would automatically invoke the PostScript interpreter so that you can read the document on the screen. If the document is contaminated with an attached virus, however, the PostScript interpreter will execute it without any warning and your local environment may be harmed.

It is well known on the Internet that the PostScript language poses a large security risk. One famous example is the "melting screen" PostScript program, which destroys screens under the control of PostScript viewers such as Ghostview. For another example, PostScript can be used to change the password on some PostScript printers with previously undefined passwords. This act denies the use of the printer until the printer's password can (somehow) be changed back. These security holes are discussed, not to encourage their exploitation, but because they exist and are well known. To protect against mischief, several safeguards are being developed and prototyped.

### EDI and MIME

The practice of assigning "mailboxes" to programs has long been a feature of the Internet's e-mail environment. Programs or processes await the arrival of messages, which they interpret and act on. Some of the programs provide access to documents or programs by sending a copy of a requested object back to the requester as an electronic mail message ("Please send a copy of document A"). Others accept messages and perform some action ("Find the e-mail address of the company B and mail it to me"). Others handle the maintenance of e-mail distribution lists ("Please add my name to or delete my name from this list"). It is therefore no surprise that one could readily contemplate business applications that accept messages containing EDI transactions and act on them, possibly responding with additional electronic mail messages as needed.

MIME becomes an important part of the EDI infrastructure, since with a MIME-capable e-mail gateway, EDI-formatted information can pass easily through the existing e-mail infrastructure. MIME recognizes EDI data just as it handles any other kind of specially formatted information. The methods of identifying EDI objects in a MIME message are being defined by IETF-EDI, a working group of the Internet Engineering Task Force (IETF).

The following example message is taken from a Internet Draft Standard on EDI over the Internet [CROC95]. In this example, the EDI message has two parts: header and body. The header contains addressing information, content description information, and type of content transfer. The body contains the EDI document based on the X.12 or EDIFACT standards.

**MIME EDI Envelope Structure**

```
TO:              <<recipient organization EDI e-mail address>>
SUBJECT:
FROM:            <<sending organization EDI e-mail address>>
DATE:
MIME-VERSION: 1.0
Content-Type: APPLICATION/EDI-X12
Content-Transfer-Encoding: BINARY
      <<standard ASC X12 EDI Transaction Message goes here>>
```

The APPLICATION/EDI part contains data as specified for electronic data interchange with the consent of an explicit, bilateral trading partner agreement exchanging the EDI-consent traffic. Two commonly used types, APPLICATION/EDI-X12 and APPLICATION/EDIFACT, contain data as specified by the respective standards. As such, use of EDI-other provides a standard mechanism for "wrapping" the EDI objects but does not specify any of the details about those objects.

In sum, all this potential puts MIME at the forefront of a whole new way of thinking about electronic messaging. The strength of MIME, other than being an industry standard, is that it is extensible and modular. MIME is an enabling technology that can be used as a basis for a whole host of exciting new applications. Once multimedia messaging becomes commonplace, the possibilities for extensive mail-enabled applications seem almost endless.

## 10.4 VALUE-ADDED NETWORKS (VANs)

A VAN is a communications network that typically exchanges EDI messages among trading partners. It also provides other services, including holding messages in "electronic mailboxes," interfacing with other VANs, and supporting many telecommunications modes and transfer protocols. A VAN's "electronic mailbox" is a software feature into which a user deposits EDI transactions and then retrieves those messages when convenient. It works much like residential personal mailboxes, and it allows everybody involved to be flexible and cost-effective.

Businesses can exchange data either by connecting to each other directly or by hooking into a VAN. Traditionally, by acting as middlemen between companies, VANs have allowed companies to automatically and securely exchange purchase orders, invoices, and payments. When a company sends an EDI transaction, it arrives at a message storehouse on the VAN to await pickup by the destination company. In this way VANs can safeguard the transaction network.

Figure 10.4 illustrates the EDI process. Company A puts an EDI message for trading partner manufacturing company B in the VAN mailbox at a date and time of its choosing. The VAN picks up the message from the mailbox and delivers it to trading partner B's mailbox, where it will remain until trading partner B logs on and picks it up. Trading partner B responds to trading partner A in the same fashion. The cycle repeats itself on a weekly, daily, or perhaps even hourly basis as needed. This service is generally referred to as mail-enabled EDI.

The disadvantage of EDI-enabling VANs is that they are slow and high-priced, charging by the number of characters transmitted. With connect time and mailbox charges factored in, companies incur charges of many thousands of dollars.

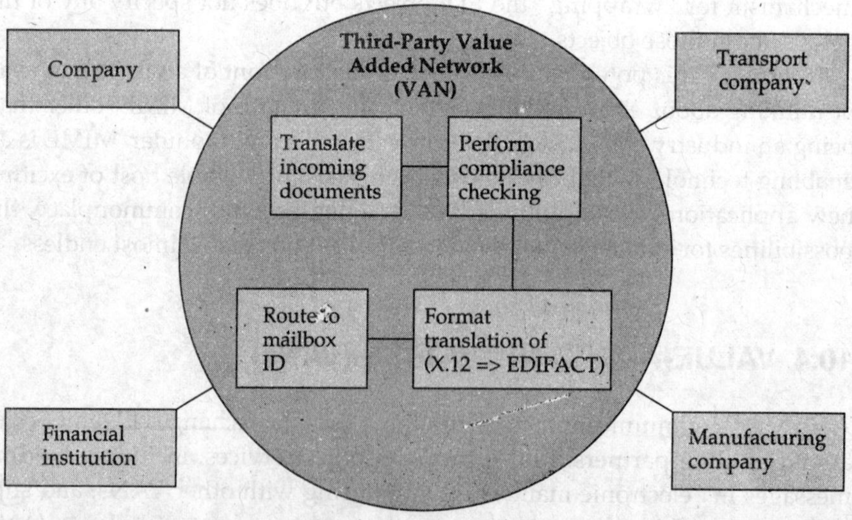


**Figure 10.4** Functions of a third-party VAN

Whether a company really needs a VAN is a question of simple logistics. For example, a business that wants to use EDI with some fifty trading partners has several communications choices:

- The company can buy a multiport modem capable of handling fifty incoming phone lines, install fifty phone lines, add communications ports for its computer system, and allow each trading partner to communicate directly at its convenience.
- The company can use a single modem with a phone line and arrange a tightly controlled schedule for each of its trading partners, for example, 12:00 A.M. for trading partner B, 12:11 A.M. for trading partner C, and so on. The problems with this alternative become obvious when a trading partner misses its turn or has too many EDI messages to fit into its ten-minute slot.
- The company can establish an electronic mailbox on a VAN and require each trading partner to use the VAN for sending and retrieving EDI messages. This alternative works well because most VANs maintain a large number of access points (known as ports, lines, nodes) to their networks and can spread the costs of maintaining these ports among their clients. Thus a large number of trading partners can access the VAN at their convenience without encountering blockage from other trading partners and at relatively low cost.

Large EDI-capable businesses and government agencies with more than a handful of trading partners almost always rely on VANs, and small organizations with six or more trading partners are good candidates for using VANs, as are organizations with minimal internal expertise regarding computers, modems, telecommunications, and EDI. Many businesses find that the decision to use a VAN is made for them by their trading partners. An organization selecting a VAN should consider the VAN's reputation and experience, level of technical support and service capacity, and ability to cope with network outages. Other factors include whether the VAN operates its own communications network or leases capacity from a network provider, what are the means of connectivity to the VAN, and what are the costs.

## VAN Pricing Structures

VANs bill in various ways for services rendered. Typically, customers can pick and choose from an array of VAN services and be billed accordingly. These services may include EDI translation software and support, EDI to fax support, e-mail capability, inter-VAN connectivity, and, most commonly, transmission of X.12 documents. Typically, VAN services entail three types of costs: account start-up costs, usage or variable costs, and VAN-to-VAN interconnect costs.

### Account Start-Up Costs

Opening an account with a VAN incurs start-up costs as well as other variable costs such as mailbox/network fees. The network usage fee is a flat monthly rate that applies whether or not the services are used. The network usage fee can also include a mailbox fee for maintaining an account and a password. Each account has a "mailbox" through which companies exchange EDI data.

The overall start-up costs vary depending on the EDI readiness of the organization and the trading partner, the number of trading partners, line attachment options (asynchronous), and software application options. These software services include EDI and/or EDIFACT transmission support, archiving, and audit trails of transactions.

### VAN Usage or Variable Costs

VANs charge session fees based on use of their services. Unlike the postal service, which charges only to send a letter, most VANs charge to both send and receive data. If a user agrees to cover all of the transaction costs, the VAN can charge twice for each transaction: (1) when the user sends or receives, and (2) when a trading partner sends or receives.

The customer pays according to volume of usage. Usage is defined as the number of transactions sent and received by the customer or the trading partner. Transaction fee assessment is not consistent or straightforward. Some VANs allow users to "bundle" several transaction sets (purchase orders, invoices, acknowledgments) into a single envelope, as though sending several invoices in one paper envelope.

Other VANs open the "interchange" and charge for each transaction set in the envelope. Interestingly enough, VANs generally charge a kilo (1000 characters) character fee according to the size of the packet. Many VANs use a sliding scale in which the first kilo character has a higher cost than subsequent kilo characters in the same exchange. Although many VANs charge in 100-character increments, the majority price in kilo characters. In addition to kilo character fees, VANs also assess envelope fees for each EDI packet or "interchange envelope" sent or received.

Other support and software costs are hidden. The session fee is a variable cost related to envelope/message fee delivery of functionally similar EDI documents. Support fee generally applies to updates to the software and telephone support for the VANs that provide software. Some VANs provide free software that works only with its sponsoring VAN. Other VANs provide customized software that may or may not operate with other VANs. The final category includes VANs that do not provide software, for which you must obtain your own EDI software that can translate data. Most of these packages are expensive and require a high level of technical expertise in your business. Table 10.2 summarizes the variable costs.

### *Interconnect Costs*

A company that exchanges EDI data with a trading partner that subscribes to a different VAN will pay a VAN interconnect fee (transaction/document fee) for the number of characters in each document. Most VANs offer interconnects, but they often charge monthly fees for using them and may have other charges as well.

If no transactions are sent, there is only the monthly charge for the mailbox and interconnect fee. Since most VANs offer volume discounts, the variable costs per transaction will decrease as the number of transactions sent increases. Table 10.3 estimates the costs of two types of EDI transactions: sending a purchase order to a trading partner on the same VAN and sending a purchase order to a trading partner on another VAN.

**Table 10.2** VAN Network Usage Fees [VA95]

| *Fee* | *Range* |
|---|---|
| *Session fee.* Fee for each log-on to network. | \$0–\$1.00 per session plus the cost to access the network (i.e., local vs. long-distance phone call) |
| *Transaction fee.* Varies depending on character volume. | \$0.07–\$0.35 per kilo characters (1000 characters) |
| *Envelope fee.* Some VANs batch non-time-sensitive transactions into one envelope and send as a single transaction. | \$0.15–\$0.37 per functional documents in one envelope |
| *Volume discounts.* May be applied to monthly variable costs or to the number ofelectronic documents sent and received. | 25%–75% of total costs. Volume discounts can be negotiated. |

**Table 10.3** Transaction Fee Structure [VA95]

| *Cost Scenario* | *Monthly Fixed Cost* | | *Variable Cost* | |
|---|---|---|---|---|
| Transmit a purchase order via VAN A to a trading partner on the same VAN. The average size of a purchase order is 1000 characters. | Mailbox,<br>Interconnect,<br>Total, | $25.00<br>15.00<br>$40.00 | Session fee,<br>Envelope fee<br>Transaction fee<br>Total | $.00<br>.15<br>.10<br>$.25 |
| Transmit a purchase order via VAN A to a trading partner on VAN B. The average size of a purchase order is 1000 characters | Mailbox,<br>Interconnect,<br>Total, | $25.00<br>15.00<br>$40.00 | Session fee,<br>Envelope fee,<br>Transaction fee,<br>Interconnect usage fee,<br>Total | $.00<br>.15<br>.10<br>.10<br>$.35 |

## VAN Service Providers

A wide range of VAN providers exist. Some provide only the network for electronic communications, and others also provide such services as customizing vendor profiles to screen procurement data. Some of the well-known EDI VAN service providers are listed here, as this information is often very difficult to find in trade magazines:

*AT&T.* Strong coverage in the United States and in the main European centers, with extensive X.400 electronic mail interconnections.

*British Telecom (BT).* Owns GNS, the world's largest VAN, combining the domestic packet switching service (PSS) and, since 1989, the Tymnet network. End-to-end GNS connection is available in thirty-six countries with gateway connections to 100 more planned.

*Cable & Wireless.* Resources in fifty countries, including Mercury in the United Kingdom. Offers its Global Digital Highway linking the world's main commercial centers. Claims an 8 percent share of the international VAN market and targets the top 2500 global companies.

*GEIS.* Very experienced; presence in fifty countries. Firmly established in e-mail and EDI services for specific business applications. Bought the remaining half of INS from ICL in January 1994, giving it strong U.K. EDI cover.

*Advantis/IBM.* Large customer base and long experience, particularly in its own systems network architecture (SNA) protocol connectivity. Known to take down its network each week for scheduled maintenance.

*Infonet.* Long-established internationally. Among its shareholders are MCI, Transpac, Singapore Telecom, and other organizations that are themselves considering VAN activity.

*Saturn.* Recently entered Europe from Australia. Concentrating initially on tailored solutions for the financial market, notably for multiple sub-64-kbps services such as analog voice tie lines, subrate voice services, and lower-speed data lines.

*Scitor.* Relatively new entrant owned by the airlines' network Sita. It has coverage in 150 countries as a result and boasts 200 help-desks, but it lacks wide commercial experience.

*Sprint.* U.S.-based, it relies heavily on joint ventures with local operators. It is known for competitive prices but lacks the "one-stop shop" appeal of some players.

*Transpac.* New to the international market, it owns the largest European domestic network (in France). It owns a part of Infonet for its overseas cover.

*Unisource.* A recent entrant, it is a joint venture between three medium-sized public telecom operators (PTTs) from the Netherlands, Sweden, and Switzerland. It relies on Sprint for non-European cover. Must overcome tariff and regulatory obstacles and keep internal controls in order to maintain cost-effectiveness and security.

## VANs and the Internet

VANs that use private networks could soon face stiff competition for EDI business. Why? With increasing cost pressures in business today, firms are looking for a more affordable way to collaborate with customers and partners on-line and may find promise in several projects underway to move EDI technology onto the Internet and away from traditional VANs. VANs are taking seriously reports that Internet access providers, with flat-rate pricing, will zero in on their value-added services business. With the Internet lurking as a potential competitor, VAN providers are repositioning themselves and their service offerings to be competitive.

After years of providing little more than rudimentary value-added services, VANs are now putting together what they are promoting as platforms for next-generation intercompany communications over the Internet. The new services go beyond the usual e-mail and EDI applications to offer a wide range of functions, including global directory services, access to information servers, and even interactive groupware sessions involving users from different organizations. In short, new services represent a way for VANs to cash in on the electronic marketplace frenzy that has made the Internet such a hot item.

The Internet might seem like an unlikely medium for delivering commercial EDI transactions, given its original design to enhance communications and file sharing among users. Yet, it is currently transporting EDI data between organizations in certain industry sectors, with many more planned in the near future. Among the Internet services offered or in the works: access to VAN services via the TCP/IP communications protocol; Internet Mail, including support for the MIME protocol designed to carry EDI and related multimedia files within the same message envelope; and World Wide Web sites for obtaining information and technical assistance. Rounding out the primary applications available are *information servers*, programs that store data in a standardized format that can be accessed by any user with the appropriate client interface.

Here is how the Internet EDI might work: Manufacturers and distributors with Internet access will be able to fill out forms-based requests for quotes (RFQs) and send them to a VAN mailbox using the Internet Simple Mail Transport Protocol (SMTP). The VAN will convert these documents to EDI RFQs (840) and forward them to shippers. EDI quotes (843) will be returned to the VAN by the shippers for transmission to the manufacturers. Awards traveling back to the shippers will undergo a similar conversion from an SMTP-based form to a contract award (836) and purchase order (850).

By cobbling together services that extend basic internetworking functions, carriers hope to attract companies that want an easy-to-use forum for electronic commerce managed by a provider that can be held accountable for all aspects of the service. Many say that VANs will continue to play an important role in electronic commerce because they give a company a single point of contact. Trading is a many-to-many relationship, which is very hard to manage from one company. Sometimes, it is an easy decision to turn it all over to a centralized company.

Even as they embrace the Internet, VANs believe that the day is a long way off when a significant portion of EDI traffic will travel the global network. The key question is not about technology but about business: Will companies consider putting EDI transactions on the Internet? VANs emphasize that their large customers are wary of the Internet, finding it short on security and lacking guaranteed delivery. They also point out that end users want security, reliability, nonrepudiation, audit trails, authentication, data integrity, and consulting, among other services. Whether the VAN using the Internet can offer these services remains a question. In addition, any price advantage now enjoyed by Internet access providers may evaporate under the burden of providing these value-added services.

In sum, it is safe to assume that even an Internet-dominated world would have plenty of room for VANs. Because a vast majority of EDI transactions are communicated today via a single VAN or through multiple VANs, it would be premature to believe that either VANs or Internet service providers will dominate in the future. Rather, we will see a mixed environment where VANs, Internet service providers, and X.400 gateways can provide a variety of services. VANs have a limited window of opportunity, however, before the Internet competition gets serious.

## 10.5 INTERNET-BASED EDI

Several factors make the Internet useful for EDI:

- *Flat-pricing* that is not dependent on the amount of information transferred. The Internet flat-rate model is better for the customer as opposed to the standard VAN approach of charges per character.
- *Cheap access* with the low cost of connection—often a flat monthly fee for leased line or dial-up access. Business users have access to commercial and noncommercial Internet services in some 140 countries providing ubiquitous network coverage.
- *Common mail standards* and proven networking and interoperable systems; another attraction is that Internet mail standards are nonproprietary and handle congestion and message routing exceptionally well. It has been noted that sometimes on a VAN network an e-mail message can take hours or days to reach its destination, while on the Internet it usually takes seconds to minutes.
- *Security*—public-key encryption techniques are being incorporated in various electronic mail systems. This will enable systems to ensure the privacy of EDI messages and give users a way to verify the sender or recipient.

Electronic commerce services on the Internet differ from earlier value-added network offerings in several respects. First, they're based on established technologies and applications available from independent vendors, whereas more traditional services are based on proprietary software and front ends. Not only does the proprietary approach limit interoperability, but it also narrows application choices.

Older services limited the customer to what the vendor was willing to provide. Nonproprietary solutions, in contrast, allow the customer to choose the level of service needed. In addition, because the Internet supplies users with a working software infrastructure, VANs can work with companies to configure their applications for interacting with business partners. For instance, a manufacturer could set up an inventory database to allow its customers to determine whether stock is on hand to meet a specific order.

Today, several organizations are exchanging EDI transactions over the Internet. Among them are the U.S. Department of Defense, which is setting up its electronic commerce system using the Internet, and other government agencies working with private companies.

### Internet EDI and the U.S. Department of Defense

Using the Internet as a communications medium for the transfer of EDI data transactions has been pioneered by the U.S. government and the education community. A big user of Internet EDI is the U.S. Department of Defense (DOD). The DOD's experience suggests that VANs and Internet mail can interoperate to provide a seamless environment in which each partner can select a VAN or the Internet as their communications gateway. Lawrence Livermore National Laboratory (LLNL) has been running a pilot project called GATEC for the Wright-Patterson Air Force Base to enable its procurement process to be operated via EDI.

Procurement transactions are collected via the Defense Data Network, a private Internet network, and collected at the EDI hub gateway located at LLNL. The hub gateway connects to several commercial VANs via X.25/X.400 or Internet mail. The fact that at least some of the commercial VANs currently have gateways for Internet mail suggests that all commercial VANs will offer this feature in the near future. Internet mail currently carries EDI data in much the same way as it is carried in X.400 messages. The body of the message contains a single EDI interchange. The message is routed via the sender and receiver identifiers on the message header. In 1988 the X.400 standard was extended to allow multiple objects, or body parts, to be carried within a single X.400 message. This means that a text message, a CAD drawing, and an EDI interchange can be encapsulated in an X.400 message. The receiving application identifies the message from the identifier attached to each object and routes it to the appropriate applications.

## The SPEEDE Project

The transfer of student transcripts between educational establishments has traditionally been a source of much frustration for all the parties involved. Florida, Texas, and other pioneering states have developed their own file formats for exchanging transcripts between K–12 schools and colleges. This intrastate exchange has proved to be highly successful.

In 1988 the American Association of Collegiate Registrars and Admissions Officers appointed a task force to determine how student transcripts could be exchanged nationally. The task force later adopted the acronym SPEEDE (Standardization of Postsecondary Education Electronic Document Exchange). A parallel task force, created by the National Center for Educational Statistics to study transcript transfer for prekindergarten to 12th grade, adopted the acronym ExPRESS (Exchanging Permanent Records Electronically for Students and Schools). The two task forces then collaborated to define a single transaction set, the Student Educational Record (130), which accommodates K–12 and college transcripts. In February 1992 this transaction set, which contains the joint SPEEDE/ExPRESS format, was formally adopted as an ANSI ASC X12 standard.

## VAN-Free Internet EDI

The Internet can be used directly for exchanging EDI messages without going through a VAN. Trading partners must agree on the protocols for exchanging messages and then agree on some details with the exchange.

### *E-Mail-Based Messaging*

The simplest and most widely supported means of exchanging messages is via e-mail. Typically, the IETF-MIME encapsulation specification would be used to enclose the EDI data within the e-mail message, and the trading partners would need to agree on an encryption method for secure e-mail, typically PEM or PGP (see Chapter 5). The trading partners would then exchange the following:

- The e-mail address for EDI messages and an e-mail address for personal communications related to EDI
- Agreement on the encryption and digital signature protocols, including e-mail acknowledgment (e.g., support for the "Return-Receipt-To:" e-mail header or X.400 extended e-mail header fields)

- Public keys for PEM or PGP encryption and digital signature. (or private keys for DES encryption)
- Agreement on the format of the message, e.g., X.12 or EDIFACT transaction sets

An example of e-mail-based EDI is Templar, a UNIX-based software package that can dispatch commercial trading transactions over the Internet as e-mail messages. Taking advantage of the Internet's peer-to-peer connectivity, Templar is designed to provide users with the advantages of electronic data interchange (EDI) without incurring the third-party overhead of value-added networks.

To provide a similar level of security while removing the high costs of a VAN, Premenos Corporation, the developer of Templar, adopted e-mail as a transaction carrier because it can connect companies directly. To solve the encryption problem, Premenos licensed RSA Data Security's public-key encryption standard to bring the protection available within VANs to the Internet. Although Templar is a low-cost and secure EDI solution, it will not provide the same level of administration or control as a VAN.

### *FTP-Based Messaging*

To exchange EDI messages via FTP, some set-up information must be included in the trading partner agreement. Typically, an account would be created for each trading partner for a FTP log-in, including a password. Typically, each X.12 or EDIFACT message would be stored in a file, and the trading partner agreement would define the conventions for naming files and directories for the messages.

The trading partner agreement would include:

- FTP log-in name and password; machine(s) from which the login will be accepted
- Directory and file-naming conventions
- File encryption protocols and keys
- Wrappers around EDI data, e.g. MIME/EDI headers, PEM/PGP wrappers
- Agreement on message format, e.g., X.12 or EDIFACT transaction sets.

Several compression routines and utilities are available for virtually any computer system that uses the Internet. Many of these utilities will convert across platforms (say UNIX to Mac, UNIX to PC, and visa versa) and are available at no cost from one of several FTP archive servers.

### EDI Gateways

The increase in transaction volumes and types of standards and communication protocols possible between organizations has brought to the fore the issue of managing communication among a multitude of ad hoc and often incompatible application systems, protocols, communications methods, and data standards. In response, EDI gateways are being built that act as communication hubs between different sections of the same organization or with outside trading partners.

Gateways are necessary when using multiple standards. Common gateway facilities include [SS93]:

- EDI message construction and translation
- Translation between application software package standards and some agreed-on in-house standard
- Translation between the in-house standard and the various EDI document formats (such as ANSI X.12 or UN/EDIFACT)
- Queue management for both inbound and outbound documents
- Compliance checking of arriving messages to ensure correctness
- Transmission between the organization's internal data communications standards (X.400 or a local area network standard such as IEEE 802.3) and those of the recipient, who may be a value-added network service provider (in which case X.25 would be the most likely standard) or a trading partner (who might well be using X.400 messaging)
- Session management and directory services maintenance
- Full delivery audit facilities
- Security and management features
- Call-logging facilities designed to enable operation of a service desk
- The creation of trading partner relationships and the establishment of trading partner profiles
- A variety of optional additional services, such as support for interactive database queries

While many U.S. companies operate on a single standard, an increasing number of global trading partners are realizing that some use of EDIFACT will be a requirement in the near future. Discovering that you need to use multiple standards should not present a significant roadblock to implementing EDI. Many companies select translation software that accepts a variety of standards.

For example, company X uses one translator for communication with affiliates across the globe. U.S. departments use ANSI, some European departments use EDIFACT, and other European facilities use a different standard, such as TRADICOMS. One EDI translation application allows company X to send and receive documents in any standard. Another answer is gateways. A gateway provides a trapdoor for documents that require a different standard. It transforms an ANSI transaction into an EDIFACT message.

## 10.6 SUMMARY

In the past two chapters, we have discussed in some detail various aspects of existing and potential EDI applications and a variety of implementation scenarios. After all this, the decision to implement EDI comes down to a cost–benefit analysis.

The discussion of EDI would not be complete without mentioning manpower and skill requirements. Responsibility for managing EDI gateways and partnerships tends to fall on IS professionals. Of course, titles and positions vary with company size. For example, firms with only a few trading partners may have one EDI coordinator responsible for mapping and translation, application programming, and day-to-day operations, including linking to new partners. Conversely, companies with thousands of partners may have one or two EDI coordinators, several programmer/analysts or business analysts, and an EDI team leader. The following job descriptions provide a perspective of the talent required for EDI implementation:

*EDI coordinator.* Acts as technical liaison between the company and its trading partners; responsible for day-to-day operations; establishes trading partner agreements and service levels; tracks the status of document transmittals and translations; provides on-site and phone support to EDI users; keeps up with state-of-the-art developments in EDI and monitors vendor progress; reports to EDI team leader.

*EDI programmer/analyst.* Integrates EDI translation software with business applications; maps translated EDI data into the appropriate applications; develops and tests new maps; establishes EDI disaster recovery plan; may be responsible for the communications links; reports to EDI coordinator or team leader.

*EDI team leader.* Manages the overall EDI effort from the technical side; advises business units on EDI software and hardware selection and choosing communications protocols; spearheads new development projects in electronic commerce.

Finally, to determine whether new EDI technologies or automation strategies are worth what they will cost, it is important to keep four questions in mind: Will the application or technology reduce costs and improve productivity? add value to customer services? improve reliability of service and operations? strengthen needed management controls? A viable EDI-based technological answer should rate a decisive yes in at least one or more of these categories.

Chapter 11

# Intraorganizational Electronic Commerce

Electronic commerce cannot reach its full potential as a stand-alone concept addressing mainly customer-organization, interorganizational, or disconnected internal automation activities. For companies to be fully effective, these three activities must be integrated and the corresponding software applications developed together.

Earlier, we elaborated on "public" commerce built on a foundation of World Wide Web and other technologies over which firms, suppliers, and consumers engage in on-line transactions. The press tends to assume that electronic commerce is restricted exclusively to activities external to the organization. Reality refutes this assumption. The technologies and methods associated with electronic commerce are already used extensively within firms, where the focus is on operations and other aspects of efficiency-gaining activities. These activities are known by various names: enterprise integration, process control systems, business process reengineering, and work-flow management.

Internal commerce is the application of electronic commerce to processes or operations. Specifically, we define internal commerce as using methods and pertinent technologies for supporting internal business processes between individuals, departments, and collaborating organizations (see Fig. 11.1).

Private commerce is significant because it is closely related to market orientation toward creating superior value for customers. This requires that a company understands a customer's business value chain and tàilor its operations, products, or services to deliver better value. A company can create customer value at any point in the chain by being more efficient in its operations, delivering better quality, and being flexible.

To achieve better performance, a business must develop and sustain competitive advantage. Competitive advantage was once based on structural characteristics such as market power, economies of scale, or a broad product line. Today, the emphasis has shifted to capabilities that enable a business to consistently deliver superior value to its customers through better coordina-

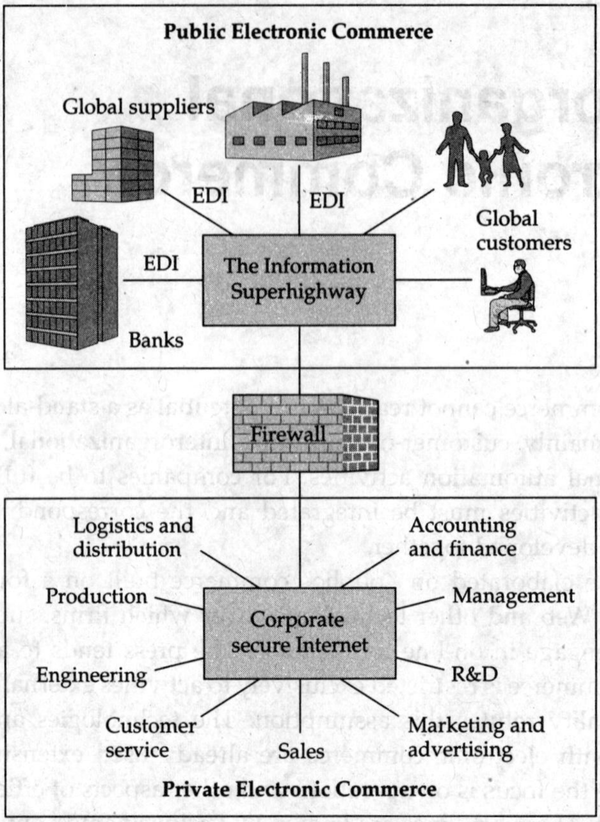


**Figure 11.1** Private and public electronic commerce

tion and work-flow management, product and service customization, and supply chain management.

### *Work-Flow Management*

Companies have spent millions of dollars to reengineer work flows in order to improve coordination within the enterprise. The use of work flows for task coordination is important because people do not work in isolation but collaborate to accomplish tasks. Companies have developed methods to optimize work flows by pruning unneeded operational steps and moving much of their internal paper handling onto computer networks. The most common work flows are administrative—time-consuming, unexciting tasks such as processing a trip request from initiation, through approval, to issuing the ticket, cutting a check for the cash advance, and debiting an account.

These work flow reengineering efforts have been mostly localized to a few departments or tasks. Extending this effort to coordinating enterprise processes using electronic commerce methods is the logical next step for most organizations. Many organizations are asking, If we can distribute a document electronically, shouldn't we also be able to have it reviewed and approved electronically? Shouldn't the system track the document status and monitor its progress through the labyrinth of that work process? If we become confused and want to know what step comes next, shouldn't we be able to ask the system? If the usefulness of work flow automation is granted, the next step is to use new technology to improve it. But several tricky questions remain unresolved: What technology is involved? How to implement it? How to benchmark it? In short, we see work flow as a gold mine for new electronic commerce application software.

### *Product or Service Customization*

Consumer demand and expectations are forecasted to drive made-to-order or customized products with rapidly shrinking lead times. Products will come configured as customers want them and provide a high level of reliability, excellent quality, and longer life spans. We are already witnessing customization in the area of consumer electronics and computers, where "bundled" features expressly tailored for each order are increasing.

Customization is often associated with agile manufacturing. Since the early 1980s, concerns about global competitiveness have popularized the terms *world-class manufacturing*, *lean production*, and *agile manufacturing*. These terms connote essentially the same things: elimination of inventory and other forms of "waste," greater flexibility in production scheduling, shortened lead times, and advanced levels of quality in both products and customer service.

Customization focuses on two issues: time-to-market and flexible operations:

*Time-to-market* depends largely on gathering the specific consumer preferences and using these preferences to custom design products or services. Custom designing any product or service requires tremendous coordination between various departments and functions. For instance, if engineering wants to use a specific part in the design, it must coordinate with purchasing to determine whether the part is in supply and with manufacturing to design the process needed for production. In other words, an implicit assumption in successful time-to-market is cross-functional coordination built on the communications infrastructure.

*Flexible operations* depend largely on implementation details or working practices that make time-to-market a reality. A company convinced of the value of being just-in-time triggers production automatically on customer orders, rather than stockpiling inventory. The key idea is to avoid tying up time and capital in terms of setup costs and inventory.

A key point to remember is that in customization, it is customer demand that drives product or model varieties. The motto is simple: If the customer does not want it, don't produce it. Now compare this philosophy with the traditional paradigm where engineering and R&D ingenuity enables the creation of new products and sales and marketing attempt to convince customers that they really need them.

The concept of customization has been around for a while but we still do not know how to do it effectively. The technology requirements for supporting customization are becoming the primary of focus of internal-commerce.

### Supply Chain Management

A *supply chain* is the network of suppliers and customers within which any business operates. For example, a computer manufacturer has a chain of suppliers for its microprocessors, disk drives, video monitors, power supplies, systems software supplies, and so on, and a chain of customers in its retailers, resellers, and ultimate consumers.

Supply chain management is important as it is becoming impossible for companies to compete at the business or industrial level as isolated entities. For competitive reasons, it is likely that one tightly aligned and coordinated network of companies—a group of suppliers, distributors, retailers, manufacturers, and other support providers—will compete against other networks of companies. The result will be a blurring of corporate boundaries, with significant implications for management practice.

Before we get into the features of the changing organization, let's examine the information systems that are currently implemented in organizations. This will provide a framework for the ensuing discussion.

## 11.1 INTERNAL INFORMATION SYSTEMS

As noted earlier, the business forces driving internal commerce are the economic and competitive market forces. These forces are commanding a rethinking of the importance of networks—computer and communications—and their role in the better utilization of corporate information in operational and analytical decision making. Peter Drucker [PD70] stated, "Communications and information are totally different, but information presupposes functioning communications (infrastructure)."

What exactly do we mean by "information in business organizations"? Information usually begins with corporate data. Corporate data provide the building blocks to form the information and knowledge that underlie the operations of all enterprises regardless of industry, size, or country. Corporate information is created, managed, and stored in many forms and places, and its value is contingent on the ability of workers to access, manipulate, change, and distribute it.

So the challenge of enabling internal commerce is plain and simple: How do we integrate the distributed corporate data using a high band-width network? What tools do we need to turn this corporate data into a cohesive information infrastructure that is essential to the smooth functioning of the firm? And, because usage is dependent on the task being performed, how do we deliver this information to the worker at the right place (in the office or in the field—mobile worker) at the right time?

Getting a handle on corporate data is not exactly a new problem. Many interesting concepts have been floated over the last three decades in the race to deliver information to the manager and line worker.

## Proprietary Systems as Differentiators

The old paradigm was captured succinctly in 1984, when Warren McFarlan published an influential article in the *Harvard Business Review* on the competitive potential of information technology. He asked managers to consider how information systems might benefit their companies. Could technology build barriers to competitive entry? Could it increase switching costs for customers? Could it change the balance of power in supplier relationships? He went on to argue that for many companies the answer was yes. The result was a focus on proprietary systems. Today, every MBA student is taught to recite the success stories of the 1970s and 1980s that are considered candidates for the Information Technology Hall of Fame.

The following well-known computer systems are representative of an important chapter in the application of computing to build competitive advantage and enhance organizational effectiveness:

SABRE, American Airlines's reservation system, which eventually became a computerized reservation system (CRS), and United Airlines' Apollo systems, the other leading CRS, transformed ticket booking, marketing, and distribution in the airline industry.

COSMOS, Federal Express's customer service system, tracks every movement of every package in the network through hand-held computers carried by all employees who handle packages. It has become the basis for the firm's continuing ability to differentiate itself in an increasingly competitive market.

American Hospital Supply's ASAP order-entry and inventory-control system generated huge sales increases for the company's medical products and turned it into an industry leader.

McKesson, the pharmaceutical wholesaler, implemented its pioneering ECONOMOST system by placing terminals in drugstores and tying them into McKesson's central computer. Originally designed to expedite order processing and to control inventory, the system rejuvenated the wholesale drug distribution industry and eliminated dozens of competitors.

United Service Automobile Association (USAA) used its Automated Insurance Environment to outperform its insurance industry rivals in service quality, premium growth, and profitability.

Mrs. Fields Cookies relied on its Retail Operations Intelligence system, an automated store management network, to build and operate a nationwide chain of 400 retail outlets without a costly and stifling bureaucracy.

In all these cases, a proprietary infrastructure was put in place first and then the organization went beyond the technology to view the management of "infrastructure" itself as an asset to gain competitive advantage. For instance, American Airlines enjoys a very steady cash flow from selling its SABRE system services to other airlines, an outcome that was not envisioned when the system was developed.

For every successful system listed, however, at least fifty costly failures resulted from trying to emulate the strategy. Increasingly, companies are refraining from introducing proprietary architecture and systems. Managers are realizing that while it is more dangerous than ever to ignore the power of information technology, it is even riskier still to believe that on its own, an information system can provide an enduring business advantage. In other words, the old models no longer apply. It is time to turn the page.

## A New Paradigm: Information Architecture

The focus of the new paradigm lies in creating an information architecture that enables cross-functional systems and better information utilization.

**Cross-Functional Systems.** Early on in business computing, unifunctional automation was the norm; applications were focused on automating discrete business tasks. This can be seen in the early data entry, payroll, and invoicing systems. Today, systems tend to be more broadly focused and tend to cut across functional boundaries.

Cross-functional automation with emphasis on integrating the enterprise, with information flowing from one business area to another, is rapidly becoming the norm. Cross-functional integration has shifted the entire thrust of corporate computing from monolithic mainframes toward client-server systems connecting corporate databases, workers, and tasks via the networking infrastructure.

We can see the genesis of this process in supply chain management where electronic mail, electronic data interchange (EDI), facsimile, and other communications applications are rapidly becoming interrelated and interdependent. Also in the same vein, the merging of data processing information management with document-oriented office publishing (or electronic publishing broadly speaking) has been evident for some time.

**Information Not Data.** The focus of competitive differentiation today is not on building better systems than those of the competitors, but is based on the use of corporate information. Why? While the information systems and applications may have to change periodically to cope with changes in business operations, the information has a longevity of 10–25 years. Simply stated, the corporate systems of the future will be built around information and companies are attempting to become information architects rather than systems builders.

Other trends have contributed to this paradigm shift. First, computers have become a substitutable commodity and as such are as much a part of the business environment as telephones. Organizations can easily automate and capture the efficiency benefits of information technology, sometimes by buying off-the-shelf packages. As a result, companies find it harder to differentiate themselves simply by automating faster than the competition.

Another factor is the dramatic change taking place in the technology management arena. Many companies, whose IS managers have spent thirty years handcrafting computer systems, pride themselves at being better than most in functions like hardware evaluation, project management for software development, and systems integration. Unlike proprietary systems of the past, information architecture today is based on the widespread adoption of standards and protocols in hardware, software, and telecommunications. The day has come when customers can buy hardware and software from different vendors and tailor their systems to their needs. They don't have to reinvent the wheel every time.

Finally, technology is changing faster than ever. It would be naive to assume that any information system that takes five years to develop will not be outdated by the time it is put into place. Today, changes in technology are both radical and rapid. It is well known that in the past two decades, price–performance ratios for computers have improved exponentially. For instance, Intel's 486 evolved from 25 MHz, to 33 MHz, to 66 MHz in just two years. The Intel Pentium is currently running at 90–150 MHz, and the next generation P6 is expected to run at 250–300 MHz. This improvement changes how computers generate and process information. Already, desktops are a ubiquitous presence in offices and factories, and organizations use them far more creatively than in the past. But do we understand how to harness this power in developing better applications? The answer is an emphatic no. Most firms lack the vision needed to make use of technological innovations in building applications for supporting business operations.

In short, we are at the crossroads of a major paradigm shift that will change the way we have viewed business information systems for over three decades. What is making us change the way we designed information systems is the revolutionary change in the business environment.

## 11.2 MACROFORCES AND INTERNAL COMMERCE

This section highlights the changes taking place in organization structure and explores how technology and other economic forces are molding arrangements within firms.

The business case for internal commerce can be made by the broad macroforces affecting organizations: an increasingly competitive global marketplace, shrinking middle management functions, changing customer demand and preferences, and pressures to reduce expenses. These needs have brought about myriad management strategies for efficient operations identified by the popular buzzwords: *total quality management*, *business process improvement*, or *business process reengineering*. The common focus in most of these modern management practices is the use of technology for improving efficiency and eliminating wasteful tasks in business operations.

The words *improvement* and *reengineering* are often used interchangeably, creating confusion. Although the goals of these two efforts are similar—productivity gains, cost savings, quality and service improvements, and cycle-time reductions—the two differ dramatically. Process improvement is a systematic method that seeks to simplify and streamline existing business processes. Process improvement follows the 80–20 rule: 20 percent of the work flow consumes 80 percent of the effort. The goal in process improvement is to streamline this 20 percent to improve results. Process reengineering aims at creating new processes, making radical and innovative changes to business methods to achieve dramatic improvements. Reengineering occurs when 70 percent to 100 percent of work processes are altered.

People also confuse reengineering with *downsizing*, when in fact the two functions are quite different. Generally, reengineering results in more work accomplished by fewer people; productivity improves and/or profits increase. Downsizing (or corporate restructuring) reduces the work force or modifies the organizational structure to meet the same workload or to cut personnel costs. Reengineering often uses automation to reduce the workload and increase efficiency and quality. Reengineering may not lead to downsizing and sometimes even leads to a bigger work force.

One main reason for reengineering is to better compete in global markets. Global networking is underpinning the evolution of a single global marketplace, where the importance of national borders is greatly diminished.

## Global Markets: Definition and Characteristics

Today the competition for goods, services, and ideas pays no respects to national borders or the old geopolitical divides that supposedly separate East from West, North from South, G-7 from Third World nations. A single world market exists for products ranging from cars, consumer electronics to carbonated drinks. Build a better product in Bombay and buyers will be there from London to Johannesburg. Before going further, the distinction between global and international needs to be made clear: *International* typically means that a company has an office in a foreign country; *global* goes beyond that, to autonomy and decentralization of operations.

The primary catalyst for the growing global economy is the dissemination of communication-related technologies. Technological advances have propelled once isolated and so-called Third World societies into contact with the products of modernity. Access to speedy and efficient information technology has facilitated the instantaneous flow of financial and industrial activities once hampered by national governmental controls. The result is a new commercial reality—the emergence of global markets for standardized consumer products on a previously unimagined scale.

Global markets are not new to the multinational corporation (MNC), which, by definition, does a substantial portion of its business in countries other than its home country. To qualify as a "true multinational," at least 25 percent of an organization's business must come from abroad; most large multinational companies do anywhere from 25 percent to 75 percent of their business outside their home country. Certain types of businesses have traditionally extended themselves to many countries: petroleum firms, motor vehicle manufacturers, pharmaceutical firms, computer companies, communications companies, some food and beverage/consumer products companies, and certain kinds of financial services firms.

During the late 1990s and the early 2000s, the trend toward globalization of business is expected to accelerate and the number and size of multinational companies are expected to grow, for a variety of reasons. First, the world is witnessing greater economic integration due to free trade agreements in Europe and North America. This is coupled by the emergence of new market-oriented economic systems in eastern Europe, Russia, and a number of Asian and Latin American nations. Second, businesses in the advanced countries face saturated, mature markets at home and are forced to pursue opportunities abroad. Finally, corporations in advanced countries are burdened with very high labor and production costs and so must seek cheaper sources of production in developing countries to remain competitive and viable.

Although familiar to MNCs, global markets represent a totally new ballgame for small companies now dealing with global marketing, logistics, and distribution issues associated with global sourcing: buying from suppliers worldwide; meeting customized demands of global customers; and tailoring selling, advertising, and marketing in these global markets. If you belong to a firm that has traditionally done business only within national borders and are apprehensive of the future, this is enough to throw your hands up in despair and seek the protective umbrella of bankruptcy courts to save your assets. If, on the other hand, you are aggressive, you will realize that this is an opportunity of a lifetime. The challenge is to understand the nuances of doing business in global markets using the tools and methods made possible by electronic commerce.

Many questions must be resolved before global markets become efficient. For instance, what are the implications of increasing business globalization on management practice? How must businesses adjust their administrative and information management systems to operate successfully throughout the world? What is the role of the Information Superhighway in the global marketplace? Clearly, there are more questions than answers. One main issue that businesses must resolve: What is the most effective organizational structure for the global marketplace?

## Organizational Structure: Vertical Versus Horizontal

The traditional approach views the organization as a collection of vertical departments or business units. More recently, horizontal or team-based organizations have come into vogue. These organizational forms emphasize implementing a smooth business process that cuts across functional boundaries. In the future, we can expect to see another organization form (software brokerage-based), where human agents and software agents work in tandem as internal business partners.

### The Vertical Organization

The vertical approach to corporate management poses two problems to smooth operations. First, it creates boundaries that discourage employees in different departments from interacting with one another. Second, departmental goals are typically set in a way that could cause friction among departments. For instance, goals for sales are typically set to maximize sales and pay little attention to account collection or service delivery. If a customer is unable to pay for the sales or if the correct quantity is not delivered on time to the right location, that is not a problem for sales; from its perspective, sales did its job and met its goals. Meanwhile, there is a disputed item in the company's accounts receivable. Is accounting or transportation the culprit? Are they the only losers in this situation? The question remains: How can such an organization achieve or sustain superior performance?

The vertical organization allows gaps to exist between employees from different departments and lacks a channel to facilitate interaction and communication. The lower the level in the hierarchy, the larger the gap. These gaps expand with geographic dispersion and corporate growth. Problems can result when a need arises for two departments to communicate at the lower level. Typically, resolving an issue originating at a lower level requires communication with a higher management authority, and after resolution the decision is then passed back down to the lower level. This structure consumes time and resources, and the lack of communication channels and practices clearly contributes to misunderstanding and frustration among departments.

Finally, three key ingredients are missing from the vertical organization chart: the product, the process, and the customer. Operating in a fast changing environment without a clear picture of such components, it would be difficult for top management to run a business effectively.

In short, a major drawback of the vertical organization is its failure to provide an environment that fosters understanding and cooperation between departments. To achieve this, many firms have begun to look at the organization structure from a horizontal perspective, by examining how work actually flows through the organization.

### The Horizontal Organization

The principal goal of horizontal management is to facilitate the smooth transition of intermediate products and services through its various functions to the customer. This is achieved by empowering employees, improving communication, and eliminating unnecessary work. The importance of having a clear view of how products and services flow from one department to another, and eventually, to the customer is apparent. Without a good understanding of the business process, it is almost impossible for management to function effectively. The marketplace may have been more tolerant of the inefficiency in the past, but this is clearly not acceptable in the current competitive environment.

The structure of a horizontal organization is two-tiered instead of multilayered, as seen in vertical organizations: a core group of senior management responsible for strategic decisions and policies, and a stratum of employees in process teams. The objective of a horizontal structure is to change the staff's focus from coordinating and reporting to improving flow management and work quality and increasing value for customers. The key is to align market needs, corporate strategies, and each of the core business processes; to identify the "disconnects"; and to ensure that each process adds value from the customer's perspective. Any process identified as nonessential to the attainment of business goals or customer satisfaction should be eliminated. Although the objectives seem reasonable on paper, they become rather vague and elusive during implementation because every group has a different view of what the goals should be and what information is needed to achieve them.

Information in the horizontal organization is processed at the local level by process teams. Team members are typically from the respective functions working in the process. Process teams can resolve problems quickly, and in this way permit the company to operate with flexibility and responsiveness in a continuously changing business environment. If successfully implemented, increased interaction of employees across departments fosters close working relationships and better communication. Employees from varied functions can obtain better understanding of one another's responsibilities, thus reducing costly conflicts arising as a result of misunderstanding and disagreement. The horizontal structure eliminates the need to devote resources to vertical communication. However, there is an increased need for coordination of the various parties involved.

## New Forms of Organizational Structure

As noted earlier, electronic commerce applications can alter how data are collected, how transactions are completed, and even what work humans do. It can also impact the way organizations are structured. Two new forms of organizational structure are becoming prominent—virtual or network structures and brokerage structures.

### Virtual or Network Organizational Structure

In recent years, virtual enterprises have gained much attention as more and more such firms have emerged in industries ranging from computer chip manufacturing to aircraft manufacturing. Today, the virtual label is used to describe everything from virtual reality to virtual offices to virtual communities. It is enough to confuse virtually any prospective manager. The concept of the virtual corporation is proving to be much more than another catchy phrase, however. With most companies already striving to do things better, faster, and smarter, the virtual model challenges managers to think about things that aren't even possible today.

What is the virtual corporation? The *virtual organization* is defined as being closely coupled upstream with its suppliers and downstream with its customers such that where one begins and the other ends means little to those who manage the business processes within the entire organization. In simplest terms, it is an organization having the essence or effect of a traditional corporation without the structure or appearance of one.

In the virtual organization, each separate firm retains authority in major budgeting and pricing matters and functions as part of a greater organization coordinated by a core firm acting as integrator of the actions done by the various partners. Interdependence among partners differentiates the virtual corporation from the traditional hierarchy. Experts say the virtual corporation offers the most extreme model of the externally focused organization, powered by time-based competition. Companies adept at coordinating and maximizing the capabilities of suppliers will gain more control over key elements of time—from overall order-to-shipment lead time to product-specific cycle time. In addition, full-fledged alliances that tap the resources of multiple parties will effectively slash product- or process-development time.

Virtual organizations have been variously referred to as network organizations, organic networks, hybrid arrangements, and value-adding partnerships. This phenomenon has been driven by the effort to achieve greater effectiveness and responsiveness in an extremely competitive environment marked by increasing globalization, technological change, and customer demands.

Examples of companies experimenting with the principles of virtuality have begun to surface in the real industrial world. One of the most successful is Cisco Systems, a maker of internetworking equipment (routers) that has experienced rocketing growth since the mid-1980s. The company attributes this success to a manufacturing strategy that has provided flexibility, huge capacity, and access to other firms' production expertise. Called "the extended factory," this strategy consists of carefully developing and managing relationships with manufacturing partners who handle all production except for final assembly, testing, and configuration. Partner firms are selected based on performance and work quality. They are reviewed quarterly and involved early on in the design of new products to take advantage of their manufacturing expertise. The result is a network of firms, with Cisco at its core, giving Cisco such competitive advantages as high quality, low inventory, rapid expansion capability, and low cost.

Aerospace giant Boeing is another virtual organization. In building its new 777, the company assembled a virtual network of partners that may remain intact for several years as its product, the airplane, may serve its market for ten to twenty years. In the auto industry, the virtual organization can be seen in GM and Ford, which once were so integrated that they made their own steel but are now outsourcing the fabrication of more than half the components for their cars. Such changes have often been referred to as a "return to core competencies."

### Understanding the Structure of Virtual Enterprises

Two major approaches are used to form virtual organizations: downward and lateral. Downward networking is initiated by a large, vertically integrated company seeking to reduce its overhead by outsourcing. Outsourcing has two purposes: to reduce costs associated with fixed assets and to maintain a focus on key operations. Outsourcing breaks down the company's vertical structure; for instance, a manufacturer once making all crucial parts now establishes a network of suppliers to provide needed parts. A company that successfully outsources becomes economically slimmer and more adaptive. To the extent that it cultivates long-term relationships with suppliers (rather than short-term, price-oriented contracts), the company functions as the core firm of a virtual enterprise.

The lateral approach is observed in small, specialized firms that, in the interest of seeking strategic alliances, form partnerships along a value-added chain (e.g., suppliers, manufacturers, and distributors). McKesson Corporation, a major distributor of pharmaceuticals and health care products in the United States, has been highly successful in developing value-adding partnerships that include manufacturers, distributors, and third-party insurance suppliers. Without acquiring the ownership headaches, the core firm of such a network can increase profits and reduce risks. Each such core firm can benefit by modeling the adaptivity and responsiveness of a small, specialized company and the scale economies of a large and integrated firm.

Some networks emphasize reliable supply and close cooperation in scheduling and quality requirements. This requires that firms thoroughly adapt to one another, strengthening the bonds between the core firm and other firms and stabilizing the network. For example, Ford and its supplying firms have formed a stable network in order to ensure a steady supply of parts. By their nature, some industries (fashion, toys, publishing) do not promote a stable customer–supplier relationship, resulting in a more dynamic relationship between the core firm and other firms in a network. This tends to occur when the competition is keen, the product development cycle is relatively short, and the rate of change is fast. The core firm of a dynamic network may simply operate as a brokerage that puts everything together by identifying and assembling assets owned by various firms in the network.

Naturally, virtual enterprises run risks of their own. For example, the firms with limited loyalty to the core firm are constantly exploring opportunities in other networks or markets. On the other hand, the core firm with a stable network of cooperating and committed partners must avoid becoming passive due to its strong relationships with its partners. Stagnation may prevent the core firm from eliminating unsatisfactory partners and injecting new blood into its network. When dealing with firms that are more opportunistic, as seen in a dynamic network, it is important that the core firm maintain an up-to-date, unbiased assessment of the value of each potential and existing partner in order to facilitate new product ideas and to open up new markets in a timely and appropriate manner.

### *Electronic Organizations and Brokerages*

Technological support for managing the creation and functioning of virtual firms is a special, but unexplored, aspect of electronic commerce. The specific issue is both complex and important because a poorly structured or managed virtual organization quickly degenerates into a chaotic entity. A consensus is emerging that the future "organization architecture" will be built and managed by electronic information brokerages staffed by software agents. In fact, with these new developments, the fully automated or "lights-out" office may only be a few years away.

The goal of electronic brokerages is to increase the efficiency of the internal marketplace. Internal markets are beginning to appear not only in corporations but even in nonbusiness institutions like the government. They are created inside organizations, allowing firms, suppliers, and government agencies to meet the new challenges of a fast-changing environment. A glimpse of this can be seen in what is happening in a number of large organizations that are decentralizing into autonomous business units to capture the dynamism of the marketplace. Many enterprises are abandoning their central-planning apparatus in favor of internal markets to foster internal competition, reduce costs, and increase efficiency.

In short, internal markets aided by computing will be replacing the organization structure of the past: vertically and horizontally integrated organizations. The changeover to internal markets is difficult even with the best planning, yet more organizations are moving in this direction because economic realities demand it. Corporations must master an intensely competitive global economy that requires massive technical and management innovation. These corporations, however, require a clear organizational structure to manage these work flows and the agents (or brokers) carrying out the work flow in the virtual organization.

To understand how the brokerage concept works, consider the following example in the retail industry. In Chicago and San Francisco, a company called Peapod is delivering groceries, liquor, prescriptions, and even subway tokens to more than 10,000 households. Using a PC, shoppers can browse through virtual aisles based on the way they want to shop—searching for foods offered as specials or scanning the dairy counter. After a customer types in an order, a Peapod employee sets forth with a wagon to pick up supplies and delivers them within three hours. Peapod is breaking barriers, as the company is getting people on computers who were not users before; some 75 percent of customers are women. They ring up big numbers too, five times higher than the $18 the typical walk-in customer spends. Teleshoppers pay an extra 12 percent on average for service, including delivery. Theoretically, when this pool of teleshoppers becomes substantial, a fancy grocery store situated on high-priced real estate becomes unnecessary. A warehouse will do.

Once we accept the premise that the future organizational structure will be an internal marketplace populated by specialized brokerages, questions surface about the structure of this marketplace. We chose the notion of brokerage to describe the internal marketplace because in the real world, brokerages are widespread (realtors, stockbrokers, tax accountants) and play an important role in facilitating efficient markets. Our working definition of an *electronic brokerage* is: multiple services provided by a single interface with a single point of accountability on an order-by-order basis. Brokerage service providers are intimately involved in the details of customer operations, end to end, in order to understand customer needs and deliver better service.

One such striking trend can already be seen in production and operations management (POM). In POM, we see the appearance of internal brokers for customer order management and for logistics and supply chain management. Figure 11.2 depicts an organization structured as an internal marketplace around the concept of brokerages. The focus of this internal market is to process a custom order as fast as possible and deliver it. The issues related

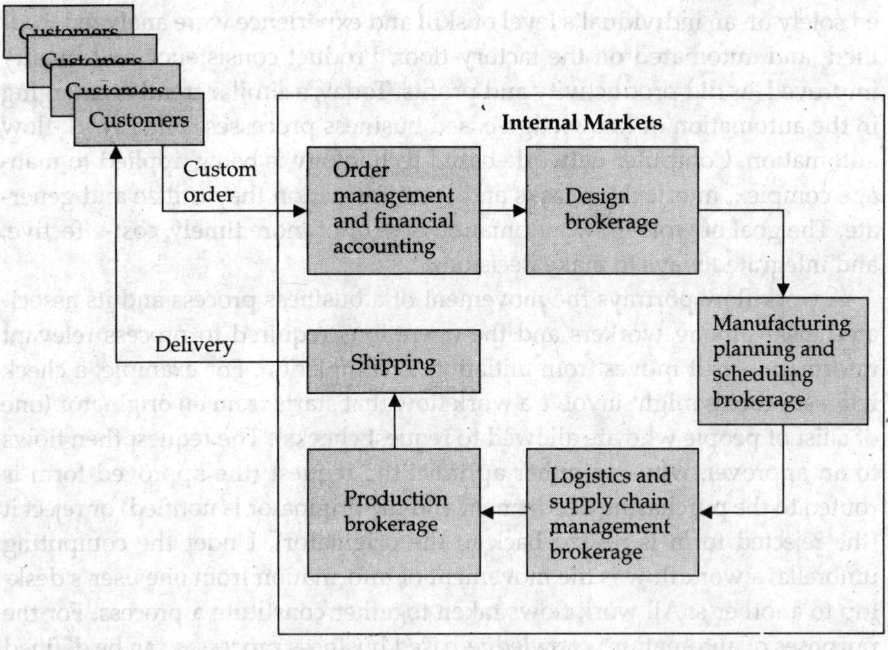


**Figure 11.2** Types of electronic brokerages in internal markets

to customization require that the firm be organized as a collection of electronic brokerages that coordinate among themselves to provide the best service to the customer.

Several important issues must be resolved before electronic brokerages become commonplace. For instance, how are these brokerages built in an electronic environment? How are they internally organized? What technology components are needed for a "good" brokerage? What language do brokerages use to coordinate internally and among themselves? What languages do they use to communicate with customers? These issues need to be addressed before efficient electronic markets can be created. Of these, work-flow automation and coordination issues are especially crucial.

## 11.3 WORK-FLOW AUTOMATION AND COORDINATION

In the last decade, a vision of speeding up or automating routine business tasks has come to be known as *work-flow automation*. This vision has its roots in the invention of the assembly line and the application of Taylor's Scientific Management Principles. Mechanical processes that had previously depended solely on an individual's level of skill and experience were analyzed, codified, and automated on the factory floor. Product consistency and quality improved, as did productivity and profits. Today, a similar trend is emerging in the automation of knowledge-based business processes called work-flow automation. Computer network–based technology is being applied to manage complex, interlocking tasks and the information they utilize and generate. The goal of work-flow automation is to offer more timely, cost-effective, and integrated ways to make decisions.

A work flow portrays the movement of a business process and its associated tasks among workers and the operations required to process relevant information as it moves from initiation to completion. For example, a check request process might involve a work flow that starts from an originator (one of a list of people who are allowed to request checks). The request then flows to an approver, who can either approve the request (the approved form is routed to the purchasing department and the originator is notified) or reject it (the rejected form is routed back to the originator). Under the computing umbrella, a work flow is the movement of information from one user's desktop to another's. All work flows taken together constitute a process. For the purposes of automation, knowledge-based business processes can be defined as sets of rules and milestones that define and control the flow of information.

Typically, work flows are decomposed into steps or tasks, which are then task ordered to determine which should be done first, second, and so on. Work flows can be simple or complex. Simple work flows typically involve one or two tasks, for example, an intelligent mail application helps prioritize and route a user's mail. On the other hand, a work-flow application that can move a purchase order through the approval process and track the actual delivery of the product from the supplier to the warehouse is a complex task. A complex work flow may involve several other work flows, some of which may execute simultaneously.

Another way of looking at work flows is to determine the amount of cross-functional activity. Old-fashioned managers, or "traditionalists," tend to manage most business functions as a series of independent and unrelated activities, or what has come to be known as "functional silos." However, current market forces are so compelling that one can no longer accept worn-out variations of the same basic approach.

Clearly, it is time to adopt a new business model, or "a paradigm shift," treating the overall business operations as an "extended enterprise" centered on the customer. In other words, companies must adopt an integrated process view of all the business elements. This view cuts across traditional departmental boundaries and manages the entire operational flow from start to finish. If successful, results include enhanced customer relationships, increasing leverage in the marketplace, reduced costs and inventories, and faster and more reliable deliveries of material and services.

Organizational integration is extremely complex and typically involves three steps: (1) improving existing processes by utilizing technology where appropriate; (2) integrating across the business functions after identifying the information needs for each process; (3) integrating business functions, application program interfaces, and databases across departments and groups. The ultimate goal is to ensure that all departments and end users have access to organizationwide data, rather than relying on proprietary data.

Organizations must consider the inevitable transformation that integration will force on the traditional relationships as departments move from an adversarial position within the firm to one of mutual cooperation. Companies must also look beyond the traditional organization boundaries to integrate processes and data with their customers, suppliers, other business partners, and regulatory agencies.

## Work-Flow Coordination

The key element of a market-driven business is the coordination of tasks and other resources throughout the company to create value for customers. To this end, effective companies have developed horizontal structures around small multifunctional teams that can move more quickly and easily than businesses that use the traditional function-by-function, sequential approach.

Some of the simplest work-flow coordination tools to understand and implement are electronic forms-routing applications such as Lotus Notes. These packages offer a network-based, automated alternative to paper documents (such as expense reports, purchase orders). A department manager, for example, might design an expense report form that is initiated by account executives, routed to an administrative assistant for error checking, then sent back to the manager for approval. After approving the report, the manager can print it out and send it to accounting for final settlement. The manager could also include an accounts payable person in the work flow, thus extending the routing process outside the sales department.

As the number of parties in the work flow increases, good coordination becomes crucial. To facilitate better work flow coordination, companies are using software agents (see Chapter 16).

## Work-Flow-Related Technology

Managerial talk paying homage to the team-based concept and cross-functional coordination alone is not sufficient unless it can be backed up with implementation. In other words, technology must be the "engine" for driving the initiatives to streamline and transform business interactions. Unfortunately, we are far from having any single toolkit that replicates a range of functions necessary for work-flow management.

Pressures for more comprehensive work-flow systems are building rapidly. Large organizations are realizing that they have a middle-management vacuum after all the downsizing and reorganization of the past few years. And it is now becoming clear what all those middle managers used to do: They were the organization's memory. At their best, middle managers knew how to get things done. They were the essence and means of coordination. They were the energy and activity of work flow. The hope is that information systems in general, and work-flow tools in particular, will supplement the organizational memory, the coordination, and the process support needed in the zone of the missing manager.

For now, work-flow systems are limited to factorylike work processes. For the foreseeable future, moreover, wide-scale work flow does not seem practical for all work environments. Realistically, then, work-flow systems will play a useful role in the important but boring world of repetitive, periodic work processes, especially relating to managing documents and images. Work flow in an unstructured context remains elusive, and the notion of comprehensive work-flow systems must be regarded as nothing more than a dream. It is best to focus attention on today's realities and the actual market trends that show some promise. Among them are the following:

- *Middleware is maturing.* Users or third-party providers need to learn how to develop work-flow applications within the middleware environment. For instance, Lotus Notes, to date the most successful groupware product, is more accurately described as "middleware"—not an application itself but an environment within which applications can be developed. But this is a proprietary environment. On the other hand, work-flow applications built on the Internet or public domain tools remain elusive.
- *Organizational memory is becoming practical.* The new tools for organizational memory are advancing toward what can be called the "corporate digital library." These tools are based on the premise that information is not a finished product but something that can be refined in new ways that are useful to different people at different stages in the work process.

Users, as usual, are caught in the middle. The great uncertainties surrounding work-flow environments mean hard choices must be made. What platform to choose? What environment to build from? What tools to invest in? The vendors are experimenting on corporate users, by necessity, because nobody really knows yet how to scale work-flow systems. And the users have no choice but to participate in this real-life experiment.

In sum, work-flow software electronically supports real-world collaborative activity. Work can be routed in ways that correspond to interoffice communications, in sequential routes, alternative routes, routes with feedback loops, circular routes, and more. A good work-flow package lets users specify acceptance criteria for moving work from one stage to the next. So, work flow brings the information to the people (and programs) who can act on it. It can also coordinate existing software and track processes to make sure the work gets done by the right people.

## 11.4 CUSTOMIZATION AND INTERNAL COMMERCE

Technology is transforming consumer choices, which in turn transform the dynamics of the marketplace and organizations themselves (see Fig. 11.3). Technology embodies adaptability, programmability, flexibility, and other qualities so essential for customization. Together they have created the promise of "any thing, any way, any time." Customers can have their own version of virtually any product, including one that appeals to masses rather than individuality if they so desire.

Think of a product or an industry where customization is not predominant. The car? Originally, Henry Ford's goal was to place a simple, all-black Model T in front of every home. His famous words were, "The customer can have any color as long as it is black." Today's models come in more than several thousand permutations and combinations, with options running the

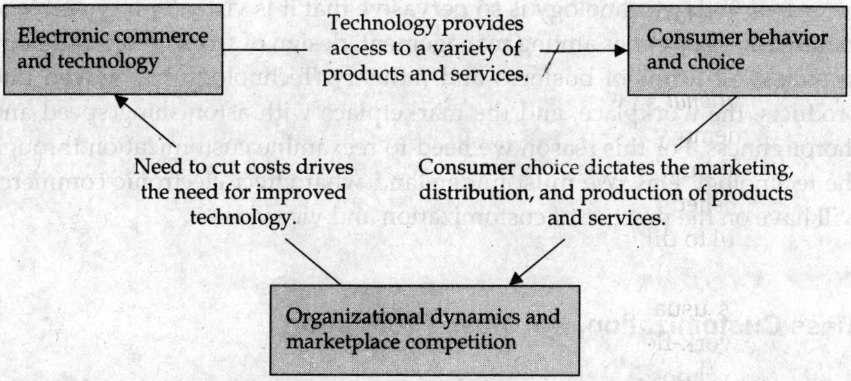


**Figure 11.3** The technology, choice, and marketplace triad

gamut from different colors and features to cellular phones as well as a variety of maintenance options.

How about a venerable product like the bicycle? According to an article in the *Washington Post*, the National Bicycle Industrial Company in Kokubu, Japan, builds made-to-order bicycles on an assembly line. The bicycles, fitted to each customer's measurements, are delivered within two weeks of the order. The company offers 11,231,862 variations on its models, at prices only 10 percent higher than ready-made models [RM91].

Customer-driven customization is becoming crucial because of too much choice. In 1800, the typical consumer in the United States had access to fewer than 300 products and about 500 square feet of retail space. In 1993, the consumer had access to more than one million consumer products and 15 million square feet of selling space. Purchasing decisions have become so complex that people spend, on average, more than 9 percent of their nonworking, nonsleeping time gathering information on products. Many predict that this continuing trend will give rise to a new occupation—an independent information broker who collects information and advises consumers on what to order or buy [AM93].

Not all markets are well suited for the application of the customization principles. Customers of really innovative products representing engineering breakthroughs (wireless technology) do not (yet) demand distinctive features because they have no idea what the product is all about. Similarly, customers of such commodity products as soybeans, oil, gas, and wheat, do not ask for product differentiation. In public utilities, government services, and other regulated markets customization can work both ways. It can make knowledgeable customers very happy by giving them a breadth of choice, or it can confuse customers into making choices they don't want or need.

Most of the written material and thinking about customization has neglected technology: It has been about management and the design of work processes. Today technology is so pervasive that it is virtually impossible to make clear distinctions among management, design of work, and technology in almost all forms of business and industry. Technology has moved into products, the workplace, and the marketplace with astonishing speed and thoroughness. For this reason we need to reexamine customization through the technology lens. We must understand what effect electronic commerce will have on the practice of customization and vice versa.

## Mass Customization, Not Mass Production

Today the walls that separated functions in manufacturing and service industries alike are beginning to fall like dominoes. As management takes a hard look at reducing cost and increasing productivity, the lines between functions may eventually blur and many organizational structures as we know them today will dissolve. The mass production mentality of the 1950s and 1960s has evolved into a surge toward mass customization. Shifting the focus from product development and manufacture onto the shoulders of market opportunity requires an unprecedented level of flexibility and radical responsiveness.

Customization need not be used only in the production of cars, planes, and other traditional products. It can also be used for textiles and clothing. For instance, Textile/Clothing Technology Corporation (TC2), a U.S.-government-funded textile industry research and development group based in Cary, North Carolina, used information taken at point-of-sale (POS) terminals to provide manufacturing instructions to computerized sewing machines and assembly-line workstations. Within four hours of placing orders, customers receive one-of-a-kind garments that were monogrammed to order. The POS scanner data also trigger rapid inventory replenishment systems (quick response systems) and indicate hot-selling items to retailers.

These capabilities are believed to hold the key to reviving the $202-billion textile and apparel industries. These industries have eroded steadily as manufacturers have moved offshore in search of cheap labor. By supplying retailers with information about what is selling quickly, U.S. apparel and textile firms may be able to counter foreign labor costs. Currently the average U.S. apparel manufacturer takes eleven weeks to mass produce a garment, and another fifty-five weeks goes into procuring raw materials, shipping, handling and storing inventories. All told, that's more than a year for production when retailers further up the value chain are looking to turn over inventories every few days in anticipation of customer demand.

Technology is also enabling new forms of customized production in the apparel industry. One process being explored is infrared body scanning, whereby a customer's measurements are taken with infrared signals and converted to digital information, which is fed into automated manufacturing equipment. When deployed, this particular technology could significantly change the way clothing is bought and sold. In one scenario, manufacturers could bypass retailers entirely by selling directly to customers whose measurements would be maintained in a computerized database. Customers could call and order what they want in their exact size, and their data would in turn be fed into automated manufacturing equipment capable of producing custom clothing. Another technology is radio frequency tags, which would eliminate the need for bar-coded labels and thus significantly reduce the time shippers and retailers now spend inputting this information into computer-based inventory systems. In one scenario, an RF tag about the size of a grain of wheat will be embedded in each and every garment, to give garments a unique fingerprint. RF tags could also be used for security at retail stores and even identify specific components so that a dry cleaner would know how to clean the garment. Other promising technologies include ultra-high-speed laser cutters, which cut single plies of fabric for customized garments at speeds of up to 200 inches per second, and a belt-printing system that allows customized designs to be screen-printed directly onto precut custom garment parts [CW94].

Clearly, the changes in agile apparel manufacturing extend well beyond the introduction of technology. Instead, a completely reengineered textile/apparel/retail pipeline is foreseen that will revolutionize the way clothing is designed, manufactured, and sold. We're talking about fundamentally changing the pipeline itself so that a garment can be digitally designed, sent to a retailer for approval, then printed and manufactured at the apparel company, all using a digital format in a matter of hours.

## Customization of Services

Customization is also becoming important in service industries, where product differentiation holds the key for attracting and retaining customers. Unlike manufacturing firms, organizations that provide services (banks, retail outlets, hospitals), as opposed to manufacturing products, have unique characteristics that warrant special attention. For example, service firms are more people-oriented and customers tend to participate actively in the service process. The operations function cannot be divorced from the marketing function, given that production and consumption occur simultaneously and that services cannot be inventoried. The resulting variations in demand present a challenge to the operations manager to use service capacity effectively.

An excellent example of customization of services is the entertainment industry. Take the Rolling Stones' 1994–1995 world tour, Voodoo Lounge. The so-called "CEO" and lead singer, Mick Jagger, noted in an interview with the CBS "60 Minutes" program (November 13, 1994) that his group is an example of a virtual organization with worldwide revenues of $300 million delivering customized entertainment services. The Voodoo Lounge is less a traditional corporation than a virtual corporation, because its staff of 250 full-time employees (except for the core group of five individuals) will disband after the tour ends.

What makes the Voodoo Lounge different from other organizations in the concert business is its sheer size and complexity. For instance, the stage, a futuristic monster with a 924-square-foot Sony video screen and a 92-foot-high cobra-shaped lighting tower, requires fifty-six trucks to haul from city to city. Because the set takes four days to set up, three stages leapfrog each other from city to city around the United States. Offshore, the stage is ferried around in two 747 cargo jets and a Russian military cargo plane.

Speed and concurrent activity are essential for success in any customized service. Like any large organization, several teams are working simultaneously to supply the stage, lighting, sound, and other elements of the Voodoo Lounge show. For instance, while workers were completing the stage at Veteran's Stadium (New York), a second crew was putting up the steel skeleton of the stage for the show three days later in Columbia, South Carolina, and a third crew was prepping the Liberty Bowl in Memphis. With labor costs reaching $300,000 per city, a network of portable computers and fax machines track costs in a budget operation as sophisticated as in any company.

Voodoo Lounge's fluid organization allows it to shift gears rapidly. For example, only 42 shows were scheduled before the tour opened, partly out of concern that the concert season was glutted with other big names such as Barbra Streisand. Once the tour was underway, they were able to add 23 more shows. With 65 shows in the United States and Canada, it is predicted that the tour will gross 25 percent more than the Stones' 1989 Steel Wheels tour, which earned a record $ 98 million [BWa94].

Odd as it may seem, the Stones' tour offers an excellent primer for executives eager to understand how to translate *virtual enterprises* into reality . One thing appears certain: The "virtual corporation" is not somewhere in the future, it is happening right now.

## 11.5 SUPPLY CHAIN MANAGEMENT (SCM)

Today, there is a growing realization that product excellence does not guarantee competitive advantage and profits. Many firms have been seeking a way of increasing profits through better management of their supply chain (network of partnerships) using technology and avoiding the extremes of either internalizing it or of outsourcing most functions. In the interest of acquiring an edge, these companies are beginning to use the supply chain network to reduce costs and complement their products with basic and value-added services [RSW95].

But supply chains need to be managed. Essentially, *supply chain management (SCM)* is an integrating process based on the flawless delivery of basic and customized services. Simply put, SCM optimizes information and product flows from the receipt of the order, to purchase of raw materials, to delivery and consumption of finished goods. SCM plays an important role in the management of processes that cut across functional and departmental boundaries. SCM goes beyond organizational boundaries, reaching out to suppliers and customers.

SCM is in stark contrast to the traditional approach, whereby executives think in terms of component activities such as forecasting, purchasing, production planning, or warehousing. Typically, these activities were managed in a fragmented manner, and so it was not uncommon to find them under separate functions that do not share information. Firms are now realizing that in a world of rapid response and order fulfillment, a company that is incapable of managing cross-functional processes may become extinct. For instance, new product development today invariably integrates diverse areas including R&D, marketing, engineering, manufacturing, logistics, finance, and law.

SCM is important in retailing because it helps manage the demand and supply functions. It is safe to say that many manufacturers have not reacted well to innovations in the distribution chain, where consolidation has shifted power to the hands of big supermarket chains and discount stores, as well as a few mega-wholesalers. These retailers and wholesalers, not to mention consumers, have forced brand-name companies to reengineer their marketing and logistics in an effort to strip out costs and add more value.

In electronic commerce, supply chain management has the following characteristics:

- An ability to source raw material or finished goods from anywhere in the world
- A centralized, global business and management strategy with flawless local execution
- On-line, real-time distributed information processing to the desktop, providing total supply chain information visibility
- The ability to manage information not only within a company but across industries and enterprises
- The seamless integration of all supply chain processes and measurements, including third-party suppliers, information systems, cost accounting standards, and measurement systems
- The development and implementation of accounting models such as activity-based costing that link cost to performance are used as tools for cost reduction
- A reconfiguration of the supply chain organization into high-performance teams going from the shop floor to senior management.

Figure 11.4 shows the two primary models of supply chain management: push versus pull. These models contain three primary elements:

1. *Logistics and distribution (integrated logistics).* Logistics is a relatively new discipline that deals with the integration of materials management and physical distribution. Although logistics and SCM are sometimes interchanged, think of SCM as an umbrella that incorporates the logistics function. Over the years areas such as materials management and distribution have evolved into logistics, which in turn has become one integral component of SCM.

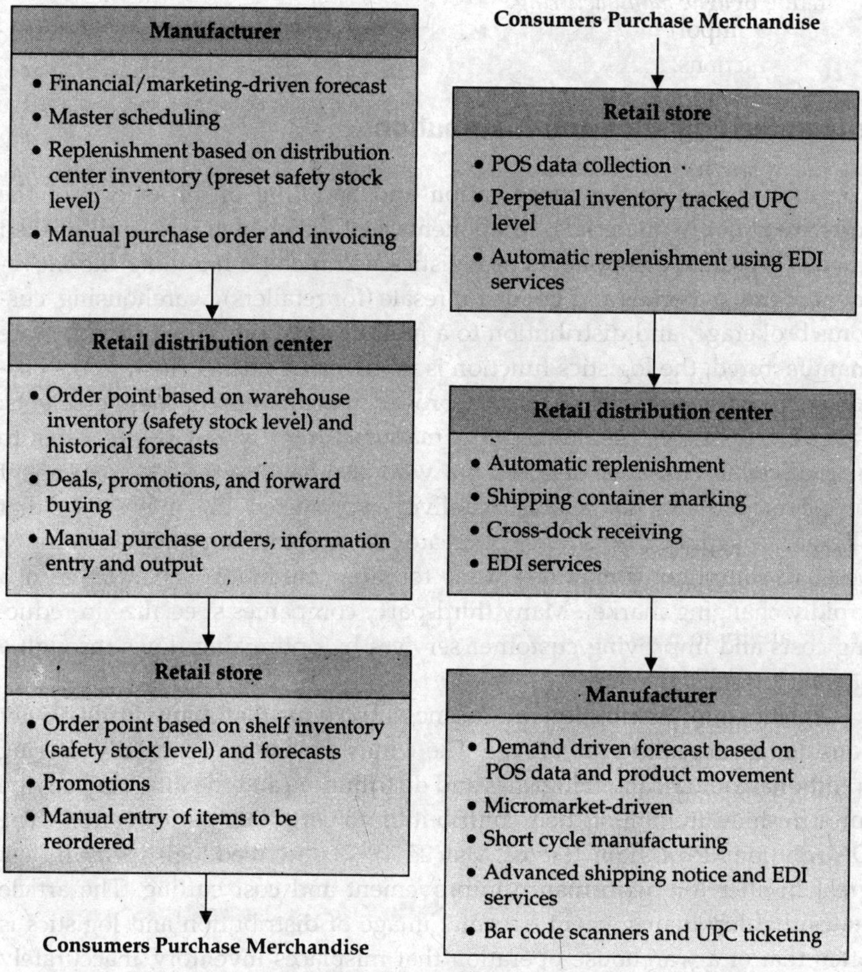


**Figure 11.4** Push-based supply chain vs. pull-based supply chain

2. *Integrated marketing and distribution.* Most managers often do not realize that order processing and fulfillment processes may exceed 15 percent of the cost of sales. Traditionally, the customer order process is initiated by sales personnel, who have an in-depth understanding of the customers' product and service requirements. In electronic commerce, the order process could be initiated by marketing information systems such as point-of-sale systems. Today, with the aid of technology, we are able to integrate the customer directly and react to changes in demand by modifying the supply chain.

3. *Agile manufacturing.* Consumers and manufacturers are stressing quality and speed. One of the most influential visions of production goes by the name of *agile manufacturing.*

## Integrated Logistics and Distribution

Logistics applies to the coordination and handling of all aspects of the movement of raw materials, components, semifinished goods, and finished goods. Typically, components of logistics will include handling the movement of raw materials and goods for resale (for retailers), warehousing, customs brokerage, and distribution to a final destination. When products are manufactured, the logistics function is involved in getting them to the customer. Huge savings result from improved coordination of these elements. Take, for instance, customized PC manufacturers who have to cater to unpredictable customer demand but who also have to rely on component suppliers who may not be able to deliver as promised. The inference is that alternative supply chains must be created to deal with supplier uncertainty, because computer companies want to carry minimum inventories in a rapidly changing market. Many third-party companies specialize in reducing costs and improving customer services by optimizing flows through a client's logistics pipeline.

Logistics and distribution are business functions that many firms do not consider a competitive advantage. The winds of change are rapidly altering traditional thought about logistics and distribution, and the time may be ripe for a fresh evaluation of their contribution to corporate performance. "The Distribution Revolution" (*Forbes*, May 25, 1992) described logistics as the last great frontier for performance improvement and cost cutting. The article states that top management's mental image of distribution and logistics is often that of a warehouse operation that misplaces inventory, inaccurately picks and ships products, and wastes manhours. Enlightened companies, however, are now discovering creative methods of adding value, cutting costs, and increasing speed throughout their entire supply and manufacturing/operations distribution chain. Logistics and distribution can add up to as much as 30 to 40 percent of total cost for some businesses. Wal-Mart, United Parcel Service, Compaq Computers, and others have made innovative distribution and logistics processes a cornerstone of their competitive strategy.

Why has logistics become so important? Companies are finding it difficult to predict demand and on this basis to plan production and materials procurements, due to variations in consumer demand and the unprecedented numbers and variety of products on the market. As a result, inaccurate demand forecasts are increasing and, along with them, the costs of those errors. Many managers, believing speed to be the solution, are turning to production-scheduling systems. These tools tackle only the visible part of the problem iceberg, however, and leave the other hidden 90 percent untouched.

What's really needed is a way to improve forecasts and simultaneously redesign logistics processes to minimize the impact of inaccurate forecasts. Supply chain management provides a way to view the entire forecasting, planning, and production process, beginning with figuring out what forecasters can and cannot predict well. Then supply chains must be made fast and flexible so that managers can postpone decisions about their most unpredictable items until they have some market signals (like early-season sales results) to use in matching supply with demand. Supply chain management enables companies to use the power of flexible manufacturing and shorter cycle times much more effectively. Logistics is the heat that forges the supply chain.

## Purchasing and Inbound Logistics

Logistics is now replacing the classic supply chain for procuring materials—planner to buyer to salesman to supplier plant—with a more streamlined process whereby the "in-plant" planner operating directly from the computer system sends the purchase orders to the supplier plant, in effect eliminating the middlemen on both sides.

We have already described the EDI process between the buyer and the supplier (see Chapter 10). The EDI process works very well when everything is going well. To illustrate EDI, let's look at a traditional usage, supplier scheduling. This process begins when the planner requisitions the buyer. The buyer then sends the purchase order to the supplier's sales department via EDI, and the sales department then communicates the order to the planner in the supplier's plant. This process is summarized in the following figure:

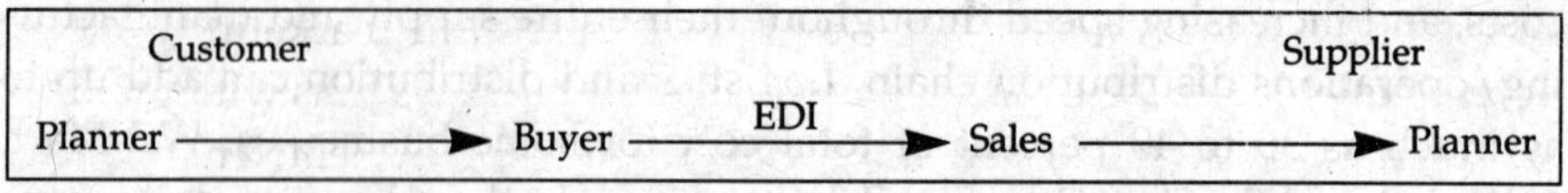


If a problem occurs on the supplier's side due to labor problems or whatever, the planner at the supplier's end notifies the sales department, which in turn passes the information to the buyer. The corporate buyer then passes this information back to the original requester. This reverse flow of information is as follows:

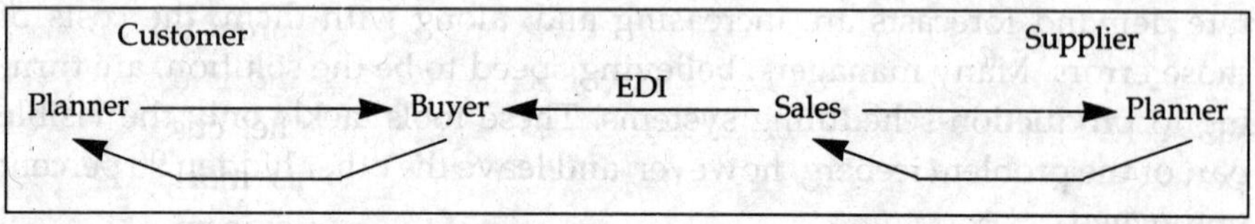


Now let's say that the revised delivery dates are not satisfactory because the buyer will incur financial hardships, so the planner informs the buyer:

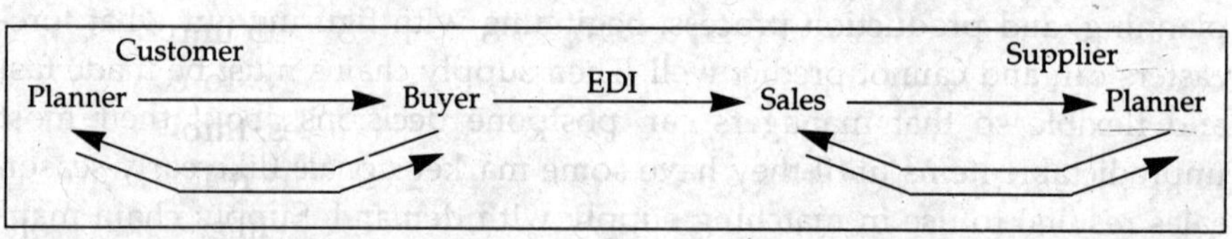


This inefficient communication flow would be unnecessary if all the information were available on-line to the planner before the communication chain started forming. Efficient decision-making requires that the customer planner have access to pertinent information that the supplier is willing to publish and use it to perform activities such as negotiation, value analysis, rescheduling, and capacity planning. This form of information sharing can take place only with the development of digital corporate libraries (see Chapter 12).

## Integrated Marketing and Logistics

The highly competitive environment of the 1990s means that marketing must do more than sell. Marketing must define the way a company does business. For instance, in any customer-oriented industry, supply chain management begins with information obtained at the checkout counter, but getting cost-conscious customers to the checkout line depends a great deal on marketing promotions such as coupons for consumer packaged goods in grocery and drugstores. Promotion has traditionally been part of the marketing function, which may not see the need to integrate its computer systems with the logistics planning systems to perform supply chain management. This philosophy is no longer viable in a market-driven environment. In this time of exploding choice, cutthroat competition, and unpredictable shifts in demand, integrated marketing could be the key to survival.

Sales, advertising, and marketing are fast emerging as hot subjects for technology-oriented business professionals. Spurred on by the desire to use information technology more competitively, companies have begun to scrutinize the interface with their customers and are realizing that they do not understand marketing at all in the electronic age. It is apparent that marketing is a virgin territory from a technological viewpoint and is underdeveloped and underutilized as a business weapon in the customization paradigm. Broadly speaking, technology is changing firms' marketing edge in several areas: in manufacturing and logistics planning; in management analysis of new markets; in identifying and targeting customers; in promotion of the allied areas of direct marketing and telemarketing; and finally in postsales (keeping the customer happy through on-line customer service).

The challenge for marketing arises from the fact that with unprecedented choice, companies face the end of customer brand loyalty. To combat that threat, they often increase their sales and marketing forces, throwing costly resources at the market as a way to retain customers. The real solution, of course, is not more marketing but more intelligent marketing. That means marketing must find ways to integrate the customer into the company, to create and sustain a relationship between the company and the customer, and use the information garnered from the customer for downstream activities.

Today, order processing starts with influencing the customer to buy a product. To understand this change, let's focus on one area where technology is having a major impact: retailing. For many retailers, strident competition has forced a restructuring. This is a consolidating industry, and experts predict that 20–35 percent of existing supermarkets may disappear in the next five years, for two main reasons: cutthroat pricing and innovation.

Supermarkets that plan to survive on price have to compete with giants like Wal-Mart, which is building 180,000-square-foot supermarket/discount supercenters at a rate of 100 a year. (A large supermarket, by comparison, runs 60,000 square feet.) In developing supercenters, Wal-Mart has unearthed a secret: The supermarket industry is not particularly good at distributing products. For years the standard assessment of the industry was something like: "Wow, they can operate at a 1-percent net profit on a 24 percent gross profit margin. They must be geniuses." Wal-Mart, which makes three times as much on a gross margin of 21 percent, arrived at another conclusion: "Traditional supermarkets take home a penny on every 24 cents of gross profit? They must be really inefficient" (*Fortune*, May 15, 1995). That gap between what supermarkets earn and what Wal-Mart and other big superstores earn creates a vacuum that cannot be ignored. Wal-Mart sees it as an opportunity to build efficient superstores based on superior distribution called efficient customer response.

## Efficient Customer Response (ECR)

The retail industry is pinning its hopes for better margins on *efficient consumer response* (ECR). Theoretically, ECR is expected to reduce costs by $30 billion, about 10 percent of the total, by reforming the retailing industry's buying habits and moving toward continuous product replenishment (CPR) to get inventory into the stores faster. The average grocery product takes more than 100 days to replenish inventory. In contrast, customers can get a car custom built and delivered in 42 days.

To really understand how a large ECR system is implemented, let us look at a data architecture developed to make transaction-level data from point-of-sale systems useful and legible to front-office buyers, logistics personnel, and senior managers. Effective inventory management—having just the right amount of the right merchandise on the shelves for just the right amount of time—minimizes overstocking and markdowns, and so boosts profitability.

We have chosen an integrated logistics system implemented at Mervyn's department stores [DBMS94] to illustrate the ECR concept. Mervyn's is a division of Dayton Hudson, the Minneapolis-based retailing giant whose holdings also include Target, and Marshall Field. Today, Mervyn's accounts for approximately 25 percent of Dayton Hudson's annual sales. It is managed as a promotional department store focused on "trend-right" clothing and home fashions at competitive prices. This finely tuned business required that inventory management and buyers have an identical view of the performance (both in units sold and sale prices) for some 300,000 stock-keeping units (SKUs) in 286 stores.

The data collection process proceeds as follows:

1. POS data from retail stores "trickle" into an IBM mainframe in a data center several times a day via a satellite-based network.
2. The data—transaction-level detail from each store's POS controller, summarized by SKU store—are downloaded on a daily basis from the mainframe to the UNIX server.
3. On the UNIX server, the raw production data (approximately 500 Gigabytes (GB)) are loaded into database tables. The parallel loading and

index-building features of modern databases are used to handle the huge influx of information.

4. Once updated, managers at their desktop PCs linked by TCP/IP networks can access the database.

Although the database/UNIX combination provides the necessary query processing performance, the heart of the environment—from the business user's perspective—is a sophisticated client decision support application. The client application focuses on trend analysis, merchandise performance analysis, and inventory stock management and provides users with the ability to customize their views of information and ways of performing their analyses through custom filters that save sales, inventory, financial, and vendor criteria of interest to the user. In addition, the application will use agent alerts and capabilities to sift through the data warehouse for exceptions and notable trends and will notify appropriate users of significant data changes. In addition, the client application enables the integration of data into desktop applications, simplifying the sharing and distribution of analyses.

Another fascinating example of efficient ECR comes from the world of toys. Bad forecasting could result in the stockpiling of large toy inventories in distribution centers, tying up both money and space. Let's examine one successful company in this area: U.S. toy giant Toys "R" Us, with over 900 stores and $9–$10 billion in sales. Toys "R" Us also has over 350 international toy stores.

Toys "R" Us avoids direct competition with wholesale clubs by not carrying the same items, and it has been particularly successful versus discount stores, in part due to very good marketing programs. For instance, a major catalog coupon promotion allowing 20 percent discounts recently distributed a total of 52 million books in newspapers and another 3 million through its stores in one month alone. The strategy worked extremely well because of an effective supply chain management system built around a satellite communication system linking all its domestic stores.

The system also links suppliers with EDI for purchase orders and receives advance shipping notices from many. All sales information is captured at the cash register and communicated by satellite. Labor scheduling is on-line, and Toys "R" Us is linking new systems for personnel and payroll management with its supply chain system. Toys "R" Us has also been increasing the size of its distribution centers (DCs) and upgrading their capabilities. The company believes that a mere fifteen to seventeen DCs in the United States will be able to handle 900 stores. Toys "R" Us has been involved in a program of reducing its inventories and wants just-in-time service everywhere it does not have long dating—products (e.g., batteries) that must be sold quickly.

To summarize, the advantages of ECR are obvious. Buyers and inventory analysts can now look on-line and see, by advertising zone, how sales of products peak and trough over a season or how they vary across regions or stores. In the past, this was a long process that required the analyst to consult both on-line and off-line data sources. Today, better in-house systems enable managers and buyers to do three things: analyze the performance of standard and trend items in stores; spot, on a daily basis, upswings and downturns in the performance of trend merchandise; and replenish or authorize markdowns for trend items, as necessary, to take advantage of the buying trends in the stores. In addition, these managers and buyers acquired the ability to associate that information with in-store, print, and television advertising campaigns and advertising zones, as well as perform trend analysis across a reasonable period of time (ideally, sixty weeks). Other uses include detailed analysis of item performance, what-if scenario evaluation, and exception reporting and handling.

## Agile Manufacturing

Promotions must be closely tied to agile manufacturing capability. Agile manufacturing calls for flexibility and quick response to changing market conditions, customer demands, and competitor actions. In an ever-changing environment, people, processes, units, and technology reconfigure to give customers exactly what they want. Managers coordinate independent, capable individuals, and an efficient linkage system is crucial. Result: low-cost, high-quality, customized standard goods and services.

At first glance, agile manufacturing may sound like another way of describing the lean/flexible manufacturing approach, which calls for the elimination of inventory and other forms of "waste," greater flexibility in production scheduling, shortened lead times, and advanced levels of quality in both products and customer service. Result: efficient use of resources. Lean production is regarded by many as simply an enhancement of mass-production methods. The traditional mass-production company is bureaucratic and hierarchical. Under close supervision, workers repeat narrowly defined, repetitious tasks. Result: low-cost, standardized goods and services.

Agility implies breaking out of the mass-production mold and producing highly customized products—when and where the customer wants them. In a product-line context, it amounts to striving for economies of scope—ideally serving ever-smaller niche markets, even quantities of one, without the high cost traditionally associated with customization—rather than economies of scale Also, agile manufacturing requires an enterprisewide view, whereas lean production is typically associated only with the factory floor. Agility also embodies such concepts as rapid formation of multicompany alliances to introduce new products to the market.

Recall that the actual manufacturing process is increasingly being absorbed into the larger infrastructure. Just as concurrent engineering dropped the walls between design and manufacturing through the sharing of information, people, and tasks, the agile manufacturing model emphatically declares that organizations "drop all walls." In short, agile manufacturing requires an integrated applications environment with common access to services for users. Such integration can extend beyond an organization to include business partners—customers and suppliers.

Agility is essential in a future that requires new and innovative manufacturing practices, among them the following:

- Customers "custom design" products such as automobiles and clothing, electronically transmitting their requirements to remote locations capable of quickly manufacturing and distributing these products.
- Companies rapidly and easily form alliances to produce new products, employing advanced manufacturing concepts such as agile and virtual manufacturing.
- Small and medium-sized companies advertise their manufacturing capabilities over computer networks and efficiently bid on projects required by other companies.
- "Software system brokers" connect users who need temporary access to sophisticated manufacturing tools that would normally be too expensive to acquire.
- Manufacturers and suppliers use "intelligent" procurement systems to facilitate and speed parts procurement, billing, and payment transactions, reducing costs, improving accuracy, and meeting customer demands in a timely manner.

Agile manufacturing requires companies to have more than just the fast, lean, and proactive virtues of the 1980s. Agility resides in the provision of a product, rather than in any single company. The "agility" visionaries like to talk of virtual enterprises, ad hoc coalitions built around a promising new idea. An idea is born, a design is made, a design is verified, parts are built, a product is assembled, marketed, shipped: A need is fulfilled. Each step could be done by someone different; the last step is the product of the whole.

There are various preconditions for success in an agile venture. One is clear communication channels between involved parties. Most important, however, is predictability through management. The essence of agility is sensitivity to time, to knowing a company's capabilities and the time it needs exactly. New factory management technologies make this possible. When a product is being assembled, management must know precisely the dimensions of its parts—not in breadth, length, and depth—but in terms of such things as process time and quality. At present, few companies can accurately measure themselves in many of these dimensions.

In summary, the agile manufacturing enterprise seeks to achieve the following:

- *Greater product customization,* or manufacturing to order, would come at relatively low unit cost.
- *Rapid introduction of new or modified products*—in some cases, through quick formation of temporary strategic partnerships—takes advantage of brief windows of opportunity in the marketplace. These alliances would blend together talents or "core competencies" of the partners, combining pieces of each organization into a new virtual enterprise or virtual corporation.
- *Interactive customer relationships* transform the physical product into a platform for providing an evolving set of value-adding services.
- *Dynamic reconfiguration of production processes* would accommodate swift changes in product designs or entire new product lines.

## 11.6 SUMMARY

The explosion in electronic commerce methods and technology will impact all aspects of workflow/transaction management, customization, and supply chain management, from the tools available to make decisions to the automation of processes. As clearly evident, the stakes are high. Companies that understand the workings and business issues of electronic commerce will find ways to use them to their advantage. Those that don't will drop behind. It is not a simple matter of whether to implement electronic commerce but one of reexamining strengths, weaknesses, and options and developing strategic plans that will link the business firmly to the future.

Once businesses move toward internal commerce, management, business processes, and market structure will be irrevocably altered. To maximize the effectiveness of systems for supporting internal commerce, these structures must be well integrated with the other functional policies of the firm and affect all production sources. This requires cooperation between management and employees, for these business processes will change from the traditional, hierarchical structure to a more virtual or network structure that meets the needs of three broad business needs: demand creation, demand fulfillment, and support activities. That change will not be bounded by company boundaries.

Today, alliances and partnerships between companies are springing up and changing market and organizational structures almost overnight. As competition and cooperation are rapidly becoming the norm, companies realize they must find partners or perish.

An increasingly sophisticated technology is coming to the desktop, but a delicate balance must be struck between the centralization of decision making and the decentralization of execution. For this, the sharing of the information among workers will be crucial. To promote this sharing of information, a primary player will be a networked digital library.

Chapter 12

# The Corporate Digital Library

Today, most internal electronic commerce systems, whether centralized or dispersed, concentrate on business transaction data. This focus is essential and few companies of any size can keep pace without automating routine transactions. Yet transactions barely affect key strategic decisions, and managers are likely to view them as clerical in nature. Strategic and operational decisions, and the implementations of those decisions, are the lifeblood of every organization. In fact, it is safe to speculate that the next wave of internal commerce will be aimed at decision support.

Whether managers can conduct effective, coordinated operations depends on their ability to access and utilize the right information at the right time. Managers and workers need to obtain information regarding their own situation, including the customers, suppliers, and other departments in the areas of interest and, of course, the disposition of a competitor through market intelligence. The totality of the information relevant to a manager can be referred to as the *operational picture*. The challenge is to provide managers with the most accurate, comprehensive, and consistent operational picture that technology will allow, under the presumption that an improved operational picture will improve the ability of the company to conduct operations effectively and efficiently [RSW95].

Companies are generating a lot of data but lack the tools to analyze that information for better decision making. Future data acquisition capabilities will be able to collect enormous quantities of information regarding conditions in distribution channels. This information, together with the vast information resources linked to the highly interconnected computer networks, represents a data mining, filtering, and display problem of substantial magnitude. The challenge is twofold: (1) to pull together the technology for amassing operational information and (2) to maximize the utility of existing information to managers. In addition to conventional sources of information such as text messages and data, managers will have access to the burgeoning "infosphere" of publicly accessible and proprietary data repositories of scanner data, technical documentation, on-line inventory, and market intelligence analyses.

Clearly, there is a large demand for tools to help corporations manage the information overload. Several solutions have been proposed. The following is a multiple-choice test for the reader: Which of the following is/are expected to help improve a company's competitive position in the 1990s? Please check the correct answer(s).

a. Decision Support Systems (DSS)
b. Management Support Systems (MSS)
c. Visual Information Access and Analysis (VIAA)
d. Data/Information Warehouses
e. Structured Document and Imaging Databases
f. Executive Information Systems (EIS)
g. Business Intelligence Systems (BIS)
h. On-line Analytical Processing (OLAP)
i. Multidimensional databases (MDD)
j. All of the above

If you checked (J), then you've been doing your homework. If you look at these options closely, you will notice that in a majority of the cases the focus of information processing is on analysis of data for the purpose of strategic and operational decision support. Vendors and industry analysts are using all these choices to describe the three key decision support trends:

1. Digital information infrastructure consisting of documents and data
2. Better utilization of information in strategic and operational decision making, which involves effective on-line information search and retrieval in a distributed environment
3. Architecture for implementing decisions through work-flow automation and business process integration

These trends are converging, and the result is a very novel decision support systems (DSS) architecture. In fact, DSS represents one of the key technologies of electronic commerce, allowing corporations to unlock useful information hidden away in operational databases to make more timely and better informed decisions. Companies are increasingly implementing separate decision support systems, distinct from their operational systems, to more effectively manage decision-enabling information. Organizations as diverse as banks, retail chains, and telecommunications companies are architecting unified decision support databases—in the form of data warehouses and document libraries—as repositories of historical data from which to do analysis as well as to support such decision support applications as executive information systems and micromarketing database solutions.

This chapter will provide a framework for understanding the various parts of an internal electronic commerce system that is tailored for decision support, but first we will examine the dimensions of the information systems for supporting on-line commerce. From the ensuing discussion of the requirements of the basic architecture, we will develop the underlying information systems that contain the data and documents needed for effectively supporting commerce and decisions pertaining to commerce.

## 12.1 DIMENSIONS OF INTERNAL ELECTRONIC COMMERCE SYSTEMS

Imagine a future electronic organization, with on-line suppliers, departments, workers, information brokerage services, and more. Electronic agents will roam the network, carrying out orders and negotiating with other agents. Millions of transactions and oceans of multimedia data will flow through the network every day, creating an "infosphere."

One main key to effective utilization of the infosphere is to provide managers with automated aids able to discover, retrieve, and display information relevant to the operations being conducted, regardless of whether the manager is aware of the existence of such information or able to explicitly direct that such information be retrieved from specific sources. Ideally, a good human–machine interface would facilitate discovery, acquisition, and analysis of useful information, filter information for relevance and importance in the context of current or projected operations, and then portray the resulting information in a rational and understandable fashion.

The volume and complexity of transactions, and the richness of the data on which they operate, will create the need for new enabling technologies:

- *User modeling and interaction layer.* Empowering workers of any enterprise to provide insight relevant for crucial decisions will be the key indicator of success in the electronic marketplace. In a competitive environment, where change is the only constant, workers must cultivate the ability to anticipate and quickly respond to market dynamics.

- *Mobile agents.* Consumers will have personal agents that look after their interests. Businesses will deploy agents to sell their wares on the network. "Sniffer" agents will look for trends and gather statistics. Agent technologies include cross-platform scripting engines, work-flow engines, and an infrastructure that lets agents live on any machine on the network.
- *Rich transaction processing.* Transactions will span servers for information search and retrieval, execute over long periods of time as they travel from server to server, and move securely between departments. Servers will handle massive transaction loads as more and more people come on-line.
- *Document and data management.* From anywhere on the network, workers will create, store, view, and edit structured and compound documents with multimedia content, and of course, relational data (e.g., SQL databases). Servers will provide repositories for storing and distributing massive numbers of documents.

The emergence of an infosphere will provide massive amounts and diverse types of digital information. That infosphere will require new, more powerful methods and organizational structures or institutions for finding and using information. One such electronic institution is an information brokerage, which mediates between the users and the vast information resources. This new institution will be staffed by workers in the form of software agents.

The foregoing trends are expected to help corporations gain a competitive edge through better access, analysis, and delivery of business information. The architecture for supporting internal commerce, shown in Fig. 12.1, can be divided into five key areas:

1. Modeling of users and tasks so that intelligent software can decide what to search for and how to integrate search results
2. Developing an efficient technology architecture to utilize information
3. Agent and work-flow architecture that acts as a broker in searching, retrieving, and analyzing the information
4. Navigation and retrieval methods that locate and filter multimedia information appropriate for a particular user and task; also, methods of portraying information that are appropriate for the task and for the environment in which it is carried out
5. An information infrastructure layer that represents the vast network of information resources

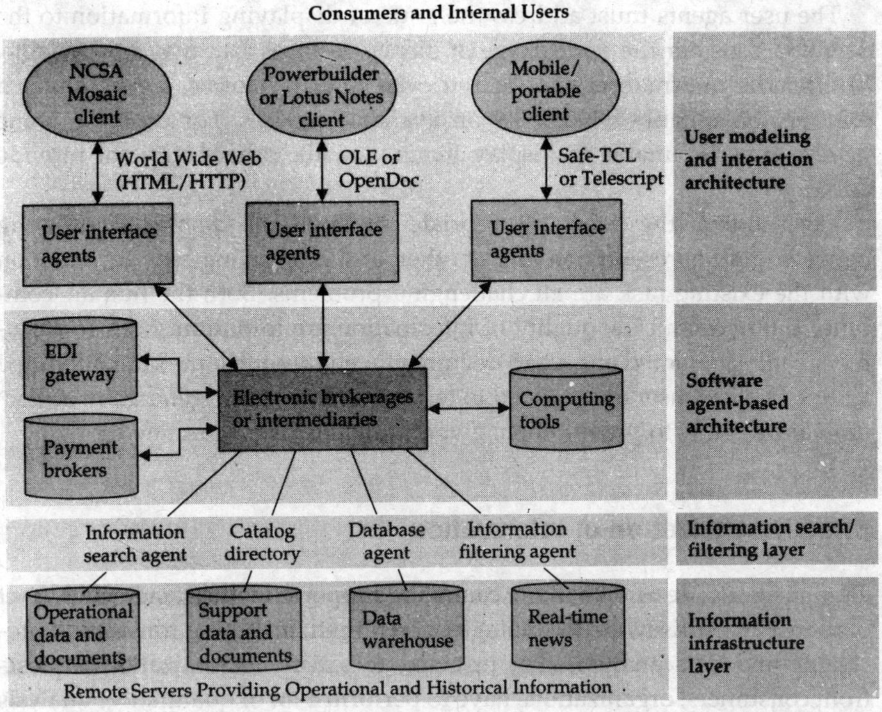


**Figure 12.1** Technological architecture for internal commerce

## User Modeling and Interaction

User models are interposed between the user interface and information sources to filter the available information according to the needs of the task and the user. Of necessity, then, these models must be customized, because what is important for one task and worker at a given time may be irrelevant to another.

Associated with each task or each person is a user agent or set of user agents. The agents maintain the models and the current state of the task and are responsible for determining what information is needed at each step of the task. The agents initiate searches, which may be performed by other agents, for the information. When information is returned, it must be appropriately combined with other information and displayed to the user. Depending on the task, it may also be necessary to communicate with other agents or users to request or provide information or to collaborate on a task. It then becomes necessary to provide a means of ensuring that the common information and task models are consistent.

The user agents must address the issue of displaying information to the user and consider the wide range of display devices that may be available. Multimedia information may be retrieved in many forms, some of which may not be suitable for display on available devices. For example, some devices may be unable to display pictures, while others may not provide audio.

Determining the most appropriate methods of display, translating between one representation and another, and integrating new information with the existing task are all challenging problems. Both the human–computer interface and the quality of information are important (a good document badly presented and a bad document well presented are both of limited value). In short, user agents need to tackle two issues: the generation of documents and how to present them given the available output devices.

## Effective Utilization of Information

Organizational decision making cannot be supported with a single tool. A set of robust enterprisewide technologies is required, including transaction processing and data analyses. For instance, to satisfy customization requests from consumers, organizations have to perform a lot of quantitative analysis for verifying whether (1) an on-line order can be met; (2) an on-line order would be profitable for the firm; and (3) what resources need to be committed to the order. Answering these questions requires decisions to be made quickly based on analysis of information.

Let's assume that Tom is in the on-line marketplace and wants to order a customized product. On the on-line order form on his NCSA Mosaic browser, he selects various features that he wants in the product and inputs the price range that he is willing to pay. This request spawns an order that must be analyzed by the organization for (1) design (Can all the requested features be designed; do the parts fit together properly?); (2) production (If the design is feasible, can it be produced with the existing machines or parts?); (3) logistics (What parts need to ordered from whom?); and (4) profitability (Is it profitable to produce the product given such variables as back orders and inventory?). Based on answers to these questions, the firm can accept or reject the order. To figure out on-line the viability or suitability of the order, the firm must gather information from various sources (servers).

### *Types of On-line Transactions*

Two types of information processing often take place in electronic commerce: on-line transaction processing (OLTP) and on-line analytic processing (OLAP). There are fundamental differences between these kinds of processing. OLTP involves the detailed, day-to-day procedures such as order entry and order management, in which data can be updated and for which clerks demand short response time. OLTP also incorporates access to operations data. Operational access refers to the current state of specific instances of data for problem solving. For example, operational access implies understanding the state of the company by answering questions such as: What is the status of order ABC? Has that order shipped on time? Has the customer been invoiced? Has the customer paid for the shipment? During production, how many times has part XY failed to meet the necessary quality criteria? Most organizational applications have been designed to handle this type of operational activity. EDI and consumer order processing systems fall under the OLTP umbrella.

Analytic processing refers to the activities involved in searching the wealth of data residing throughout an enterprise for trends, opportunities, or problem areas. To spot trends and exceptions in business conditions, managers need tools that can access a wide variety of data—quickly. On-line analytical processing enables decision makers to slice and dice data quickly, allowing for easy identification of trends and exceptions.

In the past two decades, the focal point of corporate computing has slowly shifted from a purely operational arena to an analytical one. Analytic access implies access to large volumes of data for higher-level assessment, planning, and strategic decision support activities. Typically, analytic access deals with questions such as: How many orders did we ship this past quarter by product line and by sales channel? If we decide to reduce our direct sales force by 30 percent in favor of more telemarketing and direct mail, what would be the likely impact by product line? If we decide to produce XYZ, how should the supply chain be designed and managed? What are the underlying reasons for product KLM costing more than initial estimates?

In the absence of on-line documents and data from which to deduce answers to these informational access questions, decision makers have relied on manual data gathering, talking to knowledgeable people, and more often than not, intuition. These nontechnical approaches are slowly being usurped by OLAP. OLAP is the hidden element of electronic commerce that is key to its success and allows corporations to unlock useful information hidden away in operational databases to make more timely and better informed decisions. These decisions can vary from customization decisions (Is it profitable to customize product XYZ with features A, B, and C?), logistics decisions (Should we order more of product XYZ and keep it in stock as the holiday season approaches?), and micromarketing (Is it effective to target product XYZ at population segments M, N, and O?).

## Navigating the Infosphere

Navigating the infosphere involves two related activities: (1) information search, discovery, and retrieval; and (2) presentation or visualization of the retrieved information.

### Search, Discovery, and Retrieval

In the past, information retrieval has been studied as though it were a self-contained problem (e.g., user searching for documents in a library database). Yet from the user's and organization's point of view, information retrieval is almost always part of some larger work process. This view is changing in three ways. First is the characterization of accessible information in terms of its structure. Second is the application of search concepts from the information science literature. Third is the development of information filters that reduce the problem of information overload.

Information filters reduce the amount of information that a user receives as the ever-growing availability of data can "drown" a user. One of the limiting forces for the assimilation of information, especially in an information-rich world, is simply the available time or cost spent accessing information. Information filtering is related to "sensemaking," which articulates the methods by which raw information is combined to produce new information products and insights. The goal is to enable users to profit from the amount of available information by providing them with tools that simplify the retrieval of information in an acceptable amount of time and with reasonable ease.

### Presentation and Visualization

Information that is "visual" and easy to understand can be simply presented and, more importantly, acted upon. Thus organizations must predefine rules for visual analysis and interpret business data in that context. This process will highlight trouble spots and areas of opportunity. The use of presentation tools increases companies' abilities to access, collect, query, organize, and present information in a usable and readable format, ultimately improving decision making.

The research in electronic commerce is focusing on building better information work spaces for retrieving, visualizing, manipulating, understanding, and in general, making sense of larger amounts of information. One major thrust of work is in three-dimensional visualization, to provide better navigation than would otherwise be possible using conventional WIMP user interfaces (Window, Icons, Mouse, Pointer). This work is based on the premise that many complex information tasks can be simplified by offloading complex cognitive tasks onto the human perceptual system.

For presentation, it is important to examine the relationships among trends and variances to separate reality from perception. Decision support systems enable high-level analysis of business data. Typically, Operations Research and Statistical tools are used for sophisticated and powerful analysis for financial modeling, project planning and cost analysis, forecasting from multivariate models, and analytic procedures for Total Quality Management (TQM). Knowledge workers in electronic commerce require a full range of functions. In Chapter 14, we describe the emerging area of Virtual Reality Modeling Languages, which allow users to visualize and navigate through information in 3D.

## Electronic Brokerages and Work-Flow Automation

In today's flattened, downsized, networked organization—in which cycle times have been reduced—responsibilities have been pushed downward and important information that was once the property of an elite few must be accessible to a greater number of lower-level staff. The "on-line" knowledge workers of the neo-enterprise must have access to vital information for making more and more independent decisions. To do so they need not only information and autonomy but also a comprehensive vision of the organization's direction and goals. And they must have constant access to all the resources they need, and to one another, without the mediation or coordination of disappearing middle managers.

Workers cannot be expected to spend time searching for information. Future organizations will create specialized information brokers to get workers information and to coordinate work flows. Think of the information brokerage as command and control center in the organization tailored for work-flow management. Information brokerages will play a key coordination role in a distributed system consisting of information sources, user interfaces, and sets of processing agents.

Most of the actual services required from the system will thus be performed by these information agents. They will be responsible for the following tasks: (1) processing end users' queries and displaying retrieved information; (2) searching, filtering, and summarizing large volumes of data; (3) translating or passing on search requests to databases or other agents; (4) maintaining directories about a particular data repository; and (5) monitoring usage patterns and information changes to initiate reorganization of data.

At a very high level, the internal electronic commerce system links users through their user-interface (UI) agents to document or database repositories through data-interface (DI) agents. In a simplistic system, the UI agents and DI agents could be tied together, allowing UI agents to query databases directly. This simple solution has many disadvantages, however, such as the duplication of effort in having UI agents determine the subset of DI agents relevant for meeting a particular request, or the complexities of terminating the search once one of the DI agents has answered the user's query [RSWB95].

Embedding specialized information agents (brokers) into the infrastructure to act as mediators between users and data collections can alleviate these problems and provide additional useful services to users and publishers of information. Different types of mediating broker agents for finding, processing, and delivering information are distinguished by their specific knowledge and expertise.

Roughly speaking, brokerages have the following knowledge: understanding requests of users; the effective strategies for processing requests and searching over the network; the contents and organization of data collections; the relationships among collections, data formats, and processing tools; the availability, capabilities and usage of network resources; the information usage patterns of particular users or user groups; alternative methods for summarizing and displaying information; the capabilities and effectiveness of other agents.

The knowledge and computational resources available to particular information agents dictate the range of information services they can provide to users or other agents. Each individual service offered by an information agent is a building block from which to construct complex information-processing strategies. Combinations of cooperative agents can collectively implement the more complex tasks required from the digital library system, such as information storage tasks (caching and indexing schemes), access strategies (browsing options and traversal paths), and so on. To realize the benefits of populating the infrastructure with a community of diverse information agents requires that the agents be able to team together dynamically to provide a particular information service on demand.

## Digital Library Layer

Many corporations are finding that the most effective way to manage their business information is through a corporate library that provides the architecture to model, map, integrate, condense, and transform scattered information housed in digital documents and legacy databases into meaningful business information.

Today, the term *digital library* is widely used as the generic term for diverse information structures that provide organizations and workers access to the vast amount of internal information encoded in multimedia formats. It creates a unified repository of consistent business data for information processing. Companies can perform more substantive, accurate, and consistent analyses using the digital library as a foundation for decision support systems.

The digital library is not a monolithic entity but a loose collection of distributed on-line information sources—databases and electronic documents—organized in a meaningful way. The term *library* is apt in this context because the fundamental mission of any library is to provide storage and physical access to the published document.

Digital libraries are of two types: electronic document-based digital libraries and structured data or database-oriented warehouses.

### Document Digital Libraries

In the last four years, document processing and management has emerged from obscurity to challenge traditional notions of business data processing. We use the term *document* in the broadest sense, to denote all nondata records, including books, reports, paper materials, electronic files, video, and audio.

The revolution of digital documents has been spurred by the availability of inexpensive networking technology and applications. It is also quite clear that new information generated outside of the relational database realm is done in digital document forms (word processing, spreadsheets, CD-ROMs, audio recordings, digital video, and others) and the rate of retrospective conversion (from paper to electronic form) is also growing.

From an electronic commerce perspective, a document digital library is simply a distributed network of interlinked information that is tailored for electronic publishing. It encompasses new types of information resources; new approaches to acquisition (especially with more sharing and subscription services); new methods of storage and preservation; new approaches to classification and cataloging; new modes of interaction with information; and shifts in organizational practices.

### Data Warehouses

Data warehouses are designed as central information repositories for combining and storing vast amounts of historical and reference data from a number of different sources. These corporate data sources include mainframe databases, client–server relational databases, spreadsheets, text reports, flat files, and proprietary systems.

A data warehouse, simply stated, is a physical separation of an organization's operational data systems from its decision support systems. It includes a repository of information that is built using data from the far-flung and often departmentally isolated systems.

Building a data warehouse allows companies to optimize query times and enables managers to be consistent in their analysis.

Clearly, the approaches to developing and manipulating document libraries versus data warehouses are substantially different. The differences exists at the underlying content level and at the actual application level. Although the digital library promises to make it easy to conduct electronic commerce, building the digital library itself is a challenging undertaking. That challenge can be broken down into three areas;

1. A need for a data model that provides an organization or schema
2. A strategy for populating that model with data
3. A way for users to get useful information out of the digital library

In the following sections we delve into each area.

## 12.2 MAKING A BUSINESS CASE FOR A DOCUMENT LIBRARY

This section highlights the role that documents play in today's organizations and explores how businesses can better meet their customers' needs by improving document management support.

Organizations create and archive millions of memos, contracts, engineering drawings, and other documents (see Fig. 12.2). Unquestionably, the document is mission-critical to any complex enterprise. That is, the document is the lifeblood of the enterprise, the integrating mechanism for all significant business operations. It's not surprising, then, that documents consume 20–45 percent of a company's labor costs and as much as 12–15 percent of revenues. It is estimated that American businesses create over one billion documents a day, and that office workers spend 40–60 percent of their time preparing, handling, filing, copying, and faxing documents. The average business document gets copied nineteen times and executives spend about four weeks per year waiting for documents to be located so that decisions can be made (*Computer Dealer News*, October 4, 1993).

For some industries, the rationale for generating documents is imposed by state and federal government regulation; for others, this effort is intended to support tax audits, court cases, legislative compliance issues, and legal claims; for still others, it is done because it always has been done. So how big

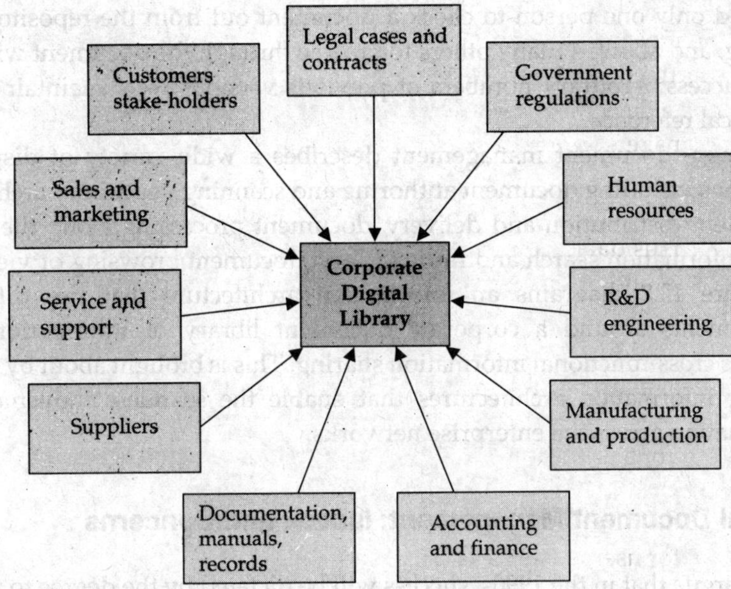


**Figure 12.2** Corporate digital library as core of document management

is the business problem created by mismanaged documents? It is huge.

As the document becomes increasingly digital, the problem of managing documents becomes very important. The digital document is the container that melds information—that is, multimedia content—with the context and appearance necessary for effective communication. Traversing all organizational functions and departments, the digital document is the means by which an organization's members interact with one another and with customers. What is the solution to the complex problem of managing digital documents? Many see document management as the answer.

Document management broadly refers to the ability to automate and streamline document-based processes—from authoring to approval, distribution to viewing, searching and retrieval, and finally storage. Document management attempts to leverage the value of corporate information by providing tools that let everyone in the organization have access to information contained within documents from any node on the network, no matter what type of computer they're using.

Initially, document management meant the ability to track files and documents. If someone needed access to a document, early management systems tracked the request and provided the document. The system, usually allowed only one person to check a document out from the repository for editing, and allowed many others to browse through the document with the write access. Arbitrary numbers of previous versions were maintained for historical reference.

In sum, document management describes a wide variety of disparate functions including document authoring and scanning, repository archiving, document distribution and delivery, document processing along the work flow, information search and retrieval, and document browsing or viewing.

Figure 12.2 diagrams an information architecture that ties different departments around a corporate document library of information that enables cross-functional information sharing. This is brought about by establishing information architectures that enable the seamless movement of information across the enterprise networks.

## Digital Document Management: Issues and Concerns

Some argue that in the 1990s, success will be dictated by the degree to which a firm analyzes and improves key document management schemes:

- *Ad hoc documents*—such as letters, financial reports, manuals—usually are initiated by managers and professionals who create content, but most elements of content and appearance of ad hoc documents, as well as the work of distributing them, have been in the hands of support staff. The content, context, and appearance of ad hoc documents are generally not well defined and can vary widely.
- *Process-specific documents*—such as invoices or purchase orders—typically are created, constructed, and distributed by support personnel. These are often forms-based: context and appearance undergo virtually no alteration and content varies only slightly according to well-articulated rules.
- *Knowledge-oriented documents* encompass technical documentation, catalogs of product information, and design documents.

Although corporations and users have become sophisticated with the management and manipulation of structured data stored in corporate database servers, few have a comparable strategy for dealing with vital corporate documents representing a breadth of organizational knowledge ranging from interactive electronic technical manuals (IETMs), regulatory documents, electronic meetings, and product information. In short, the proliferation of documents, from e-mail to news feeds, is conspiring to create environments rich with electronic documents that are not being managed effectively.

## 12.3 TYPES OF DIGITAL DOCUMENTS

Our concept of a document and its content is undergoing radical attack as we employ multimedia and other technologies in the document creation and distribution process. The emerging spectrum of documents types, shown in Fig. 12.3, range from the inflexible (imaging formats) to the most flexible or customizable (virtual documents).

In the first part of the document continuum, content is treated as a monolithic whole. Not until the second part does the structure of content become more important. In the third part, content is not assumed to be in one place but distributed on the network. And finally, as documents become more flexible they need to become smarter. They have to provide a framework for managing all the different pieces—data and applications—that are present. These smart documents are known generically as active documents or document-oriented computing.

### Document Imaging

Document imaging emulates microfiche and microfilm. An imaging system passes a paper document through a scanner that renders it digital and then stores the digital data as a bit-mapped image of the document. Keywords for each document that help in indexing and retrieval are entered during scanning. The problem with the imaging approach is that the output contains only images, not encoded text. Consequently, searching the text of a document's image is possible only using the keywords that categorize that docu-

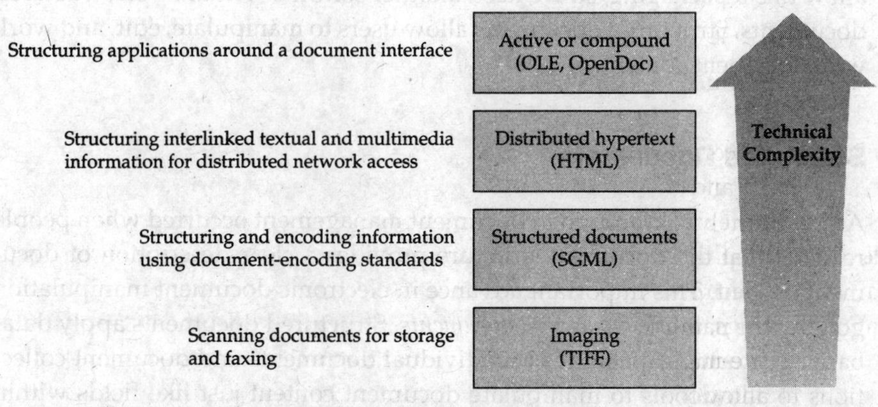


**Figure 12.3** The four types of digital documents

ment. And without a specific, well-designed list of keywords, a large library of imaged documents would be created but not used effectively.

This class of documents is characterized by little or no formal "internal" structure and provides limited freedom to use documents in a nonsequential manner. But imaging systems have their place. Insurance companies and other large firms often use imaging systems for processing high volumes of routine yet critical documents such as claims forms and supplier invoices. The benefit of being able to retrieve paperwork instantly instead of in days is obvious—time is money.

The following imaging standards are prominently used:

1. *TIFF (tag image file format).* Format for interchange of bit-mapped images. It was developed through an industry effort initiated by Aldus Corporation and has achieved de facto standard status.
2. *ITU-TSS (International Telecommunication Union—telecommunications standardization sector) Group IV T.6 Facsimile.* This standard is used for compression and exchange of bit-mapped files.

The future of document imaging lies in its ability to manipulate and package information for customized delivery. As more and more organizations realize that the usefulness of their information (document content) will outlive the formats and computers that hold it today, they are actively seeking ways to preserve their investment in information content by creating sophisticated document content manipulation tools (text retrieval, document management, and document routing).

All of the foregoing underline the importance of viewing information as a raw resource that needs to packaged or repackaged depending on the market needs and technology used for distribution. Document imaging does not allow this repackaging, so we need another solution. The answer: structured documents. Structured documents allow users to manipulate, edit, and work with document content.

## Structured Documents

A significant breakthrough in document management occurred when people realized that the document structure provides a clear description of document content. This important advance in electronic document manipulation goes by the name of *structured documents*. Structured documents apply database structuring capabilities to individual documents and document collections to allow tools to manipulate document content just like fields within database tables.

In the past, most document manipulation tools dealt with content as large monolithic structures (files, for example). This was fine as long as content was homogeneous. Today, however, the problem of document manipulation is compounded by the fact that documents are often lengthy, complex, cross-referenced, and encrusted with new information types ranging from accounting spreadsheets, to computer-aided design, to graphics, to multimedia. To work effectively with the digital document, a database approach seems to be most appropriate.

A simple example of the new approach can be illustrated with the familiar table of contents (TOC). Think of the TOC as a database schema that provides the overview structure for a book, namely, chapters and sections. A TOC can also define abstracts, subsections, captions, bulleted or numbered lists, copyright notices, bibliographies, and other document elements easily and reuse them in other contexts. The TOC allows users to navigate through an entire document or to narrow the search to specific parts or elements, which greatly improves query precision and recall. In short, the TOC provides a structure that serves as an effective index to underlying document content.

Structured documents provide the following capabilities:

1. Document formatting and rendering suits different information delivery vehicles or media. For example, companies are beginning to give their customers CDs containing electronic manuals in addition to providing hardcopy materials for those who prefer the more traditional. The reasons for this trend include reduced printing and packaging costs and faster updates of critical information.

   Document rendering and presentation affects how users interact with onscreen help, educational materials, and documentation. For example, the audio rendering of documents opens up a new world for the visually handicapped.

2. The ability to create easily modifiable structures allows more dynamic documents and user interaction and manipulation, such as the ability to create bookmarks, highlight text, and write notes.

   In other words, documents are no longer stagnant, but can be edited, cross-referenced, and linked to other items, such as graphics, video, photo, or voice scripts. These features bring the document to a multiuser, networked platform with the ability to collaborate with other users on the document.

3. Given the right structure and interface, electronic documents can be easier to search and query than its hardcopy counterpart or image counterpart. Multiple-word (Boolean) and string searches are often used to

locate and retrieve the information, either as parts of the document or the entire document itself.

A large array of standards and products are available to help create and manage structured documents, depending on the goal and task at hand. If document interchange between platforms and fidelity to document format is the main concern, a compound document architecture (ODA, RTF, or CDA) may suffice. If document structure and manipulation are paramount, then the overwhelming choice is SGML.

- *SGML (standard generalized markup language)*—an ISO standard for interchange and multiformatting description of text documents in terms of their logical structure. SGML's biggest and most powerful supporter, the Department of Defense, has mandated SGML as the standard for electronic publishing in the Computer-Aided Acquisition and Logistics Support (CALS) program. As one of the most important advances in making text more useful, SGML is covered at length in Chapter 21.
- *ODA (office document architecture)*—an ANSI and ISO standard for interchange of compound office documents. In contrast to SGML, which describes document structure, ODA specifies both content and format. Despite all the work that went into the standard, ODA is not considered to be a major player in the future of electronic publishing.
- *CDA (compound document architecture)*—Digital Equipment Corp. CDA defines a set of ground rules—content and format—and services for the interchange of compound documents between applications. CDA-compliant applications can revise each other's documents even if the applications are written in different languages, run under different operating systems, and are located on the far corners of a distributed network. The most prominent use of CDA can be found in Lotus Notes, the popular groupware software.
- *RTF (rich-text format)*—initially developed by Microsoft for interchange of text between Microsoft desktop products, RTF has become widely used by other text-processing applications.

Table 12.1 compares the advantages and disadvantages of these standards. Of all these, the SGML standard seems to have the most momentum. SGML can "make text into a database," rendering it useful in the same way traditional databases are useful. It can provide editing, interchange, and search and retrieval capabilities. SGML provides these capabilities through the concept of descriptive or generalized markup. See Chapter 21 for a detailed look at structured documents.

**Table 12.1** Comparing Structured Document Formats

| *Technology* | *Advantages* | *Disadvantages* |
|---|---|---|
| Document interchange formats (ODA, CDA, or RTF) | Generate platform- and application-independent information; keep format and styling; some even support audio graphics, and full-motion video. | Complex standards that require expertise to use; formats make users dependent on applications that can recognize the encoding used. |
| Document structure languages (SGML) | Allows the creation of document-type definitions that are like software programs specifically for document manipulation. | SGML does not support nontext elements. Extensions such as HyTime provide this capability. |

## Hypertext Documents

The value of information increases when it moves to areas where some entity—individual or software program—can make use of it. Hypertext is a way of making document-based information more mobile. Mobility of information is necessary for the following reasons:

- Information in enterprises is seldom located on one node or server but is distributed throughout the organization.
- Accessing and retrieving large monolithic documents is time consuming. A good management strategy is to split them into smaller pieces to reduce user waiting and network utilization time. For users who spend time referencing very long documents, searching for information, and looking for interrelated documents, the simple viewing/browsing, such as scrolling up and down pages, is certainly out of the question. Support for hypertext functionality, enabling cross-referencing and conditional branching to related parts of an electronic document, is an essential requirement.
- Reuse of document fragments for composing new documents is more effective when information stored on individual systems and servers across an enterprise can be accessed from remote locations.

Relationships between documents can be represented through hypermedia links (hyperlinks) that allow the production of complex, richly connected and cross-referenced bodies of knowledge. This structuring and navigation mechanism has been used effectively to deal with the presentation of large amounts of loosely structured information, such as on-line documentation or computer-aided learning.

New developments in the area of distributed hypermedia are showing the vast technological potential of a global digital library linking many document servers. However, mobility, high availability, and scalability may well be the most difficult aspects of a document management system with regard to development and successful deployment. Mobility is perhaps the most difficult of the three due to factors such as media failure, machine failure, and network partitioning or organization. See Table 12.2 for a list of hypertext document standards.

## Active Documents

Active documents (or compound documents) represent what is known as document-oriented computing. Active documents provide an interactive interface where all documents, applications, and data related to a particular task are assembled, arranged, and interlinked in such a manner that the user can focus on the task at hand and be shielded from nontask-related issues like access, storage, data formats, location, computing, or delivery mechanisms.

Active documents share the common goal of making the user's computing experience as easy and productive as possible, a goal that has remained an elusive but tantalizing prospect. As people use PCs for more and more complex tasks, often involving multiple programs and even a variety of media, they need to have better integration of various documents created by the diverse applications. This trend is evident in the shift taking place in the software development community from stand-alone, application-based computing toward integrated document-based computing.

**Table 12.2** Hypermedia Standards in a Nutshell

*HyTime.* ISO/IEC standard 10744 is an extension of SGML to multimedia, hypertext, and hypermedia. It adds time-based relationships like synchronization and supports multimedia objects.

*HTML (hypertext markup language).* Developed by the World Wide Web (WWW) community to support distributed hypermedia, it is a small subset of SGML developed to support hypertext and multimedia.

*MHEG.* An evolving standard for presenting objects in a multimedia environment, it was developed by the Multimedia/Hypermedia Encoding/Experts Group.

In addition, people are increasingly working together on computer-based projects. In the context of work-group computing, the document becomes much more of a networked entity, allowing users to access, manipulate, analyze, store, and disseminate information from a variety of sources in a multiplatform network environment. This means that the earlier, individual desktop computer model is shifting to one of shared, collaborative computing resources—a shift that demands new capabilities. To meet these demands, corporations are trying to do more integration of information and applications using the notion of active documents to allow business teams to develop and exchange information.

Active documents are especially powerful because they combine the notion of composition of information with the distributed nature of information. For example, active documents will allow spreadsheet, word-processing and other multimedia objects belonging to different applications to be dragged and dropped into a single file. Each object knows what application is capable of manipulating it. For instance, an end user may link the distance between two points in an AutoCAD drawing to a cell in an Excel spreadsheet, and whenever the end user changes the cell's value in the spreadsheet, the AutoCAD drawing changes automatically.

Active documents allow users to create interfaces that are dynamically updated from remote data and computation objects that may be stored in the document libraries on the network. These composite entities do not simply display static results from a query but also incorporate linkages to remote elements to build a structure. The active document uses links to reference distributed objects or documents instead of making a local copy of each entity. Linking enables composite documents that are portable across multiple operating systems that can "intelligently" evaluate and act on network data.

The increased role of the active document is tied directly to the emergence of distributed network computing and object-oriented application environments. Examples of active documents technology include Microsoft's Object Linking and Embedding (OLE), Apple's OpenDoc, and Object Management Group's CORBA (Common Object Request Broker Architecture). (See Chapter 22.)

## 12.4 ISSUES BEHIND DOCUMENT INFRASTRUCTURE

Creating a digital library poses many hurdles and challenges. What starts out as a conceptually simple exercise can quickly turn into a jungle of incompatible platforms, software applications, databases, and document formats.

Some of the characteristics of the corporate digital library posing special challenges include: variance in end users' needs and sophistication; diversity in hardware performance; large, both in size and number, information resources that are physically distributed; heterogeneous types of information resources and multimedia data types created by a variety of departments; and the need for extendibility to add new collections (e.g., a new database system) as well as new data types (e.g., voice).

The true challenge is to find ways and means for overcoming the preceding obstacles and create an information infrastructure that enables fast decision making and information sharing across the enterprise. In particular, the infrastructure needs to provide information anytime and anyplace; to provide access to collections of multimedia information built upon the integration of text, image, graphics, audio, video (and other continuous media); to support user-friendly personalization of information access and representation, including support for the "mining" of relevant information; and to be the heart of new technology-mediated electronic commerce such as EDI and interaction with consumers.

To make this vision a reality, the following questions must be addressed:

- What is the proper architecture for the corporate digital library?
- What are appropriate models for representing documents (and, more generally, information) and library services?
- What protocols for interoperation between repositories, libraries, and services are required?
- What are the best human interfaces to such an integrated library?
- How does one locate information of interest in a very large, distributed, and possibly disconnected collection of repositories?
- How does one represent and manipulate the information processing "activities" that occur or will occur in a digital library?

So what will corporate digital libraries be like? It is too early in the process of speculation, research, and development to answer this question. But whatever they turn out to be, they will inevitably share many properties with current libraries and will differ from them in innumerable ways as well. In technological and business practices there is always an interplay, a tension, between the forces of status quo and innovation. Business cultures do not, and should not, let go lightly of structures and practices in which they have invested heavily. The task in the years ahead will be to decide which of the existing practices and structures to cast off and which to retain, and which innovations to reject or adopt.

## Document Constituencies

The emerging document processing and management strategies must address three constituencies:

1. *End users.* End users want to do more with the information in their documents than merely store them to disk or occasionally print them. They need systems to access distributed repositories and to manipulate them in a number of ways.
2. *Developers.* Developers need a framework to prevent ad hoc system design and assure the longevity and flexibility of documents and the information they include in the face of new technological advancements. Also, methodologies are required that can guide the document development and deployment process in organizations.
3. *Document librarians.* Developers and information providers acquire and maintain materials at one end of the spectrum, and at the other end, end users utilize the information. We have also observed an interesting middle ground: librarians who manage the dissemination and maintenance of information. This new role will alter the process by which workers create, find, and use information they need in the networked environment.

The processing of retrieved documents, through validation, abstraction, integration, and presentation, is also a candidate for services by brokers and brokerages. Most decision makers need more than rapid access to documents—they also need analysis, abstraction, and value-added processing. To transform data from a digital library to information, brokers would first find references to candidate documents, using indexes provided by directory services. The essence of a document may then be abstracted for the customer, and the quality of documents validated.

Today these tasks are performed by librarians, consultants, and others. It is unclear how such processing will be done in the future. Speed is likely to be a major concern, and the on-line brokers will have to compete on the ability to provide comprehensive services to customers. It is obvious that brokers will all be on-line and accessible through networks.

Processing data into information requires that the brokers be responsive to the customer. One approach is to design processing methods that are specific to a type of customer. A more general approach would be to interpret a model of the customer's needs and match that against available data to maximize relevance.

The overall integration of the key business operations around digital documents has not itself occurred, although that's changing: Organizations have begun integrating key aspects of document creation, production, distribution, storage, and retrieval.

## Document-Oriented Processes

Although electronic technologies have reshaped how documents are created, produced, distributed, stored, and retrieved, these important developments for the most part have been undertaken separately and discretely. The components of this effort, called integrated document management, include the following:

- *Document creation* End users want to be able to create mission-critical documents cooperatively on disparate systems and applications, so links between these systems need to be seamless. For instance, a document created in WordPerfect on a DOS-based PC may be transmitted via a LAN to a Macintosh system running PageMaker so that a graphic designer can prepare it for presentation.
- *Document media conversion.* End users are looking for systems that accept multiple forms of input—hardcopy, image, text, numeric data, video, and sound—from either paper originals, a network, or magnetic media.
- *Document production and distribution.* End users need interfaces between document creation, document production, and document distribution systems. They want to (1) direct document output via networks to print on demand systems; (2) exploit just-in-time document production using page description languages, image retrieval, and network storage technologies; and (3) simplify document production by integrating finishing into high-speed production processes.
- *Document storage and retrieval.* End users seek integrated archival storage and retrieval support with easy access to whole documents as well as document elements such as text passages and illustrations. They need document inventory techniques that can generate substantial savings in document storage costs and near-elimination of document obsolescence while assuring easy document access.

End user departments and functions can benefit greatly from the integration of document creation, production/distribution, and storage and retrieval capabilities. These technologies produce cost savings and alter the way end users think about and use documents. This triggers new ideas about tasks and organizational work flow, which can result in redesign of work, reallocation of resources, and cost advantages.

### Document-Based Work Flows

The previous section described how documents move in and out of the library. Work flow is the process that moves those documents. To respond to changing business needs, document libraries are constantly changing, along with their data encoding and structures. So managing the library involves continuous incremental refinement that must track both changing technology and the changing business environment.

Four activities make up document-based work flow:

1. *Document modeling* defines structures and processes of operational systems, both internal and external to the enterprise.
2. *Transformation* creates modules for capturing, validating, transforming, and applying key operational concepts.
3. *Synthesizing* creates value-added informational objects from the combination of two or more documents.
4. *Business modeling* defines the structures and processes of the business environment, both internal and external to the enterprise.

Business modeling should lead the library effort, driving the data requirements backward all the way to document creation. However, too much focus is placed on document modeling to the detriment of business modeling. Sometimes, it is not practical to model an entire enterprise, either from a document or business process perspective. The challenge of managing document-based work flows is to provide immediate payback from the library and to initiate a continuous process of successive refinement toward a single image of business reality.

## 12.5 CORPORATE DATA WAREHOUSES

Companies are focusing on developing data warehouses to leverage existing businesses and generate new growth opportunities. Today virtually every transaction and minute business detail in the corporate environment is recorded in databases in the hope that it will enable more effective decision making throughout the organization. Unfortunately, most of the corporate emphasis has been on storing data, while tools for accessing and transforming data into meaningful information have been somewhat ignored. As a result, business managers are forced to spend more time navigating the myriad sources of enterprise data than analyzing the information.

Take, for example, financial systems. In many companies, financial consolidation is done manually, with sales information from each outlet keyed into individual computer systems every night. The information is then sent to the corporate office, where it is posted to the mainframe accounting system, which has no analysis capabilities. Any analysis has to be completed via a second system by downloading the data, thus proving the process to be labor intensive and slow. Clearly there is a need for a central data warehouse that is populated with data automatically and provides effective retrieval and use of information.

The organizations buying into data warehousing for decision support exhibit the following characteristics:

- An information-based approach to decision making
- Involvement in highly competitive, rapidly changing markets with a large, diverse customer base for a variety of products
- Data stored in many systems and represented differently
- Data stored in complex, technical, difficult-to-decipher formats, making conversion for analysis difficult

Data warehouses are necessary as enterprisewide data increase in both volume and complexity, making it important to establish an information systems architecture that transforms scattered legacy data into useful information. The data warehouse performs the following functions:

- Allows existing transaction and legacy systems to continue in operation
- Consolidates data from the various transaction systems into a coherent set
- Allows analysis of vital information about current operations for decision support

Once the data are stored in the warehouse, companies can slice it several different ways, performing detailed, multidimensional "what-if" scenarios on various aspects of the companies' operations. This capability enables users to gain insights into corporate performance and customer behavior that are not possible using disconnected operational computing systems.

## Types of Data Warehouses

The term *data warehouse* is currently being used to describe a number of different facilities each with diverse characteristics. Some companies use all of the following components of data warehousing in combination, others just one:

*Physical data warehouse.* This is an actual, physical database into which all the corporate data for the data warehouse are gathered, along with the schemas (information about data) and the processing logic used to organize, package, and preprocess the data for end user access.

*Logical data warehouse.* This contains all the metadata, business rules, and processing logic required to scrub, organize, package, and preprocess the data. In addition, it contains the information required to find and access the actual data, wherever it actually resides.

*Data library.* This is a subset of the enterprisewide data warehouse. Typically, it performs the role of a departmental, regional, or functional data warehouse. As part of the data warehouse process, the organization builds a series of data libraries over time and eventually links them via an enterprisewide logical data warehouse.

*Decision support systems* (DSSs). These systems are not data warehouses but applications that make use of the data warehouse. They are also called executive information systems (EIS).

## Building an End-to-End Data Warehouse

Decision support requires processing, summarizing, and aggregating large databases, including legacy and operational data. Hence, building a data warehouse architecture is the first step many companies are taking to respond to the inadequacies of existing decision support systems. It involves developing a separate database designed explicitly for data-intensive, decision-support applications. It moves much data and informational processing out of transaction systems and into an analytic environment equipped to handle it. The net effect is that the transaction systems environment is cleaned up and shrunk. By reducing the stress on the transaction systems environment, the data warehouse architecture streamlines systems so that users can perform both operational and informational processing more efficiently.

Three elements are crucial to having a complete data warehouse that will truly optimize business analysis (see Fig. 12.4):

1. *Back end.* Accessing and organizing data easily from disparate sources
2. *Preparing data for analysis.* Querying, searching, and governing the data
3. *Front end.* Providing means for effective analysis of the information

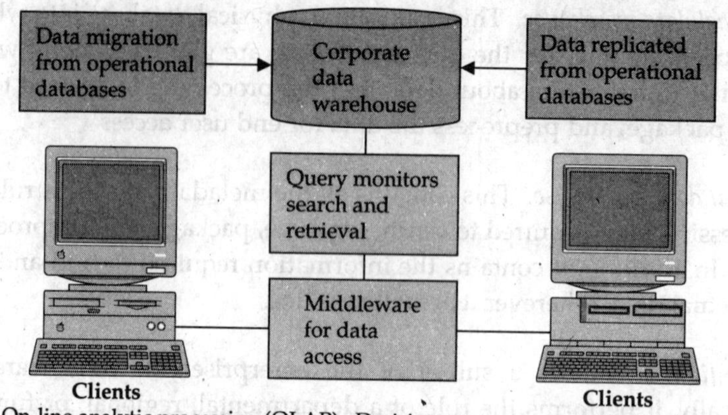


**Figure 12.4** Data warehouse architecture

## The Back End: Building a Data Warehouse

The first step in building a data warehouse is to access operational data from wherever the information resides—and in whatever format—for placement into the repository. This process consolidates operational data from on-line transaction-processing systems into the informational data of the warehouse. Data are not only consolidated but also restructured, because the tasks accomplished with the information in the data warehouse differ from those in the production transaction databases that feed it.

Industry experts agree that more than 70 percent of corporate data still reside in legacy systems' nonrelational databases. Easily accessing these sources is crucial. Just consolidating inflows from legacy data can become complex and massive, given the scale of legacy systems in most enterprises. Today, very large databases are now considered at the 500-Gigabyte level and above. The granularity of the inflow data is rapidly approaching that of the detailed transaction data in the operational systems. Those data rates and data sizes push the limits of our communication networks and database systems.

Operational data for decision support can be accessed in two primary ways:

1. The data can be loaded into another database for information access. The data are not updated in real time, but are refreshed from operational systems on a regular basis when the data transfer will not adversely affect the performance of operational systems. In addition, the warehouse repository is created to be read from, not written to or altered. In short, the data are collected over time and used for comparisons, trends, and forecasting.

2. The data can be accessed where they reside on the legacy or operational database. Software tools circumvent data access barriers by allowing users to view an arbitrary collection of files and tables, regardless of their organization, as a single, coherent relational database.

Both methods are often necessary. For example, a purchasing manager may need to access a data warehouse to determine historical demand for a product, as well as access an operational database to determine on-hand inventory. Often, enormous time and effort is devoted to inflow from legacy systems only to find that business managers also want to use data from other sources that were not considered earlier. To avoid that problem, companies need to model the information flows needed to run the business and let that model drive the inflow.

## Managing Data: Preparing for Business Analysis

Once accessed, data must be transformed into a consistent, integrated form. Often, data in the warehouse are organized by subject rather than application, so the warehouse contains only the information necessary for decision support processing. This stage is vital for decision support, as it creates a standard organization and language by which data are recognized, queried, and reported. It pays to keep in mind that the users of the data warehouse are not data entry personnel; they are business managers making quick decisions based on the existing data.

In reality, data must be transformed into a more useful resource with the following steps:

1. *Translation*. Prior to analysis, data might require translation because data loaded into the warehouse are from many separate applications and may be encoded differently. For instance, in one application, 'm' and 'f' may designate male and female; in another, '0' and '1' may be the designations. Once data are loaded into the warehouse, consistent naming conventions need to be assumed.

2. *Summarizing*. In this step, relational data are grouped into views more convenient and useful to managers. Summarizing extends beyond simple relational operators to sophisticated statistical analyses (trends, clustering, sampling).

3. *Packaging*. The detailed or summarized data is put into more usable formats, such as spreadsheets, text documents, charts, other graphical presentations, personal databases, and animation. Investing in quality

templates of spreadsheets, documents, and presentations has huge potential paybacks for consumers of warehouse information.

4. *Distributing.* The warehouse data is distributed to appropriate groups to increase availability and accessibility. As distributed environments mature, centralized databases will migrate to distributed ones in support of geographically dispersed units. The typical case today is distributing portions of a centralized DB2 warehouse to regional LAN database servers.

5. *Garbage collection.* A data warehouse becomes cluttered if useless data are ignored. To help maintain the vitality of the warehouse data, older data, which can no longer be economically maintained within the core warehouse, must be sent off to a hierarchical storage archive (such as tape cartridge or optical disc). The key activity in garbage collection is moving out data whose business value has declined with age so that the warehouse doesn't slow down.

The business analysis preparation process adds value to the informational data contained in the warehouse. It's tempting to think that, once data have been consolidated from legacy systems and other sources, the job of warehouse management is finished. A common trap is to believe a good query tool that accesses all data is sufficient when in reality a lot of careful groundwork is required.

## Exploiting Data: The Front End

The finale for data in the warehouse is the front end through which it becomes available to business consumers. With the proliferation of computing, corporations are awash with a flood of data, putting the spotlight on the effective retrieval and use of information. In fact, a data warehouse without sophisticated access, analysis, and reporting capabilities is like a library without a proper catalog.

Two key activities make up the front end:

1. *User retrieval.* End users request the data they need. The primary issue is to establish the environment for using effective query tools. In accessing, the requests can range from ad hoc (one-time) to routine (daily/weekly) to real time (continuous) in nature. In all cases, access to the warehouse should be driven by the consumer, rather than the warehouse.

2. *Proactive delivery.* Often in rapidly changing decision settings, data must be proactively delivered to end users' workstations. This is a new area and is usually based on some type of publish-and-subscribe mechanism.

> The warehouse publishes various "business objects" that are revised on a periodic basis. Consumers subscribe to the set of business objects that best meet their needs. By monitoring usage patterns, intelligent guesses can be made about what business objects to publish and which consumers should be subscribing to those objects.

The front end software also offers a robust set of decision support tools, including financial and multidimensional modeling, statistical and scientific analysis, and project management tools—to name a few. In addition, a number of predefined and customizable objects should be available. These objects provide customers with a clear, easy path for manipulating and analyzing crucial data; allowing multidimensional viewing; and more.

While the majority of today's data warehousing solutions provide data analysis that merely identifies trends in past performances, the new types of tools provide a wide range of analytical functions that enable business managers to drill down through layers of information, analyze historical data, and forecast future performance, thus solving business problems before they become crises.

The potential value of front end tools is just being recognized by many enterprises. The information analyst must be proactive in marketing the warehouse data to consumers. The challenge is dealing with the broad spectrum of ad hoc (one-time) to real-time (continuous) requests in a fluid manner.

## Advantages of Data Warehouses

The benefits of data warehousing are extensive. Timely and accurate information becomes an integral part of the decision-making process. Users can manage and access large volumes of information in one cohesive framework. Managers can distribute subject-oriented information on a variety of platforms, enabling faster decision making.

Data warehousing has widespread applicability. Consider sales and marketing functions. Instead of waiting for individual end-of-day reports, the warehouse system automatically polls sales data from the point-of-sale terminals at each outlet and consolidates it in the relational database. This information is used to consolidate and speed up end-of-day reporting, analyze sales, and monitor regulatory compliance. This enables corporate management to perform the kind of in-depth analysis that allows them to fine-tune their product mix, reduce administrative overhead, and ultimately increase profit margins. The sales tracking and analysis enables management to better correlate labor productivity and inventory forecasts with actual sales.

Because data in the data warehouse are integrated, have historical perspective, and are stored at both summary and detail levels, the data warehouse architecture provides a solid basis for DSS processing. A unified view of enterprise information over a five- to ten-year time frame provides the enterprise with an excellent comparative analysis, trending, and forecasting tool. Informational inquiries are satisfied without disrupting the performance of operational applications. And, most important, the information analyst looking out for the best interests of the corporation finds that productivity and effectiveness increase.

In sum, organizations are beginning to see data warehousing as a way to facilitate the business analysis needs of decision makers quickly and easily. A data warehouse provides data pertinent for on-line analytic processing (OLAP), which supports decision makers with business information on their desktop resulting in faster, better decision making and a more flexible, responsive organization. It provides a foundation for analytical processing by separating operational data and processing from decision support system (DSS) data and processing.

## 12.6 SUMMARY

The primary emphasis of the new paradigm of internal electronic commerce systems is the effective utilization of information and data. Many large companies, in particular, have come to realize (or are in the process of realizing) that information is a strategic asset. This information is often scattered around the organization and stored in machines, places, and formats not easily accessible and often requiring tremendous technical expertise to even get to them. This is a drag on the productivity of the corporation, especially in an age when efficiency is the watchword.

To rectify this problem, almost overnight (compared to the decades that change to organizational practice usually takes), an entirely new and potentially massive field of corporate digital library is emerging around the Internet and distributed networking. Corporate digital library creation usually takes place as a set of related phases within the organization. The early phase focuses on the introduction of information technology to add functionality and operational effectiveness (automate business processes) by connecting computers and applications with electronic tools such as bulletin board systems, groupware, databases, e-mail, electronic directories, imaging, and graphics.

The second phase moves beyond automation to integration of the business processes. Corporate digital libraries facilitate business process integration by reducing time and distance constraints, leading to improved productivity. It is important to understand that obtaining benefits of electronic commerce or corporate digital libraries is more like a journey than a destination. With each increase in the efficiency of business processes, new bottlenecks are identified, studied, and overcome, yielding a new organizational environment.

Finally, creation of the corporate digital library is not enough. Companies must find ways to use the information it houses. In an increasingly competitive environment, lacking network connectivity and employees with skill sets to use the available tools is a major liability that's quickly reflected in either diminishing market share or lost opportunities. To break down both internal and external barriers to effective usage, corporations have to embark on a journey to introduce document technologies to their employees.

Chapter 13

# Advertising and Marketing on the Internet

Instead of merely transforming commerce from a nonelectronic world to an electronic platform, electronic commerce demands radical changes in the marketing process, product sales and pricing strategies, and advertising and promotion campaigns. Misunderstandings about the nature of marketing in electronic markets are rampant. Many think that on-line marketing is equivalent to publishing a World Wide Web page with product information that shoppers can browse through. This fallacy is already evident as the initial euphoria about the WWW fades.

Recently, several companies announced that their attempt at on-line marketing was not doing as well as anticipated. For instance, the Vermont Teddy Bear Company set up a WWW page in the summer of 1994 with Digital Equipment Corporation. Within four hours of public availability, the page received 13,000 visits. Six months later, the page is gone, and the toymaker is concentrating on more traditional marketing (*Computerworld*, January 23, 1995). The company, like many others, noticed that many visitors were trekking through their "virtual" malls but very few customers were buying products. For small companies this situation is intolerable, resulting in some pulling out of the electronic marketplace.

It is clear that these firms lacked a clear marketing strategy for the electronic marketplace. What is the best strategy? How can companies create an on-line marketing approach that works? How can firms create attractive digital content in the context of a business process? How do companies get customers to look at content? How should firms advertise their products to the rest of world? These and other related issues provide the motivation for this chapter.

Very simply, real savings can be gained by using technology to do marketing-related activities that used to require expensive people-directed field operations. For example, marketers are learning that valuable information can be collected from the customer on-line with minimum effort and low cost that otherwise would take months and at least several hundred thousand dollars to gather.

Before delving into the details related to on-line advertising and marketing, it is important to note that there is a tendency in the technology literature to confuse marketing with sales and advertising. The three are certainly complementary, but are separate. To clarify the terminology used in this chapter, we provide definitions for these terms.

*Marketing* is a way of managing a business so that each important business decision is made with full knowledge of the impact it will have on the customer. It deals with all the steps between determining customer needs and supplying them at a profit. It entails drawing a management plan that views all marketing components as part of a total system that requires effective strategic planning, organization, leadership, and control.

Marketing has two underlying assumptions: (1) all company policies and activities should be aimed at satisfying customer needs and (2) profitable sales volume is a better company goal than maximum sales volume.

*Selling* is often used as an equivalent term for marketing, although this is not the case. The sales approach almost always focuses on volume, while the marketing approach focuses on profit. In short, under the sales approach the customer exists for the business, while under the marketing approach the business exists for the customer.

*Advertising* is the process of reaching the customer using a broadcast or direct mail campaign orchestrated to influence purchasing behavior. Advertising plans are conceived within the confines or parameters set by a marketing plan. With the advent of electronic commerce, a new type of interactive advertising is emerging whereby customers can choose the information they wish to access.

Traditionally, mass and direct (one-way) advertising have aimed at broadcasting a message to a large number of customers. Most business continues to operate under the classic broadcast approach—"Come buy this great product we have created for you or this fantastic service we are offering." Interactive (two-way) advertising, on the other hand, aims at allowing customers to browse, explore, compare, question, and even custom design the product configuration.

It has been said that "comparing mass-advertising to interactive advertising is like comparing shotgun buckshot to sniper fire. In the interactive environment time is taken to take aim and really penetrate the customer. Ideally, you want someone to spend 20 minutes drilling down into product information. You can't do that when they are channel surfing or flipping the pages of a magazine" [IA94]. In contrast to the traditional approach in which the company "pushes" its product, in an interactive marketing situation the company creates forces that entice customers to "pull" down the information that they are interested in. The goal is to educate and provide utility to the customer rather than to confuse.

In short, the new model of advertising aims at "putting the customer first"—a phrase that has mostly been given lip service in the past. Interactive marketing using such new media technologies as computer-based on-line services or CD-ROMs will not supplant, at least initially, conventional marketing techniques, but will augment them as a new, low-cost means of reaching customers. Table 13.1 summarizes the contrasts among the three approaches to marketing: mass, direct, and interactive.

**Table 13.1** Nature of Marketing in Electronic Commerce Environments

| | *Mass Marketing* | *Direct Marketing* | *Interactive Marketing* |
|---|---|---|---|
| Distribution Channel | Broadcast and print media (consumer is passive) | Postal service using mailing lists (consumer is passive) | The Internet (consumer is active and is the catalyst for what is shown on screen) |
| Market Strategy (and sample products) | High volume (food, beer, autos, personal and home-care products) | Targeted goods (credit cards, travel, autos, subscriptions) | Targeted audience (services and all types of product information) |
| Enabling Technology | Storyboards and desktop publishing | Databases and statistical tools | Information servers, client browsers, bulletin boards, and software agents. |
| Authors of Marketing Material | Ad agencies | Ad agencies and companies | Companies and consumers |
| Expected Outcome from Successful Implementation | Volume sales | Bounded sales, data for analysis | Data for analysis, customer relationships, new product ideas, volume sales |

## 13.1 THE NEW AGE OF INFORMATION-BASED MARKETING

Interactive marketing brought on by electronic commerce will change the roles of small business, retailers, manufacturers, and media companies. For discussion purposes, we differentiate these changing roles into four areas: retailers versus manufacturers; target and micromarketing; small business versus large business; and regulatory and legal implications of cyberspace marketing.

### Retailers Versus Manufacturers

The roles of retailers and manufacturers are fast reversing in electronic commerce. Nowadays, retailers have an advantage over manufacturers because they can measure customer response and get first crack at the broadest range of information. Indeed, point-of-sale (POS) scanning systems have played a major role in shifting power from manufacturers to retailers, as large innovators like Wal-Mart have amply proven.

The attraction of POS systems is that they record each sale in a central database, using a scanner which reads the bar code on the product, so that retailers no longer have to wait for a periodic inventory check to find out what they need to reorder. Through centralized buying that ensures lower prices through volume purchasing and efficient distribution chains, Wal-Mart and others have turned up the pressure on large manufacturers who used to dictate when, how much, and where they would deliver. Many retailers are also targeting new product possibilities with lines of private-label goods, further reducing the power of brand manufacturers.

Information-based marketing can offer manufacturers and retailers a means to do market research and customer prospecting; to establish brand loyalty, market presence, and distribute redeemable coupons; and to create customized product bundles.

#### *Market Research and Customer Prospecting*

Conventional high-tech methods of collecting prospect data often cost millions of dollars, and that's before the first piece of direct mail gets printed. For a fraction of these costs, companies can put up Internet information servers and launch discussion lists on topics that their customers care about. The lesson that advertisers are learning is that these information vehicles must provide genuine value or they simply won't be visited. The feedback alone is worth a fortune in an era when market dynamics are approaching the speed of light and when companies that can be credible—not just clever—will win enormous advantages. Presence and intelligent interaction, not advertising, is the key that will unlock the commercial opportunities on-line.

In the future, marketing research will reward customers for listening to or watching commercials. An inkling of this is evident in a phone service that is dangling money in front of customers to entice them to listen to commercials. This optional phone service, called FreeFone, is provided to US West customers in Seattle for a small fee. Customers who make a call have the option of hitting a button to hear a short commercial message, such as, "Your call is being sponsored by Pizza Hut. Press the star key for a coupon." The caller receives 15 cents for listening to the first message, and an additional 15 cents for pushing the button for the coupon. The commercial messages are then tailored to consumers' interests, based on a questionnaire they fill out. What's in it for the company? It collects information about customer preferences that enables it to further refine its marketing strategy. And, the marketers might turn around and sell the detailed information they collect to others.

### *Market Presence*

The art of value-added corporate presence as opposed to "in-your-face" advertising will distinguish the new winners in the networked millennium. Let's paint a scenario. Suppose the automotive companies were to put up WWW servers. People shopping for a new car could save time by perusing product information, mileage data, and comparative costs on-line. They could read what the critics had said in *Consumer Reports*. Granted, companies might not be inclined to post negative reviews, but given the Internet's penchant for completeness, somebody surely would. This would give the company a chance to defend itself by raising another side of the issue or—hard as it may be to believe—by admitting it had made a mistake and committing to fix the problem in the next model.

Market presence can be intelligently choreographed through promotions. Customer information systems that collect detailed consumer purchase patterns will change the practice of promotional discounts, reducing across-the-board promotions and providing steeper but highly targeted discounts. Procter & Gamble and other manufacturers have already been replacing promotional discounts with "everyday low prices" in target markets. With emerging customer information technologies, it's possible for both manufacturers and retailers to offer discounts only to those customers for whom it pays, to those who are cost sensitive enough to switch brands or change shopping habits permanently.

### Product or Services Bundling

*Bundling* is a classic marketing strategy in which two or more complementary products and/or services are offered as a package at a discounted price. Examples of bundling include two-for-the-price-of-one airline tickets, computer hardware and software combinations, season tickets for sports, and meal specials in restaurants.

A seller must choose to adopt one of the following bundling strategies:

- *Only components.* The seller prices and offers the component products or services only as separate items.
- *Only bundles.* The seller prices and offers the component products or services only as a bundle.
- *Mixed strategy.* The bundled as well as the individual component products or services are priced and offered as options.

To evaluate the desirability of these alternative strategies for marketing products on-line, the seller must address four related questions: What are the prices of the bundle or components under each strategy? For each strategy, what are the levels of revenues and profits? For each strategy, which portion of the potential market is attracted? How sensitive are revenues to variations in price? Addressing these questions in tandem is crucial for any product manager to understand the impact of adopting any of the three strategies.

In the on-line world, information bundling becomes especially easy because of hyperlink capability. For instance, a computer video card could be linked to compatible or complementary products such as software that runs best on it, hardware that optimizes video performance, and so on. This raises issues such as: On what basis do we bundle products? Does bundling decrease information search cost? How do we sell bundled products that may be comprised of elements from different countries? How do we price these bundles in a global marketplace? Finally, what are the guidelines for implementing successful bundling strategies? Our lack of experience in online marketing is compounded by the fact that product bundling is a fairly new topic in the context of electronic commerce.

### Information-Based Products: Pricing and Priority

A new commodity, the information product, is emerging enabled in part by the global networking infrastructure. Examples of information products are software, entertainment, electronic books, information databases, and product catalogs. We can also include in this category secondary or derived information about products (such as on-line problem reports, frequently asked questions) that used to be part of customer service operations but today are emerging as a competitive differentiator in the on-line environment.

Two important information-based marketing-related issues are pricing and priority. On-line customers must pay for both products and services. They also need to pay for the infrastructure services associated with connectivity and for other services such as brokerages providing support for navigating through the information space and financial institutions supporting functions like payment and settlement. These competitive institutions will set charges as well. How are prices determined in a multi-participant world? What are the characteristics of supply and demand functions and what technology do we use to obtain information useful for price estimation?

Information products will most likely be priced based on speed of availability. For example, financial information from various sources such as currency, commodity, and over-the-counter markets may well have different prices associated with them depending on the speed and accuracy that the end user needs. A trader might place a higher premium on speed and tolerate a few errors in the process, whereas a researcher might be more oriented toward quality of data. To tailor the product to a variety of markets, a range of prices may be set based on the priority assigned by customers. For instance, a customer who needs product information in one-hour guaranteed delivery to meet a product design deadline might be charged more than a customer who is satisfied by an overnight delivery at off-peak hours. How to set prices for the different priority sets, how to specify sets, and how to take into account price competition will be questions that need to be readdressed in the context of electronic commerce.

Finally, in many information services it is unrealistic to assume that consumers know the total cost before they buy. The hiring of virtually any kind of services on a "per hour" basis must usually be arranged prior to knowing the final cost. Variable metered information services unrealistically assume that the consumer knows the cost of the information prior to purchase. More generally, whenever exact cost information is sufficiently difficult to obtain before purchase, consumers might proceed with a consumption decision in partial ignorance of the cost of what they are buying. This often results in "price shock" when the final bill is shown. For many on-line services, many customers never returned after getting the first bill. Improved metered information services will require more research to develop better ways of collecting and presenting pricing information about services.

## Target and Micromarketing

In electronic commerce, technology has put target and micromarketing within the reach of the small business. Computers have armed micromarketers with more knowledge, not only about their own business but also about the customer, to develop and exploit niche markets. Traditional mass marketers continue as if the population were homogeneous, whereas micromarketers not only have discovered various segments but are mining these profitable niches by targeting customers. Customer targeting is one way to get closer and to create and sustain a two-way flow of communication between the seller and the buyer. In today's world, getting close to the customer is particularly important when one considers that the average consumer is bombarded with a multitude of commercial messages daily.

Direct mail and telemarketing are two fast-growing ways to micromarket. Both methods are able not only to find prospects but to qualify them. Because both direct mail and telemarketing can be easily measured and quickly adjusted to appeal to the needs and expectations of a customer, they have been proven to be very effective sales tools. There are two main types of micromarketing:

1. *Direct-relationship micromarketing* is aimed at stimulating sales at retail establishments through direct contact with consumers in their homes.

2. *Direct-order micromarketing* is focused on selling products directly to consumers in their homes or businesses. Catalogers are in this segment of marketing.

Technology is an essential tool in micromarketing. Take, for instance, printing. Despite postal rate increases and changing markets, one publisher, Donnelley & Sons, has used technology to rack up strong sales increases and growth in its largest segments: catalogs, advertising inserts, and magazine printing. The company offers a range of services that go far beyond the traditional business of printing. It will manage a customer's database, or supply Donnelley's own consumer and life-style data to customers. The company offers services that segment and target customers' mailing lists. And it offers specialized "selectronic" printing facilities that make it possible to produce highly customized individual publications and allow a catalog marketer to offer different merchandise to different households or a magazine publisher to offer different editorial and advertising content to different subscribers.

In the past, direct marketing was prohibitively expensive for small businesses. But new technologies like Donnelley's Selectronic Services help control the costs. One of the first customers to take advantage of the selectronic process was the *Farm Journal*. This publication began collecting in-depth reader information decades ago, including demographics, farm size and ownership type, crops, and type and quantity of livestock. Today this information allows the magazine to provide tailored editorial and advertising content to small groups of subscribers. Donnelley now prints as many as 8000 different editions of the *Farm Journal* each month.

As new on-line technologies become feasible and as more customer information is gathered over the next decade, marketers will build databases of great scale and depth. There will also be advances in the degree to which targeted promotions and advertising become automated. Consider what's likely to evolve: with a wealth of fresh consumer data analyzed in powerful new ways, retailers and manufacturers will be able to define their target customers not just by demographic characteristics but also by complex clusters of actual purchasing behavior. They'll be able to probe almost continuously and test for new product opportunities. Promotions, discounts, and advertising will be highly tailored to different consumers. The customer will see a level of service that's impossible today, one that offers the broadest selection of specialized products yet also makes shopping a less burdensome task by serving the needs of the individual.

## Small Versus Large: The David Versus Goliath Syndrome

The key distinction between small business and large firms remains access to national and international markets for advertising purposes. Today, exorbitant advertising costs ($1.2 million for a 30-second spot during SuperBowl XXVIII) represent the barrier to reaching the customer effectively. The high costs of advertising have served to ensure that small businesses rarely grow beyond local markets.

With the advent of electronic commerce, small businesses can now bridge this gap. As the Internet and other public networks come of age, the privileged access to global audiences previously held by large companies can no longer be counted on to ensure market domination, since international audiences can be effectively reached by the use of innovative Internet-based advertising.

The major differences between the Internet and other I-way advertising media are ownership and membership fees. Ownership of the interactive media of tomorrow will rest in the hands of consortia consisting of telecommunications, cable, and entertainment industries. Advertising will most likely be restricted and/or expensive. In contrast, the Internet has no primary owners, no content controllers, and almost insignificant entrance fees. For these reasons, unlike the Internet, interactive television may not have a significant immediate impact on small to medium-sized enterprises. Instead, interactive television will consist of entertainment services controlled by multinationals as the cost of entrance into this consumer utopia will remain out of reach of the typical small business. Even traditional television advertising has never provided more than local advertising capability to small businesses. There is little reason to believe that the next generation of interactive TV advertising will be less expensive or more effective [IM94].

Due to the empowering effect of Internet-facilitated advertising, however, the balance of power between large and small companies may fundamentally change in the future. Recall the upheaval in the office supplies business, once dominated by giants like 3M, in the early 1980s. The smaller upstarts built around focused stores such as Office Max and Office Depot quickly took market share from department stores and other large companies and successfully forced a change in the power structure and a paradigm shift in the way office supplies are sold. With an ever-increasing percentage of the economy and job creation tied to the rise of global business, the distinct possibility exists that the balance of power may shift from inefficient, slow-moving corporate bureaucracies to highly adaptive companies. In sum, on-line advertising on public networks is expected to level the playing field for small to medium-sized businesses and enable them to compete with large corporations on a global stage. The corporate world will experience a rude awakening when it discovers that tens of thousands of small businesses are gaining an increasing share of the international delivery of products and services.

## Gray Areas: Regulatory and Legal Implications

The I-way brings to the fore a number of interesting regulatory questions: Should tobacco, pornography, or pharmaceutical companies be allowed to market in cyberspace? Many consumer goods firms base their direct marketing and promotional programs on databases of extensive customer information. Some manufacturers, such as the tobacco companies, will be able to build substantial customer information systems that may help them to create increased consumer demand for their products. In the case of certain products (like cigarettes), this may not meet with legal (or public) approval.

U.S. cigarette makers cannot advertise on television and are constantly threatened with losing their access to print media. To overcome these market barriers, they have developed some of the most advanced database marketing programs. For many years, the tobacco companies have offered discount coupons, prizes, and free merchandise in exchange for consumer questionnaires. Using this information, cigarette marketers have built extensive databases on the demographics and preferences of most American smokers. This information helps marketers anticipate market-segment changes, test new products, and target promotions aimed at increasing brand loyalty or encouraging competitors' customers to switch. For example, in 1987 Philip Morris conducted a blind taste test in which advertisements and flyers offered two free packs of an unnamed brand. Two million smokers responded by filling out a questionnaire. They each received two packs of Philip Morris's Merit brand and follow-up mailings. As a result, the company found that half a million smokers had been converted to Merit cigarettes [JBHBR93].

Another illustrative arena is prescription drugs. Upjohn's Rogaine, a product aimed at promoting hair growth, is not allowed to directly market to the consumer. The product's main ingredient, Monoxodil, can be prescribed only by an authorized doctor. The company employs an indirect method to reach the customer, where the customer is asked to call to get more information without ever being told what the product is. This example raises an incredible specter in the area of marketing health-related products. Can companies have a web server and place all the information on-line so that everyone can download it? Can they directly reach customers and offer promotions to buy their products?

And what about cyber sex. Any person with a modem can connect to *Playboy's* server or to *Penthouse* on the Internet and download images of nude centerfolds or playmates. While there are laws that forbid anyone under the age of 18 from buying this information in the store, there are no restrictions on accessing this information on-line. What, if anything, should be done?

In sum, the rules for regulating cyberspace marketing, advertising, and sales are still in the early stages. This is a gray area that will without doubt continue to be the focus of heated exchange.

## 13.2 ADVERTISING ON THE INTERNET

Regardless of the turmoil and uncertainty, the genie is out of the bottle. The topic of advertising on the Internet has become contentious and divisive. The notion of advertising and marketing became inevitable after 1991 when the Internet was opened for commercial traffic and it became clear that the U.S. government would not continue to finance its infrastructure, in essence privatizing the infrastructure.

The issue of how to advertise, just like many others, remains unresolved due to the lack of a specific policy and an authoritative body to enforce it. In their absence, the business community will need to be sensitive to the Internet user, and vice versa. Considering the kind of dialogue the Internet makes possible, however, there is no reason why Internet advertising could not peacefully coexist with any other aspect of doing business, and not degenerate into the mass mailouts that everyone hates.

The topic of Internet advertising provokes extreme opinions in many. One of the questions still discussed on some Internet forums (see INET-MARKETING discussion group archives at http://www.einet.net/) is whether advertising should be allowed on the Internet at all. Some who are not comfortable with any commercial activity in cyberspace have started Adbusters and other organizations that spread postings claiming that the Internet should not be soiled by advertising. This view presumes that the Internet is a haven from commercialization. It ignores the fact that business is already being conducted on the Internet and that advertising usually goes hand-in-hand with business. Everyone acknowledges, either publicly or privately, that advertising is a necessary evil, profits from which can subsidize other activities such as network improvements and cheaper access. On the individual level, however, many people are outraged at the thought of receiving unsolicited junk mail in their e-mail boxes.

Equating all advertising with junk mail is not fair to advertising in general. Advertising also serves many other purposes such as educating customers about "what's out there," introducing new products or alternatives to existing products, and stimulating a desire to buy by increasing consumer confidence. There are two very good reasons for embracing the inevitability of a growing amount of commercial advertising on the Internet:

1. *Advertising conveys much needed information*. Appropriate ways and means for conveying product or service information need to be devised, much as we already have for conveying the same through print and other media. This advertising should be interesting, message-oriented, and creative.

2. *Advertising generates significant revenue* and defrays the costs of infrastructure (commercial underwriting) and some existing research and education publications. We need to devise appropriate ways and means for such revenue generation.

Regardless of the polarity of various views, the question concerning whether advertising should be allowed on the Internet is rapidly becoming a moot point. What the business community needs to decide is how to do it properly and what etiquette needs to be followed.

A number of interesting proposals have come forth. Some have suggested the establishment of separate lists or newsgroups devoted to advertising, to which users could subscribe if interested in being kept up to date on new products and services. This would avoid the problem of receiving unwanted mail, though of course it would restrict the advertiser's ability to target potential customers. Another suggestion is that all e-mail advertisement messages have distinguishing characters in their subject lines so that users could easily identify them as such. This would allow advertisers to target potential customers, but would enable users to decide whether they are interested, and if not, remove the advertisement with the push of a button.

In addition, a host of key questions must be resolved before the Internet can compete effectively with commercial advertising:

- *Advertising process.* How can advertising be offered in a way that meets the needs of both advertisers and potential buyers without becoming the digital analog of junk mail?
- *Core content.* What kind of advertising content is most useful to both advertisers and potential buyers?
- *Supporting content.* What additional services (inquiries, orders, buyer support) can meet the information needs of advertisers?
- *Market and consumer research.* How can the needs of advertisers be met without either interfering with or invading the privacy of other on-line consumers?
- *Repeat customers.* How can viable, sustainable, and mutually beneficial relationships be created between information publishers, advertisers, and consumers?

At the heart of all these questions is the fact that users and advertisers must come to an agreement. The on-line marketplace is in a unique position to redefine the relationship between advertisers and consumers. Never before has it been so easy for users to contact an advertiser who is annoying them with a poorly conceived advertising campaign. Never before has it been so easy for advertisers to deliver advertising right to a consumer. These communication lines between Internet users and advertisers should be used to strike a balance between the needs of both groups. In fact, many Internet users believe that this reciprocal form of communication will effectively regulate advertising, since the members of the Internet community are able to collaborate and effectively undermine any particular advertising campaign. This process should not be seen so much as a policing force as a moderating one. The Internet user can help advertisers become more effective (and less offensive), and advertisers can do a better and more efficient job of promoting their products.

In the haste to explain the restraint of the Internet community to embrace the real and obvious value of advertising or direct marketing via the unsolicited distribution of marketing information, it is easy to overlook the important question of who pays. In the non-Internet world, the marketeer is responsible for the costs of direct marketing. Marketing communication is not cheap, as anyone who has had to send out thousands of copies of a direct mailing will attest. In the Internet world, in contrast, this cost is borne by the consumer and subsidized by the service providers. Many users pay for their connection to the Internet by the byte or character, and we all, in one form or another, pay for the "advertising pipe" or network infrastructure through indirect taxes. These facts may well drive the development of advertising guidelines for the Internet.

## On-Line Advertising Paradigms

Despite these unresolved issues, advertising on the Internet is inevitable. The next question logically becomes, What is the right paradigm for on-line advertising?

The temptation to send unsolicited advertising via electronic mail is strong, for two reasons. First, the cost of a 10-piece mailing on the Internet is the same as a 100,000-piece mailing. Of course, this does not take into consideration the actual bearer of the costs of distribution: the infrastructure providers that need to store the e-mail and transport it. Research has shown that this is substantial given that the message can easily reach 100 countries and be replicated in thousands of service providers' databases; second, it is easy to generate a list of leads from the vertical market segments that are easily identified within the network community. Users themselves support this segmentation by creating and participating in discussion groups either via USENET newsgroups or mailing lists.

Despite these advantages, traditional direct marketing via the unsolicited distribution of information is not the right model for Internet advertising. Two different advertising paradigms are emerging in the on-line world: active or push-based advertising and passive or pull-based advertising. Active or passive refer to the activity on the company's side. Push-based advertising's prime example is infamous broadcast or spamming (the Internet term for unsolicited advertising). Pull-based advertising is more discourse oriented and content driven and as such promotes interactivity between customers and firms.

## Active or Push-Based Advertising

In the context of most media today, advertising is inherently intrusive, even invasive. Print and TV ads are constant in-your-face reminders of who's paying the lion's share for information services. Prodigy tried to promote a similar form of on-line advertising but retreated when it brought howls of protest from users unwilling to share precious screen space with digitized messages. On the Internet, overt, sometimes even subtle, advertising often results in the unmerciful flaming (sending electronic hate mail) of the perpetrator.

Push-based advertising is of two types: the broadcast model and junk e-mail (direct and unsolicited advertising).

### The Broadcast Model

Broadcasting messages provides a means for reaching a great number of people in a short period of time. The broadcast model basically mimics the traditional model, in which the customer is exposed to the advertisement during TV programming.

Broadcast models typically use direct mail, spot television, or cable television. A spot television ad runs on one station in one market. The number of viewers who see, the ad depends on how many viewers are tuned into the television station at a specific time. The number of people reached by advertising depends on the penetration and channel/program viewership in a given market. Beyond television's reach, an additional advantage is its ability to convey the message with sight, sound, and motion. The disadvantages of television advertising are relatively high cost of production; limited exposure time; short air time (making it difficult to present a complex or detailed message); and the clutter of many other ads. Television ads may require multiple exposures to achieve message retention and consumer action. Many commercials are considered intrusive, moreover, prompting viewers to switch channels to avoid them.

Text-based broadcast messages can be seen in advertising posted in USENET news groups. Although frowned upon in most serious groups, it is becoming commonplace as more people come on-line. People do get flamed, even when asking for names and addresses of businesses or information about pricing of a product or service. To protect themselves from needless flaming, there is a tendency to answer with disclaimers of affiliation with the businesses whose information they are providing. We have seen people flamed for replying to a relevant question with "I own a business that offers what you want. We sell XX for $YYY." Commercial signatures with a company name, phone, and description of business sometimes get flamed, too. One way to avoid this is to reply to the person who is asking the question rather than broadcasting the reply back to the entire news group.

In general, the broadcast model is intrusive and resource intensive when implemented in on-line environments. Its principal drawback is that it requires active choice on the part of the customer to watch the program or read the message.

### *The Junk Mail Model*

Direct mail advertisers use targeted mailing lists to reach highly specialized audiences. In addition to low waste in ad exposure, direct mail provides an advertiser with great flexibility in the message presentation. Disadvantages of direct mail include relatively high cost per contact, the need to obtain updated and accurate mailing lists, the difficulty in getting the audience's attention, and the possible cost to customers who pay for e-mail, plus of course the noise factor. As an old marketing joke goes, junk mail is just poorly targeted direct mail. Junk mail is the most intrusive of all forms of Internet advertising, because it is easily implemented using electronic mail.

The electronic equivalent of direct mail is "junk e-mail." An e-mail message full of promotions engenders fear and loathing in the hearts of users and leads to the most vicious flaming. While the very openness of the Internet makes it possible to flood e-mail addresses with electronic flyers, the culture of the Internet stands squarely against it. Internet users see themselves as part of a great experiment, all sharing their knowledge freely without imposing on their fellow netters.

Junk mail creates an unwanted expense as well as an annoyance. Some people pay usage fees based on time on-line, or storage charges for mailboxes, and probably would not want to receive unsolicited junk mail. Even the post office charges the mailer, not the recipient, for direct mail. Even so, some advertisers will try sending junk mail to lists of e-mail addresses gathered openly or covertly. These advertisers believe that even if most of the recipients throw away the message (and hate the advertiser), those few users who are induced to buy will more than make up for papering the net with unwanted mail.

One infamous example of junk-mail spamming occurred in early 1994 when a firm specializing in immigration law in Arizona flooded the news groups with advertisements for its green-card services. Outraged Internet users responded by flaming. One effective method that knocked the perpetrators' computer system off-line was to bomb their mailbox with large files ranging from 1 to 10 Megabytes. The service provider who was providing access to these lawyers, NETCOM, had to initiate damage control as they too were being affected as a result of their client's actions. The following is a public apology from John Whalen, President, NETCOM Online Communication

Service, that was sent to many news groups. Since this incident, many other service providers have followed the same policy.

> Dear Fellow Network Providers and other interested parties:
>
> NETCOM Online Communications has taken the step of cancelling the service of Laurence Canter of Canter and Siegel, the lawyer commonly referred to as the "Green Card Lawyer." Mr. Canter had been a customer of NETCOM in the past. He had been cautioned for what we consider abuse of NETCOM, system resources and his systematic and willful actions that do not comply with the codes of behavior of USENET. Mr. Canter has been widely quoted in the print and on-line media about his intention to continue his practice of advertising the services of his law firm using USENET newsgroups. He has also widely posted his intention to sell his services to advertise for others using the newsgroups. We do not choose to be the provider that will carry his messages.
>
> NETCOM believes that we can and will refuse service to people who have demonstrated that they do not respect the guidelines preventing posting advertisements to inappropriate USENET newsgroups. As a commercial Internet service provider, NETCOM encourages commercial activity on the Internet and believes it to be an important part of a complete service. However, NETCOM also believes that commercial activities need to be undertaken in an orderly and thoughtful manner, with attention to appropriate usage and sensitivity to the cooperative culture of the Internet community. Our position is that NETCOM can be compared to a public restaurant where a customer may be refused service if the customer is not wearing shoes. For the health of the other customers and the good of the restaurant, that customer may be turned away. NETCOM believes that being a responsible provider entails refusing service to customers who would endanger the health of the community. Customers, commercial or not, who will contribute to the health of the community, respect the laws of the land, and the rights of others, will be welcome.
>
> With best regards for an expanded Internet community, I am,
> John Whalen, President, NETCOM Online Communication Service

## Passive or Pull-Based Advertising

Apart from the negative response it evokes, push-based advertising simply misses the fundamental point of interactive marketing—adaptability, flexibility, and responsiveness. Effective marketing requires a feedback loop leading back into the organization. It is this element that is missing from the monologue of advertising but that is built into the dialogue of pull-based marketing. Pull-based advertising provides a feedback loop, connecting company and customer: This is central to the definition of a truly market-driven company, a company that adapts in a timely way to the changing needs of the customer. This stands in sharp contrast to traditional mass marketing where the target audience is constantly exposed to advertisements in which they have no interest. Of questionable effect even in traditional media, such methods would be downright detrimental in the new on-line medium, given the ability of "flaming" to turn public opinion against the perpetrator.

The Internet offers more than the same old paradigm of advertisers bludgeoning passive consumers. The main difference is discourse, a word not much used in the business world but that sums up much of the Internet's core value. Discourse simply means people talking to other people. And on the Internet, this discourse is free—not just in the sense of "free speech" (though, importantly, it is that as well) but in the sense of costing next to nothing.

Why is discourse important? On the Internet, content providers and audience are not separate. The people who "consume" someone else's information may themselves provide new content in the next moment. They do it because they are enthusiastic or angry, turned on or livid about any of the topics, many of which involve commercial products and services. A classic example is the furor over the Intel Pentium chip, which caused some mathematical computations to go haywire. Jokes about the Intel company flew around quickly on the Internet and were widely reported by the media, forcing the company to recall and fix the faulty Pentium chip. As you read this, it is not farfetched to imagine that someone, somewhere is posting a rave or a flame about your company. If it's a rave, it'd be nice to know about it so you could tell your other customers how cool you are. If it's a flame by some disgruntled user, you can't afford not to know about it because a negative word can decimate your market reputation.

This is where the tables get turned. All those consumers to whom companies have beamed their ads for years have suddenly found their collective voice. But why would businesses participate in anything this terrifying? The answer is simple: They have no choice. This form of exchange will continue whether companies decide to participate or not. And choosing not to could have extremely damaging consequences.

On the positive side, entering into genuine discourse with customers can be rewarding, in terms of the bottom line. Companies like to say that they are customer-oriented but often they are not. They pay millions for advertising, then staff a single 800 number for complaints. This is a poor substitute for a dialogue involving thousands. Today, on-line interactions are not only possible, but expected. Many companies today are fielding questions, providing detailed answers and pointers to additional information, even engaging in useful debates on industrywide issues. Do customers and potential customers notice this? Of course they do. Are they more likely to remain or become customers as a result? Wouldn't you?

On-line pull-based advertising includes:

- *Billboards.* An example of pull-based advertising is the Web pages set up by many different commercial ventures.
- *Catalogs or yellow pages directories.* These directories are searchable or browsable databases of advertising.
- *Endorsements.* Specific postings are made to subject-oriented Internet discussion forums. Often recommendations from users are offered in other types of communications such as product-oriented or service-oriented Internet discussion forums.

### *The Billboard or World Wide Web (WWW) Model*

The billboard model refers to information placed where it will come to the attention of customers in the course of other activities and does not require active search. Billboard advertising is often used to reinforce or remind the consumer of the advertising messages communicated through other media. This is not so easy to implement without cooperation from others who link into your content and make you part of the World Wide Web.

The advantages of billboard advertising are ability to completely cover a market and maintain high levels of viewing frequency. The advantage of this model lies in its having no cost to customers. Also, it is readily implemented in the current environment by WWW, Gopher, and similar mechanisms.

The disadvantages of billboard advertising are related to viewing time. Because target consumers are typically surfing or moving, a billboard advertisement must communicate with a minimum of words. Messages must be simple, direct, and easily understood [EB94].

### *Catalog and Yellow Pages Directory Model*

The catalog model is the least intrusive model but requires active search on the part of the customer. Catalog services are becoming an essential tool for organizing information on computer networks as the ability to interact with a company is only possible if one can locate the people or organizations with whom they need to work. In fact it is widely acknowledged that one of the limitations imposed on the effective use of the network will be determined by the quality and coverage of directory services available. The term *directory services* refers not only to the types of services provided by the telephone companies' White Pages but to electronic resource location and services, yellow pages services, mail address lookup, and the like.

In an era so concerned with productivity, it is surprising that the demand for better electronic directories has not prompted more action, since the need for such services is everywhere as tens of thousands of new users subscribe to Internet every month and new resources are added almost every day. Several research groups are actively trying to develop directories. One early effort mimics the Yellow Pages model.

Traditionally, the most visible directory services for advertisers is the Yellow Pages. Big users of the Yellow Pages are emergency buyers, comparison shoppers, buyers of infrequently purchased items, newcomers to the area, and customers unhappy with a producer or distributor. The advantages of the Yellow Pages include ad permanence (the directories are kept as a regular reference) and the ability to target a well-defined area, ranging from a neighborhood to an entire metropolitan area. In addition, the Yellow Pages support other advertising by providing a convenient way for consumers to contact sources and obtain information on the products or services desired. Finally, the Yellow Pages are relatively low in cost in terms of both ad production and placement.

The disadvantages of the traditional Yellow Pages include lack of timeliness (ads can be changed only once per year and, as a result, there is no opportunity for "price advertising"), potential clutter in some classifications, and little creative flexibility. These disadvantages can be alleviated or even eliminated to some extent in the electronic world. This raises the issue of which technology is useful for creating these directories. Due to the importance of directories in electronic commerce, we discuss business directory creation and structuring in Chapter 14.

### Customer Endorsements

Endorsements, where people tell of their experiences with products and services—both positive and negative—represent one unique aspect of advertising on the Internet. As one participant on a stock news group (misc.invest.stocks) said:

```
There are many discount stockbrokers around in the Austin
area. The most accessible one I've found is First Stock
Broker on Interstate 35 and Airport Blvd.
```

```
(Here's the standard disclaimer: I am in no way affiliated
to the above broker except being a satisfied customer :-).
[From: tom@xxx.COM (Tom Smith) Date: Thu, 28 Oct 94
00:22:21 -0400]
```

Endorsements might be exempted from the "advertising" category, because they often come in the context of a question answered ("Does anyone know where I can get . . .") or an experience shared ("My service provider offers . . ."). Even when the endorsement comes from someone who works for the company, the promotion is accepted when it is not blatantly commercial and is a reasonable answer to a question posed by someone else.

Endorsements are among the most effective advertisements on the Internet, because they are offered publicly in an interactive medium. Anyone who disagrees can post his or her own opinions, and such debates often form the best—and most unbiased—analyses of products and services. Advertisers whose products and services are discussed positively by others gain customers and loyalty. And when an advertiser participates in the debate, the power of the Internet really comes through. Advertisers whose products are panned can learn first hand about customers' problems—and solve them and let others know that those problems have been solved.

## Some Guidelines for Internet Advertising

Understanding the right way to advertise on the Internet is extremely important as the negative or downside potential is extremely great for a small start-up or medium-sized firm. To avoid problems, Martin Nisenholtz of the advertising firm Ogilvy & Mather has come up with six guidelines for tasteful advertising on the Internet (*New York Times*, August 3, 1994, p. C16):

1. Don't send intrusive messages. People should not receive a commercial message they either haven't asked to receive or do not want to receive.

2. Don't sell consumer data without the express permission of the user. Unlike some commercial services where users generally understand that their names will be sold to other businesses, Internet data should remain the user's private property.

3. Advertising should appear only in designated news groups and list servers. The most objectionable advertising is unrelated commercial postings to newsgroups, which are usually cross-posted to hundreds of groups.

4. Conduct promotions and direct selling only under full disclosure. Marketers should be free to offer promotions on the network. But users should be given an opportunity to review the rules, guidelines, and parameters of an offer before they commit.
5. Conduct research only with the consumer's informed consent. Marketers should be able to conduct consumer research so long as respondents are made fully aware of the consequences of answering the research questionnaire.
6. Never use Internet communications software to conceal activities. Marketers should never gather data from users without asking for permission.

These guidelines seek a middle ground between being completely noncommercial and a complete free-for-all. However, in many ways they are very similar to those laid down for direct marketing.

## 13.3 CHARTING THE ON-LINE MARKETING PROCESS

Contrary to the hype, marketing on the Internet is neither as easy nor as straightforward as it appears at first glance. Our goal in this section is to unravel the "mystery" of Internet marketing. We describe the process of creating a marketing plan, distributing an advertisement, and interacting with customers in a clear step-by-step manner.

Let us assume that your company has decided to launch a direct marketing campaign on the Internet for a new product, a new store, or a whole new venture and you are put in charge of the marketing campaign. Numerous questions immediately come to your mind. What is my first step? What advertising process should I follow? What electronic material should I create? If I decide to set up a customer database, how can I segment the population of potential customers? When I have built up a database of potential customers, what can I do with it?

All companies must address these questions in the world of on-line marketing. Creating a successful marketing plan that fulfills these expectations under the given financial, time, and human resource constraints is a monumental task indeed. The primary goal is to design a marketing campaign well enough up front that leads to cost savings and revenue increases downstream.

Early Internet marketing efforts were oriented toward technology and consequently placed emphasis on the product and its associated information.

In recent years there has been a shift in Internet marketing from only complex, information-heavy products such as software and hardware with their multitude of features to more commodity-like items like stock quotes, newsletters, flowers, or lingerie. This has resulted in the emphasis shifting from the product focus to the marketing process of reaching and getting close to the customer. It is this elusive transition from product to process that firms must understand and adapt to in the emerging marketplace.

The product way of thinking is succinctly captured in Internet artifacts such as the Frequently Asked Questions (FAQs), which has been very successful. For instance, in the comp.os.windows FAQ, consumers can find valuable information about the Microsoft Windows operating system—such as tricks for enhancing speeds, productivity, and so on. More recently, we witnessed hypertext publishing that enables the creation of information webs of associated products. The information web is a more process-oriented tool. The change in technology requires a change in marketing philosophy. The popular direction that most companies adopted takes the stand that in hypertext publishing environments, Internet marketing is equivalent to creating a home-page on the WWW with an underlying assumption that "create it and the hordes will come." The fallacious assumption is that the product or service stands by its technical superiority and will be recognized by the customers as being superior. Little or no attempt is made to design, package, or communicate product information meaningfully to the target audience from their point of view.

The Internet in recent years has been used successfully by start-up companies in promoting and disseminating their new products. A notable example of this strategy, Netscape Communications, is emerging as a dominant player in the WWW marketplace by creating really new products called browsers. *Really new products* are defined as products or services that create, or at least substantially expand, a category rather than merely reallocate shares. These products are hard to forecast in terms of target customer, customer interest, or advertising strategy. They often require customer learning, and the development of infrastructure, and complementary products before they are successful. Let us explore the marketing strategy for introducing really new products.

## Marketing Strategy for New Product Introduction

Developing and introducing a marketing plan for a really new product is a process that demands imagination and sound judgment and almost always calls for a great deal of experience. This process is even more challenging for start-up companies, which must gain this experience quickly and cost effectively. Start-up firms do not usually have sufficient staff for the traditional market research (segmentation, product positioning, relationship marketing) conducted by large, established companies and seldom have sufficient funds to hire consultants skilled in these areas. Nevertheless, their success in today's highly competitive marketplace may well hinge on their understanding of the dynamics of the market, their ability to reach and interact with potential customers on a worldwide basis, and their ability to collect and analyze data that provide constant feedback about the soundness of their marketing strategy.

Difficult as this process is in all cases, start-up companies that are based on a really new product most often find that the difficulty of developing and implementing an effective marketing plan is compounded by the need to create an awareness of the product in the minds of both end users and distributors. "Priming the market" through a preliminary "educational" stage of marketing increases both the cost of introducing the product and the sales cycle, either of which can lead to the untimely death of start-up businesses with limited financial resources.

The unique characteristics of the Internet environment can assist start-up companies in this monumental task. The ability to reach global markets at no extra cost alone has the potential to break down the prevailing cost barrier separating small businesses from large corporations. Exorbitant advertising costs have traditionally represented the final barrier to growth for small businesses that could not afford national, let alone international, advertising. With no hyperbole intended, the development of effective methodologies for using the Internet as an international marketing tool could well revolutionize the new product introduction process.

## Adaptation of the New Product Introduction Process to the Internet

Any on-line marketing program has a better chance of being productive if it is timed, designed, and written to solve a problem for potential customers and is carried out in a way that the customer understands and trusts. All companies face the crucial task of developing the most effective method of getting their products to their target market. The critical decision of which distribution channels and marketing tools to use are a function not only of standard practices in the particular industry but also of the expertise and financial resources available to the company.

In the nascent world of electronic commerce, traditions and norms are few and far between and the basic issues are just beginning to be addressed. A totally new approach is required to address the fundamental marketing issues that need to be resolved for success in the electronic marketplace. These issues are far-ranging. How to position and differentiate the product in the eyes of the growing Internet population estimated at 20 to 30 million with a 10-percent monthly growth rate? How to generate pull forces emanating from the company that attract and lure the potential customer into visiting the company's server? How to effectively communicate on-line with the interested customer? How to innovate continuously so the customer returns?

These basic issues permeate the entire six-step interactive marketing process outlined in Table 13.2 and described in detail in the following sections.

### *Step 1: Segment and Identify the Target Audience*

Market segmentation is the process of dividing the market into separate and distinct customer groups. Its purpose is to determine differences among customers that may be of consequence in choosing whom to target and how—a prerequisite for product positioning.

**Table 13.2** Interactive Marketing Process on the Internet

| | |
|---|---|
| **Step 1.** | Segment and identify potential customers<br>(Initial market research done by reaching relevant groups—WWW servers, listservs, news groups) |
| **Step 2.** | Create promotional, advertising, and educational material<br>(WWW page with multimedia effects—audio and video)<br>(Product information and complementary products, order forms, and questionnaires) |
| **Step 3.** | Put the material on customers' computer screens<br>Push-based marketing—direct marketing using news groups, listservs and e-mail<br>Pull-based marketing—indirect (static) marketing—WWW pages |
| **Step 4.** | Interacting with customers<br>Dialogue with the customer; interactive discussion among customers about various features offering endorsements, testimonials, questions/answers |
| **Step 5.** | Learning from customers (repeat customers are 80 percent of the customer base)<br>Incorporating feedback from customer in advertising, marketing strategy<br>Identifying new markets, using experience in new product development |
| **Step 6.** | On-line customer service |

It is a widely accepted tenet that a marketing strategy for new product introduction focuses on customer satisfaction. But all too often the focal point, namely the customer, is missing in the calculations. This is especially true in start-up firms where the atmosphere is often oriented toward engineering issues and the attitude toward marketing lies more in the line of "build a better mousetrap and the customers will beat a path to the door." Segmentation allows companies to identify their target audience, all of whom need to know about the existence of a better product and still need to be convinced that they need one!

Typical segmentation approaches that need to be reengineered and carried out on the Internet include the following [WIND78]:

- *Demographic approaches* categorize the market in terms of population characteristics such as age, sex, income, occupation, race, family size, or religion. For example, banks associate deposit sources with demographics and create programs to focus on the elderly or workers over fifty, because these groups are perceived to be savers. Focusing on "upper income" groups, the 25–44 age group of heavy borrowers, or the 18–25 credit risk groups is also segmentation marketing. The goal is to find the relationship between profits or volume and the identifiable demographic characteristics and to use those characteristics for formulating the marketing programs. How do we do this when there is no centralized directory or organization keeping tabs on Internet users?
- *Benefit or behavioral approaches* divide the market according to how people behave, their attitudes, or the benefits they seek. For instance, in the case of financial products, one can use behavioral segmentation to distinguish needs according to a customer's position in her financial life cycle—whether she needs to borrow, save, invest, protect, manage her cash flow, or control her tax position. Another type of behavioral segmentation is based on differentiating between people who use on-line firms primarily for transactions versus those who use them primarily for prospecting and discovering information.
- *Volume approaches* distinguish heavy, medium, light, or nonusers of a product category and, after determining the profitability of the product and whether its users differ in some special way, focus product sales on the right volume target. For example, marketing programs focused on business users are a response to volume segmentation.
- *Business specialization approaches* categorize the market by type or size of industry or institution. This form of segmentation applies primarily to business or institutional markets. Special programs for small business are an example of business specialization segmentation.

The key question remains: How to accomplish all these segmentation strategies on the Internet's 20–30 million users? Because the interactive marketing strategy hinges on customer satisfaction, careful identification and segmentation of the population on the Internet is vital. Segmentation analysis is based on the premise that large markets such as the Internet that appear to be heterogeneous can actually be divided into smaller homogeneous segments. These smaller segments provide opportunities for developing highly customized marketing strategies designed to elicit particular responses from the target audience.

News groups on the Internet provide a convenient starting point. An estimated 6000 news groups are organized into a hierarchy that provides a loose form of a priori segmentation. It is very important to further reduce these news groups into segments that are interested in specific areas and thus could benefit from target products. For instance, to sell a medical device related to infection control, it makes no sense to post the product information to a software news group, but it may well make sense to post it to a cat or dog aficionado's list where a veterinarian might read it and discover a new use for the product not envisioned earlier.

Advertisers should start by reading the FAQ (Frequently Asked Questions) files associated with many news groups to determine the exact nature of the forum and acceptable use policies. Within some Internet forums, commercial activity, no matter how subtle, is considered inappropriate and will be met with strong disapproval. The next step for advertisers is to understand the selected newsgroups in order to tailor the product information.

Sorting through the hundreds of newsgroups is extremely labor intensive. For the immediate future, at least, the costs of Internet-facilitated marketing will most probably be a function of the labor involved in the segmentation phase, especially as Internet growth pushes the number of forums to the tens of thousands.

In sum, segmentation means "picking your spots," focusing more on business in one part of the market than another, in the hope of gaining a more profitable mix. Success will depend on selecting the right segment and creating an appropriate package with the image, products, and services required to meet those needs. It is this last step that creates perceived extra value and institutional distinctiveness in electronic markets.

**Product Differentiation and Positioning.** Central to all businesses is product differentiation—success in appealing to desirable market segments so as to maintain visibility and create defensible market positions. Differentiation has become almost gospel among the early Internet pioneers who set up very successful WWW servers such as HotWired and O'Reilly's Global Network Navigator (GNN). These firms realized that the key to their survival as part of the new electronic marketplace was "finding and addressing a niche." Unfortunately, for every one company that has realized this there are at least ten others that took the wrong path in thinking that simply creating a home page on the WWW is effective marketing.

Differentiation is based on the view that charging a better price or achieving higher profit on products or services is dependent on the ability to differentiate oneself from the pack and forge an institutional identity. To better capture this notion of effective marketing, we state our "Law of Differentiation": As the blurring of distinctions among firms in electronic markets increases, survival requires that you identify your unique role in the marketplace in terms of value to the customer.

This law is based on that fact that although there is relatively little differentiation among on-line firms today, most will have to choose their niche in the market rather than "trying to be all things to all people." This implies that there should be some extra value in doing business with the on-line firm. Thus differentiation is the process of focusing on the identification of tangible and intangible customer needs (for both consumer and corporate markets) and creating an appropriate superior cluster of products, value-added services, and image to meet those needs.

While the notion of differentiation is easy to articulate, it is often difficult to execute. Added to that, there is much confusion about what differentiation really means in the context of electronic markets and how to go about finding your best market niche. Segmentation is only one technique for creating value-added differentiation. Differentiation goes beyond segmentation to other techniques—product bundling and packaging, price, service quality, delivery systems and organization, and strategic themes like rewarding customer loyalty—that create perceived extra value in the eyes of the customers and thereby establish the institutional distinctiveness required for survival.

### Step 2: Create a Coherent Advertising Plan

The product differentiation plan should carefully lay out the advertising campaign. On-line advertising is a form of investment similar to other investments to improve and expand business. The returns depend on the planning and thought that precede the actual commitment and expenditure of advertising dollars. By first developing an effective advertising plan, firms increase the likelihood of a positive return on the advertising investment. The basic premise of an advertising plan requires firms to analyze the answers to four key questions: What is the ad meant to accomplish? Who should the ad "talk" to? What should the ad say? What advertising medium would be effective? In a specific business situation, each of these questions has any number of potential answers. As you think about each question do not settle on any answer until you have considered and explored the full range of possibilities.

The first step in developing your advertising plan is to specify your advertising goals. Why are you advertising on line? What do you want to achieve? Everyone wants advertising to increase business, but for your advertising plan to work you must be precise. Goals for your advertising include increasing awareness of your business, attracting competitors' customers, increasing the likelihood of keeping current customers and developing their loyalty, and generating immediate sales or sales leads.

You may want your advertising to achieve all of these goals plus some others. What is important is that you prioritize your goals. Keep in mind that advertising works best when it is developed to meet one specific goal at a time.

Once you have determined your advertising goals, select the target audience for your message. Advertising that tries to reach "everyone" rarely succeeds. Successful advertising is written with a specific customer in mind. Try to picture the customer you must reach in order to achieve your advertising goals.

Once you know who your target audience is and what they are looking for in terms of the product or service you offer, you can decide what your advertising will say. Your advertising should "speak" convincingly to your target audience, explaining the important benefits your product or service offers. In deciding how to discuss the major benefits of your product or service in your advertising, keep AIDA in mind: attract *a*ttention, hold *i*nterest, arouse *d*esire and motivate *a*ction.

New advertising options are becoming increasingly available. Using the "traditional" approach, you can place ads in airports, on ski lifts, and on television monitors in the front of grocery carts. In the "on-line" approach, you can place ads in news groups, bulletin boards, Yellow Page directories, and WWW pages. Where you place your advertising should be guided by a simple principle: Go where your target audience will have the highest likelihood of seeing or hearing it. Many advertising media work well to reach a diverse range of target consumers. No single medium is inherently good or bad. A good medium for one product or service may be a poor medium for another. As you consider media choices, look for one that fits your advertising goals, reaches your target efficiently and cost effectively, and is within your budget.

Once an advertising campaign has been devised, corresponding promotional materials specially tailored for each particular target audience need to be developed. This includes both traditional advertising materials and knowledge-oriented material. This raise the question: How to create effective content on the Internet? Effective content, in general, remains a puzzle to those who create it and to those who sponsor it. Often, the ad that generates record-breaking volume for a product or service one month is repeated the following month and turns out to be a disaster. A campaign designed by the best ad agency may elicit a mediocre response. The same product sells like hotcakes after a thirty-word classified ad, with poor grammar, appears on page 23 of a catalog sent via third-class mail! The conundrum eludes solution but demands attention, given the billions of dollars spent every year on advertising.

**Interactive Advertising.** Traditional advertising copy tends to be *linear* in nature and typically assigns the customer a passive role. The interactive form of advertising, in which the customer has control over what he or she sees is known as *nonlinear advertising*, is made possible through the use of hypermedia that allows the reader to "click" on specially highlighted items to immediately access more information. In fact, documents can and often are linked to others submitted by completely different authors. This closely resembles footnoting in the traditional print media, but with instantaneous retrieval of any number of multimedia possibilities ranging from still images, animation, digital video, and audio.

The challenge in this new environment is the creation of appropriate interactive content that is compelling, informative, and nonlinear. Several variations of hypermedia documents need to be developed and experimented with to determine overall guidelines for the development of effective promotional materials tailored specifically for this medium. Keep in mind that documents are like TV advertisements. They contain video, audio, and still images.

**Content-Oriented Advertising.** Interactivity is not enough. To support it, value-laden content is essential. The Internet community appreciates quality, information that adds value, since nothing is more obvious than empty promises. So do not expect product advertising alone to be sufficient. To support content-oriented marketing, companies often publish or mail electronic newsletters that report relevant innovations or news. This way, each customer can quickly learn about and assess the comparative advantages of various products in the news In addition, companies also focus on informing customers about their own product-related developments, information on country-specific usage, and testimonials from customers. By making the transfer of information easy through the use of a conversational format, a company can leverage the ideas of its staff and spread organizational values in addition to subtly promoting a desired image of excellence and relevance.

Content-oriented marketing requires a company to master a broad range of knowledge: the technology in which it competes, its competition, its customers, new sources of technology that can alter the competitive environment, and its own organization, capabilities, plans, and way of doing business. Armed with this mastery, companies can put it to work in three essential ways: integrate the customer into the process to guarantee a product that is tailored not only to the customer's needs and desires but also to the customer's strategies; generate niche thinking to use the company's knowledge of channels and markets to identify segments of the market that the company can own; and develop the infrastructure of suppliers, vendors, partners, and users whose relationships will help sustain and support the company's reputation and technological edge.

### Step 3: Get the Content to the Customer

As discussed previously, companies need to implement a combined push and pull strategy of content delivery. Dissemination of information about the company and its products via various news groups, listservs, and e-mail will constitute a cost-effective method to reach large numbers of individuals in various target audiences. Although on the surface this closely resembles a traditional push strategy, an important difference lies in the ability to build in valuable feedback loops.

Alongside this approach, however, a strong pull-based marketing ("marketing by invitation," not intrusion) is a more effective method of marketing on the Internet. One of the essential ingredients of pull-based marketing is the skilled management of customer information and their activities on the Internet so that the most responsive customers can be identified through the use of predictive models. These models will enable us to send the right message, at the right time, to the right people in the right form (news group postings, e-mail, newsletters).

Feedback loops should be incorporated in the strategy to help continuously drive the marketing program to greater and greater efficiencies and productivity. These loops will capture and store respondent names, response rates to various mailings, and customer activity in terms of access logs of the interactive content stored on the WWW page.

Companies must explore the accumulation of customer data through nonintrusive means. Under traditional circumstances, it is difficult for most companies, and particularly so for start-ups where contact costs are high, to obtain data on their customers, their interests, and demographic variables. Even if this were feasible, feeding the results back into the marketing strategy and cleaning up and restructuring the ad campaign could cost exorbitant amounts in traditional advertising. It is often stated that it takes six months to change a catalog advertisement because a large number of parties have to be coordinated. In contrast, once acquired and analyzed, on-line information can be immediately used to feed the modeling process and change the interactive content for greater effectiveness. The expected results of this vastly increased flexibility are greater market share, cross-selling successes, and improved customer retention and satisfaction.

### *Step 4: Correspond and Interact with Customers*

One of the most powerful features of Internet-facilitated marketing is the wide variety of potential interactions possible. We restrict the discussion to four levels of interaction with potential customers:

1. *Passive interaction via anonymous FTP sites.* A broad variety of information about the company, product, and other related material can be placed in a public area accessible by any interested party by simply dialing in and using the user name: anonymous and password: guest. This is a well-known method used on the Internet for the dissemination of research papers, software programs, photographs, videos, and other material. The goal is to provide a channel where the customer is completely unfettered to do as he/she pleases with no sales pressure.
2. *Direct interaction* (one-on-one) via electronic mail (e-mail) or chat facility. Talk allows two parties to hold a discussion on-line. The goal of direct interaction is to answer questions, answer requests for more information, and follow up on a customer.
3. *Group dialog* between company and customers through bulletin boards, news groups, and other forums. The goal of group interaction is to encourage discussion among customers, provide an easy way to answer questions about unanticipated problems that may occur during product usage, and simply build a database of long-term experience-based knowledge about the product and its usage. How do you go about this? Create a USENET news group for discussion of your products. By creating your own forum, moderating the submissions (filtering out irrelevant postings), and providing high-quality information, not only about your products but about your particular commercial sector, you can establish a growing readership in much the same way that newsstand magazines function.
4. *Video conferencing* on the Internet using the Multicast Backbone (MBone) facility where several distributed parties can actively participate and monitor product-related activities. In the case of medical products, for example, companies could broadcast actual medical procedures being

conducted in the field. MBone allows the digital broadcast of live audio, video, and text with interaction among the participants through a common blackboard (actually white-board in computing terms). MBone is a relatively new tool and shows us a glimpse of the potential of digital video broadcasts to subscribing audiences (see Chapter 18).

### Step 5: Learn from Customers

Since good ideas are often a company's scarcest resource, efforts to encourage and reward their generation, dissemination, and application in the further development of products will build both relationships and profits. One part of learning is evaluation. A real-world test of the marketing plan will provide estimates of marketing-plan productivity, suggestions for improving the plan's productivity, and a disaster check.

The market provides measures of consumers' responses to those elements that have been pretested—the product, the price, and the communication plan. It also measures the acceptance of these measures. By measuring levels of consumer awareness, product trial, repeat purchase, market share, and sales volume, the market gives some indication of the productivity of the elements of the marketing plan.

The information regarding the tracking of accesses to the company's materials over the Internet can be compared with any tangible results obtained through other channels (inquiries, contacts with distributors, end sales, references in literature). This analysis will be used to determine how the company's promotional and marketing strategy and materials can be altered to better suit the needs of the target groups they are reaching as well as to determine how best to reach the target groups not yet responding.

### Step 6: Provide Customer Service and Support

On-line customer service is an essential part of the electronic commerce chain, where people are more in touch with one another than in any other type of market. This has both good and bad consequences. Word about a new product from a small company can spread quickly and widely if there is excitement; conversely, problems can be reported with equal speed and breadth. Thus companies must be constantly on their toes when it comes to customer service.

When problems confound users, good vendors know the support they provide must run the gamut of phone, fax, CD-ROM, third-party, and on-line services. On-line services can include bulletin boards and knowledge bases provided directly by the vendor, public forums or special interest groups (SIGs) on commercial services such as CompuServe, or news groups and archives on the Internet. Increasingly, however, vendors and users alike are turning to on-line support over other options for a variety of reasons. Going on-line may seem impersonal, but it's often less hassle than phoning up a technician who may or may not be there, explaining your problem to a voice-mail machine, providing documentation for your symptoms, and then waiting for a reply.

Brand loyalty through customer service needs to be cultivated among on-line customers so that they can come back for repeat purchases. Few consumers seem to demonstrate lack of brand loyalty quite like those on-line. When information is needed, the customer is more interested in the source than in a particular brand or even small variations in price. So there is a definite need to develop loyalty-building methods in the electronic marketplace. The question is how and in what form.

Loyalty and service quality are often interrelated and involve several questions: What does service quality mean in on-line environments? What are the dimensions of service quality? Is it based on the quality and speed of delivery, presentation/interface clarity and ease of usage, organization of various products on electronic shelves, and speed of transaction and settlement?

## 13.4 MARKET RESEARCH

Electronic commerce has brought to the fore the question, How do we know that we are being effective in the electronic world? What are the metrics or yardsticks for measuring effectiveness? Effectiveness is primarily measured via market and consumer research. Market research is extremely important for companies in terms of how they allocate their advertising dollars in sales promotions, how they introduce new products, and how they target new markets. Broadly speaking, we can divide market research into three phases: data collection, data organization, and sense making. Each phase shows a different level of maturity in adapting to electronic commerce.

### Data Collection

Traditionally, marketing has relied on source databases for understanding consumer behavior. Source databases mainly comprise numeric information and are directed at the business and economic sectors for market research purposes. Delivery of source database services follows two main patterns.

Either a database producer will collect and collate data, making it available, as does Dow Jones, through its own computer facility, or central hosts like CompuServe, America Online, Prodigy, and other data centers will provide customized access through specialized software packages.

Source databases can also be created directly from WWW usage. For instance, every WWW server keeps a detailed audit log of what files were accessed, how frequently they are being downloaded, what user domains are accessing these files, and so on. This information is in many ways similar to the scanner data obtained at POS terminals. It gives us the ability to systematically piece together how consumers are viewing the published. information, what paths they are navigating, how much time they spend on each page of information, and so on. This knowledge can be effectively used to tailor the information that customers interact with. From a marketing perspective, several questions need to be addressed. How do we collect and aggregate this information over several sites? How do we effectively use this information? For creating better content or for creating better strategies?

## Data Organization

The ability to refine and customize information for select business customers is one of the key abilities in this environment. It also enables the company to (1) leverage its established databases into customized offerings aimed at different audiences and markets; (2) leverage its established databases in terms of horizontal growth by cross-selling into a different market that may be in another industry or region; and (3) grow vertically by selling to the same customer through bundling additional or new value-added information, in terms of fulfilling a need that the customer never anticipated.

Everyone is collecting data in electronic commerce, but very few are organizing it effectively for developing a marketing strategy. The challenge sounds simple, but for retailers and others who are interested in consumer data the task has become almost impossible. In retail chains with hundreds of stores, thousands of store-level employees are expected to formulate a companywide buying plan. The retail stores cut across geographical and cultural boundaries, as do the goods put on the shelves. But centralized planning and buying have difficulty acknowledging all the regional differences and rarely take advantage of short-lived selling opportunities. In short, the ability to repackage, customize, and organize customer information into a sensible strategy is an area of electronic commerce where more work is requred.

### Data Analysis and Sense Making

Initially, source databases, particularly numeric databases, were considered to have a very narrow market area. The ability to link databases to analytic tools like econometric programs and forecasting models has greatly increased the potential market. Examples can be found in trading and brokerage houses where historic stock data are analyzed in (possibly futile) attempts to predict the future trends in the stock market and certain stocks.

In short, market research is undergoing major changes. The next generation of source databases will definitely include multimedia information that we do not know how to use effectively. For example, scanner data obtained from supermarket checkout counters are primarily numbers and are often used to count how much of the product was sold in which store. Now imagine a camera taking digital images and relaying them back to the data collection company, and a whole new range of possible areas of research opens up. By looking at images, we can see how placement of products affects customer buying by answering important marketing questions. Are women buying products in greater numbers than men in certain geographic regions? Are women more impulsive buyers and do they take less time than men in evaluating the product? Such questions can dictate how advertising budgets are allocated regionally or locally. However the issue of customer privacy looms large. Achieving a balance between gaining market intelligence and intrusion will be a hotly debated issue for the long term.

## 13.5 SUMMARY

The integration of electronic commerce and marketing should bring with it a renaissance of advertising, sales, and marketing functions as it presents an opportunity to get close to the customer, to bring the customer inside the company, to explore new product ideas and pretest them against real customers. In short, the paramount scope of the company—including all the attributes that concurrently define how the company does business—becomes the function of marketing. This chapter addressed several on-line marketing related issues (see Table 13.3).

Advertising and marketing are both a means to finance the infrastructure and a powerful tool for electronic commerce. With the pressure for advertising comes a need for guidelines if order is to be maintained. These guidelines can be created, and they will be welcomed by advertisers and users alike. Two broad suggestions should be followed to achieve successful on-line advertising: Provide quality information and don't impose on people.

**Table 13.3** Issues in Marketing and Advertising

| | |
|---|---|
| Product and price-related topics | Nature of consumer-product interface<br>Information-based products—creation and bundling<br>Information pricing and priority |
| Promotion-related topics | Electronic market segmentation and product positioning<br>Cultivating brand loyalty<br>Broadcast vs. narrowcast advertising<br>New product introduction |
| Market research methods and tools | Market research using WWW access-logs<br>Market research using source databases |
| Managing the search space (see also Chapter 14 and 16) | Interactive catalogs and directories<br>Electronic institutions or brokerages<br>Software agents |

It is conceivable that in the future every human with access to a computer will interact with companies. However, that ability will be useful only if users can locate the people or organizations with whom they need to work. This inability to find the product or service of interest quickly is the biggest barrier to effective advertising. The problem becomes more acute as tens of thousands of new services and companies come on-line monthly. Thus, as electronic commerce grows, one of the limitations imposed on the effective use of the network will be determined by the quality and coverage of directory services available (see Chapter 14).

Today, consumers are fairly passive. That will change very slowly, as consumers need to be educated and behavior has to be modified to adjust to electronic commerce. It's important to be forward-looking as marketing communications have become more complex and interesting. Business professionals have to be ahead of their customers and make sure they have the answers to questions when clients pose them. In other words, we have to be prepared for the future of interactive marketing.

Chapter 14

# Consumer Search and Resource Discovery

If you've ever tried looking for a specific bit of information on any of the on-line services or on the Internet, then you have undoubtedly experienced the frustration of knowing that what you want is available but buried somewhere. Either you don't know how to find it, or you've spent hours digging through piles of data just to get one helpful piece of intelligence. In short, finding what you want on-line is not easy. But take heart: Help may be on the way with the steady advancements in search and discovery technology that bode well for electronic commerce.

Two fundamental goals of electronic commerce have been to increase the *availability* and *accessibility* of useful information. Availability is accomplished through improved publishing tools that provide ready access to a voluminous amount of product information, including descriptive information from sellers (price, features, availability, and other "search" qualities) and rating information from third parties (on "experience and credence" qualities such as performance, reliability, and ease of use). The publishing aspect of WWW, for example, offers a solution to the availability problem.

The second goal, accessibility, might be enhanced through search and retrieval tools. With thousands of databases, it can often take consumers hours or days to navigate the vast web of information. The goal of search tools is to utilize the information-processing power of the computer to improve decision making without increasing the time and the effort expended in making choices. This is not to suggest that the aids necessarily substitute for human information processing, but rather that they augment it by either reducing the amount of "superfluous" information to be processed or by organizing the information in a way that enhances its usefulness.

Hence, designing flexible ways of navigating, searching, and retrieving pertinent information from on-line databases is important in light of its implications for individual and organizational decision making. This need affects both individual consumers as well as organizations. In the case of consumer-oriented electronic commerce, consumers search on-line stores (or databases) for the best product in terms of price, functional or aesthetic characteristics. In the case of organizations, search is a process through which an organization adapts to changes in its external environment such as new suppliers, new products, and new services.

## Information Search Challenges

Information search can be very complex and unfortunately remains one of the least understood in electronic markets. Being lost in cyberspace is a very common and vexing problem. Today, the average Joe Consumer is discovering that finding information in the on-line world can be tricky, for several reasons.

First, turnover of information is rapid, given that electronic market environments tend to be information intensive and constantly changing. Consumers also experience frequent turnovers in their general stock of knowledge and so must engage in extensive search efforts to keep up to date. The fact that information gathering is costly and in some cases time sensitive (e.g., stock quotes), however, can motivate consumers to curtail search processes and act on the acquired information before it becomes obsolete.

Electronic markets impose different types of information processing demands on consumers due to the rate of information change. The challenge is to design search and retrieval processes that maximize an individual's value in terms of time, cost, and information needs. In addition, the rapid turnover of information makes information filtering and data mining tools very important. These tools allow users to conquer and manage the copious amounts of information flowing in their direction and evaluate various products based on attributes and specified criteria.

Information overload is the second factor contributing to long search times. Users must be able to find a small number of products that form the best alternatives to suit their individual search needs (or preferences). For instance, if you go to a store and ask a sales representative to guide you to a certain product with characteristics or attributes (a, b, c), the salesperson will be more than willing to take you to the shelf or show you a substitutable product. The electronic environment currently offers no similar service, although software agents that mimic store clerks are a definite possibility in the future.

Suggesting substitutes is very difficult unless we can understand the customer's needs. While consumers may know their individual preferences, they lack knowledge of which products have which attributes. Consumers need to refine initial preferences as they learn more about the environment they are working in. Learning about the environment involves knowing "what is where," by organizing or structuring the information space through the use of directories and catalogs. Directory and catalog structures allow consumers to navigate and browse through the product information spaces and learn about complementary or substitutable products and services.

Finally, the focus is on the human–technology interface features that would enhance the customer's ability to make decisions and interact with the on-line environment. The next generation of user interfaces has to recognize and accommodate the fact that customers want information about the products and services they buy; they want to make intelligent choices based on "complete" information. They want to know as much as they can about these products and services, and they want to be able to access that information quickly and easily when they need it. The challenge is how to represent this information on the screen in an effective manner. New interfaces developed using virtual reality modeling languages promise to open new avenues for exploration.

Fortunately, a number of methods are being developed to help users search, discover, and filter the on-line information. The purpose of this chapter is to examine some of the tools and techniques associated with information search and retrieval interfaces. Specifically, we explore buyers' and organizations' search efforts and the specific search methods they employ. Using this as the backdrop, we describe various technological tools and techniques that are being developed for enabling and managing search in electronic commerce.

## Scenario: Integrating Search and Purchasing

Before delving into the specifics of search and retrieval, it is necessary to understand the search process involved in on-line purchasing. Research has shown that as the number of items in a choice set reaches four or five brands, consumers are forced to adopt a two-step process. The first step is an elimination of brands that are deficient on some attribute, and the second phase is a careful evaluation of the remaining brands. Let us consider this two-step process in a on-line scenario of buying a car.

Joe and Jane Consumer agree it is time to buy a new car. They have held on to their old vehicle in part because they hated their last car buying experience—the hours spent at the library going through various Blue Books evaluating specific cars; the seemingly endless trips to car dealers where they got little information other than glossy brochures; the hassles of getting a car loan and new insurance; and the disappointment upon later learning that one of their friends bought the same car with more options for much less.

This time, they think, maybe their PC and Internet connection can help. They know they need a larger vehicle for their growing family, but which is best—a minivan or a four-wheel drive utility vehicle? An on-line search pulls up independent reviews by various magazines that outline the advantages and disadvantages of each model. Still not sure which they would prefer, Joe and Jane Consumer review safety and performance reports on four minivans and four utility vehicles, chosen from their initial search. The reports provide information on consumer satisfaction, reliability, and the estimated maintenance and operating costs of each model.

To get a car owner's perspective, the couple decides to access the on-line news groups dedicated to discussion about these cars. They initially peruse the Frequently Asked Questions (FAQ) to get an idea of the news group and then read the various postings. They come across dealer information, warranty information, and other insights about the various features that are often invaluable in decision making. The couple also posts specific questions and receive answers, often within minutes. Based on this interaction, the couple prune their list to two minivans and two four-wheel utility vehicles.

The couple now decides to take a look at the candidate cars—the automobile manufacturer's server allows them to see a digital video of the car, as well as view different colors, interiors, upholstery, and other options. The interactive display allows them to select options such as engine size, sound system, rear passenger air bags, and customized climate controls, while at the same time showing the estimated cost for these options and the impact on fuel consumption. Some companies even allow the couple to custom design their car, choosing power brakes, for example, while bypassing power windows if they prefer. The availability of a car with the chosen options is shown at the bottom of the screen, along with an estimated delivery time for special orders. Reviewing the various choices available, the couple narrows their choice to two models.

While Joe and Jane could order their car directly from the manufacturer, like most drivers they want to experience for themselves how the car feels and handles and find a reputable dealer near their home who can perform routine maintenance and repairs.

Using electronic yellow pages, they search for information on which dealers of the two models are located within a ten-mile radius of their home, have service hours on Saturdays and until at least 8 P.M. on weeknights, and offer shuttle service to and from public transportation or work. This information is displayed on a computer-generated map. Using the computer mouse to click on a specific dealer, information is displayed on the length of time the dealer has been in business, whether loaner cars are offered, customer satisfaction rates, and other considerations.

Joe and Jane notify two dealerships via e-mail that they would like to make appointments for test drives on Saturday morning. Using an electronic brokering service, the couple checks information on the best advertised price for the cars and whether it is best to lease or buy. The broker also checks for the best loan terms available for a new car purchase and offers electronic loan application forms that can be filled out, then sent electronically to the chosen lender. Another click and the couple compares insurance rates for the two cars. Is one more likely to be stolen and therefore more expensive to insure? How much can they save on insurance rates by investing in an alarm system? What company offers the best rates for their particular driving history and needs? Which has the greatest level of customer satisfaction in processing claims?

On Saturday morning, Joe and Jane test drive the two cars. That afternoon, they issue an electronic bid, which is answered by an electronic brokerage service. Upon acceptance of the best offer, they activate a process that orders their new car from the factory. Electronically generated loan and insurance procedures are carried out as well, so that a week later, when the dealer's courtesy van comes to pick them up at their home, the couple signs the papers and drives home in their new car.

Much of the technology described in this example of electronic commerce is available today, but on a fragmented basis. Currently users are left to integrate the various fragments. In the future, this integration would be offered by companies as they see the benefits of providing consumers a well-thought out and integrated business process.

## 14.1 SEARCH AND RESOURCE DISCOVERY PARADIGMS

Broadly speaking, three information search and resource discovery paradigms are in use: information search and retrieval, electronic directories and catalogs, and information filtering [RD92].

### Information Search and Retrieval

Search and retrieval begins when a user provides a description of the information being sought to an automated discovery system. Using its knowledge of the environment, the system attempts to locate the information that matches the given description. Application of information retrieval methods has traditionally been in domains such as libraries, where users have been highly focused (or motivated) in their information-seeking behaviors. For instance, when users enter a library, they know roughly what they are looking for. In these cases the solution is to find the closest matches based on certain keywords, for instance, to find all books by author Clarke, Arthur. This will return all matches in the database that fit a given description.

The challenge is to develop retrieval and search strategies that help the naive or unfocused user in domains such as electronic shopping. For instance, finding the five closest products matching criteria A, B and C could require going to many servers and evaluating several products. The challenge is to minimize the cost and time of executing the query and maximize customer satisfaction. Thus search and retrieval methods that refine queries through various computing techniques such as nearest neighbors, term variants of original query, and other methods may be useful.

## Electronic Directories and Catalogs

Information organizing and browsing is accomplished using directories or catalogs. Organizing refers to the human-guided process of deciding how to interrelate information, usually by placing it into some sort of a hierarchy (e.g., the hierarchy of products in a electronic catalog). Browsing refers to the corresponding human-guided activity of exploring the organization and contents of a resource space.

The main weakness of information organizing is that it is typically done by "someone else" and is not easy to change. Ironically, this is also its main strength, because people prefer a fixed system they can get used to, even if it is not the most efficient. Maintaining a well-organized database when large amounts of data are continuously changing is difficult.

The notion of "well organized" is highly subjective and personal; what one user finds clear and easy to browse may be difficult for users who have different needs or backgrounds. Moreover, because there are few barriers to publishing information, a great deal of organized information may be useful to few users, and often for only a short period of time.

Information browsing depends heavily on the quality and relevance of the organization. Browsing can lead to navigation problems and disoriented users. To some extent, this problem can be alleviated by systems that support multiple views of same information. Yet, providing views really pushes the navigation problem "up" a level—users must locate appropriate views, which in itself is another discovery problem.

## Information Filtering

The goal of information filtering is to select all and only that information that is relevant and reduce it to a manageable and understandable set. The focus here is on providing efficient access to the constantly changing information for a specific task. In most cases, information relevant to a given task is a small subset of the total information accessible at any given time. Therefore, given a user request for information, the challenge is to proactively collect a small relevant subset and present it to the user.

This access is controlled through software filters that only allow pertinent information to pass through in a form that enables the decision maker to have more choice and flexibility in responding to a volatile business environment. Filters are of two types: local and remote. Local filters work on incoming data to a PC, such as news feeds. Remote filters are often software agents that work on behalf of the user and roam around the network from one database to another.

Software filters must search and retrieve information in a manner that conserves scarce network bandwidth and processing capabilities. For this purpose, filters must be cognizant of the wide variety of multimedia information types available, including text, pictures, maps, and sensor information. In many cases it may be more appropriate to gather metadata (summary information about data) rather than downloading the data itself.

The relevance of retrieved information is a function of time in that the importance of a document depends on the task and conditions in the environment. Various costs are associated with information from different sources, some of which might be more reliable than others. Depending on the urgency, consumers may be willing to pay various prices (even premium) to get at information. Software filters must be aware of the above issues.

## 14.2 INFORMATION SEARCH AND RETRIEVAL

Information search is sifting through large volumes of information to find some target information. Search and retrieval systems are designed for dealing with unstructured or semistructured data, in contrast to database applications involving only very structured data, such as employee records. The notion of structure being used here is not only that the data conform to a format such as a record type description, but also that the record fields consist of simple data types with well-defined meanings. E-mail messages are an example of semistructured data in that they have well-defined header fields and an unstructured text body.

The process of searching for text strings in a large collection of documents can be divided into two phases: end-user retrieval and publisher indexing phase. The *end-user retrieval phase* consists of three steps that the user performs during the text search. First, the user formulates a query, specifying in some way the material for which the text database is to be searched.

Second, the server interprets the user's query, performs the search, and returns to the user a list of documents meeting the search criteria. Text systems usually perform the search by comparing search terms with an index file containing a sorted list of words found in the document database. The list of matching documents returned to the user is generally called a hit list. Third, the user selects documents from the hit list and browses them, reading and perhaps printing selected portions of the retrieved documents.

To illustrate, if the user specified a query to find all documents containing the string "electronic commerce," the system would apply a string-matching algorithm to all the documents that it can reach to extract the goal or target set. The result might be a retrieval of multifold documents, as many documents in the world contain the term "electronic commerce." To reduce the number of documents retrieved, some systems allow users to specify the number of documents that they would like to see in any one search, typically based on the location of the data, with limited per-item (e.g., find only forty closest hits) or per-location (e.g., maximum ten hits from this location) searching facilities. In short, the goal is for the user to obtain a limited set of information from an on-line source to solve some need or problem.

The *publisher indexing phase* consists of entering documents into the system and creating indexes and pointers to facilitate subsequent searches. This process often takes place during off-hours so that system performance is not degraded during working hours. Some systems, such as those used by news agencies, add documents to the database constantly with a live data feed. The process of loading documents into the system and updating indexes is normally not a concern to the user.

Clearly these two phases are highly interdependent. The user interface should provide a way of entering search queries and for browsing matched documents. The index should be structured to expedite the type of searching permitted by the queries, and the data-entry procedures must work within the structure of the documents and the search indexes.

Text search based on string comparison is widely available in many Internet systems, such as Gopher and Web. To reduce the scope of the search, users browse to identify the server or an archive before initiating a search. Searching can be comprehensive throughout the archive (for example, WAIS servers provide full-text indexes) or limited to certain key words.

## Wide Area Information Service (WAIS) Engine

The program Wide Area Information Service or WAIS (pronounced ways) enables users to search the contents of files for any string of text that they supply. An extremely versatile service, WAIS uses an English-language query front end to a large assortment of databases that contain text-based documents.

What does WAIS do? WAIS lets users search the full text of all the documents on a server. Users on different platforms can access personal, company, and published information from one interface—text, pictures, voice, or formatted documents. Since the system uses a single computer-to-computer protocol, information can be stored anywhere on different types of machines. Anyone can use this system, because it uses natural language questions (not complicated query languages like SQL or vendor proprietary systems) to find relevant documents. Relevant documents can be fed back to a server to refine the search. Successful searches can be run automatically to alert the user when new information becomes available.

How does WAIS work? The servers take a user's question and do their best to find relevant documents. The user then enters a query, which can be a list of keywords such as X.500 and Directory (see Fig. 14.1) or even a sentence in plain English, such as, What musical instruments do West Indians use? After inputting the search string and the target database, the user specifies the maximum number of hits WAIS can return for a given query (this step saves valuable time and bandwidth). The WAIS servers, at this point, do not understand the user's English language question; rather they try to find doc-

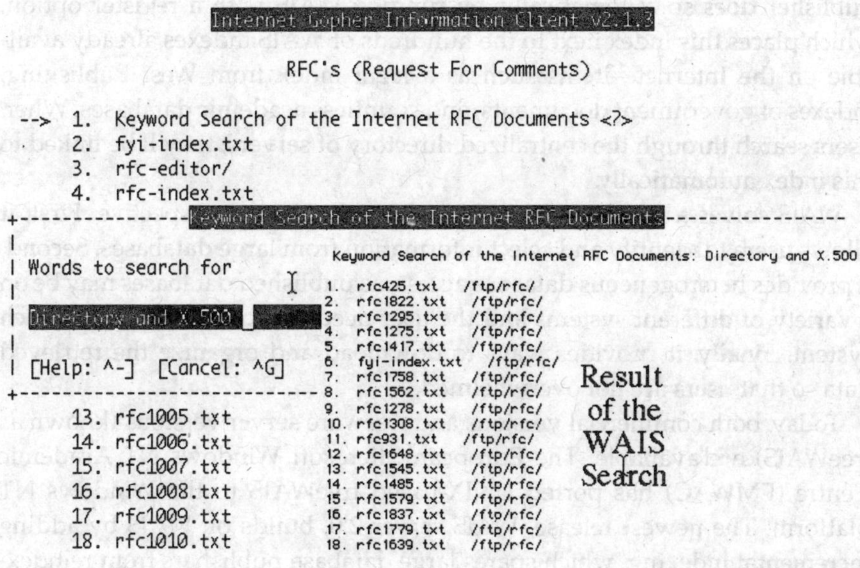


**Figure 14.1** A WAIS search of the Internet RFC database

uments that contain those words and phrases and ranks them based on heuristics.

The WAIS server returns a list of documents that contain the specified phrases and key words. Each document title contains a score, from 1 to 1000, indicating how often WAIS found the search terms in the document. At that point in the session, the user can reenter a more specific query, retrieve one of the documents, or mark the documents that come closest to what was requested and tell the server to research the selected data sources for documents that have similar content (phrases in headings, title, and text).

The WAIS client interface has changed tremendously in the last few years. Today, the NetScape or NCSA Mosaic browser with the forms capability is often used as a front-end to talk to a WAIS server. The advantage of this approach is the familiarity of the interface and ease of use.

Technically speaking, WAIS has three elements: a client, a server, and an indexer. Here's how the pieces work together: First, the indexer takes a list of files the publisher wants to index and generates from it several index files. These indexes include a directory of all words appearing in the database, a list of documents and files that constitute the database, and the "headline" of the documents contained in the database (a short summary for users who search the database).

With the index created, the user must tell the rest of the world about it. The publisher does so automatically, by running WAIS with a register option, which places this index next to the hundreds of WAIS indexes already available on the Internet—items such as a legal index from West Publishing, indexes of government documents, and countless academic databases. When users search through the centralized directory of servers, they'll be linked to this index automatically.

WAIS solves a number of problems from the user's perspective. First, it allows users to identify and select information from large databases. Second, it provides heterogeneous database access, as published databases may be on a variety of different systems and the user need not know how to use each system. Finally, it provides ways to download and organize the retrieved data so that users are not overwhelmed.

Today, both commercial versions and freeware server versions (known as freeWAIS) are available. The European Microsoft Windows NT Academic Centre (EMWAC) has ported UNIX-based freeWAIS to the Windows NT platform. The newest release, WAIS server 2.0, builds on WAIS by adding incremental indexing, which spares large database publishers from reindexing an entire database after it is amended. It also integrates WAISgate, which lets WAIS receive search requests from many more clients.

How is WAIS used? Some publishers create the WAIS indexes of files that they serve through the World Wide Web or Gopher. These indexes enable users to search the contents of those files. Several companies use WAIS to sell information over the Internet. One can associate a cost directly with WAIS sources, unlike many other Internet services. Some sources, for example, charge a certain amount for each document, while others charge an hourly rate to search them and an additional fee for the documents themselves.

## Search Engines

WAIS is a sophisticated search engine. The purpose of a search engine in any indexing system is simple: to find every item that matches a query, no matter where it is located in the file system. The trick for the software designer is to create a search engine that carries out this job quickly and accurately while taking up as little disk space as possible.

What users need, however, is a tool to help determine which data are really relevant. Why? Because the problem with a large collection of documents is that it is easy to find too many answers to any single query. Search engines are now being designed to go beyond simple, broadband searches for which WAIS is so popular.

One of the more popular approaches is used by Topic, a search engine used in Lotus Notes, Adobe Acrobat, and a variety of other products. It uses both key words and information searching to rank the relevance of each document. Topic might return a list of a hundred documents that match the user's criteria, but they would be listed in order of the relevance that Topic assigns.

A different approach is offered by context-based searching. As exemplified by Architext, these tools let the user enter a query and then come up with the relevant data based on the context of the documents themselves. The system tries to figure out the content of the documents based on the context of the words, not the words per se. The result is that the system might find stories that don't have any of the words in your search but that do have the same general meaning. For instance, you might look for "electronic commerce" and find an article that references "digital money." In theory, the system finds documents with the right meaning. This engine is probably not for everyone, but its approach is certainly promising.

Other approaches to data searching on the Web or on other wide-area networks are available. The most compelling is Oracle's Context, which can go through a variety of documents and create its own summary, pulling about three key sentences from each document it selects. For those companies that have invested heavily in Lotus Notes, tools exist that turn Notes databases into HTML documents that can be published on the Web. Folio Views lets users publish "infobases" on the Internet and search those documents with relevance-based search tools. Both Folio and Lotus are aimed at companies that want to publish corporate data for their own customers.

## Indexing Methods

To accomplish accuracy and conserve disk space, two types of indexing methods are used by search engines: file-level indexing and word-level indexing.

*File-level indexing* associates each indexed word with a list of all the files in which that word appears at least once. A file-based index does not carry any additional information about the location of words within files. Such an index uses disk space economically, usually taking up about 10 percent of the size of the main text that it indexes.

*Word-level indexing* is more sophisticated and stores the location of every instance of a word. These indexes enable users to search for complete phrases or words that are in close proximity. For instance, say you entered a query on electronic commerce into a file-level index. Such an index might return the sentence "Commerce is increasingly becoming electronic." A word-level index, on the other hand, contains the location of each word in your file system, so it avoids such mistakes by ensuring that *electronic* and *commerce* are adjacent.

The disadvantage of word-level indexing schemes is that all the extra information they contain gobbles up a lot of disk space—anywhere between 35 percent and 100 percent of the size of the original text. They also can be slower than file-level indexes because they have more information to search through.

The process of indexing data is a simple one in theory. While software designers go through many different iterations to determine the best way to create the smallest, fastest indexes, your best bet is to evaluate indexing software based on the type of storage medium you intend to use and the amount of disk space you can allocate to index your data.

Recently, a large number of indexing packages have become available for UNIX-based workstations. They take advantage of workstation speed and multitasking capability and often feature networking and distributed database capability. These packages fall into three categories:

1. The *client–server* method is based on the distributed approach in which the document database and the text search and retrieval software reside on a central server, while sophisticated data presentation and user-interface software reside on the user's workstation. The power of the server is

used for the data-intensive job of comparing search terms with text files or indexes, while the workstations are best suited for graphical interfaces.

In this approach, the index file can be split into pieces corresponding to work groups and maintained on separate servers. This approach provides fast response time for documents "owned" locally. Searches of portions of the index stored on other servers can be performed in the background while the user is retrieving and studying locally owned documents. One disadvantage of this approach is that each subindex has to be updated individually each time the master file is updated.

2. The *mainframe-based* approach is generally more expensive and less flexible than the previous architectures, but it provides for large amounts of storage, fast response time, and standard data management and configuration control. The mainframe may also handle query and display formatting, enabling searches to be conducted from nonintelligent character-based terminals.
3. The *parallel-processing* approach allows many processing units to conduct searches simultaneously. Typically, the file to be searched is broken up into many pieces, and each processor searches its segment of the index file. The processors may or may not share memory and storage. If the processor and the segments are balanced, each processor can operate independently of the others, and all processors complete processing at approximately the same time. The results are merged before being presented to the user.

The indexing and retrieval method deployed in practice depends on answers to the following questions: How much text is to be searched? Will the system be used by a single user, or will many users share the same data? What are the cost and storage constraints? What are the response time requirements? What is the degree of user sophistication? Managers will have to juggle the various options to arrive at a satisfactory solution.

## Search and New Data Types

Turning our PCs into intelligent information appliances capable of finding the data user's need will involve combining the features of many of these products—from hypertext systems and indexing programs to electronic document packages, browsers and communications packages, intelligent agents, and multimedia databases. Even though we have not solved all the problems associated with searching and retrieving information in traditional environments, we are increasingly forced to address the challenges of new technology. It is clear that we have a long way to go.

Over the past few years, new technologies have become incorporated into systems that provide additional possibilities for, but also challenges to, effective search. These include:

- *Hypertext*. Richly interwoven links among items in displays allow users to move in relatively ad hoc sequences from display to display within multimedia database (or hypermedia) applications.
- *Sound*. Speech input and output, music, and a wide variety of acoustic cues include realistic sounds (earcons) that supplement and/or replace visual communication.
- *Video*. Analog or digital video input from multiple media, including videotape, CD-ROM, incorporated broadcast video tuners, cable, or satellite downlinks, provide video imagery that supplement and/or replace traditional computer-generated graphics.
- *3D images*. Virtual reality displays offer a 3D environment in which all portions of the user interface are 3D. 3D special effects already exist in existing interfaces using techniques that overlap planes, cast shadows on other objects, highlight surfaces, and so on.

Searching through these new types of information poses interesting challenges that need to be addressed soon. In the coming years, more information in a variety of forms will be available on-line as Web publishing proliferates.

## WWW Robots, Wanderers, and Spiders

Finding information can be tricky because few directories are available to guide you to your destination. The global WWW database is growing dramatically, resulting in an explosion of information and thousands of databases. It can take years to fully navigate the vast web of information. Fortunately, a number of useful databases are linked together with hypertext and significantly reduce the pain of *trawling* (a combination of crawling and traveling) the information space.

The challenge of searching through hypertext is being addressed through software agents and techniques for building indexes to help users direct their search.

Robots, Wanderers, and Spiders are all programs that traverse the WWW automatically gathering information. The terms *robot* and *spider* are often used in reference to automated tools for access to publicly accessible databases on the Internet for the purpose of building indices of documents.

For electronic commerce, agent-based resource discovery is becoming increasingly important as the number of sellers increases. In the absence of a centralized directory, how can firms locate the trading partners and products/services they wish to acquire? One solution is to have resource discovery programs (spiders) walk the WWW and record the appearance and disappearance of resources. This search might be a general one, such as building a key word index of the titles or full contents of a set of Web documents, or it might be a recording of the universal resource locator (URL) of the relevant documents.

Resource discovery may require more than merely following hyperlinks. A resource discovery program might fill out a form, or supply a user name and password, to access the data of interest. Once you can fill out forms and supply passwords, you are no longer limited to searching for public data: You have built a program that may be employed as an agent to pay for information.

How do these programs work? A software agent views the World Wide Web as a graph. It starts at a set of nodes (.HTML) and traverses the hypertext links in these nodes to a certain depth (typical default is set to five links) beginning at a URL passed as an argument. Only URLs having "." suffixes or tagged as "HTTP:" and ending in a slash are probed. Unsuccessful attempts and document leaves are logged into a separate table to prevent revisiting. This method results in a limited-depth breadth-first traversal of only HTML portions of the Web. Another table provides a list of pruning points for document hierarchies to avoid because of discovered problems, or hierarchies not wishing to be probed.

In sum, because of time constraints and the heterogeneity of the information and of the repositories, it will not be possible to perform exhaustive searches throughout the Internet, and it will most likely be necessary to conduct multiple searches in parallel. This leads to the possibility of multiple software agents that cooperate and conduct separate searches for information. Because software agents will operate in a heterogeneous networked environment with different protocols and database systems, further research will be required into transportable agents and database access methods. Today, research is being done on controlling multiple agents, negotiation among agents, maintaining consistency, dealing with payment, security and reliability issues, efficiently searching for and transmitting information, minimizing redundancy, and ensuring adequate coverage of the information sources.

## Specific Models of Information Retrieval

Researchers have long considered ways to retrieve information efficiently from databases. This section gets into the gory details of the theory behind the three major search methods: Boolean, vector space, and probabilistic retrieval models [BC92].

The Boolean model is based on the "exact match" principle and is the standard for most popular information retrieval systems. The term Boolean is used because the query specifications are expressed as words or phrases, combined using the standard operators OR, AND, and NOT—for instance, get all documents in database with: INTERNET and COMMERCE. This model retrieves all text files containing the combination of words or phrases specified in the query, but it makes no distinction between any of the retrieved documents. Thus the result of the comparison operation is a partition of the database into a set of retrieved documents and a set of not-retrieved documents. One disadvantage of this model is that it does not allow for any form of ranking of the retrieved document set. Presenting documents to the user in presumed order of relevance would result in more effective and usable systems. Similarly, excluding documents that do not precisely match a query specification results in lower effectiveness.

Vector space and probabilistic models, based on best-match retrieval models, have been formulated in response to the problems of Boolean models. The most widely known, the *vector space model*, treats texts and queries as vectors in a multidimensional space, the dimensions of which are the words used to represent the texts. The vector model processes queries and texts by comparing the vectors, using, for example, a method called the cosine correlation similarity measure. The assumption is that the more similar a vector representing a text is to a query vector, the more likely that the text is relevant to that query. An important refinement in this model is the ability to weight terms (or dimensions) of a query, or text representation, to take account of their importance. These weights are computed on the basis of the statistical distributions of the terms in the database and in the texts.

*Probabilistic information retrieval models* are based on the probability ranking principle. This states that the function of a retrieval system is to rank the texts in the database in the order of their probability of relevance to the query. This principle takes into account that representation of both information need and text is uncertain, and the relevance relationship between them is also uncertain. The probabilistic retrieval model suggests that a variety of sources could be used to estimate the probability of relevance of a text to a query. The most typical source of such evidence is the statistical distribution of terms in the database and in relevant and irrelevant texts. It should be noted that both of the best-match models mentioned here can rank documents using Boolean queries. The distinction between the form of the query and the underlying retrieval model is an important one.

## 14.3 ELECTRONIC COMMERCE CATALOGS OR DIRECTORIES

Directories perform an essential support function that guides customers in a maze of options by enabling the organization of the information space. Finding things (users, resources, data, or applications) in a distributed network is the task of the directory service. Directories inform a potential customer or software agent about available services, providers, prices, quality, and other important characteristics necessary for making purchasing decisions. For instance, you can consult a stock brokerage directory to find the brokerage offering the cheapest stock quote, get a quote, and then feed your bid into a program trading software application that automatically trades in the NASDAQ stock market.

Why directories? Directories are essential for conducting electronic commerce. Although directory services are one of the most fundamental components of electronic commerce, technically they are the least understood and have been an invisible component in network architectures. What is interesting is that the notion of directory services as an independent network application that offers a set of value-added capabilities in its own right and is accessible to a wide range of user applications is a relatively new one. What makes directories crucial to the successful implementation of electronic commerce is that only through the use of distributed, replicated information in the form of directory services is it possible to grant users transparent access to all network resources.

Directories are of two types: the White Pages and the Yellow Pages. White Pages are used to locate people or institutions; the Yellow Pages are oriented toward consumers who have decided to buy a product or service.

Consider the following situations:

- The owner of a stereo system finds that it needs servicing, but not just any servicing. "Where is the nearest factory-authorized service center?"
- A family wants to buy a new car within their budget of $13,000, "Where can we find information that can help us in making comparisons between different models?"

These not-so-unusual situations are preludes to the use of the Yellow Pages, a low-profile advertising medium. These consumers demonstrate needs that the right kind of advertiser may be able to satisfy through the use of the Yellow Pages. In each case, the consumer has (1) already decided to make a purchase and is in the process of finding the right outlet and (2) is in the process of marshaling information needed to make a purchasing decision. The Yellow Pages over the years have built up in the consumer a degree of faith and trust in terms of providing factual information and little if no advertising puffery.

The electronic yellow pages can go way beyond the services that have been traditionally provided by the print-based Yellow Pages. The goal is to build directories that serve as interfaces to resources and are accessible from electronic commerce applications that have extensive directory requirements. An effective directory service must be readily accessible by all network components, provide quick response times, and accurately reflect changes in network configurations and resources as they occur.

The challenge is to create a directory representation that can be accessed by different types of networks (wired and wireless), different types of interfaces (TV plus set-top, mobile units, or PCs), different types of access applications (e-mail, procedure or function calls, or dial-up), and various applications (home shopping, home banking, electronic stock brokers).

What are the implementation problems? Directory services must map large numbers of objects (users, organizations, groups, computers, printers, files, processes, and services) to user-oriented names. The problem is difficult enough in a homogeneous LAN environment, given document and equipment moves and changes to names, locations, and so forth. In a heterogeneous global WAN environment, the task becomes considerably more complex, given the need to synchronize information in different directory databases.

Furthermore, as distributed applications appear on the network, the directories have to begin tracking all those objects and their components as well. Hence directories and naming tend to go hand in hand. A good name service makes use of a distributed computing environment transparent to the user. Users should not have to know the location of a remote printer, file, or application, for example, nor should they have to key in the mail address for a distant colleague.

In sum, a directory or catalog is an information base about a set of real-world objects. Users often scan directories for telephone numbers or addresses, facts, or organizations or persons. Directories must therefore be organized in a manner that facilitates easy access to information, and the directory user must be able to locate "entries" in the directory where the actual information is stored or presented. The trend has been toward the integration of directories with network operating systems such as Novell NetWare that are designed to hold network configuration information and provide a quick mapping between network names and addresses. Directories are also being slowly integrated with messaging services such as e-mail and EDI applications.

## Overview of the Directory Business

The White and Yellow Pages directory business in the United States is quite complicated. A basic overview of the industry structure would help in understanding how this business would transform itself in an electronic marketplace.

Since its humble beginnings, the telephone directory has evolved into a huge business. Advertising in the Yellow Pages was estimated at $10 billion in 1994. The first telephone directory, published in 1878, was a single page containing the names of customers of the New Haven District Telephone Company. It didn't even list telephone numbers. Listed alphabetically were residences, physicians, dentists, stores, factories, meat and fish markets, stables, the local police, a publisher, and a lawyer. Instead of dialing a number or giving it to an operator, the subscriber simply gave the operator the name of the party sought.

According to the American Association of Yellow Pages, the first use of yellow paper for the classified section of early telephone directories can be traced to Cheyenne, Wyoming, where in 1883 a printer ran out of white paper and substituted the yellow paper that was to give this advertising medium its name. The first official Yellow Pages was published in 1906 by the Michigan State Telephone Company in Detroit.

Since the divestiture ruling of AT&T in 1983, the publishers owned by the Bell operating companies have begun to compete in each other's regions and upset the previously stable Yellow Pages telephone directory business. The Bell breakup led a number of directory publishers to publish new books to compete with marketplace incumbents.

Dynamic change and deregulation frequently stimulate an industry's revenue growth and the multibillion-dollar directory industry was no exception. The Yellow Pages directory industry holds great attraction: It caters primarily to local advertisers, demand is relatively price-inelastic, and the annual or semiannual publishing cycle virtually compels the local merchant to advertise or miss out until the next directory is published. Most important, return on investment is supposed to be high.

Today, all the major directory publishers are moving on-line. France Telecom was the first to introduce electronic directory services. Minitel was instituted in the 1970s when the company faced a logjam of directory assistance calls, only 55 percent of which were answered. Instead of investing in labor, the company opted for electronic directories, providing consumers with free Minitel terminals to access the system.

U.S. electronic directory services first aimed at the heavy spender: the business traveler. Bell Atlantic started a service, Info Travel, that offers an interactive version of the Yellow Pages, pared to certain core listings for travelers that hotel guests can use through the television sets and remote controls in their rooms. The goal of Info Travel, or a similar program called City Key, introduced in 1993 in San Francisco by a Bell Atlantic rival, US West, is meant to eventually supplant conventional directories.

Guests can obtain information on participating advertisers, from restaurant hours to opera performance schedules, by using compact disk-interactive technology hooked up to the rooms' existing video systems. They can request maps, printed at the hotel's front desk, be connected by telephone to advertisers, even order merchandise from electronic catalogs. There are no charges other than the hotel charges for local calls.

The advertisers participating in Info Travel are mostly local marketers, with a smattering of national companies. They are grouped into categories bearing simple labels: places to eat, things to see and do, services, and getting around. Info Travel is emblematic of the way advertisers and media companies are gingerly exploring their places in the rapidly changing communications landscape.

Even a medium as prosaic as telephone directories must determine what lies ahead; after all, marketers in 1994 spent $10 billion advertising in the Yellow Pages, according to estimates—a figure that exceeded by $100 million estimates of spending on radio. So, it is clear that it is a market segment that cannot be ignored.

## Electronic White Pages

Analogous to the telephone White Pages, the electronic white pages provides services from a static listing of e-mail addresses to directory assistance. The Internet directory assistance service can be more extensive than the one provided by the phone companies, as the technology provides the ability to publish important information that an individual may make publicly available, such as photographs, home mailing addresses and fax numbers, office information, and job descriptions.

White pages directories, also found within organizations, are integral to work efficiency. The problems facing organizations are similar to the problems facing individuals. The original intention behind organizational directories was to reduce the amount of duplication as corporations spend money maintaining identical lists in several sites—for phones, security, payroll, faxes, computers, e-mail, and other reasons—each with almost identical information.

Faced with rapidly growing corporate networks on the verge of getting out of control, IS managers are looking for a solution that will let them consolidate their directory services activities. However, in an era so concerned with the productivity of workers, it is surprising that the demand for better directories has not provoked more action, given the need for such services everywhere.

What functions should a white pages directory perform? Searching and retrieving. Searching is the ability to find people given some information about them, such as "Find Ravi Kalakota in New York." Searches may often return a list of matches. Searching is accomplished by looking up an index. While the idea of indexing has been around for some time, a new acknowledgment of its importance has emerged recently. Users want fast searching across the cyberspace on attributes different from the traditional database structure. Precomputed indices satisfy this desire, though only for specified searches. Retrieval is obtaining additional information associated with a person, such as an address, telephone number, e-mail mailbox, or security certificate.

Which approaches will provide us with a white pages directory? It is evident that there are and will be several technologies in use. To establish a white pages directory service that accommodates multiple technologies, we should promote interoperation and work toward a specification of the simplest common communication form powerful enough to provide the necessary functionality. This "common ground" approach aims to provide the ubiquitous WPS (white pages service) with a high functionality and a low entry cost. One such WPS implementation is X.500.

## White Pages Through X.500

One of the first goals of the X.500 project has been to create a directory for keeping track of individual electronic mail address on the Internet. X.500 offers the following features [SOLL89]:

- *Decentralized maintenance.* Each site running X.500 is responsible only for its local part of the directory, so updates and maintenance can be done instantly.
- *Searching capabilities.* X.500 provides powerful searching facilities that allow users to construct arbitrarily complex queries. For example, in the white pages, you can search solely for users in one country. From there, you can view a list of organizations, then departments, then individual

names. This represents a tree structure with successive descent to the terminal nodes or instances.

- *Single global name space.* X.500 provides a single name space to users.
- *Structured information framework.* X.500 defines the information framework used in the directory, allowing local extensions.
- *Standards-based directory.* X.500 can be used to build directory applications that require distributed information (e-mail, automated resource locators, special-purpose directory tools). These applications can access a wealth of information in a uniform manner, no matter where they are based or currently running.

The X.500 standard talks about three models required to build the X.500 directory service: the directory "architecture" model, the information "architecture" model, and the security model. The X.500 directory is composed of a collection of servers termed directory system agents (DSAs). A DSA is essentially a server that stores information according to the X.500 standard and can, when necessary, exchange data with other DSAs. The DSAs cooperate to provide the overall directory services to directory user agents (DUAs).

More formally, a directory is a collection of servers (DSAs) cooperating among themselves to hold information about a variety of objects, thus forming the directory information tree (DIT). The DIT is a hierarchical data structure consisting of a *root*, below which *countries* are defined. Below the countries (usually) *organizations* are defined, and below an organization *persons*, or first additional *organizational units*, are defined. Figure 14.2 is a simplified illustration showing only three countries and no organizational units. The DIT is a representation of the global directory [X92].

Each DSA holds a part of the global directory and is able to find out, through the hierarchical DIT structure, which DSA holds which parts of the directory. The standard does not describe how to distribute different parts of the directory among DSAs, but information corresponding to a single node of the DIT (i.e., a country, an organization, a person) cannot be distributed

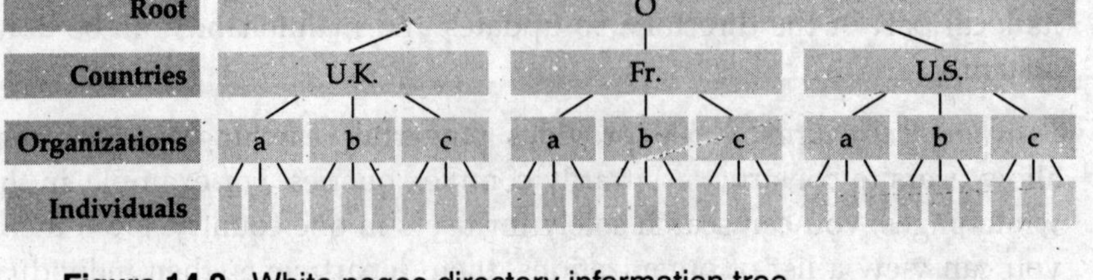


**Figure 14.2** White pages directory information tree

over several DSAs. In practice, a large organization will maintain one or more DSAs that hold its part of the directory. Smaller organizations may share a DSA with other organizations.

Figure 14.3 shows the output of a X.500 query for a person (Kalakota) on the University of Texas at Austin X.500 server. The directory user agent is the multipurpose Gopher client. The directory server agent contains information on about 100,000 students, faculty, and staff in the university.

A user of the directory can be a person or a computer program. The organization and distribution of information among the DSAs is totally transparent to the users. A user accesses the directory through a so-called directory user agent (see Fig. 14.4). The DUA automatically contacts a nearby DSA by

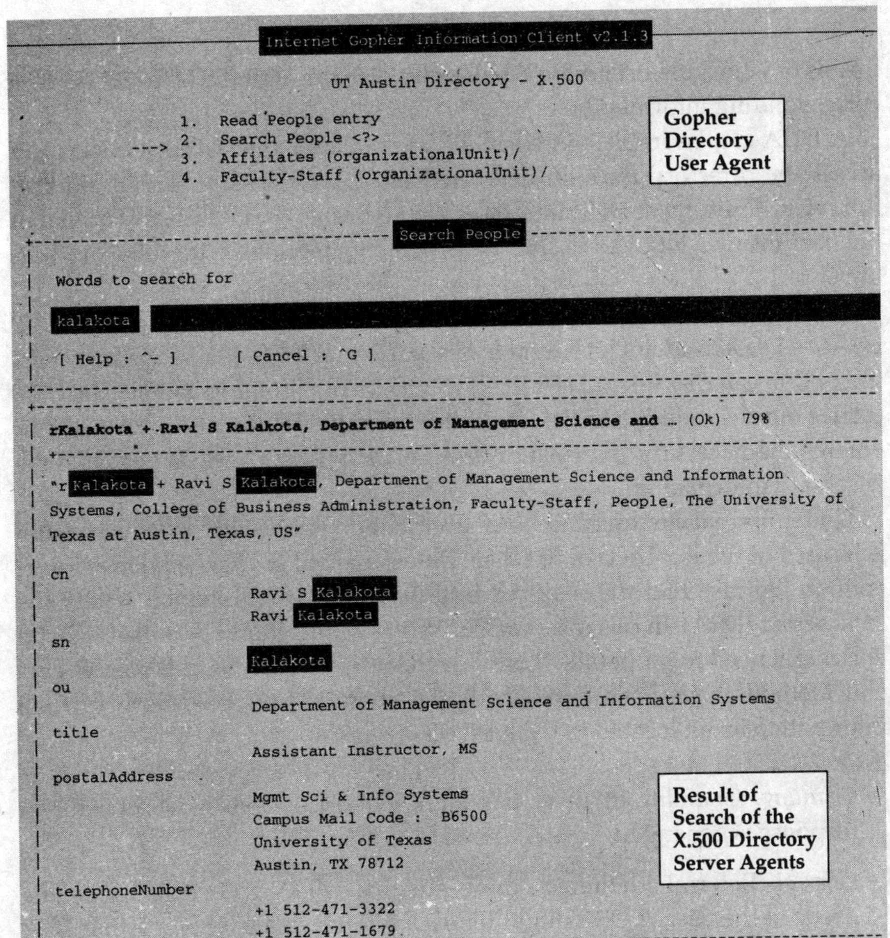


**Figure 14.3** X.500 query output

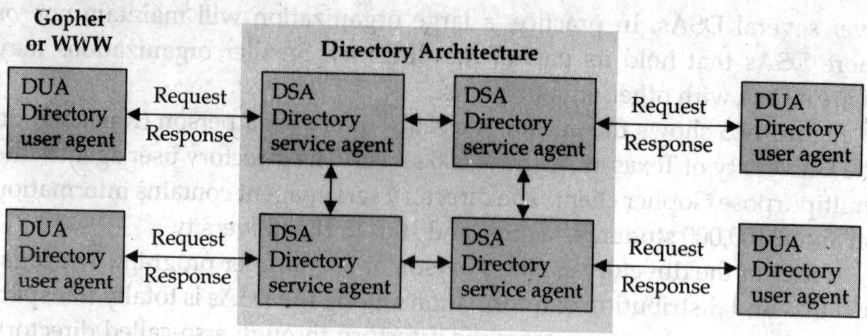


**Figure 14.4** Directory services architecture

means of which the user may search or browse through the DIT and retrieve corresponding information.

A DUA can be implemented in all sorts of user interfaces, so users can access the directory through dedicated DUA interfaces or e-mail applications. Currently, most DUA interfaces are dedicated, but it is expected that in the near future a lot of DUA interfaces will be integrated with other applications.

The DUA interacts with the directory by communicating with one or more DSAs. A DUA need not be bound to any particular DSA. For instance, a DUA in London can dial into a DSA in New York to obtain information. The DSA carries out the requests of the DUA. It returns the requested information or obtains the necessary information from other DSAs if it does not have the necessary information.

Under normal circumstances, the information requested by the user agent is located in the local server to which the user agent is attached. However, it is often the case that the required information is not contained within the local server (DSA). In this case, various server agents might become involved and might need to cooperate to provide the information. For this reason, several methods have been defined for the operation of the directory when information is not located in the local server agent:

- *Chaining.* Chaining involves passing a request to several DSAs before a response is generated.
- *Referral.* Referral identifies "more suitable DSA" who can satisfy the needs of the user. A DSA might return a referral to a user or another DSA if the request cannot be performed.

- *Multicasting.* Multicasting involves passing the same request by a DSA to two or more DSAs.
- *Hybrids.* Chaining, referrals, and multicasting can be combined as necessary to perform the intended request.

What are the problems to be overcome? It must be much easier to be part of the Internet white pages than to bring up a X.500 DSA or make good use of the already deployed X.500 DSAs. X.500 is too complicated and simpler white pages services must be defined to promote widespread implementations. To promote reliable operation and consistency of data, there must be some central management of the X.500 system. A common naming scheme must be identified and documented.

In sum, the X.500 service, while extremely useful in concept, has many technical hurdles to cross before usage becomes widespread.

## Electronic Yellow Pages

Users are increasingly turning to directory databases rather than printed Yellow Pages. For instance, on-line directory databases give much greater access to companies than a collection of printed financial directories. You may get additional information, such as employee size, sales, and ownership information, that are omitted from Yellow Pages listings. Just as importantly, directory databases expand your ability to find companies beyond your local Yellow Pages. They take up little or no shelf space, unlike the Yellow Pages, and they are easier to search.

Competition in the Yellow Pages industry has grown markedly in nearly every major market in the United States. Independent publishers continue to produce numerous specialized directories in markets they see as viable. Among these are industrial buying guides, product catalogs, corporate information directories, and college information directories. Third-party directories can be categorized variously:

- *Basic yellow pages.* These directories could be organized by human-oriented product and service listings, unlike the archaic SIC codes, and accept advertising.
- *Business directories.* These directories might take the form of extended information about companies, financial health, news clippings, or whatever. People are often likely to pay to use this kind of directory rather than pay to be in the directory. There could be many of these directories, suited to different research tasks (investment, foreign trade, manufacturing).

- *State business directories.* Every business in a state is arranged by type and by city, and there is a directory for each of the fifty states. The alternative to using one of these directories is to order phone books in the state and compile a specialized list of names. This type of directory is useful in businesses that operate on a state or geographic basis.
- *Directories by SIC.* SIC (standard industrial classification) directories are compiled by the government. More than two thousand different directories are available. For example, if your company's marketing effort is directed to all dentists, or all grocery stores, this approach would be useful.
- *Manufacturers directory.* If your goal is to sell your product or service to manufacturers, then this type of directory would be most useful.
- *Big-business directory.* This directory lists companies of 100 or more employees. If your goal is to reach this group, this is an attractive directory to have.
- *Metropolitan area business directory.* These guides, developed as sales and marketing tools for specific cities, are designed as comprehensive directories listing companies and influential contacts at each business, along with phone number, address, number of employees, and so on.
- *Credit reference directory.* This directory provides credit rating codes for millions of U.S. companies. Credit data are used for a variety of purposes such as qualifying new customers, suppliers, and so on.
- *World Wide Web Directory.* This directory lists the various hyperlinks of the various servers scattered around the Internet. Examples include Yahoo (see Fig. 14.5).

Publishers of yellow pages directories can be divided into two categories. The first is utility-related publishers, or companies that publish yellow pages directories for the telephone companies. The second category consists of independent publishers, many of whom produce directories tailored to specific market segments.

There is a huge potential for specialty directories that is waiting to be exploited in the on-line marketplace. The design and implementation of directory services for niche segments is definitely going to become a big growth industry. Examples of on-line directories include: Yahoo (See Fig. 14.5) and EINet Galaxy.

While directories such as Yahoo are restricted to keeping track of URLs, other directory implementations go even further and sometimes even index the full text of Gopher, FTP, and World Wide Web documents and other doc-

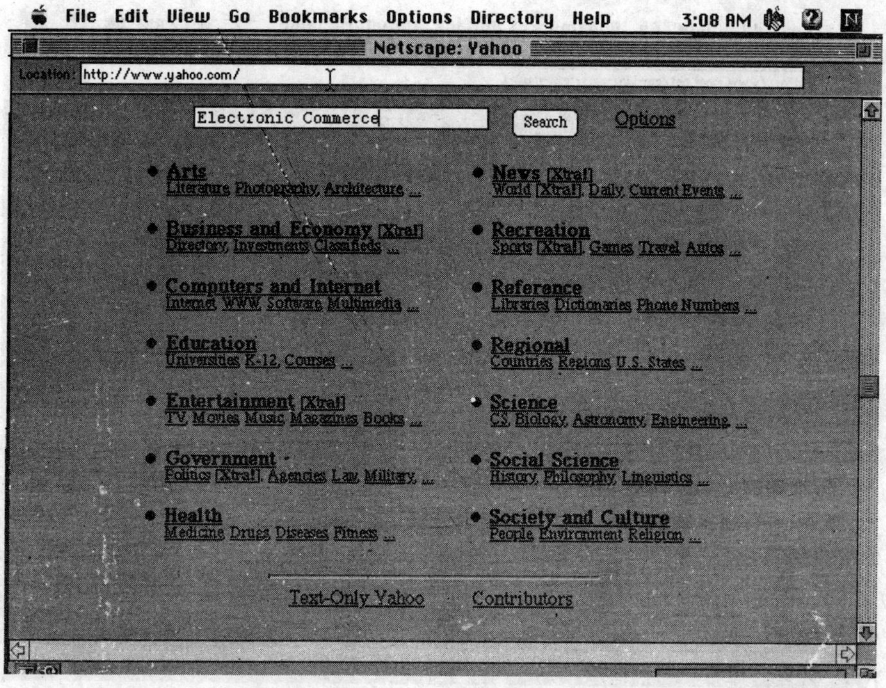


**Figure 14.5** The Yahoo World Wide Web directory of URLs

uments. An example of this type of approach is EINet Galaxy. Figure 14.6 shows a WAIS search screen where we look for the first 120 WWW documents that include the term "electronic commerce." Also next to each document, the WAIS server lists the score on the relevance index and the number of times the word has occurred in the document.

## Interactive Product Catalogs

Companies will compete through on-line directories and catalogs to promote various merchandise. They are especially important in electronic commerce as they tend to provide a one-stop center for satisfying the consumers' curiosity as to what's out there and where to get it. The goal of interactive catalogs is simple: to enable customers everywhere to buy goods from anywhere in a virtual mall open twenty-four hours a day, seven days a week. Customers simply look through the on-line merchandise and interact with the company using several methods, such as e-mail, form-based secure messaging systems, interactive desktop video, and other methods. Directories, in

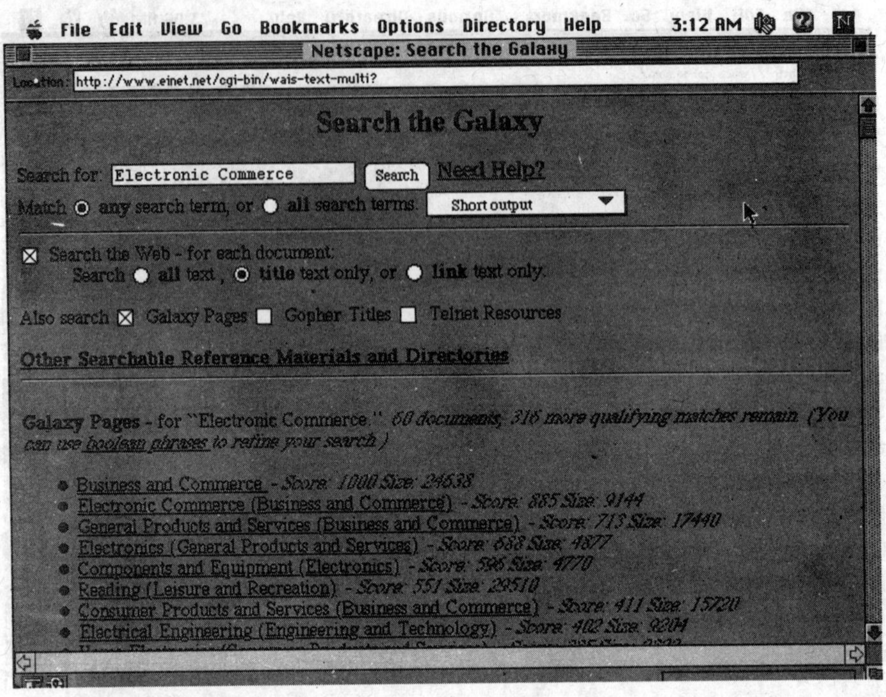


**Figure 14.6** WAIS search on the Galaxy Directory

contrast to catalogs, are usually compiled by third parties and play an influential role in guiding customers in the information space to reach catalogs.

Remember, electronic yellow pages are organized by product and services and becomes necessary as businesses move toward electronic commerce. The goal of yellow pages is to organize the vast amount of information so that customers can quickly locate desired and alternative products and services through eye-catching advertisements. In other words, yellow pages catalogs are a reactive medium, in that they satisfy a need but do not create a need. However, it must be noted that yellow pages work only when someone is looking for some particular information, not when advertisers are trying to interest people who may never have heard of their company or their product. That is the job of interactive catalogs, which are based on the idea that effective marketing relies on a two-way information flow between the marketer and the customer.

Interactive catalogs are ideally suited for small businesses, because they enable them to effectively utilize their limited marketing, support, and sales staffs with potential customers around the world. In other words, rather than a fancy storefront or an expensive research staff, cyber entrepreneurs can do business with a computer, modem, and hookup to the Internet or commercial on-line services. These businesses must collect detailed demographic and life-style information about large numbers of consumers in order to determine effective market segments. Then they must integrate this mass of information into a concrete understanding of what products different consumers want and what they're willing to pay.

Catalogs must support product/service bundling, coordinated purchasing, and associated financing. For instance, a customer purchasing a computer from a virtual storefront may customize her own personal computer with such add-ons as sound-cards, video boards, and other components from several manufacturers. To complete the purchase, she may fill out an on-line form requesting the store for financing in the form of a store credit card. This application should be approved or disapproved within a few minutes (almost real time).

Although interactive catalogs have a lot of appeal, they are extremely tricky to create. For instance, creating large on-line catalogs is a challenging task given the information overload. Consider one market segment, the retail food industry. The average supermarket stocks around 20,000 new items, with larger stores carrying two or three times that amount, and 10,000 new items are introduced each year. The average supermarket now carries roughly twice the number of items it carried ten years ago [JBHBR93]. Given the enormous variety of weights, flavors, colors, and sizes, the interactive catalog for the retail food industry may run to several hundred thousand items. Moreover, buyers have to deal with several hundred thousand price changes every year. This enormous volume of information creates an information crisis in the buying process for customers, retail managers, and manufacturers.

That this complexity exists and is almost unmanageable in traditional environments is good news for electronic commerce. The silver lining in the dark clouds exists in the form of technologies such as virtual reality or networked 3D and software agents, which have the potential to help organize, sort, and customize massive amounts of information. But we still have a long way to go.

### Interactive Catalogs—Examples

Interactive catalogs are increasingly being seen in real life. Applications take the form of unattended touch-screen kiosks, electronic brochures, and catalogs. Such applications are being developed by automobile showrooms, banks, investment brokers, travel agents, home improvement centers, department stores, real estate realtors, computer stores, beauty salons, and various retail stores. For instance, airport kiosks allow frenzied travelers not only to whisk through the video and audio menus of area hotels, restaurants, and museums but also to purchase air tickets, confirm hotel reservations, or rent convertibles.

Technologically, a kiosk catalog is designed for easy use and low-cost construction. At the heart of the system is a standard low- to mid-range PC clone–usually a 386- or 486-based machine—with a color touch screen or color monitor and keyboard. More complex systems include laser printers, credit card readers, receipt printers, and product dispensing units. Multimedia functionality in a kiosk can include full-motion video, digitized sound, graphics, and animation. Peripherals vary, too. Some kiosks include special circuit boards, CD-ROM drives, and laser disk players. Custom software running under OS/2, DOS, UNIX, or Windows controls the peripherals and interface.

A diverse group of companies have found that interactive multimedia programs housed in free-standing displays efficiently deliver a tailored sales pitch or product. Kiosks are portable, allowing them to go where the customers are, be it a bank lobby, a grocery store, or a company cafeteria. The time needed to acquaint users with the kiosk concept is virtually nil. The software is interactive, so information can be customized for such individual needs as foreign languages. Kiosk software also records every transaction, helping companies build customer databases.

The Prevue Channel on cable TV is a good example of a product catalog in the entertainment business. This simple on-screen television guide tells viewers what is on and when. It has been in business since 1985 and currently serves over 30 million cable homes. It costs a typical cable operator about $800 per month and provides a much-needed service for viewers. Prevue installs a CPU and memory unit at the local cable head-end and updates over 6000 individual program lineups in real time via satellite from a remote location in Tulsa, Oklahoma. What's significant is that Prevue and some of the other services offered have developed completely from the bottom up. Prevue began by offering needed retransmission services to WGN Chicago and then realized that cable operators needed other services. The net result is a low-cost program service that uses extra transmission capacity. Costs, in fact, are so low that it will be very difficult to implement a competitive system. This is a business that shouldn't exist; similar services should have been introduced by the cable company or by *TV Guide*. In fact the business opportunity was created because the management of Prevue understood exactly what the customer needed.

Many of the catalogs offered on the Internet are experimental. We can compare this technology with the early days of the "Computer Shopper" catalog, which has become a phenomenal success in computer products marketing. The "experts" soundly condemned the idea of what was, in fact, a catalog disguised as a monthly magazine and produced as cheaply as possible. Today it is produced in process color, in unprecedented size (usually well over 800 pages), and sold for $2.95 at every supermarket, obviously an enormous success. The moral: We never know what the public wants or how it will react.

The design of catalogs as we know it is undergoing a major revolution as transactions (buying and selling), directories, information programming, and advertising increasingly overlap. In general, effective catalogs mean reaching the consumer with information that includes positioning information to establish image, brand, and detailed product specifications. In particular, marketing new products via on-line catalogs requires an effective communication flow to inform the consumer about features and benefits. The objective of interactive catalogs is to promote, sell, and provide customer service for specific products and services.

## 14.4 INFORMATION FILTERING

*Information filtering* describes a variety of processes involving the delivery of information to people who need it. This technology is needed as the rapid accumulation of information in electronic databases makes it imperative that consumers and organizations rely on computing methods to filter and disseminate information.

Although this term is appearing quite often in articles describing applications such as electronic mail, multimedia distributed systems, and electronic office documents, the distinction between filtering and related search processes such as retrieval, routing, categorization, and extraction is often not clear. To distinguish information filtering, it becomes necessary to list the typical features of this process:

- Filtering systems involve large amounts of data. Typical applications would deal with gigabytes of text, or much larger amounts of other media.
- Filtering typically involves streams of incoming data, either being broadcast by remote sources (such as newswire services) or sent directly by other sources (e-mail). Filtering is often meant to imply the removal of data from an incoming stream, rather than finding data in that stream. In the first case, the users of the system see what is left after the data are removed; in the latter case, they see the data that is extracted. A common example of the first approach is an e-mail filter designed to remove junk mail. Note that this means profiles may not only express what people want, but also what they do not want.
- Filtering has also been used to describe the process of accessing and retrieving information from remote databases, in which case the incoming data are the result of a search query. This scenario is also used by the

developers of systems that generate "smart agents" for searching remote, heterogeneous databases.

- Filtering is based on descriptions of individual or group information preferences, often called profiles. Such profiles typically represent user interests. The use of user profiles is common in the library community where the process is known as the selective dissemination of information (SDI). SDI is defined as the service that attacks the information overload problem by keeping individuals informed of new documents published in their area of specialization so that they can keep abreast of new developments.
- Filtering systems deal primarily with textual information. The problem is more general than that and should include other types of data such as images, voice, and video that are part of multimedia information systems. None of these data types are handled well by conventional filtering systems, and all have representations and meanings that are difficult to filter.

Intelligent filters have the potential to solve information search and retrieval in large information spaces. In ten years, we will be hooked up to more than a trillion objects of useful knowledge, and no direct manipulation interface can handle that. People are not going to sit down with a super query application and start fishing around the entire world for things that might be of use to them. Instead, the interfaces are going to be twenty-four-hour retrievers that are constantly firing away doing things.

How does this work? Software filters process a document, interpret the information, and give the user capabilities such as speed/scan reading (highlights the most important segments of text to allow the reader to skim it), text summarization (paraphrases the document and reduces the content of the original by one-half to one-quarter), generation of abstracts (creates a new document approximately one-tenth as long as the original and covering all its themes), and information extraction (allows the creation of information retrieval agents to extract specific information from textual databases, such as expected trends in the stock market based on quoted analyst predictions, or information about mergers and acquisitions).

### Mail-Filtering Agents

Users of mail-filtering agents can instruct them to watch for items of interest in e-mail in-boxes, on-line news services, electronic discussion forums, and the like. The mail agent will pull the relevant information and put it in the user's personalized newspaper at predetermined intervals. An example is Apple's AppleSearch software, which enables creation of personal search agents called reporters to search incoming mail messages and documents obtained from on-line feeds or residing on servers. The user can schedule reporters to run at preset intervals or on demand. AppleSearch uses reporters to scan the available content, employs a relevance-ranking algorithm to select the information of most value to the user, then allows the user to view the text of the selected documents.

### News-Filtering Agents

These deliver real-time on-line news. Users can indicate topics of interest, and the agent will alert them to news stories on those topics as they appear on the newswire. Users can also create personalized news clipping reports by selecting from news services. Customers can receive their news stories through the delivery channel of their choice—fax, e-mail, WWW page, or Lotus Notes platform. For instance, one can create a user agent that, based on the categories selected, will daily download news clips on the computer, business, financial, or medical industries. Currently, news filtering services are primarily targeted to executives who need to keep current concerning their areas of interest.

## 14.5 CONSUMER-DATA INTERFACE: EMERGING TOOLS

Many of the electronic commerce applications require complex interfacing between humans and vast information resources. These applications must understand their environment and react to it. High-level user interfaces are needed to satisfy the many requirements and preferences of vast numbers of consumers in the on-line marketplace. Work being undertaken in building better consumer-data interfaces can be broadly classified into the following categories:

- *Human-computer interface.* A broad range of integrated technologies will allow humans and computers to interact effectively and naturally. Technologies will be developed for speech recognition and generation; graphical user interfaces will allow rapid browsing of large quantities of data; user-sensitive interfaces will customize and present information for particular levels of understanding; people will use touch, facial expressions, and gestures to interact with machines; and these technologies will adapt to different human senses and abilities. These new integrated, real-time communication modalities will be demonstrated in multimedia, multisensory environments.

- *Heterogeneous database interfaces.* Methods to integrate and access multiple structured databases composed of multiformatted data will be developed. In a future I-way environment, a user could issue a query that is broadcast to appropriate databases and would receive a timely response translated into the context of the query. Examples of multiformatted data include plain text, data that are multicolumn such as spreadsheets, and complex data types such as video.

- *User-centered design tools/systems.* New models and methods that lead to interactive tools and software systems for architecture or such as design will be developed. Ubiquitous, easy-to-use, and highly effective interactive tools combine data-driven and knowledge-based capabilities. One example of user-friendly tools is the document-oriented computing interfaces.

- *Virtual reality and telepresence.* Tools and methods for creating synthetic (virtual) environments to allow real-time, interactive human participation in the computing/communication loop will be addressed. Participation can be through sensors, effectors, and other computational resources. In support of electronic commerce application areas, efforts are focused on creating shared virtual environments that can be accessed and manipulated by many networked users.

Today, the basic infrastructure necessary for consumer interface experimentation is available in terms of the WWW and the Mosaic browser. The latter is the basis of a "universal" interface that can be used to access diverse distributed information databases and resources. With the creation of the universal resource locator, or URL, it became possible to tell users "where to go and how to get there" for all forms of data on the Internet. In short, the URL created a standard addressing mechanism for the data hidden in cyberspace. In essence, it turned the entire Internet into the equivalent of a single (very large) library and made it possible to create documents that could encompass data from many different parts of the Internet, binding them together into a cohesive whole.

URL-based addressing does need to be improved, as it is computer-centered rather than user-centered. URLs are quite cryptic and do not convey additional information required for human processing, such as relationships, proximity, and so on. In short, the URL mechanism leaves a lot to be desired, particularly for human beings. Today, several sorts of information about resources are specified and divided among different sorts of structures, mostly along functional lines. To access information, a user must be able to discover or identify the particular information desired and determine both how and where it might be used or accessed.

In the future it is expected that functionality will be partitioned into uniform resource names (URN), uniform resource characteristics (URC), and uniform resource locators (URL). A URN identifies a resource or unit of information. It may identify, for example, intellectual content, a particular presentation of intellectual content, or a distinctly namable entity. A URL identifies the location or a container for an instance of a resource identified by a URN. The resource identified by a URN may reside in one or more locations at any given time, may move, or may not be available at all. Of course, not all resources will move during their lifetimes. As such, a URL is identifying a place where a resource may reside, or a container, as distinct from the resource itself identified by the URN. A URC is a set of meta-level information about a resource. Some examples of such meta-information are owner, encoding, access restrictions (perhaps for particular instances), and cost of downloading.

In parallel to work on uniform resource names, research into "sensualized" user interfaces has received a lot of attention in the industry. Technologies, which collectively came to be known as virtual reality (VR), began a fundamental change in the nature of the user interface, moving it to a human-centered design where the space around the user became the computing environment and the senses become part of the interface. All of this was an effort to make computers more responsive to the humans who used them and focused around a basic realization: If something is represented sensually, it is possible to make sense of it.

## Virtual Reality and Consumer Experience

One of the many exciting developments is the growing universe of real time, WWW-based 3D environments. The next generation development in browsers uses 3D scenes as a user interface metaphor for navigating the Internet and visualizing relationships and clusterings of documents. Virtual reality interfaces provide a powerful data visualization tool that makes it possible to display clustering of documents, which is not feasible on either a menu or a flat page. Combining virtual reality with servers that categorize and cluster collections of documents will make it possible to visualize complex relationships within document collections. To be effective, moving about the document clusters must be fast and fluid.

Even at a time of dizzying technological change, this is a quantum leap. Consumers will be able to wander through whole virtual shopping malls. They will be able to cruise through representations of a map, visiting shops simply by "walking" down a corridor and checking on the door. Can't find a particular store? Just ask for directions. There on the left, you might be told, just past the Computer Store. The possibilities are intriguing. Let's say you're interested in buying something from a virtual boutique. You can pick it up, examine it, turn it around to see all sides. Or say you're reserving a ticket to a concert or baseball game. Usually you have to hope your view is not obstructed by a post. With 3D, you can check it out in advance. You can virtually go 'sit' in your seat, test it out.

One can envision even more ambitious uses in on-line communications. For instance, CompuServe is deploying an application developed by Fujitsu called WorldsAway. With WorldsAway, users will be able to move beyond anonymous text-based "chat rooms." Instead, users will appear "live," as a cartoon character—what Fujitsu calls an "avatar." When a user talks, a little balloon appears over his head on the computer screen, containing words. Users can pick or design their own visual on-screen avatar and opt for whatever sex or garb suits their mood. Instead of typing "LOL" (laughing out loud) to show appreciation of someone's joke, users can make their cartoon avatar smile. Users may socialize on-line by inviting other networkers over to their place, furnished to their tastes, possibly even with wall hangings of their favorite art or images of their own real furniture. Users may even go for a walk in the virtual woods, with whomever they've befriended on-line. In short, we are only at the beginning of a new era in social computing—people chatting, communicating, traveling to meet like-minded folk who share their interests, all in 3D.

What else might come along? As virtual reality takes off, companies will scramble to create 3D environments on the Web. With the exponential increase in Web sites, competition for the potential customer's attention has gotten fierce. Interactive 3D worlds offer an extraordinary way to differentiate and dazzle customers. Not only are 3D graphics stunning, but the user experience of navigating through a 3D world in which no two experiences are identical is too powerful an opportunity to ignore. Possible applications in advertising and marketing are: 3D shopping malls; product catalogs that can show off products in 3D (users can choose different styles and colors and see the results instantly); and vicarious experiences such as vacation resorts, leisure, and other recreation services that provide users with a rich and accurate 3D experience from the computer itself.

In creating 3D environments, designers must keep in mind that customers come in many different shapes and varieties. Basically, there exist three types of shoppers and shopping environments. Those in the first category, the go-for-price shoppers, care not a whit that a store might stock three kinds of products and display them in 3D or 2D. This is a pure price carnivore who simply has one priority: price. The second category is replacement shoppers, a more evolved species that sees no reason to hunt far and wide. This consumer typically attempts to minimize shopping time, so the virtual environment for this customer focuses on getting the closest possible product in the category the customer is interested in. The third category of shoppers is also the most numerous and sophisticated: shoppers who prize quality above all else. Winning their hearts and minds is where the real battle will take place.

The virtual environment must be sophisticated enough to highlight the diverse qualities of the product. The possibilities are endless. The opportunity for education, experiments, story telling, and exploration using 3D interactive worlds is mind boggling. The worlds can be designed to appeal to specific or general audiences.

## Virtual Reality and Consumer Choice and Behavior

The ability to guide consumers and their choices will be a significant factor for successful electronic business. In business, VR is seen as the future of advertising and marketing on the Internet. However, very little is known about the additional or modified features that support effective marketing or influence consumer behavior. One reason for this could be a lack of understanding of the basic technology in the research community and virtually no contact between developers and marketing researchers.

Research—theoretical and applied—is being conducted on the effect of context on consumer choice in relation to position in information space and technological capabilities such as hypertext, advanced graphical user interfaces, and multimedia including digital video. Several hypotheses related to consumer choice that have been looked at earlier in other environments need to be retested. Take, for instance the problem of alternative trade-offs: Which product characteristics in terms of content and presentation enhance or hinder a customer's ability to choose a substitute?

Consumer choice research is very important, because electronic commerce environments are not well organized and technologically inexperienced customers need to be guided with subtle cues. For instance, relationships between product documents can be easily represented by pointers or hyperlinks extensively used in the Web. The hyperlinks enable consumers to navigate through the information space by simply pointing and clicking on a link. This action results in their being transported to a terminating link anchor located in another region of the information space. To what extent can this technology aid marketing professionals in understanding consumer behavior and decision making in large market spaces?

The implications of research in consumer choice is potentially enormous, as it will in turn dictate the design and implementation of the next generation of electronic commerce user interfaces. The research findings can be used to enhance technology in two ways:

1. Enhance structured document markup languages such as HTML (HyperText Markup Language) or develop VRML (Virtual Reality Modeling Language) so they are more attractive to customers. The VRML allows the creation of multiuser network environments which allow interaction with 3D models and virtual "worlds" on the Internet.
2. Incorporate domain-specific custom characteristics by encapsulating the choice knowledge in "applets" (reusable code fragments expected to be widely available in the next generation of computing tools), which are used to customize the consumer's client browser environment (see Chapter 16).

Other relevant features that will influence choice research include issues of privacy and security and the design of smart software agents to guide users through electronic stores and product shelves.

The next generation of Web browsers will understand and interpret VRML. One such tool that has been released is the GopherVR (ftp://boombox.micro.umn.edu). Early releases of Macintosh and UNIX Gopher clients display 3D scenes. Although still under construction, you can browse Gopher directories by driving around Gopherspace, navigate between Gopher servers by driving through a series of 3D scenes, open items by clicking on them, get overviews of the neighborhood you are in, and view metainformation about items.

## Virtual Reality Modeling Language (VRML)

The Virtual Reality Modeling Language is currently a specification for adding 3D data to the Web. VRML 1.0 was meant to be a starting point for a much broader vision of networked 3D. VRML was designed to meet three criteria: platform independence, extensibility, and the ability to work over low-bandwidth (14.4 Kbps modem) connections. Early on, the designers decided that VRML would not be an extension to HTML, which is designed for text, not graphics.

How does this work? Programmers and developers can create 3D Web sites, also known as *home pages*. When users encounter a 3D link on a Web page, the software automatically kicks in—and up pops whatever 3D world has been created there, along with easy instructions on how to get around. The software isn't just for high-end users, either. It doesn't require big new investments in hardware and other paraphernalia. Any standard 486 PC with Windows can run the software, though it does help to have a fast modem say, 28.8 K or better. But even the lack of that won't slow users down much. There is a rich set of materials on *http://vrml.wired.com*, which is considered the primary VRML site.

## 14.6 SUMMARY

The growing data volume, user base, and information diversity is creating problems for the current set of search and retrieval tools. An information search system in electronic commerce will have to employ a combination of paradigms, depending on the situation.

Searching and filtering is more flexible and general than organizing/browsing, but it is also harder for the user. Forming good queries can be a difficult task, especially in an information space unfamiliar to the user. On the other hand, users are less prone to disorientation; the searching paradigm can handle change much better; and different services can be connected by searching more easily than by interfacing their organizations. As the volume of information continues to grow, organizing and browsing using directories are not effective because they have to be updated constantly.

As the number of users increases, new technical solutions will be required to react to the significantly increased load on network connections and servers. To balance the load, replicated servers and more significant use of data caching will be required.

New tools that can scale up with the diversity of information systems, number of users, and size of the information space have to be built. With growing information diversity resulting from multimedia, techniques are needed to gather data from heterogeneous sources and sort through the inherent inconsistency and incompleteness. Efforts in this realm focus on software agents for extracting, analyzing, and cross-correlating information.

In sum, the issue of being lost in cyberspace and navigating in cyberspace will remain with us for some time.

# Chapter 15

# On-Demand Education and Digital Copyrights

Education is in a state of flux. Within this changing environment, five characteristics are especially pertinent to electronic commerce applications. First, education is no longer considered something that one acquires during youth to serve for an entire lifetime. Modern education lacks age homogeneity, so in a physical or virtual class we would find young adults, middle-aged careerists, and retired seniors.

Second, because knowledge, like a product line, can become obsolete every few years, education must focus on creating an environment that facilitates continuous learning. To this end, continuous business education is becoming a necessity as companies educate their employees about competitors, events, news, and emerging products in a fast-changing global marketplace. What better environment than twenty-four hour on-line education and training in virtual classrooms rather than the more traditional notion of sending employees to expensive seminars?

Third, education and entertainment are converging. For instance, educational software is becoming an increasing part of the entertainment business and is often called "edutainment." Broadly, *edutainment* is defined as software, electronic books, and interactive games that have an educational component for children aged three and above. This new form of education is considered more effective because the user gets totally immersed in a learning experience so different from the old "lecture and drill" forms of computerized instruction that tend to bore students. The edutainment industry also capitalizes on the well-known fact that parents gladly pay a premium to ensure the quality of their children's education.

Fourth, the delivery of educational instruction has changed. Instruction will be increasingly conducted electronically and at times in small, informal meetings between faculty and students. The student will be the one who dictates when and where he or she wants to listen or participate, however. Students, both residential and nonresidential, will attend lectures broadcast to their homes, residence halls, or workplaces and draw reference materials from distant locations using computers. Local and wide area networks will enable universities to integrate many aspects of education that have long been segregated in separate buildings. The teacher's role will shift from lecturing to advising or coaching students on tough, messy issues, such as choosing materials, topics, and career paths.

Finally, electronic access to on-line databases and library catalogs will eliminate the need for much book or reference space but probably will increase the need for computer disk space. In recent years, access to CD-ROM and bibliographic databases has had considerable impact on the learning process in major universities. This revolution is expected to diffuse to every nook and cranny of the educational world.

Clearly, a new educational paradigm is called for, and we believe that it is emerging through on-line applications. The use of the on-line medium for education holds great potential and appears to be moving in that direction, but the path is rocky because of the many unknowns.

During the course of this chapter, the notion of on-line education and education on-demand will be developed further, and the electronic commerce applications and technology needed to support and deliver both will be examined in detail.

## 15.1 COMPUTER-BASED EDUCATION AND TRAINING

For a number of years, educators and employers have been talking about the enormous potential for computer-based education and training, but change has been very gradual. One reason is the heavy capital expenditure for computers in schools and offices that have been installed without an understanding of the educational processes required to take advantage of the new technology. In many cases, information technology investments have been geared toward automating old learning processes instead of designing, discovering, or enabling dramatically new ones. Although technology-based education is impressive, knowing how to use it effectively is still an art that few people understand clearly or possess the necessary skills for.

Explosive growth in technology is fueling a new wave of teaching tools: computer-aided video instruction (CAVI), hypermedia, multimedia, CD-ROMs, LANs, Internet connections, and collaborative software environments. Because we do not know how to use this emerging technology, there is an ever-widening disparity between technology and its proper use in the educational context. On the bright side, this new generation of technology promises more than just an improvement in educational productivity: It may finally deliver a qualitative change in the nature of learning itself.

Fundamental changes in computer-assisted teaching echo a new way of thinking in education theory. Instead of a one-way information flow—typified by a teacher addressing a group of passive students (broadcast)—new teaching techniques involve more student–teacher interaction (two-way), collaboration between students, and interdisciplinary approaches. There are two broad types of teacher–student interactions:

1. Synchronous, face-to-face instructor–student interaction, either classroom-based (traditional) or distance-based via tele-conferencing
2. Asynchronous interaction between faculty and students via e-mail, bulletin boards, and electronic publishing (e.g., CD-ROM, Gopher, World Wide Web)

Active learning and other new learning approaches are being developed to educate both workers and students. The shift to an information-based economy in which workers are manipulating information, rather than performing physical labor, and companies are downsizing means that on-the-job training is essential. The changing nature of companies and the work they do requires flexible and well-trained workers. Organizations are linking on-the-job learning to productivity, and are requiring schools to teach students a different set of skills than those emphasized in models based on earlier pedagogy.

The role of the teacher in the neo-education process is also changing. Students need a "guru" or guide to maneuver and explain the wealth of information available on-line. Teachers are becoming more like coaches, leaving students free to discover knowledge on their own. In short, with technology, the role of teacher is more that of facilitator, guide, and resource broker.

These tectonic shifts in education pose numerous challenges for the educator. The dilemma is three fold. First, understanding what is relevant content (subject material) in a rapidly evolving technological and business environment is not as simple as it appears. The subject matter has changed tremendously over the last decade and brought about an educational crisis. Most subject matter is interlinked, so teaching without the proper prerequisites or fundamentals can cause turmoil. We are forced to rethink the very fundamentals of course design and ponder, What exactly are the fundamental topics that lay a foundation for continuous learning in the future?

The second challenge for the educator lies in understanding the degree of change required. Is our present curriculum and course material so out-of-touch that we need major surgery, or would a simple band-aid do? Patching existing courses would merely address the symptoms, not the underlying root causes. In our opinion, we need to radically reengineer the curriculum in several areas to mirror the business and technological changes. For instance, few subjects have not been influenced in the last decade by computing, yet most college education material dates from the 1960s and 1970s, a fact that is more evident in fast-moving areas such as business education and engineering. Without a proper learning foundation, on-line education is bound to create chaos and future problems.

Finally, we must discover the right balance between the depth and breadth that should be covered in a fourteen-week semester or any other new timeframe. For instance, there need to be clearly defined start and stop boundaries to each educational activity. Without proper targets and goals, students easily get confused and demotivated. In other words, unless the education process is controlled, the effectiveness can be severely dampened. This raises the question: What is the right balance between control versus exploratory freedom?

Computer-based training is one area of electronic commerce that is slowly getting the recognition it deserves. The outcomes are far from clear, but the potential impact on the future of the information economy is enormous. Table 15.1 summarizes some of the educational models and resulting issues.

## On-Line Education and Virtual Classrooms

On-line instruction is the most recent form of what is generically termed *distance education*, which includes satellite courses, computer-based programs, video instruction, educational television, correspondence, or home-study

**Table 15.1** Changing Educational Paradigm [BYTE95]

| *Traditional Model* | *Emerging Model* | *Technological Aspects* |
|---|---|---|
| Information delivery—classroom lectures | Individual initiative and self-exploration | CD-ROMs, networked computers with access to on-line databases |
| Passive absorption | Learning by doing or apprenticeship | Requires simulations for skills development |
| Emphasis on individualism | Emphasis on collaboration and team learning | Requires collaborative tools and e-mail |
| Teacher knows all | Teacher as guide | Provides access to experts over network and USENET |
| Stable content | Rapidly changing content | Requires access to real-time news and publishing tools |

courses. These methods attempt to move educational opportunities out from a traditional, centralized classroom to students unable to attend classes at a central site because of schedule or physical problems or because a university cannot offer such classes.

On-line education is more than a long list of possible media. Early implementations of on-line education focused on creating costly high-tech classrooms with a PC on every student's desk. This philosophy assumed that placing computing at the student's fingertips would have a big impact on the quality of education. The conclusion reached after investing millions of dollars in these high-tech classrooms is that without integrating technology into the education process, there are no significant benefits. In other words, throwing the technology bucket at education is not the solution. The emphasis should be on finding the appropriate mix of "educational content" and "mode of delivery."

On-line education represents a learning domain unlike any other technology-based academic delivery system. It incorporates the group qualities of interactive classroom-based learning while providing individual students the flexibility to participate in an undergraduate or graduate degree program at their own time and place. PCs and modems are the vehicles for communication. Computer conferencing software defines the boundaries of the "virtual classroom." Our discussion of issues related to on-line education will be organized around the attributes that define its unique learning mode: place and time independence and many-to-many communication.

### Place and Time Independence

One of the advantages of on-line communication is that it is place independent. Students can complete homework assignments and prepare "classroom" responses on laptop computers while traveling by plane, then upload (or download) their work after enjoying dinner from a hotel room in a distant location. Place independence has enabled students living in remote areas to attend accredited college programs. On-line education is developing into a viable, cost-effective solution to the dilemma of delivering education to remote areas.

On-line communication also can be time independent. We say "can be" because it is possible to communicate on-line in real time using a "talk" or "chat" mode found in most communications programs. This type of synchronous communication is similar to talking on the telephone, except that communicators write (or type) rather than speak. The chat mode inhibits lengthy responses and is relatively clumsy due to network delay and typing errors. On the other hand, electronic mail (asynchronous) alleviates many problems of "chat" and "talk" programs.

The benefits of asynchronicity are significant. Group members have the opportunity to reflect on issues and to prepare responses off-line. The delay between receipt of a message and a response in an asynchronous environment appears to contribute favorably to critical thought. It also means no group member need worry about going "unheard" or otherwise being left out. All members of a group have the opportunity to contribute to a conversation. Nontraditional schedules can be accommodated because the asynchronous classroom operates virtually twenty-four hours a day. The graveyard shift worker, for example, can schedule school time in a manner that accommodates her schedule rather than that of the institution.

The place and time independence qualities of on-line education are particularly attractive to busy working adults. The asynchronous quality of communication is not synonymous with an "open-ended" course, however. It is necessary to establish clear deadlines for submitting coursework and for participating in classroom discussions. Otherwise, classroom communication would lose a sense of closure and quickly degenerate into chaos.

### *Team or Group Learning*

One of the most interesting and powerful dynamics in on-line communication is its "many-to-many communication" quality that facilitates group learning. While private communications are possible, any member can also communicate with all members of a given group, network, or conference. Each member, in turn, can reply not only to the sender but to everyone else in the network. This process is considerably different than the traditional professor-to-student exchange that tends to be one-way—with the professor lecturing and students passively absorbing information.

A democratic element is inherent in many-to-many on-line communication: The opportunity for every student to have an equal chance to participate, regardless of otherwise inhibiting status and role differences, is a strength of on-line education. In addition, students cannot "hide" by sitting in the back row. Social loafing or lack of student involvement becomes much more conspicuous because an uninvolved group member literally disappears. A student cannot physically attend class and be somewhere else mentally. For these reasons, interaction in on-line groups tends to be more evenly distributed relative to face-to-face groups.

In short, as a practical matter, a traditional professor-to-student demeanor does not work well in an on-line course. The dynamics of many-to-many communication, as described, defeats any attempts to channel communication "downward" from professor to student.

### Challenges in On-Line Education

On-line education is not without its challenges and obstacles, as well as a myriad of unanswered questions:

- How does on-line education differ from regular classroom instruction in terms of quality of student learning?
- Are there modes of educational delivery that, bundled or taken together, will have an impact that exceeds any one delivery method?
- What impact does on-line education have on other outcomes of classroom education, such as development of social behavior, attitudes, and values?
- What effect does the lack of personal contact have on teaching and learning?

The notion of administrative systems also requires examination and improvement in the context of on-line education. Administration of exams and grades, for instance, are good examples of the unique challenges of managing on-line education. Other administrative standards also pose problems, for example, a standardized curriculum with specific, even prescriptive, weekly deadlines for uploading homework and comments to classmates and the instructor. Another potentially vexing issue concerns monitoring student identity. How do we know that Jane and Joe Student are, in fact, who they say they are? The on-line medium does not allow the opportunity to compare a face to a name.

On-line education holds an advantage over traditional on-campus education for several segments of the population. For instance, the senior and disabled community benefits enormously from the medium. When participating in an on-line class, it does not matter how long it takes to answer a question or type at a keyboard. Such a class meets on the student's own timetable. Professionals who have little time to attend evening classes but seek to upgrade their education can dictate the time and place as well as learn from an expert in the field. In fact, the use of technology for the delivery of educational services to working adults is a growing area and is termed *training on-demand*.

## Training On-Demand

A revolution is under way in training aimed at upgrading employee skills for more complex, changing jobs. In fact, the fastest-growing segment of education is within industry, which is faced with the pressing question of how to keep the work force up to speed. One answer, *training on-demand,* involves bringing information to employees rather than sending employees to the information source. The primary motivations for introducing training on-demand for businesses are to reduce training costs and to increase productivity. Consistency in training delivery, greater flexibility, and learner-controlled pacing are often secondary motivations.

The old paradigm of training as a separate, centralized department is now dead. Companies believe that it is not feasible to put employees through classroom training that is slow, enormously expensive, and notoriously inefficient in terms of retention and recall. Many experts argue that the traditional training department is out of step with the times. Several factors are at work here. Training departments, viewed as overhead, are often among the first victims of layoffs even though the changing nature and growing diversity of the work force require constant training. Employees are more geographically dispersed than in the past, and turnover is higher because companies and employees are less loyal to each other. Technology is evolving so quickly that skills require frequent refreshing. In light of this, businesses are moving to decentralize training services and make them distributable to the PC.

The new education model, learning while working, is based on the assumption that workers learn at the moment they need to know it. It is similar to learning to ride a bike; if you fall off, you don't need others to give you a lecture about the physics of motion and gravity. You need quick instruction about what you're doing wrong and how to right yourself quickly. The result is that rather than teaching employees fundamental skills (especially since workers sometimes bolt to competitors), companies are instead trying to link learning to the job itself. This can take many forms. It may be as simple as putting self-paced employee-orientation materials on a network server instead of making the employee take a six-week course.

Training on-demand is a phenomenon that is common to industries ranging from high tech to grocery chains because the cost of software has come down significantly in recent years. Hewlett-Packard, for instance, is reported to have developed one such solution that cut some of its sales training costs from $2 million to $200,000 per year. In the past, the company held training classes in twelve cities that took four to five weeks per quarter. Now, through a satellite network, training sessions require just two days, and nobody has to travel. Furthermore, the message and delivery are more consistent, and there is a shorter lag time between distribution and utilization of information. In another case, Burlington Northern Railroad has reportedly boosted its training productivity and improved quality by the use of advanced simulators. In the past, new engineers had to spend most of their training time in locomotives, which presented logistical challenges and limited the range of experiences encountered during training. Now, with 3D images generated on silicon graphics workstations, engineers experience a full range of real-world scenarios, including emergencies and varying weather conditions [BYTE95]. As companies customize training, they incur added costs. But, customized or not, computer-based instruction programs bring systemwide consistency to training.

In service industries, employees' willingness to work with computers, coupled with competitive pressure to reduce operating costs and increase customer service, has made the PC a powerful training tool. Computer-based training systems for retail store-level staff are delivering on their promise to slash costs for large chains employing many employees and experiencing high rates of turnover. To keep pace with the competitive environment, smaller retailers are increasingly turning to PCs to do their teaching. For retailers the benefit lies in a significant reduction in training time. Additional benefits have also been documented [SMN95]:

- *Productivity gains in the checkout lane.* Computer-trained cashiers consistently scored better than new cashiers trained at an off-site learning center. Better skills lead to speedier transactions and less trainee supervision needed at the front end.
- *Programming flexibility.* Training programs can be customized to meet a retailer's changing requirements, and the software is portable, eliminating the expense and inefficiency of sending new cashiers off-site for training.
- *Uniformity.* Standard training formats ensure that all employees are presented the same instructions, whether they are located within a single market area or across the country. An automated testing function objectively reflects trainees' proficiency levels.
- *Cross-training opportunities.* Because the PC "trainer" is resident in-store, employees can acquire new skills when they have the time.
- *Reduced turnover.* Many workers, if not trained well enough, may be less motivated and get frustrated with their jobs and ultimately quit.

Despite the clear advantages, computer-based training is not necessarily well suited for all companies. To decide whether your business can benefit, answer these questions: Do you have large numbers of personnel to train? Do you have remote personnel to train? Do you have high personnel turnover (trainees and trainers)? Do you need to provide frequent retraining? Do you need rapid updating and modification of training materials? Do you need consistent, standardized training and evaluation? Do you need to reduce management involvement in training? Do you need to decentralize delivery and eliminate training and educational costs? Do you need to reduce distribution and ongoing training costs? Do you need training on-demand?

If even some these factors are present in your situation, training on-demand could well be a cost-effective method. On the other hand, if staff turnover is very low or the environment changes very little, computer-based training may not prove cost-effective. Of course, the type of training is also a determining factor. Leadership training or team building, for example, would not rely on it primarily but could use it as a supporting tool.

## Changing Roles of Institutions

Merging education and electronic commerce will change not only the way courses are taught and the way students learn, but the very institutions and individuals involved—universities and colleges, publishers, and authors or courseware developers.

### *Universities and Colleges*

The on-line education revolution could fundamentally change universities, colleges, and schools. It might become common practice to study at several universities rather than at a single location. Imagine a course with lectures at Oxford on Mondays, tutorials at Stanford on Tuesdays, hands-on practice with industry experts in a simulated factory, and the use of any library needed to carry out enhanced learning for the rest of the week. Students from Mexico, Australia, Burundi, India, and Belgium could all participate in a Sociology 101 lecture presented by a professor at the University of Italy and run by a university in Texas.

Faced with scenarios like these, universities in effect will become large courseware publishing houses that have the knowhow and ability to construct instructional material. Techniques such as electronic mail, conferencing, and groupware already allow students to work in groups with peer and teacher support. Teaching will be delivered via a range of electronic media, allowing students to take lectures in their own time and at their own pace. Lectures will be cross-linked to references in the library, so students can do further research at their leisure.

This vision will require several stages to implement. In the early phases, the system would consist of an extensive network, with a central hub surrounded by access points throughout the campus. Ultimately, this hub could be extended beyond the campus into the community through emerging networking techniques made possible by the I-way. Many universities worldwide are already experimenting with an embryonic form of such computerized courseware.

Longer-term, we will see even more dramatic changes as universities start to look for new sources of income such as course franchising. There is no reason why colleges should not operate through courses franchised by other institutions. Education establishments may begin to charge for intellectual property—information now given freely in lectures and tutorials. More immediately, academic institutions should be encouraged to secure and retain intellectual property rights for data, sound, video, and course material.

### Publishers

The publishing world is rapidly beginning to realize the implications of an educational world connected by networks. While desktop publishing rang a wake-up call for traditional publishers, the convergence of computing, communications, and electronic documents will have an even more dramatic effect. Two significant trends will dramatically alter publishing: the shift in emphasis from words to images and video in communications and the development of a high-bandwidth telecommunications infrastructure for the distribution of electronic documents.

Electronic documents are more appropriate than publication on physical media (paper, CD-ROM, etc.) for the following reasons:

- The document content may change frequently, and electronic publication facilitates updates. In other words, implementing corrections and improvements to the document content is much easier in electronic form.
- It is more readily available to the data user—no lengthy purchase/delivery cycle need exist. Assuming widespread availability of computers and networking, access for large communities can easily be established without requiring each user to purchase an expensive media peripheral (such as a laser disk player). This is particularly helpful in home usage.
- Publication on physical media may not be cost-effective except for very large volumes of documents. (Of course, there is a cost attached to networking, but with the rapid improvement in technology and price–performance ratio, the user is getting a better deal.)
- It may require less effort from the publisher to make documents available over a network, rather than to set up traditional distribution channels for delivery of the physical media. A good example of this is Addison-

Wesley's electronic document center (gopher.aw.com). Also, if related documents from many different sources are to be published, it may be more efficient to leave the documents in one place and simply publish the network addresses of the server holding these documents.

- Linking and navigating over related documents is easy with concepts such as hypermedia and hypertext. The only thing that comes close to this is the notion of cross referencing in traditional print publishing, a far more cumbersome method.

Counter-reasons exist that may make physical media distribution the preferred choice, for example: (1) The use of physical products is easier to price and charge, and (2) it is easier to prevent copyright infringement, using traditional copy protection techniques.

Both concerns are being addressed. Charging mechanisms do exist in some network information systems (see Chapter 8). It may be that potential information providers need to be made more aware of this. Likewise, digital copyright and copy protection schemes are being developed for electronic documents.

### Authors and Courseware Developers

The role of author is changing in the world of electronic publishing. Before answering the why and how questions, we need to understand that several types of authors exist: educators who create courseware, writers who write electronic books, creators of CD-ROMs, and third-party value-added businesses (often called secondary publishers). Electronic authoring is defined as the use of computers and associated products and paraphernalia such as printers, scanners, multimedia kits to facilitate the production of a product—print, video, electronic documents, or multimedia presentations. The scale and magnitude of the operation could be an individual, a group of individuals, or a large corporation.

Today, a wide range of authoring practices exist. In the simplest case, the author creates a word processing file and ships it to the publishing firm, which may typeset the document and create a hardcopy output. Some on-line companies simply accept any work that is submitted on diskette, list it in an on-line catalog, and transmit it to customers. The more sophisticated form of authoring is to add hypertext links to the various segments—text, graphics and video—that allow readers accessing the work through the World Wide Web or CD-ROM by clicking on "hot spots" to call up related passages from other works or even bits of audio or video.

Hypertext publishing—whereby some parts of the material are owned by someone else—raises a gamut of legal and copyright issues. In fact, downloading of copyrighted material is considered to be a major threat to the nascent electronic publishing industry. These issues are already being tackled by full text on-line services and other sophisticated document delivery systems that are fast changing the role of the publisher. The role of author is still not very clear in the digital copyrighted world.

The National Writers Union (NWU) is trying to address some of the author concerns about electronic commerce, but most of that work has been in the area of contracting. As part of its ongoing effort to assert writers' rights in all new media, NWU released a document on the Internet called Recommended Principles for Contracts Covering On-line Book Publishing. The NWU position is that the terms of the on-line book contract should reflect the amount of value added by the on-line publisher. Because on-line companies that do no editorial work and transmit plain-text versions are in effect acting as mere distributors, they should receive a small share of the income from on-line sales. Those that enhance the work through the addition of hypertext links are entitled to a much larger portion of the revenues. The main points in the NWU's recommended principles are as follows:

- Writers should retain the copyright on their works, although on-line publishers adding hypertext links may claim copyright on those added elements.
- Because on-line publishing is still underdeveloped, authors should grant publishing rights of limited duration.
- The division of revenues between authors and on-line publishers should reflect the factors discussed above, but in no case should the author receive less than 50 percent of the money collected from customers. This reflects the absence of the manufacturing, warehousing, and other costs associated with the publishing of traditional print books.
- Contracts for on-line books should specify how the work will be made available and what promotion efforts the publisher will undertake.
- Given that traditional "out of print" procedures do not apply, contracts for on-line books should terminate when the publisher stops promoting the work.

In the long term, contract and other copyright issues need to be resolved, because it is in the best interests of the information industry to avoid lawsuits over copyright infringements.

## 15.2 TECHNOLOGICAL COMPONENTS OF EDUCATION ON-DEMAND

The primary technological component of education on-demand is electronic publishing. Electronic publishing can be categorized broadly into four major classifications:

1. *On-line full-text publishing* uses various on-line databases for storage and distribution of information on-demand to consumers. Examples of this type of publishing include bibliographic databases seen in libraries, on-line public databases, and news on-demand. The scale of operation is huge and typically involves large investments. Examples of organizations in this line of publishing are Dow Jones, CNN, and Elsevier.

2. *CD-ROM publishing* uses a variety of compact disc repository media such as CD-interactive (CD-I), CD-read-only memory (CD-ROM), and CD-R (recordable CDs) for storage and distribution of specialized information such as books, encyclopedias, games, and other forms of education and entertainment. Examples of this type of publishing are Compton's Encyclopedia, Microsoft's Encarta, Sega, and Nintendo games.

3. *Collaboratories, USENET*, and *conferencing* have been demonstrated to be extremely useful for knowledge dissemination and informal education. Their usefulness for more traditional educational purposes is still virtually undocumented, however.. Examples of this type of publishing are the USENET news groups, which are emerging as an important part of interactive collaborative education.

4. *Video* is another emerging area of electronic publishing. This technology involves the use of video cameras, camcorders, and computers to capture imagery in digital form and distribute it to others or paying subscribers over the network. A significant step forward in this form of publishing is the ability to archive digital images in a library and access them multiple times later for reference, annotation, and learning. Examples of this type of publishing can be seen in new forms of work and education: telecommuting, collaborative work, and distance education using desktop video conferencing.

Though separate, these classifications do interrelate and are beginning to converge through the underlying infrastructure that is used to implement them (see Fig. 15.1). An example can be seen with the use of databases to provide print publications, on-line services and CD-ROM output.

Electronic publishing is emerging as the knowledge dissemination media of the future for a number of reasons. Over the last quarter of a century, the

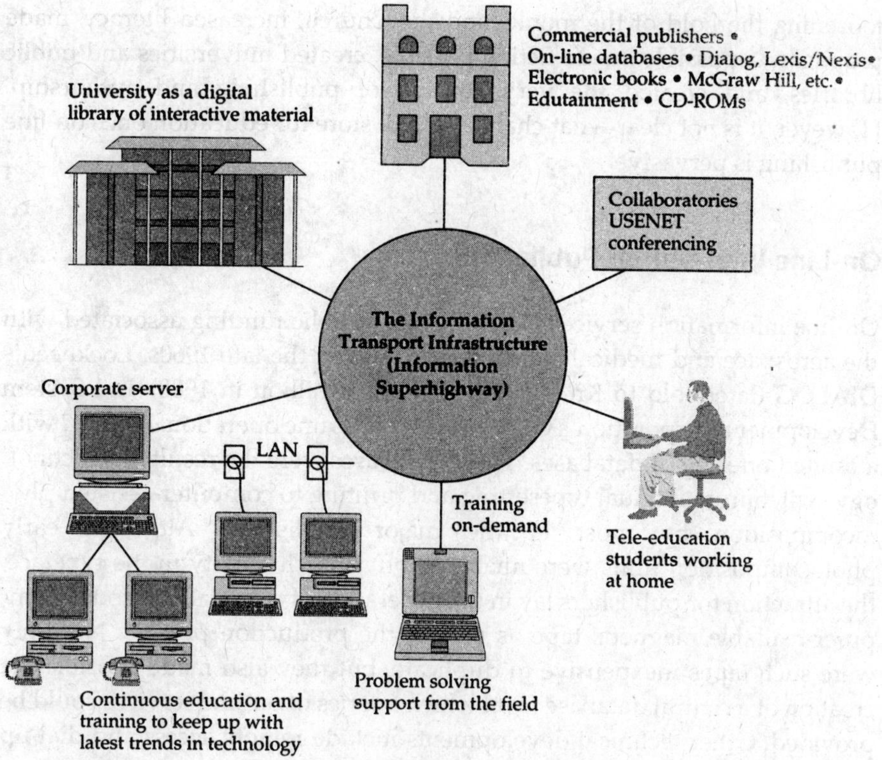


**Figure 15.1** Components of education on-demand

cost of paper and newsprint, printing, and delivery rose while their digital counterparts—memory and storage, processing power, and network communication costs—decreased dramatically. Both trends are expected to continue well into the next decade, paving the way for a digital takeover of the publishing industry. The last time an event of similar magnitude occurred was in the fifteenth century when Guttenberg's printing press, using the cheaper, newly available paper, replaced traditional parchment and scribes and revolutionized the manuscript market.

The long-term influence of electronic publishing on education is not yet clear. On the other hand, the influence of print has been well documented. The printing press, aided by the development of movable type, caused an explosive increase in the number, variety, and quality of available books and led to widespread dissemination of previously restricted knowledge and caused a social revolution. The availability of books forced people to learn the alphabet and become literate, and they used this new information source for improving the quality of life. In short, print democratized knowledge by loosening the hold of the monks and the Church, increased literacy, made propaganda possible, made fiction possible, created universities and public libraries, and created the very concept of publishing and authorship. However, it is not clear what changes are in store for education once on-line publishing is pervasive.

## On-Line Information Publishing

On-line information services evolved out of public funding associated with the aerospace and medical research programs of the late 1960s. Lockheed's DIALOG (later sold to Knight-Rider for $353 million in 1988) and System Development Corporation's ORBIT services became operational in 1972 with a limited offering of databases. These databases were the result of a technology switch from manual typesetting and printing to computer-assisted photocomposition by most of the major publishers. Although early photocomposition units were unable to offer much variety in the typeface, the attraction for publishers lay in the generation of a digitally encoded computer-readable magnetic tape as part of the production process. Not only were such tapes inexpensive to duplicate, but they also made possible the creation of a central database from which a series of on-line services could be provided. Other technical developments include remote access and dial-up database systems, improved magnetic storage devices, improved telecommunications networks, and the availability of low-cost terminals.

The on-line information services market is comprised of three main sectors: bibliographic databases full-text services, and real-time news delivery.

### *Bibliographic Databases*

Most libraries have replaced traditional card catalogs with sophisticated electronic on-line bibliographic databases offering an incredible range of functions. Bibliographic databases represent an important part of the digital library of the future. At revenues of over a billion dollars a year, bibliographic databases represent a sizable chunk of the on-line database market. An example of a bibliographic database is MEDLINE, developed by the National Library of Medicine (NLM), which caters to an increasing number of physicians who rely on on-line and CD-ROM medical databases to keep up to date with the latest developments and literature. The spread of PCs has enabled physicians to directly search databases used only by librarians in the past. MEDLINE and other medical databases are available on-line on the Internet free of charge.

Citation index databases form another segment of the bibliographic database market. Citation indexes provide librarians with an effective tool for gauging the impact of various publications on society. Publications that receive large numbers of citations are considered to be valuable. This measure is sometimes used for promotions in the academic field. Despite the shortcomings of this approach, citation indexes have proven very useful for examining journal articles and assessing the effects of research on the activities and beliefs of other scientists. Among the various activities wherein citation indexes have been employed successfully are the prediction of Nobel Prize winners, the flow of research to development, and the impact of one country on another's research.

Access to corporate documents is fast becoming a major segment of the bibliographic database market. One of the best known of this category on the Internet is the Securities and Exchange Commission (SEC) EDGAR, arguably the world's most valuable collection of financial data. EDGAR is part of an experiment on how to electronically disseminate enormous volumes of computerized government records.

**Securities and Exchange Commission's EDGAR**. EDGAR (Electronic Data Gathering, Analysis, and Retrieval) is an experimental database designed to automate the estimated 12 million pages of financial documents that public U.S. companies are required to file each year. The SEC uses the annual reports called 10Ks, quarterly reports called 10Qs, shareholder proxy statements, and many other forms filed by almost 15,000 publicly held companies to police the financial markets and prevent investor fraud. The primary users of these filings are the financial and investor community, brokerage houses, law firms, and institutional investors.

The SEC began studying methods to automate its filing process in the early 1980s, out of concern that someday the agency would be swamped by the ever-growing flood of paper. What emerged was EDGAR. Originally budgeted at $51.5 million, the project fell more than three years behind schedule. In 1992 a government analysis of the project put its ultimate cost at more than $78 million. After a three-year delay and a $20-million cost overrun, EDGAR began operating in April 1993, with 540 companies beginning mandatory electronic filing of documents. Currently, about 4000 companies are on the system, and approximately 15,000 publicly traded companies are expected to be phased in by 1997. These companies file more than 100,000 reports with the SEC every year.

EDGAR was designed to speed up not only the collection but also the dissemination of data to the public. Under the older, paper-based system, accessing the documents can take more than a week, although people who visit SEC headquarters in Washington, D.C., can get them within a day or two if they place an order in advance and camp out in a reference room. Before EDGAR, it took up to six weeks to get documents entered and transmitted electronically. In 1994, EDGAR was made available on the Internet thanks to a National Science Foundation (NSF) grant and the efforts of a few consumer groups. When it is fully completed, anyone will be able to access the legally required filings of all publicly traded companies twenty-four hours after they have been received by the SEC.

Access to EDGAR on the Internet takes several forms. User choice depends as much on technology as on data use. The more efficient, and more popular, method is to access EDGAR directly over the Internet using the World Wide Web(http://www.townhall.org/). Gopher can also be used—type gopher town.hall.org to get a menu of items. Another way is to send e-mail requesting specific files. This method is fine if all you need is the occasional document or two, but it is inefficient if you want to see a lot of material. To retrieve files this way, you first send a message to the EDGAR system's server computer at the Internet Multicasting Service (mail@town.hall.org). This message should request an index of EDGAR documents and a list of the commands for retrieving them. After that, you're ready to request specific files. The server automatically processes the requests and sends the documents back via e-mail, usually within a few hours.

An EDGAR document downloaded from the Internet site costs nothing in contrast to a paper copy of the same document (more than $50 from a leading SEC data vendor, Disclosure). In total, Wall Street brokerage firms, corporate lawyers, and others are estimated to have paid $250 million a year to be wired into this information. Easy Internet access to EDGAR has fundamentally changed a business that was closed, costly, and profitable to an open, inexpensive and competitive market.

### Full-Text Databases

This part of the on-line publishing industry is the fastest growing sector. In addition to international sources, trade publications, and newspapers, there are news broadcast transcripts, professional journals, magazines, loose-leaf services, and newswires going on-line every month. This category also includes customized news services using dedicated lines to deliver information directly to the desktops of end users, to consumer on-line services (e.g., America Online), and in multimedia formats on CD-ROM.

In full-text electronic publishing, several brand names dominate: LEXIS/NEXIS, DIALOG, Dow Jones, and NewsNet.

**LEXIS/NEXIS.** Launched in 1973, LEXIS provides the full text of U.S. legislation and court proceedings as well as U.K. and French law and statutes; NEXIS provides text of news, magazines, newsletters, and journals and other information sources. Combined, they include the full text of more than 150 million documents, ranging from Supreme Court decisions, to business, scientific, and financial information from around the world. These databases are supposed to have more than a quarter of a million customers around the world. Mead estimates that more than 10,000 customers dial into their databases every day in search of answers. In fact, the electronic publishing arm of Mead grew from $6 million in 1968 to an estimated market value of $1.6 billion in 1994, when it was bought by Elsevier and Reed International.

LEXIS is used by many students, large law firms, law libraries, financial institutions, and government agencies (see Fig. 15.2). LEXIS has become the norm in legal research; law students are given a free subscription as an introduction to the service. NEXIS also has a broad spectrum of users, with the news media and researchers—academic and professional—being the largest user categories. LEXIS /NEXIS is available via Internet: *telnet lex.meaddata.com*.

Academic LEXIS/NEXIS users are usually students with an insatiable thirst for information. Its usage is growing rapidly, especially among researchers and students who need access to its vast up-to-date database to do research. The company expects the business or professional user to remain the primary user of information services, however. How is it used by

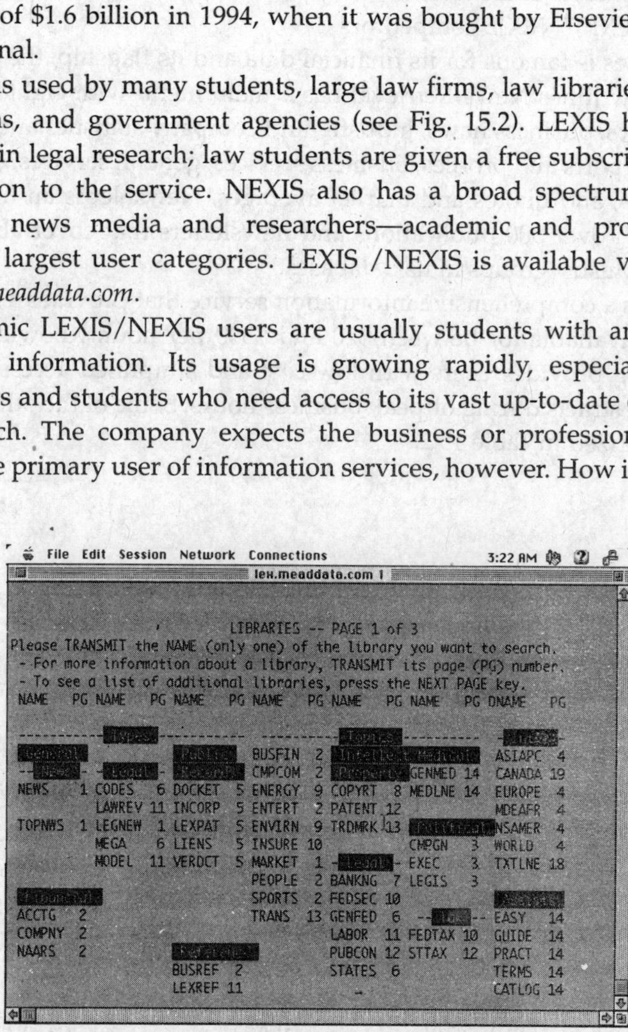


**Figure 15.2** Screen shot of LEXIS/NEXIS listing various databases

professionals? Take, for instance, CNN and other news organization that often get hot leads and need to get the background information for the story right away. Since they do not have all the necessary information themselves, they contract with companies such as Mead to do the research for a story, which requires searching for the information and packaging it in terms of a report.

**Competitors in the Full-Text Database Marketplace.** Dow Jones News-Retrieval, NewsNet, and Dialog Information Services, as well as smaller, more specialized databases, are major on-line data services that are the principal LEXIS/NEXIS competitors.

Dow Jones is famous for its financial data and its flagship, the *Wall Street Journal*. Dow Jones News-Retrieval has a main menu with eight selections: general news, business news, industry and company statistics and forecasts, company reports and profiles, business services, general services, on-line reference tools, and quotes and market averages. NewsNet is an information service with over 300 publications and newsletters that cover almost forty separate industry groups in its databases.

Dialog is a comprehensive information service that provides a number of databases available for between $20 and $500 per hour. Knowledge Index from Dialog provides users with low-cost and simplified access to Dialog database abstracts during offpeak business hours. Some of the other services are summarized in Table 15.2.

**Table 15.2** Leading On-Line Information Distributors

| *Parent Company* | *On-Line Publishing Service* | *Parent Company* | *On-Line Publishing Service* |
|---|---|---|---|
| Mead Data Central | LEXIS/NEXIS | Allied Corp | Bunker Ramo, etc. |
| DIALOG | DIALOG | IP Sharp | Financial Services |
| Dow Jones | Telerate, News/Retrieval | McGraw Hill | DRI, Standard and Poor's |
| Reuters | Monitor | ADP | Financial Services |
| Quotron | Quotron | Knight-Ridder | Commodity News Service |
| Dun & Bradstreet | Dunsprint | SDC | SDC ORBIT |
| TRW Inc | TRW Credit | BRS | BRS |

In sum, the full-text services play an important role in on-demand education. The future of full-text publishers lies in their ability to create products to suit different customer needs. To meet the needs of the busy professional, sophisticated information research facilities have to be developed. The individual user, for the intermediate term, is likely to be limited to college students who do not want or need information research in a packaged form and, most important, cannot (or are not willing to) pay for the more expensive services. Unlike the business user with deep pockets, an individual or a small business requires flexible pricing.

The main complaint about full-text services is their high price. Ignoring the vast market of users who cannot afford the expensive services represents a market gap that needs to be filled with low-cost providers. This weakness is being exploited by CompuServe, America Online, and on-line service providers teaming up with content providers to offer news, magazines (e.g., *The New York Times, Time*), and on-line stock market information. We have to wait and see which companies step in to offer competitive pricing to services similar to those offered by Mead. The next step of the competitive battle lies in acquiring customers on the Internet.

### Real-Time News, Retrieval, and Delivery Services

Essentially, real-time news, retrieval, and delivery services come under the category of news on-demand, which is rapidly becoming an important segment of the information publishing industry.

News on-demand is in essence a personalized electronic news magazine that delivers customer-selected information on a customer-specified schedule. Residential customers seeking information for entertainment or educational purposes and professional customers seeking information are seen as primary users. Already, several companies are collaborating to define and develop a system that can deliver news on-demand to corporate and financial services professionals. The service combines video, audio, text, and graphics in a format that permits browsing, searching, and user-notification on breaking news. These systems will attempt to deliver late-breaking news with minimal delays. Users are able to retrieve the information they need at any time.

All news on-demand applications have a number of "dynamic" requirements that distinguish them from conventional "static" multimedia publishing efforts:

- *Time critical alerts.* The timeliness of the information is paramount. It is absolutely necessary that users be alerted or notified of an interesting event a few seconds after it is approved by the editor.

- *Delivery control.* Because several gigabytes of information are generated every day, the information provider must be able to target each news story to a particular group of authorized subscribers and be able to monitor the delivery.
- *Dynamic user preferences.* Users have ever-changing information needs and must be able to vary their "interest profiles" at any time. The information must be coded and categorized by the provider for maximum retrieval flexibility.
- *Aging and archival.* Certain stories are discarded at the end of the day while others are retained for several months. Some information may even be archived permanently.

As shown in Fig. 15.3, a basic news on-demand implementation uses I-way multimedia servers incorporating compression techniques (MPEG for video, JPEG for still images). The information is viewed on clients with integrated browsers. This architecture will offer a selection of text, headlines, and pictures, but these features will not be the static objects they are in print. As

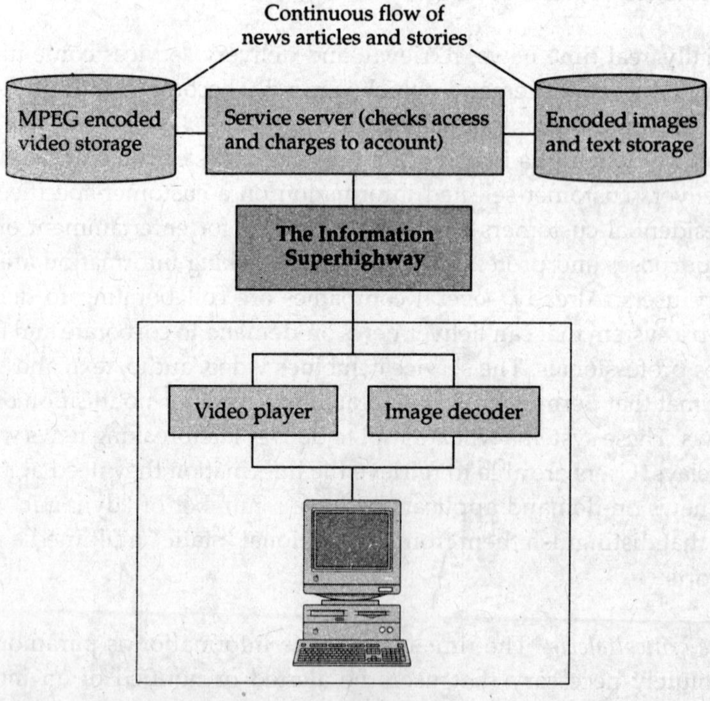


Figure 15.3 News on-demand architecture

readers delve into one story, they may be able to access more photos or hear from the participants themselves. One avenue might lead to TV coverage from NBC or CNN or other organizations. Another avenue will lead to background information and, perhaps most importantly, to the original statements of those involved in the story and their response to the coverage.

The benefits of news on-demand do not stop with rapid dissemination of information. News cries out for hypertext and other forms of linking, grouping, and classification that are not possible on paper. Although hypertext (text that contains easily followed links to other text and other media) has been discussed a great deal, serious hypertext applications have been few in number.

These new possibilities signal the end of one-sided distribution (publisher to customer) but can easily accommodate two-way interaction (publisher to/from customer). One side effect may be reduced media influence, because customers will no longer get all their information from only one source. As already noted, readers might find a menu of video clips and written reports on a specific topic, all from different news agencies and might view one or several of them. A number of solutions will allow for fair compensation to the providers of the information without requiring the subscriber to deal with each one independently. Information packagers (such as ClariNet, discussed in the next paragraph, which buys almost all of its coverage from other traditional sources such as news wires) and editors will build services for the subscriber providing them with high-quality interfaces and access to news from different sources.

As an added bonus, the distinction between local and global news will blur, with each reader having access to news and views from all over the world and editorial selections from all perspectives. In the past, newspapers had to decide what, among all the news, was fit to print. Today electronic newspapers can provide all the news before it's printed and classify it so that readers find just what they want. A major change in the nature of the news media is just beginning, and the on-line environment is the place that is giving birth to, and will nurture, that change.

**Personalization and Packaging of the News.** Fundamental to real-time news delivery is the concept of the personalization, a package of news and advertising tightly tailored and customized to the wants and needs of individual readers and advertisers and made available across the whole spectrum of consumer devices (like a waiter or waitress who knows what you want even before you order it). Customization could be used in innovative ways. Say you are living in LA but you were born in Seattle and have family there and you went to college in New York and have friends there. You can create a customized newspaper that has local news from Seattle and sports news from New York because you are a big Yankees fan. You follow college football in the ACC conference. You can call up aircraft, television, and weather schedules from LA, video clips from CNN and international news, especially from China because your spouse is Chinese. And your personal gazette will be available on the consumer equipment of your choice: computer, television, personal digital assistant, or even the car audio while you are driving to work. The possibilities are mind-boggling.

To meet the needs of personalization, publishers must understand and gain expertise in the information packaging business, which has traditionally been the purview of news media. News media strength stems largely from its unrivaled ability to package and present a vast amount of information in a compact format. This is not the first time that the newspaper industry has faced challenges. Newspaper people bemoaned first the introduction of radio and then of television. For years, many newspapers refused to provide television listings of any kind, let alone coverage of what television had to offer. Now, untold numbers of newspapers have taken on the trappings of a television sensibility. *USA Today*, with newspaper boxes that literally mimic television screens and coverage that is pithy, shows just how far the pendulum can swing in a very short time.

Newspaper, magazine, and newsletter publishing are different in many ways:

- *Speed.* Electronic newspapers, radio, and television are much faster at delivering volume information than magazines ever could be.
- *Interactivity.* Both television and radio are interactive through call-in programming; and both deliver information to targeted audiences, either large or small, that are regionally and demographically defined, making them appealing to advertisers.
- *Distribution.* It costs more to deliver a well-packaged magazine than it does to deliver the same information in piece-by-piece form electronically.
- *Advertising.* Unlike newspapers, magazines are heavily dependent on advertising for survival.

In short, magazines have access to the same information as newspapers but need to be more creative in both information presentation and reporting/packaging to capture the reader's attention. Customers love magazines and seem to feel that they deliver information more effectively than newspapers. Asked to choose which is "the most effective medium for knowledge and usable ideas," 45 percent of respondents to a 1991 survey preferred magazines. By comparison, only 18 percent chose TV, 20 percent newspapers, and

2 percent radio; 15 percent were undecided. People seem to trust magazines more than TV, radio, and newspapers.

Why do consumers consider magazines effective? The answer will shape news delivery. The answer is niche or focused markets and credibility due to reputation for accurate reporting. That credibility comes from two sources: good editorial content constantly defined and redefined by feedback from the marketplace, and the impression of an unbiased atmosphere that is unregulated and free of external influence.

Information gathering and packaging are strengths that electronic magazines are ideally suited for. The packaging comes from interacting with readers and getting marketplace feedback from advertisers. The new multimedia advertising mix is profoundly different from the business model of just a few years ago. For instance, newspapers initially defined their advertiser-supported audiotext activity as a way to enhance the print product and to stake claim as the primary information provider in their markets. Now audiotext—both advertiser-supported and pay-per-call—is seen as one of several complementary techniques to meet the needs of readers and advertisers. Instead of audiotext-as-print-enhancement, the new newspaper model includes consumer on-line services, fax publishing, and CD-ROM. These new techniques and devices are now seen as methods for reaching new customers rather than as mere adjuncts to print distribution.

With the customers in control, advertisers have to rethink what to sell, how to sell it, and how to attract customers' attention. News of the future will have to deliver clever interactive advertisements or, even, infomercials that entice viewers to "experience" test-driving a car, the look and feel of a new line of designer clothes, or a view from the suite reserved on a cruise ship. In other words, the concept of advertising in newspapers and traditional broadcast media such as television is probably going to merge to create one entity that can be customized on the fly to the medium of delivery.

Newspapers have reached a key moment in their history—and the newspaper executives, managers, and editors know it. Recognizing that readership trends are slowly declining and that technology will change the way information is delivered and accessed, the news industry is moving to decrease its reliance on cash flow from paper-based segments. Instead, companies have come to depend more on other media businesses or forms of electronic publishing such as interactive television and Internet publishing, each with its own risks.

In sum, far-sighted news executives no longer define their mission by the limitations and constraints of ink and paper. Several news organizations already offer electronic versions to experiment with the emerging media and expand their influence and reach. Many newspapers are doing their best to use modern technology. Electronic mail is rapidly becoming common for the letters-to-the-editor section. Cable and telephone companies are also moving rapidly. They are joining on-line computer companies to deliver classifieds and newspaper editions that will be augmented with images, audio, and video. The future for news on-demand is shaping up to be exciting indeed.

**Successful Electronic News Businesses—ClariNet.** ClariNet Communications Corporation, founded by Brad Templeton, is the first company to distribute wire service news and columns over the Internet. Distributed in USENET form, ClariNet stories and columns are organized into several hundred news groups. The general news and sports come from Reuters, Associated Press, and United Press International, and the computer news from the NewsBytes service.

ClariNet began by providing news to universities and major research labs on the Internet. Providing educators and researchers useful information was acceptable under the NSFNET acceptable usage policy. ClariNet achieved most of its growth through the word-of-mouth. Nonetheless, there was some initial resistance. Customers would often e-mail asking how ClariNet could offer a for-pay service over what they viewed as a non-commercial net.

ClariNet delivers its services in two ways: in the USENET format or over the point-to-point phone lines using modems. In offering news over the Internet, ClariNet exploited one of its most important features—virtual connectivity. The Internet gives users the illusion that the information of interest is actually on their desktop, not somewhere far away and difficult to access. Even if the speed of an Internet connection is slow, this virtual connectivity allows information to flow unattended into a computer. Subscribers do not need to connect to ClariNet's computers to read the news; rather it is piped into their machines and they can then read it using the subscriber's choice of reading software.

ClariNet has been successful by organizing material so that people can access it with ease. ClariNet often takes news found in a daily newspaper and places it in one or more categories. Readers can use the news groups to build a personal profile of the information and topics they find interesting. Categorization is both by priority, so that people can identify front page news in various areas, and by topic, so that readers can follow all the news in topics of interest to them, ranging from computer industry sectors to financial markets to women's rights.

ClariNet presents a good example of the newspaper of the future. But a lot of work remains to be done, and three issues need consideration: presentation, editorial, and pricing. On the presentation front, there is still a long way to go. As more sophisticated browsers are created and as the popularity of the electronic newspaper concept grows, fancier and more labor-intensive features will come into play. The balance between effective presentation of information and ease of use is tricky. Value-added editorial work will become the key aspect of news delivery, with editors filtering, classifying, and adding useful links to the information surplus. Finally, flexible pricing is vital for attracting customers.

In the long term, technology will have a significant impact as competing media and other news information delivery services may siphon away readers and, ultimately, advertisers. Companies least affected will be those that leverage their traditional strength in gathering, processing, and disseminating information to develop their own electronic news systems and/or maintain a diversified portfolio of electronic publishing businesses.

## CD-ROM-Based Publishing

CD-ROM or "compact disc read-only memory" is a technology used for the storage and retrieval of large amounts of information from a plastic 12-centimeter disc onto a PC. Today, nearly every PC comes equipped with a CD-ROM drive, which add about $300 or more to the final price of the machine. This has helped boost worldwide installations of CD-ROM drives to more than 5 million. The storage capacity of each disc is impressive, with over 650 Mb of information. This translates into an equivalent of 300,000 printed pages, one hour of music, or 15,000 photo images, all for a few dollars. CD-ROM provides capabilities far beyond the print method, such as search and retrieval based on user queries that can be very time-saving and increase research productivity tremendously.

Improvements in CD-ROM technology and the advent of new high-speed CD-ROM players for PCs allow it to be used in three ways: for competing with existing full-text database business, for electronic books, and in the edutainment business.

### *CD-ROM and Full-Text Databases*

The combination of CD-ROM and full-text databases allows low-cost access to an immense quantity of information. Let's look at a specific example, CD-ROM-based legal publisher On Point Solutions Incorporated of Marietta, Georgia, which publishes compilations of local, state, and supreme court decisions. Started in 1990, this form of publishing is fast becoming essential to law firms as a research tool in case preparation. On Point Solutions is competing and even upstaging West Publishing Company, which has published court rulings for 117 years. West's bound volumes are staples in law offices across the country.

One area where CD-ROM full-text databases dominate is libraries. The hardcopy printed books, journals, and reference markets are already seeing competition from CD-ROM-based publishing. Speaking from our personal experience, it was amazing to watch from the sidelines as our research library changed dramatically in the last few years. CD-ROM databases are rampant in all areas: scientific, technical, and medical. In short, the use of CD-ROMs in the library and networked information systems across the campus, or indeed between universities, is an important growth area.

### CD-ROM and Electronic Books

Traditional books are expected to face some challenge from CD-ROM-based information delivery. The book market is highly varied and ranges from adult and children consumer books, educational, academic and professional, and reference books. One distinct feature sets the book market apart from other types of publishing. In terms of revenue sources, this market generates circulation revenue exclusively—advertising is carried to a lesser extent only in some directories/reference products.

The penetration of electronic books is still expected to be fairly high in education markets where reduced budgets, constant change in material, and increased use of computers creates an ideal market. Supporting this trend are increasing numbers of school-aged children at upper elementary and high school age levels who are far more computer literate than the previous generation. Also aiding the trend is the continued use of supplemental books, an increased percentage of educational spending.

Adult trade and mass paperbacks are projected to be among the leading markets for electronic books. Just as adult videos gave a boost to the VCR market in the late 1970s, adult electronic material is likely to have a similar effect in the on-line world. This is borne out by the fact that adult bulletin boards are rampant, and the CD-ROM put out by *Penthouse* magazine in 1993 was among the best-sellers.

Growth of the electronic book market hinges on a distribution method. Over the last decade, book sales have benefited from the growth of book clubs, the growth and success of superbookstores, and the expanded product lines of other direct mail marketers. These superstores are larger and have improved their marketing to target an expanded market. But what will a superstore for an electronic book club look like on the I-way? The jury is still out on this one.

### Edutainment = Education + Entertainment

*Edutainment*—a combination of entertainment, education, and games—combines interactive learning products with an entertaining format. Once dismissed as a fad, this category has taken on a new level of importance as a result of the imaginative and successful products created by such companies as Broderbund, Electronic Arts, and Software Toolworks. Because they prefer to emphasize the educational experience of their products, some developers of edutainment titles take exception to being included in the same category as video games. However, this software niche makes use of technology similar to that of games. Many products are available with photorealistic images, full-motion film clips, digitized voices, and sound in CD-ROM formats.

An important quality of edutainment systems is that they engage users in an interactive learning experience that mixes video, graphics, music, voice narration, and text. Their goal is to control the learning experience so that a student becomes an active rather than a passive learner. Edutainment programs are designed for specific age groups and cover a range of subjects including mathematics, reading, early learning, writing, history, and geography. The degree to which edutainment software actually teaches literary, numerical, and science skills has not been determined; however, parents (the purchasers) prefer that their children's software have some educational component—and the consumer is always right.

Edutainment is marked by changing technology, evolving industry standards, and frequent new product introductions. Let us consider the evolution of technology in one category, the video game industry. The progression and innovation of technology in the video game market has been phenomenal. Nintendo introduced its first 8-bit video game system in 1985. This 8-bit system had superior audiovisual qualities and was more sophisticated than other models in the marketplace. Four years later, Nintendo introduced Gameboy, a hand held system that has enjoyed tremendous success and widespread consumer acceptance. In 1990, Sega took a technological leap and introduced the U.S. industry's first 16-bit system. With twice the processing power of 8-bit cartridges, 16-bit games are faster, more sophisticated, and produce better sounds and colors. In August, 1991, Nintendo retaliated with its own 16-bit system called the Super Nintendo. Not to be outdone, Sega introduced a 16-bit accessory to the Sega Genesis game system that has 100 times more memory than earlier 16-bit cartridges. It features human actors, compressed full-motion video, special effects, high fidelity sound, and complicated plots that let the player control the action interactively. In 1994, 3DO introduced a 32-bit CD-based interactive multimedia game unit that plugs into a television monitor and incorporates three-dimensional animation, high fidelity audio and cinematic special effects that promises a higher level of realism than do currently available video games. To push the envelope even further, in early 1995 Atari introduced a 64-bit player called the Jaguar that promises even better and more realistic interactivity.

In ten short years, we have witnessed the growth of a huge industry created primarily by technology. The edutainment market is expected to enjoy explosive growth because of favorable demographics and the recent proliferation of home computers. Market research indicates that this segment is now a multibillion-dollar industry and growing rapidly. Take, for instance, the video game industry. In 1993 video games were a $6.5-billion-a-year business—bigger than the total U.S. domestic movie box-office take—and the industry is projected to grow to more than $7.5 billion in 1994. NPD Research, a firm that analyzes the toy industry, reports that of the 20 best-selling toys in 1993, 17 were video games (*Digital Media*, February 1994). With the growing sophistication of game software and their appeal to adult sensibilities, the average game player is getting older. It has been estimated that 75 million individuals play a video game at least once a week. Over 45 percent of these game players are over the age of 18 and 37 percent are female. This segment will grow even further as the quality of games gets better. Games of the future will be delivered via CD-ROM technology because of the economics. A video game cartridge has approximately 1 Mb of storage capacity and costs about $15.00 to produce, compared to a 650 Mb and $1.00 manufacturing cost for a CD.

Interestingly, the use of the on-line medium as an edutainment distribution channel has been minimally exploited. It is a well-known fact that interactive role-playing games such as MUD (Multi-user Dungeons) are played by millions of people on-line. Games such as ID Software's DOOM, DOOM II, and Heretic are examples of very successful games that were initially distributed on the Internet. So many copies of these games have been sold that ID Software engineers have become quite wealthy. Clearly, a business opportunity exists; the challenge is to create a strategy for developing, distributing, and supporting on-line edutainment.

## Collaboratories, USENET, and Real-Time Conferencing

A *collaboratory* is an on-line "virtual" laboratory where people from all walks of life come together to experiment and share experiences. In growing numbers, people are turning to the Internet for the kind of value-added information and knowledge they would never get in their university library, classroom, or on-line databases. The on-line publishing model, while important, aims at providing information to the paying customer and, through its content, limits the scope of interaction. For instance, the customer cannot add to existing content so that other customers can see the modified content. In this way, it restricts and even prohibits customer-to-customer interaction, a significant drawback of the model. This too is changing.

Collaboratories, chat lines, and bulletin boards have become very popular because their two-way interaction enables people to influence and contribute to what others can read. This two-way-interaction model forces us to rethink the traditional notions of what content is and how it should be served to the customer. For example, we can have books or movies on-line that are annotated by customers refuting claims and even providing supporting evidence to certain claims. If the customer desires to make these annotations public, other customers can read them and even comment on these annotations. In other words, we are now creating an environment where the customer can go beyond simply viewing the information to a more dynamic or interactive mode and in the process also have a social interaction with other readers.

### *Real-Time Conferencing with Internet Relay Chat (IRC)*

Another form of collaboratory is the Internet Relay Chat (IRC). IRC is a multiuser implementation of the rudimentary UNIX "talk" program. Developed by Jarkko Oikarinen in Finland in the late 1980s, IRC was originally intended to work as a better substitute for "talk" on his bulletin board. IRC allows several users to simultaneously participate in a discussion over a particular "channel," or even multiple channels. There is no restriction on the number of people that can participate in a given discussion or on the number of channels that can be formed over IRC. All IRC conversations occur in real time. This remains one of the strengths of IRC and also distinguishes it from USENET.

IRC has been used extensively for live coverage of world events, news, and sports commentary. It also serves as an inexpensive substitute for long-distance calling. IRC became very popular during its live coverage of the Gulf War, and its growth has been exponential since then. Reports of the Russian coup and the California earthquake were carried live over IRC, with locals bringing in the eyewitness reports. The IRC in effect creates a global system that permits people to send messages live to other users.

The utility of the IRC for information distribution in cases of extreme need or urgency has already been demonstrated. For instance, when the devastating earthquake hit Kobe, Japan, many people around the world joined the #kobe channel for the latest news. In fact, the first news of and reaction to the unfolding disaster was on the USENET and IRC, and as the news spread globally more and more people joined in. Some users had access to up-to-date news including one person in Tokyo who was entering messages while listening to the radio as was a user in London who was watching NHK TV News coverage. As the full scale of the disaster slowly became apparent, more and more people joined IRC for the latest news, including those with family in Kobe who were desperate for any news. Meanwhile, local TV stations around the world were only just starting to get the news.

How does IRC work? The IRC network itself consists of multiple interconnected servers. It is usually best to select a server close to the site that you IRC from. A server address, countrycode.undernet.org, usually gets you to one of the servers in your region. To find out which server is closest to you once you're on IRC, use the /links command to get a list of servers. To switch to the closest server, try /server servername. To get on, you need a software program called IRC client. IRC client reads in your commands, and your PC filters them, performs the appropriate actions, and, if necessary, passes them on to a server. The server holds information about the channels and people on IRC and other information. It is also responsible for routing messages to other people on IRC. It is beyond the scope of this book to get into the details of IRC. More information is available from the frequently asked questions from *rtfm.mit.edu* under /pub/usenet/alt.irc/.

### Electronic Conferencing and USENET

Electronic conferencing in its various forms—bulletin boards, on-line forums, mailing lists, and USENET news groups—has become one of the most popular and important Internet applications. On the Internet, ARPANET mailing lists in the 1970s were the first form of electronic conferencing. In the 1980s, USENET news groups became the de facto standard for discussion and community cooperation. News groups can be something of a misnomer. They can be very interesting, informative, and educational, but they are often not just news, at least not the way most people would think of them.

What will you typically see on the USENET? For instance, in comp.lang.pascal, Tuomask from Helsinki is looking for someone who knows how to debug a complex program he has written. In soc.culture.indian, a New Jersey college student is seeking real-life terrorists or their supporters for help with a paper she is writing. If you want to discuss movie soundtracks, you can get involved with the group rec.music.movies. Ecological issues? You can start with talk.environment and move on to sci.environment or sci.bio.ecology. On a lighter note, there are news groups that cater to various types of sports, hobbies, and sex. From auto repair to Zen Buddhism, it's all there, though far beyond the scope of this book. For more on USENET, we refer the interested user to several excellent books [KROL 92] and [KEHO93].

## 15.3 DIGITAL COPYRIGHTS AND ELECTRONIC COMMERCE

It is clear that the speed of technological development has outpaced the legal system and that digital copyright issues need to be resolved with some urgency. As customers zip down the I-way, protecting intellectual property rights and collecting dues from the copyright users promise to be challenging issues.

The scope and magnitude of the problem is clear. The degree of potential copyright infringement on-line vastly surpasses the damage that can be inflicted with a photocopy machine. Anyone with a computer can make and distribute countless copies of anything digital, be it a book, a TV or computer program, or a piece of music. Even worse, the digital version can be sent to friends or even a bulletin board system (BBS) for "downloading" by anyone with a modem.

Advances in technology have raised the stakes considerably. Virtually any work can readily be "digitized," archived, and used in the digital format. This increases the ease and speed with which a work can be reproduced, the quality of the copies, the ability to manipulate and change the work, and the speed with which copies, (authorized and unauthorized) can be "delivered" to the public. Works also can be combined with other works into a single medium, such as a CD-ROM, causing a blurring of the traditional lines. The establishment of high-speed, high-capacity networking makes it possible for one individual, with a few key strokes, to deliver perfect copies of digitized works to scores of other individuals—or to upload a copy to a bulletin board or other service where thousands of individuals can download it or print unlimited "hard" copies on paper or disks.

In sum, the emergence of the I-way is dramatically changing, and will continue to change how people and businesses deal in information and entertainment products and services; and how works are created, owned, distributed, reproduced, displayed, performed, licensed, managed, presented, organized, sold, accessed, used, and stored. This leads to a clarion call for changes in the law.

### Digital Copyright Basics

Before proceeding further, let's review the basics of copyright. Copyright is a form of protection provided by U.S. laws (Title 17, U.S. Code) to the authors of "original works of authorship" including literary, dramatic, musical, artistic, and certain other intellectual works. This protection is available to both published and unpublished works. Section 106 of the Copyright Act generally gives the owner of copyright the exclusive right to do and to authorize others to do the following [USCO95]:

- To reproduce the copyrighted work in copies or phonorecords
- To prepare derivative works based on the copyrighted work
- To distribute copies or phonorecords of the copyrighted work to the public by sale or other transfer of ownership, or by rental, lease, or lending
- To perform the copyrighted work publicly, in the case of literary, musical, dramatic, and choreographic works, pantomimes, and motion pictures and other audiovisual works
- To display the copyrighted work publicly, in the case of literary, musical, dramatic, and choreographic works, pantomimes, and pictorial, graphic, or sculptural works, including the individual images of a motion picture or other audiovisual work

Copyright law seeks to protect "original works of authorship" that are fixed in a tangible form of expression. The fixation need not be directly perceptible as long as it can be communicated with the aid of a machine or device. Copyrightable works include the following categories: literary works; musical works, including any accompanying words; dramatic works, including any accompanying music; pantomimes and choreographic works; pictorial, graphic, and sculptural works; motion pictures and other audiovisual works; sound recordings; and architectural works. These categories are quite broad; for example, computer programs and most "compilations" are "literary works"; maps are "pictorial, graphic, and sculptural works."

Section 106 does not mention digital copyrights, and to correct this several amendments to the original law have been proposed. The advent of the I-way is not the first nor the last technological challenge to copyright owners' ability to prevent unauthorized uses of their works. For instance, the photocopying machine caused great fear among copyright owners of printed works. But time, cost, and quality were on the copyright owner's side. It proved to be more efficient and less expensive to buy a copy of most books than to photocopy them—and the quality of a book from the original publisher is typically higher than that of a photocopy. The introduction of audio tape recorders also posed problems for copyright owners. Again, however, the physical attributes of the work made reproductions less expensive, but lower in quality—until, of course, the introduction of digital audio recorders, which reproduce sound recordings both cheaply and with no degradation of sound quality. This threat to sound recordings was answered with the enactment of the Audio Home Recording Act of 1992, which combined legal and technological safeguards.

## Digital Copyright Wording in On-Line Databases

The stakes are indeed high. Owners of copyrights will not be willing to put their interests at risk if appropriate systems—both in the United States and internationally—are not in place to permit them to set and enforce the terms and conditions under which their works are made available. Likewise, the public will not use the services available and create the market necessary for its success unless access to a wide variety of works is provided under equitable and reasonable terms and conditions, and unless the integrity of those works is assured.

Look closely at the following extracts from copyright/contractual schemes that attempt to govern the area of the on-line database world affecting most educational activities. Most terms and conditions prohibit (or appear to prohibit) on-line searchers from sharing the results with others, at least without prior written permission. They can be categorized into no downloading at all; no electronic storage; no copies or distribution, even internally; no copies or distribution to third parties; and specific limitations on various types of use. After reading these statements, visualize how you would perform searches if the clauses were strictly enforced. Often, these provisions are widely ignored by users, and known by the industry to be widely ignored [SEAR94].

### *No Downloading at All*

> Downloading is only permissible with the written permission of Elsevier Science Publishers B.V. [Elsevier Science Publishers B.V.]
>
> No part of Westlaw transmission may be copied, downloaded, stored in a retrieval system, further transmitted or otherwise reproduced, stored, disseminated, transferred or used, in any form or by any means, without West's prior written agreement. [West Publishing Company]

### *No Electronic Storage*

> These databases may not be reproduced, stored in machine-readable form, or transmitted in any means, electrical, mechanical, photocopy or otherwise without written permission of the publisher. [Generic Terms and Conditions of approximately 20 DIALOG databases]

Customer may print out one (1) copy of Information contained in the Database from the display thereof on Customer's terminal(s), for backup/archival purposes only. . . . The downloading of information onto computers, disks, diskettes or any other media, other than in temporary storage for purposes of printing such backup/archival printout is strictly prohibited. [Teikoku, Ltd.]

### No Copies or Distribution, Even Internally

You agree not to reproduce, retransmit, disseminate, sell, distribute, publish, broadcast or circulate the information received through the Service to anyone, including, but not limited to, others in the same company or organization, without the express prior written consent of Dow Jones. [Dow Jones News/Retrieval User Agreement]

You agree that information will not be sold, reproduced, revealed or made available in whole or in part to anyone else unless required by valid subpoena or court order or without prior written consent from D&B. [Dunn & Bradstreet, Inc.]

### No Copies or Distribution to Third Parties

The information contained in HEALTH PERIODICALS DATABASE is provided for use inside customer's organization only and may not be duplicated or redistributed in any form without the prior written permission of Information Access Company. [Information Access Company]

The Customer may not disseminate the DISCLOSURE DATABASE or any part thereof for any purpose whatsoever unless authorized by DISCLOSURE in writing except that limited reproduction of printed output up to 25 copies is permitted within the subscriber organization. [Disclosure Incorporated]

### Specific Limitations on Various Types of Use

The generation of mailing labels or any kind of mailing list from the directory records in the Database is not permitted. Resale or free distribution of any data to third parties is expressly prohibited. [BioCommerce Data Limited]

Customers shall not use computer-readable search results as a database or part of a database from which hits are selectively retrieved by programmed search. Customer may create one printed copy of search results from a computer-readable file of search results provided that Recipient destroys the computer-readable search results upon creation of the printed version. [Predicasts]

It is quite obvious that the current restrictions are largely unenforceable and inhibit only the very scrupulous. It is time for the information industry as a whole to rethink the legal framework under which searching and retrieval takes place. This framework must be enforceable and not simply a set of guidelines.

## Enforcing Digital Copyrights Using Technology

Several new research efforts are aimed at curbing copyright violations [COPY95]. These efforts aim to use technology to help protect copyrighted works against unauthorized access, reproduction, manipulation, distribution, performance, or display. Authentication of copyrighted works and management and licensing of the rights are also areas of active research.

Technology-based protection of digital works can be implemented through hardware, software, or a combination thereof. It can be implemented at the level of the copyrighted work or at other, more distant levels. It can be used to prevent or restrict access to a work, as well as reproduction, adaptation, distribution, performance, or display of the work.

### *Controlling Access to Copyrighted Works*

Unauthorized access can be denied in two general ways: by restricting access to the source of the work, and by restricting manipulation of the electronic file containing the work [COPY95].

*Controlling server access.* Nearly all information providers, including commercial on-line services such as America Online and dial-up private bulletin boards, not only control access to their systems but also vary it depending on the information a user wishes to access (e.g., access to certain data is conditioned on paying a higher fee, having greater access rights).

On the other hand, Internet users can connect to public servers through protocols such as Gopher, file transfer protocol (ftp), TELNET, or the WWW. Some information providers on the Internet grant full unrestricted access to all the information contained on their servers, so that anyone can access any data stored on the servers. Other information providers restrict access to users with accounts or grant only limited access to unregistered users. For example, using ftp a user can often log on as an "anonymous" user (e.g., a user for whom no account has been created in advance), but access through anonymous ftp is limited to certain data. Of course, this requires the implementation of appropriate security measures.

Thus control over access to a server may be used as one of the first levels of protection for the works found on it. Access to servers can vary from completely uncontrolled access (the full contents of the server are accessible without restriction) to partially controlled access (unrestricted access is granted to only certain data on the server) to completely controlled access (no uncontrolled access in any form is permitted). Access control is effected through user identification and authentication procedures (log-in name and password) that deny access to unauthorized users to a server or to particular information on a server. But access control does not preclude copies from being made once this initial layer of protection is breached.

*Controlling document access.* A second level of control can be exerted through measures tied to the electronic file containing the work. One type of restriction can be implemented through "rendering" or "viewing" software. Such systems require (1) a proprietary or unique file format that can be read only by certain software and that is developed or controlled by the information provider and (2) software that incorporates both a "control" measure to prevent viewing or use of a work without authorization from the information provider and "manipulation" functions to permit the user to view or use the work. Rendering or viewing software can be written to deny access if the user enters unauthorized identification or an improper password. Rendering software can also be written to deny access if the work is not an authorized copy (provided that sufficient information regarding authorized use is included in header information and it is sealed with a digital signature).

Another method of access restriction is encryption. As noted in Chapter 5, encryption amounts to a "scrambling" of data using mathematical principles that can be followed in reverse to "unscramble" data. Encryption technologies can be used to deny access to a work in a usable form. File encryption simply converts a file from an editable file format (e.g., a word processor document) to a scrambled format. Authorization in the form of possession of an appropriate password or "key" is required to "decrypt" the file and restore it to its manipulatable format [SCHN96].

Encryption techniques use "keys" to control access to data that has been "encrypted." These keys are actually numbers that are plugged into a mathematical algorithm and used to scramble data. Scrambling simply means that the original sequence of binary digits (the 1s and 0s that make up a digital file) is transformed using a mathematical algorithm into a new sequence of binary digits. Anyone with the key (the number used to scramble the data according to the specified mathematical algorithm) can decrypt the work by plugging the number into a program that applies the mathematical algorithm in reverse to yield the original sequence of digital signals. Of course, once the work is decrypted by someone with the key, there may be no technological protection for the work if it is stored and subsequently distributed in its "decrypted" or original format.

### Controlling Use of the Work

Hardware and/or software can provide protection against unauthorized uses of copyrighted works. For instance, the Audio Home Recording Act requires circuitry in digital audio recording devices and digital audio interface devices that controls serial copying. Based on the information it reads, the hardware circuitry will either permit unrestricted copying, permit copying but label the copies it makes with codes to restrict further copying, or disallow copying. The serial copy management system implemented by this circuitry allows unlimited first-generation copying—digital reproduction of originals—but prevents further digital copying using those reproductions.

Such systems can be implemented through hardware, software, or both, using the concepts discussed above (e.g., rendering software and encryption technology). For example, files containing works can include instructions used solely to govern or control distribution of the work. This information might be placed in the "header" section of a file or another part of the file. In conjunction with receiving hardware or software, the information, whether in the header or elsewhere, can be used to limit what can be done with the original or a copy of the file containing the work. It can limit the use of the file to read-, view-, or listen-only. It can also limit the number of times the work can be retrieved, opened, duplicated, or printed [COPY95].

### Authenticating the Work

Mathematical algorithms can be used to create digital signatures that, in effect, place a "seal" on a digitally represented work. These algorithms can be implemented through software or hardware, or both. Digital signatures can play an important role in ensuring data integrity [SCHN96].

A digital signature is a unique sequence of digits that is computed based on (1) the work being protected, (2) the digital signature algorithm being used, and (3) the key used in digital signature generation. Generating a digital signature uses cryptographic techniques but is not encryption of the work; the work may remain unencrypted so it can be accessed and used freely. In fact, digital signatures and encryption can be used simultaneously to protect works. Generally, a signature is computed for a copyrighted work first and then it (including the seal) is encrypted. When the work is to be used, the work is decrypted, then the signature (the seal) is verified to be sure the work has not been modified (either in its original or encrypted form). If the work is never changed, the seal need never be removed. If the work is changed, a new seal must be computed on the revised information.

Generating a digital signature is called "signing" the work. Both the digital signature and the public key are often appended to signed copyrighted works (or they may be stored in a header). The signature serves as a "seal" for the work because the seal enables the information to be independently checked for unauthorized modification. If the seal is verified (independently computed signature matches the original signature), then the copyrighted work is a bona fide copy of the original work—nothing has been changed in either the header or the work itself [CACM94].

### Implementing Electronic Contracts

Software-based systems for tracking and monitoring uses of copyrighted works are being contemplated. Software-based systems may also be used to implement licensing of rights and metering of use. A combination of access controls, encryption technologies, and digital signatures can be used by copyright owners to protect, license, and authenticate information. These security measures must be carefully designed and implemented to ensure that they protect the copyrighted works and are not defeated.

Information included in files can be used to inform the user about ownership of rights in a work and authorized uses of it. For instance, information can be stored in the header of a file regarding authorship, copyright ownership, date of creation or last modification, and terms and conditions of authorized uses. It can also support search and retrieval based on bibliographic records.

Electronic licenses may be used in connection with information sold. Providers may inform the user that a certain action—the entering of a password, for instance, to gain access to the service or a particular work, or merely the use of the service—will be considered acceptance of the specified terms and conditions of the electronic license. The Library of Congress' Electronic Copyright Management System may be instrumental in rights management. The proposed system, which is under development, has three distinct components: (1) a registration and recording system, (2) a digital library system with affiliated repositories of copyrighted works, and (3) a rights management system. The system will serve as a testbed to gain experience with the technology, identify issues, develop a prototype of appropriate standards, and serve as a working prototype if full deployment is pursued later.

Eventually most digital copyright systems will use encryption—up to a point. Turning computer files into essentially unbreakable codes would guarantee protection, of course. But it would also defeat the purpose of on-line information: to make it possible to quickly sift vast storehouses of knowledge. To buy protected information, a customer would purchase a cryptographic key to decode the document. The price could depend on what the buyer wanted, from one-time personal rights to an unrestricted license. A cypher, scheduled for completion in late 1995, could be hidden in the document, identifying its owner and the buyer. Thus, if the information should leak onto a BBS, it would be possible to nail the offending party. We can even think of embedded cyphers that contain a program to prevent unauthorized use. If a person purchased one-time rights, the document would turn into gibberish when transmitted via electronic mail to a third party.

In sum, protection and management methods must be based on non-proprietary technologies, given that they may have broad usefulness. Furthermore, if the systems developed are too cumbersome or complicated, consumers may reject works protected under them. Whether various measures are useful in protecting copyrighted works, however, the ultimate judge will be the consumer and the marketplace.

## 15.4 SUMMARY

In summary, it is fair to say that growing interest in electronic media and a squeeze on time are forcing educators to reappraise their traditional markets. On-line education represents incredible strengths in terms of time and place independence and the potential "reach" of educational programming.

The changing needs of educational content is also influencing the publishing market. To date, electronic products supplement rather than supplant demand for printed products, but inroads by these electronic media are becoming more evident every day. Gains by the electronic media are well perceived by leading publishers, several of whom have established facilities to produce electronic materials such as on-line databases and compact disks for their customers.

Many publishers are wary because of the lack of adequate copyright protection. Most publishers have defined the task of building copyright protection as primarily technical. How can the protections they have in today's on-line environment be improved in tomorrow's on-line environment of millions upon millions of users with almost unbelievably powerful technology at their fingertips? Current efforts range from encryption with decoder devices for paid subscribers and information usage meters on add-in circuit boards, to sophisticated document headers that, much like the late unlamented copy protection schemes of many software vendors, would monitor how and how often the text was being used.

While users may welcome the ability to log into massive worldwide data networks from their desktop, the single most important factor for any student must be easy access to relevant information. The implementation of new information search and retrieval tools will help to address this issue.

# Chapter 16

# Software Agents

The competitive business environment and the growing complexity of work and personal lives create demands to perform many (often simultaneous) tasks efficiently and promptly. To support these imperatives, new computing tools are needed. One such emerging tool is the notion of an intelligent autonomous software agent. The underlying vision behind the development of software agents involves a paradigm shift from the traditional software-as-tool to software-as-assistant.

In the existing tool-based model, a user initiates various actions that are passively facilitated by the software. This is a "do what I say" model. For instance, a user instructs a software program to download files from the Internet, browse the WWW, or compute a spreadsheet column in a more efficient fashion, but the commands themselves issue directly from the user's mouse clicks or keyboard input.

In the new agent-based model, the user informs an agent about the various actions to be performed or tasks to be accomplished. This is a "do what I imply" model. The agent takes these requests and actively performs tasks on behalf of the user, such as comparing prices in on-line shopping malls or monitoring incoming electronic mail messages and organizing an agenda—even when the user is on vacation. In short, the traditional model is reactive, whereas the new model is proactive.

In many ways, software agents mimic real-world roles of a highly competent secretary, reference librarian, personal and relentless world events watcher, news-clip agency, office and personal "assistant," personal on-line shopper, personal investment adviser, or decision-making counselor. These capabilities, of indisputable value, will bring about a service-model shift in the software world that will touch and shape all of our lives significantly.

Recently, the term *software agent* has become a marketing buzzword to describe everything from a spreadsheet's macro functions to complex mobile code that can roam networks to do our bidding. Beyond the hype, nevertheless, is an emerging understanding of the nature of agent software that can help solve business and scientific problems. It is this understanding of autonomous agents and smart software that we focus on in this chapter.

### *Types of Software Agents*

Two types of human agents function in the workplace: office-bound workers and mobile field workers. Similarly, two types of software agents function: static (computer bound) and mobile. The static software agent simply sits on the server or PC and actively monitors the environment. For instance, a user mail agent executes in the background and is activated when there is an incoming mail message. After processing the mail, the agent becomes dormant again until another event requires processing. In short, stationary agents do not roam around the on-line world but use embedded knowledge to assist in filtering and processing the volume of incoming information.

Advanced forms of agents incorporate the mobility that allows a software agent to execute commands while living on a remote server, only reporting back to its home base when the given task is accomplished. Figure 16.1 shows a mobile agent that has been sent over the Internet to the server to carry out one or more tasks. Mobile or roaming agents promise to create a new computing environment in which software assistants perform a plethora of tasks for consumers. The consumer will be able to use his client (PDA or PC) to give the agent instructions—find the cheapest flight to Bermuda, or all news stories on the Internet, for instance—and then launch it into the network. Not only can the agent find the information, but it also can be programmed to make purchase decisions.

What is different about mobile agents is that they can carry out transactions without further input from the consumer—and can do so hours or days after being unleashed. Imagine a scenario in which a user dispatches a software agent off to a financial service to monitor the fluctuations of a given stock, instructing the agent to sell once the stock reaches a certain price threshold. The agent attaches itself to the financial server, where it follows the stock for weeks or months without communicating back to the user. Once the stock reaches the preordained value, the agent executes the sell command and deposits the proceeds into the user's bank account.

**Figure 16.1** Mobile agent interaction

Agents can also coöperate with other agents to accomplish a common activity such as meeting scheduling. Imagine a scenario where the agent travels to an on-line travel agency in search of the cheapest round-trip ticket to Hawaii. The agent buys the most economical fare and returns to the user's computer, entering the flight itinerary and checking the monthly planner for any potential conflicts. If a meeting is scheduled during the vacation, the agent promptly notifies the other participants via e-mail and arranges a new time that is amenable to all.

To accomplish complex tasks, static agents and mobile agents may actually work together. Take, for instance, "intelligent messaging" whereby incoming messages need to be filtered and routed intelligently to recipients on the move. Assume that you are out of the office when an important message arrives. The agent on your PC processes the incoming message and understands its significance. It immediately initiates several mobile agents to track you and deliver the message content in the most appropriate way—through a digitized voice over the telephone or to the cellular car phone, by fax or via electronic mail to the home, or even by paging you.

Software agent technology has the potential to affect peoples' lives in many ways. And, the agent technology looks set to radically alter not only the way in which we interact with computers, but also the way we conceptualize and build complex systems.

### Why Software Agents?

Here are some typical reasons why we need software agents. The basic premise is that software agents are autonomous, background software processes that execute on behalf of the user:

*Managing the information overload*. Users are overwhelmed by the huge amount of information available and the effort—time and cost—required to find the specific information they need. Agent support is needed to sort and filter an incoming data stream automatically into a manageable amount of high-value information.

*Decision support*. There is a need for increased support for tasks performed by "knowledge workers" (such as managers, technical professionals, and marketing personnel), especially in the decision-making area. Timely and knowledgeable decisions made by these professionals greatly impact their effectiveness and the success of their businesses in the marketplace.

*Repetitive office activity*. There is a pressing need to automate tasks performed by administrative and clerical personnel in functions such as sales or customer support to reduce labor costs and increase office productivity. Today, labor costs are estimated to be as much as 60 percent of the total cost of information delivery.

*Mundane personal activity.* In a fast-paced society, time-strapped individuals need new ways to minimize the time spent on routine personal tasks like booking airline tickets so that they can devote more time to other activities. One specific form of smart agents is voice-activated interface agents that reduce the user's burden of having to explicitly command the computer.

*Search and retrieval.* Because it is not possible to manipulate directly a distributed database system in an electronic commerce setting with millions of data objects, users will have to relegate the task of searching and cost comparison to agents. These agents perform the tedious, time-consuming, and repetitive tasks of searching databases, retrieving and filtering information, and delivering it back to the user.

*Domain experts.* We need to model costly expertise and make it widely available. Examples of "expert" software agents could be models of real-world agents such as translators, lawyers, diplomats, union negotiators, stockbrokers, and even priests.

In short, software agents can improve the productivity of the end user by performing various tasks, the most important being gathering information, filtering information, and using it for decision making.

## 16.1 HISTORY OF SOFTWARE AGENTS

The agent metaphor has its roots in work done in the early 1960s. The artificial intelligence (AI) community first coined the term *software agent* to refer to programs that act on behalf of people. These "intelligent" programs know something about user tastes, budget, and schedule and take care of personal jobs centered on managing information. Typical tasks include locating and retrieving information, filtering electronic mail, scheduling appointments, alerting the user to investment opportunities, and making travel arrangements. Individuals are, of course, capable of handling these routine tasks and have been doing so for years, but intelligent agent technology holds the promise of easing the burdens on users by automating such tasks.

Apple Computer got the industry thinking about user interface agents with a 1988 video about its vision of a "Knowledge Navigator." The film depicted a professor working in the year 2010 with a laptop computer that displayed a software agent—a male human face adorned with a bow tie—named Phil. The scene set in a professor's office portrays him using his agent to carry out a variety of tasks, including answering e-mail messages, replying to phone messages, and interacting with colleagues at distant locations. Phil also did other tasks such as gathering and analyzing research data, keeping track of appointments, generating maps, and even interrupting the professor. Communication with the agent was through voice recognition technology to interpret spoken commands and a touch-sensitive screen to point to menu choices shown on displays.

In 1993 Apple created the first commercial product with on-screen agents, a selection of cartoon figures that appear on the screen. Through voice-recognition technology, the agents are programmed to understand a set of spoken computer commands such as "print" or "restart." But there is more to it: When the computer has successfully deciphered a spoken command, an agent nicknamed Jay winks and clicks his tongue to signal understanding, creating an illusion that he has taken a command from the user, then passed it onto the processor inside. If the command is unclear, he says, "Pardon me?" Initially, many users used it for amusement rather than as a useful tool. The voice recognition was faulty and failed to understand commands. The technology problems are being solved rapidly and potential is great. One area of serious use is with disabled programmers who cannot use their hands.

Other companies have also contributed to the agent technology. In 1991 HP NewWave incorporated agent support for simple work-flow automation tasks like forms routing. This was used in a office automation system called Cooperation developed by NCR. More recently, IBM has developed Charlie, a more advanced agent with three-dimensional graphics so realistic that, from across the room, it might be mistaken for a real person. Microsoft has become a player by introducing its user interface agent called Bob.

On the Internet, Robert Kahn and Vinton Cerf proposed an architecture in 1988 for a set of information retrieval agents called "knowbots." Knowbots are agents that search a variety of information sources to find an answer to a query. For example, a knowbot working to satisfy a user's query, "Why is the sky blue?" may return a poem, a physics article, or a snippet from an encyclopedia. The goal is to let the knowbot do the searching, not have the user navigate cyberspace. This work is still under progress.

In sum, recent developments in computing, information management, miniaturization and human–machine interface (pen- and voice-based interfaces) are at the core of a trend toward the production of new kinds of computers and software that are more natural to use and exhibit smarter and more personalized behavior. While demands on people's professional and personal lives have made the creation of software agents necessary, these technological developments have made them possible. The goal and challenge is to offer a computing environment that supports and helps people perform their work more effectively.

## 16.2 CHARACTERISTICS AND PROPERTIES OF AGENTS

Recall that software agents can be "static," they reside on the PC, and provide expert advice or services locally. In other cases, the agent is mobile and acts as an emissary, executing on remote computers, perhaps even generating multiple clones, then returning results to users. The technical and operational characteristics of mobile and static software agents are quite different and raise diverse issues and concerns.

### Properties of Mobile Software Agents

Mobile and distributed agents raise a number of issues, among them:

- *Programming.* The agent must be programmed or instructed in some manner. The language (or other means) must be powerful enough to express the rules and concepts required.
- *Safety.* Remote hosts must be assured that the agent can cause no damage, obtain no secrets, or commit other illegal acts.
- *Resource usage.* As an owner, you want to be sure your agent does not exceed its budget; as a host, you want to be sure agents do not consume disproportionate resources.
- *Navigation.* Agents must be able to find the resources they need. They should coordinate with one another so as to traverse the infosphere efficiently.
- *Privacy.* The agent's internal state and program should not be visible to others. Visiting agents should not discover more information than they are entitled to.
- *Communication.* Agents must be able to communicate with users and one another, even if the network is not always connected.

Of all these issues, safety is by far the greatest concern, given that software agents can run amok, creating the network equivalent of an epidemic as agents are similar in many ways to the dreaded computer viruses. Despite their many uses, many computer and legal experts are concerned that the mobile software agent technology will definitely bring with it thorny technical, legal, and ethical problems. Some experts also fear the potential for criminal mischief, because the software agents are technically similar to the computer viruses and "worms" that computer hackers have used to invade corporate and government computer systems. It remains to be seen what safeguards can be developed.

## General Characteristics of Software Agents

Software agent technology is relatively new on the computing scene, so there is no firm consensus on what constitutes an intelligent agent. However, the following capabilities are often associated with the notion of an intelligent agent.

### *Independent Agency*

Agency independence is the ability to handle user-defined tasks autonomous of the user and often without the user's guidance or presence. The user does not become directly involved in executing the task. Once the user specifies how and when a task should be performed, the software agent is delegated to perform it when the right conditions are met. Note that the agent can execute the task immediately while the user waits for a response ("Tell me the best route to get to my hotel from the airport") or at a time when the user is not present ("Place any incoming e-mailed requests for meetings on my calendar").

Independent agents are usually created via scripting languages (for example, AppleScript, Telescript, or Safe-Tcl). Interpretable scripts guide agents in their movement across computing platforms with multiple architectures, a major factor in the popularity of scripting languages for agents. Additionally, communications-oriented scripting languages such as Telescript may facilitate construction of agents that communicate with other agents residing on different processors.

### *Agent Learning*

Agency learning is the ability to mimic the user's steps when normally performing a task. For example, learning agents would learn the user's habits and preferences over time and either respond to requests or act on the users' behalf based on their experience. The simplest form of this type of agent is a user interface agent that records the user's actions as he or she opens files. It may learn that, on Monday, the user deals only with reports X, Y, and Z and on Tuesday with reports A, B, and C. So the agent automatically brings these reports from the remote locations before the user arrives at the office and opens the file with a word processor or spreadsheet.

Agent learning usually occurs through observation, user feedback, or training. One of the techniques used when learning by observing is to track the user's actions and memorize the situations that prompted those actions ("situation-action pairs"). When a new situation occurs, the system computes the similarity between the new situation and previous situation-action pairs, to decide the course of action. The agent may suggest the action to the user or act directly without further intervention. In the user-feedback learning method, users can instruct the agent how to act directly ("never perform that action again") or indirectly by, for example, ignoring a suggestion given by the agent. The system stores the feedback actions. In user-training learning, the user inputs hypothetical situations and actions to the system, building a database of scenarios for the agent to use when deciding future actions.

### Agent Cooperation

Cooperative behavior is the ability to engage in complex patterns of two-way interaction with users and other agents. Agents are usually developed to provide expertise in a specific area and can, through cooperative work, jointly accomplish larger and more complex tasks. For example, in a messaging environment, an agent carrying a message from Peter to Jane marked "urgent" interacts with Jane's mailbox agent to find out how Jane wants urgent messages to be handled. The mailbox agent, knowing that Jane is on vacation, instructs Peter's agent to deliver the message by fax to Jane's secretary. Here both agents take into account the desires of the user they represent. Cooperative behavior of computing entities has been studied by researchers in the area of "distributed artificial intelligence." This field of research studies how agents, each with partial knowledge of a situation, can jointly communicate and cooperate to perform nontrivial tasks. Interagent cooperation between mobile agents is a new topic of interest.

### Agent Reasoning Capability

This is the ability to operate in a decision-making capacity in complex, changing conditions. This property is usually associated with making inferences, having the competence to choose among different strategies, or being capable of planning a task. The following three approaches are used to build agents with reasoning capabilities:

1. The *rule-based approach* employs user-scripted controls for information handling. Users must recognize where an agent would be useful; program the agent with rules or their profile of preferences, and update the rules or profiles as preferences change.
2. The *knowledge-based approach* uses an expert to compile a large amount of information, and then passes that information to an agent to deduce proper behavior. This method requires a substantial amount of work from the expert and is not applicable to all types of tasks.
3. The *learning approach* enables agents to learn as they are used, acquiring statistical history and new knowledge that will guide their future behavior.

### Agent Interface

The notion of a software agent that can effectively help humans perform daily tasks is even more powerful when users think of the agents as some sort of humanoids. Some researchers believe that computer users will be more likely to trust and feel comfortable with a system that presents a humanlike interface—an anthropomorphic interface. Apple's Knowledge Navigator is an example of this type of interface. Natural language and voice interfaces are other examples of agent interfaces, as is a pictorial representation of the agent as a human face. Some systems go as far as having the face express feelings. Expressions of confusion, satisfaction, and surprise can be used by a learning agent to denote its reaction to actions taken by the user.

Although software does not necessarily need to have all these qualities to be classified as an intelligent agent, it is reasonable to say that the intelligence level of agents can be correlated with the degree to which they implement these properties. On one end of the spectrum are agents that simply record the sequence of actions taken by a user and try to mimic those actions when invoked. On the other end are agents with the ability to learn from user behavior, adapt to new situations, plan tasks, make decisions, infer what behavior is expected based on past history or information context, and so on. Thus it is better to think of agents as providing a range, or different levels, of intelligence.

## 16.3 THE TECHNOLOGY BEHIND SOFTWARE AGENTS

In this section we will examine the various technical features behind mobile agents. Generally speaking, these software agents are mobile pieces of code that travel the networks to do the bidding of the person who sends them. Current technological issues in this area will center on answering questions pertaining to infrastructure and information:

- What are the components of a software agent?
- What are the components of the computing environment that supports software agents?
- How are software agents released or launched into an information medium?
- How might a user stop or control a released software agent?

## Components of a Software Agent

A software agent is composed of the embedded knowledge that drives its actions. This knowledge is described in the form of goals that lay out both the objectives for the agent and the manner in which it will perform its tasks. A software agent could contain the following features:

- *Owner*—parent process name, or master agent name. Agents can have many owners. Humans can spawn agents, processes can spawn agents (such as stock brokerage processes using agents to monitor prices), or other agents can spawn their own digital assistants.
- *Author*—development owner, service, or master agent name. Intelligent agents may be created by people or processes and then supplied as templates for users to personalize. This information is necessary for debugging the agent code if anything goes wrong.
- *Lifetime*—time to live (TTL). Some agents might exist only for a short duration and die after some task is completed. Others might live longer.
- *Account*—billing information, electronic addresses. Agents must have an anchor to an owner's account and an address for billing purposes or as a pointer to their origin. The agents must be charged for services so that scarce resources can be used effectively. For this purpose, links to the owner's account are essential.
- *Goal*—goal statements representing the measures for success. Crisp statements of successful agent task completion will be necessary, as well as metrics for determining the task's completion and the value of the return. Measures of success may include simple completion of a transaction within the boundaries of the stated goal (find a price as close to $10.00 as pos-

sible within three days) or a more complex measure of returned information (document meets 75 percent of my needs).

- *Subject description*—topic name, topic description attributes. The subject description will detail the goal's attributes. These attributes will provide the boundaries of the agent task, possible resources to call on, and class of need (such as stock purchase, airline price, decrease notification, and so on). These descriptors can be interrogated by the servers, which can then make a decision whether to service the agent or refuse service to it.
- *Background*—supporting information. This could include the type of data the agent understands, the languages that it can understand and so on.

A software agent will probably not have any "moving parts" that it uses to perform its tasks. Instead the agent will rely on the processing environment for most of its services.

## Components of the Agent Computing Environment

An agent will rely on supporting facilities that help it assist the user in reaching a stated goal. At a high level, these facilities will provide the "intelligence" for agent action, the "process" of agent interaction, and the "interconnection" to the world. Figure 16.2 shows the components of the computing environment that supports an intelligent agent.

Users can represent their preferences in many different areas. Within the computing environment a user can store, in knowledge bases, the informa-

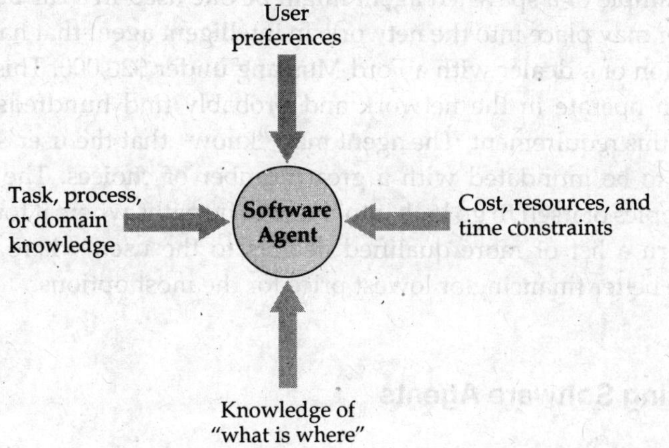


**Figure 16.2** Components of an agent's computing environment

tion and preferences that affect how an intelligent agent performs its tasks. This knowledge will be used at the client interface in the form of user-defined report formats, multimedia requirements, and so on. The user's preferences for interaction in the network also can be represented in a knowledge base. For example, a user may not wish to use certain sources or may have greater respect for other sources. This knowledge will be represented as guidelines for interactions in the network.

Task or domain-specific knowledge can consist of guiding principles for tasks such as stock market interaction, retail catalog use, accounting practices, human and other agent resources, and many other collections of knowledge about specific topics in the network. This knowledge will be used by the agent to guide how it goes about accomplishing its tasks.

The process by which an agent performs its designated duties will be guided by knowledge of a domain or the user's preferences, as well as by a model of behavior described by the constraints imposed either by the environment (resource management) or the user (cost and time). A model of behavior represents a generalized process for agent operation within the confines set forth in the user preferences and task domain.

To put the accumulated knowledge into use, the agent must know the terrain in which it is operating. This knowledge is vital if it is to perform effectively and takes the form of directories that tell the agent where information is located in the vast electronic commerce environment.

Other agents operating in the computing environment may be accessed or even spawned by intelligent agents. For this to occur, the environment must provide for agent tasks to query and access other agents performing required or similar activities.

An example of a spawned agent might be one used in a car-buying activity. A user may place into the network an intelligent agent that has as its goal the location of a dealer with a Ford Mustang under $20,000. This intelligent agent can operate in the network and probably find hundreds of dealers meeting this requirement. The agent may "know" that the user's preference was not to be inundated with a great number of choices. The agent may spawn copies of itself to go look into the specific paths where it found the hits and return a list of more qualified dealers to the user, where "qualified" might be better financing or lowest price for the most options.

## Launching Software Agents

Launching an agent into the network will ultimately be a very simple task. Agents will operate as though they are "live" entities. Intelligent agents will be pointed in the general direction of the resources needed and will proceed to query and test the available resources. Active or mobile agents will be directed to move in and out of various sources. Examples include resource discovery and search agents. On the other hand, simple agents—for example, today's information filters—operate by sitting in memory and connecting with an information source every so often to determine whether some condition has been met (such as a stock price dropping to $40). Future intelligent agents will require appropriate "living conditions" in the network so that they can exist and operate outside the user's client workstation—instead of being controlled and run from a single computer.

In a client–agent–server model, anyone (a client agent) interested in a particular resource on a network (a server) uses a formally defined application protocol to find and request a service. The technology behind agent requests is divided into three camps: RPC-based, message oriented, and database middleware.

1. *Synchronous communication-oriented remote procedure call (RPC).* An RPC is a generalization of the traditional procedure call. The client sends a request to a server and waits for a reply, completing the "request-reply cycle." The nature of the RPC communication is often synchronous, with the client waiting for the server to send a response. This is not necessary, though. Application protocols may also be designed to support asynchrony if necessary. An RPC allows the calling and the called procedures to be in different locations.

2. *Asynchronous message-oriented agents.* Message-oriented software extends process-to-process communications in distributed environments by providing the agent passing model where the messages (or agents) can contain anything—data or control. This method is also known as remote programming (RP). In short, the messaging approach permits the distribution of data or control through the use of messages.

3. *Intermediaries or database middleware.* This is a software layer that provides transparent access to homogeneous and heterogeneous relational or other databases across multiple protocol environments. It may also provide access to nonrelational data sources and even be able to provide communication protocol conversion.

Applications that have a strong synchronous flavor—for example, a client makes a request to the server and has to wait for the request before it moves on—are ideal candidates for RPCs. The messaging model fits applications that pass information onto another without necessarily waiting for a response to continue processing. The messaging is often carried out using electronic mail.

Synchronous RPC programming is by far the most common solution that forces the programmer to make decisions when writing the program. The code is then compiled, making it very efficient. Most programmers find compiled solutions too restrictive. As a rule of thumb, compiled solutions tend to be the most efficient, requiring the least amount of system resources. The inflexibility of this approach, however, makes it inappropriate for many uses. Asynchronous RPC is being developed by several companies to get around the restrictions imposed by compile time solutions. For more on RPC, see Chapter 22.

An alternative is remote programming (RP) or agent-assisted middleware, which is more flexible. With agent-assisted middleware, changes can be made to the system without requiring that each of the programs in a system be recompiled. Although agent-assisted middleware is a powerful new aid to developing distributed systems, its use has some important limitations. Its reliability is vital because applications depend on their support to run. In addition, each agent adds another component to the distributed system that may require management and can complicate the already difficult task of network management. Finally, communication between applications and these programs typically imposes performance penalties.

## Remote or Agent Programming

Remote programming changes the way network communications operate from the current distributed computing model that uses RPCs. In most RPC-based client–server systems, retrieving information from an on-line server requires a direct connection between client and server. Because the information content of the server is subject to constant change, there's no way of telling in advance what the latest data are without contacting the server and browsing through the available files. Obviously, this is a very inefficient system for both user and network. A user waiting for a particular piece of data must stay in contact continuously with the server until the desired information is located or uploaded, wasting time and money in the process. The network itself is consequently forced to handle increased traffic, as countless users prowl about the server waiting for their requests to be processed (see Fig. 16.3).

The remote programming model does away with these redundancies. Instead of logging on every fifteen minutes, the user communicates with the network in short but efficient sessions (or messages). To call up the latest news on the Internet, users dial up their remote programming–compliant on-line news server and quickly upload an agent that has been instructed to find

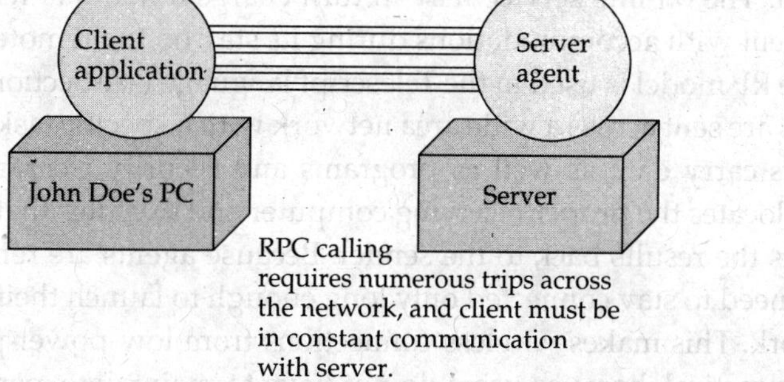


**Figure 16.3** RPC communication

any bulletins containing the key word *Internet*. This agent is not an inert document like an e-mail message, but rather a miniprogram of sorts, one that will continue to run on a remote server long after the user has disconnected from the service and returned to more pressing matters. The agent monitors the news feed twenty-four hours a day while residing in its new host environment. The moment an Internet-related story arrives, the agent dials the user's computer, deposits the story on the hard drive, and announces a successful conclusion to its mission (see Fig. 16.4).

In this scenario, the entire exchange between client and server unfolds in two brief moments of direct communication—a request and a reply. From the user's perspective, the processing time between the initial instruction and the desired result (the agent returning with the story) takes place entirely behind the scenes. No time is wasted searching for files that have yet to

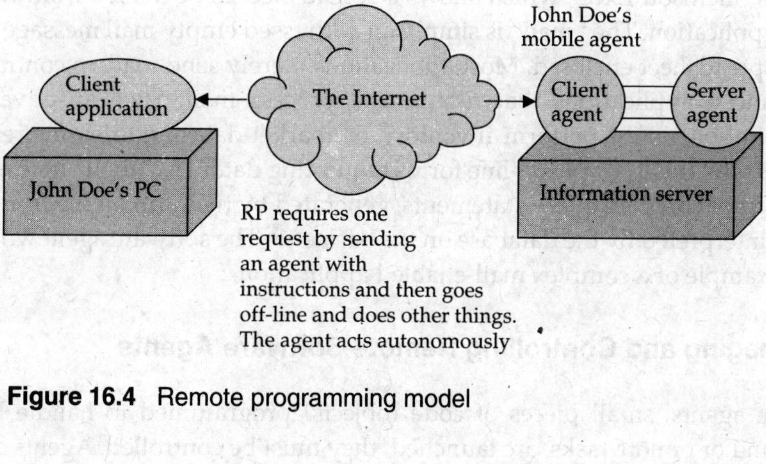


**Figure 16.4** Remote programming model

appear. The on-line service may in turn charge a nominal fee for providing the agent with accommodations during its stay on the remote server.

The RP model is used in the Telescript language (see Section 16.4) in which agents are sent across a wide area network with a specific task to accomplish. Agents carry data as well as programs and security clearances. When the agent locates the proper receiving computer and executes that task, the agent reports the results back to the sender. Because agents are remote programs, users need to stay connected only long enough to launch their agent onto the network. This makes wireless connections from low-power portables much more practical, because users do not have to maintain expensive wide area on-line connections. In contrast to most connection-based dial-up services, Telescript is transaction-based—that is, a busy user could ask a question and get an answer without going through a lengthy connection process.

The RP model uses a loosely coupled approach whereby, instead of multiple messages between clients and servers, a single client-to-server call is used to store and retrieve data and operate at a high level of abstraction (transactions rather than procedures as seen with RPC calls). There are three typical characteristics of an RP environment: (1) the environment is typically heterogeneous and multivendor; (2) the hardware platform and operating system of client and server are not usually the same; and (3) client and server communicate through a well-defined set of standard application program interfaces (APIs) and agent languages such as Telescript and Safe-Tcl [AGEN95].

Remote programming can be accomplished using electronic mail. Mail-enabled computing, also known as messaging-based or mail-based computing, is asynchronous because the responses take as long as mail takes to be delivered. Consequently, messaging is not well suited when instantaneous responses are required.

Mail-enabled applications range from simple to complex. A simple example is Microsoft Excel, which allows a spreadsheet to be mailed from within the application. The "mail" is simply an addressed empty mail message with the spreadsheet enclosed. Most applications merely send mail, in contrast to advanced applications that receive *and* process mail. Such an advanced application might perform inventory or market-data inquiries for remote users who fill in simple on-line forms requesting data. The "mail" here might consist of complex query statements, generated by the form on the front end and interpreted by the database on the back end. The software agent world is an example of a complex mail-enabled application.

## Managing and Controlling Remote Software Agents

Once agents, small pieces of code (objects) programmed to handle background or remote tasks, are launched, they must be controlled. Agents could become harmful in some way, since no program can be tested for all possible situations. This raises the issue of control. That is, once an agent is placed in the network, how can it be controlled? The challenge today is to figure out how to best implement agents so they boost productivity rather than create chaos. Without management and control, agents could become a management nightmare because users might potentially write a bad agent program. Or they could populate a network with so many agents that they initiate conflicting procedures.

Agents responsible for purchasing and selling will have to be controlled particularly closely. Consider the case of an agent created for a duration of one day to purchase a stock when it goes down to $50 and the stock fluctuates between $49 to $51 numerous times within one trading day. The user or the environment in which the stock operates must enforce controls so that the stock purchasing agent does not buy stock each time the price goes back to $50. One basic control is to give the agent an ending point through an attribute such as "Duration." Stronger controls could be placed on the agent through environmental restraints, such as a set of abort commands.

Other control issues emerge when scarce resources have to be allocated among many competing agents. Telescript uses a very interesting notion of money called Teleclicks to enforce control. Servers use Teleclicks to regulate the consumption of resources such as computation time, memory, or communication bandwidth. When an agent hitches a ride to another machine or executes some local command, it spends some of its allotment of Teleclicks, depending on the local cost of services. To better enforce control, the servers can also limit the amount of Teleclicks that a visiting agent consumes. This feature is important because a host cannot really know what a visiting agent is doing, even as the agent is caught in an infinite loop. Teleclicks provide the means for the host machine to stop memory or CPU hogs.

Control is also necessary from a user's perspective, and money limits the action of an agent. When an agent is created, the user gives it a certain amount of money, Teleclicks, to do its job to prevent it from spending too much time or resources in its search for a solution. A limitation is important because, in many cases, the user will end up paying in one way or another for the resources that the Telescript agent uses. If a user sends a request to a big text database asking for information with a certain key word, the user will probably be charged based on the CPU time that the agent consumes. Teleclicks can prevent unwelcome surprises on credit-card bills.

If users are to benefit from agents, the electronic environment must fully support their use. We must work to create languages and standards for defining intelligent agents and the processing facilities required to operate those agents. Telescript and Safe-Tcl are emerging examples of robust agent languages.

## 16.4 TELESCRIPT AGENT LANGUAGE

Telescript is primarily oriented toward creating a common communications language for wireless communications. Wireless equipment such as Personal digital assistants (PDA) are meant to be more than simply notepads; such equipment is meant to be gateways to the world, letting users send and receive mail, make appointments, access data repositories, and perform a host of other intelligent tasks to make life easier.

To reduce the time needed for interactivity between client and server, Telescript lets users bundle messages, requests, and preferences into an intelligent program that travels to a distant computer, retrieves answers to all the queries, and then returns with the answers. This results in just two trips across the network—a big saving in time, bandwidth, and money. In the more traditional case, each simple question travels in a small packet across the network to a server that will often respond with a small burst of information corresponding to a reply. Therefore, answering $N$ questions would take $2N$ times the network travel time. Hence it makes sense to bundle the $N$ questions into one request and reduce the network traffic to 2 times the network travel time.

In Telescript, an *Agent* is a program the user creates and sends across a network. An *Agent* carries out transactions on a Telescript-aware network in *Places*. *Places* are locations on the network—an electronic shopping center or a directory of services—that correspond to a Telescript Engine. *Places* can be nested, or contain other places inside themselves. Think of a *Place* as a provider of services and the agent as a consumer of services [WHIT95].

*Agents* travel from local *Places* to remote *Places*. Travel is enabled by the Telescript Go instruction, which indicates that the next instruction should be executed at the *Agent's* destination. *Agents* can have meetings with other *Agents* in the same *Place* or in two different *Places* via the notion of *Connections and Meetings*. Finally, a *Portal* is a gateway *Place* where an *Agent* can access systems and services that are not part of the Telescript network.

Let's put the process together. Telescript Agents can perform all different kinds of tasks, from electronic shopping to financial reporting, in Places on Telescript-enabled networks. The Agent program can also contain contingency plans, if is unable to do the task as first specified. For example, a user might send an Agent to the on-line florist to buy a dozen roses, as long as the buds cost less than $75. If the shop has roses for $80 a dozen, then the Agent would order whatever the user's contingency plan called for, such as a bouquet of daffodils. Or the user could tell the Agent to opt for chocolates if flower prices came in over the limit. Then it would consult the network directory for the nearest on-line chocolate store and go to work again (see Fig. 16.5).

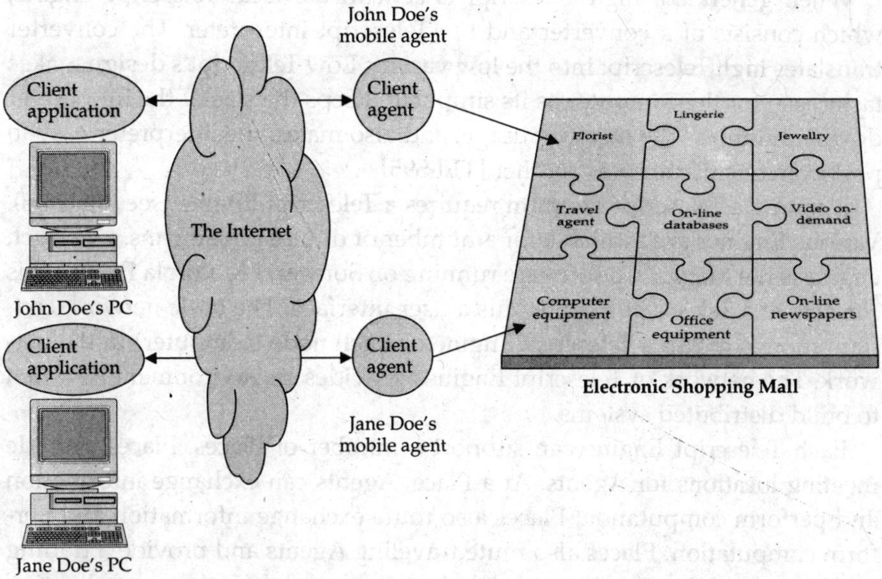


**Figure 16.5** Telescript agents and shopping malls

## How Telescript Works

Telescript is an interpreted language. The idea of using an interpreted language to transfer data is not new. PostScript revolutionized printing by using programs to control the layout of text and graphics on a page, a more flexible and efficient approach than sending images to the printer. PostScript is also machine independent; the same program will execute on printers of different capabilities, letting a user render a page at the best available resolution.

Telescript aims to bring the same interoperability to the networked world. Like PostScript, it is an interpreted language. In other words, the user won't have to worry about binary-level incompatibilities when a Macintosh-produced Telescript Agent finds itself running on a PC. Just as you can use PostScript without ever seeing PostScript code, you will rarely, if ever, see either of the Telescript languages. The applications developer will create templates in high Telescript and add an interface to collect the parameters for the agent. This interface can be written in any language.

Telescript comes in two types: high Telescript for users and programmers and low Telescript for computer processing. High Telescript has a computer language syntax and is compiled to low Telescript just like normal computer languages. Low Telescript is like assembly language used in normal computers and is harder for humans to read but much easier for computers to work with.

When generated, high Telescript is sent to the local Telescript Engine, which consists of a converter and the Telescript interpreter. The converter translates high Telescript into the low variety. Low Telescript's design makes tasks easy for the computer as its simplicity keeps the size of the interpreter down, minimizes the memory usage, and also makes the interpreter easy to port from one platform to another [TELS95].

Running a Telescript program requires a Telescript Engine (see Fig. 16.6). Various Engines are available for a number of different platforms. One such engine is the Magic Cap software running on Sony and Motorola PDAs. This consists of a Telescript Engine plus a user interface. The basic network configuration is to run a Telescript Engine on each node (computer) in the network. The network of Telescript Engines provides an environment in which to build distributed systems.

Each Telescript Engine can support a number of Places. Places provide meeting locations for Agents. At a Place, Agents can exchange information and perform computation. Places also route exchange information and perform computation. Places also route traveling Agents and provide a trading service to local Agents. A more global trading service (perhaps a federation of the local Place trading services) is also a possibility.

An Agent object can migrate between Places. An Agent can move between Places on the same Engine or between Places that exist on different Engines. Hence the Telescript notion of a distributed system is a number of distinctly located Places and a number of Agents that move between these Places.

## Mobility and Telescript Agents

When the Telescript Engine commences execution, most Agents will promptly ask to go somewhere on the network. The key command, called Go, initi-

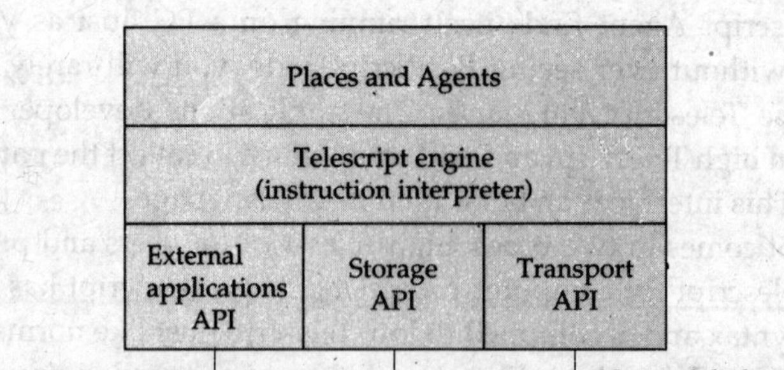


**Figure 16.6** Layered model of telescript engine

ates the move. When an Agent executes this command, the local Engine bundles up the Agent, finds its destination, and sends it on its way.

The Telescript Engine saves an Agent state by bundling up the Agent's low-Telescript code, the program counter, the stack, and any of the memory-based objects that the Agent owns. These states are captured into one file and then sent to a destination.

An Agent can specify a destination—a Place—in one of four ways. The first two, providing a name or an address, are similar. The name consists of the authority and identity of the Place, and the address consists of the authority and location of the Place. This scheme provides flexibility as the nature of the network changes with the introduction of new services and new offerings. Of course, an Agent has to first acquire the name or address of a destination before it can use them. Some names and addresses will be included with Agents that service providers supply; others will be learned by Agents themselves as they cruise the network.

The third way an Agent can specify a destination is to ask to be sent to a machine offering a particular class of service. The Telescript Engine would find the closest or least expensive service offering a particular class of information and then ship the Agent off to it. One common service will be a directory that matches real-world names, addresses, and phone numbers with Telescript addresses.

The fourth method used to designate a destination is called "the way." In this method, the interpreter not only details the address of the destination but also specifies how to get to the address. For example, it might specify that the address can be reached through only the public telephone network and will provide the appropriate telephone number. This final method marries the destination with a specific means of communication.

Telescript includes another version of the Go command called Send. This instruction lets an Agent create Subagents and send them every which way in search of parts of the final answer. In this case, the entire Agent does not move to a new location—it simply spawns versions of itself.

## Security Issues to Consider in Telescript Architecture

The biggest danger of any agent system is that some agents may run amuck. As noted earlier, agents have much in common with viruses. The only real difference between viruses and Telescript Agents is that Telescript Agents have invitations and can execute on a system only after presenting the correct credentials.

Running Telescript on an interpreter may be slower than using compiled code, but it is important for security reasons. The Telescript interpreter can check the identity of each computer sending a request and then allow access to preauthorized users only. When running an Agent, the interpreter can limit the amount of CPU time that a particular Agent consumes by counting the number of Teleclicks it uses. Intrusive or nosy Telescript Agents can also be stopped because the Telescript interpreter can limit the access to files.

Invitations are criteria that the local Telescript Engine uses to decides how visiting Agents can use local features, memory, and services. Being interpreted, Telescript acts as an intermediary that examines and executes each Agent instruction. It can stop a visiting Agent that tries to insert instructions into a Place where they don't belong. In fact, a visiting Agent cannot read from and write to memory or the file system directly. It can only create objects and access their contents. The interpreter intercepts calls to objects that do not exist or do not belong to the visiting Agent.

Other security features also exist. Agents have "attributes" such as "identify" and "owning authority" that uniquely identify the Agent and the entity responsible for it. These attributes may be used for authentication. Telescript objects also have a "permit" attribute that may be used to limit the amount of resources they may consume. A secure "permits" feature is crucial to stop Agents from creating a crash-limited number of clones of themselves, exhausting resources, or other such antisocial behavior. These measures are important security features that will stop most problems. The only danger is that there will be some hole in the Telescript Engine that mistakenly allows an Agent to access memory directly.

Telescript also includes a third aspect of security: identity. Each Telescript Agent comes sealed with a secure signature constructed by taking a secure checksum of the data and then signing it with a digital signature. The Telescript host can use this signature to verify that the packet of instructions and objects arrived securely from its owner. The signature is also important for billing purposes. Networks offering Telescript services will need a secure way to ensure that the agent is operating for someone who will pay the bills.

Telescript is a novel idea that has a lot of potential. What makes Telescript different from other computer languages is its built-in intelligence about how to interact with other systems. A Telescript-ready machine will be able to understand any arbitrary Telescript program that arrives over the network. The user employs this built-in intelligence to create messages that aren't just requests but smart programs that can make decisions based on preferences.

## 16.5 SAFE-TCL

Safe-Tcl is another agent-oriented language that is based on Tcl (Tool Command Language, pronounced "tickle"). Tcl, which is distributed as public domain, has become very popular in the Internet community and is a scripting language developed by John Ousterhout at the University of California at Berkeley [TCL90]. Many people use Tcl to develop prototype software for UNIX and Windows applications because it offers a flexible way to bind small C programs (the tools) into a large application.

Safe-Tcl has as its antecedent a project called ATOMICMAIL headed by Nathaniel Borenstein at Bellcore [SAFE94]. This featured a Lisp-like language that provided secure and portable active-messaging capabilities. An active message contains a program, which the recipient can execute on receipt. Two important developments came out of this project: Metamail and MIME.

Metamail is a portable MIME implementation designed to be called by mail-reading programs. It is bundled with many public domain and commercial mail systems and brings with it multimedia capabilities. Borenstein wanted to go beyond ATOMICMAIL's capabilities, but the language it used was limiting, and he was reluctant to develop yet a new language. When he and Marshall T. Rose (another developer) found Tcl, they were happy to adopt it and created an active mail-based agent language called Safe-Tcl.

The structure of Safe-Tcl is simple. The original Tcl is distributed as libraries that build a small interpreter for the language. It links one interpreter into the user's code, and it executes the code for controlling the basic tools built into the system. Each tool responds to some of its own Tcl commands, and the scripting language is responsible for executing the code and sending off the commands to the tools. There are two Tcl interpreters in Safe-Tcl. One is a local interpreter that has full access to the tools that do "dangerous" things, such as read and write files, peek and poke the memory, or start and stop processes. The other is a crippled interpreter that runs the incoming agent written in Tcl.

To create an information server that would respond to particular queries, the tools for answering the queries in Tcl would be built to run in the local, unprotected interpreter. Then small instructions for the incoming agent would be created and would be available in its protected space. This builds a firewall to prevent any trouble from spreading. For more sophisticated protection against infinite loops or time-wasting agents, time management functions exist in the evaluation loop of the Tcl interpreter running the agent. This evaluator checks the time used by the agent before each instruction is interpreted and executed (see Fig. 16.7).

There are limitations to this approach. The scripts can run locally, but they cannot autonomously roam from host to host like the agents in Telescript. There is no way to save all the local data and state, and there are no simple and clean ways to add these capabilities.

Originally, Safe-Tcl was meant to enable enhanced e-mail called active mail. The incoming mail message wouldn't be just a pile of text, an encoded

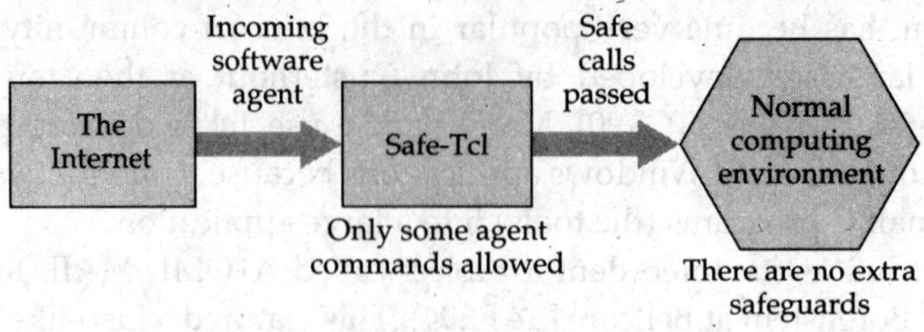


**Figure 16.7** Safe-Tcl environment

image, or even a compressed application waiting to be run. It would be a Tcl script that a user could execute in a safe mode. The script would display data on the screen and perhaps add functional buttons and other GUI devices, but it wouldn't be able to gnaw its way into the operating system like a virus. The system might ultimately be used to distribute forms, surveys, or other interactive material.

The security threat with active mail is clear. The need for mail-based virus protection is illustrated by a harmless Christmas tree virus, which made its way throughout the Internet a few years ago. The virus arrived as a shell script, and when it ran, the recipients would see a Christmas tree. The script also accessed the users' local book of e-mail addresses and sent a copy of itself to each of the entries. Most people who received the message believe it was mailed by a friend, so they executed it without taking any security precautions. Against more harmful programs, security measures are definitely needed. These measures must be robust so that even the nonexperts can use them with ease.

In sum, Safe-Tcl is promising, but much more work remains to be done.

## 16.8 APPLETS, BROWSERS, AND SOFTWARE AGENTS

Today, client applications such as Web browsers allow users to manipulate information spread across the Internet as a whole. Web browsers integrate the function of fetching the remote information, figuring out what format it is, and displaying it. These browsers contain detailed, hard-wired knowledge about the many different data types, protocols, and behaviors necessary to navigate the Web (see Fig. 16.8).

The next generation of browsers currently under development (e.g., HotJava) will extend the functionality of client browsers significantly using the notion of applets [GOS95]. *Applets* are external applications (think of

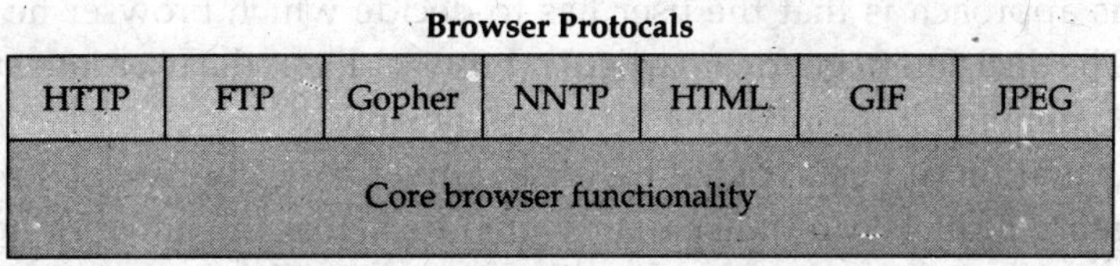


**Figure 16.8** Integrated browsers

them as software agents) that expand the capabilities of a core browser, to invoke specialized applications that range from interactive shopping applications, educational material, and games.

In the case of the Web, the core file type that most browsers understand is the Hypertext Markup Language (HTML). HTML allows text documents to embed simple formatting information and references to other objects. In short, the data viewed in existing WWW browsers are limited to text, graphics, low-quality sounds, and videos.

Today, specialized applications are being implemented using proprietary protocols. For instance, many vendors are providing new Web browsers and servers with added capabilities such as billing and security. These capabilities most often take the form of new protocols. Each vendor implements something unique, a new style of security for example, and sells a server and browser that speak this new protocol.

Figure 16.9 shows that if a user, given this situation, wants to access data on multiple servers each having a proprietary new protocol, the user needs multiple browsers. Needing several browsers is clumsy and defeats the universal readership purpose that makes the WWW so useful. Another problem

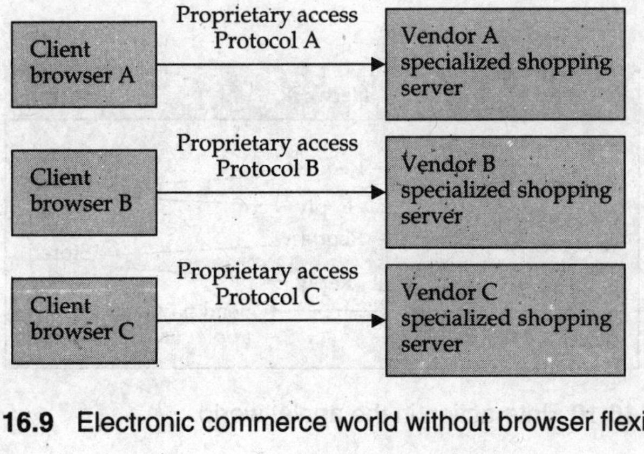


**Figure 16.9** Electronic commerce world without browser flexibility

with this approach is that the user has to decide which browser he or she wants. The decision to go for a particular browser locks the user into an environment, denying him or her the necessary flexibility.

This situation can be avoided by using applet-based browsers. Like software agents, applets can transparently migrate across the network. In other words, there is no such thing as "installing" applets. They are invoked transparently when needed. The advantage is that content developers for the WWW do not have to worry about whether some special piece of software is installed in a user's computer; the applet is automatically transported with the requested material. This transparent acquisition of applications frees content developers from the confines of a limited set of media types and lets them do innovative things.

Figure 16.10 shows the interaction between a browser and server in negotiating for an applet. The user clicks on a remote object on the screen. The browser takes the URL for the object and retrieves the object from a remote server. The browser then attempts to display the object. It realizes that the format (or type) of the object is something that it does not have the ability to interpret, so it sends another message to the server and fetches the applet suitable for the format in question. The applet executes on the client and displays the retrieved object. All this interaction is done automatically and behind the scenes. After the applet is fetched, payment must be made for the services rendered.

Using applets, the browser becomes a coordinator of resources resulting in flexibility and the ability to add new capabilities easily. The result of becoming a coordinator is the ability to exude dynamic behavior for understanding different types of objects. For example, most Web browsers can understand a small set of video formats (typically MPEG). If they see some other type (say QuickTime), they have no way to deal with it directly.

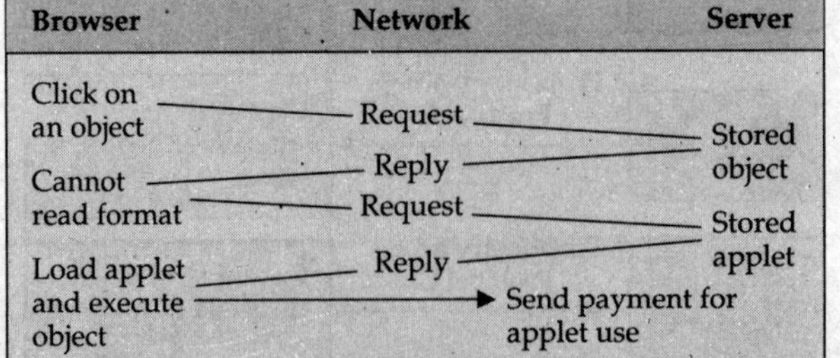


**Figure 16.10** Interaction in the applet world

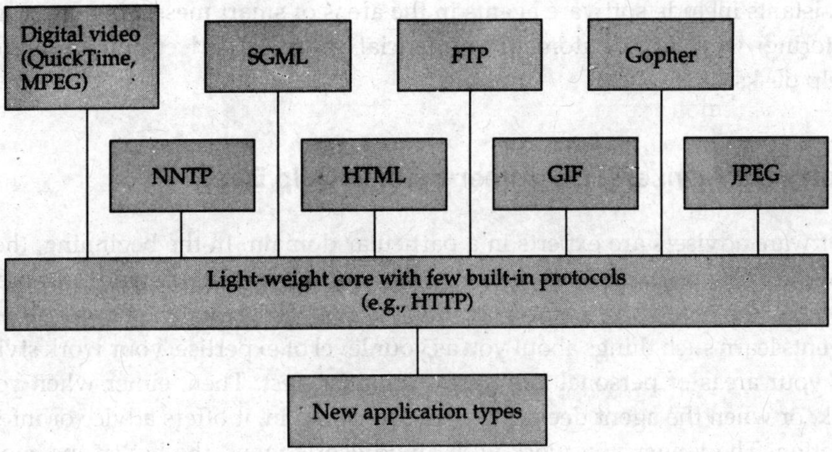


**Figure 16.11** Core browsers with surrounding applets

The applet-based browser, on the other hand, can dynamically install the necessary agent code from the server that has the QuickTime video, allowing it to play the new format. If someone invents a new video format, therefore, the inventor simply ensures that a copy of the agent code is installed on the server that contains the video the inventor wants to publish. In the old model of integrated browsers, all the browsers in the world would have to be upgraded to display the new format. The applet-based browser upgrades itself on the fly when it sees this new type (see Fig. 16.11).

The dynamic incorporation of applets has special significance to how business is done in electronic commerce environments. With applet-based browsers as a base, vendors can produce and sell exactly the piece that is their added value to what exists and integrate it smoothly with the products of other vendors. This seamless integration creates a final result that is very convenient for the end user, a necessary condition of electronic commerce.

## 16.7 SOFTWARE AGENTS IN ACTION

The software agents being designed and developed cross a number of application boundaries. They are designed to filter and gather information from commercial data services and public domains like the Internet and to automate message-based work flows. Because the range is broad, it helps to separate software agents into three main categories: event monitors, work-flow assistants, and Internet data gathering and retrieval agents. The work-flow assistants include software agents in the areas of smart messaging, message filtering, work-flow automation, financial services, and customer service help desks.

## Software Advisers: Customer Service Help Desk

Software advisers are experts in a particular domain. In the beginning, they have only rudimentary knowledge of you, your work patterns, and your preferences for managing your work life. As you go about your work, these agents learn such things about you as your level of expertise, your work style, or your areas of personal and professional interest. Then, either when you ask, or when the agent decides it's time to chime in, it offers advice or information. The longer you work with an advisory agent, the better and more timely its advice becomes. At its best, such an agent could anticipate your goals and offer to complete a task in the same way you've done it in the past.

An example of software agents is customer service advisers. With an increasing emphasis on quality customer service as an important differentiator of services, firms are turning toward technology to automate help desk functions—better data collection, retrieval, and reporting. Ideally, help desks should be able to resolve 80 percent of problems on the first call. Now a new generation adds software agent capabilities that are designed to allow nonexpert help desk personnel to home in on solutions—a big change from the days when the industry joke was that help desk professionals better have good memories. The goal is to use smarter software agents to handle 20 percent more work with 20 percent fewer people.

The heavy investment required to start a help desk is focusing attention on software that raises the desk's productivity. Much of the newer help desk software builds on that, with additional capabilities: (1) hypertext, which allows the help desk person to easily follow a chain of information or questions; (2) multimedia, particularly animation or videos, that help representatives walk callers through that process; and (3) interagent communication, which enables the help desk to be multitiered and distributed. This organization of the help desk incorporates collaborative agents for passing trouble tickets automatically to technicians for resolution.

The most powerful feature of any help desk package is its capability to bring closure. Traditional approaches have increasingly been able to cross-reference material about known problems and solutions and to intelligently search for answers, but problem resolution is where expert systems shine. Several such systems incorporate methods such as decision tree logic, which is a rule-based system; case-based reasoning (CBR), which correlates problems with known solutions; and neural networks, which attempt to go beyond decision trees and cases to mimic the flexible-learning ability of the human brain.

The next generation of help desk software will go far beyond the capabilities we envision for agents to embrace sophisticated decision-making capabilities that are hidden from the users. In other words, we can think of the help desk operators as the drivers who don't have to understand how the engine works. They can just concentrate on driving or helping customers.

## Event Monitors: System and Network Management

Agents, however, have big potential when it comes to providing a more cost-effective means of running distributed applications and managing networks of far-flung equipment. Many agent pioneers are using the technology to run background tasks on servers or remote systems that in the past were handled only by humans. Event monitors are agents that watch the environment and offer instruction and advice to help a user do some specialized task. Example of event monitors are found in complex domains such as network management.

Here, agents provide central operations and problem management of multivendor distributed networks. This agent approach gives the customer a single, central display of all enterprise problems and a consistent process-oriented method for problem resolution. This integration allows automated problem resolution of customers' backup-, storage- and print-management needs—through one console. For example, a printer queue problem can be solved automatically at a local site by intelligent agent software, or an alarm may be sent to a remote operator's enterprise-management console with a request to take further action.

On the system management front, almost any user who deploys probes on a network is technically using agents today, primarily to gather information on network conditions. The solution increases the uptime of computing resources, decreases the time to resolve system problems and helps reduce the cost of managing enterprise-wide, multivendor computer systems. Most operational systems are a distributed client–server solution that operates from a central management station and interacts with intelligent software agents installed on managed systems.

These agents gather information, messages, and monitoring values originating from sources such as system or application log files. The agent is capable of monitoring whether a given piece of equipment on the network is functioning. It also allows the companies to distribute software releases and ensure version control. Through the use of filters and thresholds, only relevant messages and alerts are forwarded to the central management system, which reduces network traffic and provides greater scalability to manage large, distributed networks.

In addition, agents can initiate automatic actions without operator intervention upon receiving crucial events enabling management by exception and let personnel focus on vital information. Long-term agent technology could be a big boost to distributed systems management by providing remote monitoring, diagnostics, and job initiations on remote servers, workstations, and other equipment that is part of the client–server network. Systems management software providers all indicate that they are working to provide smarter and more responsible agents that would not only monitor activity but also initiate corrective actions. Eventually, these agents could reduce the need for humans at remote locations [RC94].

## Work-Flow Assistants and Smart Messaging

Assistant agents can be more ambitious than advisory agents because they often act without direct feedback from users. Although this feature allows them to be much more powerful, it also raises a host of technical issues that have yet to be resolved. The concerns you might have over privacy and stifled creativity with an agent that is only offering advice become much more acute when your agent is actually doing work for you.

Agent languages can facilitate communication in many other ways. Today's electronic mail, for example, is passive and rather dumb. If you aren't sitting at your computer, or you're out of town, when you get an e-mail message, it will sit there forever until you retrieve it, no matter how important it is. But in an agent world, the sender can send a message that's imbued with intelligence. Wrapped around that message are instructions that say, "If he doesn't see this message by 2.00 P.M., send it to his assistant. If his assistant doesn't get it, signal his pager, then ring the cellular phone." Conversely, my colleague's agent-based e-mail system can say, "I'm mad at Tom. Ignore anything he sends me." Any computer software application can be made agent-aware. For example, any address book, calendar, or database program could be set up to send and receive messages automatically. An entire series of transactions could take place without human intervention.

Work-flow agents are used to offload dull; repetitive work. For instance, most tracking systems use host-based databases that contain information on customers' packages. The software agent application sits on a server along with the database, but it essentially plays the role of client. When a caller requests package information via a touch-tone telephone, the package number is submitted to an agent on the server, which translates the information into data. The software application then launches an agent to perform the query against the back-end databases, seeking the package's status. The application returns the query information to the caller as a voice response. If the package has a problem, the application automatically forwards the caller to a live customer service representative, who then discusses the problem with the caller. Workers are less frequently stuck with the task of querying the database and instead have more time to work with customers. The goal is for customer service reps to answer the more difficult questions and interpret information that the agent retrieves [RC94].

## Software Agents and Resource Discovery

The problem of information discovery within on-line networks is very complex and necessitates the use of software agents. While it is impossible to get a completely accurate picture of the number of documents available via the WWW, it is clear that it contains millions of documents. It is simply no longer practical for users to wander around on-line looking for information.

As a result, users have come to depend on agents and information brokerages (search engines). A number of different search engines are available that use a variety of methods to build their underlying databases. Some engines rely entirely on individual servers providing self-indexing information. This approach has very much fallen out of vogue lately, due largely to its requirement of cooperation from every server. As many server managers are not willing to put in the required effort, databases produced by this method are far from complete. On the other hand, there are proactive engines, which use software robots to index large portions of the WWW, such as Lycos. Engines of this class tend to have more complete databases, but even the most comprehensive does not provide full indexing. The reason for this is simple: resource constraints.

If discovering information is a big problem, indexing the entire WWW is enormous. Not only must every document be retrieved, but some portion of each document must be stored as a way of summarizing its contents for later retrieval. The problem created by indexing is this: How to manage such a vast amount of information. If, say, 1/2 kilobyte is saved for each document, the resulting index exceeds several gigabytes. The trade-off becomes one of quality of index versus coverage of documents. Saving more information per document reduces the number of documents than can be covered, and vice versa. This trade-off implies that a database will be inadequate either in scope or quality.

To summarize, the design of software agents for resource discovery entails three challenges [SIRD94]:

1. *The scale of problem.* Information discovery is currently too large a task. There are thousands of servers, with more coming on-line every day. Add to this the growing number of users on the web, and the challenge quickly becomes unmanageable.
2. *Need for cooperative brokerages.* Creating a single brokerage does not solve the information discovery problem, but rather exacerbates it, making that one site a bottleneck for all users.
3. *Need for resource sharing.* It is undesirable for multiple agents to examine the same sites. Exploring the WWW is complex enough without having a number of noncooperating and redundant searches. Not only does it cause unnecessary load on the servers, but it fails to provide a reasonable service to the user. This is, in fact, almost what we have now.

Clearly, we have a long way to go in developing software agents to solve the resource discovery problem.

## 16.8 SUMMARY

Work is underway to create a software robot called software agent, one of the most important and exciting concepts to emerge in computer science in the 1990s. This is the beginning of the science fiction robot or android, able to do extraordinary tasks like Commander Data of *Star Trek—Next Generation* navigating a space ship or performing mundane tasks like scrambling an egg or sweeping a floor. Many see this kind of technology as the "killer application" needed to usher in the age of interactivity.

Today, as plenty of business is being done on-line, the information brokerage staffed by software agents is expected to gain ground. The software agent vision is seductive: a common entity, the *lingua franca* of communications networks that will let different devices talk to each other turns communications networks into electronic trading pits, where buyer agents (demand) meet seller agents (supply) to do business with maximum efficiency.

Technology aside, many social questions need to be addressed in the agent world: How should the agent be represented on the screen? Male or female? Realistic or cartoon character? Natural voice? What happens if the agent is destroyed in the midst of an important task? Who bears the responsibility—the network service provider, the information provider, or the user himself?

In sum, the technology's potential for easing the burden of the average working professional seems to be unlimited. Although they are still in their infancy, the promise of software agents is an appealing one. The agents of tomorrow will relieve users of the burden of time-consuming and tedious searches through a massive, intricate, and globally dispersed web of electronic information. Agents will find, assemble, and analyze information that users need to solve problems, become better informed, and make more intelligent decisions.

# Chapter 17

# The Internet Protocol Suite

For any network to exist, there must be connections between computers and agreements (or protocols) about the communication language. However, setting up connections and agreements between disparate computers (from PCs to mainframes) is complicated by the fact that over the last decade, systems have become increasingly heterogeneous in both their software and hardware, as well as their intended functionality.

Before the establishment of industry standards, proprietary standards ruled the roost. These "islands of adherence" prevented communication and information exchange between different manufacturers' products and led to many "closed systems" incapable of sharing information. Although these proprietary systems proliferated, the potential advantages of "open systems" was recognized by academia and some segments of the computer industry. Out of their efforts, a range of standards for networking, called protocol stacks, were introduced.

*Protocol stacks* are software that perform a variety of actions necessary for data transmission between computers. Stated more precisely, protocol stacks are a set of rules for inter-computer communication that has been agreed upon and implemented by many vendors, users, and standards bodies. Ideally, a protocol standard allows heterogeneous computers to talk to each other.

The protocol stack works by residing either in a computer's memory or in the memory of a transmission device like a network interface card. When data are ready for transmission, this software begins executing by preparing data for transmission and then puts the data on the wire. At the receiving end, it takes the data off the wire and prepares the data for the application, taking off all the error control information that was added by the transmission end. Two protocol stacks in use today are ISO/OSI and TCP/IP.

This chapter provides an overview of the of TCP/IP Protocol Suite and other emerging developments in this area, namely, next generation IP (IPng), mobile IP for mobile computing applications, and IP multicast for broadcast video. Our goal is to present the big picture without getting into detailed technical information. What remains is a minimum of information that must be understood by the business professional.

## 17.1 LAYERS AND NETWORKING

Over the years, the data networking community has found it very useful to design protocol stacks in terms of layers. The notion of layered architecture helps to clarify the roles of the various elements and delineates responsibilities clearly. This delineation helps define how protocols interact with each other and also defines the boundaries of this interaction in various networks.

The advantages of layering are numerous:

- Any given layer can be modified or upgraded without affecting other layers. Functions, at the lower level which are closest to hardware, are affected by rapid technological change. The use of layering shields the higher-level functions. In short, different mechanisms can be substituted without affecting more than one layer.
- Modularization by means of layering simplifies the overall design. Common lower-level services may be shared by different higher-level users. Layering facilitates plug-in compatible connections between different machines of different manufacturers.
- The relationships between control functions can be better understood when they are split into layers. This is especially true with the control actions that occur sequentially in time from layer to layer.

To illustrate how layering can be used in an architecture, Fig. 17.1 shows the seven-layer OSI and five-layer TCP architectures. Both architectures build up from the hardware layers (physical layer which is the electro/optical signaling media over which data are sent) to the software layers (application layer that contains the various executable applications).

### OSI Protocol Stack

The International Standards Organization (ISO) reference model for Open Systems Interconnection standard (OSI) describes the complete communication subsystem within each computer (see Fig. 17.1). The goal of this protocol stack was to allow an application process in one computer to communicate

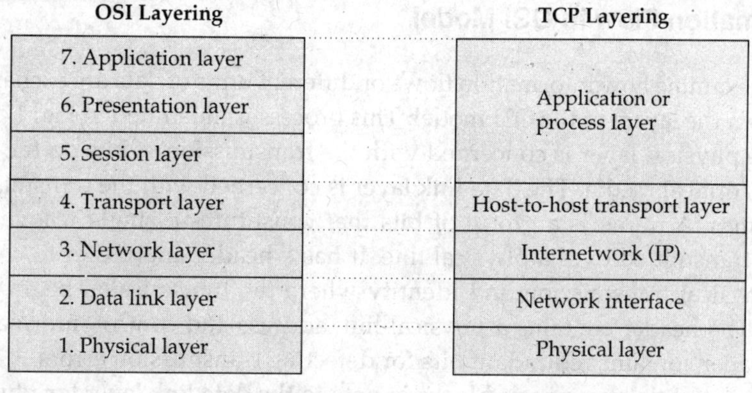


**Figure 17.1** OSI and TCP layers

freely with an application process in any other computer that supports the same standards, irrespective of its origin of manufacture.

The *physical layer* of the ISO model deals with electrical issues—namely, establishing consistent and proper voltage levels, establishing end-to-end signal paths, ensuring that energy is traveling in the right direction, and so on.

The *data link layer* is concerned with information transmission over a single channel or link. Among its functions are acknowledgment of transmissions, error detection, sequencing, and related operations.

The *network layer* is concerned with enabling simultaneous use of multiple links to increase information transmission performance. Among the issues addressed here are routing, flow control, end-to-end acknowledgments on the network for multilink paths, and host-to-network interfaces.

The *transport layer* deals with end-to-end issues such as network addressing, establishment of virtual circuits, and procedures for entering and departing from the network. It is only when we get beyond this layer that we start to discuss issues that are directly visible to the user.

The *session layer* is concerned with establishing communications between given pairs of users and in starting, stopping, and controlling communications.

At the *presentation layer*, we are concerned with the display, formatting, and editing of inputs and outputs for a user.

At the *application layer*, we are concerned with what the user is trying to do, namely, perform a business function.

Although the seven-layer model is well understood, few present day computers and networks are completely compliant to all seven layers of the OSI protocol stack.

## Information Flow in OSI Model

Let us examine how information flows or different units of data are exchanged between the layers in the OSI model. This process is illustrated in Fig. 17.2.

The physical layer is concerned with the transmission of bits on the electronic/optical media. The data link layer is concerned with the transmission of frames. A frame is a group of bits that constitutes a single recoverable block transmitted over a physical line. It has a header and trailer to control the physical transmission and identify where the transmission begins and ends. The header contains a physical link address and control information. The trailer contains redundant bits for detecting transmission errors.

The network layer passes blocks of data to the data link layer for physical transmission. They are called packets. They don't contain the frame header and trailer because this information is of no concern to the network layer. A packet may be defined as a group of bits addressed to a network destination, which is routed to that destination as a composite whole; the packet may contain data and control signals, while some packets contain only control signals. A packet is routed to its destination by means of packet switching.

The concept of a packet is of general value independently of whether packet switching is used. It is a grouping of data that travels to a destination. It must carry a destination address like the address on a letter, which is dif-

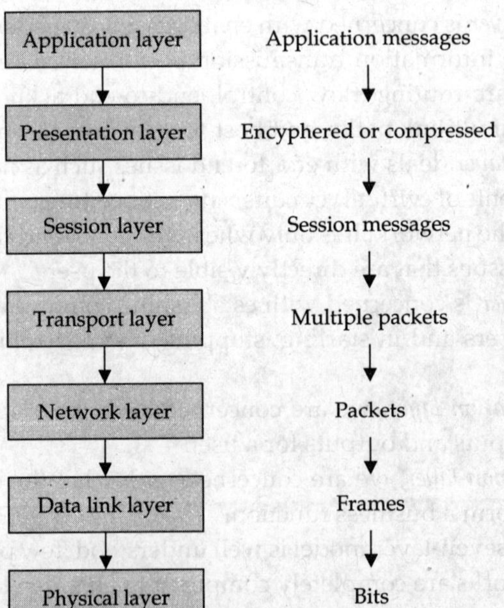


**Figure 17.2** The transfer of information in OSI protocol stack

ferent from the address of the physical nodes through which it may be routed. Like a letter it also contains a source address so that it may be returned to its sender if something goes wrong and it cannot be delivered. Packets contain control information that regulates the end-to-end delivery.

The transport layer on the source machine communicates via the common network with the transport layer of the target machine in a session. The messages that are transferred are called session messages. If a session message is too large to be transmitted as a single packet, the transport layer may slice the message received from the session layer into multiple packets and transmit them individually. The transport layer of the receiving machine would then reassemble all the packets to reconstruct the session message. Some session messages may be small and so, for efficiency, several of them can be combined into one packet before transmission.

At the application level, users may exchange messages via electronic mail. A user message would then be changed by the presentation layer into a session message. The presentation layer may encipher or compress it before transmission.

## 17.2 INTERNET PROTOCOL SUITE

TCP/IP is a family of protocols. Samples of these protocols are UDP, IP Multicast, and Mobile IP. The most accurate name for this set of protocols is the "Internet protocol suite," as these protocols define how certain applications are to be accomplished on the Internet: electronic messaging, on-line connections, and the transfer of files. The development of TCP/IP began in the early 1970s, when the potential of packet-switched technology was understood for heterogeneous system connectivity.

The TCP/IP suite of protocols was initially used to interconnect hosts on ARPANET, PRNET (packet radio), and SATNET (packet satellite). The design of the Internet protocols explicitly accounted for the fact that the networks being tied together were heterogeneous in nature. They each supported different speeds, error characteristics, data unit sizes, and information formats. All three of these networks have since been retired, but TCP/IP flourishes as an integral part of the Internet architecture. Today, the TCP/IP protocols are the most widely implemented multivendor protocol suite in use.

The TCP/IP protocol stack (Fig. 17.1) has five layers:

1. *Application or process layer* is an application protocol such as e-mail.
2. *Transport layer* is a protocol such as TCP that provides services needed by many applications.

3. *Internetwork layer* provides the basic service of getting datagrams to their final destination.

4. *Network layer* takes care of IP addressing and domain name service (DNS).

5. *Physical layer* includes the protocols needed to manage a specific physical medium, such as Ethernet or a point-to-point line. At the lowest level of the physical layer is the actual physical infrastructure, for example, the telephone network, dedicated links, and satellite circuits.

The layering is called TCP/IP because TCP and IP are seldom seen apart (see Fig. 17.1). They are separate layers that address discrete functions. This is illustrated by the few cases where IP is used without its TCP counterpart. IP handles functions of routing and addressing, essentially making sure that each data packet put on the network is sent to the right destination node. TCP handles end-to-end transport-layer connectivity between communicating processes. It ensures that all data associated with the connection are sent in the right sequence and that its corresponding TCP segment has correctly received and passed the data to the appropriate process or entity.

While TCP can't exist without an underlying IP entity, IP can live without TCP. In this case, there is a simple, nonconnection-oriented protocol called the User Datagram Protocol (UDP) that takes the place of TCP. Data packets sent without a high-level session control are called datagrams. While this can result in faster throughput, there's no way to be certain the datagrams were actually delivered. The analogy is that TCP is a mailing with an attached "acknowledge delivery" card, whereas UDP is simply a postcard with no guarantee of delivery. We don't know if it has been delivered.

Most often IP and TCP operate inseparably. Let us consider an example of the TCP/IP stack sending and receiving electronic mail. At the application layer is an application protocol for mail (e.g., *RFC 822*). Mail, like other application protocols, simply defines a standard set of commands and messages to be sent that one e-mail application sends to another (commands to specify who is the sender, who is the receiver, and then the body of the message). However, this application protocol assumes reliable communication between the two computer services provided by lower-level layers of TCP and IP.

TCP is responsible for making sure that the e-mail messages get through to the other end. It keeps track of what is sent and retransmits anything that did not get through. If any message is too large for one datagram (a datagram is an envelope containing message text and destination address), TCP will split it up into several datagrams and make sure that they all arrive correctly.

Because the network is made up of several computers, datagrams must be routed from the source to the destination. Routing requires several services that have been collectively put together into IP. Because these functions are common to many applications, they are put together into a separate protocol, rather than being part of the specifications for sending mail. You can think of IP as forming a library of procedures that applications draw upon for reliable delivery.

Like OSI, TCP/IP does embrace the fundamental concept of independent layers, thus allowing the flexibility for computers operating with similar protocol stacks to communicate with one another. To understand the inner workings of TCP/IP, however, you must first understand the logical structure, as shown in Fig. 17.3.

The name of a unit of data flowing through the layers depends on where it exists in the protocol stack. If it is in an application, it is called a message; if it is between the IP and the TCP layers, it is called a TCP segment (more generally, a transport message); if it is between the IP and the UDP layers, it is called a UDP datagram; if it is between the packet driver and the IP layer, it is called an IP packet; if it is on a packet driver (e.g., Ethernet), it is called a frame.

TCP/IP protocol suite fits within a five-layer communications framework. It is based on a simple model of data communications—application processes, hosts, intermediate networks, network interface, and the actual physical layer.

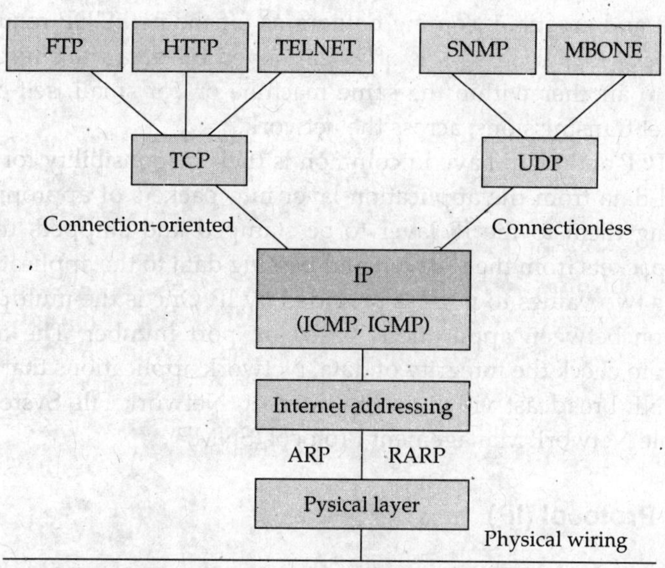


**Figure 17.3** Logical structure of Internet protocol suite

## Transmission Control Protocol (TCP)

The Transmission Control Protocol (TCP) is a connection-oriented transport protocol that sends data as a stream of bytes. TCP establishes and maintains a connection between the requesting port and the port providing services. By using sequence numbers and acknowledgment messages, TCP can provide a sending node with delivery information about packets transmitted to a destination node. Where data have been lost in transit from source to destination, TCP can retransmit the data until either a time-out condition is reached or until successful delivery has been achieved.

TCP also provides data-integrity checking, packet sequencing, flow control, and packet-retransmission request services. TCP can also recognize duplicate messages and will discard them appropriately. If the sending computer is transmitting too fast for the receiving computer, TCP can employ flow-control mechanisms to slow data transfer. TCP can also communicate delivery information to the upper-layer protocols and applications it supports.

## User Datagram Protocol (UDP)

The User Datagram Protocol (UDP), an alternative to TCP, is a connectionless datagram delivery service that does not guarantee delivery. It offers service to the user's network applications but performs none of the TCP management services itself. In other words, UDP does not maintain an end-to-end connection with the remote UDP module; it merely pushes the datagram out on the net and accepts incoming datagrams off the net. UDP requires a lot less overhead than TCP, so it is often employed for data transmission from one port to another within the same machine or, for small, self-contained data packet transmissions, across the network.

What TCP and UDP have in common is their responsibility for dividing outbound data from the application layer into packets of appropriate size; transferring them to the IP layer to be stamped and shipped; unpacking inbound packets from the IP layer; and passing data to the application layer. UDP adds two values to what is provided by IP. One is the multiplexing of information between applications based on port number. The other is a checksum to check the integrity of data. Network applications that use UDP are MBONE broadcast video on the Internet, Network File System (NFS), and Simple Network Management Protocol (SNMP).

## Internet Protocol (IP)

IP represents the heart of the Internet protocol suite. The IP layer provides services that permit data to traverse hosts residing on multiple networks. In addition to inter-network routing, IP provides error reporting and fragmentation and reassembly of information units.

In addition to IP, the inter-network layer also incorporates two other protocols: the Internet Control Message Protocol (ICMP) and the Internet Group Management Protocol (IGMP). ICMP provides diagnostic, error-messaging, and demand-reply functions, such as replies to packet Internet groper (ping) requests. IGMP is responsible for User Datagram Protocol (UDP) broadcasting or multicasting, such as sending UDP packets to all IP machines or to multiple machines on the same inter-network.

At the inter-network layer, IP provides both packet addressing and best-effort forwarding services. Essentially, it functions like a mailroom. It addresses and transfers data packets from the transport layer to the physical link layer; passes back incoming packets that have destination addresses (sockets) within the machine from the physical link layer to the transport layer; and forwards packets without final addresses in the machine to a router.

The sending host provides the network with the network address of the receiving host to ensure that the network routes the data properly. The Internet routing protocol runs not only on "local" hosts, but also on gateways that connect two networks. A gateway's primary responsibility is to relay data from one network to the other, making sure it gets to the appropriate destination host. However, once those packets leave the IP mail room, it disclaims responsibility for their fate. If they don't arrive or are damaged, some authority farther up the chain of command must order a reshipment. Thus IP doesn't assume it has a connection to another IP machine (it is "connectionless"), and it accepts no responsibility for delivery of your data.

## IP Addresses

IP addresses are unique numbers (32-bit) assigned by the Internet Network Information Center (InterNIC). Globally unique addresses permit IP networks anywhere in the world to communicate with each other. The conventions of IP addressing may appear difficult to comprehend, but they are fairly straightforward. IP addresses consist of four groups of decimal numbers with values between 0 and 255 (for example: our machine address is 128.83.112.95). IP addresses are read from left to right, with the digits on the left defining a network's class and address, and the digits on the right defining a machine's address on that network.

There are three major classes of IP network: A, B, and C. Class A networks require only the leftmost group; class B networks are defined by the two leftmost groups; and class C net addresses require all but the rightmost group.

If you are bringing up a new IP network, you are most likely going to be dealing with a class C or class B net. All legal class A networks have long since been assigned or reserved by the Internet Assigned Numbers Authority (IANA). This brings up a key point: If you plan to connect your IP network to the global Internet, you must obtain both an IP network assignment and a unique domain name assignment from the IANA.

The IP address space defines a pool of available network numbers. Ignoring some special cases, such as multicast addresses, every network number on the Internet came from this pool of available network numbers. A large subset, although not every number in this pool, has been assigned to a requester, typically on behalf of a company, university, or other institution, for active duty. The InterNIC Registrar, on behalf of the Internet community, now formally registers these assigned network numbers in a database that also includes mappings to address information of the institution responsible for the network.

## Domain Name Service (DNS)

The DNS is a system whereby difficult-to-remember IP addresses are mapped to names. For instance, the TP address could be 128.151.246.98, and the name could be *commerce.cc.rochester.edu*..

DNS provides important address resolution methods in wide area networks. Simply stated, DNS says to higher-level protocols, "When you give me this IP address, you really mean this name: ZZZ"; or "When you ask for this name, you are looking for this IP address: YYY."

DNS performs the name resolution activity on a very large scale. Fully qualified domain names, like the IP addresses they represent, are hierarchical and are read from left to right. In addition, names must also be unique, Internet-wide. However, unlike IP addresses, DNS addresses become more specific to the left and more general to the right. The rightmost part of a domain name is the name of the machine or account. Machine or subdomain names are separated from the more general domain name by dots.

## Routing in IP Environments

To move information efficiently between two points on a network, routing becomes essential. Routers within the Internet are organized hierarchically. Some routers are used to move information through one particular group of networks under the same administrative authority and control. Routers that exchange information within autonomous systems, called interior routers, use a variety of interior gateway protocols (IGPs). Routers that move information between autonomous systems, called exterior routers, use the Exterior Gateway Protocol (EGP) or Border Gateway Protocol (BGP).

Routing protocols used with IP are dynamic in nature. Dynamic routing requires that software in the routing devices calculate routes. Dynamic routing algorithms adapt to changes in the network and automatically select the best routes. In contrast with dynamic routing, static routing calls for routes to be established by the network administrator. Static routes do not change until the network administrator changes them. IP routing tables consist of destination address/next hop pairs. In the sample routing table shown in Fig. 17.4, the first entry is interpreted as meaning "to get to network 34.1.0.0 (subnet 1 on network 34), the next stop is the node at address 128.34.23.12."

As we have seen, IP routing specifies that IP datagrams travel through an inter-network one router hop at a time. The entire route is not known at the outset of the journey. Instead, at each stop, the next router hop is determined by matching the destination address within the datagram with an entry in the current node's routing table. Each node's involvement in the routing process consists only of forwarding packets based on internal information. IP does not provide for error reporting back to the source when routing anomalies occur. This task is left to another Internet protocol: the Internet Control Message Protocol (ICMP).

ICMP performs a number of tasks within an IP inter-network. In addition to the principal reason for which it was created (reporting routing failures back to the source), ICMP provides a method for testing node reachability across networks (the ICMP Echo and Reply messages), a method for increasing routing efficiency (the ICMP Redirect message), a method for informing sources that a datagram has exceeded its allocated time to exist within a network (the ICMP Time Exceeded message), and other helpful messages. All in all, ICMP is an integral part of any IP implementation, particularly those that run in routers.

## Physical Layer

The physical layer provides signaling rules, frame formats, and physical media-access layer protocols. The network layer operates on top of the phys-

| Destination address | Next hop |
|---|---|
| 34.1.0.0 | 128.34.23.12 |
| 78.2.0.0 | 128.34.23.12 |
| 147.9.5.0 | . |
| 17.12.0.0 | . |
| . | 120.32.12.10 |
| . | 128.32.12.10 |

**Figure 17.4** An IP routing entry

ical layer and provides connectivity between already-existing networks. Connections can consist of any of a variety of communication media or methods: metal wires, microwave links, packet radio, or fiber optic cables. The specific physical- or media-access protocol used to put data on the wire is independent of TCP/IP's top three layers. This means that TCP/IP can operate over virtually any media-access protocol, including Ethernet, Token Ring, or ARCnet.

The separation of the physical-layer functions from the higher layers means that the services provided by the Internet are not affected by the specifics of the underlying network protocol used. The same software can function properly regardless of the network type to which a host is connected. Divorcing the physical layers from the higher-level layers enables easy adaptation of the model to new developments. This is evident in the fact that in the last two decades, the heterogeneity of physical media-access protocols has expanded with the deployment of Ethernet, Token Ring, Fiber Distributed Data Interface (FDDI), X.25, Frame Relay, Switched Multimegabit Data Service (SMDS), Integrated Services Digital Network (ISDN), and most recently, Asynchronous Transfer Mode (ATM). TCP/IP can run on all of them.

## 17.3 DESKTOP TCP/IP: SLIP AND PPP

Even though point-to-point communication is among the oldest methods of interconnectivity for data applications, surprisingly few hosts were connected to the Internet with simple point-to-point serial links prior to 1990. Point-to-point communication permits users to connect directly to the Internet via a modem connection to the host system of a public-access provider that in turn is wired to the Internet. This solution requires that the PC and the host computer be running one of the serial communications protocols—Serial Line Interface Protocol (SLIP) or Point-to-Point Protocol (PPP). Although both were developed for the Internet protocols and were designed with IP in mind, SLIP is pretty much limited for use with IP, while PPP may be used with other protocols.

SLIP and PPP have become very popular, as they allow individuals to dial up over a phone line and directly connect their workstation to the Internet. Unlike non-IP services, where users dial into a system with "dumb" terminal emulation on their PC, Dialup IP service allows a customer's computer to become a fully functional host on the Internet. The advantages include the ability to use all of the graphical display technology with Macintosh and Windows front-end applications. Such flexibility comes with a price, however. SLIP/PPP requires that users have the expertise to install and manage their own TCP/IP software. Running TCP/IP on the PC requires the following equipment:

- Appropriate hardware, such as Modem/Serial Port, Ethernet card, or Token Ring card
- Packet drivers for the hardware, which provide a software interface that is independent of the interface card but not independent of the particular protocol stack
- The TCP/IP protocol stack that runs on top of the driver software, and uses it to access your hardware

First, users must run the TCP/IP stack on their computer, along with a SLIP or PPP program and, if they are running Windows, a Winsock (as in Windows Socket) program that manages the application's interface to TCP/IP. The Windows Socket is intended to provide a single interface to which application developers can program and multiple network software vendors can conform. With all this in place, users call into the SLIP/PPP server on their modem; once the connection is made they are on the Internet and can access any of its resources (see Fig. 17.5).

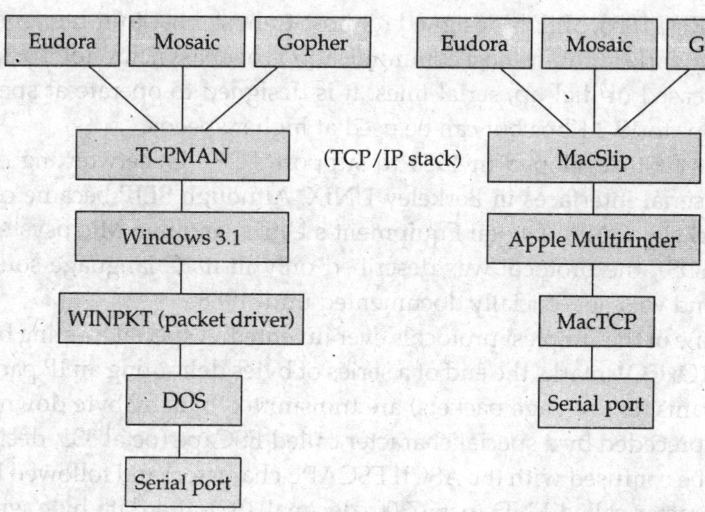


**Figure 17.5** Stick diagram of Windows and Apple's TCP/IP implementation

The benefit of a SLIP/PPP connection is that the PC becomes a part of the Internet as a peer, with full access to all services The limitations occur primarily in terms of the bandwidth available using a modem connection. The faster the modems (at least a 14.4-Kbps modem) are on both ends of the connection, the more satisfactory the Internet experience will be.

Local SLIP/PPP accounts can be purchased for around $30 a month or less from service providers. Be forewarned that not every Internet site supports SLIP and PPP. And, compared to terminal-emulation accounts, SLIP and PPP accounts are often more expensive. SLIP and PPP accounts are more likely to be billed on an hourly basis than are terminal-emulation accounts, so you may pay a higher monthly fee (more than $30 a month) plus a per-hour charge (as opposed to a flat fee of $20 a month for a terminal-emulation account).

One reason for the small number of point-to-point IP links has been the lack of a common encapsulation protocol (e.g., SLIP or PPP) that was widely accepted as either a de facto or Internet standard on which products can be developed, even though several such schemes exist for the transmission of IP datagrams over nearly every type of LAN, MAN, and WAN. This is changing as nearly every computer on the Internet supports simple point-to-point communication.

## Serial Line Interface Protocol (SLIP)

Defined in RFC 1055, SLIP is designed for host-to-host, host-to-router, router to-router, or workstation-to-host communications over asynchronous or synchronous, leased or dial-up, serial lines. It is designed to operate at speeds from 1200 bps to 19.2 Kbps but can be used at higher speeds.

SLIP was first developed in 1984 to support TCP/ IP networking over low-speed serial interfaces in Berkeley UNIX. Although SLIP became common on Berkeley UNIX, Digital Equipment's Ultrix, and Sun Microsystems' UNIX (SunOS), the protocol was described only in its C language source-code files and was not officially documented until 1988.

SLIP is one of the simplest protocols ever invented. A special framing byte, SLIP END (OxCO), marks the end of a series of bytes delimiting an IP packet. The datagrams (or message packets) are transmitted byte by byte down the serial line, preceded by a special character called ESCape (octal 333, decimal 219, not to be confused with the ASCII ESCAPE character) and followed by a special character called END (octal 300, decimal 192). If a data byte within the IP datagram has the same value as the END character, it is replaced with the two-byte sequence ESC and octal 334 (decimal 220); a byte with the same value as ESC is replaced with the two-byte sequence ESC and octal 335 (decimal 221 ). This scheme prevents the receiving SLIP software from incorrectly interpreting a data byte as the end of a network packet.

SLIP is simple to implement and works well in many environments. SLIP does have serious shortcomings, however, including an inability to detect errors on noisy telephone lines because no frame checksum is provided for comparison by the receiver. Any error detection must be handled by higher layers of the TCP/ IP protocol stack. SLIP was designed solely to handle IP, so other protocols (IPX or AppleTalk, for example) can't be multiplexed with IP over a single serial link. SLIP also lacks any method for negotiating parameters to control the connection. Decisions such as whether to employ header compression and which IP addresses to use for each endpoint must somehow be explicitly specified when using SLIP. Specifically, SLIP deficiencies include the following:

- *Addressing.* SLIP does not provide any mechanism for hosts to communicate addressing information with each other; thus both computers in a SLIP connection must know each other's IP addresses for routing purposes.
- *Protocol identification.* SLIP has no protocol-type field, so only a single protocol may be used over a SLIP connection. For example, if two hosts running both TCP/ IP and OSI are connected over a SLIP connection, the multiple protocols cannot share one SLIP line. As an aside, although SLIP was designed for use with IP, SLIP frames do not have to contain an IP datagram; any higher-layer protocol information can be carried by SLIP. The restriction is that only a single network-layer protocol may be used over a single SLIP line.
- *Error correction and detection.* SLIP provides no error-correction or error-detection mechanism. This deficiency is potentially expensive, in a protocol sense, for several reasons. First, SLIP will be used primarily over low-speed lines, so transmission time is an important consideration. Second, although IP will, in fact, detect bit errors, such errors are far more efficiently detected and corrected at lower protocol layers than at higher layers. Clearly, some form of error correction at the physical layer would add to the efficiency of the communication. Furthermore, some applications may ignore the TCP and IP checksums, assuming instead that the network has detected damaged packets before handing them up to higher layers.
- *Compression.* SLIP provides no mechanism for packet compression. Such a mechanism could provide significant performance improvements, particularly since SLIP is associated with low-speed lines. As a solution to this problem, in 1989 Van Jacobson of Lawrence Berkeley Labs proposed a

method for compressing TCP/IP headers for low-speed serial links. Jacobson wrote a much-revised version, CSLIP (Compressed SLIP), targeted to Berkeley UNIX and later ported to SunOS. The original Berkeley SLIP and this CSLIP strain form the basis for most of the freely available and commercial implementations of SLIP.

Despite its weaknesses, SLIP is used widely. It is bundled with workstations and is sold as part of the networking add-ons for several versions of the UNIX operating systems. Versions of SLIP are also supplied with most MS-DOS and Windows TCP/ IP applications. Apple's MacTCP and several third-party vendors support SLIP on the Macintosh. The SLIP protocol is supported by most router vendors and in terminal servers.

## Point-to-Point Protocol (PPP)

The Point-to-Point Protocol (PPP) was designed to overcome SLIP's shortcomings and provide a mechanism for transporting multiprotocol datagrams over point-to-point links. The first implementations of PPP were by Russ Hobby of the University of California at San Diego and Drew Perkins of Carnegie-Mellon University. Numerous other versions are derived from these early implementations.

PPP was designed to define a standard encapsulation protocol for the transport of different network layer protocols (including, but not limited to, IP) across serial, point-to-point links. PPP also describes mechanisms for network-protocol multiplexing, link configuration, link-quality testing, authentication, header compression, error detection, and link-option negotiation.

PPP addresses the limits of SLIP using three main components:

1. *Method for encapsulating datagrams.* A method for encapsulating datagrams over serial links is based on the ISO High-level Data-Link Control (HDLC) protocol. PPP's data link layer is a slightly modified version of the HDLC format extensively used by IBM and others for synchronous data transfer. HDLC was modified by adding a 16-bit protocol field that allows PPP to multiplex traffic for several network layers (NCPs). This encapsulation frame has a 16-bit checksum, but the size of this field can be negotiated.

2. *Link control protocol (LCP).* The Link Control Protocol (LCP) establishes, configures, authenticates, and tests the data link connection. LCP allows negotiating various parameters dynamically, including whether compression is enabled and which IP addresses will be used.

3. *Network control protocols (NCPs).* A family of network control protocols (NCPs) establishes and configures different network layer protocols. Several NCPs have already been defined for major networking protocols including IP, Novell's Netware IPX, DecNet, OSI, and AppleTalk.

Aside from running several protocols over a single line, PPP provides well-defined link control negotiation with standard commands and responses. LCP also supports several schemes for authentication, link-quality monitoring, and compression. These features significantly ease the difficulties in debugging PPP connections compared with debugging SLIP. Some problems remain, however, since a serial line might be used for both remote log-in and PPP use. While the promise of multiple protocols over a single line is enticing, few of the existing PPP implementations support more than a single NCP (usually IP). A large body of work related to PPP has been written within the Internet community for which there are several RFCs. See RFC archives (e.g., ftp://ds.internic.net/).

## 17.4 OTHER FORMS OF IP-BASED NETWORKING

The applications that use the TCP/IP protocol suite continue to evolve. The next set of applications will include those that use mobile communication, and video/audio information.

Current TCP/IP implementations are adequate to accommodate mobile computing. But several proposed technological innovations are coming together to make roaming a reality. The Mobile Working Group of the Internet Engineering Task Force (IETF) has done considerable work in defining how the new architecture should look. This group is extending the Internet Protocol (IP) by building in features that would accommodate mobile computers. This extension is called Mobile IP.

To support video broadcasts on the Internet, the IP protocol needs to be extended from a unicast mode to a multicast mode. Traditional IP packets are *unicast*; that is, one computer is sending to another specific single computer designated by an IP address. In contrast to this one-to-one, *multicasting* is when one host sends to a group of hosts or one-to-many.

Multicasting on a small scale already occurs in an Ethernet LAN, when one computer broadcasts packets to all computers on the same LAN or subnet. However, the routers between one subnet and another subnet will not let broadcast packets pass through. To get around this problem, the IP packets are labeled as multicast packets so that routers that support that capability will let them through. This extension is called IP multicast.

## 17.5 MOBILE TCP/IP-BASED NETWORKING

Mobile computing is defined as using a computing device with either wired or wireless interfaces, at dynamic locations that cannot be predicted beforehand. Mobile computers, such as notebook, palmtop, or portable workstations, cannot work easily due to the existing implementation of Internet addressing and routing algorithms.

The Internet presents interesting problems for mobile computing. Existing networking protocols generally assume that each computer attaches to the network at a fixed physical location with a logical address. These protocols assume that host movement occurs so rarely that it can be handled manually.

For example, consider the following host movement scenario where a user moves from his desk to a conference room or any other room. If the user's desk and the conference room have direct access to the same subnet, then the movement process is fairly easy.

Otherwise, users must acquire a new IP address on the conference room subnet from the appropriate local authority, which may not be an easy task. Numerous configuration files on the host, on multiple-name servers, and on other hosts (that use the original IP address to identify the host) must be modified to reflect the new address [JMP94].

The above process achieves network connectivity but only after a slow, error-prone configuration procedure that a typical user does not have the skills or desire to carry out. In addition, the moving computer has a completely different identity after these changes, and all existing network applications must be restarted. Figure 17.6 shows the architecture of an integrated information architecture linking both Internet-based fixed computing and mobile nodes.

### Problems with Traditional Internet Architectures

Existing IP is oriented towards fixed computers. Thus, in a traditional Internet, a given computer, be it a PC or a mainframe, is assigned a network address that ties that computer to a specific local network or "subnet." An IP subnet corresponds to a set of nodes that are on the same physical network, such as a LAN segment.

An IP network address consists of two fields: a subnet (subdomain) identity and a host identity. Therefore a given LAN has a certain subnet identity and all hosts that attach to that LAN must bear that subnet identity in their IP addresses.

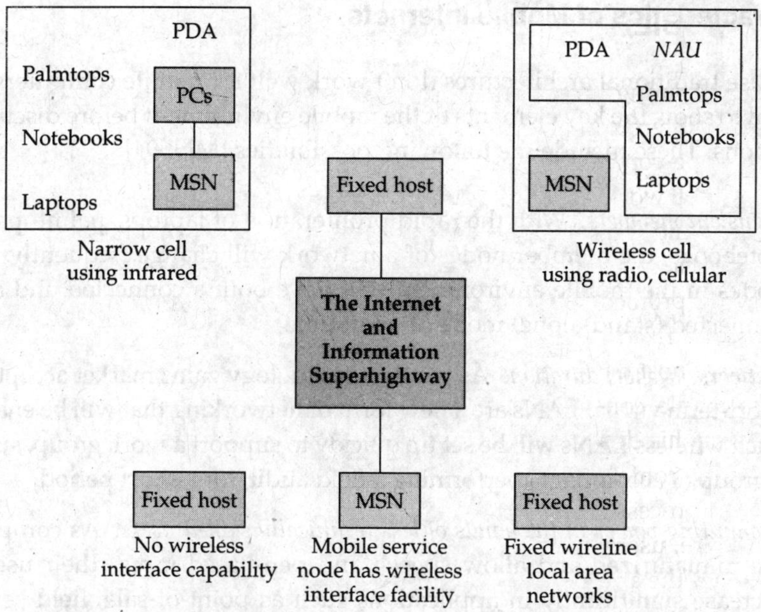


**Figure 17.6** Model of Internet-based mobile computing

This association of addresses to computers creates problems when mobile users are introduced. A mobile user needs to be able to freely detach the host from the LAN at his usual office, travel to some remote site, and reattach the host to a LAN at that site. Because the current IP address assigned to a laptop has a unique subnet identity that ties it to a given LAN, this architecture does not support the mobility of a host between the "home" location and the "remote" location.

The addressing problem becomes even more acute in the wireless scenario, because a mobile user could quickly change IP subnets by roaming from one cell to another. In short, the problem of mobile computing is not at the media level but lies at the network architecture level. Clearly, the IP layer expects to be able to route a packet to a host based on the host's IP address. If a host changes its point of connection to the Internet and moves to a new domain, IP packets destined for it will no longer reach it correctly because the address is invalid. Changing the IP address of the host is almost impossible, especially while keeping existing transport level connections open. Thus a more flexible solution is needed for routing packets to mobile hosts.

## Characteristics of Mobile Internets

Because traditional architectures don't work well for mobile computers, it is useful to show the key elements of the mobile environment before discussing solutions. These include the following possibilities [MNS94]:

- *Transient members.* With the rapid proliferation of laptops, palmtops, and notebooks, the member nodes of a network will change frequently. Also, nodes in the mobile environment will have both a connected and a disconnected (stand-alone) mode of operation.
- *Networks of short duration.* As wireless technology gains market acceptance, short-term virtual LANs are a new form of networking that will be enabled. Such wireless LANs will be set up quickly to support a work group, such as a group of accountants performing a field audit, for a short period.
- *Computing power in the hands of less technically skilled users.* As computers are miniaturized and allow speech and pen-based input, their use will increase significantly in applications such as point-of-sale, field service, and logistics by people perhaps less well versed in computers than traditional PC users. This shift in the skill level of users implies a heightened importance of user-friendly technology.
- *Partial responsibility for support moves to users.* This requirement has implications for the ease of use and fault tolerance of the technology. In a mobile environment where users will work at places far removed from sites where support personnel are located, more of the support function will be put upon the user. To some extent, this scenario conflicts with the possible lessening of the technical skills of users in a mobile environment.
- *Security becomes paramount.* A stronger level of authentication will be needed in a mobile environment where network nodes can potentially join or leave a network at will. Whereas account passwords have sufficed in the past, security devices such as smart cards will need to be employed.
- *Variety of access media.* A variety of media will be used by mobile computers. Some will use the cellular modems and others, infrared adapters to link to the LANs.

Ease of movement will become even more important as wireless network interfaces become widely available. Once the user is unconstrained by cable, it is likely that frequent network movement will become commonplace. Protocols to support host mobility will not only have to be transparent, they will also have to be efficient so that they can handle rapid host movement.

## Registering a Mobile Agent

The most important mobility support function on the Internet is the reliable and timely registration of a mobile node's current location to other computers that need to send packets to it.

A *mobile node* is a host or router that changes its point of attachment from one network or subnetwork to another. A mobile node has to communicate its location to a home agent. A home agent is a router that maintains a registry of the mobility bindings for a mobile node and encapsulates datagrams for delivery to the mobile node while it is away from home [P94].

When the mobile node is away from home, it needs to register a forwarding or care-of address with a home agent. Home agents communicate with foreign (or field) agents to reach the mobile node. A foreign agent is a router that assists a locally reachable mobile node that is away from its home network. A foreign agent (a local router) must also know that the mobile node is visiting in order to deliver arriving packets to the mobile node (see Fig. 17.7).

Home agents and foreign agents advertise their availability in the domain for which they provide service. A new mobile node can send a solicitation on the link to learn whether any prospective foreign agents are present. Depending on its method of attachment, the mobile node will register either directly with a home agent or through a foreign agent that forwards the registration to the home agent. The home agent then uses a care-of address to reach the mobile unit. Depending on the foreign network configuration, the care-of address may be either assigned to the mobile node or associated with a foreign agent.

In the case of a mobile worker, the home agent (corporate computer) keeps the location registration information in order to forward intercepted packets from the home network to the mobile node in the field; foreign nodes who might be working with the field person in other organizations need this information in order to send their own packets directly to the mobile node (see Fig. 17.8).

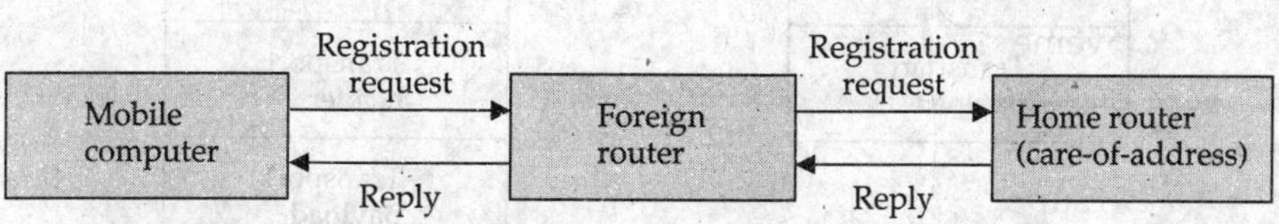


**Figure 17.7** Mobile computer registration

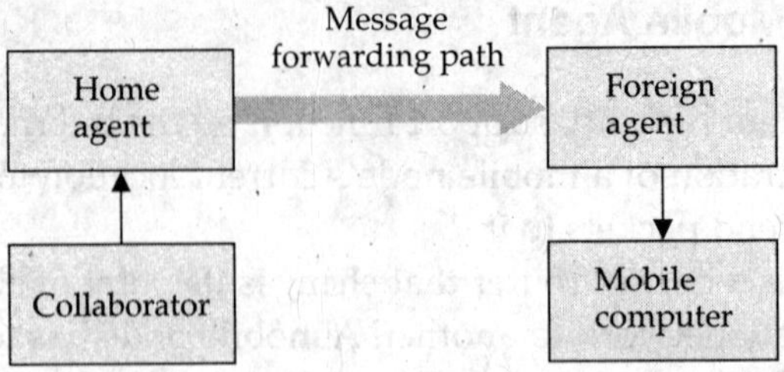


**Figure 17.8** Logical structure of mobile network

## Creating and Forwarding Mobile IP Packets

Once a mobile node has registered a care-of address with its home agent, that home agent intercepts any datagram destined for the mobile node, builds another datagram with the intercepted datagram enclosed within, and forwards the resulting datagram to the entity at the care-of address. At the care-of address, the enclosed datagram is extracted and forwarded to the mobile host.

The IP encapsulation process produces a datagram structured as shown in Fig. 17.9; the IP header of the original datagram is modified, then followed by the forwarding header and finally by the unmodified transport payload of the original datagram.

The destination field in the modified IP header is replaced by the care-of address of the mobile node (foreign agent plus field address). When decapsulating a datagram, the fields in the forwarding header are restored to the original IP header, and the forwarding header is removed from the datagram.

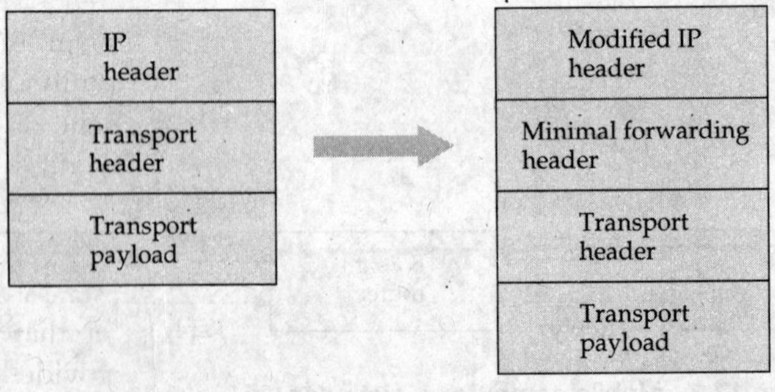


**Figure 17.9** IP encapsulation

## 17.6 MULTICAST IP

Today, potential uses for high-speed networks include combinations of audio and video such as video conferencing. These programs fall into the category of one-to-many broadcasting (or multicasting)—a single host or a few hosts broadcast to a large number of other sites. Traditionally, Ethernet LANs support multicasting. Here, a message is broadcast in the local network with a special destination address that is interpreted and read by all local clients. Except for the designated client, the other computers discarded the message. Multicasting is also found in satellite networks where receivers or receiving sites can hear all transmissions in the surrounding air.

The challenge has been to extend multicast capabilities to the Internet. To meet this challenge, an experimental protocol called IP multicasting has been developed to allow broadcasting from one or a few sources to many receivers. IP multicasting is the ability to send IP packets selectively to multiple nodes in a logical group. IP multicasting permits a source node to send one copy of data to an intermediary that in turn relays the data to multiple recipients.

This staggered relay system allows multicasting to be more efficient than sending individual copies of data to each recipient downstream. Without multicasting, some network links (Internet backbones, for example) would have to carry the same information packet over and over again for delivery to multiple receivers. With multicasting, only one copy of the data will pass over any network link (see Fig. 17.11).

The justification for using IP multicasting is that it is efficient and uses less bandwidth than TCP connections. For networked multimedia applications running over the Internet, this efficiency becomes crucial. Invariably, these applications require the ability to multicast packets across the entire enterprise in a timely and efficient way. For instance, group video teleconferencing requires the ability to send video information to multiple sites efficiently. If one IP multicast datagram containing video information can be sent to an intermediate point that would then redistribute the datagram, network bandwidth is saved.

In short, IP multicasting is the transmission of an IP datagram to a set of hosts identified by a single IP destination address. IP multicast plays an important role in the emerging high-bandwidth environment.

### IP Multicast Transport Protocols

IP multicast uses User Datagram Protocol (UDP) rather than the usual Transport Control Protocol (TCP). As noted earlier, TCP provides a point-to-point connection-oriented protocol, whereas UDP is just a transport-level

**Figure 17.10** Transport Protocols in MBONE

envelope around an IP packet with basically no control. One reason for not using TCP is that the reliability and flow control mechanisms are not suitable for broadcasting.

Occasional loss of an audio packet (as when using UDP) is usually acceptable, whereas a retransmission delay (when using TCP) is not acceptable in a interactive conference. In addition, TCP does not lend itself easily to multicasting. One problem that must be resolved is that UDP packets may be duplicated and reordered (beside being dropped) when transmitted over the Internet (see Fig. 17.10).

On top of UDP, most broadcast applications use the Real-Time Protocol (RTP) developed by the Audio-Video Transport Working Group. Each RTP packet is stamped with timing and sequencing information. With appropriate buffering at the receiving hosts, this procedure allows the applications to achieve continuous playback in spite of varying network delays. At the application level, each form of media can be encoded and compressed in several ways. Audio is usually encoded using PCM (pulse code modulation). Video is usually encoded using the CCITT standard H.261. Other video encodings are also being tested (see Chapter 18).

## How Does IP Multicast Work?

The Internet Protocol (IP) is based on transmitting packets in a point-to-point connection between one host and another. Of course, a number of routers may lie between one host and another host, so a packet destined for a distant

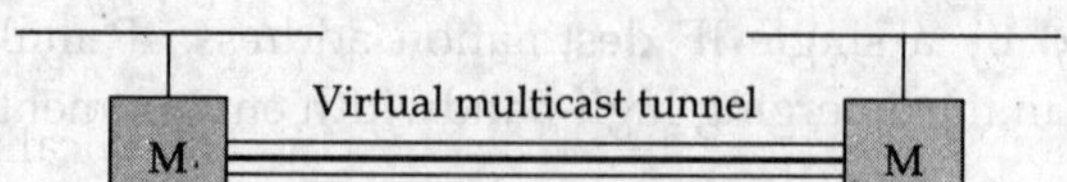


**Figure 17.11** Multicast tunneling

network must be sent to a router or gateway machine that will pass it along to the next router in the journey to its ultimate destination. For this transport, IP multicast packets are encapsulated (wrapped) for transmission through tunnels, so that they look like normal unicast datagrams to intervening routers and subnets (see Fig. 17.11).

A multicast router that wants to send a multicast packet across a tunnel will prepend another IP header (tunnel source and tunnel destination). The multicast router at the other end of the tunnel receives the packet, strips off the encapsulating IP header, and forwards the packet to the downstream groups as appropriate.

As noted earlier, IP is based on unique 32-bit addresses assigned to each node or host. IP address space is divided into class A, B, and C networks based on the upper bits of the IP address. To differentiate between normal and multicast packets, a special class of addresses has been defined (from 224.0.0.0 to 239.255.255.255) and set aside as special multicast addresses.

Class D addresses, whose IP address's first four bits are set to 1110, are handled differently from normal IP addresses. When a router that supports muiticasting gets a datagram destined for a class D address, the router examines its routing table to determine how it would transmit data.

Membership in a tunnel group is dynamic—hosts may join and leave groups at any time. Most groups have no restriction on the location or the number of members permitted, and a host can be a member of as many host groups as desired. In addition, a host can send datagrams to a group without being a member of a group. Host groups can be permanent, using a dedicated IP address administratively assigned, or transient.

Forwarding IP multicast datagrams across internetworks is handled by multicast routers that may be separate from or incorporated into normal Internet gateways. A multicast datagram is delivered to all members of this destination host group using the same methods as a regular unicast IP datagram.

## Multicast Packet Routing

The simplicity of this scheme allows routers to dynamically generate the routing path used for transporting from the sender to all the recipients. Efficient routing is crucial to multicast applications (e.g., video), because they can consume significant amounts of bandwidth. To ensure that these applications get enough bandwidth, efficient routing and resource management schemes must be deployed.

A variety of routing protocols have been developed to construct a path from source to group members. These include Distance Vector Multicast

Routing Protocol (DVMRP), Multicast Open Shortest Path First (MOSPF), and Protocol Independent Multicast (PIM). While traditional routing algorithms have struggled with multicast packets, these protocols have been designed with this task in mind.

These protocols have been tailored for a number of applications, including multisite video conferences and commercially distributed information databases such as in financial environments where stock quotations generated in a central location are delivered to many traders. Other features include the ability to automatically reroute multicast traffic around net failures and provide type-of-service routing—for example, forwarding high-bandwidth multicast traffic over paths other than those used for delay-sensitive applications.

Extensions to the standard routing protocols are defined to let individual networks advertise whether they wish to receive datagrams sent to a particular multicast group. This option is also available at the local host level to learn which groups are present on attached subnets using the Internet Group Management Protocol (IGMP) [RFC1112]. In short, IGMP is used to define which TCP/ IP hosts are in which multicast groups.

## 17.7 NEXT GENERATION IP (IPng)

The Internet architecture based on the TCP/IP protocol suite was developed and deployed in the late 1970s. Except for the addition of subnetting and the domain name system in the early 1980s and IP multicasting implementation in the 1990s, it stands virtually unchanged. Even with the understood benefits of a multilayer protocol stack, all steps taken to enhance the Internet and its services have been very incremental and narrowly focused.

Exploding Internet growth has caused a need for new services capable of supporting addressing and routing processes for scenarios of future growth. The reasons for the change from IP to IPng (IP next generation) can be described in terms of problems for which the current IP will simply become inadequate and unusable in the future. These problems are the exhaustion of IP class B address space, the exhaustion of IP address space in general, and the nonhierarchical nature of address allocation leading to a flat routing space.

One of the fundamental causes of this problem is the lack of a class of network addresses appropriate for a mid-sized organization. The class C address, with a maximum of 254 unique host addresses, is too small, while class B, with a maximum in excess of 65 thousand unique host addresses, is too large. As a result, class B addresses get assigned to organizations even though nowhere near that number of available addresses will ever get used. This fact, combined with a doubling of class B address allocations on a yearly basis, led the Internet Engineering Steering Group (IESG) to conclude in

November 1992 that the class B address space would be completely exhausted within two years. At that point, class C addresses would have to be assigned, sometimes in multiples, to organizations needing more than the 254 possible host addresses [IPNG94].

Besides address space growth, there are several issues that need consideration in any next generation Internet protocol. Some are very straightforward—for example, the new protocol must be able to support large global networks. Others are less obvious. There must be a clear way to transition from the current installed base of IP systems. It doesn't matter how good a new protocol is if there isn't a practical way to transition the current operational systems to the new protocol.

## Emergence of New Markets

Currently, IP serves what could be called the computer market. The computer market has been driving the growth of the Internet. The focus of this industry is to connect computers together in the business, government, and education markets, which have been growing at an exponential rate.

One measure of this growth is that the number of computers hooked to the Internet is doubling approximately every year. The computers used at the endpoints of Internet communications range from PCs to supercomputers.

The next phase of growth will probably not be driven by the computer market. Nomadic computing devices are bound to be ubiquitous as their prices drop and their capabilities increase. A key capability is that they will be networked. Unlike the majority of networked computers, they will support a variety of types of network attachments (RF wireless, infrared networks) and, when docked, they will use physical wires. This feature makes them an ideal candidate for internetworking, as they will need to transfer information over a variety of physical networks.

These types of devices will become consumer devices and will replace the current generation of cellular phones, pagers, and PDAs. In addition to the obvious requirement to support large-scale routing and addressing, the next generation IP needs to impose low overhead and support dynamic configuration and mobility as a basic element. Other requirements include built-in authentication and confidentiality.

Another emerging market is networked entertainment. The first signs of this emerging market are the proposals being discussed for 500 channels of television, video on-demand, and shopping. This is clearly a consumer market. The possibility is that every television set will become an Internet host. As the world of digital high-definition television approaches, the differences between a computer and a television will diminish. As in the previous market, this market will require an Internet protocol that supports large-scale routing and addressing and auto configuration. This market also requires a protocol suite that imposes the minimum overhead to get the job done. Cost will be the major factor in the selection of a technology.

Another market that could use the next generation IP is telemetry and device control. This consists of the control of everyday devices such as lighting equipment, heating and cooling equipment, motors, and other types of equipment currently controlled via analog switches and in aggregate consuming considerable amounts of power. The size of this market is enormous and requires solutions that are simple, robust, easy to use, and very low cost.

## Transition Challenges

At some point in the next three to seven years the Internet will require a deployed new version of the Internet protocol. Two factors are driving this need: routing and addressing. Global Internet routing based on the 32-bit addresses of IP is becoming increasingly strained. IP addresses do not provide enough flexibility to construct efficient hierarchies that can be aggregated.

Even if the routing can be scaled to support a gigantic Internet, the Internet will eventually run out of network numbers. There is no question that an IPng is needed, but only a question of when.

The deployment strategy for an IPng must be as flexible as possible. The Internet is too large for any kind of controlled rollout to be successful. The importance of flexibility in an IPng and the need for interoperability between existing IP and IPng cannot be understated.

The key is to ensure interoperability during the transition period. The challenge for an IPng is for its transition to be complete before existing routing and addressing methods break. The transition will be much easier if IP address are still globally unique.

The two most important transition requirements are flexibility of deployment and the ability for IP hosts to communicate with IPng hosts. There will be IPng-only hosts, just as there will be IP-only hosts. The capability must exist for IPng-only hosts to communicate with IP-only hosts globally, while IP addresses are globally unique.

## Backward Compatibility

In the product world, backward compatibility is very important. Vendors that do not provide backward compatibility for their customers usually find they do not have many customers left. For example, chip makers put considerable effort into making sure that new versions of their processor always run all of the software that ran on the previous model. It is unlikely that Intel would develop a new processor in the x86 family that did not run DOS and the tens of thousands of applications that run on the current versions of x86s.

Operating system vendors go to great lengths to make sure new versions of their operating systems are binary compatible with their old version. For example, the labels on most PC or MAC software usually indicate that they require OS version XX or greater. It would be foolish for Microsoft to come out with a new version of Windows that does not run the same applications as the previous version. Microsoft even provides the ability for Windows applications to run on their new OS NT. This is an important feature. They understand that it was very important to make sure that the applications that run on Windows also run on NT.

The Internet has a large installed base of software; hence compatibility with existing methods and software programs is a must for IPng. As with processors and operating systems, IPng must be backward compatible with existing IP, and features need to be designed into an IPng to make the transition as easy as possible.

In the past, other protocols have tried to replace TCP/IP, for example XTP and OSI. One element in their failure to reach widespread acceptance was that neither had any transition strategy other than running in parallel (sometimes called dual stack). New features alone are not adequate to motivate users to deploy new protocols. IPng must have a good transition plan and provide added functionality to satisfy future needs.

In sum, the challenge in the selection of an IPng is to pick a protocol that meets the emerging requirements of the I-way. If the IPng is a good match for these new markets, it is likely to be used. If the IPng is not appropriate for use in these markets, it is probable that these markets will each develop their own protocols, perhaps proprietary. These new protocols would not interoperate with one another.

The opportunity exists to select an IPng with a reasonable chance to be used in several emerging markets. This would have the very desirable outcome of creating an immense, interoperable, worldwide information infrastructure created with open protocols. The alternative is a world of disjoint networks with protocols controlled by individual vendors.

## 17.8 SUMMARY

The Internet owes much of its success to TCP/IP technology, which was developed in 1973 to link ARPANET with other packet-switched networks using satellite and mobile radio technology. The goal was to develop a confluence of networks that would be connected at one point. IP (the Internet

Protocol) was made very simple and undemanding in terms of computer resources and it can be supported by just about any kind of communications infrastructure.

Dramatic improvements have been made in the last few years in accessing the Internet and other TCP/IP hosts and networks via the use of serial point-to-point connections. While SLIP continues to be widely used, PPP is gaining ground because of its additional features and flexibility and is expected to be more dominant in the future.

IP has to adapt to new challenges. The network market will continue to grow at significant rates due to expansion into other markets. These markets are extremely large and bring with them a new set of requirements not as evident in the early stages of IPv4 deployment. The new markets are also likely to happen in parallel with others. It may turn out that in a decade we will have 100–500 million Internet hosts. The challenge for the next generation IPng is to provide a solution to today's problems that is attractive in these emerging markets.

Chapter 18

# Multimedia and Digital Video

In the future world of electronic commerce, imagine the following: Your 21-inch monitor displays a rotating 3D graphic of a car you want to purchase in one window; a video of a news anchorwoman reporting on an impending storm in another; an open window for real-time video conferencing with your client is in a third; and a fourth window flashes information about your stock portfolio as the stock market goes through its daily gyrations.

A typical scenario? Well, not quite. This image has more to do with the future of electronic commerce applications than today's reality. While some networks and systems can support the sophisticated multimedia depicted in this scenario, most of today's installed base of desktop computers and networks cannot. The challenge is to build the kind of networking and systems infrastructure that will support multimedia-based electronic commerce applications.

These information types share many common features: All are digital data, flow through the same networks, and display on the same workstations. Combined and shaped by a competent "information surgeon," multimedia information has the power to inform, persuade, and enlighten. But the tools and training needed for "information surgery" are not very clear. What is certain is that a solid understanding of the technology behind various multimedia types is necessary.

Multimedia information is more than plain text. It includes graphics, animation, sound, and video. Like many other technology terms, multimedia means different things in different circles. Many vendors cloud the horizon by using the term in association with products whose claim to multimedia status is tenuous at best. To limit the scope of discussion, our focus will be on one type of multimedia that is becoming a key technology for electronic commerce: digital video. Typical applications of digital video include video conferencing, video on-demand, and distance education. We will concentrate on the technology—compression, storage, and transport—and use of digital video in desktop video conferencing.

Regardless of its type or transport means, a multimedia entity (e.g., video image) must pass through a series of stages from inception to display, including:

- *Image capture/generation.* The image is captured by a sensor such as a television camera or is generated by an electronic device such as a computer.
- *Compression.* The volume of information in the raw image may be too large to be sent through an affordable transmission channel. Therefore the data must be compressed to reduce its volume in such a way that the picture can be reconstructed without degradation at the receiving end.
- *Storage.* The compressed data are stored on CD-ROM or network storage servers until ready for transport or display.
- *Transport.* The data representing the image are prepared for transmission. Each component of a video program such as picture, sound, and associated data is separately organized into packets of data. Address and descriptive information is included in each packet. Packets are aggregated into a single bit stream for transmission. This bit stream is then transmitted through a data communications network. The speed of transmission depends on the characteristics of the medium. Protection against loss or corruption of the signal is provided by adding extra bits to the data stream (see Chapter 19).
- *Desktop processing and display.* Once the image is received, the earlier steps are reversed; the bits that were added to aid in transmission are removed. The video, audio, and data streams for each program are separated. The data stream containing the images may be stored until ready for display. The images are then decompressed and formatted for display on a television, computer monitor, or other appliance.

In the following section, we will delve into multimedia compression, processing, and storage issues. These issues are crucial to the development of electronic commerce application.

## 18.1 KEY MULTIMEDIA CONCEPTS

Recall the technical definition of multimedia: The use of digital data in more than one format, such as the combination of text, audio, and image data in a computer file. The theory behind multimedia is this: digitizing traditional media—words, pictures, sounds, motion—and mixing them together with elements of database technology that provide data storage, management, and control—enables the creation of a new generation of applications.

One of the problems and challenges for multimedia developers is the size of new data types and the demand for time synchronization required for video and audio. The size of multimedia data types affects storage, network bandwidth, compression/decompression schemes, data content manipulation techniques, and even processing power.

## Multimedia Data Compression

Data compression attempts to pack as much information as possible into a given amount of storage space and ranges from as little as 2:1 to as much as 200:1, depending on the compression/decompression scheme and level of quality desired.

Compression methods in use include the following:

- *Sector-oriented disk compression.* Integrated into the operating system, this form of compression is invisible to the end user (e.g., DoubleSpace feature of MS DOS 6.2). Another example is the compression of help files in Windows 3.1, which are decompressed on the fly without causing much of a delay.
- *Backup or archive-oriented compression.* Programs such as PKZIP are often used to compress files before they are downloaded over phone lines or stored on floppy disk.
- *Graphics and video-oriented compression.* Graphics data in particular can effectively overwhelm any system's on-line storage capability. Compression techniques designed especially for graphics reduce storage requirements by a factor of 100 and can alleviate the flood of data.
- *Compression of data being transmitted over low-speed networks.* V.42bis compression in modems, as well as techniques used by routers, can reduce the bottleneck caused by sending data over low-bandwidth phone lines.

### Data Compression in Action

Data compression works by eliminating redundancy. Each block of data has an underlying information content, usually expressed as a number of bits. A block of text data containing 1000 bits may only have an underlying information content of 100 bits with the rest being white space. The goal of data compression is to make the size of the 1000-bit message as close as possible to the 100 bits of underlying information.

The need for compression is apparent to users who are often amazed at how rapidly digitized video and sound fill up a disk. An 8-bit digitized sound track sampled at 11 kHz requires just 660 Kbps for a one-minute recording. A 16-bit stereo track sampled at 44 kHz (CD-quality) requires nearly 11 Mb of disk space for a full minute. While sound files may appear a little hungry for disk space, video images are positively ravenous. (See Table 18.1 for multimedia storage requirements.)

Suppose you store a full-screen video image of size 640 × 480 pixels, in full color (i.e., 24-bit color), and at a rate of 30 frames per second. One second of this video will require 27.6 Mb of disk space. Go for a full minute and the requirement exceeds a mind-boggling 1.6 Gb. Not only is this more than would fit on two CD-ROM discs, but also keep in mind that this is just the image portion; the sound track would take additional storage.

To understand the challenge better, let's consider the following. The picture on your screen is made up of dots called pixels. For each pixel in the picture there is a corresponding byte of information that describes the pixel's color. So if the picture is 200 × 200, then the picture has 200 times 200 pixels, or 40,000 pixels or 40 Kb of information for just one frame of video. A desktop video is 200 × 200 pixels (matchbox size picture) in size, not that big considering most monitors today support at least 1024 × 768 displays.

Motion video is made up of many contiguous frames. A TV picture displays about 30 frames every second. This means that we would like to send 30 frames through the communications channel each second. That's 40 Kb times 30 pictures per second or 1200 Kb per second. Now consider the fact

**Table 18.1** Storage and Transmission Requirements for Multimedia

| | *Text* | *Image* | *Audio* | *Video* |
|---|---|---|---|---|
| Multimedia Object Type | ASCII plain text | Bit-mapped graphics, still photos, faxes | Digitized audio or voice | TV digital images at 24–30 fps |
| Memory Storage and Bandwidth Requirements | 2 Kb per page | Simple: ≥64 Kb/image (uncompressed) Detailed: ≥5 Mb/image (uncompressed) | Voice/phone, 8 kHz/8 bits, 6–44 Kbps Audio CD, 44.1 kHz/ 16 bits, 176 Kbps | 27.7 Mbps for 640*480*24 pixels (24-bit color) and 30 fps |

that transferring a 1 megabyte file across a telephone line would take about 125 seconds. Now it is obvious why bandwidth is the bottleneck and compression a dire necessity. These tremendous data requirements make animation and full-motion video difficult to achieve. The most obvious problem is the time to transfer that much data from storage to the display. Nearly 30 Mb per second is enough to choke almost any I/O port or data bus. Other problems include both storage and processing.

The solution lies in the compression of data. Compression is very important for both data storage and data transmission. Most computer users are familiar with text compression as it applies to saving space on disks. Since an enormous quantity of data (several terabytes) will be sent and received as a result of the various commercial activities on the Superhighway, understanding the various compression approaches is vital.

### *Compression Techniques*

Compression techniques can be divided into two major categories: lossless and lossy. These terms refer to the state of a given block of data after it has undergone a complete cycle of compression and decompression. Each is appropriate under certain circumstances.

- *Lossy.* Lossy compression means that a given set of data will undergo a loss of accuracy or resolution after a cycle of compression and decompression. This type of compression is usually performed on voice, graphics, or video data. Lossy compression often yields a tremendous reduction in space—sometimes on the order of 1000:1. The trade-off for more compression is generally a loss of resolution and clarity.
- *Lossless.* Lossless compression produces compressed output that is exactly the same as the input. Lossless compression is used on text and numeric data. Text always requires lossless compression because a perfect reconstruction of the original is required. Lossless compression yields approximately a 2:1 reduction in space.

Lossy compression is by far the more challenging and important because of benefits offered by a high compression factor that can be modified to allow more or less compression of data. While not being able to accurately recreate an exact copy of the input image after compression may sound like an unacceptable compromise, the loss of resolution can be adjusted to be completely undetectable. But it simply isn't suitable for most compression applications. It wouldn't be appropriate to compress a spreadsheet to 10 percent of its original size if the data changed just a little bit.

Two popular standards for lossy graphics compression are known as MPEG, for the Motion Picture Experts Group, and JPEG, for Joint Photographic Experts Group. As the names imply, JPEG is used to compress single graphics images, while MPEG is used for motion pictures. These algorithms are capable of compressing photographic images to ratios of 10 to 1 or greater with no visible loss of resolution, despite the fact that the compression is lossy. By giving up varying degrees of resolution, compression ratios of as much as 250 to 1 or greater are possible.

As data compression becomes imperative, users will have to sort through a plethora of incompatible compression standards and products. Getting it all to work together could become a full-time job. In addition, data compression is CPU-intensive and may depend on the multimedia server.

## Multimedia Servers

A *server* is a hardware and software system that turns raw data into usable information and then provides that information to users when they need it. It captures, processes, manages, and delivers text, images, audio, and video. Electronic commerce applications will require a server to manage application tasks, storage, security, transaction management, and scalability—whereas client devices handle only the user interface aspects, other critical elements are housed in the multimedia server (speed, connectivity, security, and critical applications).

The challenge facing server selection, design, and deployment presents itself when you realize that traditional models of information management don't lend themselves to the new paradigm. First, the data are radically different; we are no longer dealing with only structured, alphanumeric (ASCII) data. Second, the computing platforms that we are familiar with pose potential bottlenecks when trying to deliver large pieces of complex data to users through new interactive applications. For instance, so-called "mainframe" platforms are costly, slow, and unable to handle these new data types. On the other hand, PCs lack scalability and the ability to manage a large number of transactions. Hence, the gap is expected to be filled with multimedia servers. Clearly, the choice of platform is a key element of the solution. Currently, for true multimedia information management, platform choices include multiprocessing, multitasking, and multithreaded systems.

### *Multiprocessing*

*Multiprocessing* is defined as the ability to support the concurrent execution of several tasks on multiple processors. This implies the ability to use more than one CPU for executing programs. The processors can be tightly or loosely coupled. In loosely coupled systems, each processor has its own local memory. In tightly coupled systems, a more popular architecture, the processors share common memory. Processors interact with memory using a special memory bus. However, each processor has its own RAM cache, which reduces the traffic on the memory bus. This requires synchronization procedures to ensure that the data in these RAM caches are consistent across the different processors.

The hardware world has been toying with multiple processor architecture designs for some time, but without overwhelming success in the marketplace. Part of the problem is that software, as always, has lagged behind hardware. Some of the more successful early efforts involved attempts to add multiprocessing capabilities to UNIX. Vendors are implementing multimedia servers on multiple processors to increase multimedia processing speed and performance. Multiple processors permit servers to do either symmetric or functional multiprocessing.

### Symmetric Multiprocessing

*Symmetric multiprocessing* treats all processors as equal; in other words, any processor can do the work of any other processor (see Fig. 18.1). Applications are broken down into tasks, processes, and threads, to be run concurrently on any available processor. The goal of this approach is to maximize processor usage or total throughput. A processor does not sit idle if there is work to be done. Symmetric multiprocessing allows a task to be dynamically assigned to any processor that might be free. This task assignment is usually performed by the network operating system or the server operating system. OS/2 and Window NT are capable of symmetric multiprocessing.

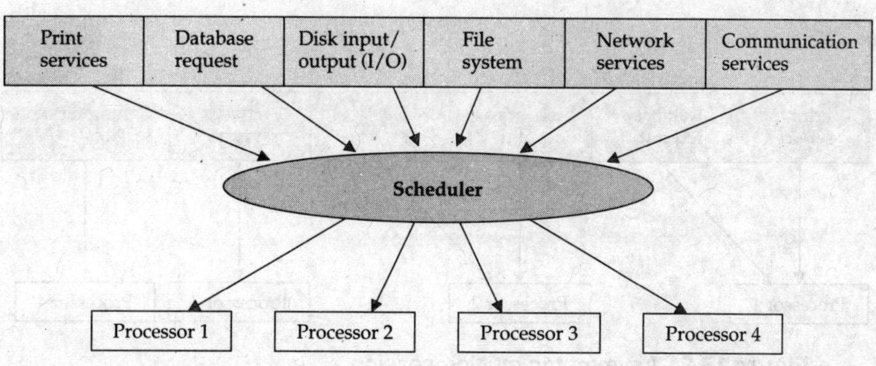


**Figure 18.1** Symmetric multiprocessing

*Asymmetric multiprocessing* (ASMP), in contrast, assigns each task to a specialized processor. For example, network services are assigned to one processor, disk I/O is assigned to another, and database storage and manipulation is assigned to a third. The problem with ASMP is that work is not evenly distributed across the separate CPUs (see Fig. 18.2). Users might reasonably expect that a six-processor machine could run six programs as well as a three-processor machine could run three. Unfortunately, the operating system can become a bottleneck because it can run only on a specific CPU on the machine. Although this restriction limits the scalability of the multiprocessor architecture, it relieves the operating system architect of a great many synchronization problems, since the operating system only does one thing at a time.

### Multitasking

*Multitasking* means that the server operating systems can run multiple programs and give the illusion that they are running simultaneously by switching control between them. Two types of multitasking are used: preemptive and nonpreemptive. Advanced server operating systems such as Windows NT offers preemptive multitasking, which means that it can distribute CPU time among programs with or without their consent.

### Multithreading

*Multithreading* is a sophisticated form of multitasking and refers to the ability to support separate paths of execution within a single address space (process). Older operating systems achieve multitasking by creating multiple processes, which creates a great deal of overhead. In a multithreaded environment, a process is broken into independent executable tasks called threads.

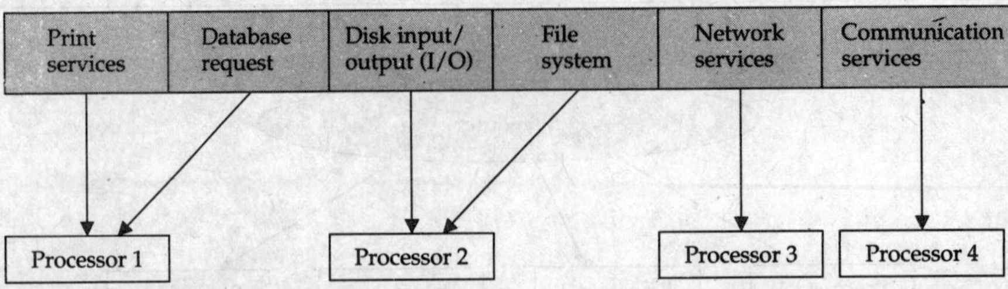


**Figure 18.2** Asymmetric multiprocessing

In multitasking, a process is the smallest unit of execution that a system can allocate resources to or schedule to run. A process consists of several threads (paths of execution). In multithreading, a thread is the smallest unit of execution that a system can schedule to run. Each thread consists of a stack, an instruction pointer, a priority queue, a CPU state, and an entry in the system scheduler about its state. The state of a thread can be blocked for input, scheduled for execution, or executing.

## Multimedia Storage Technology

Storage technology is becoming a key player in electronic commerce because the storage requirements of modern-day information are enormous. The important characteristic of next generation storage systems is not only the amount of storage but the rate at which data can be read from the disk. In the case of CD-ROM, that rate is currently anywhere from 150 Kbps (single speed) to 600 Kbps (quadruple speed). This is sufficient for all data but uncompressed, full motion color video. This goes to show that storage and input/output (I/O) throughput go together in designing electronic commerce applications.

Storage technology can be divided into two types: network-based (disk arrays) and desktop-based (CD-ROM).

### *Disk Arrays*

Disk arrays store enormous amounts of information and are becoming an important storage technology for firewall servers and other electronic commerce servers. Small arrays run from 5 to 10 gigabytes, and larger systems provide 50–500 gigabytes of storage. The technology behind these disk arrays is called RAID (redundant array of inexpensive disks). Unfortunately, this technology is quite complex, and we will describe it in a very general fashion.

The main point of RAID is that it offers a high degree of data capacity, availability, and redundancy. Current RAID systems use multiple 5½-inch disks to provide what appears as a single virtual disk to the host or the user. RAID achieves availability through the notion of fault tolerance; if something goes wrong, the system will still be able to serve the customers without any downtime. The actual degree of fault tolerance varies depending on the RAID level the user chooses. RAID technology has many levels. These levels often cause confusion, for not only do we have RAID 0 through RAID 5 but also RAID 5 Plus, 6, and 7. These labels mostly reflect vendor attempts to improve I/O throughput or data availability. At higher levels, users get extremely high data availability (three disks must simultaneously fail for the data to be lost) and increased throughput. However, there is also a severe write performance penalty, as two parity blocks must be written for each data block. But all RAID levels (except RAID 0) can reconstruct the data stored on any single failed disk in the array from the information stored on the remaining disks. In many cases, reconstruction can proceed with only minor fluctuations in end-user service.

Yet nearly six years after its conceptual debut, RAID still faces barriers to wide acceptance. Its expense, which can be several times greater than an equivalent amount of single-drive storage, is a hurdle as is its inherent complexity and the lack of general awareness about the technology. But all that could change. Not only are RAID prices going down, but RAID interest is increasing as applications require more disk space and multimedia servers become more popular.

### CD-ROM

The premiere desktop storage technology for electronic commerce applications is CD-ROM. The main advantage and also the prime reason for its success is an incredible storage density that allows a single CD-ROM disc to contain 530 Mb (audio CD)–4.8 Gb (video CD) of data, compared to 1.44 Mb for the more common 3.5-inch floppy disk. In addition, CD-ROMs are read-only (the data can only be retrieved and no new data can be added). To read the CD-ROMs a special drive (the CD-ROM drive) is required.

The origins of the CD technology date back to 1978, when optically stored data first appeared in the form of the LaserVision videodisc. Although LaserVision used an optical storage method, the encoded data followed an analog format. Thus LaserVision did not eliminate the background "noise" familiar to analog recording. Although the LaserVision product failed to meet retail sales expectations, its technical success encouraged work on an audio version of optical disc storage. In 1981, Sony and Philips agreed to a common audio CD standard that includes error correcting code ("noise" elimination). In 1983, the first audio CD was introduced.

Today, two new innovations are breaking into the market: recordable CD, which allows users to repeatedly record and erase digital data, and CD-video, which is expected to replace videocassette movies. In addition to storage benefits, CD-ROM-based electronic publishing is booming because it represents a new avenue of distribution. At present, content travels segregated distribution paths from its respective producers to its respective consumers. For instance, movies, books, magazines, newspapers, and records are each produced and distributed via separate channels and sold through separate retail outlets. CD-ROM publishing offers a new distribution channel and offers the ability to have a common platform or a standardized format for all forms of multimedia content.

CD-ROM technology exhibits the following characteristics:

- *High information density.* With optical encoding, the CD can contain some 600–800 megabytes of data on a disc less than 5 inches in diameter.
- *Low unit cost.* Because CDs are manufactured by a well-developed process similar to that used to stamp out LP records, unit cost in large quantities is less than two dollars.
- *Read-only medium.* CD-ROM is read-only; it cannot be written on or erased. It is an electronic publishing, distribution, and access medium; it cannot replace magnetic disks. But read/write CD technology may be around the corner.
- *Modest random access performance.* Due to optical read head mass and data encoding methods, random access ("seek time") performance of CDs is better than floppies but not as good as magnetic hard disks. But performance is improving every year.

CDs use a different method to record data compared to analog methods. Analog means that a device actually scribes a pattern of the original wave form onto a recording surface. A separate device, the stylus, physically connects with that surface to "read" the data. For example, a record album is created by a device that actually carves grooves into the surface of vinyl. Those grooves mimic the actual sound waves. The stylus "reads" those grooves and returns them to electronic signals into which sound is generated. Unlike a vinyl record, there is no physical contact between the recording, storage, and reading devices in CD technology. Instead, digital data storage converts electronic signals into a series of bits and bytes, and this code is read by a laser and processed by a computer into audio and visual communications.

Storing data on a CD may be thought of as occurring through a data-encoding hierarchy with each level built on the previous one. At the lowest level, data are physically stored as pits on the disc. It is actually encoded by several low-level mechanisms to provide high storage density and reliable data recovery. At the next level, the data are organized into tracks, which may be digital audio or CD-ROM. The process proceeds as follows:

1. The CD-ROM spiral surface contains shallow depressions called *pits* and spaces between indentations called *lands.* Binary information is encoded by the lengths of these pits and the lengths of the lands. Pits scatter light; lands reflect light.

2. The laser projects a beam of light, which is focused by the focusing coil.
3. The laser beam penetrates a protective layer of plastic and strikes the reflective aluminum layer on the surface.
4. Light striking a land reflects back to the detector and passes through a prism that deflects the beam to a light-sensing diode.
5. Light pulses are translated into small electrical voltages that are matched against a timing circuit to generate 1s and 0s.

A CD-ROM drive operates at a constant linear velocity. The motor varies the spin rate of a CD-ROM disk so that the portion being read is always moving past the laser at the same speed. A noncontact head that scans radially from the center to the outer edges reads the spiral track optically as the disk spins just above it. The scanning velocity is constant, thus assuring a constant data rate. This requires the disc to rotate at a decreasing rate as the spiral is scanned from its beginning near the center of the disc to its end near the disc circumference. During reading, a low-power laser beam from the optical head focuses on the reflective surface of the spiral layer and reflects back into the head. Due to the optical characteristics of the plastic disc and the wavelength of light used, the quantity of reflected light varies depending on whether the beam is on a land or on a pit. A photodetector in the optical head converts the modulated, reflected light to a radio frequency, raw data signal.

Tomorrow's CD is expected to have five times more capacity thanks to shorter-wavelength lasers, better error-correction code, and tighter formatting. We'll soon see more than 3 Gb on a single CD-ROM. Tomorrow's 3-Gb drives increase their capacity by moving from infrared to the shorter wavelength red laser. With a shorter wavelength, the disc can have smaller pits, tracks can be closer together, and more data can be recorded in the same space. The thinking goes: If a move from an infrared laser to a red one boosts capacity so much, why not continue down the spectrum—to a shorter beam called blue laser. As demonstrated in test labs, blue lasers promise 6-Gb CDs and may become feasible by the end of the century (*PC-Computing*, November 1994).

## 18.2 DIGITAL VIDEO AND ELECTRONIC COMMERCE

Desktop video has changed from an avant garde technology to a practical communication tool in a very short time. Digital video is binary data that represents a sequence of frames, each representing one image. The frames must be shown at about 30 updates per second to fool the eye into perceiving them as continuous (or smooth) motion. Digital video may contain a synchronized sound track. Our discussion of digital video data types can be generalized to audio and still images, as an audio file can be a digital movie with just a sound track and no video track and a still image can be a digital movie of just a single frame.

Figure 18.3 shows that digital video is a core component in various electronic commerce applications. What is interesting is the fact that as corporate developers become accustomed to working with text documents as a data type, they will face ever-increasing demands from end users to store and manipulate digital video. Desktop computing power has finally reached the point where you can display images with photographic resolution and color fidelity, play stereo sound to rival a CD, and display video on any monitor.

Digital video first appeared in teleconferencing applications in the early 1980s. In the initial stages, it was centered on high-definition television (HDTV). The business use of video expanded in the 1980s when compression technology improved such that video transmission over high-speed data lines became economically viable.

In 1993 the only digital video systems on the consumer market were the Philips CD-I interactive CD player and a few Japanese karaoke players pow-

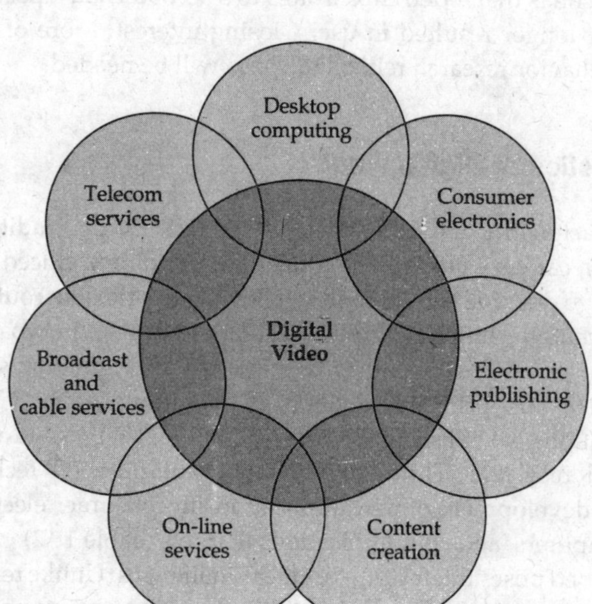


**Figure 18.3** Digital video as a core element

ered by C-cube chips. Just one year later, hundreds of thousands of PC add-in cards for video-CD playback, along with the 400,000 DirecTv systems, changed the attractiveness of digital video drastically. Virtually all the top computer-system vendors are now actively exploring the market for digital video–based set-top boxes.

In the PC market the changes have been phenomenal. In early 1994, 15-frame-per-second (fps) video at quarter-screen resolution was state of the art, and video-editing tools were immature and incomplete. By the end of 1994, advances in capture boards, processors, and graphics technologies made 30 fps, full-screen video playback achievable.

The conversion in the 1980s from audio cassettes and LPs to digital CDs is an example of how technological advances and cost reductions in digital technology can change an industry. The most significant barrier to a similar changeover from analog to digital video has been the vast amount of data that digital video requires. An hour-long video in digital form would require about 100 CDs to be stored, and transmission of an uncompressed digital video program requires an impractical amount of bandwidth.

In short, it is expected that digital video will take sometime to penetrate the marketplace. While overcoming technological barriers is a crucial starting point, it is not enough to solidify digital video's role in corporate or consumer markets. Several lessons will be learned about using it appropriately. One such lesson is that video clips from 3 to 5 seconds had a positive impact, but anything longer resulted in users' losing interest. More of this type of consumer behavior research related to video will be needed.

## Characteristics of Digital Video

Several characteristics of digital video differentiate it from traditional analog video. First, it can be manipulated, transmitted, and reproduced with no discernible image degradation. Second, it allows more flexible routing through packet switching technology. Typical analog video seen in broadcast television is sent over a one-way path from camera and originating station to the television receiver—primarily a one-way medium. Digital video enables new applications, such as collaborative planning, that would use multiple senders and receivers. Third, digital video compression technology has enabled the development of new applications in consumer electronics, multimedia computers, and communications markets (Table 18.2).

Digital video poses interesting technical challenges. Unlike text or images, video and audio are known as a constant rate, continuous time media. That is, they incorporate an interesting new dimension of data, namely time. The

**Table 18.2** Applications of Digital Video in Electronic Commerce

| *Consumer Market Applications* | *Communications Market Applications* | *Computer Market* |
|---|---|---|
| Digital movie players | Video-on-demand services | Add-in cards for video CD playback |
| Video karaoke | Cable television channel multiplexing automated ad insertion | Video game playback |
| Video games | Video telephony | High-color image editors |
| Digital cameras | Professional video editing | Desktop video editing |
| Digital video cassette recorders | Direct broadcast satellite (DBS) | Multimedia presentation authoring |
| Digital television receivers | | Image databases |
| Desktop video conferencing | | Color scanners, printers, copiers |

real difference is that video and audio have constant rate outputs requiring audio/visual synchronization that cannot be changed without significantly and negatively impacting the user's ability to extract and understand information. Their temporal nature is bounded between certain limits due to the requirements of the viewer/listener. Time is not a crucial factor in text and image understanding, whose temporal nature only comes to life in the hands of the user.

The difficulty in providing any continuous media (e.g., video and audio) from remote servers is the ability to sustain sufficient data rates from the server and over the network in order to provide pleasing audio and video fidelity (e.g., frame rate, size, and resolution) on playback for the receiving user. The ability to transmit 30 frames/second of television quality images continuously, even to a single user, is limited by network bandwidth and allocation. For current compression ratios yielding 10 Mbytes/min. of video, a minimum dedicated link of 1.3 Mbps would be required to deliver continuous video, which is not commonly achievable across the Internet. The ability to deliver the same video material simultaneously to a number of users is further limited by data storage issues.

The use of digital video in electronic commerce raises many questions: What kind of technological infrastructure—compression standards and storage servers—should be in place? What personal computer software and hardware are required? What kind of applications will benefit from digital video? The following sections delve into each of these questions.

## Digital Video Compression/Decompression

Digital video compression takes advantage of the fact that a substantial amount of redundancies exist in video. Typically, only a portion of the image changes from moment to moment. Cost-effective techniques to detect these redundancies, eliminate them during transmission and storage, and then recover them for viewing are needed to make digital video practical. The hour-long video that would require 100 CDs would only require one CD if video is compressed. The process of compression and decompression is commonly referred to as just compression, but it involves both processes.

Early attempts at video compression ran into problems. Compression was done with expensive hardware that was impractical for many applications. The process typically took a long time, usually from 10 to 100 times the length of the video itself. This made real-time and near-real-time applications impractical. Decompression had to be inexpensive to make widespread usage possible. Once encoded, a digital video can be stored and decoded many times, meaning that some applications would need only limited encoding capability but would require easy and inexpensive widespread decoding.

Furthermore, for digital video to really take off, stored video needs to be compatible across applications and among competitive manufacturers' equipment. This last requirement was addressed by the adoption of international compression standards called *codecs.* Codecs aren't products per se, but rather algorithms that determine how video and audio information is compressed and stored. Most sophisticated codecs today use lossy compression. This means that some part of the original image is lost during compression—hopefully, not enough to make the resulting decompressed image visually flawed. Because they use lossy compression, codecs have a wider selection of data-shrinking techniques available to them and can achieve much higher compression ratios than lossless technology.

Codecs attempt to solve the storage problem. While the standard frame rate for NTSC video is 30 frames per second (fps), it is generally understood that 15 fps is the bare minimum for smooth video playback on the PC. Even at 15 fps the storage requirements are amazing. At a quarter-screen resolution (usually 320 × 240 pixels) and 256 (16-bit) colors, the space required to store uncompressed video would be about 50–100 Mb per minute. And that is a modest example. Use 24-bit color and a full-size screen, and you're quickly confronted with gigabytes of data. But here's the real problem: Even if you have a lot of storage, your computer couldn't possibly retrieve the data fast enough to keep up with the frame rate (this is known as the input/output [I/O] bottleneck). For realistic video, your system's storage subsystem would have to receive or retrieve data at a rate of 1–2 Mbps to keep up. Remember that a double-speed CD-ROM drive is probably rated at only 300 Kbps. Also, most wide area networks are T-1 lines (1544 Kbps) serving thousands of people simultaneously. Here's where codecs become really important.

Codecs also solve throughput problems. Aside from squashing the data down to reasonable sizes, codecs are tuned to throughput limitations to ensure that video runs unimpeded on specific target platforms. If the video requires more bandwidth than the storage system can provide, frames will be dropped or there might be small breaks in the audio.

## Types of Codecs

Many different schemes have been developed over the past few years by industry associations and individual vendors. Most codec schemes can be categorized into two types: hybrid and software-based.

Hybrid codecs use a combination of dedicated processors and software. In general, the best compression ratios are enabled by complex algorithms that require significant processing power. This power can be attained only by using dedicated hardware chips or boards. MPEG is an example of a popular codec that's always hungry for CPU cycles. An MPEG board can decompress the video at the same rate and quality as that of a VCR tape, which is why it is used in many digital satellite broadcast systems. The problem with hybrid codecs is that they require specialized (and expensive) add-on hardware in the playback computer in order to work. This cost requirement has kept MPEG growth on the desktop slow, but hardware vendors have become interested in bringing MPEG devices to market as the processor speeds, local buses on motherboards, and high-speed CD-ROM drives have nudged the average system onto a new tier of performance. In sum, the downside of hardware codecs is the additional cost of the board and potential inflexibility as viewers are tied to a single format.

While hardware MPEG has been struggling to gain a hold in the desktop market, most of the other codec activity has been in the software arena. While each of these codecs provides some advantages for certain types of motion video, Cinepak and Indeo have emerged as the two most commonly used codecs on the PC platform. These software-based codecs come bundled in application products such as Apple QuickTime or Microsoft Video for Windows. The user is not even aware that they exist. These are inherently 24-bit codecs that provide 16.7 million colors. While true color is certainly preferable, playback on a system with 8-bit color (256 colors or less) can be flawed, since the colors out of reach of the 256-color palette must be dithered or approximated.

Three hybrid standards are used: JPEG for compression of still images; MPEG I for compression of video to CDs; and MPEG II for compression of video in real time. These standards specify the syntax in which the compressed data must be presented for multivendor equipment compatibility, but they do not specify the specific compression methodology. Thus, although image compatibility was obtained with the standards, image quality and compression efficiency were not addressed. Therefore, different compression solutions may be able to share video data, but there may be differences in quality and cost.

The following is a quick look at some of the most popular formats:

- *JPEG.* Developed by the Joint ISO/CCITT Picture Experts Group based on a file compression/decompression algorithm for individual still images
- *MPEG-1 and MPEG-2.* Open standards developed by the ISO/CCITT Moving Pictures Experts Groups for providing digital motion video with sound
- *Cinepak and Indeo.* Proprietary standards for the PC, which have been widely adopted

Two basic types of compression are done in a video sequence: interframe and intraframe. As the prefixes imply, intraframe techniques compress a frame using only the data contained within that frame. Intraframe compression is generally used to generate periodic "key" frames that provide sanity checks on the compressed output compared to the original video. Interframe compression generates compressed frames that are based on only the differences between two frames, otherwise known as delta frames (i.e., the characters are running, but the background scenery remains the same). Whereas some lower-quality codecs may use only one of these techniques, recent codecs use both.

Unlike image compression methods (e.g., JPEG), which primarily condense information within each frame, the video standards (e.g., MPEG) compress information between frames, such as a background that doesn't change. This lets users digitize and play back video and audio sequences at compression ratios as high as 160:1 while still retaining fairly good (often compared to standard VHS) quality. Because of this high compression ratio and the even higher compression promised in the MPEG-2, MPEG is a desirable delivery format for applications that require the digital video stream to be transferred over narrow bandwidth systems such as CD-ROM, telephone networks, and video conferencing. MPEG will most likely be the method of choice for video on-demand applications over cable TV. However, the huge number of calculations that MPEG requires makes it difficult to implement, and effective desktop solutions for full-screen, full-rate, real-time compression remain very expensive.

## Moving Pictures Experts Group (MPEG)

Moving Pictures Experts Group is an ISO (the International Standards Organization) group whose purpose is to generate standards for high-quality compression of digital video (sequences of images in time) with sound. When the MPEG began its work to develop a standard for digital video compression, its goal was to develop an algorithm that could compress a video signal and then be able to play it back off a CD-ROM or over telephone lines at a low bit rate (less than 1.5 Mbps). The goal was to achieve a quality level that could match that of a VHS video tape. Two standards have been defined by the committees, MPEG-1 and MPEG-2.

### *MPEG-1*

MPEG-1 defines a bit stream for compressed video and audio optimized to fit into a bandwidth (data rate) of 1.5 Mbps. This rate is special because it is the data rate of (uncompressed) audio CDs and DATs. The standard consists of three parts—video, audio, and systems—where the last part gives the integration of the audio and video streams with the proper time stamping to allow synchronization of video and audio.

The MPEG-1 implemented in commercial chips allows users to compress and play back MPEG-1 video. C-Cube Microsystems, the leader in manufacturing chips for the MPEG standard, supplies the chips on most of the MPEG video cards on the market. The MPEG-1 standard is primarily intended to process video at SIF (source input format) resolution: 352 × 240 pixels at 30 frames per second. This is one-fourth the resolution of the broadcast television resolution standard (CCIR 601), which calls for 720 × 480 pixels. (Both of these figures are for NTSC television; MPEG is also compatible with PAL, the European television format.) It is possible to display SIF-resolution video at the CCIR standard level by interpolating additional pixels, but interpolation cannot restore the detail lost in the original down-sampling.

How much does MPEG-I compress? As mentioned earlier, audio CD data rates are about 1.5 Mpbs. One can compress the same stereo program down to 256 Kbps with no loss in discernible quality. That's about a 6:1 compression. So, a MPEG I stream would have about 1.15 Mbps left for video with the rest for the system data for synchronization. The video compression ratio from the numbers here calculates to about 26:1. If you step back and think about that, it's little short of a miracle. Of course, it's lossy compression, but it can be hard sometimes to see the loss when comparing the original to the decompressed video.

The quality of decompressed digital video is measured by the number of displayable colors, the number of pixels per frame (resolution), and number of frames per second. Each of these elements can be traded off for the benefit of another and all can be traded for better transmission rates, but it is impossible to combine all of them at the television broadcast quality at low transmission speeds.

### MPEG-2

A second MPEG specification, known as MPEG-2, compresses signals for broadcast-quality video. The interest in broadcast digital video is apparent. With the work of the MPEG-2 complete, many companies with proprietary compression schemes are now becoming deeply involved in bringing their technology in line with the rest of the industry.

MPEG-2 incorporates a compression algorithm that processes video at full resolution, even at low data transmission rates. This second phase of the MPEG work concentrates on optimizing the specifications for the needs of broadcasters by providing better performance, fully supporting interlaced video sources (which were not supported in the first algorithm) and, driven by semiconductor advances, lower manufacturing costs to meet the price range of consumer set-top decoders.

Technically, MPEG-2 specifies the coded bit stream for high-quality "entertainment-level" digital video. As a compatible extension, MPEG-2 builds on the completed MPEG-1 standard, by supporting interlaced video formats and a number of other advanced features, including features to support HDTV. The MPEG-2 Main Profile is defined to support digital video transmission in the range of about 2 to 15 Mbps over cable, satellite, and other broadcast channels, as well as for digital storage media and other communications applications. This specification calls for 720 × 480 resolutions at 60 fps. It also calls for data rates of 4 to 8 megabits per second, which puts it well out of reach of ordinary desktop PC applications.

MPEG-2's future is promising, however, in the rapid evolution of cable TV's new set-top boxes. MPEG-2 decoder chips appear to be providing hardware support for the proposed "500-channel" cable networks. If interactive television and video on-demand services become reality, MPEG-2 is expected to play a crucial role. Because MPEG-2 devices are, by definition, downward compatible to MPEG-1, these advanced applications may have a trickle-down effect on the cost of MPEG in the desktop PC market.

Where do we go from here? Two other MPEG standards are currently under development: MPEG-3 and MPEG-4. MPEG-3 has been dropped and incorporated into the MPEG-2 high-level 1440 specification. It was focused on HDTV with sampling dimensions of 1920 × 1080 at 30 frames per second. The standard was to address bit rates between 20 to 40 Mbps. It was discovered that with a little bit of tweaking MPEG-2 can work very well at the HDTV rate. MPEG-4 is currently in the application-identification phase with a target of November 1998 for the official sanction of the proposed standard. Intended for very narrow bandwidth, MPEG-4 is exploring new ideas in frame reconstruction. MPEG-4 is considering speech and video synthesis, fractal geometry, and computer visualization to build accurate pictures from minimal data.

## Joint Photographic Experts Group (JPEG)

JPEG is a still-image compression algorithm defined by the Joint Photographic Experts Group and serves as the foundation for digital video. JPEG is used in two ways in the digital video world: as a part of MPEG or as motion JPEG. In both these methods, each image frame is compressed as though it were a still image.

The JPEG standard has been widely adopted for video sequences because its compression chips are relatively inexpensive and motion JPEG allows easy access to any frame in a digitized sequence. JPEG compression is fast and can capture full-screen, full-rate video, although the image degrades noticeably if the compression exceeds 20:1.

JPEG was designed for compressing either full-color (24-bit) or gray-scale digital images of "natural" (real-world) scenes. JPEG does not handle black-and-white (one bit/pixel) images, nor does it handle motion picture compression. JPEG is lossy, meaning that its compressed image isn't quite identical to what was input. The algorithm achieves much of its compression by exploiting known limitations of the human eye, notably the fact that small color details aren't perceived as well as small details of light and dark. Thus JPEG is intended for compressing images that will be looked at by humans. If you plan to machine-analyze your images, the small errors introduced by JPEG may well be a problem for you, even if they are invisible to the eye.

JPEG is a highly sophisticated technique that uses three steps. The first step, a technique known as discrete cosine transformation (DCT), carefully analyzes 8 × 8 pixel matrices. Next, a process called quantization manipulates the data and compresses strings of identical pixels by using run length encoding (RLE) techniques. Finally, the image is compressed even further using a variant of Huffman encoding that replaces redundant series of bits with shorter token values from a token table that is dynamically re-created during the decoding process. A useful property of JPEG is that the degree of lossiness can be varied by adjusting compression parameters. This means that the image maker can trade off file size against output image quality. You can make extremely small files if you don't mind poor quality; this is useful for indexing image archives, making thumbnail views or icons, and so on. Conversely, if you aren't happy with the output quality at the default compression setting, you can raise the quality until you are satisfied, and accept lesser compression.

## Cinepak and Indeo

Cinepak performs well with motion videos and is widely used for distributing movies on CD-ROM. Like MPEG, Cinepak is an asymmetrical codec, which means that while compression is fairly slow (about half an hour per minute of video compressed), playback is very quick and efficient. Cinepak can easily play 15 fps of video back in a 320 × 240 pixel window and still stay within the lowest common denominator of CD-ROM transfer rates—150 Kbps.

Despite Cinepak's entrenchment in multimedia distribution, Intel's Indeo codec technology is gaining momentum in different circles. Indeo is a symmetric codec that spends an equal amount of compression and decompression time. Indeo is becoming a major player in video conferencing, a technology that requires real-time compression and decompression.

Early versions of Indeo had problems with performance and compression ratios between key frames (intraframe compressed) and delta frames (interframe compressed). The recently introduced Indeo 4.0 greatly improved performance and transfer-rate requirements and may have a bright future in the CD-ROM world. Since teleconferencing generally involves low-motion video—meaning it contains a high degree of redundancy between frames with relatively little movement—Indeo is optimized for this type of input.

## Codecs of Tomorrow

There is no doubt that desktop video will play a major role in both the home and business computing scenarios of tomorrow. Trends to assure this outcome are appearing even now. Many companies are releasing video boards that contain onboard video accelerators that speed up the image scaling—a central component of video playback. Other manufacturers are building video-acceleration features into their 64-bit chips. They will undoubtedly be a boon for software codecs.

How the codec war of standards will play out is uncertain, but a likely scenario is emerging. Since Indeo has the head start in the video conferencing arena, it may become the de facto business standard for video conferencing.

Multimedia title distribution via CD-ROM is a little more uncertain. Here, software codecs like Cinepak become more useful each time processor speeds get a bump, and they are already widely used in existing titles.

There is no doubt that MPEG-2 will be big in broadcast video. In fact, satellite dish systems using MPEG-2 are already appearing. Eventually, support for both MPEG and the various software codecs should become cost-effective for hardware vendors to include as a standard feature on graphics accelerator boards, and such support will be essential to future versions of popular operating systems.

## 18.3 DESKTOP VIDEO PROCESSING

Video on the desktop is a key element in turning a computer into a true multimedia platform. However, digital video isn't what one would call a "natural fit" when it comes to desktop computers due to their inability to process the compression and decompression of video satisfactorily. The pace of technological change in this area has been rapid, and the PC has steadily become a highly suitable platform for video. In particular, significant improvements have occurred in the graphics capabilities of PCs (in terms of resolution, colors, and refresh rates) and color images can now be photo realistic.

The world of digital video is quite complicated. This section seeks to provide a general overview of the various desktop components needed for digital video processing and production. They include upgrade kits, sound cards, video playback accelerator boards, video capture hardware and editing software, and desktop video software (Apple QuickTime and Microsoft Video for Windows). Microphones, speakers, joysticks and other peripherals are also needed, but we will not discuss them here.

### Desktop Video Hardware for Playback and Capture

Serious desktop video means a serious financial investment as digital video requires substantial amounts of disk space and considerable CPU horsepower. It also requires specialized hardware to digitize and compress the incoming analog signal from videotapes, laser discs, cameras, and so on, and to accelerate the computation of the transitions and special effects.

Although digital video is one of the key ingredients of multimedia content—and is arguably as important as text, graphics, and sound—the late-1980s industry standard architecture of the PC has not been able to cope with the data volumes underlying video and with the requirements of video processing.

This has changed recently, as two lines of video playback products became available in the marketplace: video ASIC (application specific integrated circuits) chips and board level products, which improve the ability of PCs to carry multimedia. Both chips and board products can be integrated into the PC (with the chip fitting in at motherboard level), and board products are installed into the PC as a separate card.

### Video Playback

Existing PC architectures preclude full-screen, full-motion video. As a result, most desktop video has been extremely disappointing—the postage stamp-sized video window (160 × 120 pixels) playing at 30 fps retreats to 3 frames per sec as the window is expanded to 640 × 480 pixels and the resulting quality is generally regarded as unacceptable. There is a direct relationship between the size of the video window and the number of lost frames that affects quality.

In 1993 the VESA Media Channel architecture was announced as a solution to the problem—the absence of a dedicated highway for multimedia within the PC. This architecture is usually embedded into a video board. A video board enables a PC to display full motion video on the computer screen. Effectively, it converts the signal from one form to another, as the video display for television is different from that of the computer. Most video boards also incorporate basic sound capabilities, enabling them to behave almost like a TV.

Broadly speaking, two types of accelerator boards are available: video and graphics. One common misconception is that the terms *video acceleration* and *graphics acceleration* are interchangeable. Technically speaking, they're not. Graphics accelerators concentrate on moving graphics data (e.g., GIF or JPEG files) as swiftly as possible from the display adapter's on-board DRAM or VRAM (dynamic and virtual random access memory) to the computer monitor. These adapters incorporate graphics acceleration processors; the chips use on-board 32- and 64-bit data paths to speed graphics data—not motion video—to the monitor.

Video accelerators, on the other hand, concern themselves with improving the playback speed and quality of captured digital video sequences, and in most cases their only goal is to improve motion-video playback. Just as with graphics processors, specific video processors exist for enhancing playback of digital video.

Improvements in technology are blurring the distinction between the two. It used to be that separate boards were required to do graphics and video, but board vendors have found ways to consolidate video functions on the graphics processor, freeing up space on the board for other elements. Today, combined graphics/video accelerator boards provide that function. Increased functionality is expected to be the coming trend in video/graphics accelerators. Today, the video function is combined with 2D graphics capability. Soon, companies will be adding 3D graphics capability.

### Video Capture and Editing

Video capture boards are essential for digitizing incoming video (NTSC, PAL, S-video) for use in multimedia presentations or video conferencing. Video capture boards are also responsible for handling interpolation tasks in resizing images and sending the VGA and video signals out to the monitor so that users can see what is happening. Once the incoming raw video is digitized, it is handed over to the video compression board via an internal connector. The compression board may use a variety of compression methods (MPEG, Motion-JPEG, Indeo), depending on the manufacturer.

The video capture program also includes video-editing functions that lets users crop, resize, and convert formats and add special effects for both audio and video such as fade-ins, embosses, zooms, and echos. Developers are creating next generation video-editing tools designed to meet the wide-ranging needs of professional producers, business presenters, and video enthusiasts.

To deliver tools that are powerful, affordable, and easy enough to use, a video-editing program must support standard digital video and audio formats, cost less than $1,000, and employ a graphical interface. The last point is crucial, as video-editing packages should have more than pull-down menus and Windows compatibility. The best graphical editing tools make complex procedures accessible even to novice users. Thumbnail representations of video and audio clips can be arranged along a time line. And multiple video tracks let users see transitions between video clips (referred to as an A/B roll) and superimpositions (or overlays).

The video capture software for compression and playback is a key ingredient for creating application assets that are usable on multiple platforms. Cross-platform development is the process of capturing, editing, compressing, and converting digital video files for playback on diverse platforms and environments supporting the chosen video standard. After creating video content, the developer has the choice of using QuickTime or Video for Windows to create an end-user application. Some developers will create their application twice; once on Windows and again on a Macintosh platform. This could mean recreating the application assets (video, audio, and other art) for each platform. This duplication increases the development time and cost. If the assets can be created once and reused on multiple platforms, a significant savings would be realized.

## Desktop Video Application Software

Any PC that wants to handle digital video must have a digital-video engine available. Two significant desktop digital-video engines are Apple's QuickTime (and QuickTime for Windows) and Microsoft's Video for Windows. For the Mac, this comes as an integral part of the operating system. For Windows, it's not so simple. Users must install the playback engine, either QuickTime for Windows or Video for Windows. While other technologies are available, these software programs are the serious contenders for dominance on Macintosh and X86-based personal computers.

QuickTime and Video for Windows are "software only," meaning that no special hardware is required to playback digital movies. Although hardware-assisted playback is possible, few desktop computers are outfitted with the necessary hardware.

### *Apple's QuickTime*

QuickTime is a set of software programs from Apple that allows the operating system to play motion video sequences on a PC without specialized hardware. QuickTime has its own set of compression/decompression drivers (codecs), similar to those found in Video for Windows, and plays video files with the MOV extension.

QuickTime is a leader in many ways for desktop video; it plays the same role that PostScript played for print publishing. Few users would want to look into the data structures of a QuickTime file (nor would they want to write PostScript code by hand), but everyone appreciates what it offers: resolution and device independence, multivendor support, and a standard interface between system components.

QuickTime was the first widely available desktop video technology to treat video as a standard data type. Prior to QuickTime, video data could not be cut, copied, and pasted like text in a page composition program. QuickTime thus introduced a whole new paradigm for playing and editing movies on a personal computer. What is nice about QuickTime is that digital movies are playable on both Mac and Windows machines without conversion. The downside is that Apple markets QuickTime for Windows through the Apple Developers program, which has resulted in near invisibility in the Microsoft Windows marketplace.

QuickTime has been around for a while and has been through two upgrades. It has grown up to include some elegant and useful features. One such feature is multiple tracks. A QuickTime movie can have multiple sound tracks (for example, in different languages) and multiple video tracks (helpful in video editing). QuickTime also supports synchronized text (such as subtitles) that can appear in the movie. QuickTime's maturity makes it a robust platform for video development and playback.

### Microsoft's Video for Windows

Video for Windows is a set of software programs from Microsoft that allows Windows to play motion video sequences on a PC without specialized hardware. Video for Windows has its own set of compression/ decompression drivers (called codecs), similar to those found in QuickTime for Windows, and plays video files with the AVI extension, short for Audio/Video Interleaved.

Video for Windows is sometimes incorrectly referred to as AVI (Audio Video Interleaved), referring to the name of its file format. Microsoft introduced Video for Windows to catch up with Apple's QuickTime. It is not available on the Macintosh, but it comes with a Macintosh program that will convert QuickTime movie files to Video for Windows movie files, which then can be played on Windows.

Microsoft chose a frame-based model, in contrast to QuickTime's time-based model, which limits Video for Windows to a subset of QuickTime's features. For example, you can't have a frame (or group of frames) remain on the screen for a variable amount of time with Video for Windows as you can with QuickTime.

Omitted from our discussion of video software is Autodesk's FLI/FLC animation standard, because it doesn't have integrated audio and doesn't support the latest compression algorithms. Likewise, DVI from Intel is a hardware-assisted video standard that is being slowly eclipsed by more flexible software-based technologies. Another product in the market is IBM's digital-video technology, UltiMotion, meant for the OS/2 market.

## 18.4 DESKTOP VIDEO CONFERENCING

Thanks to the increasing digital video capabilities of PCs, desktop video conferencing is gaining momentum as a communications tool. For many business users, face-to-face video conferences are already a common practice, allowing distant colleagues to communicate without the expense and inconvenience of traveling.

Early video conferencing utilized costly equipment to provide room-based conferencing in which all participants at a location gather in a specially equipped conference room and view monitors displaying similar rooms at remote sites. For instance, if product design engineers in Los Angeles want to talk about product design ideas, they would arrange a video conference so other engineers around the country could see the product design in real time and comment on it.

The old "room" paradigm is fast becoming obsolete due to desktop video conferencing. In the new paradigm, participants sit at their own desks, in their own offices, and call up others using their PCs much like a telephone. Internetworking and compression technologies enable business users to replicate the meeting environment on the desktop. Three or four credit-card-size windows appear on the computer screen. One of these is shared space—equivalent to a meeting table—where everyone can interact to edit a commercial in real time or revise a spreadsheet. Each participant also has a private workspace window for writing notes, analyzing data, reading electronic or video mail, or even doodling during a meeting. Finally, each participant has a mute control—similar to stepping out of the meeting room into the corridor—for private conversations.

**The Economics.** Three factors have made desktop video conferencing a viable solution for business and personal communications today:

1. *Price.* The cost of video conferencing equipment has fallen dramatically, from $500,000 for a system in the early 1980s to $5000 for a room-size system today—and just $500–$1000 for a desktop system. Digital video capture and playback boards are enabling better capture and processing of desktop video at a very low price.
2. *Standards.* A worldwide standard for video conferencing is slowly emerging, allowing interoperable communications between machines from different vendors.
3. *Compression.* Bandwidth has traditionally been the limiting factor (or bottleneck). Sending video through a communications channel requires a lot of bandwidth. Better and faster compression methods are reducing the overhead associated with video conferencing.

Video conferencing is quickly leaping from corporate systems to desktops. By leveraging the power of faster processors along with new advancements in video-, sound-, and data-compression techniques, vendors have introduced packages that turn PCs into videophones for as little as $1,000. Once the PC is equipped, users can place long-distance video calls over regular

POTS lines for the price of a regular telephone call. Viability does not mean widespread usage, however. Because video conferencing requires significant investments in equipment and technical skills and often entails the use of dedicated facilities with special communications lines, its applicability and appeal to business have been limited.

## Data or Document Conferencing

Basic video conferencing systems enable groups to see and hear each other. However, these systems are often not geared to share on-line information such as spreadsheets, word processing documents, databases, and scanned or moving images. Because much of today's information is on-line, there is a disconnect between sharing verbal information and sharing documents. Recognizing this problem, several vendors of dedicated video conferencing equipment are incorporating the data elements into their desktop systems, even though most of these systems today suffer from video compression bottlenecks and require relatively expensive, high-speed communications interfaces.

Data conferencing is a form of screen sharing. Instead of having full control of a local system a remote user shares one or more designated windows with a local user. Most solutions use a whiteboard model. After establishing a desktop-to-desktop connection, the session presents a whiteboard window that both participants view and manipulate. The whiteboard software includes drawing, painting, and annotation tools for brainstorming and sketching, enabling users to emulate the interactive discussions that often take place in real meeting rooms. Bitmaps of the whiteboard are compressed before being sent over the wire, and users can save snapshots of the whiteboard for future reference.

Making existing information from a spreadsheet or other file available, however, requires "cutting" from the application and "pasting" onto the common whiteboard. The whiteboard data are static—changes made in the collaborative window do not affect and are not affected by the "real" data. The next step in terms of capabilities is interactive file or application sharing. Here, the user selects a window or file that a remote partner can access, and then both can review and modify the document. The main advantage is that both users can directly modify source data.

Various technical approaches can be used to enable application sharing. One approach captures the Windows GDI (Graphical Device Interface) screen drawing commands and sends these commands over the phone line to the receiving system, where they are executed in the background transparent to the user. Sending drawing commands and not images makes efficient use of the communications bandwidth while granting the remote and local users access to the same screen.

## Types of Desktop Video Conferencing

Most desktop video conferencing systems coming onto the market today are divided into one of three communication camps: plain old telephone lines (POTS), ISDN, or the Internet.

### *Using POTS for Video Conferencing*

POTS systems are especially attractive for point-to-point conferencing because no additional monthly charges are assessed and special arrangements with the phone company are unnecessary. The drawback with a POTS solution is a restriction to the top speed of today's modems—28.8 Kbps—to transmit all the multimedia data (see Fig. 18.4).

Most POTS solutions come complete with an external 28.8-Kbps V.fast fax/modem, a color video camera, a combination earpiece/microphone, and two expansion boards. One board captures and compresses the outgoing video. Incoming video is often decompressed through software, relying on the system's CPU horsepower. The other card is a communications board for handling audio compression and decompression.

Once properly installed, the video conferencing software allows users to pipe video, audio, and data down a standard telephone line. So making a video conference call is as easy as making a phone call. An on-screen keypad is used to dial the number, and the system is flexible enough to allow the call

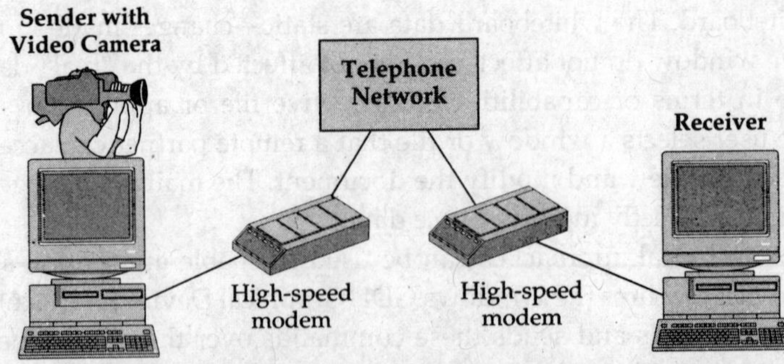


**Figure 18.4** Point-to-point video conferencing using POTS

recipient to answer on a regular telephone, then switch over to his or her own system. There's no need to call in advance to set up the video conference. Most packages also offer full application sharing, as well as a whiteboard that enables you to scan in any document so that you can edit the image together over the phone. A snapshot utility also allows users to take quick pictures, then highlight certain areas or attach electronic sticky notes. Users can even zoom in on details, which can be particularly handy when discussing a detailed AutoCAD drawing, for example.

To shrink the video to analog POTS size, many vendors use a proprietary codec as it serves a product differentiator. For instance, Creative Labs uses a codec it calls VATP (Vector Adaptive Transform Processing). VATP uses such techniques as discrete cosine transforms, silence detection, and vector quantization to squeeze the information down to a size that will fit through the 28.8-Kbps pipeline. The codec dynamically assigns the available bandwidth depending on the changing information demands. Top priority is automatically given to audio, secondary priority is given to data (such as application sharing), and the last spot goes to video.

### *Using ISDN for Video Conferencing*

ISDN lines offer considerably more bandwidth—up to 128 Kbps—but require the installation of a special hardware, assuming ISDN service is available in an area. The use of ISDN has been restricted to companies, given the obstacles associated with getting ISDN service, especially in private residences. Also, given the pervasiveness of POTS lines, it's no surprise that the majority of video conferencing newcomers are POTS products. In fact, it's the proliferation of PC-based POTS solutions that is fueling the current video conferencing explosion.

Figure 18.5, shows the basic architecture for tele or video conferencing using ISDN network transport and switching. This architecture is commonly found in videophones. The videophone is essentially a scaled-down, limited functionality, residential video conferencing service. Videophone combines a voice telephone with a video camera and monitor in a single desktop unit. Network requirements for the videophone are mainly fiber optic cable or analog POTS.

For video compression and decompression, the ISDN network uses the H.261 video compression technology. The International Telegraph and Telephone Consultative Committee (CCITT) has specified the H.261 video transmission protocol for use in real-time video information delivery at bandwidth increments of 64 Kbps. The image quality delivered by H.261 increases with bandwidth and supports so-called *graceful degradation*. This

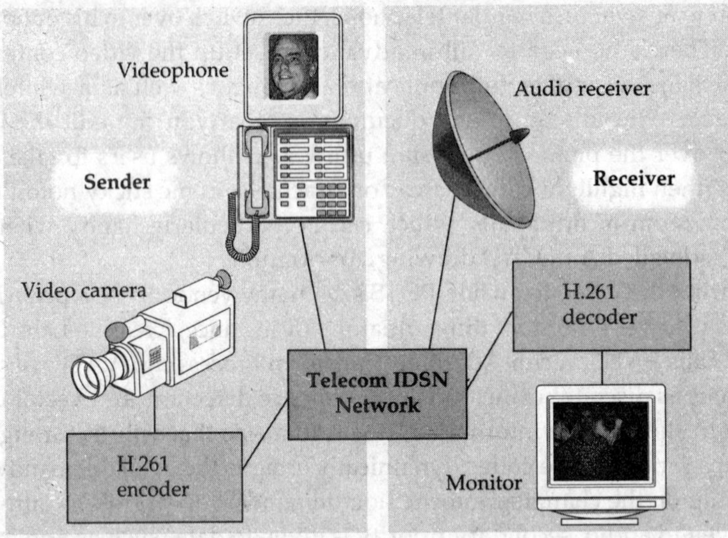


**Figure 18.5** ISDN video or teleconferencing architecture

term refers to the behavior of a system using a packet-switched channel that is heavily loaded. As the load on the channel increases and the bandwidth available to the video system decreases, how does the video performance behave? Some compression schemes, including H.261, use a scheme that sends very coarse information about the video picture across the channel first, then successively refines the picture if it has enough bandwidth left to do so. Others do things like starting from the top of the picture and leave it incomplete if time runs out. That can be very annoying.

Although H.261 is a very good compression algorithm and performs very well, it is very computationally intensive and as such requires special-purpose hardware in order to function. For this reason many companies have created their own proprietary algorithms. The problem is the lack of interoperability between the various schemes as each company strives to make its method the standard.

### Using the Internet for Video Conferencing

Two video conferencing programs are available on the Internet: CU-SeeMe and MBONE.

**CU-SeeMe.** CU-SeeMe is the first software available for the Macintosh and Windows platforms to support real-time multiparty video conferencing on the Internet. CU-SeeMe provides a one-to-one conference, or by use of a

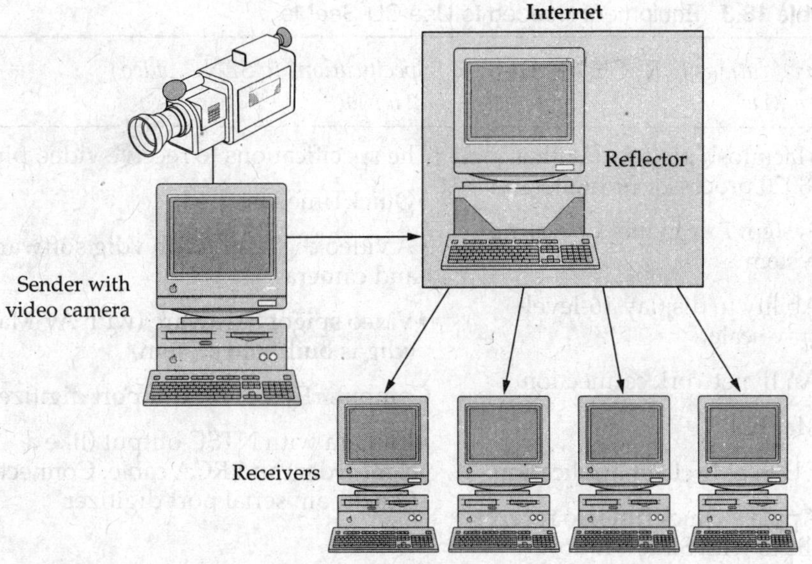


**Figure 18.6** One-to-many video conferencing

reflector (see Fig. 18.6), a one-to-many, a several-to-several, or a several-to-many conferencing depending on user needs and hardware capabilities. It displays 4-bit gray-scale video windows at 160 × 120 pixels (postage stamp-sized) and also includes audio.

CU-SeeMe is intended to provide useful conferencing at minimal cost. Receiving requires only a Mac with a screen capable of displaying 16 grays and a connection to the Internet. Sending requires the same plus a camera and digitizer (see Table 18.3), which can cost as little as $100.

A digital camera, such as a 4-bit gray-scale camera, that attaches to the Macintosh's serial port is a requirement for sending video. Examples of such cameras include Apple's QuickTake and the QuickCam—a racquetball-sized sphere—that can capture images. The QuickCam is recommended by the CU-SeeMe group; its low price and versatility make it quite a tempting impulse buy for those who want to explore the video conferencing frontier.

The QuickCam's full-motion video signal is specially designed for QuickTime video format and requires at least a System 7.0 operating system and QuickTime 2.0. Video can be recorded at a variety of frame rates: up to 30 fps at 80 × 60 pixels, but only 4 fps at 320 × 240 pixels. The recording of sound through the QuickCam and the speed of the computer also affect the frame rate. The grainy pictures and video output with the low-cost camera make them unsuitable for serious video, but its low price (~$200) makes it perfect for quick-and-dirty video conferencing.

**Table 18.3** Equipment Needed to Use CU-SeeMe

| *Specifications to RECEIVE video on a Mac* | *Specifications to SEND video on a Mac* |
|---|---|
| •Macintosh platform with a 68020 processor or higher<br>•System 7 or higher operating system<br>•Ability to display 16-level-gray-scale<br>•An IP network connection<br>•MacTCP<br>•CU-SeeMe client application<br>•Apple's QuickTime, to receive slides with SlideWindow | The specifications to receive video plus<br>•QuickTime installed<br>•A video digitizer (with vdig software) and camera<br>•Video spigot hardware (with Av-Macs, vdig is built into system)<br>ComputerEyes/RT SCSI port digitizer<br>•Camera with NTSC output (like a camcorder) and RCA cable. Connectix QuickCam serial port digitizer |

In addition to the point-to-point video conferencing, CU-SeeMe allows one-to-many broadcasts using the notion of a reflector. (see Fig. 18.6). Users can dial into a particular computer on the network designated as a reflector and receive the broadcasts that emanate from that site.

CU-SeeMe is gaining in sophistication, and many of its ideas are being incorporated into commercial products. CU-SeeMe is available as freeware from Cornell University (ftp://gated.cornell.edu/pub/video/).

***MBONE.*** The MBONE is a virtual network that has been in existence since early 1992. It originated from an effort to multicast audio and video from meetings of the Internet Engineering Task Force. The MBONE shares the same physical media as the Internet. It uses a network of routers (mrouters—multicast routers) that can support IP multicast. MBONE set-up is not for the faint of heart and is time consuming because a lot of learning and fixing are involved. However, all the tools are documented, and help is available from the MBONE community.

To understand broadcasting on Internet better, MBONE, a research Multicast Backbone, was created. This experiment was also intended to understand how IP multicast extensions (see Section 17.8) worked, as without an infrastructure for testing multicasting, it would have been another interesting theory. Over the last few years, MBONE has helped researchers understand efficient multicasting and also develop the necessary software to facilitate audio and video broadcasts.

Packetized video is a good application for multicast. In a packet-based video conference, images are continuously digitized, compressed, and sent to all remote sites. Even when compressed, the amount of data can be considerable. In such a situation, IP multicasts can keep the amount of data traversing network links to a minimum by sending only a single video stream over the line.

You may be surprised to learn that work on multimedia broadcast within the Internet community has been underway for well over two decades. In 1974 the first experiments on voice transmission across a packet network (ARPANET) were carried out. By 1976 low bit rate voice conferences were conducted. The first voice-packet protocol was proposed in 1977, and a packet video standard was proposed in 1981.

The MBONE adds video to earlier work on audio. It was first used to broadcast Internet Engineering Task Force (IETF) meetings to destinations around the globe. Today, the MBONE is a massive virtual network layered on top of parts of the physical Internet. This virtual network was necessary since IP multicasting has not yet been fully integrated into most Internet routers and gateways.

In sum, MBONE is composed of islands that support IP multicasting to local clients. These islands are connected by virtual point-to-point links called tunnels. Routing software called mrouted (multicast routed) has been developed to let UNIX workstations act as multicast routers. Between these routers, the multicast IP packets are tunneled (encapsulated into regular IP packets) with the mrouted machines as destination sites (see Fig. 18.7).

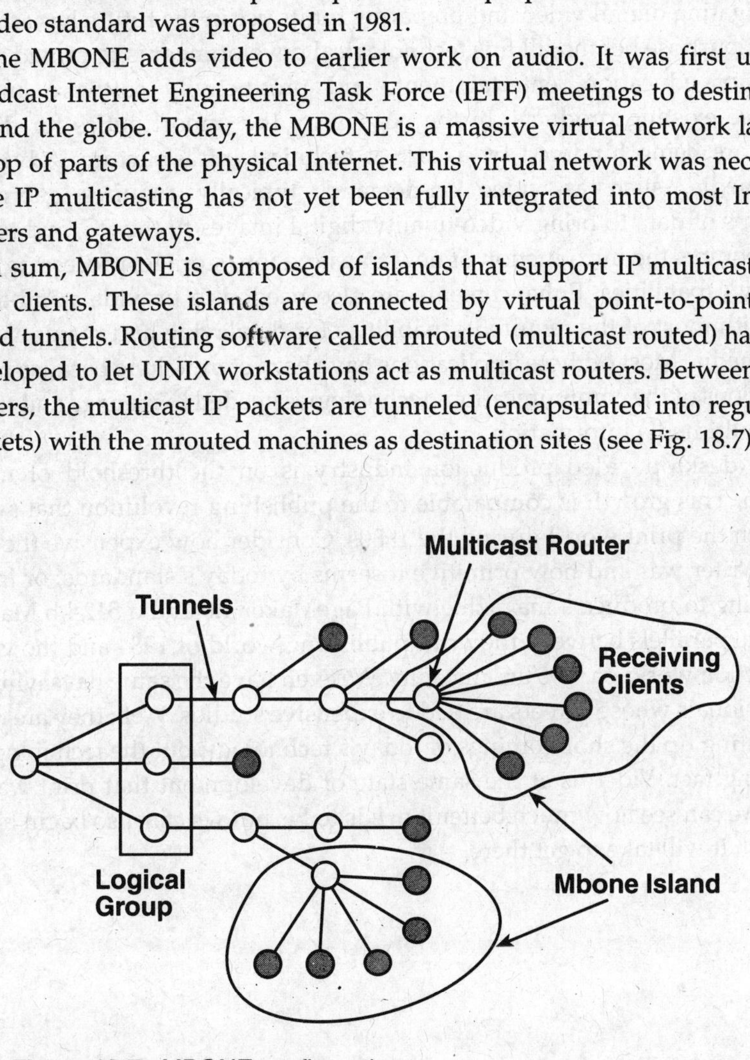


**Figure 18.7** MBONE configuration

## 18.5 SUMMARY

Multimedia—a combination of text, images, sounds, and animation to provide a comprehensive, interactive environment—is a key element of electronic commerce. In general, multimedia is of two types: desktop and network-based. Both are important in developing electronic commerce applications.

One key aspect of multimedia is digital video. Today, PCs, networks, and database storage systems are becoming capable of handling digital video, and with decreasing price-to-performance ratios. The advantages of digital video are compelling, and it can become an accepted data type. While digital video will require significant increases in bandwidth and storage, the time to begin investigating digital video and preparing for its use in the future has arrived.

The purpose behind all this technological development is to provide new forms of education, entertainment, and productivity software and to enhance existing products. In the near term, the opportunities for digital video are being hindered by a lack of technical infrastructure. Advanced multimedia, such as video on-demand, typically requires enormous amounts of data to bring video-quality digital images to the PC, and television requires the introduction of new transmission, storage, processing, and display capabilities. Enhancements are also needed to provide stand-alone PCs with most of the required capabilities for displaying and manipulating multimedia. Most of these applications have been stand-alone because of the limitations of the communications technologies needed to manage and transport multimedia information.

The desktop video production industry is on the threshold of major growth. This growth is comparable to the publishing revolution that swept through the print world during the 1980s. Consider how expensive the first LaserWriter was and how primitive it seems by today's standards; or imagine trying to produce a magazine with PageMaker 1.0 and a 512-kb Mac. In fact, the parallels between the print publishing world of 1984 and the video production world of 1995 are uncanny. We even have the same naysaying by professionals whose careers are tied to expensive studios. Well, they are right in pointing up the shortcomings of today's technology, but the technology is changing fast. Video is at the same state of development that print was in 1984: We can see how much better it needs to be, but we can also begin to see the path it will take to get there.

# Chapter 19

# Broadband Telecommunications

As we move to multimedia-based electronic commerce applications, traditional packet switching techniques may not be adequate to meet the new transmission and switching needs. Electronic commerce applications tend to differ greatly in the areas of traffic volume and required bandwidth, nature of the information, degree of burstiness, need for error control, and real-time sensitivity for transmittal, as in the case for voice. For this purpose, new fast packet-switching methods—frame relay and cell relay—are aimed at the following:

- Offering better methods for high-speed data transport
- Providing support for pricing, priority, and multicasting services or the ability to handle group broadcasts to permit delivery of the same data to multiple recipients
- Reducing the number of transport networks for various services (e.g., voice, data, video, and image) by providing better integration services

The need for integrating these features into viable communication systems has led to the concept of broadband networking—which provides new ways to achieve these functions. High-capacity broadband networks transform how information is processed, effectively eliminating the age-old restriction of distance that isolates computers and storage devices into groups like local area networks (LANs) and wide area networks (WANs).

It is clear that the emerging broadband networks for electronic commerce services will be based on fast packet switching, which combines the best of LANs and WANs to transmit voice and data. Such networks will unite users across the entire spectrum of topologies—local, campus, city, global—at blazing speeds. The flexibility and services will be unprecedented, far beyond anything available with today's relatively primitive networks.

Over the next few years, vendors are expected to unleash a tremendous array of broadband equipment, much of it with new features and performance characteristics. Invariably, the rapid development of new protocols, standards, and products is accompanied by an obscure terminology that must be mastered such as ATM, cell relay, frame relay, and fast switches. This chapter is an introduction to broadband technology, in particular ATM-based fast packet switching. The goal is to illustrate the range of capabilities and present the general concepts without inundating the reader with technical detail.

## 19.1 BROADBAND BACKGROUND CONCEPTS

Before getting into the details, some definitions need to be clarified. They include ISDN, Broadband ISDN, B-ISDN versus ATM, LAN versus WAN, and connection oriented versus connectionless communications. But first, what is the difference between narrow and broadband networks?

### Narrowband Versus Broadband Networks

In the analog world, *broadband* refers to the ability to stack frequencies on a single transmission medium, providing multiple channels on the same wire. In the digital world, broadband has come to mean any data rate greater than or equal to T-1 speeds (i.e., 1.544 Mbps).

With broadband, the physical cabling is conceptually divided into several different channels, each with its own unique carrier frequency, using a technique called *frequency division modulation*. These different frequencies are put or multiplexed onto the network cabling in such a way to allow multiple simultaneous "conversations" to take place. The effect is similar to having several virtual networks traversing a single piece of wire. Network devices "tuned" to one frequency can't hear the "signal" on other frequencies. Cable-TV is an example of a broadband network: Multiple conversations (channels) are transmitted simultaneously over a single cable; the user picks one of the frequencies being broadcast by selecting a channel.

In contrast to broadband, we have narrowband networks. A *narrowband* network is one that provides a single channel for communications across the physical medium (e.g., cable), so only one device can transmit at a time. Devices on a narrow band network, such as Ethernet, are permitted to use all of the available bandwidth for transmission, and the signals they transmit need not be multiplexed onto a carrier frequency. An analogy is a single phone line: Only one person can talk at a time—if more than one person wants to talk, everyone has to take turns.

## Integrated Services Digital Network (ISDN)

ISDN is by far the most recognized acronym of the emerging technologies and stands for Integrated Services Digital Network. It is the forerunner of B-ISDN or Broadband ISDN. ISDN was designed to utilize the preexisting copper wiring that runs from the telephone exchange to telephones on the customer premises. ISDN operates by increasing the calling capacity of the existing telephone line. This additional capacity is achieved when special electronic components are added to the ends of the telephone line, making it an ISDN compatible line. These components digitize voice or data and place them into special channels called channels for information transport. It is important to understand that these channels are not physical channels—one cannot see them as wires inside a telephone cable—rather they are "derived" channels created by the ISDN electronic components installed on the telephone line.

Three types of ISDN channels are defined: B, D, and H. The B channel is a 64 Kbps clear channel that can carry any digitized data (like the modem, only much faster) and voice (like the telephone). A clear channel means that no signaling information is sent and is meant to be an open communications line. There are 2 B channels on each ISDN line and so two kinds of information can be exchanged simultaneously. With the proper equipment, both B channels can be used to transmit data simultaneously, thus doubling the data capacity of the ISDN line. In other words, a person can be speaking to another on one B channel (a voice call) and looking at that person on the other B channel (a video call). Or a person can be speaking to someone on the phone using one B channel and transmitting or receiving data using the computer on the other B channel.

The D channel, used for signaling information, can operate at either 16 Kbps or 64 Kbps. The D channel can be used for what is known as common-channel signaling useful for synchronization, monitoring, and alarm signals. This channel can also transport digital data at speeds up to 9600 bits per second. This channel can be used for such applications as e-mail, remote login and small file transfers. This channel uses a long established format, X.25, for data transfer.

There are three H channels, all providing higher-speed transmissions than the D channel. The H0 channel operates at 384 Kbps and can be used for video conferencing, high-speed fax, or packet-switched data. Up to four H0 channels can be multiplexed into a single H1 channel, which operates at 1.544 Mbps. The H1 channel can be used for high-speed data communications or LAN interconnection. The H2 channel, which operates at 1.9 Mbps, is available only in Europe.

Although ISDN has various capabilities, it is primarily used to transmit and receive data at high speeds. Today, ISDN is positioned as the way to provide simultaneous voice and data service to the desktops of residential users, home offices, and small businesses. ISDN can provide video, dial-up data services, desktop teleconferencing, and advanced call management to the many users who work at home or out of small business offices. It can also deliver bandwidth to LAN users who do not need the constant connection provided by a leased-line service.

ISDN has recently been divided into ISDN over copper wire (narrowband ISDN) and ISDN over fiber optic (broadband ISDN or B-ISDN). The main difference is speed. Whereas ISDN offers data rates of perhaps hundreds of kilobits per second, B-ISDN gives the user data rates ranging from hundreds of megabits per second to more than two gigabits per second. Today, B-ISDN has stolen the limelight from ISDN and has the attention of the world's telephone companies as well as most computer users. A vital component of B-ISDN is called SONET in North America and SDH in the rest of the world.

## SONET and SDH

SONET, or Synchronous Optical NETwork, is a set of standards that govern synchronous fiber optic data transmission at rates ranging from 51.8 Mbps to 2.5 Gbps (see Table 19.1). The specifications were developed by the ANSI-accredited Committee of the Exchange Carriers Standards Association and

**Table 19.1** Digital Signal Hierarchy

| *Level* | *Line Rate (Mbps)* |
|---|---|
| OC-1 | 51.84 |
| OC-3 | 155.52 |
| OC-9 | 466.56 |
| OC-12 | 622.08 |
| OC-18 | 933.12 |
| OC-24 | 1244.16 |
| OC-36 | 1866.24 |
| OC-48 | 2488.32 |

adopted by the CCITT in 1989 under the name Synchronous Digital Hierarchy (SDH). Unfortunately, due to vendor politics, SONET and SDH are not identical because each has features the other lacks. The reason for this is that until the B-ISDN effort got rolling in the late 1980s, the European and American telephone companies pretty much ignored each other's telephony standards; there is a lot of legacy equipment that must be accommodated.

However, there is a subset of mutually compatible specifications that permit the American SONET to interoperate smoothly and nearly effortlessly with the European SDH. Most specifically, they are the specifications for OC-3, OC-12, and OC-48 in America; or STM-1, STM-4, and STM-16 in Europe. The good news is that virtually every implementation of either SDH or SONET complies with these three specifications, Thus, for all practical purposes, SONET and SDH are basically the same thing—if the specifications are followed.

SONET holds three attractions. First, bandwidth available with fiber optic technology is virtually limitless. SONET's current maximum data rate of 2.5 Gbps is the equivalent of 48 T-3 (45-Mbps) lines. Second, along with its massive amounts of bandwidth, SONET allows switches to add or drop individual DS-1 or T-1 (1.544-Mbps) channels. High-speed (T-3) users generally do not have such access to individual lower-speed channels. To extract an individual T-1 channel from a T-3 bundle, a network manager usually needs to unravel (demultiplex) the entire T-3 line, pull out the channel, and then rebundle (or remultiplex) the whole T-3—a process that requires a lot of equipment at every point node. SONET's third advantage is that it is an international standard; T-3 standards are defined only in the United States. Because SONET's specifications are universally applicable, SONET equipment from different vendors theoretically should be able to interoperate.

## B-ISDN Versus ATM

Another frequently confused pair of terms are B-ISDN and ATM, Asynchronous Transfer Mode. Strictly speaking, B-ISDN is underlying technology at the fiber optic level that can transport information at high-speeds. ATM is simply a service that can run over B-ISDN. It is literally little more than the specification for a 48-byte packet or cell of information with a five-byte header that tells the telephone system where that packet is going. ATM can run over a number of different physical media, ranging from UTP (copper wire (unshielded twisted pair) to the B-ISDN fiber optic network.

Think of ATM cells as a line of pickup trucks, each capable of carrying 48 bytes of data, driving over the B-ISDN highway, and you will have an understanding of both concepts. ATM deals with the issues of truck design, routing (signs on the highway), and management of delivery. B-ISDN deals with the nature of the highway surface. If it is dirt (copper wire), the truck (ATM cell) can only go at 20 mph. If it is high-quality tar (fiber optic), the truck can race along at 150 to 200 mph. B-ISDN worries about lanes sizes (frequencies), lane markings, and other low-level issues.

The introduction of a standard transport method is useful in making the LAN/WAN dichotomy completely transparent to the user. For years we have looked at the type of network and used that as the criterion for judging whether a particular network is local or wide area. For example, we all know that Ethernet is synonymous with LAN. On the other hand X.25 is a WAN—right? Perhaps this might have been true in the past. Today, the divisions are not clear. For example, we ourselves think nothing of using TELNET to log in into a system literally on the other side of the world and then proceed to work on it as though it was in the same room with us. Obviously, because TELNET is a member of the TCP/IP services, and TCP/IP is an Internet protocol, we are working over a wide area network. Or are we? From one point of view, we could be working on a LAN—an Ethernet LAN to be specific.

Okay, you might say, let's look at the type of wire and use that to classify the type of network. If it uses a phone wire or microwave or other communication service typically supplied by a company such as the telephone company, it's a WAN. Conversely, if the only physical media involved is a fiber cable, or twisted pair, then we are dealing with a LAN. This classification system works, at least for the present. However, one of the likely long-term (perhaps in five years or less) results of the introduction of B-ISDN and ATM will be the elimination of even this dichotomy.

## Connectionless Versus Connection-Oriented Networks

All network services belong to one of two broad categories, connectionless and connection-oriented. Probably no other concepts in networking cause more confusion than these because there is a continuum between the two.

- You send an electronic mail message to a friend in China. The e-mail software takes the message and breaks it down into tiny pieces. Each piece is sent separately to the destination computer and may take different routes to get there. Once all the pieces have arrived, the e-mail software will assemble them together to re-create the original.
- Your fax machine senses the ring of an incoming call and takes its phone line off-hook. After exchanging several packets of information with the fax

machine that made the call, your fax machine begins producing several sheets of an important document your attorney's fax machine is sending you. When the two fax machines are finished, they hang up.

The first scenario, the mailing of letters, illustrates connectionless communication. You send a letter, but there is no guarantee that it will be delivered. And unless you get a letter back saying that your letter was received, you don't know if it got to its intended recipient. Now let's extend the analogy and pretend that you've sent a letter every day for three days. Not only is there no guarantee that your letters will arrive, but there is also no guarantee regarding what order they might arrive in. That is to say, the third letter might arrive first, the first letter might arrive two days after the first, and the second letter might even get lost.

There is nothing profound in all this, for this is the way the e-mail system works, although it is highly probable that the letters will get to their intended recipient. Our point is that there is no guarantee in connection-less communciation.

In the networking world, such "letters," known as datagrams, are generally "mailed" to one or more addressees. There is no way of knowing whether the datagram reached any of the intended recipients unless they choose to send a reply. And if they don't choose to send a reply, it's the sender's responsibility to check.

The second scenario, a fax or a telephone call, is the classic example of a connection-oriented protocol. First, a connection is made between two parties. Unless that is accomplished, communication cannot occur. That is to say, both parties must pick up the phone and say "Hello" when the phone rings. Second, there is an exchange of packets, which in a conversation amounts to sentences, giving a step-by-step acknowledgment that the communication is occurring between the intended parties. A party who has nothing to say will usually make a sound or grunt to indicate that he or she is still connected.

Computers also use connection-oriented communication. Since computers cannot speak like humans, they use sequence numbers instead. Typically, each connection-oriented packet is numbered, and the recipient acknowledges receiving them either individually or in groups. There is also error recovery. If the line experiences noise, the listening party asks the sender to repeat what was sent earlier and retransmission occurs almost immediately. This is also typical of other connection-oriented communications.

Generally, connection-oriented communications are reliable for these reasons: The information is transferred only when a connection between the two (or more) active parties is known to exist, and the packets are exchanged in such a way that the order is preserved and quick error recovery is possible.

## Switching Techniques

Network services are provided through two primary switching technologies: circuit and packet. Traditionally, circuit switching is used for voice and packet switching is used for data. In circuit-switched networks, each link is dedicated to a predetermined number of users during a particular period and each user receives a predetermined amount of bandwidth. The most frequently cited example of a circuit-switched network is the telephone system.

In a packet-switched network, information is split into packets of data, each with its own built-in address label. They speed across the available links to meet up again at a destination node, or packet switch, along a communications path. Packet-switched networks allow end stations to dynamically share the network medium and the available bandwidth.

Packet switching can be divided into slow packet and fast packet switching. An example of a slow packet switching standard is X.25. X.25 is synonymous with packet-switched networking and is usually drawn as a cloud on network diagrams. X.25 is an aging standard, defined back in 1972 by the CCITT, the international telephone standards body.

X.25 provides access to public data networks at data rates up to 64 Kbps. What X.25 has got going for it is that a lot of people use it—and it's reliable, relatively error-free, and reasonably secure. It is an excellent technology for developing low-speed networks to support a variety of data applications, including terminal-to-host connection, point-of-sales systems, automatic teller machines, and facsimile machines. However, X.25 has been discounted as a technology for higher-speed services because of the amount of protocol overhead encountered in the network.

With electronic commerce applications demanding increasing bandwidth and speedier performance, the X.25 network world is migrating to faster technologies known, for obvious reasons, as fast packet switching. These technologies provide switching capabilities (256 Kbps to 2.4 Gbps or greater) that were unthinkable only a few years ago.

Fast packet switching comes in two varieties: frame relay and cell relay (see Fig 19.1). The term *relay* refers to the fast packet conveyance of frames or cells through the intermediate switches to their destination. Frame relay covers the range from 1.5 Mbps to 34 Mbps, whereas cell relay allows for 34 Mbps to 155 Mbps throughput at the user interface, and 600 Mbps between switching nodes.

Fast packet switching differs from the traditional circuit switching in the following three aspects:

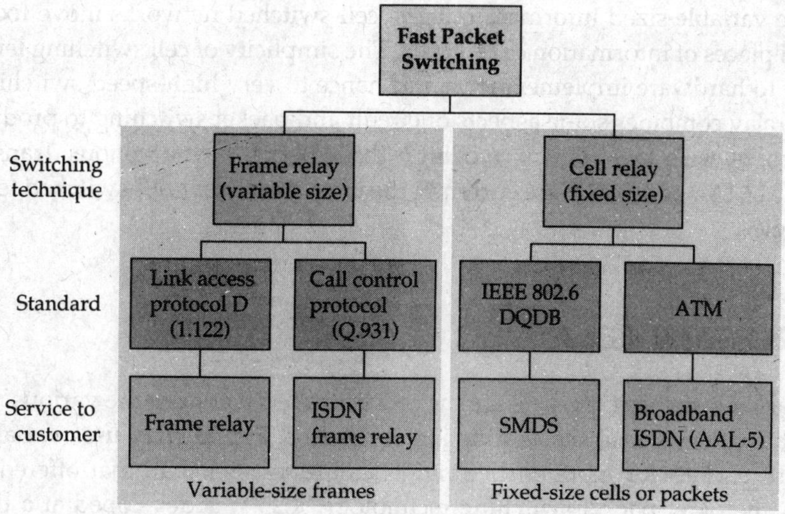


**Figure 19.1** The fast packet switching hierarchy

1. *Call set-up.* In fast packet switching, call paths are established dynamically based on the individual packet address and not permanently through a set matrix paths.
2. *Traffic management.* Each call in the circuit switching area is assigned a fixed bandwidth irrespective of its use. In fast packet switching, the bandwidth is dynamically assigned based on the need of the call.
3. *Switching.* Circuit switching takes place based on a preassigned path via the time or space switch, whereas in fast packet switching, the individual packets can be switched by the hardware based on the address field at fairly high rates (higher than conventional packet switching rates due to switching by hardware, not software).

Each switching technique has advantages and disadvantages. For example, circuit-switched networks offer users dedicated bandwidth that cannot be infringed upon by other users. On the other hand, packet-switched networks have traditionally offered more flexibility and used network bandwidth more efficiently than circuit-switched networks. The use of one over the other depends on organizational and individual needs rather than on technological superiority.

Of all the fast packet-switching technologies, cell relay is considered to be the future of high-speed networking. Unlike frame-relay networks, which move variable-sized information units, cell-switched networks move fixed-sized pieces of information called cells. The simplicity of cell switching lends itself to hardware implementation and hence to very high-speed switching. Cell relay combines some aspects of circuit and packet switching to produce networks with low latency and high throughput. Asynchronous Transfer Mode (ATM) and SMDS are currently the most prominent cell-switched technologies.

## 19.2 FRAME RELAY

In packet switching, packets are moved (switched) between the various network segments until the destination is reached. Frame relay uses variable-length packets for more efficient and flexible transfer than that offered by X.25, the older packet-switching technology. X.25 was developed at a time when network transmission facilities were more susceptible to noise and bit errors than modern digital networks are. As a consequence, X.25 includes a substantial overhead processing that is performed at each router in order to ensure that transmissions are error-free.

Frame relay cuts down on the protocol overhead contained in X.25's error-checking features, making it faster. Proponents of frame relay claim that X.25 was designed to cope with noisy analog links that needed a lot of error recovery, but that today's digital and fiber networks have far lower error rates, thus obviating the need for some of the error control procedures of X.25. If the node's processing time for every packet can be reduced, the individual packet's delay through the network can be reduced and the packet-processing capability of the node increased.

Frame relay works by transferring data using frame envelopes and can perform routing functions at the frame level. In contrast to X.25, there are neither error- nor flow-control functions (such as frame retransmission and acknowledgment). Frame relay packets, called frames, may contain a varying amount of data, which are arranged in eight-bit groups called octets. Each frame is variable in size and so may differ from any other (see Fig. 19.2).

**Number of Octets**

| 1 | 2 | Variable | 2 | 1 |
|---|---|---|---|---|
| Frame-begin flag | Address | Information | Frame check sequence (FCS) | Frame-end flag |

**Figure 19.2** Structure of a frame

Frame relay is a "connection-oriented" protocol. It establishes a logical connection for the duration of the transmission and it is implemented as a permanent virtual circuit (PVC) or leased line service. To enable PVC-type services, the frame contains a field acting as a logical channel identifier at frame level, called the data link connection identifier (DLCI), allowing permanent virtual circuits to be set up. This feature allows routing functions to be performed at the data link layer. For endpoints to communicate in a frame relay network, each origination and destination combination of pairs must be assigned and stored in the network databases setting up a permanent virtual circuit assignment. Based on these endpoint pairs and paths, originating routers activate the PVCs to "call" destination routers, using bandwidth only when data are sent.

The operation of frame relay is simple: Because the frame is likely to be correct, the router starts to pass on the frame as soon as the destination is known. In a frame relay network, a router may forward a frame immediately after receipt of the header that contains the destination address and the performance of six or so error-checking steps. This means that the node is forwarding some part of the frame while still receiving it, clearly streamlining the process. The problem with this approach is that when an error does occur, it cannot be detected by a router until the entire frame has been received. By the time the router knows about the error, most of the frame has already been forwarded on to the next router.

The solution is rather simple: The router that detects the error immediately aborts the transmission. When the abort indication arrives at downstream routers, they interrupt their transmission of this frame and eventually the frame disappears from the network. Even if the frame arrived at the destination computer, the abort does not cause irreparable damage; in either case, the original transmitter will resend the frame later when a higher protocol layer, IP in the Internet's case, so requests. In short, the frame relay network requires a little more time to recover from a bit error than a traditional packet network, but these errors will not occur frequently due to the quality of transmission.

Frame relay has two benefits:

1. *Speed.* It is no longer necessary to carry out error controls and corrections between each node due to the improvements in transmission media. As a result, frame relay offers fast switching capability, about five times faster than X.25, because the procedure has been considerably simplified. Result: Reduced processing time within the switches.

2. *Sharing costly bandwidth.* Frame relay allows users to share costly, high-throughput channels by allowing multiple communications links to operate over a single access line, and it uses a "hubbing" approach to distribute traffic over a wide area. Thus frame relay can reduce the number

of leased lines needed to support a network and in this way simplify the job of network management.

Frame relay has two drawbacks:

1. *No error correction.* Error correction is left to higher-level protocols such as TCP/IP. Erroneous frames are discarded, as there is no frame repetition within this procedure. In poor-quality physical links, service and performance can be affected.

2. *No congestion control.* Frame relay does not include a flow-control mechanism that reduces transmission windows on detecting congestion in the network. Instead, frame relay signals congestion problems by discarding the few frames that have caused the traffic congestion and leaves it to the higher-level protocol to retransmit the corresponding messages.

However, the lack of error correction may cease to be a problem. Physical links have benefited from enormous improvements in quality of service, both in optical fiber lines, which are not affected by interference, and also in copper lines due to advances in line repeater electronics. What is viewed as a drawback has proved to be an asset because end-to-end error correction, instead of internode correction, relieves the node switching software of error recovery activity, thus allowing much faster switching.

The main application of frame relay is the interconnection of LANs. Indeed, LAN users increasingly need long-distance communications. Users, accustomed to the short transit delays of the LAN, are demanding better WAN response times. Other uses are in high throughput applications such as medical CAD/CAM, where the common feature is the "bursty" character of the traffic. Frame relay can support this type of traffic, since it uses the bandwidth only when necessary while providing instantaneous high throughput. It allows optimal use of transmission media and provides high-quality services to existing applications, thus preserving the durability of current investments in local networks.

It should be noted that frame relay is not merely a temporary solution until cell relay is in general use. It will continue to be used in parallel with cell relay as a means of data distribution to remote subscriber interfaces, or to users who have retained their former equipment.

## 19.3 CELL RELAY

One of the most important trends in networking today is known as cell relay, cell switching, or cell networking. A well-known form of cell relay is

Asynchronous Transfer Mode (ATM), a switching technology for mixed voice and data networks.

The basic premise of cell relay is that all data should be transmitted in fixed-length packets, called cells. Traditionally, senders and receivers of data organized their data in packets with control information (header and trailer data) attached to them. To transmit packets over cell networks, a sender must break the incoming packet into small cell-sized chunks and transmit the cells over the network to the receiver, which must reassemble the data in the cells into a packet (see Fig. 19.3).

The cells are filled at the router by data packets that arrive in an asynchronous way, at irregular intervals, depending on the quantity of data sent by the application. At the receiving side, the cells are emptied of their data packets, which can then be taken over by an X.25 or frame relay module. These cells form a continuous flow of transport carriages that are filled as required. In this respect, the cell-switching technique belongs to the family of packet techniques. The switching function is realized in the hardware rather than the software, enabling rapid switching at rates in excess of 600 Mbps.

Why cells? Before delving into details of cell-relay, it is useful to see why cell-based networking is regarded as a more appropriate solution than ISDN or frame relay. ISDN is a circuit-based system of fixed bandwidths (e.g., 16-Kbps D channels, 64-Kbps B channels, and 384-Kbps to 1.920-Mbps H channels). Depending on the application, it generally results in the allocation of either too much or too little bandwidth. Too large a circuit means bandwidth is being wasted, and one too small means that transmission is sandwiched with other signals [GIGA94].

In short, because traffic moves in the form of digital pipes, the internal bandwidth of ISDN switches has to be an aggregate of all the connections to be fair (nonblocking). Thus 1000 10-Mbps connections would require a 10-Gbps bandwidth network.

Although frame relay allocates bandwidth more efficiently and is easier to build than an ISDN switch, it creates a problem known as serialization delay, or the time it takes to put packets onto the transport medium. Serialization delay is important for three reasons. First, in mixed-traffic networks (text, audio, and video packets), latency or packet delivery time is important to

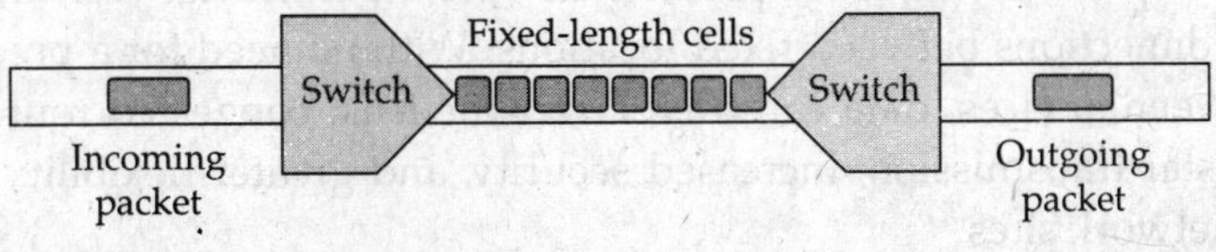


**Figure 19.3** Cell relay structure

ensure quality at the endpoints. If video packets are not sent quickly, picture quality suffers. Likewise with audio. For example, a 16-byte voice packet trapped behind a much larger data packet would suffer a delay equal to its own delay (the time taken on the circuit to deliver the complete packet) plus that of the larger data packet. It was found through research that having a small cell size minimizes delay. In short, the problem with the variable packet option is that traffic can suffer from random serialization delays due to packets of differing sizes.

In sum, circuit-switched ISDN is both inefficient and unscalable for broadband networking. Meanwhile, conventional packet switching, at fast packet switching speeds, cannot support isochronous applications (regularly scheduled deliveries), such as voice, without potentially introducing delays. The best solution, cell-based communications, allows for bounded delay times, efficient use of bandwidth, and the potential to build very fast hardware switching networks (or fabrics). The basic merits of cell networking are that cells are always the same size, take up only as much bandwidth as they need, and can be routed individually.

Cell relay is of two types: SMDS and ATM.

## 19.4 SWITCHED MULTIMEGABIT DATA SERVICE (SMDS)

Switched Multimegabit Data Service (SMDS) is a connectionless, high-speed, packet-switched data service. SMDS is used to interconnect distributed corporate LANs and WANs through the public telco networks. Because it is connectionless, SMDS eliminates the need for carrier switches to establish a call path between two points of data transmission.

SMDS uses the IEEE 802.6 protocol, which has developed as a metropolitan-area-network solution. The IEEE 802.6 standard is often described as a cell relay technology. The IEEE 802.6 packets, called cells, have a fixed size of 53 octets—48 octets for payload (user data) and five octets for address header (data that contain routing and other control information).

SMDS access devices pass 53-byte cells to a carrier switch. The switch reads addresses and forwards cells one by one over any available path to the desired endpoint. The benefit of this connectionless service is that it reduces the need for precise traffic flow predictions over the entire network and relies only on connections between fixed locations. With no need for a predefined path between devices, data can travel over the least congested routes, providing faster transmission, increased security, and greater flexibility to add or drop network sites.

SMDS defines a three-tiered architecture:

1. A switching infrastructure comprising SMDS-compatible switches
2. A delivery system made up of T-1 and T-3 circuits called subscriber network interfaces (SNIs)
3. An access-control system for users to connect to the switching infrastructure

Connecting a LAN to an SMDS network requires only a router and an SMDS-compatible network-interface card. The LANs connect to the SMDS carrier switch via a subscriber network interface (SNI) to a T-1 or T-3 circuit. A fractional T-3 circuit can be used to access intermediate-speed SMDS offerings. Interface guidelines enable the service to support the networking protocol architectures found in organizational networks such as Novell's IPX, AppleTalk, DECnet, SNA, and TCP/IP.

SMDS specifies connectionless, connection-oriented, and isochronous protocols. SMDS makes use of the connectionless capability, meaning it doesn't set up a logical, ongoing connection for the duration of the call. Instead of destination pairs and PVCs as in frame relay, only the service parameters (such as the address and billing arrangements) of each destination are input into the network. Without the need for call set-up or a permanent virtual circuit, the network routes each packet based on its address information. In small private networks (five to ten routers), this difference between SMDS and frame relay is not overly important, but in large networks serving many customers, it becomes crucial.

Networking can also involve broadcast or "multicast" communication—a message sent from one location to all or a predetermined group of other endpoints. Being connection-oriented, a frame relay network must replicate each packet once for every destination endpoint and deliver it on every virtual circuit path defined in the network. In contrast, because SMDS is connectionless, switches can be designed to include broadcast/multicast delivery as an integral part of their architecture, thus requiring little message replication.

The advantages of SMDS are clear. Consider a network with 5000 endpoints (obviously larger than most private LAN-to-LAN networks today, but modest for a shared telecom service). To add or "provision" one new endpoint where all 5000 existing endpoints must communicate with it, a frame relay network requires adding information for 5000 virtual circuit origination and destination pairs. However, adding this new endpoint to an SMDS network requires adding only the new endpoint parameters. If we consider the increased likelihood that in larger networks people, addresses, and endpoints will periodically move around and thus require reprovisioning, the difference in SMDS and frame relay administration can be significant.

Many think of SMDS as simply a transitional technology, to fill in the gap while the ATM technology was implemented. Today, it is clear that telcos are committed to an ATM-deployment approach, preparing the way for a transition.

## 19.5 ASYNCHRONOUS TRANSFER MODE (ATM)

ATM is a high-speed, connection-oriented, cell-based transmission scheme that offers bandwidth on demand for voice, data, and video telephony applications. It is currently being deployed by the world's public network service providers as the underlying switching technology for the next decade. ATM networks are being created to switch integrated voice, data, and video signals at multiples of 155 Mbps through multigigabit "hubbing devices"—ATM switches [ATMa95].

ATM builds on SMDS. Initially implemented on a subset of the IEEE 802.6 standards, SMDS is being migrated to an Asynchronous Transfer Mode (ATM) switching fabric as ATM matures and becomes widely deployed. ATM cells are 53-byte fixed cells. The 802.6 cell of SMDS is the same size and is similar in format. The alignment of SMDS's IEEE 802.6 cell and the ATM cell is important, because the SMDS networks can easily become components of the ATM networks.

ATM appears to be the future of high-speed networking for several business and technical reasons:

- The technology appears to make sense both from an application viewpoint (one pipe for everything) and from a technology viewpoint (fast transmission and switching).
- Many powerful players are making it happen—manufacturers, telcos, and big users.
- A remarkable amount of industry standardization has occurred at a very fast pace. This togetherness contrasts sharply with most new areas of telecommunications, such as ISDN, which remains a mess. Standardization means interoperability. XYZ's ATM equipment works with ABC's ATM applications without any problems.

- ATM equipment is becoming available for purchase and companies are deploying it widely. While ATM equipment is high speed, it is also very expensive by the box. But the cost is cheap by the byte—if large number of bytes are needed to move and switch quickly.

The ATM market is thriving and can be divided into five categories: (1) giant backbone switches for the Internet, telcos, and interexchange carriers; (2) medium to large switches for big private networks such as multinationals or for hubs into public networks; (3) smaller switches that are the centers of local work groups and which function like routers and hubs interconnecting LANs; (4) local access devices such as network adapter cards; and (5) ATM test equipment.

The telecoms are pushing ATM because they see it as a way to integrate all the traffic they might carry: voice, video, and data. One architecture would allow them to sell the equivalent of leased lines through software. On the corporate front, things seem a little clearer. The big benefit for corporate users is that the bandwidth at the ATM switch, even 25 Mbps, is available to each connected workstation enabling sophisticated applications.

In short, ATM offers a high-bandwidth service capable of carrying data, voice, and video over great distances. ATM can provide interfaces to transmission speeds ranging from 1 Mbps to 2.4 Gbps. It offers low latency, making it suitable for time-sensitive or isochronous services such as video and voice. In addition, it is protocol and distance-independent.

## Why All the Interest in ATM?

ATM was developed primarily to answer the need for variable bandwidth. If you think about ATM as a string of cells, each with some destination stamped onto its header, you can see several interesting possibilities. One is bandwidth allocation. If Mr. XYZ needs ten times as much bandwidth as Ms. ABC, then he is given ten times as many cells per unit of time. The idea is commonly known as bandwidth on-demand and is the key for emerging applications like video on-demand. For instance, video on-demand will not be continuous streams of data from the vendor to the customer. Instead, the vendor will download the movie to the set-top box in a large burst in fixed time intervals and so must have access to a network that provides bandwidth on-demand.

The reasons for the enormous interest in the ATM can be classified into several areas.

### Need for Equipment Interoperability

ATM has grown out of the need for a worldwide standard to allow interoperability of information, regardless of the end system or type of information. For instance, ATM is not based on a specific type of physical transport. In other words, ATM cells can be transported over twisted pair, coaxial, or fiber optic networks.

The goal of ATM is one international standard. The information systems and telecom industries are focusing and standardizing the different architectural elements that make up an ATM network. But, from the onset, ATM has been designed to be scalable and flexible in geographic distance, number of users, access, and trunk bandwidths (the speeds range from megabits to gigabits). In short, with ATM we are seeing a fast-moving technology being driven by international consensus, not by a single vendor's view or business strategy.

### Integrate Local and Wide Area Networks

ATM is the purported solution to the LAN–WAN integration quandary and the complex problem of multiple network management. Historically, separate information packaging and transport methods have been used for LANs versus WANs. This situation has added to the complexity of networking as corporate need for connectivity stretches from the LAN to metropolitan, national, and finally worldwide connectivity.

Companies are looking for an efficient and cost-effective method of integrating their dispersed multiprotocol LANs. Technologies such as frame relay and SMDS are vying as contenders. So far, none has been wholly successful. LAN technologies, with their ability to carry large amounts of data over limited distances, are inherently unsuitable in a geographically large network. WAN services, although able to efficiently carry voice and to a lesser extent data over long distances, offer limited bandwidth.

In short, ATM is evolving into a standard technology for local, campus backbone, and public and private wide area services. ATM promises to simplify network management by using the same technology for all levels of the network. As ATM continues to be deployed, the line between local and wide networks is expected to blur.

### Need for Data and Application Interoperability

Today, in most instances, separate networks are installed to carry voice, data and video information—mostly because these traffic types have different characteristics. For instance, data traffic usually travels on connectionless networks, because they tend to be "bursty"—not needing to communicate for an extended period of time and then needing to communicate large quantities of information quickly. Voice and video, on the other hand, tend to travel on connection-oriented networks because they are fairly constant in the amount of continuous information sent back and forth and are very sensitive to when and in what order the information arrives.

With ATM, separate networks will not be required. ATM aims to provide an architecture that serves all traffic types—voice, data, and video. ATM is one of the few international standards-based technologies designed from the beginning to accommodate the simultaneous transmission of data, voice, and video. Due to its high speed and the integration of traffic types, ATM expects to enable the interoperability of new applications.

### *Pricing and Priority*

ATM aims to provide a way to prioritize and price the transport of information. As each connection is established, the network allocates enough capacity to ensure that sufficient resources are available. To garner and preempt resources, the notion of priority becomes important.

To communicate information, the sender negotiates a "requested path" with the network for a connection to the destination. When setting up this connection, the sender specifies the type, speed, and other attributes of the call, which determine the end-to-end quality of service. An analogy for this negotiation of qualities would be similar to determining a method of delivery using the postal service. One can choose first-class, overnight, two-day delivery, or registered or certified mail.

One of the basic problems with ATM is pricing. In a system that provides bandwidth on-demand and that can carry all media, how should different types of information or data be priced? Pricing by the smallest denominator, the ATM cell, would require adjustment for the huge disparity in bandwidth requirements between, for example, voice telephony, video conferencing, and video on-demand. Variable rates for the length of the video conference would be feasible, but not for video on-demand. Customers would like to see a fixed price ($2.99) per movie rather than have to deal with variable prices depending on the length of the movie. Differentiating between types of information for pricing purposes is a tricky issue and has public policy implications such as subsidies for the poor.

## Types of ATM Traffic and Switching

Different types of connection-oriented traffic require different levels of service—referred to as QOS (quality of service). The types of QOS can be classified according to three characteristics: bandwidth, latency, and cell-delay variation. Bandwidth is the amount of network capacity required to support a connection. Latency is the amount of delay associated with a connection. Requesting low latency in the quality of service profile means that the cells need to travel quickly from one point in the network to another. Cell-delay variation is the range of the delays experienced by each group of associated cells. Low cell-delay variation means a group of cells must travel through the network without getting too far apart from one another.

An ATM network provides different QOS levels to different traffic types. ATM networks carry three types of traffic: constant bit rate (CBR), variable bit rate (VBR), and available bit rate (ABR) [ATMb95]:

- *Constant bit rate (CBR).* CBR traffic includes voice and video. To handle this traffic, the ATM network can act as a dedicated circuit. It provides a sustained amount of bandwidth, low latency, and low cell-delay variation.
- *Variable bit rate (VBR).* VBR traffic is handled similar to CBR except that the bandwidth requirement varies. An ATM network supporting a video conferencing application guarantees that a certain amount of bandwidth will always be available during a conference, but the actual bandwidth used can vary.
- *Available bit rate (ABR).* ABR traffic requires no specific bandwidth or delay parameters and is acceptable for many data applications. ABR connections support traffic such as e-mail and file transfers.

**ATM Switching.** *Switched-based* implies that ATM networks are connection-oriented, that cells move through the network on a route determined at call set-up. In this respect, ATM differs from traditional connectionless data networks, in which packets may be routed several different ways and thus can arrive out of order. Connection-oriented networks use a deterministic method to allocate resources. Deterministic is the opposite of probabilistic; it guarantees access regardless of the number of devices attached to the network. In other words, the network is determined to get you access.

ATM offers two circuit types, the switched virtual circuit (SVC) and the permanent virtual circuit (PVC). SVC's strong suit is that a network's bandwidth needs are negotiated before the circuit is established; the bandwidth is released when the circuit is no longer necessary. SVC is the basis of all modern telephony-based networking.

PVCs use a dedicated line and require the user to specify both committed information flows and data burst characteristics. PVC service providers commonly bill subscribers based on the number of PVCs and on the committed information rate (CIR) of each PVC, even if PVCs are idle some or most of the time. Even usage-based services include a provisioning fee and recurring charge for each PVC. Because PVC services require provisioning to all possible destinations, intermittent or sporadic communication between locations or entities may be penalized by PVC-based charges.

## ATM Cell Structure

ATM networks package traffic into cells of uniform length and manage the flow of these cells through the network. Using ATM, information to be sent is segmented into fixed length cells and transported to and reassembled at the destination. The fixed length allows the information to be transported in a predictable manner and so accommodates different traffic types on the same network.

Recall that in ATM, data associated with a service (i.e., telephone, television, data) are transferred in a sequence of fixed-length data units called cells. The ATM cell has a fixed length of 53 bytes. Each cell has a 5-byte header that manages the routing of the cell and an information field that can carry 48 bytes of payload data (see Fig. 19.4). The rate at which cells are generated is determined by the bandwidth available. Cells are transferred in a cell stream of fixed-bit rate.

In the absence of any traffic, a cell stream comprises only unassigned and possibly idle cells. Successive cells of the cell stream are sent without gaps. When service traffic is present, it occupies assigned cells, which are transferred in place of unassigned cells. Unassigned and idle cells have certain reserved header values and information field values.

The story behind the number of bytes in ATM cells, 53, is an interesting one. Initially, the computer networking experts wanted cells to carry a payload of 128 bytes and voice networking experts wanted smaller cell sizes—16 bytes. The networking group countered with 64, and the voice group responded with 32. Finally, they agreed to split the difference at 48 with an additional 5 bytes of header.

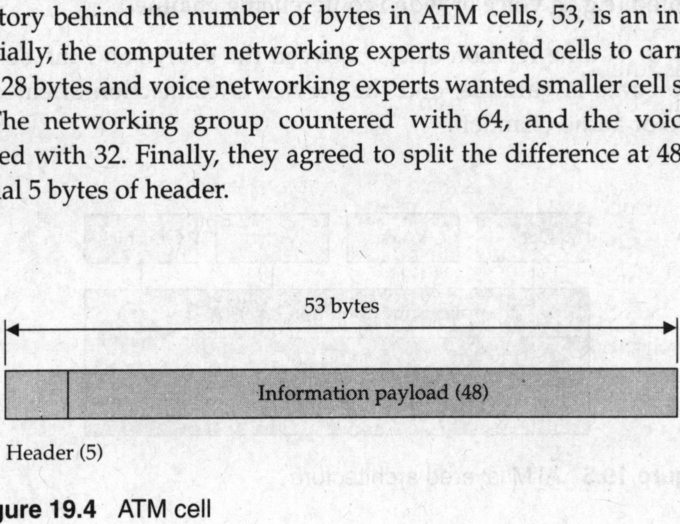


**Figure 19.4** ATM cell

## ATM System Architecture

ATM is a layered architecture allowing multiple services such as voice, data, and video to be mixed over the network. Three lower-level layers have been defined to implement the features of ATM (Fig. 19.5). The adaptation layer (AAL) assures the appropriate service characteristics and divides all types of data into the 48-byte payload that will make up the ATM cell. The ATM layer takes the data to be sent and adds the 5-byte header information that assures the cell is sent on the right connection. The ATM layer is equivalent to the data link layer of a TCP/IP protocol stack. The physical layer (PHY) defines the electrical characteristics and network interfaces. This layer "puts the bits on the wire." In general, ATM is not tied to a specific type of physical transport. Figure 19.6 shows another view of the layered architecture.

### *Application Adaptation (AAL) Layer*

The AAL defines some details of the ATM cell and how it is used and dictates how data are segmented into and reassembled from these cells. The purpose of the AAL is to provide a link between the services required by higher application layers and the generic ATM cells used by the ATM layer. Four service classes have been defined. The classification is performed according to three parameters: time relation between the source and the destination, constant or variable bit rate, and connection mode. The service classes follow:

1. *Class A.* A relation based on time exists between the source application and the destination, the bit rate is constant, and the service is connection-oriented (e.g., a voice or video conferencing channel).
2. *Class B.* A time relation exists between the source and the destination, the bit rate is variable, and the service is connection-oriented (e.g., a video or audio channel).

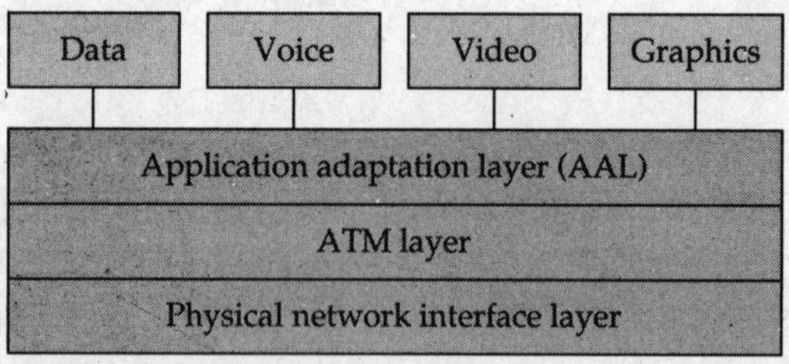


**Figure 19.5** ATM layered architecture

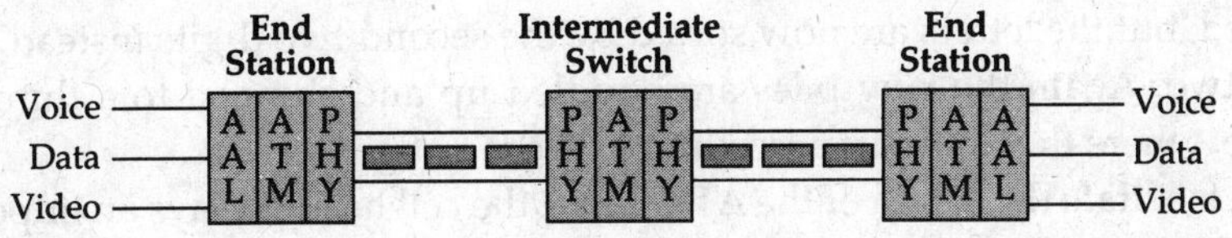


**Figure 19.6** Integrated ATM network

3. *Class C.* No time relation exists between the source and the destination, the bit rate is variable, and the service is connection-oriented (e.g., a connection-oriented file transfer).

4. *Class D.* No time relation exists between the source and the destination, the bit rate is variable, and the service is connectionless (e.g., LAN interconnection and electronic mail).

Four types of AAL protocol, types 1, 2, 3, and 4, support the four service classes defined. Types 3 and 4 have been merged into a single type (called AAL type 3/4), since the differences between them are minor. A fifth AAL type has also been proposed, due to the complexity of AAL type 3/4. The AAL type 5 protocol is sometimes called the simple and efficient adaptation layer (SEAL). Thus class A traffic will use the AAL type 1 protocol, class B traffic the AAL 2 protocol, and class C and D traffic either AAL 3/4 or AAL 5.

The AAL consists of a sublayer that provides cell segmentation and reassembly to interface to the ATM layer and also more service-specific functions to interface to the user services. The AAL also plays a key role in the internetworking of different networks and services.

### ATM Layer

An ATM layer takes the incoming frame, splits it open, and sorts all the ATM cells into groups according to where they are headed. Then on the output part of the cycle, it packages each group of ATM cells in a new physical transmission frame and sends it on its way. This all happens very fast, often in 1/8000 of a second.

A good analogy is the way postal mail is handled. You drop your letters in a mailbox. The postman comes along, collects them, and takes the bag of letters to the local post office. There, the clerk opens the bag and sorts all the letters by, say, the first two digits of the five-digit Zip Code. Eventually each pile of letters is bundled up, packed into a bag, and sent to another post office closer to the ultimate destination of those letters. There the process is repeated, but the letters are now sorted by the second two digits instead of the first two. Again the new piles are bundled up and shipped to a third post office, where the final sort according to the last digit occurs.

To facilitate the action of the ATM layer, the cell header plays an important role. In the case of ATM networks, the cell is broken into two main sections, the header and the payload. The payload (48 bytes) is the portion that carries the actual information—either voice, data, or video. The header (5 bytes) is the addressing mechanism.

The internal details of the ATM header, shown in Fig. 19.7, follows:

- *GFC (generic flow control).* Basically, this was put into the specification to support such things as the Metropolitan Area Network. By and large, it is not used, or it is used only to expand the VPI.
- *VPI (virtual path indicator).* This is a virtual path through the series of ATM switches an ATM cell has to follow. In many ways, it is the same as the virtual circuit number of X.25. The actual VPI changes from one node to the next, and the actual values are local to each ATM switch the virtual path traverses.
- *VCI (virtual channel indicator).* This is a bit more subtle than a virtual circuit. It is more like a lane number on the VPI roadway and usually remains the same from one ATM switch to the next. In fact, a number of VCIs are predefined. This field permits many channels of information to be concurrently transmitted over the same virtual path. Some of these channels are used for user data, and others are used for network control, much as the D channel in ISDN was used. However, there are a large number of OAM (overhead, administration, and maintenance) and control channels in ATM instead of just the one (i.e., the D channel) used in ISDN. They usually have preallocated VCIs.
- *PT (payload type).* These three bits define a number of features that help sort out the various OAM features in ATM. If the first is 0, the cell is carrying user data. If 1, the cell is carrying OAM—operations, administra-

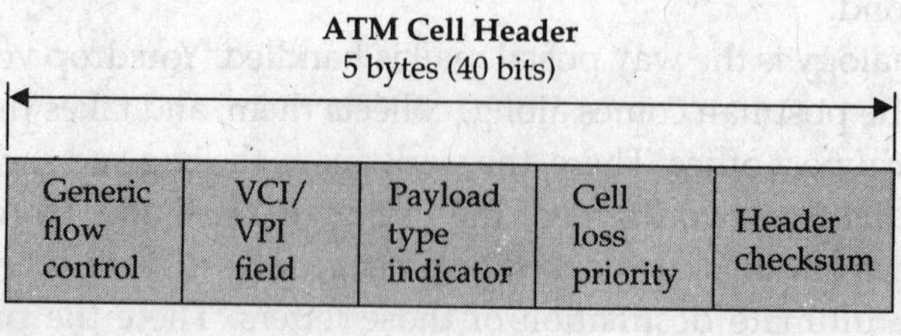


**Figure 19.7** ATM cell header structure

tion, or management data. For user cells, the second PLT bit is set if congestion was encountered by the cell in transit. The third PLT bit is reserved as a user signal.

- *CLP (cell loss priority).* Following PLT are two bits for CLP. The CLP bit set at 1 indicates that an ATM switch can discard the cell if the network is congested. If set to zero, then the ATM switches should not toss the cell, although they still might due to other circumstances. The network switch can set the CLP in cells sent above the rate agreed on at set-up time.
- *HEC (header error control).* This is the last byte in a 5-byte cell header is an 8-bit cyclic redundancy checksum (CRC) computed over the header.

Below this cell format is the physical frame structure in which ATM cells are transmitted. Above the cell format are higher layer ATM adaptation layers (AALs) that define how cells are collected to carry higher-layer protocols.

### Physical Layer

The ATM physical layer encodes and decodes the cell into the target electrical/optical waveforms for transmission and reception on the communication medium used. The physical layer also provides cell delineation functions, header error check (HEC) generation and processing, performance monitoring, and payload rate matching of the different transport formats used at this layer.

ATM does not have a specific physical layer associated with it and runs over Ethernet, Token Ring, copper fiber, and optical fiber. An ATM cell can also be packaged into various physical frames such as SONET/SDH, fiber channel, T-3 or DS-3, and T-1. Although a number of them may be repackaged by an intermediary in the conversion from a DS-3 transmission frame to an OC-3C transmission frame, the individual cell is not changed.

This feature is very efficient because an ATM cell can start off on a relatively low-speed interface and travel through a double pair of twisted wires to a local hub. There it can be easily inserted into a high-speed fiber optic system and shoved out on the Information Superhighway for a trip anywhere in the world. The trade-off associated with traveling across multiple networks is that the cell must be repackaged at every media change—and that is overhead which results in delay.

Today, many ATM physical media have been defined by the ATM Forum. One of the most prominent is the SONET/SDH. Here the ATM cells are herded into a SONET/SDH transmission frame and are shipped in bulk. It is potentially the highest bandwidth media because OC-48 (STM-16 in Europe) is rated at over 2.4 gigabits per second. However, for now, ATM over SONET/SDH is limited to OC-3C, or 155 megabits per second.

Technically, the physical layer can be divided into three functional levels: transmission path, digital section, and regenerator section (see Fig. 19.8). The *transmission path* level extends between switching elements that assemble and disassemble the transmission system's payload. For end-to-end communication, the payload is end-user information. For communication involving voice or video dial tone, the payload may be call-control signaling information (call set-up and termination). Cell delineation and header error-control functions are required at each transmission path's endpoints.

The *digital section* level extends between switching elements that assemble and disassemble a continuous information stream. This refers to the exchange, or signal transfer, points in a network that are involved in switching data streams. The *regenerator section* level is a repeater portion of the digital section. An example is a repeater used to regenerate the signal along a transmission path that is too distant to be used without signal regeneration.

## Sending Computer Data via ATM

The question addressed here is: How does data gets from sender through ATM and into the recipient's system? This is done in several steps. The example we'll use is a TCP/IP transmission. The sender's application program tells the TCP/IP stack that the program wishes to send data out on the network. TCP accepts the incoming data, and IP sends the frame of user data wrapped up in a TCP and IP headers to the ATM driver (see Fig. 19.9). The entire package of encapsulated user data is usually referred to as a packet or a frame. We'll use the term *frame*.

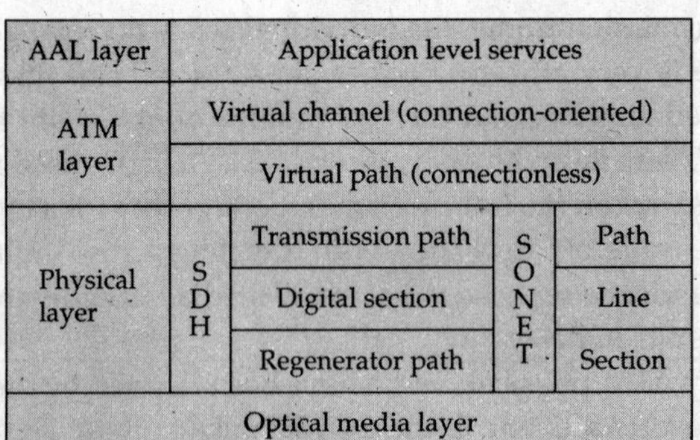


**Figure 19.8** Integrated B-ISDN transport layered model

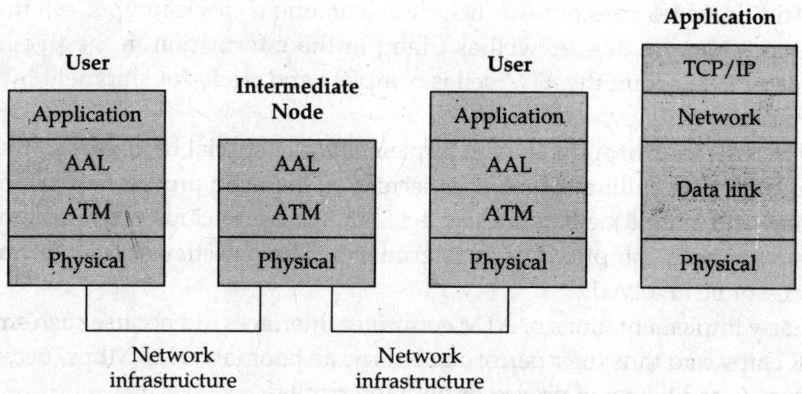


**Figure 19.9** ATM layers for application services

These encapsulated frames are about 64 Kbytes long when delivered to the ATM layer. In ATM terminology, the layer of ATM that first sees the frame is called the convergence sublayer. All it really does is to add its own header and trailer so that the overall appearance of the frame looks something like a well-wrapped parcel with the ATM layer, the IP layer, the TCP, and finally the user's actual data being layered from the outside to the center.

```
| ATM Header | IP Header | TCP Header | Payload Data | TCP
  Trailer | IP Trailer | ATM Trailer |
```

In the case of ATM, the actual format of the header and trailer information varies according to AAL type. In the case of ATM AAL type 5, the trailer information for the frame includes a 32-bit code for error detection, which covers the entire data frame.

In short, the convergence sublayer wraps whatever it is given by higher layers in a header and trailer so that the receiving system can determine whether there were any transmission errors. In the case of AAL type 5, this also includes the calculation of a 32-bit checksum, which is almost exactly the same function found in the code that handles the encapsulation of packets.

The next stop down the chain is the segmentation and reassembly layer of ATM. This layer of ATM is usually handled in special hardware for a number of reasons. Generally, the functions of this level are to slice and dice the ATM frame delivered by the convergence sublayer into neat little 48-byte cells. It also does the reverse procedure, gluing a large number of ATM cells back into an ATM frame. For these reasons, this layer of ATM is called segmentation and reassembly (SAR).

Additional features of SAR include calculating a checksum per cell in the case of AAL type 3/4, as well as filling in the information in the five-byte header. At this point the ATM cell is complete and ready for shipment by the physical layer.

The SAR level of ATM is often implemented in special hardware so that it does not create millions of calls per second on the main processor. This activity can and should be handled by the SAR hardware chips. Only when the frame has been completed or is determined to be defective should the main processor be involved.

Early implementations of ATM computer interfaces did not use such smart SAR chips, and thus their performance is quite poor (about 20 Mbps) because they overload the main processor with interrupts.

Today, a lot of research is being done on developing better techniques for segmentation and reassembly.

## Managing the ATM Connection

Different traffic types may call for different traffic management techniques. When a high-speed network is moving huge numbers of small cells through the network, traffic control is essential. This is especially vital in a network that implements ATM, in which connections for each call may be routed through any number of intermediate switches. Each switch must be able to handle all pass-through traffic.

The ATM switching process works as follows. The ATM end station (the calling party) asks the ATM network for a connection to another ATM end station (the destination) by initiating a connection request that leads to a negotiation with the ATM network. This process is called the connection establishment procedure. The parameters that must be negotiated are specified by the ATM Forum UNI (User-to-Network Interface) 3.0 standard and include traffic type, sustained and peak bandwidth, burst length, and QOS class.

This process secures a "contract" between the ATM network and the end station. The network promises to deliver a QOS, and the ATM end station promises not to send more traffic than it requested during the connection procedure. Such contracts must be enforced, and it is the job of traffic management functions to ensure that users receive the QOS they were guaranteed.

When congestion occurs, traffic management provides the mechanisms that allow the network to recover. ATM networks use three techniques: traffic policing, traffic shaping, and congestion control.

### Traffic Policing

ATM networks ensure that traffic on each connection remains within the negotiated parameters. ATM switches use a "leaky-bucket" algorithm to police traffic. Imagine a wooden bucket with a hole in the bottom. Water leaks (traffic flows) out of a bucket (buffer) at a constant rate (the negotiated rate), regardless of how fast it comes in. The need for police action occurs when traffic flow exceeds the negotiated rate and the buffer overflows.

Each ATM cell header has a CLP (cell loss priority) bit used to identify cells as either conforming (to the contract) or nonconforming. If cells are nonconforming—for example, more cells than the contract allows—the ATM switch sets the CLP bit to one. This cell can now be transferred through the network only if there is sufficient network capacity. If not enough bandwidth is available, the nonconforming cell is discarded and may need to be retransmitted.

CBR traffic needs a single leaky bucket because it uses a sustained-rate parameter in its network contract. VBR traffic uses dual leaky buckets to monitor both the sustained rate over a discrete time period and the maximum (peak) bandwidth used during the connection. If either value exceeds the contract parameters, the ATM switch polices the VBR traffic by manipulating the CLP bit.

### Traffic Shaping

Similar to traffic policing, traffic shaping is performed at the user-network interface. Traffic is manipulated so that flow rates obey the contract using a mechanism such as the dual-leaky-buckets algorithm. Devices that implement traffic shaping are typically ATM network adapters in PCs or workstations, hubs, bridges, routers, and DSUs (digital service units).

### Congestion Control

Congestion can occur in any network, whether it uses shared media or ATM, whenever an application sends more data than the network can transmit with the available bandwidth. Also, as more applications send data over the same network, the bandwidth available to any one application changes over time. Most networks fail to tell applications how much bandwidth is available at any given instant. As a result, applications have no basis on which to control the amount of data they send. When applications send more data than the network can handle, the network buffers fill up and can overflow. The application must then retransmit the data, which adds more traffic and further congests the network. An ATM network performs congestion control so that ABR traffic can efficiently use the bandwidth that has not been guaranteed to CBR and VBR traffic. Effective congestion control reduces the need to retransmit data due to congestion.

Congestion problems occur when the input rate of traffic into a switch exceeds that switch's available link capacity. Long-duration congestion is not necessarily a function of switch design; it just might be better handled with improved network design or increases in overall network capacity. Short-duration congestion can often be alleviated simply by configuring the switch to buffer inbound data.

While the problem of congestion control is still under discussion in the ATM community, it is expected that the final solution will use a variety of techniques, including end-to-end, link-by-link, rate-based, and credit-based traffic-flow control.

- *End-to-end*. A network can control congestion over an entire connection path or by sublinks. With end-to-end control, the network measures the minimum available bandwidth along the connection and communicates the amount of bandwidth to the application, which then transmits at the appropriate rate. Each link in the network simply forwards the data as fast as it receives it.

- *Link-by-link*. Under the link-to-link technique, each link along the network connection controls its traffic flow independently. Each link buffers data as needed to adjust the incoming speed to the outgoing speed.
- *Rate-based*. The rate-based traffic-flow technique constantly tells the application what transmission rate (the currently allowed rate) the sending device should use. For example, the network can tell an application that it can send 1000 cells per second. If the network becomes congested, it reduces this rate and notifies the application; when the network is no longer congested, the rate is increased. Technically speaking, the rate-based scheme provides end-to-end control using feedback mechanism. The switch monitors the congestion in the network by way of these feedback methods and, when a lot of traffic is detected, adjusts the data rate until the problem goes away.
- *Credit-based*. The credit-based technique is slightly different. Here, the network indicates to the sending device the amount of buffer space (credits) available in the network. For example, the application may be allowed to transmit 100 cells, after which it must wait. The network periodically replenishes the application's credits. If the network becomes congested, the application gets fewer credits and they're replenished less often. This forces the application to slow the sending of data. When the congestion

clears, the number of credits is increased and replenished fast enough that the application can transmit at full speed.

Technically speaking, the credit-based scheme requires flow control on a per-link, per-virtual connection (VC) basis. Each link has a sender node and a receiver node that maintain a separate queue for each VC. The receiver determines the number of cells the sender can transmit by monitoring the queues on each VC, then issues a "credit" that determines how much data the sender can transmit.

The credit-based approach allows for zero cell loss, while the rate-based approach requires that the switch be capable of sufficient buffering to prevent cell loss. The demand for a queue per VC in the credit-based approach requires additional management complexity and cost.

An integrated proposal is currently under consideration that provides for an end-to-end, rate-based scheme as the default method, with the link-by-link scheme as an option where more precise control is needed. When a connection is made from an end-to-end device, the link-by-link device would simply perform the end-to-end flow control when talking to that device. This would preserve existing equipment, while providing for future growth.

ATM channels are set up between users exchanging cells with their network. Thereafter, users send their varied data intermixed as a series of cells. The network carries the cells hop by hop through the switches set up to carry them to their destinations. ATM assumes cells will be carried quickly, in order, and with very few errors.

## ATM Switches

Providing connectivity through an ATM switch (instead of a shared bus) offers several benefits: dedicated bandwidth per connection, higher aggregate bandwidth, well-defined connection procedures, and flexible access speeds. An ATM switch must have a number of key features to make broadband networks feasible:

- ATM switches should be nonblocking in design to allow time-sensitive traffic like audio and video. A blocking switch wipes out the benefit of using small cell sizes to avoid serialization delay.
- Cell loss must be avoided even under the heaviest traffic conditions. As every cell is part of a much larger message, the loss of a single cell, say, from an IP packet, will have an effect on network congestion and necessitate retransmission of the entire packet.

- Switches need to support multicasting essential components of video on-demand services. For instance, if 100 viewers are watching the same movie, it may be more efficient to multicast the signal to all 100 viewers rather than to set up 100 virtual channels to carry the same signal. This technique could be used to offer staggered viewing times of a small selection of films.
- Routing software and network signaling protocols should allow easy and reliable call set-up. Widespread use of ATM will require that thousands of connections be set up across networks and reestablished seamlessly through multivendor platforms in case of network link failure.

ATM switches and network routers relay information in different ways. Switches forward information without knowledge of the overall path from host to host. Routers, unlike switches, understand the network-layer protocols used between the hosts.

Routers attempt to meet user needs by providing intelligent path selection and security. Switches have no understanding of the network layer protocol(s) used by the hosts. Take for instance, telephone switches. In a long-distance call the intermediate switch simply forwards the message from country A to country B. It does not do any extra processing in between. Another computer related example is a long-distance video conference. An intermediate switch will have to relay video frames from point A to point B as fast as possible. Otherwise, the audio/video synchronization will be affected and quality will be reduced.

ATM switching is an exciting area that is undergoing phenomenal changes as new developments are occuring constantly.

## 19.6 SUMMARY

In this chapter, we examined some of the emerging telecommunications services including SONET, frame relay, Switched Multimegabit Data Service, ISDN, Broadband ISDN, and Asynchronous Transfer Mode, ATM. Some of these services are currently being defined by standards committees, developed as products, and tested in trials around the world. The service that is expected to have the most impact is cell relay.

Cell relay, incorporating both SMDS and ATM, is similar in concept to frame relay. In addition to technical likenesses, cell relay and frame relay have similar histories. Frame relay was developed as part of the work of ISDN but is now finding wide application in private networks and other non-ISDN applications, particularly in bridges and routers. Cell relay was

**Table 19.2** Comparing Fast Packet Switching Technologies

| | *Frame Relay* | *SMDS* | *ATM* |
|---|---|---|---|
| Type of Data Service | Connection oriented | Connectionless | Connection-oriented or connectionless |
| Access Speeds | 9.6 Kbps to 34 Mbps | T-1 to 155 Mbps | T1-2.4 Gbps |
| Standards | CCITT/ANSI | Bellcore specification | CCITT/ANSI under the ATM forum |
| Packet Size | Variable | Fixed cell (53 bytes) | Fixed-cell (53 bytes) |

developed as part of the work in broadband ISDN but is beginning to find application in non-ISDN environments that require very high data rates. Both frame relay and cell relay take advantage of the reliability and fidelity of modern digital lines to provide faster packet switching than X.25. But cell relay has even more streamlined functionality and can support data rates several orders of magnitude greater than frame relay. Table 19.2 summarizes the various features of these services.

Clearly, the future lies in a high-speed network that not only brings voice, data, images, and video to the desktop but also has minimal delays (latencies) of no more than a few milliseconds. Now imagine this network stretching across the continent—with no appreciable increase in latency end to end. This scenario is not futuristic but is happening right now with fast packet switching networks—frame and cell relay—technologies that promise to be the fundamental building blocks for high-speed networks.

# Chapter 20

# Mobile and Wireless Computing Fundamentals

Mobile computing means different things to different people. It goes by many names—nomadic, tetherless, ubiquitous, wireless, and remote computing. Whatever the term used, mobile computing has become a key topic in electronic commerce as the size, cost, and power requirements of equipment goes down. Furthermore, services for the mobile user are maturing rapidly and are poised to change the nature and scope of communication. The key feature of the mobile computing environment is that the user need not maintain a fixed position in the network. This feature allows access to personal or business information for persons who travel away from their primary workplace.

It should be noted that the terms *wireless* and *mobile* are not synonymous. Wireless is a transmission or information transport method that enables mobile computing. It covers many approaches to communications without wires. Take, for instance, wide area cellular systems, which promise to make integrated networks a reality. The goal of wireless is to enable distributed and mobile computing, thus bringing an end to the tyranny of geography.

Growth in several market segments of wireless communications has been explosive and has stimulated activity in all the related areas including technical, regulatory, security, legal, and business. This revolution is bringing fundamental changes to telecommunication and computing, integral parts of electronic commerce.

Mobile computing, on the other hand, focuses on the applications side. It builds on the concept of being able to compute no matter where the user is. Once users begin to think about mobile computing for the local and wide area network environment, they must consider specific issues, including what type of transport service to utilize. Choices for mobile computing include infrared, cellular, packet radio services, microwave, or some type of satellite service.

The goal of mobile computing is to work toward true computing freedom (free from the tyranny of location) whereby users can connect to the network from anywhere, anytime—and operate as if they were sitting in the "home" office. For instance, consider the following scenarios:

> A salesman from the field accesses the corporate server with the mobile computing device to find out the production schedule and manufacturing lead times for a product. The ability to communicate from the field eliminates the need to go on site to find the information. The user can dial in for the information from wherever he is, in the field office or at a client's office.
>
> A business professional is working on a project with a colleague who is traveling across the country. A short time after making some crucial edits to the new product design, she plugs in the laptop, hits a few keys, and sends the updated version. This is true team computing that provides the most current data—no matter what the location is.

Mobile users will be consumers as well as producers of data. The employee in the field could be initiating production activity by taking orders and performing the order entry role. This fits nicely with the current business demands of reduced cycle times and flexibility.

A worker is an ideal candidate for mobile computing if he or she fits any of the following profiles: needs to send and receive e-mail while on the road; needs constant access to the office's internal bulletin-board system while on the road; needs real-time access to software applications such as corporate databases; moves continually from one floor to another but always in the same building; or is constantly on the road and needs a fast way to update the desktop when back at the office. These profiles have different requirements concerning technology, equipment, and software applications.

What gets lost in the discussion of mobile computing is how complex the mobile environment is. For instance, there are a number of ways to build wireless data networks, and each approach relies on different products and is ideal for a specific subset of applications. Some schemes are most appropriate for paging and one-way data broadcasts; still others are designed for short, bursty messaging rather than sustained file transfers. The wireless network that lets salespeople clinch a deal in the field may not be the best one for roving support personnel.

In sum, mobile computing requires new ways of thinking about networks and information management because of two trends: need for increased mobility and location independent data management. To understand the mobile computing issues better, a framework is necessary that succinctly analyzes the various dimensions.

## 20.1 MOBILE COMPUTING FRAMEWORK

Mobile computing is expanding in four dimensions:

1. *Wireless delivery technology and switching methods.* These deal with the rapidly expanding delivery technology of cellular, radio, paging, satellite, and wireless LAN communications and promise to furnish information to mobile users anywhere at anytime.

2. *Mobile information access devices.* In addition to the changing delivery technology, we are seeing an explosion in the variety of access equipment ranging from large units—laptops, notebooks, and other portable computers with large memories and powerful processors—to hand-helds or palmtops—personal digital assistants or personal communicators that run on AA batteries and often have no memory storage capability.

3. *Mobile data internetworking standards and equipment.* Voice-oriented cellular systems were not designed with data transmission in mind. The weak connections, frequent noise, and momentary dropouts that cellular phone users routinely experience as users move from one cell to another or encounter physical obstructions such as bridges and tunnels are an inconvenience for voice calls. But these same pitfalls can easily corrupt data calls. Add to this the problem of insufficient capacity in terms of the number of available frequencies. To solve these problems, work is being done in the area of digital cellular standards that support data communications over cellular lines.

4. *Mobile computing-based business applications.* Mobility and portability are creating an entire new class of applications and new markets, combining personal computing and consumer electronics. A number of vertical, niche applications of mobile computing are already available, including vehicle dispatch and routing, inventory and package tracking, and retail point of sale. Organizational applications are not widespread yet, but two types of applications most frequently mentioned include mail-enabled applications and information or data services to mobile users.

We will use these dimensions for structuring the rest of the discussion in this chapter.

## 20.2 WIRELESS DELIVERY TECHNOLOGY AND SWITCHING METHODS

Wireless communications are evolving in several directions. In virtually all these cases, evolution has proceeded from analog systems to digital systems having more versatility and capacity. The many approaches seen in wireless industry evolution are aimed at different consumer needs, yet a number of underlying technical concepts are common to the different activities. Network managers need to understand the technology alternatives, since they're the ones who have to evaluate wireless equipment and services and match them to their company's specific profiles. They must use the technology to accomplish the broad objective of giving mobile users the freedom to access people and information without being tethered to a wire.

In short, the wireless industry has become very complicated to understand as it splits into a number of subsets. Before the best wireless method can be chosen, it's important to understand how they differ. These methods include radio-based (land-based wireless systems and satellite-based wireless systems) and light-based wireless systems.

### Radio-Based Systems

Wireless communications services—radio, cellular, satellite, and paging—involve radio frequency (RF) signals that travel over frequencies from 100 KHz to 20 GHz (see Table 20.1). Most wireless data services are based on RF transmission in the 800-to-900 MHz range. RF signals come in two flavors: local area RF and wide area RF. Local area RF signals range from 902 to 908

**Table 20.1 Frequency Ranges and Band Classifications**

| *Name of Frequency Band* | *Frequency Range* |
|---|---|
| Very low frequency (VLF) | <30 KHz |
| Low frequency (LF) | 30 KHz–300 KHz |
| Medium frequency (MF) | 300 KHz–3 MHz |
| High frequency (HF) | 3 MHz–30 MHz |
| Very high frequency (VHF) | 30 MHz–300 MHz |
| Ultra high frequency (UHF) | 300 MHz–3 GHz |
| Super high frequency (SHF) | 3 GHz–30 GHz |

MHz and from 2400 to 2483 MHz. Wide area RF signals are broadcast at about 940 MHz, the same range in which narrowband Personal Communications Services (PCS) are licensed to operate (see Section 20.7).

RF communications are of three types: one-way, two-way, and local. One-way RF transmits a signal that covers up to 10 miles. Digital pagers, for example, rely on this technology. Two-way RF uses transceivers to send and receive data and typically covers six miles. Local area RF has a maximum range of a quarter-mile. Typically, local area RF equipment operates in the industrial, scientific, and medical (ISM) bands, which are the radio frequencies that don't require a broadcasting license; such equipment must nevertheless heed the power and bandwidth restrictions enforced by the government. The average range for local area RF equipment is from 30 feet to about 100 yards, though some equipment can reach 600 feet to one quarter-mile (1300 feet).

Radio-based services can be grouped into two main categories: *land-based*, cellular communications, packet data networks, and specialized mobile radio (SMR); and *satellite-based*, paging systems and very small aperture satellites.

Land-based radio systems send and receive data using low-power transmitters and receivers. These systems include private packet networks, circuit-switched cellular services, packet-over-cellular technology, and several schemes being deployed as wireless WANs, including spread-spectrum and trunk radio. On the other hand, recent technological advances have resulted in a series of satellite-based networks, some optimized for data networking applications and others enabling the expansion of voice networks into areas lacking a basic telecommunications infrastructure.

## Cellular Communications

Cellular radio was originally targeted at vehicular subscribers in urban areas. Today, the industry is moving simultaneously in three directions:

1. *Increasing capability and widespread coverage for cordless telephones.* Cellular technology is evolving toward taller base station antennas and larger cells to provide economical coverage of sparsely populated areas. The extreme case of this large cell evolution is the development of satellite systems.

2. *Decreasing cell size (microcells) and power levels for hand-held and vehicular cellular radio.* Cellular cells are also moving toward smaller cells having low base station antennas, or even antennas within buildings to provide higher overall capacity and to provide better coverage to the lower power cellular pocket phones that are now in increasingly widespread usage.

Cordless telephones have evolved from primarily home usage, then free roaming (e.g., car phones) applications toward widespread "universal" low power systems aimed at pedestrians, exemplified by the Personal Communications Systems (PCS).

3. *Specialized wireless data systems.* Specialized systems are also emerging although they are not yet as prominent as wireless telephony. These data-oriented wireless systems are also emerging through cellular packet data systems and smaller area coverage: High-data-rate wireless LANs using infra-red and radio technology.

In cellular systems, the areas of coverage are divided into hexagonal cells that overlap at the outer boundaries (see Fig. 20.1). Communication takes place through a grid of transmitters and receivers (transceivers), each one called a cell. A signal from a cellular handset is handled by the nearest cell, which passes the signal along normal telephone lines. The average cell is 2–10 miles across, with actual size depending on the number of users in the cell. The greater the number of users, the closer the transmitters and hence a reduction in cell size.

Frequencies are divided into cell bands with a buffer zone to prevent interference or jamming of neighboring cells' frequencies. As a cellular device, such as a portable phone, moves from one spot to another, the signal may drop off momentarily due to movement from the area covered by one cell into the area covered by a different cell. This process is called a *handoff*. As a cellular device moves into the range of a new cell, its signal is picked up by another transceiver. Usually this is the cell base nearest the device; however, if a signal is blocked, a cell base farther from the device is used (see Fig. 20.2).

Cellular communication requires careful monitoring and switching of calls from cell to cell as the user moves between them. Without dynamic switching to facilitate a smooth transition (or handoff), the calls would be ter-

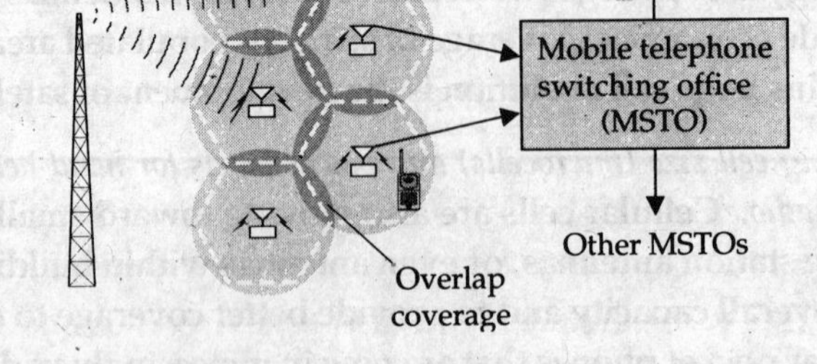


**Figure 20.1** Cell structure with radio transceivers

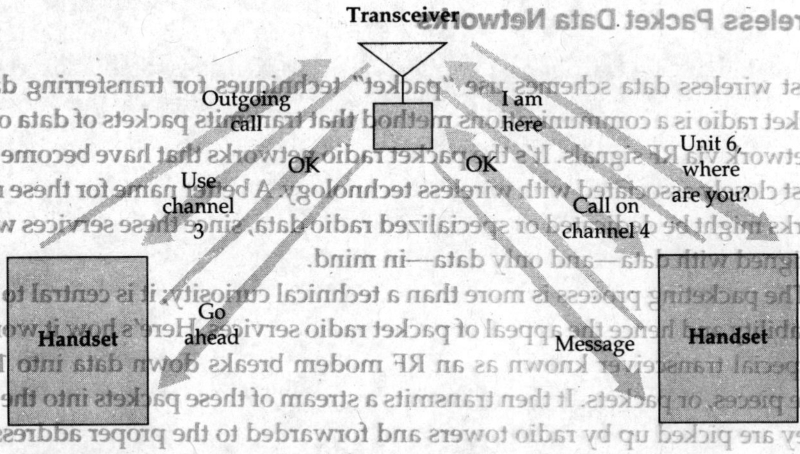


**Figure 20.2** Outgoing and incoming call handshake between transceiver and handset

minated as the user crosses the boundary of a cell. Here's how the cellular communications process works:

1. *Log-on.* Each cellular handset is assigned a unique identity or numeric arrangement module (NAM). This identity is based on its home area. Messages are often sent to the handset through separate control channels to verify that it is operating within the home area. Handsets operating outside the home area have to reregister by informing the control unit of its location. As the mobile unit moves across cells, it must continuously send messages to the mobile telephone switching office (MTSO) to confirm its location so that new calls can be directed to that traffic area.
2. *Monitoring.* Once the handset is powered on, it monitors the control channels to get information on local paging channels. It selects an available channel and goes into an idle state. In the idle state it listens to the data being transmitted over that channel.
3. *Incoming calls.* When an incoming call is received by the MTSO, it sends a signal to all the cells in that traffic area. The set receives the signal and responds to the MTSO. The MTSO will inform the set to use a specific channel to receive the call, and the set will retune itself to the new frequency.
4. *Outgoing calls.* To make a call, the user enters the telephone number and transmits it to the MTSO by an available access channel. The MTSO either agrees to the handset request or asks the set to change frequency to another available channel.

## Wireless Packet Data Networks

Most wireless data schemes use "packet" techniques for transferring data. Packet radio is a communications method that transmits packets of data over a network via RF signals. It's the packet radio networks that have become the most closely associated with wireless technology. A better name for these networks might be dedicated or specialized radio data, since these services were designed with data—and only data—in mind.

The packeting process is more than a technical curiosity; it is central to the reliability and hence the appeal of packet radio services. Here's how it works: A special transceiver known as an RF modem breaks down data into 128-byte pieces, or packets. It then transmits a stream of these packets into the air. They are picked up by radio towers and forwarded to the proper addressee. Each packet is numbered, so that the message can be reassembled at the receiving end. If a packet is not received in good condition, the receiving service automatically asks the sending modem to resend the missing or corrupted packet while continuing to receive other packets. That way, accuracy is ensured but error correction does not hold up transmission.

Packet radio technology has the following advantages. The frequencies are less susceptible to interference and noise than cellular signals. Transmission costs are based on data packets, not connect time. And there are no roaming charges. Transmissions are digitally encoded for greater security than cellular communications offer.

Packet radio has disadvantages as well. Communication is slow. Because all users share bandwidth over a particular network, throughput is often less than 2400 bps. Radio modems can be used only with electronic-mail applications; there is no fax capability. In addition, radio modems are expensive and rather bulky; for instance, the Intel Wireless Modem is the size of a brick. Batteries are good for 2 hours of use and can take up to 12 hours to recharge.

Two major packet providers in the United States are Ardis and RAM Mobile Data. These companies own and operate their own networks, licensing frequencies from the FCC and selling subscriptions to users. Both are nationwide, two-way data services used primarily to exchange e-mail messages and short- to medium-length files. These packet services parcel data bits into specific-byte-length packets before sending them off into the airwaves at radio frequencies.

How are packet networks organized? The RAM Mobile Data Network, for instance, divides metropolitan areas into cells. Within each cell is a base station—a radio tower capable of sending and receiving data packets. The base station receives and routes e-mail to other mobile users, or dispatches it to the local switch. The message travels from the switch to a regional or national switch, then to a base station near the receiving radio modem. From that base station, the packets are transmitted to the receiving modem.

Both networks stretch across the country, covering all the major metro areas and more than 80 percent of the population. In addition, RAM Mobile Data automatically locates the user as he or she travels from one transmitter area to another, so the user need not reregister location while in motion. These networks can store messages sent to the users while they are out of range and then forward them later.

Indeed, the mere fact that Ardis and RAM Mobile Data exist and work dependably—in a world that currently speaks about wireless data services in the future tense—is their most appealing feature. And the price of subscribing to these networks is already falling in anticipation of more competition in this budding market. To provide a rough estimate of costs, service plans start as low as $25, and one often can get unlimited messaging for less than $100 a month. But connection requires an RF modem—and that isn't cheap.

## Satellite Networks

Satellite networks allow global communications and serve thousands of locations all over the world. While it's possible to develop an equivalent land-based network using leased lines, local telephone company facilities, and/or public data networks, the logistics of constructing, managing, and maintaining such a network can become a nightmare. For this reason, companies large and small are using satellite communication as a cost-effective solution to the problem of sending data around the world—or even around the block. Satellite networks are ideal for broadcast applications, such as paging, cable TV, news wires, and stock tickers.

Satellite networks are useful in any situation where data need to be dispersed to, or gathered from, many remote nodes, and where end-to-end delay is not a primary concern. The station at the receiving end need only have a very inexpensive, receive-only dish pointed at the right place in the sky. Two-way satellite links are also an excellent choice when many remote sites need to report in to a central database—for instance, when each store in a large chain needs to send accounting data to headquarters at regular intervals. Airline reservation systems, ticket outlets, and other transaction-oriented services are also prime candidates for satellite links.

Satellite communications are reliable. There are no cables that can be dug up or destroyed by fire, flood, earthquakes, or other natural disasters, and a solar-powered satellite is highly unlikely to quit due to a power failure. Finally, systems that must reach remote areas with poor or nonexistent phone service, or uncooperative phone companies, may be feasible only if satellites are used. However, satellite networks are a poor choice for systems that require a high degree of security. Any signal that passes through a satellite may be broadcast to an area as large as 5000 miles [BG89]. For security purposes, signals have to be encrypted.

How do satellite networks work? Think of a satellite as a microwave relay station mounted on a very long pole. Each satellite receives signals on a particular frequency (or set of frequencies), amplifies them, and retransmits them on another frequency. The length of the link poses problems. Suppose that radio signals were able to travel in and out of the atmosphere at the speed of light in a vacuum, and that the round trip was only around 44,000 miles. The delay to get from one ground station to another would be 44,000 miles divided by 186,000 miles per second, or nearly a quarter of a second. Allow another quarter of a second for an acknowledgment, and we have a half-second to 1-second round-trip delay. Clearly, this is too slow for an interactive service. The software must be aware of, and adapt to, the long delay in the link. (A file transfer protocol such as Xmodem, which "times out" if there's even a one-second delay in the wrong place, will undoubtedly fail over such a network.)

For discussion purposes, we can divide satellite networks into very small aperture terminals (VSATs) and paging networks.

### Very Small Aperture Terminals (VSATs)

The two ground stations that communicate with one another via the satellite need not be the same size or transmit data with the same amount of power. Many satellite networks use a large number of small dishes, called VSATs (very small aperture terminals), for the outlying nodes and one central hub with a big dish that can transmit very powerful signals and is very sensitive to incoming ones. This system minimizes the cost of the majority of the ground stations at the expense of maintaining one big one, which can be shared by several users. However, this approach can cause additional delays, because the VSATs aren't powerful enough to talk to one another directly through the satellite; messages must pass through the hub and make two trips into space before reaching their final destination, incurring a double delay.

VSATs are typically used by organizations, such as oil companies, that require data or voice communications between sites distributed over a wide geographical area. Terrestrial links are economical over short distances; their cost climbs quickly as the distance between locations increases. In addition, terrestrial data and voice links, while readily available in cities, are often difficult, if not impossible, to obtain in smaller urban and remote local areas using these links. VSAT networks are often used in countries where telephone links are overloaded, unreliable, or difficult to obtain.

VSAT networks have a number of strategic advantages, including an average availability of 99.5 percent and ease of rapid deployment in remote or hard-to-reach areas. In addition, with a VSAT network, organizations have control over and insight into their entire network from a single point, an especially important feature for an organization with remote locations distributed over a large area.

### Paging and Satellite Networks

Paging is the oldest form of mobile telecommunications. The paging industry came into existence in 1949, when the FCC allocated some spectrum frequencies (or radio waves) for one-way mobile communications services. Today, paging has come a long way since the simple beep alerting the user of a message. Not only has paging expanded from the business arena to personal applications, it has also increased dramatically in capabilities and performance.

Paging is a wide area, wireless communications method in which brief alphanumeric messages are transmitted using radio frequencies to an electronic pager. When a subscriber's designated telephone number is dialed, the paging switch sends information to a radio transmitter that broadcasts a signal in the service area, which in turn delivers a tone, or numeric, alphanumeric, or voice message to the subscriber's specific pager. The subscriber is alerted either by a beep or, inconspicuously, by a vibration of the pager itself.

Here is a more detailed description of how the paging system works. When dialing a pager phone number, a caller is actually dialing into the paging terminal of the paging system owner/operator. The call reaches the paging terminal over telephone company lines in much the same manner as when a telephone call is placed across town. The tone a caller hears after dialing the pager number is the paging terminal telling the caller that it is ready to accept the page. Pressing the pound sign (#) after entering the message lets the terminal know that the message is complete. The paging terminal is linked to numerous transmitters throughout the paging coverage area. When the destination terminal receives a message (for a specific pager), it converts the message into a pager code and relays this code to the transmitters. The transmitters send out the code (as a radio signal) throughout the entire coverage area. The code is picked up by all of the pagers within the coverage area on that particular frequency. Only the pager with the proper code is activated and will display the message.

Pagers can also download the messages to a notebook or palmtop computer for display. Messages are transmitted quickly, often in less than one minute. Users can also receive news, sports, weather, and stock information at scheduled intervals. However, messages transmitted when radio signals are weak frequently contain errors.

The paging industry was highly fragmented from its beginnings until the 1980s, when local telephone companies began to assemble small paging companies into larger regional entities. By the end of 1993, there were still 585 paging companies in the United States providing service to more than 15 million pagers. It is expected that further industry consolidation will occur.

## Infrared or Light-Based Mobile Computing

Instead of climbing over the desk to attach a cable from the notebook to the printer, or bending and stretching in other ways to reach the plug, users can point the notebook computer in the direction of the printer and press a key to transfer information by infrared waves.

Infrared works by sending pulses of light from a light-emitting diode (or LED) to a photo sensor that decodes the signals. Unlike rudimentary infrared devices like TV remote controls, which can only send signals, computing devices typically can both send and receive infrared signals. Because the information is carried by lightwaves, the system will not work if any physical obstruction is placed between the sending and receiving devices.

Most infrared equipment falls into two categories: low-speed devices, which range from 115 Kbps to 250 Kbps, and high-speed devices, which transfer data at a rate of about 1.25 megabytes per second. Most infrared products come with RF transceivers that attach to the serial port on the PC; these devices transfer data within a 10-meter range. They allow the infrared link on any portable system to exchange files with other computers or to access their resources. The software allows these cigarette pack-size transceivers to synchronize files between the desktop and notebook, for example or to form a two-node network in which one machine (typically a portable device) can access resources available to the other unit, such as a printer or a disk driver [WS94].

The best feature of infrared is price. Building infrared into a new product adds only a few dollars to the cost of a system, whereas adding a radio-frequency card, itself a popular wireless data transfer method, can add $500 or more. Also, infrared is capable of sending data at many times the speed of radio waves while using very little power.

Infrared is still not as fast as many cable connections, but it is fine for updating files, downloading the day's schedule, or transmitting other data. Because it only works at distances of a few feet, however, infrared isn't a wireless technology that will compete with cellular communications or similar longer-distance techniques. But it does eliminate the cables that would otherwise be needed to connect computing devices within the same room—the same cables that are tripped over or misplaced when not in use.

Until recently, infrared has been limited to exchanging small amounts of data between identical devices. But the goal is compatibility between personal digital assistants, notebooks, and desktop computers as well as peripherals such as printers, fax machines—even telephones. The development of infrared products had been held up by the lack of common technical standards, as vendors sought industry backing for their own standards. In 1994 a common approach was hammered out by the Infrared Data Association, IRDA, which voted to adopt the Infrared Serial Data Link standard to ensure that products will work together and interchangeably [LF94].

## 20.3 MOBILE INFORMATION ACCESS DEVICES

Information can be sent over a coaxial cable or a telephone line in many forms—e-mail, data files, video, and other information. For utilizing this information, there are a wide variety of information access devices: portable computers, hybrid pen computers, personal digital assistants, and data communication equipment.

### Portable Computers

Portable computers are divided into three distinct types—laptops, notebooks, and handhelds—that vary broadly by their method of entering, storing, displaying, and processing data. Laptops are useful for running applications that demand very powerful hardware, such as computer-aided design (CAD) and video presentations. Notebooks serve the more traditional general-purpose user who wants to do a large amount of word processing and manipulate sizable spreadsheets. The hand-held systems have less powerful versions of these capabilities combined with more intuitive functions, such as phone lists and messaging.

There has been tremendous progress in the portable computer development. Laptops rapidly replaced the old "luggables." Even the early laptops with their fold-down displays weighed less than twelve pounds, and technological advances rapidly produced seven-pound and now less than five-pound subnotebook computers.

The subnotebooks have become the mainstream of mobile computing, and they provide a close approximation of the desktop computing experience. Virtually all Intel- or Intel-clone-based subnotebooks run Microsoft Windows and the applications built on top of it. Many models are available with color displays, and all have the disk capacity and integral pointing device (usually a trackball or small joystick-like device) that Windows requires. Among the more novel approaches to subnotebook design are those that include Windows software and applications in ROM.

### Hybrid Pen Computers

While keyboards traditionally have been the standard interface for many types of computers, a pen-based interface is clearly more appropriate in many situations. One of the initial applications envisioned for pen computer was that of insurance adjusters creating charts of an accident or pointing out which parts of a car were damaged. Pen computers are often equipped with wireless communications.

Ironically, one of the recent developments in pen-based computing systems is the addition of a keyboard, which seeks to harness the best of both world. It is provided in two ways: When open, it reveals a full-size keyboard and the pen can be used as a mouse. When the display is closed, the user is presented with a tablet-size writing pad.

All of these machines run standard operating systems and offer a broad range of options, including internal modems.

### Personal Digital Assistants (PDAs)

Think of a personal digital assistant (PDA) as a PC reduced in size to fit inside the coat pocket. PDAs reflect the never-ending quest to build the smallest possible useful computer. Inevitably optimizing for size and weight means limiting functionality.

The PDA market is dividing up into three functional segments:

1. *Digital assistants.* Market segment where the hand-held device captures data and digitizes it (like the Apple's Newton)
2. *Personal communicators.* Cellular telephone with an LCD screen integrated into it (like Simon)
3. *Palmtops.* Large storage segment (probably on CD-ROM) for the user who wants to carry a lot of data and be able to retrieve it easily

### Digital Assistants

Digital assistants combine personal information management with wireless voice, data, and fax communications. These devices attempt to replace personal organizers with a more flexible and more natural means of processing personal information. They rely on a pen-based user interface in place of a keyboard, and make heavy use of handwriting recognition. Handwriting recognition is a difficult technology, and it depends on sophisticated pattern-recognition algorithms. The handwriting-recognition issue remains controversial as it is not very accurate

Digital assistants include a wide array of information-management tools (e.g., file management, address book, calendar) and notepad and sketchpad functionality, and they can serve as front ends to communications services. In this sense, they use a pen-based interface to address the same needs as personal organizers and palmtop computers.

Wireless communication is widely believed to be essential for digital assistants to enjoy broad demand. At present, receive-only paging and one-way messaging are supported via adapters that plug into a PDA's PCMCIA slot. Over time, the digital assistants and the personal communicator will merge and will be available in a number of forms, from those designed for non-portable use to highly mobile, shirt-pocket-size units.

### Personal Communicators

Personal communicators couple a cellular telephone with a pen computer's user interface. Simon, designed by IBM, is packaged as a cellular phone with a small pen-based display instead of a standard keypad. This allows Simon to take on many functions, including fax transmission and reception and limited personal information management. Personal communicators will be ideal for the user who wants two-way communication and an all-in-one device. Many find the fact that the LCD screen is attached to the cellular phone difficult because a user cannot read the screen and talk on the phone at the same time. The screen is long and narrow (1.5 inches by 5 inches), which means that only a limited amount of text can appear when it is being used. However, being able to fax and send e-mail without all the attachments that digital assistants require is appealing.

Compaq and Microsoft are working on a "mobile companion," which will run a version of Microsoft Windows and access a huge base of third-party software. The ability to provide a software environment identical (or close) to that on the desktop may be one of the decisive factors as vendors battle for market share.

### *Palmtops*

Palmtop computers attempt to provide higher functionality and more closely resemble what's available in desktop computers. HP's 100LX, for example, runs MS-DOS—but not Windows—and comes with a wide variety of software for both personal automation and communications.

Palmtops called personal organizers—Sharp's Wizard line and the Casio Boss series—are designed to be fully self-contained but special-purpose machines. They provide support for such personal tasks as diary maintenance, simple note taking, expense tracking, and a variety of calculator functions. These devices, which are derivative of the pocket calculator, offer only limited expansion capability via proprietary programming cards and represent the lower bound on keyboard and screen size.

In palmtops, software is built into the ROM (read-only memory). In the case of the HP's palmtop—MS-DOS 5.0, Lotus 1-2-3, an appointment manager, a calculator, a text editor, a phone book, a stopwatch/alarm clock, a world time database, a terminal emulator, a general-purpose database, a note taker, a file manager, a keyboard macro editor, and cc:Mail. Third-party software for palmtops, while available, is limited, and the marketplace is moving to applications that are oriented to big screens and graphical user interfaces.

Palmtops offer the combined functionality of a personal organizer and communications terminal to provide access to e-mail. An interesting variation of the palmtop computer is called an application-specific personal computer (ASPC). They are mobile computers that are optimized for a limited number of tasks, such as language translation or sending faxes. These can be reprogrammed by inserting electronic "modules," each smaller than a box of matches, into the back of the machine. Figure 20.3 shows a schematic of a hand-held mobile computing device.

## Cellular Modems and PCMCIA Adapters

Like most computer and communications products, wireless modems have undergone extensive evolution. Originally designed for vehicle installation, the wireless modem has evolved into an integrated transceiver/receiver and data modem in a portable, compact format. Capable of sending or receiving data, these wireless modems now rival their wireline cousins in speed and efficiency. Modem makers have also tried to tame cellular networks with modems that use advanced error-correcting protocols to try to compensate for signaling problems.

Getting connected can be tricky, because not all cellular modems and online services support the same protocols. Some modems rely on standards,

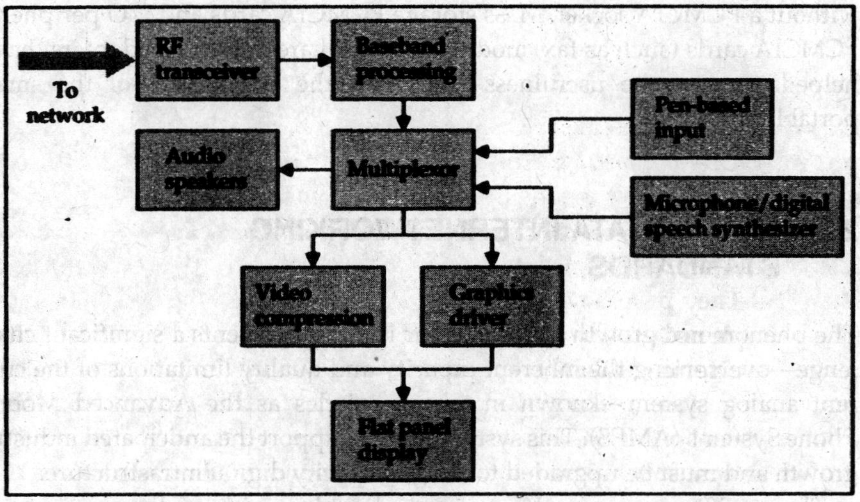


**Figure 20.3 Simplified architecture of a RH hand-held device**

MNP 10 or V.42 bis, for example, while others use proprietary schemes. There are other drawbacks as well. For instance, once on-line, the speed and reliability of cellular's circuit-switched voice channels can vary widely. And the cost of using today's cellular system for data can be high, as users are being billed at the same rates as cellular phone calls.

There are two major market sectors for cellular modems:

1. *Industry-oriented applications*. They include areas such as retailing, warehousing, manufacturing, and health care in which products are used for the collection of data. They tend to be low speed and typically connect hand-held devices to a corporate system.

2. *General-purpose applications*. Mobile computer users require LAN connectivity while they move from location to location within a given environment, and applications are typically used to send and receive electronic mail, access databases, and transmit files. They tend to have higher transmission speeds.

Connecting today's portable PCs and cellular phones often requires an awkward and costly interface device—assuming that the cellular phones support such a connection at all. This interface is a PCMCIA device. PCMCIA (Personal Computer Memory Card International Association) is the industry group that determines the standards for all credit card-size peripherals, including modems. Today, no notebook computer design is complete without a PCMCIA socket. Mass storage PCMCIA cards and I/O peripheral PCMCIA cards (such as fax, modem, and local area network adapters) have helped increase the usefulness—and thus the popularity—of the small portable computers.

## 20.4 MOBILE DATA INTERNETWORKING STANDARDS

The phenomenal growth in the cellular industry presents a significant challenge—overcoming the inherent capacity and quality limitations of the current analog system—known in telecom circles as the Advanced Mobile Phone Systems (AMPS). This system cannot support the anticipated industry growth and must be upgraded to a high-capacity digital infrastructure.

The specific reasons for the analog-to-digital transition follow:

1. *Limited available bandwidth.* Only a limited broadcast spectrum (bandwidth) is designated for cellular communications. Because the allocated cellular spectrum is fixed, a more efficient use of this spectrum has long been seen as the only practical solution.

2. *Overcrowding.* As more and more people use the cellular services, overcrowding in this already limited spectrum occurs. This overcrowding manifests itself as quality degradation due to blocked calls, dropped calls, and the particularly annoying effect of overlapping telephone conversations, or "cross-talk."

The challenge is quite clear. A more efficient spectrum use must be achieved without expending more resources. In the process of maximizing spectrum usage, other issues must be considered: bringing mass market electronic commerce applications to market, developing new services, and lowering operating costs. Efficient spectrum use is also seen as the key to the creation of the "next-generation" personal communications services (PCS) (see Section 20.7).

Many feel that digital technology provides the key to spectrum efficiency. As early as 1988, the Cellular Telecommunications Industry Association (CTIA) established a set of User Performance Requirements (UPR) stating the need for a digital cellular telephone system that could provide an immediate tenfold increase in cellular capacity. The UPR also expressed the need for better voice and service quality, greater flexibility and privacy, and higher speed data transmission capabilities.

The current analog system divides the available spectrum into 30-KHz-wide channels. This method of channelization (division of the spectrum into multiple channels) is commonly called FDMA, frequency division multiple access. Alternative means of channelization are being developed to allow more users in the same region of the spectrum. Two dominant methods are CDMA and TDMA. CDMA, or code division multiple access, is a class of modulation that uses specialized codes as the basis of channelization. These codes are shared by both the mobile station and the base station. TDMA, or time division multiple access, uses the same 30-KHz channels as FDMA but adds a time sharing of three users on each frequency. All other factors being equal, this results in a threefold increase in capacity.

## Code Division Multiple Access (CDMA)

Qualcomm's code division multiple access (CDMA) is not a new technology. It has been used in military satellite systems for decades because it is secure, but more important, it enjoys significant spectrum efficiencies, permitting great channel capacity. Recognizing CDMA's wireless potential, Qualcomm developed the innovations necessary to refine a satellite communications technology into a mobile cellular system. CDMA is called *spread spectrum*.

Unlike the present analog system and other digital systems, which divide the available spectrum into narrow channels and assign one or more conversations to each channel, CDMA is a wideband spread-spectrum technology that "spreads" multiple conversations across a wide segment of the cellular broadcast spectrum. Each telephone or data call is assigned a unique code that permits it to be distinguished from the multitude of calls simultaneously transmitted over the same broadcast spectrum. As long as the receiving device (in this case, the other phone) has the right code, it can pick its conversation out from all the others. The situation is analogous to two people conversing at a crowded restaurant. Although surrounded by people carrying on conversations in many different languages, these people are able to "tune out" the other conversations and understand each other because they are speaking the same language.

Technically, CDMA works as follows. Assume a voice signal is sampled and encoded at a base station at 9.6 Kbps. Instead of this sampled signal or bitstream (each bit of which is about 50 microseconds long) modulating a radio frequency carrier, it is mixed with a separately coded string of bits, each 0.8 microsecond long. This mixed bitstream is then spread across a 800-MHz carrier, resulting in a 1.25-MHz signal. We are "spreading" the spectrum—hence CDMA's other moniker. Some 35 encoded messages in this 1.25-MHz channel go out simultaneously, each with its own identification code embedded in the stream. The base station sends a pilot signal to all mobile units with paging information to let a particular unit know when it is about to receive a message, what code will be used, and its digital timing. With this information in hand, the mobile unit runs the appropriate code stream into an adder with the 1.25-MHz signal, yielding the original signal.

Because as many as thirty-five other subscribers occupy the channel simultaneously, their signals raise the noise floor; in effect they jam each others' signals. The effective data rate, determined empirically for simulated conversations, is 3700 bps. Channels need not be separated because all signals occupy the same channel, adding capacity.

Complicated, yes, but quite feasible, given the power of modern digital signal processors. CDMA could well become the modulation technique of choice in a wireless world.

## Time Division Multiple Access (TDMA)

TDMA is the first digital system standardized in North America. It uses time division multiplexing technology that squeezes three calls onto a single 30-KHz transmission channel. In this system, several users time-share a common carrier frequency to communicate with a base station. Calls are given separate time slots on a frequency, layered in between other signals, and transported from cell site to cell site. Each user transmitting digitized voice or data is allocated one or more time slots within a frame in the downstream (base to users) or upstream (users to base). The upstream and downstream use different frequencies for differentiation purposes (see Fig. 20.4).

In TDMA, the radio channel is divided so users transmit information in unique time slots, letting multiple users share a channel. CDMA employs a wider channel, and all users transmit a signal simultaneously. Each signal is encoded uniquely so the recipient can distinguish the correct signal; other signals seem like noise. TDMA offers the advantage of operating within

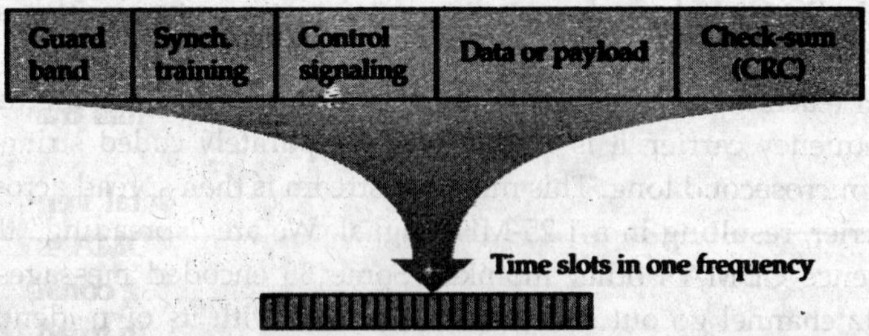


**Figure 20.4** TDMA frames and time slots

existing channel structure. Digital can be introduced as needed for each market, without affecting the existing network.

## Comparing TDMA and CDMA

Neither technology has an inherent advantage. Performance depends more on effective system implementation than basic technology. Hence, the industry (operators and manufacturers alike) must analyze real-world implementation scenarios to determine the best course of action.

Time slots, dynamic channel allocation, and microcell use are TDMA's advantages. CDMA's advantages are more difficult to determine. Because CDMA depends on recovering the correct signal from a multitude of transmissions in a a spectrum band, it is susceptible to interference from other users. Hence CDMA units require continuous power control and a spectrum clear of other signals, including analog users. A single analog user or CDMA unit out of sync can affect traffic on many CDMA sectors, reducing capacity.

CDMA systems use sectorization to realize a gain, making the technique best suited for very dense applications. Also, CDMA monitors unit power in several cells or sectors simultaneously, choosing the cell that allows the lowest transmit power for each user. Considering the need for guardbands and compensation for other CDMA signals, a fully loaded CDMA unit offers six to ten times analog's capacity in comparison to a threefold increase for the TDMA system.

In deployment, components become crucial issues for cost-effective networks. TDMA's advantage: Multiple users share the same network equipment (base stations). In high-capacity TDMA, a single channel unit can serve ten or more subscribers. CDMA's gains come with a penalty: complexity. Each coded call requires a separate base station modem. Further, resources must be dedicated to power control to monitor mobile unit power from several cells. So whereas TDMA shares equipment, CDMA increases equipment required per call. CDMA also increases network costs by constantly comparing and selecting voice paths from multiple cells for the low-power signal. Both techniques demonstrate power consumption efficiency. CDMA transmits continuously at low power. TDMA transmits only during assigned burst periods. Both also practice power control, so that units transmit only needed power levels.

The cellular industry is analyzing the benefits of digital versus analog cellular. The consumer will prove the ultimate judge. TDMA and CDMA already have entered the marketplace and are undergoing consumer scrutiny. Both standards are planned with an evolutionary path to add capacity and capabilities as needed, culminating with high-capacity gains. The final winner will be the one that provides a complete answer for compatibility, cost, capacity, and service quality.

## 20.5 CELLULAR DATA COMMUNICATIONS PROTOCOLS

Cellular uses two alternative methods for transmitting data: circuit switching and packet switching. Circuit switching is the technology behind current telephone systems. Typically, when you make a call, you establish a connection; for each connection, you receive a dedicated, two-way telephone line circuit. Unlike circuit-switched communications, in which voice and data flow continuously from connection to termination, packet-switched transmissions are like sending a document, one page at a time, with each page mailed in its own envelope. An envelope is broken into individual packets, each containing the necessary addressing information. Each packet is discrete and transmitted independently. In the event a packet is corrupted during transmission, it is automatically resent. Packets are reassembled in the proper order on the receiving end.

### Circuit-Switched Cellular Transmission

Why circuit-switched cellular? In wireless cellular communications, a cellular phone is connected to a cellular modem, which in turn is linked to a mobile unit via a data terminal equipment cable. A cellular phone transmits analog radio signals to the nearest cell. From there the call travels to its destination along analog telephone lines. When a caller moves, the signal can momentarily weaken as it is handed off to the cell closest to the caller's new location.

The advantage of this method is that users should be able to use a cellular modem as they would any modem. Because the charge for a cellular call is by the minute and also for set-up, cellular modems can be more cost-effective when used to send large messages.

The disadvantage of this method is that cellular calls are prone to static and interference. Cellular signals are easily intercepted and make data security difficult to ensure. Although many cellular modems offer speeds of up to 14.4 Kbps, most cellular transmissions occur at a default speed of 7200 bps (the faster the speed, the greater the chance of transmission errors). Cellular modems work only with a select group of cellular phones.

To alleviate some of the problems, several circuit-switched digital cellular systems exist, of which GSM is the system that is achieving some recognition.

*GSM*, or Global System for Mobile communication, originated as the European standard for digital cellular telephone systems and has been in operation since 1992. GSM offers teleservices and carrier wireless data services. Teleservices include fax, videotex, teletex, and short message services (SMS). SMS is a means of sending short alphanumeric messages of up to 160 characters over GSM from and to mobile devices.

The power of GSM lies in its robustness and flexibility from an end-user point of view. But this comes at a cost, and there are certain reservations to be considered when looking at GSM as a viable wireless service provider when it comes to short, bursty messages. These shortcomings include the following:

- Logistical obstacles include the necessity of roaming agreements between networks.
- Circuit-switched GSM systems are less reliable than, and not as cost-effective as, packet-switched systems for transactions involving shorter and much more frequent two-way messaging in such applications as dispatching, data base inquiry, or AVLS (automatic vehicle location system).
- The higher efficiency per channel on packet-switched systems is more suitable than older batch-processing systems for current interactive computing systems and can efficiently support multiple sessions and group broadcasting.

GSM is viable for wireless data transmission when applications supporting large-file transactions are required. In general, these applications focus on the vertical market. GSM can be a viable solution for some services once GSM data services are available and tested.

## Cellular Digital Packet Data (CDPD)

Cellular service providers are in the process of recasting their analog, voice-centric network as a digital, voice-and-data system with a blueprint called cellular digital packet data (CDPD). CDPD is a digital data transmission system that overlays existing analog cellular networks and provides packet data services needed for mobile computing.

One reason CDPD is gaining prominence over other cellular data technology is that it utilizes much of the cellular infrastructure currently in place for the voice network, allowing for quick implementation and reduced network infrastructure investments. Another reason is that it is being championed tirelessly by the major U.S. telcos. In the near term, CDPD is seen by many as the best hope for a wide area wireless data network.

The system operates at 19.2 Kbps per channel. CDPD provides maximum connectivity by using idle times between cellular voice calls or transmitting in a dedicated channel environment. With CDPD, a document being transferred is broken into packets, which are sent over cellular networks during the natural pauses that occur in voice conversations.

Adapting a circuit-switched voice network to send and receive data requires some technical gymnastics. CDPD is essentially similar to the packet radio networks, moving data in small packets that can be checked for errors and retransmitted as necessary to ensure accurate deliveries. However, because CDPD does this within the current cellular voice network, it uses a technique known as *channel hopping* to quickly locate idle voice channels and weave data packets into them. CDPD takes advantage of the momentary silences before, during, and after cellular phone conversations to transmit data packets. Using these methods, CDPD can achieve transfer speeds up to 19.2 Kbps, according to its technical specifications.

When data are sent in packets, CDPD communications should be more reliable—and secure—than circuit-switched analog cellular transmissions. CDPD should cost less than standard circuit-switched cellular or land-line modem transmissions, since consumers are billed by the packet. Also, CDPD combines voice and data capabilities in one device. However, the technology is extremely complex, causing some to worry that it won't work as well as promised. CDPD providers won't have an easy time getting cellular service providers, application software developers, and device manufacturers to work together for seamless operation. And the service is still not widely available.

Critics of the CDPD system say heavy system traffic could pose serious performance problems because voice calls always take priority over data transfer. CDPD proponents contend the system will perform well even under heavy traffic, and they note that the digitalization of cellular networks with CDMA and TDMA now underway will substantially increase capacity. Cellular providers could also simply add more transmitters within their regions if needed to handle heavier traffic.

Both technically and strategically, CDPD's most remarkable feature is that it works within the existing cellular systems. That's a critical factor to CDPD service providers, because it means they will not have to construct an entirely new network. It's a big plus, too, for potential hardware makers because many of the parts needed to make CDPD communicators are already being used in today's cellular phones.

In sum, wireless data dedicated systems offer a complete range of features and flexibility required by all levels of users. These systems are dedicated to wireless data, utilize highly efficient RF protocols, and fit general requirements. Unlike circuit-switched systems, a session with a user can be maintained via continuous access to a radio channel. When the channel is idle, other users can transmit data. When more messages are to be transmitted, a subscriber will have radio-channel access without the time-consuming overhead associated with establishing, breaking, and reassigning a dedicated circuit between a single mobile computing device and the network infrastructure. This is achieved through contention schemes imbedded in the RF protocol that allow for maximum capacity on the system since the channel utilization is high.

## 20.6 MOBILE COMPUTING APPLICATIONS

While constructing the right wireless infrastructure is a necessary enabler of the new environment, mobile computing will be truly realized only when application and computing services required for working while away from the office are provided over the mobile network. Today's competitive business climate demands tools that allow users to work and communicate at their own convenience and discretion. It is not enough to have the newest tool. The investment in new technology should yield an immediate benefit to its buyers without asking them to radically alter the way they live or do their work. This is the vision of mobile computing applications. And it is resulting in two changes: remote communications and data access.

*Remote communications.* Being "untethered" is not merely about the absence of wiring. It's a fundamentally different way of communicating. Traditionally, real-time communication has required people to structure their work and personal lives around a predetermined meeting place. This "communication hub" has taken many forms—be it a home, office, trading floor, school, hospital, or warehouse. When you remove constant attachment to a physical space, people are free to be more strategic, creative, and flexible about how they make decisions and get things accomplished.

True mobility heightens the value of business communication and allows it to be better leveraged for competitive advantage. It allows the work environment and hours to be established by balancing the needs of the organization with the desires of the individual. In short, this new way of working means better business for companies and more personal and professional satisfaction for the people who make them run.

*Remote data access.* While a number of applications such as spreadsheets and word processors will reside locally in the laptop, the mobile user must nevertheless have access to various applications and data files that reside on serves in the enterprise network, such as corporate accounting or personnel packages. Similarly, mobile workers such as field sales personnel will need access to libraries of reference files containing product and price information.

An important requirement of the mobile computing environment is to allow workers to be as effective while at remote locations as they are in their usual offices when fully connected. This implies that traditional applications that assumed continuous connectivity must be redesigned to allow a disconnected mode of operation. Take, for instance, a scenario where a sales representative fills in an order on her laptop at a customer site. The client software in the laptop should store the transaction until the user is able to reconnect the laptop to the network. Upon reconnection, the transaction is forwarded to the application server in the network.

In short, mobility and portability will definitely enable a new class of business applications and open new opportunities combining personal computing with consumer electronics. The disconnected mode of operation inherent to the mobile computing environment will present new challenges in terms of maintaining synchronization between individual replicas of corporate data carried around in laptops and the integrated data repository maintained on the enterprise network.

Today, a growing list of applications are being built on the mobile computing infrastructure. They include point of sale, inventory tracking, sales force automation, package tracking and delivery services, and police and taxi dispatching. Three groups of applications are most frequently mentioned: tracking and dispatching applications, mail-enabled on-line transaction processing (OLTP) providing information, and data services to mobile users.

## Tracking and Dispatching

Most prevalent applications for mobile data already encompass customized solutions in long-haul trucking, public safety, courier services, and taxi dispatch. A few years ago, two-way wireless data communication was available only to those who had vast resources and were able to lay out big bucks to get some needed competitive edge. For instance, one of the biggest users of wireless data is shipping giant United Parcel Service. The Atlanta-based company spent six years and $1.5 billion investigating and implementing wireless communications before settling on circuit-switched cellular, according to International Data Corporation. The company invested more than $150 million to stitch together a national cellular service led by four major carriers—McCaw Communications, Southwestern Bell, PacTel, and GTE. Every UPS truck has been equipped with electronic devices that immediately alert the company's central computer in New Jersey when a package is delivered. Under the old UPS system, package deliveries were recorded only after the drivers returned to headquarters. Customers like this instant-tracking system because it enables them to keep tabs on their packages. UPS attributes a 25 percent increase in air shipping volume in 1994 to its tracking system.

Since Federal Express Corporation had gotten the jump in real-time package tracking and mobile data communications, it was do or die for UPS. But UPS had to fight some wireless battles that may be too daunting for smaller firms. For example, to get cellular coverage for the top 100 U.S. markets, UPS had to negotiate with twenty-three vendors (and twenty-three different rate structures, billing increments, and billing systems). For a long time UPS, and only UPS, has had a consolidated billing arrangement with those vendors under which it receives a single bill and makes a single remittance each month. UPS made the requisite investment in wireless under the assumption that it would pay for itself in new business and customer retention. This is true of most early adopters of wireless, including the transportation industry and field service.

## On-Line Transaction Processing

The use of laptop PCs and personal digital assistants (PDAs) is rapidly becoming commonplace in business-critical applications such as field sales automation, distribution, and customer service. Mobile systems are accessing information from corporate databases and submitting mission-critical transactions, such as customer orders, back to the system. This enables businesses to operate in real time, integrating mobile users into existing corporate information systems.

Major software vendors are bringing wireless access to the mainstream. These products, called client–agent–server applications, connect users of wireless devices to a back-end relational database. The offering typically comprises three components. The UNIX server-based message gateway moves requests and data between mobile users and databases and client systems. The message manager on the mobile device relays messages between users and software agents. The agent event manager tracks the agents, which relay information between mobile users and the server.

Building and operating large-scale systems with thousands and tens of thousands of mobile clients involve complex issues that need to be addressed. Managers must ensure scalability and performance of client–server applications to support a rapidly growing number of mobile clients. These mobile devices possess smaller memory and less processing power than their desktop counterparts. That requires the "thin client" software approach in which applications are simple, small, and easy-to-use, and in which changes in evolving server applications are easy to deploy, minimizing the impact on the mobile client. Therefore organizations must learn how to develop applications specifically for the mobile devices.

In addition, mobile clients must be integrated with existing systems that often involve interactions with multiple server platforms, databases, and transaction monitors. Applications need independence from this infrastructure as well as the flexibility to support different communications options. Traditional, session-oriented network protocols, such as TCP/IP, that are used for desktop applications are poorly suited to the low-bandwidth, intermittent, and nonguaranteed nature of current wireless communications. Hence, effective mobile use must support both real-time and store-and-forward functionality for transactions and queries.

As users start implementing mobile systems in crucial business activities, such as taking customer orders, reliable queuing of client requests and messages and secure operations are top priorities. In addition, positive client identification and application-level security become essential parts of the system design. The operational requirements include management services such as peak load management (server load balancing), application performance monitoring, error notification and information logging, and event and process management [IB94].

Once deployed, applications and other system components often need to be changed dynamically and redeployed without bringing the whole system down. New technologies being developed to address these requirements combine proven transaction monitor and database products with new transactional middleware and agent-based technology. For example, middleware offloads much of the application logic and complex client APIs to server agents and gateways. This enables mobile client applications to use simple function calls to invoke application logic on the server and process database queries.

The same application logic on the server can be used by desktop applications and mobile applications communicating over the network. These types of middleware shield developers from the complexities and dependencies of communication options, transaction monitors, and databases. They also enable IS to leverage existing and mobile technologies and focus on streamlining the business process and increasing productivity.

New mobile applications are being developed in the following areas:

- *Health care.* Patient record management and point-of-care computing
- *Retail.* Point-of-sale and point-of-service applications
- *Field service.* Remote data entry of customer orders
- *Traveling professionals.* So-called "road warriors," who need a convenient way to transfer files to and from the corporate LAN before and after business trips

- *Sales and service.* People who visit branch offices and need to exchange information with the corporate LAN when they arrive
- *Members of work groups.* Exchanging electronic documents and spreadsheets and accessing information via database servers
- *Stock and commodity trading.* Traders using mobile devices to get up-to-date information about the stock market and use the information to place orders

By developing customized vertical applications for business tasks involving forms-based data collection, signature capture, and image annotation, doctors, nurses, inventory clerks, delivery people, and stock traders now are using PDAs, personal communicators, and mobile companions to help them reduce costs and to gain competitive advantages.

## Common Communications Mobile API

Mobile communication requires the purchase of a special modem and software designed for a particular wireless network. Switching to a different wireless service means the user must purchase a different modem and new software. A wireless standard is required that would give users greater flexibility to switch between wireless service providers. A wireless API that hardware and software vendors were encouraged to comply with would also increase the selection of wireless modems and software packages available to wireless users.

This standardization is similar to the one that took place in the early modem world. When modems first were developed, different vendors' modems did not work with each other. However, the AT command set developed by Hayes eventually became the de facto standard to which modem vendors now adhere. Today when users buy a modem or use communications software, they needn't be concerned with whether it will work with other modems or software. That is what is needed for building interoperable wireless software applications and hardware products.

In a move designed to make life easier for wireless users, a group of wireless service providers, along with hardware and software vendors are collaborating to develop a common set of APIs to ensure that mail-enabled applications will work with different wireless networks. Currently, software developers must bear the burden of writing multiple versions of their software to work with wireless networks such as Cellular Digital Packet Data, RAM Mobile Data, and Ardis. The group is called the Mobile Computing Alliance [MM94].

A fully standardized API set would help many corporate users' application development plans. Earlier, vendors such as RadioMail Corporation and Motorola have attempted to address the incompatibilities among wireless networks with their own API sets, but each set is slightly different. Other vendors, such as Racotek, have found a niche by creating their own APIs and network operating systems to hide the technical differences between the wireless networks. The Mobile Computing Alliance hopes to go beyond those efforts.

The development of an API set that will give software and hardware vendors the ability to write one application and have it work across all of the different wireless networks is crucial. This standard should be global and take into account all of the wireless technologies and services that are being worked on around the world.

## 20.7 PERSONAL COMMUNICATION SERVICE (PCS)

Industry analysts believe that the personal communications service (PCS) will be the driver of the wireless market in the future. The FCC has defined the PCS broadly as a family of mobile or portable radio services that can be used to provide service to individuals and businesses and may be integrated with a variety of competing networks [NWa94].

Personal communications service was originally conceived of consisting of small, low-power, very light weight, two-way wireless communications "hand sets" that could readily be carried on one's person. Presumably, systems will be available that allow these handsets to communicate within the home or office in a manner similar to that used with "cordless" telephones today. Outside the home, however, these hand sets would access the public wireless networks to be operated by the cellular companies. The current concept is that PCS systems will consist of a large number of low-power transmitters strategically located throughout the given service area. The very-low power nature of the system will have several operational advantages:

- Low power will minimize the need for bulky batteries in the subscriber units and will greatly extend the operational lifetime of one battery charge.
- The very low power will permit frequent "reuse" of the PCS spectrum within a given service area, thereby multiplying the number of subscribers that can be served by a given PCS licensee.

- The very low-power nature of PCS will prevent interference with other service providers or with existing users of the same spectrum for highly directional point-to-point wireless service.

PCS encompasses a broad variety of wireless and mobile technologies, including cellular, paging, mobile packet radio, and satellite-based systems and wireless LAN including infrared transmission. PCS is really a kind of complementary set of solutions for a lot of the existing wireless services that we are seeing out there today.

## Why PCS?

PCS services are expected to increase business productivity and significantly enhance wireless communications and mobile computing. They could do this, for example, by alerting subscribers that a message or page is waiting and by allowing those subscribers to respond and interact by transmitting voice, data, and graphic images.

In the case of mobile computing, PCS will enable wireless client–server computing, where mobile workers in the field can query, search, and interact with corporate databases. In short, PCS is targeting the consumer seeking more advanced, more efficient, and less expensive means of communicating.

Demand studies suggest that if the FCC licenses new PCS providers during 1994, there could be well over 20 million new subscribers by 1997. However, the sobering fact is that the design and technical specifications of PCS are, at present, extremely vague. Although numerous "trials" are underway by various potential PCS providers, including a number of major telephone companies, actual deployment is some time away.

The FCC cannot mandate uses for this spectrum, but it anticipates that these licenses will be used to provide such new services as advanced voice paging, two-way acknowledgment paging, and data services. The FCC has also stipulated that these licenses may not be used to provide traditional broadcasting services or fixed services unless such services are reasonably ancillary to mobile services [FSB94].

## PCS Infrastructure

PCS mobile units will connect with the network via "microcells," or very small receivers similar to those used for cellular phones. While a cellular network uses cells with up to an 8-to-10-mile radius, PCS networks will use microcells located on every street corner and in every building.

The call set-up information for a PCS call would include the microcell identifier—a very specific means of locating the user. These phones are also likely to "feature" automatic registration: Whenever the PCS mobile unit is on (in use or able to receive calls), it will automatically register itself with the nearest microcell. Routers, able to track this registration, would have the equivalent of an automatic, free, instantaneous, and global positioning locator for mobile users.

It is important to understand that PCS is not just another wireless service that is focused directly on cellular-type services, but PCS would be, from the customer's point of view, the integration of all telecommunications systems both wireline and wireless. Because of the current situation with multiple types of service providers, the PCS landscape is becoming a mosaic of many islands of mobility [IEEE92].

The PCS core network is seen as an integrator of the islands of mobility that currently exist. The challenge will be to provide users with a degree of uniformity across multiple islands toward the goal of ubiquitous service (see Fig. 20.5).

## Categories of PCS Services

The spectrum will be divided up to support two major categories of PCS service: narrowband PCS and broadband PCS. Frequencies above one GHz are generally considered to be "microwaves" and the prior allocations of these

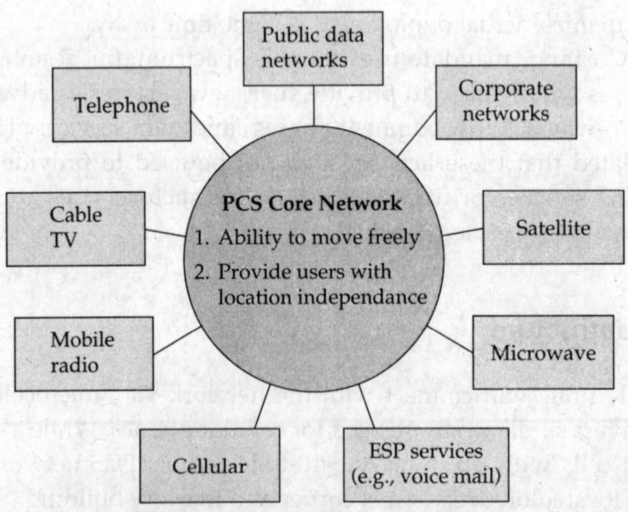


**Figure 20.5** Personal communication core network

channels were to short-haul, point-to-point "microwave" communications links. Typical uses are for private intercompany communications links, distribution of broadcast signals to networked broadcast stations, or the linking of paging transmitters, cellular cell sites, and the like.

### Narrowband PCS

Narrowband PCS has been allocated spectrum at 900 MHz to 901 MHz, 930 MHz to 931 MHz, and 940 MHz to 941 MHz. It is envisioned that this space will be used to offer new services that extend the capabilities of current pager (or beeper) technology. Such concepts as wireless voice messaging and two-way or acknowledgment paging have been discussed by suppliers.

Ten nationwide narrowband Personal Communication Service (PCS) licenses were auctioned in July 1994, for a total of $617,006,674 [FCC94]. The Federal Communications Commission ("FCC") held a simultaneous multiple round auction for 30 regional personal communications service (PCS) licenses in the 900 MHz band ("narrowband PCS").

### BroadBand PCS

Broadband PCS is what most people think of when PCS is mentioned. This refers to the services that will be provided on spectrum allocated for these services in the 1.850–2.2 GHz band. It is anticipated that this band will be used to provide new mobile services based on new mobile devices that will include multifunction portable phones, portable facsimile and other imaging devices, new types of multichannel cordless phones, and advanced paging devices with two-way data capabilities. Broadband PCS systems will be capable of interfacing with PDAs, allowing subscribers to send and receive data and/or video messages without connection to a wire.

This category can be split into licensed and unlicensed PCS. The FCC has reallocated a total of 160 MHz of spectrum between 1850 and 2200 MHz for PCS use. Frequencies in this band were previously reserved for other uses, primarily point-to-point, short-haul private communications links. These frequencies can also be referred to as lying between 1.85 and 2.2 gigaHertz (GHz). Of the 160 MHz of spectrum, 120 MHz will be licensed for PCS users and 40 MHz will be reserved for "unlicensed personal communications devices."

- *Licensed broadband*. Allocation of 120 MHz in the 1850-MHz to 1990-MHz band represents a considerable amount of spectrum—by comparison, the current cellular phone system, known as the Advanced Mobile Phone

System, occupies only 50 MHz. This type of PCS is widely believed to be the successor to cellular and will likely be used to implement an all-digital integrated voice/data infrastructure. Also possible for this service will be advanced intelligent network functionality, such as the "one person, one number" concept pushed by carriers for some time now.

- *Unlicensed broadband.* Outside of narrowband and broadband options, there is the unlicensed portion of PCS spectrum. Basically, a 40-MHz block of spectrum has been allocated from 1890 MHz to 1930 MHz. This service is designed to allow unlicensed operation of short-distance wireless voice and data devices, including wireless LANs and wireless private branch exchanges. These applications today are relegated to the industrial/scientific/medical bands, which are notorious for noise and interference. Unlicensed PCS should make better use of the radio spectrum and allow for more simultaneous users and better signal quality. But a big unanswered question is performance.

In the broadband category, seven licenses were awarded for each of the specified service areas throughout the United States. With some modifications, the service areas to be licensed are defined by the 1993 Rand McNally Commercial Atlas and Marketing Guide. Throughout the United States, the FCC will award licenses in 51 "major trading areas (MTAs)" and 492 "basic trading areas (BTAs)." In any event, it may be of interest to note that both the major trading areas and the basic trading areas vary greatly in geographic extent and population.

In summary, PCS offering high-quality voice and data services, then migrating toward higher-quality multimedia communications and advanced intelligent network services for all market segments, is expected to satisfy customer needs. A host of new voice and data services will begin their journeys toward reality as the FCC auctions off coveted slices of the radio-frequency spectrum. These frequency allocations are intended to spawn a number of loosely defined services known as personal communications services (PCS). While much of the focus so far has been on creating more competition among cellular phone services, PCS also has plenty of potential for low-power data delivery.

## 20.8 SUMMARY

The dominant wireless carriers today clearly will not be the only choices in the years ahead. Studies have shown that there is demand for mobility. Market research by Northern Telecom [FBC94] shows that over 50 percent of businesses that are utilizing existing products such as analog, cordless, SMR, paging, and cellular to meet mobility needs have varying degrees of dissatisfaction based on functionality or price. This dissatisfaction will lead to competition.

From a business point of view, wireless communication is a supplement today that may be more of a necessity ten to fifteen years from now. The first generation of applications is likely to focus on serving mobile professionals with feature-rich integrated voice and data services, with mass market demand for esoteric applications being several years away.

Cellular operators have a tremendous advantage in this coming competition. They've got an installed base, they've got quite wide coverage, they've made their investments, they didn't have to pay for their spectrum, and they've got the brand name, the marketing, administrative systems all set up. Also, many of the services envisioned with PCS can be done at 800 MHz in a cellular spectrum. However, cellular operators will have to be very aggressive and innovative in their services and pricing and provide competition to the new entrants.

From a business viewpoint it's even more important, therefore, to make sure that the new entrants have a level playing field, have the spectrum, the 30 MHz, and the regions that they need to avoid the incumbent microwave users initially. They must build up the capacity to match the cellular operators and have the power and the transmitters they need to get the same coverage at lower propagation. The challenge is going to be to create this level playing fields. If the new entrants are to gain a sizeable chunk of the market, they must overcome the starting advantage of the cellular operators.

To bolster the preceding argument, it is worth noting that the history of wireless communications has been one of slow, steady progress. Cellular took many years to become established, but PCS is on a relatively fast track. Nonetheless, given the inherent difficulties of wireless, especially involving data communications, potential customers should not be surprised if PCS service is not exactly around the corner.

Chapter 21

# Structured Documents

Today, no matter what type of on-line publishing, chances are great that structured document languages, and in particular the Standard Generalized Markup Language (SGML), are used in the process. The Hypertext Markup Language (HTML), used to create documents for the Internet's World Wide Web, is a subset of SGML [GOLD90]. SGML is an international document standard [ISO86], officially recognized since 1986, and is especially popular among government agencies and organizations that deal with large, complex, and frequently revised documents. SGML is considered to be more flexible and better suited to long and complex documents than HTML which provides a very limited set of elements (such as heading, title, paragraph) for constructing on-line documents. SGML, in contrast, lets publishers create their own elements—a feature necessary for complex publications such as technical documentation, electronic books, and product specification information (see Section 21.2).

Adoption of the SGML standard was affected by its reputation as a complex and difficult discipline. The publishing industry was replete with shining examples, but for many others there was relatively little incentive to get involved with SGML. The obstacles to involvement—developing a document type definition (DTD), investing in authoring software, figuring out document conversions, and paying to train employees—seemed too daunting. The benefits, while understandable, were not overwhelming. Lacking compelling motivation, and under pressure to buy easy-to-use tools, companies that were not zealots of the standard were reluctant to adopt specialized publishing technology that required top-level commitment and long-range vision. Despite the obstacles, the use of SGML has grown steadily, migrating from military technical manuals and a few commercial publications in the mid-1980s to its present representation at publishers in a wide variety of disciplines: reference works; textbooks; scientific, scholarly, and medical journals; government agencies' newspapers; telecommunications;

heavy equipment and computer-related documentation; and legal and financial publishing.

Today, SGML is becoming a mainstream computer and publishing technology. Indeed we may very well look back on 1993–1994 as the period when SGML finally started to achieve critical mass as a broad-based publishing standard. The driving force behind the change has been electronic delivery and the business need to publish in many electronic formats. Recently, both the installed base of CD-ROM drives and the market penetration of on-line services and the Internet have made publishers anxious to explore alternatives to paper publishing. To exploit these new opportunities and to avoid having to maintain different versions for each medium, publishers are looking for neutral formats in which to create, edit, and store their material. SGML makes an excellent neutral format. For text-intensive documents at least, it is well suited for conversion into print, CD-ROM content, or on-line hypertext files.

In this chapter, we begin with fundamental concepts behind structured documents. We then describe the key features of SGML.

## 21.1 STRUCTURED DOCUMENT FUNDAMENTALS

The structured document is a data encoding method that allows the information in documents to be shared—either by other document publishing systems or by applications for electronic delivery, database management, computer-aided design, or manufacturing. This method recognizes that data, structure, and format are separable elements. It preserves the data and structure, but does not specify the format of the document—recognizing that format should be optimized to user requirements at the time of delivery.

Why structured documents? The primary reason for increased use of structured documents in business is heterogeneity in the workplace. Three key benefits of the architecture that employs structured documents are investment protection, document reusability, and interoperability of applications.

*Investment protection.* Protecting their investment in documents is rapidly becoming a top priority for companies. Today's computing world encourages ever-increasing complexity in successive releases of most applications, because vendors are under constant competitive pressure to add more features to their products. The result is paradoxical: As applications become more awesome in terms of features, companies grow more concerned about their existing investment in information. For instance, it is not easy for companies to move from word processor A to word processor B because of the cost involved in converting all the documents created in word processor A. In addition, new programs require time and effort to develop, enhance, and maintain. By putting strategic documents into a structured format, organizations protect their information investment from being locked into a single vendor's technology or methodology.

*Document reusability.* Document reuse among sites, programs, and computers is a major stumbling block in developing an integrated architecture. In the mixed-computer environment that is the norm, the ever-increasing multitude of file formats requires an endless array of import and export filters for every program (see Fig. 21.1). Exchanging documents with other people is a hassle unless they have the same programs. In the past, exchanging documents meant file translation (transforming from one word processing format to another). The easiest approach is to transform all the data to a common format that can be read by all applications. By tagging data with their role and any other useful identifiers, structured documents allow information to be readily located and reused.

*Interoperability of applications.* Today's word processors and desktop publishing programs routinely include graphics with their documents. Computer users can create documents containing various media, such as text, tables, movies, sound, and graphics, in a variety of file formats. Currently, each medium requires users to work in different ways, and often in separate applications or editors, demanding a labor-intensive series of actions to move data from each creators application to the final document.

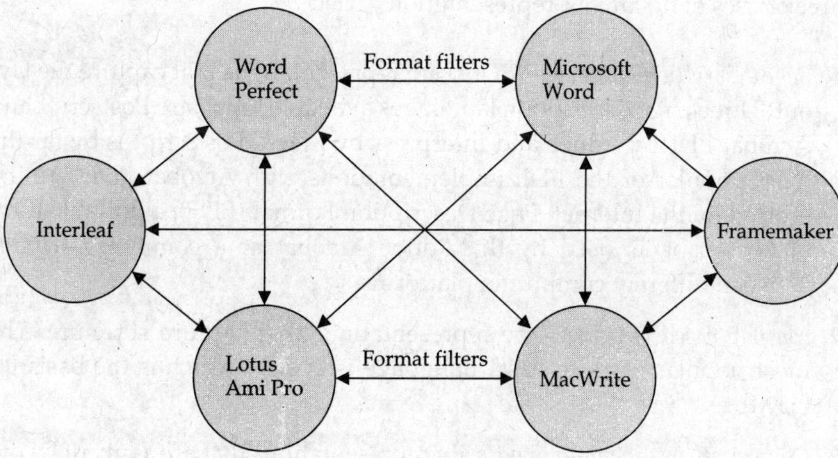


Multiple format filters required for document interchange between word processing applications

**Figure 21.1** Document interchange problem

This lengthy and cumbersome process tends to be error-prone and frustrating, and moving between applications without a standard file format for interchange is becoming increasingly difficult.

Integrating sound, images, and video into documents will only exacerbate the interchange conundrum. To solve the integration problem and the problem caused by new data types, the *structured documents* solution, is appealing.

Yet, as we explore this topic, it is important to note that there aren't any easy answers. Integrating multiple data types and distributing them on-line is a complex task and will remain so for years to come.

## Document Interchange Representations

Given that electronic documents exist in different data formats, one solution is to convert all of them to a common format that is the least common denominator capable of being manipulated by any operating system, platform, or printer. This can be done by converting the documents to plain ASCII or pure text. However, this alternative has severe shortcomings. First, converting to ASCII loses layout structure. Because the only way of representing logical structure in a formatted document is by using layout, this form of conversion loses valuable information.

Another solution to the interchange problem is to convert the document to a representation format that captures the layout and structure (see Fig. 21.2). This representation is then exchanged between systems over the network. Three classes of document representations exist:

1. *Page description languages (PDLs)* are representations that capture the layout. Three page description languages available today are Postscript and Acrobat PDF by Adobe and Interpress by Xerox. Postscript is by far the most popular of the PDL implementations with Acrobat PDF gaining ground on the Internet. Page Description Format (PDF), a portable form of Postscript, is used by the Adobe Acrobat as a common currency between different computing platforms.

2. *Markup-based languages* are representations that capture structure. The most popular markup based language is SGML, which is the basis for HTML.

3. *Compound document languages* are representations that are a mix of layout and structure. Examples include CDA and RTF.

Our focus in the remaining part of this chapter will be on structured documents and their characteristics.

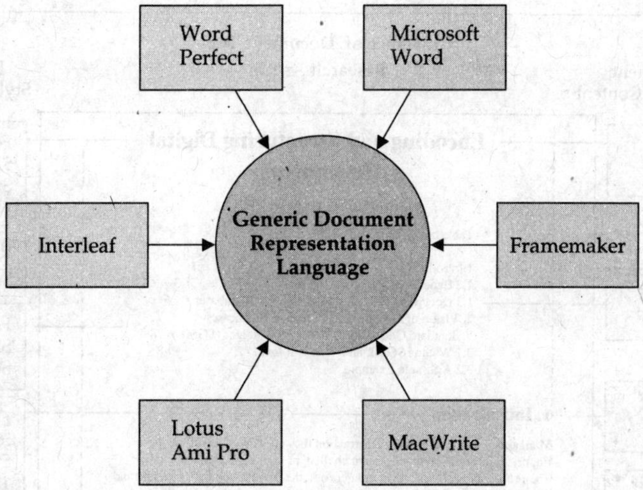


**Figure 21.2** Generic document representation approach

## Separating Logical Structure from Physical Structure

Electronic documents contain three types of information: data, logical structure, and physical format.

The data in a document may include text, graphics, images, and even multimedia objects such as video and sound. Interestingly, data may also include information that does not itself appear on the printed page. For example, a particular graphic of a machine component may have hidden data about what class of machinery uses it, what the tolerances of the component are, and who manufactures it.

The logical structure of a document refers to the relationship among the data elements. For example, the logical structure includes subheadings, paragraphs, and bulleted lists.

The physical format of a document is its appearance. In Fig. 21.3, subheadings are printed in boldface text flush against the left margin. They could also have been italicized and centered without affecting the structure of the document.

Figure 21.3 shows the distinction between the logical structure of a document and its physical presentation. On the left hand side are descriptors that indicate the logical structure of the document—the title, paragraph, and so on. On the right hand side are formatting or style instructions that convey how these logical elements (e.g., paragraph) should appear on the output.

Structured document languages describe the document in its logical terms rather than as a function of its physical presentation. For instance, SGML and

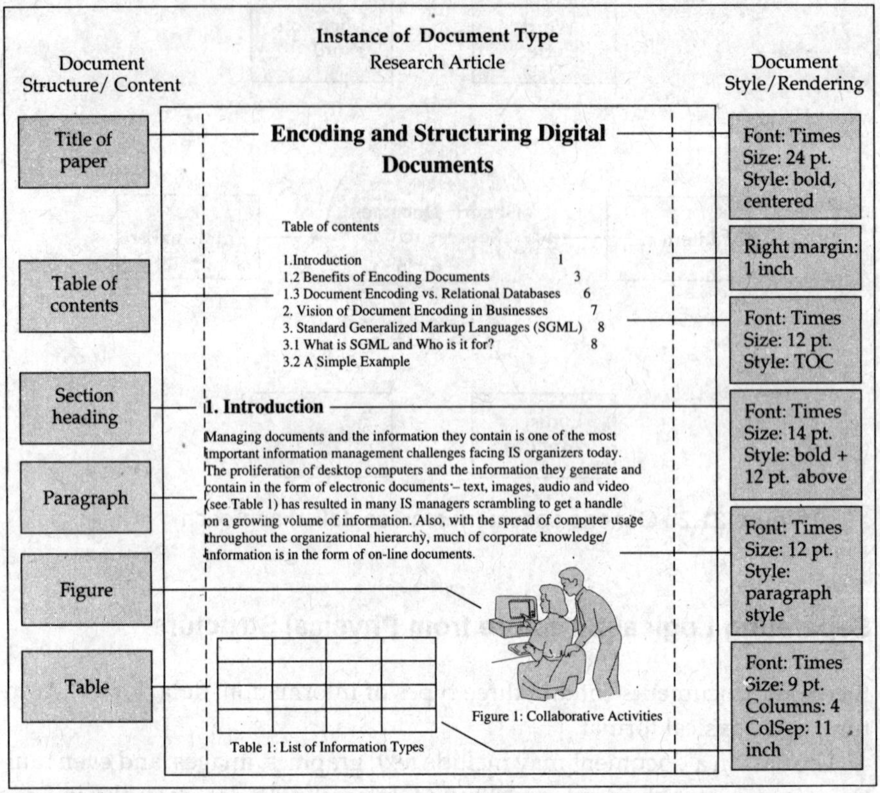


**Figure 21.3** Separating document structure from content and formatting

HTML define tags embedded in documents to identify various document elements. Most tags are set off from regular text with angle brackets; ending tags start with a slash character. Thus "<h1>First Heading</h1>" causes the interpreting application (browser) to identify the text "First Heading" as a first-level heading, which then presents it in a larger font size than the normal text, centered and boldface.

In other words, the browser decides how the logical tag "<h1>" should be formatted. This concept is revolutionary, as multiple layouts for different output media can be easily generated from a single logical description.

## Document Markup

Markup, or tagging, refers to the extra information that is interspersed between the text of the document being processed. This additional information serves two purposes: (1) It specifies the logical elements of the document, such as headings, section markers, and so on; and (2) it specifies the processing functions to be performed on these elements. For instance, in old word processors *.ce* stood for "center the following line."

Why markup? Markup allows heterogeneous equipment (printers, computer displays) to be driven from common text files without rekeying device-specific codes. Markup has its origins in the world of printers, where it refers to the instructions for the typesetter that were written on a typescript or manuscript copy by an editor. In publishing systems for which formatting can be quite complex, a typesetter specially trained for the task does the markup.

How is markup entered? Markup is entered via word processors. This appears in the form of codes or other instructions for a formatting or typesetting program, which in simple cases is also the editor or word processor, such as Microsoft Word. These programs actually hide the use of markup codes from the user by showing the text as it is formatted, and by letting the users set these formatting instructions by choosing appropriate menus, buttons, and so on (the markup codes are still there in the document but hidden). For more complex tasks, however, specialized markup languages are essential.

There are four main types of markup: Punctuational (spaces, punctuation, tabs), presentational (font choice, font size, style), procedural (layout, formatting commands), and descriptive (mnemonic labels for document elements) [CACM87]. The first two types are quite easy to understand; the last two are discussed in the next section.

## Document Markup Languages

A *markup language* is a set of instructions to express how a document should be processed or handled. Unlike most other computer languages, markup languages have to deal with embedded data and have the knowledge to differentiate between what is markup and what are data. Take, for instance, the popular language LaTeX [LAMP94]. The backslash (\) implies that subsequent input is LaTeX instructions. Most markup languages offer additional, administrative language constructs with which to define other language constructs (such as macros). Broadly speaking, electronic publishing uses two classes of markup languages: low-level procedural markup and high-level generalized markup.

### *Procedural Markup*

Procedural markup employs commands within the document description to produce changes of font, spacing, different types of justification, and so on.

Procedural markup emphasizes preserving the appearance or layout of a document. Examples of this approach include Adobe's Acrobat and Postscript.

Procedural markup preserves the look and feel of a document regardless of the hardware platform, operating system, application software, or typeface specifications used to create the original. The marked-up document can be displayed with its original layout on various computing platforms without employing the software used to produce the original document. This solution does allow users to exchange documents without losing any layout information.

Procedural markup has a number of drawbacks:

1. It is inflexible. If a user decides to change the style of his document (as he is using a different output device), he will need to repeat the markup process to reflect the changes and add the necessary codes for the new output device. This will prevent him, for example, from producing a high-quality finished copy of an annual report and also from producing a double-spaced draft on an inexpensive line printer at home. And if he wishes to distribute his documents, he is restricted to those people who use identical text processing systems, unless he is willing to do the extra work (and incur the extra cost) of repeating the markup process.

2. It is a very low-level activity akin to programming in assembly language and requires a high degree of expertise, particularly when complex typographic results are desired. This is true even when the text processing system allows macros or higher-level functions. The powerful TeX system, for example, which is widely used for mathematical typesetting, includes hundreds of primitive controls and macros as part of its processing language.

3. Despite the processing they carry out and their high typographic quality, procedural markup languages are often criticized for their lack of interactivity. This also means that the information and its inherent structure can be accessed in only one way: by a human looking at the information. We lose the principal advantage of having information on-line, that is, the ability to manipulate it. It is often said that procedural markup is one step better than exchanging printed paper; that is, exchanging PostScript files is like exchanging electronic paper, and the information present in the document cannot be processed electronically.

4. Another drawback, albeit a small one, is the inability to incorporate additional useful attributes into a document. Users cannot, for instance, add security permissions—to specify who can look at parts of the document—or context information such as author and date or even assumptions made when creating the document.

Some of the disadvantages of the procedural markup scheme can be avoided by using a descriptive or generalized markup scheme.

### Generalized or Descriptive Markup

A generalized or descriptive markup works on the basis of a logical description of documents. Generalized markup is based on two assumptions:

1. Markup should describe the logical structure and attributes of the document rather than specify layout processing to be performed on it.
2. Markup should be flexible so that techniques such as search and retrieval can be used for processing documents.

With generalized markup, the user tells the system what the structure of a document is, rather than how it should look. This is often done by putting a label (or tag) around the text. For instance, to indicate that certain text is a heading, two labels would surround the text, for example, <HEADING> This is a Heading </HEADING>.

Generalized markup has the curious property that it does not specify how things should look. For instance, <HEADING> and <PARA> can be used to denote section headings and text in each section, respectively, but not to specify how headings should look in a typeset edition of this document (e.g., all the headings could be formatted in boldface).

In other words, the author indicates the structure of various parts of his document (in case of a book, chapters, sections, subsections, heads) and leaves the presentation (style) details, which depend on the viewing platform, to the document formatter. This property in particular makes it possible to guarantee a high degree of homogeneity in the appearance of documents and makes documents portable across views, applications, and systems.

Of course, there is a clear correlation between tags and how various elements appear. Tags are placed at the start and at the end of text when special typographic features are desired, such as styling, change of typeface, etc. For example, to indicate that some text should be boldfaced, we would use the following: <BOLD>Make this statement boldface</BOLD>.

Generalized markup minimizes cognitive demands: An author needs to only recall (or recognize in a menu) a tag for the desired element, rather than also decide how it is currently to appear or recall how to obtain that appearance. Thus authors can focus on authorship.

Perhaps the most attractive feature of generalized markup is that the encoded document can be used in many ways without conversion or manual intervention of the data. A variety of output requirements can be overlaid on the logically structured document to serve the most diverse needs.

## 21.2 STANDARD GENERALIZED MARKUP LANGUAGE (SGML)

This section provides an introduction to the basics of ISO 8879, Standard Generalized Markup Language (SGML). SGML started out as GML, the Generalized Markup Language, created by Charles Goldfarb, Edward Mosher, and Raymond Lorie (G, M, and L, respectively) in 1969 at IBM for storing and retrieving legal documents. GML became the basis for the SGML Standard with aid from a project predating GML, GenCode, started by the Graphics Communications Association (GCA) in 1963. The GenCode project attempted to standardize names of commonly used elements in publishing. SGML was published as International Standard 8879 in October 1986 [BRY89].

The initial goal of SGML was to reduce the confusion caused by the many incompatible, proprietary document typesetting systems that caused publishers to expend effort and money in rekeying and copyediting information. Each document typesetting system had its own hardware, file formats, and languages for marking document content elements such as headings, numbered lists, references, and footnotes. SGML was developed to bring order to this chaotic situation by establishing a nonproprietary standard for information description that would enable easy interchange of documents between diverse systems.

Nearly a decade old, SGML is only now being discovered by companies that require text and document management. You may be asking yourself. "If this SGML stuff is so important, why haven't I heard about it before?" That's a good question. SGML has been a well-guarded secret despite its adoption as an official International Standard (ISO/IEC 8879:1986) for the electronic interchange of information by the aerospace, automotive, semiconductor, defense, and other industries.

But somehow, despite all this acceptance, it remains one of the quietest revolutions around [HERW90]. Granted, it used to have a reputation as being somewhat complicated, but the success of HTML—which is in fact a simple application of SGML—shows the importance of the ideas behind SGML. Perhaps the surest sign that it has "arrived" is the widespread acceptance of the World Wide Web, which uses SGML as the basis for its HTML language.

### Who Is SGML For?

Although started as a solution for the information processing needs of the publishing industry, SGML has much wider applicability and is being viewed with a growing interest from broader quarters. Its applications have rapidly expanded to a variety of industries and information management problems. Among the most visible examples outside traditional publishing are the initiatives and standards in developing electronic manuals for the defense, aerospace, and telecommunications industries.

The biggest backer of SGML was the Department of Defense (DOD). In 1988 the DOD mandated that, for eventual use in interactive electronic technical manuals, contractors must deliver all documentation for future weapons systems in electronic form, with the textual portions in SGML. The Computer-aided Acquisition and Logistics Support (CALS) program requires the use of SGML to maintain documentation, contracts, and contract proposals and governs a vendor's interaction with the DOD. The goal is to manage the flow of millions of pages of information in hundreds of sites using SGML for structuring information exchange, to model not only document data but also inter-document linkages and information flows between departments and weapon systems.

In 1987 the Association of American Publishers (AAP) designed a SGML tag set for books and journals. In 1989 the Aircraft Industry and Air Transport associations followed the DOD's lead and developed SGML tag sets for aircraft maintenance and operations manuals. This process helped to unify and streamline operations in the industry, because many vendors sell both commercial and military aircraft. In 1990 the Telecommunications Industry Forum (TCIF) developed SGML applications for systems documentation, information interchange between vendors, and several other applications.

In business, the Securities and Exchange Commission (SEC) is accepting corporate financial disclosure information in the form of SGML documents as part of its EDGAR (Electronic Data Gathering and Retrieval) project. LEXIS/NEXIS, which provides on-line retrieval services, is in the midst of converting 180 million documents (the equivalent of 450 Gb of text) to SGML. This will enable the company to present information as more than just a stream of linear text. Customers will be able to refine searches using not only key words or phrases but also their context in the hierarchy of the document.

In 1991 the computer industry geared up, too, when various UNIX system vendors agreed to develop SGML encoding for on-line documentation. In 1993 the electronics industry (Pinnacles Group) began developing an SGML-based directory of electronic component information whose purpose was to reduce the time to market by making available the most up-to-date information at the design phase itself. At the same time, academic researchers also adopted SGML: The TEI (Text Encoding Initiative) is an international effort to standardize the encoding of literary and research texts. Various working groups are preparing collections of texts (totaling gigabytes of data) tagged according to the TEI guidelines. In addition, both the Institute of Electrical & Electronic Engineers (IEEE) and the American Mathematical Society publish their journals using SGML.

SGML application is expanding beyond its current niche role to a much wider audience on the World Wide Web. SGML on the Web allows publishers to lift the shackles imposed by HTML. For example, SGML gives publishers greater control over display styles (font, size, color, indents, spacing, auto-numbering, and invisibility of text); the ability to search for content based on structural element (for example, searching for text within a heading, title, or table); more sophisticated linking (two-way linking, one-to-many linking, graphic-to-graphic hotspot linking); and linking to specific content within documents owned by others. When these requirements are crucial, SGML is the answer.

Ultimately, SGML is strongly positioned to become the *lingua franca* of text and document management. This is possible because SGML is, by its very nature, platform-independent and is implemented on virtually all computer operating systems.

## What Does SGML Do?

SGML provides a method for describing the relationship between a document's structure and its content. It also enables documents to be stored and exchanged independent of formatting, software applications, and computing platforms. A document encoded using SGML specifies nothing about the representation of the document on paper or a screen. A presentation program must merge the SGML document with local style information in order to produce output, such as a printed copy. This is invaluable when it comes to interchange of documents between different systems, providing different views of a document, extracting information about it, and for machine processing in general.

Conceptually, SGML is very simple: It is a standard syntax for building "structured" documents. SGML enables the markup of information content of documents. This markup provides information about the logical structure of the document in a way that is understandable or interpretable by other software applications that have SGML data interpretation capability.

Central to SGML are document type definitions (DTDs), which define in great detail the valid and expected components for documents. That is, DTDs define how many heading levels a chapter can have but not their presentation (their font and style). That's the job of an output-formatting package. DTDs are designed to identify structural elements such as titles, authors' names, captions, key words, footnotes, copyrights, illustrations, list items, and tables.

Developers can also create special tags such as industry names in securities filings and cross reference them to data sources. Once identified, these elements can then be parameters for search queries or other processes. For example, tagging all the key words in a document greatly simplifies generating an index or a cross reference. So is generating a table of contents to any arbitrary depth once the headings and subheadings are tagged. So is applying visual formatting.

Let's walk you through a simple example to show the SGML way. First, we must analyze a document and categorize its elements according to its logical structure. For example, the logical structure of a simple memo could include the from-address, to-address, subject heading, body of the message as a set of paragraphs. A sample of such a memo follows:

```
From: Ravi Kalakota
To:   Andrew Whinston
Subject:     Meeting on Monday

I am scheduling a meeting on Monday, 9:30 a.m., with the
  VP of Marketing to discuss the ad campaign for the new
  product.

Is this time convenient for you?
```

Once the key elements of this memo are identified, we produce a document type definition (DTD) for the memo. The DTD is a detailed collection of rules and instructions that define all the component elements of a document and the conditions for their use. In publishing applications, the DTD also controls the typographic style and placement of material.

Defining a DTD is similar to defining the fields in a database. A properly designed DTD does not permit data to appear where it should not appear, just as a properly designed database application will not allow a person's name to be entered into a field designated to contain a telephone number.

A DTD for the preceding memo would look like the following:

```
DocType Memo [
<! Element MEMO - - (FROM, TO, SUBJECT, BODY)>
<! Element BODY - - (para)+ >
<! Element (FROM | TO | SUBJECT | para) - 0 #PCDATA>
<! Element para - - #PCDATA>
]
```

The + sign after the para element indicates that the body of the message must contain at least one paragraph. The #PCDATA stands for parsed character data. This DTD description of the document is similar to a program written in computer language such as Pascal or C. What we have done here is describe the structure of a simple DTD in a clear and unambiguous manner.

In other words, we can think of a DTD as a program that solves a specific problem and SGML as a programming language that provides the constructs for writing this program.

Once the memo DTD is completed, every memo—typically a plain ASCII text file—is tagged; that is, every element within the file is marked to describe its function as defined in the DTD. SGML tags mark the beginnings and ends of logical document elements, such as headings, subsections, or captions. An example follows:

```
<MEMO>
<FROM> Ravi Kalakota
<To> Andrew Whinston
<Subject> Meeting on Monday
<BODY>

<para> I am scheduling a meeting on Monday, 9:30 am with
  the VP of Marketing to discuss the ad campaign for the
  new product.</para>
  <para> Is this time convenient for you?</para>
</BODY>
</MEMO>
```

In sum, SGML document instances are pure ASCII files, with no formatting information. Instead, they include descriptive coding for later processing. SGML is entirely descriptive, leaving procedures and formatting to the devices that read and interpret the tagging systems defined in an SGML document-type definition. As a language for text description, SGML is not concerned with outputting documents on a variety of devices like PostScript or other page description languages (PDL). In other words, the encoding tags do not determine how the actual output will look—whether "Subject" is to be printed or displayed as 10-point Helvetica or 12-point Times Roman. This is a matter of style, and style is the job of the output specification—a separate file that can be attached to the document. Freeing content from formatting information permits a document to be used for different delivery media: Document instances can be processed for Braille delivery, on-line screen delivery, audio delivery, machine-to-machine delivery, paper delivery, or all of these purposes. It has no biases toward or against the description of tabular material, mathematical formulae, or other complicated textual constructs.

## Creating a Corporate Digital Library Using SGML

Workers in any organization create documents. The challenge for the organization is to create a process and an architecture that protects the knowledge embedded in these documents. Figure 21.4 shows the SGML digital library creation process.

Generally, this process can be divided into six phases: Document analysis and DTD development, document creation and authoring, document parsing and conversion, document library creation and management, formatting and page composition, and electronic delivery and distribution. In the following sections, we present an overview of these areas.

### Document Analysis and DTD Development

The SGML digital library creation process begins with a *document type definition (DTD)*, generated through analysis of the documents in that domain. Document analysis and DTD creation are essentially manual operations performed by trained SGML analysts. An SGML analyst first analyzes a document and categorizes its elements. Once these elements are identified, the

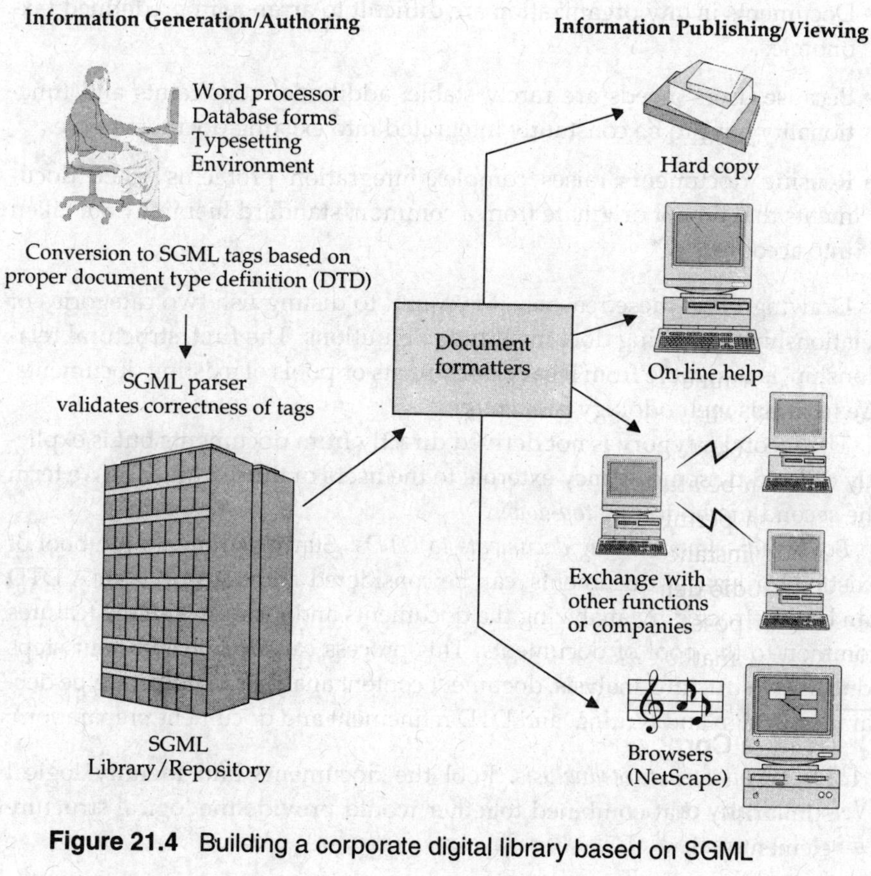


**Figure 21.4** Building a corporate digital library based on SGML

analyst produces a DTD. The DTD allows specific mappings between document templates and the logical structure in business documents. The content structure of the DTD provides the mapping application that links the DTD with the various parts in the template that the end user deals with or enters information into. A properly designed DTD will not permit data to appear where it should not appear, just as a properly designed database application will not allow the end user to enter a person's name into a field designated to contain a telephone number. When the DTD is completed, the electronic document—typically an ASCII text file—is tagged; that is, every element within the file is marked to describe its function as defined in the DTD.

DTDs frequently undergo considerable growing pains before they become readily reusable in a wide range of applications or domains. There are a number of reasons for this phenomenon:

- It is often the case that stable, reusable document type definitions are not designed from scratch, but are "discovered" through an iterative process of testing and improvement.
- Documents in any organization are difficult to arrange in predefined taxonomies.
- Because users' needs are rarely stable; additional constraints and functionality have to be constantly integrated into existing document types.
- Reusing documents raises complex integration problems when documents that do not originate from a common, standard hierarchy are taken into account.

Drawing upon these reasons, it is useful to distinguish two categories of relationships involving document type definitions. The first, structural relationship, is derivable from legacy documents or pools of existing documents. We term this methodology *bottom-up*.

The second category is not derived directly from documents but is explicitly defined by some agency external to the users of the documents. We term the second methodology *top-down*.

*Bottom-up—from existing documents to DTDs.* Starting from a large pool of existing (or legacy) documents, can be considered a bottom-up task. A DTD can be constructed by analyzing the documents and including all the features common to the pool of documents. This process can be split into four steps (document structure analysis, document content analysis, document type declaration design and writing, and DTD refinement and document preparation):

1. *Document structure analysis.* Pool the documents and identify logical similarities that combined together would provide the logical structure elements.

2. *Document content analysis.* Identify the common or recurrent components in the logical structure elements that could provide the basis for the content structure.

3. *Document type declaration design and writing.* Using the logical and content structure elements identified in the document analysis phase, create a formal grammar in the form of a DTD that can describe almost all the documents in the initial pool. Formally defined document types make it possible to check that the document instance adheres to the rules defined for its type category and to flag any errors by using the parser.

4. *DTD refinement and document preparation.* Modify and tune the DTD by examining either new documents outside the initial pool of documents or end-user applications that must use these DTDs to process documents.

The DTDs that result from the bottom-up process tend to be specific, practical, and domain-oriented as long as the initial pool of documents used in the analysis are homogeneous in nature.

This methodology has many weaknesses, however. First, the approach tends to create document definitions that may be too specific. For instance, a DTD created for corporate law must also include descriptions of cases that have elements of patent or international law. The DTDs cannot be isolated or exclusionary but must be capable of being linked together. The second weakness is the difficulty of managing a large number of DTDs that would be needed in a large organization to deal with a wide variety of documents.

The bottom-up methodology is very much an ad hoc approach and does not encourage the conceptual order required for integration and management of DTDs.

*Top-down—from generic DTD to specific domains.* The organization, and in particular the document management guru beginning work on the conceptual design of a repository of computer-based documents, needs to answer two important questions before beginning the top-down design: What are the document types that the system will deal with? What properties and relationships do these document types have with one another?

In this method, specific domain-oriented DTDs are carefully constructed to be refinements of more general DTDs, with the following advantages for the user:

1. The relationship between the different DTDs is made explicit, allowing organized library creation and update.

2. A DTD can evolve from several unrelated DTDs or even from functional areas, allowing a document to be customized or "viewed" as having different structures in domain areas.

3. DTDs with content-oriented tags (e.g., <report>) are gradual refinements of purely structural DTDs (e.g., <para>) and hence the advantages of a content orientation can be combined with those of a structural orientation.

By top-down decomposition we mean breaking the representation of a document into a number of interrelated components. In choosing a decomposition for documents, users can be guided by the usage or constructs provided by that environment. So if the domain requires both content and structural tags, the representation should contain document type components corresponding to both content and structure.

However, there is a trade-off between the granularity of structural decomposition and the simplicity of the representation: As the representation becomes more finely detailed or fine-grained, its use by tools such as SGML editors for automatic marking becomes more complex.

Not all components of the document type representation need to be derived from structural features. The representation should allow the users to attach components corresponding to contextual or descriptive attributes. Possible descriptive attributes that need to be added to structural features such as sections, chapters, or even paragraphs include the author of that logical element, the date it was written, version and release information, security information, and other comments or documentation for fellow authors. For retrieval purposes it is useful to attach textual descriptions to logical elements.

While the top-down method is more disciplined, it will work best in well-defined classes of documents.

### Document Creation and Authoring

Once the DTD is ready, end users can mark up their documents according to the DTD specifications. Document tagging is generally accomplished by using editors, although "intelligent" software is now available to assist in the automation of the tagging operation.

Users author a markup/tagged document through an application of their choice, but they must use a style guide to assure automated quality control over adherence to that structure through the extensive use of document templates. If the application (e.g., MS-Word) supports SGML as a native file format, the user directly saves the file as an SGML markup file. Otherwise, the user must employ a format converter to convert the user file format into an SGML markup.

We are also witnessing a shift in the SGML authoring market. It used to be the case that to get a decent tool for creating SGML markup, one had to buy a specialized product. This is true no longer. The arrival of SGML add-ons to

Microsoft Word and WordPerfect integrate SGML markup into basic word processing. Also, Frame Technology's FrameMaker+ SGML and Interleaf's SGML integrate SGML markup into WYSIWYG (What You See Is What You Get) page composition.

To illustrate the inner workings of an authoring tool, consider SGML Author from Microsoft. This add-on to Microsoft Word makes it possible for many potential users to develop SGML applications without having to persuade their managers to invest in special-purpose editing software. Authors need not know anything about SGML, provided they use Word's text styles in a carefully specified way. SGML Author supplies a conversion facility that automatically converts styles to SGML tags (or vice versa, when an SGML file is imported). This kind of integration makes SGML authoring much more palatable to many organizations, because it reduces the training and support costs.

Another trend in the SGML authoring market can be seen in the stampede of vendors to capitalize on the popularity of the World Wide Web. Because the Web's HTML is an SGML subset, any SGML editor is easily capable of doubling as a Web editor.

We expect SGML, enhanced by the widespread distribution of free viewers such as SoftQuad's Panorama (an SGML viewer for the World Wide Web), to start cropping up more often. The Panorama viewer is being distributed free along with NCSA Mosaic and packaged with commercial browsers such as Spyglass's Enhanced Mosaic. SoftQuad will also offer Panorama Pro a commercial version of the software that includes the ability to create SGML documents for the Web.

The use of SGML browsers will let Web publishers control typefaces and sizes, color, and position and associate multiple style sheets with any set of documents. It will let users customize their displays and navigate through long, complex documents on the Web. It will also let publishers add detailed annotations, links, navigation tools, and control over display formats to their documents.

### *Document Parsing and Conversion*

The next step in the process is to check for document conformity using a parser—software that reads the DTD and then examines the tagged document. A parser can be a stand-alone program or integrated into the editing software. The former, usually executed in a batch mode, is generally used to check material that is mass-converted from existing text files. The latter, usually executed in a interactive mode, is usually provided to authors to ensure at the time of input or editing that the tags being used are legal.

The parser makes certain that the tagged document corresponds to the rules specified in the DTD. For example, a DTD might require that a textbook always have an abstract that immediately follows the chapter head. If the parser encounters a chapter in which a plain-text paragraph follows the head, it will flag an error and inform the user that an <abstract> tag must follow the <chapter-begin> and </chapter-end> pair and that <para> tag is not correct. Parsers help to enforce proper use of styles and help clean up any remaining problems in files after they have been converted to SGML.

### Document Library Creation and Management

Document libraries and accompanying management software are the heart of any document repository. In the past, vendors provided functionality by developing their own proprietary database technology. Today, customers are looking for SGML document management that is layered on top of commercial database technology.

Most document management systems work at the file level; the smallest unit a user retrieves is a file. That approach works well with most applications, which work on whole files, and it is fine for handling metadata, information about the documents, such as status, version, and configuration.

SGML-encoded documents make it possible to break the documents down into smaller, discrete chunks that can be retrieved independently of other document parts. By breaking down the document, users can apply a finer degree of control in managing different configurations and versions of document elements and documents as a whole. The typical example is a document chunk that is part of many different documents; in an SGML-aware system, this chunk can be stored once and all documents that use it will include it by reference, ensuring that the latest version is always in the document. Queries can be based on the DTD element structure or attributes. Retrieval of an element implies retrieving all of that element's content, including subelements.

Today, the most popular method of managing document components is to employ an object-oriented database design. For instance, Astoria from XSoft is written on top of Object Design's ObjectStore. Object-oriented databases are controversial, in that performance of these databases is not yet well proven, but there are many advantages from the standpoint of database design, execution, and administration, especially when users want to manage components, not files.

### Formatting and Page Composition

A tagged SGML file and DTD make up only half the equation. Now that we have them, what do we do with them? Traditionally, composition system programmers have used DTD to write the necessary software to typeset the document. The software interprets and translates the tags into typesetting or publishing-system-specific coding that produces the output document in the desired format and typefaces.

Although SGML and DTD are portable, translation programs are necessary to convert the DTD and tagged files into each system that must display the document. This situation has the distinct advantage of permitting the data to be stored in application-independent form. The same SGML files used to produce a technical manual can be used to generate a CD-ROM hypertext application or a searchable on-line database. Only the original DTD and tagged SGML files must be altered to update the information on the various platforms being "driven" by the common data.

### *Electronic Delivery and Distribution*

Interest in on-line delivery is skyrocketing as the Internet draws millions of people onto the worldwide Information Highway. Organizations, including advertisers and publishers, desiring or are being pressured to distribute information on-line are keen to get up to speed.

Electronic delivery media tend to overlap, so to simplify matters, we can think of three groupings: (1) single-document viewers and delivery (PostScript and Acrobat viewers); (2) document collections or libraries (SGML browsers and CD-ROM browsers); and (3) hyperlinked documents on the Internet (HTML browsers).

**Single-document Viewers.** The problem with single-document viewers, or page turners as they are sometimes called, is that they are page-oriented and so the page dimensions must be determined at the time of creation. This implies that since the viewing screen might be any size, shape, and color depth, any page design decisions made a priori will necessarily be wrong for some fraction of the audience.

An example of a single-document viewer is Adobe's Acrobat. Acrobat brings two important things to the Web. First, it allows the display of arbitrary layouts, including maps, tables, mathematical equations, and rotated text. Zooming, for greater magnification, is a given, a functionality that is sorely lacking in current Web documents. Second, Acrobat lets would-be Web publishers create their pages in any environment that has a free Acrobat viewer. This feature permits users to generate Web material without learning new tools.

The year 1994 marked the introduction of products aimed at ad hoc distribution of single documents. This market is taking a little longer than expected to get rolling among consumers, but commercial publishers are taking advantage of the low cost of these products. Advertisers, for example, are testing the use of Acrobat for electronic delivery of print advertisements for newspapers. Acrobat, in fact, exemplifies the principle that technologies that succeed must play across the entire spectrum of consumer and business requirements. Digital delivery of advertising presents a very different context for electronic delivery using single-document technology to transmit ads destined for print. Retailers are anxious to reduce their lead times on run-of-press ads in newspapers, and Acrobat looks as though it may work in the future for this application.

**Document Collections or Libraries.** Unlike print, the on-line medium does not allow publishers of document collections to control the presentation. Users often want to access the same information in different ways—sometimes by topic, sometimes alphabetically by name and dynamic formatting enables publishers to give their readers that kind of flexibility. Dynamic formatting of information to the screen, rather than display of preformatted screens, has great appeal when publishers are not sure what the size of the screen will be. It also cuts down considerably on the volume of information that needs to be sent over a network and provides greater interaction between the reader and the material.

SGML allows publishers to display the same content on-screen, publish it in paper manuals, or publish it on CD-ROMs. As noted earlier, SGML brings database capabilities to document collections. It enables users to manipulate fields within large documents. They easily can define and find abstracts, subsections, captions, bulleted or numbered lists, copyright notices, bibliographies, and other document elements and reuse them in other contexts. Users can limit text searches to specific parts or elements of a document and thus greatly improve query precision and recall. SGML also smoothes text exchange between organizations with dissimilar computer systems.

The greatest use of SGML has been in vertical markets where certain organizations need to exchange well-specified kinds of information with each other, or where a dominant buyer—say, the Department of Defense or General Motors—requires SGML for new documentation. With SGML, the U.S. military has streamlined the way it manages documentation, from procurement to training and maintenance. Pharmaceutical companies store volumes of drug-test information marked up so that they can be easily searched and scanned.

**Hyperlinked Documents.** This is where we are today. The previous chasm between electronic publishing and multimedia has been bridged, leaving us with a continuum. On the one side are unformatted and static text documents, such as e-mail messages. At the other extreme are dynamic, interactive document collections that handle dynamically changing information. For example, in Interactive Electronic Technical Manuals (IETMs) there are no prebuilt screens; all screens are generated on the fly according to the user and the task.

SGML has not attracted much attention in the general-office publishing or consumer retail markets. As part of the Internet's World Wide Web, however, it has attracted a great deal of attention from companies interested in on-line publishing and communications. The Web allows people to publish "pages" of information containing mixed, highly linked text, graphics, and sounds. To do so, the Web uses the Hypertext Markup Language (HTML), a simplified and stylized, application of SGML.

Exploring the differences between SGML and HTML, by examining the designers' intents, is insightful. SGML began as a way to gain efficiencies and power in document creation, distribution, and reuse. Only later did its creators expand the original scope to an abstract representational scheme that would allow them to manipulate and reuse components of large documents for various purposes across many industries and many document types. Initially, documents were self-contained: They could contain complex structures, subdocuments, and many internal references, but they were not linked directly to other documents.

HTML, in contrast, was meant to create a way to share information over the Internet. Tim Berners-Lee designed HTML from scratch and with the specific intent to avoid much of SGML's complexity. SGML was used as a starting point because it was already mature and offered a useful framework, but he stripped out many of SGML's features and added hyperlinking capabilities. More importantly, he ignored some of the SGML community's assumptions. He restricted the number of features they would support, a decision that made the browsers easier to create. If a browser hits an unknown tag, it will ignore it instead of stopping or crashing the program. This feature made the system easily extensible and even planned for an evolutionary dynamic that might lead to HTML's replacement over time should other protocols prove more useful and popular.

Thus HTML is a specific, simple instance of a SGML DTD created for a purpose. In a way, SGML was designed to constrain the universe of documents for a task; HTML was designed to extend the universe of documents through the notion of hyperlinks. Many people have experimented with HTML, so there are some incompatible variants in use. Standards committees seem to be well on their way to setting a new baseline for HTML.

HTML is not the only extension of SGML, simply the most well known. For example, attempts to extend SGML with multimedia, hyperlinks, and prescriptive markup have met with limited success. Two such efforts, HyTime and DSSSL, are well-organized efforts but have been criticized as too complex. Few commercial software tools are available for either standard. It is possible that HyTime and DSSSL offer a functionality that will be necessary several years from now.

## 21.3 SUMMARY

In many respects, SGML is a database definition language for documents. A properly designed DTD and its tags describe not only how a document is supposed to look but also what each tagged element contains. With appropriate processing, they can generate hypertext documents, searchable databases, or even programming-language translations. Many multimedia publishers are investigating the potential of SGML to solve their format conversion needs. Indeed, most experts believe the biggest impact SGML will have is in the production and maintenance of huge repositories of on-line data.

To take advantage of SGML, users must conform to its conventions and have all documents properly tagged and in conformance to the DTD files for that class of documents. Previously, markup tasks were done by experts, but growing numbers of users means that support is needed for automating tagging/markup tasks and making it more transparent. To enable increased SGML use in organizations, IS departments must develop document type definitions as well as document templates so that the end user is freed from having to delve into the specifics of markup coding.

In conclusion, as we move toward storing greater amounts of information in documents rather than in relational databases, it is becoming clear that the strength of structured document markup languages in supporting information reuse, cross-platform reformatting, intelligent navigation, and executable interactive documents will make them an integral part of the future of information services.

Markup-based documents have several advantages:

- Easy document interchange allows users to integrate text and graphics files from various word processors, spreadsheets, and databases into a global document that maintains active links to the original files/tables that may be stored in remote sites.

- Platform and application independence gives users a method for describing the relationship between document structure and content, enabling documents to be stored and exchanged independent of formatting, platforms, and software applications. SGML answers one of the key objections to electronic document distribution by eliminating the need to store multiple copies of the same document tailored for individual platforms.

- The technology protects users' investment in information, reformats and reconstitutes information for new delivery vehicles and customization requirements, and speeds work flow by facilitating collaboration

All the signs suggest that structured document standards SGML and HTML are poised for growth. Interest is growing rapidly and the supporting technologies are now in place.

Chapter 22

# Active/Compound Document Architecture

At the software end, electronic commerce demands that PCs be integrated with an information exchange and collaboration infrastructure—mail, messaging, shared databases—to support greater work-group and organizational productivity. This view forces us to fundamentally change the meaning of the term *computing*. The PC—once viewed only as a platform for the creation, management, and analysis of information in isolation—now must support information exchange and collaboration.

The key to making this functional leap is integration: among applications on the desktop and with applications on remote servers. To meet the integration demand, the computing industry is re-engineering the desktop environment to support an information-centric environment featuring "boundaryless" applications. The redesign involves a distribution of functionality—from operating system services through application functionality—into components or objects that may be shared within the context of a user's task [CIR94].

Why do we need this? Imagine the following situation. You are creating a monthly regional sales report using PageMaker running on PowerPC. You require other key accounting and marketing information to complete your report, but there's one snag. The accounting department workers have their information in Lotus 1-2-3, and their graphs are in a Microsoft Windows format that your PowerPC software refuses to recognize. To exacerbate the problem, the sales department personnel store all their customer information and order data in an Oracle database on a Novell NetWare server.

The problem is clear: How do you import the information from all these software sources without rekeying any of it? The answer lies in seamless distributed access and dynamic format interchange capability provided by active document architectures (ADAs).

In many organizations, this nightmarish mix of different file types, applications, and platforms is the norm rather than the exception. Much of the information collected by a company is used for operational purposes: to keep credit/debit balances, maintain customer accounts, and keep track of inventory. In these applications, the users of the information have specific requirements for the data and a narrow sphere of decision making. There is no special need to accompany the information with interpretations or package it in an attractive manner. Today, companies are attempting to utilize the core information in other contexts requiring information repackaging, sharing, and distribution.

In fact, the same data can support many documents. For instance, when an annual report is prepared at the end of a fiscal year, it contains information from several different sources. This material is viewed by many different individuals, each with a different mind-set and requirements. A glossy version with upbeat text may be released to the shareholders. A condensed statement that stresses progress and company image may be released to the press. A dry and professional version is provided to the federal government as a part of the annual 10-K and 10-Q disclosures. Clearly, it is the document (or interface) that is the final product of any work activity, not the raw data. This concept, known in computing circles as the *document-oriented interface* (DOI), utilizes the integration capability of active documents.

In this chapter, we will explain the fundamental ideas behind active documents. We will also describe, albeit briefly, some of the important developments taking place. In what follows, you should be aware that many of the ideas and protocols were never designed specifically for active documents or electronic commerce. Each vendor had, and has, much broader objectives in mind, mostly toward putting object-oriented programming to good use. Today, this focus is rapidly shifting toward facilitating electronic commerce.

## 22.1 DEFINING ACTIVE DOCUMENTS

Active documents represent a new approach to computing. *Active document architecture* integrates multimedia information from multiple sources on a network in a disciplined manner. Built on, and intimately tied to, client–server and object-oriented techniques, the ADA is a more powerful and intuitive way to work with data than any other available computing interface. ADA emphasizes that the complete task (producing a quarterly report or the specification for a new design) is of greater importance than the sum of the individual pieces (software programs that execute specialized tasks).

For this vision to occur, the ADA must orchestrate transparent access to the necessary software programs. It must also ensure cooperation in a daunting world of multiple formats and incompatible programs. From an end user's standpoint, ADA computing is the logical extension of the client–server and object-oriented revolution to a much broader audience of electronic commerce.

Active documents change the way users interact with applications. Today, users start up a software application, then open a document. Most documents (or data) can be viewed and modified only by the application that created them. In contrast, the active document mode begins by activating a task-specific document (annual report, financial analysis, or product design) rather than individual applications.

The operating system, viewing software, and the network conspire to provide the necessary knowledge for viewing and/or modifying the embedded contents—text, graphics, sound, or full-motion video. Objects can be copied or moved anywhere in the document, placed in another document, sent over a network, or printed on paper. In other words, the active document changes the structure of computing across the network, from what is seen on-screen to the actual behavior of the software.

Active documents enable a high degree of resource and network integration. The integration of diverse on-line resources is quickly becoming the focal point of all forms of application development. Creating computing platforms that enable integration is the top priority for software suppliers: integration among elements on the desktop (e.g., applications with applications, applications with operating system services) and integration of desktop resources with remote resources (e.g., data, procedures, objects, mail/messaging services). While the true challenge lies in providing hooks to remote resources, it is first necessary to become more proficient at integrating the many resources that reside on the desktop itself.

Figure 22.1 illustrates an active document with a letterhead template created using a graphics editor. On the left side of this template, a chart section from one vendor overlaps a table part from another vendor to illustrate financial information. A clock part has been embedded in the top right corner over a text part that contains a button part. An embedded part is fundamentally distinct from ordinary content elements such as simple shapes, characters, or cells. The various types of data can be or should be able to link to the source, so that change in the source also is reflected in the document [AAPL94].

## Applets, Not Applications

Computing with an active document would replace stand-alone applications, as we know them today, with tools called applets. For instance, instead

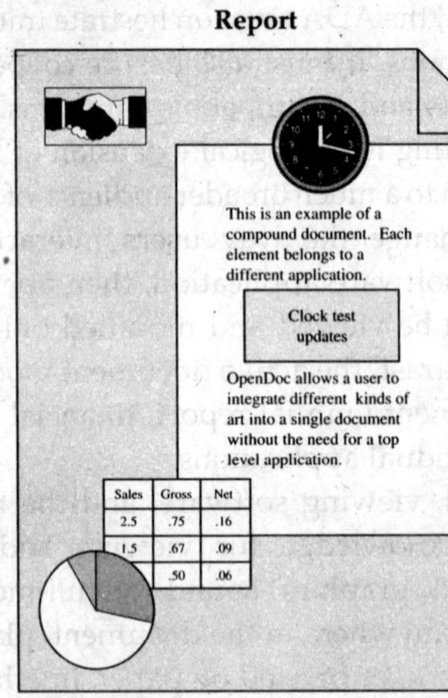


**Figure 22.1** An example of an active document

of working in a word processing application with a long list of features, a collection of word processing tools (e.g., applets) enable users to perform the same functions in a text object.

Text objects could be any size (as large as a book or as small as a graph's label), and all would use the same text-editing tool. Of course, any text applet (e.g., an editor, a spelling checker, or a style sheet editor) would work with any format of text anywhere, including text in a spreadsheet or graph. A page-layout applet would handle the formatting of text objects for the printed page.

Active document architecture enables users to mix and match applets. For example, if you like your Quattro Pro spreadsheet text-editing features but need more flexible search-and-replace features of Microsoft Excel applet, you would simply change the search-and-replace applet and keep the text-editing applet. Do you need to put mathematical equations in a graph? Add an equation tool. For a portable computer with limited storage and RAM, you would install just the essential tools rather than large toolkits or complete applications.

In any document, when you select an object, the appropriate tools would become available. The system might first look for the application that created the object; if that tool was not installed in your computer, the system would look for compatible tools with similar functionality. If you had several tools with overlapping functions, such as word processing software, you could tell the system which one you prefer to use. If no appropriate tools were available, you'd have to settle for only being able to view the contents of an object.

For a given document object type, there can be several levels of tools. The simplest is a viewer, and basic viewers will probably be built into the system software. For rare object types, the document might include a viewing tool. A software developer might give away viewing tools to promote the sale of a full-fledged editing tool that can create and modify objects. An intermediate class of tool might be able to view and extract static or dynamic information from an object but wouldn't have the ability to modify the object.

Objects will support and maintain links among themselves. For example, a global search-and-replace function could apply not only to the text object on-screen but to any other text object on a network—if a company changed its name, a user could replace every instance of it, even in the titles in a presentation video sequence.

## Elements of Active Document Architectures

This section presents a functional model (Fig. 22.2) of the emerging active document architectures and the object models and services that support them. The model assists in the prediction of how the elements of the component desktop will fill in and which competing technologies will set the standards for those elements.

The emerging active document model can be viewed as composed of three interrelated elements: single process local containers/workspaces, shared containers/workspaces, and network-distributed objects [CIR94].

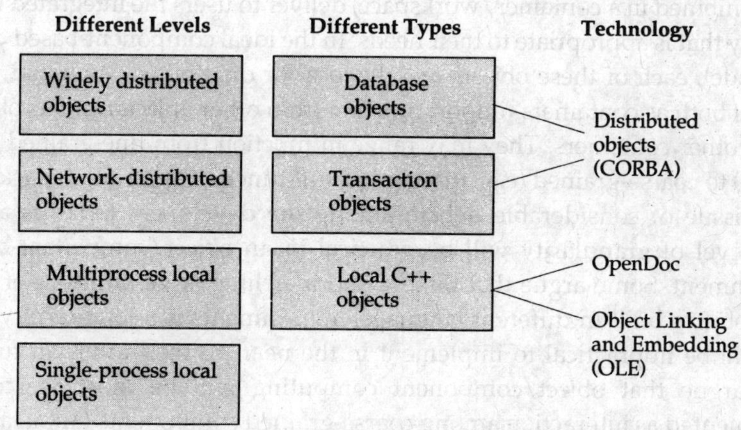


**Figure 22.2** The different levels, types, and technology in active documents

These categories are somewhat arbitrary divisions. Application services will likely be implemented as components within local object libraries, but there will be a blurring of the line between local application objects and network object services. Also as underlying operating systems become more object oriented, the line between the object services layer and the base operating system will fade into a common services layer.

### Single Process Local Containers/Workspaces

Users work with the "application" view when manipulating information. The document interface in which the user is working may consist of a "container" application, which includes built-in capabilities that map on to the user's information manipulation needs.

The container application may import functionality from other applications/objects as well. For example, if a user frequently performs mathematical functions on information, a matching container might be a spreadsheet package. For purposes of editing text within the spreadsheet, the developer or user may choose to import functions from a word processing package or import a simple text editor object into the spreadsheet environment.

Many containers may not only import component functions from other objects on the desktop (or remotely), but also may export functions to other containers.

### Shared Containers/Workspaces

Applications and application components are the functional building blocks that, combined in a container/workspace, deliver to users the integrated functionality that is appropriate to their needs. In the ideal component-based desktop model, each of these objects may be local or distributed. As noted, they may act both as containers (import function from other objects) and as objects within other containers. They may range in function from fine-grained (e.g., widget) to coarse-grained (e.g., monolithic, full-function application package).

An issue of considerable debate among the developers today is about what level of granularity will be practical in an object/component-based environment. Some argue that mixing and matching large numbers of very small objects built in different language environments is a long-term vision that will be impractical to implement in the near- to medium-term future. They argue that object/component computing will be most practically implemented as interaction among coarse-grained components (applications or major application components).

Ideally, objects written in different languages could work with one another, so a shared library could include components written in C++, SmallTalk, Basic, or COBOL. Today, these components are developed using developer workbenches, typically including foundation classes or building on a major vendor's foundation class. Many of these environments include their own proprietary component models/run-time environments. In the ideal desktop, object/component models and services are not built into the toolset level, but are made available across all objects in a network object services layer.

### *Network Object Services Layer*

This layer of services and interfaces to those services supports the creation, storage, activation, and binding of components/objects, as well as other object services. The services are built around a specific model of what objects/components are and how they behave. As already noted, the goal in having such a systemwide layer is to drive common object services out of multiple disparate language and language-specific run-time environments and into the system software, in order to facilitate integration and interoperability of heterogeneous components. Among the products that embody some or all of the object/component services are the following:

- Microsoft Component Object Model
- IBM System Object Model (SOM)
- Hewlett-Packard Distributed Object Management Facility
- SunSoft Distributed Object Environment (DOE)
- DEC Object Broker
- Object Management Group (OMG) Common Object Request Broker Architecture (CORBA)

Not all these vendors and technologies map exactly onto one another. For instance, IBM's SOM presents a programming model (language-independent) that supports interaction among objects within a single address space (in-process) [SOM94].

In contrast to the programming-model-focused SOM, object broker products focus more on object distribution and interoperability through the concept of brokering. Further complicating the picture are vendors such as Microsoft and IBM that have added distribution features to their COM and SOM that provide capabilities for objects to communicate across address spaces (out-of-process) and across systems (distributed).

An object (or component) programming model is a fundamental starting point for any desktop component software model. Some would argue that such a model is purely the domain of language (e.g., C++, SmallTalk) vendors.

## 22.2 APPROACHES TO ACTIVE DOCUMENTS

Software vendors are exploring two distinct approaches to active document architectures, depending on the basic types of interaction with external objects or applications. They include single-platform integration and multi-platform integration.

### Single-Platform Integration

Single-platform integration is the interaction between multiple objects or processes within one computer. Local objects focus on the benefits of document-centric (as opposed to today's mostly application-centric) desktop computing. This technology incorporates multiple types of data from different applications into a single dynamic document.

These solutions support the integration of certain other applications or objects but do not directly address the integration of documents across different platforms. Recipients of this form of document must have the same set of applications (or object manipulation tools) as the sender. The emphasis on integration, however, creates a document that is more responsive to the information needs of the user albeit in a restrictive domain. The single-application approach is useful for passing complete documents to those who want to edit them with their own local tools.

The most widely discussed single platform document architectures vying for developers' attention are Microsoft's Object Linking and Embedding (OLE) and the Component Integration Labs' (CIL's) OpenDoc. CIL's primary backers are Apple, IBM, WordPerfect, and other industry heavyweights opposed to Microsoft. These container architectures ride on top of more generalized object/component models—OLE on Microsoft's Component Object Model (COM) and OpenDoc on top of IBM's System Object Model (SOM).

### Multiple-Platform Integration

In the multiple-application (or distributed objects) models, a compound document is composed of objects created by different applications executing on different machines on the wide area network. The applications needn't know much about those objects. The document application creates a link to each remote object it contains, but the display and editing of the object are handled by another application on the network.

Multiplatform integration is far more complex and involves a distributed library of objects that can be accessed and used as easily as local objects. This process is very difficult to design and implement but remains an extremely important technological component of electronic commerce. An example of this architecture is CORBA (Common Object Request Broker Architecture), which is based on distributed objects.

What's a distributed object? A C++ or Smalltalk object contains instructions and data but cannot cross language or address-space boundaries. In other words, a C++ object cannot talk to a Smalltalk object. To get around this problem, distributed objects are packaged as binary components accessible to clients by means of procedure calls. Clients neither know nor care which language or compiler built a server object, or where on the network the object physically resides. They need to know only its name and how to call it.

Why distributed objects? We want electronic commerce components that not only interoperate but collaborate. For example, agents roaming the network should be able to communicate with other agents. In a homogeneous programming environment, interagent communication is easy, but the world of software components is heterogeneous and we need standards that set the rules of engagement among different types of components. In short, the distributed-objects approach is useful when information must be integrated but a program that understands that information is not available locally. This approach provides this capability by enabling communication among application programs.

Distributed objects is a very complex area and has as its foundation the development of a common messaging standard for objects. This technology holds the promise of a flexible wide area network–based active document architecture. Why? It encapsulates data and instructions in objects that can roam anywhere on networks, run on different platforms, talk to legacy applications by way of object wrappers, and manage themselves and the resources they control.

## Object-to-Object Calling Mechanism

Calling between objects is crucial to the active document architecture. The reason is quite simple: Although the desktop offers the user interface and the integration capability, all code and data do not reside there. To the contrary, for large analytical and transaction-oriented applications, the desktop is the worst place to put code and data. Instead, applications are described as a set of embedded, linked objects. The links tell the receiver (client) how to invoke editors (object implementation) (see Fig. 22.3).

The object-oriented approach enables active documents to be assembled without knowing anything about the external data. A desktop publishing program, for example, might incorporate sounds, even though the program doesn't understand audio. Activating a sound (clicking on its icon, for example) launches the program for playing back or editing the sounds. In short, the object-oriented model makes compound document editors out of all kinds of applications.

The object-oriented approach to creating active documents takes the idea of links one step further, to enable users to incorporate information that their application does not recognize. It, too, relies on the basic communication protocols of the operating system, but it does so for a different reason. Instead of using a link to paste in a data file, it links to an object that has its own editor and data format associated with it. The display of the object within the document and the editing of that object are handled by this other application. The link serves as a tool for the receiving application to send requests, or messages, to this external application, asking it to respond to a user request within a document.

In the single-application model, the document processor must be able to process the linked information. It is important to note, however, that in both OLE and conventional links, the links are not "persistent": They may not stay valid if the document or some of the linked objects are moved to a new location. Conventional single-application compound document processors rely on the user to help find a file after it has been moved (or renamed or deleted). For instance, OLE works this same way because its links are not tied to the file system and there is no system-level link manager.

The limitation of this approach is that it is impossible for the document processor itself to convey the structure of objects whose content it knows

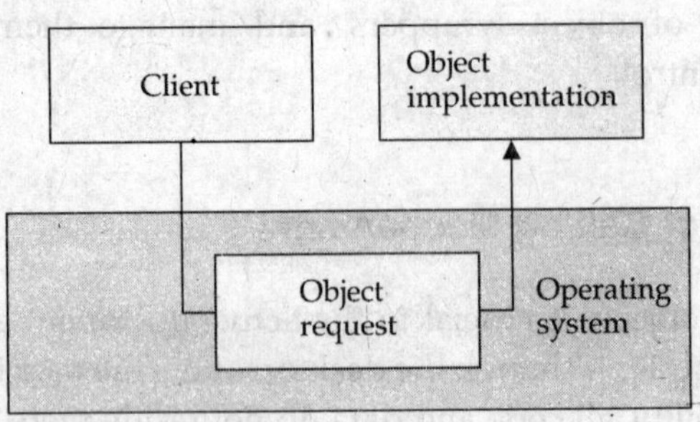


**Figure 22.3** Communication between processes

nothing about. It presumes the user will have the requisite programs to make sense of that information. A receiver of such a document who did not have all of the required applications would be unable to edit, and maybe even to display or print, that document.

The three most prominent types of object-to-object calling mechanisms are Microsoft's Dynamic Data Exchange, OpenDoc's System Object Manager, and Remote Procedure Call (RPC).

### Microsoft's Dynamic Data Exchange

In Windows 2.0, Microsoft added Dynamic Data Exchange (DDE), a communication protocol for two applications to talk to each other. It presumes that both applications are running because if they aren't, there is no communication—hence the term dynamic, as opposed to static, links. In other words, there is no dynamic data exchange once one of the applications is closed. In DDE, the receiver, or target program, of the data initiates a link with the originator, which must be running with the document open at the same time on the same workstation. As long as both programs are running, they may communicate, and changes to the referred-to source file will automatically trigger an update in the other document. Again, this scenario presumes understanding of the file format of the original data. Although it originally designed DDE for the single-application model (Microsoft Excel applications with embedded external objects), Microsoft is building on DDE concepts for its more generic application-to-application communication model: Object Linking and Embedding (OLE) [OLE93].

One big difference between OLE links and DDE links is that OLE links remain in the document even after it is closed. Of course, as long as documents are using DDE, the link cannot be updated unless the external application is also running, but at least the user can be assured that the linked object knows it is linked. OLE links are like external references in the single-application model, except that the link relies entirely on another program to understand the information object.

To summarize the distinction between DDE and OLE: In both DDE and OLE, before linking to an object, users must first launch the external application. The difference is that DDE is a two-way communication for establishing a data link. A requester can ask for a specific format for his or her data; the external application complies with the request or denies it; if denied, the user can continue the dialogue to try a new format the external application understands. In OLE, there is still a two-way communication, but no longer does the requester worry about the format of the data (although it can request a preferred method). The presentation of the object for the user is handled by the external application. Clearly, OLE is more flexible than DDE and is expected to be the dominant application-document linking mechanism. For more on OLE, see section 22.3.

### IBM's System Object Manager

System Object Model (SOM) architecture is a platform and language-independent run-time mechanism for dynamic object linking. OpenDoc uses SOM as its object-calling mechanism. Some of SOM's key features are local and remote interoperability for OpenDoc objects; a language-independent protocol for objects that communicate in a single address space or across address spaces on the same machine; and object communication across networks.

From a technical standpoint, SOM supports both static- and dynamic-method invocations. Static invocations are for objects that know about each other at compile time; dynamic invocations are for objects that know nothing about each other at compile time and end up discovering each other's services at run time. SOM provides an efficient, flexible binary standard for object interfaces that conforms to the CORBA industry standard (see Section 22.5) for distributed-object messaging. SOM lets developers create parts in a wide range of languages and lets these parts call each other with no additional effort. SOM also allows developers and users to take advantage of distributed services provided through CORBA-compliant application programming interfaces (APIs) [SOM94].

### Remote Procedure Call

In UNIX, the communication protocol is typically the Remote Procedure Call (RPC), a synchronous transmission in which the application issues a request and the serving application issues a reply (or the operating system denies the request). The RPC mechanism handles all kinds of messages including those relating to getting remote information into your document. Figure 22.4 illustrates the RPC mechanism between a caller (document) and callee (remote procedure). This interaction takes place over the network. CORBA uses a modified form of RPC calls.

Most of today's client–server systems and networking are based on RPC. Because you might encounter RPC technology on-line, we will provide a quick technical overview. These systems are tightly coupled in the sense that they use multiple client-to-server calls to store and retrieve data and operate at a lower level of abstraction (at the procedure level).

An RPC system works by automating the production of code called "stubs" that connects the procedure call on one machine to the entry point of the procedure on another and connects the return of the procedure back to the caller.

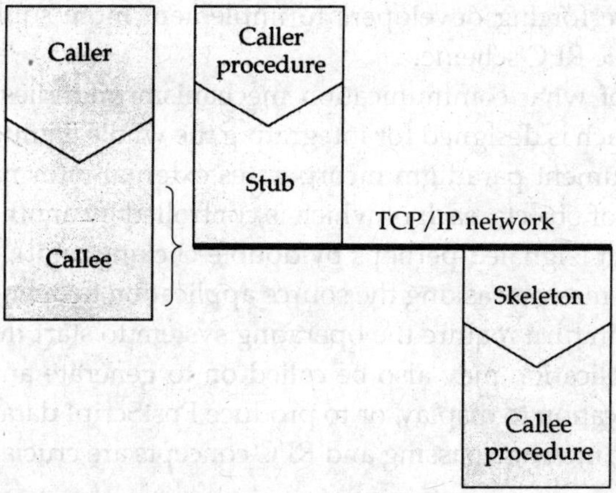


**Figure 22.4** RPC communication between two procedures

This procedure is shown in Fig. 22.5, where the client on remote machine A initiates a request message (procedure with certain arguments) aimed at a server, remote machine B", on the network. The server executes the requested procedure and responds with a reply.

Remote procedure calls provide tightly coupled, synchronous interactivity, but at the price of flexibility. RPCs are hard-coded to particular network transport protocols and topologies; changing either requires changes to applications. RPCs also create persistent links between client and server processes; if the server is busy, the client has to wait. Such constraints, which may prove to be impractical in today's wide area, heterogeneous, interenter-

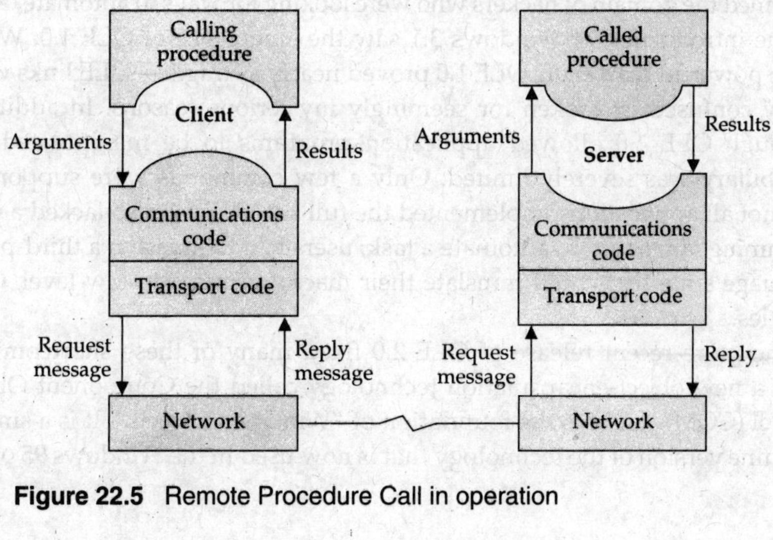


**Figure 22.5** Remote Procedure Call in operation

prise world, are forcing developers to implement more sophisticated versions of the basic RPC scheme.

Regardless of what communication mechanism underlies it, the object-oriented approach is designed for integrating the whole gamut of data types. The active document paradigm incorporates external information by referring to a series of objects, each of which is controlled by another application. To edit an object (signaled perhaps by double-clicking on it), an application simply issues a message asking the source application to open this particular file. (This may in turn require the operating system to start the application.) The source application may also be called on to generate an image for the receiving application to display, or to produce PostScript data to be sent to a printer. Clearly, message passing and RPC concepts are crucial.

## 22.3 OBJECT LINKING AND EMBEDDING

In 1990 Microsoft introduced Object Linking and Embedding (OLE) technology as its basic strategy for integrating multiple applications and multimedia data types within an active document framework. OLE was built on top of DDE. When an application was launched from within a compound document, it was given its window, and the data it needed were copied into its address space.

As noted earlier, DDE was a limited, interprocess communications (IPC) mechanism designed to allow applications to communicate with each other during execution. Unfortunately, DDE was fragile—links between applications were easily broken as files were moved or application software was updated. Few applications took advantage of DDE, and serious DDE usage remained the domain of hackers who were looking for ways to automate tasks.

The introduction of Windows 3.1 saw the emergence of OLE 1.0. While more powerful than DDE, OLE 1.0 proved nearly as fragile—OLE links were easily confused or broken for seemingly mysterious reasons. In addition, although OLE 1.0 allowed application programs to be manipulated, its vocabulary was severely limited: Only a few commands were supported, and not all applications implemented the full set. OLE 1.0 also lacked a programming language. To automate a task, users had to invest in a third-party language suite that could translate their macro wishes into low-level, OLE realities.

The more recent release of OLE 2.0 fixed many of these shortcomings with a new object-encapsulation technology called the Component Object Model (COM). COM is the foundation of "Windows Objects." It is a single-machine version of the technology that is now used in the Windows 95 operating system and allows objects to be shared among multiple systems on a network [COM94].

How does OLE work? In OLE, an application or document interface includes external information by linking or embedding an object. Linking means that it merely keeps a pointer to the object. Embedding means that it not only points to the object, but it also becomes the owner of the content associated with that object. Each object has associated with it an editing application. The object might or might not contain presentation information.

If developers follow the API approach, they write "display methods" that are attached to their objects. Applications, such as word processors, can embed objects created by other applications and, when such objects need to be displayed, can invoke the "display method." To illustrate the point, consider a sound editing program. The developer creates a suitable display method—maybe a picture of lips—that is shown within the word processing file. Double-clicking on the lips activates the sound program, which will play back the recording. All of this may be done without any sound support in the word processing program.

A limitation of the OLE approach is that the application has no way to display a linked file if the external application is not running—presentation is in the hands of the external application. The control that the receiving application has over the external object is limited to placing it and sizing it. But the receiving application has no control over the appearance of the object itself—that process is handled by the external application's display method. The same is true if a file is imbedded. Even though the data for an object are placed within a document, by default, the application will not be able to read, print, or edit the data if the source application is not available. It is possible for a developer to write code that does read embedded data, but that is not Microsoft's recommended procedure. For more specific details on OLE, see [ORFA94].

## 22.4 OPENDOC

In OpenDoc, document parts are the fundamental building blocks. They replace today's monolithic applications with smaller units of content dynamically bound with related functionality. Every document part contains data—for example, text parts contain characters, graphics parts contain lines and shapes, spreadsheet parts contain spreadsheet cells with formulas, and video parts contain digitized video. The particular type of data that each part contains is defined by the developer and is known as the part's intrinsic content [AAPL94].

In addition to its intrinsic content, a part may be able to contain other parts. Every document has a single part at its top level, the root part, into which all other parts are embedded. Again, the part developer determines whether to support the capacity to contain other parts; however, a key characteristic of multiapplication architectures is that if a part can contain one type of part, it can contain all types of parts. This is in stark contrast to the small number of standard data types supported today, such as text, JPEG, and TIFF.

Document parts have associated editors. Part editors are independent programs that manipulate and display a particular kind of content. Part editors can serve as components for solution building as well as document building. Plug-and-play solutions assembled from several parts will replace today's monolithic applications. Parts will allow developers to create new applications in a manner similar to that of constructing a document template in today's world.

Parts can also be viewed as the boundaries at which one kind of content in a document ends and another begins. A key element of the concept of parts is that each part of a document has its own content model—the model of objects and operations that is presented to the user. The content model changes at the frame between parts. Frames are areas of the display that represent a part. Frames provide a handle onto parts, allowing them to be manipulated as a whole, as well as allowing the user to see and edit a part's contents [AAPL94].

Although this description of a frame sounds much like that of a standard application window, it is not. Where windows are transitory views, only visible when the part is being edited or its content viewed, a frame is persistent. When a frame is opened into a window, the frame remains visible. When the window is closed, the part returns to the representation from which it was opened. In addition, a frame can often show only a portion of the entire content of a part. Opening a large part into a window allows the entire part to be viewed and edited.

In the OpenDoc architecture, part handlers are the rough equivalents of today's applications. When a part is being displayed or edited, a part handler is invoked to perform those tasks. A part handler is responsible for the following tasks:

- Displaying the part both on the screen and for printing purposes.
- Editing the part. The part handler must accept events and change the state of the part so that the user can edit and script the part.
- Storage management for the part. The part handler must be able to read the part from hard disk into main memory, manage the run-time storage associated with the part, and write the part back out to the hard disk.

Part handlers are dynamically linked into the run-time environment, based on the part types that appear in the document. Because any sort of part might appear in any document at any time, the part handlers must be dynamically linked to provide a smooth user experience.

Part handlers can be divided into two types, editors and viewers. An editor displays a part's content and provides a user interface for modifying that content. This user interface may include menus, controls, tool palettes, rulers, and other modes of interaction. A viewer offers a subset of an editor's functionality; it allows users to display and print a part's content, but not to edit it. Viewers can be useful in two situations: when the recipient of a document does not hold a license to some kinds of parts included in the document, or when the person sending the document does not want the recipient to alter it.

Both editors and viewers can interpret the contents of the part and display that content for the user. The idea is that, eventually, developers will create both kinds of handler for every part. The editor would be sold, but the viewer would be freely distributed, to enable and encourage document interchange.

Storage is a major feature of the OpenDoc architecture. The existence of multipart documents necessitates a persistent storage mechanism that enables multiple part handlers to share a single document file effectively. The OpenDoc storage model, based on Apple's Bento standard, assumes that the storage system can effectively give each part its own data stream—an individual area inside document files specific to part content—and that reliable references can be made from one stream to another, enabling parts to be integrated into a single document [OPEN95].

Because OpenDoc is designed to support cross-platform capabilities, it must also support the ability to write multiple representations of a given part. Because many pieces of code may need to access a given part, the storage system must support a robust annotation mechanism—one that allows information to be associated with a part without disturbing its format. The storage system also yields another advantage: collaborative access. OpenDoc provides an architecture that allows developers to create part handlers that let users collaborate on document creation. For more on OpenDoc, see [BYCS95] and [OPEN95].

## 22.5 CORBA: DISTRIBUTED OBJECTS

Single-platform objects and components currently live only on the desktop. To be useful, they need to talk to networks. This raises a question: How will OLE and OpenDoc talk to network servers? To solve this communication problem, the Object Management Group (OMG) has proposed a common object communication bus called CORBA (Common Object Request Broker Architecture). CORBA is a specification for a common messaging standard for distributed objects. The OMG envisions a common interconnection bus that hosts client components, core services needed by all components (including security, naming, persistence, events, and transactions), and common facilities for component collaboration (see Figure 22.6).

There are four key elements of the OMG's architecture:

1. *The ORB (object request broker).* The ORB is the object interconnection bus. Clients are insulated from the mechanisms used to communicate with, activate, or store server objects. CORBA defines an IDL (interface definition language) and APIs that enable client–server object interaction within a specific implementation of an ORB. It also specifies how ORBs from different vendors can interoperate.

2. *Object services.* Packaged as components with standard interfaces, these services extend the capabilities of the ORB. The common object services are naming, event notification, persistence, life-cycle management, transactions, concurrency control, relationships, and externalization. Other services include query, licensing, properties, security, and time.

3. *Common facilities.* These components define the rules of interaction for application objects. These address four disciplines: user interface, information management, systems management, and task management. The user-interface services govern on-screen activities. The information-management services support document storage and data interchange. Systems management services define interfaces used to manage, install, configure, operate, and repair distributed objects. Task management ser-

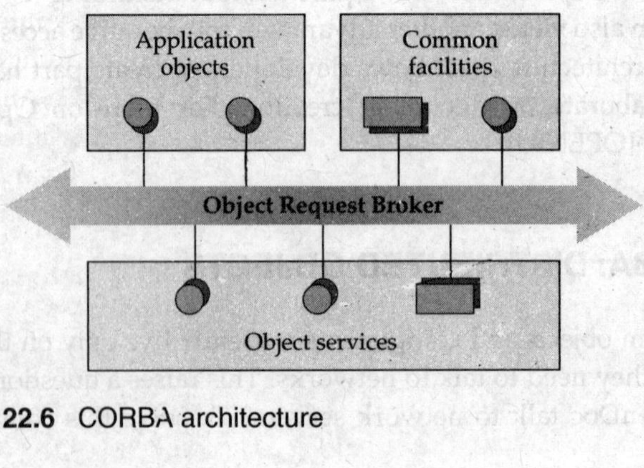


**Figure 22.6** CORBA architecture

vices include things like work flow, long transactions, agents, scripting, and rules.

4. *Application objects.* These objects are components specific to end-user applications. To participate in ORB-mediated exchanges, they too must be defined using IDL. Application objects, of course, build on top of services provided by the ORB, common facilities, and object services. Application objects will have IDL-defined interfaces and support interacting objects specialized for health, retail, finance, and other domains.

In sum, CORBA provides the universal plumbing we need to promote electronic commerce on a wide scale. However, the detailed description of CORBA is beyond the scope of this book. The interested reader may see [BYCS95] for a good overall description.

## 22.6 SUMMARY

Active document architectures change the meaning of the term *document*. In today's computing environment, a document has a type, which is tied to the application that will let the user view, edit, and print its content. With active architectures, a document is no longer a single block of content bound to a single application, but is instead composed of smaller blocks of content, or parts. Active documents present an innovative approach to the problem of dealing with data in a multiple-application environment: they associate data with the external application that created it in the first place. External applications may have created the graphics or images, but the active document must know how to import, edit, display, format, and print each external object.

Active document architectures will create environments in which applications and system services are seamlessly linked in support of the user's work. Such a change will demand a restructuring of monolithic system software and applications into components that may be easily integrated with one another and therefore incrementally enhanced. Accordingly, the battle over how the desktop will be integrated into the enterprise, and over what the desktop software environment itself will look like, is intensifying. As usual, the battleground is control of de facto standards by various vendors and competing consortiums. The prize will be the ability to control the lucrative electronic commerce marketplace.

# References


[AAPL94] Kurt Piersol, "A Close-Up of OpenDoc," *Byte*, March 1994.

[AB94] Diogo Teixeira, "Management Strategies," *The American Banker*, November 7, 1994.

[ABS94] "Communications Overview—Industry Report," Alex. Brown & Sons, Inc., July 11, 1994.

[AGEN95] Peter Wayner, *Agents Unleashed* (Cambridge, MA: Academic Press, 1995).

[AJL94] Andrew Johnson-Laird, "Smoking Guns and Spinning Disks," *The Computer Lawyer*, August 1994, p. 1.

[AL95] David Post, "E-Cash: Can't Live with It, Can't Live without It," *The American Lawyer*, March 1995.

[AM93] Richard J. Babyak, "Designing the Future; Home Appliances Design," *Appliance Manufacturer*, July 1993, p. 31.

[ATMa95] Ronald J. Vetter, "ATM Concepts, Architectures, and Protocols," *Communications of the ACM*, February 1995.

[ATMb95] B. G. Kim and P. Wang, "ATM Network: Goals and Challenges," *Communications of the ACM*, February 1995.

[AW94] "Paving the Highway; The Information Revolution Is Coming, and Part of It Is Here," *Asiaweek*, September 14, 1994.

[BC92] N. J. Belkin, and W. B. Croft, "Information Filtering and Information Retrieval: Two Sides of the Same Coin," *Communications of the ACM*, December 1992.

[BRY88] Martin Bryan, *SGML: An Author's Guide to the Standard Generalized Markup Language*, (New York: Addison-Wesley. 1988).

[BW94] "Bill Gates Is Rattling the Teller's Window," *Business Week*, October 31, 1994, p. 50.

[BWa94] "It's Not Only Rock 'n' Roll," *Business Week*, October 10, 1994, p. 83.

[BY94] "Building the Data Highway," *Byte*, March 1994.

[BYCS95] "Client/Server Computing—Special Report," *Byte*, April 1995. p. 108.

[BYTE95] "New Ways to Learn," *Byte*, March 1995, p. 50.

[CACM87] James Coombs, Allen Renear, Steven J. DeRose, "Markup Systems and the Future of Scholarly Text Processing," *Communications of the ACM*, November 30, 1987, pp. 933–947.

[CACM94] Lance J. Hoffman, Faraz A. Ali, Steven L. Heckler, and Ann Huybrechts, "Cryptography Policy," *Communications of the ACM*, September 1994, p. 109.

[CERN93a] "Basic Protection Scheme." (http://www11.w3.org/hypertext/WWW/AccessAuthorization/Basic.html)

[CIR94] "The Emerging Component-Based Desktop: The Object Is Integration," *Computer Industry Report*, December 9, 1994, p. 1.

[COM94] Microsoft, "The Component Object Model: Technical Overview," White Paper, October 1994.

[CONG94] Transcript of Testimony by Jim Williams to Committee on Science, Space, and Technology, U.S. House of Representatives, Federal News Service, October 4, 1994.

[COPY95] Copyright Act of 1976, As Amended (1994) (including the Semiconductor Chip Protection Act of 1984 and the Audio Home Recording Act of 1992). (http://www.law.cornell.edu/usc/17/overview.html)

[CROC95] D. Crocker, "MIME Encapsulation of EDI Objects," RFC 1767, March 1995.

[CW94] Alan R. Earls, "Agile Manufacturing Finds Firmer Ground," *Computerworld*, February 28, 1994, p. 93.

[DBMS94] Marc Demarest, *"Leading-Edge Retail," DBMS*, December 1994, p. 78.

[DFN88] D. Chaum, A. Fiat, and N. Naor, "Untraceable Electronic Cash," *Proceedings of Crypto '88*, 1988.

[DH76] W. Diffie and M. E. Hellman, "New Directions in Cryptography," *IEEE Transactions on Information Theory*, IT–22: 644–654, 1976.

[EB94] "Electronic Billboards on the Digital Superhighway, a Report of the Working Group on Internet Advertising," The Coalition for Networked Information, March 18, 1994.

[ECA94] "Benchmarking Comparative Payment Methods." a study by the Food Marketing Institute, *The American Banker*, July 26, 1994.

[ECON94] "Electronic Money; So Much for the Cashless Society," *The Economist*, November 26, 1994 (special edition), p. 21.

[FBC94] Federal Communications Commission, "Presents En Banc Meeting on PCS Issues," April 11, 1994. (http://fcc.gov:70/0/Panel_Discussions/940411_PCS.txt)

[FM94] Martin M. Singer, "Superhighway a Mystery to Most," *Folio: The Magazine for Magazine Management*, June 15, 1994, p. 20.

[FRAN94] Frances Williams, "Taking the Paper Out of Trade—The Quest for More Efficient Commerce," *Financial Times*, October 13, 1994.

[FRB87] Federal Reserve Bank of New York, "A Study of Large Dollar Payment Flows Through CHIPS and Fedwire," December 1987.

[FSB94] "Interim Report of the Federal Communications Commission," April 21, 1994 (Source: Lexis/Nexis).

[GAO91] Comptroller General of the United States, "Matter of National Institute of Standards and Technology—Use of Electronic Data Interchange Technology to Create Valid Obligations," December 13, 1991, File B-245714.

[GAO94] "Information Superhighway: Issues Affecting Development" (GAO/RCED-94-285), September 30, 1994.

[GCN94] "Network Break-Ins Reveal the Chinks in Systems Security," *Government Computer News*, August 8, 1994.

[GIGA94] Craig Partridge, *Gigabit Networking*, (Reading, MA: Addison-Wesley, 1994).

[GOLD90] Charles F. Goldfarb, *The SGML Handbook*, edited and with a foreword by Yuri Rubinsky (Oxford: Oxford University Press, 1990).

[GOS95] J. Gosling and H. McGilton, "The Java Language Environment: A White Paper," (http://java.sun.com/WhitePaper/)

[HAF96] Katie Hafner, *Where Wizards Stay Up at Night: The Story Behind the Creation of the Internet* (New York: Simon and Schuster, 1996).

[HBB94] Nancy E. Grant, "Home Sweet Home, Special Report; Home Banking," *U.S. Banker*, May 1994, (national edition).

[HCFA93] Health Care Financing Administration, Office of the Actuary, October 21, 1993, personal communication.

[HERW90] Eric van Herwijnen, *Practical SGML* (Hingham, MA: Wolters Kluwer Academic Publishers, 1990).

[HSN94] "Home Shopping Network—Company Report," Hanifen, Imhoff Inc., July 20, 1994 (Source Database: InvesText).

[HT91] George W. Henderson and Anthony R. Torrice, "Vendor Express: A New Era in Government," *EDI Forum*, vol. 4 (1991), p. 40.

[HTTP95] A. Schiffman Rescorla, "The Secure HyperText Transfer Protocol," Internet Draft, May 1995.

[IA94] "Interactive Advertising in an Online World," *Information Week*, October 3, 1994, p. 28.

[IB94] Imielinski and Badrinath, "Wireless Computing: Challenges in Data Management," *Communcations of the ACM*, October 1994.

[IBD95] "Quickresponse Services Inc.," *Investor's Business Daily*, September 20, 1994, p. A6.

[IEEE92] Special Issue on PCS, *IEEE Communications*, 1992.

[IM94] Laurie Peterson, "Interactive Advertising," *Inside Media*, October 19, 1994.

[IPNG94] M. Hinden, "IP Next Generation Overview," Internet Draft, October 1994.

[ISO86] International Organization for Standardization, "Information Processing—Text and Office Systems—Standard Generalized Markup Language (SGML)," Ref. No. ISO 8879:1986 (E), Geneva/New York, 1986.

[IW94] Ravi Kalakota and Andrew Whinston, "Firewalls Are Not Foolproof," *InformationWeek*, December 1994.

[IWK94] *Informationweek*, November 7, 1994, p. 8.

[JBHBR93] Jim Bessen, "Riding the Marketing Information Wave," *Harvard Business Review*, September–October 1993, p. 150.

[JMP94] David B. Johnson, Andrew Myles, and Charles Perkins, "The Internet Mobile Host Protocol (IMHP)," Internet Draft, February 14, 1994. (draft-johnson-imhp-00.txt)

[JS94] "The Information Superhighway—Separating Hype from Reality," Joseph Segel speech; Media Management; Transcript, *Direct Marketing Magazine*, February 1994, p. 18.

[KEHO93] Brendan P. Kehoe, *Zen and the Art of the Internet: A Beginner's Guide*, 2nd ed. (Englewood Cliffs, NJ: Prentice Hall, 1993).

[KROL92] Ed Krol, *The Whole Internet User's Guide and Catalog*, (Sebastopol, CA: O'Reilly & Assoc., 1992).

[KWY94] Scott Knudson, Jack K. Walton, II, and Florence M. Young, "Business-to-Business Payments and the Role of Financial Electronic Data Interchange," *Federal Reserve Bulletin*, April 1994, p. 269.

[LAMP94] Leslie Lamport, *LaTEX: A Document Preparation System* (Reading, MA: Addison-Wesley, 1994).

[LF94] Laurie Flynn, "The Executive Computer; Cutting the Data Umbilical Cord with Infrared Sensors," *The New York Times*, October 23, 1994 (Late Ed. Section 3), p. 9.

[MCN94] "Wireless Access Technology Gains Favor; Wireless Cable Television," *Multichannel News*, June 27, 1994, p. 36.

[MCOM94a] "White Paper on Security," Netscape Communications Corporation. (http://home.mcom.com/info/security-doc.html)

[MH81] R. C. Merkle and M. E. Hellman, "On the Security of Multiple Encryption," *Communications of the ACM*, July 1981.

[MM94] Michael Moeller, "Group Pushes Common API for Wireless Nets; Mobile Computing Alliance," *PC Week*, August 1, 1994, p. 47.

[MMa94] Mike Moeller, *Communications International*, February 1994, p. 14.

[MN93] Gennady Medvinsky, and B. Clifford Neuman, "NetCash: A Design for Practical Electronic Currency on the Internet," *Proceedings of the First ACM Conference on Computer and Communications Security*, November 1993 (Anonymous FTP: /pub/papers/security/netcash-cccs93.ps.Z)

[MN94] "Manufacturing and the NII," Draft for Public Comment, May 3, 1994. (http://iitf.doc.gov/)

[MNS94] Charles E. Perkins and Pravin Bhagwat, "A Mobile Networking System Based on Internet Protocol," *IEEE Personal Communications*, First Quarter, 1994. pp. 32–40.

[MSLA94] Michael Schrage, "Gates' Brave, New World of Finances," *Los Angeles Times*, October 21, 1994, p. 9.

[MW94] "Special Report on Consumer Interests," *Macworld*, October 1994.

[NAS93] "Realizing the Information Future," National Research Council, National Academy Press, Washington, D.C. 1993. (http://www.nas.org/)

[NCSA93a] "Using PGP/PEM encryption." (http://hoohoo.ncsa.uiuc.edu:80/docs/PEMPGP.html)

[NII93] "National Information Infrastructure—agenda for action." (http://sunsite.unc.edu/nii/toc.html)

[NIST92] National Institute of Standards and Technology (NIST), "The Digital Signature Standard," proposal and discussion, *Communications of the ACM*, July 1992.

[NS94] "Video on Demand," Industrial report, Nikko Securities Co., June 29, 1994. Source: InvesText CD-ROM database.

[NSF92] NSF 93-52—Program Solicitation: Network Access Point Manager, Routing Arbiter, Regional Network Providers, and Very High Speed Backbone Network Services Provider for NSFNET and the NREN Program." (gopher://stis.nsf.gov/)

[NW94] Craig Mathias and Peter Rysavy, "The ABCs of PCS," *Network World*, November 7, 1994, p. 53.

[OLE93] Kraig Brockschmidt, "Introducing OLE 2.0, Part I: Windows Objects and the Component Object Model," *Microsoft Systems Journal*, August 1993.

[OO91] T. Okamoto and K.Ohta, "Universal Electronic Cash," *Proceedings of Crypto '91*, 1991.

[OPEN95] "OpenDoc Technical Summary and White Paper," Component Integration Laboratory, Apple Computer Inc., 1995.

[ORFA94] Robert Orfali, Dan Harkey, and Jeri Edwards, *Essential Client/Server Survival Guide* (New York: Van Nostrand Reinhold, 1994).

[P94] C. Perkins, ed., "IP Mobility Support," Internet Draft, October 1994. (draft-ietf-mobileip-protocol-07.txt, 21)

[PD70] Peter F. Drucker, *Technology, Management and Society* (New York: Harper & Row, 1970).

[PD94] Peter F. Drucker, "The Theory of the Business," *Harvard Business Review*, September–October 1994.

[PGP94] Philip Zimmermann, "Pretty Good™ Privacy, Public Key Encryption for the Masses, PGP™ User's Guide," revised October 11. 1994. (http://draco.centerline.com:8080/~franl/pgp/pgp-2.6.2-doc1.html)

[PHB94a] Phillip M. Hallam-Baker, "SHEN: A Scheme for the World Wide Web," CERN Programming Techniques Group. (http://www11.w3.org/hypertext/WWW/Shen/ref/security_spec.html)

[PHB94b] Phillip M. Hallam-Baker, "SHEN: Requirements," CERN Programming Techniques Group. (http://www11.w3.org/hypertext/WWW/Shen/ref/requirements.html)

[PNMAY94] Peter G. Neumann, "Inside Risks; Approaches for Developing Secure, One-Time Passwords," *Communications of the ACM*, May 1994, p. 146.

[PRNW94] "Verifone Introduces the 450 Smart Card Reader/Writer," *PR Newswire*, November 29, 1994.

[PW94] "Motion Picture Theatrical Exhibition—Industry Report," Painewebber Inc., September 20, 1994.

[QUILL94] Michael Murriee, "Interactive Television," *The Quill*, March 1994, p. 28.

[RC94] Rosemary Cafasso, "Going Undercover with Agents of Change," *Computerworld's Client/Server Journal*, November 1, 1994, p. 21.

[RD92] Michael F. Schwartz, Alan Emtage, Brewster Kahle, and B. Clifford Neuman, "A Comparison of Internet Resource Discovery Approaches," *Computer Systems*, 5(4), 1992.

[REB94] Richard Chang, "Businesses Promote Smart Card as Computer in Wallet," *The Reuter European Business Report*, September 14, 1994.

[RFC1112] Steve Deering, "Host Extensions for IP Multicasting," Network Working Group, Request for Comments: 1112, August 1989.

[RFC1192] Request for Comments: 1192, "Commercialization of the Internet," B. Kahin, Ed., November 1990, Harvard University.

[RFC1510] J. Kohl and C. Neuman, "The Kerberos Network Authentication Service (V5)," *ISI*, September 1993.

[RJ94] Rebecca Jones, "Dialing for Dollars: Your Checkbook May Soon Be Obsolete as Computers Allow You to Tap into On Line Banking," *Rocky Mountain News*, May 18, 1994.

[RKBY94] Russell Kay, "Distributed and Secure," *Byte*, June 1994.

[RM91] Regis McKenna. "Marketing Is Everything," *Harvard Business Review*, January–February 1991, pp. 65–80.

[RSW95] Stallaert J. Ravi Kalakota, and A. B. Whinston, "Supply-Chain Management for Electronic Commerce," working paper, University of Texas at Austin 1995.

[RSWB95] Stallaert J. Ravi Kalakota, and A. B. Whinston, "Electronic Brokerages and Intermediation," working paper, University of Texas at Austin 1995.

[SAFE94] Nathaniel S. Borenstein, "E-Mail with a Mind of Its Own: The Safe-Tcl Language for Enabled Mail," submitted to ULPAA '94.

[SBS94] Smith Barney Shearson, "Personal Computing Trends—Industry Report," February 15, 1994.

[SCHN96] Bruce Schneier, *Applied Cryptography*, 2nd ed., (New York: John Wiley & Sons, 1996).

[SEAR94] J. S. Rosenberg, "Copyright of Way on the Information Highway," *Searcher*, March 1994, p. 36.

[SIMBA94] "The Future of Electronic Commerce Explored at EM 2000," SIMBA Information Inc's Electronic Marketplace 2000 trade show, *Electronic Marketplace Reports*, March 15, 1994, p. 4.

[SIRD94] C. M. Bowman, P. B. Danzig, U. Manber, M. Schwartz, "Scalable Internet Resource Discovery: Research Problems and Approaches," *Communications of the ACM*, August 1994.

[SMN95] "Computers as Tutors," *Supermarket News*, February 27, 1995, p. 11.

[SOLL89] Karen Sollins, "Plan for Internet Directory Services," Internet RFC 1107, M.I.T. Laboratory for Computer Science, July 1989.

[SOM94] IBM Corp. Object Technology Products Group, "The System Object Model (SOM) and the Component Object Model (COM): A Comparison of Technologies from a Developer's Perspective," White Paper, May 1994.

[SS93] Danielle C. Fowler, Paula M. C. Swatman, and Paul A. Swatman, "Corporate EDI Gateways: Rationale and Requirements," EDI Research Group School of Computing Curtin University of Technology.

[TBW94] Jan Spalding, "Crumpling the Paper Trace," Tribune Business weekly, July 13, 1994.

[TCL90] John K. Ousterhout, "Tcl: An Embeddable Command Language," 1990 Winter USENIX Conference Proceedings.

[TD95] "Reengineer Warehousing," *Transportation & Distribution*, January 1995, p. 98.

[TELE94] S. Ronald Foster, "CATV Systems Are Evolving to Support a Wide Range of Services; Delivering Voice and Other Services over Cable Television Systems," *Telecommunications*, January 1994, p. 95.

[TELS95] Peter Wayner, "Free Agents," *Byte*, March 1995, p. 105.

[TN93] Nanci A. Tangeman, "The International Logistics of Freight Forwarding: Performance Measurement at the Harper Group; Harper Group Inc.," *National Productivity Review*, December 22, 1993, p. 107.

[UN94a] Trade and Development Board, Ad Hoc Working Group on Trade Efficiency Third Session, Geneva, May 2, 1994. (gopher://gopher.undp.org/)

[UN94b] The Trade Point: Concept and Implementation, Special Programme for Trade Efficiency, United Nations Conference on Trade and Development. (gopher:// gopher.undp.org/)

[USCO95] "U.S. Copyright Office General Information: Copyright Basics." (http://lcweb.loc.gov/copyright/)

[USI94] Mary Smolenski, Shelagh Montgomery, Vera A. Swann, and Mary Davin, "Computer Software and Networking; Industry Overview," *U.S. Industrial Outlook*, U.S. Department of Commerce, January 1994.

[USIO94] Mary C. Inoussa, and Robert G. Atkins, "Information Services; Industry Overview," *U.S. Industrial Outlook*, U.S. Department of Commerce, January 1994.

[USITC94] Daniel W. Edwards, Stephanie W. McCullough, and Linda L. Gossack, "Telecommunications Services; Industry Overview," *U.S. Industrial Outlook*, U.S. Department of Commerce, January 1994.

[VA95] Walt Houser, "The EDI Business Case for VA, Department of Veterans Affairs." (ftp://ftp.sterling.com/edi/VA)

[WEDI93] Workgroup for Electronic Data Interchange (WEDI) reports on Health-Care EDI, 1993.

[WHIT95] Jim White, "Telescript: White Paper," General Magic, Inc., 1995.

[WIND78] Y. Wind, "Issues and Advances in Segmentation Research," *Journal of Marketing Research*, August 1978, pp. 317–37.

[WP94] "Fleet-Footed Firms Reshape Economy," *The Washington Post*, July 4, 1994, Final Ed.

[WS94] Chris Devoney, "The Unwired Nation," *Windows Sources*, April 1994, p. 106.

[WSJ94] "Sega Launches Online Games," *Wall Street Journal*, February 14, 1994.

[X92] C. Weider, J. Reynolds, and S. Heker, "Technical Overview of Directory Services Using the X.500 Protocol," For Your Information (FYI) 14—RFC 1309, ANS, USC/Information Sciences Institute, JvNC, March 1992.

[XIWT94] "Electronic Cash, Tokens and Payments in the National Information Infrastructure," XIWT (Cross-Industry Working Team) Report on Electronic Cash in the NII, Corporation for National Research Initiatives (CNRI), Reston, Virginia.

# Index

AAL (application adaptation layer) in ATM, 730–731
AAP (Association of American Publishers), 789
ABR (available bit rate) in ATM, 728
Academic Internet, 101–102
  EBONE on, 131–133
  globalization of, 129–134
Accelerators, video, 694, 696–697
Acceptable Usage Policy (AUP)
  with Internet service providers, 159
  with NFSNET, 147–148
  with NREN, 122–123
Access. *See also* Security
  to copyrighted works, 603–605
  to information highway, 93–96
  to Internet-based EDI, 409
Access equipment, network, 65
  computer-based telephony, 68
  set-top boxes, 66–67
  switches, 68–70
Accessibility
  of information, 527
  of set-top boxes, 67
Account/payment management, 306
Accounts
  for electronic cash, 317
  for software agents, 318
ACH (automated clearinghouse) transfers, 365–368
Acrobat markup language, 786, 799–800
Active advertising, 502–505
Active document architectures (ADAs), 805
  active documents in, 806–807
  applets for, 807–809
  elements of, 809–812
  multiple-platform integration in, 812–813
  Object Linking and Embedding in, 818–819
  object-to-object calling mechanism in, 813–818
  OpenDoc in, 819–821
  single-platform integration in, 812
Active documents, 474–475
Active learning, 569
Active mail system, 631–632
Ad hoc documents, 468
ADAs. *See* Active document architectures (ADAs)
Addresses
  IP, 134, 651–652
  in mobile networking, 660–661
  in multicast TCP/IP, 667
  next generation IP for, 670
  in OSI model, 646–647
  in SLIP, 657
  of Web objects, 248–250, 560–561
Adleman, Leonard, 213
Administration in education, 573
ADSL (asymmetrical digital subscriber line), 77–78
Advanced Mobile Phone Systems (AMPSs), 760
Advanced Network & Services (ANS), 114, 156
Advantis/IBM VAN service provider, 407
Advertising, 489–491, 499–502. *See also* Marketing
  Acrobat for, 800
  active, 502–505
  billboard, 507
  broadcast model for, 503–504
  catalogs for, 507–508
  content in, 518–520
  costs of, 41, 502
  customer contacts in, 520–521
  customer evaluation in, 521
  endorsements for, 508–509
  guidelines for, 509–510
  interactive, 490–491, 518. 520–521
  junk mail model for, 504–505
  in news retrieval and delivery services, 590
  on-line paradigms for, 502
  passive, 505–509
  plans for, 516–519
  on Prodigy, 154
  service and support in, 521–522

Advertising (*Cont.*)
by small and large firms, 497–498
softads, 278
in supply chain management, 447
Agents
directory system, 548–550
mail-filtering, 559
software. *See* Software agents
user, 397–398, 459–460
user-interface, 463–464
Agile manufacturing, 419, 450–452
AI (artificial intelligence), 612
Alerts, news, 587
All-talk radio, 38
Allocation issues, 93
AlterNET Internet service provider, 160–161
America Online
as Internet service provider, 155–156
privacy issues with, 94
American Hospital order-entry system, 422
Ameritech, 75
AMPSs (Advanced Mobile Phone Systems), 760
Analog systems
for mobile computing, 760
for telephone systems, 71
Analysts in EDI, 414
Analytic transaction processing, 460–461 486
Analytical buyers, 291
Anchors in hypertext, 245–246
Annual reports, corporate, 583–584
Anonymity in electronic payment systems, 341–342
with electronic cash, 318, 323
with smart cards, 330
token-based, 314
Anonymous FTP, 141–142, 520
ANS (Advanced Network & Services), 114, 156
ANSI X.12 standard, 350–351, 385–388
API for mobile computing, 771–772
Apollo reservation system, 421
Apparel industry
customization in, 439–440
new economy in, 47–48
AppleSearch program, 559
Applets
in active document architectures, 807–809
in browsers, 633–635
Application adaptation layer (AAL) in ATM, 730–731
Application interoperability with ATM, 726–727
Application layer
in OSI, 645, 647
in TCP/IP, 647
Application objects in CORBA, 823
Application services, 232–233
business-to-business transactions, 234
consumer-to-business transactions, 233
intraorganizational transactions, 234
Application-specific personal computers (ASPCs), 758
Applications
boundaryless, 805
collaborative, 53–54
in electronic commerce, 18–19
Archie tool, 142–143
Architectural framework for electronic commerce, 231–234
Architext search engine, 537
Archive-oriented compression, 675
Archives in news retrieval and delivery services, 588
Ardis packet provider, 750–751
ARPANET, 103–106
Artificial intelligence (AI), 612
ASAP order-entry system, 422
ASCII text in HTML, 253
ASMP (asymmetric multiprocessing), 680
ASPCs (application-specific personal computers), 758
Associated Communications, 63
Association of American Publishers (AAP), 789
Astoria, 798
Asymmetric multiprocessing (ASMP), 680
Asymmetrical digital subscriber line (ADSL), 77–78
Asynchronous modems, 184
Asynchronous software agents, 621
Asynchronous teacher-student interaction, 569
Asynchronous transfer mode (ATM), 69 724–725
application layer in, 730–731
ATM layer in, 731–733
vs. B-ISDN, 713–714
benefits of, 725–727
cell structure in, 729
connection management in, 736–739
data transfer in, 734–736
for gigabit networks, 129
physical layer in, 733–734
switching in, 728–729, 739–740
traffic types on, 727–728
for vBNS, 124
Atari games, 596
ATM. *See* Asynchronous transfer mode (ATM)
ATMs (automated teller machines), 270–271
ATOMICMAIL project, 631
AT&T VAN service provider, 406

Attributes of Telescript agents, 630
Audiences, targeting, 48, 496–497, 513–516
Audio Home Recording Act, 601, 605
Audio-Video Transport Working Group, 666
Audiotext, 33, 39, 591
AUP (Acceptable Usage Policy)
  with Internet service providers, 159
  with NFSNET, 147–148
  with NREN, 122–123
Aurora NREN testbed, 128
Authentication, 20
  of copyrighted works, 605–606
  of credit cards, 331
  digital signatures for, 216–217
  of electronic checks, 325
  in electronic payment systems, 314
  in financial EDI, 368
  in message security, 208–209
  with PGP, 223–224
  with SHEN, 264
  third-party, 218–220
  token, 218
  on World Wide Web, 259–264
Authorization, 193
Authors
  for education, 578–579
  in SGML, 796–797
  of software agents, 618
Automated clearinghouse (ACH) transfers, 365–368
Automated Insurance Environment, 422
Automated search tools, 540–541
Automated teller machines (ATMs), 270–273
Automation of work-flow, 433–437
Autonomy of software agents, 615
Availability of information, 527
Available bit rate (ABR) in ATM, 728
Avatars, 562
AVI format, 699

B channel in ISDN, 711
B-ISDN, 711–714
Back ends for data warehouses, 482–483
Backbones
  ATM for, 725
  EBONE, 131–132
  for Internet service providers, 178–180
  NFSNET, 113–115
  NREN, 121–125
Background information for software agents, 619
Backup-oriented compression, 675
Backward compatibility, 670–671
BAI standard, 369
Bandwidth
  in analog phone systems, 760
  in ATM, 725
  in cell relay, 721
  and costs, 174–175
  in frame relay, 719
  with Internet service providers, 179–180
  in quality of service, 727–728
  in SONET, 713
  for video, 81
Bandwidth on-demand, 725
Bank checks, 363–364
Banking, home, 269–270
  advanced services, 273–275
  basic services, 270–571
  intermediate services, 272–273
Banks in EDI, 384
BankWire funds transfer service, 365
Baran, Paul, 103
Bargaining, 287
BARRnet, 120
Basic rate interface (BRI) with ISDN, 176
Behavioral approach in audience targeting, 514
Bell Atlantic, 75
BellSouth, 63
Benefit approach in audience targeting, 514
Berners-Lee, Tim, 241, 801
BGPs (Border Gateway Protocols), 652
Bibliographic databases, 582–583
Big businesses, Yellow Pages directory for, 552
Bilateral electronic cash transactions, 319
Billboard advertising, 507
Billing and account/payment management, 306
Binary files with MIME, 399
Biometric security systems, 195–196
Birds of a feather (BOF) sessions, 136
BITNET, 101, 105, 130
Blanca NREN testbed, 128
Blinding with electronic cash, 318
Block Financial, 332
Blockbuster Video, 36, 42
BOF (birds of a feather) sessions, 136
Books, CD-ROM-based, 594. *See also* Publishing
Boolean searches, 471–472, 542
Border Gateway Protocols (BGPs), 652
Borenstein, Nathaniel, 631
Bottom-up method in DTD development, 794–795
Boundaryless applications, 805
Boundaryless relationships, 348
BOV (business operational view), 380
Brand, Stewart, 164
Brand loyalty, 522
BRI (basic rate interface) with ISDN, 176
British Telecom (BT), 63–406

Broadband ISDN, 711–714
Broadband PCS, 775–776
Broadband telecommunications, 709–710
 ATM. *See* Asynchronous transfer mode (ATM)
 B-ISDN vs. ATM, 713–714
 cell relay, 720–722
 connectionless vs. connection-oriented, 714–716
 frame relay, 718–720
 ISDN, 711–712
 vs. narrowband, 710
 SMDS, 722–724
 SONET and SDH, 712–713
 switching in, 716–718
Broadcasting, 69
 advertising model for, 503–504
 with SMDS, 723
Brochures, electronic, 278
Brokers, 431–433
 for document management, 477
 in electronic commerce, 234–236, 343
 for infosphere, 463–464
 in prepurchase preparation phase, 295–296
Browsers
 with applets, 633–635
 for Web, 143, 243–244
BT (British Telecom), 63, 406
Buffer zones in cellular communications, 748
Bulletin boards
 for collaboration, 140
 as Internet service providers, 165–166
Bundling, 494
Business application layer in EDI, 389–390
Business modeling of documents, 479
Business operational view (BOV), 380
Business specialization approaches in audience targeting, 514
Business-to-business transactions, 234
Businesses and business issues. *See also* Corporate digital libraries; Electronic commerce; Internet service providers (ISPs)
 EDI standards, 387
 electronic cash, 320–321
 encryption, 225–226
 goals in, 230–231
 on Internet, 101–102, 108, 147–150
 smart cards, 330–331
 Yellow Pages directories for, 551–552

Cable
 content of, 25–26
 costs of, 40–41, 283
 as information route, 32
 for last mile, 78–83
 wired, 79–81
 wireless, 81–83
Cable & Wireless VAN service provider, 406
Cable companies
 information highway plans by, 61
 as Internet service providers, 150–152
 mergers with telcoms, 63
 movie production house purchases by, 282–283
Calls
 in cellular communications, 749
 in packet switching, 717
CALS (Computer-aided Acquisition and Logistics Support) program, 789
Cameras for CU-SeeMe program, 705
Campus networks, 118–119
Canter, Laurence, 505
Capstone project, 215–216
Capture, image and video, 674, 697–698
Car purchase, search scenario for, 529–231
Card readers, 329
Cartoon characters in chat rooms, 562
CASA NREN testbed, 128
Cash, 298
 electronic. *See* Electronic cash
 slippage in, 330
Casual RSA key-size option, 223
Catalogs, 532, 543–545
 for advertising, 507–508
 for home shopping, 277–278
 interactive, 236, 553–557
 multimedia, 48
CBR (constant bit rate) in ATM, 728, 737–738
CCD standard, 369
CCD+ standard, 369
CD-ROMs
 for books, 594
 for full-text databases, 593–594
 as information route, 33
 for multimedia, 682–684
 operation of, 683–684
CD-video, 682
CDA (compound document architecture), 240–472
CDMA (code division multiple access), 761–764
CDPD (cellular digital packet data) protocol, 765–767
Cell-delay in quality of service, 728
Cell loss priority (CLP) in ATM headers, 733, 737
Cell relay, 720–722
Cell structure in ATM, 729
Cellular communications, 84–85, 747–749
 circuit-switched, 764–765

infrastructure for, 85–87
mobile data networks, 87–88
modems for, 758–459
operation of, 749
protocols for, 764–767
SMR, 87
Cellular digital packet data (CDPD) protocol, 765–767
Cellular Telecommunications Industry Association (CTIA), 760
Censorship
by local-level service providers, 164
by Prodigy, 155
Centralized management with hardened firewall hosts, 204
Cerf, Vinton, 613
CERFnet, 116, 130–131
CERN, 241–242
CGI gateway services, 255–257
Chaining in X.500 project, 550
Challenge-response systems, 217–218
smart cards, 218
third-party authentication, 218–220
Change for electronic cash, 320
Channel hopping in CDPD, 766
Channel management in supply chain management, 53
Chat rooms, avatars in, 562
CheckFree service, 272–273
Checks
vs. credit cards, 338
electronic, 324–326
in financial EDI, 363–364
Checksums
in ATM, 736
in Kerberos, 220
CHINAPAC network, 131
CHIPS (Clearing House Interbank Payments System) service, 364–365
Christmas tree virus, 632
Cigarettes, marketing, 498–499
Cinepak format, 690, 694
Ciphers. *See* Encryption
Ciphertext, 209–210
CIR (committed information rate) in ATM, 728–729
Circuit-switched networks, 716, 764–765
Citation index databases, 583
City Key program, 546
CIX (Commercial Information Exchange), 123, 157, 171–174
Claims processing, EDI in, 370–371
Clarinet news service, 592–593
Classes
in ATM AAL layer, 730–731
of IP networks, 651–652
Clear channels in ISDN, 711
Clearing House Interbank Payments System (CHIPS) service, 364, 365
Cleveland Freenet, 167
Client-agent-server applications, 769
Client-server architecture
for indexing, 538–539
for multimedia storage servers, 27–28
security in, 191–199
for Web, 243–244
Clients in Wide Area Information Service, 536
Clinton, Bill, 38
Clipper chip, 215–216
Closed systems, 643
CLP (cell loss priority) in ATM headers, 733, 737,
CNN network, 37
CNPAC network, 131
CNSSs (core nodal traffic switching substations), 115, 120
Co-makership concept, 50
Code division multiple access (CDMA), 761–764
Codecs, 688–689
Cinepak, 694
future of, 694–695
Indeo, 694
JPEG, 693–694
MPEG, 691–693
types of, 689–690
for video conferencing, 703
Collaboration on Internet, 107–108, 140
Collaborative applications, 53–54
Collaboratories, 596–597
Colleges, new roles for, 576–577
Collision-proof checksums, 220
COM (Component Object Model), 811–812, 818
Commercial Information Exchange (CIX), 123, 157, 171–174
Commercial on-line services
applications of, 88–89
information highway plans by, 62
as Internet service providers, 150, 152–156
for last mile, 88–90
Commercial RSA key-size option, 223.
Commercialization of Internet, 108, 147–150. *See also* Internet service providers (ISPs)
Committed information rate (CIR) in ATM, 728–729
Common Business Services, 20
Common facilities in CORBA, 822–823
Common Object Request Broker Architecture (CORBA), 475, 813, 816, 821–823
Common signaling channels in ISDN, 711
Communication by software agents, 614

Communication modes in contract law, 375
Communications layer in EDI, 391–392
Comp-U-Card shopping service, 48
Compatibility issues
  in mercantile models, 302
  in next generation IP, 670–671
Competitive advantage, 417–418
Competitive intelligence, 374
Competitive strategies, time-based, 45
Component Object Model (COM), 811–812, 818
Compound document architecture (CDA), 240, 472
Compound document languages, 782
Compound documents. *See* Active document architectures (ADAs)
Compression
  for cable transmissions, 80
  Cinepak, 694
  for digital video, 688–695
  Indeo, 694
  JPEG, 693–694
  lossy and lossless, 677–678
  MPEG, 691–693
  in multimedia, 675–678
  operation of, 675–677
  with PGP, 224
  in SLIP, 657–658
  for video conferencing, 700, 703–704
CompuServe on-line service, 153–154
Computer-aided Acquisition and Logistics Support (CALS) program, 789
Computer displays for set-top boxes, 66–67
Computer Shopper catalog, 557
Computerized reservation systems (CRSs), 421
Computers
  as information route, 32
  portable, 755–756
  for set-top box control, 66–67
  for telephony, 68
Concentration of security with hardened firewall hosts, 204
Conferencing
  in education, 597–598
  video. *See* Video conferencing
Confidentiality, 258. *See also* Security
  of messages, 207–208
  with PGP, 223–224
Congestion management
  in ATM, 736–739
  in frame relay, 720
Congestion-network upgrade cycle, 114
Connectionless vs. connection-oriented networks, 714–716
Connections
  in ATM, 736–739
  for local-level service providers, 184
  in Telescript language, 626
Connectivity
  for Internet service providers, 171–174
  for news services, 592
Consignment tracking systems, 49
Constant bit rate (CBR) in ATM, 728, 737–738
Constant linear velocity devices, 684
Constituencies for documents, 477–478
Consumer-data interface for searches, 559–565
Consumer-interactive platforms, 37
Consumer-oriented electronic commerce, 267–268
  features of, 286–287
  home entertainment, 279–283
  home shopping, 275–278
  mercantile models for. *See* Mercantile models
  microtransactions in, 283–286
  personal finance and home banking management, 269–275
Consumer-to-business transactions, 233
Consumers and consumer applications, 36–39. *See also* Customers
  access devices for, 33–36, 64–65
  consumer wants in, 39–40
  delivery of products in, 42
  research for, 42–44
  service provider targeting of, 188
  and virtual reality, 561–565
Containers in active document architectures, 810–811
Content
  in advertising, 518–520
  convergence of, 22
  in DTD development, 795
Context-based searches, 537
Contract law with EDI, 375–376
Contracts
  in ATM, 736
  electronic, 606–607
Control issues with software agents, 624–625
Controls for set-top boxes, 67
Convenience factor, 40
Convergence, 21
  in ATM, 735
  media, 21–23
Conversion of documents, 478, 797–798
Converter boxes, 66–67
  as brokers, 35
  MPEG-2 for, 692
Cooperation by software agents, 616, 640
Coordination of work-flow, 435
Coordinators for EDI, 414

Copyright Act, 599–600
Copyright issues, 258, 599
  access control, 603–605
  authentication, 605–606
  for databases, 601–603
  electronic contracts, 606–607
  in hypertext, 579
  overview of, 599–601
  use control, 605
CORBA (Common Object Request Broker Architecture), 475, 813, 816, 821–823
Cordless telephones. *See* Cellular communications
Core Internet, 101–102
  EBONE on, 131–133
  globalization of, 129–134
Core nodal traffic switching substations (CNSSs), 115, 120
CoREN (Corporation for Regional and Enterprise Networking), 118
Corporate digital libraries, 436, 455–457
  active documents in, 474–475
  creation and management of, 468, 798
  data warehouses for, 479–486
  document creation and authoring for, 796–797
  document imaging in, 468–470
  document infrastructure issues in, 475–479
  document parsing and conversion in, 797–798
  document type definitions for, 793–796
  electronic delivery and distribution in, 799–802
  formatting and page composition in, 798–799
  hypertext documents in, 473–474
  need for, 466–468
  SGML for, 792–802
  structured documents in, 470–473
Corporate documents, publishing, 583–584
Corporation for Regional and Enterprise Networking (CoREN), 118
COSMOS customer service system, 422
Costs
  of advertising, 41, 502
  of cable service, 283
  of CD-ROMs, 683
  of cellular technology, 85
  of credit card transactions, 300–301
  of EDI, 392–393, 409
  of electronic purchases, 301
  of firewalls, 205
  of information-based products, 494–495
  of information highway, 92–93, 96
  of international networks, 133–134
  of light-based mobile computing, 754
  of local-level service providers, 180
  in mercantile models, 303–304
  of microtransactions, 283–286
  in NFSNET, 114–115
  of training, 574
  of value-added networks, 403–406
  of video conferencing, 700–701
Couriers in contract law, 375
Courseware developers, 578–579
Court proceedings, database for, 585
Credit-based flow control in ATM, 738–739
Credit cards, 298–301, 331–332
  encryption for, 332–334, 339
  infrastructure for, 339–340
  pros and cons of, 338–339
  third-party processors for, 334–337
Credit electronic tokens, 313
Credit references, Yellow Pages directory for, 552
Credit risk in electronic payment systems, 342–343
Credit transfers with ACH, 365–367
Critical mass for electronic commerce, 286
Cross-functional information systems, 422–423
Cross-media convergence, 22
Cross-references in hypermedia, 247
Cross-training opportunities, 575
CRSs (computerized reservation systems), 421
CSNET, 105–106, 130
CTIA (Cellular Telecommunications Industry Association), 760
CTP standard, 369
CTX standard, 369
CU-SeeMe video conferencing program, 704–706
CUC International, 48–49
Currency servers, 317–318
Custom translators in EDI, 390–391
Customer premises equipment (CPE), 65
  computer-based telephony, 68
  for independent service providers, 157–158
  set-top boxes, 66–67
  switches, 68–70
Customer service and support, 301–302
  in advertising, 521–522
  in EDI, 355
  efficient customer response for, 448–450
  by local-level service providers, 164, 180, 186–188
  software agents for, 636–637
Customers. *See also* Consumers and consumer applications; Mercantile models
  in agile manufacturing, 452

Customers (*Cont.*)
with EDI, 355–356
endorsements from, 508–509
evaluations by, 521
in information-based marketing, 492–493
interaction with, 520–521
service provider targeting of, 188
Customization
agile manufacturing for, 452
in intraorganizational electronic commerce, 419–420, 437–441
of services, 440–441
Customs clearances in international trade, 360–361
Cyber sex, marketing, 499

D channel in ISDN, 711
Danmont consortium, 330–331
Data
categories of, 258–259
compressing. *See* Compression
in EDI, 387–388
interoperability of, in ATM, 726–727
libraries of, 481
market research, 522–524
remote access of, 767
security of. *See* Security
in Transmission Control Protocol, 650
Data conferencing, 701–702
Data Encryption Standard (DES), 210–211
Data-interface (DI) agents, 464
Data link connection identifiers (DLCI) in frame relay, 719
Data link layer in OSI, 645–646
Data warehouses, 465–466, 479–480
advantages of, 485–486
back ends for, 482–483
building, 481–485
data preparation for, 483–484
front ends for, 484–485
types of, 480–481
Databases
access to, 302
bibliographic, 582–583
CD-ROM-based publishing for, 593–594
copyright issues for, 601–603
directory services, 236–237
for electronic payment systems, 343
full-text, 584–587, 593–594
interfaces for, 560
in market research, 522–523
for software agents, 621
Datagrams
with PPP, 658
with SLIP, 656
in TCP/IP, 648–649
David vs. Goliath syndrome, 497–498
DBS (direct broadcast satellite) systems, 81–82
DCTs (discrete cosine transformations), 693
DDE (Dynamic Data Exchange), 815–816
Debit cards, 328, 330
Debit electronic tokens, 313
Debit transfers with ACH, 365–368
Decentralized maintenance in X.500 project, 547
Decision support systems (DSSs), 456–457, 481, 611, 616. *See also* Corporate digital libraries
Dedicated Internet connections, 117
Delayed communication in contract law, 375
Delays in satellite networks, 752
Deliberation, purchase, 290
Delivery
of data warehouse data, 484–485
of information, 31–33
of products, 42
in SGML, 799–802
Demographic approaches in audience targeting, 514
Department of Defense (DOD), 99, 73
Internet-based EDI for, 410
SGML for, 789
DES (Data Encryption Standard), 210–211
Descriptive document markup, 787
Desktop publishing, 577
Desktop video
applications for, 698–699
capture and editing hardware for, 697–698
conferencing. *See* Video conferencing
playback hardware for, 695–697
Destination addresses in OSI model, 646–647
Devaluation of electronic cash, 321
Developers
of courseware, 578–579
of documents, 477
DFN network, 130
DI (data-interface) agents, 464
Dial-up connections, 117, 175
DIALOG information service, 582, 596
Dictionary comparisons for password detection, 195
Digest function with Kerberos, 220
DIGEX (Digital Express Group), 165
DigiCash, 317
Digital assistants, 757
Digital cameras, 705
Digital compression. *See* Compression
Digital documents
active, 474–475
constituencies for, 477–478
hypertext, 473–474

imaging of, 469–470
infrastructure of, 475–479
management issues in, 468
processes for, 478
structured, 470–473
in work flows, 479
Digital Equipment Corporation, 46
Digital Express Group (DIGEX), 165
Digital libraries. *See* Corporate digital libraries
Digital payment systems. *See* Electronic payment systems
Digital public-key certificates, 214–215
Digital section level in ATM, 734
Digital Signature Algorithm (DSA), 216–217
Digital Signature Standard (DSS), 216–217, 376
Digital signatures
for authentication, 216–217
for copyrighted works, 605–606
in EDI, 376–377
for electronic cash, 316–317
for electronic checks, 325
public-key encryption for, 212
in RSA encryption, 213
Digital switches, 68–70
Digital video, 684–686
characteristics of, 686–687
compression for, 688–695
space requirements for, 676–678
Diller, Barry, 58
Direct broadcast satellite (DBS) systems, 81–82
Direct-dial EDI systems, 391
Direct interaction in advertising, 520
Direct marketing, 40, 48, 496–497
Direct Satellite System (DSS) service, 83
Directories, 532, 543–545
for advertising, 507–508
overview of, 545–546
white pages, 546–551
yellow pages, 551–553
Directory architectural model, 548
Directory information trees (DITs), 548, 550
Directory services databases, 236–237
Directory system agents (DSAs), 548–550
Directory user agents (DUAs), 548–550
Discipline-specific Internet stage, 107
Discounts in information-based marketing, 493
Discourse in passive advertising, 506
Discovery in infosphere, 462
Discrete cosine transformations (DCTs), 693
Disk arrays, 681–682
Disney, 36
Display methods for Object Linking and Embedding, 819
Displays for set-top boxes, 66–67
Disputes
in electronic commerce, 287
in electronic payment systems, 341
Distance education, 570–571
Distance Vector Multicast Routing Protocol (DVMRP), 667–668
Distributed component catalogs, 278
Distributed computing applications, gigabit networks for, 126–127
Distributed objects, 813
with CORBA, 821–823
management and services for, 240–241
Distribution
of data warehouse data, 484
of documents, 478
in news retrieval and delivery services, 590
in SGML, 799–802
in supply chain management, 52–53, 444–445
DITs (directory information trees), 548, 550
DLCI (data link connection identifiers) in frame relay, 719
DNS (domain name service) in TCP/IP, 652
Document access to copyrighted works, 604
Document conferencing, 701–702
Document exchange, 237–238
Document-oriented computing, 240
Document-oriented interfaces (DOIs), 806
Document tracking and transport, 391
Document type definitions (DTDs) in SGML, 253, 790–796
Documentation from local-level service providers, 186
Documents
active, 474–475 *See also* Active document architectures (ADAs)
constituencies for, 477–478
EDI for. *See* EDI (electronic data interchange)
encryption for, 221–224
hypermedia, 246–248
hypertext, 473–474
imaging of, 469–470
infrastructure of, 475–479
investments in, 780–781
libraries for. *See* Corporate digital libraries
management issues in, 468
processes for, 478
structured. *See* Structured documents
in work flows, 479
DOIs (document-oriented interfaces), 806
Domain experts, software agents as, 612
Domain name service (DNS) in TCP/IP, 652
Domain-specific knowledge for software agents, 620

Donahue, Phil, 38
Donnelley & Sons, selectronic services by, 496–497
Double bagging in EDI envelopes, 394
Double spending of electronic cash, 316, 319
Dow-Jones News-Retrieval service, 586
Downloading, copyright issues in, 601
Downsizing, 46, 425
Downward networking, 430
Drucker, Peter, 46, 421
Drugs, marketing, 499
DS-1 channels with SONET, 713
DSA (Digital Signature Algorithm), 216–217
DSAs (directory system agents), 548–550
DSS (Digital Signature Standard), 216–217, 376
DSS (Direct Satellite System) service, 83
DSSs (decision support systems), 456–457, 481, 611, 616 *See also* Corporate digital libraries
DTDs (document type definitions, 253, 790–796
Dual stack strategies, 671
DUAs (directory user agents), 548–550
DVMRP (Distance Vector Multicast Routing Protocol), 667–668
Dynamic Data Exchange (DDE), 815–816
Dynamic organization in hypermedia, 247
Dynamic preferences in news retrieval and delivery services, 588
Dynamic reconfiguration of products, 452
Dynamic routing in TCP/IP, 653

E-cash. *See* Electronic cash
E-commerce. *See* Electronic commerce
E-mail, 20, 139, 169
  vs. EDI, 351
  encryption for, 221–224
  filters for, 559
  interconnectivity for, 393
  for Internet-based EDI, 411–412
  junk, 504–505
  for letters-to-the-editor, 592
  for software agent programming, 624, 631–632
  software agents for, 638–639
  with TCP/IP, 648–649
E-mail to fax Internet services, 139–140
EARN network, 130
East Coast Federal Interagency Exchange, 116
Eavesdropping, 198, 342
EBONE network, 102, 131–133
Echo service, 166
ECONOMOST drug distribution system, 422
ECR (efficient customer response), 448–450
EDGAR (Electronic Data Gathering, Analysis, and Retrieval) database, 583–584, 589
EDI (electronic data interchange), 15–16, 20 347–349, 383–384
  architecture of, 349–352
  benefits of, 354–356
  business application layer in, 389–390
  communications layer in, 391–392
  costs in implementing, 392–393
  defining, 349
  in electronic commerce, 377–381
  envelopes for, 393–401
  financial, 362–369
  gateways for, 413–414
  in health care industry, 369–371
  history of, 386–387
  for information and product design, 373–374
  information flow in, 352–354
  in international trade, 357–358
  Internet-based, 409–414
  job descriptions for, 414–415
  legal issues in, 375–376
  new, 378–380
  old, 378
  open, 380–381
  in procurement, 371–374
  security in, 376–377
  software for 389–393
  standards in, 350–351, 368–369, 378–379 384–388
  traditional, 377–378
  transactions in, 387
  translation layer in, 390–391
  value-added networks in, 401–409
EDIFACT standard, 369, 385–389
Editors
  for HTML, 253
  for OpenDoc parts, 820–821
  for video, 697–698
Education, 567–570
  authors for, 578–579
  bibliographic databases for, 582–583
  CD-ROM-based publishing for, 593–594
  challenges in, 573
  collaboratories in, 596–597
  copyright issues in, 599–607
  corporate documents on-line, 583–584
  edutainment, 567, 595–596
  fill-text databases for, 584–587
  news retrieval and delivery services in, 587–593
  publishers in, 577–578
  real-time conferencing in, 597–598
  technical components of, 580–582
  training on-demand, 573–576

university roles in, 576–577
virtual classrooms for, 570–573
Edutainment, 567, 595–596
Efficient customer response (ECR), 448–450
EFT (electronic funds transfer), 284, 310, 312, 364, 378
EGPs (Exterior Gateway Protocols), 652
800 toll-free service, 38–39
820 standard, 369
823 standard, 369
EINet Galaxy, 552–554
EISs (executive information systems), 481
Electronic books, 594
Electronic brokers, 431–433
Electronic cash, 313–315
business issues in, 320–321
currency servers for, 317–318
digital signatures for, 316–317
legal issues in, 322–324
properties of, 315–316
risk in, 322
using, 318–320
Electronic checks, 324–326
Electronic commerce, 15–17, 229–231
application services for, 232–234
consumer access devices in, 33–36
consumer applications of, 36–44
consumer-oriented. *See* Consumer-oriented electronic commerce
digital video in, 684–695
EDI in, 377–381
framework of, 17–21
information brokerage and management in, 234–236
information delivery and transport in, 31–33
interface and support services in, 236–237
intraorganizational. *See* Intraorganizational electronic commerce
and media convergence, 21–23
middleware services in, 238–241
multimedia content for, 23–27
multimedia storage servers in, 27–31
organizational applications of, 44–54
searches in. *See* Searches
secure messaging and structured document exchange in, 237–238
Electronic contracts, 606–607
Electronic Data Gathering, Analysis, and Retrieval (EDGAR) database, 583–584, 789
Electronic data interchange. *See* EDI (electronic data interchange)
Electronic directories and catalogs, 532, 543–545
interactive catalogs, 553–557
overview of, 545–546
white pages, 546–551
yellow pages, 551–553
Electronic funds transfer (EFT), 284, 310, 312, 364, 378
Electronic mail. *See* E-mail
Electronic payment systems, 309–310, 313–314
cash, 314–324
checks, 324–326
credit card-based, 331–340
designing, 343–344
digital token-based, 313–326
privacy in, 342
risk in, 340–343
smart cards, 326–331
types of, 310–313
Electronic purses, 328
Encoding in structured documents. *See* Structured documents
Encrypted passwords, detection of, 195
Encryption, 20, 209–210
business and legal issues in, 225–226
clipper chip for, 215–216
for copyrighted works, 604–607
for credit cards, 332–334, 339
Data Encryption Standard, 210–211
digital public-key certificates, 214–215
for documents and e-mail, 221–224
for eavesdropping, 198
in EDI, 376–377
for electronic cash, 316–318
PGP, 222–224, 259
public-key, 211–214
in satellite networks, 752
secret-key, 210–211
Secure Hypertext Transfer Protocol for, 262–263
Secure Sockets Layer for, 261–263
SHEN for, 263–264
on World Wide Web, 259–261
End-to-end flow control in ATM, 738
End-user retrieval phase in search and retrieval, 533–534
End users of documents, 477
Endorsements for advertising, 508–509
Engines
search, 537–538
Telescript, 628–630
Enhanced Mosaic browser, 797
Enhanced specialized mobile radio (ESMR), 87
Enhancements by local-level service providers, 186
ENSSs (exterior nodal switching substations), 115, 119–120

Entertainment
  home. *See* Home entertainment
  next generation IP for, 669–670
Entirely unplanned purchases, 291
Entrepreneurs, convergence driven by, 23
Envelopes
  in EDI, 393–401
  in frame relay, 718
  MIME-based, 396–401
  X.400 and X.449, 393–395
Error detection and correction
  in frame relay, 719–720
  in SLIP, 657
Escrowed keys, 215
ESMR (enhanced specialized mobile radio), 87
ESNET, 116
EUNET, 130, 170–171
Europe, Internet service providers in, 170–171
EurOpen group, 170
Evaluation in advertising, 521
Event monitors, software agents as, 637–638
Exact match models in information retrieval, 542
Executive information systems (EISs), 481
Experimental networking Internet stage, 107
Experts, software agents as, 612
Export regulations on security, 224–225
ExPRESS task force, 411
Exterior Gateway Protocols (EGPs), 652
Exterior nodal switching substations (ENSSs), 115, 119–120

Facilitation centers in international trade, 362
FAQs (Frequently Asked Questions) for advertising, 511, 515
Far East, Internet service providers in, 168–170
Fast packet switching, 68, 716–717
Fault tolerance with RAIDs, 681
Faxes
  encryption for, 221
  services for, 139–140
FDMA (frequency division multiple access), 761
Federal Communications Commission (FCC), 74
Federal Express
  customer service system, 422
  package tracking by, 769
Federal Interagency Exchange (FIX), 116, 123
FedWire funds transfer service, 364–365
Fee-based information, 138
Feedback loops in advertising, 519
Fiber optics
  for cable transmissions, 81
  for ISDN, 712
  for last mile, 72, 77–78
  for satellite networks, 91–92
  for SONET, 712–713
Field service, mobile applications for, 770
File-level indexes, 538
File transfer protocol (FTP), 141–142
  for advertising, 520
  eavesdropping on, 198
  for Internet-based EDI, 412
  with local-level service providers, 185
  URL format for, 249
Files, searches for, 142–143
Filtering
  for infosphere, 462
  mail-filtering agents for, 559
  news-filtering agents for, 559
  in searches, 532–533, 557–559
Financial EDI, 362–363
  automated clearinghouse transfers in, 365–366
  checks in, 363–364
  interbank transfers in, 364
  payments in, 366–368
  standards in, 368–369
  types of, 363
Financial management in supply chain management, 53
Fingerprints, digital, 213
Firewalls, 199–201 *See also* Security
  hardened firewall hosts, 203–204
  IP packet screening routers, 201–202
  management of, 204–206
  proxy application gateways, 202–203
First Digital Bank, 317
First Virtual service, 332, 335–336
FIX (Federal Interagency Exchange), 116, 123
Flaming from advertising, 503–505
Flexibility
  in customization, 420
  as PC training benefit, 575
Float with bank checks, 364
Flow control in ATM, 736–739
Folio Views search engine, 537–538
For Your Information (FYIs) from IETF, 136–137
Forbes, Walter, 49
Foreign agents in mobile networking, 663
Format/content negotiation in HTTP, 252–253
Formatting in SGML, 798–799
Forms with HTML, 254–255
Fractional T-3 circuits, 723
FRAME-Net network, 153

Frame relay service, 158–159, 718–720
FrameMaker+ SGML, 797
Frames
in ATM, 734–735
in OSI model, 646
in TCP/IP, 649
Free information on Internet, 138
Free-nets, 166–167
Freedom of expression, 164
FreeFone service, 493
freeWAIS servers, 536
Frequencies in cellular communications, 748
Frequency division modulation, 710
Frequency division multiple access (FDMA), 761
Frequently Asked Questions (FAQs) for advertising, 511, 515
Front ends for data warehouses, 484–485
FSV (functional service view), 380–381
FTP (file transfer protocol), 141–142
for advertising, 520
eavesdropping on, 198
for Internet-based EDI, 412
with local-level service providers, 185
URL format for, 249
Full-text databases, 584–587, 593–594
Functional service view (FSV), 380–381
Functional silos, 434
FYIs (For Your Information) from IETF, 136–137

GAB (Group Access Bridging), 39
Games, 279, 595–596
Garbage collection of data warehouse data, 484
GATEC project, 410
Gateways
CGI, 255–257
for EDI systems, 391–392, 413–414
proxy application, 202–203
in Telescript language, 626
teletext, 44
GCA (Graphics Communications Association), 788
GEIS VAN service provider, 406
GenCode project, 788
General Instrument, 66
General Motors Corporation, 368
General-purpose cellular modem applications, 759
General research networking Internet stage, 107
Generalized markup in structured documents, 787
Generalized Markup Language (GML), 788
Generally planned purchases, 291
Generic flow control (GFC) in ATM headers, 732
Geosynchronous orbit (GEO) satellites, 92
GES (Global Enterprise Services), 163
GFC (generic flow control) in ATM headers, 732
GIF (graphics interchange format), 154
Gigabit networks
applications for, 126–127
architecture for, 125–126
research testbeds for, 127–129
Global bulletin boards, 140
Global Digital Highway, 406
Global Enterprise Services (GES), 163
Global hypertext publishing concept, 243–248
Global information distribution networks, 65
long-distance, 90–91
satellite, 91–92
Global issues for information highway, 93–95
Global markets in electronic commerce, 425–426
Global names spaces in X.500 project, 548
Global System for Mobile (GSM) communications, 765
Globalization of Academic Internet, 129–134
GML (Generalized Markup Language), 788
Go instruction in Telescript language, 626, 628–629
Goals
business, 230–231
for software agents, 618–619
Goldfarb, Charles, 788
Gophers
with local-level service providers, 185
URL format for, 249
GopherVR tool, 564
Government
and electronic cash, 323–324
as Internet service provider, 166–167
and security, 224–226
Graceful degradation with H.261, 703–704
Graphics accelerators, 696–697
Graphics Communications Association (GCA), 788
Graphics-oriented compression, 675
Green Card Lawyer, 505
Group Access Bridging (GAB), 39
Group dialogs in advertising, 520
Group learning, 572
GSM (Global System for Mobile) communications, 765
GULFNET, 130

H.261 compression, 703–704
H channels in ISDN, 711

Handheld computers, 755–756
Handheld password generators (HPGs), 218
Handoffs in cellular communications, 748
Hardened firewall hosts, 203–204
Hardware
for desktop video, 695–698
for multimedia, 25
Hash function with Kerberos, 220
Hauser Communications Systems, 63
HDLC (High-level Data-Link Control) protocol, 658
HDTs (host digital terminals), 78
HDTV (high-definition television), 685
Header error control (HEC) in ATM headers, 733
Headers, 68
in ATM, 729, 732–733
in EDI envelopes, 394
in MIME, 397
in OSI, 646
Health care industry
EDI in, 369–371
marketing products for, 499
mobile applications for, 770
HEC (header error control) in ATM headers, 733
Hedonic shopping behavior, 294–295
Help desk, software agents for, 636–637
Heterogeneous database interfaces, 560
Hewlett-Packard, training by, 574
HFC (hybrid fiber-coax) systems, 77–78
High-definition television (HDTV), 685
High-level Data-Link Control (HDLC) protocol, 658
High performance computing and communications (HPCC) programs, 109–110
High-speed infrared devices, 754
High Telescript language, 627–628
Hobby, Russ, 658
Home agents in mobile networking, 663
Home banking, 269–270
advanced services, 273–275
basic services, 270–271
intermediate services, 272–273
Home entertainment, 279–280
impact of, 282–283
market size for, 280–282
Home pages, 565
Home shopping
catalog-based, 277–278
television-based, 275–277
Home Shopping Network (HSN), 63, 275–276
Hong Kong, Internet service providers in, 169–170
Horizontal organizational structures, 426–428
Host digital terminals (HDTs), 78
Host protocols for local-level service providers, 182–183
HPCC (high performance computing and communications) programs, 109–110
HPGs (handheld password generators), 218
HSN (Home Shopping Network), 63, 275–276
HTML (Hypertext Markup Language), 253–254, 474, 779
for browsers, 633
CGI gateway services for, 255–257
forms for, 254–255
vs. SGML, 801–802
HTTP (hypertext transfer protocol), 249–253
HTTPD servers, 251–252
https access method, 262
Hubs for video programming, 69–70
Huffman encoding, 693
Human-computer interfaces, 560
Hybrid codecs, 689
Hybrid fiber-coax (HFC) systems, 77–78
Hybrid pen computers, 756
Hybrids in X.500 project, 551
Hyperlinked documents, 800–801
Hypermedia
benefits of, 246–248
vs. hypertext, 245–246
Hypertext, 243–245, 473–474
benefits of, 246–248
vs. hypermedia, 245–246
in news retrieval and delivery services, 589
in publishing, 578–579
searches in, 540
Hypertext Markup Language (HTML), 253–254, 474, 779
for browsers, 633
CGI gateway services for, 255–257
forms for, 254–255
vs. SGML, 801–802
Hypertext transfer protocol (HTTP), 250–253
HyTime hypertext standard, 474

IAB (Internet Architecture Board), 134–135
IANA (Internet Assigned Numbers Authority), 652
IBM and mainframe computers, 46
ICMP (Internet control message protocol), 651, 653
IDEA (international data encryption algorithm), 223
Identification
in message security, 208–209

in on-line transaction processing, 770
of Telescript agents, 630
IEEE 802.6 protocol, 722
IESG (Internet Engineering Steering Group), 136, 668
IETF (Internet Engineering Task Force), 136–137, 401
IETMs (Interactive Electronic Technical Manuals), 801
IGMP (Internet Group Management Protocol), 651, 668
IGPs (interior gateway protocols), 652
Image capture for multimedia, 674
Imaging systems for digital documents, 469–470
Impulsive buyers, 291
Inbound logistics in supply chain management, 445–446
Incoming calls in cellular communications, 749
Inconsistent usage security holes, 193
Indeo format, 690, 694
Independence of software agents, 615
Independent Internet service providers, 150, 156–160
PSI, 161–162
UUNET/AlterNET, 160–161
Indexes
in imaging systems, 469–470
for information search and retrieval process, 538–539
in Wide Area Information Service, 536
for World Wide Web, 639–640
Individual-to-group Internet communications, 138–139
Industry-oriented cellular modem applications, 759
Info Travel service, 546
Infonet VAN service provider, 407
Information. *See also* Corporate digital libraries; Documents; Infosphere
access devices for, 22
content of, 19
delivery and transport of, 31–33
EDI for, 373–374
hiding, 204
overload of, 528, 611
processing, 16, 139
searching for. *See* Information search and retrieval process
sharing, 107–108
Information architectural model, 548
Information-based marketing, 492–495
Information brokers, 463–464
in electronic commerce, 234–236
in prepurchase preparation phase, 295–296
Information databases on Internet, 138, 140–141
Information flow
in EDI, 352–354
on NFSNET, 119–120
in OSI, 646–647
Information highway, 15–20, 57–59. *See also* Internet
access to, 95–96
components of, 64–65
equipment for, 65–70
global, 90–92
last mile in. *See* Last mile
market forces on, 60–64
public policy issues for, 92–97
standards for, 96–97
strategic alliances for, 62–64
subsidies for, 95–96
Information search and retrieval process, 531–534
indexes for, 538–539
models of, 542–543
new data types in, 539–540
in prepurchase preparation phase, 292
robots for, 540–541
search engines in, 537–538
WAIS in, 534–537
Information Services division in CompuServe, 153
Information transfer and delivery Internet services, 138–139
Infosphere, 457–459. *See also* Corporate digital libraries
brokers for, 463–464
digital library layer for, 464–466
effective use of, 460–461
navigating, 462–463
on-line transactions, 460–461
user modeling and interaction layer for, 459–460
Infrared Data Association (IRDA), 755
Infrared mobile computing, 754–755
Infrastructure, 18–19
INRIA network, 130
Instantaneous communication in contract law, 375
Insurance, EDI in, 369–371
Integration
in active document architectures, 812–813
of applications, 805
of messaging, 237
in supply chain management, 443–448
Integrity
in message security, 208
in TCP/IP, 650
Intel Pentium chip, 506
Intelligent filters, 559–560

Intelligent messaging, 611
Interaction
in advertising, 490–491, 518, 520–521
in consumer applications, 38–39
in customer relationships, 452
in learning, 595–596
in news retrieval and delivery services, 589–590
Interactive catalogs, 236, 553–557
Interactive EDI, 379
Interactive Electronic Technical Manuals (IETMs), 801
Interactive marketing, 48, 491
information-based, 492–499
legal issues in, 498–499
micromarketing in, 496–497
small vs. large firms in, 497–498
Interactive media, 59
Interactive publishing, 143
Interactive Transactions Partners, 332
Interactive TV, 22, 33–34, 43, 64–65
Interads, 278
Interbank electronic funds transfer, 364
Interconnect costs for value-added networks, 405
Interest on electronic cash, 321
Interexchange carriers (IXCs), 74, 90–91
Interfaces
for browsing, 34–36
document-oriented, 806
in electronic commerce, 236–237, 287
for electronic payment systems, 343
pen-based, 756
for searches, 559–565
for software agents, 617
Interference
in cellular communications, 764
in packet radio, 750
Interframe compression, 690
Interior gateway protocols (IGPs), 652
InterLock service, 159
Intermediaries for software agents, 621
Internal information systems, 420–421
architecture of, 422–424
proprietary systems, 421–422
International business, 49
International currencies and electronic cash, 321
International data encryption algorithm (IDEA), 223
International markets vs. global markets, 425
International networks, 130–131
barriers to, 133–134
EBONE, 131–133
International trade
components in, 358–360
customs clearances in, 360–361
EDI in, 357–362
trade points in, 361–362
transport logistics in, 361
Internet, 99–100 *See also* World Wide Web (WWW)
advertising and marketing on. *See* Advertising; Marketing
application overview for, 137–144
commercialization of, 108, 147–150. *See also* Internet service providers (ISPs)
data and transaction categories on, 258–259
EBONE on, 131–133
globalization of, 129–134
governance hierarchy of, 134–136
growth of, 107–110
history of, 103–111
international networks, 130–131
network structure of, 110–111
and NFSNET, 112–120
and NREN, 120–129
terminology of, 100–103
for video conferencing, 704–707
Internet Architecture Board (IAB), 134–135
Internet Assigned Numbers Authority (IANA), 652
Internet Backbone Access Providers, 152
Internet-based EDI, 409, 413–414
for Department of Defense, 410
SPEEDE project, 411
VAN-free, 411–412
Internet control message protocol (ICMP), 651, 653
Internet-Drafts, 137
Internet Engineering Steering Group (IESG), 136, 668
Internet Engineering Task Force (IETF), 136–137, 401
Internet Group Management Protocol (IGMP), 651, 668
Internet Protocol (IP), 159, 650–651
Internet protocol suite. *See* TCP/IP (Transport Control Protocol/Internet Protocol)
Internet Relay Chat (IRC), 597–598
Internet service providers (ISPs), 147, 150–151
backbone access for, 178–180
commercial on-line services, 152–156
connecting to, 174–177
connectivity for, 171–174
in Europe, 170–171
in Far East, 168–170
local-level, 164–168
national independents, 156–162
regional-level, 162–163
telephone and cable companies, 151–152

Internet Society (ISOC), 134
InternetMCI service, 152
Internetwork layer in TCP/IP model, 648
InterNIC, 134
Interoperability, 21, 241. *See also* Standards
  with ATM, 724, 726–727
  with documents, 781–782
  in EDI, 385
  of electronic cash, 316
  of interpreted languages, 627
  in mobile computing, 771–772
Interorganization commerce, EDI in. *See* EDI (electronic data interchange)
Interpress page description language, 782
Interpreted languages
  security issues with, 629–630
  Telescript, 627–628
Interprocess communications (IPC) mechanisms, 818
Intraframe compression, 690
Intraorganizational electronic commerce, 417–418
  customization in, 419–420, 437–441
  global markets in, 425–426
  internal information systems in, 420–424
  macro forces in, 424–433
  organizational structures in, 426–433
  supply chain management in, 420, 441–452
  work-flow management in, 418–419, 433–437
Intraorganizational transactions, 234
Intuitive interfaces, 343
Inventory management
  just-in-time manufacturing, 49–50
  in mercantile models, 301–302
  quick response retailing, 50–51
  in supply chain management, 52
Invitations for Telescript agents, 629–630
IP (Internet Protocol), 159, 650–651
IP addresses, 134
  in mobile networking, 660–661
  in multicast TCP/IP, 667
  in TCP/IP, 651–652
IP multicast extension, 659
IP packet screening routers, 201–202
IP packets in TCP/IP, 649
IPC (interprocess communications) mechanisms, 818
IPng (next generation IP)
  compatibility in, 670–671
  for new markets, 669–670
  transition challenges in, 670
IRC (Internet Relay Chat), 597–598
IRDA (Infrared Data Association), 755
ISDN (integrated services digital networks)
  with ADSL, 77
  for Internet connections, 176–177
  operation of, 711–712
  for video conferencing, 703–704
ISOC (Internet Society), 134
ISPs. *See* Internet service providers (ISPs)
ITU-TSS imaging standard, 470
IXCs (interexchange carriers), 74, 90–91

Jacobson, Van, 657
JANET, 130
Japan, Internet service providers in, 168–169
JIT (just-in-time) manufacturing methods, 15–16, 49–50, 371–372
JPEG (Joint Photographic Experts Group) compression, 678, 689–690, 693–694
JUNET, 130
Junk mail advertising model, 504–505
Just-in-time (JIT) manufacturing methods, 15–16, 49–50, 371–372
JvNCNet, 163

Kahn, Robert, 613
Kerberos authentication protocol, 219–220, 325
Key management with PGP, 223–224, 226
Keys. *See* Encryption
Keywords in imaging systems, 469–470
Kiosk catalogs, 278, 556
Knowbots, 613
Knowledge bases for software agents, 617, 619–620
Knowledge Navigators, 612–613, 617
Knowledge-oriented documents, 468
KREONet, 131

Land-based RF communications, 747
Lands in CD-ROMs, 683
LANs (local area networks), 100–101
  ATM for, 726
  frame relay for, 720
  routers for, 69
Laptop computers, 755–756
Large vs. small in marketing, 497–498
LaserVision videodiscs, 682
Last mile, 70–71
  cable-based, 78–83
  commercial on-line services-based, 88–90
  radio-based, 83–88
  telecom-based, 71–78
LATAs (local access transport areas), 74
Latency in quality of service, 728
Lateral networking, 430
LaTeX markup language, 785
Launching software agents, 620–622
Law. *See* Legal issues
Layers
  in OSI model, 644–647
  in TCP/IP model, 647–649

Layout, procedural markup for, 786
LCP (link control protocol), 658
Leaky-bucket algorithm, 737
Lean production, 419
Learning. *See also* Education
  active, 569
  group, 572
  interactive, 595–596
  by software agents, 615–617
LECs (local exchange carriers), 74
LEDs in mobile computing, 754
Legal issues
  in copyrights, 599–607
  in EDI, 375–376
  in electronic cash, 322–324
  in encryption, 225–226
  in hypertext, 579
  in interactive marketing, 498–499
Legislation, database for, 585
LEXIS database, 585, 789
Liberty Media, 63
Librarians for documents, 477
Libraries
  corporate. *See* Corporate digital libraries
  as Internet service providers, 166–167
Licensed PCS, 775–776
Licenses, electronic, 606
Lifetime of software agents, 618
Light-based mobile computing, 754–755
Limited VANs, 391
Linear advertising, 518
Link-by-link flow control in ATM, 738
Link control protocol (LCP), 658
Linking
  in documents. *See* Hypertext
  in OLE, 814
  in publishing, 578
LinX module, 66
Local access transport areas (LATAs), 74
Local area networks (LANs), 100–101
  ATM for, 726
  frame relay for, 720
  routers for, 69
Local containers in active document architectures, 810
Local exchange carriers (LECs), 74
Local filters in searches, 533
Local infrastructure, access to, 95
Local-level Internet service providers, 151, 164–165
  bulletin board and niche services, 165–166
  challenges for, 167–168
  customer targeting by, 188
  free-nets, libraries, and government, 166–167
  infrastructure for, 181–185
  software for, 185–186
  technical support by, 186–188
Local loops, 71–72
Local RF communications, 747
Local roads. *See* Last mile
Log-ons in cellular communications, 749
Logical data warehouses, 481
Logical structure in structured documents, 783–784
Logistics
  in international trade, 361
  in supply chain management, 443–448
Long distance carriers, 74
Long-distance networks, 90–91
Loosely coupled multiprocessing systems, 679
Lorie, Raymond, 788
Lossless compression, 677
Lossy compression, 677–678, 688
Lotus Notes, 351
Low-speed infrared devices, 754
Low Telescript language, 627–628

Macmillan, 63
Magazines
  effectiveness of, 590–691
  on-line, 34–35
MAGIC NREN testbed, 128
Mail-enabled computing, 624, 631–632
Mail systems. *See also* E-mail
  computing components of, 398–399
  filtering agents for, 559
  with Internet-based EDI, 409
  security problems in, 196
Mailbox rule in contract law, 375
Mailing list services, 185
Mainframe computers
  for indexing, 539
  in multimedia, 27
Maintenance
  in EDI, 392–393
  in X.500 project, 547
Malicious code, security problems from, 196–197
Management
  of digital documents, 468
  of distributed objects, 240–241
  of firewalls, 204–206
  of software agents, 624–625
Manufacturers
  in information-based marketing, 492–495
  Yellow Pages directory for, 552
Manufacturing
  agile, 419, 450–452
  EDI in, 371–373
  new economy in, 47–48

Many-to-many communication in virtual classrooms, 572
Market-driven transactions, 234
Market forces on information highway, 60–64
Market-link transactions, 234
Market presence in information-based marketing, 493
Market research, 42–44
 data analysis in, 524
 data collection in, 522–523
 data organization in, 523
 in information-based marketing, 492–493
Marketing, 489–491
 audience targeting in, 513–516
 charting progress of, 510–522
 in electronic commerce, 48–49
 information-based, 492–499
 legal issues in, 498–499
 micromarketing in, 496–497
 new products, 511–512
 product differentiation and positioning in, 515–516
 small vs. large firms in, 497–498
 in supply chain management, 444, 446–448
Marketplace transactions, 233
Markup languages, 784–788
Maryland government as Internet service provider, 167
Massive parallel systems, 29–30
MasterBanking, 332
MBONE video conferencing program, 706–707
McFarlan, Warren, 421
MCI, 63, 152
McKesson, drug distribution system by, 422
MCSNet, 165
Media convergence, 21–23
MEDLINE database, 582
Meetings in Telescript language, 626
Melting screen PostScript program, 400
Memory, organizational, 436
Mercantile models, 287–289
 cost estimation and pricing in, 303–304
 order billing and payment management in, 306
 order fulfillment and delivery in, 306
 order planning and generation in, 303
 order receipt and entry in, 304–305
 order scheduling in, 305
 order selection and prioritization in, 305
 postpurchase interaction phase, 301–302
 postsales services in, 306
 prepurchase preparation in, 290–296
 purchase consummation phase, 296–301
Mervyn's department stores, 448
Message-enabled work-flow solutions, 238
Message security
 authentication/identification in, 208–209, 368
 confidentiality in, 207–208
 digital signatures in, 216–217
 encryption in, 209–216
 integrity in, 208
Message transfer agents (MTAs), 398
Messages. *See also* E-mail; Mail systems
 in EDI, 368, 384
 in electronic commerce, 237–238
 overloading of, 198–199
 passing, 27–28
 software for, 20
 in TCP/IP, 649
Messaging-based computing, 624, 631–632
Messaging systems in contract law, 375–376
Metamail system, 631
Metered information services, 495
Metropolitan area businesses, Yellow Pages directory for, 552
MHEG hypertext standard, 474
Microcells in personal communications systems, 773–774
Micromarketing, 496–497
Microsoft Network, 89–90
Microtransactions, 283–286
Mid-level regional networks in NFSNET, 115–118
Middleware services, 238–239
 distributed object management and services, 240–241
 maturation of, 436
 for software agents, 621–622
 transaction security and management, 240
 transparency in, 239
Military RSA key-size option, 223
MILNET, 116
MIME system, 631
 with EDI, 396–401
 with HTTP, 252–253
Minicomputers, 46
Minitel system, 545–546
MMDS (multichannel multipoint distribution service), 82
MNCs (multinational corporations), 425–426
Mobile agents. *See* Software agents
Mobile computing, 85, 87–88, 743–745. *See also* Wireless communications
 API standard for, 771–772
 applications for, 767–772
 cellular communications for, 747–749, 764–767
 cellular modems in, 758–759
 code division multiple access for, 761–764

Mobile computing (*Cont.*)
hybrid pen computers in, 756
infrared, 754–755
for on-line transaction processing, 769–771
packet radio, 750–751
PCMCIA adapters in, 759–760
personal digital assistants in, 756–758
portable computers in, 755–756
standards for, 760–764, 771–772
time division multiple access for, 762–764
for tracking and dispatching, 768–769
Mobile Computing Alliance, 771–772
Mobile nodes, 663
Mobile TCP/IP-based networking, 660
addresses in, 660–661
characteristics of, 662
packets in, 664
registering in, 663
Mobile telephone switching offices (MTSOs), 749
Mobile Working Group, 659
Mobility in document management, 474
Models
of documents, 479
of information retrieval, 542–543
mercantile. *See* Mercantile models
OSI, 130, 644–647
Modems
cellular, 758–759, 764
for local-level service providers, 184–185
multiport, 403
RF, 750–751
Modified Final Judgment (MFJ), 74
Mondex card, 316, 330, 341
Monitoring in cellular communications, 749
Mosaic browser, 797
Mosher, Edward, 788
MOSPF (Multicast Open Shortest Path First) protocol, 668
Motion Picture Experts Group (MPEG) compression, 678, 689–690
MPEG-1, 691–692
MPEG-2, 692–693
Motorola, 772
Movie on-demand, 279
Movies
computer space requirements for, 676–678
home entertainment impact on, 282–283
MPEG (Motion Picture Experts Group) compression, 678, 689–690
MPEG-1, 691–692
MPEG-2, 692–693
Mrs. Fields Cookies management system, 422
MSOs (multiple systems operators), 80
MTAs (message transfer agents), 398
MTSOs (mobile telephone switching offices), 749
Multicast mode in TCP/IP, 659
operation of, 666–667
packet routing in, 667–668
transport protocols for, 665–666
Multicast Open Shortest Path First (MOSPF) protocol, 668
Multicasting
in SMDS, 723
in X.500 project, 551
Multichannel multipoint distribution service (MMDS), 82
Multimedia, 18, 673–674
in catalogs, 48
CD-ROMs for, 682–684
compression in, 675–678
content of, 19–20, 23–27
servers for, 27–31, 678–681
storage for, 27–31, 674, 681–684
Multinational corporations (MNCs), 425–426
Multiple-platform integration, 812–813
Multiple systems operators (MSOs), 80
Multiple-word searches, 471–472
Multiport modems, 403
Multiprocessing, 678–681
Multitasking, 680–681
Multithreading, 680

Name services for directories, 544
Names spaces in X.500 project, 548
NAMs (numeric arrangement modules) in cellular communications, 749
NAPs (network access points) in NREN, 121–123
Narrowband telecommunications
vs. broadband, 710
ISDN, 712
PCS, 775
National independent Internet service providers, 156–160
PSI, 161–162
UUNET/AlterNET, 160–161
National Information Infrastructure (NII), 15
National Research and Education Network. *See* NREN
National Writers Union (NWU), 579
Natural language interfaces, 617
Navigation by software agents, 614
NCPs (network control protocols), 659
nCube video server, 30
Nectar NREN testbed, 128
Negotiation in electronic commerce, 287
NetCash system, 220
NetCheque system, 220, 326

NETCOM, junk mail advertising on, 504–505
Netscape Communications
browsers by, 511
Secure Sockets Layer by, 261–263
Network access points (NAPs) in NREN, 121–123
Network control protocols (NCPs), 659
Network externality, 94
Network infrastructure, 57–59
access to, 95–96
components of, 64–65
equipment for, 65–70
global, 90–92
Internet. *See* Internet
last mile in. *See* Last mile
market forces on, 60–64
public policy issues for, 92–97
standards for, 96–97
subsidies for, 95–96
Network layer
in OSI, 645–646
in TCP/IP, 648
Network management, software agents for, 637–638
Network object services layer in active document architectures, 810–811
Network operation centers (NOCs), 116–117, 187
Network organizational structures, 429–431
Network Services division in CompuServe, 153
Network topology criteria for Internet service providers, 178–179
Networks
for automated teller machines, 270–271
firewalls on, 205
gigabit, 125–129
as information route, 32
international, 130–134
layers in, 644–647
local area, 100–101
packet-switched, 716–717
paging, 753–754
publishing on, 18
regional, 115–118
satellite, 91–92, 751–754
security for. *See* Security
wide area, 100–101
Neumann, Clifford, 326
New Economy, 46
New EDI, 378–380
New products
agile manufacturing for, 452
in electronic commerce, 287
marketing for, 511–512
News groups
advertising on, 509, 515, 520
for collaboration, 140
URL format for, 249
News retrieval and delivery services, 587–589
Clarinet, 592–593
filtering agents for, 559
personalization in, 589–592
NewsNet service, 586
Newspapers
changes in, 591–592
on-line, 34–35
NEXIS database, 585, 789
Next generation IP, 135, 668–669
compatibility in, 670–671
for new markets, 669–670
transition challenges in, 670
NFSNET, 102, 105–111
Acceptable Use Policy on, 147–148
backbones of, 113–115
information movement on, 119–120
mid-level regional networks in, 115–118
state and campus networks in, 118–119
structure and components of, 112–120
Niche services as Internet service providers, 165–166
NII (National Information Infrastructure), 15
900 phone service, 39
Nintendo games, 595–596
Nisenholtz, Martin, 509
NOCs (network operation centers), 116–117, 187
Noise
in cellular communications, 764
in packet radio, 750
Nonlinear advertising, 518
Nonpreemptive multitasking, 680
NORDUNET, 130, 170
Notarized time-stamping in EDI, 376
NREN, 120–121
backbones of, 121–125
gigabit research for, 125–129
network access points in, 121–123
routing arbiters in, 123–124
vBNS service in, 124–125
NSI network, 116
NT-1 equipment with ISDN, 176
Numeric arrangement modules (NAMs) in cellular communications, 749
NWU (National Writers Union), 579
NYNEX, 75
NYSERnet, 161

Object Linking and Embedding (OLE), 475, 812, 818–819
vs. Dynamic Data Exchange, 815–816
linked information in, 814

Object Management Group (OMG), 822
Object orientation, 240
Object request brokers (ORBs) in CORBA, 822
Object services in CORBA, 822
Object-to-object calling mechanisms in ADAs, 813–815
  dynamic data exchange, 815–816
  Remote Procedure Calls, 816–818
  System Object Model, 816
OC-3 specification, 713
OC-12 specification, 713
OC-48 specification, 713
Octets
  in frame relay, 718
  in SMDS, 722
Office Depot stores, 498
Office document architecture (ODA), 472
Office Max stores, 498
Oikarinen, Jarkko, 597
OLAP (on-line analytic processing), 460–461, 486
Old EDI, 378
OLE (Object Linking and Embedding), 475, 812, 818–819
  vs. Dynamic Data Exchange, 815–816
  linked information in, 814
OLTP (on-line transaction processing), 460–461, 769–771
OMC (order management cycle), 303–304
OMG (Object Management Group), 822
On-line analytic processing (OLAP), 460–461, 486
On-line catalog-based shopping, 277–278
On-line games, 279
On-line information in prepurchase preparation phase, 295–296
On-line newspapers and magazines, 34–35
On-line services
  applications of, 88–89
  information highway plans by, 62
  as Internet service providers, 150, 152–156
  for last mile, 88–90
On-line third-party processors (OTPPs), 334–337
On-line transaction processing (OLTP), 460–461, 769–771
On Point Solutions databases, 593
One-way RF communications, 747
Open checks for electronic cash, 320
Open EDI, 380–381
Open Market service, 335
Open systems, 643
OpenDoc technology, 475, 812, 819–821
Operating systems, 34, 125–126
Operational picture, 455
Oracle's Context search engine, 537
ORBIT information service, 582
ORBs (object request brokers) in CORBA, 822
Order management cycle (OMC), 303–304
Order processing in supply chain management, 447
Orders in mercantile models, 306
  billing and account/payment management, 306
  fulfillment and delivery, 306
  planning and generation, 303
  receipt and entry, 304–305
  scheduling, 305
  selection and prioritization, 305
Organizational applications, 44–45
  changing environments in, 45–47
  inventory management, 49–51
  marketing, 48–49
  retail industry, 47–48
  supply chain management, 51–53
  work group collaborative, 53–54
Organizational memory, 436
Organizational search process, 292–294
Organizational structures
  electronic, 431–433
  vertical vs. horizontal, 426–428
  virtual, 429–431
Organizational units in X.500 project, 548
Organizations in X.500 project, 548
OSI protocol stacks, 130, 644–647
Ousterhout, John, 631
Out-of-territory RBOC expansion, 76–77
Outgoing calls in cellular communications, 749
Owners of software agents, 618

Packaging of data warehouse data, 483–484
Packet radio, 750–751
Packet sniffing, 207
Packet-switched networks, 716–717
Packet transfer mode (PTM), 129
Packets
  in cell relay, 721–722
  Internet Protocol, 159
  in mobile networking, 664
  modification of, 199
  in multicast TCP/IP, 667
  on NFSNET, 119–120
  in OSI model, 646–647
  replaying, 199
  routing, 68–70
  screening, 201–202
  security of, 199, 207
  in TCP/IP, 649
PACOM network, 130
Page composition in SGML, 798–799
Page Description Format (PDF), 782

Page description languages (PDLs), 253–257, 782
Page turners in SGML, 799
Paging networks, 753–754
Palmtop computers, 758
Panorama viewer for SGML, 797
Paper savings from EDI, 355
Parallel-processing indexing method, 539
Paramount, 26, 63
Parsing of documents in SGML, 797–798
Parts in OpenDoc, 819–821
Passive advertising, 505–509
Passive customer interaction, 520
Passwords, 193–195
  for anonymous FTP, 142
  for copyrighted works, 606
  handheld generators for, 218
Patient buyers, 291
Payload type (PT) in ATM headers, 732–733
Payments, 296–298
  cash, 298
  credit card, 298–301
  electronic. *See* Electronic payment systems
  in financial EDI, 366–368
  in supply chain management, 53
PBXs (private branch exchanges), 68
PCMCIA adapters, 759–760
PCSs (personal communications systems), 32, 748, 772–773
  benefits of, 773
  infrastructure of, 773–774
  service categories in, 774–776
PDAs (personal digital assistants), 756–758
PDF (Page Description Format), 782
PDLs (page description languages), 253–257, 782
Peapod company, 432
PEM (Privacy Enhanced Mail) standard, 221–222, 259, 334
Pen-based interfaces, 756
Pentium chip, 506
Performance Systems International (PSI), 161–162
Perkins, Drew, 658
Permanent virtual circuits (PVCs)
  in ATM, 728–729
  in frame relay, 719
Permits for Telescript agents, 630
Perot, Ross, 38
Personal communications systems (PCSs), 32, 748, 772–773
  benefits of, 773
  infrastructure of, 773–774
  service categories in, 774–776
Personal communicators, 757
Personal digital assistants (PDAs), 756–758
Personal finance and home banking management, 269–270
  advanced services, 273–275
  basic services, 270–271
  intermediate services, 272–273
Personal identification numbers (PINs), 195
Personal organizers, 758
Personalization in news retrieval and delivery services, 589–592
PGP (Pretty Good Privacy) encryption, 222–224, 259, 334
Physical data warehouses, 481
Physical layer
  in ATM, 733–734
  in OSI, 645–646
  in TCP/IP model, 648, 653–654
Physical security holes, 193
Physical structure in structured documents, 783–784
PIM (Protocol Independent Multicast), 668
PINs (personal identification numbers), 195
Pipelines for set-top boxes, 67
Pixels, 676
PKZIP program, 224
Place independence in virtual classrooms, 571–572
Places in Telescript language, 626, 629
Plaintext in encryption, 209–210
Plans for advertising, 516–519
Playback, video, 696–697
Point-of-sale (POS) systems
  benefits of, 492
  with EDI, 372–373
Point-to-multipoint communication, 69
Point-to-point file transfers, 20
Point-to-point protocol (PPP), 175–176, 654–656
  with local-level service providers, 183, 185
  operation of, 658–659
Points of presence (PoPs), 157, 179
Policy issues for information highway, 92–97
POM (production and operations management), 432–433
PoPs (Points of presence), 157, 179
Pornography
  on bulletin boards, 166
  on information highway, 94
Portability. *See* Mobile computing
Portable computers, 755–756
Portals in Telescript language, 626
Ports for local-level service providers, 183
POS (point-of-sale) systems
  benefits of, 492
  with EDI, 372–373
Postpaid electronic tokens, 313
Postpurchase interaction phase, 301–302

Postsales services in mercantile models, 306
PostScript language
as page description language, 782, 786
portability of, 627
security problems in, 400
POTS (plain old telephone lines) system
with ADSL, 77
for video conferencing, 702–703
PPP (point-to-point protocol), 175–176, 654–656
with local-level service providers, 183, 185
operation of, 658–659
Preemptive multitasking, 680
Prepaid electronic tokens, 313
Prepurchase preparation phase, 290–292
information brokers in, 295–296
information search process in, 292
organizational search process in, 292–294
search experiences in, 294–295
Prescription drugs, marketing, 499
Presentation layer in OSI, 645, 647
Presentation of infosphere, 462–463
Presentational markups in structured documents, 785
Pretty Good Privacy (PGP) encryption, 222–224, 259, 334
Prevue Channel, 556
Price
in ATM, 727
in cellular technology, 85
in electronic payment systems, 344
of information-based products, 494–495
in light-based mobile computing, 754
in mercantile models, 303–304
of video conferencing, 700
Price shock
with on-line services, 495
with video on-demand, 40
Primary rate interface (PRI) with ISDN, 176
Prime Cable, 63
PrimeStar DBS service, 82–83
Print publishing, content of, 26
Priorities
in ATM, 727
of information-based products, 494–495
of orders in mercantile models, 305
Privacy, 6. *See also* Encryption; Security
in electronic payment systems, 342–343
on information highway, 94
with software agents, 614
Privacy Enhanced Mail (PEM) standard, 221–222, 259, 334
Private branch exchanges (PBXs), 68
Private circuits for Internet connections, 177
Privatization stage of Internet, 108, 147–148
Privileges, access, 193
Probabilistic models in information retrieval, 542–543
Problem resolution with EDI, 355
Procedural markup in structured documents, 785–787
Procedure calls for distributed objects, 813
Process-specific documents, 468
Process teams in horizontal organizational structures, 428
Processes in multiprocessing, 679–680
Processors for multimedia, 678–679
Procurement, EDI in, 371–374, 410
Prodigy, 332
advertising on, 503
as Internet service provider, 154–155
Production and operations management (POM), 432–433
Production of documents, 478
Productivity increases from PC training, 575
Products
bundling, 494
designing, in EDI, 373–374
differentiating and positioning, 515–516
interactive catalogs for, 553–557
Programmers for EDI, 414
Programming with software agents, 614, 621–624
Promotional materials, 517–518
Promotions in information-based marketing, 493
Proprietary information systems, 421–422
Proprietary protocols for browsers, 633–634
Protection. *See* Security
Protocol Independent Multicast (PIM), 668
Protocol stacks, 643
Internet. *See* TCP/IP (Transport Control Protocol/Internet Protocol)
OSI, 644–647
Protocols
for browsers, 633–634
for cellular communications, 764–767
for gigabit networks, 126
for Internet, 101
for local-level service providers, 182–183
Proxy application gateways, 202–203
PSI (Performance Systems International), 161–162
PSTN (public switched telephone network), 84
PT (payload type) in ATM headers, 732–733
PTM (packet transfer mode), 129
Public data, 258
Public information on Internet, 138
Public-key certificates, 214–215
Public-key encryption, 211–214
Public policy, 18, 92–97

Public switched telephone network (PSTN), 84
Public utility commissions (PUCs), 74
Publisher indexing phase in search and retrieval, 534
Publishing
  bibliographic databases for, 582–583
  CD-ROM-based, 593–594
  copyright issues in, 599–607
  corporate documents, 583–584
  in education, 577–578
  full-text databases, 584–587
  hypertext. *See* Hypertext
  interactive, 143
  network, 18
  news retrieval and delivery services, 587–593
  on Web, 248
Pull-based advertising, 505–509
Punctuational markups in structured documents, 785
Purchase consummation phase, 296–298
  cash payments in, 298
  credit card payments in, 298–301
Purchase deliberation, 290
Purchasing
  search scenario for, 529–531
  in supply chain management, 445–446
Push-based advertising, 502–505
PVCs (permanent virtual circuits)
  in ATM, 728–729
  in frame relay, 719

QOS (quality of service) in ATM, 727–728 736
QR (Quick response) retailing, 50–51, 372–373
Quality control in JIT manufacturing, 50
Quality of service (QOS) in ATM, 727–728, 736
Quantum system for video on-demand, 36
QUBE Cable Network, 44
Quick Response (QR) retailing, 50–51, 372–373
QuickCam cameras, 705
Quicken program, 272
QuickTake cameras, 705
QuickTime programs, 698–699
QVC, 26

Racotek company, 772
RADB (routing arbiter database), 124
Radio-based systems
  for last mile, 83–88
  for mobile computing, 746–747, 750–751
Radio frequency apparel tags, 439–440
RadioMail Corporation, 772
RAIDs (redundant arrays of inexpensive disks), 681–682
Rain fade, 82
RAM Mobile Data Network, 750–751
Rankings in searches, 537
RAs (routing arbiters) in NREN, 123–124
Rate-based flow control in ATM, 738
RBOCs (Regional Bell Operating Companies), 74–77
Readers, smart card, 329
Real-time conferencing, 597–598
Real-time electronic tokens, 313
Real-time processing, gigabit networks for, 126–127
Real-Time Protocol (RTP), 666
Reconfiguration of products, 452
Record keeping
  for credit cards, 338
  in electronic payment systems, 341
Recordable CDs, 682
Redundancy and compression, 675–676, 688
Redundant arrays of inexpensive disks (RAIDs), 681–682
Reengineering vs. downsizing, 425
References in hypertext, 245–246
Referrals in X.500 project, 550
Regeneration section level in ATM, 734
Regional Bell Operating Companies (RBOCs), 74–77
Regional Internet service providers, 150, 162–163
Regional networks in NFSNET, 115–118
Regulations
  convergence driven by, 23
  and electronic cash, 323–324
  for information highway, 93
  in interactive marketing, 498–499
  for security, 224–226
Relationship-based smart cards, 327–328
Relevance rankings in searches, 537
Reliability of satellite networks, 751–752
Religious issues, 94
Reminder purchases, 291
Remote communications, 767
Remote filters in searches, 533
Remote Procedure Calls (RPCs), 621–623, 816–818
Remote programming (RP), 621–624
Rendering software for copyrighted works, 604
Repetitive activity, software agents for, 611–612
Reports, corporate, 583–584
Requests for comments (RFC) from IETF, 136
Research, consumer. *See* Market research

Research testbeds for gigabit networks, 127–129
Reservation systems, 421
Resource discovery, software agents for, 639–640
Resource-sharing Internet services, 139
Resources for software agents, 614
Restructuring of businesses, 46
Retail industry
  EDI in, 371–373
  in information-based marketing, 492–495
  mobile applications for, 770
  new economy in, 47–48
  supply chain management in, 447–448
Retail Operations Intelligence system, 422
Retrievability of electronic cash, 316
Retrieval
  of data warehouse data, 484
  of documents, 478
  from infosphere, 462
Returns and claims, 301–302
Reusability of documents, 781
Reverification costs, 285
RF communications
  for last mile, 83–88
  for mobile computing, 746–747, 750–751
RF modems, 750–751
RFC (requests for comments) from IETF, 136
RFC 822 protocol, 396
Rich-text format (RTF), 472
Right of way for last mile access, 70–71
Riordan, Mark, 222
RIPE network, 130
RIPEM program, 222
Risk. *See also* Security
  in electronic cash, 322
  in electronic payment systems, 314, 340–343
  in JIT manufacturing methods, 50
Rivest, Ron, 213
RLE (run-length encoding), 693
rlogin security hole, 193
Roaming in cellular technology, 86
Robots for searches, 540–541
Rolling Stones, 440–441
Rose, Marshall T., 631
Routers, 68–70
  in ATM, 740
  in cell relay, 721
  IP packet screening, 201–202
  for local-level service providers, 182
  in mobile networking, 663
  in multicast TCP/IP, 666
  for NFSNET, 114, 119–120
Routing
  of datagrams, 648–649
  with MBONE program, 707
  next generation IP for, 670
  in TCP/IP, 652–653, 667–668
Routing arbiter database (RADB), 124
Routing arbiters (RAs) in NREN, 123–124
RP (remote programming), 621–624
RPCs (Remote Procedure Calls), 621–623, 816–818
RSA digital envelope, 214
RSA encryption, 213–214, 222–223
RSAREF routines, 222
RTF (rich-text format), 472
RTP (Real-Time Protocol), 666
Rule-based approaches with software agents, 617
Run-length encoding (RLE), 693

S-HTTP (Secure Hypertext Transfer Protocol), 262–263
S/T interface with ISDN, 176
SABRE reservation system, 421
Safe-Tcl language, 630–632
Safety of software agents, 614–615
Sales
  mobile applications for, 771
  in supply chain management, 447
Sales force productivity in supply chain management, 53
Salk, George, 45
SAR (segmentation and reassembly) layer in ATM, 735–736
Satellite networks, 91–92, 751–752
  and paging, 753–754
  VSAT, 752–753
Saturn VAN service provider, 407
Savings from EDI, 355
Scanning velocity with CD-ROMs, 684
Schools. *See* Education
Scitor VAN service provider, 407
SCM. *See* Supply chain management (SCM)
Scrambling. *See* Encryption
Screen phones, 329
Scripts, CGI, 256–257
SDH (Synchronous Digital Hierarchy), 713, 733–734
SDN network, 130
Seamless interfaces, 287
Seamless roaming in cellular technology, 86
Search engines, 537–538
Searches, 527–528
  challenges in, 527–528
  directories and catalogs for, 532, 543–557
  filtering in, 532–533, 557–559
  in imaging systems, 469–470
  indexes for, 538–539
  in information search and retrieval, 531–543

infosphere, 462
models of, 542–543
new data types in, 539–540
in prepurchase preparation phase, 292–295
robots for, 540–541
scenario for, 529–531
search engines for, 537–538
in structured digital documents, 471–472
tools for, 142–143, 559–565
WAIS, 534–537
white pages for, 546–551
SEC (Securities and Exchange Commission)
corporate documents from, 583–584
and SGML, 789
Secret data, 258
Secret-key encryption, 210–211
Sector-oriented disk compression, 675
Secure Hypertext Transfer Protocol (S-HTTP), 262–263
Secure messaging, 237–238
Secure Sockets Layer (SSL), 261–263
Securities and Exchange Commission (SEC)
corporate documents from, 583–584
and SGML, 789
Security, 20
of active mail, 632
biometric systems for, 195–196
challenge-response systems in, 217–220
client-server, 191–199
of credit cards, 331
data and message, 206–217
digital signatures in, 221–224
for documents, 216–217
in EDI systems, 368, 376–377, 391, 409
in electronic payment systems, 314, 343
encryption in, 209–216
in financial EDI, 368
firewalls for, 199–206
and government regulations, 224–226
in Internet-based EDI, 409
with Internet service providers, 158–159
in MIME, 382
in mobile networking, 662
through obscurity, 194
in on-line transaction processing, 770
passwords for, 194–195
radio frequency apparel tags for, 439–440
of satellite networks, 752
Secure Hypertext Transfer Protocol for, 262–263
Secure Sockets Layer for, 261–263
for servers, 197–199
SHEN for, 263–264
from software agents, 196–197
in Telescript language, 629–630
in Templar EDI, 412
trust-based, 194
on Web, 257–264
in X.500 project, 548
Sega games, 595
Segel, Joseph, 40
Segmentation and reassembly (SAR) layer in ATM, 735–736
Selectronic services, 496–497
Selling vs. marketing, 490
Semantic layer in EDI, 349–350
Send instruction in Telescript language, 629
Senders, authenticating and identifying, 208–209
sendmail security hole, 193
SERI network, 131
Serial copy management systems, 605
Serial Line Internet Protocol (SLIP), 175–176, 654–656
with local-level service providers, 183, 185
operation of, 656–658
Serialization delay, 721–722
Servers, 20
for copyrighted works, 603–604
for electronic cash, 317–318
HTTPD, 251–252
for local-level service providers, 182
for multimedia, 27–31, 678–681
security threats to, 197–199
for video, 29–31
for Web, 248
in Wide Area Information Service, 536
Service overloading, 198–199
Service providers
Internet. *See* Internet service providers (ISPs)
for value-added networks, 406–407
Services, customization of, 440–441
Session layer in OSI, 645, 647
Sessions for local-level service providers, 183–184
Set-top boxes, 66–67
as brokers, 35
MPEG-2 for, 692
Sexual material
on bulletin boards, 166
on information highway, 94
marketing, 499
SGML. *See* Standard Generalized Markup Language (SGML)
SGML Author tool, 797
Shamir, Adi, 213
Shared containers in active document architectures, 810–811
SHEN security, 263–264
Shopping
behaviors in, 294–295
home, 275–578
teleshopping, 432

Short message services (SMSs), 765
SIC (standard industrial classification) Yellow Pages directory, 552
Signatures, digital. *See* Digital signatures
Simon computer, 757
Simple Mail Transport Protocol (SMTP), 396–399
Simultaneous overlapping supply problem, 29–30
Single-document viewers in SGML, 799
Single-platform integration, 812
Single process local containers, 810
Situation-action pairs with software agents, 616
Skipjack algorithm, 215–216
SLIP (Serial Line Internet Protocol), 175–176, 654–656
  with local-level service providers, 183, 185
  operation of, 656–658
Slippage in cash, 330
Slow packet-switched networks, 716
Small-fee transactions, 283–286
Small vs. large in marketing, 497–498
Smart Card Forum, 329
Smart cards, 218, 326–327
  business issues in, 330–331
  readers for, 329
  relationship-based, 327–328
Smart messaging, 638–639
Smart phones, 329
SMDS (Switched Multimegabit Data Service), 722–724
SMR (specialized mobile radio), 87
SMSs (short message services), 765
SMTP (Simple Mail Transport Protocol), 396, 399
Snapshots for video conferencing, 703
Sniffers, 207
Social interaction in consumer applications, 38–39
Social issues for information highway, 94
Society for Worldwide Interbank Financial Telecommunications (SWIFT) funds transfer service, 365
Softads, 278
Software
  content of, 26
  for EDI, 389–393
  for local-level service providers, 185–186
  security holes in, 193
Software agents, 235–236, 540–541, 609
  and applets, 633–635
  benefits of, 611–612
  characteristics of, 615–617
  components of, 618–619
  for customer service, 636–637
  as distributed objects, 813
  environments for, 619–620
  as event monitors, 637–638
  history of, 612–614
  launching, 620–622
  managing and controlling, 624–625
  programming, 621–624
  properties of, 614–615
  for resource discovery, 639–640
  Safe-Tcl language for, 630–632
  security from, 196–197
  for smart messaging, 638–639
  Telescript language for, 626–630
  types of, 610–611
  as work-flow assistants, 638–339
Software Products division in CompuServe, 153
Software Publishers Association (SPA), 225
SOM (System Object Model), 811–812, 816
SONET (Synchronous Optical NETwork)
  with ATM, 733–734
  and SDH, 712–713
  for vBNS, 124
Sound
  with digital video, 685
  searches in, 540
  space requirements for, 676
Source databases in market research, 522–523
Southwestern Bell, 63
SPA (Software Publishers Association), 225
Spawned software agents, 620, 629
Specialization approaches in audience targeting, 514
Specialized mobile radio (SMR) communications, 87, 747
Specifically planned purchases, 291
Speed
  in frame relay, 719
  in news retrieval and delivery services, 590
SPEEDE project, 411
Spiders for searches, 540–541
Spoofing, 198
Spread spectrum technology, 761
Sprint VAN service provider, 407
SSL (Secure Sockets Layer), 261–263
Standard Generalized Markup Language (SGML), 472, 779–780, 788
  for corporate digital libraries, 792–802
  document creation and authoring for, 796–797
  document parsing and conversion in, 797–798
  document type definitions in, 253, 790–796
  electronic delivery and distribution in, 779–802

formatting and page composition in, 798–799
library creation and management in, 798
purpose of, 788–790
Standard industrial classification (SIC) Yellow Pages directory, 552
Standards, 19–21
in ATM, 724, 726–727
in EDI, 350–351, 368–369, 378–379 384–388
in electronic payment systems, 344
for encryption, 226
for hypertext documents, 474
for imaging, 470
for information highway, 96–97
in Internet, 134–135
for mobile computing, 760–764, 771–772
protocol stacks, 643
for structured documents, 472–473
for video conferencing, 700
in X.500 project, 548
Start-up costs for value-added networks, 404
Start-up firms, marketing by, 512
State backbone nodes, 117
State business Yellow Pages directory, 552
State government as Internet service provider, 167
State networks in NFSNET, 118–119
Static routes in TCP/IP, 653
Static software agents, 610
Sticker shock
with on-line services, 495
with video on-demand, 40
STM-1 specification, 713
STM-4 specification, 713
STM-16 specification, 713
STO (security through obscurity), 194
Stock trading, mobile applications for, 771
Storage
of documents, 478
of electronic cash, 316
of multimedia, 27–31, 674, 681–684
in OpenDoc, 821
Strategic alliances for information highway, 62–64
String searches
in search and retrieval, 534–537
in structured digital documents, 471–472
Strong authentication with SHEN, 264
Strong encryption with SHEN, 264
Structure analysis in DTD development, 794
Structured documents, 470–473, 779–782
in electronic commerce, 237–238
interchange representations for, 782
logical and physical structures in, 783–784
marking up, 784–785
markup languages for, 785–788 *See also* Standard Generalized Markup Language (SGML)
Stubs in Remote Procedure Calls, 816–817
Student Educational Record, 411
Student transcripts, SPEEDE project for, 411
Subject descriptions for software agents, 619
Subjects of certificates, 215
Subnotebook computers, 756
Subsidy issues
for information highway, 93, 95–96
for international networks, 133–134
Summarizing data warehouse data, 483
SUNET, 130
Supercomputing centers, 112, 124–125
Suppliers
in EDI, 355–356
in supply chain management, 52
Supply chain management (SCM), 51–53, 441–442
agile manufacturing in, 450–452
characteristics of, 442–444
efficient customer response in, 448–450
integrated logistics and distribution in, 444–445
integrated marketing and logistics in, 446–448
in intraorganizational electronic commerce, 420
purchasing and inbound logistics in, 445–446
Support
in advertising, 521–522
in electronic commerce, 236–237
by local-level service providers, 164, 180, 186–188
Support Services division in CompuServe, 153
SURAnet, 116
SVCs (switched virtual circuits) in ATM, 728–729
SWIFT (Society for Worldwide Interbank Financial Telecommunications) funds transfer service, 365
Switched Multimegabit Data Service (SMDS), 722–724
Switched virtual circuits (SVCs) in ATM, 728–729
Switching, 68–70
in ATM, 728–729, 739–740
in broadband telecommunications, 716–718
in gigabit networks, 126
Symmetric multiprocessing, 679–680

Synchronous Digital Hierarchy (SDH), 713, 733–734
Synchronous modems, 184
Synchronous Optical NETwork (SONET)
  with ATM, 733–734
  and SDH, 712–713
  for vBNS, 124
Synchronous procedures with software agents, 621–622
Synchronous teacher-student interaction, 569
Synthesis of documents, 479
System management, software agents for, 637–638
System Object Model (SOM), 811–812, 816

T-1 lines, 72
  for NFSNET, 114
  for NREN, 120
  for SMDS, 723
  for SONET, 713
T-3 lines
  for NREN, 120
  for SMDS, 723
  for SONET, 713
T-carrier telecom systems, 71–72
TA (terminal adapter) equipment with ISDN, 176
Tables of contents, structure in, 471
Tags in structured documents, 784–785, 787, 790–791
Talk shows, 38
Targeting audiences, 49, 496–497, 513–516
Task-specific knowledge for software agents, 620
Tasks in multiprocessing, 679–680
Taxes and electronic cash, 323
TCI cable operator, 80, 282–283
TCIF (Telecommunications Industry Forum), 789
Tcl (Tool Command Language), 630–631
TCP/IP (Transport Control Protocol/Internet Protocol), 101–102, 130, 175–176, 647–649
  domain name service in, 652
  Internet Protocol in, 650–651
  IP addresses in, 651–652, 667
  mobile, 659–664
  multicast, 665–668
  next generation, 668–671
  physical layer in, 653–654
  routing in, 652–653, 667–668
  SLIP and PPP in, 654–659
  Transmission Control Protocol in, 650
  User Datagram Protocol in, 650
TCP packets, 175
TDCC (Transportation Data Coordination Committee), 386
TDI (trade data interchange), 378
TDMA (time division multiple access), 762–764
Teaching. *See* Education
Team leaders for EDI, 414–415
Team learning, 572
TEI (Text Encoding Initiative), 789
Tele-Communications (TCI), 80, 282–283
Teleclicks money, 625
Telecommunications, content of, 25–26
Telecommunications Industry Forum (TCIF), 789
Telecoms
  ATM for, 725
  information highway plans by, 61
  as information route, 32
  as Internet service providers, 150–152
  for last mile, 71–78
  mergers with cable companies, 63
  RBOC strategy, 75–77
  structure of, 74–75
Telemarketing, 496
Telemetry and control, next generation IP for, 670
Telephone lines for video conferencing, 702–703
Telephone support by local-level service providers, 186
Telephones
  market penetration by, 38
  smart, 329
Telepresence, 560
Telescript language, 624–626
  agent mobility in, 628–629
  operation of, 627–628
  security issues in, 629–630
Teleservices, GSM for, 765
Teleshopping, 432
Teletext services, 44
Television
  advertising on, 503
  high-definition, 685
  for home shopping, 275–277
  interactive, 22, 33–34, 43, 64–65
  market penetration by, 38
TELNET
  eavesdropping on, 198
  from local-level service providers, 183
  URL format for, 249
Templar EDI, 412
Templates for HTML, 253
Terminal adapter (TA) equipment with ISDN, 176
Terminal equipment, 65
  computer-based telephony, 68

for independent service providers, 157–158
for local-level service providers, 182–184
set-top boxes, 66–67
switches, 68–70
Testbeds for gigabit networks, 127–129
TeX system, 786
Text-based broadcast messages, 503
Text Encoding Initiative (TEI), 789
Text searches, 534–537
Textile industry, 439
Theaters, home entertainment impact on, 282
Theory of the business, 46
Third-party authentication, 218–220
Third-party processors (TPPs), 298–299, 334–337
Third-party service providers, 391
Threads, 679–681
3D environments, 562–563
3D images, searches in, 540
TIFF (tag image file format), 470
Tiger architecture, 30–31
Tightly coupled multiprocessing systems, 679
Time-based competitive strategies, 45
Time critical news alerts, 587
Time division multiple access (TDMA), 762–764
Time independence in virtual classrooms, 571–572
Time stamps
in EDI, 376
for electronic cash, 322
Time-to-market in customization, 419
Time Warner, 36, 63, 80
TN3270 protocol, 183
Token authentication, 218
Token-based electronic payment systems, 313–326
Tomlinson, Roy, 104
Tool Command Language (Tcl), 630–631
Tools
applets, 807–809
for decisions. *See* Corporate digital libraries
for searches, 142–143, 559–565
Top-down method in DTD development, 795–796
Topic search engine, 537
Total Quality Management (TQM), 463
Toys "R" Us stores, 449
TP (transaction processing), 240
TPPs (third-party processors), 298–299, 334–337
TQM (Total Quality Management), 463
Tracking and dispatching, mobile computing for, 768–769
Trade data interchange (TDI), 378
Trade points in international trade, 361–362
Trading partners in EDI, 384
Traditional EDI, 377–378
Traffic management
in ATM, 736–739
in fast packet switching, 717
Trailers in OSI model, 646
Training. *See also* Education
by local-level service providers, 186
training on-demand, 573–576
Transaction processing (TP), 240
Transactions, 16–17, 296–298
in application services, 233–234
cash payments in, 298, 319
categories of, 258–259
credit card payments in, 298–301
in EDI, 387
in electronic payment systems, 314
information handling for, 460–461
microtransactions, 283–286
on-line transaction processing for, 769–771
security of, 207–209
Transcripts, SPEEDE project for, 411
Transformation of documents, 479
Translation
of data warehouse data, 483
in EDI, 383
Translation layer in EDI, 390–391
Transmission, convergence of, 22
Transmission path level in ATM, 734
Transpac VAN service provider, 407
Transparency in middleware services, 239
Transport
in ATM, 727
of information, 31–33
in international trade, 361
of multimedia, 674
Transport layer
in EDI, 351
in OSI, 645, 647
in TCP/IP model, 647
Transport messages in TCP/IP, 649
Transportation Data Coordination Committee (TDCC), 386
Trapdoor primes, 217
Travel. *See* Mobile computing
Trawling in searches, 540–541
Trilateral electronic cash transactions, 319
Triple DES encryption, 211
Trojan Horses, 197
True multinational corporations, 425–426
Trust-based security, 194
Tunnels
with MBONE program, 707
in multicast TCP/IP, 667
Turnover of information, 528

Turnover reductions as PC training benefit, 575
TV Guide On Screen, 279
TWBNet, 116
Two-way RF communications, 747
Two-way satellite links, 751–752

U interface with ISDN, 176
UA (user agents)
in MIME, 397–398
in user modeling, 459–460
UDP (User Datagram Protocol), 648, 650–651, 665–666
UFRJ network, 130
UI (user-interface) agents, 463–464
Underground economies, 323–324
Unicast mode in TCP/IP, 659
Uniform resource characteristics (URCs), 561
Uniform resource locators (URLs), 248–250, 337, 560–561
Uniform resource names (URNs), 561
Uniformity as PC training benefit, 575
UNINET, 130
Unisource VAN service provider, 407
United Parcel Service (UPS), 768–769
United Service Automobile Association (USAA) insurance system, 422
Universal access issues, 93–96
Universal browsers
with applets, 633–635
for Web, 143, 243–244
Universal interfaces, 560–561
Universal readership concept, 243–244
Universities, new roles for, 576–577
Unlicensed PCS, 776
UPRs (User Performance Requirements) for cellular systems, 760
UPS (United Parcel Service), 768–769
URCs (uniform resource characteristics), 561
URLs (uniform resource locators), 248–250, 337, 560–561
URNs (uniform resource names), 561
US West, 63, 75
[i]USA Today[i], 590
USAA (United Service Automobile Association) insurance system, 422
Usage costs for value-added networks, 404–405
USENET
for Clarinet news service, 592
for collaboration, 140
in education, 598
User agents (UAs)
in MIME, 397–398
in user modeling, 459–460
User-centered design tools, 560
User Datagram Protocol (UDP), 648, 650–651, 665–666
User-interface (UI) agents, 463–464
User interfaces. *See* Interfaces
User modeling and interaction in information handling, 459–460
User Performance Requirements (UPRs) for cellular systems, 760
Utilitarian shopping behavior, 294
UUCP network, 130, 186
UUNET Internet service provider, 160–161

V.32 modem standards, 184
V.34 modem standards, 184
Value-added networks (VANs), 366–368, 391–393, 401–403
and Internet, 407–409
as Internet access providers, 65
pricing of, 403–406
providers of, 406–407
Value of electronic cash, 316
Variable bit rate (VBR) in ATM, 728, 738
Variable costs in value-added networks, 404–405
VATP (Vector Adaptive Transform Processing), 703
vBNS (very high speed backbone network service), 109, 124–125
VBR (variable bit rate) in ATM, 728, 738
VCI (virtual channel indicator) in ATM headers, 732
VDT (video dial tone) systems, 76–78
Vector Adaptive Transform Processing (VATP), 703
Vector space models of information retrieval, 542
Vendor Stock Replenishment (VSR) service, 355
Verification in credit card transactions, 338
Vermont Teddy Bear Company, 489
Vertical markets, SGML in, 800
Vertical organizational structures, 426–427
Very high speed backbone network service (vBNS), 109, 124–125
Very small aperture satellites (VSAT), 92, 752–753
VESA Media Channel architecture, 696
Viacom, 26, 63, 80
Video, 684–686
applications for, 698–699
capture and editing hardware for, 697–698
characteristics of, 686–687
compression for, 688–695
desktop, 695–699
digital switches, routers, and hubs for, 68–70

in education, 580
playback hardware for, 695–697
searches in, 540
servers for, 29–31
space requirements for, 676–678
Video conferencing, 54, 699–700
in advertising, 520–521
costs of, 700–701
document conferencing, 701–702
Internet for, 704–707
ISDN for, 703–704
POTS for, 702–703
Video dial tone (VDT) systems, 76–78
Video for Windows program, 699
Video games, 595–596
Video on-demand, 29, 35–36
ATM for, 725, 727
billing for, 40
Video-oriented compression, 675
Video pumps, 30
Video rentals, 281
Videophones, 703
Viewers
for copyrighted works, 604
for OpenDoc, 821
for SGML, 797, 799
Viewtron service, 44
Virtual channel indicator (VCI) in ATM headers, 732
Virtual classrooms, 570–571
place and time independence in, 571–572
team learning in, 572
Virtual connectivity with news services, 592
Virtual enterprises, 440–441
Virtual laboratories, 596–597
Virtual networks, 239
Virtual organizational structures, 429–431
Virtual path indicator (VPI) in ATM headers, 732
Virtual reality (VR), 560–565
Virtual Reality Modeling Language (VRML), 564–565
Viruses, 197, 615, 629
VISA Interactive, 332
VISTAnet NREN testbed, 128–129
Visualization of infosphere, 462–463
Voice interfaces, 617
Volume approach in audience targeting, 514
Voodoo Lounge tour, 440–441
VPI (virtual path indicator) in ATM headers, 732
VR (Virtual reality), 560–565
VRML (Virtual Reality Modeling Language), 564–565
VSAT (very small aperture satellites), 92, 752–753
VSR (Vendor Stock Replenishment) service, 355
WAIS (Wide Area Information Service), 534–537
Wal-Mart
QR systems by, 51
supply chain management by, 447–448
Wanderers for searches, 540–541
WANs (wide area networks), 100–101
ATM for, 726
routers for, 69
Way, the, in Telescript, 629
Weak authentication with SHEN, 264
Web. *See* World Wide Web (WWW)
WELL, The, 164–165
Whalen, John, 504–505
White Pages directory
electronic, 546–551
telephone, 543, 545
X.500 project for, 547–551
Wide Area Information Service (WAIS), 534–537
Wide area networks (WANs), 100–101
ATM for, 726
routers for, 69
WIDE network, 168
Windows 95 operating systems, 34
Winsock programs, 655
WIRE on-line service, 166
Wireless communications, 32–33. *See also* Mobile computing
for cable, 81–88
cellular communications, 747–749
infrared, 754–755
vs. mobile, 743
packet radio, 750–751
personal communications systems, 772–776
radio-based systems, 746–747
satellite networks, 751–754
Wireless Modem, 750
Wiring infrastructure in market penetration, 38
Wolff, Stephen, 147
Women on Internet, 166
Word-level indexes, 538
Work-flow
automation of, 433–437
coordination of, 435
document-based, 479
in intraorganizational electronic commerce, 418–419, 433–437
software agents for, 638–639
technology for, 435–437
Work groups
collaborative applications for, 53–54
mobile applications for, 771

Workshops by local-level service providers, 186
Workspaces in active document architectures, 810–811
World-class manufacturing, 419
World Wide Web (WWW), 143, 231, 241–243
  for advertising, 507
  authentication features on, 259–261
  Hypertext Markup Language for, 253–257
  hypertext publishing on, 244–248
  hypertext transfer protocol for, 250–253
  indexes for, 639–640
  with local-level service providers, 185
  parts of, 243–244
  Secure Hypertext Transfer Protocol for, 262–263
  Secure Sockets Layer for, 261–263
  security on, 257–264
  SGML for, 790, 797
  SHEN security for, 263–264
  uniform resource locators for, 248–250
  Yellow Pages directory for, 552
WorldsAway program, 562
Worms, 197
Writers, copyrights for, 579

WYSIWYG pages with SGML, 797
X.12 standard, 350–351, 385–388
X.25 format, 711, 716
X.400 and X.435 envelopes, 393–395
X.500 project, 547–551

Yahoo directories, 552–553
Yellow Pages directory, 507–508
  electronic, 551–553
  telephone, 543–546

Zimmerman, Phillip, 222, 224